CW01019626

GRK

A GREEK GRAMMAR OF
THE NEW TESTAMENT AND
OTHER EARLY CHRISTIAN
LITERATURE

A
GREEK GRAMMAR
OF THE
NEW TESTAMENT
and Other Early Christian Literature

F. BLASS AND A. DEBRUNNER

A Translation and Revision
of the ninth–tenth German edition
incorporating supplementary notes of A. Debrunner
by

ROBERT W. FUNK

THE UNIVERSITY OF CHICAGO PRESS
Chicago and London

This work was published originally as *Grammatik des neutestamentlichen Griechisch* by Vandenhoeck & Ruprecht, Göttingen, Germany

International Standard Book Number: 0-226-27110-2
Library of Congress Catalog Card Number: 61-8077

THE UNIVERSITY OF CHICAGO PRESS, CHICAGO 60637
THE UNIVERSITY OF CHICAGO PRESS, LTD., LONDON

89 88 87 86   13 14 15

CONTENTS

CONTENTS

CONTENTS

CONTENTS

FROM THE PREFACE TO THE FOURTH EDITION

The candid confession which Blass makes, at the opening of his preface to the first edition, regarding his competence in the linguistic field, permits us to presume that it was entirely in conformity with the author's intent when the publisher assigned the revision to a linguist who devoted his major effort to precisely this aspect of the work. As a matter of fact, philology and even theology were satisfactorily incorporated into the first and second editions, and I found it necessary to question the numerous text-critical and exegetical notes only in rare cases where I was certain I could offer better. In doubtful cases I did not shy away from a small *sacrificium intellectus*—which one can surely justify *vis-à-vis* a Blass!

The linguistic revision was to contribute primarily, of course, to the sections on phonology and accidence, since it was in this area (besides lexicography which plays a marginal role in grammar) that Hellenistic studies had made the most progress since the second edition, and that results lay most conveniently to hand (Mayser, Helbing, Crönert, etc.). For this reason, the first two parts have undergone the most change. The saying πολὺς μὲν ὁ θερισμός, οἱ δὲ ἐργάται ὀλίγοι unfortunately still applies to the study of Hellenistic (and Medieval as well as Modern) Greek syntax, and the meager and scattered publications in the area are just sufficient to make the immense gaps which remain painfully conspicuous. The major emphasis in the treatment of NT syntax must, therefore, fall where Blass had demonstrated his mastery, namely on the comparison of NT with classical syntax—an area all too greatly neglected today. I have striven all the more, at least as far as it is presently possible, to extend these comparisons to the syntax of the LXX, the Apostolic Fathers, the papyri and inscriptions, as well as of Modern Greek. (I hope I am not misunderstood when I use the expression 'right' or 'correct' here and there, or occasionally designate a form as 'better'.) But I beg the reader, in his assessment of the work, to observe the following considerations: it was my intention that the book should retain the character indicated by the title without growing into a Hellenistic grammar, or into an exhaustive handbook, but should remain a practical tool in which theologians, philologians and linguists, pastors and scholars, and students can find, not everything, but as much usable data, analysis and interpretation, and as many bibliographical leads as possible (cf. Table V). Whether the continued existence of this grammar is justified in view of the three NT Greek grammars which have appeared in German since the second edition (Moulton, Radermacher, Robertson–Stocks), let others decide.

A. DEBRUNNER

PREFACE TO THE ENGLISH EDITION

The question which Albert Debrunner submitted to public judgment in his preface to the fourth edition (1913), as to whether the continued existence of Blass's *Grammatik* was justified, has been answered affirmatively by the reception accorded the six editions which followed. The modesty of Professor Debrunner would not permit him to predict that the work, under his hand, would come to occupy an even more central position among the basic tools found on the shelves of linguists, theologians and students; that it has achieved this status is due in no small measure to his untiring efforts to keep the work fully in the wake of the rapid advances being made during the first half of this century in the fields of comparative philology and the history of the Greek language.

Friedrich Blass, Professor of Classical Philology at the University of Halle-Wittenberg, published the first edition of his *Grammatik des Neutestamentlichen Griechisch* in 1896. It was rendered into English by H. St John Thackeray in 1898, who included the alterations of the second German edition (1902) in two appendices in a second edition (1905).

Albert Debrunner, Professor of Indo-European and Classical Philology at the University of Bern during most of his academic life, succeeded to the editorship upon the death of Blass. His initial contribution took the form of a thorough revision, particularly with reference to the sections treating phonology, accidence and word-formation (s. *supra*, Preface to the fourth edition). In addition, he transformed the rather cumbersome arrangement of the material into a much more perspicuous and legible order by collecting statements and principles into main sections and relegating the wealth of detail, mostly in the form of notes, to subsections (printed in reduced type). This revision appeared as the fourth edition (1913).

Debrunner found it necessary, owing to the stress of the times, to alter the format of the work once again in the seventh edition (1943), while at the same time thoroughly revising and augmenting the text. Many of the notes were now taken out of the text and collected into an appendix at the end of the book, making it possible to issue both a complete and an abbreviated edition without appendix; aside from the inconvenience caused by this arrangement, the work was again a substantial advance over previous editions. It was in this edition that the author worked in important new manuscript material: the Chester Beatty Biblical Papyri ($\mathfrak{P}^{45}$, $\mathfrak{P}^{46}$, $\mathfrak{P}^{47}$), the Washington (Freer) Gospels (W) and the Washington Manuscript of the Pauline Epistles (I), $\mathfrak{P}^{13}$, the Unknown Gospel (Papyrus Egerton 2), and, finally, new manuscript material for Hermas (the Michigan Papyrus, the Hamburg parchment fragment, and the small papyrus fragments).

The appendix which was created out of the notes for the seventh edition was retained in the eighth (1949), but in the ninth (1954) it was broken up and inserted in the text at the appropriate points in a mechanical fashion, thus providing most sections with *two* subsections. The tenth edition (posthumous) is a reprint of the ninth with typographical corrections.

The history of the work may thus be summarized in tabular form:

First edition, by F. Blass	1896	Second edition, with corrections and additions	1902
First English edition, trans. H. St John Thackeray	1898	Second English edition	1905

PREFACE TO THE ENGLISH EDITION

Third edition	1911	Seventh edition, thoroughly revised and	
Second English edition (reprinted)	1911	augmented	1943
Fourth edition, revised by A. Debrunner	1913	Eighth edition	1949
Fifth edition, corrected	1921	Ninth edition (with new pagination)	1954
Sixth edition, with new appendix	1931	Tenth edition (corrected)	1959

While both format and content have been radically transformed since Blass created the work, the basic principles upon which it is based have remained substantially the same. The conviction of Blass that the isolation of the NT from its historical setting is detrimental to its understanding (Preface to the first edition) was fully shared by Debrunner. Blass had developed extensive and illuminating comparisons with the norms of Classical Greek and had drawn lines from the NT to texts contemporary with it, e.g. Barnabas, Hermas and the Clementine literature. While retaining these, Debrunner moved still further ahead in the direction of a fuller treatment of the ties of the NT also with the LXX, the other Apostolic Fathers, the NT Apocrypha, the papyri and inscriptions, as well as with Medieval and Modern Greek. The development of the *Grammatik* along these lines has been its strength, i.e. it has afforded an external check, so to speak, for theologians and exegetes working more narrowly within the field of NT interpretation. Yet neither Blass nor Debrunner can be said to have been unacquainted with NT research proper and the *Grammatik* reflects the specialized literature in the field as much as any work of its type. On the other hand, both Blass and Debrunner recognized the peculiar position of the NT over against other ancient literature and, in particular, the special demands of textual criticism and theological exegesis; the latter, they believed, could only be met by a special treatment of 'NT Greek' (s. §1).

While he in no way desired to belittle the work of the great textual critics such as Lachmann and Tischendorf, Westcott and Hort, Blass was of the opinion that a modern *textus receptus*, even a critical one, could not help but obscure the diversity of the manuscript tradition and hence the possibilities open to the interpreter of the text. Consequently, he cited the manuscript evidence itself rather than the editions, even at points where he was not interested in establishing the text. Although some of Blass's text-critical practices and hypotheses failed to gain general acceptance and his conclusions as noted in the *Grammatik* had to be modified at many points, his practice of working with the manuscripts rather than the editions was wisely retained and even expanded by Debrunner.

Debrunner, more than Blass, regarded the *Grammatik* from its practical aspects and believed, consequently, that it ought to provide as many bibliographical leads as possible for those wishing to pursue a given point. Those who occasionally find the numerous references annoying will be correspondingly compensated by the ease with which a subject may be followed up. Debrunner managed to keep the literature canvassed down to 1943 (seventh edition) and had planned to bring it up to date in a revision which he was not to complete.

A word should perhaps be added with reference to the style of the *Grammatik*. Blass's text was deliberately laconic in order to conserve space and Debrunner undertook to shorten what was already extremely terse. The reason for this policy is the cost factor: a grammar containing roughly the same content could easily extend to a thousand pages or more if presented in expansive prose (cf. A. T. Robertson's *A Grammar of the Greek New Testament in the Light of Historical Research*!). Consequently, the Greek text is often abbreviated—the reader will have his text at hand in any case—and other abbreviations and symbols are employed. Add to this the German predilection for abbreviating at will and the reader will understand the dismay of the translator confronted with the necessity of rendering a terse statement packed with abbreviations into tolerable English—equally brief!

The translation of Walter Bauer's monumental lexicon into English by W. F. Arndt and F. W. Gingrich made it increasingly imperative that the *Grammatik* follow suit. That the English counterpart to Blass–Debrunner, begun by Thackeray, was never continued, can be excused only on the ground that English language theologians, during the early decades of this century, were in an even worse state with respect to lexicography; grammatically, they had the work of J. H. Moulton and A. T. Robertson upon which to rely, but for a lexicon they were still dependent upon Thayer. The work of Arndt–Gingrich altered the latter aspect of the situation and the failure to extend the work of the Anglo-Saxon grammarians made the former critical. The choice of Blass–Debrunner as the vehicle for an advanced grammar in English was obvious once it had been determined that a wholly new work was not a practical option; for such a work, if undertaken afresh, would be many years in the making and it is not at all certain that the present situation in philological and NT studies would support such an undertaking.

The work on the English version was begun with the intention of producing a fairly straightforward translation, making such rearrangements and revisions as were necessary to adapt the work to English practices. The latter included a modest number of references to the scholarly literature in English which had been overlooked by or were inaccessible to Debrunner.

Professor Debrunner, in approaching what, as it now appears, he must have known to be the end, determined to discharge his scholarly responsibility by placing in the hands of the translator an extensive set of notes which he had prepared for a new German edition, the completion of which his untimely death in 1958 made impossible. As a consequence, the original intent of the translator had to be considerably modified and the work, as a matter of course, projected over a greater period of time. With Debrunner's own notes as the base, it was decided to embark upon a limited revision of the ninth–tenth German edition, making such deletions, corrections and additions as were indicated by the notes, or which clearly fitted into the plan and purpose of the work as the author had conceived it. The work, therefore, was to remain substantially that of Debrunner: alterations which could not be referred to Debrunner were often so indicated, e.g. as dissenting opinion (cf. §477(2) on *Chiasmus*), or they were made in the belief that Debrunner himself would have taken note, in due course, of new light and of recent informed opinion. It must be added that the translator hesitated to lay hands on any part of the text and that a small *sacrificium intellectus* in some instances was little enough tribute to pay to Debrunner—as he says with respect to his predecessor!

In many minor particulars, too, the English version has been considerably modified. Cross-references have been provided to standard works in English whether or not they contribute materially to the discussion; this applies especially to the mammoth work of A. T. Robertson. Occasional references to H. W. Smyth's *Greek Grammar* and to Goodwin and Gulick, *Greek Grammar*, have been inserted for the benefit of those who may not be as familiar with classical norms as the original authors assumed. Recent works in English, e.g. C. F. D. Moule, *An Idiom Book of New Testament Greek*, have been consulted and often cited as well as the more recent German literature; the references to a few works have been brought up to date, e.g. Brugmann–Thumb has been replaced where possible by references to

PREFACE TO THE ENGLISH EDITION

Eduard Schwyzer, *Griechische Grammatik*, the syntax volume of which Debrunner himself brought to conclusion. German and English works with a counterpart in the other language have been cited in both versions, the reference to the original coming first, with the corresponding reference to the translation following in brackets, e.g. J. H. Moulton, *Grammar of New Testament Greek*, vol. I *Prolegomena*, Deissmann, Jeremias, etc. (s. Table V). In some cases finer distinctions were necessary, e.g. in references to Bauer: the Arndt–Gingrich translation and adaptation is cited simply as Bauer and this refers also to Bauer[4] where the two are identical (the vast majority of instances), but it was occasionally necessary to refer to either Bauer[4] or Bauer[5], indicating that the point in question could be found only in the German editions.

With respect to external features, it is to be noted that the disorder produced by the reintroduction of the appendix to the seventh edition into the text (ninth edition, 1954) has been overcome by rearranging the material within the sections: all notes relevant to a given section are therefore to be found appended to that section in some reasonable order. It is also hoped that some degree of regularity has been brought into the vast array of forms in which citations were given as well as into the complex and not always perspicuous system of abbreviations, the diversity of which was doubtlessly occasioned by the frequent and not always thorough revisions. The new format, designed by the Cambridge University Press, adds to the legibility and hence the utility of the work. The double-column page, which is a departure from the historic format for grammars, and the arrangement of the material within the sections denote the kinship of the *Grammar* and Bauer's *Lexicon*: they are twin tools for the study of the language of the primitive church.

In response to requests from many sources, a new set of indices has been prepared. The Index of Greek Words and Forms and the Index of References were both begun anew; the Index of Subjects has not been as radically revised and expanded owing to the fact that it does not bear the weight which the first two do in a work of this type. In every case the new index has been checked against the old to insure that the new will be at least as complete.

This English edition, like the German, is the work of many hands. A complete list of those who have contributed directly and indirectly to its preparation would embrace many teachers, colleagues and students—far too many to name here. This is to say nothing of the readers who, it may safely and hopefully be predicted, will contribute in the future to its improvement. It is both appropriate and a privilege, however, to mention here those who have participated substantially in the work and without whose assistance such merit as the work may possess would not have been easily possible.

Professor Debrunner was able, prior to his death, to read some of the sections in translation and to offer suggestions for their improvement, and it is to him, of course, that primary credit must go for the revised form of the text. Professor Kendrick Grobel of Vanderbilt University graciously placed at my disposal his wide knowledge and experience as linguist and translator. He served as a discerning critic through the early stages of the manuscript and it was due to his constant encouragement that the work has come to fruition.

The Rev. Dr W. P. M. Walters (Peter Katz) of Cambridge agreed to assume Debrunner's role in checking the translation and advising on matters pertaining to revision and expansion. I was indeed fortunate to have as a collaborator one who had been a close associate of Debrunner for many years. As was evident in his notes, Professor Debrunner had intended to incorporate in a new edition much of the work which had been flowing steadily from the pen of Dr Katz; the happy circumstance of having the latter as collaborator thus made it possible to revise and increase substantially the references to the LXX and to the secondary literature in this highly specialized field. In this respect the work has been greatly enriched. Among the sections to which Dr Katz has made a more substantial contribution are the following: §§ 6 (βάϊς), 11 (πλήμυρα), 13, 23 (δανίζειν etc.), 111(5), 128(5) (ἵλεώς σοι), 143 (ὁ ὤν), 146 (the whole), 148(4) (causative active), 165 (H 12: 15), 185, 203, 245a (new: comparative expressing exclusion), 248(3), 298(4) (Mk 14: 60 par.), 300 (the whole), 338(3), 431(3). It needs to be added, on the one hand, that this list by no means exhausts the measure of his assistance and, on the other, that I alone must be held responsible for the final form of the material. Moreover, the incentive to advance the revision as far as possible within the limits outlined above was stimulated by Dr Katz and his desire to honor Professor Debrunner by keeping the work alive.

I should also like to express my gratitude to the Rev. Dr J. A. Fitzmyer, S.J., of Woodstock College who was kind enough to read portions of the manuscript and to provide suggestions, especially with respect to Semitic languages; to the Rev. Dr C. H. Hunzinger, *Dozent* at the University of Göttingen, who extended very considerable help with respect to the nuances of his native tongue; to my colleague, Dr Karlfried Fröhlich, who was never too busy to discuss a translation problem or to go in quest of obscure bibliographical data; and to Dr James F. Ross, another colleague, who checked the citations of Semitic languages.

I am also very much indebted to the German publishing house of Vandenhoeck and Ruprecht, and especially to Mr Hellmut Ruprecht, for prompt and courteous response to all my requests; to the University of Chicago Press for its patient understanding and concern for quality work; and to the University Press, Cambridge, whose editors and readers are blessed with both a sense of humor and an almost unerring eye for detail.

Grateful acknowledgment is also made of the services of Mr Wayne A. Blakely who assisted with textual citations, of Mr Daniel Bechtel who read the galleys, and of Miss Caroline Becker who helped with the Index of Greek Words and Forms, as well as of many other students who did yeoman's service in the attention to many details. And finally, but without reference to rank, notice must be taken of my wife, Micki, who patiently typed the original manuscript and who often willingly, but I trust regretfully, managed without a husband during its preparation.

One is tempted to append an apology in advance for the limitations to which this work is subject. The reader will surely understand the restrictions which had to be invoked upon the process of revision: the task is never ending and can hardly be said to be completed. It goes without saying that all recent technical works such as the later parts of the *Theologisches Wörterbuch*, the periodical literature and the newer commentaries, could not be perused and given notice. It would be in order to boast that the German text had been freed from many errors were it not certain that a new set had been added; it is only to be hoped that the latter are not more grievous than the former. The choice of technical language will doubtless afford the basis for disagreement, but it is assumed that the reader will be tolerant of conventional terminology and will accept the use of such words as 'vulgar' and 'vulgarism' in a technical sense. The peculiar features of this grammar, now supported by a long tradition, will not strike every reader as informed by the same degree of wisdom: it is a moot question whether

PREFACE TO THE ENGLISH EDITION

too many or too few parallels are cited in the notes, whether too much or too little is presupposed by way of an elementary knowledge of Greek, and whether the resolution of one crux with sweeping authority is justified over against the suspension of judgment in the case of another. Yet these are features which help to make Blass–Debrunner what it is, and that is apology enough.

ROBERT W. FUNK

The Theological School
Drew University

TABLES OF ABBREVIATIONS

(A) PRIMARY TEXTS

I. The New Testament, the Apostolic Fathers, and the other early Christian literature treated in this grammar

This grammar is concerned primarily with the language of the Greek NT, but the other early Christian literature which has been examined for the purpose of placing the NT within the development of Greek as the language of the church is justifiably included in this category.

(1) *The New Testament (NT)*

Mt = Matthew	E = Ephesians	H (Heb) = Hebrews
Mk = Mark	Ph = Philippians	Ja = James
Lk = Luke	C = Colossians	1 P = 1 Peter
Jn = John	1 Th = 1 Thessalonians	2 P = 2 Peter
A = Acts of the Apostles	2 Th = 2 Thessalonians	1 Jn = 1 John
R = Romans	1 T = 1 Timothy	2 Jn = 2 John
1 C = 1 Corinthians	2 T = 2 Timothy	3 Jn = 3 John
2 C = 2 Corinthians	T = Titus	Jd = Jude
G = Galatians	Phm = Philemon	Rev = Revelation

(2) *The Apostolic Fathers (Ap. Frs.)*

Barn = Barnabas	Ign = Ignatius
1 Clem = 1 Clement	IEph = Ephesians
2 Clem = 2 Clement	IMag = Magnesians
Did = Didache	IPhld = Philadelphians
Diogn = Diognetus	IPol = Polycarp
Herm = Hermas	IRom = Romans
Man = Mandates	ISm = Smyrnaeans
Sim = Similitudes	ITr = Trallians
Vis = Visions	MPol = Martyrdom of Polycarp
	Pol Ph = Polycarp to the Philippians

(3) *New Testament Apocrypha (Apocr.)*

Acta Barn(abae)	?v AD	ApocP = Apocalypse of Peter . first half ii AD
L.–B. II 2, 292–302		Kl. T. 3 (1933) 8–13
Acta Joh(annis)	ii AD	Evang(elium) Evae . . . . ii AD
L.–B. II 1, 151–216		Only fragments in quotation (Epi-
Acta Pauli et Theclae . . .	ii AD	phanius)
L.–B. I 235–72		Ev(angelium) Thom(ae Graece)
Acta Petri et Pauli . . .	?iii AD	original form ?end ii AD
L.–B. I 178–222		Tischendorf, Evangelia Apocrypha²
Acta Phil(ippi) . . not earlier than iv/v AD		140–63
L.–B. II 2, 1–98		Gesta Pil(ati), s. Acta Pil(ati)
Acta Pil(ati)	?iv AD	GNaass = Gospel of the Naassenes
Tischendorf, Evangelia Apocrypha²		E. Preuschen, Antilegomena² (1905)
210ff.		12f.
Acta Thom(ae)	iii AD	GP = Gospel of Peter . . . . mid. ii AD
L.–B. II 2, 99–291		Kl. T. 3 (1933) 4–8

TABLES OF ABBREVIATIONS

Mart(yrium) Paul(i) . . . . ii AD
   L.–B. I 104–17

Mart(yrium) Petri et Pauli . . . ?iii AD
   L.–B. I 118–77

Paradosis Pilati . . . . medieval
   Tischendorf, Evangelia Apocrypha²
   426–31

Passio Andreae . . . . after 400 AD
   L.–B. II 1, 1–37

Protev(angelium) Ja(cobi) . second half ii AD
   Tischendorf, Evangelia Apocrypha²
   1–50

UGosp = Fragments of an Unknown
   Gospel and other Early Christian
   Papyri, ed. H. I. Bell and T. C.
   Skeat (1935)

(4) *The Pseudo-Clementine Literature (Ps.-Clem.)*

Diamart(yria)
   Rehm 2ff.

Ep(istula) Clem(entis) ad Jac(obum)
   Rehm 5–22

Ep(istula) Petri ad Jac(obum)
   Rehm 1f.

Epit(omae)
   Ed. A. R. M. Dressel (Leipzig, ²1873)

Homil(iae) Clem(entinae)
   Rehm 23–281

II. The Septuagint (LXX)

The other versions of the Greek Old Testament are designated by the addition of Aqu(ila), Symm(achus) or Theod(otion).

Am = Amos
Bar = Baruch
Bel = Bel and the Dragon
1 Chr = 1 Chronicles
2 Chr = 2 Chronicles
Da = Daniel
Dt = Deuteronomy
Eccl = Ecclesiastes
EpJer = Epistle of Jeremiah
1 Esdr = 1 Esdras (apocr.)
2 Esdr = 2 Esdras (Ezra–Nehemiah)
Esth = Esther
Ex = Exodus
Ezk = Ezekiel
Gen = Genesis
Hab = Habakkuk
Hg = Haggai
Hos = Hosea
Is = Isaiah
Jdth = Judith
Jer = Jeremiah
Jo = Joel
Job
Jon = Jonah
Josh = Joshua
Judg = Judges

1 Km = 1 Kingdoms (1 Samuel)
2 Km = 2 Kingdoms (2 Samuel)
3 Km = 3 Kingdoms (1 Kings)
4 Km = 4 Kingdoms (2 Kings)
La = Lamentations
Lev = Leviticus
1 Macc = 1 Maccabees
2 Macc = 2 Maccabees
3 Macc = 3 Maccabees
4 Macc = 4 Maccabees
Mal = Malachi
Mi = Micah
Na = Nahum
Num = Numbers
Ob = Obadiah
Pr = Proverbs
Ps = Psalms
PsSol = Psalms of Solomon
Ruth
Sir = Jesus Sirach
SSol = Song of Solomon
Sus = Susanna
Tob = Tobit
Wsd = Wisdom of Solomon
Zech = Zechariah
Zeph = Zephaniah

(A) PRIMARY TEXTS

III. Greek and Latin Texts and Authors

The tables in Liddell–Scott, Bauer(–Arndt–Gingrich), and the Abkürzungs-Verzeichnis to the Theologisches Wörterbuch zum Neuen Testament (1960) will serve as guides to the standard editions of works here listed. Editions are specified where the authors quote from those not customarily employed or where ambiguity might arise; recent editions are occasionally noted even though they are not utilized. Dates are assigned to authors and works wherever possible, although in some instances these must be regarded as approximate; a question mark (?) indicates that the date is in dispute, a blank that the date is, for one reason or another, indeterminable.

Acta Carpi, ed. Harnack, TU iii, 3–4
  (1888) 433–66 . . . .   ii AD
Acta Marinae et Christophori (H.
  Usener, 1886)
Aelian(us) . . . . .   ii/iii AD
  VH = Varia Historia
  NA = De Natura Animalium
Ael(ius) Aristid(es), s. Aristid(es)
Aeneas Tact(icus) . . .   iv BC
Aeschin(es) . . . . .   iv BC
Aeschyl(us) . . . . .   vi/v BC
  Agam(emnon)
  Ch(oephoroe)
  Eu(menides)
  Pers(ae)
  Supp(lices)
  Th. = Septem contra Thebas
Aesop(us)
  C. Halm (Leipzig, 1889) (Teubner);
    A. Chambry (Paris, 1925); A.
    Hausrath, Corpus Fabularum Aeso-
    picarum i 1 (1940), i 2 (1956)
    (Teubner); Ursing s.v. v
Alciphro(n) . . . . .   c. 200 AD
Alex(ander) Aphr(odisiensis) . .   c. 200 AD
  De An(ima liber)
Alexis . . . . . .   iv BC
Anacreontea . . .   ii BC–vi AD
Anal(ecta) Boll(andiana) 1882ff.
Anaximenes. . . . .   vi BC
Andocides . . . . .   c. 400 BC
Anec(dota) Gr(aeca)
  Bekker, Anec. Gr. = Anec(dota)
    Gr(aeca), ed. I. Bekker, 3 vols.
    (Berlin, 1814–21)
  Cramer, Anec. Ox. = Anec(dota)
    Gr(aeca), ed. J. A. Cramer, 4 vols.
    (Oxford, 1835–7)
Anth(ologia) Pal(atina)
  Ed. F. Dübner (1864–72), Appendix
    ed. E. Cougny (1890); ed. H.
    Stadtmüller (1894ff.); ed. H.
    Beckby (1957ff.)
Antiatt(ici) [Bekker, Anec. Gr.]

Antig(onus of) Car(ystus) . . .   iii BC
Antipho(n) (Orator) . . . .   v BC
Apollonius Dysc(olus) . . . .   ii AD
  (De) Synt(axi)
  (De) Pron(ominibus)
Apollonius of Rhodes . . . .   iii BC
Appian(us) . . . . . .   ii AD
  Hist(oriae) Rom(anae)
    Praefatio
    Hisp. = Ἰβηρική
    Pun. = Λιβυκή
Apuleius . . . . . .   ii AD
  Metamorphoses
Arat(us) . . . . . .   iii BC
  Phaenom(ena)
Aristeas Judaeus . . . . .   ii BC
  Ed. Swete, Introduction 551–606
(Ps.-)Aristides
  Ars rhet(orica)
Aristoph(anes) . . . . .   v/iv BC
  Ach(arnenses)
  Aves
  Eccl(esiazusae)
  Eq(uites)
  Frag(menta)
  Lys(istrata)
  Nu(bes)
  Pax
  Pl(utus)
  Ra(nae)
  Thesm(ophoriazusae)
  Vespae
  Scholia
Arist(otle) . . . . . .   iv BC
  (De Republica) Ath(eniensium) =
    Ἀθηναίων Πολιτεία
  Eth(ica) Nic(omachea)
  Frag(menta)
  Poet(ica)
  Rh(etorica)
  [Rhetorica ad Alexandrum]
Arrian(us) . . . . . .   ii AD
  An(abasis)
  Epicteti Dissertationes

TABLES OF ABBREVIATIONS

Arrian(us) (*cont.*)
  Ind(ica)
  Ep(istula) ad Trai(anum)
Artem(idorus) . . . . . ii AD
Athanasius . . . . . . iv AD
Athen(aeus) . . . . . ii/iii AD
Batr(achomyomachia) . . . . ?
Bekker, Anec. Gr., s. Anec(dota)
  Gr(aeca)
Caesar . . . . . . i BC
  B(ellum) G(allicum)
Callim(achus) . . . . . iii BC
  Frag(menta)
  Hymn(us) in Art(emidem)
Callinicus . . . . . . v AD
  Vita S. Hypatii
Cass(ius) Dio, s. Dio Cass(ius)
Cat(alogus) Cod(icum) Astr(ologo-
  rum)
  Ed. F. Boll, F. Cumont *et al.*
  (1898 ff.)
Cebes . . . . . . ?i AD
  Tab(ula)
Choerob(oscus) . . . . iv/v AD
Chrysippus (Tyanensis) . . i AD
  (Fragments in Athenaeus)
Chrys(ostomus) . . . . d. 407 AD
Cicero . . . . . . i BC
  (Epistulae) ad Atticum
  (De) Orat(ore)
  Tusc(ulanae Disputationes)
Cleanthes (Stoicus) . . . iv/iii BC
  Hymn to Zeus
Clem(ens) Alex(andrinus) . . . ii/iii AD
  Paed(agogus)
  Strom(ata)
Cleomedes . . . . . ii AD
Com(icorum) Att(icorum) Frag(menta)
  Ed. T. Kock, 3 vols. (Leipzig, 1880–
  8); J. Demiańczuk, Supplementum
  Comicum (Cracow, 1912)
Constit(utiones) apost(olorum) . . c. 380 AD
Corp(us) Herm(eticum) . . imperial times
  Ed. W. Scott I–IV (1924–36); ed.
  A. D. Nock and A. J. Festugière,
  Hermès Trismégiste (1945–54)
Cramer, Anec. Ox., s. Anec(dota)
  Gr(aeca)
Cratinus (Comicus) . . . . v BC
Ctesias . . . . . . v/iv BC
Cyrill(us Alexandrinus) . . d. 444 AD
  (Commentary on Haggai)
(Ps.-)Demetrius . . . . c. 100 AD
  (De) Eloc(utione) = Περὶ ἑρμηνείας
Democritus . . . . . v BC
Dem(osthenes) . . . . . iv BC
Dinarchus . . . . . iv BC
Dio Cass(ius) . . . . . ii/iii AD

Dio Chrys(ostom) . . . . i/ii AD
Diodor(us) (Sic[ulus]) . . . . i BC
Diodorus Tars(ensis) . . . iv AD
Diog(enes) L(aertius) . . . . iii AD
Diog(enes) Oen(oandensis) . . ii AD
Dionys(ius of) Hal(icarnassus) . . i BC
  Ant(iquitates Romanae)
  (De) Comp(ositione) Verb(orum)
  (De) Orat(oribus) Vet(eribus)
  (De) Thuc(ydide)
Diosc(urides) . . . . . i AD
Ducas = Michael Ducas Nepos . . xv AD
Empedocles . . . . . v BC
Enoch
  Ed. C. Bonner (1937)
Epicharmus (Comicus) . . . v BC
Epict(etus) . . . . . i/ii AD
  S. Melcher s.v. v
  Ench(iridion)
Epicur(us) . . . . . iv/iii BC
Epimenides . . . . . vi BC
Epiphanius . . . . . iv AD
  Haer(eses)
Etym(ologicum) Mag(num) . . . medieval
  Ed. T. Gaisford (Oxford, 1848)
Eur(ipides) . . . . . v BC
  Ba(cchae)
  Cyc(lops)
  HF = Hercules Furens
  Hec(uba)
  IA = Iphigenia Aulidensis
  IT = Iphigenia Taurica
  Ion
  Med(ea)
  Supp(lices)
  Troades
  Frag(menta), ed. A. Nauck[2]
Eus(ebius) . . . . . d. 330
  H(istoria) E(cclesiastica)
  Onom(asticon)
  Praep(aratio) Ev(angelica)
    Ed. K. Mras I, II (1954, 1956)
    (GCS 43, 1–2)
  (Liber de) Mart(yribus) Palaest(inae)
Eustathius . . . . . xii AD
  Odyss. = Commentarii in Homeri
    Odysseam
Euthalius . . . . . (iv to vii AD) ?
Galen . . . . . . ii AD
Geopon(ica)
Georg(ios) Hamartolos . . . ix AD
  Chronicon Syntomon
Gorg(ias) . . . . . v BC
Grammatici Graeci
  recogniti et apparatu critico instructi
    I (Leipzig, 1889), II (1894)
Hdt. = Herodotus . . . . v BC
Hermetica, s. Corpus Hermeticum

Hermogenes . . . . . ii AD
De Inventione
Herodian(us) Gramm(aticus) . . ii AD
Ed. A. Lentz (Leipzig, 1867–70)
Hero(n)das (Mimographus) . . . iii BC
Hes(iod) . . . . . vii BC
Opera (et Dies)
Scut(um Herculis)
Hesych(ius Lexicographus) . . . v AD
Hippiatr(ica) = Corpus Hippiatricorum
Graecorum, ed. E. Oder and C.
Hoppe I (1924), II (1927)
Hippoc(rates) . . . . v/iv BC
Ed. E. Littré, 10 vols. (Paris, 1839–
61)
Epid(emiae)
(De) Morb(o) Sacr(o)
Hipponax . . . . . vi BC
Hist(oria) Laus(iaca), s. Pallad(ius)
Hom(er) . . . . . viii/vii BC
Il(ias)
Od(yssea)
Hom(erici) Hymn(i) . . . . beg. vii BC
Horace . . . . . i BC
Sat(irae)
Hyperid(es) . . . . iv BC
(adv.) Ath(enogenem)
(pro) Eux(enippo)
(pro) Lyc(ophrone)
(adv.) Phil(ippum)
Iambl(ichus) (Philosophus) . . . iii/iv AD
VP = De Vita Pythagorica
Isaeus . . . . . . iv BC
Isid(orus) Pelus(iota) . . . . iv/v AD
Isocr(ates) . . . . . v/iv BC
Jos(ephus) . . . . . i AD
Ed. B. Niese (1885–95); ed. H. St John
Thackeray–R. Marcus (1926–43)
Ant(iquitates Judaicae)
Bell(um Judaicum)
C(ontra) Ap(ionem)
Vit(a)
Justin (Martyr) . . . . ii AD
Apol(ogy)
Leont(ius) Neap(olitanus) . . vii AD
Vita Joann(is Eleemosynarii)
Lob. Phryn., s. Phryn(ichus)
Longus . . . . . ii or iii AD
Past(oralia)
Lucian(us) . . . . . ii AD
Amor(es)
Cat(aplus)
Charon
D(ialogi) Deor(um)
D(ialogi) Mar(ini)
Herm(otimus)
Jud(icium) Voc(alium)
Lex(iphanes)

(De Morte) Peregr(ini)
Pisc(ator)
Prom(etheus)
Sol(oecista)
(De) Syr(ia) D(ea)
Trag(odopodagra)
Ver(ae) Hist(oriae)
Scholia
Lycophron . . . . . iii BC
Lycurgus . . . . . iv BC
Leocr(ates)
Lysias . . . . . . v/iv BC
Malalas(, Johannes) . . . . vi AD
S. Wolf s.v. v
Manetho (Astrologus) . . . . i AD
M(arcus) Ant(oninus) = Marcus Aurelius ii AD
Martial(is) . . . . . i AD
(Epigrammata)
Maximus Tyr(ius) . . . . ii AD
Melinno . . . . . ?i AD
(Fragments in Stobaeus)
Men(ander) . . . . . iv/iii BC
Ed. A. Körte and A. Thierfelder[3]
(1938–53)
Epit(repontes)
Her(os)
Perik(eiromene)
Mimnermus . . . . . vii BC
Moeris . . . . . . ii AD
Ed. J. Pierson (Leiden, 1759)
Musonius . . . . . i AD
Nicander . . . . . ii BC
Ther(iaca)
Oracula Sibyllina . . . . ?
Origen . . . . . . ii AD
De Oratione
Ep(istola) ad Rom(anos)
Pallad(ius Helenopolitanus) . . v AD
Hist(oria) Laus(iaca)
Passio Perpet(uae) et Felic(itatis) . iii AD
Ed. J. A. Robinson (1891) = Texts
and Studies I (Cambridge); ed. van
Beek I (Nimwegen, 1936)
Paulus Silentiarius . . . . vi AD
Paus(anias) . . . . . ii AD
[Pelagia]: Legenden der (heiligen)
Pelagia, H. Usener, 1879; Marty-
rium Pelagiae (part of the above
work) (Cited as: Usener, Legenden
der Pelagia)
Περὶ ὕψους (De Sublimitate) . . . i AD
(formerly attributed to Longinus)
Periplus Maris Rubri . . . . i AD
Philemo (Comicus) . . . . iv/iii BC
Com. Att. Frag. II
Philetas [Philitas] . . . . iv/iii BC
Philo Byz(antius) (Mechanicus) . . iii BC
S. Arnim s.v. v

TABLES OF ABBREVIATIONS

Philo (Judaeus) . . . . . i AD
    Ed. Cohn–Wendland (1896–1930); ed.
      Colson–Whitaker (1929–41)
    (De) Abr(ahamo)
    (De) Conf(usione Linguarum)
    (De) Cong(ressu Eruditionis Gratia)
    (De) Decal(ogo)
    (In) Flacc(um)
    Her. = Quis Rerum Divinarum Heres
      sit
    L.A. = Legum Allegoriarum Libri III
    (De) Leg(atione) ad Gaium
    (De) Post(eritate) Caini
    (De) Praem(iis) et Poen(is)
    (De) Sacr(ificiis) Abel(is et Caini)
    (De) Sob(rietate)
    (De) Somn(iis)
    (De) Spec(ialibus) Leg(ibus)
    (De) Vita Cont(emplativa)
Philodemus . . . . . . i BC
    (Volumina) Rh(etorica)
Philostorg(ius) . . . . . v AD
    Hist(oria) Eccl(esiastica)
Philostr(atus) . . . . . ii/iii AD
    (De) Gym(nastica)
    Her(oicus)
    VA = Vita Apollonii
Photius . . . . . . ix AD
    Bibl(iotheca)
Phryn(ichus) . . . . . ii AD
    Ed. C. A. Lobeck (Leipzig, 1820);
      ed. W. G. Rutherford (London,
      1881)
Pind(ar) . . . . . . v BC
    Frag(menta)
    Pyth(ian Odes)
    Scholia
Plato . . . . v/iv BC
    Ap(ologia)
    Ax(iochus)
    Charm(ides)
    Crat(ylus)
    Critias
    Crito
    Ep(istulae)
    Gorg(ias)
    Lg. = Leges
    Menex(enus)
    Meno
    Parm(enides)
    Phaedo
    Phdr. = Phaedrus
    Phil(ebus)
    Protag(oras)
    Re(s)p(ublica)
    Symp(osium)
    Theae(tetus)
    Tim(aeus)

Plato Comicus . . . . . v/iv BC
Plut(arch) . . . . . . i/ii AD
    Agis
    Alc(ibiades)
    Arist(ides)
    Caesar
    Cato Min(or)
    C. Gracch(us)
    Demetr(ius)
    Mor(alia)
    Per(icles)
    Publ(icola)
    Quaest(iones) Conv(ivales)
Pollux (Grammaticus) . . . . ii AD
Polyb(ius) . . . . . . ii BC
    S. Schoy s.v. V
Porph(yry) . . . . . . iii AD
    VP = Vita Pythagorae
Posidippus . . . . . . iii BC
Proclus . . . . . . v AD
    Chrest(omathia)
Ps.-Callisth(enes) . . . . c. 200 AD
Ptolem(aeus) . . . . . ii AD
    Geog(raphia)
Rhianus . . . . . . iii BC
Simon(ides of Ceos) . . . . vi/v BC
Soph(ocles) . . . . . . v BC
    Aj(ax)
    Ant(igone)
    El(ectra)
    Frag(menta)
    OC = Oedipus Coloneus
    OT = Oedipus Tyrannus
    Ph(iloctetes)
    Tr(achiniae)
Stephanus (Byzantius) . . . ? v AD
Stob(aeus) . . . . . . v AD
    Ecl(ogae)
Strabo . . . . i BC/i AD
Suidas . . . . x AD
Tatian . . . . . . ii AD
Teles . . . . . . iii BC
Test(aments of the) 12 Patr(iarchs)
    Ed. R. H. Charles (1908)
    Test(ament of) Gad
    Test(ament of) Jos(eph)
    Test(ament of) Levi
    Test(ament of) Naphth(ali)
Theoc(ritus) . . . . . iii BC
Theognis . . . . . . vi BC
Theophanes . . . . . viii AD
    Chron(ographia)
Theophr(astus) . . . . iv/iii BC
    S. Hindenlang s.v. V
    Char(acteres)
    Hist(oria) Pl(antarum)
    (De) Lap(idibus)
Theophyl(actus) . . . . . xi AD

(A) PRIMARY TEXTS

Thom(as) Mag(ister)	xiv AD	Xen(ophon)	v/iv BC
Thuc(ydides)	v BC	Ages(ilaus)	
Timo(n) Phliasius	iii BC	An(abasis)	
Timotheus (Lyricus)	v/iv BC	[Ath. = Republica Atheniensium]	
(Persae)		Cyr(opaedia)	
Tzetzes(, Joannes)	xii AD	HG = Historia Graeca	
Varro, M. Terentius	i BC	Hiero	
Ed. R. G. Kent² (London, 1951)		Mem(orabilia)	
De Lingua Latina		Oec(onomicus)	
Vett(ius) Val(ens)	ii AD	Xen(ophon) Eph(esius) . . .	i/ii AD

IV. Papyri and Inscriptions

Additional sources will be found under v, e.g. Deissmann, Mayser, Meisterhans, Moulton–Milligan, Preisigke, etc.

Audollent, Defix. Tab. = A. Audollent, Defixionum Tabellae (Paris, 1904).

Benndorf–Niemann, Reisen in Lykien = O. Benndorf und G. Niemann, Reisen in Lykien und Karien (Vienna, 1884).

Berl(iner) Klassikertexte], hg. von der Generalverwaltung der königlichen Museen zu Berlin, I–VII (Berlin, 1904–23).

BGU = Ägyptische Urkunden aus den königlichen Museen zu Berlin: Griechische Urkunden, I–VIII (1895–1933).

CIG = Corpus Inscriptionum Graecarum, I–IV (Berlin, 1828–77).

CIL = Corpus Inscriptionum Latinarum (Berlin, 1863–1909).

Corp. Gloss. Lat. = Corpus Glossariorum Latinorum (Leipzig, 1888–1923).

CPR = Corpus Papyrorum Raineri Archiducis Austriae, I Griechische Texte, ed. C. Wessely (Vienna, 1895).

Dialekt-Inschr. = Sammlung der griechischen Dialekt-Inschriften, ed. H. Collitz and O. Hoffmann, 4 vols. (Göttingen, 1884–1915).

Dit., Or. = Orientis Graeci Inscriptiones Selectae, ed. W. Dittenberger, 2 vols. (Leipzig, 1903–5 [reprinted 1960]).

Dit., Syll.³ = Sylloge Inscriptionum Graecarum, ed. W. Dittenberger³, 4 vols. (Leipzig, 1915–24 [reprinted 1960]); ed. W. Dittenberger², 3 vols. (1898–1901).

Edict(um) Diocl(etiani)], ed. T. Mommsen and H. Blümner, Der Maximaltarif des Diocletian (Berlin, 1893).

Ephemeris Epigraphica], Corporis Inscriptionum Latinarum Supplementum (Berlin, 1872 ff.).

Epigr. Kaibel = Epigrammata Graeca ex lapidibus conlecta, ed. G. Kaibel (Berlin, 1878).

IG = Inscriptiones Graecae (Berlin, 1873 ff.) (s. L.-S.)

IG² = Inscriptiones Graecae, editio minor (Berlin, 1913 ff.).

Inschr. v. Magn. = Die Inschriften von Magnesia am Mäander, ed. O. Kern (Berlin, 1900).

Inschr. v. Perg. = Die Inschriften von Pergamon (in Altertümer von Pergamon VIII), ed. M. Fraenkel (Berlin, 1890–5).

Inschr. v. Priene = Die Inschriften von Priene, ed. F. Hiller von Gärtringen (Berlin, 1906).

Inscrip. Délos = Inscriptions de Délos, ed. F. Dürrbach et al. (Paris, 1926–37).

Inscrip. Ponti = Inscriptiones antiquae orae septentrionalis Ponti Euxini graecae et latinae, ed. M. B. Latyschev (Petersburg, 1885–1901); I² 1916.

Milligan = G. Milligan, Selections from the Greek Papyri edited with translations and notes (Cambridge, 1910).

Mitteis, Chr. and Gr., s. v.

Monum. Ancyr. = Monumenti Ancyrani versio Graeca (Res Gestae Divi Augusti, ed. E. Diehl³) (Bonn, 1918).

MPER = Mitteilungen aus der Papyrussammlung der Nationalbibliothek in Wien (Papyrus Erzherzog Rainer) (N.S. 1932 ff.).

PAmh = The Amherst Papyri, ed. B. P. Grenfell and A. S. Hunt, 2 vols. (London, 1900–1).

Pap. Soc. Arch. Ath. = Papyrus Societatis Archaeologicae Atheniensis.

PBasel = Papyrusurkunden der öffentlichen Bibliothek der Universität zu Basel, I Urkunden in griechischer Sprache, ed. E. Rabel (GGAbh., n. F. 16, 3) (Berlin, 1917).

PCairo = Cairo Papyri cited by catalogue no. from B. P. Grenfell and A. S. Hunt, Greek Papyri, Catalogue général des Antiquités égyptiennes du Musée du Caire (vol. X, nos. 10001–10869; Oxford, 1903).

PEleph = Elephantine-Papyri, ed. O. Rubensohn (BGU Sonderheft, 1907).

Petersen–Luschan, Reisen = E. Petersen and F. von Luschan, Reisen in Lykien, Milyas und Kibyratis (Vienna, 1889).

TABLES OF ABBREVIATIONS

PFay = Fayûm Towns and Their Papyri, ed. B. P. Grenfell, A. S. Hunt and D. G. Hogarth (London, 1900).

PFlor = Papiri Fiorentini, documenti pubblici e privati dell'età romana e bizantina, I ed. G. Vitelli (Milan, 1906), II ed. D. Comparetti (1908–11), III G. Vitelli (1915).

PGenève = Les papyrus de Genève transcrits et publiés par Jules Nicole, I (Geneva, 1896–1906), II (1909).

PGiess = Griechische Papyri im Museum des oberhessischen Geschichtsvereins zu Giessen, ed. O. Eger, E. Kornemann and P. M. Meyer (Leipzig, 1910–12).

PGM = Papyri Graecae Magicae, hg. und übersetzt von K. Preisendanz, 2 vols. (Leipzig and Berlin, 1928, 1931).

PGrenf I = An Alexandrian Erotic Fragment and other Greek Papyri, chiefly Ptolemaic, ed. B. P. Grenfell (Oxford, 1896).

PGrenf II = New Classical Fragments and other Greek and Latin Papyri, ed. B. P. Grenfell and A. S. Hunt (Oxford, 1897).

PHib = The Hibeh Papyri, ed. B. P. Grenfell and A. S. Hunt, I (London, 1906).

PHolm = Papyrus Graecus Holmiensis, ed. O. Lagercrantz (Uppsala, 1913).

PIand = Papyri Iandanae, ed. C. Kalbfleisch et al. (Leipzig, 1912ff.).

PLeid = Papyri Graeci Musei antiquarii publici Lugduni-Batavi, ed. C. Leemans, I (Leiden, 1843), II (1885).

PLeipz = Griechische Urkunden der Papyrussammlung zu Leipzig, ed. L. Mitteis, I (1906).

PLille = Institut papyrologique de l'Université de Lille: Papyrus grecs publiés sous la direction de Pierre Jouguet, I (Paris, 1907–28), II (1912).

PLond = Greek Papyri in the British Museum, ed. F. G. Kenyon and H. I. Bell, I–V (London, 1893–1917).

PMagd = Papyrus de Magdola, réédité par Jean Lesquier (Paris, 1912) (= PLille II).

PMasp = Papyrus grecs d'époque byzantine, ed. Jean Maspéro in Catalogue général des antiquités égyptiennes du Musée du Caire, I (Cairo, 1911), II (1913), III (1916).

POsl = Papyri Osloenses, ed. S. Eitrem and L. Amundsen (Oslo, 1925–36).

POxy = The Oxyrhynchus Papyri, ed. B. P. Grenfell and A. S. Hunt, 1ff. (London, 1898ff.).

PPar = Notices et extraits des papyrus grecs du musée du Louvre et de la bibliothèque impériale, XVIII (2), ed. W. Brunet de Presle (Paris, 1865).

PPetr = The Flinders Petrie Papyri, ed. J. P. Mahaffy and J. G. Smyly, I–III (Dublin, 1891–1905).

PPrinceton = Papyri in the Princeton University Collections. 1 ed. A. C. Johnson and H. B. van Hoesen (= Johns Hopkins University Studies in Archaeology, no. 10; Baltimore, 1931), II ed. E. H. Kase (= Princeton University Studies in Papyrology, no. 1; Princeton, 1936).

PRainer = Corpus Papyrorum Raineri, ed. C. Wessely (Vienna, 1895).

PRev. Laws = Revenue Laws of Ptolemy Philadelphus, ed. B. P. Grenfell (Oxford, 1896).

PRoss-Georg = Papyri russischer und georgischer Sammlungen, hg. Gregor Zereteli, bearbeitet von G. Zereteli, O. Krüger, P. Jernstedt (Tiflis, 1925–35).

PRyl = Catalogue of the Greek Papyri in the John Rylands Library at Manchester, I ed. A. S. Hunt (Manchester, 1911), II ed. Hunt, J. de M. Johnson and V. Martin (1915), III ed. C. H. Roberts (1938).

PSI = Pubblicazioni della Società italiana: Papiri Greci e Latini, I–XI (Florence, 1912–35).

PStrassb = Griechische Papyrus der Kaiserlichen Universitäts- und Landesbibliothek zu Strassburg, ed. F. Preisigke, I (Leipzig, 1906–12), II (1920).

PTebt = The Tebtunis Papyri, ed. B. P. Grenfell, A. S. Hunt, E. J. Goodspeed and J. G. Smyly, I–III (London, 1902–38).

PTheb. Bank = U. Wilcken, Aktenstücke aus der königlichen Bank zu Theben (ABA, 1886).

(E.) Schwyzer, Dial(ectorum) Graec(arum) Exempla epigr(aphica)] potiora (Leipzig, 1923).

(F.) Solmsen, Inscr(iptiones) Graecae (ad illustrandas dialectos) selectae], ed. E. Fraenkel[4] (Leipzig, 1930).

Supp(lementum) Epigr(aphicum)] Graecum, ed. J. J. E. Hondius et al. (Leiden, 1923ff.).

Tab(ulae) Heracl(eenses)] = IG XIV.645.

Tituli Asiae Minoris], II, 1 ed. E. Kalinka (Vienna, 1920), II, 2 (1930).

UPZ = Urkunden der Ptolemäerzeit, ed. U. Wilcken, I (Berlin and Leipzig, 1922–37), II (1935ff.).

Wessely, Stud. Pal. = C. Wessely, Studien zur Paläographie und Papyruskunde (Leipzig, 1901–24).

Wilcken, Chr. and Gr., s. v.

R. Wünsch, Antike Fluchtafeln, ausgewählt und erklärt (Kl. T. 20; Bonn, 1907).

R. Wünsch, Sethianische Verfluchungstafeln (Leipzig, 1898).

ZenP Cairo = Zenon Papyri, ed. C. C. Edgar, I (Cairo, 1925), II (1926), III (1928), IV (1931).

(B) LITERATURE

V. Modern Literature, including Series and Editions

Where appropriate, works that have appeared in both German and English are cited, first in the original language, then the corresponding reference is added in brackets, e.g. Deissmann, LO⁴ 96 (LAE 120).

Abbott = Edwin A. Abbott, Johannine Grammar (London, 1906).

Abel = P. F.-M. Abel, Grammaire du grec biblique suivie d'un choix de papyrus (Paris, 1927).

Allen = F. H. Allen, The Use of the Infinitive in Polybius compared with the Use of the Infinitive in Biblical Greek (Diss. Chicago, 1907).

Almqvist = H. Almqvist, Plutarch und das NT. Ein Beitrag zum Corpus Hellenisticum Novi Testamenti (Acta Seminarii neotestamentici Upsaliensis xv [1946]).

Anagnostopulos = Γ. Π. Ἀναγνωστοπούλου Συμβολὴ πρώτη εἰς τὴν ἱστορίαν τῆς Ἑλληνικῆς γλώσσης. Περὶ τοῦ ἄρθρου (Athens, 1922) (From Ἀθηνᾶ 34).

Arnim = M. Arnim, De Philonis Byzantii dicendi genere (Diss. Greifswald, 1912).

Audollent, s. iv.

Bănescu = N. Bănescu, Die Entwicklung des griechischen Futurums von der frühbyzantinischen Zeit bis zur Gegenwart (Diss. Munich; Bucharest, 1915).

Bardenhewer = O. Bardenhewer, Geschichte der altkirchlichen Literatur, 5 vols. (Freiburg i. Br., 1902–32).

Bauer = W. Bauer, Griechisch-Deutsches Wörterbuch zu den Schriften des Neuen Testaments und der übrigen urchristlichen Literatur (Berlin, ⁴1952, ⁵1958) [A Greek–English Lexicon of the New Testament and Other Early Christian Literature, trans. and adaptation by W. F. Arndt and F. W. Gingrich from the 4th ed. (Cambridge and Chicago, 1957)] [Bauer refers to Bauer⁴ or Bauer–Arndt–Gingrich; Bauer⁵ to the 5th German edition].

Bechtel–Fick, Griech. Personennamen = Die griechischen Personennamen, nach ihrer Bildung erklärt und systematisch geordnet von A. Fick. 2nd ed. with F. Bechtel (Göttingen, 1894).

Bechtel, Gr. Dial. = F. Bechtel, Die griechischen Dialekte, 3 vols. (Berlin, 1921–4).

F. Bechtel, Die historischen Personennamen des Griechischen bis zur Kaiserzeit (Halle, 1917).

Beginnings = F. J. Foakes Jackson and Kirsopp Lake (eds.), The Beginnings of Christianity, i–v (London, 1920–33).

Benndorf–Niemann, s. iv.

Bezdechi = S. Bezdechi, Vulgarismes dans l'épopée de Nonnos, Anuarul Institutului de studii clasice iii (1936–40; Sibiu, 1941) 34–74.

Billerbeck = H. L. Strack and P. Billerbeck, Kommentar zum Neuen Testament aus Talmud und Midrasch, i–iv (Munich, 1922–8), v Rabbinischer Index (1956).

Björck, Alpha imp. = G. Björck, Das Alpha impurum (Uppsala, 1950).

Björck, Die periphr. Konstruktionen = G. Björck, Ἦν διδάσκων, die periphrastischen Konstruktionen im Griechischen (Skrifter K. Hum. Vet.-samf. i Uppsala 32, 2 [1940]).

Black, Aramaic Approach = M. Black, An Aramaic Approach to the Gospels and Acts (Oxford, 1946, ²1954).

Blass (on Acts) = F. Blass, Acta apostolorum... editio philologica (Göttingen, 1895).

Blass (on Matthew) = F. Blass, Textkritische Bemerkungen zu Matthäus (Beiträge zur Förderung christlicher Theologie iv 4; Gütersloh, 1900).

Blass, Aussprache³ = F. Blass, Über die Aussprache des Griechischen³ (Berlin, 1888) [Pronunciation of Ancient Greek, Eng. tr. by W. J. Purton (Cambridge, 1890)].

Bonaccorsi = Giuseppe Bonaccorsi, Primi saggi di filologia neotestamentaria, i (Turin, 1933), ii (1950) (Without vol. no. = i).

Bonhöffer = A. Bonhöffer, Epiktet und das NT (Giessen, 1911) (Religionsgeschichtliche Versuche und Vorarbeiten hg. R. Wünsch und L. Deubner, x).

Bonner = A Papyrus Codex of the Shepherd of Hermas (Similitudes 2–9) with a Fragment of the Mandates, ed. Campbell Bonner (Ann Arbor, 1934) (University of Michigan Studies, Humanistic Series xxii).

Brockelmann, GVG = C. Brockelmann, Grundriss der vergleichenden Grammatik der semitischen Sprachen, i (Berlin, 1908), ii (1913).

Brockelmann, Hebräische Syntax = C. Brockelmann, Hebräische Syntax (Neukirchen Kreis Moers, 1956).

Brockmeier = Wilhelmine Brockmeier, De Sancti Eustathii episcopi Antiocheni dicendi ratione (Diss. Münster, 1932).

Br.-Th. = K. Brugmann, Griechische Grammatik. 4. Auflage bearbeitet von A. Thumb (Munich, 1913) (Handbuch der Altertumswissenschaft ii 1).

Brugmann, Dem. = K. Brugmann, Die Demonstrativpronomina der indogermanischen Spra-

Brugmann, Dem. (*cont.*)
chen (Abhandlungen der sächsischen Gesellschaft der Wissenschaften, phil.-hist. Klasse 22, 6; 1904).

Brugmann, Grundriss² = K. Brugmann, Grundriss der vergleichenden Grammatik der indogermanischen Sprachen², I, II 1–3 (Strasbourg, 1897–1916).

Buck, Dictionary = C. D. Buck, A Dictionary of Selected Synonyms in the Principal Indo-European Languages: A Contribution to the history of Ideas (Chicago, 1949).

Buck, Greek Dialects = C. D. Buck, The Greek Dialects (Chicago, 1955).

Bultmann = R. Bultmann, Der Stil der Paulinischen Predigt und die kynisch-stoische Diatribe (Göttingen, 1910) (Forschungen zur Religion und Literatur des Alten und NTs, hg. W. Bousset und H. Gunkel, 13).

R. Bultmann, Das Evangelium des Johannes (Meyer Kom.) (Göttingen, ¹⁰⁻¹⁶1941–59).

Burkitt = F. C. Burkitt, The Syriac Forms of NT Proper Names (Proceedings of the British Academy 1911–12, 377–408).

C. F. Burney, The Aramaic Origin of the Fourth Gospel (Oxford, 1922).

Burton = E. de Witt Burton, Syntax of the Moods and Tenses in NT Greek (Chicago, 1893).

Buttmann = A. Buttmann, Grammatik des neutestamentlichen Sprachgebrauchs (Berlin, 1859).

Buturas = A. Buturas, Ein Kapitel der historischen Grammatik der griechischen Sprache (Leipzig, 1910).

Chantraine = P. Chantraine, Histoire du parfait grec (Paris, 1927).

P. Chantraine, Études sur le vocabulaire grec (Paris, 1936).

P. Chantraine, La formation des noms en Grec ancien (Paris, 1933).

H. Conzelmann, Die Mitte der Zeit = Hans Conzelmann, Die Mitte der Zeit: Studien zur Theologie des Lukas (3., überarbeitete Auflage, 1960) [H. Conzelmann, The Theology of Saint Luke (1960; trans. from the 2nd ed. 1957)].

Cramer, Catenae = J. A. Cramer, Catenae graecorum patrum in Novum Testamentum, III (Oxford, 1844).

Cremer–Kögel = H. Cremer, Biblisch-theologisches Wörterbuch der neutestamentlichen Gräcität, bearbeitet von J. Kögel (¹¹1923).

Crönert = W. Crönert, Memoria Graeca Herculanensis (Leipzig, 1903).

Cuendet = Georges Cuendet, L'ordre des mots dans le texte grec et dans les versions gotique, arménienne et vieux slave des Évangiles. I, Les groupes nominaux (Paris, 1929).

Curme Volume of Linguistic Studies = Language Monographs 7 (Baltimore, 1930).

Dalman = G. Dalman, Grammatik des jüdisch-palästinischen Aramäisch² (Leipzig, 1905).

Dalman, Jesus = G. Dalman, Jesus-Jeschua (Leipzig, 1922) [Jesus-Jeshua (London, 1929), tr. by P. P. Levertoff].

Dalman, Worte = G. Dalman, Die Worte Jesu (Leipzig, 1898, ²1930) [The Words of Jesus (Edinburgh, 1902), tr. by D. M. Kay].

R. M. Dawkins = Modern Greek in Asia Minor (Cambridge, 1916).

Debrunner = A. Debrunner, Griechische Wortbildungslehre (Heidelberg, 1917) (Sprachwissenschaftliche Gymnasialbibliothek 8).

A. Debrunner, Das Augment ἠ-. Festschrift für Friedrich Zucker (Berlin, 1954) 85–110.

Deissmann, BS = A. Deissmann, Bibelstudien (Marburg, 1895).

Deissmann, NBS = A. Deissmann, Neue Bibelstudien (Marburg, 1897).

Deissmann, [BS] = Bible Studies, tr. by A. Grieve (Edinburgh, 1901) (Embraces both BS and NBS).

Deissmann, LO⁴ = A. Deissmann, Licht vom Osten⁴ (Tübingen, 1923).

Deissmann, [LAE] = Light from the Ancient East, tr. by L. R. M. Strachan (from the 4th ed.) (New York, 1927).

Denniston = J. D. Denniston, The Greek Particles (Oxford, 1934).

Diels, Vorsokr.⁵ = H. Diels, ed., Vorsokratiker (5th ed. by W. Kranz, I–III, 1934–7).

Dieterich = K. Dieterich, Untersuchungen zur Geschichte der griechischen Sprache von der hellenistischen Zeit bis zum 10. Jahrhundert n. Chr. (Leipzig, 1898) (Byzantinisches Archiv 1).

Dieterich, Mithr. = K. Dieterich, Eine Mithrasliturgie erläutert (Leipzig, 1903).

Dit., Or. and Syll., s. IV.

Dodd Festschrift = The Background of the NT and its Eschatology, ed. W. D. Davies and D. Daube (Cambridge, 1956).

Döttling = C. Döttling, Die Flexionsformen lateinischer Nomina in den griechischen Papyri und Inschriften (Diss. Basel; Lausanne, 1920).

DuCange, Charles DuFresne, Glossarium ad Scriptores mediae et infimae Latinitatis, 6 vols. (Paris, 1733–6).

Eakin = F. Eakin, 'The Greek Article in First and Second Century Papyri', AJPh 37 (1916) 333–40.

Ebeling = H. Ebeling, Griechisch-deutsches Wörterbuch zum Neuen Testamente (Hanover and Leipzig, 1913).

Egli, Heterokl. = J. Egli, Heteroklisie im Griechischen... (Diss. Zurich, 1954).

Enoch, ed. Bonner = Campbell Bonner, The Last Chapters of Enoch in Greek (Studies and Documents 8, Kirsopp and Silva Lake eds.) (London, 1937).

(B) LITERATURE

J. A. Fabricius, Bibl. Gr. = J. A. Fabricius, Bibliothecae Graecae (Hamburg, 1716–28).

Festschrift Kretschmer = Festschrift für Paul Kretschmer, Beiträge zur griechischen und lateinischen Sprachforschung (Berlin, Vienna, etc., 1926).

Festschrift Wackernagel = ΑΝΤΙΔΩΡΟΝ. Festschrift Jacob Wackernagel...gewidmet...(Göttingen, 1923).

Fischer, Vitia lexicorum NT = J. F. Fischer, Prolusiones de Vitiis Lexicorum Novi Testamenti (Leipzig, 1791).

Fraenkel = E. Fraenkel, Geschichte der griechischen Nomina agentis auf -τήρ, -τωρ, -της (-τ-), I (Strasbourg, 1910), II (1912) (Untersuchungen zur indogermanischen Sprach- und Kulturwissenschaft I, IV).

Frisk, Wortstellung = Hjalmar Frisk, Studien zur griechischen Wortstellung (Göteborgs Högskolas Årsskrift XXXIX 1 [1933]).

C. F. A. Fritzsche, Pauli ad Romanos epistola, 3 vols. (1836–43).

Funk = R. W. Funk, The Syntax of the Greek Article: Its Importance for Critical Pauline Problems (Diss. Vanderbilt Univ. 1953).

GCS = Die Griechischen Christlichen Schriftsteller der ersten drei Jahrhunderte (Berlin, 1897ff.).

Gersdorf = Gersdorf, Beiträge zur Sprachcharakteristik der Schriftsteller des NT (Leipzig, 1816).

Gesenius–Kautzsch = H. F. W. Gesenius and E. Kautzsch, Hebräische Grammatik[28] (Leipzig, 1909) (Tr. by A. E. Cowley; Oxford, [2]1910).

Ghedini, Lett. crist. = Giuseppe Ghedini, Lettere cristiane dai papiri greci del III e IV secolo (Milan, 1923) (Supplementi ad 'Aegyptus', serie divulgazione, sezione greco-romana N. 3 = Pubblicazioni della Università Cattolica del Sacro Cuore, sezione filologica, vol. 1).

Ghedini, Vang. ap. = G. Ghedini, La lingua dei vangeli apocrifi greci. Pubblicazioni della Università Cattolica del Sacro Cuore V 16 (Milan, 1937) 443ff.

Gild. = B. L. Gildersleeve, Syntax of Classical Greek from Homer to Demosthenes, I (New York, 1900), II (1911).

Goodwin and Gulick = W. W. Goodwin and C. B. Gulick, Greek Grammar (Boston, 1930).

Gregory = Novum Testamentum Graece, ed. C. Tischendorf, Editio octava critica maior. III, C. R. Gregory, Prolegomena (Leipzig, 1884–94).

Gromska = Daniela Gromska, De sermone Hyperidis (Lemberg, 1927) (Studia Leopolitana III).

Haenchen = Ernst Haenchen, Die Apostelgeschichte (Meyer Kom.) (Göttingen, [10]1956, [11]1957, [12]1959).

Hahn = L. Hahn, Rom und Romanismus im griechisch-römischen Osten (Leipzig, 1906).

Hanhart, LXX 3 Macc, s. Septuaginta.

Harsing = C. Harsing, De optativi in chartis Aegyptiis usu (Diss. Bonn, 1910).

Harvard Studies in Class(ical) Phil(ology) (Cambridge, 1890ff.).

Hatzid. = G. N. Hatzidakis, Einleitung in die neugriechische Grammatik (Leipzig, 1892) (Bibliothek der indogermanischen Grammatiken V).

M. Haupt, Opuscula, I (Leipzig, 1875), II–III (1876).

Hauser = K. Hauser, Grammatik der griechischen Inschriften Lykiens (Diss. Zurich; Basel, 1916).

Havers = W. Havers, Untersuchungen zur Kasussyntax der indogermanischen Sprachen (Strasbourg, 1911) (Untersuchungen zur indogermanischen Sprach- und Kulturwissenschaft III).

Havers, Erkl. Synt. = W. Havers, Handbuch der erklärenden Syntax (Heidelberg, 1931).

Hawkins, Horae Synopt. = J. C. Hawkins, Horae Synopticae[2] (Oxford, 1909).

Hdb. = Handbuch zum NT, ed. Hans Lietzmann.

Helb. = R. Helbing, Grammatik der Septuaginta. Laut- und Wortlehre (Göttingen, 1907).

Helb., Kas. = R. Helbing, Die Kasussyntax der Verba bei den Septuaginta. Ein Beitrag zur Hebraismenfrage und zur Syntax der Κοινή (Göttingen, 1928).

Hering = J. Hering, Lateinisches bei Appian (Diss. Leipzig, 1935).

Hermann = E. Hermann, Die Nebensätze in den griechischen Dialektinschriften im Vergleich mit den Nebensätzen in der griechischen Literatur (Leipzig, 1912) (Griechische Forschungen I).

Hiller–Crusius = E. Hiller and O. Crusius, Anthologia Lyrica sive Lyricorum Graecorum veterum praeter Pindarum reliquiae potiores (Leipzig, 1903).

Hindenlang: L. Hindenlang, Sprachliche Untersuchungen zu Theophrasts botanischen Schriften (Diss. Strasbourg, 1909) (Published in part; complete in Dissertationes philologicae Argentoratenses 14).

O. Hoffmann, Griech. Dial. = O. Hoffmann, Die griechischen Dialekte, I–III (1891–8).

O. Hoffmann, Gr. Spr. I = O. Hoffmann, Geschichte der griechischen Sprache I. Bis zum Ausgange der klassischen Zeit[2] (Leipzig, 1916) (Sammlung Göschen 111).

E. Hofmann, Ausdrucksverstärkung (Göttingen, 1930).

Horae Soederblomianae (Travaux publiés par la Société Nathan Söderblom), I–IV (Uppsala, 1944–57).

Horn = R. C. Horn, The Use of the Subjunctive and Optative Moods in the nonliterary Papyri (Diss. Philadelphia, 1926).

TABLES OF ABBREVIATIONS

Huber = K. Huber, Untersuchungen über den Sprachcharakter des griechischen Leviticus (Diss. Zurich; Giessen, 1916).

Humbert = J. Humbert, La disparition du datif en grec (du ıer au xe siècle) (Paris, 1930).

I.C.C. = International Critical Commentary.

Jannaris = A. N. Jannaris, An Historical Greek Grammar (London, 1897).

Jeremias, Die Abendmahlsworte Jesu = J. Jeremias, Die Abendmahlsworte Jesu (1935; ²1949; ³1960) [The Eucharistic Words of Jesus, trans. by A. Ehrhardt from the 2nd ed. 1955].

Joachim Jeremias, Die Gleichnisse Jesu (³1954; ⁵1958) [The Parables of Jesus, trans. by S. H. Hooke (1954)].

Johannessohn I = M. Johannessohn, Der Gebrauch der Kasus und der Präpositionen in der Septuaginta, I Gebrauch der Kasus (Diss. Berlin, 1910).

Johannessohn II = M. Johannessohn, Der Gebrauch der Präpositionen in der Septuaginta (Berlin, 1926) (Mitteilungen des Septuaginta-Unternehmens III 3 = NGG 1925, Beiheft).

Josephus(, Flavius), opera, ed. et apparatu critico instruxit B. Niese (editio maior), I–VII (1885–95; reprinted 1955).

Josephus, ed. (with English translation) H. St John Thackeray and Ralph Marcus, I–VII (LCL, 1926–43).

Käser = J. Käser, Die Präpositionen bei Dionysius von Halicarnassus (Diss. Erlangen; Borna, 1915).

Kapsomenakis = Stylianos G. Kapsomenakis, Voruntersuchungen zu einer Grammatik der Papyri der nachchristlichen Zeit (Munich, 1938) (Münchner Beiträge zur Papyrusforschung 28).

Katz, Philo's Bible = P. Katz, Philo's Bible (Cambridge, 1950).

Katz, Recovery = Peter Katz, 'The Recovery of the Original Septuagint: A Study in the History of Transmission and Textual Criticism', Actes du Premier Congrès de la Fédération Internationale des Associations d'Études Classiques... à Paris Août—2 Septembre 1950 (Paris: Librairie C. Klincksieck, 1951) 165–82 [= TZ 5 (1949) 1–24 (with few changes)].

Kautzsch = E. Kautzsch, Grammatik des Biblisch-Aramäischen mit einer kritischen Erörterung der aramäischen Wörter im Neuen Testament (Leipzig, 1884).

K.–Bl. = R. Kühner, Ausführliche Grammatik der griechischen Sprache, I Elementar- und Formenlehre, 3. Auflage von F. Blass (in 2 vols.) (Hanover, 1890–2).

K.–G. = *Op. cit.* II Satzlehre, 3. Auflage von B. Gerth (in 2 vols.) (Hanover and Leipzig, 1898–1904; reprinted 1955).

Kenyon = F. G. Kenyon, The Chester Beatty Biblical Papyri, I–II (London, 1933), III (1934), III Supplement (1936).

Kieckers, Stellung des Verbs = Ernst Kieckers, Die Stellung des Verbs im Griechischen und in den verwandten Sprachen, I (Strasbourg, 1911) (Untersuchungen zur indogermanischen Sprach- und Kulturwissenschaft II).

Kl. T. = Kleine Texte für Vorlesungen und Übungen, ed. H. Lietzmann, K. Aland (1902ff.).

Knuenz = J. Knuenz, De enuntiatis Graecorum finalibus (Innsbruck, 1913) (Commentationes Aenipontanae 7).

Kock = Comicorum Atticorum Fragmenta, ed. T. Kock, 3 vols. (Leipzig, 1880–8).

Kretschmer = P. Kretschmer, Die Entstehung der Κοινή (Sitzungsberichte der Wiener Akademie 143, 10 [1901]).

Krüger = K. W. Krüger, Griechische Sprachlehre für Schulen. 1. Teil: Über die gewöhnliche, vorzugsweise die attische Prosa⁵ (Berlin, 1875).

Kuhring = W. Kuhring, De praepositionum Graecarum in chartis Aegyptiacis usu (Diss. Bonn, 1906).

Künnecke = H. Künnecke, De Latinorum vocabulorum Graece transcriptorum, quae sunt apud priorum saeculorum historicos scriptores, rationibus grammaticis (Diss. Münster, 1923) (Only an extract published).

Lademann = W. Lademann, De titulis Atticis quaestiones orthographicae et grammaticae (Diss. Basel; Kirchhain, 1916).

Lagarde, Mittheilungen IV = Paul de Lagarde, Mittheilungen IV (Göttingen, 1891).

Lautensach = O. Lautensach, Die Aoriste bei den attischen Tragikern und Komikern (Göttingen, 1911) (Forschungen zur griechischen und lateinischen Grammatik I).

L.–B. = R. A. Lipsius and M. Bonnet, Acta Apostolorum Apocrypha, I (1891), II 1 (1898), II 2 (1903) (reprinted 1959).

LCL = Loeb Classical Library (1912ff.).

E. Lerch, Hauptprobleme der französischen Sprache, 2 vols. (Berlin, 1930–1).

Libistros and Rhodamne = Le roman de Libistros et Rhodamné, publié d'après les manuscrits de Leyde et de Madrid, avec une introduction, des observations grammaticales et un glossaire par J. A. Lambert (Amsterdam, 1935).

Lindhamer = Luise Lindhamer, Zur Wortstellung im Griechischen. Eine Untersuchung über die Spaltung syntaktisch eng zusammengehöriger Glieder durch das Verbum (Diss. Munich; Borna–Leipzig, 1908).

Ljungvik = Herman Ljungvik, Studien zur Sprache der apokryphen Apostelgeschichten (Uppsala Univ. Årsskrift 1926) (Filosofi...8).

Ljungvik, Syntax = H. Ljungvik, Beiträge zur Syntax der spätgriechischen Volkssprache (Skrifter K. Hum. Vet.-samf. i Uppsala 27, 3 [1932]).

(B) LITERATURE

E. Löfstedt, Philologischer Kommentar zur Peregrinatio Aetheriae (Uppsala, ¹1911, ²1936 [reprint]).

L.–S. = A Greek–English Lexicon compiled by H. G. Liddell and R. Scott. A new edition rev. by H. S. Jones (Oxford, 1925–40).

Magie = D. Magie, De Romanorum iuris publici sacrique vocabulis sollemnibus in Graecum sermonem conversis (Halle, 1905).

Martin, s. 𝔓⁶⁶.

A. Matthiae, Ausführliche griechische Grammatik³ (Leipzig, 1835).

Mayser = Edwin Mayser, Grammatik der griechischen Papyri aus der Ptolemäerzeit, ɪ (Leipzig, 1906; ɪ² Berlin, 1923), ɪɪ 1 (Berlin, 1926), ɪɪ 2 (1934), ɪɪ 3 (1934); 2nd ed.: ɪ 2 (1938), ɪ 3 (1936).

Meillet = A. Meillet, Aperçu d'une histoire de la langue grecque (Paris, 1913, ³1930).

Meinersmann = B. Meinersmann, Die lateinischen Wörter und Namen in den griechischen Papyri (Leipzig, 1927) (Papyrusinstitut der Universitätsbibliothek in Heidelberg, ɪ 1).

Meister = M. Meister, De Axiocho dialogo (Diss. Breslau, 1915).

Meisterhans = K. Meisterhans, Grammatik der attischen Inschriften (Berlin, ¹1885; ²1888). Dritte Auflage von E. Schwyzer (Berlin, 1900) (Unless otherwise specified, the edition quoted is the 3rd).

Melcher = P. Melcher, De sermone Epicteteo quibus rebus ab Attica regula discedat, Pars prima (Diss. Halle, 1905) (complete in Dissertationes philologicae Halenses 17, 1).

Meuwese = A.-P.-M. Meuwese, De rerum gestarum Divi Augusti versione Graeca (Diss. Amsterdam; Buscodici, 1920).

Meyer Kom. = Kritisch-exegetischer Kommentar über das Neue Testament. Begründet von H. A. W. Meyer.

W. Meyer-Lübke, Grammatik der romanischen Sprachen, 4 vols. (Leipzig, 1890–1902).

M.–H. = J. H. Moulton and W. F. Howard, A Grammar of New Testament Greek, ɪɪ Accidence and Word-Formation (Edinburgh, 1919–29).

Michaïlov = G. Michaïlov, La langue des inscriptions grecques en Bulgarie, ɪ Phonétique (Sofia, 1940; ²1943) (Studia hist.-phil. Serdicensia, Suppl. vɪ).

Miller = C. W. E. Miller, 'Note on the Use of the Article before the Genitive of the Father's Name in Greek Papyri', AJPh 37 (1916) 341–8.

Milligan, s. ɪv.

Mitsotakis, Chrestom. = J. K. Mitsotakis, Chrestomathie der neugriechischen Schrift- und Umgangssprache (Lehrbücher des Seminars für orientalische Sprachen zu Berlin xɪv; Berlin, 1896).

Mitteis, Chr. and Gr. and Wilcken, Chr. and Gr. = L. Mitteis and U. Wilcken, Grundzüge und Chrestomathie der Papyruskunde (Leipzig, 1912): ɪ Historischer Teil, ɪ 1 Grundzüge (Wilcken, Gr.), ɪ 2 Chrestomathie (Wilcken, Chr.); ɪɪ Juristischer Teil, ɪɪ 1 Grundzüge (Mitteis, Gr.), ɪɪ 2 Chrestomathie (Mitteis, Chr.) (Gr. are cited by page, Chr. by number).

Mlt. = J. H. Moulton, A Grammar of New Testament Greek, ɪ Prologomena³ (Edinburgh, 1908) [Einleitung in die Sprache des Neuen Testaments, tr. by A. Thumb from the 3rd ed. (Heidelberg, 1911)] (References will occasionally be found to only one edition due to the fact that the German edition was also a revision).

R. Morgenthaler, Die lukanische Geschichtsschreibung als Zeugnis, 2 vols. (Zurich, 1949).

Moule = C. F. D. Moule, An Idiom Book of New Testament Greek (Cambridge, 1953).

Moulton, ClR 15, 18 = J. H. Moulton, 'Grammatical Notes from the Papyri', ClR 15 (1901) 31–8, 434–42; 18 (1904) 106–12, 151–5.

Moulton–Milligan = J. H. Moulton and G. Milligan, The Vocabulary of the Greek Testament Illustrated from the Papyri and other Non-literary Sources (London, 1914–29).

MPG = J. P. Migne, Patrologia, Series Graeca (Paris, 1857 ff.)

Nachmanson = E. Nachmanson, Laute und Formen der magnetischen Inschriften (Uppsala, 1904).

Nachmanson, Beiträge = E. Nachmanson, Beiträge zur Kenntnis der altgriechischen Volkssprache (Uppsala, 1910) (Skrifter K. Hum. Vet.-samf. i Uppsala 13, 4).

Nägeli = T. Nägeli, Der Wortschatz des Apostels Paulus (Göttingen, 1905).

Nauck = A. Nauck, Tragicorum Graecorum Fragmenta² (Leipzig, 1889).

E. Nestle, Philologica Sacra. Bemerkungen über die Urgestalt der Evangelien und Apostelgeschichte (Berlin, 1896).

Norden = E. Norden, Agnostos Theos, Untersuchungen zur Formengeschichte religiöser Rede (Leipzig, 1913) (reprinted 1956).

E. Norden, Die antike Kunstprosa⁵, 2 vols. (Stuttgart, 1958).

Obrecht = J. Obrecht, Der echte und soziative Dativ bei Pausanias (Diss. Zurich; Geneva, 1919).

Oldenburger = E. Oldenburger, De oraculorum Sibyllinorum elocutione (Diss. Rostock, 1903).

Olsson = Bror Olsson, Papyrusbriefe aus der frühesten Römerzeit (Diss. Uppsala, 1925).

𝔓⁶⁶ = Victor Martin (ed.), Papyrus Bodmer ɪɪ: Évangile de Jean, chap. 1–14 (Bibliotheca Bodmeriana, Geneva, 1956). Victor Martin (ed.), Papyrus Bodmer ɪɪ, Supplément. Évangile de Jean, chap. 14–21 (Bibliotheca Bodmeriana, Geneva, 1958).

Pallis, Notes = A. Pallis, Notes on St Mark and St Matthew (London, 1932).

TABLES OF ABBREVIATIONS

Palm = J. Palm, Über Sprache und Stil des Diodoros von Sizilien (Lund, 1955).

Palmer = L. R. Palmer, A Grammar of Post-Ptolemaic Papyri, I Accidence and Word-Formation, Part 1 The Suffixes (London, 1946) (Publications of the Philological Society XIII).

Passow–Crönert = F. Passow's Wörterbuch der griechischen Sprache völlig neu bearbeitet von W. Crönert, 3 Lieferungen (ἀ–ἀνά) (Göttingen, 1912–13).

Pauly–Wissowa = Pauly's Realencyclopädie der classischen Altertumswissenschaft, new revision in progress since 1892 by G. Wissowa, then by W. Kroll, K. Mittelhaus, et al.

Percy = E. Percy, Die Probleme der Kolosser- und Epheserbriefe (Lund, 1946) (Skrifter K. Hum. Vet.-samf. i Lund 39).

Pernot, Études: Hubert Pernot, Études sur la langue des Évangiles (Paris, 1927).

Petersen–Luschan, s. IV.

Philo, ed. Cohn–Wendland = L. Cohn and P. Wendland, Philonis opera quae supersunt, editio maior, I–VII (Berlin, 1896–1930).

Philo, ed. with English translation, F. H. Colson and G. H. Whitaker, I–IX (LCL, 1929–41).

Preisigke = Friedrich Preisigke, Wörterbuch der griechischen Papyrusurkunden mit Einschluss der griechischen Inschriften, Aufschriften, Ostraka, Mumienschilder usw. aus Ägypten. Vollendet und hg. Emil Kiessling (Berlin, 1914–27).

Preisigke, Namenbuch = F. Preisigke, Namenbuch, enthaltend alle griechischen, lateinischen, ägyptischen, hebräischen, arabischen und sonstigen semitischen und nichtsemitischen Menschennamen, soweit sie in griechischen Urkunden (Papyri, Ostraka, Inschriften, Mumienschildern, usw.) Ägyptens sich vorfinden (Heidelberg, 1922).

Preisigke, Sammelbuch = F. Preisigke, Sammelbuch griechischer Urkunden aus Ägypten, I (Strasbourg, 1915), II (1922), III–v ed. by F. Bilabel (1927–50).

Preuschen = Erwin Preuschen, Vollständiges griechisch-deutsches Handwörterbuch zu den Schriften des NT und der übrigen urchristlichen Literatur (Giessen, 1910).

Psaltes = St. B. Psaltes, Grammatik der Byzantinischen Chroniken (Göttingen, 1913) (Forschungen zur griechischen und lateinischen Grammatik 2).

Psichari = J. Psichari, 'Essai sur le grec de la Septante', Revue des Études juives 55 (1908) 161–208 = Travaux 831–91.

J. Psichari, Travaux = J. Psichari, Quelques travaux de linguistique, de philologie et de littérature helléniques 1884–1928, I (Paris, Société d'édition 'Les Belles lettres', 1930).

Raderm(acher) = L. Radermacher, Neutestament-

liche Grammatik. Das Griechisch des Neuen Testaments im Zusammenhang mit der Volkssprache (Tübingen, 1911; ²1925) (Hdb. 1).

Raderm., WSt 31 = L. Radermacher, 'Besonderheiten der Koine-Syntax', WSt 31 (1909) 1–12.

Ramsay, Luke = Sir Wm. Mitchell Ramsay, Luke the Physician, and other Studies in the History of Religion (London, 1908).

Regard = Paul F. Regard, La phrase nominale dans la langue du Nouveau Testament (Paris, 1919).

Regard, Prép. = Paul F. Regard, Contribution à l'étude des prépositions dans la langue du NT (Paris, 1919).

Rehm = Bernhard Rehm, Die Pseudoklementinen, I Homilien (Berlin, 1953) (GCS 42).

B. Reicke, The Disobedient Spirits = Bo Reicke, The Disobedient Spirits and Christian Baptism (1946) (Acta Seminarii Neotestamentici Upsaliensis XIII).

Reinhold = H. Reinhold, De graecitate Patrum Apostolicorum librorumque apocryphorum Novi Testamenti quaestiones grammaticae (Dissertationes philologicae Halenses XIV 1 [1898]).

Harald and Blenda Riesenfeld, Repertorium Lexicographicum Graecum: A Catalogue of Indexes and Dictionaries to Greek Authors (Coniectanea Neotestamentica XIV [1953]).

Riggenbach (on Hebrews) = E. Riggenbach, Der Brief an die Hebräer (Kommentar zum NT) (¹1913, ²,³1922).

RLV = Reallexikon der Vorgeschichte, 15 vols. (1924–32).

Rob. = A. T. Robertson, A Grammar of the Greek New Testament in the Light of Historical Research⁴ (Nashville, 1923).

C. H. Roberts, The Antinoopolis Papyri, ed. with translations and notes, Part I (London: Egypt Exploration Society, 1950).

Rossberg = C. Rossberg, De praepositionum Graecarum in chartis Aegyptiis Ptolemaeorum aetatis usu (Diss. Jena, 1909).

Rouffiac = J. Rouffiac, Recherches sur les caractères du grec dans le NT d'après les inscriptions de Priène (Paris, 1911) (Bibliothèque de l'École des Hautes-Études, Sciences religieuses 24, 2).

Rudberg = G. Rudberg, Neutestamentlicher Text und Nomina sacra (Uppsala and Leipzig, 1915) (Skrifter K. Hum. Vet.-samf. i Uppsala 17, 3).

Rüsch = E. Rüsch, Grammatik der delphischen Inschriften, I Lautlehre (Berlin, 1914).

Sacco = Giuseppe Sacco, La koinè del Nuovo Testamento e la trasmissione del sacro testo. Lezioni preliminari per lo studio del NT greco con introduzione e crestomazia (Rome, 1928).

Sanders = H. A. Sanders, A Third-century Papyrus Codex of the Epistles of Paul (Ann Arbor, 1935) (University of Michigan Studies, Humanistic Series XXXVIII).

(B) LITERATURE

Sanders, Wash. = H. A. Sanders, The Washington Manuscript of the Four Gospels (New York, 1912) (University of Michigan Studies, Humanistic Series IX 1).

Sanders, Wash. II = H. A. Sanders, The Washington Manuscript of the Epistles of Paul (New York, 1918) (University of Michigan Studies, Humanistic Series IX 2).

Scham = J. Scham, Der Optativgebrauch bei Klemens von Alexandrien in seiner sprach- und stilgeschichtlichen Bedeutung. Ein Beitrag zur Geschichte des Attizismus in der altchristlichen Literatur (Diss. Tübingen) (Published in part; complete in Forschungen zur christlichen Literatur- und Dogmengeschichte 11, 4 [Paderborn, 1913]).

Schekira = R. Schekira, De imperatoris Marci Aurelii Antonini librorum τὰ εἰς ἑαυτόν sermone quaestiones philosophicae et grammaticae (Diss. Greifswald, 1919).

Scherer = A. Scherer, Zur Laut- und Formenlehre der milesischen Inschriften (Diss. Munich, 1934).

Schlageter = J. Schlageter, Zur Laut- und Formenlehre der ausserhalb Attikas gefundenen attischen Inschriften. Ein Beitrag zur Koine (Programm Freiburg i. Br. 1908).

Schlageter, Worschatz = J. Schlageter, Der Wortschatz der ausserhalb Attikas gefundenen attischen Inschriften. Ein Beitrag zur Entstehung der Koine (Strasbourg, 1912).

Schmid = W. Schmid, Der Attizismus in seinen Hauptvertretern, I–V (Stuttgart, 1887–97).

Schmidt = W. Schmidt, De Flavii Iosephi elocutione. Fleckeisens Jahrbücher für klassische Philologie, Suppl. XX (1894) 341–550.

Schniewind = J. Schniewind, Euangelion (Gütersloh, 1927, 1931) (Beiträge zur Förderung christlicher Theologie II 13, 25).

Schoy = A. Schoy, De perfecti usu Polybiano (Diss. Bonn, 1913).

Schürer = E. Schürer, Geschichte des jüdischen Volkes im Zeitalter Jesu Christi, I³,⁴ (Leipzig, 1901), II⁴ (1907), III⁴ (1909), IV⁴ (1911).

Schulze, Graeca Latina = W. Schulze, Graeca Latina (Programm Göttingen, 1901).

W. Schulze, Kl. Schr. = Kleine Schriften von Wilhelm Schulze, zum 70. Geburtstag am 15. Dezember 1933. Hg. vom Indogermanischen Seminar der Universität Berlin (Göttingen, 1934).

Schwab = Otto Schwab, Historische Syntax der griechischen Comparation in der klassischen Literatur, II (Würzburg, 1894), III (1895) (Beiträge zur historischen Syntax der griechischen Sprache hg. von M. Schanz. Heft 12 und 13 = Band IV Heft 2 und 3).

Schweizer = E. Schweizer, Grammatik der pergamenischen Inschriften (Berlin, 1898).

Schwyzer I, II = Eduard Schwyzer, Griechische Grammatik, I (Munich, 1939), II Syntax und syntaktische Stilistik, vervollständigt und hg. von A. Debrunner (Munich, 1950).

Schwyzer, Jahrb. = Eduard Schwyzer, 'Neugriechische Syntax und altgriechische', NJklA 21 (1908) 498–507.

Septuaginta (LXX) = Septuaginta. Vetus Testamentum Graecum, Societatis Litterarum Gottingensis editum (1931–).

　IX 1 = Maccabaeorum liber I, ed. Werner Kappler (1936).

　IX 2 = Maccabaeorum liber II, ed. Robert Hanhart (1959).

　IX 3 = Maccabaeorum liber III, ed. Robert Hanhart (1960).

　X = Psalmi cum Odis, ed. Alfred Rahlfs (1931).

　XIII = Duodecim Prophetae, ed. Joseph Ziegler (1943).

　XIV = Isaias, ed. Joseph Ziegler (1939).

　XV = Ieremias, Baruch, Threni, Epistula Ieremiae, ed. Joseph Ziegler (1957).

　XVI 1 = Ezechiel, ed. Joseph Ziegler (1952).

　XVI 2 = Susanna, Daniel, Bel et Draco, ed. Joseph Ziegler (1954).

Septuaginta, ed. A. Rahlfs (1st ed. 1935, reprinted 1944, 1949, 1950).

Slotty = F. Slotty, Der Gebrauch des Konjunktivs und Optativs in den griechischen Dialekten, I Der Hauptsatz (Göttingen, 1915) (Forschungen zur griechischen und lateinischen Grammatik 3).

Smyth = H. W. Smyth, Greek Grammar, rev. by Gordon M. Messing (Cambridge: Harvard University Press, 1956).

Smyth, Ionic = H. W. Smyth, The Sounds and Inflections of the Greek Dialects. Ionic (Oxford, 1894).

v. Soden = H. von Soden, Die Schriften des NT in ihrer ältesten erreichbaren Textgestalt, I Untersuchungen (Berlin, 1902–10).

Solmsen = F. Solmsen, Beiträge zur griechischen Wortforschung (Strasbourg, 1909).

Solmsen–Fraenkel, Indog. Eigennamen = F. Solmsen, Indogermanische Eigennamen als Spiegel der Kulturgeschichte, hg. E. Fraenkel (Heidelberg, 1922).

F. Sommer, Handbuch der lateinischen Laut- und Formenlehre² (Heidelberg, 1914).

Sophocles, Lexicon = E. A. Sophocles, Greek Lexicon of the Roman and Byzantine Periods (Boston, 1870).

Spengel = L. Spengel, Rhetores Graeci, 3 vols. (Leipzig, 1853–6).

Stahl = J. M. Stahl, Kritisch-historische Syntax des griechischen Verbums der klassischen Zeit (Heidelberg, 1907).

Stephanus–Dindorf, Thesaurus Graecae Linguae, 8 vols. (Paris, 1831–65).

TABLES OF ABBREVIATIONS

Stolz–Schmalz, Lat. Gr.⁵ = M. Leumann and J. B. Hofmann, Stolz–Schmalz, Lateinische Grammatik⁵ (Munich, 1926–8).

Svensson = A. Svensson, Zum Gebrauch der erzählenden Tempora (Lund, 1930).

Swete, Introduction = H. B. Swete, An Introduction to the Old Testament in Greek, rev. by R. R. Ottley (Cambridge, 1914).

Tabachovitz = David Tabachovitz, Sprachliche und textkritische Studien zur Chronik des Theophanes Confessor (Diss. Uppsala, 1926).

Tabachovitz, Die Septuaginta = David Tabachovitz, Die Septuaginta und das Neue Testament; Stilstudien (Lund, 1956) (Acta Inst. Ath. Regn. Suec. 4).

Test. 12 Patr., ed. R. H. Charles, The Testaments of the Twelve Patriarchs, translated from the Editor's Greek Text and edited with Introduction, Notes, and Indices (London, 1908; reprinted 1960).

Thack. = H. St J. Thackeray, A Grammar of the Old Testament in Greek according to the Septuagint, I Introduction, Orthography and Accidence (Cambridge, 1909).

H. St John Thackeray, The Septuagint and Jewish Worship (London, 1921, ²1923).

Thes. ling. Lat. = Thesaurus Linguae Latinae editus auctoritate et consilio academiarum quinque Germanicarum Berolinensis Gottingensis Lipsiensis Monacensis Vindobonensis (1900 ff.).

Thieme = G. Thieme, Die Inschriften von Magnesia am Mäander und das NT (Göttingen, 1906) (Diss. Heidelberg, 1905).

Thumb² = A. Thumb, Handbuch der neugriechischen Volkssprache² (Strasbourg, 1910) [Handbook of the Modern Greek Vernacular, tr. by S. Angus (Edinburgh, 1912)] (The two editions are paragraphed identically).

Thumb, Hell. = A. Thumb, Die griechische Sprache im Zeitalter des Hellenismus (Strasbourg, 1901).

Tischendorf, Evangelia Apocrypha = C. Tischendorf, Evangelia Apocrypha (Leipzig, 1853); 2nd ed. by F. Wilbrandt (Leipzig, 1876).

Trunk = J. Trunk, De Basilio Magno sermonis Attici imitatore (Programm Ehingen a. D. 1907–8 and 1910–11) (Stuttgart, 1911).

Tschuschke = A. Tschuschke, De πρίν particulae apud scriptores aetatis Augusteae prosaicos usu (Diss. Breslau; Trebnitz, 1913).

TU = Texte und Untersuchungen zur Geschichte der altchristlichen Literatur, ed. O. v. Gebhardt and A. v. Harnack; K. Aland, W. Eltester, and E. Klostermann (1883 ff.).

TW = Theologisches Wörterbuch zum NT, hg. G. Kittel und G. Friedrich, I (Stuttgart, 1933), II (1935), III (1938), IV (1942), V (1954), VI (1959), VII (1960–).

Ursing = U. Ursing, Studien zur griechischen Fabel (Diss. Lund, 1930).

H. Usener, Epicurea (Leipzig, 1887) (Epistulae, Fragmenta, Sententiae of Epicurus).

Viereck = P. Viereck, Sermo Graecus quo senatus populusque Romanus magistratusque populi Romani usque ad Tiberii Caesaris aetatem in scriptis publicis usi sunt (Göttingen, 1888).

Viteau = J. Viteau, Étude sur le Grec du NT. Le verbe: Syntaxe des propositions (Thèse, Paris, 1893).

Viteau, Sujet = J. Viteau, Étude... comparé avec celui des Septante. Sujet, complément et attribut (Paris, 1897).

Völker = F. Völker, Syntax der griechischen Papyri, I Der Artikel (Programm Münster i. W., 1903).

Vogeser = J. Vogeser, Zur Sprache der griechischen Heiligenlegenden (Diss. Munich, 1907).

Wackernagel, Anredeformen = J. Wackernagel, Über einige antike Anredeformen (Programm Göttingen, 1912) (= Kl. Schr. 970–99).

Wackernagel, Hell. = J. Wackernagel, Hellenistica (Programm Göttingen, 1907) (= Kl. Schr. 1034–58).

Wackernagel, Homer = J. Wackernagel, Sprachliche Untersuchungen zu Homer (Göttingen, 1916) (Forschungen zur griechischen und lateinischen Grammatik 4; pp. 1–159 also = Glotta 7, 161–319, the rest as a Beiheft to Glotta 7).

Wackernagel, Kl. Schr. = J. Wackernagel, Kleine Schriften, 2 vols. (Göttingen, 1953).

J. Wackernagel, Studien zum griechischen Perfektum (Programm Göttingen, 1904) (= Kl. Schr. 1000–21).

Wackernagel, Syntax = J. Wackernagel, Vorlesungen über Syntax mit besonderer Berücksichtigung von Griechisch, Lateinisch und Deutsch², I (Basel, 1926), II (1928).

J. Wackernagel, Vermischte Beiträge zur griechischen Sprachkunde (Programm Basel, 1897) (= Kl. Schr. 764–823).

Walde–Hofmann³ = Lateinisches etymologisches Wörterbuch von Alois Walde, 3. Auflage von J. B. Hofmann (Heidelberg, 1930–8).

Waldis = J. Waldis, Sprache und Stil der grossen griechischen Inschrift vom Nemrud-Dagh in Kommagene (Nordsyrien). Ein Beitrag zur Koine-Forschung (Diss. Zurich; Heidelberg, 1920).

Warning = W. Warning, De Vettii Valentis sermone (Diss. Münster, 1909).

Wellhausen, Einl.² = J. Wellhausen, Einleitung in die drei ersten Evangelien² (Berlin, 1911).

Wessely, s. IV.

Westcott–Hort, App. = B. F. Westcott and F. J. A. Hort, The NT in the Original Greek. Appendix to the 1st ed. (Cambridge and London, 1881).

Wettstein = J. J. Wettstein, Novum Testamentum Graecum etc., 2 vols. (Amsterdam, 1751, 1752).

Molly Whittaker, Die Apostolischen Väter, I Der Hirt des Hermas (Berlin, 1956) (GCS 48).

(B) LITERATURE

Widmann = H. Widmann, Beiträge zur Syntax Epikurs (Stuttgart, 1935) (Tübinger Beiträge zur Altertumswissenschaft 24).

Wilcken, Chr. and Gr., s. Mitteis.

Wilke, Rhetorik = C. G. Wilke, Die neutestamentliche Rhetorik. Ein Seitenstück zur Grammatik des neutestamentlichen Sprachidioms (Dresden and Leipzig, 1843).

Wilke–Grimm = C. G. Wilkii Clavis Novi Testamenti philologica. Lexicon Graeco-Latinum in libros NT auctore C. L. W. Grimm. (Leipzig, ³1888, ⁴1903) (reprinted).

Winer = G. B. Winer, Grammatik des neutestamentlichen Sprachidioms⁷ (Leipzig, 1867).

Winer-M.³ = Winer–Moulton, A Treatise of the Grammar of New Testament Greek³ (Edinburgh, 1882) (Cited as the English counterpart of Winer).

Witkowski, Bericht = St. Witkowski, Bericht über die Literatur zur Koine aus den Jahren 1903–6. Jahresbericht über die Fortschritte der klassischen Altertumswissenschaft 159 (Leipzig, 1921) 1–279.

Witkowski, Epistulae = St. Witkowski, Epistulae privatae Graecae quae in papyris aetatis Lagidarum servantur² (Leipzig, 1911).

Wittmann = J. Wittmann, Sprachliche Untersuchungen zu Cosmas Indicopleustes (Diss. Munich; Borna, 1913).

Wolf I, II = K. Wolf, Studien zur Sprache des Malalas, I (Programm Munich, 1910–11), II (Programm Munich, 1911–12) (Also as Diss. Munich, 1912).

W.–S. = G. B. Winers Grammatik des neutestamentlichen Sprachidioms, 8. Auflage neu bearbeitet von P. W. Schmiedel, I Einleitung und Formenlehre (Göttingen, 1894), II 1 (1897), II 2 (1898).

Wuthnow = H. Wuthnow, Die semitischen Menschennamen in griechischen Inschriften und Papyri des vorderen Orients (Leipzig, 1930) (Studien zur Epigraphik und Papyruskunde I 4).

Zerwick = Max Zerwick, Untersuchungen zum Markus-Stil (Rome, 1937).

Zerwick, Graec. bibl. = Max Zerwick, Graecitas biblica exemplis illustratur. Ed. altera et aucta et emendata (Rome, 1949; ³1955) (Scripta Pontif. Inst. Bibl. 92).

J. Ziegler, Beiträge zur Jeremias-Septuaginta (Göttingen, 1958) (Mitteilungen des Septuaginta-Unternehmens VI).

Ziegler, LXX Daniel, s. Septuaginta.

Ziegler, LXX Isaiah, s. Septuaginta.

Ziegler, LXX XII Prophetae, s. Septuaginta.

Zilliacus, Familienbriefe = H. Zilliacus, Zur Sprache griechischer Familienbriefe des III. Jahrhunderts n. Chr. (P. Michigan 214–21) (Helsinki, 1943) (Societas Scientiarum Fennica, Comm. Hum. Litt. XIII 3).

Zorell = F. Zorell, Novi Testamenti Lexicon Graecum² (Paris, 1931).

Zuntz = G. Zuntz, The Text of the Epistles (London, 1953).

VI. Periodicals

ABA = Abhandlungen der Königlich-Preussischen (Deutschen) Akademie der Wissenschaften zu Berlin (philosophisch-historische Klasse) (1804 ff.).

Abh. Ak. München = Abhandlungen der bayerischen Akademie der Wissenschaften zu München (philosophisch-philologische und [since 1911] historische Klasse) (1835–1929, N.S. 1929 ff.).

Acta et comm. Univ. Tartuensis = Acta et commentationes Universitatis Tartuensis (B. Humaniora 1921 ff.).

Aegyptus = Aegyptus, Rivista Italiana di Egittologia et di Papirologia (Milan, 1920 ff.).

AEM = Archäologisch-epigraphische Mittheilungen aus Oesterreich-Ungarn (Vienna, 1877–97).

Aevum = Aevum, rassegna di scienze storiche, linguistiche e filologiche (Università Cattolica del Sacro Cuore) (Milan, 1927 ff.).

AJPh = The American Journal of Philology (Baltimore, 1880 ff.).

AJSL = American Journal of Semitic Languages and Literature (Chicago, 1884–1941).

AJTh = The American Journal of Theology (Chicago, 1897–1920).

Ἄγγελος = Ἄγγελος, Archiv für neutestamentliche Zeitgeschichte und Kulturkunde (Leipzig, 1925–32).

Annales Acad. Sc. Fennicae = Annales Academiae Scientiarum Fennicae (Sarja B. Humaniora 1909 ff.).

APF = Archiv für Papyrusforschung und verwandte Gebiete (Leipzig, Berlin, 1901–41).

Arbeiten und Mitteilungen = Acta seminarii neotestamentici upsaliensis (Arbeiten und Mitteilungen aus dem neutestamentlichen Seminar zu Uppsala) edenda curavit Anton Fridrichsen (1935 ff.).

Arch. f. Religionswiss. = Archiv für Religionswissenschaft (Freiburg, Leipzig, Tübingen, 1898–1941).

Archiv f. lat. Lexikogr. = Archiv für lateinische Lexikographie und Grammatik (Leipzig, 1884–1908).

Archivo glott. it. = Archivio glottologico italiano (Rome, 1873 ff.).

Arch. Stud. n. Sprachen = Archiv für das Studium der neueren Sprachen (und Literaturen) (Brunswick, 1846 ff.).

TABLES OF ABBREVIATIONS

'Aθηνᾶ = 'Aθηνᾶ. Σύγγραμμα περιοδικὸν τῆς ἐν 'Aθήναις ἐπιστημονικῆς ἑταιρείας (Athens, 1889ff.).

ATR = Anglican Theological Review (New York; Evanston, Ill., 1918ff.).

Atti Ist. R. Veneto = Atti dell'Istituto Reale Veneto (1857ff.).

Bayerische Blätter für das Gymnasialschulwesen (Bamberg, Munich, 1864–1935).

BCH = Bulletin de correspondance hellénique (Paris, 1877ff.).

Biblica = Biblica (Pontifical Biblical Commission) (Rome, 1920ff.).

BPhW = Berliner Philologische Wochenschrift (1881–1920) (S. also PhW).

Bull. of the Bezan Club = Bulletin of the Bezan Club (Leiden, [1926]–37).

Bull. Soc. Ling. = Bulletin de la Société de Linguistique de Paris (Paris, 1868ff.).

Byz.-neugr. Jahrb. = Byzantinisch-neugriechische Jahrbücher (Berlin, Athens, 1920ff.).

ByzZ = Byzantinische Zeitschrift (Leipzig, 1892ff.).

BZ = Biblische Zeitschrift (Freiburg, 1903–39; N.S. Paderborn, 1957ff.).

Chronique d'Égypte = Chronique d'Égypte (Brussels, Musées royaux d'art et d'histoire. Fondation égyptologique reine Élisabeth) (1925ff.).

Classica et Mediaevalia = Classica et Mediaevalia. Revue danoise de philologie et d'histoire (Copenhagen, 1938ff.).

Class. Journ. = Classical Journal (Classical Association of the Middle West and South; Classical Association of New England) (Chicago, 1905ff.).

Class. Phil. = Classical Philology (Chicago, 1906ff.).

ClQ = Classical Quarterly (London, 1907ff.; N.S. 1950ff.).

ClR = Classical Review (London, 1887ff.).

Con. Neot.: Coniectanea Neotestamentica curavit Anton Fridrichsen, a XIII H. Riesenfeld (Uppsala, 1936ff.).

Denkschr. Wien. Ak. = Denkschriften der Akademie der Wissenschaften in Wien (Phil.-hist. Klasse) (1850ff.).

Didaskaleion = Didaskaleion. Studi filologici di letteratura cristiana antica (Torino, 1912–17, N.S. 1923–31).

DLZ = Deutsche Literaturzeitung für Kritik der internationalen Wissenschaft (Leipzig, 1880ff.).

Emerita = Emerita. Boletín de lingüística y filología clásica (Madrid, 1933ff.).

Eranos = Eranos. Acta Philologica Suecana (Gothenburg, Uppsala, 1896ff.).

ET = The Expository Times (Edinburgh, 1890ff.).

Exp. = The Expositor (London, 1875–1925).

Geistige Arbeit = Geistige Arbeit. Zeitung aus der wissenschaftlichen Welt (Berlin, 1934–44).

Germ.-Rom. Monatsschrift = Germanisch-Romanische Monatsschrift (Heidelberg, 1909ff.).

GGA = Göttingische Gelehrte Anzeigen (1739ff.).

GGAbh. = Abhandlungen der Gesellschaft der Wissenschaften zu Göttingen (Philologisch-historische Klasse) (1896ff., N.S. 1932ff.).

Giorn. Soc. As. It. = Giornale, Società Asiatica Italiana (Florence, 1887–1920, N.S. 1925–35).

Glotta = Glotta. Zeitschrift für griechische und lateinische Sprache (Göttingen, 1909ff.).

Gnomon = Gnomon. Kritische Zeitschrift für die gesamte klassische Altertumswissenschaft (Berlin, 1925ff.).

Hermes = Hermes. Zeitschrift für klassische Philologie (Berlin, 1866ff.).

HTR = Harvard Theological Review (Cambridge, Mass., 1908ff.).

IF = Indogermanische Forschungen (Berlin, 1892ff.).

IF Anz. = Anzeiger für indogermanische Sprach- und Altertumskunde (Strasbourg, 1892–1930).

Indog. Jahrb. = Indogermanisches Jahrbuch (Strasbourg, Berlin, 1914ff.).

IZBG = Internationale Zeitschriftenschau für Bibelwissenschaft und Grenzgebiete (Düsseldorf, 1951–2ff.)

Jahresb. Altertumsw. = Jahresbericht über die Fortschritte der klassischen Altertumswissenschaft (Berlin, Leipzig, 1873–1944).

JBL = Journal of Biblical Literature (New Haven, Boston, Philadelphia, 1881ff.).

JHS = The Journal of Hellenic Studies (London, 1880ff.).

JTS = The Journal of Theological Studies (Oxford, 1900ff., N.S. 1950ff.).

Judaica = Judaica: Beiträge zum Verständnis des jüdischen Schicksals in Vergangenheit und Gegenwart (Verein der Freunde Israels) (Zurich, 1945ff.).

K. Hum. Vet.-samf. i Lund, Årsber.: K. Humanistiska Vetenskapssamfundet i Lund, Årsberättelse (1918–19ff.).

K. Hum. Vet.-samf. i Uppsala, Årsbok = K. Humanistiska Vetenskapssamfundet i Uppsala, Årsbok (1937ff.).

KZ = Zeitschrift für vergleichende Sprachforschung auf dem Gebiet der indogermanischen Sprachen, begründet von K. Kuhn ([Berlin, Gütersloh,] Göttingen, 1852ff.).

Language = Language. Journal of the Linguistic Society of America (Baltimore, 1925ff.).

Lexis = Lexis. Studien zur Sprachphilosophie, Sprachgeschichte und Begriffsforschung (Lahr, Germany, 1948ff.).

The Link = The Link. A Review of Mediaeval and Modern Greek (Oxford, 1938–9).

Mededeel. Akad. Amsterdam, Afd. Letterk. = Mededeelingen K. Akademie van Wetenschappen, Amsterdam, Afdeeling Letterkunde (Since 1920 [vol. 53] published in two series: A. Letteren..., B. Geschiedenis...).

(B) LITERATURE

Mnemosyne = Mnemosyne. Bibliotheca philologica Batava (Leiden, 1852–62, N.S. 1873–1933, N.S. 1934 ff.).

Museum Helveticum = Museum Helveticum. Schweizerische Zeitschrift für klassische Altertumswissenschaft (Basel, 1944 ff.).

Neophilologus = Neophilologus. A Modern Language Quarterly (The Hague, 1916 ff.).

NGG = Nachrichten der Gesellschaft der Wissenschaften zu Göttingen (Philologisch-historische Klasse, 1894–1933).

N. Jahrb. = Neue Jahrbücher für Philologie und Paedagogik (Leipzig, 1831–97).

N. Jahrbücher Suppl. = Neue Jahrbücher für Philologie und Paedagogik, Supplement (Leipzig, 1855–1903).

NJklA = Neue Jahrbücher für das klassische Altertum (Leipzig, 1898–1924).

NKZ = Neue Kirchliche Zeitschrift (Erlangen, 1890–1933).

NT = Novum Testamentum (Leiden, 1956 ff.).

NTS = New Testament Studies (Cambridge, 1954 ff.).

Philol. = Philologus. Zeitschrift für das klassische Altertum (Leipzig, Göttingen, 1846–1948).

PhW = Philologische Wochenschrift, incorporating the Berliner Philologische Wochenschrift and the Wochenschrift für klassische Philologie (1921–43).

Πλάτων (Athens, 1949 ff.).

Πρακτ. ̓Ακ. ̓Αθ. = Πρακτικὰ τῆς ̓Ακαδημίας ̓Αθηνῶν (Athens, 1926 ff.).

Proceedings of British Ac. = Proceedings of the British Academy for the Promotion of Historical, Philosophical and Philological Studies (London, 1903 ff.).

Prot. Monatshefte = Protestantische Monatshefte (Berlin, 1854–96, N.S. 1897–1921).

RB = Revue Biblique (Paris, 1892 ff., N.S. 1904 ff.) (= Vivre et Penser. Recherches d'exégèse et d'histoire, 1941–4).

Rev. crit. = Revue critique d'histoire et de littérature, recueil hebdomadaire (Paris, 1866–75, N.S. 1876–1935).

Rev. d'hist. eccl. = Revue d'histoire ecclésiastique (Louvain, 1900 ff.).

Rev. Ét. gr. = Revue des Études grecques (Paris, 1888 ff.).

Rev. Ét. juives = Revue des Études juives (Paris, 1880 ff., N.S. 1937 ff.).

Rev. Ét. lat. = Revue des Études latines (Paris, 1923 ff.).

Rev. Phil. = Revue de Philologie, de Littérature et d'Histoire anciennes (Paris, 1845–7, N.S. 1877–1926, Troisième Série 1927 ff.).

RhM = Rheinisches Museum für Philologie (Bonn, Frankfurt a. M., 1827–9, N.S. 1833–9, N.S. 1842 ff.).

RHPR = Revue d'Histoire et de Philosophie religieuses (Publiée par la Faculté de Théologie protestante de l'Université de Strasbourg, 1921 ff.).

RSR = Recherches de Science Religieuse (Paris, 1910 ff.).

SAB = Sitzungsberichte der Preussischen (Deutschen) Akademie der Wissenschaften zu Berlin (Philosophisch-historische Klasse) (1882 ff.).

Schweizerische Rundschau (Stans, 1900 ff.).

Skrifter K. Hum. Vet.-samf. i Lund = Skrifter, K. Humanistiska Vetenskapssamfundet i Lund (1920 ff.).

Skrifter K. Hum. Vet.-samf. i Uppsala = Skrifter, K. Humanistiska Vetenskapssamfundet i Uppsala (1890 ff.).

Sokrates = Sokrates. Zeitschrift für das Gymnasialwesen (Berlin, 1847–1924) (Entitled Zeitschrift für das Gymnasialwesen from 1847 to 1912).

StKr = Theologische Studien und Kritiken (Hamburg, Gotha, 1828–1942).

Studia Theol. = Studia Theologica (Lund, 1947 ff.).

Stud. Ital. = Studi Italiani di filologia classica (Florence–Rome, 1893–1915, N.S. 1920 ff.).

Stud. Pal. = C. Wessely, Studien zur Palaeographie und Papyruskunde (Leipzig, 1901–24).

Svensk Exeg. Årsbok = Svensk Exegetisk Årsbok (Uppsala, 1936 ff.).

Symb. Osl. = Symbolae Osloenses (Oslo, 1922 ff.).

Syria = Syria. Revue d'art oriental et d'archéologie (Paris, 1920 ff.).

ThBl = Theologische Blätter (Leipzig, 1922–42).

ThLZ = Theologische Literaturzeitung (Leipzig, 1876 ff.).

ThR: Theologische Rundschau (Tübingen, 1898–1917, N.S. 1929 ff.).

ThSt = Theological Studies (New York, Woodstock, Md., 1940 ff.).

ThStudiën = Theologische Studiën (Utrecht, 1883 ff.).

ThZ = Theologische Zeitschrift der Theologischen Fakultät der Universität Basel (Basel, 1945 ff.).

Trans. Am. Phil. Ass. = Transactions of the American Philological Association (Boston, etc., 1869 ff.).

Verbum Domini (Rome, 1921 ff.).

Verhandelingen Ak. Wet. Amsterdam, Afd. Letterk. = Verhandelingen K. Akademie van Wetenschappen, Amsterdam, Afdeeling Letterkunde (1858–91, N.S. 1892 ff.).

Vet.-Soc. i Lund, Årsbok = Vetenskaps-societeten i Lund, Årsbok (1920 ff.).

Vig. Christ. = Vigiliae Christianae (Amsterdam, 1947 ff.).

Vox Theol. = Vox Theologica. Interacademicaal theologisch Tijdschrift (Assen, 1930 ff.).

VT = Vetus Testamentum (Leiden, 1951 ff.).

Die Welt des Orients = Wissenschaftliche Beiträge zur Kunde des Morgenlandes (Wuppertal, 1947 ff.).

Wien. Sitzb. = Sitzungsberichte der (kaiserlichen) Akademie der Wissenschaften in Wien (Phil.-hist. Klasse) (1849 ff.).

WkP = Wochenschrift für klassische Philologie (1884–1920) (S. also PhW).

WSt = Wiener Studien. Zeitschrift für klassische Philologie (Vienna, 1879 ff.).

ZAW = Zeitschrift für die alttestamentliche Wissenschaft (Berlin, 1881 ff.).

ZDMG = Zeitschrift der Deutschen Morgenländischen Gesellschaft (Wiesbaden, 1847 ff.).

ZDPV = Zeitschrift des Deutschen Palästina-Vereins (Leipzig, Stuttgart, 1878–1945; resumed 1949 as Beiträge zur biblischen Landes- und Altertumskunde).

Zeitschrift f. d. Gymnasialwesen = Zeitschrift für das Gymnasialwesen (Berlin, 1847–1912) (Continued to 1924 as Sokrates, q.v.).

Zeitschrift f. österr. Gymn. = Zeitschrift für die österreichischen Gymnasien (Vienna, 1850 ff.).

Zeitschrift f. Ortsnamenf. = Zeitschrift für Ortsnamenforschung (Munich–Berlin, 1925 ff.) (From 1925 to 1937 entitled Zeitschrift für Namenforschung).

ZkTh = Zeitschrift für katholische Theologie (Innsbruck, 1877 ff.).

ZNW = Zeitschrift für die neutestamentliche Wissenschaft und die Kunde des Urchristentums (Giessen, Berlin, 1900 ff.).

ZThK = Zeitschrift für Theologie und Kirche (Tübingen, 1891–1917, N.S. 1920 ff.).

Ztschr. f. deutsche Wortf. = Zeitschrift für deutsche Wortforschung (Strasbourg, 1900–14).

Ztschr. f. rom. Phil. = Zeitschrift für romanische Philologie (Halle, 1877 ff.).

ZWTh = Zeitschrift für wissenschaftliche Theologie (Jena, Leipzig, 1858–1914).

(C) GENERAL AND SPECIAL ABBREVIATIONS

VII. General Abbreviations

acc. = accusative, according
act. = active
AD = Anno Domini
add. = addendum, -a
adj. = adjective(s)
ad loc. = on the passage (under consideration) (*ad locum*)
adv. = adverb
al. = others (*alii*)
aor. = aorist
Apocr. = Apocrypha
Ap. Frs. = Apostolic Fathers
Aq. = Aquila (Greek trans. of the OT)
Aram. = Aramaic
art. = article
Att. = Attic
attrib. = attribute, -ive
augm. = augment
BC = Before Christ
beg. = beginning
biblio. = bibliography
Byz. = Byzantine
c. = about (*circa*)
c(hap). = chapter
cf. = compare (*confer*)
class. = classical (Greek)
cod. = codex
comp. = comparative
conj. = conjunction
constr. = construction(s)
dat. = dative
decl. = declension

depon. = deponent
Diss. = Dissertation
Dor. = Doric
ed. = edited (by), edition
e.g. = for example (*exempli gratia*)
esp. = especially
et al. = and others (*et alii*)
ex(x). = example(s)
f. = for
f., ff. = following
fem. = feminine
f.n. = footnote
frag. = fragment
fut. = future
gen. = genitive
Gos. = Gospel(s)
Gr. = Greek
Hdb. = Handbuch zum NT, ed. Hans Lietzmann
Hebr. = Hebrew
Hell. = Hellenistic
hg. = herausgegeben (von) (edited by)
ibid. = in the same place (*ibidem*)
i.e. = that is (*id est*)
impera. = imperative
impf. = imperfect
indecl. = indeclinable
indic. = indicative
inf. = infinitive
in loc. = in the place (*in loco*)
inscrip. = inscription(s)
instr. = instrumental
interrog. = interrogative

(C) GENERAL AND SPECIAL ABBREVIATIONS

intr(ans). = intransitive
intro. = introduction
Ion. = Ionic
irreg. = irregular
KJV = King James Version
l. = line
Lat. = Latin
lit. = literally, literature
loc. cit. = in the place cited (*loco citato*)
LXX = Alexandrian Version of the Greek OT
masc. = masculine
MGr = Modern Greek
mid. = middle
minusc. = minuscule(s)
MS(S) = manuscript(s)
MT = Masoretic Text
n. = note
neg. = negative
neut. = neuter
n.F. = neue Folge (New Series)
no(s). = number(s)
nom. = nominative
N.S. = New Series
NT = New Testament
obj. = object
om. = omit
op. cit. = in the work cited (*opere citato*)
opp. = opposed (to)
opt. = optative
OT = Old Testament
p., pp. = page(s)
pap. = papyrus (-i), papyrological
par(s). = parallel(s)
pass. = passive
perf. = perfect
pers. = person
Pesh. = Peshitta
pf. = perfect
pl(ur). = plural
plupf. = pluperfect
pred. = predicate
prep. = preposition
pres. = present

pron. = pronoun
Ps.-Clem. = Pseudo-Clementines, s. I (4)
ptcp. = participle
Ptol. = Ptolemaic
q.v. = which see (*quod vide*)
redupl. = reduplication
reflex. = reflexive
rel. = relative
RSV = Revised Standard Version
s. = see
scil. = supply (*scilicet*)
Sem. = Semitic
sg. = singular
sic = so, thus, indicating an error transcribed as it
    stands in the original
sing. = singular
subj. = subjunctive, subject
subst. = substantive(ly)
superl. = superlative
suppl. = supplement
s.v(v). = under the word(s) (*sub voce*)
syll. = syllable
Symm. = Symmachus (Greek trans. of the OT)
synon. = synonym(ous)
Syr. = Syriac
Tdf. = Tischendorf
Theod. = Theodotion (Greek trans. of the OT)
t.r. = textus receptus
Trag. = Tragedy, Tragedians
trans. = transitive
tr(ans). = translated (by), translation
translit. = transliteration
t.t. = technical term
vb(s). = verb(s)
viz. = namely (*videlicet*)
voc. = vocative
vol. = volume
Vulg. = Vulgate
v(v). l(l). = variant reading(s) (*varia[e] lectio[nes]*)
v(v). or vs(s). = verse(s)
w. = with
w.o. = word order

VIII. Special Abbreviations

Dates are given either by century or year: lower-case Roman numerals designate the century,
Arabic numerals the year, e.g.

v BC = fifth century BC
i AD beg. (mid., end) = beginning (middle, end) of
    the first century AD

70 AD, *c.* 200 BC, etc.

Citations of textual evidence for the NT follow the sigla of Tischendorf or Nestle. The
following are to be noted:

S = Sinaiticus
046 = B in Rev
add. = addendum

al. (alii) is used loosely in some instances, i.e. with-
    out the qualifications customary in Nestle
it, vg, lat and latt are used as in Nestle

TABLES OF ABBREVIATIONS

minusc. = one or more minuscules
t.r. = Textus Receptus
The Fathers are cited in a shorter form in textual citations (as in Nestle), e.g. Chr(ysostomus), Cl(emens Alexandrinus), Ir(enaeus), Non(nus), Or(igenes), etc.

To be noted for Hermas:

A = Codex Athous
PBer = Berlin Pap. 5513 (Sim 2.4–10, 4.2–5)

PMich = Michigan Pap. 129 (s. Bonner s.v. v)
Further, s. M. Whittaker ix–xvi

For textual sigla for the Pseudo-Clementine Literature s. Rehm xxiii f.

Textual evidence for the LXX is cited according to Rahlfs or the Göttingen edition.

The Dead Sea Scrolls are cited by the customary designations, e.g.

1QS = Rule of the Community
1QH = Thanksgiving Hymns

Further, s. Discoveries in the Judean Desert I, 46 f.

INTRODUCTION

(1) 'NEW TESTAMENT GREEK'

1. Special treatment of the grammar of New Testament Greek has been prompted for the most part by purely practical needs. Theological exegesis and textual criticism have always required an exact analysis of the language of the NT, more exact than was afforded by the classical grammars of the language as a whole. When pursued independently, the 'NT language' as a special idiom could more easily be divorced from developments in the language elsewhere, just as, analogously, the content of the NT was separated from its intellectual and religious environment. Since, however, both the language and the content of the NT have been set so emphatically in their contemporary context, a special grammar of NT Greek may appear to some to be a reversal of a sound trend. But the NT, in spite of all its historical ties—with its own period and preceding and subsequent periods—is a historical unity; to that extent a special treatment of its language, as of its content, is justified, provided, of course, that it is assigned its correct place within the general history of the Greek language.

Bonaccorsi xxxiiiff.; J. Ros, De studie van het Bijbelgrieksch van Hugo Grotius tot Adolf Deissmann (Nimwegen and Utrecht, 1940). On the language of Christianity, Ed. Meyer, Ursprung und Anfänge des Christentums III (Stuttgart, 1923) 11. For a historical survey and material relevant to §§1–7, s. Mlt. 1–41; Rob. 1–30, 49–75, 76–139.

(2) THE KOINE

2. The higher unity to which the language of the NT belongs is the Greek lingua franca of its time. The brisk political and commercial relations of Athens in the v and iv centuries BC had already procured for the Attic dialect a certain diffusion across Attic borders as the language of diplomacy and commerce; but not until the Macedonian conqueror had pressed the Greeks into unity with a heavy hand and carried the Attic vernacular along with Greek ways into the 'barbaric' lands to the East, were the conditions provided for a common Greek culture and a *universal Greek vernacular*, a *Hellenistic*[1] *language*. The old Greek dialects did not capitulate unconditionally, however, to the Attic idiom. *On the lips of other Greeks, Attic gradually lost the peculiarities* which set it off from all or most other dialects: ττ rather than σσ, ρρ rather than ρσ, the optative, dual, etc. (s. Subject Index under *Atticisms*). But the non-Attic dialects have also left traces in other ways. The extremely sparse *Aeolicisms* do not appear in the NT. Doric has contributed more[2] (cf. *Doricisms* in the Index).

From the NT may be mentioned, in addition to those listed: the ᾱ of μεγιστᾶνες (the ᾱ from αο like Doric ᾶς from *ᾶος, Ionic ῆος, Attic ἕως; adaptation of middle Persian *mahistān 'great men' H. H. Schaeder in Schwyzer I 521 n. 5) and λᾱτομεῖν (cf. Latin *latomia, lautumiae*), λᾱξευτός (Lk 23: 53, cf. λαξός 'stone-mason' in the papyri [Mayser I² 2,

---

[1] The expressions 'common Greek', 'Koine' (ἡ κοινὴ διάλεκτος) and 'Hellenistic' are here used as synonyms corresponding to the now current usage.

[2] Only those phenomena are considered here which are common to the whole Hellenistic world. Instances where localized dialecticisms appear in an original dialect area or among people from regions where a particular dialect was spoken (local and individual dialecticisms) are, of course, not treated. New dialecticisms are naturally to be expected within Koine in view of its wide geographical extension and the great diversity of Greek and foreign idioms which it either absorbed or repressed; and in fact the ancient grammarians already have much to say about an 'Alexandrian dialect'. Research has not yet, however, arrived at positive results. Among the NT authors themselves, certain distinctions appear which have nothing to do with the divergence of their cultural status. Some, for example, confuse εἰς and ἐν, especially Lk, while the author of Rev distinguishes these prepositions properly. Furthermore, Hermas, certainly a representative of the vulgar language, quite often uses the superlative forms in -τατος and -ιστος in an elative sense, while the NT authors have almost completely lost those in -τατος, and those in -ιστος are also used very little (s. §60). Such diversity may go back to local differences within Koine although the mapping of their diffusion can no longer be carried out; but it may equally well be just a question of individual preference for a stylistic feature (Meillet, Bull. Soc. Ling. 19 [1914] 69). S. §285(1) on ἐμός, §388 on the inf. after verbs of motion. Recent inadequate attempts to demonstrate local differences of the Koine in the NT: M. Wellmann, Die Schrift des Dioskurides περὶ ἁπλῶν φαρμάκων (Berlin, 1914) 69f. (dat.-instr. with 'to be filled', ὅτι with inf.); Pernot, Études 177 (ἄν τις; but cf. Debrunner, Gnomon 4 [1928] 444f.).

165]); on λᾶ- s. Björck, Alpha imp. 69, and for μᾱρυκᾶσθαι and the α–η shift s. §29(3). Further, ἀλέκτωρ (Ionic–Attic ἀλεκτρυών [according to Fraenkel I 154ff. ἀλέκτωρ is also Ionic; but the Batrachomyomachia stems from the Hellenistic period, and in Herondas a Koine-Doricism is not impossible]), βουνός (designated as Cyrenaic by Hdt. 4.199), the forensic sense of κριτής and κριτήριον (Attic κριτής 'critic, umpire'; Wackernagel, Hell. 10f. = Kl. Schr. 1041f.; Fraenkel II 32f.), καταδίκη in the sense of 'condemnation' (Schlageter, Wortschatz 21), ὁρκίζειν (Fraenkel I 180), ὁρκωμότης (NT only -οσία, ibid. 200).

Attic mixed most intensively with the dialect to which it was most closely related, the Ionic. A very large number of *Ionicisms* have been noted in phonology, inflection, and principally in vocabulary (s. *Ionicisms* in the Index). Of course, some Ionicisms might prove to be of a general non-Attic character if the other dialects were better known. But whenever specific peculiarities of Attic appear in Koine, we are justified in speaking also of *Atticisms* (s. Index) as in the case of βορρᾶς, ττ in certain words, and κατάβα. *The Hellenistic language is thus by and large a compromise* between the claim of the strongest (Attic) and that of the majority. The method of handling the primitive Greek ᾱ in Koine affords a good illustration of this point: because the non-Attic dialects here part company (Ion. η, otherwise ᾱ), Attic, which took a middle position (ᾱ after ι, ε, ρ, otherwise η), was destined to prevail (for exceptions s. §43). It is not a full-fledged dialecticism when a tendency previously present in Attic (and in other dialects) is fostered by a dialect; thus, for example, the mutation of ει to ῑ is not a 'Boeotianism', although it was already fully developed in Boeotian in V BC; Boeotian ῑ merely encouraged the development of close Attic ει to ῑ (Witkowski, Bericht 181). Likewise the gender of ἡ λιμός may have been formed independently following ἡ πεῖνα, ἡ δίψα, and then have been supported by Doric (Mayser I¹ 8; I² 2, 18.43ff.; Solmsen 109f.); cf. §49(1).

---

[1] As is well known, the contrast between MGr vernacular, the direct descendant of Koine, and classicism (the καθαρεύουσα) still governs the Greek world.
[2] Lk is compared with Mt and Mk in Norden, Die antike Kunstprosa (Leipzig, 1898; 2nd ed. 1909) 486ff.; and in Agnostos Theos 357ff. S. Schrenk, TW III 229.23ff. on the style of the shorter ending to the Gospel of Mk.
[3] The frequently doubted MS reading is defended and conjectures like γυναῖκες νεάνιδες παιδίσκαι rejected by A. Plummer, ET 26 (1914/15) 560-2, likewise

(3) THE PLACE OF THE NT WITHIN HELLENISTIC GREEK

3. Literary position. Cultural differences naturally had great influence on the oral and written use of the new common language. An Egyptian donkey-driver spoke a more 'vulgar' tongue than a scholar or a royal official. When a common man wrote he could certainly strive to be somewhat more painstaking in diction, but he could never achieve the finesse of one brought up on Plato and Demosthenes, especially after the artificial return to Attic, known as Atticism, increasingly became the ideal of the educated.[1] Where between the two extremes do the NT documents belong, to the everyday idiom reflected in the papyrus letters, or to the Atticized literary monuments? By and large it may be said that *the language of the NT authors is nearer to the simple popular language*, as found—apart from the LXX and primitive Christian literature—in the non-literary papyri and perhaps Epictetus, than to the refined literary language. But there are differences which are quite noteworthy: the author of Rev writes in the most colloquial style and Luke in the most painstaking,[2] especially in the prologues of the Gospel and Acts and in the speeches of Paul, as does the author of Hebrews; Paul exhibits a good, sometimes even elegant, style of vulgar Greek. However, almost nothing of proper classical education appears in these authors, although Clement of Rome soon afterward reveals an entirely different character with his γυναῖκες Δαναΐδες καὶ Δίρκαι (1 Clem 6.2)[3] and his tale of the Phoenix (1 Clem 25). Yet many a good classical form and construction and many a word from the cultured literary language (often beside corresponding vulgar expressions), indicate that Paul and Luke and the author of Hebrews must have had some kind of grammatical and rhetorical education.[4] See also §126(3).

---

by R. Knopf in his commentary *in loc.* (Tübingen, 1920). Δαναΐδες καὶ Δίρκαι is supported by the Coptic version: W. L. Lorimer, JTS 42 (1941) 70. Cf. also ἀέναοί τε πηγαί 1 Clem 20.10. The letter to Diognetus and the Martyrdom of Polycarp are also written in a rather elevated literary Koine.
[4] In Paul's speech before Agrippa (A 26) cf. the true superlative κατὰ τὴν ἀκριβεστάτην αἵρεσιν (26: 5) and Att. ἴσασι (26: 4; otherwise οἴδασιν, e.g. Lk 23: 34). The style of Paul displays many affinities with the popular preaching of the Stoics and Cynics; thus μὴ γένοιτο, τί οὖν, τί ὄφελος; cf. in addition to the book of Bultmann, J. Weiss, Die Aufgaben der nt. Wissenschaft in der Gegenwart (Göttingen, 1908) 11ff.; P. Wendland, Die hellenistisch-römische Kultur² (Tübingen, 1912) 357 n. 1. On the Areopagus speech

For the language of the individual NT authors see the Subject Index under their names. Ed. Schweizer, 'Eine hebraisierende Sonderquelle des Lukas?', ThZ 6 (1950) 161–85. For summary and literature, s. Rob. 116–37; Bonaccorsi xcvi–clxvii; M.-H. 18–34.

The question as to the extent the MSS transmit the original orthography is still little clarified. For cod. D cf. G. Rudberg, Ntlicher Text und Nomina sacra (Skrifter K. Hum. Vet.-Samf. i Uppsala xvii 3, Uppsala and Leipzig, 1915). For the early period of textual history one has rather to reckon with (unintentional) vulgarization, especially with itacistic errors (§§ 22 ff.). Individual MSS and recensions, however, were also subject to Atticistic influences (Michaelis, ZNW 22 [1923] 121; the LXX recension of Lucian is also Atticistic): the Chester Beatty papyri of the NT strive after better Greek (M. J. Lagrange, RB 43 [1934] 22, 169 ff.; G. Kümmel, ThR 10 [1938] 299); 𝔓⁴⁷ especially attempts to smooth the rough language of Rev (Lagrange, op. cit. 491 f.; Kümmel, op. cit. 301). The most extensive MS of the Shepherd of Hermas (cod. Athous) also Atticizes; the older, more vulgar form is to be found in cod. Sinaiticus and PMich (ii AD; s. Bonner).

4. Non-Greek elements.
A vulgar idiom is normally more susceptible to foreign influences; consequently loanwords in the NT, too, are an index of its relation to the popular language.

In this connection the question of *Semitisms* is uppermost (s. *infra* for literature). This is not the place to go into this vexed question in detail; the following brief considerations may suffice.[1]

(1) Many expressions which a Greek would not have used were bound to creep into a faithful written translation of a Semitic original. Such *translation Semitisms* include (a) those universally recognized for the LXX and accordingly those in quotations in the NT; (b) those to be expected in the NT books which probably rest on an Aramaic original (parts of the Synoptics and Rev).[2]

(2) Frequent hearing and reading of the OT in the Greek translation influenced the language of the Jews ('*Septuagintisms*', '*biblicisms*') in two ways: (a) the language of the LXX appeared to be very appropriate to a solemn and dignified style; the two hymns in Lk 1: 46–55 and 68–79, both couched entirely in the style of the OT, afford the best examples of this; also such instances as καὶ ἰδού (Johannessohn [s. §442(7)], especially KZ 67, 49) and οὐαί (transcription of אוֹי, הוֹי; LXX; prophetic style; at the same time, however, also a Latinism = vae, thus e.g. in Epictetus, cf. §190(2)) belong here; (b) all terms which were connected with Judaism were drawn from the LXX and some of these were certainly widely used in religious texts and speech,[3] e.g. αἰῶνες and οὐρανοί (§141(1)).

(3) Finally, there was certainly a *spoken Jewish-Greek* in the sense that even his *secular* speech betrayed the Semitic mind of the Jew, and such Semitisms are to be expected in the Jewish-Christian authors of the NT.[4]

Yet the distribution of Semitisms into the above categories and the decision for or against a Semitism in a specific instance often create difficulties.[5]

---

s. Norden, especially pp. 55, 333 ff.; on the prologue to the Gospel of Lk, *ibid.* 316.1. On Atticisms in the NT s. W. Michaelis, ZNW 22 (1923) 91–121, Björck, Die periphr. Konstruktionen 123; on the Atticism of 2 P s. M.-H. 5 f.

[1] Such Semitic loanwords as βύσσος, κύμινον, μνᾶ, χιτών and the like do not come under consideration, for some have long since been naturalized and some at least belong to the whole contemporary language.
[2] Often the cod. Cantabrigiensis (D) alone has an Aramaizing variant in the Synoptics (original? Wellhausen, Einl.² *passim*). Lk has eliminated many a Markan Aramaism. A. J. Wensinck, 'The Semitisms of Codex Bezae and their Relation to the non-Western Text of the Gospel of Saint Luke', Bull. of the Bezan Club 12 (Leiden, 1937); Un groupe d'aramaïsmes dans le texte grec des Évangiles (Mededeel. Akad. Amsterdam, Letterkunde 81 A 9). Black, Aramaic Approach, chap. viii, app. c and *passim*. Contrast Haenchen¹² 47–50 (earlier ZThK 51 [1954] 153–67).—P. Kahle, 'Das zur Zeit Jesu in Palästina gesprochene Aramäisch', ThR 17 (1949) 201–16 [acc. to more recent discoveries]: p. 212: *Rabbuni* found for the first time in a Palestinian targum on the Pentateuch; also in the Samaritan targum; cf. Black, Aramaic Approach 21. Thack. 36 ff. and Katz, ThLZ 1957, 113 f. also note errors in trans-

lation due to Semitic words which are phonetically reminiscent, e.g. ἵλεώς σοι (s. §128(5)).
[3] When a clergyman in Switzerland today gives religious instruction in dialect, he borrows his religious terms from the literary German of the Bible and liturgy (as is true of English-speaking clergy!).
[4] E.g. ἀνέβη ἐπὶ τὴν καρδίαν αὐτοῦ A 7: 23 (the speech of Stephen!) 'The thought came to him', cf. 1 C 2: 9 (inserted in a quotation from the LXX!), also Lk 24: 38; Herm several times; LXX; Is 65: 16 (cf. 17 with ἐπελθεῖν); Jer 3: 16, 51: 21; 4 Km 12: 4 v.l.; also θάνατος 'pestilence' (Rev) according to Knopf-Lietzmann-Weinel, Einf. in das NT³ (1930) 17. Norden, Die antike Kunstprosa³, ii Nachtr. 3, also favors accepting a Jewish-Greek (against Thumb).
[5] E.g. σκάνδαλον מִכְשׁוֹל transferred to the moral realm (and σκανδαλίζειν derived from it) or πρόσωπον λαμβάνειν נָשָׂא פָנִים 'to show partiality or favoritism to somebody' (of which προσωπολήμπτης, -λημπτεῖν, -λημψία, ἀπροσωπολήμπτως are derivatives from the religious terminology of the LXX (Thack. 43 f.). Lk even makes the newly converted Philippian jailor speak 'biblical Greek' (A 16: 36); s. Foerster, TW ii 409.36 ff. Phrases like ἀρέσκειν ἐνώπιόν τινος (A 6: 5) instead of ἀ. τινί and πρὸ προσώπου τῆς εἰσόδου αὐτοῦ (A 13: 24) 'before his coming' are, on the other hand,

It is important, therefore, to guard against two opposing errors: not everything which conforms to Semitic idiom is a Semitism, nor is everything which appears somewhere or sometime in Greek genuine Greek. In numerous instances a phenomenon not unheard of in Greek, but yet unusual, has become a living expression and has replaced the customary idiom because it coincided with Semitic usage. This appears to be the case with instrumental ἐν = בְּ. In such instances one may speak of Semitism even though the author believed himself to be writing genuine Greek. The Semitic element has often supported the tendencies of the more popular levels of the language and abetted them in Jewish-Christian circles; the frequency of the periphrastic construction with ἐστίν, ἦν etc. with participle in place of the simple tenses is probably to be so understood. Here too, of course, the diversity of the cultural levels of the authors betrays itself. The less cultured an author is, the more the influence of Aramaic emerges; again Revelation and Hebrews are the two extremes.

On the problem of Semitisms in general s. Abel xxv–xxxiii; Sacco 64–119; M.-H. 411–85; Bonaccorsi lxix, lxxxi–xci; G. Rudberg, Teol. Stud. E. Stave (Uppsala, 1922) 184ff. (Nachmanson, Glotta 8 [1932] 551); Debrunner, GGA 1926, 137–43; Gnomon 4 (1928) 443f.; ThBl 1929, 237; IF 48 (1930) 100f.; 52 (1934) 253; Geistige Arbeit 3, 5 (1936) 6. On Aramaisms s. the account of the literature by Debrunner, Jahresb. Altertumsw. 240 (1933) 24f.; 261 (1938) 207f.; in addition R. H. Connolly, JTS 37 (1936) 374–85; W. C. van Unnik, Vox Theol. 7 (1936) 123–31; A. J. Wensinck, Mededeel. Akad. Amsterdam 81 A 5 (1936); J. de Zwaan, JBL 57 (1938) 155–71; Rob. 88–108. J. Munck, 'Les sémitismes dans le NT. Réflexions méthodologiques', Classica et Mediaevalia 6 (1944) 110–50. H. F. D. Sparks, 'The Semitisms of the Acts', JTS 1 (1950) 16–28 (cf. his earlier article, 'The Semitisms of St Luke's Gospel' 44 [1943] 129–38). Acc. to J. Schniewind, ThR 2 (1930) 147, the Semitizing sections in Lk are now attributed to Semitic sources. Ed. Schweizer, ThZ 5 (1949) 231:

Semitisms in Lk beyond the use of sources; perhaps even a Semitizing of his sources! See Moule 171–91 for summary and bibliography.

5. *Latinisms* are not so strongly represented in the NT as the Semitic element (s. *infra* for literature).

(1) In addition to a fairly numerous group of proper names, a number of expressions were *taken over directly* from Latin: (*a*) from military terminology: πραιτώριον, λεγιών, κεντυρίων, κουστωδία;[1] (*b*) from legal and administrative parlance: Καῖσαρ, κῆνσος, κολωνία, λιβερτῖνος, σικάριος, σπεκουλάτωρ, τίτλος (from vulgar Latin *titlus = titulus*), φραγέλλιον (Jn 2: 15; vulgar Latin *fragellum = flagellum*) and from the last φραγελλοῦν, for which Lk 23: 16, 22 has παιδεύσας;[2] (*c*) designations for measures: (λίτρα Jn 12: 3 = *libra*, a loanword of long standing), μόδιος, ξέστης (back-formation from *ξεστάριον which was felt to be a diminutive; Schwyzer I 269; according to Etymologicum Magnum 610.5b euphonic for *σέξτης [unattested; ξτ is foreign to Greek]), μίλιον Mt 5: 41 formed as a singular to μίλια (= *milia*), and for coinage: ἀσσάριον, δηνάριον (frequent, even Lk; δραχμή only Lk 15: 8 twice), κοδράντης = *assarius, denarius, quadrans*; (*d*) expressions from business and commercial life: λέντιον (= *linteum*), σιμικίνθιον (= *semicinctium*), σουδάριον, ῥεδῶν gen. plur. Rev 18: 13 (= *rēdārum*),[3] εὐρ-ακύλων (= *eur-aquilo*), χῶρος 'north-west (wind)' = *caurus* or *cōrus* (also *chaurus* and *chōrus*, cf. Thes. ling. Lat. III 658), μεμβράνη. For οὐαί s. §4. Many of these loanwords are shown to be in general usage by their frequent appearance elsewhere in every type of Hellenistic literature; some like μόδιος, ξέστης, σουδάριον, κουστωδία, μίλιον, δηνάριον, μεμβράνη, τίτλος, φραγέλλιον, are shown by their MGr descendants[4] to be words belonging to the common language.[5] The fact that Lk is inclined to remove Latinisms is a further indirect proof of their popularity; thus he replaces κεντυρίων of Mk (15: 39) with ἑκατοντάρχης (23: 47; also Mt 27: 54), κῆνσος

---

expressions from spoken Jewish-Greek. Formal and tautological expressions like ἀποκριθεὶς εἶπεν, ἐξῆλθεν καὶ ἀπῆλθεν in the Synoptics are probably translation Aramaisms (Wellhausen, Einl.[2] 14f.). For further examples of Semitisms, s. Index.

[1] περπερεύεσθαι etc. from Latin *perperam* etc. (Walde-Hofmann[3] II 291; περπ. from military language *miles gloriosus*)? There are no derivatives in Latin and the meaning is not identical. Cf. TW VI 92.26ff.

[2] γερμανε Ph 4: 3 FG gloss on γνήσιε.

[3] Lat. *reda* is in turn a loanword from Celtic. Ῥαίδια BGU III 815.18 [ii AD; it is questionable whether it =

'carriage'], ἐπὶ ῥαιδίου (v.l. ῥεδίου) Acta S. Marinae 17.11 Usener, ῥαῖδα Edict. Diocl. 15.33. S. also §41(1).

[4] G. Meyer, Ngr. Studien III (Wien. Sitzb. 132 [1895]); M. Triantaphyllidis, Die Lehnwörter der mittelgriech. Vulgärlit. (Strassburg, 1909); Buturas 65f.

[5] Some also because they have gone over into other languages: ἀσσάριον, δηνάριον, κεντυρίων, κῆνσος, κοδράντης, κολωνία, λεγιών, λέντιον, μίλιον, ξέστης, πραιτώριον, σικάριος, σουδάριον, σπεκουλάτωρ, φραγέλλιον have penetrated Palestinian Aramaic from Koine (Dalman 182–7 and Aram.-neuhb. Wb. [Frankfurt a. M., 1901]). German *Zins* is *census*. Latinisms in Hermas: Bardenhewer I (1902) 564.

Mt 22: 17 = Mk 12: 14 (ἐπικεφάλαιον D in Mk) with φόρος (20: 22), μόδιος Mt 5: 15 = Mk 4: 21 with σκεῦος (8: 16, but μόδιος in the doublet in 11: 33, where, however, 𝔓⁴⁵L and several minusc. omit οὐδὲ ὑπὸ τὸν μόδιον), κοδράντης Mt 5: 26 with λεπτόν (12: 59); cf. also ἐπιγραφή Lk 23: 38 against τίτλος Jn 19: 19, 20.[1] Latin *macellum* is probably original to Latin, although it has been proposed that it is a loanword from μάκελλον which in turn had a Semitic origin (s. J. Schneider, TW IV 373f.; Walde-Hofmann[1] II 1f.); according to Bauer s.v. it is attested in an inscription from Epidaurus *c.* 400 BC in the sense of 'enclosure, grating', therefore a loanword in Latin which re-entered Hellenistic Greek with the Latin meaning. Φαιλόνης (φαινόλης) may also be a Latin loanword (*paenula*; cf. §§25; 32(2); Bauer s.v. [Buck, Dictionary 417, holds that the Latin word is derived from Greek]; M.-H. 106). Θρίαμβος 'hymn to, or procession for, Dionysus and epithet of Dionysus' went over from Etruscan into Latin as *triump(h)us*, and from there θρίαμβος took over the meaning 'triumph' and formed the derivative θριαμβεύειν = *triumphare* (C 2: 15, cf. 2 C 2: 14); cf. Delling, TW III 159f.

(2) Certain *Latin suffixes* also became current in Greek and were added to Greek words. This is limited in the NT to proper names, especially ethnic names: πλοῖον Ἀλεξανδρῖνον[2] A 27: 6, 28: 11 (but Ἀλεξανδρεύς 6: 9, 18: 24), Ἡρῳδ-ιανοί (Mt, Mk), Χριστ-ιανός[3] (Acts, 1 P), Φιλιππ-ήσιοι[4] (Ph).

(3) Also to be reckoned among Latinisms are *translations* of Latin terms and phrases: (*a*)[5] Official terminology of the chancellery, above all for offices:[6] ἀνθύπατος *proconsul* (Acts) and ἀνθυπατεύειν (v.l. A 18: 12), ἡγεμών *procurator* (Pilatus, Felix, Festus) and *legatus Augusti* (Mt 10: 18 par., 1 P 2: 14) and ἡγεμονεύειν (Lk 2: 2, 3: 1), στρατηγοί *duoviri coloniae* (A 16), ἐπίτροπος *procurator* (Lk 8: 3, -εύειν v.l. Lk 3: 1), ἔπαρχος *praefectus* (1 Clem 37.3), ἐπαρχεία and ἡ ἐπάρχειος (§23) *provincia*, ῥαβδοῦχος *lictor* (A 16: 35, 38); χιλίαρχος *tribunus militum*, ἑκατόνταρχος (and -άρχης) *centurio*, σπεῖρα *manipulus* (Debrunner, IF 48 [1930] 244), *cohors*; ἀπογραφή *census* (Lk 2: 2, A 5: 37), προστάτις *patrona* (R 16: 2), συμβούλιον *consilium* 'decision' (result of consultation) and 'council' (as a body) (s. *infra* (*b*) and Mommsen, Hermes 20 [1885] 287); ὁ Σεβαστός *Augustus* (A 25: 21, 25, but Καίσαρος Αὐγούστου as a proper name Lk 2: 1), σπεῖρα Σεβαστή *cohors Augusta* (A 27: 1), κύριος *dominus* (A 25: 26), κράτιστος (s. §60(2)) (*vir*) *egregius*,[7] ἡμέρα *dies* (*forensis*) 1 C 4: 3 (cf. Zorell 570). The following formations were strongly supported by Latin: διετία = *biennium* (A 24: 27; 28: 30; Thieme 26; Deissmann, NBS 86 [BS 258]; Wilke-Grimm 102), τριετία *triennium* (A 20: 31).[8] (*b*) Phraseological Latinisms are scarce and used mostly in connection with Roman authorities and the like. Clearly belonging here are δὸς ἐργασίαν[9] (Lk 12:

---

[1] In IPol 6.2 δεσέρτωρ, δεπόσιτα, ἄκκεπτα are found side by side, ἐξεμπλάριον three times in Ignatius' other letters (-άριον is a new sing. from the pl. -άρια = -*aria*; cf. §5(1) on μίλιον. In Hermas (who wrote in Rome!) συμψέλ(λ)ιον *subsellium* (pap. also, s. Bauer s.v.), κερβικάριον *cervical* Vis 3.1.4 (the same phenomenon: -*al* -*alia* was taken over into Greek as -άριον -άρια), στατίων *statio* Sim 5.1.1 and 2 (Hell. also elsewhere); Sim 1.1, 2 ἑτοιμάζειν = *comparare* 'to purchase' [so Lk 23: 56; 24: 1?], Vis 2.3.4 ἐάν σοι φανῇ = *si tibi videtur* (Chr. Mohrmann, Vig. Christ. 3 [1949] 75); στατίων = *statio* in the sense of *ieiunium* (*ibid.* 76). Hermas also λέντιον.

[2] Cf. κλάση Ἀλεξανδρίνη in pap. = *classis Alexandrina*; s. Preisigke III 212f., Wilcken, Gr. 379. Barytone by analogy with Ἀκραγαντῖνος, Ταραντῖνος.

[3] On -ᾱνός s. Hahn 263.9; cf. *Pompeiani, Caesariani* etc. -ιανοί is later much used for names of sects. R. A. Lipsius, Ursprung des Christennamens (Jena, 1873). Also cf. §24. E. Peterson, Schweizerische Rundschau 51 (Jan. 1952) 611–13: 'Christ*ians*' coined by the Romans as a counterpart to Herodians who were pro-Roman: partisans of Christ.

[4] Hellenization of -*ē(n)sēs* following ethnica in -ήσ(σ)ιος, which belong to names of cities in -ησσός; cf. also Ἰθακήσιος. Φιλιππεῖς is good Greek; also Φιλιππηνοί (Steph. Byz.) with the 'Asia Minor' termi-

nation -ηνός (cf. Dittenberger, Hermes 41 [1906] 102 for the treatment of foreign ethnica). Philippians was perhaps written in Rome.

[5] David Magie, De Romanorum iuris publici sacrique vocabulis sollemnibus in Graecum sermonem conversis (Leipzig, 1905).

[6] On the one hand, good Greek official terminology (often from lower Italy or Macedonia) was used with precision for analogous Roman offices, e.g. χιλίαρχος, σπεῖρα, ἡγεμών; on the other hand, the terms are sometimes literally translated, e.g. Σεβαστός.

[7] Several of these like χιλίαρχος and σπεῖρα also passed over into Aramaic.

[8] Τριετία and τετραετία Theophr., τετραετία in an Att. inscrip. of 335 BC (also once in Roman times, Meisterhans 158), πενταετία inscrip. *c.* 300 BC (Schlageter, Wortschatz 71), ἑπταετία Philo, Her. 294, Jos., Ant. 1.302, δεκαετία Arist., Ath. 3.1, πενταετία and εἰκοσαετία Wilcken, Gr. 223.3, πολυετία Philo, Sob. 7 and elsewhere.

[9] Weizsäcker's translation 'give him his due' is impossible. Δὸς ἐργασίαν also Dit., Or. 441.109 (senatorial decree, 81 BC), POxy IV 742.11 (2 BC, letter to a certain Faustus), s. Viereck 83; Deissmann, LO⁴ 93 [LAE 116 n. 8]; Witkowski, Epistulae 128; ὡς δυναμένῳ σοι ἐργασίαν δῶναι 'since I am able to render a service to you' PGiess 11.16 (118 AD); ἐ. διδόναι in the letter of one Σατορνῖλος = *Saturninus* Class. Phil. 22 [1927] 250.7. Entirely different is [Hermogenes] *de inventione* 3.6.7 (not 3.5.7 as Deissmann cites) = Walz, Rhetores Graeci

58 = *da operam*, τὸ ἱκανὸν (§ 131) ποιεῖν[1] Mk 15: 15 (cf. Herm Sim 6.5.5) = *satisfacere*, λαβόντες τὸ ἱκανόν A 17: 9 = *cum satis accepissent*,[2] συμβούλιον λαμβάνειν (Mt five times, Mk σ. ποιεῖν twice) = *consilium capere*, ἄξιός ἐστιν ᾧ παρέξῃ τοῦτο Lk 7: 4 = *dignus est cui hoc praestes*, probably also τιθέναι τὰ γόνατα Mk 15: 19, Lk 22: 41, Acts four times (Herm Vis 1.1.3; 2.1.2; 3.1.5) = *genua ponere* (poetic Eur., Troades 1307), ῥαπίσμασιν αὐτὸν ἔλαβον Mk 14: 65 = *verberibus eum acceperunt* (§ 198(3)), συνεσταμένον (παρῃτημένον) ἔχειν (§ 157(3)), ἀγοραῖοι (scil. σύνοδοι or ἡμέραι) ἄγονται A 19: 38 = *fora (conventūs) aguntur*,[3] κρατεῖν (*memoria*) *tenere* Mk 9: 10, αἰτία 'relationship, case' = *causa* Mt 19: 10 (minusc. Mk 5: 33?) and ὅμοιός τινος (§ 182(4)). However, ἐκ (τοῦ) μέσου αἴρειν 1 C 5: 2, C 2: 14 (= *de medio tollere*; yet ἐκ μέσου ἐξελθεῖν, ἁρπάσαι, γίνεσθαι also appear in the NT) and the passive in ἐκέλευσεν αὐτὸν ἀχθῆναι (= *duci eum iussit*, § 392(4)) and the like may just as well be good Greek. For Latinisms in cod. D s. Nestle[24], p. 67*.

For Latinisms in the NT (and elsewhere in Koine) and especially for Latinisms in Mk as (alleged) evidence for a Latin original, s. the report of Debrunner, Jahresb. Altertumsw. 240, 18ff.; 261, 205f.; in addition, Hahn, esp. 257–66; Wohlenberg, Markus 24f.; Witkowski, Bericht 57; Raderm.[2] 15–17; Abel xxxiii–xxxvi; C. H. Turner, JTS 29 (1928) 346–61; Zilliacus, Familienbriefe 35f.

6. The few assured *loanwards from other languages* may be mentioned in a supplementary

fashion: τὰ βάϊα Jn 12: 13 (Test Naphth 5: 4; Thumb, Hell. 114; Bauer s.v.; Katz, ThLZ 1954, 240f.; 1957, 112) stems from Coptic, ἀγγαρεύειν (Mt, Mk), γάζα (in γαζοφυλάκιον Mk, Lk, Jn) and παράδεισος (Lk, 2 C, Rev; LXX also, Hebr. פַּרְדֵּס) come from Persian (Mayser I[1] 42f.).

Τὸ βάϊον is a Grecizing of Coptic *bāi* 'palm-leaf', as is ἡ βάϊς. This is a case of heteroclisis, but it is not necessary to assume with Schwyzer I 582 that it is due to the acc. βάϊν misunderstood as βάϊον. The correct accents are found in Field's Hexapla (ἄλλος Lev 23: 40), Schwyzer I 154, 209, 582, and L.-S.; the acc. βάϊν requires them (Katz, ThLZ 1936, 284), as does the late Jewish loanword באגון (Schwyzer I 209). The accents βαΐα, βαΐς are mistaken; also in the pap., see Mayser I[2] 2, 31f. who overlooks the fact that βάϊς has the same inflection as the other Egyptian loanword ἶβις, which differs both from the Ionic which retains -ι- throughout and from πόλις with its gen. plur. πόλεων; Preisigke; Bauer. Βαΐων Symm. SSol 7: 8(9) can be derived from βάϊς or from βάϊον. In 1 Macc 13: 51 βαΐων belongs to βάϊς; cf. 13: 37 τὴν βάϊν[ην] ἥν (dittography). Hell. ἀγγαρεύειν -εία Mayser I[2] 3, 139; Preisigke; Bauer s.v. Hell. γάζα (A 8: 27) and γαζοφυλάκιον Bauer.

7. To sum up contemporary opinion regarding the language of the NT, the definition which Székely[4] gives of the LXX '*Dialectus vulgaris melior hebraizans*' applies also on the whole to the NT, provided that '*hebraizans*' is understood as 'Semitizing here and there, sometimes more, sometimes less'.

III 121.6; 123.19 = H. Rabe, Rhetores Graeci VI 150.11 (chap. 6 is missing here), where ἐργασία is a technical term in rhetoric.
[1] Also Polyb. 32.7.13; Appian, Hist. Rom. 8.74 (1.260.4 Mendelssohn); Diog. L. 4.50; BGU IV 1141 several times (13 BC, letter of a freedman); POxy II 293.10 (28 AD); Mitteis, Chr. 377.5f. (Constitutio Antonina, 212 AD); Diodor., Exc. Vatic. (3.97.9 Din-

dorf). Further, Preisigke s.v. ἱκανός 1; ποιήσει τὸ ἱκανόν in the letter of Jesus to Abgar (in an inscrip.; SAB 1914, 825). S. Bauer s.v. ἱκανός.
[2] Cf. Dit., Or. 484.50 (Roman), 629.100 (136/7 AD).
[3] Jos., Ant. 14.10.21(245) ἄγοντι τὴν ἀγοραῖον, Strabo 13.4.12 p. 629 τὰς ἀγοραίους ποιοῦνται, Ephemeris Epigraphica VII p. 436.10 (Apamea, ii AD) ἡ ἀγοραῖος ἤχθη.
[4] In Hermeneutica biblica generalis. Freiburg i. Br. 1902 (according to Psichari 174).

PART I

PHONOLOGY

1. ON ORTHOGRAPHY

(1) VOWELS

8. The diphthong υι was limited from earliest times to the one case where another vowel follows, and even here it became ῡ in Attic from v BC on. Nevertheless in Hellenistic, probably because of learned restoration and the influence of dialects other than Attic, it reappeared, even frequently being written υει (i.e. ü-i) in papyri and inscriptions, while, on the other hand, the inflection -υῖα, -υίης (§43(1)) seems to presuppose the quiescence of the ι.

The NT uncials have υι throughout. The diphthongal character is occasionally emphasized by such orthography as ὕϊος (cod. A and 𝔓⁴⁶ sporadically), προβεβηκυῖα (Lk 1: 18 D), εληλυθειαν (Mk 9: 1 W) and word division like υ/ιον (thus sometimes the first scribe of B). Ps.-Herodian in Cramer, Anec. Ox. III 251.21 objects to trisyllabic μυῖα, υἱός.—Schwyzer I 199f.; Crönert 123–5; Lademann 37ff.

9. υ diphthongs. Ηυ (§67(1)) has the diaeresis as a rule in some MSS (SA). The spelling εου for ευ appears rarely in χαλκεούς 2 T 4: 14 D (also inscriptions and papyri: Crönert 128f.; Schwyzer I 197. Εου for ευ also N. Müller, Die Inschr. der jüd. Katakombe am Monteverde zu Rom [hsg. von N. A. Bees, Leipzig, 1919] no. 98.2).

(2) CONSONANTS

10. Z for σ. Only a few examples are found in NT MSS of the spelling ζβ, ζμ for σβ, σμ (mostly at the beginning of a word), widespread in the Hellenistic period, by means of which the soft (voiced) s-sound was supposed to be indicated.

Thus Ζμύρνα Rev 1: 11 and 2: 8 S, lat in part; but ζμύρνα is less well attested, e.g. Mt 2: 11 D; σζμ, also attested elsewhere, in σζμύρνης Jn 19: 39 S (ζμ- WD^supp); ζβεννύναι 1 Th 5: 19 B*D*FG, Mt 12: 20 D, 25: 8 D; ἄζβεστον Mk 9: 43 N.— Mayser I¹ 204; Buturas 21; Rüsch 205f.; Lademann

56f.; Meuwese 19; Gromska 18f.; Schwyzer, RhM 81 (1932) 196.1 (Syr. *zm* for σμ). Ζμ, ζβ were rejected by the grammarians, but only gradually disappeared from iv AD onwards (C. Wendel, Pauly-Wissowa 18 I [1942] 1455).

11. Gemination. Uncertainty often prevailed in the Roman period regarding the doubling of consonants. (1) The old Greek rule that the origin of an 'aspirated' ρ arising from σρ or Ϝρ, when it was moved from an initial to an inner position (through inflection or composition), was indicated by doubling was no longer observed without exception even in Attic orthography. Later the effort was obviously made to do away with special treatment of initial ρ in orthography; the pronunciation had probably approached that of mediate ρ so that the reduplication ρε-ρ- could be tolerated (§68). The doubling cannot be carried out in the NT without doing strong violence to the oldest MSS.; only the older rule, however, provides a definite norm. (2) Only scattered instances of the single spelling of the other liquids appear in the NT.

(1) The NT MSS, like the pap., keep ρρ in obscure compounds and traditional words: ἄρρωστος, ἔρρωσο, ἄρρητος, χείμαρρους, ἐρρέθη. Elsewhere there is vacillation: ἄραφος Jn 19: 23, ἐπιράπτει Mk 2: 21, ἀπορίψαντας A 27: 43, etc.; s. Gregory 121, v. Soden 1365. For Att. ρρ and ρ s. Meisterhans 95. Syriac still transcribes ῥ as *rh: rhwm'* Ῥώμη; cf. Agnes Smith Lewis, Studia Sinaitica no. IX, p. 𝔑; further Schwyzer I 155, 212. On παρησία in inscrip., MSS (NT also) and pap. for παρρησία (from παν-ρ-) s. Crönert 79, Helb. 15.

(2) λλ–λ: metrically well-founded βαλλάντιον (difficult to explain!) prevails in the MSS against βαλάντιον (Helb. 15f.). 𝔓⁴⁶ often has αλ for ἀλλ'. The gemination in ἐννενήκοντα and ἔννατος (Mayser I¹ 214) is not original; it derives from its model ἐννέα. Γέννημα only of living beings (from γεννᾶν); however, the MSS predominantly, the pap. exclusively (Deissmann, BS 105f., NBS 12 [BS 109f.,

184]; Mayser ɪ¹ 214), employ γένημα (from γενη- in γενήσομαι etc.) of vegetative products; Phryn. 286 censures the use of γεννήματα (he means γενήματα) for καρποί as un-Attic. The doubling in πλήμμυρα and its cognates is an inveterate mistake found in MSS of many authors from Homer on, due to the false etymology πλην + μύρομαι, influenced by πλημμελής, -εια, -έω which are true compounds. In Lk 6: 48 DW al. have the correct -μ-. M.-H. 101 considers this a literary correction, but the correct form does not appear among the Atticists' precepts any more than e.g. ἑόρακα. The noun πλήμυρα is a retrograde formation from the verb πλημύρομαι and as such is possible only on the basis of a simple verb, and not of a compound; cf. Debrunner §§ 24, 224 (Katz, ThLZ 1956, 604; 1958, 315). On χύννω and κτέννω s. § 73.

(3) WORD DIVISION

12. Word division was generally not customary in writing in the period of the rise of the NT and for a long time thereafter, although the grammarians often debated what was ἐν μέρος τοῦ λόγου and what was not, on account of the use of diacritical marks. There is no word division in the oldest extant MSS; it remains imperfectly developed even in late MSS (to xv AD). As the dispute among grammarians shows, word-unity in Greek as in all languages is not something which is obvious in all instances. Words originally separated gradually amalgamated without the moment of transition being recognized. Certainly some external criteria for the subsequent inner coalescence have been established: (1) when the constituent elements can no longer be separated by another word; (2) when a new accent is created; (3) when a new meaning for the whole arises. These criteria are, however, by no means universally applicable nor without exception, and many doubtful instances remain; e.g. τοῦτ᾽ ἔστιν 'that is' is almost a formula in the NT so that one may write τουτέστι(ν), although τοῦτο δέ ἐστιν appears once (R 1: 12).

(1) Ὅταν δέ, not ὅτε δ᾽ ἄν, but ὃς δ᾽ ἄν. Τὸ δ᾽ αὐτό, τῷ γὰρ αὐτῷ NT also, but ὡσαύτως δέ (also pap.; Mayser ɪ² 2, 67), while Homer, Hdt. and the Attic authors (and even Philodemus, Rh. 2.97 Sudhaus) write ὣς δ᾽ αὔτως. The following are accordingly one word: ὅστις, καίπερ, τοίνυν, μέντοι, οὐδέ, οὔτε, οὐδέποτε, οὔπω, μήτι, μήτιγε, ὡσεί, ὥσπερ, ὡσπερεί. Att. still divides ὅστις, οὐδέποτε, οὔπω, even οὐδείς in instances like οὐδ᾽ ὑφ᾽ ἑνός, where the NT has only ὑπ᾽ οὐδενός.

(2) Ἐπέκεινα, ὑπερέκεινα from ἐπ᾽ (ὑπέρ) ἐκεῖνα, οὐδείς from οὐδ᾽ εἷς, ἔκπαλαι from ἐκ πάλαι.

(3) Παραχρῆμα is no longer = παρὰ χρῆμα, καθόλου no longer = καθ᾽ ὅλου; ἐξαυτῆς (very frequent in pap.; Preisigke s.v.) for ἐξ αὐτῆς τῆς ὥρας (αὐτῆς ὥρας BGU ɪɪ 615.6 [ii AD]) or for ἐξ αὐτῆς τῆς ὁδοῦ (Wackernagel, Homer 41.4); ἱνατί from ἵνα τί γένηται. Ἐξαυτῆς as early as Cratinus, Frag. 34 (1.22 Kock), Aeneas Tact. 22.29 (conjecture); perhaps an Ionicism (E. Fraenkel, Baltoslavica [Göttingen, 1921] 28.1).—For combinations like ἀναμέσον, κατιδίαν, ὡσαύτως s. M. Reil, ByzZ 19 (1910) 479f., 501f., 507f. 𝔓⁴⁶ divides at the end of the line του/τεστιν, ου/κεστιν, ου/κανηγγελη, ου/κακυροι; Sanders 19.— Prepositions before adverbs may be written separately if the combination is still analogous to that of prepositions with their case, otherwise together, especially if the combination corresponds to a compound verb or adj. Therefore perhaps ἀπὸ πέρυσι, ἐφ᾽ ἅπαξ (like ἐπὶ τρίς), but ἐπάνω, ὑποκάτω, ἐπαύριον ('tomorrow'), ἀπέναντι, παρεκτός, παραυτίκα, ὑπερλίαν, ὑπερ(εκ)περισσῶς (cf. ὑπέρογκος, ὑπερπερισσεύειν and the like; in ὑπερεκπερισσοῦ E 3: 20, 1 Th 3: 10, 5: 13 [v.l. -ῶς], ἐκπερισσοῦ is already a *single* concept and is kept together moreover by ὑπέρ); however, there is still sufficient latitude for the preference of the editor. Moreover, the decision between εἴπως and εἴ πως and the like is purely a matter of taste. Ἀπ᾽ ἄρτι 'from now on' is in at least some places to be taken as ἀπαρτί (Ion., popular Att.) 'exactly, certainly' (A. Fridrichsen in a letter); e.g. Rev. 14: 13 (where the traditional connection of ἀπ᾽ ἄρτι with the preceding ἀποθνήσκοντες is mistaken) ἀπαρτὶ λέγει τὸ πνεῦμα 𝔓⁴⁷S* (the other MSS add the gloss ναί before or after λέγει); cf. τὸ πνεῦμα ῥητῶς λέγει 1 T 4: 1. A comparison of the equivocal απαρτι of Mt 26: 29, 64 with its Synoptic and Johannine parallels leads to far-reaching conclusions about a source common to Mt and Jn 13: 19, 1: 52: ἀπαρτί = ἀμήν 'definitely' (Debrunner, Con. Neot. 15 [1947] 45–9).—On καθεῖς or καθ᾽ εἷς s. § 305.

(4) ACCENT

13. The system of symbols to help in reading aloud (accents, breathings, etc.) was developed by the Alexandrian grammarians and was first employed in older (dialectal) poetic texts. It was applied systematically to prose texts for the first time in the period of the minuscules. Euthalius had already employed these symbols in his edition of the NT and they are found in individual uncials from vii AD on (Gregory 99f.). In B they originate with a corrector of the x or xi century; the accent is found only once in 𝔓⁴⁶ (H 6: 16 πέρας; Sanders 19). For accent the norms given by the ancient grammarians are to be applied to the NT, except where, for Hellenistic Greek, there is authority for a deviation from Attic or where a difference in quantity from Attic requires another accent.

Some of these grammarians' norms have been traditionally neglected. The proparoxytone voc. ἄδελφε is inherited from Indo-European (as is Ζεῦ Λητοῖ compared with nom. Ζεύς Λητώ, Schwyzer I 547) and is rightly postulated by the grammarian Trypho (i BC) and is still alive in MGr ἄδερφε; it was rescued from oblivion first by K. W. Krüger's Grammar (1842ff.) and is slow in being introduced even into modern classical editions. Wackernagel, Kl. Schr. 756–64; Katz, ThLZ 1958, 316. It should be restored in Acts 9: 17, 21: 20; GP 2: 5. Herodian 1.150 expressly distinguishes between the biblical word ὁ, ἡ φάρμακος 'poisoner, sorcerer, magician' Ex 7: 11 (masc.), Mal 3: 5 (fem.), Oracula Sibyllina 3.225 (masc.), Jos., Ant. 9.118 (fem.), and ὁ φαρμακός 'scapegoat', classical from Hipponax onward (L.-S. s.v.; Katz, ThLZ 1958, 316). Therefore φαρμάκοις Rev 21: 8, φάρμακοι Rev 22: 15. According to Herodian ἰχθῦς, -ῦν, ὀσφῦς, -ῦν (but ἰσχύς) are universal, not merely Attic, and should accordingly be received into our editions of the NT. On the other hand, Herodian 1.140 is mistaken in postulating the regular φαγός. Paroxytone φάγος takes its accent from original compounds such as ὠμοφάγος (Schwyzer I 459). Paroxytone διέτης etc. is designated as especially Attic (Herodian 2.687.11 Lentz), hence NT διετής, τεσσαρακονταετής, ἑκατονταετής. Furthermore μῶρος is a special Att. accent instead of μωρός, ἄχρειος instead of ἀχρεῖος, ἱμᾶντος instead of ἱμάντος, χιλιαδῶν instead of χιλιάδων, ἰδέ λαβέ instead of ἴδε λάβε (s. §101 under ὁρᾶν). Ἐρῆμος, ἑτοῖμος, ὁμοῖος are distinctly ancient and also foreign to Koine; one would have concluded from Herodian's words (2.938.23, 26 Lentz) that ἔρημος and ἔτοιμος were special late Att. forms; however MGr also accents ἔρημος (romance ermo etc., Meyer-Lübke, Rom. etym. Wb.³ no. 2891), ἔτοιμος, ὁμοιος in contrast to ἀχρεῖος. Ἀγοραῖος or ἀγόραιος (s. M.-H. 57)? Hell. κρίμα (like θέμα, πόμα § 109(3); earlier κρεῖμα Aeschyl., Supp. 397 [not κρῖμα]), thus also κλίμα (only since Arist.; NT only plur.); cf. Wackernagel, Homer 76.1. Otherwise χρίσμα (like the LXX and usually late pap.; Crönert 228.3), cf. χρεισμα 1 Jn 2: 20, 27 in B*, and χριστός. Μίγμα Jn 19: 39 is doubtful (possibly μεῖγμα; μῖγμα is impossible); ψύχος probably also NT, not ψῦχος (but ψῦγήσομαι §76(1)), although πνῖγος, ῥῖγος instead of πνῖγος, ῥῖγος are attested as popular (Lob. Phryn. 107).—Herodian advocates the general shortening of ι and υ before ξ, from which arise Φῆλιξ, κῆρυξ, κηρύξαι (cf. Gregory 101); we have no reason at all to extend this to ι and υ before ψ, thus θλῖψις (B θλειψις). Ῥῖψαν Lk 4: 35 (B ρειψαν) from ῥίπτειν is certain, while κύπτειν is not established and therefore neither is κύψαι (ἀνα- Lk

13: 11, παρα- 1 P 1: 12). Κράζειν has ᾱ, thus κρᾶζον A 21: 36 (v.l.), G 4: 6. Τρίβειν ἔτριψα (B with ει before ψ, διέτρειβεν Jn 11: 54 𝔓⁴⁵ADΘ), also συντετρῖφθαι Mk 5: 4 (-ει- B). In the case of σπίλος 'spot' the quantity of ι is unattested; cod. B gives only indirect evidence for ῐ since it has σπίλος (also 𝔓⁴⁶ E 5: 27) ἄσπιλος σπιλοῦν everywhere. Γαζοφυλάκιον, not -εῖον, is found throughout in B and also has the support of analogies like σιτομέτριον (§111(4)); cf. ἀργυρωματο-, ρισκο-, σκευο-φυλάκιον in pap. from the middle of iii BC. However, εἰδώλιον 1 C 8: 10 (§111(5)), though better attested in the NT (SAB etc.) than -εῖον, is itacistic. At times it is difficult to decide between competing spellings even when they involve difference of accent. Thus Katz favors τελωνεῖον 'customs office' (thus spelled in Suidas), since in Strabo and others there is a different τελώνιον 'customs duty'. Γαζοφυλάκιον etc. may be different because they are compounds. Some inconsistency, which is not due to itacism, as in ἐπαρχεία but συναρχία, must be frankly accepted (Katz, ThLZ 1957, 111). On the whole cf. M.-H. 51–60.

(5) BREATHING

14. The same principle must be followed in determining breathing as in the case of accent, yet with concessions to the MSS in the use of voiceless stops or aspirates with elided vowels and with οὐκ οὐχ. Rough breathing made some further gains in Hellenistic, for which the MSS of the NT are also among the witnesses. Some of these to be sure (e.g. D in the Gospels and Acts) are generally unreliable with reference to voiceless stops and aspirates and never agree on non-Attic smooth breathing or on non-Attic rough breathing. But in the case of ἐλπίς, ἰδεῖν, ἴδιος, ὀλίγος, ἐφιορκεῖν, alone, where aspiration in the NT is frequent and strongly attested, aspiration is supported by other MS tradition, by inscriptions and papyri (seldom pre-Christian [Crönert 148–53; Helb. 25f.; Hauser 60]). The basis of the phenomenon in any case is to be sought in analogies (Schwyzer I 305): ἀφιδεῖν following ἀφορᾶν, καθ᾽ ἰδίαν following καθ᾽ ἑαυτόν, οὐχ ὀλίγος following οὐχ ἥττων, οὐχ ἥκιστα; ἐφιορκεῖν has arisen from ἐπιορκεῖν (ibid. 219). There is, on the other hand, no recognizable rationale for the infrequent omission of aspiration before vowels which were aspirated in Attic; they are, therefore, to be ascribed to scribal errors which point to Ionic-MGr psilosis (de-aspiration).

The use of *spiritus asper* in the MSS originally served to distinguish between synonyms: 𝔓⁴⁵ has it occasionally, especially with the article and rel.

pron. (Kenyon II p. ix), and αὐτοῖς A 5: 35; 𝔓⁴⁶ twelve times with εἶς and rel. pron. (Sanders 19); W in the Gospels has it eighty times, always correctly (Sanders, Wash. 18).—'Ελπ-: e.g. ἐφ' ἐλπίδι in 𝔓⁴⁶ R 8: 20, 1 C 9: 10 (twice erroneously ἐφ' ἐλπίζει), ἀφελπίζοντες Lk: 6: 35 DP. 'Ιδεῖν: e.g. 𝔓⁴⁶ ἀφίδω Ph 2: 23, οὐχ εἶδον G 1: 19, S οὐχ ἰδού A 2: 7, in addition οὐχ ὄψεσθε Lk 17: 22 AW, οὐχ ὄψεται (-τε) Jn 3: 36 DW, αὐθόπται Lk 1: 2 W. Καθ' ἰδίαν: e.g. G 2: 2 𝔓⁴⁶, Mt 24: 3 SB*, Mk 4: 34 B*DWΔ. Οὐχ ὀλίγος: in 𝔓⁴⁵ A 17: 12, in S 12: 18, 14: 28, 19: 23, 24; οὐκ ὀλ. without v.l. only 15: 2. Hell. often καθ' ἔτος, καθ' ἐνιαυτόν, ἐφ' ἔτος (LXX, pap. ἐφέτειος instead of ἐπέτειος [Katz]; MGr ἐφέτο(ς) 'this year') following καθ' ἡμέραν etc.; but NT only καθ' ἔτος Lk 2: 41 only in W and καθ' ἐνιαυτόν H 9: 25, 10: 1, 3 only in 𝔓⁴⁶. 'Εφιορκεῖν: -κήσεις Mt 5: 33 S, ἐφιόρκοις 1 T 1: 10 D*P. —Isolated scribal errors: οὐχ 'Ιουδαϊκῶς G 2: 14 S*ACP, οὐχ ἠγάπησαν Rev 12: 11 A, καθείδωλον A 17: 16 M, καθηχ- twice G 6: 6 𝔓⁴⁶, and the reverse οὐκ εὖρον (D several times), οὐκ εὑρίσκω Lk 13: 7 𝔓⁴⁵ (cf. B in LXX: Thack. 129), οὐκ ἕνεκεν 2 C 7: 12 SCDE, οὐκ ὁ Lk 11: 40 𝔓⁴⁵, 1 C 7: 12 𝔓⁴⁶, κατ ις (= καθ' εἶς) R 12: 5 𝔓⁴⁶. However Jn 8: 44 provides especially strong attestation for οὐκ ἕστηκεν (SB*DLWX al.); it has taken over the smooth breathing of the aorist ἔστην ἔστησα like the not infrequent ἀπέστηκα etc. in the pap. and inscrip. (Crönert 146; Mayser I¹ 203; cf. Thack. 127f.), s. also §97(1).—On the whole s. Gregory 90–2; v. Soden 1363; M.-H. 98ff.; Rob. 221–6.

(6) OTHER DIACRITICAL MARKS

15. The *diaeresis*, which was commonly used since early times to designate an initial vowel of a word or syllable, especially ι and υ, is necessary or helpful when ι or υ could be combined with a preceding vowel into a diphthong and when the accent does not preclude misinterpretation: 'Αχαΐα, 'Αχαϊκός, 'Εβραϊστί, Πτολεμαΐς. S. §37.

For ϊ and ϋ in the Chester Beatty Papyri s. Kenyon II p. ix; III p. xii; Sanders 19. The 'hypodiastole', e.g. τό, τε to distinguish it from τότε, is superfluous as in the case of ὅ, τι, where it is in part still common; writing ὅ τι serves just as well. Cf. M-H. 50.

(7) PUNCTUATION AND COLOMETRY

16. It is certain that the authors of the NT could have used punctuation just as other people did at that time, not only in MSS, but sometimes also in letters and documents. However, whether the NT books were punctuated no one knows, and it is unknown, moreover, where and how they were punctuated, since no authentic traditions have been handed down. Modern editors are compelled to provide their own punctuation and hence often their own interpretation. The latter is very definitely the case, e.g. when a mark of interrogation occurs (found in MSS in ix AD at the earliest). It is probably most correct to adhere to modern habits of punctuation without being economical in their use and with due consideration for the peculiarities of Greek sentence-structure (circumstantial participle, etc.).

The earliest MSS of the NT, 𝔓⁴⁵, 𝔓⁴⁶ (not 𝔓⁴⁷), 𝔓⁶⁶, S and B, have already received some punctuation by the first hand (Kenyon II p. ix; III p. xii; III Suppl. p. xiv; Sanders 16f.; Gregory 345, 358; Tischendorf, NT Vat. xixff.). In B, among other marks, the point above the line (στιγμή) is used for a full stop, the lower point (ὑποστιγμή: e.g. AYTON.) for pauses after thoughts which are as yet incomplete. A very practical device for reading is the arrangement of the text in sense-lines (στίχοι) with a break for each rather obvious unit of thought which requires a pause in reading. It is met from iv AD onwards, although not often carried through perfectly, e.g. in D of the Gospels and Acts, D of the Pauline corpus, but consistently used in the Chester Beatty Papyrus of Sirach (iv AD end); it is used particularly by Euthalius (vii AD according to v. Soden 643; v AD according to earlier opinion) in his edition of the NT. See Gregory 113–15 (Norden 360ff. favors a colometric edition of the NT). For more recent work on colometry in the NT s. Debrunner, Jahresb. Altertumsw. 236 (1932) 208ff., also §487; James A. Kleist, The Gospel of Saint Mark presented in Greek Thought-Units and Sense-Lines, With a Commentary (Milwaukee, 1936). Improvement of the sense by alteration of the accepted punctuation: Ch. Bruston, Rev. Ét. gr. 38 (1925) 16–28.—On the whole cf. Rob 241–5; M.-H. 46ff.

2. PHONETICS IN COMPOSITION

(1) ELISION

17. In line with the scribal tendency of the period towards greater isolation of individual words, there is little to note regarding elimination of hiatus by elision or crasis in the NT MSS. From this it is by no means to be concluded that there was a similar disposition in the spoken language. Rather, it is clearly evident from the agreement in practice of other MSS and inscriptions of not designating elision which was required by metre (χρηστὰ ὁμιλίαι instead of χρήσθ' ὁμ. in the verse from Menander 1 C 15: 33), that the spoken language was more elided than the written (on τετραάρχης and the like s. §124). The NT MSS never indicate elision in nominal and verbal forms, seldom in pronouns, frequently in the most common particles, customarily in prepositions in current formulae and with following pronouns. Proper names following prepositions were preferably kept independent and more readily identifiable by *scriptio plena* of the preposition. In all of these practices the NT MSS follow the prevailing custom (Mayser 1¹ 155–8; Helb. 12f.; Thack. 136f.).

Elision in pronouns: only τοῦτ' ἔστιν or τουτέστιν (§12), therefore a fixed formula; τοῦτ' εἰπών Jn 20: 22 in the POxy. In particles: ἀλλά, acc. to Gregory 93f., is elided in 215 instances among 345 where a vowel follows (it should be remembered along with these statistics that the standard MSS are not always in agreement); preference for elision is greater before articles, pronouns and particles than before nouns and verbs because an accumulation of unaccented short words requires more rapid pronunciation. Δέ: often δ' ἄν, otherwise seldom δ' (Ph 2: 18 δ' αὐτό ACDE al., δὲ αὐτό 𝔓⁴⁶SBP). Οὐδ' ἄν H 8: 4, οὐδ' οὐ Mt 24: 21, H 13: 5, οὐδ' οὕτως 1 C 14: 21 (οὐδ' ὡς 𝔓⁴⁶), οὐδ' ὅτι R 9: 7 (οὐθ' ὅτι 𝔓⁴⁶); οὐδ' ἵνα H 9: 25, but οὐδέ 𝔓⁴⁶C, still more variation in οὐδ' εἰ A 19: 2, οὐδ' ἡ H 9: 18; otherwise οὐδέ. Τε, οὔτε, μήτε, ἅμα, ἄρα, ἄρα etc. are not elided.—Prepositions in formulae and with pronouns: ἀπ' ἄρτι, ἀπ' ἀρχῆς, ἀπ' αὐτοῦ, ἀπ' ἐμοῦ, δι' αὐτῆς, δι' οὗ, ἐπ' αὐτῷ, κατ' ἐμέ, κατ' ἰδίαν, κατ' οἶκον, μετ' ἐμοῦ, παρ' ὧν, ὑφ' ἡμῶν, ὑφ' ὑμῶν, ὑπ' οὐδενός (1 C 2: 15). Ἀντί is elided only in the stereotyped ἀνθ' ὧν (§208(1)). Elision is most frequent with διά in order to avoid three successive vowels, e.g. δι' ὑπομονῆς R 8: 25, δι' ἐσόπτρου 1 C 13: 12; but with proper names this is not always followed, e.g. διὰ Ἰησοῦ R 16: 27, διὰ Ἠσαίου Mt 8: 17 (before Ἀβραάμ H 7: 9 the MSS are divided

between διά and δι'). On διά cf. Zimmer, ZWTh 24 (1881) 487. 𝔓⁴⁶ also has ἵν' ἔχῃ E 4: 28, ὁποῖοί ποτ' ἦσαν G 2: 6.—On the whole, v. Soden 1377–80; for the *symbol* for elision in 𝔓⁴⁶, Sanders 19. Cf. also Rob. 206ff.; M.-H. 61ff.

(2) CRASIS

18. Crasis is still more limited in the NT, entering into only a few combinations with the article and καί which have become fixed; it is the same with the papyri etc., s. Mayser 1¹ 158–60.

Article: τοὐναντίον (adverbial, one word, therefore τοὐναντίον δέ); τοὔνομα 'by name' Mt 27: 57 (D τὸ ὄνομα); κατὰ ταὐτά (γάρ) Lk 6: 23, 26; 17: 30, but even in this formula not without strong evidence for τὰ αὐτά. A 15: 27 D ταυτα for τὰ αὐτά as τοῦτο sometimes for τὸ αὐτό. 1 Th 2: 14 A ταυτα (with coronis, i.e. an apostrophe over the contracted syllable), Ph 3: 1 S*FGP ταυτα, 1 P 5: 9 all MSS τὰ αὐτά. With conjunction τὰ γὰρ αὐτά, τὸ δὲ αὐτό. **Καί:** κἄν 'if only' is fixed (MGr κἄν 'at least'), fairly often κἄν 'even if' (e.g. Mt 21: 21 [D καὶ...ἐάν], 26: 35, Jn 8: 14 [yet in 16 only S has κἄν]), but for καὶ ἐάν 'and if' κἄν appears only sporadically ([Mk] 16: 18; Lk 13: 9 [D καὶ ἐάν], 6: 34 D, Ja 5: 15; καὶ ἐάν all MSS Mt 5: 47, 10: 13 etc.). In most places the overwhelming testimony is for κἀγώ, κἀμοί, κἀκεῖνος, κἀκεῖ(θεν). S. the statistics in Gregory 96f.; Zimmer, ZWTh 24 (1881) 482; v. Soden 1380f. Κἄλεγεν and the like need scarcely be considered; the single example of that type is κἀπεθύμει Lk 15: 16 D*.— **Προε-** never becomes προὐ-, hence προεχόμεθα, προέκοπτε, προέγραψα etc. (LXX has only the literary προυφάνησαν 4 Macc 4: 10 SA; Thack. 206 n. 3).—Cf. Rob. 208; M.-H. 63.

(3) ASSIMILATION AND NON-ASSIMILATION

19. Assimilation of a ν to a following consonant appears in the classical period not only in compounds but also between words, especially with ἐν, σύν and other monosyllabic proclitics. But the contrary tendency began to make itself felt at an early time *in writing* which avoided not only the assimilation of the final ν in words, but even set aside assimilation in composition for the sake of etymological perspicuity. An Attic inscription of 425 BC already has ἔνγραφοι (Meisterhans 1¹ 111). Even ἐκ was assimilated at one time to ἐγ before voiced stops and liquids and to ἐχ before aspirates;

here, however, non-assimilation has been more radically carried out and has asserted itself as the norm for compounds also. In the widespread spelling of ἔπενψεν, ἐνγύς, ἐγρανμάτευεν, etc. ν is probably simply a general sign for a nasal (ἐνγύς appears as early as an Attic inscription of *c.* 600 BC; Meisterhans 113). The NT MSS fit in by and large with this development: (1) only traces of the assimilation of ν between words are found with ἐν and σύν; (2) non-assimilation of ἐν and σύν in composition is frequent, more so with σύν than with ἐν; (3) ἐγ- for ἐκ- before voiced consonants is more frequent in 𝔓⁴⁶ alone; (4) πένψω and the like is extremely rare.

(1) Ἐγ γαστρί Lk 21: 23 A (A also often in LXX, Thack. 131), ἐγ Κανᾶ Jn 2: 11 AF; ἐμ μέσῳ several times as v.l. (never SBD), ἐμ πραΰτητι Ja 1: 21 S, ἐμ πολέμῳ H 11: 34 𝔓¹³. Σὺμ Μαριάμ Lk 2: 5 AE al., σὺμ πᾶσι(ν) 24: 21 EGW al., A 16: 32 𝔓⁴⁵.

(2) Outside of σύν and ἐν, only παλινγενεσία Mt 19: 28 and T 3: 5 as a good variant. Also the ν of σύν, which acc. to phonetic law is supposed to disappear before ʒ and σ, is for the most part restored before ʒ (συνʒητεῖν, σύνʒυγε), and often before σ. LXX συμ- before labials, but συν- before gutturals (Thack. 132f.); NT similarly (Westcott-Hort, App. 149). On the tendency not to assimilate in general s. §§ 17 and 124.

(3) Only ἐγλογή 𝔓⁴⁶ R 9: 11, 11: 5, 7, 28 (without example to the contrary), ἐγλεκτόν 𝔓⁴⁶ R 16: 13, ἐγλελυμένοι H 12: 3 𝔓¹³𝔓⁴⁶D*, ἐγλύου 5 𝔓¹³𝔓⁴⁶, ἐγλέλησθε 5 𝔓⁴⁶, ἀνέγλιπτος Lk 12: 33 D, ἔγδικος R 13: 4 𝔓⁴⁶AB, ἀπεγδύσει C 2: 11 B*, ἔγβασιν H 13: 7 𝔓⁴⁶. Cf. Lat. *egloga* = ἐκλογή, MGr γλυτώνω 'save' from ἐκλυτ-. Thus also ἔγγονα 1 T 5: 4 D* for ἔκγονα (cf. Rüsch 270f.; pronunciation probably *eggonos*, s. Blass, Aussprache des Griech.³ 123 [Lk 3: 25 Ναγγαι = Naggai]; but MGr ἔγγονος ἐγγόνι 'grandchild' with nasal; s. W. Schulze, KZ 33 [1895] 376 = Kl. Schr. 288f.).

(4) 𝔓⁴⁵ ἐνγίʒει Lk 12: 33, 𝔓⁴⁶ ἐνγύς E 2: 13, 17, Ph 4: 5, H 8: 13. Otherwise only cod. D Clarom. πένψω 13 times, ἔλανψεν 2 C 4: 6, μεμιανμένοις T 1: 15, etc.; cf. Rudberg 17 for cod. D.—On the whole, cf. Mayser ɪ¹ 224–36; Gregory 73–8; Rob. 215ff.; M.-H. 104f.; C. Wendel, Pauly-Wissowa. 18 ɪ (1942) 1455.

(4) MOVABLE FINAL CONSONANTS

20. Movable ν (mistakenly called ν ἐφελκυστικόν) appears in Ionic-Attic inscriptions of the classical period without definite rule (the other dialects use it first under the influence of Koine). Its particular place, however, is the pause, i.e. the

end of a sentence or clause. Moreover, from the v BC on the tendency to employ ν to avoid hiatus, and therefore to comply with the modern rule which stems from the Byzantine period, betrays itself in an increasing degree. It is very popular in the Hellenistic language, but e.g. in the papyri of the Ptolemaic period (Mayser ɪ¹ 236–40) it is *omitted* often before vowels and *appears* still more often before consonants. In MGr, dialectal forms like ἔδεσεν, ἤκουενε (= ἔδησεν, ἤκουεν; Thumb² §214(4)) perhaps contain traces of the old movable ν. On the whole question cf. finally Schwyzer ɪ 405f. The standard MSS of the NT almost always employ it, whether a consonant or vowel follows, or the word stands at the end of a sentence.

It is omitted here and there (never, however, before a vowel and in pause) following ε (e.g. Lk 1: 3 ἔδοξε SBCD al., -εν AEKSΛ) and with ἐστί, somewhat more often after the -σι of the 3rd pl. (the witnesses favor e.g. χαλῶσι Mk 2: 4, ἔχουσι Lk 16: 29, τιμῶσι Jn 5: 23 twice), most frequently by comparison after the -σι of the dat. plur.; for more examples s. Westcott-Hort, App. 146ff.; Gregory 97–9. On cod. W. s. Sanders, Wash. 25. The LXX is like the NT (Thack. 134f.).—For 'twenty' the NT has only εἴκοσι (12 times); εἴκοσιν οὖσιν Homil Clem 10.26.4. Εἴκοσιν is also extremely infrequent elsewhere: in pap. only once (305 AD; Mayser ɪ¹ 239f.), seldom in inscrip. (Sommer, Festschr. z. 49. Vers. d. Philol. [Basel, 1907] 19f.; Lademann 82). Likewise only πέρυσι 2 C 8: 10, 9: 2 (D*FG πέρου, Dᵇ πέρισυ), Herm Vis 2.1.1 twice (once πέρσι S*, the second time πέρυσιν A), but 2.1.3 πέρυσιν A (πρότερον S). Πέρυσι is found in pap. beg. iii BC (Mayser ɪ¹ 239, 240; Preisigke s.v.), πέρυσιν Schol. Aristoph. Thesm. 1060. Lex. rhet. in Reitzenstein Ind. lect. Rostock 1892/3 p. 6: πέρυσιν οἱ Ἀττικοὶ μετὰ τοῦ ν̄, φωνήεντος ἐπιφερομένου. Πέρου Supp. Epigr. ɪv 707.6 (Cyzicus; Roman period), POxy x 1299.8 (iv AD; Kapsomenakis 64). Cf. Herm Vis 3.10.3 περσυνῆ S, περισυνῆ A for περυσινῆ. Περσυνός and περισυνός for περυσινός s. Dieterich 37; Crönert, Zeitschrift f. d. Gymnasialwesen 52 (1898) 580; Schwyzer, Glotta 5 (1914) 196; L.-S.; Preisigke; Kapsomenakis 64f. n. 2 (where also πέρισυ and πέρυσυ from late pap.). MGr πέρσι περσινός.—Always ν with -θεν, ἕνεκεν, πάλιν as in the pap. of the Ptolemaic period (Mayser ɪ¹ 240–2).—v. Soden 1381; Rob. 219ff.; M.-H. 113.

21. Movable σ. The σ with οὕτως is fixed for the most part in the NT, before consonants as before vowels. Ἄχρι and μέχρι are mostly without σ as in Attic, even before vowels; the most frequent exception is μέχρις (ἄχρις) οὗ as in the LXX and Aristeas. Always -κις, never -κι (ἑπτάκις, πολλάκις, ὁσάκις etc.); likewise only χωρίς. Εὐθύς (usually εὐθέως; v. Soden 1391) as adverb, never εὐθύ. Once ἀντικρύς (or ἄντικρυς?).

Οὕτω is more strongly attested only in A 23: 11 (before σε), Ph 3: 17 (before π-), H 12: 21 (before φ-), Rev 16: 18 (before μ-); H 6: 15 𝔓⁴⁶ (before μ-). Μέχρις οὗ Mk 13: 30 (S -ρι, D ἕως), G 4: 19, ἄχρις οὗ G 3: 19, H 3: 13 (-ρι M); a greater vacillation be-

tween ἄχρις (μέχρις) οὗ and the form without σ, e.g. 1 C 11: 26, 15: 25. Ἀντικρὺς Χίου A 20: 15 (-υ B³HP etc. Atticistic correction) 'opposite Chios' like Hell. for Att. καταντικρύ (ἄντικρυς in Att. 'direct'); ApocP 21, 26 (κατ-)ἀντικρὺς ἐκείνου, αὐτῶν, 29 καταντικρὺ τούτων.—On the whole cf. Mayser I¹ 242ff.; Rüsch 273f.; Lademann 86f.; Hauser 74; Brockmeier 7f.; Bauer s.vv.; Preisigke s.vv. Also Rob. 221; M.-H. 112f.

3. MAJOR VOWEL CHANGES

(1) INTRODUCTION

22. MGr exhibits, as is well known, radical differences in the pronunciation of vowels compared with ancient Greek: ι, ει, η (ῃ), οι, υ (υι) are all pronounced like *i* ('itacism'), αι like ε; the quantitative distinction between ο and ω, α and ᾱ etc. has disappeared, as well as iota-subscript. The beginning of these phenomena goes back to the period of the old dialects (as early as v BC Boeotian inscriptions show ι for ει, in iii BC υ for οι; regarding ι = ει in an Argolic inscription of v BC and a similar thing in Corinth s. Kretschmer, Glotta 4 [1913] 319f.; Schwyzer I 192); the process was largely completed in the Hellenistic period. The learned grammarians labored zealously, of course, for the preservation of the historical spelling, corresponding to the general trend of the period which sought to revive the old classical language. In spite of ever increasing difficulties, they succeeded in giving an appearance of life to the old orthography for which they —above all Herodian of Alexandria (under Marcus Aurelius)—constructed countless artificial rules according to the best of their knowledge. They made their influence felt in the schools —as even today in Greece. For the first two post-Christian centuries, the following come under consideration: the change of ει to ῑ (η to ῑ), αι to ε, α η ω to ᾱ η ω and the leveling of quantity; the interchange of οι and υ (Meisterhans 58f.; Mayser I¹ 110f.; Thack. 93f.) e.g. in 𝔓⁴⁵ ἀνυγή-σεται Lk 11: 9, 10 (ἀνυγ- in pap. as early as ii BC), μεμψίμυροι Jd 16 SAL; further Sanders, Wash. 20.—A. H. Forster, The Pronunciation of Greek in NT Times (ATR 5 [1922] 108–15). Cf. Rob. 177–81; M.-H. 64–5, 93–7.

(2) ει–ῑ (ῐ)

23. The phonetic leveling of ει and ῑ betrays itself by the *rather frequent* confusion in usage in

the early Hellenistic period, in Attic inscriptions from ii BC end, in Egyptian papyri from iii BC mid.; the confusion of ει and ῑ is much less frequent. Cf. Mayser I¹ 87ff.; Rüsch 66ff., 93ff.; Lademann 31ff.; Hauser 31f., 35f. The possibility is accordingly precluded that even Lk and Paul employed the correct historical spelling of ι and ει; how they actually wrote is unknown to us. Our earliest MSS treated the scholastic regulations much more freely than the later, i.e. they frequently wrote phonetically ι instead of ει or (like Vaticanus and the great Hermas papyrus [Bonner 20]) ει for ῑ to distinguish it from ι (thus especially in ii AD, cf. Lademann 32f.; Hauser 32). Consequently, the only possible procedure for an editor of the NT is, of course, to carry through Attic spelling without any regard to the MSS.

The following peculiarities are worthy of mention: Θυάτιρα (not -τειρα); οἰκτίρω not -είρω (accordingly also οἰκτίρμων οἰκτιρμός despite the fact that B almost always has ει). On the other hand, (μειγνύναι) ἔμειξα etc. (μεῖγμα § 13); (τίνειν) τείσω; φιλόνικος -κία (from νίκη, but with νεῖκος in mind [pronounced *nīkos*]; § 51(1)); πανοικεί, παμπληθεί, but Ἑλληνιστί Λυκαονιστί etc. (§ 122). Δανίζειν with -ι- instead of Att. -ει- is strongly attested, likewise δανιστής Lk 7: 41 (Gregory 87). The future δανιῶ (also in Philo) and δανιοῦμαι in the LXX (Helb. 87) could derive from -ίζω only (Wackernagel, ThLZ 1908, 637) and the metrical measurement δανίσας is additional proof for its existence. There are two explanations: either transition from -ει- to -ι- by itacism (Wackernagel, *loc. cit.* and Debrunner in the earlier editions of this grammar) or the explanation which Debrunner communicated by letter to Katz (ThLZ 1936, 281f.), according to which δανείζω as derived from δάνειον and δανίζω as derived from δάνος existed side by side. Complete analogies from Homer onward are found in Debrunner § 258 and IF 40 (1922) 107. Katz, ThLZ 1957, 111 prefers the latter. The distinction is difficult between -εια (with adj. in -ής) and -ία (with other adj.) because both formation types are already partially crossed in Att.

as is proved by poetry and the inscrip. (κακοπαθία Meisterhans 53); thus κακοπαθία (Ja 5: 10 B*P) besides -πάθεια, ὠφελία besides ὠφέλεια (R 3: 1, Jd 16), αὐθαδία (Ap. Frs.) are attested for Att. -είᾱ is certain if it belongs to -εύειν; thus λογεία 'collection' 1 C 16: 1, 2 (codd. -ία, only 2 𝔓⁴⁶B λογειαι) from λογεύειν (both in pap., cf. Mayser I² 3, 7f., 139, also Thieme 16f.; Deissmann, LO⁴ 83ff. [LAE 104ff.], στρατείας 2 C 10: 4 (𝔓⁴⁶B?) from στρατεύειν, μεθοδεία (E 4: 14 B^cCD^cE al., 6: 11 B³D^cP al.; -ία also 𝔓⁴⁶ 6: 11, 12) from Hell. μεθοδεύειν, φαρμακεία (Rev 9: 21 S, 18: 23 B, G 5: 20 FG) from class. φαρμακεύειν. Ἐπαρχεία (A 25: 1 B*, al. -ία, S*A ἐπαρχ(ε)ίῳ; 23: 34 -είας and -ίας) is shown to be the correct form by the inscrip.; cf. Magie 59 (-εία and ἡ -ειος). For (ὀφθαλμο-) δουλία cf. §115(1); ἐθελοθρησκία §118(2); εἰδωλολατρία §119(2); εἰλικρίνεια §119(4); -ιον and -εῖον §13; αει = αϊ §41(1); ει in Semitic words §38. Acc. to Herodian ἀναίδεια (from ἀναιδής; or ἀναιδεία from ἀναιδεύεσθαι?), ἀναιδία fluctuate and thus Lk 11: 8 ἀναιδίαν SCDLΔ, al. -ειαν as Sir 25: 22 ἀναίδεια. Ἡ ἐπαρχεία is a remodeling of ἡ ἐπάρχειος (scil. χώρα) following ὑπατεία and the like. On δοκίμιον, δοκιμεῖον s. M.-H. 78; Grundmann, TW II 259. -ει- is proved to be correct not only in τὸ δοκιμεῖον 'means of testing' Ja 1: 3, but also in the substantivized adj. τὸ δοκιμεῖον 'genuineness' by P. Chantraine, La formation des noms en Grec (1933) 53: the suffix -εῖος expresses a higher degree of the quality expressed by the simple adjective; he compares μεγαλεῖος and καθάρειος (accent?). This is accepted by L.-S. and Katz, ThLZ 1958, 314f.; cf. §263(2). Further on -εια and -ια v. Soden 1372. On the fluctuation of spelling in territorial names in -ία like Φρυγία and city names like Ἀντιόχεια, Φιλαδέλφεια (but φιλαδελφία), s. v. Soden 1370 and for Σαμάρεια §38. Εἰδέα is incorrect Mt 28: 3 (weaker v.l. ἰδέα), Lk 9: 29 D (al. εἶδος), Herm Sim 6.1.6 and 2.5 in PMich, LXX (Helb. 9) for ἰδέα. 2 P 2: 4 σιροῖς S (σειροῖς ABC) 'to pits' or σειραῖς KL 'with ropes'?

(3) η–ῑ (ει)

24. H was leveled to ι later than ει (Blass, Aussprache³ 37); sporadic examples of the confusion appear first in Attic inscriptions (Meisterhans 19) from 150 AD on; in the Ptolemaic papyri Mayser (I¹ 82–5) finds no entirely certain example. The NT MSS are therefore almost entirely free of this interchange.

A parallel form to ἦ μήν (not itacism) is εἶ μήν (H 6: 14 𝔓⁴⁶SABD*), which appears also in the LXX (Thack. 83) and beg. 112 BC in the pap. (Mayser I¹ 78; II 3, 146f.); on εἶ μάν in dialectal inscr. (first time IG IV 840.15, Argolis, c. iii BC end) s. Hermann 312. Γυμνιτεύομεν 1 C 4: 11 (with η 𝔓⁴⁶L) is probably correct (γυμνίτης formed after ὁπλίτης along with

γυμνήτης is conceivable). The distinction between κάμηλος 'camel' and κάμιλος 'rope' on account of Mt 19: 24 pars. (s. Suidas s.v., Schol. Aristoph. Vespae 1035) is a later artificial rationalization (dissenting, Boisacq, Dict. étym. p. 403.1 and Bröndal, s. BPhW 1918, 1081f.); s. Bauer; Michel, TW III 598 n. 5. The spelling Χρηστιανός in S* (A 11: 26; 26: 28; 1 P 4: 16) depends on an interpretation of the name Χριστός based on the similarly sounding χρηστός, which was also frequently used as a proper name; cf. Blass, Hermes 30 (1895) 465ff.; v. Harnack, SAB 1915, 762; A. Jacoby, Byz.-neugr. Jahrb. 1 (1920) 148ff. (Indog. Jahrb. 9, 106); H. Fuchs, Vig. Christ. 4 (1950) 71 n. 7, 74 n. 13. Unexplained ἀναπείρους Lk 14: 13, 21 ABDW al., -πιρ- S for class. -πηρ-; cf. LXX (Thack. 83), ἀναπειρία Arist., Rh. 2.8.1386a 11 cod. A^c; also [Phryn.] in Bekker, Anec. Gr. I 9.22 attacks ἀναπειρία with ει as barbarous; Radermacher, Wien. Sitzb. 224, 5 (1947) 23. Κειρία κηρία 'bandage' likewise fluctuates: Jn 11: 44 κειρίαις 𝔓⁴⁵SBW (κιρ-) al. (v.l. κηρ-); κειρία Aristoph., Aves 816, LXX Pr 7: 16; Plut., Alc. 16.1, κηρία medical papyri, ed. Kalbfleisch, Index lect. Rostock 1902 aest. p. 5 n. on col. II l. 24 (s. L.-S. s.v.), κιρία and ἡμικίριον in pap. iii BC (Preisigke s.vv.). M. Scheller, Die Oxytonierung der griech. Subst. auf -ιᾱ (Diss. Zürich, 1951) 57f.— Κυρήνιος = Quirinius s. §41(1). On cod. D s. Rudberg 13.

(4) αι–ε

25. The confusion of αι and ε began in ii BC according to the testimony of the papyri. The earliest MSS (not however D), though still far more correct here than in the case of ει–ι, cannot, however, serve as a standard in doubtful cases.

Thus, in spite of the tradition, κεραία, ἐξαίφνης and the like are to be so spelled, but also φαιλόνην (Greek, s. §32) 2 T 4: 13 (-ε- all uncials except L) due to paenula; conversely συκομορέαν Lk 19: 4 (AE*F al. -αίαν), s. §45. Ἀνάγαιον Mk 14: 15, Lk 22: 12 with αι entirely preponderates; s. §44(1). Κταίνειν = κτένειν s. §73. P. Chantraine, The Link, no. 1 (June 1938) 7–10 seeks pre-Hellenistic traces of ε for αι; cf. Debrunner, IF 48 (1941) 188.

(5) IMPROPER DIPHTHONGS

26. The loss of the second element of improper diphthongs is attested in the Egyptian papyri, for ᾱι from ii BC, for ηι and ωι from iii BC on (Mayser I¹ 120, 123, 132f.). According to the statement of Strabo (14 p. 648: πολλοὶ γὰρ χωρὶς τοῦ ι γράφουσι τὰς δοτικὰς καὶ ἐκβάλλουσι δὲ τὸ ἔθος φυσικὴν αἰτίαν οὐκ ἔχον), many omitted the ι even in the dative where rules were easily given, and so it is omitted for the most part in the older NT MSS. The editor is to follow the Attic norm everywhere.

𝔓⁴⁵ usually writes ι after η and ω, but not after ᾱ (Kenyon II p. ix), 𝔓⁴⁶ and 𝔓⁴⁷ not at all; it does not appear in Pap. Egerton 2 ('The Unknown Gospel') at all (only examples of ω and η but not α).—The improper diphthong is to be written, in addition to the recognized cases, in μιμνήσκειν and θνήσκειν (from -η-ίσκειν), πανταχῇ πάντη, ἀθῷος ζῷον (compounds with ζωο- as the first element are to be distinguished: ζωο- [or ζω-] from ζωός [ζωή] 'living' [*lebendig*], e.g. ζωο-ποιεῖν; ζωο- from ζῷον 'living being' [*Lebewesen*], e.g. ζῳοτροφία. Cf. L.-S. 758–61; contrast Bauer 342). Πατρῷος ὑπερῷον ᾠόν, Τρῳάς Ἡρῴδης (from Ἡρω-ίδης), πρῷρα. Ἀντιπέρα εἰκῇ κρυφῇ λάθρα πεζῇ are instrumental in -ᾳ -η or dative in -ᾳ -η (Manetho 4.188 elides the α in καταντιπέρα). It is uncertain in the case of σῴζειν (from σω-ίζειν) to what extent the ι has been carried over from the present into the other tenses (formed on the stem σω-). Σέσῳσμαι is certain, yet σέσωται A 4: 9 SA (v.l. σέσωσται; σεσωσμένοι E 2: 5, 8 [8 only σεσωμένοι P]) and ἐσώθην; cf. Mayser I² 2, 154, 196. Ῥαθυμεῖν without ι is established (Wackernagel, Hell. 25; L.-S. s.v.) and likewise πρᾶος (Mayser I¹ 121; Debrunner, IF 40 [1922] Anzeiger 13f.); the NT however has only πραότης (as v.l. to πραΰτης); always πραΰς instead of πρᾶος; cf. Crönert 290.2; Thack. 180f.; Egli, Heterokl. 100–6: πράέως > πράαος, from which Att. πρᾶος). In the case of δώην γνώην (Opt.; §95(2)), πατρολῴαις μητρολῴαις 1 T 1: 9, in which ω appears for οι for the first time in Hellenistic Greek, it is doubtful whether an ι was ever present (§35(2)); it may be written for the sake of analogy.

27. η–ει. Before the change of ῃ to η and partially parallel with it, a change to ει took place (i.e. long, close *ē*), principally in Attic where it is attested from *c.* 400 BC on. Soon, however, -η reappeared where it was restorable by analogy, i.e. above all in augment, dative, subjunctive, and this new -η then became η according to § 26 (Meisterhans 39; Schweizer 64f.).

There have been preserved in the NT (as in Hell.) only isolated instances of κλείς κλείειν, λειτουργός -γία etc. (older Att. κλῇς κλῄειν λῃτ-) and βούλει (Lk 22: 42 from literary language [in folk language θέλεις, §101], but βούλῃ FGR al., βούλῃ Herm Sim 9.11.9, βούλει apparently in Vis 5.5; cf. Mayser I² 2, 90f.). NT as Hell. generally ἀποθνήσκω and λῃστής from -θνη-ίσκω λῃ-ιστής with restoration of the old formation; cf. Mayser I¹ 122. Att. also has θνείσκω λειστής with this change (Meisterhans 36f.; Lademann 13f.).

(6) LEVELING OF QUANTITATIVE DISTINCTIONS

28. There are only a few traces of the leveling of quantity in the NT. Of the interchange of ω and ο, which appeared the earliest (iii/ii BC, Mayser I¹ 97), the only examples worth mentioning are variants like ἐκφευξώμεθα H 2: 3 𝔓⁴⁶, καυθήσωμαι 1 C 13: 3 C, κερδηθήσωνται 1 P 3: 1 minusc., because they have furnished the occasion for the impossible acceptance of a future subjunctive (W.-S. §13, 7). S. also §373(2) and Bănescu 17; on ἔχομεν or ἔχωμεν R 5: 1 s. Lietzmann, Hdb. *in loc.*

4. OTHER SOUND CHANGES

(1) SIMPLE VOWELS

29. (1) α > ε before ρ. Τέσσερα τεσσεράκοντα are Hellenistic (MGr τέσσερις τέσσερα). Καθερίζειν rather often in MSS, but always καθαρός. (2) **Interchange of -ια- and -ιε-** (-υα- and -υε-). Χλιερός (Ionic) Rev 3: 16 only S. Φιάλη and ὕαλος ὑάλινος (but ὑελίνην Rev 15: 2 𝔓⁴⁷) like Attic; Ionic and, according to Phryn. 309, Hellenistic φιέλη and ὕελος, but MGr γυαλί = ὕαλος, ὕαλος LXX Job 28: 17, ὑάλινος PPetr III 42 H 7.3 (*c.* 250 BC). Μυελός H 4: 12 like Attic and LXX (yet μεμυαλωμένα Ps 65 [66]: 15); cf. Crönert 101. Doricisms in Koine include ἀμφιάζει Lk 12: 28 B for -έζει, ἠμφιασμένον Mt 11: 8 D for

-ιεσμ- (§73) and πιάζειν 'seize' (§§101 and 73). (3) ᾱ–η: μᾱρυκᾶσθαι Barn 10.11 from the LXX, s. Bauer; Björck, Alpha imp. 298f.; Katz, Philo's Bible 157–9. Doric ὁδᾱγός ὁδᾱγεῖν (occasionally Attic and Hellenistic) D Mt 15: 14, Lk 6: 39, B* A 8: 31; Νικᾱνορα A 6: 5, Μνᾱσωνι 21: 16 (proper names; cf. Mayser I¹ 7); cf. §2 and P. Chantraine, Études sur le vocabulaire grec (Paris, 1936) 88ff.; Björck, Alpha imp. 291–4. (4) **Interchange of ε and ο.** Ἀπελλῆς S* A 18: 24, 19: 1 for Ἀπολλῶς (D in the first instance Ἀπολλώνιος) like Doric Ἀπέλλων for Ἀπόλλων. (5) **Dissimilation of ι to ε** to avert contraction (§31(2)). Ἀλεεῖς (-*eîs* from *iîs*) is a good variant of ἁλιεύς (Mt 4: 18, 19, Mk 1: 16, 17, Lk 5: 2).

(6) **Prothetic vowels.** Ἐχθές (also predominant in Att. and Hell.), weaker v.l. χθές; LXX likewise, Thack. 97.

(1) Schwyzer I 255; Scherer 37f. Τέσσερα Jn 19: 23 SALM, Rev 4: 6 A, 4: 8 SA, etc., τεσσεράκοντα throughout acc. to the earliest witnesses ($\mathfrak{P}^{46}$ also; LXX likewise; pre-Christian pap. seldom τεσσερ-, Mayser I² 2, 74; L.-S. s.v. not common in pap. before ii AD, apart from Ion.). Always τέσσαρες, -άρων, -αρσι; acc. τέσσαρες, not τέσσερας, s. §46(2). Τεσσε- also Ion., but universally Hell. only before α (dissimilation; but cf. M.-H. 66f.). P. Kretschmer, Festschr. Wackernagel 194f., also refers to MGr dialectal σεράντα for σαράντα. Ἐκαθερίσθη Mt 8: 3 B*EL al., Mk 1: 42 AB*CG al. (all MSS have καθαρίσθητι καθαρίσαι etc. along with it); and -ερ- at times elsewhere, especially in A (Gregory 82). The LXX is quite like the NT (Thack. 74). Also cf. μυσερός 1 Clem. 14.1; 30.1 in A; LXX Lev 18: 23 ABF. Καθερίζω also Byz. and MGr (dialectal); Psaltes 2.—Cf. ρε > ρα in ἐραυν- (§30(4)) and δράπανον (Rev 14: 14–19 $\mathfrak{P}^{47}$ and in an epigram Berl. Klassikertexte 5(1) p. 77; δραπανίδες Hesychius).

(2) Schwyzer I 243f. LXX has only πιάζειν for 'to seize' (SSol 2: 15, Sir 23: 21 SB), 'to press' πιέζειν, seldom -πιάζειν (Judg 6: 38 AB, 1 Km 12: 3 A), s. Thack. 282. MGr πιάνω ἔπιασα; the corresponding Att. πιέζειν is retained in Lk 6: 38 πεπιεσμένον 'pressed down'. On ἀμφιάζειν K.-Bl. II 366; Schmid IV 600; Reinhold 39; Thack. 75; Psaltes 10f.; Pernot, Rev. Ét. gr. 44 (1931) 167ff.; Vett. Val. 266.16, 333.30; Dit., Or. 200.24 (iv AD). Πιάζειν and λῃστοπιαστής in pap., s. Preisigke II 305, III 131; Wünsch, Sethianische Verfluchungstafeln 49.58, 59; further Crönert 102.1; Psaltes 10f.

(3) D also has ὁδηγ- in other places. Cf. further Lob. Phryn. 429. Χορηγεῖν like Att. (here -ηγ- from στρατηγός etc.) and Ion.-Hell. Hell. διηνεκής (Heb 4 times) belongs to ἐνεγκεῖν, therefore primitive Greek ē; Att. διᾱνεκής (but Plato also διην-, Mayser I¹ 13) is an Attic hypercorrection (cf. Hauser 23.1) or a new interpretation in connection with διά. Πρηνής 'head first' A 1: 18 (since Arist.; Att. πρᾱνής) by analogy after ἀπ-ηνής and the like (Schwyzer I 189); some however accept another πρηνής for A 1: 18 'seized with an inflammatory swelling' (from πίμπρημι with primitive Greek ē); s. Bauer s.v. For Νυμφαν s. §125(1).

(4) Although Ἀπελλῆς and Ἀπολλῶς are etymologically related, two different persons seem to be involved since Ἀπολλῶς has been introduced into Acts from 1 C 1: 12 etc.; the scholia (Cramer, Catenae 309f.) also appear to regard the distinction between persons as possible.

(5) Schwyzer I 243. In LXX nearly always ἁλεεῖς (Meister, Zeitschrift f. österr. Gymn. 60 [1909] 19); ἁλεεῖς PFlor II 127.15 (256 AD), Pap. Soc. Arch. Ath. no. 35 (PhW 1940, 647, 648; besides ἁλιεύ(ε)ιν).

(6) On ὁμείρεσθαι and (ἐ)θέλειν s. §101.

(2) DIPHTHONGS

30. (1) **αι and α.** In Attic from v BC on α appears for αι before open vowels. From forms arising thus, ἀετός ἀεί (Ionic and older Attic αἰετός αἰεί) prevailed in Koine; on the other hand ἐλάα (because of ἔλαιον), κάειν κλάειν (because αι was preserved phonetically before ω and ο also in Attic) do not appear. (2) **ει > ε.** The Attic change of ει to ε before vowels has left few traces in Hellenistic. In the NT it is always δωρεά (as in the papyri etc.: Mayser I¹ 68; Arnim 19; Rouffiac 32; vulgar Attic according to Thumb, Hell. 207; Attic inscriptions until 402 BC only δωρειά), Ἀρεοπαγίτης, Αἰνέας (Mayser I¹ 67), πλεονάζειν πλεονέκτης etc., occasionally πλέον. (3) **Dialectal variation between ε and ει, ο and ου.** Hellenistic always ἔσω (Ionic also, formed after ἔξω; Attic εἴσω) and ἔσοπτρον (Doric? s. Fraenkel, IF 32, 134; Attic κάτοπτρον, cf. κατοπτριζόμενοι 2 C 3: 18), but εἰς. Εἵνεκεν besides ἕνεκεν (both are Ionic and Hellenistic). Διόσκουροι (Ionic) A 28: 11 (Attic -κορ- Phryn. 235) as occasionally in Hellenistic (Crönert 130; Schlageter 7; Rüsch 211f.; Hauser 29; but also Plato and Thuc., s. Lob. Phryn 235). (4) **Hellenistic change of ευ to αυ after ρ.** (ἐξ-)ἐραυνᾶν ἀνεξεραύνητος besides ἐρευνᾶν etc. (5) Always υἱός and -υῖα; s. §8.

(1) On ἐλαία cf. Schweizer 78, on κ(λ)α(ι)ειν Mayser I² 2, 119. Ἀχαΐα Ἀχαϊκός Πτολεμαΐς etc. (αϊ from αιι) are understandable.

(2) Ἠχρεώθησαν R 3: 12 OT (SAB*D*G; also LXX SA², cf. Thack. 82), otherwise ἀχρεῖος; τελεῶσαι H 10: 1 D^c (similarly in LXX etc., s. Thack. 82; Arnim 19; Schekira 132; Scherer 47), otherwise τέλειος τελειοῦν (Philo sporadically τελεώτερος besides a more general τελειο-); πλέον e.g. Lk 3: 13 (πλεῖον C), A 15: 28 (πλεῖον D), therefore literary language (cf. LXX, Thack. 81f.; Philo Byz., Arnim 18f.), but always πλείων πλείονος etc. Ἐπιρεάζειν Lk 6: 28, 1 P 3: 16 as in Att. and Hell. from Att.-Hell. ἐπήρεια IMag 1.3 (in nouns in -εια the ι is retained). Like Att. NT Ἀρεοπαγίτης—Ἄρειος πάγος. Θειότης —θεότης (R 1: 20, C 2: 9); cf. H. S. Nash, JBL 18 (1899) 1–34; Stauffer, TW III 120; Kleinknecht, TW III 123. As ει > ε, so οι > ο: χρόα 'color' Herm several times as in Plato et al. (χροία Aristoph., χροιή Homer et al.). Only στοά like Att. and Hell., but Aristoph. στοιά: Crönert 122; Rüsch 101; Hauser 38. Always ποιεῖν etc. (regularization; cf.

Scherer 48), never ποεῖν etc. except in ποισαι Lk 11: 42 S, ποισας Jn 5: 11 W (ιη = *ĭ ĭ* > *ī*, cf. §31(2)).

(3) Είνεκεν Lk 4: 18 OT (also LXX Is 61: 1), A 28: 20 S*A, 2 C 3: 10 (preponderating evidence including 𝔓⁴⁶). S. also §35(3).

(4) Ἐραυνᾶν not in D, always in 𝔓⁴⁶, for the most part in S and B*, in part in A and C, likewise LXX in SAB* (Helb. 7; Thack. 79) and Barn 4.1 in S, ἐραυ[νᾶτε] UGosp 1.7f., ἀνηραύνων Homil Clem 12.17.1. Ἐραυν- in pap. beg. 22 AD, inscrip. beg. i BC (IG XII 5.653.21; cf. Wackernagel, ThLZ 1908, 37); ἐραυν-, ἱεραύς (Delphi i BC end) and other places. Rüsch 136; Nachmanson, Eranos 11 (1911) 239; Lagercrantz, PHolm p. 81.—Ἀγουστ- s. §41(1).

(3) CONTRACTION AND RELATED PHENOMENA

(apart from contraction in inflection)

31. (1) **Non-contraction.** Hellenistic generally σεαυτοῦ ἑαυτοῦ etc. (§64(1)), ἐάν (§107), (φρέαρ) φρέατος; νεομηνίας (Ionic and again only after 150 AD) C 2: 16 only in BFG for Attic νουμηνίας; ἀγαθοεργεῖν 1 T 6: 18 s. §124. (2) **Non-Attic contraction.** A new Hellenistic contraction which appeared about 100 BC (Mayser I¹ 92, 1) of -ιει- = -*ĭ ĭ*- to -*ī*- (-ει-) is found in the NT in ταμεῖον = ταμιεῖον, πεῖν = πιεῖν (§101). M.-H. 89f. Ἱερωσύνη (Heb) is Ionic-Hellenistic, ἱερεωσύνη Attic (Mayser I¹ 154; I² 3, 7₁, from *ἱερηϝ-ο- > ἱερεύς). On λα- from λαο- s. §2. (3) **Syncope** (loss of vowel before a vowel) (Hermann, BPhW 1917, 742). Ionic-Hellenistic νοσσός Lk 2: 24 SBE al., νοσσιά 13: 34, νοσσίον Mt 23: 37, but always ἑορτή as in Attic and Hellenistic.

(1) LXX occasionally νεομηνία as v.l. (Thack. 98), later more frequently (Wackernagel, KZ 28 [1887] 138, 143 = Kl. Schr. 641, 646). Ἀγαθουργῶν A 14: 17 (v.l. ἀγαθοποιῶν), always κακοῦργος, ἱερουργεῖν etc. For τετραάρχης s. §124, for προε- §18, Θευδᾶς §125(1, 2).

(2) Also ἐπείκεια A 24: 4 B*, ἐπικές (= ἐπιεικές) Ph 4: 5 𝔓⁴⁶, otherwise always ἐπιεικής ἐπιείκεια. Even ἀνασῖ Lk 23: 5 S for -σείει. On ἀφεῖς s. §94(2). Ταμιεῖον in NT only Mt 24: 26 as a weak variant, πιεῖν more frequently (§101). Hell. often ὑγεια (accent?) for ὑγίεια; this word does not appear in the NT. Katz, ThLZ (1957) 111 would like to establish the Att. norm ταμιεῖον, ὑγίεια, πιεῖν. In the case of ἐσθίει(ς), the analogy of ἐσθίω etc. prevented contraction (but not in the case of the half-substantivized πεῖν in spite of πίω πιών and the like). Ps.-Herodian condemns πεῖν and ὑγεια in Cramer, Anec. Ox. III 261.3; 251.13.

(3) Ελεινος Rev 3: 17 AC, ελεινοτεροι 1 C 15: 19

FG is probably not ἐλεινός (Att.) but ελεϊνος = ἐλεεινός. Phryn. 206 is against νοσσός νοσσίον. Homer and Ion. inscrip. also ἑορτή; is therefore the ὀρτή of the Herodotus tradition an artificial Ionicism? (F. Hartmann, KZ 60 [1933] 99). Cf. also W. Schulze, Zeitschrift f. d. Gymnasialwesen 47 (1893) 164f. = Kl. Schr. 690; Bechtel, Gr. Dial. III 93.

(4) REMOTE ASSIMILATION OF VOWELS AND METATHESIS OF CONSONANTS

32. (1) **Remote assimilation.** (ἐξ-)ὀλοθρεύειν is preponderantly attested along with a well established ὄλεθρος; cf. MGr ξολοθρεύω. Ὀχυρά Herm Vis 2.3, ὀχύρωμα 2 C 10: 4; papyri also only ὀχυρ-, not ἐχυρ- (Mayser I¹ 96). Βιβλίον is assimilated from βυβλίον, and βίβλος βιβλαρίδιον accordingly; but accented υ is retained: τρύβλιον (Mayser I¹ 102). (2) **Metathesis** and related phenomena. Φαιλόνης (§25) from φαινόλης; cf. MGr φελόνι 'surplice'. Lk has φάτνη four times as in Homer and Attic; it likewise preponderates in the LXX (besides πάθνη and πάθμη; Thack. 106). Cf. Rob. 189f., 1210.

(1) Ἐχυρός (not NT) (ἐ- kept or reintroduced following ἔχειν) appears to be Att., cf. ἠχυρωμένος IG II 1.167.42, 68, 73 (iv BC); ὀχυρός probably from ἐχυρός like Κόρκυρα from Κέρκυρα. (Ἐξ-)ὀλοθρεύειν A 3: 23 OT (-ε- AB*CD), H 11: 28 OT (-ε- 𝔓⁴⁶ADE), ὀλοθρευτής 1 C 10: 10 (-ε- D*[FG]). LXX also mostly ὀλοθρεύειν B^corr (Buresch, RhM 46 [1891] 216f.; Thack. 88); ὀλοθρ- in Homil Clem (ὀλοθρεύσει 10. 13.1) and Acta Phil., Reinhold 40. For assimilation cf. Att. ὀβολός from ὀβελός. Βιβλίον βίβλος in Att. inscrip. beg. 400 BC (Meisterhans 28), in pap. beg. ii BC end increasingly often (Mayser I¹ 102); acc. to P. Kretschmer, KZ 57 (1930) 253 n. it is not a question of assimilation, but perhaps different reproductions of a Semitic vowel. Βύβλῳ Ph 4: 3 𝔓⁴⁶.

(2) Evidence for φαινόλης φαινόλιον φαιλόνης φαιλόνιον in Dibelius, Hdb. on 2 T 4: 13 (pap.), Psaltes 68f.; 118.1 (Byz. Chron.). On the formation of φαινόλης s. Hahn 10.8; Fraenkel, KZ 42 (1909) 115.1 (M.-H. 106 differ); C. D. Buck, A Dictionary of Selected Synonyms in the Principal Indo-European Languages (1949) 417 treats *paenula* as a Greek loanword. S. also Ed. Schwyzer, Museum Helveticum 3 (1946) 49ff.; Walde-Hofmann³ II 235. Acc. to Moeris 212.9 the Hell. form was πάθνη, not φάτνη; MGr presumes πάθνη. Ἐνδυδισκ- = ἐνδιδυσκ- s. §73. Ion. κύθρα 1 Clem 17.6 in an apocryphal quotation, LXX as v.l. (Thack. 103); Att. χύτρα; both in pap. (Mayser I¹ 184).

(5) INTERCHANGE OF SIMPLE CONSONANTS

33. Attic πανδοκεῖον πανδοκεύς for later -χεῖον -χεύς (χ from δέχεσθαι whose earlier form is also δέκεσθαι) is found in Lk 10: 34, 35 in 𝔓⁴⁵S* (35 also D*). Later Attic οὐθείς μηθείς (inscriptions beg. 378 BC, Meisterhans 258), under the influence of the old dialects and Atticism, was again gradually displaced by οὐδείς μηδείς in the Hellenistic period (MGr δέν = οὐδέν); the NT MSS still have -θ- along with -δ-. The relation of μόλις to μόγις is not yet settled; both are attested in the NT as in Attic authors and the papyri. On ποταπός s. §298(3); ὗς = σῦς §126(1 a α); δηλαυγῶς–τηλαυγῶς §119(4).

Hell. inscrip. have mostly πανδοκεῖον (Nachmanson 81); Phryn. 307 warns against -χ-; cf. εὐδοκεῖν §119(1). Always οὐδεμία μηδεμία; therefore οὐθείς does not = οὔτε plus εἷς. NT also οὐδαμῶς μηδαμῶς, but 1 Clem 33.1, 45.7, 53.4 μηθαμῶς as sometimes in the pap. (Mayser I¹ 182); οὐθέτερος Homil Clem 19.12. NT μηθέν A 27: 33, οὐθέν 5 times, οὐθενός Lk 22: 35, 2 C 11: 9, but nowhere unanimously transmitted. Yet ἐξουθενεῖν is the predominant form (-δενοῦν and -θενεῖν prevail in the LXX, Thack. 105); only Mk 9: 12 BD -δενηθῇ (W -θενηθῇ, S -θενωθῇ, ACX al. -δενωθῇ), 2 C 10: 10 B ἐξουδενημένος. Μηθέν as early as an Argive inscrip. of v BC beg., IG IV 1607.8f., 10. On the whole s. Wackernagel, Hell. 23 (= Kl. Schr. 1054); Meillet³ 263ff.; Gromska 16ff.; Schwyzer I 408; M.-H. 111f.— Μόλις 5 times, μόγις Lk 9: 39 (μόλις BW), 23: 53 add. D, A 14: 18 D; μόλις appears to be popular, μόγις is accepted as Att. (Helladius in Photius, Bibl. 530a 38, Schol. Lucian p. 28.21 Rabe); cf. Crönert 98; Mayser I¹ 17, I² 3, 120.6. On μο(γ)γιλάλος cf. §34(6).

(6) CONSONANTS IN COMBINATION

34. (1) **σσ and ττ.** The Hellenistic language did not in general accept ττ in place of σσ, the former being found almost exclusively in Attic. Individual instances, however, were introduced from literature, especially with the rise of the Atticistic movement and in words especially Attic. There appear in the NT accordingly, γλῶσσα, θάλασσα, νοσσός (§31(3)), περισσός, τέσσαρες; βδελύσσεσθαι, κηρύσσειν, ἐκπλήσσεσθαι (-ττ- only A 13: 12 B, Mt 7: 28 S, 13: 54 KMSΓ), πράσσειν, ταράσσειν, φυλάσσειν etc. Accordingly also σήμερον (Attic τήμερον); ἧσσον 1 C 11: 17, 2 C 12: 15. Ἡττᾶσθαι (2 P 2: 19, 20) and ἥττημα (R 11: 12, 1 C 6: 7) only with -ττ- because this formation was solely

Attic; Paul is acquainted with the related Ionic forms: ἡσσώθητε 2 C 12: 13 𝔓⁴⁶S*BD* (v.l. ἡττήθητε and ἐλαττώθηται) from Ionic ἑσσοῦσθαι. The Attic derivatives ἐλαττοῦν (H 2: 7, 9 OT, Jn 3: 30, 2 C 12: 13 FG) and ἐλαττονεῖν (2 C 8: 15 OT) always have -ττ-; accordingly ἐλάττων often appears along with ἐλάσσων and the antonym κρείττων along with κρείσσων. (2) **ρσ and ρρ.** The situation is the same as in the case of σσ–ττ. Ἄρσην appears to be the rule; θάρσος θάρσει θαρσεῖτε, but θαρρεῖν (Paul, Heb). Πόρρω(θεν) is established because πόρσω was not Ionic. Πυρρός 'red' in the NT as in the LXX (Thack. 123), papyri (Mayser I¹ 221) and Delphic inscriptions (Rüsch 244f.). (3) **Attic ρρ from ρε before a vowel.** Βορρᾶς (-ᾶ Lk 13: 29, Rev 21: 13) like Attic and Hellenistic. (4) **Omission of consonants.** Γίνεσθαι γίνώσκειν are Ionic-Hellenistic for γιγν-; MGr also γίνομαι. Ἄρκος (for ἄρκτος) Rev 13: 2 LXX (all uncials, also 𝔓⁴⁷) is an old by-form, attested also e.g. in the LXX (Helb. 21f.; Thack. 116); cf. M.-H. 112. Ἄμμος, known in the papyri and earlier to Xenophon and Plato, is a mixed formation from ἄμαθος and ψάμμος; s. Mayser I¹ 202. (5) **Other consonant changes** (except σσ–ττ and ρσ–ρρ). Κλίβανος Mt 6: 30, Lk 12: 28 is Doric, Ionic (Hdt.) and Hellenistic; Attic κρίβανος; cf. Mayser I¹ 7. Ὀσμή (ἡδύοσμον) in the NT (from *ὀδ-σ-μή or ὀδμή? Schwyzer I 208, 494) as in Attic-Hellenistic, not ὀδμή; cf. Crönert 136. On the other hand, Ionic-Hellenistic βαθμός (1 T 3: 13) ἀναβαθμός (A 21: 35, 40) for Attic βασμός (Smyth, Ionic §358; Thumb, Hell. 73) from *βα-θ-σ-μός. Γναφεύς is Hellenistic Mk 9: 3 (all uncials), κναφεύς early Attic and perhaps also Ionic, cf. Mayser I¹ 169f. The aspiration after σ in σφυρίς σφόγγος (v.l. σπυρίς σπόγγος) and μασθός (v.l. μαστός and μαζός) is unexplained. (6) **Insertion of a consonant** appears to have taken place in σφυδρόν (A 3: 7 σφυδρά S*AB*C*) for σφυρόν; cf. Schwyzer I 239. Μογγιλάλος 'speaking in a hoarse or hollow voice' is weakly attested in Mk 7: 32 (WLNΔ al.): a remodeling of μογιλάλος (= μόγις λαλῶν; §119(4)) 𝔓⁴⁵SAB*DGK al. after μογγός 'hollow, hoarse' the attestation for which is late (Thack. 121; Psaltes 71). Πτολεμαΐς A 21: 7 could not be pronounced any other way as an official name (Mayser I¹ 167) in spite of πόλεμος.

(1) Βασίλισσα also has σσ and never appears with ττ because of its non-Att. origin (§111(1); Mayser I¹ 10). The LXX (except 2–4 Macc) agrees with the NT (Thack. 122). Ἐλάσσων Jn 2: 10, R 9: 12 OT, ἐλάττων 1 T 5: 9, H 7: 7; Hermas ἐλάττων and

ἐλάττωμα along with ἐλάσσων, Diogn 10.6 ἐλαττούμενον. Paul has κρείσσων acc. to overwhelming testimony, Heb κρείττων (variation only 6: 9 [𝔓⁴⁶ also -σσ-] and 10: 34 [𝔓¹³ also -σσ-]) as in Peter (1 P 3: 17, variation in 2 P 2: 21). Somewhat more literary are 1 Clem (ἥττονα 47.4, γλώττης 57.2 C, θᾶττον 65.1) and MPol (κρειττόνων 11.1, ἐκπλήττεσθαι 7.2, θᾶττον 13.1); ἐκπληττόμενος A 13: 12 B, ἔλαττον ἥττονα ἥττων addition in D to Mt 20: 28. Always -ττ- in Ἄτταλος (Ign) Ἀττάλεια (Acts), a name from Asia Minor. On the whole cf. Wackernagel, Hell. 13–23 (= Kl. Schr. 1044–54); Rosenkranz, IF 48 (1930) 143 ff.

(2) Ἄρσην with ρσ in the Gospels, otherwise ρρ several times as v.l., especially in S, but only ἀρσενοκοίτης. Πόρρω(θεν) only Lk, Heb (Mt 15: 8 = Mk 7: 6 OT) for popular μακράν (already class.), (ἀπὸ) μακρόθεν; μακρὰν καὶ πόρρω Barn 20.2 (μακρὰν alone Did 5.2), μακρὰν ῥιπτομένους... πόρρω ἀπερίφησαν Herm Vis 3.6.1. Βυρσεύς (Acts) as βύρσα always in Att. (foreign word). In the quotation from Gen 1: 27 (G 3: 28 and Rev 12: 5 also have this reference in view) ἀρσ- is almost uniformly attested in the NT, because the LXX is acquainted almost exclusively with this form; the variant ἀρρ- is much stronger in R 1: 27. v. Soden 1364.—MGr θαρῶ (not θαρρῶ): Medieval Greek dissimilates ἐθάρσησα etc. to ἐθάρρησα etc. (G. N. Hatzidakis, Byz.-neugr. Jahrb. 2 [1921] 157 f.).—Ion. also πυρρός (Hdt., Hippoc.; Smyth, Ionic §334; Schlageter, Wortschatz 57); πυρσός 'firebrand' (since Homer) along with πυρσεύειν is to be kept distinct.—Δέρρην (= δέρριν) Mk 1: 6 D (pm. τρίχας): δέρσις is not found in Greek at all. On the whole cf. Wackernagel, Hell. 12–22 (= Kl. Schr. 1043–53); Meillet³ 297; Rosenkranz, op. cit. 145 f.

(3) But στερεός (Att. στερρός) as e.g. pap. (Mayser I¹ 221) and LXX. Correspondingly Att. νν from νε before a vowel (Schwyzer I 274) in γεννᾶν γέννημα (NT also and Hell. otherwise; γέννα [Pindar and the Tragedians] is a back-formation from it, Schwyzer I 475), but the NT like Ion.-Hell. γενεά (γενεή) and class.-Hell. γενεαλογία.

(4) NT like Hell. always μικρός, never σμικρός (Att. inscrip. along with μικρός). Hell. and NT only σύν (ξύν is especially Att.). Γιν- from iv BC beg. in Att. also (Rosenkranz, op. cit. 146 f.); γιγν- in W several times (Sanders, Wash. 23).—Σάλπιγξ λάρυξ s. §46(4).

(5) Σπυρίς and σφυρίς in pap. (Mayser I¹ 173); Att. also varies in the cases of σπυρίς and σπόγγος between σπ- and σφ- as does MGr (Hatzidakis, IF 36, 299 f.). Σφυρίς Mt 15: 37 D, 16: 10 BD, Mk 8: 8 SA*D, 20 D, A 9: 25 SC; σφόγγος Mk 15: 36 D (only with σπ- Mt 27: 48, Jn 19: 29).—Μασθός appears to be Dor. (K.-Bl. I 157). Μαστοῖς Rev 1: 13 CP 046 (-σθ- S, -ȝ- A), μαστοί Lk 11: 27 (-σθ- DFG), 23: 29 (-σθ- D*FG, -ȝ- C); -σθ- in two Egyptian

magical pap. (Crönert 86.2), 3 times as v.l. in the LXX (Thack. 104), also in Byz. (Psaltes 97). Acc. to Walde-Hofmann³ II 7 μαζός μαστός μασθός contain different suffixes.

(6) Σφυδρόν Corpus Gloss. Lat. II 100.28, PFlor III 391.53, 56 (iii AD), Hesychius.—Μογγιλάλος also in LXX Is 35: 6 QΓΒᵃᵇ (al. μογι-), Etymologicum Magnum under βατταρίζειν (cf. Du Cange, Glossarium s.v. μογγιλάλος); for attestation for μογιλάλος s. L.-S. and Bauer. Pallis, Notes 26 is incorrect (μογιλάλος is an atticistic correction for μογγιλ.).—On κράβαττος–κράβακτος s. §42(4).

(7) SOUND CHANGES AS A RESULT OF DIVERGENCE IN FORMATION

35. (1) **Dependent on differing formation of the final stem vowel** are πρόϊμον Ja 5: 7 (SAB*P; connected with πρό) as v.l. to the original πρώϊμον (from πρωΐ), Στοϊκῶν A 17: 18 (SAD al., connected with στοά) as v.l. to Στωϊκῶν which is correct. For ἀνάθεμα etc. s. §109(3), -γεως -γαιος -γειος §44(1), πόμα for πῶμα, -θεμα for -θημα etc. §109(3). (2) **Diversity in composition.** Ἀνάγαιον (§25), by association with ἀνά, for ἀνώγαιον (poorly attested variant; Xen., An. 5.4.29; from ἄνω). Χρε-οφειλέτης Lk 7: 41, 16: 5 is better attested than χρεωφειλέτης. In πατρολώαις μητρολώαις (§26) 1 T 1: 9 SADFGL instead of -αλοίαις (from ἀλο(ι)ᾶν) the 'composition vowel' ο is introduced following πατροκτόνος etc.; cf. Crönert 123. The reverse (i.e. α for ο) is the case in μεσανύκτιον (weak v.l.) for μεσο-νύκτιον. For ἀρχε- and ἀρχι- s. §118(2). (3) **Diversity of suffix.** Φόβηθρα Lk 21: 11 BD for φόβητρα; cf. LXX Is 19: 17 B*. Both suffixes are old; -τρον is supported in this word by aspirate-dissimilation. Ja 3: 12 uses Att. ἁλυκός (as the LXX), not ἁλικός which arose through assimilation to the known suffix -ικός. Ἕνεκεν is Ionic-Hellenistic (but also in Aristoph. and Hyperid.; Gromska 13 f.) as is εἵνεκεν (§30(3)) for Attic ἕνεκα; also εἶτεν for Attic εἶτα (Mayser I¹14).—For λήμψομαι etc. and ἐμπιπλᾶν ἐμπιπρᾶν s. §101.

(1) LXX mostly πρόϊμος (Thack. 90); on πρώϊμος Mayser I¹ 90. Att. πλόϊμος, later πλώϊμος, is different; C. Arbenz, Die Adj. auf -ιμος (Diss. Zürich, 1933) 46, 48 f. On Στοϊκός Crönert 123.1 (also Στοεικός Στοεικοῦ IG XII 3, 130.1 f. [Roman period]). On the phonetic relation of Στωϊκός to στοά (< στοιά < στωιά) Scherer 15, 48; Schwyzer I 244, 498.

(2) The original form is ἀνώγεον (so Dialekt-Inschr. II no. 1581.4; on ἀν-άγειν 'to lead up' O. Hoffmann in the same vol., p. 120).—Χρεωφειλέτης

for χρε-οφ- through assimilation to words with χρεω- (from χρηο-; Att. χρέως, Ion. χρέος from χρῆος) as χρεω-φυλάκιον in inscrip.; χρεοφιλέτας Dit., Syll.³ 742.53 (Ephesus, i BC); Herodian II 606.27 Lentz ω and ο; s. Lob. Phryn. 691, Fraenkel I 62.—Μεσανύκτιον Mk 13: 35 B*W, Lk 11: 5 D*, POxy XIV 1768.6 (iii AD), μεσάνυκτον fable from 1539 AD (Soyter, Bayerische Blätter f. d. Gymnasialschulwesen 64 [1928] 237); MGr τὸ μεσονύκτιον and τὰ μεσάνυχτα; cf. μεσαστύλιον Lob. Phryn. 195. Μεσα-connected with the adv. μέσα (M.-H. 73).

(3) Ἀλικός in the pap. and ostraca (Mayser I¹ 102).—On ἕνεκα ἕνεκεν Ghedini, Aegyptus 15 (1935) 238. Att. ἕνεκα is not to be tolerated in the NT except in ἕ. τούτων A 26: 21 (speech of Paul before Agrippa!), where all witnesses have it (but 19: 32 -κα only SAB, as v.l. also Lk 6: 22 [-κεν D al.], Mt 19: 5 OT SBLZ [LXX -κεν], Mk 13: 9 B). Philo Byz. also has τούτων ἕνεκα along with ἕνεκεν elsewhere (Arnim 15f.). For Hermas s. Reinhold 39f. For ἕνεκεν in the orators, Thuc., [Xen.], Ath. 1.10, s. Rosenkranz, IF (1930) 149. Εἶτεν only Mk 4: 28 SB*L, never ἔπειτεν; acc. to Phryn. 124 both are ἐσχάτως βάρβαρα. Εἶτεν in inscrip. s. Mayser I¹ 14; Schlageter 5; Scherer 5.—Νηφαλέος (or -αιος) 1 T 3: 2, 11, T 2: 2 (also Philo, LA 3.82 [I 131.5 Cohn-Wendland] and others) is a weak variant to νηφάλιος (beg. w. Aeschyl., inscrip. also from iv BC beg.) from which it was remodeled following adj. in -αλέος; s. Debrunner, IF 23 (1908) 17f. and Bauer.

5. ON THE TRANSLITERATION OF FOREIGN WORDS

(1) SEMITIC WORDS

(apart from old naturalized words like χιτών)

36. Introduction. In the representation of Semitic loanwords the witnesses sometimes differ considerably, partly as a result of the ignorance of the copyists, partly also, it must be admitted, because of the corrections made by those who thought they knew better. Only a selection of the rules by which transliteration takes place need be given here—they are essentially the same as in the LXX.

The variants in the Aramaic words from the Cross in Mt 27: 46 are characteristic: ηλει αηλι (ἀήλί) ελω(ε)ι(μ), λεμα λημα λ(ε)ιμα λαμα, σαβαχθαν(ε)ι σαβακτανει ζαφθανει (σαφθ-); in Mk 15: 34 ελω(ε)ι ελωη ηλ(ε)ι, λεμα λαμ(μ)α λ(ε)ιμα, σαβαχθ- σαβακτ- σιβακθανει ζα(βα)φθανει.—s. Wuthnow.

Literature: Z. Frankel, Vorstudien zu der Septuaginta (Leipzig, 1841) 90–131. C. Könnecke, Programm des Gymn. von Stargard 1885. Helbing 26–31. Kautzsch 8–12. F. C. Burkitt, The Syriac Forms of NT Proper Names (Proceedings of the Br. Ac. [1911/12] 377–408). A. Schlatter, Die hebr. Namen bei Josephus (Beitr. z. Förd. Christl. Theol. 17, nos. 3, 4, Gütersloh, 1913). F. Wutz, Die Bedeutung der Transkriptionen in der Sept. bis Hieronymus (BZ 16 [1922–4] 193–213); Die Transkr. von der Sept. bis Hieron. (Lief. 1, Stuttgart, 1925 = Beiträge zur Wiss. vom AT, n. F. Heft 9, 2) on which s. R. Kittel, DLZ 1925, 657–64; for later opinion s. P. Kahle, ZDMG 92 (1938) 276ff., H. M. Orlinsky, 'Current Progress and Problems in Septuagint Research', The Study of the Bible Today and Tomorrow (1947) 155ff. G. Lisowsky, Die Transkription der hebr. Eigennamen des Pentateuch in der Septuaginta (Theol. Diss. Basel, 1940).

37. Diacritical marks. Accentuation is based on the tradition in later MSS and old editions, in liturgies and choral songs, in the Romance languages (e.g. Italian *Gesù, Mosè, Maria, Giúda*, Spanish *Abrahán, Emaús*): Zorell xv. Diaeresis was often used in the MSS to designate a non-diphthongal pronunciation (s. §15).

Thus Καϊν Ναϊν in SBD, Ησαϊας (𝔓⁴⁵D; B for the most part, 𝔓⁴⁶S are divided), Βηθσαϊδα(ν) (with ει or ϊ D, with ι 𝔓⁴⁵B, S is divided [3 times each]). The Lat. form can often be a guide: Ἰεσσαί *Jessae* (-e), Ἐφραίμ *Ephraem* (-em, Jn 11: 54 SL also -εμ). נַעֲמָן Lk 4: 27 is Ναιμάν (-ας) in SABCDKL, for which X has Νεμαν, lat in part *Neman*; but Νεεμαν EFM al. and other Lat. witnesses, the remaining lat *Naaman*. In the case of Καιναν, αι appears to be more correct in spite of Lat. *ai* after the Semitic basic form קֵינָן, and αι stands also in SB (D ϊ). Και(α)φας is difficult: D and most of the Lat. witnesses have Καιφας (Καειφ- Κηφ-, 𝔓⁴⁵ Jn 11: 49 Καϊφας) *Caiphas*; Καϊάφας is also found in Jos.; Syriac has *qyp'*, so that Κηφᾶς *kyp'* has nothing to do with it. Cf. Lagarde, Mittheilungen IV 18; Schürer II⁴ 271 n. 12; E. Nestle, Theol. Stud. f. Th. Zahn (1908) 251ff.; Dalman 161.2; Burkitt 385. For Μωϋσῆς s. §38.

38. Vowels. The MSS and editions cling tenaciously to ει for ῑ (§23) in Semitic words. Proper names in -ίας have for the most part -ῐ- and consequently not ει; but -είας -ίας appear for Hebrew -*iyyāh(ū)* (ו)יָּה.—Αἰλαμῖται A 2: 9 B is considered the correct form, not Ἐλ-. Συμεών for שִׁמְעוֹן throughout (as in the LXX); cf. §53(2).—Μωυσῆς is the better form ($\mathfrak{P}^{46}$ and $\mathfrak{P}^{66}$ [Martin 27: 11 times] always, W always except for Lk 16: 29, I [Freer] always, and predominantly in SBDK), also in the LXX and Josephus (also cf. Dieterich 81), Μωσῆς is later ($\mathfrak{P}^{45}$ except for A 7: 20, $\mathfrak{P}^{47}$ only in Rev 15: 3 ω, corrected to ου; predominantly in AEFG); according to Thack. 163 n. 3 ου as a *diphthong* is an attempt to reproduce Egyptian pronunciation (cf. Θωῦθ, later Θῶτ).

ι or ει for Hebr. *ī* e.g. in Βενιαμιν (-ειν $\mathfrak{P}^{46}$ R 11: 1, Ph 3: 5), Δαυιδ (-ϊδ $\mathfrak{P}^{45}$ Mt 20: 31, -ειδ $\mathfrak{P}^{46}$), Ἐλισαβετ (B always -ει-, S for the most part, CD sporadically, s. Tdf. on Lk 1: 5), Ἰεριχω (-ει- Mt 20: 29 BCLZ, H 11: 30 $\mathfrak{P}^{46}$, B always, S[D] frequently), Λευι(ς) (-ει- H 7: 5 $\mathfrak{P}^{46}$), Σάπφιρα (A 5: 1; MSS ει, ι, υ; Grecizing of Aram. שַׁפִּירָה 'beautiful' [Dalman 163] with dependence on σάπφ(ε)ιρος = סַפִּיר, Katz, ThLZ 1954, 240), where ει likewise is unwarranted [Rev 21: 19 -ιρος P 046]). On Γεθσημανι s. Kautzsch in W.-S. §5, 13a (Hebr. גַּת שְׁמָנֵי 'oil-press' from -*īm* Dalman 191; on the Syrian transliteration, which evidently depends on Greek, s. Burkitt 384; -η is very weakly attested, and perhaps the η of the second syllable should be weakened to the α of the western tradition). Ἠλι, ῥαββι, ῥαββουνι (cf. p. 3, n. 2), ταλιθα, σαβαχθανι.—Also Μαριάμ Μαρία with ῑ. In -ίας (-είας): Ἠλίας (-ει- also $\mathfrak{P}^{45}$ Lk 9: 30, 33), Ἰωσίας, Ὀζίας, Οὐρίας; s. Westcott-Hort, App. 155. In the case of Οὐρείου Mt 1: 6 only B and a papyrus fragment are consistent with -ει-, in the case of Ἀβεία 1: 7 only the papyrus; Ἐζεκίας 1: 9, 10 -ει- only in Lk 3: 23 D altered acc. to Mt (no pap. evidence; CIG 8613 B 17 also Ἐζεκίας [-χίας] along with Ἰωσείας 19). Σιών צִיּוֹן (-ει- $\mathfrak{P}^{46}\mathfrak{P}^{47}$B) also belongs here. Ἐλισαῖος Lk 4: 27 אֱלִישָׁע undoubtedly has ι (B -ει); B also has Γαλειλαία, -αῖος (but $\mathfrak{P}^{45}$ -ι-), Σεινᾶ, Φαρεισαῖος ($\mathfrak{P}^{45}$ also, -ι- $\mathfrak{P}^{46}$ Ph 3: 5). Σαμάρεια follows the analogy of Ἀντιόχεια etc. (§23), therefore -ει- in any case (Herodian I 279.34 Lentz; so A 15: 3 $\mathfrak{P}^{45}$); yet the inhabitant is called Σαμαρίτης (fem. -ῖτις) as that of Μαρώνεια is Μαρωνίτης; also cf. Ἰσραηλίτης etc. §111(2).—Αἰλαμῖται from Αἰλάμ עֵילָם (but Assyrian, Egyptian, and Aramaic have no radical *i*. In Hebrew it may well be a sign of length. Cf. also ἡ Ἐλυμαΐς, -αία, οἱ Ἐλυμαῖοι [Katz]); s. Eus., Onom. p. 8.1 Klostermann; yet the LXX has Αἰλάμ and Ἐλαμῖται side by side acc. to Könnecke (s. *supra* §36).—Inscrip. and pap. Μουσ-; Μωσ- not until viii AD; Wuthnow 79f. Acc. to Joachim Jeremias, TW IV 853 n. 1 ου is upper-Egyptian, ω lower- and extra-Egyptian (Strabo). The interchange with ω speaks for the original diphthongal pronunciation of ου as does the reading ωυ (not ωϋ), e.g. in $\mathfrak{P}^{46}$, while the division at the end of the line Μω/υσης in $\mathfrak{P}^{46}$

R 10: 19 and French *Moïse* (= Lat. *Moyses*) speak perhaps for the double syllable. In the LXX and Philo the good MSS have -ου-, the inferior ones -ω-. This decides against dating -ου- late (Katz).—Schaeder, TW IV 882.39ff. understands ω as a transliteration of *šewā* in Ναζωραῖος (cf. §39(4)).—In order to preserve a Semitic final consonant perhaps -α was added (cf. §56(1, 2)): Σόδομα, Ἱεροσόλυμα, μάννα, σίκερα etc. (J. Psichari, Rev. Ét. juives 54, 1912 = Travaux I 1055ff.; qualified by Schwyzer, KZ 62 [1935] 16, who shows that Greek elsewhere appends a vowel (α or ε) to otherwise unpronounceable foreign words).

39. Half-vowels and consonants. (1) **Half-vowels**: י and ו = ι and υ; the latter coalesces with a preceding vowel into a diphthong. Initial י as ι receives smooth breathing except where there is association with a Greek word with rough breathing: Ἱεροσόλυμα, but Ἰερουσαλήμ, Ἰεριχώ. (2) **Mutes**: כ, פ, ת (unvoiced non-emphatic stops and spirants) are represented by χ, φ, θ, except where two aspirates would follow in contiguous syllables (in which case the Greeks dissimilated even in their own words). ק, ט (unvoiced emphatic stops) are rendered by the voiceless stops κ, τ. (3) **Laryngeals and Gutturals.** א, ה, ח, ע were not expressed, with some exceptions: for ח (and א) χ appears; initial ע is rendered in certain words by γ. The question where to use smooth or rough breathing with the initial sound is insoluble; it seems reasonable to employ smooth breathing for א and ע and rough breathing for ה and ח, as Westcott-Hort have done. Yet it is to be hoped that future editions will follow Lagarde, Rahlfs, and the Göttingen editions of the LXX which omit both accents and breathing in proper names and other transliterations wherever absence of terminations and inflection indicate that no Grecizing was intended (Katz). (4) **Sibilants.** ס, צ, שׁ, שׁ = σ, ז = ζ (sonant *s*). (5) **Consonants inserted to assist pronunciation.** Σαμψων, i.e. Σαμ-π-σων, H 11: 32 as in the LXX, occasionally Ἰστραήλ; S always Ἰσδρ- in Acts, cf. v. Soden 1375f. Homil Clem 9.3.2 Μεστρεμ = מִצְרַיִם, 4.1, 5.1 Νεβρωδ = נִמְרֹד. Also to be noted are (6) dissimilation, (7) the addition of a consonant and (8) the disappearance of a final nasal.

(1) Δαυίδ, Εὔα (Schmiedel prefers Ἕυα), Λευίς, Νινευῖται Lk 11: 32 (Νινευή is another reading, -ευί is poor); Δαουει[δ] pap. iii AD 2 Chr 24: 25 (UGosp p. 54) is now certain (Katz, ThLZ 1957, 111; Ziegler, LXX Daniel 78). For Σκευᾶς s. §125(2). Ἡσαΐας has lost the initial י (Syr. also *s'y*).

(2) Πάσχα (Jos. v.l. φασκα; cf. LXX פִּשְׁחוּר Πασχώρ and Φασσούρ), Καφαρναούμ כְּפַר נַחוּם (SBD, also 𝔓⁴⁵ Lk 10: 15, later MSS Καπερν- s. Tdf. on Mt 4: 13, Nestle [s. *supra* §37]), Κηφᾶς. Acc. to F. C. Burkitt, JTS 34 (1933) 385–90 Καφαρν- is old, Καπερν- Antiochian pronunciation; W has Καπερν- in Mt except 17: 24, otherwise Καφαρν- except for Lk 10: 15. However, ת is also represented by τ: σάββατα שַׁבָּת, cf. Ἀστάρτη also taken over early. T in σάββατον is an older transliteration (as in βῆτα etc.; the same transliteration is used in letters of the alphabet in the LXX [Rahlfs, Sept. II 756] and it is nearly identical in Eus., Praep. Ev. 10.5 [A. Schmitt, Der Buchstabe H im Griech. (Münster, 1952) 12–14], and accordingly in Syriac loanwords from Greek [Schwyzer I 159]): Schwyzer, KZ 62 (1935) 12. In Ἐλισαβεθ -βετ, the dental is due to corruption in the LXX. A first-century ossuary reads Ελισαβη. For אֱלִישֶׁבַע בַת- Ex 6: 23 we have Ελισαβεθ θυγατέρα in B, -βε in A*, -βετ = NT (back-reading?) in the remainder. Here an original -βεε (second ε for ע) was changed to -βεθ owing to the following θ. The best etymology is that of Hertz, ET Dec. 1933 שֶׁבַע = 'good fortune, abundance', which Köhler s.v. finds also in יְהוֹשֶׁבַע 4 Km 11: 2 'Jahweh is bliss' and בַת־שֶׁבַע 'daughter of fortune, Fortunata'. In 4 Km 11: 2 the majority reading is Ιωσαβεε. Katz, ThLZ 61 (1936) 274; 1957,111. צָרְפַת becomes Σάρεπτα Lk 4: 26 (-φθ- B²KLM) as in the LXX (-φθ- is a weak variant). Ναζαρεθ also fluctuates (so also 𝔓⁴⁵ A 10: 38), -ρετ, -ρα(θ); the Semitic form is uncertain (Dalman 152; Burkitt 391ff.; acc. to Schaeder, TW IV 882.37ff. Aram. נַצְרַת; for further biblio. s. Bauer). Γεννησαρεθ, -ρετ are incorrect, Γεννησάρ is correct in D, LXX, Jos. and elsewhere (Bauer). Χ for ק in σαβαχθάνι שְׁבַקְתָּנִי, where however there is reverse assimilation to -κτανι. Θ for ט in Λωθ Lk 17: 29 W, 32 DW, otherwise Λωτ.

(3) Χ for ח in Ῥαχήλ, Ἀχάζ, Χαρράν, πάσχα; רָחָב fluctuates between Ῥαχάβ Mt 1: 5, Ῥαάβ H 11: 31, Ja 2: 25. Γ for ע: Γομόρρα, Γάζα. Acc. to the rule regarding breathing, for example, Ἀβελ (ה), Εὔα (ח), Ἄννα and Ἀνανίας (ה), ἀλληλουια (ה) would also be written with rough breathing; but Ἑβραῖος (ע). The MSS are entirely unreliable and at variance (Gregory 106f.); Jerome avowedly puts א ה ח ע in a category in his treatment of biblical names and writes *h* for none of them. Cf. E. Nestle, Philol. 68 (1909) 457ff. Occasionally breathing appears to be controlled in relation to similar sounding Greek words (Zorell xii), e.g. Ἀλφαῖος following ἄλφα, Ἡλίας following ἥλιος.—Μεσσίας = Aramaic מְשִׁיחָא, cf. Jerome *Slias* = Aram. שְׁלִיחָא (Rengstorf, TW I 414 n. 52). Unusual χ for א: Ἀκελδαμάχ (-ά C al.) A 1: 19 = חֲקַל דְּמָא; cf. LXX Σιράχ = שִׂירָא (Dalman

202.3). The transliteration of Hebr. ע and ח is older than the leveling of old Semitic ʿ and ġ, ḥ and ḫ in Hebr.: ġ = γ, ḫ = χ, ʿ and ḥ were not expressed in Greek. S. Gesenius-Kautzsch § 6e; M. Flashar, ZAW 28 (1908) 104–20; R. Ružička, BZ 1913, 342–9; Joh. Pedersen, Reallex. d. Vorgesch. 12 (1928) 25. Inserted or prefixed α for a guttural: Ναθαναήλ נְתַנְאֵל, Ἰσαάκ יִצְחָק (but e.g. 𝔓⁴⁶ and D always Ἰσάκ), ἀήλι Mt 27: 46 L (Eus); so also LXX Ἀερμών חֶרְמוֹן, Ἀενδωρ עֵין־דֹּר; acc. to R. Meister, WSt 28 (1906) 160f. ἀ is the Hebr. article (impossible).

(4) Σ for ז in Βοες Mt 1: 5 SB, Βοος C (Βοοζ EKLM al.) for בֹּעַז; ὕσσωπος = אֵזוֹב (H. Lewy, KZ 55 [1927] 31.2). Z for צ: Ναζαρεθ (s. *supra* 2) Ναζωραῖος. Ναζωραῖος by connection with נָזִיר 'consecrated' (Burkitt 394); however, see the other exx. of ز = צ in Schaeder, TW IV 884.1ff.; s. Bauer also. Z = σδ in Ἄζωτος (LXX also) = אַשְׁדּוֹד is worth noting.

(5) Ἰστραήλ Mt 19: 28 W, Mk 12: 29 DW, Lk 2: 32 D, Acts B several times. Ἰαμ-β-ρῆς 2 T 3: 8 (Semitic basic form is uncertain; Odeberg, TW III 192f.). Cf. Σαλαμψιω(ν) שְׁלָם צִיוֹן in Jos. and on ossuaries (Abel 20); J. T. Milik, 'Trois tombeaux juifs récemment découverts au Sud-Est de Jérusalem', Studii Biblici Franciscani Liber Annuus 7 (1956–7) 240, 245, finds significant variations in spelling: שלמצין and שלמציה (the latter may be even closer to the Greek form without the final *nun*). Cf. ἀν-δ-ρός, μεσημ-β-ρία, and LXX Ἐσ-δ-ρας, Μαμ-β-ρῆ. Schwyzer I 277; M.-H. 103.

(6) Dissimilation: Βελιαρ 2 C 6: 15 (poor variants -αν, -αβ, -αλ), also Test 12 Patr, Oracula Sibyllina = בְּלִיַּעַל. Γολγοθᾶ is probably due to Greek dissimilation from Γολγολθᾶ (Mt 27: 33 Δ) = Aram. גֻּלְגֻּלְתָּא; cf. Bauer.

(7) Addition of a consonant: Ἀσάφ Mt 1: 7, 8 P¹SBCD (Ἀσά EKL ad.) = אָסָא; M.-H. 109f. 'Irrational' nasal with geminatives (Mayser I¹ 197; Schwyzer I 231f.; cf. §§41(2); 42(3)): Σαμφίρη A 5: 1 S, cf. v.l. in Jos. (W. Schulze, KZ 33 [1895] 382 = Kl. Schr. 293); Λύνδα A 9: 38 𝔓⁴⁵ (al. Λύδδα(ς), Λύδδης). According to J. A. Fitzmyer (by letter) the 'irrational' nasal may represent a phenomenon well-known in Aramaic: the resolution of doubling by the use of *nun*, e.g. *madda*ʿ, 'knowledge', appears as *manda*ʿ (whence Mandaean); *yn'l* from the root *'ll*. Without corroborating evidence, such an explanation is equivocal for Λύνδα (Λύδδα) and Σάμφιρα (Σάπφιρα). Here, as in other features, the two languages concur. In the LXX the place-name מַתָּנָה and the proper names מַתַּנְיָה and מַתַּנְיָהוּ are represented as Μανθαν- and it would not be easy to decide whether this tendency was Greek or Semitic (Katz; cf. Schwyzer I 231f.).

(8) Disappearance of a terminal nasal: γέεννα = Aram. גֵּי הִנֹּם; s. Joachim Jeremias, TW I 655.

Σαμψω H 11: 32 𝔓¹³𝔓⁴⁶D (al. -ων); cf. Σαλαμψιω *supra* 5 and -ας -ης for וֹ‎, α for ◌ַ‎ §53(2c, 3).

40. Great uncertainty prevails in the matter of **doubling consonants**. It is warranted in ἀρραβών (Hebr. עֵרָבוֹן‎) and Ἄννα (=חַנָּה‎), hardly in μαμ(μ)ωνᾶς (=מָמוֹנָא‎) and Ἰωάννης; it is doubtful in Ἰόππη.—The doubling of aspirates, which is never correct in Greek (especially Μαθθ- along with Ματθ-), appears in transliterated Semitic words.

Ἀρραβών is established by the metrically assured form in prosody –◡– and Lat. *arrha*; ρρ is also based on the Semitic form. Ἀραβῶν 2 C 1: 22 SAFGL, 5: 5 SDE, E 1: 14 𝔓⁴⁶FG; -ρρ- in an inscrip. (ii/i BC), pap. -ρρ- and -ρ-, s. W.-S. §5, 26c; Deissmann, NBS 11 [BS 183f.]; Moulton, CIR 15 (1901) 33; Mayser I¹ 40. NT only Σάρρα (except Σάρας R 9: 9 L) corresponding to the later name שָׂרָה‎ (LXX Σάρρα; שָׂרַי‎ = Σάρα). Μαμμωνᾶς is very weakly attested (assimilation to Lat. *mamma, annona,* and others? Hauck, TW IV 390 n. 1). Ἰωάνης: 𝔓⁴⁵𝔓⁴⁶ (G 2: 9) 𝔓⁶⁶ always with νν, B almost throughout with one ν, D in Lk and Acts -ν-, in Mt and Mk -νν- (Rudberg 13f.); -ν- and -νν- in inscrip. and pap. (Wuthnow 59); -νης for נָן‎ (§53(2c)). Ἰωάνα Lk 8: 3 (-ν- BD), 24: 10 (-ν- DL) (cf. Wuthnow 59) = Syr. *yōhan* is explicable in view of Σουσάννα Lk 8: 3 = Syr. *šwšn*, Μαριάμμη (Jos.) = Μαριάμ; the masc. Ἄννας (Hebr. חָנָן‎, Jos. Ἄνανος) could be influenced by Ἄννα. Ἰόππη is the spelling of the NT (and 1 Macc); Ἰόπη preponderates otherwise. Σαφφίρη A 5: 1 DE (al. Σαπφ- [Σαμφ- *supra* §39(7)], but σάπφ(ε)ιρος Rev 21: 19 universally), εφφαθα or -εθα Mk 7: 34 almost all witnesses. Μαθθαῖος (in the title SBDW), Μαθθίαν A 1: 23, 26 B*D, Μαθθάν Mt 1: 15 B(D), Μαθθάθ (-ααθ, -ατ) Lk 3: 29 S*B*; Burkitt, JTS 34 (1933) 389f.; Wuthnow 69, 74. Βαττολογεῖν (βατταλ- SBW) Mt 6: 7 is difficult: acc. to Blass from Aram. בטל‎ 'empty, inane' and -λόγος, therefore for *βατταλο-λογεῖν (syˢ '*mryn btlt*', syʰʳ '*mryn mlyn btlyn*') with haplography (Schwyzer I 262ff.); acc. to Delling, TW I 598 a remodeling of βατταρίζειν 'stammer' in connection with -λογεῖν; also cf. Lat. *bat(t)ulus* 'μογιλάλος'; Corp. Gloss. Lat. II 32.17 *garrulus* βαττολάλος, W. Schulze, BPhW 1895, 7f. = Kl. Schr. 680; more recently G. Zuntz, Gnomon 30 (1958) 20f. (review of Bauer⁵).

(2) LATIN WORDS

Cf. Dittenberger, Hermes VI (1872) 129–55, 281–313. Eckinger, Die Orthographie lat. Wörter in Griech. Inschr. (Zürcher Diss.), München, 1893. Wessely, Die lat. Elemente in der Gräzität der ägypt. Papyrusurk. (WSt 24 [1902] 99–151; 25 [1903] 40–77). Psaltes *passim*. Döttling, Künnecke, Meinersmann. The transliteration in the NT is entirely

that which was customary in the early imperial period.

41. (1) **Vowels**. Just as *Delmatia* is still found in the imperial period along with the later *Dalmatia*, so also 2 T 4: 10 Δελματίαν (C, Δερμ- A) besides Δαλμ-. ι before vowels for ě in Ποτίολοι A 28: 13 *Puteoli*, λέντιον Jn 13: 4, 5 *linteum* (assimilation to Greek -ιον); ε for ĭ in λεγεών *legio* and also λέντιον, but Τιβερίου Lk 3: 1 (earlier Τεβέριος). H for ī in Κυρήνιος Lk 2: 2 *Quirinius* is doubtful; σιμικίνθιον A 19: 12 *sēmicinctium* in all MSS (ι for ē on account of the *i* in the second syllable, cf. Wackernagel, IF 25 [1909] 330 [= Kl. Schr. 1026] and σιρικοῦ *serici* Rev 18: 12 in all uncials). Ου represents ū: Ἰούλιος, Λούκιος (earlier Λεύκιος), Λουκᾶς, Ῥοῦφος; *u* is represented in pre-Christian times by ο or υ, later also by ου: κουστωδία (κοστ- is older; Debrunner, IF 52 [1934] 228), κεντυρίων (Mk 15: 39), Τέρτυλλος (in connection with the Greek suffix -υλλος). Αι renders *ae*: Καῖσαρ, ῥαίδη hardly for *raeda* (uncials ῥεδῶν, s. §5 (1d)). *Ai* are two syllables in Γάϊος. A appears for *au* in Ἀγούστου Lk 2: 1 SC*Δ as in Latin. (2) **Consonants**. Unaccented *qua-* becomes κο- in κοδράντης *quadrans*, accented κουα- in Κούαρτος; cf. Dieterich 74. *Qui* becomes κυ in Ἀκύλας *Aquila*, εὐρ-ακύλων *aquilo*, Κυρίνιος *Quirinius*. *V* after a consonant yields Hellenistic ου or (beg. i AD) β (Schwyzer I 158); thus in the NT Σιλουανός is better attested than Σιλβανός. *Publius* is rendered, as always in the older period, by Πόπλιος. For Ἀπφία *Appia* s. §42(3). The omission of the *n* from *Clēmēns* etc. and *-ēnses* in Κλήμης (§54) Φιλιππήσιοι (§5(2)) depends upon its reduced pronunciation in Latin. There is vulgar Latin dissimilation in φραγέλλιον (POxy XXII φλαγελλα) *flagellum*; s. §5(1 b)). (3) **Accent**. *Mārcus*, where the long vowel is established in Latin, must be written Μᾶρκος; on the other hand, Κούαρτος and Σέκουνδος can also be written instead of Κουᾶρτος and Σεκοῦνδος.

(1) On *Delm-* s. Thesaurus linguae Lat., Onomast. III 15; H. Krahe, Die alten balkanillyr. geogr. Namen (Heidelb., 1925) 20; Zeitschrift f. Ortsnamenf. 7 (1931) 12f.; in pap. ii–iii AD Δελμ- and Δαλμ- (Deissmann, NBS 10 [BS 182]). Λέντιον in inscrip., pap., ostraca (Nachmanson 26; Preisigke). Most uncials have λεγεών in Mt 26: 53 (-ι- S*B*DL), Mk 5: 9 (-ι- S*B*CDLΔ), 15 (-ι- S*BLΔ; D omits), Lk 8: 30 (-ι- S*B*D*L); this constitutes the NT witness for -ι- (inscrip. and pap. -ι- and -ε-). Κυρήνιος may depend on Κυρήνη; however, B and the Latinists have Κυρ(ε)ίνου *Cyrino*; the MSS also have -ήνιος

predominantly in Jos., cf. Μᾶρκον Κυρήνιον IG III 1 no. 599. Acc. to Bonfante, Rev. Ét. lat. 12 (1934) 159f. *ae* in *raeda* represents an open Gallic *ē*. The old trisyllabic character of *Gāius* is attested by Latin poetry (Fr. Allen, Harvard Studies in Class. Phil. 2 [1891] 71ff.; Stolz-Schmalz, Lat. Gr.⁵ 109) and by the frequent Γαειος (Nachmanson 50). Ἀγουστ- also in late inscrip. and pap. (Mayser I¹ 114); pure Greek words also occasionally show α for αυ (Mlt. 47 [69f.]; Psaltes 55f.).—The omission of the initial vowel in Σπανία R 15: 24, 28 ('Ισπ. only minusc.), pap. (Wessely, WSt 24 [1902] 147), 1 Macc 8: 3, Diodor. and others (Psaltes 31) = *Hispania* (*Isp-* is better, Schulten, Pauly-Wissowa 8 [1913] 1965) probably stems directly from Iberian (acc. to Pokorny, Reallex. d. Vorgesch. 6 [1925] 6 *i* is the Iberian article); F. Sommer, Handb. d. lat. Laut- und Formenl.², Heidelb. 1914, 294 (on *Spaniae* CIL v 5835) and Psaltes 31 interpret differently; cf. also W. Sieglin, Zeitschrift f. Ortsnamenf. 10 (1934) 258 and F. Mertens, PhW 1936, 623.

(2) E.g. Σιλβανοῦ 2 C 1: 19 𝔓⁴⁶ first hand DEFG, Σιλουανοῦ 𝔓⁴⁶corr SABC. Cf. M.-H. 110. On Πόπλιος (from *pop(u)lus*) s. also Walde-Hofmann³ s.v. *poplicus*. With an 'irrational' nasal (s. *supra* §39(7)) συμψέλ(λ)ιον (p. 5, n. 1).

(3) 𝔓⁴⁶ Κρισπον 1 C 1: 14 (B ει) = *Crispum* (*i*: W. Schulze, GGAbh. v 2 [1904] 157.1), but Πρεισκαν R 16: 3, -ας (*sic*) 1 C 16: 19, therefore to be accented Κρίσπος.—Cf. M.-H. 59.

(3) WORDS FROM OTHER LANGUAGES

42. (1) Syncope of ε takes place in Macedonian Βερνίκη for Βερενίκη (= Attic Φερενίκη). (2) A variant ἐγγ- exists for the Persian loanword ἀγγαρεύειν (influenced by the preposition ἐν). (3) Some variations appear in names from Asia Minor (and related places). (4) Foreign words of unknown origin: κολλύριον Rev 3: 18 varies between -υ- (SC 046) and -ου- (AP); it is difficult to decide between the spelling κράβαττος and κράββατος; all uncials have σιρικοῦ Rev 18: 12 (Lat. *serici*).

(1) On Βερνίκη s. Mayser I¹ 146; Hauser 50; Schwyzer I 259. Φερνίκη IG XII 3.903 (Thera). Cf. M.-H. 56, 64, 92.

(2) Ἐγγαρεύειν Mt 5: 41 S, Mk 15: 21 S*B*; pap. also (Mayser I¹ 56; PLond III 1171ᵛ c [p. 107] 2 [42 AD]).

(3) Ἀπφίᾳ (Ἀφφίᾳ D*) Phm 2 does not involve Lat. *Appia* which always appears with -ππ- in the inscrip., but a name native to Asia Minor (the two names doubtless influenced each other) which appears there in inscrip. with -πφ- or -φφ- (Schweizer 110; Nachmanson 78; Thieme 39; Hauser 58; Michaïlov 54). Ἰκόνιον (*i* acc. to Etymologicum Magnum s.v.; coins ι and ει) Εἰκόνιον (A 14: 21 BD), Κολοσσαί (C 1: 2 almost all witnesses) Κολασσαεῖς (title 𝔓⁴⁶AB*K[S]). Μυτιλήνη (old) Μιτυλήνη (A 20: 14 as in late Greek), Πάταρα Πάτερα (A 21: 1 AC), Τρωγύλ(λ)ιον (A 20: 15, MSS Ptolem., Geog. v 2.8) Τρωγίλιον (Strabo *et al.*).—Φύγελος (2 T 1: 15) Φύγελλος (same, A only); inscrip. from the vicinity of Ephesus show -λ-; cf. Benndorf, Zur Ortskunde u. Stadtgeschichte von Eph. (1905) 74 and Inschriften von Milet no. 142 (iv BC 2nd half) pp. 316, 317; the place-name with incorrect -λλ- is also found in the MSS: Eustathius, Suidas (Benndorf, *op. cit.* 73). Ἀδραμυντηνῷ A 27: 2 AB* (-μυττ- SB³HP) with 'irrational' nasal, s. *supra* §39(7).

(4) Κολλούριον is later; s. Crönert 130; Thack. 92; Psaltes 60; M.-H. 78f.; Preisigke. MGr κουλλούρι, also Lat. *collurium* besides *collyrium*. Κράβαττος: the older NT MSS speak for β (ββ the corrector of B) and ττ (κτ S; simple τ only B* Mk 2: 4). Thumb, Hell. 22 infers ββ from MGr dialects; in Arrian's Epicteti Dissertationes the copies have ββ and τ throughout; Mlt. [60 n.] (cf. Bauer s.v.; M.-H. 102; Rob. 213f.) attests κράβαττος and -κτος from the pap. (in addition the not entirely certain κραβάκτιον PGrenf. II 111.32 [v/vi AD]) and κράβατος from an ostracon and conjectured dialecticisms from the MSS; cf. *grabātus* and M.-H. 102. Σιρικόν: cf. σιρικοποιός IG XIV 785.4 where *siricarium* and *olosiricum* from Lat. inscrip. are compared; σιρικάριος IG III 2, no. 3513.2 (v AD); acc. to Schwyzer I 256 σιρικ- is the result of assimilation from σηρικ-. NT like Hell. σίναπι (Mayser I¹ 43), only Lk 17: 6 W σινήπεως (cf. PLeipz 97, 33.4, 8 [iv AD]); η Ion. (Sanders, Wash. 25; M.-H. 68).

PART II

ACCIDENCE AND WORD-FORMATION

1. DECLENSION

(1) FIRST DECLENSION

43. (1) Substantives in -ρᾰ (rare) follow predominantly the analogy of those in -σσα, -λλα etc. in the early NT MSS, and frequently do so in Koine elsewhere; i.e. they have -ης -ῃ in the gen. and dat. sing. instead of Attic -ᾱς -ᾳ. The same is true of those in -υῖα (§ 8), while those in -ειᾰ (and the cardinal μίᾰ) retain ᾱ throughout. (2) Some nouns have -νᾰ -νᾰν (Hellenistic) for the old -νη -νην.

(1) Σπείρης A 10: 1 etc. (PPar 69.c9 [232 AD], BGU I 142.10 [159 AD], II 462.5 [150–6 AD], Mitteis, Chr. 372 III 7, IV 11, but σπείρᾳ V 5, 9 [ii AD]), μαχαίρῃ A 12: 2 etc., πλημύρης (cf. § 11(2)) Lk 6: 48, πρῴρης A 27: 30, Σαπφείρῃ 5: 1, συνειδυίης 5: 2. M.-H. 118. The adj. στεῖρα retains ᾱ: στείρᾳ Lk 1: 36. Against ξύστρης, γεφύρης and the like, Cramer, Anec. Ox. III 247.16. Examples like δευτέρη (Reinhold 48), παλαίστρη (Helb. 31 f.), πορφύρης (Mayser I¹ 12) etc. (Psaltes 143, 187) from subst. and adj. in -ρᾱ do not appear in the NT.

(2) Πτέρναν Jn 3: 18 OT, πρύμνα A 27: 41 (cf. πρῷρα in the same vs.), σμύρναν Mt 2: 11. Cf. Solmsen 233 f., 236.

(2) SECOND DECLENSION

44. (1) The so-called Attic second declension is dying out in the Hellenistic vernacular. The only remnant in the NT is the formula ἵλεώς σοι (v.l. ἵλεος) Mt 16: 22 (s. § 128(5)) (ἵλεως H 8: 12 OT, v.l. ἵλεος); ἀνώγεων Mk 14: 15, Lk 22: 12 is not well attested (v.l. -αιον and -εον; s. § 35(2)). (2) Θεός: in Mt 27: 46 the voc. θεέ is found as occasionally in the LXX (s. § 147(3)). 'Goddess' = ἡ θεός A 19: 37 as in Attic (θεά D*E²P), but ἡ θεά in the phrase ἡ μεγάλη θεά Ἄρτεμις 27 as in the inscriptions (s. Blass *ad loc.*; Thieme 10 f.; Wackernagel, Anredeformen 23 = Kl. Schr. 990; Stocks, NKZ 24 [1913]

689.2; Hauser 81 f.); σε ὡς θεὰν ἡγησάμην Herm Vis 1.1.7. (3) Ἄδελφε s. § 13.

(1) Ἵλεως in 1 Clem and Herm several times. Ἀνίλεως Ja 2: 13 L al. is spurious for ἀνέλεος. The same corruption is found in Is 54: 10 where Torrey emends ἵλεώς σοι to ὁ ἐλεῶν σε = מְרַחֲמֵךְ, and inversely ελεος A for ἵλεως 2 Macc 2: 7 (Katz, ThLZ 1957, 114). Dor. λαός (also Ἀρχέλαος and Λαοδίκεια) and ναός (Björck, Alpha imp. 323–5, 327–9) always for Att. λεώς and νεώς, but νεωκόρος A 19: 35 as in Hell. (Helb. 39; Schlageter, Wortschatz 15; Rouffiac 64 f.; Rüsch 164; Hauser 80), ἡ ἅλων -ωνος for ἡ ἅλως (only τὴν ἅλωνα in the NT; cf. Mayser I² 2, 14), ἀρχιερεύς (s. *infra*) for ἀρχιέρεως, αὐγή (MGr) for ἕως 'dawn', -γειος for -γεως (ἐπίγειος), πλήρης and μεστός for πλέως. Acc. of Κῶς A 21: 1 is Κῶ (as in new Att.; Meisterhans 128 f.) instead of Κῶν following αἰδώς. Ἀρχιερεύς is Hell. following ἱερεύς (Schweizer 151; Rouffiac 73 f.; Scherer 31 differs; s. also Bechtel, Gr. Dial. III 114 f.).—Scherer and F. Sommer, Abh. Ak. München n. F. 27 (1948) 129.

(2) But usually θεά in the pap. (Mayser I² 2, 8 f.; II 1, 29). Bulgarian inscrip. mostly θεά (Michaïlov² 107). On θεέ cf. Wackernagel, Anredeformen 6 f. (= Kl. Schr. 973 f.) against Helb. 34 and Thack. 145; Katz, Philo's Bible 60, 152 f.; PLond I 121.529 (p. 101) [iii AD]. MGr θεέ and θέ. E. Artom, Archivio glott. it. 35 (1950) 118–50; J. Svennung, K. Hum. Vet.-samf. i Uppsala, Årsbok 1952, 123–32.

(3) CONTRACTED FORMS OF THE FIRST AND SECOND DECLENSIONS

45. Γῆ, μνᾶ (Lk 19), Ἑρμῆς like Attic and Hellenistic; βορρᾶς (-ᾶ Lk 13: 29, Rev 21: 13) is an Atticism of Koine. On νοῦς, πλοῦς and χοῦς s. § 52. Χειμάρρου Jn 18: 1 from χείμαρρος (Helb. 34) or χειμάρρους (cf. Thack. 144). Ὀστέον remains uncontracted as often in Hell. (ὀστοῦν only Jn

19: 36 OT) as does ὄρνεον (Attic ὄρνις), συκομορέα (Lk 19: 4, from συκόμορον. Cf. MGr, e.g. μηλέα from μῆλον, Thumb, Hell. 67; but always συκῆ as in Attic [also LXX], because the cultivation of figs was native to Attica), occasionally χρύσεος. Χρυσᾶν Rev 1: 13 S*AC instead of -ῆν following ἀργυρᾶν. Homil Clem 10.8.1 χρυσέους καὶ ἀργυρέους, 3 χρύσεα ἢ ἀργύρεα ἢ χάλκεα.

Βορρᾶς has been erroneously cited as a Doricism since Thumb, Hell. 65. As in Hell. ἁπλοῦς διπλοῦς are always contracted (but διπλότερον §61(2)). Ὀστέα Lk 24: 39 (-ᾶ D), -έων Mt 23: 27, E 5: 30 DFG, H 11: 22 (-ῶν 𝔓⁴⁶, corr. by first hand); ὀστοῦν Ἀττικοί, ὀστέον Ἕλληνες Moeris; uncontracted forms have been handed down by Att. writers also. Χρυσέων Rev. 2: 1 AC, -έους 4: 4 S, -έας 5: 8 S, -εα and χάλκεα 9: 20 S, χρύσεα ἀργύρεα χάλκεα 𝔓⁴⁷; otherwise consistent contraction. Uncontracted forms in the LXX, Helb. 34f.; Thack. 173; in the Ap. Frs., Reinhold 50. Λινοῦν Rev 15: 6 𝔓⁴⁷ 046 (al. read differently). With χρυσᾶν cf. PLond I 124.26 (p.122) (iv/v AD) χρυσᾶν ἢ ἀργυρᾶν, PGM II p. 129.22 (ii/iii AD) χρυσῆν ἢ ἀργυρῆν and Psaltes 187f.; Ps.-Callisth. 94.13 χρυσᾶ, 142.8 -ᾶν, 128.19 τὴν μὲν χρυσῆν, τὴν δὲ ἀργυρῆν. Hesseling (Neophilologus 11 [1926] 224f.) wants to see in σπιλάδες Jd 12 the influence of the inflection -ᾶς -άδος etc. which proceeds from proper names (§55(2)); he therefore interprets as 'dirty persons' (cf. Hesychius σπιλαδες· μεμιασμένοι); it is otherwise interpreted as σπιλάδες 'reefs' or 'blemishes'. For names in -ᾶς s. §§55(1b), 125(1).

(4) THIRD DECLENSION

46. Endings. (1) **Acc. sing. masculine, femine**: the ending -αν (an old dialect form which gained wider currency only in the post-Christian period) for -α is sometimes found in the MSS. Barytones of the third declension in -ης have acc. sing. in -ην (borrowed from the first declension) as a rule in Koine (Mayser I² 2, 39f.; Gromska 21f.; thus Σωσθένην A 18: 17), a form not unknown in Attic (τριήρην, Δημοσθένην). Later Koine extended -ην also to the oxytones of the third declension. In the NT (as in the LXX) ὑγιῆν and the like are only occasionally attested. (2) **Acc. plur. masculine, feminine**: in Hellenistic Greek -ας of the consonant stems has intruded into the vowel stems (τοὺς βότρῡς, βοῦς) in place of the old ending -ς (from *-νς): βότρυας Rev 14: 18, ἰχθύας Mt 14: 17, βόας Jn 2: 14. The substitution of the nom. plur. -ες for -ας of the acc. plur., known from the 'Northwest' dialects, frequent in Koine and dominant in MGr (following αἱ, τὰς πόλεις etc.),

arose from τέσσαρες (Bechtel, Gr. Dial. II 416) and is attested in the NT only in τέσσαρες (following τρεῖς nom.–acc.; cf. MGr nom.–acc. τέσσερις following τρεῖς), although but weakly; in the LXX such accusatives are virtually limited to τέσσαρες (Thack. 148f.). Katz warns that numerals are frequently written out from numeral letters at a late date and therefore can never be referred to the original authors with certainty. Always τοὺς βασιλεῖς as in Hellenistic. (3) **Gen. sing. in -έως instead of -έος**: the sole examples in the NT of the gen. of adjectives in -ύς are βαθέως (following βαθέων) Lk 24: 1 (on overwhelming evidence), πραέως 1 P 3: 4 SBKL. (4) **Assimilation of the nom. sing. to the other cases**: ἡ ὠδίν 1 Th 5: 3 like Hellenistic ῥίν, Σαλαμίν, δελφίν (ἀκτίν ApocP 7). Λάρυγξ R 3: 13, AP have the older λάρυξ, the corresponding σάλπιγξ 1 C 14: 8 𝔓⁴⁶ALP, the others -ιγξ.

(1) J. Ziegler, LXX Isaiah 106. On -αν Psichari 164–70 in detail with many examples; further Psaltes 154; Mayser I² 2, 46; Ghedini, Lett. crist. 306. On -ην cf. Tischendorf on H 6: 19; M.-H. 139; Mayser I² 2, 56f. For acc. μείζων and the like s. §47(2). -αν e.g. in σάρκαν E 5: 31 𝔓⁴⁶; 𝔓⁴⁷ Rev 9: 14 σάλπιγγαν, 10: 5 χεῖραν 12: 13, γυναῖκαν (also A); ἀστέραν Mt 2: 10 S*C, τρίχαν Mt 5: 36 W, χεῖραν Jn 20: 25 S*AB, Δίαν A 14: 12 DEH, εἰκόναν Rev 13: 14, μῆναν 22: 2 A. Ἀσφαλῆν H 6: 19 ACD*, συγγενῆν R 16: 11 𝔓⁴⁶ AB*D*, ἀσεβῆν 4: 5 SD*FG, ὑγιῆν Jn 5: 11 S*, ποδήρην Rev 1: 13 A, Νηρέαν R 16: 15 AFG, al. Νηρέα.

(2) Mayser I¹ 59; I² 2, 74; II 2, 187. In the NT τέσσαρας never without v.l. -ες: τέσσαρες A 27: 29 S, Jn 11: 17 SΔ, Rev. 4: 4 SAP (A has τέσσερας the second time), 7: 1 (A twice, P once), 9: 14 S. Acc. ἀστέρες Rev 1: 16 A, ἡμαρτηκότες Herm Sim 8.6.5, POxy XIII 1599.5f. (iv AD) (A -ας), 6.6 μετανενοηκότες (A, PMich -ας). Γυναῖκας as nom. pl. H 11: 35 𝔓¹³S*AD* is an error.

(3) On -έως cf. Helb. 52f.; Mayser I² 2, 56.4ff.

(4) Ὠδίν also LXX Is 37: 3; cf. also Psaltes 152; Mayser I¹ 213; I² 2, 56.

47. Formation of the case-stem. (1) The vocalic inflection of neuters in -ας has nearly disappeared: from γῆρας only the dat. γήρει (Lk 1: 36) appears; for κέρας and τέρας the τ-stem, already customary in Attic, is used throughout in Koine; thus in the NT κέρατα κεράτων, τέρατα τεράτων τέρασιν. But the Attic plur. κρέα is retained (also in LXX) R 14: 21, 1 C 8: 13 (other cases are wanting). (2) Comparatives in -ων are usually inflected in the more recent way, 'regularly' according to the ν-stem pattern; exceptions are virtually limited to Acts and John. (3) The mixture of dental stems with vocalic stems, already old in χάριν ἔριν, is extended occasionally to the nom. and acc. plur.: νήστεις ἔρεις. Conversely, the NT exhibits traces of the later Hellenistic reversion from Attic κλεῖν κλεῖς (acc. plur.) χάριν to κλεῖδα κλεῖδας χάριτα. (4) Peculiarities: for Attic οἱ ἅλες, τὸ ἅλας τοῦ ἅλατος often appears in Hellenistic (MGr τὸ ἅλας or ἁλάτι), probably as the consequence of a new interpretation of the acc. (τοὺς) ἅλας following κρέας. From ἀρήν ἀρνός only ἄρνας Lk 10: 3 appears (literary language, πρόβατα AM al.); otherwise ἀρνίον (John), ἀμνός or πρόβατα is used; cf. Thack. 152. In ἐσθήσεσιν Lk 24: 4 ACLXΓΔ al., A 1: 10 SABC the dat. ending is added a second time, as it were, in order to make it clear (W. Schulze, KZ 42 [1909] 255 n. 2). Ναῦς only A 27: 41 τὴν ναῦν (literary language, vernacular πλοῖον). Ὄρνιξ 'hen' Lk 13: 34 SDW instead of ὄρνις Mt 23: 37, Lk 13: 34 is a Doricism in Koine; for 'bird' the NT as Hellenistic otherwise employs ὄρνεον. On indeclinable πλήρης s. §137(1). Συγγενεῦσιν Mk 6: 4 (-έσιν Sᵃ [om. S*] AB²CD* al.), Lk 2: 44 B*LWXΔΛ from συγγενεῖς is an analogous formation following γονεῖς-γονεῦσιν. From ο- (οσ-) stems only αἰδοῦς 1 T 2: 9, H 12: 28 SᶜDᵇᶜKL al. (for which ἐντροπή 1 C 6: 5, 15: 34 as in MGr) and πειθοῖ 1 C 2: 4 (all uncials have the corrupt πειθοῖς [§ 112]); ἥρως and ἠχώ (s. §50) do not appear. Πραΰς instead of πρᾶος s. §26. Ὄναρ only in κατ' ὄναρ (6 times in Mt) 'in a dream', otherwise ἐνύπνιον.

(1) Mayser I² 2, 36. Γήρους and γήρει also in the LXX and elsewhere (Thack. 149f.; Psaltes 154f.); similarly in Ionic.

(2) Πλείους nom. or acc. A 13: 31, 19: 32, 21: 10, 23: 13, 21, 24: 11, 25: 6, 14, but -νες -νας 27: 12, 20, 28: 23; John: μείζω 1: 50 neut. pl. (-ονα S; -ων MXΔ), 5: 36 acc. sg. fem. (-ων ABE al. [cf. ἀστέραν, ἀσεβῆν §46(1) and Thack. 146f.], -ονα D), ἐλάσσω 2: 10 acc. sg. masc. (v.l. -σσων and -σσον), πλείους 4: 41; otherwise πλείω or -ους Mt 26: 53. Pap. -ονα -ονες in ii/i BC are on the increase: Mayser I² 2, 59ff.

(3) In the NT usually χάριν, always as a prep.; χάριτα only A 24: 27 (-ιν SᶜEL Ψ), 25: 9 A, Jd 4 AB. Νήστεις (acc.) Mt 15: 32, Mk 8: 3 (inferior v.l. νήστῑς), ἔρεις (acc.) T 3: 9 SᶜAC al. (ἔριν S*DEW al. amidst obvious plurals), nom. 1 C 1: 11 all MSS, nom. and acc. 1 Clem (Reinhold 52), ἔρεις Ps 138: 20? From κλείς (Rev 9: 1) acc. sg. κλεῖν Rev 3: 7, 20: 1, Lk 11: 52 D (κλεῖδα al., τὰς κλεῖς Justin), acc. pl. κλεῖς Mt 16: 19 (v.l. κλεῖδας), Rev. 1: 18 (κλεῖδας 046).

On κλεῖδα and χάριτα s. especially Thack. 150, Mayser I² 2, 31.

(4) Τὸ ἅλας nom. Mt 5: 13 twice (ἅλα S twice, D once), Mk 9: 50 twice (ἅλα S* once, LΔ twice), Lk 14: 34 twice (ἅλα S*D); ἅλας acc. Mk 9: 50 (third occurrence) SᶜA²CN al., ἅλα S*A*BDLΔ; ἅλατι C 4: 6, ἁλί Mk 9: 49 D (injunction of Lev 2: 13 is missing in SBLΔ); cf. Herodian II 716.23; Nägeli 58.1; Mayser I² 2, 45. Ἅλατος Diamart. 4.3 (p. 4.16 Rehm) in P (ὕδατος O). Τὸ ἅλα (also in glosses; Dieterich 165) from ἁλατ- following σῶμα σώματ-; cf. τὸ γῆρα Artem. 211.19 (cod. Laur.). S. also M. Leumann, Homerische Wörter (Basel, 1950) 160f.; Egli, Heterokl. 97f. Ἐσθήσεσι LXX 2 Macc 3: 33, 3 Macc 1: 16, BGU I 16.12 (p. 395) (159 AD), PLond I no. 77.20, 32 (p. 241ff.) (vi AD), also as a variant in Strabo etc. (Crönert 173.1). On ὄρνιξ cf. Thumb, Hell. 90; Crönert 174.5; F. Robert, Les noms des oiseaux en grec ancien (Diss. Basel [Neuchâtel, 1911]) p. 17; Mayser I² 2, 31 (ὄρνιξ pap. iii BC); ὄρνιξι several times PLond I 131 (pp. 173ff.) (78 AD). MGr (Cappadocian) ὄρνίχ 'hen' need not be old (Thumb, Hell. 91; Dawkins, Modern Greek in Asia Minor §93). Συγγενεῦσι LXX 1 Macc 10: 89 A, inscrip. ABA 1925, 5, p. 33 (Dor. iv BC); JHS 22 (1902) 358; Petersen-Luschan, Reisen II no. 32.5; Malalas (Wolf I 29); cf. W. Schulze, KZ 33 (1895) 400 = Kl. Schr. 328; Crönert, WSt 21 (1899) 64. Συγγενέων Lk 21: 16 A; inscrip. and Ap. Frs. συγγενέα and -έας s. Thack. 153; Reinhold 52; Mayser I² 2, 57. Byzantine -εύς, -έως, -έα (Wolf I 29, Psaltes 63). Acc. to Ps.-Herodian in Cramer, Anec. Ox. III 246.7 many even said συγγενεῖσι; cf. inscrip. γονεῖσι and others (Dieterich 154; W. Schulze, op. cit. 399f.; Nachmanson 132; Mayser I² 2, 29). Even ὑεῖσι (Michaïlov² 115); γονεῖσιν (124). Κατ' ὄναρ also in an inscrip. from Pergamon (Schweizer 157); Att. expresses 'in a dream' by simple ὄναρ (cf. Phryn. 421).

48. Contraction.

Just as uncontracted gen. plurals of certain neuters in -ος are not entirely unfamiliar to Attic authors, they are found also in the NT: ὀρέων Rev 6: 15, χειλέων H 13: 15 (from LXX Hos 14: 3); but always ἐθνῶν, ἐθῶν, ἐτῶν (§165) etc. Contrary to Attic practice the following are contracted: πηχῶν (Attic πήχεων from πῆχυς) Jn 21: 8 (-εων A), Rev 21: 17 (-εων S), ἡμίσους (instead of -εος) Mk 6: 23, ἡμίση Lk 19: 8 ΓΠ (D²). Only ὑγιῆ (Jn 5: 11, 15 etc.) is found in Hellenistic, while ὑγιᾶ also in Attic.

Ὀρέων also Herm and 1 Clem (Reinhold 52); Aristeas 119. Cf. Thack. 151; M.-H. 139; Mayser I² 2, 37. Adjs. remain contracted, e.g. ἀσεβῶν; contrast συγγενέων (supra §47(4)). Hell. πηχῶν Thack. 151; Mayser I² 2, 25. Ἡμίσους and -ση appear early in Koine (Gromska 22f.; Mayser I² 2,

55f.; Schwyzer I 573), indeclinable ἥμισυ is much later (τὰ ἥ. Lk 19: 8 ARΔ [D*] W as in LXX Tob 10: 10 B [A?]; often in the Byzantine Chronicles, s. Psaltes 159) as is the neut. pl. ἡμίσ(ε)ια (Lk 19: 8 SBLQΘ; βαρεῖα etc. in MSS of the LXX, Thack. 178f., θήλεια Arat. 1068, Dialekt-Inschr. 4706.95 [c. 200 BC]; otherwise ὀξεῖα [Hesiod], Scut. 348 [metre], πλατεια Att. inscrip. 358 BC [Meisterhans 150]); cf. Hatzid. 381; Crönert 111; Helb. 53; Wackernagel, ThLZ 1908, 638; ἡμίσους and -ση as Hell. [Herodian] in Cramer, Anec. Ox. III 247.14.

(5) METAPLASM (FLUCTUATION OF DECLENSION)

49. Fluctuation of gender in the second declension. (1) Feminines of the second declension: ὁ and ἡ βάτος, ὁ λίθος (also for 'gem', where Attic used ἡ), ὁ and ἡ λιμός, ὁ ὕαλος. (2) Masculine instead of neuter: δεῖπνος for δεῖπνον only as v.l. Lk 14: 16, Rev 19: 9 (046), 17. Always ζυγός 'yoke' (predominant in Hellenistic), never Attic ζυγόν. Ὁ νῶτος R 11: 10 OT (classical τὸ νῶτον) as in Hippoc., Xen., Arist. etc.; ὁ ὦμος is the prototype: Georgacas, Class. Phil. 48 (1953) 242. (3) Fluctuation of gender in the plural: δεσμός plur. δεσμοί and δεσμά (both old); ὁ θεμέλιος (properly scil. λίθος; Attic), plur. τὰ θεμέλια and οἱ θεμέλιοι; ὁ σῖτος–τὰ σῖτα as in Attic; στάδιον plur. -οι and -α (both Attic).

(1) Ἀλάβαστρος with article only Mk 14: 3 τὸν (v.l. τὸ and τὴν) ἀλάβαστρον, Att. allegedly ἡ, Aristoph. ὁ, Menander τό. Ὁ ἄψινθος Rev 8: 11 (ὁ is wanting in S), because it is used as a name. Ὁ βάτος preponderates in Mk 12: 26, ἡ (acc. to Moeris Hell. which is incorrect; rather ἡ is Atticistic, ὁ is vulgar: Thack. 145; Katz, ZNW 46 [1955] 136 with n. 8a) Lk 20: 37, A 7: 35. Usually ἡ ληνός (following ἡ νόσος Schwyzer II 37 n.); τὴν ληνόν...τὸν μέγαν Rev 14: 19 ACP 046 is anacolouthon (ἐν τοῖς ληνοῖς LXX Gen 30: 38, 41 in minusc.). Ἡ λιμός (LXX, early in Doric) Lk 15: 14, A 11: 28 (v.l. masc.), ὁ Lk 4: 25 (fem. W); s. § 2. Ἡ στάμνος like Att. H 9: 4, ὁ LXX and Doric. Ὁ ὕαλος instead of ἡ Rev 21: 18 (cf. λίθος; ὁ ὕελος Theophr., Lap. 49). In the case of ὕσσωπος Jn 19: 29, H 9: 19 the gender is not determinable. Otherwise ἡ ἄμμος, ἄμπελος, κάμινος, ὁδός etc. as usual. On ἡ θεός s. §44(2).

(2) Late Gr. ὁ δεῖπνος (Aesop. [Ursing 23] and MGr; perhaps following ὁ σῖτος) for τὸ δεῖπνον: Lk 14: 16 B³D μέγαν, Rev 19: 9 046 τὸν, 17 minusc. τὸν, but 1 C 11: 21 only τὸ. Ζυγός as early as Hom. Hymn. Dem. 217; LXX except for nom. ζυγόν Ezk 45:10A, ζυγά Lev 19:36; also MGr ζυγός. S. Egli, Heterokl. 110f.: for νῶτον -τος 84–6.

(3) Δεσμοί Ph 1: 13, δεσμά Lk 8: 29, A 16: 26, 20: 23; θεμέλιος 1 C 3: 11, 12, 2 T 2: 19, Rev 21: 19, θεμέλιοι H 11: 10, Rev 21: 14, 19, -α A 16: 26, -ον as nom. sg. Herm Sim 9.4.2, 14.6; σῖτος Mt 3: 12 etc., σῖτα A 7: 12 HP (σιτία SAB al.); σταδίους Jn 6: 19 SᶜᵒʳʳABL al. (στάδια S*D), Lk 24: 13, Rev 21: 16 A 046 al. (v.l. -ίων). Cf. Reinhold 53, 54; Mayser I² 2, 45, 49; Helb. 46f.

50. Parallel formations in the first and second declensions. Compounds with ἄρχειν as the second member are formed in Attic in -αρχος, in (the dialects and) Hellenistic more often in -άρχης (first declension), but -αρχος is retained in proper names (Mayser I² 2, 12): Ἀρίσταρχος. New formations in Hellenistic have only -άρχης (following the type of -αλοίας -μέτρης Schwyzer I 451). Φύλαρχος Dt 31: 28 is -ης in PFuad 266 (iii BC) as in 2 Macc 8: 32. According to Moeris δυσεντέριον (A 28: 8; minuscules -ία) is Hellenistic for -ρία (cf. Lob. Phryn. 518), likewise ὁ ἦχος (and τὸ ἦχος, cf. §51(2)) for ἠχή. Ἦχος as masculine H 12: 19, as neuter Lk 21: 25 (ἤχους gen. sing., hardly to be written ἠχοῦς; M.-H. 125), Apocr. three times (Reinhold 54), indeterminable Lk 4: 37, A 2: 2; never ἠχή or ἠχώ. Ὁ μύλος is Hellenistic (and MGr) for ἡ μύλη. Μύλος Rev 18: 21, 22, as v.l. Mt 18: 6 pars. and 24: 41. Τὸ ἔνεδρον (POxy VI 892.11 [338 AD]) as v.l. (HLP) for τὴν ἐνέδραν A 23: 16, ἐνέδραν all MSS 25: 3; ἔνεδρον and ἐνέδρα are still not synonyms in the LXX (Thack. 156f.). Τὸ βασίλειον in the sense of ἡ βασιλεία is late, 2 Clem 6.9, 17.5 (LXX in hexaplaric additions; Thack. 157).

Ἐθνάρχης, πατριάρχης, πολιτάρχης, τετραάρχης (Ἀσιαρχῶν A 19: 31); also ἑκατοντάρχης Mt 8: 5 S*W, 13 (-χῳ SᵇUΔ), Lk 7: 6 BLW (-ος 𝔓⁴⁵SACD), 23: 47 S*B, and preponderant in Acts; but always χιλίαρχος (like Hell.), ἑκατόνταρχος A 22: 25 and often (but with frequent variants); στρατοπέδαρχος or -άρχης A 28: 16 in an addition (om. SAB). Cf. Thack. 156; Fraenkel II 144ff.; Mayser I² 2, 11f.

51. Neuters in -ος with parallels in the first and second declensions. (1) In the first declension: δίψα and δίψος are Attic; in the NT only δίψει 2 C 11: 27 (δ(ε)ιψη B*𝔓⁴⁶). The early Hellenistic form τὸ νῖκος is an analogical remodeling of νίκη following κράτος; s. Wackernagel, Homer 81f. Στέγη Mk 2: 4, Mt 8: 8 = Lk 7: 4 as in Attic, LXX, papyri and Philo Byz.; literary τὸ στέγος (Tragedians) 1 Clem 12.6 as LXX Ep Jer 10 (Arnim 44). (2) In the second declension: the examples of fluctuation between masculines in

-ος and neuters in -ος have increased somewhat in comparison with classical Greek. Thus τὸ ἔλεος, τὸ ζῆλος (also MGr), τὸ ἦχος, τὸ πλοῦτος (also MGr), τὸ σκότος (neuter after τὸ φάος = φῶς) as opposed to Attic ὁ (Fraenkel, KZ 43 [1911] 195 ff.); ὁ θάμβος (formed earlier) for τὸ θ.—Egli, Heterokl. 64–73; Th. St. Trannetatos, Τα εἰς -αρχης, -αρχος συνθετα ἐν τη ἀρχαια Ἑλληνικη γλωσση (Πλατων I [1949] 1–18).

(1) Τὸ νῖκος Mt 12: 20 OT (= לָנֶצַח), 1 C 15: 54 OT, 55 OT, 57, Herm Man 12.2.5, ἡ νίκη 1 Jn 5: 4.

(2) Always τὸ ἔλεος (yet v.l. ἔλεον sometimes), also gen. ἐλέους, dat. ἐλέει; the old derivative ἐλεεινός (like φάος–φαεινός) and the compound νηλεής show that the ς-stem is original. Ὁ ζῆλος also for the most part in the NT; but τὸ ζ. 2 C 9: 2 𝔓⁴⁶SB, Ph 3: 6 𝔓⁴⁶S*ABD*FG, ζῆλος as nom. 2 C 7: 11 𝔓⁴⁶, ζήλους as gen. A 5: 17 B*. Ἦχους s. § 50. Τὸ πλοῦτος as nom. acc. sg. 2 C 8: 2 𝔓⁴⁶S*BCP, R 9: 23 𝔓⁴⁶G, Herm Sim 2.7, 8, POxy IX 1172.25, 38 (here also PBer) (but 5 [1172.6] τὸν πλοῦτον, 7 [1172.28] τῷ πλούτῳ); overwhelmingly or well attested: E 1: 7, 2: 7, 3: 8, 16, Ph 4: 19, C 1: 27, 2: 2, otherwise ὁ πλ. (also E 1: 18); gen. always πλούτου. Τοῦ στρήνους Rev 18: 3 (στρήνου C), neuter as everywhere from iv bc on, except for Lycophron 438 (s. L.-S. s.v.). Τὸ σκότος universal in Hell. (ὁ is early, but τὸ appears in Pindar; moreover, the NT as Hell. frequently has σκοτία), H 12: 18 σκότῳ SᶜDᵇᶜL (σκότει 𝔓⁴⁶) spurious variant for ζόφῳ (S*ACD*P). Θάμβος only Lk 5: 9 (gender indeterminable), 4: 36 (likewise, but D θ. μέγας), -ους A 3: 10 (-ου C). Mere inadvertences: ὁ πλάτος E 3: 18 𝔓⁴⁶, σάλους Lk 21: 25 W (pm. -ου). Γνόφος H 12: 18 and ῥύπος 1 P 3: 21 only masc.

52. Other fluctuations between second and third declensions. Νοῦς and πλοῦς follow βοῦς in Hellenistic (conversely βοῦ after νοῦ Aeschyl. and Soph.). Ἡ ἄλων, -ωνος (Mt 3: 12, Lk 3: 17) replaces ἡ ἅλως, -ω (§44(1)). From δάκρυον and σάββατον the dat. plur. is formed according to the third declension: δάκρυσιν (a remnant of the old δάκρυ? probably from Attic literary language [Egli, Heterokl. 29]) and σάββασιν (following σώματα–σωμάτων–σώμασιν; cf. Schwyzer, KZ 62 [1935] 9 ff.). In Rev 12: 10 A forms a nom. κατήγωρ for κατήγορος (perhaps following ῥήτωρ arising from the gen. plur. in -όρων); Debrunner, GGA 1926, 137 ff.

Appearing in the NT: νοῦς νοός νοΐ νοῦν (νουνεχῶς Mk 12: 34), πλοός πλοῦν; in Hell. also ῥοῦς ῥοός, χοῦς χοός 'rubbish, dust' (NT only χοῦν in formal expressions); cf. Helb. 51; Mayser I² 2, 12f., 27; Reinhold 55; W. Schmid, PhW 1934, 969. Bonfante

is incorrect, Stud. Ital. 9 (1931) 77 (πλοῦς πλοός as an old declension). Homil Clem 17.10.3 νοός, 5 νῷ, 17.5 νῷ; 13.3.3 σύννοες. On νοῦς etc. Egli, Heterokl. 62–4. Δάκρυσιν Lk 7: 38, 44; always σάββασιν Mt 12: 1 etc., only Mt 12: 1, 12 σαββάτοις in B. LXX always δάκρυσι, σάββασι once, otherwise σαββάτοις (Helb. 49). With κατήγωρ (Rabbinic קַטִיגוֹר TW III 637.24) cf. κατήγορας in a late magic pap. and διάκων -ωνος -ονος etc. in pap. beg. i AD (Preisigke III 108, 400) (late Latin diacones diaconibus), s. Deissmann, LO⁴ 72 f. [LAE 93 f.]; Raderm.² 19 f.; Psaltes 175; Ursing 21 f.; Olsson 138; Michaïlov² 117.—Υἱός survives only as an o-stem as in Hell.

(6) DECLENSION OF FOREIGN WORDS

(cf. Helb. 58–60 and the literature cited in §36)

(A) Personal Names

53. Hellenization of Semitic personal names. (1) Hebrew personal names taken from the OT remain as such unaltered and indeclinable: Ἀδάμ, Ἀβραάμ, Δαυίδ, Ἰακώβ, Φαραώ etc. Exceptions are chiefly names ending in הָ‍ which are taken over as -ᾶς (and not only after ε, ι, ρ) and declined according to the first declension: Ἰούδας, Ἐζεκίας etc. In addition the following are Grecized: Μανασσῆς, Ἰαννῆς and Ἰαμβρῆς 2 T 3: 8, Λευίς, Σολομών (in the LXX an older form is Σαλωμ-, then Σαλομ- and finally Σολομ-; inscriptions and papyri Σαλωμ-, Σολομ-, Σολωμ-, Wuthnow 103, 111; Σαλαμω[ν?] Graffito Dura: Syria 20 [1939] 30), Ἰησοῦς Joshua (A 7: 45, H 4: 8, Ap. Frs.), Μωυσῆς. (2) Semitic names of the NT period are far more susceptible to Hellenization. Often the same name, if it belongs to a person of the NT period, is Grecized, and not Grecized if it designates a person of a former age or is used of a NT person in a formal manner (cf. Deissmann, BS 184.3 [BS 316 n. 1]). Exceptions: Δανιήλου Mt 24: 15 D (according to Rudberg 18 vernacular). Hellenization takes place (a) by appending -ος (Ἰάκωβος, Ἄγαβος, Λάζαρος); (b) by adding -ς in the nom. to names that terminate in a vowel (Ἰησοῦς, Λευίς etc., also Ἰούδας etc., s. supra (1)); (c) by taking the terminal ן‍ of names as acc. -ᾶν and then transposing the whole to the pattern of Ἰούδας (e.g. Ἰωνάθας Atticized Ἰωάν(ν)ης); (d) sometimes by substituting a similar sounding genuine Greek name (Ἰάσων for Ἰησοῦς, Σίμων for Συμεών, Θωμᾶς for תְּאוֹמָה [R. Herzog, Philol. 56 (1897) 51; Dalman 145.6; Wuthnow 55], Κλεοπᾶς for Κλωπᾶς; s. also § 125(2)); (e) by translation: Κηφᾶς–Πέτρος (cf. Jn 1: 42); cf. Gressmann, DLZ 1920, 308 f.; Cassuto, Giorn. Soc. As. It. N.S. 2 (1933) 209–30. Others remain unchanged and indeclinable, e.g. Ἰωσήφ (generally; in addition Ἰωσῆς s. *infra*), Ναθαναήλ (also Μιχαήλ, Γαβριήλ), Μαναήν (A 13: 1). (3) Likewise in the case of names of women: Ἐλισάβετ (cf. §39(2)), while מִרְיָם is represented both as Μαριάμ (Μαριά(μ)μη Jos.) and as Μαρία. It is no longer correct to say that Μαρία is a Hellenized form since Jerusalem inscriptions have מריה; E. Y. Kutscher, Scripta Hierosolymitana IV (1957), Aspects of the Dead Sea Scrolls, 23 f., shows that מריה is a back-formation from מרין > מרים, due to the fact that ן- was understood as an appended nasal (s. especially n. 118). Ἄννα חַנָּה (only nom. Lk 2: 36) and Μάρθα (Aram. מָרְתָא) are declinable as transliterated. The following are Hellenized by the addition of -α (ἄ?): Ἰωαν(ν)α יוחנא and יוחני Dalman 179.5), Σουσαννα (Syr. *šwšn*); by the addition of η according to the Attic rule only Σαλώμη (Syr. *šlwm*). (4) As to the gender of proper names, feminine τῇ Βάαλ R 11: 4 (from LXX 3 Km 19: 18 τῷ Βάαλ) stems from Qᵉrê בּשֶׁת αἰσχύνη (Mlt. 59 [88]; M.-H. 152).

(1) Ἀβιά (as in the LXX) does not follow the decl. in -ίας Mt 1: 7 nom. and acc., Lk 1: 5 gen. Also indeclinable are Λευ(ε)ί, e.g. Lk 3: 24, 29; H 7: 9 (-(ε)ίς SᶜBC*), Σολομών (s. §55(2)). Γαμαλιήλου A 22: 3 BΨ, -ήλ (gen.) pm.

(2) Ἰάκωβος but the patriarch Ἰακώβ. Ἰωάνης–Ἰωανάν: Ἰωάν(ν)ης for יוֹחָנָן (§40), but Ἰωανάν Lk 3: 27 (an ancestor of Christ); it is also shortened to Ἰωνᾶ (Syr. *yōnā*'; as sometimes in the LXX MSS Ἰωνᾶ, -ας, -αν for (יה)וחנן; J. Jeremias, TW III 410); Σίμων Βαριωνᾶ Mt 16: 17 = Σ. (ὁ υἱὸς) Ἰωάννου Jn 1: 42 (Ἰωνᾶ AB³ al., sy), 21: 15–17 (Ἰωνᾶ ACᶜᵒʳʳ al., sy *ywnn*, which however in Lk 11: 29 etc. stands also for the prophet Jonah); Ἰωανάν or -άμ (SBΓ, sy) Lk 3: 30, an ancestor of Christ. Σαῦλος–Σαούλ: Σαούλ only in formal address, otherwise Σαῦλος; but 𝔓⁴⁵ Σαουλʼ throughout (gen. A 7: 58, 11: 30, dat. 9: 24, acc. 13: 7). Λάζαρος–Ἐλεάζαρ (Mt 1: 15 Ἐλεάζαρ LXX Macc and 1 Esdr): Λαζαρ 𝔓⁴⁵ Jn 11: 2 probably inadvertently; Λάζαρος and Ἐλάζαρος Wuthnow 66. Συμεών (indecl.) of Peter A 15: 14 in the speech of James (but see S. Giet, RSR 39 [1951] 203 ff.) and 2 P 1: 1 (B Σίμων), of others Lk 2: 25, A 13: 1, etc., Σίμων often for different persons. Σίμων = Συμεών often in the Hell. period, one of the most frequent Jewish names in the period of the Empire (Hölscher, Beihefte ZAW 41 [1925] 150 f., 155; Wuthnow 113). Ἰάσων is also popular (TW III 285 f.). -ας for ן,: Ἄννας חנן (Jos. Ἄνανος) from חֲנַנְיָה Ἀνανίας. Ναιμας

Lk 4: 27 D*d* for Ναιμάν as Jos. Καινας for Καινάν, Ναθας for Ναθάν. Μνάσων (Κύπριος) A 21: 16 = מְנַשֶּׁה or מְנַחֵם; cf. *Mnaseas*, the father of Zenon of Cyprus, and Cyprian *ma-na-se-se* (i.e. Μνασῆς = Μνασέας) = Mnachem in bilingual Phoenician-Cyprian (Bechtel, Gr. Dial. I 414); s. also W. Schulze, Kl. Schr. (1933) 394 f.; Cadbury (Debrunner, Jahresb. Altertumsw. 261 [1938] 208). Ἰωνάθας A 4: 6 D as in Aristeas 48, 49 and in a pap. of iii BC (Mayser I² 2, 7.42), but Jos. and Aristeas 50 Hellenize it still further to Ἰωνάθης. יוסף was similarly shortened to יוסה Ἰωσῆ (as v.l. several times) or Ἰωσῆς (§55(2); Wuthnow 60); cf. ישו for ישוע Laible, ThBl 1923, 114. Σιλέας is not clear (A 15: 34 D Σειλέα *Sileae*) = Σιλᾶς (§125(2)).— On the assimilation of Jewish names s. also H. J. Leon, Glotta 19 (1931) 188 f.

(3) Μαριάμ especially for the mother of Jesus. There is great diversity in the MSS: Mt gen. Μαρίας acc. Μαριάμ 1: 20 (-ίαν BL), in chaps. 27, 28 -ία preponderates for the other Marys; Lk Μαριάμ as nom., voc., dat., acc., but τῆς Μαρίας 1: 41, ἡ Μαρία 2: 19 SBD (D otherwise more often nom. -α, dat. -α [= ᾳ], acc. -αν); A 1: 14 Μαρίᾳ SACD, -άμ BE; Paul R 16: 6 Μαριάμ for an unknown woman (-ίαν ABCP). Cf. v. Soden 1373 f.; Ed. König, ZNW 17 (1916) 257 ff.; M.-H. 144 f.

(4) Βάαλ with the fem. art. is found also in the LXX, s. Lietzmann, Hdb. on R 11: 4. Αἰσχύνη as a translation of בַּעַל LXX 3 Km 18: 19, 25, Hos 9: 10, Jer 3: 24, 25; where it denotes the divinity it should be capitalized (Katz, ThLZ 1936, 286), e.g. Jer 3: 24.

54. Hellenization of Latin personal names.

Only Agrippa Ἀγρίππας, Aquila Ἀκύλας according to the first declension are to be noted. *-ēns -entis* become -ης -εντος: (Κλήμης) Κλήμεντος Ph 4: 3, Κρήσκης 2 T 4: 10, Πούδης 21 for *Clēmēns Crēscēns Pudēns*; cf. §41(2). For Λουκᾶς etc. s. §125(2).

55. The declension of personal names.

Foreign proper names are adapted as far as possible to Greek paradigms, chiefly to the first declension and to the short names in -ᾶς etc. There is, moreover, a quite perceptible effort at simplification, since stems in long vowels maintain a uniform inflection-pattern, modeled on the original Doric but also taken over into Attic in the case of non-Ionic-Attic names: -ας -α -ᾳ -αν -α. (1) Thus there arise the following declension patterns: (*a*) Ἰούδας, -α, -ᾳ, -αν, -α, therefore following Doric-Attic Λεωνίδας Ἀβροκόμας (but gen. -ίου from -ίας following Attic Λυσίας -ίου; cf. Οἰδίπους -ου ... -ουν -ου), in the case of women

-α, -ας; (b) Σατανᾶς, -ᾶ, -ᾷ, -ᾶν, voc. -ᾶ; (c) ᾽Ιωάνης, -ου, -η, -ην (following Att. ᾽Αλκιβιάδης); (d) Μανασσῆς, -ῆ, -ῇ (unattested for the NT), -ῆ(ν), -ῆ; (e) Λευίς, gen. -ι, acc. -ί(ν); (f) ᾽Ιησοῦς, -οῦ, -οῦ, -οῦν, -οῦ; (g) ᾽Απολλῶς, -ῶ, acc. -ῶ(ν). (2) The dental inflection of names, which stems from Ionic and is found very frequently in Hellenistic (Mayser I² 2, 33 ff.), and in the widely diffused MGr -άδες with appellatives (-ᾶς -άδος or -ᾶτος, -οῦς -οῦδος or -οῦτος; papyri -τ-, almost never -δ-), is found in the NT only in the case of ᾽Ιωσῆς (§ 53 (2)): ᾽Ιωσῆτος Mk 6: 3 BDLΔ (᾽Ιωσῆ ACW, ᾽Ιωσήφ S), 15: 40 SᶜBDLΔ, 47 SᶜBLΔ. Σολομων has a gen. in either -μῶνος (therefore nom. -μών) or -μῶντος (after Ξενοφῶν, therefore nom. -μῶν).

(1) K.-Bl. I 492 ff.; on the vocatives Wackernagel, Anredeformen 17 f. = Kl. Schr. 984 f.; W. Schulze, Festschrift Wackernagel 244 f. = Kl. Schr. 86 f. (a) Gen. e.g. ῎Αννα, Καϊάφα, ᾽Ιούδα, ᾽Αγρίππα, but e.g. Οὐρίου, Ζαχαρίου, ᾽Ηλίου (᾽Ηλεία SB Lk 1: 17; LXX nearly always indeclin. ᾽Ηλ(ε)ιου; cf. Τωβ(ε)ία and the like as v.l. in LXX, Thack. 162). Μάρθα often (§ 53 (3)), -ας Jn 11: 1 (Λύδδα -ας s. § 56 (2)). Only gen. in -ου in pap. of the Ptol. period, also without preceding ι: ᾽Ιωνάθου ᾽Ιούδου ᾽Αννίβου; Mayser I² 2, 4.33 ff. (b) E.g. Βαραββᾶς, Βαρναβᾶς, Ζηνᾶς, Σατανᾶς (cf. § 58), Σιλᾶς. (c) ᾽Ιωάνου often, as v.l. to ᾽Ιωανάν already in the LXX 2 Chr 28: 12; v.l. to ᾽Ιωάνη -ει Lk 7: 18 SAB*, 22 SABL, Mt 11: 4 DΔ, Rev 1: 1 S*, cf. infra (d) Μωυσεῖ. (d) Μανασσῆς nom. Mt 1: 10 (-ῆ SᵇB), gen. -ῆ Rev 7: 6, acc. -ῆ Mt 1: 10; the LXX also fluctuates (Thack. 164). ᾽Απελλῆς A 18: 24 S*, -ῆν R 16: 10, A 19: 1 S* (§ 29 (4)). Μωυσῆς is peculiar: gen. always -έως (as if from -εύς), dat. -εῖ Mt 17: 4 SBD al. (v.l. -ῆ), Mk 9: 4 AB³DE al. (-ῆι 𝔓⁴⁵), 5 almost all witnesses, and thus elsewhere with variation between -ει and -η; acc. -έα only Lk 16: 29, 1 C 10: 2 𝔓⁴⁶, otherwise -ῆν; voc. -ῆ Barn 4.8, 1 Clem 53.1. In the LXX the inflection -ῆς, -ῆ -ῇ -ῆν -ῆ predominates; in their text of Jos. Niese and Naber adopt -έος (hardly correct; -έως is moreover a strong variant in the MSS) -εῖ -ῆν; -έως (v.l. -έος) is attested as early as Diodor. Sic. 34.1 (IV 133.22 Bekker). -εῖ is probably an itacistic reinterpretation of -ῆ which gave rise to -έως (better Greek; Thack. 164). (e) Λευ(ε)ίς Lk 5: 29 (without -ς D), H 7: 9 SᶜBC* (without -ς al.), cf. Wuthnow 67; gen. always Λευ(ε)ί, acc. Λευ(ε)ίν Mk 2: 14 (without -ν S*A al.), Lk 5: 27 (without -ν D). (g) Nom. always ᾽Απολλῶς, gen. always -ῶ, acc. -ῶ (cf. Κῶς–Κῶ § 44 (1)) A 19: 1 (-ων A²L, ᾽Απελλῆν s. supra (d)), 1 C 4: 6 (-ων S*AB), T 3: 13 (-ων SDᵇH, -ωνα FG).

(2) Σολομων- e.g. Mt 1: 6 -μῶνα (-μῶν indecl. S*); Σολομωντ- only A 3: 11 (DE -μῶνος), 5: 12 (BDEP -μῶνος), Σαλομῶντος Jn 10: 23 W (but Σολομῶνος

Mt 12: 42 W); 𝔓⁴⁵ -ῶνος Lk 11: 31 twice, -ῶντος A 5: 12. LXX -μωντ- if declined at all; -μων- has very slender support and is late (Thack. 166). Cf. Pauly-Wissowa Suppl. 8 [1956] 660.

(B) Geographical Names

56. Hellenization of non-Greek names. (1) The Hellenization and inflection of geographical proper names is still more common than in the case of personal names, even apart from prominent designations known earlier to the Greeks. For example, Τύρος, Σιδών -ῶνος, ῎Αζωτος (§ 39 (4)), Δαμασκός; ᾽Ιορδάνης -ου. ᾽Ιεροσόλυμα is strongly Hellenized by assimilation to ἱερός and Σόλυμοι (s. § 38) -ων (as early as Polyb.), which is used in addition to ᾽Ιερουσαλήμ. (2) Names in -α (whether the -α is Semitic or Greek) usually fluctuate between indeclinable usage and declension. (3) Always transliterated unaltered, e.g. Βηθλεέμ, Βηθσαϊδά(ν), Βηθφαγῆ, Καφαρναούμ, Ναζαρέθ, Αἰνών (Jn 3: 23), Σαλίμ (ibid.), Σιών, Σινᾶ, Κεδρών Jn 18: 1. (4) Gender of foreign place-names: there is not only ἡ ᾽Ιερουσαλήμ, but even πᾶσα ᾽Ιεροσόλυμα Mt 2: 3 (precursor of indeclinable πᾶσα in MGr?). Masculine Σιλωάμ (spring and pool) Lk 13: 4, Jn 9: 7, 11 is explained by the interpretation added in Jn 9: 7—ἀπεσταλμένος.

(1) ᾽Ιεροσόλυμα regularly in Mk, Jn, also in Mt except for the solemn apostrophe 23: 37; ᾽Ιερουσαλήμ regularly in Rev, Heb, and Paul except for the report in G 1: 17, 18, 2: 1; there is a mixture in Lk, yet ᾽Ιεροσ. occurs seldom in his Gospel. ᾽Ιεροσολυμῖται Mk 1: 5, Jn 7: 25 is its gentilic (cf. Thack. 171). LXX ᾽Ιερουσ-, except in 1–4 Macc and Tob; Schütz, Ιερουσαλημ and Ιεροσολυμα im NT (ZNW 11 [1910] 169–87); M.-H. 147 f. On the breathing s. § 39 (1).

(2) Showing fluctuation: Βηθανία (בֵּית עֲנָיָה) -ας -αν as a rule, but εἰς Βηθανία Mt 21: 17 B*, Mk 11: 1 B*, εἰς Βηθφαγῆ καὶ Βηθανία Lk 19: 29 S*BD*; ἀπὸ Βηθανιαμ Jn 11: 1 𝔓⁴⁵ is unique. Γολγοθᾶ Mt 27: 33, Jn 19: 17, -ᾶν as acc. Mk 15: 22 SBFG al. Γομόρρα and Σόδομα s. § 57. (Λύδδα) gen. Λύδδης A 9: 38 B³EHLP (-ας S*B*C, indecl. -α 𝔓⁴⁵SᶜA is very harsh here), acc. -α 32, 35 (-αν CEHLP) as neut. plur. or indecl.? (fluctuation likewise in Jos.). Σάρεπτα as acc. Lk 4: 26 (gen. -ων LXX Ob 20). Τὸν Σαρ(ρ)ωνα (᾽Ασσαρ-) A 9: 35 (𝔓⁴⁵ Σαρωναν) for the plain שָׁרוֹן: third decl. or indecl. with Aram. -α? Γαλιλαία (but Γαλιλα in a pap. like Aram.; Schubart, Gnomon 11 [1935] 423) following ᾽Ιουδαία etc.

(3) Jn 18: 1 τοῦ χειμάρρου τοῦ Κεδρών A (קִדְרוֹן) is correct, other MSS with dependence on κέδρος:

τῶν κέδρων SᶜBCL (v.l. as back-reading from the NT in the LXX 2 Km 15: 23, 3 Km 15: 13 [Katz]) or τοῦ κέδρου S*DW; Jos. τοῦ Κεδρῶνος; cf. Ps 82: 10 τῶν κισσῶν in inferior MSS for Κισών.

(4) Πᾶσα (ἡ) Ἱεροσόλυμα also Usener, Legenden der Pelagia p. 14.14 (cf. also p. 50); but also Ἱεροσόλυμα ἔσται ἔρημος LXX Tob 14: 4, Γάλγαλα αἰχμαλωτευομένη αἰχμαλωτευθήσεται Am 5: 5. Jos. generally ἡ Σιλωάμ (scil. πηγή), τὴν -άν and the like, but τοῦ -ᾶ Bell. 2.340; 6.363.

57. Declension of place-names. Σόδομα סְדֹם is inflected in the LXX as a neuter plur., Γομόρρα עֲמֹרָה as feminine sing. It is the same in the NT, except that the extremely rare adaptation of the inflection of Γομόρρα to that of Σόδομα in the LXX is gaining ground: Γομόρρων Mt 10: 15 (-ας CDLMP), but Σοδόμων καὶ Γομόρρας 2 P 2: 6 as in the LXX (Thack. 168). Θυάτιρα and Λύστρα are inflected -α -ων -οις -αν. On Λύδδα and Σάρεπτα s. §56(2). In the case of Σαλαμῖνι A 13: 5 SAEL have the not unprecedented variant -ίνῃ.

Γομόρρα nom. R 9: 29, Jd 7, dat. -οις Mk 6: 11 AΠ (addition). Θυάτιρα acc. Rev 1: 11 S (-αν AC 046), gen. -ων A 16: 14, dat. -οις Rev 2: 18 (-ρῃ 046, cf. §43(1)), 24 (-ρῃ Sᶜ, -ραις 046). Λύστραν acc. A 14: 6, 21, 16: 1, but dat. -οις 14: 8, 16: 2, 2 T 3: 11; cf. a similar summary Mlt. 48 [71]; M.-H. 147. Σαλαμίνης -νῃ Acta Barn. 22, 23 (L.-B. II 300.10, 15, 22), Suidas s.v. Ἐπιφάνιος in cod. A, Salamina(m) Lat. Acta ibid. Salaminae insulae Justin II 7.7, Salaminam XLIV 3.2. Cf. Wolf I 22; Psaltes 177 and the transformations like *Tarragona, Cartagena, Narbonne* in the romance languages.

(C) Appellatives

58. The few indeclinable appellatives are mostly loanwords: τὸν κορβαν Mt 27: 6 B* (correctly τὸν κορβανᾶν [Dalman 174 n. 3]; Mk 7: 11 κορβᾶν introduced as a Hebrew word), τὸ μάννα (Rev 2: 17 τοῦ μ.), τὸ πάσχα (τοῦ π. Lk 2: 41 etc., τῷ π. Jn 2: 23, 18: 39; LXX τὸ πάσχα, Jos. τὸ and ἡ [Debrunner, TW v 895 n. 1], Philo, Her. 255 [III 58.14] τὸ), σαταν instead of -νᾶ as a gen. 2 C 12: 7 Sᶜ al. (more a proper name than appellative; cf. §55(1b)), σίκερα acc. Lk 1: 15 (indeclinable in LXX). The substantival interjection ἡ οὐαί also is, of course, indeclinable (e.g. δύο οὐαί Rev 9: 12, also οὐαί...ἐστίν 1 C 9: 16, similarly LXX [s. Bauer], therefore an imitation of Hebrew [cf. also §4(2a)]), and may have taken its gender from ἡ θλῖψις and the like (cf. §§ 136(5); 248(3)).

(7) ADJECTIVES: NEW FEMININES AND COMPARISON

(A) New Feminines

59. (1) From compound adjectives in -ος there is a tendency to form a special feminine in the later period (there is a similar tendency earlier in Attic; it is the rule in MGr). Thus in the NT ἀργή, αὐτομάτη, παραθαλασσία. (2) The reverse tendency obtains in the case of several simple adjectives, especially with those which fluctuated between two and three endings in the classical period. Thus in the NT ἡ ἔρημος, ἡ κόσμιος, ἡ οὐράνιος etc. Koine conforms in general, however, to the classical language. (3) Ἡ συγγενίς Lk 1: 36 (-ής B³C*KM al., -είς W), Homil Clem 12.8.2 συγγενίδα (PE, -νῆ Oe) from ὁ συγγενής.

(1) Mayser I² 2, 50ff. Ἀργή (ἀργός from ἀ-εργος) 1 T 5: 13 twice, T 1: 12 (quotation from Epimenides), Ja 2: 20 BC* (v.l. νεκρά); Att. ἀργὸς γυνή Phryn. 104. Αὐτομάτη Mk 4: 28, A 12: 10, not unclassical. Παραθαλασσία Mt 4: 13 (-ιον D, παρὰ θάλασσαν S*W), but ἡ παράλιος Lk 6: 17 (literary language); these compounds in -ιος admit both forms.

(2) Mayser *ibid.* Ἡ ἔρημος regularly; Att. -μος and -μη. Ἡ ἕτοιμος Mt 25: 10 (A -μαι), -μη 2 C 9: 5, 1 P 1: 5; Att. -μος and -μη. Usually Ἡ αἰώνιος as customary in Att. (Gromska 41ff.), -ία 2 Th 2: 16 (-ιον FG), H 9: 12, often as v.l.; Thieme 11. Regularly ἡ βεβαία; Att. -α and -ος. Ἡ κόσμιος 1 T 2: 9 S*ADᶜᵒʳʳ al. (v.l. -ίως), cf. Thieme 11; Att. -ία. Ἡ μάταιος and -αία as in Att. Ἡ νηφάλιος 1 T 3: 11. Ἡ ὅμοιος? Rev 4: 3 (infrequent, s. Crönert 186). Ἡ ὅσιος 1 T 2: 8 all uncials; Att. -ία. Ἡ οὐράνιος Lk 2: 13 (v.l. οὐρανοῦ), A 26: 19; Att. -ία. Ἡ σωτήριος T 2: 11.

(3) Cf. συγγενίς Supp. Epigr. IV 452.4 (Roman period); BCH 24 (1900) 340.17; Benndorf-Niemann, Reisen I no. 53 E 3 (Hauser 98; πόλι συγγενί); further L.-S.; εὐγενίδων γυναικῶν Ps.-Clem., Epit. 2. 144. [Herodian] in Lob. Phryn. 451 συγγενίδα οὐ ῥητέον· οὔτε μὴν εὐγενίδα, Pollux 3.30 ἡ συγγενὶς ἐσχάτως βάρβαρον. Psaltes 152. Εἰκοσαετίς as early as Plato.

(B) Comparison

60. The decline of the superlative. (1) The system of degrees of comparison is simplified in the vernacular: in the great majority of instances the superlative disappeared and the comparative degree involving the contrast of two units has also taken over the function of the comparison of a unit with a plurality (ἀμείνων ἀπάντων 'better than all' = ἄριστος ἀπάντων 'the best of all'). In the NT the remnants of the superlative forms are used mostly with 'elative' force as in the papyri (Mlt. 77 [121 ff.]; Mayser II 1, 51, 53) and MGr, a usage already quite old (or even original?). The case of πρῶτος for πρότερος is different; s. §62. The only superlatives in -τατος in the NT are ἀκριβέστατος A 26: 5 (Paul's speech before Agrippa, literary language), ἁγιώτατος Jd 20 (elative) and τιμιώτατος (elative) Rev 18: 12, 21: 11; ἁπλούστατοι Mt 10: 16 D (for ἀκέραιοι) is a gloss which has been inserted in the text. (2) Somewhat more numerous are the remnants of the superlative in -ιστος. The majority are elative and in part stereotyped: ἐλάχιστος *perexiguus* often; ἥδιστα 'very gladly' 2 C 12: 9, 15, A 13: 8 D; κράτιστος (*vir*) *egregius* (§5(3a)); μέγιστος *permagnus* 2 P 1: 4; πλεῖστος Mt 11: 20, 21: 8 (cf. §245(1)), τὸ πλεῖστον 'at most' 1 C 14: 27; ὡς τάχιστα A 17: 15 (a genuine superlative, literary language); ὕψιστος (ὁ θεὸς ὁ ὕψιστος and ἐν τοῖς ὑψίστοις) frequently; ἔγγιστα D Mk 6: 36, 1 Clem 5.1 (Antipho 4 δ 11, Hippoc. 6.522 Littré [ἐγγιστότατα] and Hellenistic; s. Crönert 190; Hauser 98). (3) (Μᾶλλον) μάλιστα has persisted most tenaciously. Cf. §244.

(1) The use of the comparative and superlative degrees in Barnabas agrees with the NT; in Hermas, on the other hand, both types of superlatives are common in the elative sense, while the comparative is used for the real superlative. Cf. p. 1 n. 2. This (Roman?) form of the Koine compares with modern Italian which does not distinguish between the comparative and superlative, but uses the forms in *-issimo* etc. in the elative sense.

(2) Ἐλάχιστος as a genuine superlative 1 C 15: 9 (literary language or corruption? for which E 3: 8 has ἐλαχιστότερος, s. §61(2)); elative Herm Man 5.1.5 ὑπὸ τοῦ ἐλαχίστου ἀψινθίου 'by a little bit of wormwood' (in the preceding ἀψινθίου μικρὸν λίαν); a similar use occurs as early as Aeschin. 3.104. Τὸ πλεῖστον μέρος Herm Sim 8.5.6, 10.1, 9.7.4 but τὸ πλεῖον μέρος 8.1.16. Κράτιστος is the official rendering of the title *vir egregius* (cf. Magie 31, 112; Hahn 259; Seeck in Pauly-Wissowa v 2006f.); thus A 23: 26, 24: 3, 26: 25 in the address to the procurators Felix and Festus; κράτιστε Lk 1: 3 however is a polite form of address as it is used in dedications, e.g. also in Diogn 1.1 and Galen (Kühn) 10.78, 14.295, 19.8 (s. also §146(3)).

(3) Μάλιστα 12 times (Acts, Paul, 2 P). A popular substitute for μᾶλλον μάλιστα as for πλείων πλεῖστος is the adj. περισσός 'excessive, profuse' together with its adverb and comparative (MGr περισσότερος =πλείων). Τὸ περισσὸν τούτων Mt 5: 37 = τὸ πλέον τ. (cf. §244(3)); περισσότερόν (περισσόν AD al.) τι = πλέον τι Lk 12: 4, further neut. περισσότερον 12: 48

(πλέον D), Mk 12: 33 (v.l. πλεῖον), Mt 11: 9 = Lk 7: 26, Mk 12: 40 = Lk 20: 47, 1 Clem 61. 3. Περισσῶς Mt 27: 23 (on which Chrys. 7.813 B [7.918 Montfaucon]: περισσῶς τουτέστι μᾶλλον), Mk 10: 26, 15: 14 (v.l. -σσοτέρως §102(1)), but = 'very' A 26: 11; μᾶλλον περισσῶς Mk 14: 31 W. Cf. Preisigke s.v. Also combined are μᾶλλον περισσότερον Mk 7: 36 (-έρως D), -έρως μ. 2 C 7: 13 (s. *infra*); cf. §246 and pleonasms like εὐθέως παραχρῆμα. In Paul περισσοτέρως appears in part to have a still stronger force = ὑπερβαλλόντως; thus 2 C 7: 15, 12: 15, G 1: 14 (περ. μᾶλλον 2 C 7: 13 'still much more'? s. *supra*), while it can be replaced elsewhere (in Paul) by μᾶλλον or μάλιστα (περισσότερος by πλείων); so also H 7: 15 περισσότερον (= μᾶλλον) ἔτι κατάδηλον and -ρως 2: 1, 13: 19; cf. Herm Man 4.4.2; Sim 5.3.3.

61. The comparative. (1) Of comparatives in -(ι)ων the following are attested in the NT: from ἀγαθός rather often κρείσσων (§34(1)), from βελτίων (Herm, 1 Clem, Diogn) only the adv. βέλτιον 2 T 1: 18, A 10: 28 D (s. §244(2)), never ἀμείνων. From κακός never κακίων, sometimes χείρων 'worse'; τὸ ἧσσον with its antithesis τὸ κρεῖσσον 1 C 11: 17, ἧσσον adv. 'less' (of degree) 2 C 12: 15; ἐλάσσων *deterior*, as the antithesis of κρείσσων Jn 2: 10, H 7: 7 (s. *infra* (2)), as the antithesis of μείζων (like Attic) R 9: 12 OT, ἔλαττον adv. 'less' (of number) 1 T 5: 9. Μείζων and πλείων often; κάλλιον adv. A 25: 10 (s. §244(2)). The Hellenistic form τάχιον (B ταχειον) is always used. (2) Worthy of note are the popular new formations in -ότερος: ἐλαχιστότερος 'least of all' (§60(2)); μειζότερος 3 Jn 4; διπλότερον *duplo magis* Mt 23: 15; μικρότερος Mt 11: 11 'younger' (referring to Jesus[?]), O. Cullmann, Con. Neot. 11 (1947) 30 (following Franz Dibelius).

(1) Κρείσσων means 'superior', also 'mightier, of higher standing', antithesis ἐλάττων H 7: 7. Vulgar ἀγαθώτατος -τατος is not found in the NT (nor in the LXX proper, for ἀγαθώτερος Judg 11: 25, -έρα 15: 2 are found only in B and its satellites, a recension dating from early iv AD; it is neither LXX nor strictly biblical [Katz, ThLZ 1957, 113f.]; -τερος Herm Man 8.9.11, -τατος as a genuine superl. Diodor. Sic. 16.85 [iv 125.22 Fischer] = 'excellent' Herm Vis 1.2.3; Hermas also ἡδύτερος Sim 8.9.1); Helb. 54f.; W. Döllstädt, Griech. Papyrusbriefe... (Diss. Jena, 1934) 51 f. Μικρότερος means 'lesser' as in Att. Att. θᾶττον does not appear in the NT unless perhaps in A 27: 13 θᾶσσον is read for ἆσσον (Jos. also has ἆσσον); in 1 Clem 65.1 the literary construction ὅπως θᾶττον with the subj. appears side by side with the colloquial εἰς τὸ τάχιον and the inf.; MPol θᾶττον ἤ 13.1, but τάχιον 'more quickly' 13.2, 'as quickly as possible' 3.1.

(2) Double comparison is found occasionally already in the earlier period for the purpose of clarification (K.-Bl. I 573, e.g. Homer πρώτιστος and ἀσσοτέρω, Mimnermus ἀμεινότερος), and often in the Hell. period and later (Crönert 190; Mayser I² 2, 62 n. 1; Jannaris §506; Mlt. 236 n. on p. 79 [123 n.]; Psaltes 190). Διπλότερα τούτων Appian, Praefatio 10 (I 10.12 Mendelssohn) = διπλάσια τ.; ἁπλότατον Anth. Pal. VI 185.3; cf. Att. ἁπλό-της, διπλό-ω (Xen., LXX, NT) and ἁπλό-ω (Batr. 81, 106 and later), MGr ἁπλός διπλός. Dieterich 179f.; Moeris 336 on τριπλᾶ. There was, however, an old διπλός, cf. Lat. *duplus* (O. Hoffmann, Griech. Dial. III 299f.; Brugmann, IF 38 [1920] 132; Schwyzer I 598). Att. ἁπλούστερον Barn 6.5, -τατος s. §60(1). Διπλοκαρδία Did 5.1 = Barn 20.1.—Παλαιός, αἰσχρός, ἐχθρός are attested only in the positive in the NT.

62. Adjectival comparison of adverbs.

Hellenistic has retained the superlative πρῶτος; πρότερος has surrendered the meaning 'the first of two' to πρῶτος and now means only 'earlier'. The opposite ἔσχατος also appears in a comparative sense (Mt 27: 64); ὕστερος conversely is superlative. If the beginning or end of a series—the extremity—is to be emphasized, the superlative is used without reference to the number of units (πρῶτος, ἔσχατος): the category of duality is eliminated (§§2 and 64); if, however, the relative is to be emphasized, the comparative is used without reference to the unity or plurality of the comparison (ὕστερος, cf. ὑστερεῖν), cf. §60(1). —Further attested are: ἐξώτερος (only superlative τὸ σκότος τὸ ἐξώτερον Mt 8: 12, 22: 13, 25: 30; it is different in Herm Sim 9.7.5 etc.), ἐσώτερος (A 16: 24, H 6: 19), κατώτερος (E 4: 9). Only the following adverbs are Attic (the adjectives from which they are derived are not): ἀνώτερον Lk 14: 10, H 10: 8 (Attic more often -ρω), κατωτέρω Mt 2: 16 (D perhaps more correctly κάτω), πορρωτέρω (-ρον AB) Lk 24: 28, ἐγγύτερον R 13: 11 (Hellenistic more often ἔγγιον ἔγγιστα).

Πρῶτος for πρότερος: Mt 21: 28, Rev 20: 5, 21: 1 etc. (Zahn, NKZ 28 [1917] 379.1), πρῶτός μου Jn 1: 15, 30 (PGM II 113.50 [ii/iii AD] σοῦ πρῶτός εἰμι [allusion to the passage in John?], LXX, Aelian, Plutarch *et al.*; cf. Mlt. 79 [123f.]; Thack. 183; W. Bauer [Hdb.] on Jn 1: 15; inscrip. cf. Raderm. ¹185, ²70, 71f.). Τὸν πρῶτον λόγον A 1: 1: Zahn, *op. cit.* 373ff., believes it is used for the conception, 'the first of three works' (cf. his commentary on Acts [1919] 16ff.); but πρῶτος = πρότερος elsewhere in Acts: 7: 12, 12: 10 (Haenchen¹² 105 n. 5; cf. 68), thus refuting Zahn; Athen. 15.701c (Bauer⁵ is incorrect) refers to the first of the two books of Clearchus 'On

Proverbs' as ἐν τῷ προτέρῳ περὶ παροιμιῶν, but 10.457c ἐν πρώτῳ περὶ παρ.; Diodor. Sic. 1.42.1 calls the first half of a two-part work ἡ πρώτη, while in 13.103.3 he uses interchangeably ἡ πρώτη σύνταξις and ἡ προτέρα σύντ. for the first of two works (Bauer⁵ s.v.). Πρῶτος ἦλθεν Homil Clem 2.17.2, the corresponding adv. πρῶτον Mt 7: 5, 8: 21 etc. (πρῶτον ὑμῶν Jn 15: 18). Πρότερος 'earlier, formerly existing': τὴν προτέραν ἀναστροφήν E 4: 22, cf. Herm Man 4.3.1, 3 etc.; adv. πρότερον 'earlier' H 10: 32, 1 P 1: 14, τὸ πρ. (§160) Jn 6: 62, 9: 8 (7: 50, 51 spurious reading), G 4: 13, 1 T 1: 13. Πρότερον of the first of two acts H 4: 6 ('the first time' with reference to the giving of the Law; contrast πάλιν v. 7), 7: 27 (πρότερον–ἔπειτα) stems from literary language; πρότερον 2 C 1: 15 is perhaps to be struck out with S*. Ὕστερος only 1 T 4: 1 superlative (properly 'in future times'), Mt 21: 31 B comparative; adv. ὕστερον usually 'later, secondly', superl. Mt 22: 27 = Lk 20: 32. Ἔτι ἄνω, ἔτι κάτω for ἀνώτερον, κατώτερον in the apocryphal reference Mt 20: 28 DΦ are peculiar; cf. Xen., An. 7.5.9 ἔτι ἄνω στρατεύεσθαι and Dindorf on this passage.—Cf. Thack. 183f. on the whole subject.

(8) NUMERALS

63. (1) The Hellenistic inflection of the cardinal for 'two' is that of the NT: δύο nom. gen. acc., δυσίν dat. (following τρισίν); Mayser I² 2, 72f. Ἀμφότεροι, not ἄμφω, s. §64. On τέσσαρες as acc. s. §46(2); τέσσερα and τεσσεράκοντα §29(1); ὀκτα- §120(1). (2) Cardinals from 12 to 19 have δέκα as the first element in Koine: δεκαδύο etc. following the pattern of εἴκοσι πέντε etc.; the order is reversed in the case of ordinals πεντεκαιδέκατος (Ionic; Attic πέμπτος καὶ δέκατος) etc. following ἑνδέκατος δωδέκατος. (3) The NT knows only the Hellenistic -πλασίων for the proportionals (new formations from -πλάσιον [also from the acc. plur. -πλασίους?], which was understood as a comparative), not -πλάσιος.—Rev 9: 16 δισμυριάδες AP, δύο μυριάδες 𝔓⁴⁷.

(1) Δυσὶ μὴ λέγε, ἀλλὰ δυοῖν Phryn. 210. Τέτρασι(ν) A 10: 11 E, 11: 5 D, LXX Judg 9: 34 B* is literary Koine (Crönert 199).

(2) J. Wackernagel, Festschr. Binz (Basel, 1935) 37f. = Kl. Schr. 240f. Δεκαδύο A 19: 7 HLP, 24: 11 HLP, W in Mt 26: 14, Lk 2: 42, 8: 1 (but very often δώδεκα and always ἕνδεκα; MGr also ἕντεκα δώδεκα but δεκατρεῖς δεκατέσσερις etc.); δεκατέσσαρες Mt 1: 17, 2 C 12: 2, G 2: 1; δεκαπέντε Jn 11: 18, A 27: 28, G 1: 18 (δέκα καὶ πέντε Herm Vis 2.2.1 S), δεκαοκτώ Lk 13: 4 (δέκα καὶ ὀκτώ SᶜA al.), 11 (δ.κ.ὀ. AL al.), δ.κ.ὀ. 16. Ἕνδεκα and δώδεκα (δεκαδύο is weakly attested) also in the LXX (Thack. 188), but pap.

more frequently δεκαεῖς and δεκαδύο (Mayser ι² 2, 75f.). The digits in the case of larger numbers may also follow, and customarily without καί: εἴκοσι τρεῖς 1 C 10: 8, τεσσαράκοντα καὶ ἕξ Jn 2: 20; cf. MGr εἴκοσι δύο etc. A similar order is found sometimes in the earlier period (Gromska 28ff.): inscrip. as early as v BC end δέκα τρεῖς and τριάκοντα πέντε (Meisterhans 160f.). Τεσσαρεσκαιδέκατος A 27: 27, πεντεκαιδέκατος Lk 3: 1.

(3) Ἑκατονταπλασίων Mt 19: 29 SCDX, Mk 10: 30, Lk 8: 8, πολλαπλασίων Mt 19: 29 BL, Lk 18: 30 (ἑπταπλ- D). Cf. K.-Bl. ι 623; Schmidt 530; Arnim 142; Vogeser 5; Fraenkel ι 38.1; Ed. Schwyzer, Museum Helveticum 2 (1945) 137ff.

(9) PRONOUNS

64. (1) **Reflexives.** Ἐμαυτοῦ, σεαυτοῦ (not σαυτοῦ), ἑαυτοῦ (hardly αὑτοῦ); plur. only ἑαυτῶν for all three persons as generally in Hellenistic; on ὑμῶν αὐτῶν 1 C 5: 13 etc. s. §288(1). (2) **Demonstratives.** Οὗτος, ἐκεῖνος as usual; the Attic intensive -ί (οὑτοσ-ί) is unknown, but it has survived vestigially in νυν-ί Acts, Paul, Heb. (LXX) Ὅδε is virtually confined to the phrase τάδε λέγει(A 21: 11, Rev 2: 1, 8, 12, 18, 3: 1, 7, 14), otherwise only τάδε A 15: 23 D, τῇδε Lk 10: 39, τήνδε Ja 4: 13. (3) **Relatives.** Ὅς ἥ ὅ. Ὅστις ἥτις ὅ τι only in the nom. sing. and plur. as in Hellenistic, and only ὅ τι also as acc.; for the meaning s. §293. Frozen in a phrase is ἕως ὅτου Lk, Jn 9: 18, Mt 5: 25, ἀφ' ὅτου Lk 13: 25 D. Ὅσπερ only Mk 15: 6, ἅπερ 𝔓¹⁵ Jn 10: 16 and according to Marcion ἅπερ ἔκρυψας Lk 10: 21; for καθάπερ s. §453. (4) **Correlatives.** Ποῖος–τοιοῦτος (τοιόσδε only 2 P 1: 17 τοιᾶσδε, cf. *supra* (2) ὅδε)–οἷος– ὁποῖος. Πόσος–τοσοῦτος–ὅσος. Πηλίκος (G 6: 11, H 7: 4)–τηλικοῦτος (2 C 1: 10, H 2: 3, 12: 1 S*I, Ja 3: 4, Rev 16: 18)–ἡλίκος (C 2: 1, Ja 3: 5). For ποταπός s. §298(3). (5) **Indefinite pronouns.** τίς ποτε s. §303. Ὁ δεῖνα 'so-and-so' as in Attic: Mt 26: 18 τὸν δεῖνα. (6) **Pronouns and pronominal words expressing duality** (ἑκάτερος– ἕκαστος and the like) are obsolete with the exception of ἀμφότεροι (so the NT for ἄμφω) and ἕτερος (§306); πότερος only in πότερον…ἤ Jn 7: 17; cf. LXX (Thack. 192) and M. Ant. (Schekira 160).

(1) The trisyllabic forms σεαυτ- ἑαυτ- are supplanting the disyllabic in the Hell. period more and more; they were used alongside each other in the class. period; σαυτ- αὐτ- are no longer attested in the pap. beginning in i BC (Mayser ι² 2, 65; ιι 2, 71ff.). Traces of αὐτ- (cf. LXX, Thack. 190): Jn 2: 24 οὐκ ἐπίστευσεν αὐτὸν (S*A*BL, ἑαυτὸν SᶜA²P) αὐτοῖς, Lk 23: 12 reciprocal πρὸς αὐτούς SBLT (ἑαυτούς AX). The use of ἑαυτοῦ for (ἐμαυτοῦ and) σεαυτοῦ, corresponding to its use for all persons in the plural, which is only weakly established for classical prose (Rosenkranz, IF 48 [1930] 150), depends also in the NT on doubtful authority: Jn 18: 34 ἀφ' ἑαυτοῦ σὺ τοῦτο λέγεις, yet ἀπὸ σεαυτοῦ SBC*L; R 13: 9 = G 5: 14 OT ὡς ἑαυτόν FGLP and 𝔓⁴⁶FGLN*P respectively; Mk 1: 44 ἑαυτόν W (σεαυτόν pm.). Cf. Herm Vis 4.1.5 ἠρξάμην λέγειν ἐν ἑαυτῷ (S*A; ἐμαυτῷ Sᶜ), Sim 2.1 τί σὺ ἐν ἑαυτῷ ζητεῖς (lacking in S), Evang. Evae ἑαυτὸν συλλέγεις (iii AD; fragment in Epiphanius, Haer. 26.3); Herm Sim 9.2.5 (PMich ἐμ-), Homil Clem 14.10, 17.18 for ἐμαυτοῦ etc. Exx. from the pap. in Moulton, ClR 15 (1901) 441, 18 (1904) 154; Mayser ι² 2, 63f. From the inscrip. Nachmanson 144.1; Hauser 100. From later lit. Psaltes 196.

(2) On ὅδε cf. §289 and *supra* (4) τοιόσδε. Οὐδ' ὥς 'not even so' 1 C 14: 21 𝔓⁴⁶ may well be a classicism (οὐδ' οὕτως SABD, οὐδέπω FG); cf. pap. (Mayser ι² 2, 66f.; ιι 1, 58).

(3) On the confusion of ὅς and ὅστις s. §293, on demonstrative ὅς §250. There are no forms in the NT like ἄττα ἄσσα, interrog. τοῦ τῷ, indef. του τῳ etc. The pap. and inscrip. are in conformity with the NT: ὅστις only nom. and (ἕως, ἐξ, ἀφ') ὅτου; cf. Moulton, ClR 18 (1904) 154; Nachmanson 145f.; Mayser ι² 2, 68, 70. The situation is comparable in the LXX (Thack. 192). On Koine generally and the authors individually, s. Kallenberg, RhM 72 (1917/18) 481, 489ff. Ὅνπερ ἡτοῦντο Mk 15: 6 SᶜB³C al., ὃν παρῃτοῦντο S*AB* (ὃν ἧτ- W) is inferior, ὃν ἂν ἡτοῦντο DG is correct, s. §367.

(4) LXX almost exactly as the NT (Thack. 192). Οἱ τοῖοι οἱ λόγοι POxy ιv 654.1 (Logion, iii AD) is certainly spurious (read οὗτοι οἱ λ.?). On correlative adverbs s. §106. Τοιοῦτος τοσοῦτος have a neut. in Hell. in -ον or -ο (Mayser ι² 2, 66; Att. more often -ον): -ον with v.l. Mt 18: 5, A 21: 25, H 7: 22, only -ον H 12: 1, but cf. e.g. τηλικοῦτο Herm Vis 4.1.10 (2.3 with v.l.). Cf. Moeris 210.27: ταὐτὸν Ἀττικοί, τὸ αὐτὸ Ἕλληνες; accordingly NT and pap. (Mayser ι² 2, 67) τὸ αὐτό.

(6) Ἀμφότεροι 'all' A 19: 16? (s. Raderm.² 77; Bauer; Bonaccorsi 550f.). Ἑκάτερος seldom in Hell.: Thack. 192; Mayser ιι 2, 92.

2. CONJUGATION

(1) INTRODUCTION

65. The conjugational system is to all appearances not greatly altered from its earlier form, for nearly all the classical forms are found in the NT, with the exception, of course, of the dual. The most important general differences are the following: (1) The future has retreated in several ways, in that (a) alternative formations of the future are reduced to a single one, (b) the future perfect has dropped out, (c) the use of the simple future is limited almost entirely to the indicative; (2) the optative, of which Attic was so fond, persists only in vestiges; (3) the verbal adjectives are no longer a living feature; (4) the periphrastic construction is on the increase. The end results of this development are evident in modern Greek: the optative has disappeared, the future and other forms are formed periphrastically, the verbal adjective in -τέος is wanting, that in -τός is frozen into a limited group of ordinary adjectives (Thumb, 151).

(1) (a) Besides φανήσομαι which is derived from the aor. ἐφάνην, the older form, φανοῦμαι, appears only in a quotation from the LXX 1 P 4: 18. (b) Forms like ἑστήξω and μεμνήσομαι are not met; the only example of a simple (i.e. non-periphrastic) fut. perf. in the NT is κεκράξομαι etc. (Lk 19: 40 inferior reading, cf. §77) supported by ἐκέκραξα etc. (§101). A second ex. in the LXX is κεκλήσεται (certain in Lev 13: 45, nearly so in Hos 12: 1 (11: 12), and as v.l. in Ex 12: 16). In non-biblical Koine it is much the same (Cakot, De Graecorum tertio quod vocatur futuro, Diss. Breslau, 1911, 79ff.). (c) The fut. opt. does not occur, the fut. inf. is confined to Acts and Hebrews (§350), the fut. ptcp. occurs only in a few places outside the Lukan corpus (§351).

(2) The opt. appears only in the Lukan corpus with any frequency owing to the influence of literary language. Statistics for the opt. in Mlt. 194f. [307 n. 2 with table]: Paul has 31 instances, aorist only, of which 14 are γένοιτο; Lk (Gospel and Acts) 20 in pres. tense (11 are εἴη and 4 are forms of δύνασθαι and βούλεσθαι), 8 in aorist; in the rest of the NT 2 in pres. (1 P 3: 14 εἰ καὶ πάσχοιτε, 3: 17 εἰ θέλοι) and 6 in aorist. Cf. also §384. The opt. does not appear in Hermas. Statistics for the Ptol. pap. in Mayser II 1, 289 n. 1; 295f.

(3) The verbal adj. in -τέος is represented only in the literary βλητέον Lk 5: 38 (S*D βάλλουσιν, W βάλληται), Mk 2: 22 SᵃACL (addition from Mt) 'one must put'; the adj. in -τός, apart from the forms frozen into adjs. like ἀγαπητός δυνατός ζεστός θνητός ὁρατός (αἱρετώτερον Herm Vis 4.2.6; s. also §112), is retained only in παθητός 'capable of suffering' A 26: 23 (Plutarch) and in compounds like ἀκατάπαυστος (cf. §117); the pass. ptcp. may serve as a substitute for -τός: ψηλαφωμένῳ H 12: 18, σαλευομένων and τὰ σαλευόμενα v. 27 (cf. ἀσάλευτον v. 28; s. Tholuck on 12: 18, trans. James Hamilton, Edinburgh, 1842, 2 vols.). In the earlier pap. -τός is used to express possibility (only βατός and ὑπερβατός) and -τέος is limited to the official style; Mayser II 1, 357, 359f. For the LXX s. Thack. 193f.

(4) On periphrasis, cf. §§352ff.; here only the formation of the fut. perf. through periphrasis (§352) and the contrast of ἔστωσαν περιεζωσμέναι (Lk 12: 35) with πεφίμωσο (Mk 4: 39) and ἔρρωσο, ἔρρωσθε need be indicated.

(2) AUGMENT AND REDUPLICATION

66. Syllabic augment. (1) The pluperfect often lacks the augment in Koine (as also in Hdt., for example, though rarely in Attic), in the NT as a rule, especially in compounds. Exceptions occur principally in the passive (as in papyri, Polyb., Jos., LXX, Ap. Frs.; Thack. 196; Mayser I² 2, 98): ἐβέβλητο etc. (2) Syllabic augment before vowels (in addition to the temporal) has held its own poorly in the Koine: in the NT it is missing in the case of ὠθεῖν and ὠνεῖσθαι; in the case of ἀνοίγειν and καταγνύναι it is retained and has sometimes intruded, because misunderstood, into the non-indicative moods and the fut. (§101; Hatzid. 64f.; Psaltes 204). (3) Augment ἠ- instead of ἐ- is always found with θέλειν (Attic ἐθέλειν ἤθελον), never with βούλεσθαι, a word borrowed from literary language (ἠβ. A 28: 18 only HLP, Phm 13 only S, 2 Jn 12 many minuscules; ἠβούλετο Herm Sim 5.6.5); δύνασθαι and μέλλειν vacillate in the MSS between ἠ- and ἐ-. For particulars concerning augment ἠ- s. Debrunner, Festschrift Zucker (Berlin, 1954) 85–110.

(1) Kapsomenakis 27f. n. Ἐβέβλητο Lk 16: 20, ἐπεγέγραπτο A 17: 23 (ἦν γεγραμμένον D), συνετέθειντο Jn 9: 22, περιεδέδετο 11: 44 (περιδ- D*, ἐδέδετο 𝔓⁴⁵), ἐπεποίθει Lk 11: 22 (πέποιθεν D), ἐγεγόνει Jn 6: 17 (v.l.), etc.; the last two always appear in the LXX too with augment (Thack. 196f.).

(2) Ὠνήσατο A 7: 16 (Att. and pre-Christian pap. augment ἐων-), ἀπώσα(ν)το A 7: 27 etc., ἐξῶσεν v. 45 (ἐξέωσεν only S*E*). Προορώμην A 2: 25 OT (-ωρ- B³P) s. §67(2): ἑώρων (from *ἠ-ϝορ-) Jn 6: 2 SΓΔ al. may well be a misreading for ἐθεώρουν. On ἑόρακα s. §68.

(3) The origin of ἠ- is ἤθελον (s. §101); βούλεσθαι δύνασθαι μέλλειν with ἠ- do not appear in Att. inscrip. before 300 BC (Meisterhans 169). Gromska 35f.; Mayser I² 2, 93f. MGr still augments θέλω– ἤθελα (Thumb² §183).

67. Temporal augment.

(1) The absence of temporal augment is not unheard of even in Attic with initial diphthongs beginning with ε or ο; thus NT εἴξαμεν G 2: 5 (as in Attic). It was especially easy in Koine to leave οἰ- unaugmented because ῷ- (ō) was hardly more suitable as the augment for οἰ-, since in customary pronunciation it tended to be sounded like German ü. In the period of classical Attic ευ- was augmented to ηυ (especially in simple verbs); later ευ was preferred; in the NT ευ- preponderates, but ηυ- is not infrequently found. The single example of unaugmented αι- is ἐπαισχύνθη 2 T 1: 16 (-η- S*K). (2) Simple short vowels are unaugmented only where Attic reduplication is involved (ἐληλύθειν Jn 6: 17 etc. as in Attic); there are isolated instances in compound verbs. Ὄφελον is not unaugmented ὤφελον (for both s. §359(1)), but a participle with which an original ἐστίν is to be supplied (§127(2)); s. Wackernagel, Homer 199f. (3) In the case of ἐργάζεσθαι the customary Attic distribution of η- and ει- is followed: augment ἠργ- (from *ἠ-ϝεργ-), reduplication εἰργ- (from *ϝε-ϝεργ-; §68).

(1) Οἰκοδομήθη Jn 2: 20 SB*W, οἰκοδόμησεν A 7: 47 B*D, Lk 7: 5 C*D, ἐποικοδόμησεν 1 C 3: 14 (ἐπῳκ- B³C), on the other hand ᾠκοδόμησεν Mt 21: 33 all MSS, ᾠκοδόμητο Lk 4: 29 (οἰκοδόμηται D), cf. ἐνῴκησεν 2 T 1: 5 (-οι- D*), κατῴκησεν (-ισεν) Ja 4: 5, παρῴκησεν H 11: 9 OT etc.; Westcott-Hort, App. 161. Unaugmented οι- appears also in the pap. (Mayser I² 2, 102) and inscrip. (Meisterhans 172; Schweizer 172; Nachmanson 152), just as it was preferred with οἰκοδομεῖν (where οἶκος protected the οι) and was scorned by the grammarians (Phryn. 153, Cramer, Anec. Ox. III 260.19) as an Ionicism (Hdt. always οι-). Ηὑρίσκετο H 11: 5 OT 𝔓⁴⁶ SADE, προσηύξαντο A 8: 15 (-ευ- B), 20: 36 (-ευ- B*D), ηὐχόμην R 9: 3 (εὐχ- DEKL); ηὐδόκησα etc. s. Gregory 120f.; v. Soden 1396; Sanders, Wash. 23. Whether ευ as augment of αυ, as it appears here and there in inscrip., pap. and MSS (Crönert 204; Mayser I² 2, 101; Inschr. v. Priene 109.160 [c. 120 BC];

Meuwese 30), is phonetically shortened from ηυ or merely 'misspelling' (analogous to ηὗρον– εὗρον) is doubtful; NT only εὔξανε A 12: 24 D* (εὐλίζετο LXX Job 31: 32 A). The augmentation ηυ- was probably facilitated by the fact that the υ in ευ and αυ was tending to be pronounced as a spirant (f, v), leaving the ε or α a simple vowel and no longer part of a diphthong; cf. the spelling ηὔξατο ηὐλόγησεν (e.g. SA throughout) and the protest against ηυ- in Cramer, Anec. Ox. III 258.10, and finally the MGr ηὗρα (pronounced ivra) = ηὗρον. On εὐ- in indirect compounds s. §69(4).

(2) Omitted augment with compounds (cf. Hatzid. 63; Jannaris §717 n.; Mayser I² 2, 102): ἀνέθη (-ε- borrowed from the non-indicative moods instead of the regular augment -ει-) A 16: 26, ἀφέθησαν R 4: 7 OT (from Ps 31 (32): 1, where only S has -ει-; cf. ἀφέθη Ditt., Or. 435.9 [132 BC]), διερμήνευσεν Lk 24: 27 (-η EHKM al.), διεγείρετο Jn 6: 18 B al., ἐνέργησεν G 2: 8 𝔓⁴⁶D*; προορώμην s. §66(2) and Helb. 73; ἀνορθώθη Lk 13: 13 (-ω- SE al.) and others. With simple verb ὀργίσθη Rev 11: 18 𝔓⁴⁷ (§28). Here belongs also ἑστήκεισαν Rev 7: 11 C, Hermas several times; cf. Reinhold 63. (3) Ἠργάζοντο A 18: 3 S*AB*DE, ἠργάσατο Mt 25: 16 S*B*DL, 26: 10 S*B*DW, Mk 14: 6 S*B*DW, Lk 19: 16 (προσ-) S*AB*DE* al., -αντο H 11: 33 S*D*, -ασάμεθα 2 J 8 B* (s. also R 7: 8, 15: 18, 2 C 7: 11, 12: 12 [𝔓⁴⁶ also on the last two], B* has ει- only in R 15: 18, S in all four places, DE in none); Herm Sim 7.2(3) PMich ἠ-, A ει- as usual; 2.7 PBer ἠ-, A ει-; but εἰργασμένα Jn 3: 21, κατειργάσθαι 1 P 4: 3; augm. ἠργ-, redupl. εἰργ- almost consistently also in the pap. (Mayser I² 2, 95, 97) as in Att. (Meisterhans 171; Lautensach 188f.). Scherer 70 §121.

68. Reduplication.

Initial ρ is reduplicated occasionally like any other consonant, therefore with ρε- (with rough breathing?). Μεμνηστευμένη from μνηστεύω (better reading is ἐμν-) Lk 1: 27, 2: 5 by analogy with μέμνημαι. Εἴργασμαι s. §67(3). Ἑώρακα (after ἑώρων) as in Hellenistic (Crönert 272; Mayser I² 2, 203; in Attic prose only as a variant); in addition, the Attic ἑόρακα is found in the Epistles to some extent as a strong variant (from *ϝε-ϝορ-). According to Katz, ThLZ 1957, 111, ἑόρακα is found in the oldest LXX papyri, and is, therefore, to be inserted in the text (with Ziegler); he argues that the restitution of ἑόρακα was not among the points made by the Atticists and that those parts of the Bible which have it are, therefore, likely to reflect the true text; it was subsequently lost in the earlier books of the NT and should be restored. Εἰλκωμένος Lk 16: 20 (almost all MSS) after the pattern ἕλκειν εἷλκον. Occasionally reduplication from the perfect has intruded into other tenses and the formation of substantives: ἐκέκραξα s. §101 κράζειν; πεποίθησις (from πέποιθα) as in Hellenistic (s. Bauer; LXX ἐπεποίθησα etc., Helb. 82; Thack. 224f.). Γρηγορεῖν is older (§73).

Ρεραντισμένοι H 10: 22 𝔓⁴⁶S*ACD*P, περιρεραμμένον Rev 19: 13 S* (περιρεραντισμένον Sᶜᶜ), ρεριμμένοι Mt 9: 36 D*, but ἔρριπται Lk 17: 2 and the stereotyped ἔρρωσο ἔρρωσθε. The phenomenon is Ionic (Homer ρερυπωμένα) and Hell., but everywhere quite sporadic (Helb. 81f.). On ἐρ- instead of ἐρρ- s. §11(1). Μεμνήστευμαι, ρέριμμαι also in LXX (Thack. 204f.), Homil Clem 13.16, Protev Ja 19.1 (v.l. ἐμν-), -ευκώς Diodor. Sic. 18.23 (IV 35.25 Fischer). Ἑώρακα 1 C 9: 1 𝔓⁴⁶AB³ al. (-ο- SB*DᶜEFGP), Jn 1: 18 SAB³CLM al. (-ο- B*EFGHKX) etc. (v. Soden 1397); ἑορ- 𝔓⁴⁶ C 2: 1, 𝔓⁴⁵ Lk 9: 36, W more often than ἑωρ- (Sanders, Wash. 20), I only ἑορ- (ibid. II 257); 𝔓⁶⁶ ἑωρακ- 13 times, ἑόρακας 8: 57, 9: 37; in addition ἑωρακότες 11: 45. Pap. only ἑώρακα; s. Mayser I² 2, 103. It is not necessary to elaborate on Att. reduplication (ἀκήκοα, ἐγήγερται etc.).

69. Augment and reduplication in compounds (direct and indirect). (1) Compounds whose simple form is forgotten are apt to be handled in all periods as simple verbs: NT always καθεύδειν–ἐκάθευδον, καθίζειν–ἐκάθισα ἐκαθεζόμην ἐκαθήμην, while for Attic καθεῦδον etc. was still possible. Ἠμφιεσμένος Mt 11: 8, Lk 7: 25 as in Attic, but ἤφιεν is new Mk 1: 34, 11: 16 from ἀφίειν = ἀφιέναι (§94(2)), and ἤνοιγον ἤνοιξα from ἀνοίγειν (§101). (2) With double augment ἠνέῳξα (§101), but ἀνέχεσθαι with single augment. (3) Compounds with two prepositions are inclined to a double augment (to some extent an earlier development): ἀπεκατεστάθη etc. (4) Indirect compounds (παρασύνθετα, derivatives from compounds) where the first element is a preposition were treated in Attic in general as other compounds; so also in the NT (e.g. ἀπεδήμησεν, ἐνεφάνισαν, κατηγόρουν), but προεφητευ- is only weakly attested because the root word προφήτης was especially well known. Indirect compounds with εὐ- tend to augment a following short vowel: always εὐηγγελιζόμην.

(1) Ἐκάμμυσαν Mt 13: 15 OT, A 28: 27 OT is a matter of course; καμμύειν from κατ(α)μύειν is proscribed by Phryn. 339; MGr (Macedonian) καμμύω–ἐκάμμυξα (Hatzid. 136); cf. Thumb, Hell. 64; Crönert 64.4. Ἤφιεν is also attested for Att., in addition to ἀφίει ἤφιει, but is hardly correct.

(2) Ἀνεσχόμην A 18: 14 (ἠν- DEHLP), ἀνείχεσθε

2 C 11: 1, 4 (ἀνέχ- 𝔓⁴⁶BD*; in 4 ἠνείχεσθε Ψ); ἠνέσχετο Ἀττικοί, ἀνέσχετο Ἕλληνες, Moeris 198.5; nowhere has the NT any doubly augmented forms of this type; but cf. ἠνέστη Lk 9: 8 D, Jn 2: 22 W (vulgar, Rudberg 19). 𝔓⁴⁶ has the incorrect ἐπεριεπατήσατε E 2: 2, ἐπροέκοπτον G 1: 14.

(3) Ἀπεκατέστη -εστάθη Mt 12: 13 (ἀποκ- DK), Mk 3: 5 (ἀποκ- D), 8: 25 (ἀποκ- B), Lk 6: 10 (ἀποκ- BU); ἀντεκατέστητε H 12: 4 weakly attested. Earliest example: ἀπεκατεστάσαμες in the Doric tablets from Heraclea, Tab. Heracl. II 22 (IV BC end); Helb. 77; Mayser I² 2, 109.

(4) Ἐπροφητεύσαμεν Mt 7: 22 SB*CLWZ (προεφ- B²EGK al.), ἐπροφήτευσαν 11: 13 SB*CDZ (προεφ- B**EFG al.); similarly divided are 15: 7, Mk 7: 6 (ἐπροεφ- W), Lk 1: 67, Jn 11: 51 (ἐπροφ- also 𝔓⁴⁵), A 19: 6; S always ἐπρ-, also Jd 14 προεπροφήτευσεν (B* ἐπροφ-, B³ ἐπροεφ-, the others προεφ-). On this verb cf. Kontos, Κριτικαὶ καὶ γραμμ. παρατηρήσεις (1895) 70ff.; Schmidt 442; Psaltes 206; Scherer 70 §121. Παρρησιάζεσθαι–ἐπαρρ- does not belong here, because the first element is παν-, not παρα-. Un-Attic διηκόνουν from διακονεῖν, although διάκονος is not composed of δι-ἀκ-; cf. Psaltes 206; Att. ἐδιακόνουν. Περιέσσευον (proscribed by Phryn. 28 and Cramer, Anec. Ox. III 257.18; cf. Helb. 80) only in A 16: 5 E. Εὐηρεστηκέναι H 11: 5 𝔓¹³𝔓⁴⁶SDEP (εὐαρ- AKL); εὐαρεστηκότων Herm Vis 3.1.9 S (εὐηρ- A), εὐηρέστησαν Sim 8.3.5 (-καν PMich), 1 Clem 62.2.

(3) -Ω VERBS

(A) Formation of Tense (General)

70. Verb-stems ending with a vowel. (1) The short vowel is retained in Hellenistic in the formation of the tense stems of φορεῖν (Attic -η-, MGr -ε-) modeled after ἠμφίεσα (Hatzidakis, Glotta 22 [1933] 129); contrast ἐπιποθήσατε 1 P 2: 2 from ἐπιποθεῖν. From ρη- come the indicatives ἐρρέθη and ἐρρήθη, but always ρηθείς. (2) Πεινᾶν, πεινάσω ἐπείνασα Lk 6: 25 etc., but διψᾶν διψήσω ἐδίψησα. (3) With σ affixed to the stem λελουσμένοι H 10: 23 SD*P (the others, including 𝔓⁴⁶, without σ), but λελουμένος as in Attic Jn 13: 10 (-σμ- only in E); always κέκλεισμαι (Lk 11: 7 etc.) contrary to Attic -ειμαι (-ημαι), but ἐκλείσθην as in Attic. Cf. ζωννύναι, κεραννύναι §101, σῴζειν §26.

(1) Ἐφορέσαμεν and φορέσομεν 1 C 15: 49; also ἐφόρεσα in 1 Clem and Hermas, but still πεφορηκότες Herm Sim 9. 16. 1 (Reinhold 70). Elsewhere too -ε- is not found until later outside the aor. and fut. act. (Crönert 225.3); MGr φορέζω ἐφόρεσα. (Ἐπ-) ἐπόθησα also in Hdt., Xen. and LXX, therefore Ionic-Hell.; -εσα preponderates in early Greek and Att. Ἐρρέθη Mt 5: 21 SLM al., 27 SKL al., 31 SLM

al.; -ε- is found in the indic. (elsewhere -η-) as early as Hdt. (artificial? F. Hartmann, KZ 60 [1933] 106) and from Arist. on (Lautensach 286f.; Thack. 218f.; Mayser I² 2, 156; Crönert 267.7). Ἀκαιρεθῆναι Herm Sim 9.10.5 A is singular.

(2) Πεινάσω (ᾱ according to Anth. Pal. XI 402.5 and Choerob. in Grammatici Graeci IV 2 pp. 161.30f., 165.10f.; cf. Plutarch πεινᾱτικός) following κοπιάσω, for which it is often a synonym, e.g. in the LXX; cf. MGr πεινῶ (πεινάζω) ἐπείνασα, but also διψῶ (διψάζω) ἐδίψασα.

(3) Λέλουσμαι is found in the LXX as in the NT; cf. Thack. 220. Cf. κέλευσμα 1 Th 4: 16 for the customary κέλευμα (Crönert 227.5). Spurious ἐνισχύσθη A 9: 19 𝔓⁴⁵ (-ύθη BC* al.; -υσεν most other witnesses) and κεκονιασμένοις Mt 23: 27 W. Ἐκαύθην (s. §76), but κεκαυτηριασμένων 1 T 4: 2 CDE al. (-καυστ- SAL); τεθραυμένους Lk 4: 18 OT D²W (al. -σμ- as in LXX and Hell. otherwise; instances in Att. are doubtful).

71. Verb-stems ending with a stop.
Of the verbs in -ζειν, νυστάζειν and (ἐμ-)παίζειν have a guttural character, which is a deviation from Attic; the dental character of σαλπίζειν is un-Attic; ἁρπάζειν and στηρίζειν fluctuate. There is no present in the NT for ἡρμοσάμην and ἔσφαξα (Attic ἁρμόττειν, σφάττειν, Ionic-Hellenistic ἁρμόζειν [Diogn 12.9, Herm; Mayser I² 2, 118f.], σφάζειν).

Ἐνύσταξαν Mt 25: 5 as Hell. and MGr. Always ἐμπαῖξαι, ἐνεπαίχθη etc. (cf. Lautensach 195f.; Mayser I² 2, 133), also ἐμπαίκτης ἐμπαιγμός -γμονή: Doricism of Koine supported by the desire to distinguish ἔπαιξα from ἔπαισα (from παίειν); also MGr παίζω ἔπαιξα. Always σαλπίζω ἐσάλπισα σαλπιστής (derived from -ίζειν) as Hell. instead of -ι(γ)ξα (from σάλπι(γ)ξ -ιγγος). In the NT always ἐβάστασα as in Att., while in late Hell. -ξα is frequent (βαστάξαι Rev 2: 2 P, δυσβάστακτα [avoiding cacophony *-βασ-τασ-τα] Lk 11: 46 [Mt 23: 4 BDΓΔ al.]; Thack. 222; Mayser I² 2, 134f.; MGr ἐβάσταξα). Ἁρπάσω ἥρπασα ἡρπάσθην as Att., besides ἡρπάγην (§76(1)); cf. ἅρπαξ (Att.), ἁρπαγή (old and new Att.), ἁρπαγμός. Στηρίζειν is dental in fut. and aor. act. only in Lk 9: 51 𝔓⁴⁵BCL al. (-ξ- SAD al.), 22: 32 (-ξ- D al.), Rev 3: 2 ACP (-ξ- S 046), 2 Th 3: 3 B, A 15: 32 CE, otherwise -ξ- and always ἐστήριγμαι στηριγμός ἀστήρικτος. Ἐδίστασα Mt 14: 31, 28: 17, Herm Man 9.5, διστάσω Barn 19. 11, Did 4.7, but ἀδιστάκτως often in Herm, δισταγμός Herm Sim 9. 28.4, 1 Clem 46.9.

72. Verb-stems ending with a liquid.
The first aorist active of verbs in -αίνειν -αίρειν -άλλειν is formed generally in Hellenistic in -ᾶνα -ᾱρα -ᾱλα without reference to the preceding sound.

The perfect passive participle of ν-verbs usually in Hellenistic and always in the NT is formed in -μμένος (from *-ν-μένος; Attic usually -σμ-, but also -μμ-).

Ἐξήρανα as in Att., but also ἐλεύκανα (ἐκέρδανα §101), ἐβάσκανα, ἐσήμανα instead of Att. -ηνα; ἐπιφᾶναι Lk 1: 79, ἀναφάναντες A 21: 3 (inferior reading -φανέντες AB*CE al.), φάνῃ Rev (8: 12?), 18: 23; ἐξεκάθᾱρα 1 C 5: 7, 2 T 2: 21; ἀνεθάλατε Ph 4: 10 𝔓⁴⁶D* (probably correctly; the others have -λετε, s. §75). Katz, ThLZ 1957, 112: Ezk 25: 6 ἐπέχαρας, 25: 3 𝔓⁹⁶⁷ (instead of -ρητε), ἐπιχάραντες Bar 4: 31 B*A 544 (good). Attic also displays isolated forms in -ᾰν- and -ᾰρ- for -ην- and -ηρ- (K.-Bl. II 170f.; Lautensach 200, 202 etc.); in MGr -α- is found virtually throughout (e.g. ἐξεθύμανα ἔψαλα), Björck, Alpha imp. 254f.—Ἐξηραμμένην Mk 3: 3 DΓ al. parchment MPER N.S. 4, no. 32 (B al. ξηράν), 3: 1 (almost all), 11: 20. Μεμαμμένος T 1: 15. Μεμαραμμένον Herm Vis 3.11.2 (-ασμ- A), κατῃσχυμμένος Man 12.5.2; ἐκτεθηλυμμένων Homil Clem 12.6.3; σεσημαμμέναις PBer (Mnemosyne III 13 [1947] 304.24), βεβαρυμμένοι PTebt 23.5 (c. 115 BC), κατασεσημημμένα (sic) POxy I 117.14 (ii/iii AD); cf. Thack. 224. For -μμ- from -ν-μ- cf. LXX 2 Esdr 9: 1, 11 μάκρυμμα.

(B) Formation of Tense (Present)

73.
Ἀμφιέζειν (-ζει Lk 12: 28 𝔓⁴⁵DL) and ἀμφιάζειν (-ζει ibid. B) are new Hellenistic formations for ἀμφιεννύναι built on ἀμφιέσαι (-άσαι).—Γρηγορεῖν is a new Hellenistic formation taken from the perfect ἐγρήγορα (pluperfect ἐγρηγόρει formed like ἐποίει), Katz, Philo's Bible 159f.—Ἐνδιδύσκειν 'put on' for ἐνδύειν appears to be a Doricism.—Κρύβειν (only imperfect περιέκρυβεν Lk 1: 24, κρύπτειν unattested) is a new Hellenistic formation for κρύπτειν from Hellenistic aorist ἐκρύβην following ἐγράφην–γράφειν.—A variety of new forms appear in the MSS for ἀποκτείνειν: -κτέ(ν)νειν, -κτιννύναι, -κτεννύναι, -κταίνειν (αι = ε according to §25).—Νίπτειν (Mt 15: 2, Jn 13: 5, 6, 14) instead of νίζειν is a back-formation from νίψω ἔνιψα etc., likewise ῥήσσειν (§101) from ῥήξω ἔρ(ρ)ηξα.—Στήκειν is a Hellenistic formation based on ἔστηκα; both are used concurrently.—Χύν(ν)ειν (also MGr) instead of χεῖν is a Hellenistic formation from ἐχύθην κέχυμαι on the analogy of πλύνειν ἐπλύθην.—S. also §101 βλαστᾶν, γαμίζειν, δύνειν, κυλίειν, λιμπάνειν (under λείπειν), ἀνοίγειν, ὀπτάνεσθαι (under ὁρᾶν), ῥιπτεῖν, σκοπεῖν.

Ἀμφιέννυσιν Lk 12: 28 SAW al., Mt 6: 30 all MSS. On ἀμφιάζειν cf. §29(2); Cramer, Anec. Ox. II 339.2 τὸ μὲν ἀμφιέζω ἐστὶ κοινῶς· τὸ δὲ ἀμφιάζω Δωρικόν, ὥσπερ τὸ ὑποπιέζω καὶ ὑποπιάζω; ἀμφιέζειν as pres. only in Plut., C. Gracch. 2 (v.l. ἀμφιάζειν).—Γρηγορεῖν s. Thack. 224; Helb. 82, 84 (where, however, Arist. is to be omitted [Rudberg, Bibelforskaren (= der Bibelforscher) 1914, 74]); Debrunner, IF 47 (1929) 356. Ἐγρήγορα no longer in NT; but ἐγρηγορῶν Rev 3: 2 S* (perhaps already objected to by S*, with the ε deleted by Sᶜ), διεγρηγορήσαντες Lk 9: 32 𝔓⁴⁵.—Ἐνδιδύσκειν Mk 15: 17 SBC (D ἐνδυδισκ-), mid. Lk 8: 27 SᶜᵃA (D -δυδισκ- like ἐνδυδισκόμενος Dit., Syll.² 857.13 [Delphi, ii BC mid.]; after verbs in -ίσκειν al. (v.l. aor.), 16: 19, Herm Sim 9.13.5; ἐκ- and ἐν- LXX, ἐξεδίδυσκε Jos., Bell. 2.278.—Κρύβειν also LXX, Jos., later pap. and Apocrypha; s. Thack. 227; Schmidt 531; Dieterich 233f.; Reinhold 72; Psaltes 244. Homil Clem 9.17.5 συγκρύβουσιν. Cf. adv. κρυβῇ for κρυφῇ E 5: 12 𝔓⁴⁶, POxy I 83.14 (327 AD), III 465.230 (ii AD), LXX Gen 31: 26 (27) A, Ruth 3: 7 A, 1 Km 19: 2 B, 2 Km 12: 12, 3 Macc 4: 12.—Ἀποκτεννόντων Mt 10: 28 (-εν- E al., -ειν- B), Lk 12: 4 (-εν- DGW al., -αιν- M, -ειν- 𝔓⁴⁶ B), -κτέννοντες Mk 12: 5 (-ένοντες FG al., -εννύντες B, -ιννύντες Sᶜ, -αίνοντες M, -ίνοντες W), -κτέννει 2 C 3: 6 SFG 𝔓⁴⁶ second hand (-ένει 𝔓⁴⁶ first hand ACDE al., -είνει B), Rev 13: 10 (-ένει CP 046, -είνει S), -κτέννεσθαι 6: 11 (-ειν- P 046); -ειν- predominates in Mt 23: 37 (-ενν- CGK, -εν- S), Lk 13: 34 (-ενν- AK al.). For -νν- or -ν- s. under χύν(ν)ειν. Of late origin are the spellings ἀναίβεννον A 3: 1 A, ἀνέβεννον C, καταίβεννεν Lk 10: 31 A for -έβαιν-. The situation is comparable with -κτείνειν and -βαίνειν in the LXX (Thack. 225f.). -κτένω with -κτενῶ -έκτεινα on the analogy of μένω μενῶ ἔμεινα?—Νίπτειν is found outside Hell. as early as Hippocrates (and Homer?); Debrunner, IF 21 (1907) 211.—Στήκειν: virtually confined to Paul and mostly impera. στήκετε (1 C 16: 13, G 5: 1, Ph 4: 1, 2 Th 2: 15; Att. ἕστατε), otherwise στήκῃ (-ει) Mt 12: 26 acc. to Homil Clem 19.2.3, στήκετε as indic. Mk 11: 25 (§382(4)), 1 Th 3: 8 SᶜABF al. (§372(1a)), Ph 1: 27, στήκοντες Mk 3: 31 BC* (v.l. στάντες, ἑστηκότες, ἑστῶτες), στήκει R 14: 4. But οὔκ ἔστηκεν Jn 8: 44 is perf. (§§14; 97(1)); Rev 12: 4 ἔστηκεν impf. or ἕστηκεν perf.? Στήκω in W also in Mk 3: 32, 13: 14 and an impossible στηκότων Mt 27: 47. Jn 1: 26 𝔓⁶⁶ ἑστηκεν; pm. στήκει. Στήκειν LXX, Apocrypha, epigram in Epigr. Kaibel 970 (iii AD?); condemned by Phryn. 317 with Lobeck's comments; s. Helb. 82, 84; Reinhold 72; Psaltes 245. MGr στέκω.—Χύν(ν)ειν throughout except for συνέχεον A 21: 27 (-αν C, -εσχον E), ἐπιχέων Lk 10: 34 (-έας 𝔓⁴⁵), Mt 9: 17 ἐκχεῖται (interpolation?); in Rev 16: 1 ἐκχέατε is to be read with 046 instead of -έετε, Herm Sim 8.2.7 with PMich πειράσω καὶ...παραχέω (cf. §471(1)) instead of -χέειν A; only 3 Km 22: 35 ἀπεχύννετο in the LXX. The orthography of the best witnesses is -νν-: A 9: 22 SB*C, 21: 31 S*AB*D, 22: 20 SAB*, Mt 26: 28 SABCD al., similarly 23: 35, Mk 14: 24, Lk 6: 38, 11: 50, 22: 20; MGr also points

to -νν- (Thumb² §199 I 6 n. 2). Elsewhere, however, χύνειν alone is recognized (Lob. Phryn. 726), which analogy supports; συγχύννου Herm Vis 5.5 S. Psaltes 241 sees in -νν- an artificial Aeolicism.— Φρίζουσιν Ja 2: 19 𝔓²⁰ (POxy IX 1171.2; iii AD end) is spurious for φρίσσουσιν.

(C) Formation of Tense
(Future Active and Middle)

74. (1) The so-called Attic future of verbs in -εῖν, -άζειν etc. is, in general, missing from Hellenistic Greek. Thus the NT (as a rule also the papyri, Mayser I² 2, 129) has καλέσω τελέσω (ἀπολέσω §101) following the aorist ἐκάλεσα ἐτέλεσα, whereby the future was distinguished from the present καλῶ τελῶ. Verbs in -άζειν always form the future in -άσω (LXX very often ἁρπᾷ, ἐργᾶται etc.); those in -ίζειν in -ίσω. -ιῶ is virtually confined to quotations from the LXX. (2) The NT forms a future without σ for the following: πίομαι as in Attic; Hellenistic has formed a new future φάγομαι (instead of ἔδομαι) from ἔφαγον following πίομαι ἔπιον; χεῶ has appeared in place of χέω (ἐκχεῶ A 2: 17, 18 from OT). (3) Ἑλῶ from εἷλον is new (after βαλῶ from ἔβαλον), as is ἑλκύσω from ἕλκω εἵλκυσα; s. §101.—On the 'future subjunctive' s. §28.

(1) Fut. in -ιῶ: from LXX ἐλπιοῦσιν Mt 12: 21, R 15: 12, ἐδαφιοῦσιν Lk 19: 44, παροργιῶ R 10: 19, μετοικιῶ A 7: 43; cf. μακαριοῦσιν Lk 1: 48 (Hymn in OT style). Otherwise: (δια-)καθαριεῖ Mt 3: 12 (Lk 3: 17), H 9: 14, ἀφοριοῦσιν Mt 13: 49 (there was evidently a tendency to avoid the succession of sounds in -ίσουσιν), κομιεῖσθε 1 P 5: 4. Fut. in -ιῶ as v.l.: ἀφοριεῖ Mt 25: 32 SᶜABD al. (-ίσει S*LWΔ), γνωριοῦσιν C 4: 9 S*ACDᶜ al. (-ίσουσιν 𝔓⁴⁶SᶜBFGP; but in 7 all MSS have γνωρίσει, likewise E 6: 21 and γνωρίσω Jn 17: 26), ἐγγιεῖ Ja 4: 8 (-ίσει A), κομιεῖται C 3: 25 S*ACD*I (-ίσεται SᶜBDᶜ al.), E 6: 8 SᶜDᶜ al. (-ίσεται 𝔓⁴⁶S*ABD*al.), κομιούμενοι 2 P 2: 13 (v.l. ἀδικούμενοι), φωτιεῖ Rev 22: 5 S 046 (-ίσει AP), χρονιεῖ H 10: 37 OT SᶜADᶜI al. (-ίσει 𝔓⁴⁶S*D*; οὐ μὴ χρονίσῃ LXX Hab 2: 3), καταρτιεῖ 1 P 5: 10 𝔓²⁵ (POxy XI 1353.24, iv AD; -τίσει SAB, -τίσαι KLP). Always -ίσω in the following verbs: βαπτίσω, ἐμφανίσω, θερίσω, καθίσω, στηρίσω (in addition to -ίζω §71), χαρίσεται R 8: 32, χωρίσω; otherwise much variation. In the LXX -ιῶ prevails decisively, in the Ptol. pap. it rules exclusively (Mayser I² 2, 128); for the NT the tendency of scribes is obviously to use Att. forms, so that in original composition -ίσω is to be preferred as the original spelling (s. supra).

(2) Phryn. 327: φάγομαι βάρβαρον; the LXX still has ἔδομαι along with φάγομαι. That χεῶ and not χέω

is the correct accent follows, apart from the evidence of the grammarians, from ἐκχεεῖτε LXX Dt 12: 16, 24.

(3) With ἐλῶ cf. παθεῖται instead of πείσεται 2 Clem 7.5 A (Reinhold 74), formed from ἔπαθον perhaps after βαλῶ ἔβαλον.

(D) Formation of Tense (Aorist)

75. First–second aorist active and middle. Koine often used a first aorist modeled after a sigma-future in addition to, or as a substitute for, an Attic second aorist. In the NT e.g. -ῆξα in addition to ἤγαγον; ἡμάρτησα and ἤμαρτον; βιῶσαι 1 P 4: 2 (Ionic-Hellenistic transformation of Attic βιῶναι); ἐβλάστησα, never ἔβλαστον; ἔδυσα intransitive for ἔδυν; ἔκραξα (and ἐκέκραξα) along with Attic ἀνέκραγον; -έλειψα along with Attic ἔλιπον.

Ἐπάξας 2 P 2: 5, ἐπισυνάξαι Lk 13: 34, συνάξαντες A 14: 27 D; LXX also -ῆξα; inscrip. and pap. from ii BC (Helb. 91, where, however, the examples from Homer and the class. period are to be omitted; Thack. 233; Mayser I² 2, 144; Lautensach 96); MGr ἐσύναξα. Homil Clem 3.73.3 προήξαμεν 'we preceded'.—Ἡμάρτησα R 5: 14, 16 (6: 15 -σομεν is better [§77] since the aor. does not suit), H 3: 17, 2 P 2: 4, Mt 18: 15 (Lk 17: 3 and 4 v.l.), Herm Man 4.3.6, etc. Otherwise Empedocles, LXX etc.; cf. Lob. Phryn. 732 f.; MGr ἁμάρτησα.—For ἐβίων Hell. usually has ἔζησα (Ion.) A 26: 5 etc., also Herm; cf. Nachmanson 167.—Ἐβλάστησα Mt 13: 26, H 9: 4, factitive in Ja 5: 18 as in LXX, e.g. Gen 1: 11; Empedocles, Hippoc. 9.100 Littré, Hell., MGr.—Ἔδυσεν for ἔδυ Mk 1: 32 BD (ἔδυ SA al.), δύσαντος Lk 4: 40 D (δύναντος a few, most have δύνοντος); cf. §101 and Thack. 235, 265.—NT usually ἔκραξα; ἀνέκραγον Lk 23: 18 SBLT, Herm Vis 3.8.9 (-γεν); ἐκέκραξα A 24: 21 SABC (al. ἔκραξα) s. §101; all are also found in LXX (Helb. 90, 91 f.); MGr ἔκραξα.—Καταλείψαντες A 6: 2, κατέλειψαν Lk 5: 11 D, ἐγκατέλιψεν Lk 10: 40 W, καταλείψῃ Mk 12: 19 S for -λ(ε)ίπῃ. Herm Sim 8.3.5 PMich κατέλειπεν (twice), A -λειψεν and -λιπεν. Pap., LXX. Ap. Frs., Apocr. nearly always (ἐγ-)κατέλειψα (Helb. 90f.; Thack. 234; Mayser I² 2, 138; MGr ἔλειψα). Ep. Clem. ad Jac. 5.5 (p. 9.14 Rehm) καταλείψαντα. Simple ἔλειψα is rare (Anth. Pal.; s. also Helb. 91; Vogeser 13).—There is a new second aor. in ἀνεθάλετε Ph 4: 10; the first aor. is still met also, cf. §72 and Thack. 235 (in ἀναθάλοι Sir 46: 12, 49: 10, -λη Wsd 4: 4, an aorist is syntactically required, so that -λ- for -λλ- [Debrunner] is unwarranted [Katz, ThLZ 1957, 112]); on the significance s. §101.

76. First–second aorist and future passive.
(1) New second aorists (passive): in the Hellen-istic period the second aorist is very popular (more Ionic than Attic). Thus in the NT (apart from regular Attic forms): ἠγγέλην, ἡρπάγην (along with the Attic ἡρπάσθην), ἐκάην, ἐκρύβην, ἐνύγην, ἠνοίγην, ὠρύγην, ἐπάην (§78), ἐτάγην, ἐφράγην, ἐψύγην. But ἐκλίθην κλιθήσομαι (poetic) forms a first aorist following ἐκρίθην instead of the Attic ἐκλίνην. (2) An aorist passive in place of an intransitive active or middle: a new first aorist passive replaces an intransitive in ἐτέχθην Mt 2: 2, Lk 2: 11 (for Attic ἐγενόμην), and often ἀπεκτάνθην (for Attic ἀπέθανον); an intransitive root-aorist (ἔφυν ἔδυν) is being replaced by a second aorist passive built on the same stem in ἐφύην ἐδύην (cf. ἐρρύην). A. Prévot, L'aoriste grec en -θην (Paris, 1935) 178ff., especially 208-14.

(1) Ἠγγέλην (only in compounds) 1 P 1: 12, Lk 8: 20, R 9: 17 OT, A 17: 13 is probably not Att. (Lautensach 265f.).—Ἡρπάγην 2 C 12: 2, 4, ἡρπάσθη Rev 12: 5 𝔓⁴⁷ACP (-άγη S, -άχθη 046), ἁρπαγησόμεθα 1 Th 4: 17.—Κατεκάη Rev 8: 7, κατακαήσεται 1 C 3: 15, (2 P 3: 10), otherwise ἐκαύθην καυθήσομαι as in Att.; ἐκάην is Ionic (Homer, Hdt.); MGr has ἐκάηκα in addition to ἐκαύτηκα.—Ἐκρύβην Mt 5: 14 etc.; cf. κρύβειν §73; these new second aorists prefer a voiced stop (as final stem-consonant) even though, as in this case (κρυφ-), it is not original (Att. -φθην, poet. -φην); Lautensach 251.—Κατενύγησαν A 2: 37, cf. LXX (Thack. 237).—Ἠνοίγησαν Mk 7: 35 (-οιχθ- 𝔓⁴⁵ A al.), -γη A 12: 10 (-χθη EHLP), Rev 11: 19 (-χθη 046), ἀνοιγῶσιν Mt 20: 33 (-χθ- CN al.), Rev 15: 5, -γήσεται Mt 7: 7, 8 (-γεται B), Lk 11: 9 (-χθ- DEFG al.), 10 (-χθ- AEFG al., -γεται BD); in addition to ἀνεῴχθην, ἠνοίχθην and the like (§101); -χθ- is Att.; -γ- is found in the post-Christian pap. (Dieterich 211).—Διορυγῆναι (v.l. -χθῆναι) Mt 24: 43, Lk 12: 39, cf. ὠρύγη Herm Sim 9.6.7.—Διαταγείς G 3: 19, ὑπετάγην R 8: 20, 10: 3, etc., ὑποταγήσομαι 1 C 15: 28, H 12: 9, (Barn 19.7); cf. προσετάγη Herm Man 4.1.10; but ποιεῖν τὰ διαταχθέντα Lk 17: 9, 10 as in Att. (official language; cf. Jos., Ant. 5.252, 11. 138, 20.46, Vit. 109).—Φραγῇ R 3: 19, -γήσεται 2 C 11: 10; LXX ἀπ- and ἐνεφράγη, ἀποφράγητε, ἐμφραχθείη, -θήσεται.—Ψυγήσεται Mt 24: 12 (-χήσεται K; ἐψύχθη is also class.); cf. above under ἐκρύβην (ψύγω is later; cf. Lobeck on Soph., Aj.³ p. 373 n.). Lautensach 233f.—Ἐκλίθην is also found in the LXX (Helb. 96); κλιθέντα PTebt 3.4 (epigram i BC).

(2) Ἐτέχθην and ἀπεκτάνθην are found also in the LXX (Helb. 96; Thack. 238). On ἐτέχθην also cf. Schmidt 463.5; Melcher 16; Lautensach 241.—Φυέν Lk 8: 6, 8, συμφυεῖσαι 7, ἐκφυῇ Mt 24: 32 = Mk 13: 28; παρεισεδύησαν Jd 4 B. Cf. Reinhold 76; Helb. 96f.; Thack. 235; Schmidt 467 (Jos. ἔφυν and ἐφύην); Prévot, op. cit. 198; Mayser I² 2, 161. Ἐφύην AEM XIX 228.5, 11 (Michaïlov² 180).

(E) Voice

77. Future active and middle. While many active verbs form a future middle in Attic, Koine prefers the active for the most part. In the NT the middle is retained for the following (because no active sigma-aorist exists for these verbs): -βήσομαι, γνώσομαι, ἀποθανοῦμαι, λήμψομαι, ὄψομαι, πεσοῦμαι, πίομαι, τέξομαι, φάγομαι, φεύξομαι, χαρήσομαι (but Attic had χαιρήσω). Only the active form appears for the following: ἁμαρτήσω Mt 18: 21, R 6: 15 (s. § 75) (Herm Man 4.1.1, 2), ἀπαντήσω Mk 14: 13, συναντήσω (Attic Future unattested) Lk 22: 10, A 20: 22, ἁρπάσω Jn 10: 28 (οὐ μὴ ἁρπάσῃ SDLX), βλέψω Mt 13: 14 = A 28: 26 OT, γελάσω Lk 6: 21, διώξω Mt 23: 34 etc., ἐμπαίξω Mk 10: 34, ῥεύσω Jn 7: 38 (Attic ῥεύσομαι and ῥυήσομαι), σπουδάσω 2 P 1: 15 (-άζω S; Attic middle, active since Hyperides; Gromska 36 f.). The following vacillate between active and middle: ἀκούσω, ζήσω, κλαύσω, κράξω.

On θαυμάσομαι s. § 78.—Ἀκούσομαι: Acts (except 28: 26 OT -ετε), -σονται R 10: 14 S*DE al. (-σωνται 𝔓[46]) incorrectly for -σωσιν S[c]B; ἀκούσω: Mt 12: 19 OT, Jn 5: 25 (-ονται AD al.), 28 (the same), 10: 16 (-σωσιν SAG al.), 16: 13 (v.l. -σῃ, ἀκούει SL); -σω is to be preferred where the MSS vacillate since the variants do not encroach upon -σομαι in Acts. Ζήσω: Jn 5: 25 SBDLW (-ονται A al.), 6: 51 SDLW (-εται BC al.), 57 ABC² (-εται WΓΔ al., ζῇ C*D), 58 SBCE (-εται DHK al.) and at times a similar division elsewhere; ζήσομαι: Mt 9: 18 (all MSS), Jn 11: 25 ([ζήσ]ει 𝔓[45]), R 8: 13 and the frequently quoted ζήσεται from the LXX; ζήσω: συνζήσομεν 2 T 2: 11 (-ωμεν CLP is corrupt; 1 Th 5: 10 s. § 369(2)), etc.; both futures are also Att. Κλαύσω Lk 6: 25, Jn 16: 20, Rev 18: 9 (SA -ονται as in Herm Vis 3.3.2). Κράξουσιν Lk 19: 40 SBL, κεκράξονται is an inferior variant (Att., LXX; § 65(1b)) AR al., κράξονται D.

78. Aorist (future) middle and passive. The later language preferred the aorist passive in the case of deponents (where a real passive meaning is at best a possibility; deponents in MGr always form the aorist in -(θ)ηκα = -(θ)ην). Thus in the NT: ἐγενήθην (Doric, Ionic, and generally Hellenistic; Phryn. 108; Lautensach 285; Mayser I² 2, 157 f.) in addition to ἐγενόμην; ἀπ-, ὑπ-, δι-εκρίθην as in Hellenistic (Phryn. 108; Mayser I² 2, 158) in addition to ἀπεκρινάμην; ἀπελογήθην (an old form, but not good Attic) in addition to -γησάμην; ἠγέρθην (intransitive and passive as in Hdt., Xen. and others [Lautensach 249]; likewise ἐγερθήσομαι), never the Attic ἠγρόμην; ἐγαμήθην (§ 101) for Attic ἐγημάμην; ἀναπαήσομαι is a

variant for ἀναπαύσομαι (ἐπάην is to ἔπαυσα as ἐκάην is to ἔκαυσα). And especially with verbs of emotion (even those which were originally intransitive actives): ἠγαλλιάθην, (ἐνεβριμήθην,) ἐθαμβήθην, ἐθαυμάσθην (intransitive); see also § 101 ἀπορεῖν. Koine shows reverse preference for the aorist middle instead of the passive in the case of ἀρνεῖσθαι and διαλέγεσθαι of which there are examples also in the NT.

Ἐγενήθην: Mt only γενηθήτω 6: 10, 8: 13, 9: 29, 15: 28, 26: 42, ἐγενήθην 21: 42 (quotation), otherwise only -νήθησαν 11: 23 SBCD, 28: 4 SBC*DL; never in Jn; only in quotation in Mk; likewise Lk, however 10: 13 (= Mt 11: 23) -νήθησαν SBDLẔ, 18: 23 -νήθη SBL; Acts, except for the quotation in 1: 20, only 4: 4 -νήθη (all MSS); D reads it also in 7: 13, 20: 3, 16; Paul, Peter, Heb often. The papyri and LXX also have ἐγενήθην in addition to the more frequent ἐγενόμην. Prévot, *loc. cit.* 90–3 wants to carry out extensively in the NT a distinction between ἐγένετο 'was, happened, occurred' and ἐγενήθη 'became, was done'.—Ἀπεκρίθην: found generally (MGr ἀποκρίθηκα); only Lk has ἀπεκρίνατο also (Att.) 3: 16 (L correctly -νετο 23: 9), A 3: 12 (D reads differently); otherwise only with v.l.: Mt 27: 12 (D correctly -νετο), Mk 14: 61 (-ίθη D; -νετο?), Jn 5: 17, 19, 12: 23, 18: 34. Ἀποκριθήσομαι is the corresponding fut. Ὑπεκρίθην Herm Sim 9.19.3, συνυπ- G 2: 13. From διακρίνεσθαι 'to doubt' always διεκρίθην.—Ἀπολογηθῆναι Lk 21: 14, -γήσησθε 12: 11 (but -γηθῆτε following Clem. Alex., Strom. IV 9.70.4 [II 280.8 Stählin]).—Ἀναπαήσεται: in a saying of Jesus POxy IV 654.9 (iii AD), ἐπανα- Lk 10: 6 SB* (-παύσεται al., -παύσηται W), ἀναπαήσονται Rev 14: 13 𝔓[47]SAC, v.l. -παύσονται or -σωνται as in 6: 11 and the like elsewhere; Herm παῆναι Vis 1.3.3 S (παυθῆναι A), 3.9.1 S (παῦσαι A), ἐπαναπαῇ Sim 2.5 in POxy IX 1172.9 (iv AD) (A ἀναπλῇ), -ῆναι Sim 9.5.1 PMich (-παυθῆναι A). Reinhold 78; Psaltes 225; s. Dieterich 240 for inscrip. and pap.—Ἠγαλλιάσατο Lk 10: 21, Jn 8: 56 (-ᾶτο Nonnus and two Lat. MSS), A 2: 26 OT (LXX only aor. mid.), 16: 34 (-ᾶτο C*DP), ἀγαλλιαθῆναι Jn 5: 35 (-σθ- BL).—Ἐνεβριμήσατο Mt 9: 30 B²CDE al. (-ήθη SB*), Jn 11: 33, ἐμβριμησάμενος Mk 1: 43; Att. mid.—Ἐθαμβήθησαν Mk 1: 27 (-βησαν D), θαμβηθέντες A 3: 11 D; ἐθαμβοῦντο Mk 10: 24, 32, θαμβῶν intr. A 9: 6 D. Homer and other poets θαμβεῖν which is intr. and causative in the LXX; in LXX also θαμβεῖσθαι, ἐθαμβήθην (intr.).—Ἐθαυμάσθη Rev 13: 3 A (-μασεν SP 046, -μαστώθη C, -μαση 𝔓[47] is corrupt), θαυμασθήσονται 17: 8 AP (-μάσονται S 046) from the late θαυμάζεσθαι (otherwise in the NT always act.; MGr θαμάζω -ζομαι, cf. § 307); θαυμασθῆναι in a pass. sense 2 Th 1: 10 (so also in the LXX with the exception perhaps of Esth 4: 17p; s. Thack. 240 n. 1).—(Ἀπ-)ηρνησάμην always: Att. -ήθην more often; ἀπαρνῆσαι Herm

Sim 1.5 is corrupt.—Διελέξατο A 17: 2 SAB (-έχθη DE), 18: 19 SAB (-έχθη EHLP) is an incorrect variant for διελέγετο; διελέχθησαν as in Att. Mk 9: 34. Διαλέξασθαι, οὐ μόνον διαλεχθῆναι Pseudo-Phryn. in Bekker, Anec. Gr. i 37.4. Rutherford, Phryn. 186 ff.; Prévot, op. cit. (§ 76) 206–8.

79. Future middle and passive.
The conjugation -σομαι, etc. is no longer used in a passive sense, only -(θ)ήσομαι. Likewise many deponents, which in Attic had an aorist passive but a future middle, carry over the passive to the future in Hellenistic.

Thus we find in the NT: εὐφρανθήσονται Rev 11: 10 046, κοιμηθησόμεθα 1 C 15: 51, μεταμεληθήσεται H 7: 21 OT (but ἐπιμελήσεται 1 T 3: 5), φανήσομαι (φανεῖται 1 P 4: 18 OT), φοβηθήσομαι H 13: 6 OT. However, γενήσομαι, δυνήσομαι, πορεύσομαι persist.

(F) Endings: Confusion of First Aorist–Perfect with Second Aorist–Imperfect

80. Introduction.
Modern Greek has completely abandoned the distinction between first and second aorists (and imperfect) with regard to endings. An imperfect like ἔγραφα, an original first aorist like ἔγραψα or ἔστειλα, and an original second aorist like ἔβαλα are inflected exactly alike: ἔγραφα -ες -ε ἐγράφαμεν -ετε or -ατε ἔγραφαν. The roots of these paradigms reach back into the Koine. From ἔλυσεν–ἔλυσαν, ἤγγειλεν–ἤγγειλαν the transition was first made to ἔπεσεν–ἔπεσαν, εἷλεν–εἷλαν, which afforded an easy means of distinguishing the 3rd plur. from the 1st sing. ἔπεσον εἷλον; then other second aorists (like εἷδεν–εἷδαν) followed suit and at the same time the remaining forms of the second aorist indicative and imperative, and finally the imperfect and middle. The 2nd sing. in -ες and accordingly the 2nd plur. in -ετε (and the imperative in -ε -έτω -ετε) held their own under the influence of the 3rd sing. in -εν and intruded also into the first aorist. The old double forms εἷπον–εἷπα and ἤνεγκον–ἤνεγκα and the identity of the first and second aorist subjunctive contributed to the intermingling. Since, on the other hand, the first aorist and the perfect were distinguishable only in the 3rd plur., these forms were also leveled out, usually by taking -αν over into the perfect (ἑωράκαν; under the influence of ἔδωκαν and the like); thus the way for -ες to pass into the perfect was open. The NT fits well into the course of this

development. Debrunner, Festschr. Kretschmer 15–22; for details in the LXX s. Thack. 209–16.

81. First aorist–second aorist.
(1) Εἷπα: α is firmly entrenched in the forms with τ (Attic likewise), rather solidly also before μ; εἷπαν preponderates, εἷπα is infrequent; the imperative has both εἰπέ and εἷπον (Lautensach 111); εἷπας as participle seldom, εἰπόντος etc. always, likewise εἰπεῖν. (2) Ἤνεγκα has the Hellenistic α except for the infinitive. (3) Other second aorists always have an infinitive in -εῖν, participle in -ών, 2nd sing. indicative in -ες, 2nd sing. imperative in -ε. Otherwise some forms are attested which follow the first aorist, e.g. ἔβαλαν, εἴδαμεν, εἷδα and especially ἔπεσα -ατε (ἐξεπέσατε G 5: 4) -αν (because ἔπεσε was felt to be a sigma-aorist). From ἐλθεῖν, ἐλθάτω ἔλθατε predominate in the imperative (with ἐλθέ) after the pattern of ἔνεγκε ἐνεγκάτω ἐνέγκατε (Lk 15: 25 D) (Debrunner, loc. cit. 21 f.); middles like ἐξείλατο εὐράμενος and the like are also well attested.

(1) Εἴπατε, -άτω, -άτωσαν; ἀπειπάμεθα 2 C 4: 2 (a correction in 𝔓⁴⁶ has -όμεθα), προείπαμεν 1 Th 4: 6 (-ομ- AKL al.); εἷπας Mt 26: 25, 64, Lk 20: 39, Mk 12: 32 (-ες S*DEF al.), Jn 4: 17 (-ες SB*); εἷπα, e.g. Jn 10: 34 OT (-ον AD), A 26: 15; εἷπας A 22: 24 (-ών HLP), εἷπασα Jn 11: 28 (𝔓⁶⁶BC*, but εἰποῦσα occurs in the same vs. in all MSS), Herm Vis 3.2.3 S, 4.3.7 S*. Cf. Lautensach 107 ff.; Mayser i² 2, 135. The oxytone form of the impera. εἰπόν may well be only grammatical hair-splitting (Lob. Phryn. 348; Katz, ThLZ 1936, 284; 1958, 316; Wackernagel, Kl. Schr. 878 ff.; W. Schmidt, GGA [1895] 35 had taken a different view: εἰπόν is used to distinguish the impera. from indic. 1st sing. εἷπον; Helb. 62: εἰπόν following εἰπέ).
(2) Inf. ἐνέγκαι only in 1 P 2: 5 (ἀν-), Mk 2: 4 SBL (προσ-); Jos. always -εῖν (Schmidt 457). Impera. προσένεγκε Mt 8: 4 (-ον BC), Mk 1: 44 (CL has inferior spelling in -αι), Lk 5: 14 (-αι L), παρ- Mk 14: 36 (-αι SACK), Lk 22: 42 (-αι SKL, -εῖν AQ al. is better). Lautensach 101 ff.; Lademann 104 f.; Mayser i² 2, 136 f.
(3) Ἔβαλαν A 16: 37 BD, Mt 13: 48 D, Rev 18: 19 C, ἐπ- A 21: 27 S*A, Mk 14: 46 SB, ἐξ- Mk 12: 8 B, Mt 21: 39 D, Jn 9: 34 𝔓⁶⁶W. Εἷδαν Mt 13: 17 SB, Lk 20: 24 SBC al., Mk 6: 33 D, etc.; εἴδαμεν Mt 25: 37 B*I, 38 I, Mk 2: 12 CD, 9: 38 DN, Lk 5: 26 C; εἴδατε Lk 7: 22 A, Jn 6: 26 D; εἷδα Rev 17: 3 A, 6 SA; εἷδον preponderates by far in the 1st sing. Ἀνεῖλαν A 10: 39 (-ον HLP), -ατε 2: 23, εἵλατο 2 Th 2: 13 (-ετο K), Herm Sim 5.6.6, ἀν- A 7: 21 (-ετο P), ἐξ- 7: 10 (-ετο H), 12: 11 (-ετο P), ἐξειλάμην 23: 27 (-όμην HLP), but ἐξελέσθαι 7: 34 OT; ἀφειλάμην is

opposed in Cramer, Anec. Ox. III 258.16. Εὖρα is weakly attested: εὗραν Lk 8: 35 B*, Mt 22: 10 D, A 5: 10 AE, 13: 6 A, εὕραμεν Lk 23: 2 B*L al.; but the mid. is strongly attested: εὑράμενος H 9: 12 (-όμ-D*). Ἀπῆλθα G 1: 17 𝔓⁴⁶ (but in the same vs. ἦλθον and ἀνῆλθον in v. 18), Rev 10: 9 𝔓⁴⁷ A, ἤλθαμεν Mt 25: 39 D, A 21: 8 B, 27: 5 SA (κατ-), 28: 16 A (εἰσ-); -αν is often found in addition to -ον; ἐξήλθατε Mt 11: 7, 8, 9, 25: 36, 26: 55 and pars. in the best MSS, and even Lk 7: 24, 25, 26 as v.l. assimilated to the par. in Mt 11: 7–9 in place of the correct ἐξεληλύθατε. Impera. πέσατε Lk 23: 30 OT (-ετε S*ABD al.), Rev 6: 16 (-ετε SC 046). Everything else is quite sporadic: γενάμενος (MGr) e.g. H 9: 11 𝔓⁴⁶, Lk 22: 44 S, 24: 22 B, Mk 6: 26 Δ, 15: 42 Δ; ἀπέθαναν Mt 8: 32 Sᵇ, Lk 20: 31 B*, Jn 8: 53 D, ἀπεθάνατε C 3: 3 𝔓⁴⁶ (second hand); ἐλάβαμεν Lk 5: 5 A, -ατε 1 Jn 2: 27 B*, -αν Jn 1: 12 B*; ἔπιαν 1 C 10: 4 D*, etc.; ἀνάπεσον Lk 14: 10 a few minusc., 17: 7 Γ al.; v. Soden 1392f. Almost none of these forms has yet appeared in the Ptol. pap. and pre-Christian inscrip. (Mayser I² 2, 84, 144; Helb. 64); γενάμενον on an ostrakon, the later pap. have more (Mayser I² 2, 135). Cf. also Lautensach 114f.; Psaltes 210f. Michaïlov² 158, 159; γενάμενος 177.

82. First aorist–imperfect. The intrusion of first aorist endings into the imperfect has taken place seldom in the NT and is nowhere unanimously attested. The same is true for the LXX (Thack. 212), but the Fathers and Apocrypha have it more frequently (Reinhold 81); there are no certain examples in the pre-Christian papyri (Mayser I² 2, 85, 144).

Εἶχαν Mk 8: 7 SBDWΔ, 16 D, Lk 4: 40 D, Jn 15: 22, 24 D* (the others have -ον or -οσαν), A 8: 10 S (προσ-), 19: 14 D, 28: 2 SAB (παρ-), H 11: 15 𝔓⁴⁶, Rev 9: 8 SA (all MSS have -ον in v. 9); εἴχαμεν H 12: 9 𝔓⁴⁶, 2 Jn 5 SA. Ἔλεγαν Mk 3: 21 W, Jn 9: 10 S*, 16 S*, 11: 36 S*, 56 SD, A 28: 6 B. Ἐγόγγυζαν Lk 5: 30 B*R. There are more instances in D (M.-H. 194). Cf. ἔλεγας BGU II 595.9 (70–80 AD).

83. Second aorist and first aorist–perfect. (1) In the NT -αν for -ασι in the perfect is sometimes well attested; it appears also in the inscriptions and papyri beginning in ii BC (Wackernagel, Homer 191; Mayser I² 2, 84f.; Kapsomenakis 75 n. 1). (2) The NT MSS exhibit extremely weak evidence for the penetration of -ες and -ετε into the first aorist, clearer evidence for -ες into the perfect.

(1) Ἑώρακαν (ἑορ-) Lk 9: 36 𝔓⁴⁵BC²LX, C 2: 1 𝔓⁴⁶S*ABCD*P, τετήρηκαν Jn 17: 6 BDLW (ἐτήρησαν S), ἔγνωκαν 7 ABCD al. (ἔγνων S), ἀπέσταλκαν A 16: 36 𝔓⁴⁵SAB, εἰσελήλυθαν Ja 5: 4 BP, γέγοναν R 16: 7 SAB (-εν 𝔓⁴⁶), Rev 21: 6 SᶜA (-α S*P 046), πέπ(τ)ωκαν 18: 3 AC, εἴρηκαν 19: 3 SAP. In the LXX -αν is confined to a few late instances, Thack. 212.

(2) Ἀπεκάλυψες Mt 11: 25 D; into κ- aorist: ἔδωκες Jn 17: 7 SB, 8 B, ἀφῆκες Rev 2: 4 SC, ἀφήκετε Mt 23: 23 B*. Into the perf.: κεκοπίακες Rev 2: 3 AC, πέπτωκες 5 S, ἐλήλυθες A 21: 22 B, ἑώρακες Jn 8: 57 B*W, εἴληφες Rev 11: 17 C, etc. S. Rudberg 20 on D. The oldest examples of -ες appear to be ἔγραφες PSI VI 567.2 (254 BC) and εἴωθες in the Hyperides pap. (Phil. col. 4.20 ii/i BC [its pre-Christian date is now being challenged]); in any case these instances remain isolated for a long time (Mayser I² 2, 81f.). Apollonius Dysc. (Synt. I 10 p. 37, 36 p. 71) testifies that εἴρηκες ἔγραφες γράφετο are forms disputed by grammarians; MGr impera. γράψε, γράφετε; γράφε seldom in the pap. (Mayser I² 2, 89). Ἐξέθρεψες, ἐφίλησες, ἔστηκες (in epigrams) Michaïlov² 158. Very little and nothing certain in the LXX, Thack. 215f.

(G) Endings: Extension of -σαν

84. The ending -σαν has enlarged its domain still further in the Hellenistic period: (1) to the imperative (universally in Hellenistic; Gromska 33f.; Mayser I² 2, 89. For Attic beginnings, s. Lautensach, Glotta 9 [1917] 80ff., 92), then (2) to the imperfect and second aorist (competing here with the introduction of -αν and soon driven out by the latter), (3) to the imperfect of contract verbs and (4) to the optative. In cases (2)–(4), the number of syllables in the plural was thereby made uniform, in (2) and (3) differentiation of 1st sing. and 3rd plur. was also achieved.

(1) Impera. in the NT regularly -έτωσαν, -άτωσαν, the corresponding mid.–pass. e.g. προσευξάσθωσαν Ja 5: 14. Rosenkranz, IF 48 (1930) 153: Thuc. -ντων -σθων only in the treaties, otherwise -τωσαν.

(2) E.g. εἴχοσαν Jn 15: 22, 24 SB al. (εἶχαν D*, εἶχον AD², which introduces a bad ambiguity), παρελάβοσαν 2 Th 3: 6 S*AD* (-ετε BFG, -ον SᶜDᶜᵒʳʳE al., somewhat ambiguous), ἐξήλθοσαν Mk 8: 11 D, ἐφέροσαν 1: 32 D, ἐλέγοσαν 6: 14 D; v. Soden 1309; ἐτίθοσαν s. §94(1). In the LXX and pap. much more frequent. A. G. Tsopanakes, Κοινή—Ῥοδιακὰ ἰδιώματα (Rhodes, 1948; on which F. Dölger, ByzZ 43 [1950] 409: -οσαν is said to be a Doricism and lives on today in one village on Rhodes.

(3) Ἐδολιοῦσαν R 3: 13 OT, ἐθορυβοῦσαν A 17: 5 D, κατοικοῦσαν 2: 46 D* (κατ' οἴκους D²), διηκονοῦσαν Mk 15: 41 W, ἠδικοῦσαν Rev 9: 19 minusc., εὐσταθοῦσαν Herm Sim 6.2.7 A (εὐστάθει PMich), ἐδοκοῦσαν 9.9.5, εὐλογοῦσαν 1 Clem 15.3 OT A (-ουν C). Sporadic instances in pap. beginning with iii BC: ἠγνοοῦσαν 257 BC, κατηντλοῦσαν 118 BC; Mayser I² 2, 84; Papadopoulos, Πρακτ. Ἀκ. Ἀθ. 10 (1935)

154–67; inscrip. from Cos ἠξιουσαν (Herzog-Klaffenbach, ABA 1952, 1 p. 18; 242 BC). On accent cf. Herodian (Lentz) II 237.5; Wackernagel, ThLZ 1908, 638; Debrunner, IF 57 (1939) 151; MGr ἐλαλοῦσαν etc.

(4) Ψηλαφήσαισαν and εὕροισαν A 17: 27 D.—On -οσαν cf. Mayser I² 2, 83; Helb. 65–7. On -οῦσαν Thack. 214 (Katz, ThLZ 1957, 114); Psaltes 214. On -οισαν -αισαν Thack. 215; Schweizer 166; Psaltes 214.

(H) Endings: 'Aeolic' Forms of the Aorist Optative

85. Aorist optative active in the NT has -αι in the 3rd sing. rather than -ειε(ν) preferred in Attic; 3rd plur. has -αιεν rather than -ειαν. On (-οισαν) -αισαν s. §84(4).

Gromska 32f.; Mayser I² 2, 87f. -αι and -αιεν are normal in Hell. (Harsing 14f., 21), the Atticists are fond of the Aeolic forms (Scham 39f.; Brockmeier 15). Cf. ἐάσαι 1 Clem 33.1, but Diogn 7.2 has εἰκάσειεν. Ποιήσαιεν Lk 6: 11 BL (-ειεν SAW, -ειαν EKM al.), ψηλαφήσειαν A 17: 27 AB al. (-ειεν SE, -αισαν D perhaps correctly).

(I) Endings: Pluperfect

86. The pluperfect takes ει (not ε) in Koine also in the plur. (an intrusion from the sing.): ᾔδειτε Lk 2: 49, Jn 8: 19, πεποιήκεισαν Mk 15: 7 etc., ᾔδεισαν Mk 14: 40 etc. Cf. Mayser I² 2, 82f., 85; Helb. 68. Exceptions: ᾖσαν (§99(1)). 1st sing. in NT only in -ειν: ᾔδειν Jn 1: 31, 33 etc.; papyri -ειν and -ην (Mayser I² 2, 80f.). Thack. 216.

(J) Endings: 2nd Singular Middle–Passive

87. On βούλει s. §27.—The Koine has preserved in some cases the phonetically or analogically parallel termination to -μαι -ται, i.e. -σαι (δίδομαι -σαι -ται, κεῖμαι -σαι -ται etc.) and further extended it, first to πίεσαι (by means of which the monosyllabic πίη = pī was avoided), after this to φάγεσαι (cf. §74(2)) and finally to the present indicative of contract verbs. Cf. Wackernagel, ThLZ (1908) 39, 639; Glotta 14 (1925) 153. MGr φαίνεσαι κοιμᾶσαι πατεῖσαι etc.

Πίεσαι is to πίεται as ἵεσαι is to ἵεται. NT φάγεσαι καὶ πίεσαι Lk 17: 8, never φάγῃ πίῃ. Verbs in -ᾶν only -ᾶσαι: ὀδυνᾶσαι Lk 16: 25, καυχᾶσαι 1 C 4: 7, R 2: 17, 23, 11: 18 (κατακαυχᾶσαι along with impera. κατακαυχῶ such as νικῶ R 12: 21, χρῶ 1 T 5: 23); πλανᾶσαι, χρᾶσαι, ἐπισπᾶσαι Herm (Reinhold 84). Verbs in -εῖν: λυπῇ Herm Vis 3.1.9, αιτισαι i.e. αἰτεῖσαι 10.7 S

(αἰτεῖς A as in 6 SA); φοβῇ σύ Lk 23: 40 may have suggested φοβεῖσαι, POxy II 292.9 (25 AD) χαρίεσαι. Verbs in -οῦν: -οῦσαι is not found in the NT, but in the LXX (ἀπεξενοῦσαι 3 Km 14: 6 A, in a hexaplaric addition [the other witnesses ἀποξε-]; -εξ- is an error due to the preceding ἀπεξενοῦτο in v. 5) and Apocr. (Reinhold 84). -ᾶσαι, -εῖσαι, -οῦσαι Vogeser 9. Palmer, JTS 35 (1934) 172; Mayser I² 2, 91. Ἀντιποιεῖσαι Schwyzer, Dial. Graec. exempla epigr. (1923) 372 g (c. 100 BC). Thack. 216ff.

(K) Contract Verbs

88. Verbs in -ᾶν. NT has πεινᾶν διψᾶν as in Hellenistic (Attic -ῆν; M. Leroy, Festschrift Debrunner [Bern, 1954] 288: Doric πεινᾶντι Theoc., διαπεινᾶμες Aristoph. appear to prove that ᾱ was original; peculiar Homeric διψάων πεινάων [289] Aeolicism? following Epic -άων elsewhere, but ζῆν (Attic; η was retained because τὸ ζῆν was a substantive [§398]). From χρῶμαι only χρῆται 1 T 1: 8 SD al. (χρήσηται AP), otherwise no pertinent examples. On -ᾶσαι s. §87.

Cf. ἐπείνασα §70(2). MGr πεινῶ -ᾶς but ζῶ ζῆς (phonetically leveled with the type πατῶ πατεῖς). The 1st sing. ἔζην R 7: 9 B (to ἔζη following ἔβην: ἔβη, ἐλύθην: ἐλύθη) for ἔζων is also attested in the LXX, a pap. and MS of Eur. and Dem.; cf. Mayser I² 2, 114; Thack. 242, and ζῆθι K.-Bl. II 436; σύ(ν)ζηθι Herm Man 4.1.9. Lautensach, Philol. 77 (1921) 61f. The Hell. (and pseudo-Ion.: Hartmann, KZ 60 [1932] 102f.) χρᾶσθαι appears in pap. of iii BC and Ap. Frs. (Mayser I² 2, 114, Reinhold 84; Leroy, op. cit. 285–7: χρᾶσθαι is not Ion., but inscrip. and pap., LXX, NT, Ap. Frs.); in the NT only καταχρᾶσθαι 1 C 9: 18 A (-χρήσασθαι al.).

89. Verbs in -εῖν. In Koine monosyllabic stems often do not contract to ει (standardization of the paradigm), e.g. πνέει from πνέω.

Thus in the NT ἐδέετο Lk 8: 38 (ἐδεῖτο SᵃBC²LX; ἐδεεῖτο AP [cf. Thack. 243 for the LXX] corrected from ἐδέετο), Homil Clem 3.63, πνέει Jn 3: 8 L Chr; ἐκχέετε Rev 16: 1 and παραχέειν Herm s. §73. In pap. of the Ptolemaic period no examples as yet (Mayser I² 2, 113), but in the LXX etc. (Thack. 242ff.) and e.g. δέεσθαι PSI IV 299.17 (iii AD).

90. Confusion of paradigms in -ᾶν and -εῖν. There are some traces in Koine of a mixture of -ᾶν and -εῖν, resulting in a single paradigm in which ου appears for ω and the corresponding forms from -ᾶν for ει: more strongly attested only ἠρώτουν Mt 15: 23 SABCD, ἐλεᾷ R 9: 18 𝔓⁴⁶D*(E)FG (-εῖ SA²BDᶜL al.), ἐλεᾶτε Jd 22 SBC², 23 SB, ἐλλόγα

Phm 18 (-ει SᶜDᶜᵒʳʳ EKL), ἐλεῶντος R 9: 16 (-οῦ-B³K).

-εῖν for -ᾶν: κοπιοῦσιν Mt 6: 28 D; ἠρώτουν Mk 4: 10 SC, Jn 4: 31 C, 40 W, 9: 15 X (12: 21 all MSS have -ων), A 16: 39 A, κατεγέλουν Mt 9: 24 W, Lk 8: 53 D*KX, ἐπετίμουν Lk 18: 39 AΓ; τελευτείτω Mk 7: 10 D*; νικοῦ R 12: 21 A; νικοῦντι Rev 2: 17 AC, 7 A (-οντι 046), -ντας 15:2 C, προσδοκούντων A 28: 6 A, πλανούντων 1 Jn 2: 26 A, κοπιοῦσας R 16: 12 𝔓⁴⁶; ὀδυνούμενοι Lk 2: 48 W, κοιμούμενος A 12: 6 D*. C also elsewhere (M.-H. 195).—-ᾶν for -εῖν: ἐλλογᾶται R 5: 13 Sᵃ (ἐλλογᾶτο A; the verb is ἐλλογεῖν, s. Nägeli 48), φιλοτιμώμενος 2 C 5: 9 𝔓⁴⁶, θεωρῶσιν Mk 5: 15 L, ἐθεώρων Jn 6: 2 A. Koine may form here the connecting link between the old dialectal paradigms (ὁρ)έω -ᾷς -ᾷ -έομεν -ᾶτε -έουσι (O. Hoffmann, Griech. Dial. III 245f.) and MGr (ρωτ)ῶ -ᾷς -ᾷ -οῦμε -ᾶτε -οῦν(ε).—To be viewed differently is ἐνεβριμοῦντο Mk 14: 5 SC* (-ῶντο ABC²DL al.), ἐμβριμούμενος Jn 11: 33 𝔓⁴⁵𝔓⁶⁶DΘ, 38 𝔓⁶⁶SAU (-ώμ- BC³DL al.); βριμοῦσθαι (after θυμοῦσθαι) appears already in Att. in addition to (ἐμ)βριμᾶσθαι, cf. Debrunner, IF 21 (1907) 53. For the LXX Thack. 241f.

91. Verbs in -οῦν. The late Hellenistic infinitive in -οῖν instead of -οῦν is weakly attested in the NT, but the subjunctives in ου rather than Attic ω (like an indicative in appearance), which are already opposed by Pacatus (i AD; M. Haupt, Opusc. II 434) on the recommendation of χρυσῶται, are better attested (ζηλοῦτε G 4: 17, φυσιοῦσθε 1 C 4: 6).

-οῖν is a new formation to go with -οι after λέγειν—λέγει, ποιεῖν—ποιεῖ; cf. περιεκύκλοι LXX Jer 52: 21 S (Crönert 220) following ἐποίει. A few more equally precarious examples from the LXX in Thack. 244.—Subj. ζηλοῦτε like the indic. because in the sing. and in the entire -ᾶν paradigm the subj. and indic. are identical. Nevertheless, the Att. subj. εὐοδῶται 1 C 16: 2 (-δωθῇ SᶜACJ al.).—Κατασκηνοῖν Mt 13: 32 B*D, Mk 4: 32 B*, ἀποδεκατοῖν H 7: 5 𝔓⁴⁶BD*, φιμοῖν 1 P 2: 15 S*, but all uncials have πληροῦν Lk 9: 31. LXX only ὑφοῖν Tob 12: 6 B, otherwise -οῦν; pap. from i AD on also -οῖν (Mayser I² 2, 116; Mlt. 53 [79]). Psaltes 234f.; Wessely, Stud. Pal. 13 (1913) 3.—Subj.: ὅταν μαιοῦσθε LXX Ex 1: 16, ἵνα ἑνοῦται Test Naphth 6 (acc. to Helb. 112), ἐὰν εὐοδοῦται Test Gad 7, ἵνα μὴ ἐνοχλούμεθα PBasel 16.7 = Ghedini, Lett. crist. p. 59 (iii AD); Choerob. Grammatici Graeci IV 2 pp. 287.25ff.

(4) -MI VERBS

(A) Present: Transition to the -Ω Conjugation

92. Verbs in -νύναι. The gradual decline of -μι verbs, to be observed throughout the history of the Greek language, reaches its final stage in modern Greek where the entire category disappears. This decline is strongly felt in Koine as compared with classical Greek. Verbs in -νύειν are active competitors of those in -νύναι (besides ὀλλύναι) already in Attic etc.; the older athematic formation has not yet died out in the NT and entirely dominates the passive (as in Attic; therefore generally ἀπόλλυται, -ύμεθα etc.). Mayser I² 2, 121; Gromska 38ff.; Thack. 244–58 with full paradigms.

Active: δείκνυμι 1 C 12: 31 (never -ύω in the 1st sg.); δεικνύεις Jn 2: 18 (never -υς); δείκνυσιν Mt 4: 8 (-ύει S), Jn 5: 20 (-νύει D, yet D has -νυσιν for δείξει), ἀμφιέννυσιν (§ 101), ἀπολλύει Jn 12: 25 (v.l. ἀπολέσει), ὄμνυει Mt 23: 20, 21, 22 (from this verb there are no certain forms in -μι); ὀμνύουσιν H 6: 16. Imperf. only thematic: ἐζώννυες Jn 21: 18; (ὑπ-)ἐστρώννυον Mt 21: 8 (ἔστρωσαν S*D), Mk 11: 8 (the first occurrence D, the second ADN al.), Lk 19: 36. Impera.: ἀπόλλυε R 14: 15; ὀμνύετε Ja 5: 12, σβέννυτε 1 Th 5: 19. Inf.: ὀμνύειν Mt 26: 74, Mk 14: 71 (-ύναι BEHL al.), δεικνύειν Mt 16: 21 (-ύναι B). Ptcp.: ἀπολλύων Rev 9: 11, δεικνύοντος 22: 8 (-ύντος S), ὑποζωννύντες A 27: 17, ἀποδεικνύοντα 2 Th 2: 4 (-ύοντα AFG).—Some verbs in -νύναι are replaced by other thematic formations or by synonyms built on other stems: thus κορεννύναι by χορτάζειν, ἀνοιγνύναι by ἀνοίγειν, ῥηγνύναι (§ 101) by ῥήσσειν, σκεδαννύναι by σκορπίζειν. Πεταννύναι is not found in the NT, nor is the present tense of ζευγνύναι, κεραννύναι, κορεννύναι, κρεμαννύναι, μειγνύναι, πηγνύναι and ῥωννύναι.—-νύουσι -νυον -νυοντ- are perhaps more primitive than -νύασι -νυσαν -νυντ- (Schwyzer I 698f.).

93. Verbs in -άναι (-ασθαι). Here also there is transition to the -ω conjugation: an entirely new present has arisen from the infinitive ἱστάνειν, remodeled from ἱστάναι; with it is mixed the earlier ἱστᾶν developed from the subjunctive ἱστῶ. Likewise πι(μ)πλᾶν appears for πι(μ)πλάναι (usually γεμίζειν [MGr] or πληροῦν). In the passive the -μι conjugation also holds its own here; of the later ω-forms like δύνομαι (thus MGr), developed from the subjunctive δύνωμαι, there is no certain example in the NT except for δύνῃ (along with δύνασαι), which is already attested for the Attic poets.

In the act. certain examples of the -μι conjugation are confined to συνίστημι R 16: 1 (a polite social formula), συνίστησι 3: 5, 5: 8, 2 C 10: 18, G 2: 18 DEKLΨ; otherwise ἱστάνειν (primarily in inf. and ptcp.) and often in addition ἱστᾶν as a variant; στάνειν, which is yet more vulgar, is rare. E.g. ἱστάνειν 2 C 3: 1 (FG -άναι, 𝔓⁴⁶BD* -ᾶν), μεθιστάνειν

1 C 13: 2 ACKL (-άναι 𝔓⁴⁶SBDEFG); συνιστάνοντες 2 C 4: 2 𝔓⁴⁶ABP (-στάντες SCD*FG, -στῶντες DᶜEKL), similarly 6: 4 (𝔓⁴⁶ also -άντες, Sᶜ also -ῶντες), συνιστανόντων 2 C 10: 12 (-άντων 𝔓⁴⁶) (herewith are given also the more important examples of -μι forms as v.l.). Cf. μεθιστάνει Herm Vis 1.3.4, ἱστάνεσθαι Sim 8.1.6 in PBer (ἵστασθαι A), καθίστανον 1 Clem 42.4 (-ιστᾶν C), παριστάνειν Homil Clem 15.5 (v.l. -άν). LXX frequently has ἱστᾶν (Thack. 247f.), seldom ἱστάνειν; pap. have both (Mayser Iˊ 2, 123) and likewise Byzantine (Psaltes 236); καθιστᾶν Inscrip. Délos, Dürrbach 366 A 99 (iii BC end). -ιστᾶν is somewhat less vulgar than -ιστάνειν (Brockmeier 17). Στάνειν: ἀποκατα-στάνει Mk 9: 12 S*D (-τιστάνει B*), -νεις A 1: 6 D, καταστάνοντες A 17: 15 𝔓⁴⁵D (D* had καθιστάνοντες, Lagrange, RB 43 [1934] 166); ἐστάνοντο PMich Herm Sim 8.1.9–17 (A ἵσταντο, PBer ἱστάνοντο once).—Ἐμπι(μ)πλῶν A 14: 17, cf. LXX (Helb. 105) and later Greek (Psaltes 236).—Passive: περιΐστασο 2 T 2: 16, T 3: 9, καθίσταται H 5: 1 etc., (ἐμ-)πίμπρασθαι A 28: 6 (Tdf. -ᾶσθαι), κρέμαται Mt 22: 40, κρεμάμενος A 28: 4, G 3: 13 OT; so also δύνασθαι ἐπίστασθαι.—Δύναμαι -όμεθα -όμενος only B or B* Mt 19: 12, 26: 53, Mk 10: 39, A 4: 20, 27: 15; also the pap. (Mayser Iˊ 2, 125) and LXX (Thack. 249); cf. ἐξεκρέμετο Lk 19: 48 SB. Δύνη Mk 9: 22 𝔓⁴⁵SBDW al., likewise 23, 1: 40 B, Lk 16: 2 SBDPW (v.l. -ῃσῃ), Rev 2: 2, but all MSS have δύνασαι Mt 5: 36, Lk 5: 12, 6: 42, Jn 13: 36; Hermas δύνη and δύνασαι (Reinhold 95, where also ἠδύνου and the like from the Apocr. are discussed). On δύνη s. Helb. 61f.; Psaltes 238.

94. Διδόναι, τιθέναι, ἱέναι. (1) In Attic the beginning of the transition to the -ω conjugation had already been made in the imperfect ἐδίδου ἐτίθει, imperative δίδου τίθει, subjunctive τιθῶ; Ionic (as early as Homer) made further inroads (Smyth, Ionic §§691, 700), just as the Koine does. In the NT some middle–passive forms appear: -εδίδετο (aorist middle -έδετο) from the later δίδω (MGr), which were built on ἐδιδόμεθα–ἐδίδοντο after ἐλύετο–ἐλύοντο, etc. (2) In the case of ἱέναι, a new formation -ίειν is found only in the popular compounds with ἀφ- and συν-; it was developed perhaps from -ίετε, -ίεται etc.—For the present subjunctive and optative of διδόναι s. §95(2).

(1) Διδόναι, τιθέναι: Pres. indic. as in Att., also παραδίδως Lk 22: 48, διδῶ (δίδω?) only in Rev 3: 9 AC (-ωμι P 046, δέδωκα S), τιθι, i.e. τιθεῖ Lk 8: 16 D; impf. ἐτίθει ἐδίδου as in Att., but also 3rd plur. ἐτίθουν ἐδίδουν. Impera. δίδου τίθει as in Att. Διεδίδετο A 4: 35 (-οτο B³P), παρεδίδετο 1 C 11: 23 (-οτο B³LP), ἀπέδετο H 12: 16 𝔓⁴⁶AC, ἐξέδετο Mt 21: 33 S*B*CL = Mk 12: 1 SAB*CKL = Lk 20: 9

S*AB*CL; but all MSS have ἀπέδοσθε A 5: 8. Cf. Moulton, ClR 15 (1901) 37; Crönert 251, 278 n. 5; Rüsch 156; Mayser Iˊ 2, 140. Ἐτίθουν A 3: 2, 4: 35, 8: 17 𝔓⁴⁵D*EHLP (-εσαν SAD², -οσαν B from the late τίθω, -εισαν C), Mk 6: 56 ADN al. (-οσαν SBLΔ), cf. Att. Bekker, Anec. Gr. I 90.5; ἐδίδουν A 4: 33, 27: 1, Mk 15: 23, A 16: 4 HLP (-οσαν 𝔓⁴⁵ al.), Jn 19: 3 ADᵁᵖᵖˡY al. (-οσαν SBLX); in Mk 3: 6 Heikel, StKr 106 (1934/5) 314, wants to substitute (συμβού-λιον) ἐτίθουν for ἐδίδουν; ἐδίδοσαν Mk 4: 8 C for -δου. Ptcp.: ἀποδιδοῦν (instead of -όν) Rev 22: 2 A, παραδιδῶν (-δίδων?) in S Mt 26: 46, in D Mk 14: 42, Jn 18: 2, 21: 20. Hermas διδοῖ Sim 2.4 POxy IX 1172.1 (iv AD) (δίδωσιν A) (but in 8 ἀποδιδώσιν as in A and PBer), ἐπεδίδουν (but also v.l. ἐπεδίδοσαν) ἐτίθουν τιθῶ (indic.), 1 Clem 23.1 ἀποδιδοῖ (indic.). Cf. Reinhold 93, on δίδω τίθω ibid. 94, on the whole subject Helb. 104–6; Vogeser 16; Psaltes 236ff.; Ghedini, Aegyptus 15 (1935) 237; Mayser Iˊ 2, 122, 123f.—Προσετίθοντο A 5: 14 some minusc., ἐξέθοντο A 18: 26 D, συνέθοντο 23: 20 H*; cf. παρέθοντο PSI v 447.16 (167 AD), ἐπεθόμην inscrip. 202 AD (Michaïlov 8), ἐτεθόμην 202 AD, ἀνεθόμην c. iii AD (Michaïlov² 13), ὑπερτίθοντε (= -ται) BGU III 984.12 (iv AD).

(2) Ἱέναι appears only in compound form with ἀν-, ἀφ-, καθ-, (παρ-,) συν-: ἀφίημι, e.g. Jn 14: 27, -ίησιν Mt 3: 15, -ιέναι Mk 2: 7 etc., but ἀφίομεν Lk 11: 4 SᶜABCDE, Mt 6: 12 DW al. (ἀφήκαμεν S*B), -ίουσιν Mk 4: 36 𝔓⁴⁵DWΘ, Rev 11: 9 (v.l. -ήσουσιν); 2nd sing. ἀφεῖς Rev 2: 20 (Georg. Hamartolos 123.5; 124.15; s. Psaltes 237) (i.e. ἀφίεις, §31(2); ἀφιεις and τιθεις also appear in Att.). Homil Clem 19.6.3 ἀφίης (P ἀφεῖς). Impf. ἤφιεν Mk 1: 34, 11: 16; the form varies in the pass., s. ἀφέωνται §97(3). For συνιέναι there is only a single certain example of the -μι conjugation in the NT: συνιέναι A 7: 25, otherwise only as v.l. (s. infra). Other compounds: ἀνιέντες E 6: 9, καθιέμενος A 10: 11, 11: 5. Συνιέναι Lk 24: 45 (συνεῖναι B*), -ιέντος Mt 13: 19 (-ιόντος DF), -ιέντες E 5: 17 DᶜEKL al. (-ίετε 𝔓⁴⁶SABP), but also συνίειν etc. not without v.l. except for quotations: συνίουσιν Mt 13: 13 (in imitation of OT; -ιωσιν B**, cf. D), 2 C 10: 12 Dᶜ (interpolation? s. §416(2); -ῖασιν 𝔓⁴⁶SªB, συνίων R 3: 11 OT, Mt 13: 23 CEFG al. In the Ap. Frs. ἀφίουσιν, συνίω, σύνιε, συνίων, etc. (Reinhold 94) in addition to ἀφίησι -ίενται, συνιέναι -ιέντες. LXX ἀφίω, συνίω, etc. often, also ἀφεῖς (i.e. = ἀφίεις) Ex 32: 32 (Thack. 249–52); pre-Christian pap. several times (Mayser Iˊ 2, 124); ἀφείομεν Inscrip. Ponti II 401.15 (ii AD). On -ίει (or -ιεῖ?) in Homer and Hdt. s. K.-Bl. II 213; Smyth, Ionic §691(2); Schwyzer I 687.

(B) Athematic Inflection in Tenses Other than Present

95. Second aorist active and middle. (1) Koine extends the -κ- of the singular to the plural in the aorist active indicative: ἐδώκαμεν -ατε -αν, ἐθήκαμεν, ἥκαμεν (there is precedent in the class. period); the old inflection is retained in the middle. (2) The inflection of the subjunctive of ἔδωκα has entirely gone over to the pattern of verbs in -οῦν: δοῖς δοῖ (δῷ was awkward because in pronunciation it was identical with the 1st sing. δῶ) along with δῶ δῶμεν δῶσιν after the pattern ζηλοῖς ζηλοῖ with ζηλῶ etc.; likewise διδοῖς διδοῖ (present) and γνοῖς γνοῖ. The aorist optative in Hellenistic is δῴην. (3) Koine has -βα etc. (Attic from *-βαε etc.) in the imperative along with -βηθι, and accordingly also -στα etc. side by side with -στηθι.

(1) NT ἐθήκαμεν, ἐδώκαμεν, ἀφ-, συν-ήκαμεν etc.; also συνήκατε Mt 13: 51 and ἀφήκαμεν (καὶ ἠκολουθή-καμεν [BCD, -ήσαμεν al.]) Mk 10: 28 are aor., not perf.; cf. the pars. to Mk 10: 28 and ξυνήκαθ' ὃ λέγει Aristoph., Ach. 101. Προσηκάμενοι Ep. Petri ad Jac. 2.3 (p. 2.3 Rehm). Ἔδωκες and the like, s. § 83(2). Except for -έδετο (§ 94(1)), the mid. follows the -μι pattern; in the act. only παρέδοσαν Lk 1: 2 (Prooemium, literary language). The remainder of the 'root-aorists' do not differ from Att.: ἔστην ἔβην ἔγνων; for ἔδυν s. § 75, ἐφύην instead of ἔφυν § 76(2). Ἵνα...δώσῃ Jn 17: 2 ScAC al. (v.l. -σω, -σει, δῶ etc.) and ἀγοράσωμεν...δώσωμεν Mk 6: 37 SBD (v.l. -σομεν and δῶμεν) need not be examples of the late aor. ἔδωσα (Reinhold 89; Dieterich 220; Moulton, ClR 15 [1901] 38; Lautensach 119; Psaltes 239; Ghedini, Aegyptus 15 [1935] 237), s. § 369(2, 3). UGosp 1.26f. παρ[αδώ]σω[σι]ν. On Rev 4: 9 s. § 382(4). Δῶναι (after γνῶναι) Mt 26: 15 S (-νε), often in pap. (M.-H. 88).
(2) Subj. NT δῷς (e.g. Mt 5: 25), δῷ γνῷ, δοῖ γνοῖ and δώῃ. Δώῃ (until c. 300 AD only a worthless MS variant) is virtually limited to Paul, in whom the copyist often met what was to him an uncommon opt. in δῴη and took it as subj. (therefore the opt. is rather to be spelled δῴη; δῴη and δώῃ in post-Christian pronunciation are in fact identical; cf. Mlt. 193f. [305] on the subj. γνώῃ in Clem. Alex. and the protest of Phrynichus against (δι)δώῃ): δώῃ E 1: 17 (δῷ B), 3: 16 DEK al., 2 T 2: 25 S*ACD*P, Jn 15: 16 EGH al., ἀποδοίη 1 Th 5: 15 D*. It is difficult to decide between δῷ γνῷ and δοῖ γνοῖ. Opt. δῴη often in Paul (R 15: 5 etc.). Γνῷ preponderates Jn 7: 51, 11: 57 (γνοῖ D*), 14: 31, A 22: 24; γνοῖ better or equally well attested Mk 5: 43, 9: 30, Lk 19: 15; all MSS ἀποδῷ Mt 18: 30, δῷ or δώῃ E 1: 17, 3: 16, 2 T 2: 25, Jn 15: 16 (δώσει S), 13: 29 (δοῖ D); (δι)δοῖ(ς) in addition to (δι)δῷ(ς) as v.l. Mk 4: 29, 8: 37 (δώσει 𝔓45ACD), 14: 10, 11, Lk 12: 59 D, Jn 13: 2, 1 C 15: 24, 1 Th 5: 15; (δι)δοῖ(ς) γνοῖ appear in pap. beginning iii BC, but more frequently in post-Christian times (Thack. 255f.; Harsing 10f.;

Ghedini, op. cit.; Olsson, 59; Mayser I² 2, 87). Opt. δῴη cf. Thack. 255f.; Koine replaces -οίην quite often by -ῴην of the verbs in -ᾶν, e.g. φρονῴη ἀξιῴη etc. in Philodemus (Crönert 214). Βιῴη (aor.) M. Ant. 7.16 (in addition to βιῶναι), εἰ ἐπὶ πλέον βιῴη τις 3.1.1 (Schekira 140); Helbing, WkP 35 [1918] no. 23/4: the forerunner is in Aristoph., Ra. 177 ἀναβιῴην (unanimously transmitted). Further Lob. Phryn. 343; Lautensach, Glotta 7 (1916) 99f.; Nachmanson, Apophoreta Gotoburgensia (1936) 133; Mayser I² 2, 88. On the whole question, Radermacher, Glotta 7 (1916) 21ff.
(3) Ἀνάβα Rev 4: 1 (-ηθι A), μετάβα Mt 17: 20 SB, μετάβηθι Jn 7: 3, κατάβα Mk 15: 30 ACH al. (-βάς SB al.), κατάβηθι Mt 27: 40 etc., προσανάβηθι Lk 14: 10; καταβάτω Mt 24: 17 = Mk 13: 15 = Lk 17: 31, Mt 27: 42 = Mk 15: 32, ἀνάβατε Rev 11: 12 (-ητε 046); usually ἀνάστηθι; ἀνάστα A 12: 7, E 5: 14 OT, A 9: 11 B (-στάς al.); always -στήτω, -στητε.—Διάβα PFay 110.15 (94 AD), LXX -στα in addition to -στηθι but always -βηθι (Thack. 254); ἀνάστατε 2 Km 15: 14 AB. Schmidt 473f.; Arnim 62; K.-Bl. II 45; Brugmann, Grundriss² II 3, 568f.; Lautensach 4ff. and Glotta 8 (1917) 190f.; Schwyzer I 676. On account of Att. βᾶτε and MGr ἀνέβα–ἀνεβᾶτε, διάβα–διαβᾶτε etc., Hell. forms may also well be accented -βᾶτε -στᾶτε.

96. Ἕστηκα and τέθνηκα. The -μι forms of the perfect of ἕστηκα and τέθνηκα retreat still more in Hellenistic than in classical. In the NT they are confined to the infinitive and participle; δεδιέναι etc. do not appear.

Always ἑστάναι Lk 13: 25, A 12: 14, 1 C 10: 12; mostly ἑστώς, but also ἑστηκώς; ἑστῶσα 1 C 7: 26, 2 P 3: 5; ἑστός (corresponds to masc. ἑστώς as -κώς: -κός) Mt 24: 15 (v.l. -ώς), Rev 14: 1 (-ώς 𝔓47046),ἑ-στηκός 5: 6 (-ώς S). Ἑστός in pap. (Crönert 261f. n. 1; Denkschr. Wien. Ak. 45 (1897) I p. 18 no. 59.6), ἐνεστός Mayser I² 2, 147.13, PLond II 151.7 (p. 216) (ii AD). Lautensach, Philol. 77 (1921) 236f. ([το γ]εγονὼς A 13: 12 𝔓45). Indic.: ἕστηκα, ἑστήκαμεν etc. Στήκειν s. § 73. Pap. ἑστώς and ἑστηκώς (Mayser I² 2, 146f.), likewise LXX (Helb. 103).— Τεθνάναι A 14: 19 DEHLP, always τεθνηκώς; likewise LXX (Thack. 253).

(C) Remaining Tenses of Ἱστάναι, Διδόναι, Τιθέναι, Ἱέναι

97. (1) **Ἱστάναι.** Transitive Hellenistic perfect ἕστακα (ἐξεστακέναι A 8: 11 [ἐξιστ- AEHΨ, ἐξειστ- C]; since Hyperides; Gromska 37f.); intransitive future στήσομαι and σταθήσομαι, aorist ἔστην and ἐστάθην (both simple forms are intransitive, as in Ionic-Hellenistic). Mayser I² 2,

147 f. (2) Other tenses of διδόναι as in Attic. From τιθέναι, middle–passive τέθειμαι (after κεῖμαι) as generally in Hellenistic and accordingly Hellenistic active τέθεικα (Jn 11: 34, A 13: 47; Attic τέθηκα). (3) The perfect active of ἱέναι does not appear (Attic εἷκα); in the passive the NT uses the Doric-Ionic-Arcadian ἕωμαι (Smyth, Ionic §694; Mlt. 38 n. 3 [55 n. 2]; further Dit., Syll.³ 306.19 f. = IG v 2 p. xxxvi [324 BC], IG v 2.6.14 [iv BC?]). On ἀνέθη ἀφέθησαν, s. §67(2).

(1) There is not sufficient reason to attribute a pass. sense to the simple σταθῆναι in passages like Lk 21: 36 (στήσεται D). Att. ἐστάθην σταθήσομαι are pass. (exceptions since Homer: Stahl 68.1; Lautensach 283); but MGr aor. is ἐστάθηκα (to στέκω 'I stand'). The compounds in the NT form the intrans. in -έστην, -στήσομαι (so ἀνθ- ἀν- ἀφ- δι- ἐξαν- ἐξ- ἐφ-ίστασθαι etc.), the pass. with -θη-. The perf. ἕστηκα has present meaning; also οὐκ ἕστηκεν Jn 8: 44 (§73) probably means 'he has not persisted, he does not stand fast'. Ἕστᾰκα (or rather ἕστᾰκα: κατέστακα is well attested in the LXX; Thack. 128; cf. §14) is formed as a trans. act. to ἕσταμαι (and the latter from ἐστάθην): ἐξέστᾰται (mid.–trans.; cf. Crönert 263) Mk 3: 21 D* (ἐξέστη al.); ἕσταμαι (or rather ἕστᾰμαι: LXX has κατεσταμ- at times; Thack. 128) Polyb. frequently (Schoy 60 f.), pap. from iii BC, perhaps as early as Hdt 1.196 and Plato, Tim. 81D (K.-Bl. II 197; Chantraine 108 f.); Mayser I² 2, 152 f.; Rüsch 219; Psaltes 231 n. 1; Stein, Glotta 6 (1915) 134.—Passive -εστάθην, e.g. κατεστάθησαν R 5: 19 (-έστησαν 𝔓⁴⁶), ἀπεκατεστάθη (ἀποκ-) Mt 12: 13, Mk 3: 5 (-έστη C), 8: 25 (-έστη SBCLΔ), Lk 6: 10 (-έστη S*), ἀποκατασταθῶ H 13: 19, μετασταθῶ Lk 16: 4; intrans. -θη- in the simple verb also Herm Vis 3.1.6, Sim 8.4.4, 5, 5, 6 (PMich always στῆναι), 9.4.1; in compounds only D in ἐπιστασθείς Lk 4: 39, 10: 40, ἐπιστασθέντων 1 Clem 12.4, ἀνιστασθῶσιν Herm Man 12.2.3, παρεστάθην Sim 8.4.1 (Reinhold 90); ἀναστα-θεῖσα Herondas 6.2. Ἔστην also appears as a passive: Pol Ph 9.2 τὸν...ὑπὸ τοῦ θεοῦ ἀναστάντα (cf. §315), Diog. L. 8.2 συστῆναι 'be introduced', Porph., VP 1 συστάντα and in the simple verb Dit., Syll.³ 56.43 (Argos, c. 450 BC) hα στάλα ἔσστα 'was set up'.

(2) Συνετέθειντο Jn 9: 22 (W συνέθεντο) and συγκατατεθειμένος Lk 23: 51 ABP are mid.; ἦν τεθειμένος Jn 19: 41 SB is pass. (ἐτέθη al.; in the par. Lk 23: 53 ἦν κείμενος, as also elsewhere in the NT, the more sophisticated Att. κεῖσθαι is used for the perf. pass.). Τεθειμένοι pass. Herm Sim 9.15.4, also περι-τεθειμένα 1 Clem 20.6.

(3) Ἀφέωνται Jn 20: 23 (spurious variant -ίενται, -(ε)ίονται [cf. -ίοντο twice as weak v.l. in the LXX, Thack. 252]; ἀφεθήσεται S*), 1 Jn 2: 12, Lk 5: 20, 23, 7: 47, 48 (W 47 and 48 ἀφίενται); to be preferred also

in Mt 9: 2 (-ίονται D, -ίενται SB), 5 (-ίονται S*D, -ίενται SᶜB), Mk 2: 5 (-ίενται B), 9 (-ίε- SB). Hell. formed an act. ἕωκα from ἕωμαι. Ἀφέωκε ZenP Cairo III 59502.4 (iii BC), ἐπαφίωκεν PRoss-Georg III 1.20 (iii AD); cf. Wackernagel, Studien z. gr. Perf. (Göttingen, 1904) 21 f. = Kl. Schr. 1018. Παρειμένος H 12: 12 (LXX, 1 Clem 34.1, 4; literary language; this compound appears otherwise only in παρεῖναι Lk 11: 42) is entirely adjectival = 'indolent'.

(D) Other -μι Verbs

98. Εἶναι. The transition to the deponent inflection (cf. the old future ἔσομαι), completed in MGr, appears in the NT in ἤμην (always; in order to differentiate between 1st sing. and 3rd sing. ἦν) and consequently in ἤμεθα (along with ἦμεν). The imperfect 2nd sing. is ἦς as in Hellenistic, more rarely ἦσθα. Imperative, in addition to ἴσθι ἔστω ἔστωσαν, also ἤτω (Hellenistic). Ἔνι, which properly stands for ἔνεστιν (ἔνι = ἐν) as πάρα stands for πάρεστιν, and which in MGr (in the spelling εἶναι, pronounced ēnĕ) has driven out ἐστίν and εἰσίν, appears in the NT with the meaning 'there is' (always with negative).

Ἤμεθα Mt 23: 30, A 27: 37, E 2: 3 𝔓⁴⁶SB; G 4: 3 ἦμεν (all MSS)...ἤμεθα (SD*FG); otherwise ἦμεν. Ἦσθα (the ending -σθα is used in the NT only with this word) only Mt 26: 69, Mk 14: 67 (ἦς W minusc. Eus.), otherwise ἦς (which Phryn. 149 Lob. designates as a σόλοικον; only since Jos. [Meister 30], very weak in LXX [Thack. 256]). Impera. ἔστε does not appear in NT (s. however §353(6)), but 1 Clem 45.1; ἔσεσθε (Mt 6: 5) or γίνεσθε (e.g. Mt 24: 44) is used instead, or the verb is omitted (1 P 3: 8 f.); ἴσθι (Mt, Mk, Lk, 1 T) can be replaced by γίνου (e.g. Lk 19: 19, Rev 2: 10, 3: 2, Herm Sim 7.6, Did 4.5 = Barn 19.9, Epict. 1.24.20) (Wackernagel, NGG 1906, 181 n.); cf. γενέσθω R 3: 4 = ἔστω. Ἤτω 1 C 16: 22, Ja 5: 12; corresponding ἦτε 1 C 7: 5 (𝔓⁴⁶ συνέρχεσθε)? Ἔσο IPol 4.1 and Apocr. Γίνου Did 3.8 = ἴσθι 7 = ἔση Barn 19.4. Ἔνι 1 C 6: 5 (ἐστιν DFG), G 3: 28 three times (𝔓⁴⁶ always οὐκέτι for οὐκ ἔνι), C 3: 11, Ja 1: 17. Ἔνι = ἔνεστιν 'be in, present' since Homer (Schwyzer II 423.4). M.-H. 306; Dieterich 225 f. Ἔνι 'is' attested for the first time in v/vi AD; ἔνι on a Corinthian vase (vi BC) is an error for εμι = εἰμί: Debrunner, Museum Helveticum 11 [1954] 57–64. In the LXX Sir 37: 2 is corrupt; instead of ἔνι ἕως θανάτου, we should read ἐγγ⟨ιε⟩ῖ ἕως θ. = Hebr. ﬠﬦﬞ Hiph. (Katz, ThZ 5 [1949] 7).—On the whole subject cf. LXX (Thack. 256 f.), Ap. Frs. and Apocr. (Reinhold 86 f.); pap. ἤμην ἤμεθα ὦμαι (Mayser I² 2, 127), from the ii BC on ἤτω (Moulton, ClR 15 (1901) 38, 436; 18 (1904) 112).

99. Ἰέναι, εἰδέναι, φάναι. (1) ʼἰέναι is not popular in Hellenistic either in the simple or compound form (ἔρχεσθαι instead § 101); only Lk and Heb (literary language) use it in the NT, and only in compounds (cf. Epict.: Melcher 11) and then not always correctly. (2) Εἰδέναι: οἶδα -ας -εν οἴδαμεν -ατε -ασιν as in Ionic-Hellenistic; ἴσασιν A 26: 4 (Paul before Agrippa) stems from literary language; ἴστε as imperative at the most; pluperfect ᾔδειν -εις -ει -ειτε -εισαν; future εἰδήσω § 101. (3) Except for φημί φησίν φασίν (R 3: 8) ἔφη (as imperfect and aorist as in Attic), no forms of φάναι appear in the NT.

(1) Εἰσίασιν H 9: 6 for εἰσέρχονται (in Att. the pres. indic. of ἰέναι is futuristic); εἴσιθι A 9: 6 B (-ελθε al.); εἰσιέναι 3: 3, ἐξιέναι 20: 7 (4 D), 27: 43; συνιόντος Lk 8: 4 (-ελθόντος D), ἐξιόντων A 13: 42, aoristic ἐξιόντες 21: 17 D; τῇ ἐπιούσῃ § 241(2); impf. aoristic εἰσῄει 21: 18, 26, ἀπῄεσαν 17: 10, ἐξῄεσαν 15. In Jn 7: 34, 36 εἶμι is possibly to be understood as εἶμι 'I shall go'; cf. the striking frequency of εἶμι in the Apocr. written in vulgar Greek (Reinhold 87–9). 1 Clem 24.3 ἄπεισι 'departs', cf. 54.2 ἐκχωρῶ ἄπειμι; Homil Clem 3.63.1 εἰσιών = -ελθών; 9.10. 2, 13.2 εἰσ-, προσίασιν, 10.4 εἰσέρχονται, 13.2 προσ-ιέναι, 23.3 προσῄεσαν, 16.14.1 ἴμεν. (2) Εἰδῶ, εἰδέναι, εἰδώς as in Att.; impera. ἴστε H 12: 17 (indic.? literary language), Ja 1: 19 (v.l. ὥστε), E 5: 5 (v.l. ἐστε, § 353(6)). M.-H. 222. Homil Clem 9.14.1, 19.5, 10.2.2 ἴσασιν, 9.21.1 οἴδασι, 10.14.1 ἴσμεν, 16.14.4 οἴδαμεν, 12.24.2 οἴδατε, 17.16.2 ἴσμεν, 18.6.5 οἴδας. (3) Φημί 1 C 7: 29, 10: 15, 19, 15: 50; very frequent in Herm.

100. Καθῆσθαι, κεῖσθαι. From καθῆσθαι come the Atticisms κάθῃ A 23: 3 (as early as Hyperides; cf. Lautensach, Glotta 8 [1917] 186; Gromska 31 f. and δύνῃ § 93) and imperative κάθου (also new Attic, Lautensach, Glotta 9 [1918] 88) twice Ja 2: 3, five times in the quotation κάθου ἐκ δεξιῶν from the LXX. Imperfect ἐκαθήμην § 69(1). Fut. καθήσομαι s. § 101.—Κεῖσθαι as in Attic; cf. also § 97(2).

Κάθου is to κάθησο as τίθου is to τίθεσο acc. to Wackernagel, Glotta 14 (1925) 56 = Kl. Schr. 864; cf. κατάκου for κατάκεισο, Preisendanz, PGM II (1931) 13.136 (iv AD) (Kapsomenakis 66 f.).

(5) SUPPLEMENT: CATALOGUE OF VERBS

101. See also the Index of Greek words.

ἀγαλλιᾶν (a Hell. transformation of ἀγάλλεσθαι after ναυτιᾶν κοπιᾶν ἀγωνιᾶν etc.) act. Lk 1: 47 (Rev

19: 7 -ώμεθα 046 may well be more correct; 1 P 1: 8 -ᾶτε only BC*), otherwise depon. (with aor. mid. or pass., § 78).

ἄγειν: aor. ἤγαγον and infrequently -ῆξα, § 75. Pf. act. is unattested. Ὑπάγειν is the popular word for 'go, depart' (from which MGr πάγω πηγαίνω): most frequently in John, never Acts, Paul, Heb; it forms only a pres. (most frequently impera. ὕπαγε ὑπάγετε; other present forms, e.g. Jn 3: 8 ὑπάγει) and is supplemented by means of πορεύεσθαι (which is not itself defective); cf. § 308.

ἀγνύναι only with κατ- (like Att.; Lautensach 163) and only in the following forms: κατέαξαν (Att.) Jn 19: 32, 33, with misplaced augment (§ 66(2)) κατεάξει Mt 12: 20 OT (LXX is different) and κατεαγῶσιν Jn 19: 31 (κατεάξω Ps 47: 8 Symm., κατέαγμα pap. ii AD [Preisigke]).

αἱρεῖν: aor. εἶλον and εἶλα §§ 80; 81(3). Fut. ἑλῶ (§ 74(3)); LXX, pap., inscrip., Epict.; Mayser I² 2, 130) Lk 12: 18, 2 Th 2: 8 (v.l. ἀναλοῖ s.v. ἀναλίσκειν), Rev 22: 19, yet mid. αἱρήσομαι Ph 1: 22 as in Att.

ἀλήθειν instead of ἀλεῖν (Phryn. 151); only the pres. is attested. Cf. νήθειν.

ἅλλεσθαι (ἐξ-, ἐφ-) outside of Acts only Jn 4: 14. First aor. (LXX) ἥλατο A 14: 10, (Jn 21: 7 D); second aor. (a pap., s. Mayser I² 2, 135) ἐφαλόμενος A 19: 16 (ἐφαλλ- S⁽ᶜ⁾E al., ἐναλλ- D), also 3: 8 ἐξαλόμ-is better than the -λλ- of the MSS; both are also found in Att. (Lautensach 88 f., 209).

ἀμφιεννύναι: only pres. (§§ 29(2) and 73) and ἠμφιεσμένος (§ 69(1); Polyb. also knows only the ptcp. in the perf.: Schoy 22).

ἀναλίσκειν: καταναλίσκον H 12: 29 OT, ἀναλοῖ 2 Th 2: 8 S* Or (v.l. ἀναλώσει, ἀνελεῖ), ἀναλῶσαι Lk 9: 54, ἀναλωθῆτε G 5: 15; all as in Att.

ἀπορεῖν (δι-, ἐξ-): act. only Mk 6: 20 SBL (mid. W), Lk 9: 7, A 5: 24, 10: 17 (2: 12 διηπόρουν CDEI [-οῦντο SAB]), otherwise always depon. as in Hell. (§ 307; already also in class., Mayser I² 2, 116) with aor. pass. (2 C 1: 8, UGosp 1.63 f.). Correspondingly only εὐπορεῖτο A 11: 29, never the Att. εὐπορεῖν. Koine prefers -πορεῖσθαι; s. also ὑστερεῖν.

ἀρκεῖν: Hell. pass. depon. 'be satisfied with' (ἀρκεσθησόμεθα 1 T 6: 8); cf. Schmidt 464; Nägeli 55.

ἁρμόζειν: single form ἡρμοσάμην 2 C 11: 2; also ἁρμοζ- Diogn 12.9 and Herm.

αὐξάνειν: Att. αὔξειν and αὐξάνειν trans. 'cause to increase', depon. intrans. 'grow'. NT -άνειν trans. only 1 C 3: 6, 7, 2 C 9: 10, otherwise intrans. = Att. -άνεσθαι (A 6: 7 etc.); -άνεσθαι Mt 13: 30 (συν-), 32 (-ήσῃ S⁽ᵇ⁾D), Mk 4: 8 v.l., rather often in Paul, 1 P 2: 2; αὔξειν only intrans. (E 2: 21, C 2: 19; cf. Herm Vis 3. 4.1, αὐξήσας 1.1.6). Cf. Nägeli 35; Mayser I² 2, 170; 3, 149.15; and especially Katz, JTS 5 (1954) 207–9. Augm. εὔξ- s. § 67(1).

βαρεῖν (Hell.): act. attested only with ἐπι- and κατα- (Paul); usually pass.: Lk 21: 34, 2 C 1: 8, 5: 4, 1 T 5: 16 and especially βεβαρημένος (beg. w. Plato;

almost always this form in the LXX, otherwise βαρύνειν: Thack. 261): Mt 26: 43, Lk 9: 32 (Mk 14: 40 v.l. βεβ-, καταβεβ-, καταβαρούμενοι, καταβαρυνόμενοι). Βαρύνειν, which was the word common in Att., only v.l. Mk 14: 40, Lk 21: 34 (DH), A 3: 14, 2 C 5: 4 (D*FG). Βαρεῖν Apocr. Gospels, POxy x 1224 p. 6 (iv AD), Homil Clem 11.16, κατα- Herm Sim 9. 28.6. Cf. Schmid III 187; Nägeli 26; Melcher 12; Schekira 238.

βιοῦν: only βιῶσαι (§75), otherwise ʒῆν (q.v.).

βλαστάνειν: pres. (subj.) only Mk 4: 27 -άνῃ SAC² al., βλαστᾷ BC*DLWΔ (from βλαστᾶν like βλαστῶντα LXX Eccl. 2: 6, Herm Sim 4.1.2), otherwise only aor. ἐβλάστησα (§75; from which βλαστᾶν is formed).

βλέπειν: originally only of the function of the eyes, 'to look, to possess the power of sight'; thus often in the NT, also fut. βλέψω §77, aor. ἔβλεψα (as in Att.) A 3: 4, περιεβλεψάμην Mk 3: 5 etc.; βλέψωσιν Jn 9: 39 (v.l. βλέπωσιν)=ἀναβλ- 'to regain sight' as in Att.; in addition βλέπειν with the Hell. meaning=ὁρᾶν 'to see, perceive', but only in pres. and impf. (προβλέψασθαι=προϊδέσθαι H 11: 40, s. §316(1)).

γαμεῖν: act. also of the woman (Att. mid.) Mk 10: 12 v.l., 1 C 7: 28, 34, 1 T 5: 11, 14 (ἐγάμησα of the woman AEM VIII 11.4, XIX 225.4 [Bulgaria]: Michaïlov² 174; also γαμῆσαι PMich 221.16 [296 AD]), otherwise γαμίζεσθαι of the woman (v.l. ἐκ-, γαμίσκεσθαι [cf. Bauer s.v.] and ἐκγαμισκ-) Mk 12: 25 pars., Lk 17: 27, 20: 34. Γαμεῖσθαι only γαμοῦνται Lk 20: 34 D, γαμηθῇ Mk 10: 12 AC²N al., -θῆναι (Att. γήμασθαι) 1 C 7: 39 (ἐγαμήθην Plut., Demetr. 38. 1, Passio Perpet. et Felic. 2.1, Malalas [Wolf I 71]). Act. γαμίζειν 'to give in marriage' Mt 24: 38 SD (ἐκγ- JL al., γαμισκ- B, ἐκγ- W), =γαμεῖν 1 C 7: 38 (s. Lietzmann, Hdb. ad loc. and the preface to the four main Epistles p. x).—Hell. aor. act. ἐγάμησα Mt 5: 32 etc., Att. ἔγημα never without v.l.: γήμας Mt 22: 25 SBL, ἔγημα Lk 14: 20 (ἔλαβον D, ἠγάμηκα 𝔓⁴⁵), γήμῃς 1 C 7: 28 KL al. (γαμήσῃς 𝔓⁴⁶SBP, λάβῃς γυναῖκα DEFG), γήμῃ 1 C 7: 28 (γαμῇ D*FG).

γηράσκειν: aor. ἐγήρασα intrans. (Att. trans., K.-Bl. II 390): γηράσῃς Jn 21: 18.

γίνεσθαι: not γιγν- (§34(4)); fut. §79; aor. ἐγενόμην and ἐγενήθην §78; γενάμενος §81(3); often γέγονα, undisputed γεγένημαι only Jn 2: 9, v.l. R 15: 8 SAC²DᶜE al., more weakly attested in Lk 8: 34, A 7: 52; 1 Th 2: 8; cf. Polyb. (Schoy 61 f.); since Simon., Pindar etc. (Lautensach, Philol. 77 [1921] 244ff.); only this, not γέγονα, in Ion. inscr. (Chantraine 196); both in pap. (Mayser I² 2, 172).

δύνασθαι: pres. §93; augm. ἠ- and ἐ- §66(3); fut. δυνήσομαι §79; aor. ἠδυνήθην and ἠδυνάσθην; the latter in Mt 17: 16 B, Mk 7: 24 SB, H 3: 19 𝔓¹³; Epic and Ion.-Hell. (Mayser I¹ 19; I² 2, 156, 158).

δύειν: intrans. 'to go down, set' E 4: 26 (Homer; Att. δύεσθαι), for which δύνειν (non-Att., but LXX

etc.; Mayser I² 2, 119; 3, 149.37 ff.; Psaltes 223) Lk 4: 40 (§75), ἐνδύνοντες 'creeping in' 2 T 3: 6, cf. Barn 4.10; aor. ἔδυν ἔδυσα §75, ἐδύην §76(2). Ἐνδύειν trans. 'to put on': pres. only Mk 15: 17 AN, correctly ἐνδιδύσκειν §73; mid. ἐνδιδύσκεσθαι s. §73; the other tenses as in Att.: -έδυσα -εδυσάμην etc.; also ἐξέδυσα (pres. and impf. unattested).

ἐγείρειν: act. 'to raise' ('to awaken' is expressed more frequently by διεγείρειν); intrans. ἔγειρε (not -αι aor. mid.!) Mk 5: 41 etc. (cf. Eur., IA 624, Aesop. 81.5 [Ursing 80]); ἐγείρεσθαι is intrans. with aor. pass. (§78); perf. ἐγήγερται 'has arisen' (late) Mk 6: 14 SBDL, 1 C 15: 4. For the ancient grammarians on ἔγειρε and ἔγειραι s. Reitzenstein, GGA 1921, 167. Γρηγορεῖν s. §73.

εἰδέναι: §99(2); Ion.-Hell. fut. εἰδήσω (Att. εἴσομαι) H 8: 11 OT. Mayser I² 2, 130.

ἕλκειν: aor. εἵλκυσα as Att., from which Ion.-Hell. fut. ἑλκύσω (§74(3)) Jn 12: 32 (Att. ἕλξω). Mayser I² 2, 176.

ἔρχεσθαι: while ἰέναι is retreating (§99(1)), ἔρχεσθαι is being extended in Koine: ἔρχομαι (Att. ἴω), ἠρχόμην (Att. ᾖα) etc.; Hell. fut. ἐλεύσομαι (Ion.; Att. εἶμι, Phryn. 37); aor. ἦλθον and ἦλθα §81(3); ἐλθέ s.v. ὁρᾶν; pf. ἐλήλυθα as Att. In Hell. ἔρχεσθαι is confined to the meaning 'to come', consequently new verbs appear for 'to go' (πορεύεσθαι, ὑπάγειν); cf. especially Mt 8: 9. A. Bloch, Zur Gesch. einiger suppl. Verba im Griech. (Diss. Basel, 1940) 69.

ἐσθίειν and (primarily the ptcp. of) ἔσθειν (-θειν Homer, Dor. and other poets, Hell.). Fut. φάγομαι §74(2), φάγεσαι §87; aor. act. φαγεῖν; pf. βέβρωκα Jn; aor. pass. βρωθῇ Lk 22: 16 D as classical. Τρώγειν is the popular substitution for ἐσθίειν; John always, otherwise only Mt 24: 38 (for which Lk 17: 27 has ἤσθιον), Barn, Herm Sim 5.3.7 (not in the LXX). Cf. Haussleiter, Archiv f. lat. Lexikogr. 9 [1896] 300ff., where edere is compared with popular manducare. MGr τρώγω–ἔφαγα. Ἐσθίειν predominates in the NT (as in the LXX), often without v.l.; ἔσθητε Lk 22: 30 BD*T, ἔσθων Mk 1: 6 SBL*Δ, Lk 7: 33 BD, 34 D, 10: 7 BD (otherwise Mk and Lk also have -ι- without v.l.), ἔσθοντα R 14: 3 𝔓⁴⁶ (ἐσθείοντα in the same verse), ἔσθοντες 1 C 10: 18 D. Ἔσθειν also in pap. iii BC (Mayser I² 2, 178), ostraca iii BC (BGU VI 1507.14, 1508.3, 4); ἔσθεν in an inscrip. from Cos in Herzog, Arch. f. Religionswiss. 10 (1907) 400ff. (a 23, 27, 42; iii BC); κατεσθόντων Greek Enoch (Bonner) p. 9.6 (103.15), p. 9.24 (104.5). On the rise of ἔσθειν s. Thurneysen, IF 39 (1921) 189; Schwyzer I 704 n. 1.—Κατατρώγειν 'pulverize' LXX Pr 24: 22e, Ezk 23: 34 Aqu. Symm. Theod.

εὐπορεῖσθαι s.v. ἀπορεῖν.

ἔχειν: fut. as in Hell. (Mayser I² 2, 178f.) only ἕξω, never σχήσω, also from ἀνέχεσθαι only ἀνέξομαι; augm. §69(2); εἶχαν etc. §82, εἴχοσαν §84(2).

ζῆν: pres., impf. § 88; fut. ȝήσω and ȝήσομαι § 77; Ion.-Hell. aor. (MGr) ἔȝησα § 75; Att. ἐβίων s.v. βιοῦν; pf. unattested.

ȝωννύναι: pres. § 92; perf. pass. περιεȝωσμένος (Att. without σ) Lk 12: 35 etc. (Ion., LXX), cf. § 70(3).

ἥκειν: the point of transition in Hell. to the perf. conjugation on account of the perf. meaning is the 3rd plur. ἥκασιν Mk 8: 3 SADN (al. ἥκουσιν, Β εἰσίν), 1 Clem 12.2. Cf. e.g. pap. (Mayser ι² 2, 148), LXX (Thack. 269), Jos. (Schmidt 470); cf. IG xii v. 109.13 (411 bc) τῶμ παρικότων.

θάλλειν: only Ph 4: 10 ἀνεθάλετε or -ατε (§§ 72 and 75), either factitive 'you have revived your care for me' (τὸ ὑπὲρ ἐμοῦ φρονεῖν) or intrans. 'you have revived as far as your care for me is concerned' (τοῦ FG, cf. § 399(1)). Clearly intrans. ἀναθάλλει 1 Clem 36.2. Ἀνέθαλάς με Is 38: 16 Σ′ Θ′ (Katz, ThLZ 1957, 112 n. 2).

θεᾶσθαι s.v. θεωρεῖν.

θέλειν: so NT and pap. (Mayser ι² 2, 119), never Att. ἐθέλειν (Diogn 10.6 ἐθέλει), but always augm. ἠ- (§ 66(3)) and ἐθελο- in composition (§ 118(2)); in Att. drama as a rule ἠθέλησα–θελῆσαι (Lautensach 134); MGr always θέλω ἤθελα. Θέλειν (by means of aphaeresis as a result of combinations like εἰ 'θέλεις, μὴ 'θέλειν) is the popular word in Hell. for 'to wish, want' (cf. MGr); likewise βούλεσθαι without difference in meaning, but frequent only in Acts, seldom in the Gospels and Epistles. On βούλεσθαι and (ἐ)θέλειν s. Rödiger, Glotta 8 (1917) 1ff.; Fox, BPhW 1917, 597ff., 633ff.; Zucker, Gnomon 9 (1933) 191ff.; and especially Schrenk, TW ι 628–31.—A. Braun, Nota sui verbi greci del 'volere' = Atti Ist. R. Veneto 98 (1938/9) 337–55: βούλομαι more the considered will, θέλω Asia Minor and Koine (Dor. λῆν); P. Joüon, Les verbes βούλομαι et θέλω dans le NT = RSR 30 (1940) 227–38; A. Wifstrand, Die gr. Verba für wollen, Eranos 40 (1942) 16–36.

θεωρεῖν: virtually confined to pres. and impf.; fut. Jn 7: 3, aor. Mt 28: 1, Lk 8: 35 D, 23: 48 SBCD al., Jn 8: 51 (-σει S), Rev 11: 12; otherwise supplemented with θεᾶσθαι (for which the pres. and impf. in turn are missing): ἐθεασάμην, τεθέαμαι, ἐθεάθην.

ἱλάσκεσθαι (like class.) 'to reconcile with oneself' Η 2: 17; ἱλάσθητι pass. 'be propitiated = be merciful' Lk 18: 13; cf. ἐξιλασθέν 'atoned for' Plato, Lg. 9.862c. Cf. LXX (Thack. 270f.).

καθαίρειν appears seldom in the NT and means as in the vernacular 'to clean, clear away, prune': καθαίρει Jn 15: 2 (καθαριεῖ D correctly), ἐκκαθάρατε 1 C 5: 7 (on -ᾶρ- s. § 72), ἐκκαθάρῃ 2 Τ 2: 21, διακαθᾶραι Lk 3: 17 S*B (καὶ διακαθαριεῖ al.), κεκαθαρμένους Η 10: 2 L; καθάρας Diogn 2.1, κεκάθαρται Herm Sim 9.10.4, -ρμένων 9.18.3. Otherwise always καθαρίζειν (or καθερίζειν § 29(1)); cf. Nägeli 59.

καθέζεσθαι, καθίζειν, καθῆσθαι: Att. καθίζειν 'to set, cause to sit' also 'to seat oneself', otherwise -ίȝεσθαι 'to sit down'; ἐκαθεȝόμην aoristic 'I sat down'; καθῆσθαι 'to sit'. NT: 'to set' καθίȝειν, fut. καθίσω § 74(1), aor. ἐκάθισα (Att.); 'I sat down' ἐκάθισα (hence Jn 19: 13 is very ambiguous), also perf. (as in Hell.; Melcher 14) κεκάθικα Η 12: 2 (pres. καθίȝειν only trans.; for fut. s. infra); aor. ἐκαθέσθην (LXX Job 39: 27, Jos. [Schmidt 464], Apocr. [Reinhold 97] etc. [Lautensach 268], opposed by Lucian, Sol. 11 and Phryn. 269) from καθέȝεσθαι only Lk 10: 39 SABC* al. (-ίσασα 𝔓⁴⁶C³DPW etc.). 'To sit' καθῆσθαι (predominantly) and καθέȝεσθαι (rare): ἐκαθέȝετο 'sat' ('had sat down') Jn 4: 6, 11: 20, for which elsewhere ἐκάθητο (Mt 13: 1 etc.); καθεȝό-μενος = καθήμενος Α 6: 15 (-ήμενοι D) etc.; fut. καθήσομαι Mt 19: 28 (-ίσεσθε CD* al.) and Lk 22: 30 SAB³ al. (-ίσεσθε EF, κάθησθε subj. B*, καθέȝησθε D) instead of the Att. καθεδοῦμαι; καθίσει Mt 25: 31 all MSS. On καθῆσθαι 2nd sing. κάθῃ, impera. κάθου 'sit down!', s. § 100. Augm. ἐκαθ- § 69(1). Herm: καθίȝειν trans. in pres. (Vis 3.2.4), but καθιῇ 'you shall be permitted to sit' Vis 3.1.9 S (καθίσεις A), aor. trans. Sim 9.1.4, intrans. more often, perf. κεκαθίκαμεν sederamus 5.6. Ἐκαθέσθην etc. Homil Clem 19.25.1, 20.1.1, 21.3, 2.1.2, 3.63.1.

κεραννύναι: only perf. pass. κεκέρασμαι (as often Hell., Att. κέκραμαι) Η 4: 2 𝔓⁴⁶SABCD* (-κραμ- D°EK al.), Rev. 14: 10 (LXX Bel 32) and aor. ἐκέρασα Rev 18: 6, 1 C 12: 24. Cf. § 92.

κερδαίνειν: pres. and impf. unattested, aor. ἐκέρδησα (Ion.-Hell.; MGr ἐκέρδεσα) Mt 16: 26 and often; κερδάνω (§ 72) 1 C 9: 21 S*ABC al. (κερδήσω 𝔓⁴⁶S°DE al., as it is four times in 19, 20, 22); fut. pass. κερδηθήσονται 1 P 3: 1. Κερδησ- also predominates in Jos., s. Schmidt 451 and 459.

κορεννύναι: only κορεσθέντες Α 27: 38 (literary language), otherwise replaced by χορτάȝειν (§ 126(1 a β)), cf. Athen. 3.99 ε.

κράȝειν: pres. rare in Att. (κέκραγα instead), often in NT, κέκραγα only Jn 1: 15 (§ 321); fut. κράξω or (κε)κράξομαι §§ 65, 77; aor. ἀνέκραγον, ἔκραξα and ἐκέκραξα (§ 75), the last being a new formation after κεκράξομαι which was reinterpreted as a simple fut. (cf. κέκραγα in a pres. sense § 341); the reduplicated aor. then supported the reduplicated fut. 1 Clem 34. 6 ἐκέκραγον (from the LXX Is 6: 3, cf. 4 and 3 Macc 5: 23; Thack. 225) = ἔκραγον with the extension of the reduplication (§ 68).

κρεμαννύναι: besides κρέμασθαι, only κρεμάσαν-τες (A 5: 30, 10: 39), κρεμασθῇ Mt 18: 6, -σθέντων Lk 23: 39 appear. Ἐξεκρέμετο s. § 93.

κυεῖν or κύειν: only ἀποκυεῖ (-κύει) Ja 1: 15, ἀπεκύησεν 18. LXX ἐκύομεν Is 59: 13, κύουσι (κυοῦσι?) 4, ἀποκυήσασα 4 Macc 15: 17.

κυλίειν, a back-formation from ἐκύλισα, perhaps going back to Att. (K.-Bl. ιι 453; earlier form κυλίνδειν), is found in Mk 9: 20, Lk 23: 53 an addition of D (Herm Vis 3.2.9, 7.1); fut. κυλίσω Mk 16: 3, aor. (ἀπ-)ἐκύλισα, perf. pass. (ἀπο-)κεκύλισμαι as in Att.

λᾱκεῖν 'to burst' (to be distinguished from λάσκειν 'to ring, crash'—ἔλᾰκον): ἐλάκησεν A 1: 18 (Acta Thom. 33 [L.-B. II 2, 150.18]), otherwise just διαλᾱκήσασα Aristoph., Nu. 410.

λαμβάνειν: in Hell. the μ of the pres. stem has found its way into all the other tenses and derivatives (ἐπίλαμπτος 'epileptic' as early as IG IV² 1.123. 115 [iv BC 2nd half]; in the first centuries AD the forms with μ predominate; thus NT λήμψομαι (§77), ἐλήμφθην, λῆμψις Ph 4: 15, ἀνάλημψις Lk 9: 51, ἀντίλημψις 1 C 12: 28, πρόσλημψις R 11: 15, προσωπολήμπτης, -λημπτεῖν, -λημψία, ἀπροσωπολήμπτως, ἀνεπίλημπτος. Schwyzer I 761 n. 4. Later MSS prefer to omit the μ again (cf. Thack. 109); in the NT Apocr. almost no more of these forms are found (Reinhold 46f.). Ἔλαβαν etc. §81(3), ἐλάβοσαν §84 (2). The aor. act. impera. is accented λάβε (Rev 10: 8f.), not λαβέ as in Att.; cf. ἴδε under ὁρᾶν.

λέγειν 'to pick up, gather': only συλλέγω συνέλεξα (Att.), ἐκλελεγμένος (usually ἐξείλεγμαι in Att.) Lk 9: 35, cf. -λελεγμένος in the pap. (Mayser I² 2, 97), ἐκλελεγμένος LXX (Thack. 274), ἐπιλελ- and ἐκλελ-Xen. and Polyb. (Schoy 63). 'To gather': ἐκλέλεκται 1 Clem 43.4, -γμένος 50.7, IEph (Salutation), Pol Ph 1.1; Herm Vis 4.3.5.

λέγειν 'to say': ἔλεγαν §22; Att. λέξω ἔλεξα etc.; in the NT it is defective (the beginning of which goes back to Att., cf. Miller, AJPh 16 [1895] 162 n. 3) with only pres. and impf. appearing; fut. ἐρῶ, aor. εἶπον and εἶπα (§81(1)), perf. εἴρηκα, aor. pass. ἐρρέθην ῥηθείς (§70(1)), perf. pass. εἴρημαι. A certain distinction between λέγειν and εἰπεῖν was still felt, as, for example, that which emerges from the combination εἶπαν λέγοντες Lk 12: 16, 20: 2 (cf. Kieckers, IF 35 [1915] 34ff., especially 36f. and §420).—From διαλέγεσθαι aor. διελέχθην and διελεξάμην §78.

λείπειν: alternative pres. form -λιμπάνειν in διελίμπανεν A 8: 24 D, -ον 17: 13 D, ὑπολιμπάνων 1 P 2: 21, ἐγκαταλιμπανόμενοι 2 C 4: 9 FG Eus Chr; also LXX and pap., cf. Thack. 227. Aor. ἔλειψα in addition to ἔλιπον §75.

μελ-: fut. ἐπιμελήσομαι (pres. impf. unattested) §79, aor. ἐπεμελήθην as in Att. Μεταμέλομαι (Att.) and μετεμελόμην 2 C 7: 8; Att. inscrip. iv and iii BC mostly -μελεῖσθαι (Meisterhans 175; Lademann 126f.). Aor. μετεμελήθην (unattested in Att.) Mt 21: 29 etc.; fut. μεταμεληθήσομαι §79. Pap. -μέλεσθαι (and -λοῦμαι), -μεληθῆναι Mayser I² 2, 115, 158, 159. Inscrip. from the Ion. Cyclades: earlier only ἐπιμέλεσθαι, later -λεῖσθαι more often: E. Knitl, Die Sprache der ion. Kykladen (Diss. Munich, 1933) 104.

μοιχ-: in addition to the Att. μοιχεύειν (of the man, mid. of the woman [Jn] 8: 4), Doric μοιχᾶσθαι appears in Mt and Mk (of both man and woman); Mt and Mk have μοιχεύειν only outside the pres. (except for quotations): ἐμοίχευσεν Mt 5: 28, μοιχευθῆναι 32 SBDW (besides μοιχᾶται), 19: 8 BC*N. Cf. Wackernagel, Hell. 7ff. = Kl. Schr. 1038ff.

νήθειν 'to spin' (Hell.): only νήθει Mt 6: 28 = Lk 12: 27; never νῆν; cf. supra ἀλήθειν.

ξυρ-: pres., impf. unattested; aor. mid. ξύρασθαι (not -ᾶσθαι) 1 C 11: 6, ξυρήσωνται A 21: 24 AB³CH (-σονται SB*D²EP, ξύρωνται D*); perf. pass. ἐξυρημένη 1 C 11: 5 like Att. ξύρασθαι and ξυρήσασθαι are unattested in Att.

ἀν-οίγειν: as in the pap. (Mayser I² 2, 188) never -οιγνύναι (§92). Augmentation has become very involved: always διηνοίχθησαν Lk 24: 31, διήνοιγεν 32 etc.; so also without δι- always in (a new) second aor. pass. ἠνοίγην A 12: 10 (-χθη E al.) etc. (§76). In the other forms (impf. is attested only from διαν-) the old syllabic augm. is still strongly attested: aor. act. ἀνέῳξεν Jn 9: 14 (ἠνέῳξεν LX, ἤνοιξεν D), 17 KL (ἠνέῳξεν BWX, ἤνοιξεν SAD al.), likewise 32; in 21, 26, 30 also ἤνοιξεν B, which is to be preferred; cf. A 5: 19, 9: 40, 12: 14, 14: 27, Rev 6: 1, 3 etc. Perf. intrans. (Ion.-Hell., Phryn. 157) ἀνέῳγα Jn 1: 51 (ἠνεῳγότα S), 1 C 16: 9, 2 C 6: 11, otherwise ἀνέῳγμαι (like Att.) R 3: 13 OT, 2 C 2: 12 (ἠνεῳγμ- DEP), A 7: 56 (διηνοιγμ- SABC), 9: 8 (ἠνεῳγμ- SᶜCE, ἠνοιγμ-S*A), 10: 11 (ἠν- E), 16: 27, Rev 4: 1 046 (ἠν- SAP); the text vacillates between ἀν- ἠν- also in 10: 2 (ἠν-𝔓⁴⁷SCP, ἀν- 046), 8 (ἠν- SCP, ἀν- 𝔓⁴⁷ 046), 19: 11, (3: 8 ἀν- AC 046). First aor. pass. ἀνεῴχθην Mt 3: 16 (ἠν- B), 9: 30 (ἠν- BD), 27: 52, Lk 1: 64 etc.; ἠνεῴχθ-Jn 9: 10 preponderant (ἀν- AK al.); ἠνοίχθ- A 16: 26 SAE (ἠνεῴχθ- BCD, ἀνεῴχθ- HLP); Rev 20: 12 (twice) also vacillates. Inf. (with misplaced augm., §66(2)) ἀνεῴχθῆναι Lk 3: 21 (-νοι- D). Second aor. pass. ἠνοίγην s. §76(1). The LXX is in accord with the NT; Helb. 78f., 83ff., 95f., 102f.; Thack. 202ff. Ptol. pap. ἤνῳξα, ἀνοῖξαι, ἀνοίξαντες, ἀνεῳγμένος (ἤνυγμ-); Mayser I² 2, 104, 108, 188. For Plut. (Quaest. conv. 737 D ff.) ἀνοίγειν is a word beginning with α.

οἴεσθαι: only οἰόμενοι Ph 1: 17, οἰέσθω Ja 1: 7 and formally Att. οἶμαι Jn 21: 25 (LXX 4 Macc 1: 33, pap.; Mayser I² 2, 120); οἴομαι R 1: 13 D*G. It appears more frequently in the more literary patristic writers: pres. 1 Clem 30.4 OT, 2 Clem, Diogn, ᾠήθην ITr 3.3. Impf. in reports of dreams in the LXX and pap., s. Johannesohn, KZ 64 (1937) 212.

οἰκτίρειν: ῑ, not ει, s. §23; only fut. οἰκτιρήσω R 9: 15 OT, otherwise ἐλεεῖν (Ion.?).

οἴχεσθαι: only παρῳχημέναις A 14: 16.

ἀπ-ολλύναι: pres. §92; fut. ἀπολέσω (§74(1); also Herm Sim 8.7.5), the Att. fut. ἀπολῶ only 1 C 1: 19 OT (-έσω appears only in the later books of the LXX) and Mt 21: 41 W, but always ἀπολοῦμαι (as in the LXX) because the mid. does not have a σ-aorist. Mayser I² 2, 129.

ὀμείρεσθαι (or ὁμ-) = ἱμείρεσθαι: ὁμειρόμενοι 1 Th 2: 8 (all uncials; ὅμειρ- as v.l. to ἱμειρ- also in the LXX Job 3: 21 [ἱμειρ- Bᶜᵒʳʳ] and Symm. Ps 62: 2) has still not been clarified; the comparison with δύρεσθαι–ὀδύρεσθαι, κέλλειν–ὀκέλλειν (W.-S. 141) is not valid, because μείρωνται in Nicander (Ther. 402) is not the equivalent of ἱμείρωνται, cf. Debrunner, IF 21 (1907) 203, 204. An etymological connection between ομειρ- and ἱμειρ- is impossible. Cf. M.-H. 251.

ὀμνύναι: pres. §92; otherwise only aor. ὤμοσα (often).

ὁρᾶν: even pres. and impf. are in very limited use; usually replaced by βλέπειν (θεωρεῖν, θεᾶσθαι); more frequent only ὅρα ὁρᾶτε cave cavete Mt 8: 4 and often (but also βλέπετε A 13: 40 etc. may be so used); other forms only in more refined language: Lk 16: 23, 23: 49, H 2: 8, 11: 27, 1 P 1: 8, Ja 2: 24 (Mk 8: 24, Jn 6: 2, A 8: 23, Rev 18: 18) and in composition: A 2: 25 OT, R 1: 20, H 12: 2, also infrequent in the Ap. Frs. (Reinhold 98f.). Impf. s. §66(2). Perf. ἑώρακα (ἑορ-) §68. Aor. εἶδον (εἶδα §81(3)); impera. ἴδε (Att. ἰδέ, cf. supra λάβε; but ἐλθέ [Mt 14: 29, Jn 4: 16] and εἰπέ as in Att.) Jn 1: 46 etc., ἰδού as interjection with acute accent (like Att.). Fut. ὄψομαι §77, aor. pass. ὤφθην apparui, fut. pass. ὀφθήσομαι (perf. pass. ὦπται Herm Vis 3.1.2 S), from which a new pres. is formed ὀπτάνομαι A 1: 3 (LXX 3 Km 8: 8, Tob 12: 19 AB; pap. s. Mayser I² 2, 189; for later Gr. s. Psaltes 242); s. W. Michaelis, TW v 317 n. 12. Ὀπτάζῃ Num 14: 14 is closer to ὀπτασία: Katz, ThLZ 1957, 112. Cf. MGr βλέπω–εἶδα.

παίζειν: ἐμπαίξω etc. §§71 and 77. From the simple verb only παίζειν 1 C 10: 7 OT.

πείθειν: fut. πεισθήσονται most likely 'they will (not) be open to persuasion' (like Att.) Lk 16: 31 (πιστεύσουσιν DW).

πειράζειν 'to test someone' (Ion. [Homer]-Hell.) NT always for Att. πειρᾶν (only H 4: 15 πεπειραμένον CKLP), also 'to attempt something' (e.g. A 24: 6), for which the Att. πειρᾶσθαι stands in A 9: 26 EHLP al., 26: 21 (Paul before Agrippa). In Epict. πειρᾶσθαι prevails (Melcher 15). Fraenkel II 102.

πετ- 'to fly': only in Rev and except for πέτηται 12: 14 only pres. ptcp. -όμενος (four times) with the variant -ώμενος (046 and P twice each, 4: 7 only minusc.) and -άμενος (14: 6 S); LXX πέτασθαι and πέτεσθαι (and -ίπτασθαι), Apocr. πέτεσθαι, πετᾶσθαι and πέτασθαι. Cf. Thack. 281f.; Reinhold 100.

πηγνύναι: only aor. (προσ-)έπηξα A 2: 23, H 8: 2.

πιάζειν, πιέζειν: πιέζειν 'to squeeze' (like Att.) Lk 6: 38, πιάζειν (only vernacular) 'to seize' with aor. ἐπίασα (also UGosp 1.26 πιάσωσιν, 28 πιάσαι), ἐπιάσθην in Jn and Acts and once each in Paul, Rev. Cf. §29(2).

πιμπλάναι, πιμπράναι: conjugation of the pres. §93. Forms without μ, permitted in Att. in compounds with ἐμ- (dissimilation), appear in the NT as variants: ἐμπιπλῶν A 14: 17 (with μ 𝔓⁴⁵DEP), ἐμπίπρασθαι 28: 6 S* (A even πίπρασθαι; SᶜBHLP πιμπρ-). In the LXX the tradition favors the forms without μ (Helb. 22). Ἐμπιπρ-, but καταπιμπρ- Philo Byz. (Arnim 32).

πίνειν: fut. πίομαι §§74(2), 77, πίεσαι §87; aor.

ἔπιον (ἔπια §81(3)), impera. πίε Lk 12: 19 (Att. also πῖθι); inf. πιεῖν e.g. Mt 10: 22 (except W), besides πεῖν (§31(2)) Mt 27: 34 S*D twice, Mk 10: 38 D, 15: 23 D, Jn 4: 7 S*B*C*DL, cf. 9, 10 etc. Examples from the pap. in Moulton, ClR 15 (1901) 37, 434; 18 (1904) 111; monosyllabic πεῖν is certain for metrical reasons in Lucillius, Anth. Pal. XI 140.3; s. also Heraeus, RhM 70 (1915) 1ff.

πιπράσκειν: NT as Att. and Hell. πέπρακε Mt 13: 46 (ἐπώλησεν D), ἐπράθη etc. Jn 12: 5 etc., πεπραμένος R 7: 14, but also (like Hell.) pres. πιπράσκειν (-σκομένων A 4: 34 [Att. also pass.], ἐπίπρασκον 2: 45); along with it πωλεῖν (πωλῶ ἐπώλουν ἐπώλησα πωλοῦμαι like Att.) and ἀποδίδοσθαι (only aor.: A 5: 8, 7: 9, H 12: 16, therefore literary language). P. Chantraine, Rev. Phil. 14 (66, 1940) 20f.: NT compared with class. (pres. πιπρ. puristic, ἀπεδόμην is literary, only πωλέω remains a part of the living language: MGr πουλῶ).

ῥηγνύναι 'to break, tear (in pieces)': pres. pass. still ῥήγνυται Mt 9: 17, διε(ρ)-ρήγνυτο Lk 5: 6 AXΓ al.; act. ῥήσσειν (§§73; 92) (also LXX) Mt 9: 17 D, Mk 2: 22 AΓ al. (ῥήξει SBCDL; διαρρήσσονται W), Lk 8: 29, διερ(ρ)ήσσετο 5: 6 SBL (-σσοντο W) (διαρρήσσων PGM I 4.1022 [iv AD]); fut. ῥήξω, aor. ἔρ(ρ)ηξα. Barn 3.6 ῥήσσειν = ῥηγνύναι also: ἵνα μὴ προσρησσώμεθα 'in order that we be not shipwrecked' as προσρήσσεται M. Ant. 4.49. Ἀπερρηγώς 'broken up' Herm Vis 1.1.3 S (A -ρρωγ-) with -η- instead of -ω- from the other tenses; cf. intrans. ἔρρηγα in the tablets from Heraclea (Dor. or Koine?), LXX (Helb. 101f.; Thack. 283; besides the older form ἔρρωγα), Hesychius. To be distinguished is the old Epic ῥήσσειν 'to strike, stamp', to which Att. ῥάττειν (Soph. ἐπιρ-, Thuc. and Xen. συρ-, simple form Dem. 54.8) 'to dash to the ground' corresponds; this ῥήσσειν may well be found in Mk 9: 18 (ῥάσσει D), Lk 9: 42 (G 4: 27? OT), LXX Wsd 4: 19, Herm Man 11.3 (ῥάξαι A) and in προσέρηξεν = προσέβαλεν Lk 6: 48f. Perhaps the two verbs converged in Koine. Fraenkel II 40f.

ῥίπτειν (-ῑ- §13): NT the pres. stem only A 22: 23 -ούντων (-όντων DEHL): Att. ῥίπτειν and ῥιπτεῖν; cf. ἐρ(ρ)ίπτουν Herm Vis 3.5.5 (along with ἔρριπτον 2.7). Redupl. §68.

ῥύεσθαι 'to save' (Ion.-Hell.) with aor. ἐρ(ρ)υσάμην and aor. pass. ἐρ(ρ)ύσθην (also LXX, cf. Thack. 238, 284).

ῥωννύναι: limited to the epistolary formulae ἔρρωσο A 23: 30 SEL and ἔρρωσθε A 15: 29, 23: 30 HP.

σκοπεῖν forms with σκέψασθαι etc. one paradigm in Att., in that only the pres., impf. were formed on σκοπεῖν, the others on σκεπ-. NT σκοπεῖν only pres., impf., but σκεπ- does not appear at all in the simple verb; ἐπισκέπτεσθαι 'to go to see, visit' also forms a pres. (H 2: 6, Ja 1: 27, 1 Clem 25.5, Herm several times); ἐπισκοπεῖν (only ἐπισκοποῦντες H 12: 15, 1 P 5: 2 AKLP al.) = σκοπεῖν 'to look out for'. In

Att. prose ἐπισκέπτεσθαι in the pres. is very rare, more frequent in Hell.; cf. Mayser ı² 2, 120; Melcher 16; Psaltes 243f.

τρώγειν: s.v. ἐσθίειν.

τυγχάνειν: Hell. perf., if with gen., τέτευχα (Ion.) instead of τετύχηκα; cf. Phryn. 395. Thus τέτευχεν H 8: 6 SᶜBDᶜE (τετύχηκεν P, τέτυχεν 𝔓⁴⁶S*AD*KL). The latter is also sometimes found in MSS of Hell. authors; cf. Schmidt 469; Crönert 280; Mayser ı² 2, 152.

τύπτειν: defective and supplemented by other verbs as in Att.: τύπτω ἔτυπτον–πατάξω ἐπάταξα (never pres., impf. from this stem)–ἔπαισα (ditto); pass. τύπτομαι–ἐπλήγην (from this verb only ἐπλήγη Rev 8: 12; but often ἐκπλήσσεσθαι and Lk 2: 48 ἐξεπλάγησαν, Barn 7.10 ἐκπλαγῶσιν). Cf. LXX (Thack. 287f.; Wackernagel, ThLZ 1908, 640); Lautensach 168f., 223.

ὑστερεῖν and just as frequently depon. with aor. pass.; cf. s.v. ἀπορεῖν, further § 180(5); ὑστερηθῆναι Jos., Ant. 15.200.

φαυ–: s.v. φώσκειν.

φεύγειν: fut. φεύξομαι (§ 77) (Jn 10: 5, Ja 4: 7, R 2: 3, H 2: 3, Rev 9: 6) as in Plato (mostly) and Philodemus; cf. Crönert 224; ἐκφεύξεσθαι LXX 2 Macc 9: 22. Att. usually φευξοῦμαι.

φθάνειν: aor. ἔφθασα like Hell. (Mayser ı² 2, 142; already more common in Att.; Lautensach 127), never ἔφθην which is likewise Att.; perf. ἔφθακα (unattested in Att.) 1 Th 2: 16 BD*. The meaning is 'to arrive, come' as in late Greek (Vogeser 46; Wolf ıı 31; Wittmann 16) and MGr; 'to precede' only 1 Th 4: 15, for which προφθάνειν Mt 17: 25. The form and usage are comparable in the LXX (Thack. 288f.).

φύειν: the sole forms in the NT are φύουσα H 12: 15 OT (= LXX Dt 29: 18; intrans. as also in later authors) and a few forms of the aor. pass ἐφύην (§ 76(2)). In the meaning 'to beget' it is replaced by γεννᾶν -ᾶσθαι.

φώσκειν: ἐπιφωσκούσῃ Mt 28: 1, ἐπέφωσκε Lk 23: 54 (W ἐπίφαυσκεν [sic]) (δια-, ἐπι-φαύσκειν LXX, -φώσκειν only as v.l.) Ion.-Hell., but only in composition with διά, ἐπί, ὑπό and only in pres. and impf. The other tenses from φαυ-; thus NT ἐπιφαύσει E 5: 14 OT (διέφαυσε etc. LXX). The Apocr. are in accord with the NT (-φώσκω: -έφαυσα), s. Reinhold 101. -φω- for -φαυ-, secondary after φῶς Bechtel, Griech. Dial. ııı 201; Specht, KZ 59 (1932) 62; E. Fraenkel, Lexis 2, 1 (1949) 147f.

χύν(ν)ειν (only ἐκ-, ὑπερεκ- and συγ-) instead of χεῖν § 73; fut. χεῶ § 74(2); aor. ἔχεα like Att., likewise pass. κέχυμαι ἐχύθην.

ψύχειν: pres. intrans. ἀποψυχόντων Lk 21: 26; fut. ψυγήσομαι § 76(1).

ὠνεῖσθαι: augm. § 66(2). Aor. ὠνήσατο A 7: 16 (not Att., s. Lautensach 131; Att. ἐπριάμην which is still retained in the LXX; pap. ὠνήσασθαι along with the frequent πρίασθαι s. Mayser ı² 2, 142). Usually replaced by ἀγοράζειν.

3. ADVERBS

(1) ADVERBS OF MANNER

102. (1) Adverbs of manner in -ως which are formed from adjectives sometimes have a comparative in -τέρως; however -τερον still preponderates as in Attic. From adjectives in -(ί)ων the adverb is always -(ι)ον (βέλτιον etc.; Attic also -όνως). (2) From ταχύς both classical adverbs, ταχύ and the more literary ταχέως (Pernot, Études 187), are attested. (3) 'Well' is now καλῶς, hardly ever εὖ; 'better' κρεῖσσον 1 C 7: 38 (βέλτιον 2 T 1: 18, s. § 244(2)). Μάλα and πάνυ do not appear (Nägeli 57). (4) Διπλότερον (§ 61(2)) 'twice as much' Mt 23: 15 (late). (5) From an ordinal: πρώτως 'for the first time' A 11: 26 𝔓⁴⁵SBD² (πρῶτον A(D*)E al.). (6) Adverbs derived from participles, common in Koine and not unknown to classical usage, are also found in the NT.

(1) Περισσοτέρως 2 C 1: 12 and always elsewhere in Paul, H 2: 1, 13: 19, (6: 17 -ότερον, B only -οτέρως; 7: 15 -ότερον), Mk 15: 14 ENP al. (περισσῶς SAB al.), 7: 36 D (-ότερον 𝔓⁴⁵SAB al.); cf. § 60(3). Σπουδαιοτέρως Ph 2: 28 (-ότερον D*FG), τολμηροτέρως R 15: 15 AB (-ότερον 𝔓⁴⁶SCD al.). Cf. in the superlative ἐσχάτως ἔχειν (Polyb.) Mk 5: 23. Many examples of -τέρως in Crönert 193; only two in the Ptol. pap. (Mayser ı² 3, 125). Μεγίστως Aristeas 19, καλλίστως PGM ı 4.2465 p. 148 (iv AD).

(2) Τάχα 'perhaps' R 5: 7, Phm 15. Ταχύ Mt 5: 25, 28: 7, 8, Mk 9: 39, (Lk 15: 22 interpolation in SBLX [ταχέως D]), Jn 11: 29, Rev rather often; ταχέως Lk and Paul (Jn 11: 31 likely an interpolation, cf. v. 29). Mk always uses the vulgar εὐθύς (42 times) for 'immediately'; Mt only 6 times (from Mk), but 11 times the somewhat archaic εὐθέως (παραχρῆμα 21: 19, 20); Lk εὐθύς 6: 49 (v.l. εὐθέως), A 10: 16 (v.l. πάλιν), εὐθέως 6 times (Acts 9 times), the more choice παραχρῆμα 10 times (5 times for Markan εὐθύς) (Acts 6 times). Pernot, Rev. Ét. gr. 36 (1923) 400–6; Études 181ff. Εὐθύς in Mk: J. Weiss, ZNW 11 (1910) 124ff.; G. Rudberg, Con. Neot. 4 (1944) 42–6 (also in a weakened sense: Mk in part, Thuc. also, ἰθύς Hdt.; but it is used paratactically only in Mk); cf.

Tabachovitz, Die Septuaginta 29–35 (Mk uses εὐθύς with two different functions, temporal and stylistic; the former is reflected in Mt and Lk, the latter usually not). Cf. also § 484.

(3) Εὖ, except as interjection εὖ(γε) 'bravo!' (Mt 25: 21, 23, Lk 19: 17), only E 6: 3 OT, A 15: 29 (literary language), εὖ ποιεῖν 'to do good' Mk 14: 7; cf. εὐποιΐα H 13: 16 with ἀγαθοποιΐα 1 P 4: 19. More often καλῶς in the pap. than εὖ (Mayser I² 3, 126). W. Schmid, PhW 1931, 705.

(4) Homil Clem 9.4.3. On ἀνώτερον, κατωτέρω, πορρωτέρω s. § 62.

(5) Πρώτως Homil Clem 9.4, 16.20 (πρῶτος ἐφθέγξω, ἃ πρώτως ἠκούσαμεν) as in the NT. Πρώτως appears in authors beg. w. Arist.˙(also Polyb. 6.5.10, Diodor. Sic. 4.24 [I 434.3 Vogel; τότε πρώτως]), seldom in pre-Christian pap., often thereafter, inscrip. e.g. Inschr. v. Priene 117.39 (i BC), Dit., Syll.³ 797.16 (37 AD), Benndorf-Niemann, Reisen in Lykien, no. 51.2 (ii AD). Lob. Phryn. 311f.; Crönert 193; Mayser I² 3, 124.44ff.; Preisigke.

(6) Ὑπερβαλλόντως 2 C 11: 23 (Att.; Origen read according to codex Athous ἐν φυλακαῖς περισσευόντως, ἐν πληγαῖς ὑπερβαλλόντως), φειδομένως 9: 6 (Plutarch); ὄντως 'really' is old (found esp. in Paul); Crönert, Gnomon 4 (1928) 84; Bauer s.v.; Schmid IV 620; Reinhold 30f.; Crönert 240f.; Nachmanson 139; Lautensach, Philol. 77 (1921) 251ff.; Mayser I² 3, 124f. For ὄντως 2 P 2: 18 SCKLP, SᶜAB have more correctly the less frequent Hell. ὀλίγως 'hardly' (class. ὀλίγον 'little, a little'); Bauer s.v. ὀλίγως.

(2) ADVERBS OF PLACE

103. Classical Greek did not always distinguish between 'where?' and 'whither?', i.e. in the use of ἔνθα, ἐνταῦθα, ἐνθάδε, ἄνω, κάτω, εἴσω, ἔξω. The distinction has entirely vanished in the NT, just as also ἐν and εἰς (§§ 205, 206, 215(3) and 218) and the acc. and gen.–dat. with ἐπί (§ 234(2)), παρά (§ 236(1)) and πρός (§ 239(1, 3)) are beginning to be confused. Local adverbs in -η do not appear in the NT except for πάντας πανταχῇ 'everyone everywhere' A 21: 28 (-χοῦ HLP); πάντη τε καὶ πανταχοῦ 24: 3 appears to mean 'in every way and everywhere'.

Besides εἴσω (NT ἔσω, § 30(3)) and ἔξω, the Attic writers still had ἔνδον, ἐντός, ἐκτός to use in response to the question 'where?'; Phryn. 127 therefore condemns εἴσω as an answer to this question in spite of occurrences in poetry and prose. Ἔνδον never in the NT; ἐντός, ἐκτός only rarely in response to the question 'where?' (the latter mostly in Paul). Ποῦ = 'where?' and 'whither?' (ποῖ has disappeared), similarly οὗ ὅπου (s. § 293); indefinite που only in H 2: 6, 4: 4, but = 'approximately' in R 4: 19,

δήπου H 2: 16. 'Here (hither)' is expressed by ἐνθάδε in Lk, esp. in Acts, and in Jn 4: 15, 16 (never by ἐνταῦθα, although related οὗτος has driven out ὅδε [s. § 289] which corresponds to ἐνθάδε), but usually by ὧδε (Acts only 9: 14, 21), which no longer has the meaning 'thus' (also in Att. sometimes = 'hither'); Hermas at times has ὧδε κἀκεῖσε 'here and there', 'hither and thither' (Man 5.2.7 etc.). 'There (thither)' ἐκεῖ; ἐκεῖσε is more elegant A 21: 3, 22: 5 (D ἐκεῖ) = 'there'. Corresponding πανταχοῦ 'in all directions' Mk 1: 28, ἀλλαχοῦ 'in another direction' 38; Lob. Phryn. 43f. For ἐκεῖ A 18: 19 BHLP read αὐτοῦ which is otherwise attested only in Mt 26: 36 (but τοῖς μαθηταῖς αὐτοῦ SC*W), A (15: 34 minusc. and versions) 21: 4 SBCHP. Cf. Dieterich 183. Ὧδε 'here (hither)' in pap. s. Mayser I² 2, 66; II 1, 74; Keil, Hermes 43 (1908) 553 n. 1. Ἐκεῖσε 'there' LXX Job 39: 29, Homil Clem 9.5, POxy I 60.9 (323 AD), Acta Joh. 15*, 16* (L.-B. II 1, 160.13, 20, 21), Timotheos 170 (in the mouth of the Persian); Jannaris § 435; Psaltes 336. Ὁμόσε ὄντων A 20: 18 D for ὁμοῦ (cf. Polyb. 6.7.5; Vett. Val., s. Warning 19). 'Thither' always ἐκεῖ in the LXX; Johannessohn II 330 n. 1; further Olsson 105.

104. (1) Adverbs in -θεν answer the question 'whence?', thus πόθεν, ὅθεν, ἔνθεν, ἐντεῦθεν, ἐκεῖθεν, πάντοθεν, ἀλλαχόθεν, οὐρανόθεν (A 14: 17, 26: 13). (2) -θεν is stereotyped and meaningless for the most part in ἔσωθεν ἔξωθεν 'within, outside' (as already in Attic), also in κυκλόθεν (Rev; Att.), and completely so in ἔμπροσθεν ὄπισθεν (from earliest times). Contrast ἄνωθεν 'from above' (κάτωθεν does not appear). Often an intensifying ἀπό (ἐξ) is added. (3) (Ἀπὸ) μακρόθεν besides Attic πόρρωθεν (cf. § 34(2)), ἐκ παιδιόθεν Mk 9: 21 (ἐκ om. AX al., ἐκ παιδός D); cf. (ἀπ', ἐξ) οὐρανόθεν. Classical ἐγγύθεν is not found in the NT.

(1) Ποθέν and ὁπόθεν do not appear; ἔνθεν Mt 17: 20 (ἐντεῦθεν C) and Lk 16: 26 (ἐντεῦθεν ΚΠ) is unclass. = ἐντεῦθεν ἐνθένδε; conversely ἐντεῦθεν καὶ ἐντεῦθεν Jn 19: 18 = Att. ἔνθεν καὶ ἔνθεν. Πανταχόθεν (Att. prose) Mk 1: 45 EGU al. Rev. 22: 2 ἐντεῦθεν καὶ ἐντεῦθεν some minusc., ἐντ. καὶ ἐκεῖθεν A 046 al., ἔνθεν καὶ S*, ἔνθεν add. Sᶜ. Ἐκεῖθεν A 27: 6 A (al. ἐκεῖ) '(of the continuation of a journey) from there'.

(2) Ἔσωθεν ἔξωθεν 'from inside, outside' Mk 7: 15 (𝔓⁴⁵ ἔξω), 18, 21, 23, Lk 11: 7; never in response to the question 'whither?' Ἀπ' ἄνωθεν ἕως κάτω Mt 27: 51 (without ἀπ' SL), Mk 15: 38.

(3) Πόρρωθεν Lk 17: 12 (with ἔστησαν) and H 11: 13 (literary language). Ἀπὸ μακρόθεν Mt 26: 58 (without ἀπό SCF al.), Mk 5: 6 (without ἀπό AKLW al.), Mk 15: 40 etc., also with ἵστασθαι and the like; μακρόθεν without v.l. ἀπὸ μακ. only Lk 18: 13. Ἐκ

παιδιόθεν also Gen 47: 3 in A only (spurious addition). Μακρόθεν appears first in Hell. (Chrysippus in Athen. 4.137ғ, Epict. 1.16.11; often in LXX), likewise παιδιόθεν (Lob. Phryn. 93). Lob. Phryn. 46; Dieterich 183 f.; Ljungvik, Aegyptus 13 (1933) 165–8.—M. Lejeune, Les adverbes grecs en -θεν (Publications de l'Univ. de Bordeaux, no. 3, 1939).

(3) ADVERBS OF TIME

105. Πότε, ποτέ, ὅτε, ὁπότε, τότε; πάντοτε Hellenistic and MGr for ἀεί (Phryn. 103; W. Schmid, PhW 1934, 941 f.). Πηνίκα etc. do not appear; only ἡνίκα 2 C 3: 16 OT and consequently also 15.

Πάντοτε often in Paul and Jn, occasionally Mt, Mk, Lk (Acts never), H 7: 25, Catholic Epistles never; ἀεί only Mk 15: 8 ACD al. (om. SBWΔ), A 7: 51, 2 C 4: 11, 6: 10, T 1: 12 (quotation from Epimenides), H 3: 10 (OT), 1 P 3: 15 (om. A sy Eus), 2 P 1: 12.

Ὁπότε only Lk 6: 3 v.l. and Barn 12.9 (§ 455(1)); ἄλλοτε does not appear. In Hermas the use of ἀεί instead of πάντοτε is one of the indications of the forged conclusion of Simonides (Sim 9.30–10.4).

(4) CORRELATIVE ADVERBS

106. The system of correlative adverbs is waning in Koine owing to the retreat of the indefinite and indefinite relative adverbs.

Of the indefinite advs. only ποτέ is in common use (οἵῳ δηποτοῦν s. § 303); πως only in εἴπως μήπως; on που s. § 103. The indefinite relatives are being confused with the definite forms (§ 293) and in part are almost or entirely disappearing; only ὅπου and ὅπως are still common; in addition there is a remnant of ὁπότε (§ 105).

For compound adverbs s. § 122, adverbial accusative § 160, adverbial genitive § 186, adverbial dative §§ 199, 200.

4. PARTICLES

107. The language of the NT is not rich in particles as compared with the classical (cf. Mayser II 3, 115), partly because a number of old particles are not used at all, but especially because many of those that remain have only a limited function. On the other hand, some few, e.g. καί, are overworked. The usage and combinations of the individual particles are treated under syntax; here only individual statistics and formal remarks are given.

Some particles appear in the NT once only; these consist mostly of classicisms of Lk and Heb: δήπου H 2: 16, δήποτε Jn 5: 4 (ᾧ δήποτε C³EF al., οἱῳδηποτοῦν A, ὑοδήποτε L; SBC*DW omit the verse), ἐπειδήπερ Lk 1: 1, ἐπείπερ R 3: 30 S°D*°EF al., εἶ μήν H 6: 14 OT (§ 24; the only illustration for μήν), ἤπερ Jn 12: 43 ABD, νή 1 C 15: 31 (solemn asseveration), ὁπότε Lk 6: 3 (§ 105), οὐκοῦν Jn 18: 37. Cf. also ἡνίκα § 105. Hermas also has καὶ μήν (Barn also; § 450(4)) as well as γοῦν (= οὖν as also other later authors, s. Stephanus-Dindorf under γοῦν) Sim 8.8.2 (MPol 17. 2); Barnabas further πέρας γέ τοι 10.2 and frequently; Homil Clem 17.18.5 πέρας γοῦν 'finally'.— -περ appears in the NT as in Att. only in compound form: διόπερ, εἴπερ, ἐάνπερ, ἐπειδήπερ, ἐπείπερ, ἤπερ, καθάπερ, καίπερ, ὅσπερ (§ 64(3)), ὥσπερ (ὡσπερεί). Cf. Mayser II 3, 153 f. -τοι only in ἤτοι, καίτοι, μέντοι, τοίνυν, yet according to Theodoret R 4: 16 reads διά τοι τοῦτο. Τοιγαροῦν (not with the enclitic -τοι, therefore not postpositive).—The following Att. particles have no place in the NT: ἀτάρ, ἆτε, αὖ, γοῦν, δῆθεν, δῆτα, εἴθε, μά, μήτοι, μῶν, νυν, ὁπόταν (§ 381), (οὔκουν,) οὔτι, οὔτοι, τέως.—**Interchange of ἄν and ἐάν**: ἐάν, not ἤν or ἄν, is the Hell. form for 'if' (uncontracted like ἑαυτοῦ σεαυτοῦ; but MGr ἄν 'if'); ἄν is found, however, now and then in NT MSS, thus Jn 12: 32 B, 13: 20 (ἐάν DEFG al.), 16: 23 BC al., 20: 23 twice (ἐάν AD, once S*), A 9: 2 SE. This is in accord with the strong inroads which ἐάν made on the province of ἄν, which could easily have produced uncertainty for the scribe. Ἐάν appears very frequently instead of ἄν after relatives in the NT, as in the LXX and pap. (Mayser I¹ 152 f.; II 1, 263 f., 265, 267; II 3, 58 f.; the highpoint is in the i/ii AD: Thack. 67), perhaps in order to underline the conditional aspect. Ἐάν for ἄν, e.g. Mt 5: 19 ὃς ἐάν (ἐάν om. D*, ἄν Dᶜ; shortly thereafter ὃς δ' ἄν), 8: 19 ὅπου ἐάν, 10: 14 ὃς ἐάν CEF al. (ἄν SBDKLW), 42 ὃς ἐάν (ἄν BD), 11: 27 ᾧ ἐάν (ἄν D), A 7: 7 OT ᾧ ἐάν (ἄν BD), also e.g. ὅστις ἐάν G 5: 10, ἥτις ἐάν A 3: 23, but always ἕως ἄν (Gregory 96; cf. pap. and LXX, Mayser I¹ 153; II 1, 269; Thack. 65). Ἄχρι οὗ ἄν s. § 383(2); Barale, Didaskaleion 2 [1913] 443); John only ὃ ἐάν 15: 7 (ἄν B), 1 Jn 3: 22 (ἄν B), 3 Jn 5. Cf. Mlt. 42 f., 234 [62 f.] and on the very strongly vacillating orthography of the NT MSS, v. Soden 1385 f. Xen., Mem. 3.10.12 ᾧ ἐάν, Lysias 24.18 οὓς ἐάν, Arist., Ath. 30.2 (pap.) οἳ ἐάν. Langdon, AJPh 24 (1903) 447–51; Witkowski, Bericht 240 f.; Barale, op. cit. 439 ff.; on ἄν in Lk and Jn, Pernot, Études 168 f.

5. WORD-FORMATION

M.-H. 268–410; Rob. 143–76; for the papyri Mayser I² 3; Chantraine; Schwyzer I 425–544, 672–737; L. R. Palmer, A Grammar of Post-Ptolemaic Papyri. Vol. I. Accidence and Word Formation, Part I. The Suffixes [London, 1946] (too schematic and therefore not very helpful). Cf. the list in Bauer pp. xii ff.

(1) WORD-FORMATION BY SUFFIXES

Only some types of stem-formation which were productive in Koine or otherwise noteworthy will be included here; the list is representative rather than exhaustive.

(A) Verbs

108. (1) Factitives are formed with **-οῦν**, mostly from o-stems. (2) Derivatives of compounds are preferably formed with **-εῖν**, s. §§115(1); 119(1); 120(4); cf. §123(2). (3) Verbs in a variety of senses with **-ίζειν**, especially from neuters in -μα (thus -ματίζειν) and in the sense of 'to act like' and the like ('imitatives', M.-H. 409); -άζειν appears after ι where -ίζειν is expected. (4) Intransitives are formed in **-άζειν** from adjectives in -ος. (5) Most verbs with the meaning 'to follow an occupation (professionally), to be something (of vocation)' are formed in **-εύειν** from the most diverse stems (originally from nouns in -εύς). (6) Less frequently in **-ύνειν**.

(1) Ἀνακαινοῦν (class. -ίζειν). Ἀναστατοῦν. Ἀποδεκατοῦν (earlier δεκατεύειν) from ἡ δεκάτη. Δολιοῦν 'to deceive' R 3: 13 OT (from δόλιος). Θεμελιοῦν. Κραταιοῦν from κραταιός and accordingly the synonyms σθενοῦν (1 P 5: 10) from τὸ σθένος and (ἐν-)δυναμοῦν from δύναμις. Νεκροῦν. Σαροῦν (class. σαίρειν) from σάρος, cf. Lob. Phryn. 83. Χαριτοῦν from χαριτ-. Ἀφυπνοῦν intr. 'to fall asleep'; -ίζειν class. 'to awake', -οῦν and ἐξυπνίζειν are equivalent in Hell.; old forms for 'to fall asleep, sleep' ὑπνοῦν καθυπνοῦν, cf. ὑπνοῦν pap., ἐπικαθυπνοῦν Barn 4.13. Κεφαλαιοῦν Mk 12: 4 (ἐκεφαλίωσαν is the superior reading, SBL; κεφαλεώσαντες W) is usually taken to mean 'to strike on the head, treat brutally (with reference to the head)', but as such is entirely unattested (Lob. Phryn. 95); or is this a vernacular κεφαλιοῦν 'to behead, decapitate' (from κεφάλιον)?

(2) Δυνατεῖν (Paul) is a back-formation from the older ἀδυνατεῖν. On ἐξουθενεῖν and the newer ἐξουδενοῦν as in the LXX, s. §33; Mayser I² 2, 117 wants to distinguish between ἐξουδενεῖν 'to annul' and

-νοῦν 'to deem insignificant'. Ἐξουδενίζειν (-ουθ-) Plut., Jos., et al. (L.-S.).

(3) Ἀγιάζειν from ἅγιος, old form ἁγίζειν. Αἰχμαλωτίζειν. Ἀνεμίζειν, old form -μοῦν. Ἐνταφιάζειν from τὰ ἐντάφια or ἐντάφιος. Εὐαγγελίζεσθαι §119(1). Θεατρίζειν, μυκτηρίζειν, ὀρθρίζειν, πελεκίζειν. Σινιάζειν from σινίον 'sieve', also a late word; Att. διαττᾶν, later σήθειν. Σκανδαλίζειν (LXX). (Δια-)σκορπίζειν is old Ion.: Phryn. 218. Σμυρνίζειν. Σπλαγχνίζεσθαι from σπλάγχνα = Hebr. רַחֲמִים 'entrails, compassion'. Συμμορφίζειν from σύμμορφος. Φυλακίζειν from φυλακή 'prison'. Φωτίζειν. -ματίζειν: ἀναθεματίζειν (Deissmann, LO⁴ 74 [LAE 95f.]), δειγματίζειν, δογματίζειν, ἱματίζειν besides ἱματισμός, καυματίζειν. Imitatives: ἰουδαΐζειν, νηπιάζειν (Hippoc.), similarly κρυσταλλίζειν Rev 21: 11 'to look like crystal, to glisten'. Συνετίζειν Herm Man 4.2.1, Diogn 12.9 (and LXX) 'cause to understand' from συνετός like σοφίζειν 2 T 3: 15 (and LXX) from σοφός. Ἱματίζειν in pap. as early as iii BC (Mayser I² 3, 145; Deissmann, LO⁴ 65 [LAE 82f.]), from Ion. εἶμα, but with the ι of the Att. ἱμάτιον; ἱματισμός in the pap. beginning with iii BC (Mayser I² 3, 62; εἱμ- as early as PEleph 1.4 [311/10 BC]), inscrip. (Schlageter, Wortschatz 71), Polyb.

(4) Στυγνάζειν from στυγνός, πυρράζειν (in the spurious passage Mt 16: 2, 3) from πυρρός (μονάζειν Barn 4.10, Herm Sim 9.26.3 from μόνος); ἡσυχάζειν is older (also in the NT) from ἥσυχος; cf. Rutherford, New Phryn. 284.

(5) (Ἐξ-)ὀλεθρεύειν (LXX often); παγιδεύειν from παγιδ-. Γυμνιτεύειν (§24) 'to be naked' from *γυμνίτης, μεσιτεύειν 'to perform the office of mediator' (Polyb.) from μεσίτης and also ἱερατεύειν belong to a group originating with βασιλεύειν etc. (from -εύς) and κυριεύειν (from -ος): following a similar pattern ἐγκρατεύεσθαι (Arist.) 'to conduct oneself like an ἐγκρατής' (cf. class. εἰρωνεύεσθαι) and in a similar fashion περπερεύεσθαι 1 C 13: 4, παραβολεύεσθαι Ph 2: 30 (otherwise in an inscrip. from Olbia [probably ii AD, Deissmann, LO⁴ 68f. (LAE 88)]) and several times in Ps.-Callisth. 'to prove dauntless (παράβολος), expose oneself to danger', ἀναιδεύεσθαι Herm Vis 3.7.5 from ἀναιδής, ἀκριβεύεσθαι Barn 2.10 from ἀκριβής. Αἰχμαλωτεύειν (LXX, Aristeas, Diodor. Sic.; most likely a formation analogous to φυγαδεύειν) only 2 T 3: 6 as v.l. to -τίζειν; LXX more often -τεύειν; Hell. generally -τίζειν (Passow-Crönert s.v.).

(6) Σκληρύνειν (LXX often) following τραχύνειν (from τραχύς).

(B) Substantives

109. Verbal substantives. (1) Nouns expressing action are formed with **-μός**; new formations

are drawn largely from verbs in -ίζειν and -άζειν.
(2) Derivatives in **-μα**, exceedingly popular in Koine as in Ionic and arising from all sorts of verbs, specify the result of the action for the most part; (3) where the final stem vowel preceding the suffixes -σις and -της (-τος) is short, Koine extends the short stem vowel to the corresponding formations in -μα. (4) Abstracts are formed with **-σις**, but hardly ever except from vowel-stems, while -σμός is preferred for stems in -ζειν. (5) The abstract in **-εία** is formed from -εύειν. Less frequent formations are: (6) **-μονή** (arising in the first place from nouns in -μων) and (7) **-ή** in compound nouns denoting action in which the first member is nominal. (8) New *nomina agentis* retain **-της**, while -τηρ or -τωρ are no longer used; for which the feminine is **-τρια** (Attic), not -τρίς or -τειρα. (9) Place (where something happens) is designated by **-τήριον** (actually a further development from -τηρ).

(1) From -ίζειν -άζειν: ἁγιασμός, βαπτισμός, ἐνταφιασμός, ὀνειδισμός, παροργισμός, πειρασμός, ῥαντισμός, σαββατισμός (σαββατίζειν LXX), σωφρονισμός. Otherwise only ἀπελεγμός from ἀπελέγχειν, ἁρπαγμός from ἁρπάζειν, Hermas συμφυρμός Vis 2.2.2 S, πλατυσμός Man 5.2.3 (1 Clem 3.1).

(2) Ἀγνόημα 'unwitting sin', αἰτίωμα A 25: 7 (and PFay 111.8 [95/6 AD]; a striking substitute for the old form αἰτίαμα 'accusation', cf. however αἰτίωσις Eustathius, Odyss. p. 1422.21), ἀνταπόδομα (old form -σις), ἄντλημα 'object for drawing water' (otherwise ἀντλητήρ and -τήριον), ἀπαύγασμα, ἀποσκίασμα, βάπτισμα (βαπτισμός is never used of the baptism of John, of Christian baptism only C: 2 12 𝔓⁴⁶SᶜBD*FG; H 6: 2 is a different matter; -σμός expresses the act of immersion, while -σμα includes the result; Jos., Ant. 18.117 admittedly uses βαπτισμός of the baptism of John), ἐξέραμα, ἥττημα, θέλημα, ἱεράτευμα (-τεύειν § 108(5)), κατάλυμα (Hell. for καταγωγεῖον; the primary meaning may well be 'unyoke, rest', then the derived meaning 'place of unyoking, rest' i.e. 'lodge'), κατόρθωμα (Polyb.), πρόσκομμα. Hermas ματαιώματα 'vanities' Man 9.4; μέθυσμα '(an intoxicating) drink' 6.2.5, 8.3, 12.2.1, also Philo; cf. ἔδεσμα (Herm Man 6.2.5 with μέθυσμα in the same context). In Rev μεσουράνημα 'zenith' is noteworthy, from μεσουρανεῖν 'to be at the zenith' (Arist.), *μεσούρανος.

(3) Δόμα (ἀνταπόδομα) following δόσις δοτήρ δότης δοτός; θέμα (only IPol 2.3; as early as old Dor.) following θέσις θετός, hence also ἀνάθεμα (also with the meaning 'a votive offering' Lk 21: 5 SADWX [B al. -θήμασιν]) instead of Att. ἀνάθημα (cf. Moeris 188.30); πόμα (as early as Pindar) for πῶμα; κλίμα κρίμα s. § 13. Even διάστεμα A 5: 7 D (from stem

στᾰ- !); cf. ἀνά- διά- κατά- σύ- ὑπό-στεμα in MSS of the LXX (Thack. 80); but κατάστημα T 2: 3. Ὀφ(ε)ίλεμα Mt 6: 12 D, R 4: 4 D*, εὕρεμα Homil Clem 8.14. Reinhold 41; Mayser I¹ 65, I² 3, 57; Specht, KZ 59 (1932) 50f.; A. Strohschein, Auffälligkeiten griechischer Vokal- und Diphthongschreibung in vorchristlicher Zeit (Diss. Greifswald, 1940; Berlin, 1941) 114.

(4) Βίωσις, ἐπιπόθησις, θέλησις H 2: 4 (otherwise -μα), κατάνυξις R 11: 8 OT (from κατανύσσειν 'to stun' A 2: 37, LXX, Theod. Dan 10: 9; Fritzsche, Paul. ad Rom. II 558ff.), πεποίθησις (§ 68), πρόσκλισις (Polyb.), πρόσχυσις; ἁμάρτησις Herm Vis 2.2.5.

(5) Ἀρεσκεία (as early as Theophr.; from ἄρεσκος ἀρεσκεύεσθαι), ἐριθεία (Arist.), ἱερατεία (-εύειν § 108 (5), μεθοδεία (§ 23). However, ἐπιποθία R 15: 23 (it does not appear otherwise) may well be from ἐπιποθεῖν following the analogy ἐπιθυμεῖν–ἐπιθυμία. Cf. § 23.

(6) Πλησμονή (old), πεισμονή 'obedience' G 5: 8 from πείθειν (§ 488(1b)), ἐπιλησμονή 'forgetfulness' Ja 1: 25 (and LXX Sir 11: 27) from ἐπιλήσμων.

(7) Οἰκοδομή 'edification, building' (Dor. [Tab. Heracl. I 146, 150] and Hell.; Lietzmann, Hdb. on 1 C 3: 9; Schmidt 528f.; Mayser I² 3, 19) instead of -μία or -μησις (Lob. Phryn. 490) following δομή (from δέμειν)? Cf. παρασκευή (NT also) from -άζειν following σκευή, and Att. μισθοφορά instead of -ία (from -φόρος) following φορά. Προσευχή virtually limited to Jewish-Christian sources (but IG IV² 1.106 I 27 [Epidaurus] iv BC προσευχά).

(8) Βαπτιστής, βιαστής, γογγυστής, δανειστής, διώκτης, δότης (old form δοτήρ), ἑλληνιστής ('one who speaks or lives like a Greek', scil. Jew; from ἑλληνίζειν 'to speak Greek'; cf. ἰουδαΐζειν § 108(3)), ἐξορκιστής, εὐαγγελιστής, κολλυβιστής, λυτρωτής, μεριστής, προσκυνητής, στασιαστής; these words, as e.g. Mt 11: 12 (βιάζεται–βιασταί), Jn 4: 20ff. (προσκυνεῖν–προσκυνηταί) show, were formed with almost the same facility as verbal forms. With ἐπενδύτης 'outer garment' Jn 21: 7 (as early as Soph.) cf. 'overcoat' and words like ζωστήρ 'belt'. Σωτήρ, ῥήτωρ, πράκτωρ, ἀλέκτωρ ('cock', properly 'fighter') are old forms. Feminines in -τρια: μαθήτρια A 9: 39; cf. Hatzidakis 179; Psaltes 269f.; Mayser I² 3, 83. Lat. -*tōr* -*tōris* are assimilated to -τωρ -τορος: σπεκουλάτορα Mk 6: 27, δεσέρτωρ IPol 6.2.—On the whole s. Fraenkel.

(9) Ἀκροατήριον and ἱλαστήριον; σωτήριον (§ 113(1)) and ποτήριον are different.

110. Abstract substantives from adjectives (and substantives).
(1) **-ότης** (Lob. Phryn. 350) is common in the later period for formations from adjectives and substantives of the second declension. (2) **-σύνη** is used to form a few qualitative abstracts as is **-ία**, the latter less frequently.

(1) From adj.: ἁγιότης, ἁγνότης (besides the earlier form ἁγνεία from -εύειν), ἀδηλότης, γυμνότης, ματαιότης, μεγαλειότης. From subst.: θεότης (Lucian and Plut.), ἀδελφότης (1 and 4 Macc, Dio Chrys., pap.; s. Warning 48) concrete-collective 'brotherhood' 1 P 2: 17, 5: 9 (1 Clem 2.4, abstract Herm Man 8.10), κυριότης likewise 'domination' (a type of angel; as abstract Herm Sim 5.6.1). Ἀφελότης A 2: 46, Dio Chrys., Vett. Val. (otherwise ἀφέλεια) from the adj. ἀφελής 'simple, plain' following ματαιότης μεγαλειότης which are related in meaning. Θεμελιότητα H 6: 1 𝔓⁴⁶ for τελειότητα is false assimilation to θεμέλιον in the same verse.

(2) -σύνη is especially common earlier with adjs. in -(μ)ων, thus NT ἀσχημοσύνη, ἐλεημοσύνη (as early as Callim.; in the NT mostly in the concrete sense 'alms'), σωφροσύνη (Att.); instead of μνημοσύνη Ion.-Hell. μνημόσυνον. From -ος: δικαιοσύνη, ἀκεραιοσύνη Barn 3.6, 10.4; with lengthening of -ο following a short vowel: ἀγαθωσύνη, ἁγιωσύνη, μεγαλωσύνη; the model ἱερωσύνη (§31(2)) is old. In -ία: ἐλαφρία 2 C 1: 17, παραφρονία 2 P 2: 16 (from παράφρων, -φρονεῖν, cf. εὐδαιμονία); ὀρκωμοσία and the like s. §119(3). The scribe of W almost always writes δικαιωσύνη in Mt (Sanders, Wash. 21). Μνημόσυνον also in Enoch 97.7, 99.3, 103.4 (Bonner).—The old suffix -ειᾰ from adjs. in -ής is well preserved: ἀλήθεια, ἀκρίβεια, ὠφέλεια etc.; cf. §23. Συγγένεια is concrete, 'the relatives'.—Δοκιμή (seldom in Hell., s. Grundmann in TW II 259.4 ff.) 'testing, trial', not from δόκιμος, but a back-formation from δοκιμάζειν 'to put to the test'.

111. Substantives from substantives.

(1) Originating from masculines in -ιξ is the feminine form **-ισσα** (Γαλάτισσα from Γαλάται, βαλάνισσα from βαλανεύς etc. following Φοῖνιξ–Φοίνισσα, Κίλιξ–Κίλισσα etc.), which, as a general feminine form (very common in MGr; Thumb² §40(1)), spread out from Macedonia in the Hellenistic period (Witkowski, Bericht 26; Fraenkel, IF 32 [1913] 403; Buck, Class. Phil. 9 [1914] 370 ff.) with non-Attic orthography (§34(1)). (2) Names from Semitic stems are readily formed with **-ίτης**, feminine **-ῖτις**; the Hebrew gentilic suffix, ‎יִ‎, fem. ‎יִּית‎, was normative for the choice of -ίτης: Ἰσραηλίτης=‎יִשְׂרְאֵלִי‎. On the suffix, originally Latin, -ιανός s. §5(2). (3) Diminutives are not frequent in the NT because they are not suited to a language even slightly elevated. However, the NT, especially Mark (Turner, JTS 29 [1928] 346 ff.), has some especially popular diminutives denoting parts of the body and names of animals. D. C. Swanson, 'Diminutives in the Greek New Testament', JBL 77 (1958) 134–51: diminutives in -ισκο- appear first in elegiac and lyric poetry of

vi BC, forms in -ίς and -ιον in v BC; the use of diminutives comes to full flower in Attic comedy (p. 134; cf. Debrunner 147 f.). There is a statistical increase of diminutives in Koine (p. 134); the NT has more diminutives than comparable contemporary texts (pp. 150 f.). Mk exhibits the greatest frequency, but Mt and Lk have the greatest number of different words (the table p. 142 and figures p. 143 and n. 23 do not agree with the list pp. 137 ff.). Cf. W. Petersen, Greek Diminutives in -ιον (Weimar, 1910); M.-H. 344–6, 375, 380. The suffixes are mainly -ιον and -άριον. (4) Koine also has a preference for **-ιον** with non-diminutives from compounds (juristic expressions) (Lob. Phryn. 519; cf. Attic, e.g. λιποταξίου δίκη). (5) **-εῖον** and (6) **-ών** are rare. (7) **-ιά** from substantives, mostly collectives: ἀνθρακιά, θημωνιά (s. §158), λαλιά (TW IV 4.10 ff., 76.11 ff.), νοσσιά, πατριά (TW V 1017.25 ff.), πρασιά, τροχιά, τρυμαλιά. Chantraine, Form. des noms 82; Schwyzer I 469.5.

(1) Βασίλισσα (Att. inscrip. beg. 307 BC; cf. Mayser I² 2, 9; opposed by Phryn. 225), Συροφοινίκισσα (developed with -ισσα by Lucian from Συροφοῖνιξ) Mk 7: 26 (v.l. [W also] Συραφ-, i.e. Σύρα Φ.; D Φοίνισσα, lat Συροφοίνισσα; Φοίνισσα Herodian 1.268.24, 2.708.10, but Φοινίκισσα 2.455.19). Feminines in -ις from masc.: Ἑβραΐς, Ἑλληνίς (also Rev 9: 11 S); προφῆτις, προστάτις, πρεσβῦτις from -της; -ῖτις s. infra 2, -πωλις §119(2), συγγενίς §59(3); more loosely μοιχαλίς from μοῖχος.

(2) Αἰλαμῖται A 2: 9 (§38), Ἰσραηλίτης, Λευίτης, Νινευίτης, Σαμαρίτης and -ῖτις (§38), and the purely Greek Τραχωνῖτις Lk 3: 1. However, -αῖος sometimes represents Hebr. ‎יִ‎ (cf. Ἀθηναῖος, Θηβαῖος): Ἰουδαῖος ‎יְהוּדִי‎, Ἑβραῖος ‎עִבְרִי‎; perhaps the Aram. ‎יְהוּדִי‎ has been decisive (so J. A. Fitzmyer). Γαλιλαῖος may be loosely classified here (without a Semitic base in either ‎יִ‎ or ‎יִ‎).—With -έτης: συμφυλέτης 1 Th 2: 14 (IG XII 2.505.18 [ii BC], Hell.; Fraenkel II 125 n. 4), 'tribesman' from Att. φυλέτης.

(3) Names of animals, for the most part in the nature of 'hypocoristica' (s. M.-H. 344, n. 1): ἰχθύδιον Mt 15: 34 = Mk 8: 7, Barn 10.5; κυνάριον (Phryn. 180) Mt 15: 26, 27 = Mk 7: 27, 28 (κύνες are stray dogs Lk 16: 21; cf. 2 P 2: 22 OT, and designates profane men Mt 7: 6 etc.); ὀνάριον Jn 12: 14, otherwise ὄνος; προβάτιον Jn 21: 16 f.; στρουθίον. Ἀρνίον often (§47(4)). Designations for parts of the body: ὠτίον (Gospels, Moeris 205.25 as Hell.) and ὠτάριον (Mk 14: 47 SBC, Jn 18: 10 SBC*LWX; beg. w. middle comedy: Schlageter, Wortschatz 86) for 'ear lobes', while οὖς (besides ἀκοή) is used of the organ of hearing; Lk 22: 50 Atticizes when the author uses οὖς for a part of the body (ὠτίον DK and 51 ὠτίον

all MSS). In *v.* 50 οὖς in a simple asseveration, in 51 ὠτίον is emotionally charged: Niedermann, Gnomon 3 (1927) 353 with a Latin parallel. Οὖς was abandoned because of irregular inflection (Meillet, Bull. Soc. Ling. 32, 3 [1931] 102). For other reasons for change of vocabulary s. § 126. Perhaps the following come from 'nursery talk': ῥαβδίον Herm Sim 8.2.9; the names for various dishes: ὀψάριον 'fish (as a food)' Jn 6: 9, 11, 21: 9, 10, 13 (MGr ψάρι; likewise ἰχθύδιον Mt 15: 34 = Mk 8: 7), while John uses ἰχθῦς for fish as a living animal; ψιχίον Mt 15: 27 = Mk 7: 28 [Lk 16: 21] 'bread-crumbs' (NT only; from ψίξ), ψωμίον Jn 13 (W. Bauer, Hdb. on Jn 13: 26, MGr ψωμί 'bread'); further perhaps also πλοιάριον (Mk, Jn, but also already in Aristoph.) and κλινίδιον Lk 5: 19, 24 (κλινάριον A 5: 15 SABCD, v.l. κλινῶν; Lob. Phryn. 180). The following esp. common words belong together: παιδίον, παιδάριον, παιδίσκη, θυγάτριον, τεκνίον; to which add γυναικάριον (derogatory) 2 T 3: 6 and κοράσιον Mt, Mk. There remain only πτερύγιον Mt 4: 5 = Lk 4: 9 and βιβλαρίδιον Rev 10: 2, 8, 9, 10, Herm Vis 2.1.3 (v.l. in every instance βιβλιδάριον [Aristoph., cf. λιθαρίδιον in later authors and Swanson's remark, *op. cit.* p. 145], Rev 10 v.l. βιβλίον in every case; 10: 10 βιβλίδιον 𝔓⁴⁷) from a combination (conglutinate) of -άριον and -ίδιον (Crönert 293) (βιβλαρίδιον NT only). Swanson, *op. cit.* 137ff. gives a definitive list of diminutives in the NT which supplements the above list. In -ιον: ἐρίφιον, κεράτιον, νησίον, νοσσίον, σχοινίον; in -άριον: κλινάριον; in -ίδιον: πινακίδιον (v.l. only); in -ίσκος, -ίσκη: βασιλίσκος (v.l. only), νεανίσκος; in -ίς (-ίδ-): θυρίς, κεφαλίς, πινακίς (v.l. only). He appends a list of non-diminutives in -ιον and -ίς. On the possibility of Semitic influence on the diminutives s. Schulthess, ZNW 21 (1922) 222 n.—For diminutives for parts of the body cf. Lob. Phryn. 211f., MGr μάτι 'eye' from ὀμμάτιον, αὐτί (ὠτίν) 'ear', also σωμάτιον Homil Clem 5.1 (Hell.). Κοράσιον acc. to Kretschmer 18 is Doric, acc. to Solmsen, RhM 59 (1904) 503f. it is Northwest Greek; it was rejected by the Atticists (for which ἡ παῖς Lk 8: 54 is substituted). The ᾱ in κοράσια Anth. Pal. ix 39.1 may be a purely metrical lengthening.—Δηνάριον and ἀσσάριον (§5(1c)) from Lat. *denarius* and *assarius* scil. *nummus* (the ending is dependent on Greek diminutives), therefore with ᾱ; ἀσσάριον scil. νόμισμα = *assarius* scil. *nummus*: Thes. ling. Lat. ii 848.27. Cf. Herodian 2.13.23; W. Schulze, Graeca Latina 19 (who quotes an epigram on stone for δηνάριον; but Nonnus ᾰ); Schwyzer, IF 49 (1931) 25 n.

(4) Ἀποστάσιον Mt, Mk (Dem.; pap. s. Mayser I² 3, 51.34; Mitteis, Gr. 167ff.), γεώργιον 1 C 3: 9 (from γεωργός), ὀψώνιον (pap., Polyb. etc.; Thieme 31; Mayser I² 3, 52.1), Lk 3: 14 and Paul (from ὀψώνης), παραμύθιον Ph 2: 1 (Soph., Thuc. etc.; remodeled from -θία?), σιτομέτριον Lk 21: 42 (from σιτομέτρης), συμβούλιον Mt, Mk, Acts (from σύμβουλος),

τελώνιον (§ 13) Mt 9: 9 and par. (from τελώνης). Cf. also γαζοφυλάκιον § 13, εὐαγγέλιον § 119(1). These formations in -ιον, and many others, date from a period in which -ιον was not yet used in a diminutive sense (Debrunner 147 n. 2).

(5) -εῖον (MGr -ειό) is predominantly locative (Palmer 5, 12, 58), denoting a craftsman's premises or shop (χαλκεῖον, καπηλεῖον), or the shrine or sanctuary of a god (Μουσεῖον). Originally from stems in -εσ- and -ηϝ-, the suffix was extended by analogy to other types already in the class. period (Debrunner 144, 146). Hell. prefers -εῖον at the expense of earlier -ιον (e.g. Ἀπολλώνιον) and even -ι-εῖον far beyond legitimate instances such as Ἀσκληπι-εῖον. Accents differ: Θησεῖον, Ἡράκλειον (or -εῖον L.-S. s.v.). Εἰδωλεῖον 'idol's temple' (§ 13; -ιον [if not itacistic] would mean 'little idol') LXX Da 1: 2, Bel 10 and should be restored in 1 Esdr 2:9, 1 Macc 1: 47, 10: 38. From LXX cf. also Βηλ(ε)ῖον, Νανα(ε)ῖον, Ἀσταρτιεῖον, Ἀτεργατιεῖον. Some kindred expressions are based on the place or purpose of the room: εὐχεῖον PLond iii 1177.60 (113 AD) (M.-H. 344), συναγωγ(ε)ῖον = -ή Philo, Somn. 2. 127 (iii 279.6), Leg. ad Gaium 311 (vi 212.19), σαββατεῖον in an imperial decree in Jos., Ant. 16.164 whose pagan author may however have thought of Σαβάζιος. Mayser i 92; Katz, ThLZ 61 (1936) 283 and 1957, 111, TZ 5 (1949) 5 n. 6 = Recovery 186 n. 3; M.-H. 344; Palmer 56ff., 79f. Cf. Lob. Phryn. 367–72 (to be used with circumspection).

(6) Ἀφεδρών 'latrine' Mt 15: 17 = Mk 7: 19 (D softens in Mk to εἰς τὸν ὀχετόν 'through the intestinal canal' [Wellhausen takes it differently, *ad loc.*]), cf. κοπρῶν περιστερεῶν etc. (Fischer, Vitia lexicorum NT 698ff.). S. § 143 for ἐλαιών.

(C) Adjectives

112. From verbs. Many compounds (§117) occur in -τος (verbal adjectives), otherwise rarely. In -ωλός only ἁμαρτωλός Arist., Eth. Nic. 2.9, 1109 a33, LXX, NT, inscriptions (Deissmann, LO⁴ 91f. [LAE 113ff.]; Rengstorf, TW i 321f.), which may well have arisen from the substantive ἁμαρτωλή (Theognis, Rhianus); cf. φειδωλός (beg. w. Hesiod) from φειδωλή (Homer). Πειθός (like φειδός Callim., Frag. 460, Eustathius from φείδεσθαι) would have been formed from the present stem without suffix, if πειθοῖς 1 C 2: 4 (only occurrence) were not a corruption of πειθοῖ (§47(4)); Zuntz 23–5. Simple verbal adjectives: (passive) possibility only παθητός (§65(3)); = perfect passive participle: σιτιστός 'fattened' Mt 22: 4, γραπτός 'written' R 2: 15, and originally also ἀγαπητός etc. (§65(3)) and most of the compounds.

113. From nouns (and participles). (1) With -ιος: σωτήριος is old, from which τὸ σωτήριον was formed; likewise ἡ ζευκτηρία A 27: 40 (here only, ζευκτήριος is old). From the LXX λαὸς περιούσιος (TW VI 57f.) T 2: 14 = ὅς περίεστιν, ὃν ὁ θεὸς περιεποιήσατο ἑαυτῷ. Ἐπικούρειος > Latin *Epicureus* > German *Epikureer* (not -äer) and English Epicurean, Debrunner §285. On ἐπιούσιος s. §123(1). (2) With -ικός (after nouns in -ι- -ακός): πιστικός, κεραμικός, σαρκικός, κυριακός. (3) With -ινός adjectives of time (as in classical μεσημβρινός; very popular later, Psaltes 295f.): ὀρθρινός, πρωϊνός (not before Theophr. [Hindenlang 145]; πρώιος πρῷος are old forms), καθημερινός, ταχινός 'quick' (from τάχα ταχέως) 2 P 1: 14, 2: 1 (Herm 3 times).

(1) Σωτήριον in the LXX = 'thank offering' and as in the NT = 'salvation'. Λαὸς περιούσιος = עַם סְגֻלָּה lit. 'people of possession' i.e. 'belonging to Yahweh'; cf. Jerome in Tdf. *ad loc.* and Bauer.

(2) Σαρκικός 'belonging to σάρξ, of the nature of σάρξ' (in contrast to πνευματικός) is sometimes confused with σάρκινος in the MSS, 2 C 3: 3 'made of flesh' (like λίθινος ὀστράκινος [both in NT]): R 15: 27, 1 C 3: 4 ScLP (al. ἄνθρωποι), 9: 11, 2 C 1: 12 (FG -ίνη), 10: 4, 1 P 2: 11, 1 C 3: 3 S al. twice (D*FG both times -ινοι; 𝔓46 -ικοί and -ινοι once each); in similar passages, R 7: 14, 1 C 3: 1, H 7: 16, the best textual tradition favors -ινος, but the sense, because the contrast is with πνευματικός, favors -ικός. Κυριακός (with ἡμέρα Rev 1: 10, with δεῖπνον 1 C 11: 20; inscrip. and pap. from 68 AD on, s. Deissmann, LO⁴ 304 [LAE 357f.]). Πιστικός Mk 14: 3 and Jn 12: 3 (νάρδου πιστικῆς) may well mean 'genuine' and be derived from πιστός or πίστις, but it could also be an εἶδος νάρδου οὕτω λεγόμενον (Theophylact.); cf. Bauer. Σκεύη κεραμικά (v.l. -μεικά) Rev 2: 27, i.e. 'the vessels of the potter' (κεραμεικός from κεραμεύς) or more naturally 'earthen' (then κεραμικός is from κέραμος; for κεραμεοῦς Lob. Phryn. 146.

(3) Ὀρθινός Lk 24: 22 (ὄρθριαι K²P al. is an Atticistic correction; Phryn. 51), Herm Sim 5.1.1; καθημερινός 'daily' A 6: 1, Herm Vis 1.3.2 (< καθ' ἡμέραν or a remodeling of καθήμερος καθημέριος; cf. class. μεθημερινός νυκτερινός). The quantity of -ι- fluctuates in the Hell. poets; elsewhere, however, it is short in this suffix, and cod. B writes -ινος, not -εινος (§23).

(2) WORD-FORMATION BY COMPOSITION

114. Introduction. Compounds are in rather wide use in the NT; they served from the earliest times in more elevated styles as adornments of speech, but they are by no means lacking even in the simplest style. It is not proposed in the following sections to treat the subject either exhaustively or in logically flawless categories; those categories and individual cases which merit special attention are to be presented by a method of classification in which, for practical reasons, the formal and the logical principles are mixed.

The frequency of compounds in the NT may be illustrated by an enumeration of all the more striking compounds (together with their derivatives) in the short Epistle to Titus: ἀδόκιμος, αἰσχροκερδής, ἄκαρπος, ἀκατάγνωστος, ἄμαχος, ἀνέγκλητος, ἀνόητος, ἀνομία, ἀνυπότακτος, ἀνωφελής, ἀπειθής, ἀσωτία, αὐθάδης, αὐτοκατάκριτος, ἀφθορία, ἀψευδής, γενεαλογία, εὐάρεστος, ἱεροπρεπής, καλοδιδάσκαλος, ματαιολόγος, οἰκονόμος, οἰκουρ(γ)ός, παλιγγενεσία, πειθαρχεῖν, φιλάγαθος, φίλανδρος, φιλανθρωπία, φιλόξενος, φιλότεκνος, φρεναπάτης.

(A) Determinatives

The (unaltered) second element is more closely defined by means of the first.

115. A noun as the first element. (1) The simplest type is οἰκοδεσπότης. (2) The first element is seldom an adjectival stem (Schwyzer I 453): καλο-διδάσκαλος = καλὸς διδάσκαλος.

(1) Συροφοίνισσα (or -νίκισσα §111(1); Λιβυφοίνικες Polyb.); εὐρακύλων from εὖρος and *aquilo* (§5(1d)), cf. εὐρόνοτος 'south-east' Arist.; σαρδόνυξ Rev 21: 20 (σαρδιόνυξ A) from σάρδιος and ὄνυξ, likewise χρυσόλιθος. With the second element having verbal force (cf. §119): χρεοφειλέτης (or -ωφ- §35(2)) from χρέος and ὀφειλέτης; οἰκοδεσπότης (Gospels, -τεῖν 1 T 5: 14) is objected to by Phryn. 373. Νομοδιδάσκαλος, cf. the old word χοροδιδάσκαλος; ἑτεροδιδασκαλεῖν 1 T 1: 3, 6: 3, IPol 3.1 from ἑτεροδιδάσκαλος 'teacher of another (teaching)' Eus., therefore 'to teach a different doctrine'; πολυδιδάσκαλοι Ja 3: 1 following the emendation (L πολυ διδ., usually read πολλοὶ διδ. [οι for υ]; translated in old Lat. by *multiloqui*, therefore de Sande Bakhuizen πολύλαλοι; Völter, ZNW 10 [1909] 328f. conjectures ἐθελοδιδάσκαλοι [§118(2)]). Δεσμοφύλαξ A 16: 23, γαζοφυλάκιον Mk 12: 41 etc. (LXX) from -φύλαξ. In the case of ὀφθαλμο-δουλία E 6: 6, C 3: 22 (𝔓46B -εία incorrect in mistaken conformity with δουλεία; cf. -θρησκεία §118(2), -λατρεία §119(2)), ὀφθαλμόδουλος (for the first time in Constit. Apost.), the adj. may be a back-formation from the noun as an exception to the rule, in view of the late date of the Constit. Apost. and their dependence on the NT (F. W. Gingrich, JBL 52 [1933] 263).

(2) Καλοδιδάσκαλος T 2: 3, cf. κακοδιδασκαλεῖν

2 Clem 10.5, Hypothesis ι and χ in Aristoph., Nu. (ed. Bergk), -λία IPhld 2.1. Διδάσκαλος replaces the *nomen agentis* from διδάσκειν (Debrunner, TW II 151 n. 3). Cf. κακοικονόμος Philo (-μία pap., Mayser I² 3, 28), καλοσύμβουλος is late (Jannaris § 1133), further ἐλευθερολατόμος Mayser I² 3, 157, λευκόϊον Hippoc., Theoc. etc., ἀγαθοδαίμων Apollon. Dysc., further § 120(3) and names of birds like λευκερωδιός, φαλακροκόραξ (F. Robert, Les noms des oiseaux en grec ancien [Basel Diss., Neuchâtel, 1911] 86 f., 117). For δικαιοκρισία s. § 119(3). MGr λιανόβροχο 'drizzling rain', χοντρόβροχο 'heavy rain', καλόγρια ('good old woman') 'nun' (Thumb² § 41 *a*, 1 *b*).— Whether δευτερό-πρωτος (ἐν σαββάτῳ δευτεροπρώτῳ Lk 6: 1 ACDE etc., δευτ. om. SBLW) also belongs in this category is uncertain because the meaning of the word is not at all clear; cf. Tdf. *ad loc.* and the commentaries and lexica.—On ψευδ- s. § 119(5).— Νέα πόλις is not yet regarded as a compound because of Νέαν πόλιν A 16: 11 (doubly declined as in class.; but Νεάπολιν CD*EHLP, IPol 8.1); Ἱερᾷ Πόλει C 4: 13 is accordingly to be written divided. But cf. M.-H. 278; Risch, IF 59 (1949) 262 f.

116. A prepositional prefix as the first element.

(1) Koine has an fondness for composite verbs where the classical language was content with the simple forms. (2) Prepositions appear not only before verbal substantives and adjectives, but also, though far less often, before other substantives and adjectives: προσάββατον Mk 15: 42 and several compounds with συν-. (3) The later language, more than classical (Lob. Phryn. 45 ff.), forms compound adverbs (and improper prepositions) with prepositional prefixes. (4) Verbs (and verbal nouns) in Koine can be compounded with several prepositions as in the classical period.

(1) Cf. out of the large number ἐπερωτᾶν, ἀνατρέφεσθαι, ἀποκρύπτειν, ἀπαρνεῖσθαι, ἐπιδιδόναι, ἐπιζητεῖν, ἐπιστρέφειν (Gregory 126 f.). Winer wrote five occasional academic papers [Programme] De verborum cum praep. compositorum in NT usu 1834–43. M.-H. 293–328.

(2) Συστρατιώτης (class.), συμπρεσβύτερος, συγκληρονόμος. Adj.: περίπικρος 'very bitter' Herm Sim 6.2.5, ἀπόκενος 'quite vain, frivolous, completely empty' Man 5.2.1, 12.5.2 ff.

(3) Ὑπεράνω (LXX) E 1: 21, 4: 10, H 9: 5 (ἐπάνω ὑποκάτω are known in the earlier period), ἔκπαλαι 2 P 2: 3, 3: 5 (acc. to Phryn. 45 Att. ἐκ παλαιοῦ). Ὑπερεκπερισσοῦ E 3: 20, 1 Th 3: 10, 5: 13 SADᵇE al. from ὑπέρ and ἐκ περισσοῦ, besides ὑπερπερισσῶς Mk 7: 37 from ὑπέρ and περισσῶς, and accordingly remodeled ἐκπερισσῶς Mk 14: 31 SBCD (ἐκ περισσοῦ A) and ὑπερεκπερισσῶς Mk 7: 37 DU, 1 Th 5: 13 BD*FG, 1 Clem 20.11. Ὑπερλίαν 2 C 11: 5, 12: 11,

ὑπεράγαν 1 Clem 56.2 (ὑπὲρ μὲν ἄγαν Eur., Med. 627 [lyrical passage], ὑπεράγαν Aeschyl., Eur., 2 Macc 10: 34, 13: 25, Strabo 3.2.9, Aelian., NA 3.38 etc.; cf. ὑπέρφευ). Also ὑπερέκεινα 2 C 10: 16 is new (ἐπέκεινα is the old form [§ 141(2)] from ἐπ’ ἐκεῖνα; crasis rather than true composition).

(4) Special mention may be made of διαπαρατριβαί 1 T 6: 5 'constant disputations' from παρατριβή 'dispute' Polyb. Cf. A. Rieder, Die mit mehr als einer Präp. zusammengesetzten Verba (und überhaupt Wörter) des N(u.A)T, Programm Gumbinnen 1876.

117. A verbal adjective as the second element.

(1) The composition of verbal adjectives with certain particles (ἀ- privative, δυσ- with a similar meaning, εὐ- as the antithesis of both) was common in Greek in all periods. Ἀ- privative especially appears in Koine in numerous formations (stemming for the most part from compound verbs). (2) But nouns are also prefixed to verbal adjectives; these then designate the agent of the passive act: πατροπαράδοτος = ὑπὸ τῶν πατέρων παραδεδομένος.

(1) With ἀ- **privative**: as ἀναπολόγητος and ἀ(μετα)νόητος show, the meaning is not exclusively passive; cf. also the older ἄπταιστος Jd 24 and ἀσύνετος (NT several times); but ἀπείραστος Ja 1: 13 is probably pass., s. § 182(3). Ἀγενεαλόγητος, ἀδιάκριτος, ἀδιάλειπτος (pre-Christian, Nägeli 29), ἀδύνατος with ἀδυνατεῖν (both old), ἀκατάγνωστος, ἀκατακάλυπτος, ἀκατάκριτος, ἀκατάλυτος, ἀκατάπαυστος, ἀκατάστατος (old, -ασία NT, Polyb. *et al.*), ἀμετανόητος, ἀναπολόγητος, ἀνόητος (old), ἀνεξερεύνητος, ἀνεξιχνίαστος, etc. With δυσ-: δυσβάστακτος Lk 11: 46, δυσερμήνευτος H 5: 11, δυσνόητος 2 P 3: 16 (Herm Sim 9.14.4). With εὐ-: εὐάρεστος (as early as Xen.), εὐμετάδοτος 'generous' 1 T 6: 18, εὐπρόσδεκτος, εὐπερίστατος H 12: 1 (nowhere else; probably = ἡ ῥαδίως περιϊσταμένη 'easily surrounding, ensnaring'; 𝔓⁴⁶ εὐπερίσπαστον 'easily distracted, liable to distract' F. W. Beare, JBL 63 [1944] 390 f.; Zuntz 25–9); with an ordinary adj. (like class. ἄναγνος δύσαγνος etc.) εὐπάρεδρος 'constant' 1 C 7: 35, where admittedly there is more παρεδρεύειν present than πάρεδρος according to the sense.

(2) Πατροπαράδοτος 1 P 1: 18, σητόβρωτος Ja 5: 2, λιθόστρωτος (Soph.) Jn 19: 13, ποταμοφόρητος (from φορεῖν) Rev 12: 15 (-ητον ποιεῖν also Hesychius under ἀπόερσεν), θεοδίδακτος 1 Th 4: 9 (Barn 21.6), θεόπνευστος 2 T 3: 16. To these belong also the compounds with αὐτο-: αὐτοκατάκριτος T 3: 11 (αὐτόματος and αὐθαίρετος are old). The case of εἰδωλόθυτον 'sacrificed to (before) εἴδωλα' is different.—Προσήλυτος is peculiar (LXX also), containing a kind of ptcp. from ἔρχεσθαι; ἔπηλυς, ἐπηλύτης are old formations.

(B) Verbal dependent determinatives

One element is a verbal noun, to which the other stands in dependent relationship as to a verb (ἀρχέκακος, φερέοικος, δηξίθυμος). Many of these compounds undergo some mutation (cf. §120).

118. The first element 'governs' the second. Only the following types, developed strongly along particular lines, come under consideration for the NT: (1) ἰσο- in ἰσάγγελος Lk 20: 36 corresponds to a participle, in this case like 'being equal to' = ἴσος τοῖς ἀγγέλοις, formed on the old model ἰσόθεος. (2) With peculiar fluctuation between verbal and nominal function (cf. ψευδο- §119(5)): ἀρχι- (Hellenistic; older form ἀρχε-, cf. Mayser ι¹ 81 f.; ι² 3, 160 f.), ἐθελο- and φιλο-.

(1) Ἰσότιμος 2 P 1: 1, ἰσόψυχος Ph 2: 20 are different (like §120(1)).

(2) **Ἀρχι-**: ἀρχιερεύς (earlier form ἀρχιέρεως §44(1)), i.e. ὁ ἄρχων τῶν ἱερέων; this is clearly the case with ἀρχισυνάγωγος, ἀρχιτρίκλινος Jn 2: 8, 9, then in the sense of 'chief-': ἀρχάγγελος 1 Th 4: 16, Jd 9, ἀρχιποίμην 1 P 5: 4 (also elsewhere, s. Bauer; = ποιμὴν μέγας H 13: 20), ἀρχιτέκτων 1 C 3: 10, ἀρχιτελώνης Lk 19: 2. Ἀρχε- is retained in proper names also in Koine: Ἀρχέλαος Mt 2: 22. Cf. further the literary ἀρχέγονος 'progenitor' 1 Clem 59.3. **Ἐθελο-** (modeled after φιλο-): ἐθελοθρησκία (-εία B; ἐθελο-ενθρησκεία 𝔓⁴⁶ is incorrect; cf. θρησκεία and the discussion in §115(1) of ὀφθαλμοδουλεία) C 2: 23 from an assumed *ἐθελόθρησκος (θρῆσκος Ja 1: 26 is a back-formation from θρησκεία -εύειν), cf. ἐθελοδιδάσκαλος Herm Sim 9.22.2 and class., e.g. ἐθελο-κακεῖν Hdt., -δουλος Plato. **Φιλο-** (properly = φίλος 'beloved', then it was felt to belong to φιλεῖν): φιλάγαθος T 1: 8, φίλαυτος 2 T 3: 2, φιλήδονος and φιλόθεος 4, φιλοπρωτεύειν 3 Jn 9 (φιλόπρωτος Plut.), φιλόϋλος IRom 7.2. Formations with μισο- do not appear.—Λιποτακτεῖν 1 Clem 21.4 (Hell.) 'desert' from Hell. -τάκτης 'deserting the battle-line'.

119. The second element 'governs' the first. (1) The second element is most frequently an o-stem which has retained its verbal power: κακοποιός = κακὸν ποιῶν; from such compounds derivatives in -ία and -εῖν are very common (parasyntheta). (2) Some verbs (above all those in -ᾶν) prefer a masc. in -ης (fem. -ις) as the second element (often in an independent usage no longer common): εἰδωλολάτρης. (3) Compounds in -σία also belong here, since they (or rather the adjectives in -σιος which lie behind them) originally presume a second element in -της (or -τος): ὀρκωμοσία from ὀρκωμότης. (4) Occasionally

compounds end in -ής -ές without an underlying σ- stem: γονυπετής.

(1) Ἀγαθο-ποιός 1 P 2: 14, -ποιία 4: 19 (1 Clem), -ποιεῖν, e.g. 1 P 2: 15 (LXX also), -ποίησις Herm Man 8.10, Sim 5.3.4; moreover, ἀγαθοεργεῖν 1 T 6: 18, ἀγαθουργεῖν v.l. ἀγαθοποιεῖν A 14: 17; εὐποιία H 13: 16, IPol 7.3 (derivative of εὖ ποιεῖν; εὐποιός only Hesychius); καλοποιεῖν 2 Th 3: 13; κακοποιός 1 P (κακοῦργος; both are old), -ποιεῖν (old); εἰρηνοποιός Mt 5: 9, -εῖν C 1: 20; μοσχοποιεῖν NT only (A 7: 41; LXX μόσχον ποιεῖν); ἰσχυροποιεῖν and -ποίησις Hermas. Κακουχεῖν is old (ἔχειν; *κακοῦχος is not found). Πληροφορεῖν (Ctesias in Photius p. 41.28 Bekker; otherwise from the LXX onward: Deissmann, LO⁴ 67 f. [LAE 86 f.]; *πληροφόρος does not appear) and -φορία; τροποφορεῖν A 13: 18 (ἐτροφοφ-AC*E) from LXX Dt 1: 31, also in Cicero, ad Atticum 13.29.2 (= φέρειν τὸν τρόπον; *τροποφόρος does not appear); δωροφορία (Hell.) R 15: 31 BDFG from old form δωροφόρος. Θεομάχος A 5: 39, -μαχεῖν 23: 9 HLP al.; λογομαχεῖν 2 T 2: 14, -χία 1 T 6: 4 (-μάχος other later authors); θυμομαχεῖν 'to be very angry' A 12: 20 (Polyb.) from *θυμομάχος. Λιθοβολεῖν 'to stone' besides λιθάζειν, old (κατα-) λεύειν; λατομεῖν Mt 27: 60, Mk 15: 46; ἑτεροζυγεῖν 2 C 6: 14 (from ἑτερόζυγος LXX); ἀνθρωποκτόνος Jn 8: 44, Ja 3: 15; ἀνθρωπάρεσκος E 6: 6, C 3: 22 from ἀρέσκειν; of uncertain meaning δεξιολάβος A 23: 23 (a kind of troops). Ἀλλοτρι(ο)επίσκοπος 1 P 4: 15 (-επίσκοπος more nominal?). Κηπουρός Jn 20: 15 (from *κηπογορ-), but θυρωρός (from *θυρα-ϝωρ-), cf. Mayser ι¹ 15; ι² 3, 167 (θυρουρός Mk 13: 34 D*, Jn 10: 3 D, pap.). Εὐδοκεῖν (Hell.) must be derived from an imaginary *εὔδοκος (from δέχεσθαι) and not from δοκεῖν; likewise the old form καραδοκεῖν (NT ἀποκαραδοκία R 8: 19, Ph 1: 20) from the unattested *καραδόκος lit. 'stretching forth the head' (TW ι 392) (from κάρα and δέχεσθαι, earlier δέκεσθαι); on the κ cf. δοκεύειν and §33 πανδοκεύς. Εὐάγγελος (class.; not in NT) from εὖ and ἀγγέλλειν with dependence on ἄγγελος; from which already in Homer εὐαγγέλιον 'reward for good news' (cf. §111(4)); as the 'good news' it is attested for the first time only much later (beg. w. Cicero; Schniewind 116 ff.); however εὐαγγελίζεσθαι already in Att. Σπερμολόγος 'one who picks up seeds, a rook, a gossip' A 17: 18 (Att. and Hell.); συναρμολογεῖν 'join together' E 2: 21, 4: 16 (simple form Hell.) from ἁρμολόγος (glosses) 'fitting the joints together'. Ὀρθοτομεῖν 'to cut out (a path) in a straight direction; to lead straight ahead' 2 T 2: 15 (LXX) from unattested *ὀρθοτόμος.

(2) Πατρολῴας from ἀλο(ι)ᾶν, s. §35(2); φρεναπάτης 'one who deceives his own mind, i.e. conceited' T 1: 10 (and in the erotic fragment from ii BC, Mayser ι² 3, 261) along with φρεναπατᾶν G 6: 3 from ἀπατᾶν; πορφυρόπωλις A 16: 14 (masc. -πώλης

from πωλεῖν as τελ-ώνης from ὠνεῖσθαι); ἀρσενο-κοίτης 1 C 6: 9, 1 T 1: 10 from *κοιτᾶν (κοιτάζειν); εἰδωλο-λάτρης with -λατρεῖν (Hermas) and -λατρία (B has -λατρεία everywhere except for 1 C 10: 14, on account of λατρεία; cf. -θρησκεία §118(2)) from λάτρις λατρεύειν. For -άρχης besides -αρχος s. §50. Thus originally also the subst. in -της in the second element: προσωπολήμπτης A 10: 34 (with -μπτεῖν Ja 2: 9 and -μψία) is earlier than λήπτης; καρδιο-γνώστης also A 1: 24, 15: 8, Herm Man 4.3.4 (nowhere else) does not require γνώστης (A 26: 3 and Plut.) as a prerequisite; so perhaps also χρεοφειλέτης (§115(1)) and the quite conjectural κενεμβατεύειν (§154; -εύειν instead of -εῖν following ἐμβατεύειν) from a supposed κενεμβάτης (on the needlessness of the conjecture in C 2: 18 s. §154; Bauer s.v. ἐμβατεύω; Dibelius, Hdb. *ad loc*; cf. A. D. Nock, JBL 52 [1933] 132f.). Cf. e.g. the older ἱππηλάτης (Aeschyl. and Eur.), ἱπποδιώκτης (Theoc.), and following this type ἐργοπαρέκτης 'employer' 1 Clem 34.1 (otherwise unattested). Δειπνοκλήτωρ Mt 20: 28 add. D is unique.

(3) Ὀρκωμοσία H 7: 20, 21, 28 (Dor. s. §2; Att. τὰ ὁρκωμόσια, cf. γυμνάσιον συμπόσιον), ὁροθεσία A 17: 26 (Inschr. v. Priene 42.8, cf. 11, 12 [133 BC], BGU III 889.17 [ii AD]; ὁροθέσια Galen 19.348.8 Kühn, cf. τὰ ὅρια), υἱοθεσία (LXX), δικαιοκρισία 'righteous judgment' R 2: 5 (s. Bauer), αἱματεκχυσία H 9: 22 (𝔓⁴⁶ αἵματος ἐκχυσία incorrect) (παλιγγενεσία Mt 19: 28, T 3: 5). In composition with prep. already current in an earlier period, e.g. ἀποστασία (προ-στασία Att.). Another group forms abstracts with non-active meaning from verbal adjectives: ἀκατα-στασία from ἀκατάστατος §117(1).

(4) Εἰλικρινής with -κρίνεια (old) from κρίνειν; γονυπετεῖν (Polyb. also) from -πετής (Eur.); νου-νεχής Mk 12: 34 (-ῶς; Polyb., [Arist.], Rhetorica ad Alexandrum 30.1436b33) from νοῦν ἔχειν; ἱερο-πρεπής T 2: 3 (Att.). The relationship of the determining element to that governed is here very diverse; cf. further ἡμι-θανής Lk 10: 30 (Strabo etc.; Att. -θνής). Τηλαυγής is old (LXX also; -ῶς Mk 8: 25 as in Strabo 17.1.30, Philo often, POxy VI 886.24 [iii AD; the τ is uncertain], -έστερον Herm Sim 6.5.1 A), for which (by popular connection with δῆλος) δηλαυγής appears ([Democritus] in J. A. Fabricius, Bibl. Gr. IV 333, -ῶς Mk 8: 25 S*CLΔ, PGM I 4.775, 1033 pp. 98, 108; Hesychius, -έστερον Herm *ibid.* PMich), both usually in the weakened sense of 'evident'.

(5) Μογι-λάλος (§34(6)) is odd = μόγις λαλῶν (μογι- following the analogy of substantival ι-stems; Solmsen 160).—Ψευδο- occupies a special place; the point of departure is ψευδο-λόγος 'speaking falsely' (like §119(1)) 1 T 4: 2 and the like; closely related is ψευδό-μαρτυς (already in Att.) 'giving false testimony = a false witness' (Reitzenstein correctly in Hermes 52 [1917] 446ff. against Holl *ibid.* 301ff.; s. also Corssen, Sokrates 6 [1918]

106ff. and the literature in Indog. Jahrb. 5 [1918] 123f.); also in ψευδο-διδάσκαλος 2 P 2: 1 and -προ-φήτης the second element can still have some governing power; but ψευδό-χριστος, ψευδ-απόστολος 2 C 11: 13, -άδελφος 2 C 11: 26, G 2: 4 were certainly felt to be determinatives with an adjectival first element. The formation of γλωσσόκομον (or -κόμον?) is not clear: 'little box, case' (properly for the mouthpiece of a flute [γλῶτται]) Jn 12: 6, 13: 29, Hell. (Mayser I¹ 222; I² 3, 171; Bauer) for Att. γλωττοκομεῖον (Phryn. 98; W in Jn 12: 6 and 13: 29 γλωσσοκομιον); perhaps γλωσσοκόμος -ον 'to care for γλῶτται (κομεῖν, κομίζειν)' and expanded in Att. with -εῖον as χερνιβεῖον from χερνιβ-.—Ὑψηλοφρονεῖν R 11: 20 CDFG, 1 T 6: 17 ADE al., schol. on Pind., Pyth. 2.91 was certainly felt to equal ὑψηλὰ φρονεῖν (cf. ὑψηλὰ φρόνει R 11: 20 𝔓⁴⁶SAB, 1 T 6: 17 ὑ. φρονεῖν SI), but was derived (acc. to §120(4)) from class. ὑψηλόφρων Herm Sim 8.9.1 A (om. PMich) as were the old words σωφρονεῖν ὑπερφρονεῖν from σώφρων ὑπέρφρων.

(C) Attributive compounds showing mutation

The second element is a substantive, the compound, however, a possessive adjective: λευκώ-λενος = λευκὰς ὠλένας ἔχουσα.

120. (1) The first element is a noun (numeral), (2) a preposition or ἀ- privative; (3) the type of composition is sometimes obscured by substantivization; (4) occasionally only parasyntheta from compounds showing mutation have survived.

(1) Δίστομος (class.); δίψυχος Ja 1: 8, 4: 8 (Hermas often) besides -χεῖν and -χία; ἑτερόγλωσσος 1 C 14: 21 (Polyb., Strabo, Philo, Aquila); μονόφθαλ-μος Mt 18: 9 = Mk 9: 27 (Hdt. and Hell.); σκληρο-τράχηλος A 7: 51 (LXX); also πρωτότοκος (from ὁ τόκος with an adverbial first element; cf. πρωτό-γονος, παλίλλογος Schwyzer I 454) 'first born', from which πρωτοτοκεῖα H 12: 16 OT. To express the idea of distinction -εῖα, parallel to -εύω, is usual; cf. τὰ πρεσβεῖα, τὰ ἀριστεῖα, τὰ πρωτεῖα. In these instances the spelling -ία is impossible although it is found in the majority of MSS both in the LXX passages and in H 12: 16 (Debrunner, TW VI 875, n. 22), nor is τὰς πρωτοτοκείας 𝔓⁴⁶ preferable. Ὀκτα-ήμερος Ph 3: 5: Ion.-Hell. ὀκτα-, Att. ὀκτω-, Mayser I² 2, 74f.; Schwyzer I 591.

(2) Ἀνέλεος Ja 2: 13 (cf. ὁ ἔλεος §51(2); old νηλεής, Att. ἀνηλεής from τὸ ἔλεος); ἄνομος–ἔννομος 1 C 9: 21 (acc. to Marcion *et al.* R 2: 12 also ἀνόμως–ἐννόμως; cf. class. ἄτιμος–ἔντιμος, cf. ἐμπερίτομος Barn 9.6 C = ἐν περιτομῇ SG (opposed to ἀπερίτμη-τος); ἀπο-συνάγωγος 'expelled from the synagogue' Jn 9: 22, 12: 42, 16: 2, cf. ἀπόδημος. Ἔμφοβος ('afraid, terrified [of, at something]') like class. and Hell., accordingly ἔντρομος A 7: 32, 16: 29, H 12: 21

𝔓⁴⁶AC (Hell.); synonymous ἔκφοβος (back-formation from class. ἐκφοβεῖν) Mk 9: 6, H 12: 21, accordingly ἔκτρομος H 12: 21 SD* and the magical texts (Bauer).—Κατείδωλος 'full of idols' only A 17: 16; cf. Eur. κάθαιμος ('with blood all over') 'bloody', Hell. κατάχρυσος 'overlaid with gold' and the like.

(3) Ἡ ἀγριέλαιος (Hell. s. Nägeli 29; in addition ZenP Cairo II 59184.7 [255 BC]; Att. for which, acc. to Moeris 201.33, κότινος) R 11: 17, 24 (likewise ἡ καλλιέλαιος R 11: 24). Originally ἡ ἀγριέλαιος, καλλι-έλαιος ἐλαία 'olive-tree with wild, good olives'; thus ZenP Cairo ibid. (ἐλαία supplied), further I 59125.2f. and 7f. (256 BC). But ἄγριος ἔλαιος Pind., Frag. 46, πολλὸν δ' ἄρσεν' ἐκτεμόνθ' ὁμοῦ / ἄγριον ἔλαιον Soph., Tr. 1196f. Later -έλαιος was transformed into ἀγριελαία (Pollux, Diosc.) and καλλιελαία (pap. in Plasberg, APF 2, 218 [iv AD]) and on the model of ἐλαία–ἀγριελαία, ἀγριοκολοκύντη etc. were created (corresponding to the type in §115(2)); cf. MGr ἀγριόμηλο, ἀγριόσυκο etc. Τὸ δωδεκάφυλον A 26: 7, 1 Clem 55.6 (ἡ -ος Protev Ja 1.3) = αἱ δώδεκα φυλαί, cf. τὸ δωδεκάσκηπτρον 1 Clem 31.4, τὸ δωδεκα-πρόφητον Epiphanius. Τὸ ἡδύοσμον = 'mint' (garden plant) Mt 23: 23 = Lk 11: 42 from ἡδύς and ὀσμή. Χρυσόπρασος Rev 21: 20 (scil. λίθος) from χρυσός and πράσον 'leek'.

(4) Ὀρθοποδεῖν G 2: 14 (nowhere else) from the older ὀρθόπους. Μεσουράνημα s. §109(2). Σκληρο-καρδία (LXX) Mt, Mk from σκληροκάρδιος (LXX), instead of *-καρδι-ία; cf. διπλοκαρδία Barn 20.1, Did 5.1. Ἀκροβυστία may well be a distorted form (M.-H. 277) of ἀκρο-ποσθία (Hippoc., Arist.; from πόσθη) as the result of a popular etymological connection with βύειν; also therefore ἀκρόβυστος (in OT translators and in IPhld 6.1); cf. K. L. Schmidt, TW I 226f. -ιία > -ία also in the subst. ὁσίη, αἰτία, ἀξία: Frisk, Eranos 43 (1945) 220.

(D) Copulative (co-ordinative) compounds

The two elements are logically united by 'and'. There are few examples on the whole; s. Schwyzer I 452f.

121. The single example in the NT (apart from δώδεκα δεκαπέντε etc., §63(2)) is νυχθήμερον (as object) 'day and night = 24 hours' 2 C 11: 25 (later authors).

Νυχθήμερον either from ἡ νυχθήμερος (scil. περίοδος, cf. ἡ τρίμηνος and the like §141(3)) as Mitteis, Chr. 78.6 (376/8 AD) ἐπ(ε)ὶ τέσσαρας ὅλας νυχθημέρους (adj. also μετὰ δύο δρόμους νυχθημέρους Periplus Maris Rubri 15 [5.25 Frisk]), or from τὸ νυχθήμερον (Stob., Ecl. 1.21.9, Proclus in Tim. Platon. [E. Diehl's index], Galen et al.; δύο νυχθή-μερα Pratum spirit. ByzZ 38 [1938] 360.8; τριῶν νυχθημέρων Passio Andreae 12 [28.12 L.-B.]); s. L.-S.

Εἴκοσι νυχθήμερα Leont. Neap., Vita Joann. 19.9, 105.17; ἐποίει τὸ νυχθήμερον Vita S. Hypatii 95.24. Cf. also νυκτῆμαρ Wilcken, Chr. 130.12 (iv AD) and MGr μερόνυχτα 'day and night' (ἡμερόνυκτα Tzetzes, ἡμερονύχθιον Ducas 188.19, -νυκτον -νυχθον -νύκτιον Libistros and Rhodamne [ed. Lambert, 1935] pp. 228, 229, 463).

(E) Adverbial compounds

These presuppose neither an uncompounded adverb nor a compound adjective.

122. Of this type, which is rare elsewhere too, there are only two in -εί and one in -δόν in the NT.

Παμπληθεί Lk 23: 18 and πανοικεί A 16: 34 (-κί B³HLP al.) in the cultured language of Lk; cf. πανδημεί which is good Attic (ί is incorrect spelling, s. §23). Ὁμοθυμαδόν, frequent in Acts, also R 15: 6, appears already in class. Νυχθήμερον (§121) is not adverbial.

(F) Hypostasis: Combination of composition and derivation

The elements are joined and a suffix added to form the compound.

123. These are mostly derivatives from pre-positional expressions: (1) nominal: παραθα-λάσσιος from παρὰ θάλασσαν, (2) and much less frequently verbal: ἐγκακεῖν = ἔν τινι κακοὺς γενέσθαι (Thuc. 2.87.3).

(1) Ἐπιθανάτιος 1 C 4: 9 (also Dionys. Hal.) = ἐπὶ θανάτῳ συνειλημμένος, and the old forms ἐπίγειος (ἀνάγαιον also? s. §§35(2) and 44(1)), ἐπουράνιος, καταχθόνιος, παραθαλάσσιος (Mt 4: 13), παράλιος (Lk 6: 17); ἐνώπιον (neut. from ἐνώπιος) is also formed in this way; ἐντόπιος A 21: 12 from ἐν τόπῳ (ὤν). In the case of ἐπιούσιος (ἄρτος) Mt 6: 11 = Lk 11: 3, conceptually and grammatically the most plausible explanation is the assumption of a sub-stantivization of ἐπὶ τὴν οὖσαν (scil. ἡμέραν) '(deter-mined) for the day in question' ('this day' Mt, 'any day' Lk); cf. ἐπιμήνιος ἐφημέριος etc. (on the hiatus s. §124; M.-H. 91f.). A Semitizing remodeling of τὰ ἐπιούσια, attested in a pap. of the beginning of the imperial period (Preisigke, Sammelbuch 5224.20 ἐπιουσί[ων]; but s. B. M. Metzger, ET 69 [1957–8] 52–4 where reservation regarding this reading is expressed [the pap. has been lost], and the only other alleged occurrence outside the Lord's Prayer, in a Rhodian inscrip., is found to be erroneous [cf. Debrunner, Museum Helveticum 9 (1952) 60–2;

Bauer[5] omits]), = Lat. *diaria* 'daily wage, minimum for daily existence', which would have been expressed in pure Greek by ἡ ἐφήμερος τροφή (Ja 2: 15, Diodor. Sic., Dionys. Hal., Ael. Aristid., Vett. Val., PSI VI 685.9). But the notion of 'bread for the coming day' (from ἡ ἐπιοῦσα scil. ἡμέρα A 16: 11 and elsewhere in Acts) must also be considered (Debrunner: 'is perhaps to be'); cf. περιούσιος § 113(1); Origen (de oratione 27.7) knows the word neither from literature nor from colloquial speech. Literature and discussion on the ἐπιούσιος problem: M.-H. 313f.; Debrunner, ThBl 8 (1929) 212f., 259f.; Bonaccorsi 61–3, 533–9; Foerster in TW II 587–95; Bauer s.v. The following are substantivized: ἐνύπνιον, προσκεφάλαιον, ὑποπόδιον 'footstool' (also pap. from ii BC on, LXX, Lucian, s. Bauer), ὑπολήνιον 'the vessel placed under a wine-press (ληνός)' Mk 12: 1 (also LXX, Pollux, Geopon., etc., s. Bauer; as adj. Dit., Or. 383.147 [i BC]) and προσφάγιον Jn 21: 5 (acc. to Moeris 204.24 προσφάγημα is Hell. for Att. ὄψον 'side dish'; from πρός and φαγεῖν).—Nouns (adj.) also appear as the first element: ἀκροθίνια H 7: 4 (old) from ἄκρος and θιν-, likewise ἀκρογωνιαῖος λίθος 'the stone at the ἄκρα γωνία'; μεσονύκτιον (Hell., Lob. Phryn. 53; on μεσαν- s. § 35(2)); ἀλεκτοροφωνία 'time of the cockcrowing' Mk 13: 35 (Mt 26: 34 𝔓[37,45], both iii AD, accepted by Zuntz, JTS 50 [1949] 182; Mt 26: 75 in a 4th-century parchment cod. [C. H. Roberts, The Antinoopolis Papyri, part I, no. 11; cf. Katz, ThLZ 80 (1955) 737]) is not clear (vulgar, Lob. Phryn. 229; properly ἡ ἀλεκτοροφωνία scil. φυλακή 'nightwatch'?). Ἡμιώριον 'half-hour' Rev 8: 1 (ἡμίωρον AC; cf. ἡμίδραχμον, but ἡμιπόδιον, K.-Bl. II 323).— Ἐμπερίτομος Barn 9.6 (Diamart. 1.1 [p. 3.3 Rehm], Philostorg., Hist. Eccl. 3.4) = ἐν περιτομῇ SG; but ἐγκαίνια (§ 141(3)) back-formation from ἐγκαινίζειν (Schwyzer, KZ 62 [1935] 1).—Τὰν ἀκρόθινα (indisputable, s. Rüsch 216) in the Delphic inscrip. of the Labyadae (iv BC) Dialekt-Inschr. 2561 D 47 'offering of first-fruits'.

(2) Ἐγκακεῖν (inferior v.l. ἐκκακεῖν) Lk 18: 1 and Paul rather often (Herm Man 9.8.8, Polyb. 4.19.10). Ἐλλογεῖν (§ 90) = ἐν λόγῳ τιθέναι 'to charge to someone's account' Ἐνωτίζεσθαι A 2: 14 (also LXX) is explained by Hesych. as ἐν ὠτίοις δέχεσθαι, but it is rather to be explained as: ἐν with acc. following an old usage = εἰς (Schwyzer II 460.3); cf. Lk 9: 44 θέσθε ὑμεῖς εἰς τὰ ὦτα ὑμῶν. Ἐνωτίζεσθαι in the LXX formed for Hebr. Hiphil of אזן 'listen intently': Katz, ThLZ 1957, 112. Similarly ἐνστερνίζεσθαι (+ τοῖς σπλάγχνοις) 1 Clem 2.1 (Clem. Alex., Paed. 1.6 τὸν σωτῆρα ἐνστερνίσασθαι; Eus., Mart. Palaest. 8.6 τὸν λογισμὸν ἐνεστερνισμένη, 11.4 τοσαύτας μνήμας (τῶν θείων γραφῶν) ἐνεστέρνιστο; Constit. Apost. 1 ἐνεστερνισμένοι τὸν φόβον αὐτοῦ [= Ἰησοῦ]; Athanasius ἐνστηθίζειν; Jos., Longus *et al.* προσστερνίζεσθαι 'to clasp to the breast').

(G) Supplementary: Hiatus in word-composition

124. Koine often neglects euphony for the sake of etymological clarity (§§ 17 and 19). So, in an effort to achieve clear isolation of the elements, hiatus is not avoided in composition (contrary to Attic), especially in numerals.

Δεκαοκτώ § 63(2); τετρα-άρχης -αρχεῖν Tdf. A 13: 1 following S*, Lk 3: 1 following S*C etc. (s. Tdf. on Lk 3: 1); ὀκταήμερος § 120(1); τεσσερακονταετής A 7: 23, 13: 18, ἑκατονταετής R 4: 19 (also dialectal with -ετής, but due to ϝέτος; Att. -τούτης from -το-έτης). Ἐπιούσιος also belongs here if from ἐπί and ἡ οὖσα (§ 123(1)). Ἀγαθοεργεῖν 1 T 6: 18 (but ἀγαθουργεῖν A 14: 17 [§ 31(1)], ἱερουργεῖν R 15: 16 and κακοῦργος Lk 23: 32, 2 T 2: 9 etc.), ἀλλοτριοεπίσκοπος 1 P 4: 15 KLP (-τριεπ- SB). Ἀρχιερεῖς B Mt 26: 14, cf. ἀρχιερεύς PPetr III 53 p. 2 (iii BC), -ρέα Tituli Asiae Minoris II 420.2 (i AD), ἀρχιατρός POxy I 126.23 (572 AD), PLond III 1032.3 (vii BC), MSS of Origen 3.289.24 Klostermann, Tituli Asiae Minoris II 224.3 (Roman period), Trans. Am. Phil. Ass. 57 (1926) 224 no. 48.3 (Roman), ἀρχιοινοχόος LXX, Plut.; Schwyzer I 202 takes -ιι- in Asia Minor to be an indication of the native pronunciation -*iy*-; is ἀρχιγερεῖ PHib 62.8 (iii BC) also so intended (cf. Mayser I[1] 168)?—Hiatus following o: λιθοεργός Philo Byz. (Arnim 38), ὑποϊππαρχήσαντα Tituli Asiae Minoris II 420.7 (i AD), ἱπποΐατρος POxy I 92.3 (iv AD), pap. ii/iii AD ἱεροΐατρος (Gnomon 17 [1941] 334), in LXX γραμματοεισαγωγεύς, μακροημερεύειν and others (Thack. 130 n. 4), later ὁμο-ούσιος and the like. On the whole subject: Wackernagel, Homer 194f.; Immisch, NJklA 29 (1912) 34; W. Schulze, Festschrift Wackernagel 240 (n. 6) = Kl. Schr. 82; Cremer-Kögel 408.—IRom introduction ἀξιέπαινος (Xen., Dem.), ἀξιοεπίτευκτος, ἀξιόαγνος (both new), but IPhld 5.2 and 1 Clem 1.1, 21.7 ἀξιαγάπητος (likewise new).—The earlier language had already introduced the privative particle in the form ἀ- instead of ἀν- before o (the point of departure is perhaps ἀόρατος from ἀ-ϝορ-; Schwyzer I 431); thus ἀόρατος (class.) NT, ἄοκνος (class.) 1 Clem 33.8, IPol 7.2, ἀόργητος (Arist.) Ap. Frs.

(3) THE FORMATION OF PERSONAL NAMES

125. With regard to personal names in the NT, grammatically only the type of (hypocoristically) abbreviated names need be mentioned. These abbreviated names were widespread in Greek from earliest times with great variation in the suffixes (s. Bechtel-Fick, Griech. Personennamen 26ff.): -ις, -ίας, -είας, -έας (-ῆς), -υς,

-ιλ(λ)ος, -υλ(λ)ος, -ων, -ίων etc. (1) Virtually only -ᾱς is known to the NT, as to Hellenistic, and indeed not only where the full name contains an α ('Αντιπᾶς Rev 2: 13 for 'Αντίπατρος, s. W. Schulze, KZ 40 [1906] 409 n. 3 = Kl. Schr. 67, n. 3), but also when this connection is lacking. A remnant may thereby survive from the second element of a compound name ('double-stemmed abbreviated names'), e.g. Πατροβᾶς R 16: 14 for Πατρόβιος, Θευδᾶς for Θεύδωρος, or the like. Either the abbreviated names were given at birth (as when a Mantitheos named his son Manteas, a Nikeratos Nikias, a Demoletes Demon etc.), or a person was given the full name at birth but readily addressed with the nickname; thus Menodorus, the admiral of Sextus Pompeius, is sometimes called by his full name in the historians and sometimes Menas; s. Solmsen-Fraenkel, Indog. Eigennamen (Heidelberg, 1922) 120f. (2) Moreover, in the NT there is the case where a foreign name has passed over into the category of Greek abbreviated names: Κλεοπᾶς (for Κλεόπατρος) L 24: 18 = Κλωπᾶς Jn 19: 25 (Deissmann, BS 184, n. 1 [BS 315, n. 2], Dalman 179.4; the persons need not be identical).

(1) Abbreviated names in -ᾶς (frequently without definitely identifiable full names): 'Αρτεμᾶς for 'Αρτεμίδωρος (Varro, de Lingua Latina 8.21), Έρμᾶς perhaps for Έρμόδωρος, Ζηνᾶς for Ζηνόδωρος (Bekker, Anec. Gr. II 857.2), Νυμφᾶς for Νυμφόδωρος (M.-H. 71 sees in Νύμφαν a fem. which he bases on αὐτῆς C 4: 15 B), 'Ολυμπᾶς perhaps for 'Ολυμπιόδωρος; Δημᾶς for Δημήτριος? Στεφανᾶς for Στεφανηφόρος or a development from Att. Στέφανος? (Bechtel-Fick, op. cit. 253f. holds Στέφανος itself to be an abbreviation of Φιλοστέφανος or Στεφανο-

κλῆς). Παρμενᾶς for Παρμένων, cf. Πάρμενις, -νίδης, -νίσκος, -νίων (ibid. 205).—Abbreviated names in -ῆς appear less frequently: 'Απελλῆς s. infra, Έρμῆς R 16: 14 (hardly to be simply identified with the name of the god, although in the later period this type of designation also appears [ibid. 304ff.]); in -ῶς only 'Απολλῶς (s. infra). 'Ανδρέας is an old Greek name.—Double names for the same person: Σιλᾶς and Σιλουανός s. infra (2); 'Απολλώνιος A 18: 24 D and 'Απολλῶς Paul ('Απελλῆς s. §29(4)); 'Αμπλιᾶτος R 16: 8 and v.l. 'Αμπλιᾶς; 'Αντιπᾶς and 'Αντίπατρος Jos., Ant. 14.10; accordingly, 'Επαφρόδιτος Ph 2: 25, 4: 18 and 'Επαφρᾶς C 1: 7, 4: 12, Phm 23 could be one person, were it not improbable on other grounds.

(2) Θωμᾶς (cf. Θαῦμις Θαύμων Θώμων Bechtel-Fick, op. cit. 141; Bechtel, Hist. Personennamen [Halle, 1917] 199, 214) for תּאֹומָא (§53(2d)) and presumably Θευδᾶς (Ion. short form of Θεόδωρος or the like, Bechtel-Fick, op. cit. 143; Dalman 179.9; cf. Τεύφιλος as the name of three Jews in Preisigke, Namenbuch [1922] s.v.; H. Lewy, KZ 59[1932] 179). The more easily Grecized form Βαρναβᾶς for Βαρνεβοῦς (acc. to Deissmann, BS 177, NBS 16 [BS 187ff., 309f.]; ZNW 7 [1906] 91f.). Λουκᾶς (for Lucius, Lucanus or something similar; s. W. Schulze, Graeca Latina 12; Klostermann, Hdb. on Lk 1 title; Deissmann, LO⁴ 372ff. [LAE 435ff.]; cf. also §268(1)) and 'Αμπλιᾶς (s. supra) are certainly unaltered Latin names; further 'Ιουνιᾶς (= Junianus?), if ('Ανδρόνικον καὶ) 'Ιουνιαν R 16: 7 means a man (the ancients understood a married couple like Aquila and Priscilla, s. Tischendorf ad loc.; 'Ιουλίαν 𝔓⁴⁶ with several ancient versions); but Σκευᾶς A 19: 14 hardly = Lat. Scaeva.—Σιλᾶς (Acts) or Σιλέας (§53(2)) and Σιλουανός (Paul and 1 P 5: 12) are perhaps Grecized and Latinized forms of the same Semitic name (Aram. שְׁאִילָא Dalman 157.5); cf. Radermacher, ZNW 25 [1926] 293ff. and Σαούλ–Σαῦλος (§53(2))–Παῦλος.

6. VOCABULARY

The following sketch is intended merely to indicate the major headings under which the Hellenistic vocabulary of the NT may be considered. A more detailed investigation involving the whole range of materials is a subject for a comparative lexicon of the NT, for which only preliminary studies of Deissmann (BS), Rouffiac, Thieme, Nägeli and Bonaccorsi (pp. l–lxxi) are available (freely utilized in the following).

126. (1) Many words are being replaced by others

etymologically quite dissimilar (for substitution by means of words etymologically cognate but with other suffixes or endings, see examples under declension, conjugation and word-formation). (a) The reasons for the disappearance of older words lie in the efforts towards clarity and simplicity of expression; thus (α) short, especially monosyllabic, words were readily replaced by fuller-sounding words, and (β) words with more or less obsolete and troublesome inflections were shunned. (b) The substitute words (α) are sometimes derived from the dialects, especially the Ionic, (β) are sometimes based on the tendency to more drastic forms of expression; (γ) in many instances their origin is admittedly still undetermined. (2) The meaning of many words has shifted (usually faded). For special Christian recoinage of concepts (especially in Paul) see Nägeli 51 and Milligan xxx. (3) Among the NT authors there occur strong contrasts in diction which are due to cultural diversity and to the extent of their dependence on the literary language. Cf. further W.-S. 19–22 and especially A. D. Nock, JBL 52 (1933) 131–9.

Examples. (1) (*a*, α) καλῶς for εὖ (§102(3)), ἀσφαλίζειν along with κλείειν (*klīn*), ἀφιέναι (MGr ἀφήνω) for ἐᾶν (the latter virtually limited to Acts), βρέχει (MGr) for ὕει (§309(2)); πρόβατον (MGr) for οἶς and χοῖρος (MGr) for ὗς (only in the proverb 2 P 2: 22; LXX ὗς throughout, later translators χοῖρος; σῦς is not Hell., Schweizer 146; Arnim 28); also because οἶς and ὗς became alike in pronunciation (cf. Mayser ı² 2, 26, 28 n. 2). (β) ἀκολουθεῖν (MGr) for ἕπεσθαι (§193(1)), cf. χορτάζειν for κορεννύναι etc. (§92); γινώσκειν for εἰδέναι (Bonaccorsi 55 on *v.* 3). (*b*) (α) Doric βουνός (§2; MGr βουνό βουνί 'mountain') along with ὄρος (καὶ τὰ ὄρη καὶ τοὺς βουνούς Herm Vis 1.3.4); Ionic ἀπαρτίζειν καταρτίζειν (Mayser ı¹ 20 f.; ı² 2, 170; MGr) for Att. ἀνύειν (NT only διανύσαντες A 21: 7); ἐντρέπεσθαι ἐντροπή for αἰδεῖσθαι αἰδώς (MGr ντρέπομαι ντροπή); the alleged 'poetic' words are also mostly Ion.: φέγγος (also Xen., Plato and pap., Schmid, GGA 1895, 36) in addition to φῶς (MGr φεγγάρι 'moon'). (β) τρώγειν besides ἐσθίειν (§101), χορτάζειν for κορεννύναι (§101; MGr χορταίνω ἐχόρτασα). (γ) ὑπάγειν (§101 under ἄγειν) besides πορεύεσθαι.

(2) ἀσφαλίζειν 'close (fast)' (MGr σφαλῶ σφαλίζω 'close'), δέρειν 'to beat' (like MGr), ἐκβάλλειν especially often in Mt 'to take out' (thus MGr βγάλλω), ἐρωτᾶν 'to ask', ξενίζειν 'to surprise' (A 17: 20, 1 P 4: 4, 12; depon. in pap. 'to be surprised' [Mayser ı² 2, 147; Preisigke s.v.]; also MGr), ὀψώνιον 'wages', χορηγεῖν τι 'to supply something' (MGr χορηγῶ 'offer, provide').

(3) Κοράσιον only Mt and Mk; ἡ παῖς is substituted in Lk 8: 54. Cf. the division of τρώγειν and ἐσθίειν (§101), besides §5(1) for the attitude of Lk to Latinisms. In general, reference can be made to the remarks in §§2–7 which are particularly applicable to vocabulary. MGr provides valuable clues for the ascertainment of the meanings of words; thus the meaning 'rain' for βροχή Mt 7: 25, 27 is corroborated by MGr. The meaning 'stench' or 'filth' for βρώματα Mk 7: 19 has been accepted by many on the basis of MGr since Pallis (in Thumb, N. Jahr. f. Phil. 17 [1906] 248); yet this does not suit Mk 7: 19 well (s. Behm in TW ı 640 n. 1), and MGr βρόμος or rather ἡ βρόμα (not τὸ βρῶμα, Dawkins, ClR 53 [1939] 33) 'stench, filth' as a back-formation from MGr βρομῶ goes back to ancient Gr. βρόμος 'din' *crepitus ventris*, βρομεῖν 'to roar', not to βρῶμα 'food' (Hatzidakis, Glotta 22 [1934] 130 f., 132 f.).

PART III
SYNTAX

1. SUBJECT AND PREDICATE

Rob. 390–402; Smyth §§900–1017

(1) OMISSION OF THE VERB εἶναι

Regard 31–107, 186–216

The verb εἶναι as a copula can be omitted in the NT as in Greek and other Indo-European tongues from the earliest times (pure nominal sentence). Omission is the rule in Hebrew, while Modern Greek like most literary languages customarily employs it.

127. Omission of ἐστίν. As in classical Greek, the most common form of the copula, the 3rd sing. ἐστίν, is by far the most frequently omitted, though no fixed usage developed. Still a preference for omission may be observed in (1) proverbs, (2) impersonal constructions, especially those expressing possibility or necessity (cf. with ἐστίν §353(5)), (3) questions, (4) exclamations. The omission of ἐστίν, too, in the single instance of the verbal adjective in -τέος agrees with classical usage: οἶνον νέον εἰς ἀσκοὺς καινοὺς βλητέον Lk 5: 38 (§65(3)). (5) Omission is less frequent in simple assertions. Ἐστίν is even omitted in the sense of 'there are': 1 C 15: 40 καὶ σώματα ἐπουράνια καὶ σώματα ἐπίγεια which is in the midst of sentences without copula (condensed logical demonstration).—Mayser ΙΙ 3, 16 ff.

(1) Ἄξιος ὁ ἐργάτης τῆς τροφῆς (τοῦ μισθοῦ) αὐτοῦ Mt 10: 10, 1 T 5: 18. Μικρὸν καὶ τέθνηκα M. Ant. 8.2.

(2) Δῆλον ὅτι (class.) 1 C 15: 27 (1 T 6: 7 v.l.), also reversed ὅτι..., δῆλον G 3: 11; (ἔτι) μικρόν, καὶ... Jn 14: 19; 16: 16, 17, 19, ἔτι μικρὸν ὅσον ὅσον H 10: 37 OT (but LXX Is 26: 20 ἀποκρύβηθι μ. ὅ. ὅ.; cf. §304). Ὥρα R 13: 11; ἐξόν and συμφέρον §353(5); ἀδύνατον, εἰ δυνατόν ('if possible') (with ἐστιν Mt 26: 39 v.l., Mk 14: 35). Ὄφελον cf. §67(2). Ἀνάγκη (with ἐστίν Mt 18: 7, BL without) H 9: 16, 23, R 13: 5? (διὸ ἀ. ὑποτάσσεσθαι SAB, διὸ ὑποτάσσεσθε DEFG, 𝔓⁴⁶ perhaps correctly διὸ καὶ ὑποτάσσεσθε; perhaps ὀργήν has intruded from v. 4 for ἀνάγκην; cf. Isocr.

3.12: 'one must submit to the monarchy οὐ μόνον διὰ τὴν ἀνάγκην..., ἀλλ' ὅτι καί...').

(3) Τί ἐμοὶ (ἡμῖν) καὶ σοί; Mt 8: 29 etc.=מַה־לִּי וָלָךְ, but class. has a comparable construction (K.-G. ι 417). D. C. Hesseling, Τί ἐμοὶ καὶ σοί; (Donum natalicium Schrijnen, Nimwegen, 1929, 665 ff.) gives as the sense: 'Leave me in peace ! do not bother me !' and rejects a Semitism (against Schwartz, NGG 1901, 511 n.). Τί πρὸς σέ (ἡμᾶς); Mt 27: 4, Jn 21: 22, 23 = quid (hoc) ad te?; class. similarly: οὐδὲν πρὸς Διόνυσον is proverbial, οὐδέν ἐστι δήπου πρὸς ἐμέ Dem. 18.21; cf. τί γάρ μοι 1 C 5: 12 and others §299(3). Epict. τί (οὐδὲν) πρὸς ἐμέ (σέ), s. Schenkl's Index under πρός; cf. BGU ιν 1158.17 (9 BC). Τί (μοι) τὸ ὄφελος; 1 C 15: 32, Ja 2: 14, 16; cf. ἀλλὰ τί τούτων ὄφελος αὐτοῖς; Dem. 9.69. Less formulaic: Lk 4: 36 τίς ὁ λόγος οὗτος; A 10: 21 τίς ἡ αἰτία δι' ἥν...; R 3: 1 τί τὸ περισσὸν τοῦ Ἰουδαίου ἢ τίς ἡ ὠφέλεια τῆς περιτομῆς; Further 2 C 2: 16, 6: 14, Rev 5: 2, 13: 4, indirect question R 8: 27. Τί μέγα, εἰ 1 C 9: 11, 2 C 11: 15: Almqvist 98.

(4) Μακάριος ἀνὴρ ὅς...Ja 1: 12, R 4: 8 OT (Hebr. אַשְׁרֵי הָאִישׁ), thus also μακάριοι οἱ πτωχοί etc. Mt 5: 3 etc. The 3rd pers. here never with εἶναι, but conversely the 2nd pers. Mt 5: 11, 16: 17 and in an assertion: μακάριός ἐστιν Mt 11: 6=Lk 7: 23; cf. μακάριός γ' ἀνὴρ ἔχων...Aristoph., Ra. 1482. Μεγάλη ἡ Ἄρτεμις Ἐφεσίων A 19: 28, 34; ὡς ἀνεξερεύνητα etc. R 11: 33. Οὐ θαῦμα 2 C 11: 14 (s. Bertram, TW ΙΙΙ 40).

(5) Πάντα δυνατά σοι Mk 14: 36; ὅπου διαθήκη etc. H 9: 16 f.; πιστός...1 C 1: 9, 10: 13, 2 C 1: 18, 1 Th 5: 24 (πιστὸς δέ ἐστιν ὁ κύριος 2 Th 3: 3, but FG al. without ἐστιν), 1 T 1: 15, 3: 1, 4: 9, 2 T 2: 11, T 3: 8. Κεφάλαιον δέ H 8: 1 (class.). Ὁ κύριος ἐγγύς Ph 4: 5. 1 C 1: 24 Χριστὸς θεοῦ δύναμις καὶ θεοῦ σοφία 𝔓⁴⁶Cl (all others Χριστὸν δύναμιν—σοφίαν); the source to which Paul may have alluded, Theod. Da 2: 20 (J. A. Montgomery, I.C.C.), has the copula: ἡ σοφία καὶ ἡ δύναμις αὐτοῦ ἐστι (cf. Katz, ThLZ 1958, 317). The omission of ἐστίν in the sense of 'there is (are)' occurs in both classical and literary Hellenistic Greek, and occasionally in the papyri. Further

Pauline exx.: 1 Th 5: 3 εἰρήνη καὶ ἀσφάλεια, R 2: 8, 9, 10, 8: 1, 1 C 8: 6, 13: 8, Phil 2: 1, E 4: 4, 1 T 2: 5 (N. Turner).

128. Omission of other forms of εἶναι. (1) Ellipsis of εἰσίν hardly ever occurs except following ellipsis of ἐστίν and in logical deductions. (2) Εἰμί, ἐσμέν, and εἶ are not often omitted, and when they are, the personal pronoun is usually present. (3) Ἦν (3rd sing.) is always omitted in the phrases ᾧ (ἦ) ὄνομα, οὗ τὸ ὄνομα Mk 14: 32 (ᾧ C), καὶ τὸ ὄνομα αὐτῆς Lk 1: 5; cf. 27 (Hebraizing, cf. LXX 1 Km 1: 1 etc.), ὄνομα αὐτῷ (parenthetical; §144). Otherwise almost never. (4) Ἔσται and ἦ are seldom omitted. (5) The omission of εἴη (or ἔστω; Mayser II 3, 19) is normal in formulaic wishes like εἰρήνη ὑμῖν etc. In doxologies 'is' as well as 'be' can be supplied. (6) Ἔστω is almost never omitted except in the classical formula χάρις (τῷ θεῷ). For ἔστε s. §98. (7) Following the Semitic pattern a present or imperfect (also aorist or future) of εἶναι (παρεῖναι, [παρα-]γίνεσθαι) can be omitted following ἰδού = Hebr. הִנֵּה, Aram. הָא. But cf. also ἰδοὺ χελιδών on an old Attic vase (Meisterhans 203). For further ellipsis of the verb s. §§480(5) and 481; for omission of εἶναι and ὤν §§157(3); 414; 416(1, 2); 418(6).

(1) H 2: 11, R 11: 16, 4: 14; otherwise, e.g. 1 C 16: 9. Cf. also μακάριοι §127(4).

(2) Ἐγώ ὁ θεὸς Ἀβραάμ Mk 12: 26 = A 7: 32 OT (but LXX with εἰμί since אָנֹכִי = ἐγώ εἰμι, and thus Mt 22: 32, also some witnesses in Mk and Acts). Jn 14: 11 (cf. 10); Rev 21: 6 (εἰμί A), 22: 13; καθὼς αὐτὸς Χριστοῦ, οὕτως καὶ ἡμεῖς 2 C 10: 7. Without pron. 2 C 11: 6 εἰ δὲ καὶ ἰδιώτης τῷ λόγῳ (scil. εἰμί, which D*E add). On R 1: 15 πρόθυμος scil. εἰμί s. §224(1). Rev 15: 4 ὅτι μόνος ὅσιος scil. εἶ. Ph 3: 15.

(3) Mk 14: 21 καλὸν αὐτῷ BLW (al. add ἦν and Mt 26: 24). G 4: 15 εἰ δυνατόν (formulary, s. §127(2); here ἦν is to be supplied). Ὧι (ἦ) ὄνομα Lk 1: 26, 27, 2: 25, 8: 41, 24: 13 (D ὀνόματι as in Lk elsewhere and almost always in Acts [class.]; cf. §§144 and 197), 18 (SB al. ὀνόματι), A 13: 6 (𝔓45 minusc. ὀνόματι, D ὀνόματι καλούμενος); ὄνομα αὐτῷ Jn 1: 6 (ἦν S*D*W), 3: 1 (ὀνόματι S*). It makes no difference whether ἦν (with persons) or ἐστίν (with places) is to be supplied. Cf. further Dem. 32.11 Ἀριστοφῶν ὄνομ' αὐτῷ, Xen., An. 1.5.4 ὄνομα δ' αὐτῇ Κορσωτή (cf. 10). IEph 19.2 ταραχή τε ἦν, πόθεν ἡ καινότης (scil. ἦν; direct: πόθεν ἡ κ.;). Herm Vis 3.1.5 αἱ τρίχες μου ὀρθαί (scil. ἦσαν).

(4) Ἔσται (or ἐστίν): 1 P 4: 17, H 6: 8, 1 C 15: 21, cf. 22. Ἦι only Paul now and then (2 C 8: 11, 13). T. Nissen, Philol. 92 (1937) 248 conjectures for H 12:

16 μή τις πόρνος (ἦ) ἢ βέβηλος; against this P. Katz, in connection with his conjecture in H 12: 15 (s. §165), would maintain that we have an intentional 'beautiful sequence of three clauses without copula'.

(5) The traditional interpretation of ἵλεώς σοι, scil. ὁ θεὸς εἴη, Mt 16: 22 (Debrunner earlier; Bauer⁵; Mlt. 240 n. on p. 181 [285 n. 2]; Büchsel, TW III 300f.) lacks the support of the Vulg. *absit a te*, with which KJV 'Be it far from thee' incidentally agrees. Acc. to Katz, ThLZ 1957, 113f., this ἵλεως is not the Greek word for 'merciful', but one among the homonyms selected because of similarity of sound (Thack. 38) to render חָלִילָה with dat. 'profane, far be it from...'. It appears in the LXX at 2 Km 20: 20, 23: 17 = 1 Chr 11: 19, 1 Macc 2: 21 and, as a hexaplaric variant, in 1 Km 12: 33, 14: 45, 20: 2, 9, 22: 15 where it replaces the better Greek μή μοι γένοιτο or μὴ γένοιτό μοι. In Mt it is a Septuagintism, followed by the doublet οὐ μὴ ἔσται σοι τοῦτο, whereas Lk 20: 16 and Paul in many passages agree with the earlier LXX, writing μὴ γένοιτο (Bauer s.v. 3a). The Syriac has חס = ἵλεως = חָלִילָה (Mt 16: 22). The marginal version of KJV, 'pity thyself', which is taken from Luther, stands for a connotation of Syriac חס, but the comment of I. E. Rahmani, Les liturgies orientales et occidentales (1929), 108f., as quoted by Stendahl, The School of St Matthew (1954), 112 n. 2, is vitiated the moment we accept ἵλεως as a Septuagintism. For obvious reasons no secular parallels can be adduced. In an expression which is so closely modeled on the Hebrew pattern it would not be safe to speak of an omission of the copula.—Ὁ κύριος μετὰ σοῦ Lk 1: 28, ἐπικατάρατος πᾶς ὅς...(ὁ...) G 3: 10, 13. Doxologies: εὐλογητὸς ὁ θεός (2 C 1: 3 etc.) = Hebr. בָּרוּךְ אֱלֹהִים. Cf. on the one hand R 1: 25 ὅς ἐστιν εὐλ., 2 C 11: 31 ὁ ὤν εὐλ.; on the other LXX 3 Km 10: 9 γένοιτο εὐλ., Job 1: 21 εἴη εὐλ. Ἔστιν appears, however, to be in the mind of the NT authors. Also cf. G 1: 5 ᾧ ἡ δόξα with 1 P 4: 11 ᾧ ἐστιν (A om. ἐ.) ἡ δ.—Χάρις ὑμῖν καὶ εἰρήνη, ἡ χάρις...μεθ᾽ ὑμῶν etc.; cf. χ. ὑ. κ. εἰ. πληθυνθείη 1 P 1: 2, 2 P 1: 2, 1 Clem introduction, similarly in the introductions of Pol Ph and MPol (cf. εἰρ. ὑ. πληθ. LXX Dan 3: 98).

(6) Χάρις τῷ θεῷ 1 C 15: 57, 2 C 8: 16, 9: 15, R 6: 17, also 7: 25 B. Μηδὲν σοὶ καὶ τῷ δικαίῳ ἐκείνῳ Mt 27: 19 (cf. §127(3) τί ἐμοὶ καὶ σοί). H 13: 4f. τίμιος ὁ γάμος etc.; R 12: 9ff., C 4: 6.

(7) Mt 3: 17 (17: 5) καὶ ἰδοὺ φωνὴ (scil. ἐγένετο) ἐκ τῶν οὐρανῶν λέγουσα...(similarly, but without ἰδού A 10: 15); Lk 5: 18 καὶ ἰδοὺ ἄνδρες φέροντες...(scil. παρῆσαν as in 13: 1); 5: 12. Future: A 13: 11 ἰδοὺ χεὶρ κυρίου ἐπὶ σέ. Present: 8: 36, Lk 22: 38. Cf §144. Lk 9: 30 ἰδοὺ ἄνδρες δύο συλλαλοῦντες 𝔓45, the other witnesses συνελάλουν. UPZ I 78.25 (159 BC) ἐμὲ δὲ ἄφες, εἰδοὺ πολιὰς ἔχων. On καὶ ἰδού s. Johannessohn, KZ 64 (1937) 249f.; 66 (1939) 145ff.; 67 (1940) 30ff.

(2) OMISSION OF THE SUBJECT

129. Impersonalia. Of the so-called impersonal verbs expressing meteorological phenomena, only βρέχει Ja 5: 17 (Hellenistic-MGr for ὕει, Phryn. 291) is found in the NT (as in the Ptolemaic papyri: Mayser ΙΙ 3, 2).—Ὀψὲ ἐγένετο Mk 11: 19, ἦν πρωΐ Jn 18: 28.—Equally unusual (as in the Ptolemaic papyri: Mayser, *op. cit.*) are the classical impersonal expressions in which the subject is implied in the verb (ἐκήρυξε scil. ὁ κῆρυξ): σαλπίσει 1 C 15: 52 'the trumpet will sound', cf. ἐσάλπιγξε Xen., An. 1.2.17.

Βρέχει is personal in Mt 5: 45 (scil. ὁ θεός as in LXX Gen 2: 5 and also class. ὁ θεὸς ὕει) with an object τὸν ὑετόν (cf. §492 and Blass *in loc.*); ἔβρεξεν πῦρ καὶ θεῖον Lk 17: 29 is perhaps also personal (from LXX Gen 19: 24 where the subject is κύριος). Rev 11: 6 ἵνα μὴ ὑετὸς βρέχῃ, Vulgate merely *ne pluat*. Instead of βροντῆσαι Jn 12: 29 has βροντὴν γεγονέναι. Ἀστράπτειν usually 'to shine' (class.) Lk 24: 4 (περι- A 9: 3, 22: 6), otherwise only ἡ ἀστραπὴ ἀστράπτουσα Lk 17: 24.—With subj. ὀψὲ οὔσης τῆς ὥρας Mk 11: 11 (ὀψίας ABDW al.). For δέον (ἐστίν), χρή, ἔδει and the like s. §130(1).—Impersonal δοκεῖ s. §405(2).—Obscure ἀπέχει Mk 14: 41: either 'he has received his money' or more likely impersonal (Anacreontea 15. 33 Hiller-Crusius, Cyrill. on Hag. 2.9 [= MPG 71, 1048], PLond ΙV 1343.38 [709 AD]) = class. ἀρκεῖ (Mt 25: 9, Jn 14: 8), properly 'it is receipted in full, the account is settled' (DW ἀπέχει τὸ τέλος 'it is the end [of the matter]'); Bauer s.v. Pallis, Notes 47 ff. is mistaken (ἐπέστη τὸ τέλος); cf. G. H. Boobyer, NTS 2 (1955–6) 44 ff. Lk 24: 21 τρίτην ταύτην ἡμέραν ἄγει 'he is already spending the third day' (cf. the references to Galen in Bauer), not impersonal 'it is...'.

130. The indefinite subject 'one'. (1) The impersonal passive (Lat. *itur* 'one goes') is not common in the NT and was never extensively used in Greek generally. (2) For 'one' it is much more customary to employ the 3rd plur. (without subject). The range of ideas expressed by verbs so used has been enlarged under the influence of Aramaic (which is not fond of the passive; in classical Greek the construction is used primarily with verbs of saying, etc. as is the case in MGr: Thumb² §254). Οἱ ἄνθρωποι may also appear as subject. (3) In the case of formulae introducing citations, e.g. λέγει etc., ὁ θεός, ἡ γραφή or the like is understood as subject.

(1) Mt 7: 2 μετρηθήσεται ὑμῖν (pass. to avoid the divine name; Dalman, Worte Ι² 183–5 [224 f.]), cf. Mk 4: 24 and Lk 6: 38. Lk 6: 38 δίδοτε καὶ δοθήσεται ὑμῖν (cf. Mt 7: 7 and Mk 4: 25), but further on μέτρον...δώσουσιν. 1 P 4: 6 νεκροῖς εὐηγγελίσθη. R 10: 10 πιστεύεται...ὁμολογεῖται. 1 C 15: 42 f. σπείρεται...ἐγείρεται. Herm Man 3.3 ἐπιστεύθη τῷ λόγῳ μου. But the subject of ἐρρέθη Mt 5: 31 is the following clause with ὅτι (EGK al.), used just as πρέπει, δεῖ, ἔξεστιν, ἐξόν, ἐνδέχεται, ἐγένετο, γέγραπται, and the like are used; ἀνέβη ἐπὶ τὴν καρδίαν αὐτοῦ A 7: 23 has as its subj. the following inf. (impersonal Herm Man 4.1.1 μὴ ἀναβαινέτω σου ἐπὶ τ. κ. περὶ γυναικὸς ἀλλοτρίας; Hebr. עָלָה עַל־לֵב).

(2) Συλλέγουσιν Mt 7: 16, Lk 6: 44, προσέφερον Mk 10: 13, ἐροῦσιν Lk 17: 23, Mt 5: 15, Mk 15: 27, Lk 12: 20, 14: 35, Jn 15: 6, 20: 2, A 3: 2, Rev 12: 6, 1 C 10: 20 OT. With οἱ ἄνθρωποι Lk 6: 31. 3rd plur. = 'one' also in Plut. and Dio Chrys. elsewhere than with verbs of 'saying'; Wifstrand, K. Hum. Vet.-samf. i Lund, Årsber. 1930–1, ΙΙΙ 138 f. 3rd pl. used circumspectly for 'God' (Dalman, *op. cit.*): L 6: 38 δώσουσιν, 12: 20, 16: 9.

(3) Λέγει 2 C 6: 2, G 3: 16 etc.; φησίν 1 C 6: 16, H 8: 5; εἴρηκε H 4: 4. In 2 C 10: 10 φησίν (SDE etc.; φασίν B) = 'the (imaginary) opponent says' as in the diatribe (Bultmann 10, 67), cf. Homil Clem 11.9 beginning; §465(2). R 10: 8 correctly λέγει 𝔓⁴⁶SAB, λ. ἡ γραφή D, ἡ γρ. λ. FG; φησίν of God also Barn 7.11 end, φησίν 'the author (Moses) wishes to say' in illustrations in commentary style 10.3–8.—W. Schmid, Jahresb. Altertumsw. 129 (1906) 274; Wackernagel, Syntax Ι² 113; Stolz-Schmalz, Lat. Gr.⁵ 622 f.; Ed. Norden, Aus altröm. Priesterbüchern (Lund, etc. 1939) 261. Cf. late Lat. *dicit* 'one says' Lerch, Neophilologus 27 (1941/2) 3.

2. AGREEMENT

(1) AGREEMENT IN GENDER

131. In adjectival or pronominal predicate. When the predicate stands for the subject conceived as a class and in the abstract, not as an individual instance or example, then classical usage puts the adjectival predicate in the neuter sing., even with subjects of another gender: οὐκ ἀγαθὸν πολυκοιρανίη. The NT exhibits only apparent examples of this construction, none at all for the fuller form μάταιόν τι, χρῆμα σοφόν, but some good instances of the parallel phenomenon in a pronominal (or comparable) predicate: τι 'something (special)', οὐδέν '(good for) nothing', etc. In particular assertions, however, the pronoun is brought into agreement.

Adj. pred.: Mt 6: 34 ἀρκετὸν τῇ ἡμέρᾳ ἡ κακία αὐτῆς, 2 C 2: 6 ἱκανὸν τῷ τοιούτῳ ἡ ἐπιτιμία αὕτη, A 12: 3 D ἰδὼν ὅτι ἀρεστόν ἐστιν τοῖς Ἰουδαίοις ἡ ἐπιχείρησις αὐτοῦ, thus always in an unclass. way for individual cases. Ἀρκετόν and ἱκανόν appear to follow the pattern of Lat. *satis*, cf. Lk 22: 38 ἰδοὺ μάχαιραι ὧδε δύο... ἱκανόν ἐστιν, Herm Vis 3.9.3 τὸ ἀρκετὸν τῆς τροφῆς *satis cibi* (but ἀρκετὸς ὁ χρόνος 1 P 4: 3) and τὸ ἱκανὸν ποιεῖν,— λαμβάνειν §5(3b). Καλὸν τὸ ἅλας Mk 9: 50, Lk 14: 34 'salt is a good thing' (class. perhaps χρήσιμον οἱ ἅλες) is a concealed example because the subj. happens to be neut.— *Pronominal pred.* or the like: G 6: 3 εἰ δοκεῖ τις εἶναί τι μηδὲν ὤν. Δοκεῖ τις εἶναι 'He gives the appearance of being something' Ps.-Callisth. 1.37 (Kroll 41.19). Τὸ μηδὲν ὄντας Plut., Mor. 106Α from Eur.(Frag. 332): Almqvist 111. 1 C 13: 2 οὐθέν εἰμι (like class., cf. G 2: 6; however, cf. εἶναί τινα ἑαυτόν A 5: 36, 8: 9 'a great man, somebody', cf. IRom 9.2, which is not impossible even in class.: K.-G. I 664, 1; cf. Epict. 2.24.19), 1 C 15: 10 χάριτι θεοῦ εἰμι ὅ εἰμι. Particular assertions: R 11: 15 τίς (what) ἡ πρόσληψις εἰ μή..., E 1: 18 τίς (*qualis*), 1 C 3: 17 (ὁ ναὸς τοῦ θεοῦ) οἵτινές ἐστε ὑμεῖς, but 6: 11 ταῦτά (scil. κλέπται etc.) τινες ἦτε = τοιοῦτοι, which might not have been entirely clear. Herm Sim 9.5.3 τί ἐστιν ('means') ἡ οἰκοδομή; Τί εἴη ταῦτα, τί ὁ Πέτρος ἐγένετο and the like s. §§298(5); 299(1, 2); 301(1). 1 C 11: 5 (the unveiled woman) ἕν ἐστιν καὶ τὸ αὐτὸ τῇ ἐξυρημένῃ (identical in meaning but not in person, hence the fem. is inconceivable); similarly Mt 6: 25 = Lk 12: 23 ἡ ψυχὴ πλεῖόν ἐστι.

132. In pronominal subject. (1) A pronoun subject may be made to agree with the predicate noun (against both German and English usage): αὕτη ἐστιν ἡ μεγάλη ἐντολή Mt 22: 38, Φιλίππους ἥτις ἐστὶν πόλις A 16: 12. Greek is not, however, as consistent as Latin: τοῦτο χάρις 1 P 2: 19, 20 is translated HAEC *est gratia*. (2) In explanatory phrases Koine employs the neuter ὅ ἐστιν, τοῦτ' ἔστιν (τουτέστιν) 'that is to say', a formulaic phrase used without reference to the gender of the word explained or to that of the word which explains—a usage which is perhaps strengthened by the Latin *id est, hoc est*. Yet the gender is readily assimilated to the predicate where there is identification: 1 C 3: 17 (§131), E 3: 13 θλίψεσιν..., ἥτις ἐστὶν δόξα ὑμῶν, Ph 1: 28, A 16: 12 (§164(3)); but even here ὅ ἐστιν is possible (E 5: 5). For τί ἐστι ταῦτα s. §299(1).

(1) Mt 7: 12.
(2) ὅ ἐστιν: Mk 3: 17 Βανηρεγες (minusc. 700), ὅ ἐστιν υἱοὶ βροντῆς; Jn 1: 41 etc. Mk 12: 42 λεπτὰ δύο,

ὅ ἐστιν κοδράντης. Mk 15: 16 τῆς αὐλῆς, ὅ ἐστιν πραιτώριον; E 6: 17 τὴν μάχαιραν..., ὅ ἐστιν ῥῆμα θεοῦ. With continuation of the construction: ἀρχήν..., ὅ ἐστιν ἄλλου κόσμου ἀρχήν Barn 15.8. **Τουτέστιν**: Mt 27: 46 ἠλί...τουτέστιν θεέ μου...; H 2: 14 τὸν τὸ κράτος ἔχοντα τοῦ θανάτου, τουτέστιν τὸν διάβολον; 7: 9, 9: 11 etc. Mt 27: 33 τόπον λεγόμενον Γολγοθᾶ, ὅ (ὅς A al.) ἐστιν κρανίου τόπος (the repeated λεγόμενος [W-ον] either before or after τόπος is correctly om. with SᶜᵃD); Mk 15: 22 Γ. τόπον, ὅ ἐστιν μεθερμηνευόμενον (§353(4)) κρ. τ.; Jn 19: 17 (badly garbled; perhaps read with LX vg etc. τὸν λεγόμενον κρανίου τόπον, Ἑβραϊστὶ δὲ Γ.). Against Latinism: T. Hedberg, Eustathios als Attizist (Diss. Uppsala, 1935) 120f. (Plato, Phdr. 249C τοῦτο δέ ἐστιν ἀνάμνησις ἐκείνων). Ὅ ἐστιν is vernacular, τουτέστιν literary: Mayser II 1, 75, 77.—Assimilation to the antecedent: Rev 4: 5 λαμπάδες..., ἅ (v.l. αἵ) εἰσιν τὰ ἑπτὰ πνεύματα, 5: 6, indeterminable v. 8 φιάλας..., αἵ εἰσιν αἱ προσευχαί, C 3: 5. Fluctuating: C 3: 14 τὴν ἀγάπην, ὅ (v.l. ὅς, ἥτις) ἐστιν σύνδεσμος; spurious: C 2: 10 ὅ (𝔓⁴⁶BDEFG) instead of ὅς (SACK) and v. 17 ὅ (BFG) for ἅ (𝔓⁴⁶SACD al.), 1: 27 ὅς (SCDEKL) for ὅ (𝔓⁴⁶ ABFGIP). ITr 11.2 ἕνωσιν..., ὅς ἐστιν αὐτός, but IEph 17.2 θεοῦ γνῶσιν, ὅ ἐστιν Ἰησοῦς Χριστός.

(2) AGREEMENT IN NUMBER

133. Perhaps no syntactical peculiarity of Greek is more striking to us than the use of the singular verb with a neuter plural subject (neuter plurals were originally in part feminine singular collectives: Schwyzer I 581f.). The rule appears to have been most strictly followed in Attic (Schwyzer II 607); Homer and Koine are less consistent, while the plural is used exclusively in MGr. In the NT (as in the LXX and pap.: Mayser II 3, 28ff.) there is marked diversity, and often in individual instances the MSS diverge. The plural is used for the most part in Herm. (1) The plural is used especially with neuters designating persons (also class., K.-G. I 65), most frequently with ἔθνη, less often with τέκνα and δαιμόνια. (2) The singular, on the contrary, preponderates with words having non-personal meaning (even when a numeral is inserted: ἐὰν γένηται...ἑκατὸν πρόβατα Mt 18: 12), (3) and even more so with abstracts and pronouns (ταῦτα, ἅ etc.).—For stereotyped ἴδε, ἰδού, ἄγε used in spite of a plural subject, s. §144.

(1) Πνεύματα varies: plur. Mk 1: 27, 3: 11 (v.l. sing.), 5: 13 (sing. B), A 8: 7? Rev 4: 5? 16: 14 (v.l. once sing.); sing. Lk 11: 26 κατοικεῖ, 10: 20 (v.l. δαιμόνια), 1 C 14: 32 (v.l. πνεῦμα), Rev 16: 13 S

Τέκνα with plur. Mt 10: 21 (sing. ΒΔ)=Mk 13: 12 (sing. B); sing. 1 Jn 3: 10, 2 Jn 13, R 9: 8, 1 C 7: 14. Ἔθνη with plur. Mt 6: 32 (sing. EG al.), 12: 21 OT, 25: 32 (sing. AE al.), Lk 12: 30 (sing. 𝔓⁴⁵AD al.), A 4: 25 OT, 11: 1 (sing. D*), 13: 48, R 2: 14 (sing. DᶜE), 15: 12 OT, 27, 1 C 10: 20? (sing. KL, om. τὰ ἔθνη BDEF al.), G 3: 8 OT, 2 T 4: 17 (sing. KL), Rev 11: 28 (sing. 𝔓⁴⁷S*), 15: 4, 18: 3, 23, 21: 24, 1 Clem 59.4; sing. in all MSS R 9: 30, E 4: 17. Sing. preponderates with δαιμόνια: Lk 4: 41 (plur. SC), 8: 2, 30 (plur. CF, D also reads differently, cf. 31, 32), 35 (plur. Sᶜ), 38 (33 the evidence favors εἰσῆλθον, SU -εν), 10: 17; plur. Ja 2: 19.

(2) Exceptions: Mt 6: 28 (cf. § 476(2)) τὰ κρίνα πῶς αὐξάνουσιν etc. (sing. Lk 12: 27 in the same saying); Jn 19: 31 first ἵνα μὴ μείνῃ τὰ σώματα, then ἵνα κατεαγῶσιν αὐτῶν τὰ σκέλη. Πρόβατα in Jn 10: 3 ἀκούει, 4 ἀκολουθεῖ (with the addition ὅτι οἴδασιν τὴν φωνὴν αὐτοῦ, because οἶδε would have been ambiguous, and accordingly v. 5 also has pl.), 8 οὐκ ἤκουσαν (-σεν 𝔓⁴⁵L), 10 ἔχωσιν, 12 ἐστιν 𝔓⁴⁵SABLX (εἰσιν DΓ al.), and continually varying like this until v. 16; 27, 28 with indeterminate text. Herm Sim 9. 1.8 ἐβόσκοντο (A, -ετι PMich) τὰ κτήνη καὶ πετεινά.

(3) Exceptions: τὰ ῥήματα ταῦτα with ἐφάνησαν Lk 24: 11, ἔργα with δύνανται (v.l. -αται) 1 T 5: 25. ἅ εἰσιν καὶ ἃ μέλλει γενέσθαι Rev 1: 19; ἐγένοντο ἀμφότερα 1 Clem 42.2, πάντα...εἰσίν 27: 6 (Jn 17: 7 v.l.). Rev 15: 4 τὰ δικαιώματά σου ἐφανερώθησαν (-θη 𝔓⁴⁷), A 5: 12 ἐγείνοντο [σημεῖα καὶ τέρατα] πολλά parchment fragment iv AD beg. (Salonius, ZNW 26 [1927] 118) for ἐγίνετο of all other MSS. 1 C 10: 11 two vv.ll.: ταῦτα δὲ τυπικῶς συνέβαινεν and... τύποι συνέβαινον, the latter with the verb agreeing with predicate noun (as in 6, Herm Sim 5.5.2, 3), which is also found in class. (and in Lat.; K.-G. ι 75f.).

τὸν θεὸν καὶ λεγόντων; (c) even a plural verb with a singular subject is not impossible: ὁ πλεῖστος ὄχλος ἔστρωσαν ἑαυτῶν τὰ ἱμάτια Mt 21: 8. (2) Feminine or neuter personal collectives standing in the plural may be continued by a masculine plural: G 1: 23 μόνον δὲ ἀκούοντες ἦσαν refers to ταῖς ἐκκλησίαις v. 22. (3) A masculine participle referring to a neuter noun which designates a personal being: Mk 9: 20 ἰδὼν αὐτὸν τὸ πνεῦμα.

(1) (a) οἴδατε τὴν οἰκίαν Στεφανᾶ, ὅτι ἐστὶν ἀπαρχή...καὶ ἔταξαν ἑαυτούς 1 C 16: 15 (ἔταξεν ἑαυτήν would be unnatural). (b) A 21: 36 τὸ πλῆθος τοῦ λαοῦ, κράζοντες (κρᾶζον DHLP); cf. 3: 11, 5: 16. (c) A 6: 7 πολύς τε ὄχλος τῶν ἱερέων (=πολλοὶ ἱερεῖς) ὑπήκουον (-εν AE) τῇ πίστει. 25: 24 ἐνέτυχον (-χεν ΒΗΨ). Jn 7: 49, Rev 8: 9, 9: 18 ἀπεκτάνθησαν (𝔓⁴⁷ -θη) τὸ τρίτον τῶν ἀνθρώπων. Herm Vis 2.2.2 (σπέρμα), Sim 9.1.8 (γένος; ἐνέμοντο A, ἐνέμε[το] PMich). Incongruity as the result of an additional remark: 8.10.1 ἀκούσαντες...τὸ πλεῖστον μέρος... μετενόησαν, cf. 2.9 and for ἕκαστος and εἷς s. § 305.

(2) E 4: 17f. τὰ ἔθνη περιπατεῖ...ἐσκοτωμένοι (1 C 12: 2 is different). Lk 10: 13 Τύρῳ καὶ Σιδῶνι... καθήμενοι (-ναι 𝔓⁴⁵DEG al. is perhaps better because the cities as wholes and not the inhabitants are meant; cf. Mt 11: 21ff.).

(3) Mt 9: 26 κράξας καὶ...σπαράξας of a πνεῦμα (-ξαν᾽ AC²NX, cf. 1: 26 where only D has -ξας). Mk 13: 14 τὸ βδέλυγμα...ἑστηκότα (ἑστηκός D, ἑστός AEF al. as in Mt 24: 15). Referring to πνεῦμα: Lk 9: 40 αὐτὸν 𝔓⁴⁵, 11: 24 three masc. ptcp. in 𝔓⁴⁵ minusc. (CD only the 3rd).—A metaphor is dropped: IPhld 3.1 τῶν βοτανῶν, ἅστινας... αὐτούς (people are meant by βοτ.), similarly ITr 11.1. For *constructio ad sensum* with αὐτοῦ etc. s. § 282, with rel. pron. § 296.

(3) 'CONSTRUCTIO AD SENSUM'

134. The so-called *constructio ad sensum*, without following any fixed rules, was very widespread in Greek from early times and is found in the NT as in the papyri (Mayser ΙΙ 3, 25ff., 38f.). (1) The principal instance is that in which a collective, embracing a plurality of persons in a singular noun, is construed as if the subject were plural. Such collectives are masculines like ὄχλος, λαός, feminines like στρατιά, οἰκία, neuters like πλῆθος, σπέρμα (with plur. Herm Vis 2.2.2). (a) When the plural which conforms to the sense does not appear until the following clause, we feel no offense: Jn 6: 2 ἠκολούθει ὄχλος πολύς, ὅτι ἐθεώρουν; (b) a plural circumstantial participle joined to a singular noun is harsher: Lk 2: 13 πλῆθος στρατιᾶς οὐρανίου (=ἀγγέλων), αἰνούντων

(4) AGREEMENT WITH TWO OR MORE CO-ORDINATE WORDS

135. Connected by καί (ἤ). Regarding agreement with two or more subjects connected by καί, the same loose rules are valid for the NT as for classical usage. The following examples with persons as subject may be noted: (1) When the subject consists of sing. + sing. or of sing. + plur. the verb agrees (a) with the first subject if the verb stands before it, except when the subject-group is basically conceived as a whole; (b) with both subjects taken together if the verb stands after the second subject; (c) with the first if the verb stands between; (d) rules (a) and (b) can be combined when a finite verb stands before and a participle after the group, or the reverse. (2) When one of the two subjects is a 1st plur., the verb is in the 1st plur. and modifiers which refer to the subject are in the nominative plur.; such modifiers are in the masculine even when the subject group combines masculine and feminine. (3) Attributives (participles) which belong to two or more connected substantives customarily agree with the nearest. (4) The sing. is regularly used with two sing. subjects connected by ἤ (as in English but contrary to German).

(1) Mayser II 3, 23 f., 30 ff. (a) A 11: 14 and 16: 31 σωθήσῃ σὺ καὶ ὁ οἶκός σου, where the first is the main subj. ('you together with your house'); likewise Jn 2: 2 ἐκλήθη δὲ καὶ ὁ Ἰησοῦς καὶ οἱ μαθηταὶ αὐτοῦ. But also when the subjects are equal: Jn 18: 15 ἠκολούθει δὲ τῷ Ἰ. Σίμων Πέτρος καὶ ἄλλος μαθητής; 20: 3, A 16: 30. Still more so when the subjects are not persons: παρέλθῃ ὁ οὐρανὸς καὶ ἡ γῆ Mt 5: 18. Plural: Mk 10: 35 προπορεύονται αὐτῷ Ἰάκωβος καὶ Ἰωάνης οἱ υἱοὶ Ζεβεδαίου (the brothers were thought of as a pair from the start). Jn 21: 2 ἦσαν ὁμοῦ Σίμων Πέτρος καὶ..., Lk 23: 12 ἐγένοντο φίλοι ὅ τε Ἡρῴδης καὶ ὁ Πιλᾶτος, A 5: 24 ὡς δὲ ἤκουσαν...ὅ τε στρατηγὸς... καὶ οἱ ἱερεῖς (mentioned together above in 17 and 21), cf. 1: 13, 4: 27. Where such reasons are lacking and the variants are conflicting, the sg. is probably to be preferred, e.g. Lk 8: 19, A 17: 14 (R 15: 26 following 𝔓⁴⁶B?). (b) See under (d). (c) Lk 8: 22 αὐτὸς ἐνέβη εἰς πλοῖον καὶ οἱ μαθηταὶ αὐτοῦ, Jn 4: 36 (with ὁμοῦ!), etc. (d) A 5: 29 ἀποκριθεὶς δὲ Πέτρος καὶ οἱ ἀπόστολοι εἶπαν; also v. 21. Lk 2: 33; Mt 17: 3 ὤφθη (SBD, al. -ησαν)...Μωυσῆς καὶ Ἠλίας συλλαλοῦντες. The number also varies with two finite verbs: Jn 12: 22 ἔρχεται Ἀνδρέας καὶ Φίλιππος καὶ λέγουσιν. Hardly correct A 14: 14 D ἀκούσας δὲ Βαρναβᾶς καὶ Παῦλος διαρρήξαντες...ἐξεπήδησαν, 13: 46 D.
(2) Mayser II 3, 34 f. Lk 2: 48 ὁ πατήρ σου κἀγώ (Mary) ὀδυνώμενοι ἐζητοῦμέν σε; Jn 10: 30; 1 C 9: 6.
(3) Lk 10: 1 εἰς πᾶσαν πόλιν καὶ τόπον; 1 Th 5: 23. H 9: 9 δῶρά τε καὶ θυσίαι...μὴ δυνάμεναι (3: 6 βεβαίαν is missing in 𝔓¹³𝔓⁴⁶B, interpolated in the others from v. 14).
(4) Mt 5: 18 ἰῶτα ἓν ἢ μία κεραία οὐ μὴ παρέλθῃ; 12: 25, 18: 8; E 5: 5; the sg. is even more common when the verb precedes the group as in 1 C 14: 24. G 1: 8 ἐὰν ἡμεῖς ἢ ἄγγελος...εὐαγγελίζηται (impossible to embrace both by means of -ζώμεθα, which otherwise could be used with reference to ἡμεῖς). Exception: Ja 2: 15 ἐὰν ἀδελφὸς ἢ ἀδελφὴ γυμνοὶ ὑπάρχωσιν (γυμνός or γυμνή would have been harsh).

(5) MORE SERIOUS INCONGRUENCIES (SOLECISMS)

136. *Revelation* exhibits a quantity of striking solecisms which are based especially on inattention to agreement (a rough style), in contrast to the rest of the NT and to the other writings ascribed to John: (1) An appositional phrase (or circumstantial participle) is often found in the nominative instead of an oblique case (§137(3)): τῆς καινῆς Ἰερουσαλὴμ ἡ καταβαίνουσα 3: 12. Likewise with some translators of the OT (Nestle, Philologica Sacra 7). (2) Occasionally there is also a hanging accusative or genitive, e.g. τὰς ἑπτὰ φιάλας τῶν γεμόντων (instead of τὰς γεμούσας) 21: 9. (3) The masculine is often substituted for the feminine or neuter: 11: 4 αἱ δύο λυχνίαι αἱ... ἑστῶτες (ἑστῶσαι SᶜᵉP). Examples from late Greek in Jannaris §1181 b. (4) λέγων λέγοντες often appear as anacolouthon, ἔχων less often. (5) Incongruence in number: 9: 12 ἔρχεται ἔτι δύο Οὐαί (previously ἡ Οὐαί, therefore not neuter [but according to Katz, ThLZ 1957, 112 οὐαί is not a certain incongruence in number but perhaps in gender since the feminine with a neuter meaning is a Semitism (cf. §§ 58; 248 (3))]).—The participle accounts for the major part of these incongruencies; in other respects, too, its use in the later period becomes more and more uncertain, with the masculine, especially in the nominative singular, greatly preferred; in MGr the participle has only *one* indeclinable form in -ντας (nom.). Cf. the commentaries on Rev and the introductions to the NT on the whole question.

On late and MGr s. Reinhold 57 f.; Dieterich 207 f.; Jannaris §§822 f.; Radermacher² 106 ff.; Krumbacher, Das Problem der ngr. Schriftspr. (München, 1903) 50; Thumb, Hell. 131; Vogeser 40; Wolf I 54 f.; Ljungvik 8 f.; Ursing 25 f.; Kapsomenakis 30 f., 40 ff. n. 2; 78 f. n. 1; Mayser II 1 339; II 3, 22, 35. Acc. to Hatzidakis, Πρακτ. Ἀκ. Ἀθ. 3 (1928) 634 ff. MGr -ντας has arisen through assimilation to the nom. masc. sg. from the Byzantine adv. in -ντα, which goes back to the old neut. acc. pl. (indecl. -ντα several times in inscriptions from Asia Minor: Klaffenbach, DLZ 1933, 498). For incongruent nom. of the ptcp. in the pap. s. Mayser II 1, 341 f.

(1) 1: 5 ἀπὸ Ἰησοῦ ὁ μάρτυς ὁ πιστός (ὁ μ. ὁ π. quotation! below τῷ ἀγαπῶντι agreeing with αὐτῷ 6); 2: 20, 7: 4, 8: 9, 9: 14, 14: 12, 20: 2. Ποτήριον... γέμων βδελυγμάτων καὶ τὰ ἀκάθαρτα 17: 4. As Nestle (*op. cit.*) remarks, all these solecisms were later removed by educated revisers. In 1: 4 the true text is still not found in any edition; originally it certainly read: ἀπὸ τῶν ἑπτὰ πνευμάτων τὰ ἐνώπιον τ. θ. α. This jarred upon every cultured ear, hence the five variants: omission, τῶν, ἅ, ἅ ἐστιν, ἅ εἰσιν. From the LXX Nestle quotes Amos 2: 6 f. ἕνεκεν τῶν ὑποδημάτων, τὰ πατοῦντα...(τῶν πατούντων Lucian and the Catena.
(2) 7: 9 ὄχλος...ἑστῶτες...περιβεβλημένους (an

acc. to εἶδον which comes at the beginning of the verse, but after καὶ ἰδού with the nom.).

(3) 5: 6 εἶδον ἀρνίον ἑστηκὼς (S, -κὸς AP 046) ὡς ἐσφαγμένον, ἔχων (ἔχον P). 14: 19 εἰς τὴν ληνὸν ... τὸν μέγαν (τοῦ μεγάλου 𝔓⁴⁷, τὴν μεγάλην S). 17: 4 s. *supra* (1). 13: 14 τῷ θηρίῳ ὃς (S ὃ is a correction) ..., because it is a reference to the Antichrist (cf. 8 αὐτόν, but v.l. αὐτῷ; 11 ἄλλο θηρίον ἀναβαίνων 𝔓⁴⁷ [also referring to λέγων 14 almost all witnesses]); s. the commentaries and Foerster, TW III 134f. (Blass differed).—On (ἀρνίον) ἑστώς s. § 96. 9: 14 (φωνὴν ...) λέγοντα SA (λέγουσαν 𝔓⁴⁷P).—12: 5 ἄρσεν (AC, ἄρρενα 𝔓⁴⁷S 046, ἄρσενα P) is substantival and in apposition to υἱόν (ὅς refers to υἱόν), therefore correct; in addition, ἔτεκεν ἄρσεν is an allusion to LXX Is 66: 7. On the basis of PSI IX 1039.36 (iii AD) υἱὸν ἄρρενα, Olsson (Glotta 23 [1935] 112) recommends υἱὸν ἄρρενα (ἄρσενα) for Rev 12: 5.

(4) λέγων λέγοντες are, so to speak, indecl.: 4: 1, 5: 12, 11: 15 (𝔓⁴⁷SCP λέγουσαι), 14: 7 (𝔓⁴⁷ λέγονται); with v.l. 11: 1, 19: 6. A 6: 11 ἄνδρας λέγοντες SAD*; 13 S. Similarly = לֵאמֹר in the LXX (Gen 15: 1, 22: 20, 38: 13, 45: 16 etc.). Correspondingly ἔχων 10: 2, 21: 14, ἔχουσα 12. Rev 4: 1 ἀπὸ ὁ ὤν etc. s. § 143. Rob. 413–16.

137. Such incongruencies as are found occasionally in other books of the NT are to be regarded either as more excusable or as a corruption of the text. Cf. Mayser II 3, 22. (1) Indeclinable πλήρης (only with a following gen.) which appears a few times, but never without variants, was in use generally in vulgar Hellenistic from i AD onward. (2) Ph 2: 1 εἴ τις οὖν παράκλησις ... εἴ τι παραμύθιον ... εἴ τις κοινωνία ... εἴ τις σπλάγχνα καὶ οἰκτιρμοί probably ought to be written εἴ τι throughout ('if ... amounts to anything', cf. § 131, or with stereotyped adverbial τι; Dibelius, Hdb. *ad loc.*: the solecism was not so offensive, and it remains only to accept a stereotyped τις like stereotyped τι; τινα is avoided for rhythmical considerations). (3) The remaining instances are appositives or

circumstantial participles in the nominative instead of an oblique case (cf. § 136(1)).

(1) Jn 1: 14 τὴν δόξαν αὐτοῦ ... πλήρης (-ρη D) χάριτος καὶ ἀληθείας; A 6: 5 ἄνδρα πλήρης (-ρη BC²) πίστεως; 3 πλήρης (-ρεις SBCD) πνεύματος; 19: 28 πλήρης (AEL, -ρεις al.) θυμοῦ; Mk 8: 19 πλήρης (-ρεις SBCL) κλασμάτων; only 2 Jn 8 without following gen. μισθὸν πλήρης L. Cf. German '*eine Arbeit voll*' (or '*voller*') *Fehler*' (Nestle): 'a work full of errors'. Πλήρης declined without indeclinable variant, only Mt 14: 20, 15: 37, Mk 4: 28 (πλήρη σίτου or πλήρης [+ ὁ DW] σῖτος), 6: 43 (πλήρεις, v.l. πληρώματα), always without gen. Cf. Mayser I¹ 63f.; I² 2, 58; Thack. 177; Psaltes 160; M.-H. 162. On indecl. ἥμισυ s. § 48.

(2) Cf. Plato, Phdr. 260 D acc. to codex B εἴ τι ἐμὴ ξυμβουλή 'if my advice counts for anything' and Mlt. 59 [89]; Radermacher¹ 184.

(3) Ja 3: 8 τὴν γλῶσσαν ... ἀκατάσχετον κακόν, μεστὴ ἰοῦ (the editors place a semicolon before ἀκατ. so that the following becomes independent, with ἐστιν understood). Lk 24: 47 κηρυχθῆναι μετάνοιαν ... ἀρξάμενοι (-ένων D, -ενον AC³FH al.) and A 10: 37 οἴδατε τὸ γενόμενον ῥῆμα καθ' ὅλης τῆς Ἰουδαίας, ἀρξάμενος (-ενον is correct 𝔓⁴⁵LP) ἀπὸ τῆς Γαλιλαίας (ἀρξ. γὰρ AD improves nothing; perhaps ἀρξ. ἀ. τ. Γ. stems from Lk 23: 5; Beginnings IV 14, 120: there is some evidence that the nom. was used absolutely in a quasi-adverbial sense). A dangling acc. ptcp. appears in A 26: 3 ἐπὶ σοῦ ..., μάλιστα γνώστην ὄντα σε ... (ἐπιστάμενος add. SᶜAC). Mk 7: 19 καθαρίζων (referring to πᾶν τὸ ... 18 or to ἀφεδρῶνα? -ίζον KMU al., -ίζει D). 2 Th 1: 8 διδούς D*FG (the others διδόντος correctly). In the addition of W to Mk 16: 14 ὑπὸ τὸν σατανᾶν ἐστιν, ὁ μὴ ἐῶν. Cf. Audollent, Defix. Tab. 241.24 κατὰ τοῦ ... θεοῦ τοῦ καθημένου ... ὁ διορίσας ... καὶ χωρίσας; PAmh II 112.10 (128 AD) ἀπέχειν παρ' αὐτοῦ τὸν ὁμολογοῦντα (instead of τοῦ -ντος), similarly 110.17 (75 AD); 111.14 (132 AD); 113.11 (157 AD). Wilhelm, Wien. Sitzb. 166, 3 (1912) 13f.; Havers, Glotta 16 (1928) 105ff.; Ghedini, Vang. ap. 447; Mayser II 3, 190ff.

3. USE OF GENDER AND NUMBER

(1) GENDER

138. (1) The neuter is sometimes used with reference to persons if it is not the individuals but a general quality that is to be emphasized. Intensifying πᾶν or πάντα may be added: τὸ γεγεννημένον Jn 3: 6, πᾶν τὸ γ. 1 Jn 5: 4 (τὸν γεγεννημένον 1). For classical examples s. K.-G. I 14, W.-S. § 28 n. 1; πάντα τὰ συμβεβιασμένα

Dem. 8.41. H 9: 5 Χερουβίμ as neuter (κατασκευάζοντα, but AP -ζον); Bauer s.v. for discussion and bibliography. (2) The feminine is used instead of the neuter as the result of a literal translation of the quotation from Hebrew Mt 21: 42 = Mk 12: 11 παρὰ κυρίου ἐγένετο αὕτη (not to be referred to κεφαλὴν γωνίας!) καὶ ἔστιν θαυμαστή (Ps 117 (118): 23); αὕτη = זֹאת 'αὕτη, τοῦτο'. (3) Masculine for feminine and the reverse: λεγιών Mk 5: 15

masculine because it is the name of a demon, elsewhere feminine = *legio*. Ἡ Βάαλ s. §53(4).

(1) Jn 17: 2 πάσης σαρκός, ἵνα πᾶν ὅ (cf. Hebr. כָּל־אֲשֶׁר) δέδωκας αὐτῷ, δώσει αὐτοῖς (ἔχῃ D) ζωὴν αἰώνιον, where men are first subsumed under σάρξ, then under πᾶν, and finally are designated by αὐτοῖς, the commonest term. Similarly 6: 37. Η 7: 7 τὸ ἔλαττον ὑπὸ τοῦ κρείττονος εὐλογεῖται (more general than ὁ ἐλάττων or οἱ ἐλάττονες). G 3: 22 τὰ πάντα (more general than τοὺς πάντας R 11: 32). Jn 12: 32 πάντα S*D, al. πάντας. 1 C 1: 27f. τὰ μωρὰ τοῦ κόσμου...τὰ ἀσθενῆ τ. κ....τὰ ἰσχυρά (pl. because τὸ μωρόν, ἀσθενὲς τοῦ κ. would be understood, in view of v. 25 τὸ μ., ἀσθ. τοῦ θεοῦ, as 'the foolishness, weakness of the world').—To be understood differently τὸ γεννώμενον Lk 1: 35 (individual = τὸ τέκνον, which is perhaps present to the mind of the author) and τὸ δωδεκάφυλον (§ 120(3); collective).

(2) Cf. LXX Ps 118 (119): 50 αὕτη, 1 Km 4: 7 τοιαύτη, etc. Swete, Introduction³ 307; Katz, Philo's Bible 25f. More examples in F. W. Mozley, The Psalter of the Church (1905) 49; the same in the Old Latin and Vulgate: H. Roensch, Itala und Vulgata (1869) 452.—Lk 11: 33 εἰς κρυπτήν is the exact equivalent of Aram. (fem. pass. ptcp. = neut.) 'hidden' (Wellhausen: 'in a hiding-place' without basis): Torrey, ZDMG 101 (1951) 135. Bauer takes another view (εἰς κρύπτην, which Preuschen had rejected).

(2) NUMBER

(A) Singular

139. The collective (generic) singular appears several times in the NT with persons, also with ethnic names: R 3: 1 τί τὸ περισσὸν τοῦ Ἰουδαίου; i.e. of the Jew as Jew (in 2: 17–19 one is singled out as a type). This usage is not unclassical (e.g. Thuc. 6.78.1 τὸν Συρακόσιον–τῷ Ἀθηναίῳ, cf. K.-G. ι 14; Wackernagel, Syntax ι² 93f.). S. also §§ 138(1); 263.

Mt 12: 35 ὁ ἀγαθὸς ἄνθρωπος...ὁ πονηρὸς ἄ.; 1 P 4: 18 ὁ δίκαιος...ὁ ἀσεβής; R 14: 1 τὸν ἀσθενοῦντα. R 13: 3 τῷ ἀγαθῷ ἔργῳ. But Ja 2: 6 τὸν πτωχόν refers to the example in v. 2; also in 5: 6 τὸν δίκαιον denotes an individual example. 1 C 6: 5 διακρῖναι ἀνὰ μέσον τοῦ ἀδελφοῦ αὐτοῦ is an abbreviation (requiring correction?) for ἀνὰ μ. ἀδελφοῦ καὶ (ἀνὰ μ.) τοῦ ἀδ. αὐτοῦ (syᵖ). The repetition of ἀνὰ μέσον is a Semitism both in the Pesh. and the LXX. Johannessohn ιι 171ff. attempts to work out the rules according to which the second ἀνὰ μέσον can be omitted in contrast to the Hebrew text. Examples such as ἀνὰ μ. ὕδατος καὶ ὕδατος Gen 1: 6, ἀνὰ μ. ποίμνης καὶ ποίμνης Gen 32: 16 compare with 1 C 6: 5. However, more slavish translators tend to imitate the Hebrew closely; thus omission or repetition is largely a matter of difference with regard to the standards of translation. Cf. Ezk 18: 8, Dt 1: 16.

140. Distributive singular. Of the two types 'they shook their heads' and 'they shook their head' (i.e. each his own, cf. κινήσουσι τὴν κεφαλὴν αὐτῶν LXX Jer 18: 16, τὰς κεφαλάς A [the attestation is inverted in Jer 14: 4; Ziegler prefers the sing. in both instances]), the first (plur.) is normal in Greek (as in Lat.), but it is not without exceptions. The second is known to Hebrew and is preferred by Aramaic (Kautzsch § 78, 3) so that its use in the NT is thereby facilitated. Ἀπὸ προσώπου etc. is always used in the singular in conveying Semitic idioms.

A 21: 24 ἵνα ξυρήσωνται τὴν κεφαλήν (*capita* vg); Lk 1: 66 ἔθεντο πάντες ἐν τῇ καρδίᾳ (DL ταῖς καρδίαις) αὐτῶν; Mk 8: 17 πεπωρωμένην ἔχετε τὴν καρδίαν ὑμῶν.—Representing Semitic idiom: ἀπὸ προσώπου τῶν πατέρων A 7: 45, κατὰ πρόσωπον πάντων τῶν λαῶν Lk 2: 31, διὰ στόματος (πάντων) τῶν προφητῶν A 3: 18, 21; E 6: 14 περιζωσάμενοι τὴν ὀσφὺν ὑμῶν... καὶ ἐνδυσάμενοι τὸν θώρακα, Rev 6: 11 ἐδόθη αὐτοῖς ἑκάστῳ στολὴ λευκή (but ἐσθής Lk 24: 4 collective 'clothing' as usual with this word; v.l. ἐσθήσεσιν, s. § 47(4)), C 3: 16 ἐν τῇ καρδίᾳ ὑμῶν DᶜΕΙΚL (pl., al.).— Even διὰ χειρὸς ἀνόμων A 2: 23 (vg *per manus iniquorum*), but with the understandable variant χειρῶν C³ΕP; likewise διὰ χειρὸς αὐτῶν 15: 23, but διὰ τῶν χειρῶν αὐτῶν 14: 3; ἐκ τῆς χειρὸς αὐτῶν Jn 10: 39.

(B) Plural

141. Of concrete subjects. In a generalization the plural can stand for *one* person: Mt 2: 20 τεθνήκασιν οἱ ζητοῦντες τὴν ψυχὴν τοῦ παιδίου, i.e. Herod (19) and those with him etc. (allusive plural, Smyth § 1007). The plural of certain concrete substantives, originally to denote what is long or wide, or mysterious powers (Havers, Festschrift Kretschmer 40f.), is more frequent; German and English regularly employ the singular (but cf. 'heavens', 'wages', etc.): (1) In an unclassical way following the Hebrew pattern αἰῶνες 'world' H 1: 2, 11: 3 (1 T 1: 17?), 'eternity' Lk 1: 33 and often (especially εἰς τοὺς αἰῶνας τῶν αἰώνων G 1: 5 etc. as in the LXX Ps 83 (84): 5), = עוֹלָמִים. Οὐρανοί = שָׁמַיִם, yet most authors use it only in a figurative sense as the abode of God (sing. also), while the singular predominates in the literal sense, except for those instances where, according to the Jewish conception, several heavens were to be distinguished. (2) The plural for the four directions and the like is classical, as it is (3) for the names of festivals, (4) in πύλαι (only πύλαι ᾅδου Mt 16: 18, cf. LXX Wsd 16: 13) and θύραι (NT only in fixed phrases), (5) in κόλποι, (6) in αἵματα (class. poetry, Hell.; Behm, TW I 172 n. 6), (7) in ὕδατα. (8) Ἀργύρια 'pieces of money' is unusual in classical (Plato, Lg. 5.742 D, cf. Pollux 3.86, 9.89f.) Mt 26: 15, 28: 12; ὀψώνια 'wages' is Hellenistic Lk 3: 14 etc. (also plural only in LXX: Rouffiac 38; papyri sing. and plur. without distinction: Mayser II 1, 37). Κέντρα A 9: 5 t.r., 26: 14 is also classical and Hellenistic.

(1) Always ἡ βασιλεία τῶν οὐρανῶν Mt 3: 2 etc.; ὁ πατὴρ ὑμῶν ὁ ἐν (τοῖς) οὐρανοῖς 5: 16 etc.; Lk 10: 20 τὰ ὀνόματα ὑμῶν ἐγγέγραπται ἐν τοῖς οὐρ. (τῷ οὐρανῷ D); 12: 33 θησαυρὸν ἐν τοῖς οὐρ.; A 2: 34, 7: 56. In Paul: 2 C 5: 1, E 3: 15, 6: 9 (οὐρανῷ S), Ph 3: 20, C 1: 5, 4: 1 (-ῷ S*ABC), 1 Th 1: 10; 1 P 1: 4 (-ῷ S). John nowhere plur., even Rev only 12: 12 (from LXX). Several heavens: E 4: 10 ὑπεράνω πάντων τῶν οὐρ.; 1: 10, etc.; also perhaps αἱ δυνάμεις τῶν οὐρ. Mt 24: 29 pars. Plur. of the vault of heaven Mt 24: 31 ἀπ' ἄκρων οὐρανῶν ἕως ἄκρων αὐτῶν (translation Semitism?), contrast Mk 13: 27 and LXX Dt 30: 4; Mt 3: 16, 17, cf. Mk 1: 10, 11 (but Lk 3: 21, 22 sing.) and A 7: 56, is different. Οὐρανοί in the LXX especially with plur. verb preceding and in personifying invocations: Katz (s. infra). Torm, ZNW 33 (1934) 48–50 (mostly poetical). Katz, Philo's Bible 141–6; Welt des Orients II 2 (1956) 268; H. Traub, TW V 510f. (LXX), 512ff. (NT).

(2) Ἀνατολαί 'east' and δυσμαί 'west' Mt 2: 1, 8: 11, etc., but only in the phrase ἀπὸ (ἕως) ἀνατολῶν, δυσμῶν. The sing., however, in ἐν τῇ ἀνατολῇ Mt 2: 2, 9; also ἀπὸ ἀνατολῆς (B -ῶν) alongside ἀπὸ δυσμῶν Rev 21: 13; ἀπὸ ἀνατολῆς (-ῶν A) ἡλίου 7: 2 and 16: 12; δυσμή never in sing., as it is almost always plur. in class. Always ἐκ δεξιῶν, ἐξ ἀριστερῶν (εὐωνύμων); ἐν τοῖς δεξιοῖς Mk 16: 5, εἰς τὰ δεξιὰ μέρη Jn 21: 6; besides ἐν δεξιᾷ scil. χειρί (or ἐνδέξια?) R 8: 34, E 1: 20 etc. (class. also). Τὰ μέρη 'district' Mt 2: 22 etc.; in A 7: 43 ἐπὶ τὰ μέρη is a theological 'improvement' (Haenchen[12] 236) of Am 5: 27; ἐπέκεινα = מֵהָלְאָה 'beyond' also in Gen 35: 16 (21), Jer 22: 19.

(3) Ἐγκαίνια Jn 10: 22, γενέσια Mt 14: 6, Mk 6: 21; cf. class. Διονύσια Παναθήναια etc., pap. γενέθλια (§ 200(3)), Ἀρσινόεια and others (Mayser II 1, 39). Σάββατα of one sabbath Mt 28: 1 (s. § 164(4)), C 2: 16(?), especially in the dat. τοῖς σάββασι (-άτοις) Mt 12: 1, 5 etc. and ἡ ἡμέρα τῶν σαββάτων Lk 4: 16 etc. would fit into this pattern. But sing. also; both sing. and plur. for 'week'. Σάββατα = שַׁבָּת + α to make it pronounceable in Greek; accordingly first σάββατα in the Hexateuch, thereafter also σάββατον (Schwyzer, KZ 62 [1935] 10 f.). Σάββατα 'sabbath' as early as ZenP Cairo IV 59762.6 (iii BC).

Horace, Sat. 1.9.69. Pl. for a festival τὰ ἄζυμα (instead of οἱ ἄζυμοι scil. ἄρτοι) is also involved in ἡ ἑορτὴ τῶν ἀζύμων Lk 22: 1 and αἱ ἡμέραι τῶν ἀ. A 12: 3 etc. (s. Debrunner, GGA 1919, 121.3), for which the shortened τὰ ἄζυμα also appears: Mk 14: 1 τὸ πάσχα καὶ τὰ ἄζυμα (D om. κ. τ. ἄζ.). Here also γάμοι 'wedding (ceremony, feast)' Mt 22: 2 etc. (class. in poets and Isaeus 8.18 and 20, besides Arist., Frag. 549; pap. ii AD [Preisigke s.v.], further e.g. POxy I 111 [iii AD] εἰς γάμους, BGU III 909.3 [359 AD] εἰς τοὺς γ. as often in the NT: εἰς (τοὺς) γ.; Diog. L. 3.2 ἐν γάμοις δειπνῶν; pl. Latinism = nuptiae? For 'wedlock' γάμος also appears in the pap.); yet sing. Mt 22: 8 etc. (H 13: 8 'wedlock'). —Τὰ πάσχα Mt 26: 18 W for τὸ πάσχα is the same error as τὰ παταχρα Is 8: 21 for τὸ παταχρα (Aram. פִּתְכְּרָא 'idol'; Is 37: 38 τὸ[ν] παταχρον: Katz).

(4) Otherwise of one gate πύλη; likewise θύρα of one door (class. often θύραι); following αἱ θύραι πᾶσαι A 16: 26, perhaps θύραι Jn 20: 19, 20, A 5: 19, 21: 30 is to be understood as several doors. Idioms with pl.: ἐπὶ θύραις Mt 24: 33 = Mk 13: 29; also πρὸ τῶν θυρῶν Ja 5: 9 is figurative, while πρὸ τῆς θύρας A 12: 6 is literal (5: 23 ἐπὶ τῶν θυρῶν a formula or literal plural?).

(5) Lk 16: 23 ἐν τοῖς κόλποις αὐτοῦ, but 22 εἰς τὸν κόλπον. Κόλποι Theoc. 2.120, Plut., Cato Min. 33, Aesop. and others; s. Ursing 28, L.-S.

(6) Αἵματα of the shed blood of several persons (so LXX, e.g. Hab 2: 8) Rev 16: 6 S (αἷμα ACP 046), 18: 24 046 (αἷμα 𝔓⁴⁷SACP), of parents' procreative substance Jn 1: 13 οὐκ ἐξ αἱμάτων (cf. Eur., Ion 693).

(7) Ὕδατα 'water(s)' Mt 14: 28, 29, Rev 1: 15, 14: 2, 17: 1, 15 etc.; 'rivers' Jn 3: 23.

(8) Acc. to F. Smend, Ἄγγελος 1 (1925) 41 the pl. of κέντρα is from Eur. (and pl. there on metrical grounds; but elsewhere not from metrical considerations; acc. to A. Vögeli, ThZ 9 (1953) 428 with n. 50 because the goad was double-pointed. S. also K. L. Schmidt, TW III 664.18ff. Ἱμάτια mostly 'clothes' (comprising ἱμάτιον and χιτών), e.g. Mk 5: 30, but = ἱμάτιον Jn 13: 4, 19: 23 and perhaps also A 18: 6. Χιτῶνες Mk 14: 63.—The part of the temple (the tabernacle) H 9: 2, 3 τὰ ἅγια and τὰ ἅγια τῶν ἁγίων (LXX, e.g. 3 Km 8: 6) along with τὸ ἅγιον 9: 1. Also Jos. ἅγια of the temple in Jerusalem, probably a Hebraism (Flashar, ZAW 32 [1912] 245 n. 2).—Κριθῶν Rev 6: 6 SACP (class.), κριθῆς 046; sg. also Theophr. and pap. (Mayser II 1, 35).—Διαθῆκαι E 2: 12, R 9: 4 SCK (sg. 𝔓⁴⁶BDE al.) is doubtless a literal plur.; for the sing. is elsewhere always διαθήκη (as in the LXX).—Mt 21: 7 ἐπεκάθισεν ἐπάνω αὐτῶν is a text-critical problem; probably ἐπεκ. ἐπάνω (vg, Blass in loc.) or ἐπεκάθισαν ἐπάνω (αὐτόν) following Sᶜ is to be read.

142. Of abstract subjects. The plural of abstract expressions frequently serves in poetry and in (elevated?) prose in a way foreign to us as a designation of concrete phenomena (Smyth § 1000, 3): θάνατοι 'deaths', i.e. 'ways of dying'; or 'cases of death' (cf. Katz, ThLZ 1957, 112). The NT sometimes uses this plural:

Mt 15: 19 φόνοι, μοιχεῖαι, πορνεῖαι, κλοπαί, etc., cf. Mk 7: 21f. 2 C 12: 20 ἔρις (v.l. ἔρεις § 47(3)), ζῆλος (v.l. ζῆλοι), θυμοί etc., cf. G 5: 20f. 1 P 2: 1, cf. 4: 3. 1 C 7: 2 τὰς πορνείας; Ja 2: 1 προσωπολημψίαις; Jd 13 αἰσχύνας. Also θανάτοις 'deadly perils' 2 C 11: 23 (following 3 parallel plurals), θανάτων 2 C 1: 10 𝔓⁴⁶ sy

and οἰκτιρμοί in Paul R 12: 1 etc. (= רַחֲמִים sg. only C 3: 12 [pl. K]). Μνῆμαι Herm Sim 6.5.3. Mt 14: 9 ὅρκους (an oath; properly 'words of an oath'). Lk 5: 21 βλασφημίας (the words of the one blasphemy spoken in v. 20). Cf. Jeremias, ZNW 38 (1939) 115f. Ἀνάγκαι 'the means of compulsion' and 'calamities' A. Fridrichsen, Con. Neot. 9 (1949) 29.

(C) The Dual

The dual does not appear in the NT (§§ 2 and 65).

4. SYNTAX OF THE CASES

(1) NOMINATIVE

Rob. 456–61

143. Nominative used to introduce names. Names are usually cited in the case required by the construction; only very rarely are they introduced independently in the nominative (ὀνομαστική) case: Jn 13: 13 φωνεῖτέ με ὁ διδάσκαλος καὶ ὁ κύριος (actually a substitute for the vocative, s. § 147(3)) and Rev 9: 11 ὄνομα ἔχει Ἀπολλύων (ὄν. ἔχει om. vg, so that ὄνομα—scil. ἐστιν—still governs). Cf. Xen., Oec. 6.14 τοὺς ἔχοντας τὸ σεμνὸν ὄνομα τοῦτο τὸ καλός τε κἀγαθός.

Name construed: Mk 3: 16 ἐπέθηκεν ὄνομα τῷ Σίμωνι Πέτρον (Δ and lat Πέτρος); cf. § 157(2). Completely construed with ὀνόματι: A 27: 1 ἑκατοντάρχῃ ὀνόματι Ἰουλίῳ; cf. § 144. Smyth § 940; Rob. 458. LXX Thack. 23; Johannessohn I 7. Pap. K. F. W. Schmidt, GGA 1922, 113; Mayser II 2, 185ff. Further exx.: Lob. Phryn. 517 n. 1; Havers, Glotta 16 (1927) 95.—Lk 19: 29, 21: 37 τὸ ὄρος τὸ καλούμενον Ἐλαιῶν accordingly would be possible; with τοῦ ὄρους τῶν ἐλαιῶν Lk 19: 37 in view however, τὸ καλούμενον ἐλαιῶν is to be preferred. Stereotyped ἐλαιῶν was admittedly identified upon occasion with ὁ ἐλαιών (pap., s. Mayser I² 3, 87; Mlt. 49 [73]; cf. § 111(6)), hence (ὄρους τοῦ καλουμένου) ἐλαιῶνος A 1: 12, ἐλαιῶνα Lk 19: 29 W (Jos., Ant. 7.202 διὰ τοῦ Ἐλαιῶνος ὄρους); cf. Mlt. 235 n. on p. 69 [104f.], who compares Ἰβίων (properly gen. pl. of ἶβις) with the reinterpretation of the gen. of place-names in PTebt (also κώμης Ἰβίωνος PGrenf II 111.2 [v/vi AD], PAmh II 139.2 [350 AD]); in pap. of the earlier period Ἀγκυρῶν πόλις and others, in Roman pap. κώμη Ἀγκυρώνων (Bilabel, Philol. 77 [1921] 422–5). W. Petersen, Class. Phil. 32 (1937) 318ff. explains place-names in -(ε)ών generally from the gen. plur. in -ῶν.—The divine name ὁ ὢν καὶ ὁ ἦν καὶ ὁ ἐρχόμενος Rev 1: 8 'who is and was and will be' (chrono-

logically arranged 4: 8 ὁ ἦν καὶ ὁ ὢν ὁ ἐ., abbreviated ὁ ὢν καὶ ὁ ἦν 11: 17, 16: 5 [ὃς ἦν 𝔓⁴⁷]) is based on rabbinical exegesis of Ex 3: 14 ἐγώ εἰμι ὁ ὤν (אֶהְיֶה (אֲשֶׁר אֶהְיֶה)...ὁ ὢν ἀπέσταλκέ με (אֶהְיֶה שְׁלָחַנִי). Its earliest reflection points to c. 200 BC in places like Is 41: 4 ἐγὼ θεὸς πρῶτος, καὶ εἰς τὰ ἐπερχόμενα ἐγώ εἰμι. At a later date the Jeremiah LXX renders אֲהָהּ אֲדֹנָי יהוה 'Ah, Lord God!' four times as ὁ Ὤν δέσποτα κύριε, reading אֲהָה (= ὤ in vv.ll.) as אֶהְיֶה, and Hos 1: 9 renders לֹא־אֶהְיֶה לָכֶם correctly οὐκ Εἰμὶ (a tetragrammaton!) ὑμῶν, your 'AM' (Katz, ThLZ 1936, 286; cf. Ziegler, XII Prophetae ad loc. and Ziegler, Beiträge zur Jeremias-Septuaginta 40). For later rabbinical evidence s. Billerbeck III 788. This name is even used unaltered after ἀπό, a very harsh construction: Rev 1: 4 ἀπὸ ὁ ὢν etc.: Debrunner, GGA 1926, 147f.; M.-H. 154; Stauffer, TW II 342f.

144. Parenthetical nominative. The nominative in parenthetical ὄνομα αὐτῷ is to be expected, e.g. Jn 1: 6 ἐγένετο ἄνθρωπος...ὄνομα αὐτῷ Ἰωάνης (ἦν before ὄν. S*D*W). Cf. 3: 1 (but S* Νικόδημος ὀνόματι), more fully with ἦν δέ 18: 10; cf. Rev 6: 8, 8: 11, 9: 11 (ὄν. αὐτῷ AP, ᾧ ὄν. 𝔓⁴⁷, ᾧ ὄν. α. S). Similarly classical and e.g. POxy III 465.12 (ὁ δὲ κραταιὸς αὐτοῦ, ὄνομα αὐτῷ ἐστιν Νεβύ, μηνύει...). However, the phrases ᾧ (ᾗ, οὗ) ὄνομα and ὀνόματι are more common, s. § 128(3).— The nominative with designations of time is more striking: Mt 15: 32 ὅτι ἤδη ἡμέραι (-ρας S) τρεῖς (+εἰσιν καὶ D) προσμένουσίν μοι (cf. Mk 8: 2, § 201) is perhaps a mixture of ἡμέρας τρ. προσμ. and ἡμέραι τρ. (εἰσιν) (καί) προσμ. (§ 442(4)). Cf. LXX Josh 1: 11 ἔτι τρεῖς ἡμέραι ὑμεῖς διαβήσεσθε in the hexaplaric A group (ἡμ. ÷ καὶ ϒ ὑμ. διαβαίνετε in the original text; Viteau, Sujet 41), Acta Pauli et Theclae 8 (according to POxy I

6.3) ἡμέραι γὰρ ἤδη τρεῖς καὶ νύκτες τρεῖς Θέκλα οὐκ ἐγήγερται, with καὶ LXX Jon 3: 4 ἔτι τρεῖς ἡμέραι καὶ Νινευὴ καταστραφήσεται. Attic ὅσαι ἡμέραι, ὁσημέραι = 'daily' (K.-G. II 418).

With asyndetic quasi-clausal temporal designation in nom. preceding: POxy IX 1216.8f. (ii/iii AD; letter) ἐνιαυτὸς σήμερον ἐκτός σοῦ εἰμι, XIV 1764.4 (iii AD) πολλαὶ ἡμέραι προσκαρτεροῦμεν Φιλέα (cf. Olsson, Aegyptus 6 [1925] 294), PPrinceton II (1936) no. 98.17 (iv AD) ἰδοὺ δύο μῆνες σήμερον οὐδὲν δέδωκάς μοι. Similarly with temporal designation in the nom. following: Mitteis, Chr. 5.3 (iii BC) κατα[δε]-δυναστεύομαι...μῆνές εἰσιν δέκα, BGU VIII 1848.10 (i BC) διετὴς χρόνος ἤδη[ι], III 948.6 (iv/v AD) ἀσθενῖ εἰδοὺ τρῖς μῆνες (-ες = -ας acc. to §46(2)?), PSI III 177.5f. (ii/iii AD; letter) [οὐκ ἔ]φαγε σ̄ ἡμέρε (= -ραι) δ' εἰσί. Thus ἔτη Lk 13: 16 is probably also to be taken as nom. with Bengel and Winer: ἢν ἔδησεν ὁ σατανᾶς ἰδοὺ δέκα καὶ ὀκτὼ ἔτη. The nom. with ἰδού (§128(7)) and ἴδε (ἴδε ὁ ἀμνὸς τοῦ θεοῦ Jn 1: 29 and often) is explicable on the basis that these are frozen imperatives like ἄγε φέρε (ἰδού is a particle already in Att.), a conclusion which follows from their combination with the plural (e.g. ἴδε ἠκούσατε Mt 26: 65, ἄγε οἱ λέγοντες Ja 4: 13; cf. 5: 1, §364(2)). Through amalgamation with the construction ἐγένετο δὲ... καὶ...(§442(5)), Lk 9: 28 ἐγένετο δὲ μετὰ τοὺς λόγους τούτους, ὡσεὶ ἡμέραι ὀκτώ, καὶ παραλαβὼν...arises; accordingly also A 5: 7 ἐγένετο δέ, ὡς ὡρῶν τριῶν διάστημα (therefore nom.), καὶ ἡ γυνή....Finally, that such a nom. can be felt to be equivalent to a temporal acc. or dat. is shown by LXX Eccl 2: 16 ἤδη αἱ ἡμέραι ἐρχόμεναι τὰ πάντα ἐπελήσθη and PLond II 417.10 p. 299 (346 AD) ἀσχολῶ ἐλθεῖν πρὸς σὲ αὖται ἡμέραι.—The parenthesis (Schwyzer, ABA 1939, 6, pp. 20f.) and the construction 'it is...days since...' must be taken into consideration for the origin (cf. Wackernagel, Vermischte Beitr. z. gr. Sprachkunde [Basel, 1897] 27 [= Kl. Schr. 788], Schwyzer, op. cit.): Lk 13: 7 ἰδοὺ τρία ἔτη ἀφ' οὗ ἔρχομαι (cf. pap. Class. Phil. 22 [1927] 250.8f.; ii AD), where, however, A omits ἀφ' οὗ so that τρία ἔτη becomes acc.; Mk 8: 2 D (§201). D. Tabachovitz, Museum Helveticum 3 (1946) 157f. (τρίτον ἔτος τουτί and the like is nom.).—References in inscrip. are not certain (cf. Schwyzer, op. cit. 21 n.; IG I² no. 324.10).

145. The predicate nominative is used in the NT as in Attic. But occasionally εἰς with the accusative appears in its place under Semitic influence (Hebr. ל; and for the predicate acc. too, §157(5)). (1) Thus with γίνεσθαι and εἶναι (mostly with ἔσεσθαι which has a certain relationship to γίνεσθαι), but usually in quotations. (2) The non-Attic combination of λογίζεσθαι (pass.) εἰς arises

likewise from the LXX (Johannessohn I 4), but links up with the Hellenistic λογίζεσθαι 'to charge against somebody's account', and is not, therefore, limited to quotations; it has even produced, through amalgamation with ἐλάχιστόν ἐστιν (Michel, TW IV 660.8ff.), an ἐμοὶ εἰς ἐλάχιστόν ἐστιν 1 C 4: 3.

On the Semitism, G. R. Hauschild, Des en d'identité semit. Herkunft und bibelsprachl. Entwicklung (Festschr. z. Einweihg. des Goethe-Gymn. in Frankfurt a. M. 1897) 151–74; Johannessohn I 4f.; Psichari 201f.; Br.-Th. 432; Wittmann 22f.; Wolf II 35; Reiter, PhW 1925, 651; Debrunner, GGA 1926, 140f.; Helb., Kas. 60–7, esp. 64f., 66f.; M.-H. 462f.; too strongly against Semitism: Deissmann, LO⁴ 96f. [LAE 120ff.]; Raderm.² 20f.; Mlt. 71f. [110]; examples also in Jannaris §1552.

(1) Quotations: ἔσονται εἰς σάρκα μίαν Mt 19: 5 (also 1 C 6: 16 etc.; but εἰσὶν...σὰρξ μία Mt 19: 6), ἐγενήθη εἰς κεφαλὴν γωνίας 21: 42 pars., ἔσται τὰ σκολιὰ εἰς εὐθείας Lk 3: 5, ἔσεσθέ μοι εἰς υἱούς 2 C 6: 18 (εἰς χολὴν...ὁρῶ σε ὄντα A 8: 23); cf. H 1: 5, 8: 10. Not in quotations: οἱ τρεῖς εἰς τὸ ἕν εἰσιν 1 Jn 5: 8, ἐγένετο εἰς (om. εἰς D) δένδρον Lk 13: 19, ἡ λύπη ὑμῶν εἰς χαρὰν γενήσεται Jn 16: 20 (= μεταστραφήσεται, with which εἰς would not be surprising), ἐγένετο εἰς ἄψινθον Rev 8: 11, ἐγένετο εἰς τρία μέρη 16: 19 (cf. διαιρεῖν εἰς), εἰς κενὸν γένηται ὁ κόπος ἡμῶν 1 Th 3: 5 (cf. Att. εἰς κέρδος τι δρᾶν). Εἶναι εἰς 'to serve for' 1 C 14: 22, C 2: 22, Ja 5: 3, as in Inschr. v. Priene 50.39 (c. ii BC), is different.

(2) Λογίζεσθαι εἰς in quotation: ἐλογίσθη αὐτῷ εἰς δικαιοσύνην R 4: 3 etc. from Gen 15: 6. Not in quotation: εἰς οὐθὲν λογισθῆναι A 19: 27 (the same expression in LXX Is 40: 17), τὰ τέκνα λογίζεται εἰς σπέρμα R 9: 8, εἰς περιτομὴν λογισθήσεται 2: 26 (Chrys. [μετα]τραπήσεται) corresponding to ἀκροβυστία γέγονεν 25. Class. οὐδὲν εἶναι, τὸ μηδὲν εἶναι. Λογί-ζεσθαί τινι 'to charge to somebody's account' R 4: 4, 6, 11, 2 C 5: 19, Dit., Or. 595.15 (174 AD), PFay 21.9 (134 AD), and so perhaps 2 C 12: 6 μή τις εἰς ἐμὲ λογίσηται; but pap. beg. ii BC εἴς τι (not εἴς τινα!). Similarly Plato, Phil. 25A εἰς τὸ πέρας ἀπολογιζό-μενοι 'to count to the limits' and with ἐν Xen., Mem. 2.2.1 ἐν τοῖς ἀδίκοις καταλογίζεσθαι 'to reckon among the unjust', Aeschin. 3.202 ἐν ἀρετῇ...μηδεὶς καταλογιζέσθω, LXX Is 53: 12 (1 Clem 16.13) ἐν τοῖς ἀνόμοις ἐλογίσθη (translated literally μετὰ τῶν ἀνόμων Lk 22: 37 = את; cf. Herm Sim 8.9.3, §227(1)). Λογ. with the double acc. is better Att., 'to count somebody as': LXX Ps 118: 119, Is 33: 8, Wsd 5: 4 etc. as in Arist., Eur., Xen.; pass. e.g. πιστοὶ ἐλογίσθησαν LXX 2 Esdr 23: 13 (for which NT ὡς; §157(5)); also 'to be reckoned as' LXX Pr 17: 28 σοφία λογισθήσεται, Job 31: 28, therefore A alone corrects 1 Macc 2: 52 εἰς δικαιοσύνην (from Gen 15: 6)

to δικαιοσύνη. Helb., Kas. 66f.; Bonaccorsi 603f.; Mayser II 2, 362ff., 416ff.; Heidland, TW IV 287, 288 n. 4. S. also §157(5).

(2) VOCATIVE
Rob. 461–6

146. The use of ὦ (ὤ). (1) In conformity with Koine and Semitic usage vocative ὦ is frequently omitted before the vocative in the NT and always in invoking God, while it was regularly used in Attic (in the Ptolemaic papyri ὦ is found only once, in a solemn Artemisian execration [iv BC]; Mayser II 1, 55). (a) The polite, unemotional ὦ (in Attic style) is confined to Acts and almost always to instances where the address consists of a single word. (b) ῏Ω is usually employed to express emotion, either of a lesser (e.g. R 2: 1, 3) or greater degree. There is stronger emotion in Mt 15: 28 ὦ (om. D) γύναι, μεγάλη σου ἡ πίστις, which announces an immediate reward (cf. γύναι without ὦ: Lk 22: 57, Jn 2: 4, 4: 21 etc.); in 1 T 6: 20 introducing a strict command; in A 13: 10 preceding the announcement of divine punishment. The last three instances, especially A 13: 10, are closely related to (2). (2) In exclamations (usually written ὤ), expressing very strong emotion, the force of ὦ is not confined to the following vocative but dominates and colors the whole sentence (frequently a question).

Classical Greek used ὦ before the vocative to express address or invocation along with ὤ to introduce an exclamation. The traditional distinction should not be neglected (Katz).—Never ὦ πάτερ in the NT because it expresses pathos, but it is found in Hell. (Jos., often Corp. Herm.): Schrenk, TW v 985 n. 251.—Cf. Schwyzer II 60f. on the whole subject.

(1) (a) A 18: 14 ὦ (ἄνδρες) ᾽Ιουδαῖοι (Gallio speaking); 27: 21 ὦ ἄνδρες. On the other hand, ἄνδρες ἀδελφοί 13: 26 etc., ἄνδρες ᾽Αθηναῖοι 17: 22, etc. without ὦ and even simple ἄνδρες 7: 26 and often elsewhere; βασιλεῦ 26: 7 (ὦ 13 c*syʰ). ῏Ω Θεόφιλε A 1: 1, but κράτιστε Θ. Lk 1: 3: the omission of ὦ is a Latinism (cf. §60(2) also) as in Ποστούμιε Τερεντιανὲ φίλτατε and Τερ. ἥδιστε in the work περὶ ὕψους 1.1.4; but ὦ κράτιστε ᾽Αμμαῖε Dionys. Hal., Orat. Vet. 1. (b) As indicated by the context there is some emotion in ὦ ἄνθρωπε R 2: 1, 3, 9: 20, Ja 2: 20 (ἄνθρωπε alone Lk 12: 14, 22: 58, 60 is more abrupt; cf. Xen., Cyr. 2.2.7). A 13: 10 ὦ πλήρης (§147(1))...υἱὲ...ἐχθρὲ.... (2) R 11: 33 ὦ βάθος πλούτου..., which issues in the exclamation ὡς ἀνεξερεύνητα..., leads up to the rhetorical questions in the quotation vv. 34f., and

ends in the solemn ascription v. 36, introduces an act of adoration, thus excluding the possibility that an abstract quantity is being addressed (the latter is better suited to the stilted style of 4 Macc than to Paul); cf. the translation of Delitzsch: מֶה־עָמֹק עֲשֵׁר חָכְמַת אֱלֹהִים ... . Mk 9: 19 (= Mt 17: 17, Lk 9: 41) ὦ γενεὰ ἄπιστος (nom., s. §147(1)), ἕως πότε...; Lk 24: 25 ὦ ἀνόητοι, οὐχὶ ταῦτα ἔδει...; Gal 3: 1 ὦ ἀνόητοι Γαλάται, τίς ὑμᾶς ἐβάσκανεν; are rhetorical questions intended as a rebuke. These instances are to be interpreted against the background of Semitic exclamatory interjections which introduce forceful or impassioned statements, often in the form of questions; in the LXX these are rendered by ὦ as well as by οἴμοι and οὐαί (Katz).

147. Nominative instead of vocative. Even where the nominative is still formally distinguished from the vocative, there is still a tendency for the nominative to usurp the place of the vocative (a tendency observable already in Homer). In the NT this is the case (1) generally with adjectives used alone or without a substantive where the vocative is clear; (2) with additions of all kinds to the vocative (Attic σὺ ὁ πρεσβύτατος, Πρόξενε καὶ οἱ ἄλλοι), especially with participles (§412(5)) which hardly ever form the vocative. (3) Attic used the nominative (with article) with simple substantives only in addressing inferiors, who were, so to speak, thereby addressed in the 3rd person (Aristoph., Ra. 521 ὁ παῖς, ἀκολούθει). The NT (in passages translated from a Semitic language) and the LXX do not conform to these limitations, but can even say ὁ θεός, ὁ πατήρ etc., in which the arthrous Semitic vocative is being reproduced by the Greek nominative with article.

(1) Mt 17: 17 pars. ὦ γενεὰ ἄπιστος (D ἄπιστε in Mk and Lk), A 13: 10 ὦ πλήρης (cf. ὦ δυστυχής in Menander); ἄφρων Lk 12: 20 and 1 C 15: 36 with weaker variant ἄφρον.

(2) Lk 11: 39 ὑμεῖς οἱ Φαρισαῖοι, thus also 6: 25 οὐαὶ ὑμῖν, οἱ ἐμπεπλησμένοι, in which οἱ ἐμπ. has the value of a voc. Rev 18: 20 οὐρανὲ καὶ οἱ ἅγιοι. Cf. ᾽Ιησοῦ (voc.) ὁ ἱερεὺς ὁ μέγας LXX Hg 2: 4, Zech 3: 8. C 3: 18ff. αἱ γυναῖκες...οἱ ἄνδρες...τὰ τέκνα etc. = ὑμεῖς μὲν αἱ γυν.... ὑμεῖς δὲ οἱ ἄνδρες etc.

(3) Lk 8: 54 ἡ παῖς, ἐγείρου; Mk 5: 41 τὸ κοράσιον (= Aram. טְלִיתָא). ῾Ο πατήρ Mt 11: 26, R 8: 15, ὁ δεσπότης Rev 6: 10, ὁ διδάσκαλος καὶ ὁ κύριος Jn 13: 13; s. §143. Also with attributives: ὁ βασιλεὺς (S βασιλεῦ) τῶν ἐθνῶν Rev 15: 3, ὁ β. τῶν ᾽Ιουδαίων Mt 27: 29 (BD al. βασιλεῦ) = Mk 15: 18 (SBD al. βασιλεῦ) = Jn 19: 3 (S βασιλεῦ) is Semitizing, but King Agrippa in A 26: 7 etc. is addressed as βασιλεῦ

(official address). Omission of the art. only υἱὸς Δαυίδ Mt 9: 27, 20: 30, 31 (𝔓⁴⁵ υἱέ here) and A 7: 42 οἶκος Ἰσραήλ (from Amos 5: 25), because in such cases the art. does not appear in Hebr. either. Ὁ θεός Lk 18: 11, H 1: 8 OT, 10: 7 OT etc., also κύριε ὁ θεός Rev 15: 3 OT; θεέ only Mt 27: 46: θεέ μου as a translation of the anarthrous ἠλί (θεέ seldom in LXX either; Thack. 145). Wackernagel, Anredeformen 7 (= Kl. Schr. 974); Katz, Philo's Bible 59f., 152f. Κύριε ὁ θεός Epict. 2.16.13 comes from Judæo-Hell. magic (Breithaupt, Hermes 62 [1927] 255); cf. the same with ἡμῶν in the Hermetic writing Cat. Cod. Astr. 8.2, p. 172. 6.—With attributive: Ὁ κύριός μου καὶ ὁ θεός μου Jn 20: 28 (cf. Rev 4: 11), ὁ λαός μου Rev 18: 4 (voc. sg. from λαός λεώς generally not common); Lk 12: 32, Mk 9: 25.—Anarthrous πατήρ (Jn 17: 11 B, 21 BDW, 24 and 25 AB) and θυγάτηρ (Jn 12: 15 ABDW al. [OT], Lk 8: 48 BKLW, Mt 9: 22 DGLW, Mk 5: 34 BDW, etc.) are to be explained in the NT, perhaps, as scribal slips with reference to the later retreat of special forms for the voc. in the third decl. In the LXX Judg 11: 35 θυγάτηρ μου only B (a late revision); 36 both texts only πάτερ (μου); Ruth 2: 22 θυγάτηρ only BALᵃ; these passages never had an article; the revisers who changed the voc. to nom. failed to insert the article (Katz, ThLZ 1957, 113 n. 2). Cf. θυγάτηρ Melinno (i AD?), κύριέ μου πατήρ BGU II 423.11 (ii AD), μήτηρ PRoss-Georg III 2.6 and 27 (iii AD) and with adj. κύριε παντοκράτωρ LXX; there is no certain ex. in the Ptol. pap. (Mayser II 1, 55f.). On the whole Schwyzer II 59–64; W. Schulze, Festschrift Wackernagel 240ff. (= Kl. Schr. 82ff.); Havers, Glotta 16 (1927) 104; for the LXX Johannessohn I 14f.

(3) ACCUSATIVE

Rob. 466–91

(A) The Simple Accusative of the Object

148. Transitive use of original intransitives was always possible in Greek with certain verbs. Those which come into consideration for the NT: (1) denote an act. The action, originally conceived absolutely, is placed in relation to an object: ἐνεργεῖν 'to be at work' (Mt 14: 2 etc.) becomes 'to be at work at something' = 'to effect something' (1 C 12: 6 etc.; since Polyb.: Trunk 9); treated, therefore, like old transitives such as πράττειν. (2) Are verbs of emotion. Καυχᾶσθαι 'to boast of' (R 2: 17 and often), κ. τι 'to boast of something' (2 C 9: 2, 11: 30). (3) The Hellenistic transformation of intransitive actives into causatives is represented in μαθητεύειν: it meant first 'to be a disciple' (Plut., Mt 27: 57 v.l.), then became a deponent (Mt 13: 52, 27: 57 v.l.), and

from this there developed a new active 'to make a disciple of' (28: 19, A 14: 21). Cf. §309(1). (4) A variety of the causative active (= Hebrew Hiphil) is the declaratory, forensic הִצְדִּיק 'to declare just(ified)' (= δικαιοῦν LXX, NT, e.g. R 3: 20, 24, G 2: 16f., etc.) and, conversely, הִרְשִׁיעַ 'to condemn' (= ἀσεβεῖν, LXX only).

Mayser II 1, 87f.; II 2, 310ff.

(1) Συνεργεῖν intr., only R 8: 28 πάντα (πᾶν 𝔓⁴⁶) συνεργεῖ ὁ θεός acc. to AB. Ἱερουργεῖν (late word) τὸ εὐαγγέλιον R 15: 16. Ὑβρίζειν only trans. Ἐνεδρεύειν trans. A 23: 21, Lk 11: 54 (αὐτόν om. SDΘ). Πλεονεκτεῖν only trans. (Paul). Χορηγεῖν trans. 'to supply' 2 C 9: 10, 1 P 4: 11. Εὐσεβεῖν trans. A 17: 23, 1 T 5: 4 (Trag., Antipho, Hell.; Meister 40; Helb., Kas. 13). Ἐμπορεύεσθαι 'to carry on commerce' Ja 4: 13, trans. 2 P 2: 3 'to defraud' (like ἐμπολᾶν Soph., Ant. 1050) or 'to buy' (Bauer). Θριαμβεύειν only trans. 'to lead in triumphal procession; to mock, deride' (TW III 160 n. 2) C 2: 15, 2 C 2: 14 (or 'cause to triumph' here? cf. supra 3 μαθητεύειν and Lietzmann, Hdb. in loc.). Perhaps also here old μένειν 'expect' A 20: 5, 23, ὑπο- 1 C 13: 7 etc. (also 'to wait [confidently] on God' 1 Clem 34. 8 OT; LXX τὸν κύριον and the like besides τῷ κυρίῳ; Helb., Kas. 103f.), περι- A 1: 4, ἀνα- 1 Th 1: 10, and the peculiar τρίζειν τοὺς ὀδόντας Mk 9: 18 (τοῖς ὀδοῦσιν Hippiatr. 86). Καρτερεῖν trans. 'to fix one's eyes on' H 11: 27 (s. Bauer).

(2) Verbs of fearing etc. s. §149. Θαρρεῖν only intr. (class. also trans.). Θαυμάζειν usually intr., trans. Lk 7: 9 (αὐτόν om. D), (Lk 24: 12,) Jn 5: 28, A 7: 31 (τὸ ὅραμα om. A), Jd 16 (θ. πρόσωπα = נָשָׂא פָנִים, LXX e.g. Dt 10: 17, 28: 50, Job 13: 10, Pr 18: 5 etc.; = הָדַר פָּנִים Lev 19: 15; cf. (προσ-) λαμβάνειν πρόσωπον p. 3, n. 5; cf. Thack. 43f.). Ἐλεεῖν trans. Οἰκτίρειν trans. R 9: 15 OT. Κλαίειν mostly intr., trans. Mt 2: 18 OT (LXX differs), Lk 23: 28 D (al. ἐπ' ἐμέ). Πενθεῖν trans. only 2 C 12: 21 (Lk 23: 28 D). Κόπτεσθαι 'to wail' trans. (class.) Lk 8: 52 (23: 27?), with ἐπί and acc. Rev 1: 7, 18: 9. Εὐδοκεῖν 'to be pleased' trans. only Mt 12: 18 OT (S*B, al. εἰς, ἐν), H 10: 6 and 8 OT (LXX here only ἠθέλησας, but trans. εὐδ. in other places, e.g. Ps 50: 18; s. Helb., Kas. 264, also from an inscrip.[?] and a pap.[?]). In the place of it θέλειν τινά is used: Mt 27: 43 = Ps 21: 9, 40: 12, Tob 13: 8, IMag 3.2, and still more slavishly ἔν τινι (= Hebr. בְּ) in LXX (Johannessohn II 334); but hardly so in C 2: 18 θέλων ἐν ταπεινοφροσύνη (Dibelius, Hdb. in loc., Bauer θέλω 4b; more likely θέλων is adverbial 'intentionally': Riesenfeld, Arbeiten und Mitteilungen I [1935] 1ff., 15f.; II [1936] 13). (ἐξ-)εὐδοκεῖν 'to satisfy' in the pap. (Mayser II 1, 88; II 2, 317). Ἀπορεῖσθαί τι A 25: 20 SABHP (CEL with εἰς), otherwise never ἀπ., διαπ. with acc. (sometimes ἀπορεῖν as in class.), but

with ἐν or περί (both prepositions Herm Sim 8.3.1). **Ἱλάσκεσθαι** trans. 'to propitiate (God)' (class. ἐξ-) Lk 18: 13 (pass.), 1 Clem 7.7 (ἐξ-), Herm Vis 1.2.1 (ἐξ-), 'to expiate' H 2: 17 ἁμαρτίας (LXX, Philo, ἐξιλ. ἁμαρτίαν Dit., Syll.³ 1042.16 [ii/iii AD]); Helb., Kas. 213, 215). **Εὐχαρίστει** τοῦτο ('for it') τῷ κυρίῳ Herm Sim 7.5; cf. pass. §312(2).

(3) Cf. Debrunner §§197, 215, 222 and IF 21, 58ff.; Psaltes 318ff.; Rob. 801f.

(4) The decision as to whether **δικαιοῦν** is used forensically or effectively must be determined by the context. Forensically with personal object never outside the LXX and NT: Schrenk, TW ii 215.49f.; this usage is characteristic of the LXX and Paul: Schrenk, TW ii 216.13ff., 219ff.; cf. R. Bultmann, Theologie des Neuen Testaments 268–70 [Theology of the New Testament i 271–4]; H. Rosman, Verbum Domini 21 (1941) 144–7. Contrast E. J. Goodspeed, Problems of NT Translation (1945) 143–6; JBL 73 (1954) 86–91. There is no doubt that ἀσεβεῖν is used forensically in Job 9: 20 τὸ στόμα μου ἀσεβήσει '... will condemn me'; accordingly in 10: 2 μή με ἀσέβει is to be restored following the MT. Ἀνομεῖν once combined with δικαιοῦν, 3 Km 8: 32 ἀνομῆσαι (ἀνομηθῆναι BAL) ἄνομον καὶ τοῦ δικαιῶσαι δίκαιον (Katz, JTS 48 [1947] 195f.; Welt des Orients ii [1957] 271). Cf. Pr 17: 15.

149. Accusative with verbs of fearing, etc. and of swearing. In addition to the accusative, the NT also employs ἀπό with the genitive with verbs of 'fearing, fleeing, avoiding' etc., which was in part possible already in classical, but was encouraged by Semitic influence (Johannessohn ii 245 n. 7, 276f.; Helb., Kas. 24–36, 71f.). E.g. φοβεῖσθαι is usually transitive; with ἀπό (MGr; Psichari 186) only Mt 10: 28 = Lk 12: 4 (acc. immediately following). Only in Ja 5: 12 does ὀμνύναι still take the accusative of that by which one swears, while it elsewhere takes ἐν (εἰς) = Hebr. בְּ (Mt 5: 34 etc.) or κατά τινος (H 6: 13, 16, Herm Vis 2.2.5 and 8, Homil Clem 5.5, Chrysostom in Mt; already in classical), as in the LXX (Johannessohn i 77); but (ἐν-)ὁρκίζειν 'to adjure' still takes this accusative (Mk 5: 7, A 19: 13, 1 Th 5: 27, besides ἐξορκίζω [ὁρκ- D] σε κατὰ τοῦ θεοῦ Mt 26: 63, cf. Herm Sim 9.10.5; the imprecatory tablets often have [ἐν-]ὁρκίζω τινὰ κατά τινος [Audollent, Defix. Tab. 473ff.; also M.-M.], but also ἐξορκίζω σε...τὸν θεόν: Wünsch, Antike Fluchtafeln [Kl. T. 20] 4.1; cf. §155(7) also). Νή as in classical also takes the accusative (1 C 15: 31, originally scil. ὄμνυμι).

Φεύγειν trans. 'shun' (opp. to διώκειν 'strive after') 1 C 6: 18, 1 T 6: 11, 2 T 2: 22, with ἀπό 1 C 10: 14, Did 3.1; 'to flee from, take flight' (class.) only H 11: 34 ἔφυγον στόματα μαχαίρης, otherwise Hebraizing with ἀπό Mt 3: 7 = Lk 3: 7 φυγεῖν ἀπὸ τῆς μελλούσης ὀργῆς, Mt 23: 33, Rev 9: 6 (class. and MGr only local: φεύγειν ἀπὸ τῆς Σκύλλης Xen., Mem. 2.6.31; cf. Ja 4: 7, Jn 10: 5? Herm Man 11.14 φεύγει ἀπ' αὐτοῦ = flees from him) or following the Hebrew idiom entirely ἀπὸ προσώπου Rev 20: 11; ἐκφεύγειν trans. Lk 21: 36 etc., likewise ἀπο- 2 P 2: 20 (1: 4 gen.? cf. §180(2)). **Φυλάσσεσθαι** 'to (be on one's) guard against' trans. as in class. A 21: 25, 2 T 4: 15, with ἀπό Lk 12: 15 (Xen., Cyr. 2.3.9; MGr), φυλάσσειν ἑαυτὸν ἀπό 1 Jn 5: 21 (φύλαξόν με ἀπὸ παντὸς δαίμονος PGM i 4.2699 p. 158; as early as Xen.; s. Helb., Kas. 31). Similarly (δια-) **τηρεῖν** ἐξ (unclass.) Jn 17: 15, Rev 3: 10, ἐξ (ἀφ' D) ὧν διατηροῦντες ἑαυτούς A 15: 29. **Ἀποστρέφεσθαί** τινα 'to turn away from someone' as in class. Mt 5: 42 etc. **Αἰσχύνεσθαι** intr., with ἀπό 1 Jn 2: 28, but ἐπαισχ-·trans. **Λανθάνειν** trans. A 26: 26, 2 P 3: 5, 8 as in class. (but κρύπτειν τι only with ἀπό, s. §155(3)).

Other verbs for 'to be on guard' also retain ἀπό: **προσέχειν** (ἑαυτῷ) scil. τὸν νοῦν 'to give heed to oneself' = 'to take care, be on guard' Lk 12: 1, Mt 7: 15 etc. (LXX; Helb., Kas. 292); βλέπετε Mk 8: 15, 12: 38 (trans. 'to look to, heed' Mk 13: 9, 1 C 1: 26 etc.; Ph 3: 2 also? or here = φυλάσσεσθε?); ὁρᾶτε καὶ φυλάσσεσθε ἀπό Lk 12: 15 (καὶ φ. om. sy), ὁρᾶτε (+ καὶ 𝔓⁴⁵C) βλέπετε ἀπό Mk 8: 15 (DΘ om. ὁρ.), ὁρ. καὶ προσέχετε ἀπό Mt 16: 6 (ὁρ. καὶ om. lat), therefore ἀπό is hardly to be combined with ὁρᾶτε; βλέπειν ἀπό in a pap. from 41 AD (Deissmann, LO⁴ 96 [LAE 120]). **Ἐντρέπεσθαί** τινα 'to be afraid of someone' as in the comedian Alexis (iv BC), Frag. 71 (Kock ii 320; τὴν πολιάν 'people with gray hair', Kock τὴν πολιὰν (μητέρα)), Polyb. et al.; earlier 'to trouble oneself about'.—'To swear' etc. with κατά is found also in class., LXX and pap.; Helb., Kas. 72; Mayser ii 2, 304f., 430 (originally 'on somebody's head'). Rev 10: 6 ὤμοσεν (+ ἐν ACP) τῷ ζῶντι 𝔓⁴⁷S; cf. Aristoph., Nu. 248f., LXX Lev 19: 12 (τῷ ὀνόματί μου).

150. Verbs otherwise intransitive may be rendered transitive by a preposition in composition: κατά, διά, παρά, περί, πρό, ὑπέρ, ὑπό.

With **κατά** (class.): -αγωνίζεσθαι (since Polyb.) H 11: 33 'conquer' (i.e. 'to fight down'), -βραβεύειν C 2: 18, -πονεῖν (only -πονούμενος A 7: 24, 2 P 2: 7), -σοφίζεσθαι A 7: 19. Cf. §181. With **διά** (class.): -βαίνειν, -έρχεσθαι, -πλεῖν, -πορεύεσθαι Lk, Acts, Heb (besides διά and the gen. in an equivalent phrase: διέβησαν τὴν θάλασσαν ὡς διὰ ξηρᾶς γῆς H 11: 29). With **παρά**: -έρχεσθαι Lk, Acts (also Mk 6: 48). With **περί** (class.): -έρχεσθαι, -στῆναί τινα, -τρέχειν; also περιάγειν τι intr. (§308) 'to go about in an area' Mt 9: 35, 23: 15, Mk 6: 6 (v.l.

ἐν Mt 4: 23); cf. Dem. 42.5 and trans. τὴν χώραν..., ἣν περιήγαγον [ἡμᾶς] 'in which they led us around' IG ıx 2, p. 11, no. 205.2.9 (Delphi, c. 200 BC), τὴν λίμνην Hdt. 4.180. With **πρό**: -άγειν *praecedere aliquem* (§ 308), for which -έρχεσθαι Lk 22: 47 (weak v.l. αὐτοῖς and αὐτῶν; D προῆγεν); cf. Mk 6: 33 (many vv.ll., a difficult passage); R 12: 10 ἀλλήλους προηγούμενοι 'preferring' (not 'outdoing'), construed like προκρίνειν (acc. dependent on ἡγεῖσθαι) = Ph 2: 3 ἀλλήλους ἡγούμενοι ὑπερέχοντας ἑαυτῶν (cf. 1 Th 5: 13 also). With **ὑπέρ**: -έχειν Ph 4: 7 (§ 177). With **ὑπό**: -τρέχειν A 27: 16.—Helb., Kas. 80 ff.

151. Dative alternating with or supplanting classical accusative. (1) As in classical, **βλάπτειν** (Mk 16: 18, Lk 4: 35; the verb does not appear elsewhere) and **ὠφελεῖν** (especially the passive) take the accusative. But either the dative or the accusative is used with 'to do good or evil in word or deed', while the accusative is the rule in Attic. (2) **Προσκυνεῖν** more commonly takes, in addition to the Attic accusative, the more descriptive dative, which is customary in the later period (Lob. Phryn. 463; Schmidt 384; Wittmann 16; Wolf ıı 34; Helb., Kas. 296 ff.; not in Ptol. inscrip., s. Moulton, ClR 15 (1901) 436; Mayser ıı 2, 256).

(1) **Λυσιτελεῖν** τινι as Attic, but only Lk 17: 2 (συμφέρει D); **συμφέρειν** only dat. (Mt 5: 29 etc.). **Ἀδικεῖν** only with acc. Κακῶς ποιεῖν does not appear; **καλῶς ποιεῖν** only with dat.: Lk 6: 27 (Mt 5: 44 DEKL al.), likewise **εὖ ποιεῖν** Mk 14: 7 (dat. is missing in S*; acc. AXΠ al.; the acc. is still the rule in the LXX, Johannessohn ı 78); Hell. dat., Mayser ıı 2, 263 f. Cf. § 157(1). **Κακῶς λέγειν** τινά only A 23: 5 OT, otherwise **κακολογεῖν** τινα A 19: 9 etc. (= λοιδορεῖν § 152(1)); correspondingly **καλῶς λέγειν** τινά only in Lk 6: 26 (ὑμῖν D), otherwise **εὐλογεῖν** τινα Lk 1: 64 and often. (Simple λέγειν τινά 'to mention someone in speaking' is used as in class. Jn 1: 15 v.l.; 8: 27 v.l., Ph 3: 18.)

(2) **Προσκυνεῖν** with acc. only Mt 4: 10 OT (on account of LXX Dt 6: 13 for φοβηθήσῃ) = Lk 4: 8 OT, 24: 52 (om. D), Jn 4: 22 twice, 23 (αὐτῷ S*; in the same vs. all MSS τῷ πατρί), 24 (αὐτόν om. S*D*), 9: 38 D, Rev several times in addition to dat.; elsewhere dat. or absolutely, twice ἐνώπιόν τινος (§ 187(2)). Greeven, TW vı 762.34 ff. (dat. in the LXX on account of ?, but also to avoid the trans. 'kiss'; at the same time due to εὔχεσθαί τινι). J. Horst, Proskyneïn (Gütersloh, 1932) 33–9. Synonymous **γονυπετεῖν** similarly (Polyb.): acc. Mt 17: 14 (dat. very weakly attested), Mk 1: 40 AC (om. al.; dat. weakly attested), 10: 17, ἔμπροσθεν Mt 17: 14 D, 27: 29.—Helb., Kas. 1–23.

152. Accusative alternating with or supplanting classical dative is found in the NT with (1) verbs meaning 'to censure, revile, blaspheme, curse' (following the pattern of Attic λοιδορεῖν τινα Jn 9: 28, A 23: 4 and ὑβρίζειν [NT only transitive]), (2) εὐαγγελίζεσθαί τινα (probably following the pattern of εὐλογεῖν etc. [§ 151(1)]; Attic dative of person [Phryn. 266], accusative of thing), (3) παραινεῖν (absolutely A 27: 9, acc. 22 after the analogy of παρακαλεῖν; Ursing 32), (4) χρῆσθαι.

(1) **Ἐπηρεάζειν** τινά; Att. τινί. **Λυμαίνεσθαί** τινα A 8: 3; Att. dat. and acc. **Ὀνειδίζειν** τινά Mt 5: 11 etc. (27: 44 αὐτῷ is a spurious reading for αὐτόν); Att. τινί. **Μέμφεσθαι** αὐτούς H 8: 8 S*AD* al., αὐτοῖς 𝔓⁴⁶SᶜBDᶜ al.; Att. dat. and acc. (Schekira 147). **Καταρᾶσθαί** τινα [Mt] 5: 44 (D* dat.), Mk 11: 21, Lk 6: 28 (ὑμῖν EHL al.), Ja 3: 9; Att. τινι (Did 1.3). Similarly **βασκαίνειν** 'to bewitch' with acc. G 3: 1; in Attic also with dat.—by analogy with φθονεῖν? **Φθονεῖν** G 5: 26 SACDF with dat. ἀλλήλοις as in Attic, 2 Clem 15.5; with acc. (by analogy with ζηλοῦν) G 5: 26 𝔓⁴⁶BG as in Aesop. (Ursing 33; Hausrath, PhW 1931, 44).—Acc. instead of Att. εἴς τινα and the like in **βλασφημεῖν** τινα (LXX, Jos. etc.; Schmidt 388; Nägeli 44) Mt 27: 39 etc.; retaining εἴς τινα Mk 3: 29 (εἰς om. D), Lk 12: 10, (22: 65?). 2 P 2: 12 ἐν οἷς ἀγνοοῦσιν 'in matters of which they are ignorant' (more intelligible Jd 10).—Helb., Kas. 21–3.

(2) **Εὐαγγελίζεσθαί** τινα (not in LXX: Helb., Kas. 233) rather often Lk and Acts, also G 1: 9 (dat. 8), 1 P 1: 12; τινί τι Lk 1: 19 etc.; with double acc. A 13: 32, where, however, τὴν ἐπαγγελίαν is in anticipation of the ὅτι clause.

(3) Cf. **προσφωνεῖν** § 202.

(4) **Χρῆσθαι** with acc. 1 C 7: 31 οἱ χρώμενοι τὸν κόσμον 𝔓⁴⁶S*ABD*FG, dat. SᶜDᶜᵒʳʳEK al. as in 9: 12, 18 etc. For the acc. cf. Homil Clem 9.6; Rob. 473 n. 1, 476; Raderm.² 133; Ursing 33 f.; Mayser ıı 2, 312; Helb., Kas. 253 f. (acc. only 2 Macc 4: 19, Pr 10: 26 SB, κατα- 3 Macc 5: 22). **Ἐγκόπτειν** 'to hinder', originally 'to put a cut (trench) in the way of someone', therefore with dat. (pap. [Mayser ıı 2, 262]), then with acc. in NT on the analogy of κωλύειν: A 24: 4, G 5: 7, 1 Th 2: 18 (and pass. ἐγκόπτεσθαι R 15: 22, 1 P 3: 7); Stählin, TW ııı 855.

On the accusative supplanting classical genitive, see under Genitive §§ 162 ff.

(B) The Simple Accusative of Content (Cognate Accusative)

Rob. 477 ff.

153. Substantives (with and without attributive). (1) Where the accusative of content is a cognate of the verb either in etymology or meaning, it serves a purpose only when a qualifying word or phrase in the form of an attributive (adjective or genitive) is introduced: ἐφοβήθησαν φόβον μέγαν Mk 4: 41 (3 times LXX, Johannessohn I 73). A comparable idiom is found in both Hebrew and Aramaic. (2) The qualifying phrase can be introduced by a relative pronoun: τὸ βάπτισμα, ὃ ἐγὼ βαπτίζομαι, βαπτισθῆναι Mk 10: 38. (3) If the etymologically related substantive does not merely substantivize the verbal idea, an attributive is not required: φυλάσσειν φυλακάς 'to stand guard' Lk 2: 8 (classical and LXX). Cf. Mayser II 2, 318f.; Helb., Kas. 88ff.

(1) Mt 2: 10 ἐχάρησαν χαρὰν μεγάλην σφόδρα. 1 P 3: 14 OT τὸν φόβον αὐτῶν ('of them') μὴ φοβηθῆτε. C 2: 19 αὔξει ('grows') τὴν αὔξησιν τοῦ θεοῦ. Rev 16: 9 ἐκαυματίσθησαν καῦμα μέγα. The qualifying phrase for ἁμαρτάνοντα ἁμαρτίαν 1 Jn 5: 16 is μὴ πρὸς θάνατον, cf. later in the vs.: ἔστιν ('there is') ἁμαρτία πρὸς θ.

(2) Lk 1: 73 ὅρκον ὃν ὤμοσεν, cf. Ja 5: 12. Jn 17: 26 ἡ ἀγάπη ἣν ἠγάπησάς με (ᾗ D); E 2: 4. Herm Man 7.1 ὁ φόβος ὃν δεῖ σε φοβηθῆναι.

(3) Instances like οἰκοδομεῖν οἰκίαν Lk 6: 48, εὐαγγελίζεσθαι τὸ εὐαγγέλιον, ἰδεῖν (βλέπειν) ὅραμα A 10: 17, 11: 5, 12: 9, 16: 10 (cf. 2: 17 OT) are self-explanatory; in them the acc. becomes the subj. in the pass.: τὸ εὐαγγέλιον τὸ εὐαγγελισθέν G 1: 11, ὅραμα ὤφθη A 16: 9. For δήσατε (αὐτὰ) δεσμάς s. § 158.

154. Adjectives and pronouns. These are often used alone instead of a modified substantive, but seldom in such a way that the substantive is still mentally supplied as in Lk 12: 47, 48 δαρήσεται πολλάς, ὀλίγας scil. πληγάς. Rather, the adjective is usually in the neuter as in Lk 5: 33 νηστεύουσιν πυκνά (= πυκνὰς νηστείας). Although not so much as in the classical idiom, the neuters of certain pronouns and universal adjectives like τοῦτο, τί, οὐδέν, πάντα etc. are very popular; these have a strong tendency to pass over to the accusative of general reference (§ 160).

2 C 12: 14, 13: 1 τρίτον ('for the third time') τοῦτον ἔρχομαι. Ph 1: 6 πεποιθὼς αὐτὸ τοῦτο 'in just this confidence = I am sure'. 1 C 9: 25 πάντα ἐγκρατεύεται, but in Herm Man 8.2 ἐγκρ. τὸ πονηρόν is a genuine transitive (= φεύγειν § 149), where gen., ἀπό, ἐπί, and inf. also appear (Herm Man 8.1–12). 1 C 10: 33 πάντα πᾶσιν ἀρέσκω, 11: 2 πάντα μου μέμνησθε ('in all things, in every connection'). Τὸ δ' αὐτό Mt 27: 44 and Ph 2: 18 'in the same way' and accordingly pregnant τὴν αὐτὴν ἀντιμισθίαν (πλατύνθητε) 2 C 6: 13 perhaps = τὸν αὐτὸν πλατυσμὸν ὡς

ἀντιμισθίαν. A 10: 20 μηδὲν διακρινόμενος; cf. 11: 12, s. also § 156. R 6: 10 ὃ γὰρ ἀπέθανεν, τῇ ἁμαρτίᾳ ἀπέθανεν... ὃ δὲ ζῇ, ζῇ τῷ θεῷ 'the death which he died... the life which he lived...' or 'that he died, lived'. G 2: 20 ὃ νῦν ζῶ ἐν σαρκί, ἐν πίστει ζῶ. Plut., Mor. 100F ὃ καθεύδουσι. 2 C 12: 11 οὐδὲν ὑστέρησα, cf. 11: 5; but hardly correct Rev 3: 17 οὐδὲν (οὐδενὸς SP 046 [s. § 180(4)]) χρείαν ἔχω. Mt 19: 20 τί ὑστερῶ 'in what am I deficient?', contrast Lk 22: 35 μή τινος ὑστερήσατε; 'did you lack anything?' 2 C 12: 13 τί ἐστιν ὃ ἡσσώθητε;, Mk 7: 36 ὅσον ('the more', properly 'as much as', W minusc. 700 ὅσῳ) διεστέλλετο, αὐτοὶ μᾶλλον ἐκήρυσσον; cf. Herm Sim 9.1.8 ὅσον ἐβόσκοντο (-ετο) τὰ κτήνη, μᾶλλον καὶ μᾶλλον αἱ βοτάναι ἔθαλλον. C 2: 18 ἃ ἑώρακεν ἐμβατεύων, εἰκῆ φυσιούμενος 'vainly conceited over what he beheld at his initiation' (ἐμβατεύω is so used in inscrip.) acc. to Fridrichsen, ZNW 21 (1922) 135ff. (or ἃ ἑ. ἐμβ. is to be referred to ταπεινοφροσύνῃ κ. θρησκείᾳ: Riesenfeld, Arbeiten und Mitteilungen I [1935] 7f.). The conjecture ἃ ἑώρα κενεμβατεύων (§ 119(2)) is therefore unnecessary; cf. Bauer s.v. ἐμβατεύω. Percy 173 favors Lightfoot's αἰώρᾳ κενεμβατεύων 'standing on a rope suspended in empty air'.

(C) The Double Accusative
Rob. 479–84

155. Two accusatives, both of which are external objects, are used with a number of verbs which can take an object of the person and of the thing (with a different relation to the verb); in this the NT conforms for the most part to classical usage. Cf. Mayser II 2, 322f. (1) NT with 'to teach' and 'to remind' as in classical, but less frequently. (2) With 'to inquire' and 'to ask' as in classical, but αἰτεῖν may be used also with παρά and ἀπό. (3) Κρύπτειν only with τι ἀπό τινος (= Hebrew מִן). (4) 'To rob' never with double accusative. (5) 'To dress and undress' as in classical: ἐν-, ἐκ-διδύσκειν τινά τι Mt 27: 31, Mk 15: 17, 20, (Lk 15: 22); by analogy also περιβάλλειν τινά τι (unclassical) Lk 23: 11 (AD al., αὐτόν om. SB al.), Jn 19: 2. (6) Χρίειν τινὰ ἔλαιον H 1: 9 OT is a Hebraizing construction. (7) Causatives (more popular in the NT than in classical) of course take the double accusative.

(1) **Διδάσκειν**: A 21: 21 ἀποστασίαν πάντας, Jn 14: 26 ὑμᾶς πάντα, H 5: 12 τοῦ διδάσκειν ὑμᾶς τινα (not τίνα) τὰ στοιχεῖα; Mk 6: 34 αὐτοὺς πολλά: πολλά is rather an acc. of content, cf. 1: 45, 3: 12 etc. and particularly 9: 26 πολλά σπαράξας (Zerwick 123); διδάσκειν with dat. instead of acc. Rev 2: 14 (Aesop., pap. vi AD; following δηλοῦν; Ursing 39f.) depends

upon an entirely uncertain reading. Ἀναμιμνήσκειν 1 C 4: 17, ὑπο- Jn 14: 26.

(2) **Αἰτεῖν** τινά τι Mk 6: 22, 23 etc.; παρά τινος (class.) Jn 4: 9, A 3: 2, 9: 2 (mid., which never takes double acc.), ἀπό τινος Mt 20: 20 BD (v.l. παρ'), 1 Jn 5: 15 SB (v.l. παρ'). Ἐρωτᾶν ('to ask') τινά τι Mt 21: 24, Mk 4: 10. Lk 14: 32 ἐρωτᾷ (αὐτὸν) τά (om. SB) πρὸς (εἰς B) εἰρήνην 'he inquires after his well-being' as several times in the LXX ἐρωτᾶν (τά) εἰς εἰρήνην = שָׁאַל לְשָׁלוֹם (Helb., Kas. 40) or 'he greets him (and pays homage to him)' (Foerster, TW II 410.20ff.).

(3) Κρύπτειν ἀπό in LXX: Helb., Kas. 42; Johannessohn II 276f. Mt 11: 25 (ἀπ-)ἔκρυψας ἀπό σοφῶν, Herm Sim 9.11.9, still more Hebraic Rev 6: 16 ἀπὸ προσώπου τοῦ...; pass. Lk 19: 42, κεκρυμμένον ἀπ' αὐτῶν 18: 34 (as incidentally also Homer, Od. 23.110 κεκρυμμένα...ἀπ' ἄλλων), παρακεκαλυμμένον ἀπ' αὐτῶν Lk 9: 45. MGr κρυφά ἀπό 'hidden from' Thumb² §172.

(4) Ἀφαιρεῖσθαί τι ἀπό τινος Lk 16: 3 (D without ἀπό), ἀφαιρεθήσεται αὐτῆς Lk 10: 42 (ἀπ' αὐτῆς SᶜACP); ἀφεῖλεν αὐτοῦ (Lk class. αὐτῷ) τὸ ὠτίον (οὖς Lk) Mt 26: 51 and pars. Mayser II 2, 232; gen. also class. Ἀποστερεῖν usually only with acc. of person, but ἀπεστερημένων τῆς ἀληθείας 1 T 6: 5 (D* reads differently). LXX: Helb., Kas. 43ff. ('to rob' mostly τί τινος or ἀπό τινος).

(5) But **περιβάλλειν** 'to put around' with τί τινι Lk 19: 43, also χλαμύδα κοκκίνην **περιέθηκαν** αὐτῷ Mt 27: 28. LXX: Helb., Kas. 46f. περιβάλλειν τινά τι (cf. Hdt. 1.163 τεῖχος τὴν πόλιν; 'to clothe' pap., inscrip.), τινά τινι and τινί τι.

(6) But **ἔχρισεν** πνεύματι A 10: 38; Rev 3: 18 κολλύριον does not depend on ἐγχρῖσαι but still on ἀγοράσαι. LXX: Helb., Kas. 48 more frequently χρίειν (ἐν) ἐλαίῳ.

(7) **Ποτίζειν** ('to cause to drink') τινά ποτήριον Mk 9: 41, γάλα 1 C 3: 2; cf. Plato, Phdr. 247E. **Ψωμίζειν** in the NT only with one acc. (R 12: 20, 1 C 13: 3), while it also takes two in the LXX (s. Helb., Kas. 49f. on ποτίζειν, ψωμίζειν). **Φορτίζειν** τινά τι 'to cause to carry' Lk 11: 46. (ἐν-)ὁρκίζειν τινά τι 'to cause to swear = to adjure' s. §149; cf. ἐξορκοῦν τινα τὸ Στυγὸς ὕδωρ Hdt. 6.74.

156. Accusative of object and cognate accusative. There are few examples:

Jn 17: 26 ἡ ἀγάπη ἣν (D ᾗ) ἠγάπησάς με. E 2: 4 τὴν ἀγάπην ἣν ἠγάπησεν ἡμᾶς. Lk 4: 35 μηδὲν βλάψας αὐτόν. G 5: 2 ὑμᾶς οὐδὲν ὠφελήσει. G 4: 12, A 25: 10, Mt 27: 44, Mk 6: 34 (§155(1)). Rev 14: 7 δοξάσατε αὐτὸν δόξαν 𝔓⁴⁷, δότε αὐτῷ δόξαν pm. Mayser II 2, 321.

157. An accusative of object and a predicate accusative are used with the following concepts,

corresponding to classical usage: (1) 'to have as': A 13: 5 εἶχον Ἰωάνην ὑπηρέτην; 'to take as': Ja 5: 10 ὑπόδειγμα λάβετε τοὺς προφήτας; 'to make into': Jn 6: 15 ποιεῖν αὐτὸν βασιλέα (many vv.ll.), H 1: 2 ὃν ἔθηκεν κληρονόμον, Lk 12: 14 τίς με κατέστησεν κριτήν; (2) 'To designate as, call': Jn 10: 35 ἐκείνους εἶπεν θεούς, Lk 1: 59 ἐκάλουν αὐτὸ Ζαχαρίαν; 'to pretend': Lk 20: 20 ὑποκρινομένους ἑαυτοὺς δικαίους (D and lat, otherwise with εἶναι, §397(2)); 'to confess': Jn 9: 22 αὐτὸν ὁμολογήσῃ Χριστόν (with εἶναι D), 1 Jn 4: 2 (acc. with inf. B), 2 Jn 7, R 10: 9. (3) 'To regard as': Ph 3: 7 ταῦτα ἥγημαι ζημίαν (8 with εἶναι, as LXX Job 30: 1 A, Dit., Syll.³ 831.13 [117 BC]). (4) 'To prove to be': G 2: 18 παραβάτην ἐμαυτὸν συνιστάνω. (5) Εἰς with the accusative is sometimes used for the predicate accusative as for the predicate nominative (§145). Semitic influence is unmistakable, although Greek had approximations to this usage (Mlt. 71f. [110]; Raderm.² 21, 122); the same is true of ὡς which may be inserted before the predicate. S. §145.—Helb., Kas. 50–68; Mayser II 2, 320f.

(1) Herm Sim 1.4 τί ποιήσεις τὸν ἀγρόν; LXX seldom (Helb., Kas. 7), e.g. Num 24: 14 τί ποιήσεις... τὸν λαόν σου;, Mk 15: 12 (but dat. D); pass. also A 12: 18 τί ὁ Πέτρος ἐγένετο (§299(2)). 'To do something to somebody' τινί τι Mt 21: 40, Lk 20: 15, A 9: 13, Herm Sim 5.2.2, 9.11.8, Apocr. Gos. (Ghedini, Vang. ap. 450); also A 16: 28 μηδὲν πράξῃς (instead of ποιήσῃς) σεαυτῷ κακόν, cf. Mt 13: 14 and Lk 18: 31 (§188(1)); Latinism? (ne quid tibi malum feceris; cf. vg nihil tibi m. f.). The acc. would have been used in Att. throughout (cf. §151(1)), while ποιεῖν τινί τι 'to do something for somebody' (Mk 7: 12, 10: 36) is also good Att. 'To do something to somebody' is also expressed by π. τι ἔν τινι Mt 17: 12 (ἐν om. SD al.), Lk 23: 31, or εἴς τινα (Hdt.; K.-G. I 324) Jn 15: 21 (ὑμῖν AD² al.), or μετά τινος (§206(3)); cf. καλὸν ἔργον ἠργάσατο ἐν ἐμοί Mk 14: 6, εἰς ἐμέ Mt 26: 10 (cf. 3 Jn 5; Att. ἐργ. with double acc.), οὕτως γένηται ἐν ἐμοί 1 C 9: 15, cf. Lk 21: 31. LXX ποιεῖν τι with τινι, ἔν τινι, ἐπί τινα, μετά τινος, εἴς τινα (seldom; Helb., Kas. 7), acc. is virtually limited to εὖ ποιεῖν (s. supra); Johannessohn I 61f.

(2) Mk 10: 18 τί με λέγεις ἀγαθόν; Jn 15: 15. Hebraistic: καλέσεις (and other verbs) τὸ ὄνομα αὐτοῦ Ἰωάνην, Ἰησοῦν, Ἐμμανουήλ Mt 1: 21, 23, 25, Lk 1: 13, 31; pass. ἐκλήθη τὸ ὄν. αὐτοῦ Ἰησοῦς 2: 21: Buttmann 132. UGosp 1.52f. τί με καλεῖτ[ε...διδ]άσκαλον; dat. with ἐπικαλεῖν ὄνομα Mt 10: 25 B*, cf. §202. LXX καλεῖν τὸ ὄνομά τινος with nom., less often with acc. (Jer 11: 16, Tob 1: 9 S).

(3) Νομίζειν and ὑπολαμβάνειν do not appear with double acc., λογίζεσθαι only R 6: 11 𝔓⁴⁶ADEFG (the

rest with εἶναι); A 20: 24 ποιοῦμαι τὴν ψυχὴν τιμίαν with v.l.; ἔχειν with double acc. = 'regard (someone) as...' like Lat. *habere*: Lk 14: 18, 19 ἔχε με παρῃτημένον, Ph 2: 29, A 20: 24 v.l., with ὡς Mt 14: 5, 21: 26 like λογίζεσθαι ὡς 1 C 4: 1, 2 C 10: 2 (pass. s. *infra* (5)), ἡγεῖσθαι ὡς 2 Th 3: 15, 2 Clem 5.6, Herm Vis 1.1.7. Γνώσῃ (PMich ἴδε) αὐτοὺς πάντας τοὺς... 'you will recognize among them all those which...' Herm Sim 8.3.4. Λαμβάνειν εἰς 'to conceive as' Homil Clem 6.9. Τὴν τιμὴν ἀναφερομένην ἔχουσιν εἰς ἐκεῖνον 'they regard the honor as shown to him' Homil Clem 16.19, ἔχειν αὐτὸν συνεσταμένον 'to consider him recommended' POxy II 292.6 (c. 25 AD; = Olsson no. 18), IV 787 (16 AD; = Olsson no. 16 p. 63), ἔχε με συνιστάμενον PHolm p. 55 (cf. PhW 1933, 277; Olsson, Aegyptus 12 [1932] 356); these phrases are translated from Latin: *commendatum habere* (Thes. linguae Lat. III 1853.64ff.), *excusatum habeas me rogo* Martial 2.79.2.

(4) But 2 C 6: 4 συνιστάνοντες ἑαυτοὺς ὡς θεοῦ διάκονοι; on 7: 11 s. § 197.

(5) Εἰς: A 13: 22 ἤγειρεν αὐτοῖς τὸν Δαυὶδ εἰς βασιλέα (OT style), 47 OT, 7: 21 (OT style); Mt 21: 46 εἰς προφήτην (ὡς πρ. CD al.) αὐτὸν εἶχον (LXX more often; 1 Clem 42.4 καθίστανον εἰς ἐπισκόπους). Ὡς: ἐλογίσθημεν ὡς R 8: 36 OT (Hebr. ﬤ), φαίνεσθε ὡς δίκαιοι Mt 23: 28 acc. to Ir sy[s], ἐφάνησαν ὡσεὶ λῆρος Lk 24: 11. Further exx. s. *supra* (3) and (4).

158. Accusative of object and of result. The classical pattern διαιρεῖν τι δύο μέρη (μέρη is the result of διαιρεῖν; K.-G. I 323) is also represented in the NT (apart from ποιεῖν with double acc., s. § 157(1)): Mt 13: 30 δήσατε αὐτὰ δεσμάς LXΔ (εἰς δ. SBCEF al., without αὐτά D Or), Lk 9: 14 κατακλίνατε αὐτοὺς κλισίας. It survives in MGr (Schwyzer, NJklA 21 [1908] 506f., Thumb[2] § 50a; for example, Pallis translates the phrase in Mt 13: 30 with δέστε τες δεμάτια [Thumb[2] p. 265 [277]]).

The acc. of result is sometimes repeated in Hebraic fashion to indicate distribution (cf. § 493(2)): Mk 6: 39 ἀνακλῖναι πάντας συμπόσια συμπόσια, cf. δήσατε δεσμὰς δεσμάς Mt 13: 30 Epiph Or, συνήγαγον αὐτοὺς θημωνιὰς θημωνιάς LXX Ex 8: 14 (10). Cf. with intrans. ἀνέπεσαν πρασιαὶ πρασιαί Mk 6: 40, τάγματα τάγματα Herm Sim 8.2.8 and 4.2 (κατὰ τάγματα 2.8!), μέλη μέλη κατέκοψεν αὐτόν Acta Thom. 8 [L.-B. II 2, 112.11f.] (Ljungvik, Aegyptus 13 [1933] 162). LXX Helb., Kas. 63.

(D) The Accusative with the Passive

159. (1) The accusative of the thing is retained with the passive of the verbs listed in § 155: 2 Th 2: 15 τὰς παραδόσεις ἃς ἐδιδάχθητε. (2) Likewise with the passive of those in § 156: Mt 15: 5 = Mk 7:

11 ὃ ἐὰν ὠφεληθῇς. (3) Perfect passive participle with τοὺς πόδας and the like (remnant of the passive in the so-called σχῆμα καθ' ὅλον καὶ κατὰ μέρος; ἤ σε πόδας νίψει Homer, Od. 19.356; Smyth § 985; Schwyzer II 80. (4) Since the person which in the active voice appears in the dative can become the subject in the passive (§ 312(1)), such passives can also take an accusative of the thing: πεπίστευμαι τὸ εὐαγγέλιον G 2: 7; cf. R 3: 2, 1 C 9: 17 etc. Xen. and Hellenistic: Helb., Kas. 202; Mayser II 2, 326.

(1) 1 C 12: 13 ἓν πνεῦμα ἐποτίσθημεν; H 6: 9 πεπείσμεθα τὰ κρείσσονα (after class. πείθειν τινά τι). Ἐνδεδυμένος and περιβεβλημένος (properly mid.) with acc., but Rev also περιβάλλεσθαι ἐν (3: 5, 4: 4 [without ἐν AP]) and Mt 11: 8 = Lk 7: 25 ἐν μαλακοῖς ἠμφιεσμένον. Κατηχούμενος τὸν λόγον G 6: 6, cf. A 18: 25, (21: 24, Lk 1: 4,) although the act. does not appear with double acc. (but cf. διδάσκειν). Πεπληρωμένοι καρπὸν (καρπῶν PΨ) δικαιοσύνης Ph 1: 11 (cf. C 1: 9) need not be a pure Hebraism; cf. MGr in the active (Thumb[2] § 50c with n. 1) in addition to πληρώσεις με εὐφροσύνην A 2: 28 OT (stronger v.l. -σύνης, also v.l. LXX), ἐνέπλησα αὐτὸν πνεῦμα σοφίας LXX Ex 31: 3 (cf. Ps 147: 3) and γέμειν with acc. Rev 17: 3 (§ 172). Helb., Kas. 147f. (with attestation in secular Hell.).

(2) Pass. of ζημιοῦν τινα ζημίαν with a somewhat shifted meaning = 'to lose' (antonym κερδαίνειν): Ph 3: 8 τὰ πάντα ἐζημιώθην, A 16: 26 τὴν ψυχὴν αὐτοῦ ζημιωθῇ (cf. pars.) (the MSS have τοῦ ἑνός... τῇ ψυχῇ ζημιώσεαι 'you shall be punished by the life (i.e. death) of one', not τὴν ψυχήν, in Hdt. 7.39).

(3) Jn 11: 44 δεδεμένος τοὺς πόδας (in spite of δήσαντες αὐτοῦ πόδας Mt 22: 13), 1 T 6: 5 διεφθαρμένων τὸν νοῦν, H 10: 22 ῥεραντισμένοι τὰς καρδίας... καὶ λελουσμένοι τὸ σῶμα.

(4) Περικεῖσθαί τι (pass. for περιτιθέναι τινί τι): A 28: 20, H 5: 2, (Lk 17: 2 following d λίθον μυλικόν?,) Herm Vis 5.1, Sim 6.2.5. Looser acc. τὴν αὐτὴν εἰκόνα μεταμορφούμεθα 'into the same form' 2 C 3: 18. With τὴν αὐτὴν ἀντιμισθίαν πλατύνθητε 6: 13 cf. § 154 and τὸν αὐτὸν τρόπον § 160; ἀναφανέντες τὴν Κύπρον A 21: 3 is a spurious variant for ἀναφάναντες (§ 72).— R 6: 17 s. § 294(5).—Rob. 484ff.; Mayser II 2, 323ff.

(E) Accusative of Respect and Adverbial Accusative

160. The accusative of respect with adjectives (for δεδεμένος τοὺς πόδας and the like, s. § 159(3)) and the like is used in the NT in a very limited way, since its function has almost entirely passed over to the dative (§ 197). Mt 27: 57 τοὔνομα 'by name (with respect to name)' as in classical, otherwise ὀνόματι. Jn 6: 10 τὸν ἀριθμὸν ὡς πεντακισχίλιοι. Η 2: 17 πιστὸς ἀρχιερεὺς τὰ πρὸς τὸν θεόν, cf. 5: 1. But in R 15: 17 the same phrase τὰ πρὸς τὸν θεόν has now become an adverbial accusative. A 17: 28 γένος (from Arat., Phaenom. 5; cf. Cleanthes, Hymn to Zeus 4 [Stoic. I 537] ἐκ σοῦ γὰρ γένος ἐσμέν), taken up in *v.* 29 γένος οὖν ὑπάρχοντες: with Aratus it was certainly an acc. of general reference, while in Acts it was evidently felt to be subject. Cf. Bauer s.v. for bibliography. There are other remnants of this adverbial usage in the NT:

R 12: 18 τὸ ἐξ ὑμῶν... εἰρηνεύοντες, 9: 5 τὸ κατὰ σάρκα, 1: 15 τὸ κατ' ἐμέ (§ 224(1)), 12: 5 τὸ καθ' εἷς, 16: 19 τὸ ἐφ' ὑμῖν v.l.; τὰ πολλά (v.l. πολλάκις) 15: 22, τὸ πλεῖστον ('at most') τρεῖς 1 C 14: 27, τὸ πρότερον, τὸ πρῶτον, cf. § 62. With meaningless article: τὸ καθ' ἡμέραν 'daily' (class.) Lk 11: 3, 19: 47, A 17: 11, 28 D, 19: 9 D, τὸ πρωΐ 5: 21 D (LXX Ex 29: 39 and often), τὸ δειλινόν 'afternoon' 3: 1 D (LXX Ex 29: 39 etc.), s. § 161(3). Τὸ νῦν ἔχον A 24: 25 'for now' (Lucian *et al.*), τὰ νῦν Acts, e.g. 4: 29; τὸ τέλος 'finally' 1 P 3: 8, τὴν ἀρχήν 'from the beginning, at all' Jn 8: 25 (cf. § 300(2)). For the latter meaning cf. Homil Clem 11.32.1, 18.21.3, 19.6.6, 10.1; 'to begin with' 19.24.3; τί καὶ τὴν ἀρχὴν διαλέγομαι; 6.11 (s. Bauer, Hdb. on Jn 8: 25). Αὐτὸ τοῦτο s. § 290(4). Δωρεάν 'gratuitously' and μακράν (§ 161(1)) have become purely adverbial, and χάριν 'on account of' has become a preposition. (Τὸ) λοιπόν 'for the rest, more-over, now, already' rather often (E 6: 10 𝔓⁴⁶S*AB τοῦ λοιποῦ 'henceforth', s. § 186(2)); already in Att.; λοιπὸν οὖν 1 Th 4: 1 as in BGU IV 1079.6 (41 AD); pap. Mayser II 3, 145f. A. Cavallin, (Τὸ) λοιπόν, eine bedeutungsgeschichtliche Untersuchung (Eranos 39 [1941] 121–44).—Ἀκμήν 'still' Mt 15: 16, also Η 5: 13 D*E*. Hell. Phryn. 123; Krumbacher, KZ 27 (1885) 498ff.; 29 (1888) 188f.; Psaltes 334; Gromska 63f. Ἀκμήν Theoc. 4.60 resumption of ἔτι 58, ἀκμήν ἔτι Polyb. 14.4.9, 15.6.6, ἔτι ἀκμήν inscrip. 5 BC, etc. (Klaffenbach, APF 13 [1939] 213). Not in LXX; MGr ἀκόμη 'still'.—Ὃν τρόπον Mt 23: 37 and rather often (LXX often, Johannessohn I 81), τὸν ὅμοιον τρόπον Jd 7 (τὸν αὐτὸν τρ. and the like LXX, Johannessohn I 82) are related to the acc. of content; also dat. παντὶ τρόπῳ Ph 1: 18 (LXX 1 Macc 14: 35, § 198(4)) and καθ' ὃν τρ. A 15: 11, 27: 25 (LXX, Johannessohn I 82). Cf. R 3: 2, 2 Th 2: 3. Ptol. pap. τὸν αὐτὸν τρ., ὃν τρ., τίνα τρ. besides οὐδενὶ τρόπῳ and the like (Mayser II 2, 329). Οὐδὲν χρείαν ἔχω Rev 3: 17 AC (οὐδενός SP 046; cf. § 154).—Smyth §§ 1600ff., 1606ff.; Rob. 486ff.; Mayser II 2, 151, 326ff.

(F) Accusative of Extent

161. (1) The accusative of the extent of space in response to the questions 'how far? how long?'

etc. needs no amplification (Lk 22: 41 ἀπεσπάσθη ἀπ' αὐτῶν ὡσεὶ λίθου βολήν; 2: 44; Jn 6: 19). Except for stereotyped μακράν (§§ 34(2); 184), only ὁδὸν θαλάσσης Mt 4: 15 OT (Is 8: 23 where it is a back-reading from the NT as can be seen from its position in the context: Katz; LXX also else-where, e.g. Dt 11: 30, cf. Johannessohn I 75) as a literal translation of Hebr. דֶּרֶךְ, Lat. *versus*, need be considered (cf. § 166). Furthermore, the occasional replacement of the accusative by ἀπό and a genitive in response to the question 'how far away?'—a usage which corresponds to Latin (Caesar, B.G. 2.7.3 *a milibus passuum duobus*)—is proved to be good Greek by parallel appearances with πρό (§ 213) and μετά (cf. W. Schulze, Graeca Latina 15ff.): Jn 11: 18 ἦν Βηθανία ἐγγὺς τῶν Ἱερ., ὡς ἀπὸ σταδίων δεκαπέντε. A 26: 20 πᾶσάν τε τὴν χώραν (v.l. εἰς π. τ. χ.); Bonaccorsi 457f.: if correct then a Hebraistic acc. of place. (2) The accusative is used for extent of time in response to the question 'how long?' (cf. however dat. § 201): Jn 2: 12 ἔμειναν οὐ πολλὰς ἡμέρας. The distributive use is also old: Mt 20: 2 συμφωνεῖν ἐκ δηναρίου τὴν ἡμέραν *per diem* (Mayser II 2, 333). (3) In the case of ὥρα the accusative is classical, answering the question 'when?': Jn 4: 52 ἐχθὲς ὥραν ἑβδόμην; in the NT, however, it also appears in τὴν ἡμέραν τῆς πεντηκοστῆς A 20: 16 (εἰς τὴν ἡ. D) as well as in τὸ δειλινόν, τὸ πρωΐ (§ 160). Otherwise the dative has strongly en-croached upon the domain of the accusative; s. §§ 200(2); 201.—Mayser II 2, 330ff.; Smyth §§ 1580ff.; Rob. 469f.

(1) Ἀπό for 'how far away?': Jn 21: 8, Rev 14: 20, Herm Vis 4.1.5 (Diodor. Sic., Plut. etc.; cf. also Jannaris § 1513 with n.; Schmidt 394; W. Bauer, Hdb. on Jn 11: 18; Vogeser 26f.); acc. on the other hand, e.g. Lk 24: 13 ἀπέχουσαν σταδίους ἑξήκοντα ἀπὸ Ἰερουσαλήμ (cf. A 1: 12).

(2) Νύκτα καὶ ἡμέραν '(throughout) day and night' Mk 4: 27, Lk 2: 37, A 26: 7, 2 Th 3: 8 ADE al. (gen. SBFG); τὰς ἡμέρας... τὰς νύκτας 'during the days and nights' Lk 21: 37; ἡμέραν ἐξ ἡμέρας 2 P 2: 8 (class.: cf. μίαν ἐκ μιᾶς § 305). With Mt 20: 2 cf. exx. from Att. inscrip. in Meisterhans 205, from pap. in Moulton, ClR 15 (1901) 436,18 (1904) 152.—On μικρόν s. Michel, TW IV 653 n. 14.

(3) Rev 3: 3 ποίαν ὥραν, A 10: 30 τὴν ἐνάτην (add. ὥραν ΗΡΨ; but 9 περὶ ὥραν ἕκτην; also 3 περί as v.l.), 10: 3 ὥραν ἐνάτην τῆς ἡμέρας Ψ. Μεσονύκτιον s. § 186(2). Τεσσαρεσκαιδεκάτην σήμερον ἡμέραν προσ-δοκῶντες 'having been in suspense now already fourteen days' A 27: 33 is a special idiom; cf. κεῖμαι τριακοστὴν ταύτην ἡμέραν Lucian, D. Mar. 13.3,

ἐνάτην ἡμέραν γεγαμημένην 'for eight days' Xen., An. 4.5.24 and τρίτον ἔτος τουτί 'for two years' Lysias 24.6 (K.-G. I 314). Ὥραν: Aeschyl., Eu. 109 ὥραν οὐδενὸς κοινὴν θεῶν, Eur., Ba. 723 f. τὴν τεταγμένην ὥραν, Arist., Ath. 30 (at end) τὴν ὥραν τὴν προρρηθεῖσαν, Dem. 54.4 etc.; according to the sense = εἰς ὥραν 'at the hour' (ἐπὶ τὴν ὥραν A 3: 1). LXX Ex 9: 18 etc. ταύτην τὴν ὥραν αὔριον, Sus 7 Theod. μέσον ἡμέρας (LXX τὸ δειλινὸν later in the vs.), Gen 43: 15 τὴν μεσημβρίαν, etc. etc. (Johannessohn I 67: ἐχθὲς καὶ τρίτην ὥραν LXX). Sophocles, Lexicon p. 44; Dieterich 151; Jannaris § 1275; Trunk 12; Wolf I 12; Thumb² § 52. No certain exx. in Ptol. pap. (Mayser II 2, 232), but later, e.g. POxy III 477.8 (132/3 AD) τὸ πέμπτον ἔτος 'in the fifth year'.

For the accusative absolute s. § 424.

(4) GENITIVE

Rob. 491–520

(A) The Adnominal Genitive

The genitive with the function of an adjective is the commonest way in which the case is used; like the adjective it can be used either as an attributive or a predicate (dependent upon εἶναι, γίνεσθαι etc.). The *nomen regens* can also be represented by a pronoun or especially by the article. Only the more noteworthy phenomena need be mentioned here. Mayser II 2, 118 ff. Lk prefers the genitive to an adjective (according to Meillet, Bull. Soc. Ling. 31, 3 [1931] 90, Semitism); s. § 165.

162. Genitive of origin and relationship. (1) It is employed, as in classical, to identify a person by his father: Ἰάκωβον τὸν τοῦ Ζεβεδαίου Mt 4: 21 etc. The rather frequent addition of υἱός is not Attic but Semitic (and Latin, Viereck 62): Ἰωάνην τὸν Ζαχαρίου υἱόν Lk 3: 2. (2) If υἱός is omitted, contrary to classical usage a second article in the genitive is added after the first: Δαυὶδ τὸν τοῦ Ἰεσσαί A 13: 22 OT; cf. pap. (Mayser II 2, 7. 22 ff.). (3) Also to identify a mother by her son: Μαρία ἡ Ἰωσῆτος Mk 15: 47 following Μαρία ἡ Ἰακώβου τοῦ μικροῦ καὶ Ἰωσῆτος μήτηρ 40 (cf. Mt 27: 56). (4) And to identify a wife by her husband (classical also): Μαριὰμ ἡ τοῦ Κλωπᾶ Jn 19: 25. Cf. ἡ τοῦ Μετέλλου (scil. μήτηρ) Plut., Mor. 205 A. (5) The possession of slaves by a family: τοὺς (scil. brethren, Christians) ἐκ τῶν (scil. slaves) Ἀριστοβούλου, Ναρκίσσου R 16: 10, 11. (6) The use of υἱός in a figurative sense (often) is predominantly a Hebraism, Deissmann, BS

162–6 [161–6] notwithstanding. (7) Other types of relationship: attributive οἱ τοῦ Χριστοῦ 1 C 15: 23; frequently predicate: οὗτος οὐκ ἔστιν αὐτοῦ R 8: 9, also οὐχ ὑμῶν ἐστιν γνῶναι A 1: 7 'it is not your concern...'. Ἑαυτῆς γενομένη 'after she had come to herself' Homil Clem 13.6.5. Mayser II 2, 188 f. (8) Ἐν, εἰς with genitive 'in somebody's house' is not found in the NT; in place of ἐν, εἰς Ἅιδου (1 Clem 4.12) Lk 16: 23 has ἐν τῷ ᾅδῃ.

(1) Υἱοί is almost always used of the sons of Zebedee when they are mentioned together: Mt 26: 37, 27: 56, Mk 10: 35, Lk 5: 10; only Jn 21: 2 οἱ τοῦ Z. ABL al. (οἱ υἱοὶ Z. SD, οἱ υ. τοῦ Z. E).

(2) Cf. §§ 259(1); 260(2). Without art. Ἰούδαν Σίμωνος Ἰσκαριώτου Jn 6: 71 etc. and as in class. Σώπατρος Πύρρου Βεροιαῖος A 20: 4. For the genealogy Lk 3: 23 ff. (ὢν υἱός Ἰωσὴφ τοῦ Ἠλὶ τοῦ...) cf. the exact parallel from the bilingual inscrip., Palmyrene-Aramaic and Greek, in Mlt. 236 n. on p. 84 [134]. Pap.: Eakin 335 ff.; Miller 341 ff. The rule in Att. lapidary style (Meisterhans 223 f.; Meister, IF 18 [1905/6] 197; Mayser II 2, 7) is: Περικλῆς Ξανθίππου, but in the gen. Περικλέους τοῦ Ξ.; the τοῦ belongs to the preceding gen. (cf. pap. Βερενίκης τῆς Νικάνορος [254 BC] and the like; Mayser II 2, 7 f. n.). Att. literary style and the other dialects employed the art. with all cases (Περ. ὁ Ξανθίππου etc.; Wahrmann, IF 54 [1936] 60). Further exx. of ancestral lines with τοῦ...τοῦ...in Klostermann, Hdb. on Lk 3: 23 ff. (p. 419; as early as Hdt.); τοῦ τοῦ 'of the son of...' is avoided; yet 1 Clem 12.2 ὑπὸ Ἰησοῦ τοῦ τοῦ Ναυή.

(3) Μαρία ἡ Ἰακώβου Mk 16: 1, Lk 24: 10. The genitive art. is omitted except for Mt 27: 56 ἡ τοῦ Ἰακ. μήτηρ. Identification of the father by the son is impossible, therefore the explanation of the variant A 7: 16 τῶν υἱῶν Ἐμμὼρ τοῦ Συχέμ (DH; al. ἐν Σ. or τοῦ ἐν Σ.) as Ἐ. πατρὸς Σ. (following LXX Gen 33: 19) is not correct.

(4) Mt 1: 6 τῆς τοῦ Οὐρίου. It is grammatically impossible to tell whether, with the apostle Ἰούδας Ἰακώβου Lk 6: 16, A 1: 15, υἱός or, following Jd 1, ἀδελφός is to be supplied (Τιμοκράτης ὁ Μητροδώρου scil. ἀδ. Alciphro 2.2 [4.17.10 Schepers]).

(5) 1 C 1: 11 τῶν (scil. slaves?) Χλόης.

(6) 1 Th 5: 5 υἱοὶ φωτός ἐστε καὶ υἱοὶ ἡμέρας, immediately followed by a pred. without υἱός: 6 οὐκ ἐσμὲν νυκτὸς οὐδὲ σκότους and 8 ἡμέρας ὄντης; cf. H 10: 39 οὐκ ἐσμὲν ὑποστολῆς (but vg *subtractionis filii*)...ἀλλὰ πίστεως. Thack. 41 f.; Johannessohn I 32. Mk 3: 17 υἱοὶ βροντῆς 'thunderbolts' (Fridrichsen, Symb. Osl. 13 [1934] 38 ff.).

(7) On τὰ Καίσαρος etc. s. § 266(3). Εἶναί τινος 'to belong to': A 27: 23 τοῦ θεοῦ οὗ εἰμι; 1 C 1: 12, 3: 4; 6: 19 οὐκ ἐστὲ ἑαυτῶν 'you do not belong to yourselves' (cf. 20); 3: 21 πάντα ὑμῶν (= ὑμέτερα § 285(2)) ἐστιν; H 5: 14, 12: 11; Herm Sim 8.7.6. With

γίνεσθαι: Lk 20: 14 ἵνα ἡμῶν γένηται ἡ κληρονομία; 2 P 1: 20; A 20: 3 ἐγένετο γνώμης (Att. τῆς αὐτῆς γνώμης ἦσαν and the like, s. K.-G. ɪ 373; Glotta 5 [1914] 288; Homil Clem 15.10 προαιρέσεως ἐγενόμην). 1 C 14: 37 κυρίου ἐστίν DFG (+ἐντολή 𝔭⁴⁶S*AB). Jn 17: 6 W σοῦ ἦσαν (al. σοὶ ἦ.). Προθέσεώς εἰμι τοῦ ὑμᾶς κολάσαι Ps.-Callisth. 1.3 (42.6 Kroll); οὐ γὰρ ἰδίας ἐξουσίας ἐστὶν ὁ λόγος τοῦ κοιμωμένου Homil Clem 17.14.6.

(8) Εἰς ᾅδην A 2: 27 OT (ᾅδου EP and part of the LXX MSS), 31 (ᾅδου ACDEP). Ἐν τοῖς τοῦ πατρός μου Lk 2: 49. Ἐν τοῖς Ἀπολλωνίου and the like in the pap., s. Mlt. 103 [167]; Mayser ɪɪ 1, 8. Att. also (e.g. Aristoph., Vespae 1432 εἰς τὰ Πιττάλου, Lysias 12.12 εἰς τὰ τοῦ ἀδελφοῦ, Herondas 5.52 εἰς τὰ Μικκάλης); Byzantine (Tabachovitz 3 f.).

163. Objective genitive. Those instances of the objective genitive which are associated with expressions which are transitive in Greek are noteworthy: ζῆλος θεοῦ 'zeal *for* God' R 10: 2 (ὁ ζῆλος τοῦ οἴκου σου Jn 2: 17 OT) for ζηλοῦν τινα (G 4: 17, 2 C 11: 2), τὸ μαρτύριον τοῦ Χριστοῦ 1 C 1: 6 for διαμαρτύρεσθαι τὸν Χριστόν A 18: 5; and above all τὸ εὐαγγέλιον (*of, about*) τῆς βασιλείας Mt 4: 23 etc., τὸ εὐ. Ἰησοῦ Χριστοῦ Mk 1: 1 (Paul often has a similar usage), τὸ εὐ. τῆς ἀκροβυστίας (to) G 2: 7 for εὐαγγελίζεσθαι τὴν βασιλείαν Lk 8: 1, Ἰησοῦν τὸν Χριστόν A 5: 42, τὴν πόλιν A 14: 21. For dative expressions: πίστις Ἰησοῦ Χριστοῦ R 3: 22 etc. (πιστεύειν τινί), closely related to which is πίστις εἰς τὸν κύριον Ἰ. Χρ. A 20: 21 etc., ἐν Χρ. Ἰ. 1 T 3: 13 etc. (πιστεύειν ἔν τινι, εἴς τινα § 187(6)); ὑπακοὴ τοῦ Χρ., τῆς πίστεως, τῆς ἀληθείας 2 C 10: 5, R 1: 5, 1 P 1: 22 etc. (ὑπήκουον τῇ πίστει A 6: 7).

The gen. in εὐαγγέλιον τοῦ θεοῦ R 1: 1 etc. designates the originator (further defined by περὶ τοῦ υἱοῦ αὐτοῦ 3), in τὸ εὐαγγέλιόν μου R 2: 16, 16: 25, 2 T 2: 8, ἡμῶν 2 C 4: 3, 1 Th 1: 5, 2 Th 2: 14 the preacher (but εὐ. κατὰ Ματθαῖον etc. 'according to the presentation of Matthew', not τοῦ M. 'the [special] Gospel of Matthew'). Ἀγάπη τοῦ θεοῦ can be either subjective or objective; δικαιοσύνη τ. θ., τῆς πίστεως indicates the originator or the cause, therefore also ἡ ἐκ θεοῦ δικ. Ph 3: 9, ἡ ἐκ πίστεως δικ. R 9: 30, even ἡ διὰ π. δ. Ph 3: 9, can be synonymous. Mt 24: 6 ἀκοαὶ πολέμων 'reports of wars' (ἀκούσητε πολέμους Lk 21: 9); A 4: 9 εὐεργεσία ἀνθρώπου 'to a man'; Jn 7: 13 and 20: 19 'for fear of'; Mt 13: 18, 36 'the parable of, about'; 1 C 1: 18 ὁ λόγος τοῦ σταυροῦ (cf. τὸν πατέρα αὐτοῖς ἔλεγεν Jn 8: 27; Raderm.² 109). R 2: 7 is a type of obj. gen.: ὑπομονὴ ἔργου ἀγαθοῦ 'to persevere in...'; on the other hand 1 Th 1: 3 τῆς ὑπομονῆς τῆς ἐλπίδος, which is parallel to τοῦ ἔργου τῆς πίστεως and τοῦ κόπου τῆς ἀγάπης, more likely expresses subjectively the patient hope

which accompanies active faith (cf. G 5: 6) and laboring love. Loosely used: H 10: 19 εἰς τὴν εἴσοδον τῶν ἁγίων 'for entering the holy place' instead of εἰς τὰ ἅγια due to the preceding εἰς; Michaelis, TW v 109.54 ff.; τὴν τῶν ἁγίων ὁδόν 9: 8 the same (*ibid.* 77.21 ff.). C 3: 14 σύνδεσμος τῆς τελειότητος 'the bond which produces perfection' (Fridrichsen, Symb. Osl. 19 [1939] 41 ff.). Ἐξουσία 'authority over' Mk 6: 7 etc. (cf. Foerster, TW ɪɪ 563.1 ff.; class.) by analogy with 'to exercise authority over' (§ 177).—In many instances the gen. θεοῦ, Χριστοῦ in Paul is used only to express some relationship not exactly defined; it thus corresponds to an English or German adj. (cf. § 165) or to the first element in a compound: O. Schmitz, Die Christus-Gemeinschaft des Paulus im Lichte seines Genetivgebrauchs (Gütersloh, 1924; Paulusstudien 2). The division of the gen. into obj., subj. etc. is really only an attempt to set off several special types among the manifold possibilities of the general function of the adnominal gen., which is to denote a relationship (Rob. 493 f. calls it the specifying case, while Smyth uses the word *limiting* to describe its function [§ 1289]). Acc. to A. Schmitt, Natalicium Geffcken (Heidelberg, 1931) 126 ff. δικαιοσύνη θεοῦ in Paul means 'divine salvation'. A. Oepke, ThLZ 78 (1953) 257–64 δικαιοσύνη θεοῦ R 1: 17 'the righteousness which "is before God"' or 'which God awards to men' (cf. Dt 33: 21 Gad executed Yahweh's righteousness). Zerwick, Graec. bibl. § 28 genetivus 'generaliter determinans'.

164. The partitive genitive or the genitive of the divided whole, while not yet extinct, is being driven out by the use of the prepositions ἐκ (ἀπό, ἐν); s. A. Wilhelm, WSt 61/2 (1943–7) 167–89. (1) The genitive (alone) predominates with τις (except in Jn), is exclusively used with ἕκαστος (but πᾶς ἐξ ὑμῶν Lk 14: 33), often with εἷς. Ἐκ is customarily found with τίς. Other examples of the genitive (alone): Lk 18: 11 οἱ λοιποὶ τῶν ἀνθρώπων, R 15: 26 τοὺς πτωχοὺς τῶν ἁγίων, H 7: 5?; idiomatic τὰ αὐτὰ τῶν παθημάτων 1 P 5: 9 (strictly speaking incorrect). Μυριάδες μυριάδων καὶ χιλιάδες χιλιάδων Rev 5: 11 OT is a translation Hebraism (Johannessohn ɪ 20 f.; E. Hofmann, Ausdrucksverstärkung 50–2). As predicate: 1 T 1: 20 ὧν ἐστιν Ὑμέναιος, A 23: 6, with ἐκ Lk 22: 58, Jn 18: 17, 1 C 12: 15, 16, (2 Clem 14.1, 18.1,) with ἀπό Homil Clem 15.3. This ἐκ is hardly classical, although μόνος ἐξ ἁπάντων and the like appear (μόνος always by itself in NT); ἀπό is even less classical (pap. s. Kuhring 20; Rossberg 22; Mayser ɪɪ 2, 348 f.; LXX s. Johannessohn ɪ 17; MGr): Mt 27: 21 τίνα ἀπὸ τῶν δύο (τίνα alone syˢ) = Attic πότερον τούτοιν! There are, however, classical models for ἐν: τις (τινες) ἐν ὑμῖν 1 C 15: 12, Ja 5: 13, 14, 19, τις ἐν τῷ συνεδρίῳ A 5: 34 (ἐκ τοῦ συνεδρίου D); but the local significance 'in, among' is still clearly perceptible in most instances. Cf. ἐκ and ἀπό instead of the partitive genitive with verbs § 169. (2) The partitive genitive or its equivalent is also used as subject or object: Jn 16: 17 εἶπον ἐκ τῶν μαθητῶν ('some of his disciples'), Lk 21: 16 θανατώσουσιν ἐξ ὑμῶν (scil. τινας). Such expressions are quite rare in classical (K.-G. ι 345f.; Schwyzer ιι 102; Nachmanson, Beiträge 34.1; Mlt. 72f. [112]; Mayser ιι 2, 351, 352), but common in Semitic languages (Hebrew and Aramaic מן, therefore often in LXX; s. Johannessohn ι 18f.; Huber 69f.). (3) The country within which a city etc. lies also stands in the partitive genitive (always with article, § 261(6); the usage is found in class., pap.: Mayser ιι 2, 126): ἐν Ταρσῷ τῆς Κιλικίας A 22: 3; cf. § 261(6). (4) Ὀψὲ σαββάτων Mt 28: 1 according to what follows and according to Mk 16: 1 means 'after the sabbath'. (5) The classical reverse assimilation of gender and number occurs in τὰ ἡμίσεια (τὰ ἥμισυ § 48) τῶν ὑπαρχόντων Lk 19: 8; cf. classical ἡ ἡμίσεια τῆς γῆς etc. (K.-G. ι 279; Mayser ιι 2, 123).

Ptol. pap. more often ἀπό than ἐκ; ἐν is quite rare (Mayser ιι 2, 352f.). (1) The gen. πάντων in Mk 12: 28 is a frozen masc.-neut. form, ποία ἐστὶν ἐντολὴ πρώτη πάντων (πασῶν only M* al.); however πάντων is omitted in DW lat etc. and appears to belong to the following vs.: πάντων πρῶτον. Ἄκουε Ἰσραήλ (so Eus and minusc.). Τὰ ἅγια τῶν ἁγίων s. § 245(2), εἰς τοὺς αἰῶνας τῶν αἰώνων § 141(1). Εἷς with the gen. Mt 5: 29, 30 etc., with ἐκ 10: 29 etc.; τίς ἐξ ὑμῶν 6: 27 etc., with gen. for certain only A 7: 52, H 1: 5, 13, uncertain Mt 22: 28 τίνος τῶν ἑπτά (τῶν ἑ. probably spurious), Mk 12: 23 τίνος αὐτῶν (αὐ. om. Δ c k), Lk 7: 42 τίς αὐτῶν (αὐ. om. D al.), 14: 5 τίνος ὑμῶν (ἐξ ὑ. D), 20: 33 τίνος αὐτῶν (αὐ. om. S* e ff²). (2) Instead of gen.: Lk 8: 35 D παραγενομένων ἐκ τῆς πόλεως ('people from'). Hardly for the dat.: Jn 3: 25 ἐγένετο ζήτησις ἐκ τῶν μαθητῶν Ἰωάνου μετὰ Ἰουδαίου (-ων) = τισὶν ἐκ τῶν μ. (cf. A 15: 2), although sys and syp have ἑνὶ before ἐκ (due to Ἰουδαίου). As subj.: Jn 7: 40 ἐκ τοῦ ὄχλου ἀκούσαντες...ἔλεγον (ΓΔΛ al. insert πολλοί); A 21: 16 συνῆλθον δὲ καὶ (ἐκ add. E) τῶν μαθητῶν ἀπὸ Καισαρείας (τινες τῶν might have dropped out after μαθ., for one misses the expected repetition of the article before ἀπό); 19: 33, Rev 11: 9, 15: 7 ἐκ τῶν τεσσάρων (ζῴων) ἔδωκαν 𝔓⁴⁷ (-κεν S), ἐν ἐκ τ. τ. ζ. ἔδωκεν al. Cf. LXX 1 Km 14: 45 τῆς τριχός, 2 Km 14: 11 (ἀπό) τῆς τρ., 4 Km 10: 23 ἔστιν(!)...τῶν δούλων; Schulthess 226f. Pap. seldom: Mayser ιι 2, 196. As obj.: Mk 6: 43, Lk 11: 49, Mt 23: 34, 2 Jn 4, Rev 2: 10, Herm Sim 8.6.5 ἐξ

αὐτῶν (A and PMich πολλούς before or after). Mk 9: 37 ἐκ τῶν τοιούτων παιδίων WΘ (om. ἐκ D; ἐν pm.). Mayser ιι 2, 195f.

(3) Ναζαρὲθ τῆς Γαλιλαίας Mt 21: 11, Mk 1: 9, Κανὰ τῆς Γαλ. Jn 2: 1; cf. A 16: 12 ἥτις (scil. Φίλιπποι) ἐστὶν πρώτης (to be read thus instead of -η) μερίδος τῆς Μακεδονίας πόλις.

(4) Further cf. μετ' ὀλίγον τούτων Xen., HG 1.1.2 (Dindorf in the Thesaurus under μετά; K.-G. ι 391); the gen. with ὀψέ and μετ' ὀλίγον have become associated in meaning with ὕστερον τούτων, πρότερον τούτων (cf. πρό § 213). Philostr. ὀψὲ μυστηρίων 'not until after the mysteries' VA 4.18 (1.138.8 Kayser), ὀ. τούτων 6.10 (1.213.24), ὀ. τῆς μάχης Her. 12 (2.190.10), but certainly partitive ὀ. τῶν Τρωϊκῶν 'late in the Trojan war' 5.1 (2.171.4), ὀ. τῶν Ὀλυμπιάδων Gym. 13 (2.268.21), and thus the class. ὀ. τῆς ὥρας 'at a late hour' MPol 7.1, pap. (Mayser ιι 2, 533). E. Tobac, Ὀψὲ δὲ σαββάτων... (Rev. d'hist. eccl. 20 [1924] 239–43; s. Bauer s.v. ὀψέ for further lit.).

(5) Without assimilation ἥμισυ καιροῦ Rev 12: 14 OT (cf. τρεῖς ἡμέρας καὶ ἥμισυ 11: 9, 11), ἕως ἡμίσους τῆς βασιλείας Mk 6: 23; correspondingly τὸ δέκατον (scil. μέρος) τῆς πόλεως Rev 11: 13.

165. **The genitive of quality** provides in many combinations an attributive which would ordinarily be provided by an adjective: ὁ μαμωνᾶς τῆς ἀδικίας Lk 16: 9 = ὁ ἄδικος μαμωνᾶς 11. Hebrew usage is thus reflected, in that this construction compensates for the nearly non-existent adjective. Classical Greek exhibits very sparse parallels in poetry only, e.g. ὁ τᾶς ἡσυχίας βίοτος = ὁ ἥσυχος βίοτος Eur., Ba. 389 (K.-G. ι 264). Cf. Schwyzer ιι 122, 124; Johannessohn ι 27f.; Huber 55; Raderm.² 108f.; Percy 250–2. Brachylogy in technical language also contributes: C. Mohrmann, Misc. G. Mercati 1 = Studi e Testi 121 (Città del Vaticano, 1946) 17f. Combinations with σῶμα are especially favored: R 6: 6, 7: 24 (τοῦ θανάτου, cf. θνητὸν σῶμα 6: 12, 8: 11), Ph 3: 21, C 1: 22, 2: 11, as are those with ἡμέρα: R 2: 5, 2 C 6: 2 OT, 1 P 2: 12 OT, etc. The reverse: ἐπὶ πλούτου ἀδηλότητι 1 T 6: 17 = ἐπ' ἀδήλῳ πλούτῳ has classical parallels (Winer § 34, 3 [Winer-M.³ 296]).—The predicate use of the genitive of quality like ἦν, ἐγένετο ἐτῶν δώδεκα Mk 5: 42, Lk 2: 42 (D reads differently) conforms to classical usage. For ἐγένετο γνώμης etc. s. § 162(7).—Mayser ιι 2, 134ff., 218; Rob. 496f., Smyth § 1320f.

In ἡμέρα ἀναδείξεως Lk 1: 80 only the Hebraistic ἡμέρα = χρόνος is to be noted; cf. οἱ χρόνοι τῆς αἱρέσεως Aeschin. 2.58. A 1: 18 also (τῆς) ἀδικίας and

2 P 2: 15 with μισθός (here acc. to M.-H. 440 an obj. gen. as in LXX Ezk 14: 4, 44: 12 κόλασις (τῆς) ἀδικίας), Lk 16: 8 with οἰκονόμος, 18: 6 with κριτής. Further ἀπιστίας H 3: 12, βλασφημίας A 6: 11 S*D (v.l. -μα), Rev 13: 1, 17: 3, χολὴ πικρίας A 8: 23, ῥίζα π. H 12: 15: in fact, πικρίας is the only genuine variant in Heb of LXX Dt 29: 18 (17) μὴ τίς ἐστιν ῥίζα ἄνω φύουσα ἐν χολῇ καὶ πικρίᾳ, where AF have πικρίας after ῥίζα without omitting καὶ πικρίᾳ, thus as a doublet, and B*AF*…ἐνοχλῇ, but without removing ἐστιν so that the clause can no longer be construed. Both variants are therefore back-readings from H 12: 15 in which ἐνοχλῇ is a scribal corruption of ἐν χολῇ = LXX. For a full discussion see Katz, ZNW 49 (1958) 213–17; earlier ThLZ 1951, 537; Biblica 33 (1952) 525 n. 1; ThLZ 1957, 113. Σκεῦος ἐκλογῆς A 9: 15 = ἐκλεκτόν (different from σκεύη ὀργῆς, ἐλέους R 9: 22, 23, figuratively, as if 'bearers of wrath, mercy'); οἱ λόγοι τῆς χάριτος Lk 4: 22; πάθη ἀτιμίας R 1: 26; γέεννα τοῦ πυρός Mt 5: 22 etc.; ὁ οἶνος τοῦ θυμοῦ Rev 14: 10 etc. (where it was not even possible to use an equivalent adj.); βάπτισμα μετανοίας Mk 1: 4 etc. (ditto); τέκνα ὑπακοῆς 1 P 1: 14; ἀκροατὴς ἐπιλησμονῆς Ja 1: 25; κριταὶ διαλογισμῶν πονηρῶν approximately 'judges who make evil decisions' Ja 2: 4 (Schrenk, TW II 98; Büchsel, TW III 944 n. 3); ἄπειρος λόγου δικαιοσύνης 'incapable of understanding correct, normal speech' H 5: 13 (Schrenk, TW II 200.5f.). Ἐν ἀνθρώποις εὐδοκίας (S*AB*DW) Lk 2: 14 'among men to whom God's gracious approval applies' (Schrenk, TW II 745ff.): it is now clear that the gen. is the correct reading 'men of God's good pleasure', i.e. his chosen ones (the Qumran community thought of itself as the elect of God living in the end of time!) = בני רצונו 1QH iv.32f.; cf. xi.9; αὐτοῦ may be supplied: E 2: 3 τέκνα ὀργῆς; εὐδοκία = רצונו Sir 15: 15, 39: 18. Proposed by J. Jeremias, ZNW 28 (1929) 17ff.; detailed treatment in the light of the Dead Sea Scroll evidence: C. H. Hunzinger, ZNW 44 (1952/3) 85–90; 49 (1958) 129f.; cf. E. Vogt in Stendhal, The Scrolls, 114–17; J. A. Fitzmyer, ThSt 19 (1958) 225–7 (who calls attention to an Aramaic parallel); and Delitzsch's translation into Hebr. לאנשי רצונו.

For ἐτῶν with εἶναι and γί(γ)νεσθαι and as appositive (with ὤν etc. to be supplied) in the pap., s. Preisigke s.v. ἔτος; MGr Thumb² 31; ὡς ἐτῶν…as a formula describing persons is frequent in the pap. (s. also Deissmann in P. M. Meyer, Griech. Texte aus Äg., p. 26 n. 48). Also predicate Rev 21: 17 ἐμέτρησεν τὸ τεῖχος αὐτῆς ἑκατόν…πηχῶν 'as amounting to one hundred…cubits', cf. 16 (ἐπὶ…χιλιάδων); for late pars. to these passages s. Tabachovitz 6. 2 Th 1: 8 ἐν πυρὶ φλογός, A 7: 30 ἐν φλογὶ πυρός (both with the alternative reading as a variant) from Ex 3: 2 where the correct reading is ἐν πυρὶ φλογός Bhqru in spite of the Hebr. 'in a flame of fire'; ἐν φλ. π. by assimilation to the Hebr. text (Katz, ZNW 46[1955]

134–8). The inversion of the construct state is sometimes found in Hebr. and many translations (A. Schulz, ZAW 13 [1936] 270–7).

On the whole U. Holzmeister, ZkTh 41 (1917) 317–21.

166. Genitive of direction and purpose.
A genitive of purpose (or result) appears in ἀνάστασις ζωῆς, κρίσεως 'to life, judgment' Jn 5: 29, to be compared with ἀ. εἰς ζωήν LXX 2 Macc 7: 14. Direction is expressed by the genitive in combination with ὁδός and the like:

Ὁδὸς ἐθνῶν 'way to…' Mt 10: 5, τῶν ἁγίων H 9: 8, ὁδόν (as prep., § 161(1)) θαλάσσης Mt 4: 15 OT (but s. § 161 (1)); ἡ θύρα τῶν προβάτων Jn 10: 7, πίστεως A 14: 27 (but τοῦ λόγου C 4: 3 'where the word enters'). Μετοικεσία Βαβυλῶνος Mt 1: 11, 12; ἡ διασπορὰ τῶν Ἑλλήνων 'among' Jn 7: 35. But κίνδυνοι ποταμῶν, λῃστῶν 2 C 11: 26, in spite of ἐν θαλάσσῃ following, are 'dangers which spring from…', cf. ἐξ ἐθνῶν in the same vs.

167. Genitive of content and appositive genitive.
To the genitive of content belongs inter al. Jn 21: 8 τὸ δίκτυον τῶν ἰχθύων; cf. classical πλοῖα σίτου etc. (K.-G. I 333; pap. s. Mayser II 2, 122f.).—The use of the appositive genitive, i.e. of the genitive used in the sense of an appositive, conforms in the NT to classical usage: 2 C 5: 5 τὸν ἀρραβῶνα τοῦ πνεύματος 'the guarantee (earnest) which consists in the Spirit'. Cf. K.-G. I 264; Pfister, Festgabe Deissmann (1927) 72f.; Rob. 498f.

R 4: 11 σημεῖον περιτομῆς (-μὴν AC*). 2 C 5: 1 ἡ οἰκία τοῦ σκήνους. Jn 2: 21 τοῦ ναοῦ τοῦ σώματος αὐτοῦ. E 2: 14 τὸ μεσότοιχον τοῦ φραγμοῦ. With πόλις (Homer Ἰλίου πόλιν) only 2 P 2: 6 πόλεις Σοδόμων καὶ Γομόρρας; but πόλεως Θυατίρων A 16: 14 is the gen. of πόλις Θυάτιρα, cf. ἐν πόλει Ἰόππῃ 11: 5; with gen. of inhabitants 2 C 11: 32 τὴν πόλιν Δαμασκηνῶν, Rev 3: 12, 18: 10, 21, 21: 2, 10. Γῆ Αἰγύπτου s. § 261(7). E 4: 9 τὰ κατώτερα (μέρη) τῆς γῆς is not partitive (Winer §59, 8 [Winer-M.³ 666]; Sasse, TW I 679) or appositive ('the lower regions', i.e. the earth; cf. Barn 10.5 ἐν τῇ γῇ κάτω τοῦ βυθοῦ 'down there in the earth, the deep'), but 'the regions under the earth' (Büchsel, TW III 641f.).—The gen. of the names of cities is seldom found in class., and then nearly always in poetry; there is only one ex. in the Ptol. pap. (Mayser II 2, 117), more frequently in Byz. (Tabachovitz 1). The same phenomenon appears in Lat. and Romance languages (Stolz-Schmalz, Lat. Gr.⁵ 394f.).—Zerwick, Graec. bibl. §33 (Holzmeister, Verbum Domini 25 [1947] 112–17).

For the genitive with adjectives and participles used as substantives s. §263(2, 4).

168. Concatenation of genitives with different meanings is possible in the NT as in classical. (1) Two genitives dependent on the same noun—which then usually stands between them—do not occur very often: 2 C 5: 1 ἡ ἐπίγειος ἡμῶν οἰκία τοῦ σκήνους (possessive and appositive genitives). (2) Generally one genitive is dependent on another, whereby an author, particularly Paul, occasionally produces a quite cumbersome accumulation of genitives; to facilitate clarity in such cases, the governing genitive must always precede the dependent genitive (cf. pap., Mayser II 2, 143.37ff., 144), which also corresponds to Hebrew usage: 2 C 4: 4 τὸν φωτισμὸν τοῦ εὐαγγελίου ('the light emanating from the Gospel') τῆς δόξης (content) τοῦ Χριστοῦ.

(1) Ph 2: 30 τὸ ὑμῶν (subj.) ὑστέρημα τῆς πρός με λειτουργίας (obj.). Rev 7: 17. 2 P 3: 2 τῆς τῶν ἀποστόλων ὑμῶν ('apostles *to* you') ἐντολῆς τοῦ κυρίου καὶ σωτῆρος is not entirely clear; probably '…of the commandment of the Lord transmitted by the apostles' ([διὰ] τῶν ἀποστ.? Cf. sy).

(2) Rev 14: 8 ἐκ τοῦ οἴνου τοῦ θυμοῦ (§165) τῆς πορνείας αὐτῆς, unless τοῦ θυμοῦ is to be omitted here (and 18: 3; Griesbach) as an intrusion from *v.* 10; 16: 19 τὸ ποτήριον τοῦ οἴνου τοῦ θυμοῦ τῆς ὀργῆς αὐτοῦ (αὐτοῦ om. S); 19: 15 τὴν ληνὸν τοῦ οἴνου τοῦ θυμοῦ τῆς ὀργῆς τοῦ θεοῦ. The last gen. is usually possessive. Noteworthy word order: 1 P 3: 3 ὁ… ἐμπλοκῆς τριχῶν…κόσμος; H 6: 2 βαπτισμῶν διδαχῆς (𝔓⁴⁶B, certainly correctly, διδαχήν: F. W. Beare, JBL 63 [1944] 394; Zuntz 93f.) can only be 'teaching concerning baptism'. E 1: 6 εἰς ἔπαινον δόξης (a *single* idea, cf. Ph 1: 11 εἰς δόξαν καὶ ἔπαινον) τῆς χάριτος αὐτοῦ (τῆς δόξης DE, which would necessitate the interpretation 'praise of the glory of grace'; cf. E 1: 12 εἰς ἔπ. τῆς δόξης αὐτοῦ [τῆς only A], 14 [τῆς om. S]). E 1: 18, 19, 4: 13, C 2: 12. 1 Th 1: 3 τῆς ὑπομονῆς τῆς ἐλπίδος (§163) τοῦ κυρίου ἡμῶν (with variants).

(B) The Adverbial Genitive

169. The (partitive) genitive with verbs meaning 'to take from, eat of', etc., has been replaced in the NT to a still greater degree than the adnominal partitive genitive (§164) by prepositional phrases or by other cases. (1) Μεταλαμβάνειν 'to receive a share of' always takes the genitive (A 24: 25 καιρόν 'to find time later' as in Polyb. 2.16.15 is a different matter); μετέχειν with

ἐκ only 1 C 10: 17, otherwise genitive. As the genitive with these two verbs is limited to Acts, Paul, Hebrews, so κοινωνεῖν takes the genitive only in H 2: 14, while Paul, Peter, John use the dative or a preposition. Μεταδιδόναι never takes the genitive, the accusative when the whole is shared (R 1: 11, 1 Th 2: 8; classical is analogous), otherwise only the dative of person. Μετεῖναι does not appear. (2) The expressions 'to take, bring, eat of' etc. are now for the most part outside the sphere of the genitive and take ἐκ or ἀπό instead. When the action of the verb affects the whole object, the accusative is used as in classical (K.-G. I 356). Cf. MGr τρώγω ἀπό, but τρώγω ψωμί = ἐσθίω ἄρτον (Psichari 184; Jannaris §1299). (3) The genitive is still somewhat more frequently attested with related concepts like 'to satiate, eat one's fill, taste' but mostly under the influence of literary usage.

(1) **Κοινωνεῖν** with dat. of thing R 15: 27, cf. 1 T 5: 22, 1 P 4: 13, 2 Jn 11, also with dat. of person as in class. (R 12: 13 falls between). Κοινωνεῖν τινι (person) ἔν τινι G 6: 6 and εἰς λόγον δόσεως καὶ λήμψεως Ph 4: 15; cf. ὁ ἔχων μέρος ἐν…(thing) Rev 20: 6.

(2) 'To give of': Lk 20: 10 ἀπό; with simple gen. as in class. Rev 2: 17 δώσω αὐτῷ τοῦ (AC, τὸ 046, ἐκ τοῦ S) μάννα τοῦ κεκρυμμένου, is not credible. 'To take from': Mk 12: 2 ἀπό; only A 27: 36 προσελάβοντο τροφῆς (many variants) = ἐγεύσαντο (s. *infra* (3)); 33 μηδὲν προσλαβόμενοι is correct. 'To bring of': Jn 21: 10 ἐνέγκατε ἀπὸ τῶν ὀψαρίων. 'To eat, drink of': ἐσθίειν Mt 15: 27 = Mk 7: 28 ἀπὸ τῶν ψιχίων, 1 C 11: 28 ἐκ τοῦ ἄρτου (but usually ἐσθίειν ἄρτον Mt 15: 2 etc.), cf. 1 C 9: 7; πίνειν Jn 4: 14 ἐκ τοῦ ὕδατος. Ἐσθίειν with acc. correctly Mk 1: 6, 1 C 10: 25, 27, τὰ εἰδωλόθυτα 1 C 8: 10, cf. 7, Rev 2: 14, 20; τὰς θυσίας 1 C 10: 18 'to consume the sacrifices as a community'. A class. author would have used the gen. more often where the acc. is found in the NT; thus Jn 6: 53 ἐὰν μὴ φάγητε τὴν σάρκα τοῦ υἱοῦ τοῦ ἀνθρώπου καὶ πίητε αὐτοῦ τὸ αἷμα, cf. 54, 56, 57 with τρώγειν, which in the NT as in class. never takes the gen., but which would not have been used here by a classical author.

(3) **Κορέννυσθαι** (literary language) with gen. A 27: 38; **χορτάζειν** (§101 under κορεννύναι) with gen. Mk 8: 4, pass. -άζεσθαι only with ἀπό or ἐκ: Lk 15: 16 (ἐκ BDLR al., v.l. γεμίσαι τὴν κοιλίαν αὐτοῦ ἀπό, cf. §172 and MGr dialect γιομώνω ἀπό 'am filled with' Thumb² p. 290.7 [302]), 16: 21, Rev 19: 21. Ἀπολαύειν does not appear. **Μεθύσκεσθαι** s. §195(2). **Γεύεσθαι** θανάτου Mt 16: 28 and pars., Jn 8: 52, H 2: 9, τοῦ δείπνου Lk 14: 24, μηδενός A 23: 14, τῆς δωρεᾶς H 6: 4; the acc. is not class.: τὸ ὕδωρ Jn 2: 9 (acc. to Behm, TW I 675 n. 7 a Hebraism), θεοῦ ῥῆμα H 6: 5 (Antig. Car. [iii BC], a Ptol. pap. in Mayser II 2,

206, LXX, e.g. 1 Km 14: 43. Abbott 77; Helb., Kas. 135. Γλυκὺν γεύσας τὸν αἰῶνα Hdt. 7.46; but Arist., Poet. 22, p. 1458b10 conjecture). Ἐγώ σου ὀναίμην Phm 20, Ign 6 times (the word appears only here) stems from the literary language; cf. Aristoph., Thesm. 469 οὕτως ὀναίμην τῶν τέκνων (but in other combinations already in Plato, Charm. 175 E with ἀπό); K.-G. I 355f.

170. Genitive with verbs meaning 'to touch, take hold of'. (1) Verbs of touching still regularly take the genitive: ἅπτεσθαι, καθάπτειν A 28: 3, θιγγάνειν (literary language) H 11: 28, 12: 20. (2) 'To take hold of': ἐπιλαμβάνεσθαι 'to take hold of somebody (something)' always with the genitive; especially the part grasped stands naturally in the genitive: ἐπιλαβόμενος τῆς χειρὸς τοῦ τυφλοῦ Mk 8: 23, cf. A 23: 19. Κρατεῖν 'to seize, hold' ('a specific mark of Hell. usage', Wackernagel, Homer 192) on the other hand takes the accusative of the whole thing (e.g. κρατήσας τὸν Ἰωάνην Mt 14: 3) and only the genitive of the part which is grasped; in the sense of 'to hold fast' it takes the genitive (A 27: 13, H 4: 14, 6: 18; perhaps following κρατεῖν 'to rule, hold sway' with the genitive in literary language and even more ἔχεσθαι and the like [s. *infra* 3]) except for Rev 2: 14, 15 (τὴν διδαχήν). Lk also says πιάσας (=λαβών) αὐτὸν τῆς χειρός A 3: 7 like λαβὼν Πολυξένην χερός Eur., Hec. 523. (3) The figurative uses of ἔχεσθαι always take the genitive: H 6: 9 τὰ ἐχόμενα σωτηρίας 'the things which belong or lead to salvation'; ἀντέχεσθαι (Hell., Nägeli 54) = 'to cling to, hold fast to': Mt 6: 24 = Lk 16: 13 τοῦ ἑνὸς ἀνθέξεται, T 1: 9; = 'to care for': 1 Th 5: 14 ἀντέχεσθε τῶν ἀσθενῶν; ἀντιλαμβάνεσθαι 'to care for' (LXX and Hell., Nägeli 54): Lk 1: 54, A 20: 35; ἐπιλαμβάνεσθαι H 2: 16.

(1) Ἅπτεσθαι with gen. often in the Gospels (Jn only 20: 17 and 1 Jn 5: 18), Acts never, Epistles 1 C 7: 1, 2 C 6: 17 OT.

(2) Κρατεῖν with gen. of the part: Mt 9: 25 ἐκράτησε τῆς χειρὸς (τὴν χεῖρα D) αὐτῆς (also Gen 19: 16); Mk 1: 31 (not D), 5: 41 (τὴν χεῖρα D), Lk 8: 54, but ἐκράτησαν αὐτοῦ τοὺς πόδας Mt 28: 9; κρατεῖν τινά τινος not outside of Mk 9: 27 A al., but SBD have τῆς χειρὸς αὐτοῦ. Κρατεῖν with acc. Anaximenes (Diels, Vorsokr.⁵ I p. 95.18 συγκρ. 'to hold together'), Soph., OC 1380 ('hold power over', Wackernagel, Homer 192), Hell. often, MGr (Helb., Kas. 121); 'to arrest' NT with acc., e.g. Mt 21: 46 (= Mk 12: 12), Mt 26: 55 (= Mk 14: 49), avoided in Lk 20: 19, 22: 53. Δράσσεσθαι 'to seize' with acc. (Hdt., LXX, Jos. etc.; Schmidt 385): ὁ δρασσόμενος τοὺς σοφούς 1 C 3: 19 (= Job 5: 13, where LXX has καταλαμβάνων). Ἐπιλαβόμενος (-νοι) with acc. (A 9: 27, 16: 19, 18: 17 and Lk 14: 4) is only an apparent instance; the acc. actually belongs to the finite verb on which the ptcp. depends (Delling, TW IV 9 n. 3 to the contrary); in Lk 23: 26 SBCDLX have ἐπιλ. Σίμωνά τινα Κυρηναῖον ἐρχόμενον, but APWΓΔ al. the gen. Lk 20: 26 ἐπιλαβέσθαι αὐτοῦ ῥήματος 'a word of his' (for which SBL τοῦ ῥ., Θ τοῦ ῥ. αὐτοῦ). Λαβόμενος τὴν χεῖρα τοῦ τυφλοῦ Mk 8: 23 D is neither class. (τῆς χειρός Plato, Parm. beg.) nor NT; the mid. λαμβάνεσθαι does not appear at all in the NT. However, cf. χεῖρα... οὐκ ἀντελαμβάνοντο LXX Ezk 16: 49 and the scattered class. and Hell. exx. of acc. with 'to touch' in Helb., Kas. 124f. (λαμβάνεσθαι with acc. PFlor I 36.7, Dit., Or. 8.68 in M.-M. is different). Αἴρειν: Mt 22: 13 (acc. to the correct reading of D lat sy) ἄρατε αὐτὸν ποδῶν καὶ χειρῶν, Herm Vis 1.4.3 ἦραν αὐτὴν τῶν ἀγκώνων, 3.1.7 ἐξεγείρει με τῆς χειρός.

(3) Συναντιλαμβάνεται τῆς ἀσθενείας R 8: 26 v.l. for dat. (§ 202 συν-; there also on Lk 10: 40). 1 T 6: 2 οἱ τῆς εὐεργεσίας ἀντιλαμβανόμενοι (= 'to take part, share in' or better 'to devote oneself to'; s. Bauer s.v.).—Helb., Kas. 123ff.; Mayser II 2, 199ff.

171. Genitive with verbs meaning 'to strive after, desire' and 'to reach, obtain'. (1) Verbs of desiring, striving still govern the genitive. Only Mt 5: 28 ἐπιθυμεῖν with accusative according to BDEW etc. (S* weak v.l. αὐτῆς, and the case is missing in the Church Fathers); further πεινᾶν and διψᾶν with accusative τὴν δικαιοσύνην Mt 5: 6 (ἐδίψα τὴν σωτηρίαν Kosmas und Damian 10.64 ed. Deubner), instead of classical genitive, probably by analogy with ἐπιποθεῖν which is transitive in the NT as in classical (and Jos., Bell. 1.628). (2) Of the genitive with verbs of reaching, obtaining there are vestiges only in the better educated authors.

(1) Ἐπιθυμεῖν with gen. A 20: 33, 1 T 3: 1; usually absolutely or with inf.; with acc. beg. w. Plato Comicus (Helb., Kas. 138), frequently in LXX (Johannessohn I 40), further Herm Vis 1.1.4, Sim 9.9.7 (with gen. 13.8), Did 2.2. Ὀρέγεσθαι with gen. 1 T 3: 1, 6: 10, H 11: 16. Ὁμείρεσθαι (§ 101) with gen. 1 Th 2: 8.

(2) Τυγχάνειν with gen. Lk 20: 35 (τυχεῖν om. lat), Acts and Hebrews, 2 T 2: 10. Λαγχάνειν only with acc. (also more frequent in class. than gen.; analogy with λαμβάνειν!): A 1: 17, 2 P 1: 1; only apparently with gen. Lk 1: 9 (τοῦ θυμιᾶσαι = θυμ., § 400(3)). Ἐπιτυγχάνειν with gen. H 6: 15, 11: 33, but R 11: 7 τοῦτο οὐκ ἐπέτυχεν in all authoritative witnesses, οὐδέν Herm Man 9.5 (but τῆς πράξεως 10. 2.4); in class. acc. with neuter pron. or adj. (K.-G. I 350); πᾶν UPZ I 41.25 (161 BC); MGr (ἐπι-)τυχαίνω

trans. **Κληρονομεῖν** 'to inherit something' only with acc. (Mt 5: 5 etc.) as in Hell. generally (Phryn. 129; Cramer, Anec. Ox. III 262.1) for Att. gen.; also κλ. τινά 'to inherit someone', i.e. 'be a person's heir' (1 Clem 16.13 OT, Plut. etc.; Phryn. 129) is Hell. Κληρονομεῖν τι 'to acquire as a possession (through inheritance)' first in Lycurgus (iv BC), Leocr. 88 (Helb., Kas. 139; on τινα 140). 'Εφικνεῖσθαι only with εἰς 2 C 10: 14 and ἄχρι 13 (class. gen.). 'Αστοχεῖν s. §180(2).—'To put somebody to the test' mostly with gen. in the earlier period, yet πειρᾶν (-ᾶσθαι) γυναῖκα and the like appear in Pind., Lysias etc. (K.-G. I 370 n. 18) and so **πειράζειν** with acc. Apollonius of Rhodes 3.10, LXX (Helb., Kas. 143f.), NT often (pass. πειράζεσθαι also often; and with ἐκ-), Did 11.7, Aesop. p. 18 Th., πειρασθῆναι Herm Sim 7.1.—Helb., Kas. 136–44; Mayser II 2, 203ff.

172. Genitive with verbs meaning 'to fill, be full of' is well preserved: πιμπλάναι (Gospels and Acts only) and ἐμπιμπλάναι (R 15: 24 also) always take it (Mt 22: 10, Lk 1: 53 etc.). Πληροῦν, too, still takes the genitive, but in addition ἐκ (partitive, cf. §169) Jn 12: 3 (Β ἐπλήσθη) and in the passive also the dative (R 1: 29, 2 C 7: 4; cf. §195(2)), ἐν (E 5: 18, cf. R 15: 13 v.l., s. *infra*) and accusative (§159(1)) also. Γέμειν with genitive Mt 23: 37, Rev 4: 6, 8 and often; only Rev 17: 3 vulgar γέμοντα (γέμον) ὀνόματα βλασφημίας, cf. Wolf II 33 and 'to be filled' with accusative §159(1). Γεμίζειν with genitive Mk 15: 36 (D πλήσας), Jn 2: 7, Rev 15: 8, with ἐκ (cf. *supra* πληροῦν) Rev 8: 5, ἀπό Lk 15: 16 v.l. (§169(3)). Similarly περισσεύουσιν (ΑΒΡ -ονται) ἄρτων Lk 15: 17. Finally, Lk 16: 24 βάπτειν τὸ ἄκρον τοῦ δακτύλου ὕδατος (ὕδατι S) can be included here.

Πληροῦν with gen. Lk 2: 40 πληρούμενον σοφίας (-ίᾳ SᶜBL, s. *supra*), A 2: 28 OT (v.l. acc.), 5: 28, 13: 52, R 15: 13 (BFG πληροφορῆσαι ἐν [ἐν om. FG] πάσῃ χαρᾷ), 14, 2 T 1: 4. C 2: 10 ἐν αὐτῷ (Χριστῷ) πεπληρωμένοι presumably = '(fulfilled,) consummated in him (through him)'; cf. 4: 12 τέλειοι καὶ πεπληροφορημένοι (𝔓⁴⁶DᶜE al. πεπληρωμένοι) ἐν παντὶ θελήματι τοῦ θεοῦ. Γεμίζειν with gen. perhaps also Jn 6: 13 ἐγέμισαν δώδεκα κοφίνους κλασμάτων ἐκ τῶν πέντε ἄρτων etc.; however, κοφ. κλασμ. may be combined as in Lk 9: 17, cf. κόφινον κοπρίων Lk 13: 8 D. 1 Th 3: 12 **περισσεύσαι** τῆς ἀγάπης FG (acc. I, the rest dat. as δόξῃ 2 C 3: 9 𝔓⁴⁶ABC [ἐν δ. SᶜDE al.]). **Βάπτειν** with ἀπό LXX Lev 14: 16; the class. exx. of βάπτεσθαί τινος (the poet Arat. also [650 etc.], Buttmann 148) are formed by analogy from λούεσθαί τινος (Homer).—Helb., Kas. 144ff.; Mayser II 2, 205f.

173. Genitive with verbs of perception. (1) The classical rule for ἀκούειν is: the person whose words are heard stands in the genitive, the thing (or person: E 4: 21 αὐτὸν ἠκούσατε) about which (or whom) one hears in the accusative; the person can also be introduced by παρά (Jn 1: 40 and elsewhere; classical also), ἀπό (A 9: 13, 1 Jn 1: 5; §210(3)) and ἀπό (διά, ἐκ) τοῦ στόματός τινος (Lk 22: 71, A 1: 4 D, 22: 14; Hebraism, §217(3)). (2) The NT wavers between genitive and accusative in phrases meaning 'to hear a sound', while in classical it is ἀκούειν φωνῆς, βοῆς etc. The construction for 'to hear a speech' is also doubtful in classical Greek; the NT takes the accusative for the most part, but genitive in Jn 7: 40, 12: 47, 19: 13 (v.l., cf. 8); τῶν λόγων Lk 6: 47 for τοὺς λόγους Mt 7: 24. (3) 'Επακούειν 'to hear a prayer' takes the genitive 2 C 6: 2 OT, likewise παρακούειν 'refuse to hear' Mt 18: 17 (2 Clem 3.4, 6.7; Mk 5: 36 is different) and ἐπακροᾶσθαι 'to listen to' A 16: 25. 'Υπακούειν 'to obey' takes the dative as in classical. Αἰσθάνεσθαι appears only in Lk 9: 45 and then with accusative of thing αὐτό (like classical = 'to understand', for which the NT elsewhere uses συνιέναι). Πυνθάνεσθαι takes παρά with the person: Mt 2: 4 (not D), Jn 4: 52 (not B).—Helb., Kas. 150–9; Mayser II 2, 207ff.

(1) 'Ακούειν στεναγμοῦ A 7: 34 OT, συμφωνίας καὶ χοροῦ Lk 15: 25 are correct; doubtful: τὴν σοφίαν Σολομῶνος Mt 12: 42 = Lk 11: 31, τὴν βλασφημίαν Mt 26: 65, τῆς βλασφημίας Mk 14: 64 (acc. ADGW), τὸν ἀσπασμόν Lk 1: 41; incorrect: λέγοντα(ς) Rev 5: 13, λαλοῦντας A 2: 6 D. A double gen. in places like A 22: 1 ἀκούσατέ μου τῆς πρὸς ὑμᾶς ἀπολογίας, Jn 12: 47 etc., Herm Man 12.5.1 (cf. Sim 9.23.2 μου τὰς ἐντολάς) is only apparent since μου goes with ἀπολογίας; cf. §473(1).

(2) 'Ακούειν φωνῆς in John in the sense of obey: 5: 25, 28, 10: 3, 16 etc. 'Ακούειν φωνήν of perception: 3: 8, 5: 37; in Acts and Rev in this sense, both cases indiscriminately: acc. A 9: 4, 22: 9, 14, 26: 14 (gen. E), Rev 1: 10, 4: 1 etc., also 2 P 1: 18; gen. A 9: 7, 11: 7 (acc. 𝔓⁴⁵D), 22: 7, Rev 10: 4 𝔓⁴⁷, 11: 12 𝔓⁴⁷SCP, 14: 13, 16: 1, 21: 3, (3: 20 'obey',) also H 3: 7 and 15 OT, 12: 19. Both LXX (Johannessohn I 36) and the pap. (Mayser II 2, 207) take gen. and acc.

(3) **Εἰσακούειν** with gen. 'obey' 1 C 14: 21, 1 Clem 8.4 OT, 'to hear prayers' 22.7 OT, 57.5 OT; pass. Mt 6: 7 etc. The person with συνιέναι is everywhere undesignated.

174. Genitive with verbs for 'smelling of'. 'Οζειν is used only absolutely; but probably on the analogy of ὄζειν, πνεῖν, ἐμπνεῖν τινος, 'to smell of something' (K.-G. I 356f.): A 9: 1 ἐμπνέων ἀπειλῆς καὶ φόνου 'breathing threats and murder' (classical φόνον πνεῖν; K.-G. I 309). Cf. LXX Josh 10: 40 πᾶν ἐμπνέον ζωῆς 'every living thing' = כָּל־הַנְּשָׁמָה. Homil Clem 13.16 μύρου δὲ πνέει, τῆς ἀγαθῆς φήμης.—Helb., Kas. 91 f.

175. Genitive with verbs of remembering and forgetting. Μιμνήσκεσθαι (H 2: 6 OT, 13: 3), also in the aorist and perfect, always takes the genitive (predominantly also in LXX, s. Johannessohn I 37; on 1 C 11: 2 cf. §154). Μνημονεύειν mostly genitive, though accusative also, and in the sense of 'to mention' περί (all are classical, K.-G. I 364). Ὑπομιμνῄσκειν (-εσθαι) also takes all three constructions; ἀναμιμνῄσκειν (-εσθαι) is attested only with the accusative (classical more frequently genitive; LXX mostly accusative, s. Johannessohn I 37); ἐπιλανθάνεσθαι with genitive only Heb (6: 10, 13: 2, 16; ἔκλανθ. 12: 5), with accusative Ph 3: 13, H 13: 2 S* (classical occasionally; cf. POxy IV 744.11, 12 [1 BC]; UPZ I 61.10 [161 BC]).—Helb., Kas. 107ff.; Mayser II 2, 209ff.

Μνημονεύειν with acc. Mt 16: 9 (D is different), Jn 15: 20 S (τὸν λόγον) D (τοὺς λόγους, al. τοῦ λόγου; with gen. Jn 16: 4 [om. SᶜᵃD], 21), 1 Th 2: 9, 2 T 2: 8, Rev 18: 5, Herm Vis 1.3.3, 2.1.3; with περί H 11: 22 (gen. 15). Ὑπομιμνῄσκειν (-εσθαι) with acc. Jn 14: 26, 3 Jn 10 (2 T 2: 14 ταῦτα acc. of content); with gen. Lk 22: 61, with περί 2 P 1: 12.

176. Genitive with verbs of emotion. (1) The genitive of the cause of emotion no longer appears anywhere with ὀργίζεσθαι, θαυμάζειν, ἐλεεῖν; only the related ἀνέχεσθαι 'bear with' retains the genitive throughout: Mt 17: 17 ὑμῶν, etc. (classical and LXX accusative also, especially of the thing). The genitive of the cause with interjections has survived in Diogn 9.2 ὤ τῆς ὑπερβαλλούσης φιλανθρωπίας, 5 (three times) and 1 Clem 53.5; in the NT ἀπό is used instead: Mt 18: 7 οὐαὶ τῷ κόσμῳ ἀπὸ τῶν σκανδάλων (cf. §210(1)). (2) The genitive has survived with 'to care for': ἐπιμέλεσθαι Lk 10: 34, 35, 1 T 3: 5, ἀμελεῖν 1 T 4: 14, H 2: 3, 8: 9 OT, ὀλιγωρεῖν H 12: 5 OT, προνοεῖσθαι 1 T 5: 8, doubtful μεριμνᾶν. (3) Μέλει with genitive only 1 C 9: 9, but DEFG περί with genitive (not unclassical) as in Mt 22: 16 = Mk 12: 14, Jn 10: 13, 12: 6, 1 P 5: 7. For ἐντρέπεσθαί τινα s. §149.—Helb., Kas. 111f.; Mayser II 2, 211ff.

(1) Lk 16: 8 ἐπῄνεσεν ὁ κύριος τὸν οἰκονόμον τῆς ἀδικίας acc. to Sophie Antoniadis, L'Évangile de Luc (Paris, 1930) 376ff. 'on account of the damage caused' (cf. Plut., Mor. 1 D); further §165 and Bauer s.v. ἀδικία. Hebraistic σπλαγχνίζεσθαι = ἐλεεῖν (§108(3)) in Mt 18: 27 probably only appears to take the gen. of the person pitied (otherwise ἐπί τινα, ἐπί τινι, περί τινος), since ὁ κύριος τοῦ δούλου ἐκείνου (the whole phrase is om. in syˢ; unnecessary expansion? B om. ἐκ.) 'the master of that servant' is to be taken together.

(2) **Μεριμνᾶν**: Mt 6: 34 ἑαυτῆς SB al., τὰ ἑαυτῆς EK, perhaps ἑαυτῇ after Lat. sibi; cf. 1 C 7: 32–4 τὰ τοῦ..., Ph 2: 20 τὰ περὶ ὑμῶν, 1 C 12: 25 ὑπὲρ ἀλλήλων; περί Mt 6: 28, Lk 12: 26, τῇ ψυχῇ Mt 6: 25, Lk 12: 22. **Προνοοῦμεν** καλά 'we are intent on the good' 2 C 8: 21 from LXX Pr 3: 4 προνοοῦ καλά; cf. Xen., Cyr. 4.1.6 τὸ παραγγελλόμενον προνοεῖτε.

(3) A 18: 17 οὐδὲν τούτων τῷ Γαλλίωνι ἔμελεν; οὐδέν is probably subj. and τούτων partitive as sometimes in class.; likewise Herm Sim 9.13.6 πάντα σοι μέλει.

177. Genitive with verbs of ruling and surpassing. 'To rule, govern' usually with genitive: ἄρχειν Mk 10: 42, R 15: 12 OT, κυριεύειν Lk 22: 25, R 6: 9 etc., κατακυριεύειν Mt 20: 25, Mk 10: 42 etc., κατισχύειν Mt 16: 18, αὐθεντεῖν 1 T 2: 12, ἐξουσιάζειν Lk 22: 25, 1 C 7: 4, κατ- Mt 20: 25 = Mk 10: 42, ἡγεμονεύειν Lk 2: 2, 3: 1 (D ἐπιτροπεύοντος), τετραρχεῖν 3: 1, ἀνθυπατεύειν A 18: 12 EHLP. But βασιλεύειν with ἐπί τινα following Hebrew מָלַךְ עַל. Only remnants of the genitive remain with verbs of surpassing: ὑπερβάλλειν E 3: 19 (Plato, Gorg. 475 B; classical usually accusative or absolutely as in 2 C 3: 10 etc.), ὑπερέχειν Ph 2: 3 (accusative 4: 7 as in classical also; LXX genitive and accusative, s. Johannessohn I 42).—Helb., Kas. 113ff., 188ff.; Mayser II 2, 215ff.

Καταδυναστεύειν with gen. Ja 2: 6 SᶜBC al., with acc. S*A like καταγωνίζεσθαί τινα etc. (§150). On **κρατεῖν** s. §170(2). **Βασιλεύειν** ἐπί τινα Lk 1: 33, 19: 14, 27, R 5: 14; with gen. Mt 2: 22 τῆς Ἰουδαίας SB (ἐπὶ τῆς Ἰ. al., cf. LXX 4 Km 11: 3 = 2 Chr 22: 12; but ἐπὶ τῆς γῆς Rev 5: 10 = 'on earth'), Protev Ja 23.2. **Ἡγεῖσθαι** with gen. only A 14: 12 ὁ ἡγούμενος τοῦ λόγου. For ἡττᾶσθαι s. §191(5).

178. Genitive with verbs of accusing etc., used to denote the basis of the accusation, appears only in A 19: 40: ἐγκαλεῖσθαι στάσεως, just where it is un-Attic (ἀσεβείας Dio Cass. 58.4.5); otherwise περί τινος is used with the passive ἐγκαλεῖσθαι and κρίνεσθαι as in Attic (A 23: 6, 29 etc.). Ἐγκαλεῖν τινί τινος (Attic τινί τι) Plut., Arist. 10, PAmh II 66.33 (124 AD). For dative instead of genitive of penalty s. §195(2).

179. Genitive of price and value is used (1) with 'to buy' and 'to sell', also with συμφωνεῖν 'to agree on' (δηναρίου Mt 20: 13, but ἐκ δην. τὴν ἡμέραν v. 2 as in classical, §161(2)), in addition to ἐκ (papyri, Kuhring 27f.; Mayser II 2, 347f., 387f.): ἀγοράζειν ἐκ Mt 27: 7, κτᾶσθαι ἐκ A 1: 18 (cf. Lk 16: 9), and ἐν (§219(3)). (2) With (κατ-) ἀξιοῦν τινος 2 Th 1: 5, 11, 1 T 5: 17, H 3: 3, 10: 29. Ἀλλάξαι τι ἐν R 1: 23 means 'to exchange for' (from LXX Ps 105: 20; unclassical; similarly, but more strongly local, Soph., Ant. 944f.). Mayser II 2, 218ff.

(1) Mt 10: 29 ἀσσαρίου πωλεῖται, 26: 9, A 5: 8 etc.; τιμῆς 'for a price (cash-payment)' 1 C 6: 20, 7: 23 (Deissmann, LO⁴ 275 [LAE 324]), Hdt. 7.119, pap. (Bauer; Mayser II 2, 220f.); τιμῆς ἀργυρίου A 7: 16.

(2) Μεταλλάσσειν ἐν R 1: 25, εἰς 26 (Plato, Tim. 19 A 'transfer' L.-S.).

180. The genitive of separation has been driven out for the most part by ἀπό or ἐκ (both are classical in addition to the regular genitive, Smyth §1393. LXX and pap. often have ἀπό: Johannessohn I 38f.; Mayser II 2, 227ff., 234ff., 353f., 569; Helb., Kas. 159–81. MGr ἀπό, Thumb² §161(2)) with χωρίζειν, λύειν, λυτροῦν, ἐλευθεροῦν, ῥύεσθαι, σῴζειν, καθαρίζειν, λούειν. (1) 'To separate' still governs the genitive: ἀπαλλοτριοῦν E 2: 12, 4: 18; also κωλύειν τινά τινος 'to hinder somebody from doing something' (Xen., Polyb.) A 27: 43 besides κ. τι ἀπό τινος Lk 6: 29 'to refuse' (Hebraizing as in LXX Gen 23: 6). (2) 'To depart from': ἀστοχεῖν τινος (Nägeli 31) 1 T 1: 6, but περί τι 6: 21, 2 T 2: 18; ἀφίστασθαί τινος 'to fall away from' 1 T 4: 1. (3) 'To be away from': ἀπέχειν τινός Lk 7: 6 S*D; διαφέρειν τινός 'to be different' Mt 6: 26 etc. (4) The related idea 'to be in need of' takes the genitive: χρῄζειν Mt 6: 32, Lk 11: 8 (ὅσων; SᶜDE al. ὅσον), 12: 30, R 16: 2, 2 C 3: 1; προσδεῖσθαι A 17: 25; λείπεσθαι 'to lack' Ja 1: 5, 2: 15 (ἐν μηδενί 'in nothing' 1: 4). For Rev 3: 17 s. §160. (5) 'To keep away from, restrain oneself': ἀπέχεσθαι 'abstain from' with genitive or ἀπό. Φείδεσθαι always takes the genitive, but is confined to Lk (A 20: 29), Paul and 2 P 2: 4, 5. Ὑστερεῖν 'to be inferior' (cf. ὕστερος) 2 C 11: 5, 12: 11, 'to lack' Lk 22: 35, in the same sense ὑστερεῖσθαι R 3: 23 (with ἐν 1 C 1: 7, cf. supra (4) λείπεσθαι). 2 P 3: 9 οὐ βραδύνει κύριος τῆς ἐπαγγελίας 'the Lord is not holding back, delaying the fulfilment of his promise' also belongs here. (6) 'To cease': 1 P 4: 1 πέπαυται

ἁμαρτίας, but 3: 10 OT παύειν τινὰ ἀπό and Herm Vis 3.9.1 παῆναι ἀπό.

(1) Ἀποστερεῖσθαι with gen. 1 T 6: 5 with v.l. ἀπεστραμμένων ἀπό (D*), cf. 2 T 4: 4; μεθιστάναι Lk 16: 4 varies (ἐκ SBD, ἀπό LX, simple gen. APRW al.); κωλύειν for the most part only with τινά or τι. Καθαιρεῖσθαι τῆς μεγαλειότητος αὐτῆς A 19: 27 SABE (HLP τὴν μεγαλειότητα) is uncertain.

(2) More frequently ἀφίστασθαι ἀπό 'depart' Lk 2: 37 etc., but H 3: 12 probably 'fall away'.

(3) Lk 7: 6 v.l. ἀπέχειν ἀπό as in 24: 13 etc., cf. v.l. Mt 14: 24.

(4) Δεῖσθαι 'ask' also takes the gen.: Mt 9: 38, at times in Lk, 2 C 8: 4, G 4: 12; in addition πρός τινα A 8: 24, cf. LXX Is 37: 4, εὔχομαι πρός 2 C 13: 7 and λέγω πρός.

(5) Ἀπέχεσθαι with gen. A 15: 29, 1 T 4: 3, 1 P 2: 11, with ἀπό 1 Th 4: 3, 5: 22, A 15: 20 varies. Ὑστερεῖν ἀπό 'to remain away from', i.e. 'to miss' H 12: 15 (also LXX Eccl 6: 2), cf. ἀνυστέρητος ἀπό Herm Man 9.4; ὑστερεῖν = 'to fail': without case Jn 2: 3 (cf. Diosc. 5.86 [xxv 748 Kühn]), with acc. (following ἐπιλείπει, ἐκλείπει) Mk 10: 21 ἕν σε ὑστερεῖ SBCW al. (σοι AD al.), cf. LXX Ps 22 (23): 1 (LXX elsewhere dat. also, Buttmann 147; s. also §189(3)); UPZ I 20.26 (164 BC) εἰς τὸ μηθέν... ὑμᾶς ὑστερεῖν—30 εἰς τὸ μ. ἡ.... ἐγλιπεῖν. Helb., Kas. 174f.

(6) 'To rest from': ἀναπαύεσθαι ἐκ (as in class.) Rev 14: 13, κατέπαυσεν (intr.) ἀπό H 4: 4 OT, 10. Ἄρχεσθαί τινος does not appear.

181. The genitive more or less dependent on prepositions in compounds. Apart from the compounds with ἀπό treated in §180 and ἐκπίπτειν (in a figurative sense) G 5: 4, 2 P 3: 17 and ἐκβάλλειν Mk 7: 26 𝔓⁴⁵L, only κατά in the sense of 'against' or also 'down upon' ('down' with acc., §150) needs to be considered. The most common earlier compounds with κατά tend to go over to the accusative: καταδικάζειν in the NT only with τινά (Mt 12: 7, Ja 5: 6?), likewise κατακρίνειν (both with genitive in Attic). For κατακυριεύειν etc. (even the simple verb takes genitive) s. §177.—Helb., Kas. 182ff.; Mayser II 2, 237ff.; Smyth §§1382ff.

Κατα- 'against' with gen.: -γελᾶν Mt 9: 24 (D* αὐτόν), Mk 5: 40, Lk 8: 53, -γινώσκειν 1 Jn 3: 20, 21, -καυχᾶσθαι 'to boast against' R 11: 18, Ja 2: 13, -λαλεῖν Ja 4: 11, 1 P 2: 12 (Homil Clem 16.8, 19.7 καταλέγειν 'revile'), -μαρτυρεῖν Mt 26: 62 etc., -ναρκᾶν 'to burden' 2 C 11: 9, 12: 13, -στρηνιᾶν 'become wanton against' 1 T 5: 11, κατηγορεῖν often. Κατα- 'down upon, over' with gen. -χεῖν Mk 14: 3 SBC al. (others κατά or ἐπί with gen.; Mt 26: 7 ἐπί with gen. or acc.; with gen. LXX Gen 39: 21, Ps 88 [89]: 46), also -φρονεῖν Mt 6: 24 etc.

(C) The Genitive with Adjectives and Adverbs

182. The genitive with adjectives is greatly reduced compared with classical usage. (1) It is best preserved with 'taking part', etc. (§169): (συγ-)κοινωνός τινος (thing) 1 P 5: 1, 2 P 1: 4 and Paul; (συμ-)μέτοχός τινος Heb, E 3: 6; σύμμορφος τῆς εἰκόνος R 8: 29 'participating in the form of his image', cf. dative §194(2). Κοινός and ἴδιος never take the genitive. 'Following upon, touching' (§170) only in ἀκόλουθα τούτων Herm Man 8.4, 10 (classical). 'Full' (§172): μεστός τινος Mt 23: 28 etc., πλήρης Lk 4: 1 etc.; κενός and ἐνδεής nowhere with genitive, but κενὸς ἀπό Herm Man 5.2.7, 11.4, Sim 9.19.2 (§211). (2) The following belong to the genitive of price (§179): (ἀν-)άξιος Mt 3: 8, 1 C 6: 2 etc. and thus ἔνοχός τινος besides the dative which is more common in classical. (3) To the genitive of separation (§180): ξένος τινός 'strange to something' E 2: 12 (Plato, Ap. 17 D; dative 1 Clem 1.1), cf. ἀλλότριοι τοῦ θεοῦ 1 Clem 7.7. Ἀπείραστος κακῶν Ja 1: 13, if it means 'not subject to temptation, unexperienced in evil, alien to evil' (cf. πειρᾶσθαί τινος §171(2) and classical ἀπείρατός τινος, ἄγευστος κακῶν etc. [K.-G. I 401 f.], Bauer s.v. ἀπείραστος). Similarly ἀκαταπαύστους (v.l. -πάστους) ἁμαρτίας 2 P 2: 14 'not ceasing with sin' (s. Bauer s.v.) like ἄπαυστος γόων Eur., Supp. 82. 'To be free from', however, always takes ἀπό: ἄσπιλος Ja 1: 27 (ἐκ CP), ἀθῷος Mt 27: 24, καθαρός A 20: 26 (first in the oath in Dem. 59.78. Cf. Deissmann, NBS 24 [BS 196]; Kuhring 52 f.; Rossberg 15; Mayser II 2, 353, 570; Vogeser 26; Bauer s.v. for further examples). LXX has both (Johannessohn II 282), cf. καθαρίζειν ἀπό §180. Likewise ἐλεύθερος ἀπό R 7: 3 'independent of' (Plato, Lg. 8. 832 D, pap. in Preisigke, APF III 419.31 [vi AD]), with ἐκ 1 C 9: 19. Mayser II 2, 139 f. (4) Ὅμοιος ὑμῶν Jn 8: 55 SCLX (ὑμῖν ABDW al.) instead of the customary dative (9: 9, 1 Jn 3: 2 etc.) is peculiar; it is perhaps a Latinism (*vestri similis*), cf. Barn 10.3 ὅμοιοι χοίρων, Did 3.1. (5) Of the type παρασκευαστικός τινος (K.-G. I 371), H 4: 12 κριτικὸς ἐνθυμήσεων is the only example in the NT.

(1) Substantival κοινωνός with gen. of person 'an associate of someone' Mt 23: 30, H 10: 33, and 1 C 10: 18, 20 (for Lk 5: 10 s. §190(1)), μέτοχός τινος H 1: 9 OT (cf. E 5: 7?), συνεργός τινος and others, s. §194(2); συγκληρονόμος τινός E 3: 6.

(2) Ἔνοχος with dat. (pap. also; following ἐνέχεσθαί τινι) Mt 5: 21, 22, also ἔνοχος εἰς τὴν γέενναν 22 (otherwise ἐνς Ἀθαναίαν IG IV 554.7, Argos, vi/v BC); LXX gen. and dat. (Johannessohn I 43); with gen.

cf. Nachmanson, Eranos 11 (1911) 232 and synonymous ἁμαρτωλός τινος in inscrip. (Deissmann, LO[4] 91 f. [LAE 116]; Rengstorf, TW I 321 f.).

(3) Following the pattern of ἀπείραστος κακῶν (attested in the pap. also; Mlt. 235, n. on p. 74 [113 n.]), Paul has created the bold phrase ἄνομος θεοῦ—ἔννομος Χριστοῦ 1 C 9: 21 (s. §120(2)) where the gen. seems to depend on νόμος; cf. Soph., Ant. 369, Eur., Med. 737; MGr ἄφοβος τοῦ θεοῦ 'not fearing God'. Thumb[2] §45, 3.

(4) Ὅμοιος with gen. also Aelian (from Praeneste!), NA 8.1 ὁμοίως ἐκείνου (acc. to K.-G. I 413 the only certain example; Scholfield in LCL dat.), PIand VI no. 97.9 (iii AD) ὅμοιός σου, Passio Perpet. et Felic. 12.3 ὅμοιοι χιόνος, Aesop. (Ursing 37), Byz. (Jannaris §1357). The gen. with ὅμοιος in LXX Is 13: 4 is different: φωνή... ὁμοία ἐθνῶν πολλῶν 'a voice (sound) like (דְּמוּת) [the voice (sound)] of a great multitude'. In Mt 5: 45 ὅμοιοι τοῦ πατρὸς ὑμῶν Chr Epiph, ὅμοιοι is merely an explanatory interpolation for υἱοί. (Εἶδον) ὅμοιον υἱὸν ἀνθρώπου Rev 1: 13 S 046 (υἱῷ ACP al.), 14: 14 (υἱῷ C; striking adv. 𝔓[47] ὁ...καθήμενος ὅμοιον υἱῷ) is a solecism; cf. German '*er ist der ganze Vater*'=he is his father all over again (Herm Sim 9.4.5 is different ὅμοιοι ἐγένοντο λευκοί 'the stones of different colors became alike, namely white'). Reverse assimilation in κέρατα δύο ὁμοίῳ ἀρνίῳ Rev 13: 11 𝔓[47] (the others ὅμοια); 9: 10 οὐρὰς ὁμοίοις (SA, -ας pm.) σκορπίοις.

183. The genitive with substantivized verbal adjectives used to designate the agent with the passive is found also in the NT. Only in 1 C 2: 13 is it used with one not substantivized: οὐκ ἐν διδακτοῖς ἀνθρωπίνης σοφίας λόγοις (connecting ἀν. σοφίας with λόγοις as if διδακτοῖς were not there), ἀλλ' ἐν διδακτοῖς πνεύματος, unless λόγοις is spurious (Soph., El. 343 ἅπαντα γάρ σοι τἀμὰ νουθετήματα κείνης διδακτά, where σοι διδακτά = μεμάθηκας, is different). This genitive appears with a perfect passive participle only in Mt 25: 34 οἱ εὐλογημένοι τοῦ πατρός and less obviously Lk 2: 27 τὸ εἰθισμένον (ἔθος D) τοῦ νόμου.

Ἐκλεκτοὶ θεοῦ Mt 24: 31 etc., ἀγαπητοὶ θεοῦ R 1: 7 (ὁ ἀγαπητός μου 16: 5 etc., οἱ ἀγαπητοὶ ἡμῶν A 15: 25, cf. Att. ὁ ἐρώμενός τινος), διδακτοὶ θεοῦ Jn 6: 45 OT, γεννητοὶ γυναικῶν Mt 11: 11, Lk 7: 28 (LXX Job 14: 1). R 1: 6 κλητοὶ Ἰησοῦ does not belong to this category (possessive gen.; the one calling is God). Semitic influence is decisive for the NT, but an Indo-European archaism has contributed to it: Schwyzer, ABA 1940, 7, pp. 7, 8f.

184. Genitive with adverbs (improper prepositions). In addition to those treated in §§214–

16 are the following: ἐγγύς (often), πλησίον Jn 4: 5 (cf. Lk 10: 29, 36 and ὁ πλησίον σου Mt 5: 43 etc.), παραπλήσιον Ph 2: 27 (v.l. θανάτῳ, cf. §194 and *infra* ἐγγύς), μακράν Lk 7: 6 SD (ABCL al. μ. ἀπό as elsewhere), Pol Ph 3.3, 4.3, 6.1 (POxy ι 113.18 [ii AD]). Ἐντός Lk 17: 21, ἐκτός 1 C 6: 18 etc.; ἔξω Mt 21: 39 etc.; πέραν Mt 4: 25 etc. (ἐπέκεινα A 7: 43 is a spurious variant), ὑπερέκεινα 2 C 10: 16, ἀντιπέρα Lk 8: 26.

Ἐγγύς with dat. (seldom in class., but later frequently; K.-G. ι 408, Obrecht 14) only A 9: 38 ἐγγὺς οὔσης τῆς Λύδδης τῇ 'Ιόππῃ (thus with good reasons) and 27: 8 (not an entirely certain instance); cf. LXX Ps 33: 19, 144: 18. Mt 23: 25 τὸ ἔξωθεν τοῦ ποτηρίου, 26 τὸ ἐντὸς τ. π. . . . .τὸ ἐκτὸς [αὐτοῦ] with partitive gen.; likewise Lk 11: 39. Mk 15: 16 ἔσω τῆς αὐλῆς ('farther into the palace', cf. *v.* 1, thus partitive), DP ἔσω εἰς τὴν αὐλήν; vv.ll. in 14: 54 are similar. In ὁ ἔσω ἡμῶν (scil. ἄνθρωπος) 2 C 4: 16 the gen. as in the preceding ὁ ἔξω ἡμῶν ἄνθ. is possessive.

(D) The Genitive of Comparison

185. The genitive of comparison is employed as in classical usage. Thus with (1) the so-called *abbreviated comparison*: Mt 5: 20 ἐὰν μὴ περισσεύσῃ ἡ δικαιοσύνη ὑμῶν πλεῖον τῶν γραμματέων =τῆς τῶν γρ., and with περισσός (=πλείων §60): Mt 5: 37 τὸ περισσὸν τούτων, E 3: 20 ὑπερεκπερισσοῦ ὧν . . . . Πρῶτός μου, πρῶτον ὑμῶν are unclassical; s. §62. (2) As in classical and the papyri (Mayser ιι 2, 142), the *analytic comparison with ἤ* is used much more rarely. It is employed chiefly in instances where the genitive was not applicable or not sufficiently clear: with adjectives 2 T 3: 4 φιλήδονοι μᾶλλον ἢ φιλόθεοι, with temporal clause R 13: 11, with infinitive Mt 19: 24, A 20: 35 etc., with genitive A 4: 19 ὑμῶν μᾶλλον ἢ τοῦ θεοῦ, and with dative Mt 10: 15, A 5: 29 etc. (3) In addition, the *use of prepositions instead of the genitive or* ἤ still survives: π α ρ ά τινα: Lk 3: 13 πλέον παρὰ τὸ διατεταγμένον and often in Heb; cf. classical examples like Thuc. 1.23.3 (K.-G. ι 514f.), where, however, παρά cannot be simply replaced by ἤ. In MGr παρά or ἀπό is the normal substitute for the comparative genitive or ἤ. Ὑ π έ ρ τινα: Lk 16: 8 φρονιμώτεροι ὑπέρ; only beginnings of this construction are found in classical. (4) *'Than' is omitted* after πλείων and ἐλάσσων before numbers: A 4: 22 ἐτῶν πλειόνων τεσσεράκοντα. Cf. K.-G. ιι 311; Lob. Phryn. 411; Schwab ιι 84ff.; *plus quingentos*. Ἐπάνω is a vulgar substitute for πλείων: Mk 14: 5 πραθῆναι

ἐπάνω δηναρίων τριακοσίων, 1 C 15: 6 ἐπάνω πεντακοσίοις ἀδελφοῖς.—Mayser ιι 2, 140ff.

(1) Jn 5: 36 ἐγὼ ἔχω τὴν μαρτυρίαν μείζω τοῦ 'Ιωάνου is ambiguous ('than that which John had' or 'than that given by John'; however, in the latter sense μείζω ἢ τοῦ 'I. would be better). Likewise 21: 15 ἀγαπᾷς με πλέον τούτων = ἢ οὗτοι or rather (acc. to A. Fridrichsen in H. Riesenfeld, Con. Neot. 5 [1941] 3) ἢ τούτους. Rob. 516.
(2) Acc. to Schwab ιι 93 the gen. of comparison is still used more than three times as often as ἤ in the last part of the class. period. Ἤ without definite grammatical necessity: Jn 3: 19, 4: 1, 1 Jn 4: 4, 1 C 14: 5. But in 1 T 1: 4 ἐκζητήσεις παρέχουσιν μᾶλλον ἢ οἰκονομίαν θεοῦ the gen. would not be appropriate, especially since μᾶλλον ἤ is here the equivalent of a negative in meaning (=comparative expressing exclusion, s. §245*a*). Cf. Rob. 666.
(3) Παρά also Herm Vis 3.12.1, Sim 9.18.2 (for παρά = 'more than' without comparative, §245(3)). Lk 18: 14 μᾶλλον παρ' ἐκεῖνον D it sy^p, but there are many variants (cf. 245 *a* (2)). The best text is παρ' ἐκεῖνον SBL (= 𝔖); further ἢ ἐκεῖνος W 61*69, ὑπὲρ ἐκεῖνον, ἤπερ or ἢ γὰρ ἐκεῖνος (Schulthess 224: *ē gar* several times in the Christian-Palestinian translation of the Gospels, thus probably derived from the later vulgar Greek of Palestine or Antioch(?)). Ὑπέρ: H 4: 12, G 1: 14 (further Bauer s.v. ὑπέρ 2); also in the LXX = מן, e.g. Ex 1: 9, Ps 68: 32 (1 Clem 52.2), 83: 11, Judg 11: 25 B (Johannessohn ι 45); μᾶλλον ὑπέρ Jn 12: 43 v.l. SL al. for μᾶλλον ἤπερ ABD al. With elative superlative Herm Man 5.1.6, with elative comparative Barn 5.9 ὑπὲρ πᾶσαν ἁμαρτίαν ἀνομωτέρους. Details for the pap. Schwab ιι 149ff., for παρά 108f., 152f., for ὑπέρ 109f.; παρά Ursing 47, ὑπέρ 48f. Cf. Rob. 667.
(4) Πλείων without ἤ: A 23: 13, 21, 24: 11, 25: 6; with stereotyped ἔλαττον (K.-G. ιι 311) χήρα μὴ ἔλαττον ἐτῶν ἑξήκοντα 1 T 5: 9 (some relate γεγονυῖα to ἑνὸς ἀνδρὸς γυνή, but ἐτ. ἑξ. also remains a qualitative gen. in the phrase μὴ ἔλ. ἐτ. ἑξ., cf. §165 (end) and Plato, Lg. 6.755 A μὴ ἔλαττον ἢ πεντήκοντα γεγονὼς ἐτῶν [K.-G. ιι 311 n. 3]). Lk 9: 13 S* οὐκ εἰσὶν ἡμῖν πλείονες (v.l. πλεῖον ἤ, πλέον ἤ with stereotyped πλέον) ἄρτοι πέντε. Mt 26: 53 πλείους (S^cAC al., πλείω S*BD) δώδεκα (SBDL, ἢ δ. AC al.) λεγιῶνας (S^cBD al., -νων S*AC al.) ἀγγέλων.

(E) Genitive of Place and Time

186. (1) Only a few remnants of the genitive of place remain in the NT (apart from ποῦ, αὐτοῦ and the like, §103): Lk 5: 19 ποίας (scil. ὁδοῦ) εἰσενέγκωσιν, 19: 4 ἐκείνης (D ἐκείνη) ἤμελλεν διέρχεσθαι, not in the old sense in which the classical genitive of space designates the whole area within which something took place; in classical the dative ποίᾳ, ἐκείνῃ would be used here (cf. Xen., An. 3.4.37 ᾗ ἔμελλον παριέναι). (2) On the other hand, the classical genitive of time within which something takes place is not foreign to the NT: χειμῶνος Mt 24: 20 = Mk 13: 18 'during the winter', ἡμέρας Rev 21: 25 and τῆς ἡμ. Lk 9: 37 𝔓⁴⁵ 'during the day', ἡμέρας καὶ νυκτός Mk 5: 5, Lk 18: 7, A 9: 24 etc., νυκτός Mt 2: 14 etc., τῆς νυκτός 'on that night' Lk 2: 8, σαββάτου Mt 24: 20 D (§200(3)), and distributive with a numeral adverb, e.g. δὶς τοῦ σαββάτου 'twice a week' Lk 18: 12, ἅπαξ τοῦ ἐνιαυτοῦ H 9: 7 (classical). Homil Clem αὐτῆς (μιᾶς, οὐδεμιᾶς) ἡμέρας 12.1.1, 1.1, 2.2, ἡμερῶν 'for several days' 12.2.3, 3.6, 13.1.4, πλεόνων ἡμ. 'plures dies' 12.24. 1, πολλῶν ἡμ. 13.9.3. But the genitive of a *point* of time is not classical: ἡμέρας μέσης A 26: 13, μέσης νυκτός Mt 25: 6, μεσονυκτίου and ἀλεκτοροφωνίας (cf. §123(1)) Mk 13: 35 (μεσονύκτιον SBC al., cf. §161(3)), ὄρθρου βαθέως Lk 24: 1. Τοῦ λοιποῦ (scil. χρόνου) G 6: 17, E 6: 10 𝔓⁴⁶S*AB 'from now on, henceforth' is a classical formula.— Mayser II 2, 223 ff.; Rob. 494 ff.

(1) A 19: 26 οὐ μόνον Ἐφέσου ἀλλὰ σχεδὸν πάσης τῆς Ἀσίας is held by Rob. 494 f. to be a gen. of place (cf. Mlt. 73 [113]; Bonaccorsi 419, 602 f.); that would be a Latinism (*Ephesi*) and could hardly be compared with the Homeric Ἄργεος 'in the area of Argos' etc. (K.-G. I 384); however, that the gen. goes with the following ὄχλον is quite possible. (2) Doubtful τοῦ ἐνιαυτοῦ ἐκείνου Jn 11: 49, 51, 18: 13; s. Zahn, Einleitung³ II 572 n. 12. Pap. ὥρας πρώτης and the like (Mayser II 2, 225). M. Ant. 8.51 πάσης ὥρας, 53 τρὶς τῆς ὥρας, Homil Clem 19.25.3 αὐτῆς ὥρας 'immediately', 20.16.3 'just then', 16.3 αὐτῇ νυκτί 'in that very night'. Νύκτα καὶ ἡμέραν s. §161(2); ἐν τῇ ἡμέρᾳ 'in the day' Jn 11: 9 s. §200; διὰ τῆς ἡμέρας 'in the course of this day' Lk 9: 37 D. Διὰ νυκτός s. §223(1). Τεσσεράκοντα ἡμερῶν A 1: 3 D* for δι' ἡμ. τεσσ. SB al. and therefore synonymous (§223(1)); cf. the common ἡμερῶν (ὀλίγων) διατρίψας 'for … days' in Homil Clem, e.g. 1.13.3, 15.1, 3.73.1 etc., Rev 2: 10 ἕξετε θλῖψιν ἡμερῶν δέκα SACP, ἡμέρας δ. 046.

(5) DATIVE

The dative was exposed to a greater extent than either the accusative or genitive to the encroachment of various prepositions, especially ἐν and εἰς, on the function of the simple case. The complete disappearance of the dative which is evident in MGr and its replacement by (the genitive or) the accusative tallies with this and with the dis-

appearance of the use of the dative with prepositions (Schwyzer II 170 f.; Mlt. 62 f. [93]; cf. the dative for εἰς §199). In the meantime it is still retained in the NT in a wide range of usages.— G. N. Hatzidakis, Ἀθηνᾶ 41 (1929) 3–9; J. Humbert, La disparition du datif en grec (du Iᵉʳ au Xᵉ siècle), Paris, 1930; O. Merlier, BCH 55 (1931) 207–28; Mayser II 2, 240 ff.; D. Tabachovitz, Museum Helveticum 3 (1946) 147–51, 154 f.

(A) The Dative Proper: Designating the More Remotely Concerned Person

187. The following points are to be noted regarding **the dative as a necessary complement**: (1) there are almost no examples of the dative with 'to give'; (ἐπι-)χορηγεῖν τινί τι with the Hellenistic meaning 'to furnish, grant' (classical: 'to pay the expenses of a chorus *for* somebody'). 'To do good, benefit, harm' etc. with dative and accusative, s. §§151(1); 157(1) (also ἐν). (2) 'To serve' always takes dative, also δουλοῦν 'to make a slave to' 1 C 9: 19. (3) 'To show, to reveal' always takes dative as does 'to seem' (δοκεῖν, φαίνεσθαι). (4) 'To tell to' as in classical takes τινί or πρός τινα; 'to write, announce' takes dative; isolated examples of a more unusual dative with verbs of saying: ἀπολογεῖσθαί τινι ('before, with somebody') A 19: 33, 2 C 12: 19 (Lucian, Plut.), ἀποτάσσεσθαι 'to say farewell' Mk 6: 46 etc. (Hellenistic, Phryn. 23 f., Nägeli 39), καυχᾶσθαι 'boast before' 2 C 7: 14, 9: 2, ὁμολογεῖν τινι 'to praise' H 13: 15 (1 Esdr 4: 60 σοὶ ὁμολογῶ 'my confession is to thee' [Rudolph] incorrect: Katz, ThLZ 1957, 112), ψεύδεσθαί τινι (LXX) A 5: 4 (cf. 3, 'deceive by lying' τινα as in classical). (5) 'To censure' and 'to command' with dative; also κελεύειν Mt 15: 35 EFG al. (otherwise accusative as in classical), Herm Sim 8.2.8 A (PMich accusative), Homil Clem (Reinhold 30), GP 2.47, 49, Acta Thom. 77 (L.-B. II 2, 192.1), Jos. etc. (Schmidt 424; Raderm.² 132, 133; Vogeser 31; Wolf II 34; Obrecht 14 f.; Helb., Kas. 209). (6) 'To trust, obey' with dative; πεποιθέναι besides dative (e.g. Ph 1: 14) rather often with ἔν τινι, ἐπί τινι or τινα, εἴς τινα, πιστεύειν similarly; πειθαρχεῖν τινι (Acts) like Attic, not τινος like Ion.-Hell. (7) 'To be angry, envy, thank, owe' etc. with dative as usual. (8) The corresponding adjectives also take the dative: ὠφέλιμος T 3: 8, σωτήριος 2: 11, ἀρεστός (s. also under (2)), ἀρκετός, ἱκανός, φανερός A 4: 16, 7: 13, 1 T 4: 15 (v.l. with ἐν),

ἐμφανής A 10: 40, R 10: 20 OT, ὑπήκοος A 7: 39, πιστὸς τῷ κυρίῳ A 16: 15; cf. H 3: 2 (1 P 1: 21 εἰς θεόν AB, but SC al. πιστεύοντας; used for the most part absolutely), ἀπειθής A 26: 19 etc. (ἄπιστος absolute), ἐναντίος Mk 6: 48 etc. (πρός τι A 26: 9). Mayser II 2, 148f. The dative with a verbal substantive is found only in 2 C 9: 11, 12 εὐχαριστία τῷ θεῷ (by analogy with εὐχαριστεῖν τῷ θεῷ 1 C 1: 4 and often); cf. classical and papyri (Mayser II 2, 146.4ff.).—On the whole subject: Helb., Kas. 191–227; Mayser II 2, 240–68; Smyth §§1460–7, 1499–502; Rob. 538–41.

(1) Δεδομένος ἐν s. §220(1); Herm Vis 4.1.8 εἰς τὸ θηρίον ἐμαυτὸν ἔδωκα. 3.11.3 παρεδώκατε ἑαυτοὺς εἰς τὰς ἀκηδίας where εἰς expresses the result is different; similarly R 1: 24 etc. (although E 4: 19 has both dat. and εἰς). Παραδ. εἰς συνέδρια Mt 10: 17 and similar usages are justifiable. Mayser II 2, 356f.

(2) Δουλεύειν, λατρεύειν, διακονεῖν, ὑπηρετεῖν τινι; δουλοῦσθαι s. §191(4). Προσκυνεῖν dat. and acc., §151(2); in addition Hebraizing ἐνώπιόν τινος (cf. §214(6)) Lk 4: 7, Rev 15: 4 OT; likewise ἀρέσκειν ἐνώπιόν τινος A 6: 5 and ἀρεστὸς ἐνώπιόν τινος 1 Jn 3: 22 (cf. §214(6); otherwise ἀρέσκειν and ἀρεστός take dat.).

(3) Φαίνειν τινί 'shine upon' Rev 21: 23 (Sᶜ with ἐν), ἐπιφαίνειν Lk 1: 79; φανεροῦν ἐν and the like s. §220(1).

(4) Εὔχεσθαί τινι A 26: 29, πρός τινα 2 C 13: 7, προσεύχεσθαι only dat. (Mt 6: 6, 1 C 11: 13). Ἐξ-, ἀνθ-ομολογεῖσθαι R 4: 11 OT, 15: 9 OT, Mt 11: 25, Lk 2: 38, 10: 21, accordingly αἰνεῖτε τῷ θεῷ Rev 19: 5 and ᾄδειν (ψάλλειν) τῷ κυρίῳ (θεῷ) E 5: 19, C 3: 16 (Nägeli 42f.) as in the LXX Jer 20: 13 ᾄσατε τῷ κ., αἰνέσατε αὐτῷ etc. (Buttmann 153 n.); Helb., Kas. 69f., 243ff. Ὁμολογεῖν τινι 'to confess before somebody, to somebody' A 24: 14, Mt 7: 23, 'promise' A 7: 17 (v.l. ὤμοσεν, 𝔓⁴⁵DE ἐπηγγείλατο), Mt 14: 7; ὁμολ. ἐν. s. §220(2).

(5) Ἐπιτιμᾶν, ἐπιπλήσσειν, ἐγκαλεῖν with dat., ἐγκ. κατά τινος R 8: 33. On καταρᾶσθαι, μέμφεσθαι, παραινεῖν, εὐαγγελίζεσθαι s. §152. Ἐπιτάσσειν, προστάσσειν, διαστέλλεσθαι etc. with dat. Κελεύειν in class. with dat. only 'to call (encouragingly) to', yet Homer also 'to command'.

(6) Πείθεσθαι, ὑπακούειν, ἀπιστεῖν, ἀπειθεῖν with dat. as usual. Πιστεύειν often with dat., also in the sense of 'to believe in' (A 5: 14, 18: 8 τῷ κυρίῳ, 16: 34 τῷ θεῷ), for which elsewhere εἴς τινα, εἰς τὸ ὄνομά τινος, and ἐπί τινα A 9: 42 etc. are used; ἐπί τινι only with reference to LXX Is 28: 18 (Joachim Jeremias, TW IV 275f.; R 9: 33, 10: 11, 1 P 2: 6, also 1 T 1: 16; Lk 24: 25 is different [πιστ. om. D] 'on the basis of'; incorrect Mt 27: 42 EFW al. [SBL ἐπ᾿ αὐτόν, AD αὐτῷ]); πιστεύετε ἐν τῷ εὐαγγελίῳ Mk 1: 15 (LXX, s. Johannessohn I 60f.; Jn 3: 15 ἐν αὐτῷ [B], if correct,

is to be taken with ἔχῃ ζωήν). Cf. Mlt. 67f., 235 n., [102f.] and Bauer s.v. Bultmann, TW VI 203.19: πιστεύειν εἰς=π. ὅτι (e.g. 1 Th 4: 14, Jn 20: 31). Ἐλπίζειν τινί 'to hope in someone' (instead of ἐπί τινα or ἐπί τινι or εἴς τινα; Thuc. 3.97.2 τῇ τύχῃ ἐλπίσας is different: dat. of cause) is found only in Mt 12: 21 (ἐν τῷ D al., κἄν Holwerda) in a quotation from Is 42: 4 where the reading is ἐπὶ τῷ. Helb., Kas. 199, recalls θαρσεῖν ἐπί in profane Hell.; but ἐπὶ σοὶ γὰρ πεποιθὼς PSI VI 646.3 (iii BC) (Helb., Kas. 198) is uncertain because the text is incomplete.—R 4: 20 εἰς τὴν ἐπαγγελίαν τοῦ θεοῦ οὐ διεκρίθη τῇ ἀπιστίᾳ= ἐπίστευσεν (18).

(7) Also ἐμβριμᾶσθαί τινι Mt 9: 30 etc., μετριοπαθεῖν τινι indulgere H 5: 2; for μέμφεσθαι s. §152(1).

(8) Substantivized σύμφορον and συμφέρον with gen. 1 C 7: 35, 10: 33.

188. The dative of advantage and disadvantage (*dativus commodi et incommodi*) with various verbs serves to designate the person whose interest is affected. (1) Μαρτυρεῖν τινι 'to bear witness to someone' Mt 23: 31, Lk 4: 22 etc. (Ἀνα-)πληροῦται αὐτοῖς (D al. ἐπ᾿ αὐτοῖς) ἡ προφητεία Mt 13: 14, cf. Lk 18: 31 (περί with genitive D), 1 P 5: 9. Ἔκρινα ἐμαυτῷ ('for myself') τοῦτο 2 C 2: 1, cf. Herm Man 12.3.6 σεαυτῷ κέκρικας τοῦ μὴ δύνασθαι. (2) Paul uses several combinations especially loosely (often θεῷ, κυρίῳ) as 2 C 5: 13 εἴτε γὰρ ἐξέστημεν, θεῷ (it happened for God's sake)· εἴτε σωφρονοῦμεν, ὑμῖν (in your interest).—Γαμεῖσθαί τινι Mk 10: 12, 1 C 7: 39 (§101) and μνηστεύεσθαί τινι (§191(4)) also probably belong here.—Mayser II 2, 270ff.; Rob. 538f.; Smyth §§1481ff.

(1) Μεριμνᾶν Mt 6: 25 (Lk 12: 22) 'about life… body' (other constructions §176(2)). Ἀνέβη ὁ καπνὸς ταῖς προσευχαῖς Rev 8: 4 is also probably *dat. commodi*; cf. 3 (Winer §31, 6 [Winer-M.³ 270f.]; acc. to Mlt. 75 [117] sociative instrumental).

(2) R 14: 4 τῷ ἰδίῳ κυρίῳ στήκει ἢ πίπτει; ὁ ὁ φρονῶν τὴν ἡμέραν κυρίῳ φρονεῖ· καὶ ὁ ἐσθίων κυρίῳ ἐσθίει ('in honor of the Lord'). Ἐμοὶ κάμψει πᾶν γόνυ 11 OT is similar; it is to be compared with προσκυνεῖν τινι (§151(2)). Ἑαυτοῖς (-τῷ) 'for themselves' R 2: 14, 13: 2, 1 C 14: 28, Jn 19: 17, R 11: 25 ἑαυτοῖς (𝔓⁴⁶FG, ἐν ἑ. AB, παρ᾿ ἑ. SCD, both prepositions following references in the LXX) φρόνιμοι; hence 'of his own accord' MPol 3.1, 13.2. Lietzmann, SAB 1934, 779. Black, Aramaic Approach 76f., sees Aram. influence e.g. Mt 23: 9 D, Mk 7: 4 D, for which πρὸς ἑαυτόν also appears in Lk 24: 12, εἰς ἑαυτούς in 7: 30; these would correspond to a *dat. ethicus* in Aram.—In the following examples the dat. expresses more the possessor (cf. §189): R 6: 10 τῇ ἁμαρτίᾳ ἀπέθανεν… ζῇ τῷ θεῷ, 11, 14: 7 f. (ending with τοῦ κυρίου ἐσμέν,

cf. 6: 2); 7: 4, 2 C 5: 15, G 2: 19, also 1 P 2: 24. Ἀπώλοντο (A; ἀπέθανον PMich) τῷ θεῷ Herm Sim 8.6.4.

189. Dative of possession: Εἶναι, γίνεσθαι (and ὑπάρχειν Acts and 2 P 1: 8): Lk 2: 7 οὐκ ἦν αὐτοῖς τόπος 'they had no place', A 2: 43 ἐγίνετο πάσῃ ψυχῇ φόβος 'all became more and more afraid' (imperfect). (1) The classical distinction, whereby the genitive is used when the acquisition is recent or the emphasis is on the possessor (e.g. R 14: 8) and the dative when the object possessed is to be stressed, is customarily preserved. (2) Exceptions appear only occasionally: R 7: 3 ἐὰν γένηται ἀνδρὶ ἑτέρῳ, 4 εἰς τὸ γενέσθαι ὑμᾶς ἑτέρῳ (Hebraism following תִּהְיֶה לְאִישׁ, LXX Lev 22: 12 etc.). (3) Εἶναί τινι also means 'to happen to, befall': οὐ μὴ ἔσται σοι τοῦτο Mt 16: 22 (a doublet, interpreting ἵλεώς σοι, s. §128(5)), cf. Lk 1: 45; antithesis ἕν σοι λείπει Lk 18: 22, cf. T 3: 13 (Polyb. 10.18.8, Epict. 2.14.19). Mayser II 2, 269f.; Smyth §§1476ff.; Rob. 541.

(1) A 21: 23, Mt 19: 27, 18: 12. Following the pattern of ἔστιν συνήθεια ὑμῖν Jn 18: 39 also κατὰ τὸ εἰωθὸς αὐτῷ Lk 4: 16 (αὐτῷ om. D), τῷ Παύλῳ A 17: 2 (ὁ Παῦλος D). Of time: A 24: 11 οὐ πλείους εἰσίν μοι ἡμέραι δώδεκα. With verb omitted: 2 C 6: 14f. τίς γὰρ μετοχὴ τῇ δικαιοσύνῃ (always gen. as v.l., but not always in the same MSS).
(2) A 2: 39 ὑμῖν ἐστιν ἡ ἐπαγγελία probably following ἐπαγγέλλεσθαί τινι. Lk 12: 20 ἃ ἡτοίμασας, τίνι ἔσται (scil. ἡτοιμασμένα? Yet D has τίνος).
(3) Cf. the dat. with συμβαίνει Mk 10: 32 etc.; with ellipsis of the verb: Lk 1: 43 πόθεν μοι τοῦτο; on Mk 10: 21 ἕν σοι ὑστερεῖ v.l. s. §180(5).

190. Εἶναι with the dative and predicate nouns (εἶναι with the dative forms only a part of the predicate). (1) The predicate supplement is a substantive: A 9: 15 σκεῦος ἐκλογῆς ἐστίν μοι οὗτος 'I have in him...'; usually 'to the credit (discredit) of': 1 C 11: 14, 15 ἀτιμία αὐτῷ (δόξα αὐτῇ) ἐστιν, for which εἰς also is used (§145(1)). (2) The predicate supplement is an adjective: καλόν σοί ἐστιν 'it is good for you, to your advantage' Mt 18: 8 etc.; accordingly οὐαί μοί ἐστιν 1 C 9: 16. Infrequently with an adverb instead of an adjective: 1 Th 2: 10 ὁσίως... ὑμῖν ἐγενήθημεν (§434(2)). (3) The dative is used by analogy in related expressions in which it is more closely connected to the substantive: οὐκ ἔσχηκα ἄνεσιν τῷ πνεύματί μου 2 C 2: 13 = οὐκ ἦν ἄνεσις; several times with εὑρίσκειν: Mt 11: 29, R 7: 10, 21, 2 C

12: 20, Rev 20: 11 (2 P 3: 14 s. §192). (4) It is seldom found without the verb (ellipsis): G 5: 13.

(1) 1 C 1: 18 τοῖς μὲν ἀπολλυμένοις μωρία ἐστίν 'is considered as folly'; 2: 14, Mt 18: 17; Χριστοῦ εὐωδία ἐσμὲν τῷ θεῷ 2 C 2: 15. With concrete nouns: A 19: 31 ὄντες αὐτῷ φίλοι (elsewhere subst. φίλος with gen.: Jn 19: 12, etc., likewise ἐχθρός Mt 5: 44 etc.); Lk 5: 10 ἦσαν κοινωνοὶ τῷ Σίμωνι (D ἦσαν δὲ κ. αὐτοῦ) 'Simon had them as partners' (subst. κοιν. as elsewhere with gen. [§182(1)]); ὀφειλέτης εἰμί τινι R 1: 14, 8: 12 (gen. 15: 27 etc.).
(2) Οὐαί τινι often with ellipsis of verb: Mt 11: 21 etc.; Rev with acc. 8: 13 S 046, 12: 12 SACP; cf. vae me and mihi.
(3) 1 C 7: 28 θλῖψιν τῇ σαρκί (with ἐν D*FG); 2 C 12: 7; dat. with κινεῖν στάσεις A 24: 5; ἀγοράζειν εἰς ταφὴν τοῖς ξένοις Mt 27: 7 (as one can say ὁ ἀγρός ἐστιν ταφὴ τοῖς ξ.).
(4) Without verb μονογενὴς υἱὸς τῇ μητρί Lk 7: 12 = ὃς ἦν τῇ μ. μον. υἱός. Cf. μονογενής εἰμι τῷ πατρί μου LXX Tob 3: 15; cf. Judg 11: 34 A (Hdt. 7.221).

191. Dative of agent (dative with passive = ὑπό τινος) is perhaps represented by only one genuine example in the NT and this with the perfect: Lk 23: 15 οὐδὲν ἄξιον θανάτου ἐστὶν πεπραγμένον αὐτῷ (M.-H. 459 correctly reject an Aramaism [Wellhausen, Einl.² 18]; but D πεπρ. ἐν αὐτῷ, c invenimus in illo; perhaps the correct reading is ἐστὶν ἐν αὐτῷ without πεπρ., cf. A 25: 5). There are, on the other hand, several examples in the Atticizing Clementine Homilies: 3.68 θεῷ ἐστύγηται, 9.21 δαίμοσιν ἀκούεται, 19.23 ἠτύχηται τοῖς ταπεινοῖς. The remaining NT examples are of a different sort: some depend upon the similarity of the passive with the deponent meaning. Thus not only φανεροῦσθαί τινι 'to appear' Mk 16: 12 etc. = classical φαίνεσθαι (so Mt for φανεροῦσθαι), but also (1) ὀπτάνεσθαί (aorist ὀφθῆναι) τινι 'to appear', A 1: 3 and often (pap., s. Mayser II 1, 122; LXX, s. Johannessohn I 51f.), which is not to be equated with ὀφθῆναι ὑπό τινος. Cf. §313. (2) Likewise γνωσθῆναί τινι 'to become known' A 9: 24 and rather often (LXX, s. Johannessohn I 52) by analogy with γνωστὸν ἐγένετο πᾶσιν (A 1: 19) and the like; but ἔγνωσται ὑπ' αὐτοῦ 1 C 8: 3 'is known by him', cf. G 4: 9. (3) R 10: 20 OT εὑρέθην τοῖς ἐμὲ μὴ ζητοῦσιν (𝔓⁴⁶BDFG with ἐν, but Hebr. Is 65: 1 ?) is related to 'to appear' (supra (1)); cf. ἐμφανὴς ἐγενόμην τοῖς (BD ἐν τοῖς)...immediately following. (4) Μνηστεύεσθαί τινι Mt 1: 18 is the passive of μνηστεύειν τινά τινι as 2 P 2: 19 τούτῳ καὶ δεδούλωται is the passive of δουλοῦν τινά τινι (§187(2)). (5) The dative is better understood as instrumental in other cases: thus Ja 3: 7 δαμάζεται καὶ δεδάμασται τῇ φύσει τῇ ἀνθρωπίνῃ in spite of Homer's δαμῆναί τινι.— Mayser II 2, 273; Smyth §§1488 ff.; Rob. 534.

(1) Ὤφθητί μοι as early as Eur., Ba. 914, τοῖς Κερκυραίοις οὐχ ἑωρῶντο Thuc. 1.51.2, Hebr. נִרְאָה with אֶל or לְ, Syriac *'thz'* with *l*. Ὤφθη αὐτοῖς A 7: 26 is more 'appeared to' than 'was seen'. Like ὀπτάνεσθαι also θεαθῆναι τοῖς ἀνθρώποις Mt 6: 1, 23: 5.

(2) With ἀνεγνωρίσθη Ἰωσὴφ τοῖς ἀδελφοῖς αὐτοῦ 'let himself be recognized' A 7: 13 (LXX Gen. 45: 1, cf. Ruth 3: 3, Ezk 20: 5) cf. γνωρίζειν τί τινι 2: 28 and ἡ Ἰφιγένεια τῷ Ὀρέστῃ ἀνεγνωρίσθη Arist., Poet. 11 p. 1452 b 6.

(3) The dat. with εὑρίσκεσθαι R 7: 10 etc. is of another type, s. §190(3); on 2 P 3: 14 s. §192.

(4) Μαθητεύεσθαί τινι Mt 13: 52 (cf. 27: 57) is also the pass. of μαθητεύειν τινά τινι. Ja 3: 18 καρπὸς... σπείρεται τοῖς ποιοῦσιν εἰρήνην is a *dat. commodi*; cf. Lk 18: 31, 1 P 5: 9 (§188(1)).

(5) 2 P 2: 19 ᾧ τις ἥττηται is probably 'by which' since ἡττᾶν is act. in Hell. and can form the usual pass.—For συνεφωνήθη A 5: 9 s. §202 under συν-.

192. The ethical dative:

Rev 2: 5, 16 ἔρχομαί σοι could be an ethical dative (likewise BGU IV 1041. 16 [ii AD]; for classical parallels s. Havers 4, 158 etc.; pap. [Mayser II 2, 270] ἐλθέ μοι), unless it reflects incorrectly, like Mt 21: 5 OT ἔρχεταί σοι, Hebr. לָךְ לְ, 'to you' (in Hebrew with verbs of motion). Ἀστεῖος τῷ θεῷ A 7: 20 (speech of Stephen) also is a Hebraism.

Barn 8.4 μεγάλοι τῷ θεῷ 'in God's eyes', 4.11 ναὸς τέλειος τῷ θεῷ, Protev Ja 10.1 ἀμίαντος ἦν τῷ θεῷ, LXX Jon 3: 3 πόλις μεγάλη τῷ θεῷ (לֵאלֹהִים), i.e. 'very great'—an elative, cf. D. W. Thomas, VT 3 (1953) 15 ff.: אֱלֹהִים and אֵל at times expresses a superlative or an elative, a mode of speech not recognized by the LXX. For the interpretation of τῷ θεῷ in A 7: 20 as a circumlocution for the superlative, s. Bauer (Arndt-Gingrich only) s.v. θεός 3 g β; cf. Mlt. 104 [168]. But δυνατὰ τῷ θεῷ 2 C 10: 4 *dat. commodi*. 2 P 3: 14 ἄσπιλοι καὶ ἀμώμητοι αὐτῷ (God) εὑρεθῆναι probably belongs to the exx. in §190(3); in accordance with ἀμώμους κατενώπιον αὐτοῦ E 1: 4, C 1: 22, the dat. can also be equated with this circumlocution, which is indeed often used for the correct dat. (ἀρεστὸς ἐνώπιον §187(2)). On the dat. of sympathy s. §473(1). The class. dat. μοι in the address (ὦ τέκνον μοι, K.-G. I 423) has, of course, disappeared and has been replaced by the usual gen.: 2 T 2: 1 τέκνον μου, G 4: 19; τεκνία μου 1 Jn 2: 1 (3: 18 v.l., SAB al. without μου, which is the usual thing; never a pron. with παιδία); πάτερ ἡμῶν Mt 6: 9, otherwise πάτερ without pron. (correct also

Lk 11: 2 SBL; LXX Gen 22: 7 etc. translates Hebr. אָבִי simply πάτερ; and בְּנִי = τέκνον; cf. Johannessohn I 7 f.). Also θεέ μου Mt 27: 46 (Wackernagel, Anredeformen 6 n. 2 [= Kl. Schr. 973 n. 2]), cf. ὁ θεός μου and the like §147(3).—J. Wellhausen, Das Evangelium Lukae (1904) *ad loc.*; Torrey, ZDMG 101 (1951) 135 f., Black, Aramaic Approach 77 f.: Lk 7: 30 εἰς ἑαυτούς and (Torrey; contrast Black, *op. cit.* 78) 18: 11 πρὸς ἑαυτόν = Hebr. (Gesenius-Kautzsch §119 s) and Aram. ethical dat.

(B) The Instrumental-Associative Dative

193. The associative (comitative) dative with verbs.

(1) 'To follow': ἀκολουθεῖν (also ἐξ-, ἐπ-, παρ-, συν-; συνέπεσθαι A 20: 4, ἕπεσθαι never) often with dative, besides μετά τινος (classical also) Rev 6: 8, 14: 13 and Hebraizing ὀπίσω τινός Mt 10: 38, Mk 8: 34 (v.l. ἐλθεῖν) as in LXX 3 Km 19: 20. (2) 'To draw near': ἐγγίζειν Lk 7: 12 etc., also with εἰς. (3) 'To join, have fellowship with': (προσ-)κολλᾶσθαι Lk 15: 15 etc., δεδέσθαι 'to be bound to someone' R 7: 2, 1 C 7: 27 (Nägeli 44), κοινωνεῖν R 12: 13 etc.; ἑτεροζυγεῖν ἀπίστοις 2 C 6: 14 'to be unevenly yoked with...' (from ἑτερόζυγος LXX Lev 19: 19), cf. συζυγεῖν with dative in Plutarch and later authors. (4) 'To associate, have intercourse with', either friendly: ὁμιλεῖν 'converse' A 24: 26 (πρός τινα Lk 24: 14; classical also), διαλέγεσθαι (also πρός τινα as in classical), διαλλάσσεσθαι Mt 5: 24, καταλλάσσειν τινά τινι and καταλλάσσεσθαί τινι rather often; or hostile: κρίνεσθαι 'dispute' Mt 5: 40 (μετά τινος 1 C 6: 6, cf. 7), δια- Jd 9 (πρός τινα A 11: 2, classical), διακατελέγχεσθαι A 18: 28, διαβάλλεσθαί τινι (passive) 'to be made suspect with someone' Lk 16: 1 (in this instance more likely a genuine dative following λέγειν τινί). (5) 'To make use of': χρῆσθαι (acc. s. §152(4)). (6) 'To be like' etc.: ὁμοιοῦν (-οῦσθαι) Mt 6: 8 etc., (παρ-)ὁμοιάζειν (intransitive) 23: 27, ἐοικέναι Ja 1: 6.—On compounds with συν- s. §202.—Helb., Kas. 227 ff.; Mayser II 2, 274 ff.; Smyth §1523; Rob. 528 ff.

(1) Lk 9: 49 μεθ' ἡμῶν not 'follow us', but 'follow (you) together with us'.

(2) Εἰς particularly with indecl. nouns Lk 18: 35 (v.l. τῇ), 19: 29, yet εἰς Ἱεροσόλυμα Mt 21: 1, Mk 11: 1 and εἰς τὴν κώμην Lk 24: 28; with ἐπί 10: 9.

(3) Δεδέσθαι in literal sense with πρός Mk 11: 4; κολλᾶσθαι μετά τινος Barn 10.11.

(4) Μάχεσθαι (class. dat.) only with πρός τινα (Jn 6: 52); πολεμεῖν (class. dat.) only with μετά τινος ('against somebody', cf. MGr [Thumb² §162, 1 n.];

class. 'on the same side with someone') Rev 2: 16, 12: 7, 13: 4, 17: 14, likewise πόλεμον ποιεῖν μετά τινος 11: 7, 12: 17, 13: 7, 19: 19. Πολεμεῖν τινα 'to wage war on, attack somebody' ITr 4.2 as in Dinarchus 1.36 and often in Hell. (Helb., Kas. 234). On μετά Helb., Kas. 233 (Hell.; πληκτίζεσθαι μετά Aristoph., Eccl. 964?).

(5) Χρῆσθαί τινι often, καταχρ. 1 C 9: 18; συγχρ. Jn 4: 9b is a spurious addition.

194. Associative dative with adjectives and adverbs. (1) Adjectives of identity etc.: ὅμοιος often (with genitive? §182(4)), ὁ αὐτός only 1 C 11: 5 ἐν καὶ τὸ αὐτό. Ἴσος Mt 20: 12 etc. In addition circumlocutions: ἴσος ὡς καί A 11: 17, cf. in a quotation R 9: 29 ὡς Γόμορρα ἂν ὡμοιώθημεν; ὁ αὐτὸς καθὼς καί 1 Th 2: 14. H 11: 11 αὐτῇ Σάρρᾳ '(Abraham) together with Sarah' in classical style, as Westcott-Hort well conjecture in their margin and Riggenbach in his commentary *in loc.*, for αὐτὴ Σάρρα which is hardly explicable. (2) Compounds with σύν: σύμμορφός τινι Ph 3: 21, but with genitive of the thing which one possesses, R 8: 29 τῆς εἰκόνος §182(1); for classical parallels see Matthiae, Ausführl. griech. Gramm. 864 (§379 end). (3) The adverb ἅμα takes the dative only in Mt 13: 29 ἅμα αὐτοῖς τὸν σῖτον (D ἅμα καὶ τ. σ. σὺν αὐτοῖς) and Ign, otherwise ἅμα σύν 1 Th 4: 17, 5: 10. For ἐγγύς and παραπλήσιον s. §184.— Substantives do not enter into these constructions with the dative (as they occasionally do in classical, K.-G. 1 426f.): R 15: 26 κοινωνίαν ποιήσασθαι εἰς τοὺς πτωχούς, 2 C 9: 13, Ph 1: 5, κοινωνία μετά τινος 1 Jn 1: 3, 6, 7; on 2 C 6: 14 s. §189(1).—Mayser 11 2, 148.

(1) The dat. can also be used to express the owner of the same thing (κόμαι Χαρίτεσσιν ὁμοῖαι Homer): Rev 9: 10 ἔχουσιν οὐρὰς ὁμοίας σκορπίοις, 13: 11; thus also 2 P 1: 1 τοῖς ἰσότιμον ἡμῖν λαχοῦσιν πίστιν, Jd 7. Cf. the 'abbreviated comparison' §185(1).— Rob. 532.

(2) The adjectives συγγενής, συγκληρονόμος, σύμβουλος (R 11: 34 OT), συμμέτοχος (E 5: 7), συναιχμάλωτος, συνεργός, σύντροφος (A 13: 1), when substantivized, take the gen.; cf. φίλος §190(1). R 6:5 σύμφυτοι τῷ ὁμοιώματι τοῦ θανάτου αὐτοῦ is doubtful: perhaps τῷ ὁμ. is instr., the gen. going with σύμφ. (cf. the following ἀλλὰ καὶ τῆς ἀναστάσεως ἐσόμεθα [σύμφ. to be supplied, hardly τῷ ὁμ.]); yet taking the gen. with the preceding word is more natural and ὁμοίωμα elsewhere always takes the gen. in Paul.

(3) Ἅμα σύν Eur., Ion 717, Alex. Aphr., de An. 83. 19; cf. Lat. *unā cum* and ἅμα μετ' αὐτῶν Dit., Syll.³ 705.57 (112 BC, in a decree of the senate).

195. In the genuinely instrumental sense the dative has been sharply curtailed in the NT by the use of ἐν. While this is certainly not entirely foreign to Greek (K.-G. 1 464f.; Raderm.² 130 n. 4; Helb., Kas. 146f.; Humbert 99–158), for NT authors Hebrew בְּ has provided the model. This usage is not found, therefore, to the same degree in the various authors. For ἐν used to designate the personal agent, which cannot be expressed by the dative, s. §219(1); for the Hebraizing circumlocutions with χείρ, στόμα for persons, s. §217. (1) The following take ἐν besides the simple dative: (a) 'with the sword (kill, die etc.)', (b) 'to a season with something', (c) 'burn with fire' (ἐν πυρί literally 'in the fire' as it means even in the chance phrase ἐν πυρὶ καίειν Hom., Il. 24.38), (d) 'baptize with', (e) 'vindicate by', (f) 'mix with', (g) 'measure with'. (2) The instrumental is sometimes used where classical used the genitive construction as a rule: μεθύσκεσθαι οἴνῳ E 5: 18, as in LXX Pr 4: 17 etc. (Helb., Kas. 150); πληροῦν τινι or (E 5: 18) ἔν τινι, besides genitive (§172); Mk 10: 33 κατακρινοῦσιν αὐτὸν θανάτῳ (-ου D*)=Mt 20: 18 (CD al. here, εἰς θάνατον S, om. B) 'they will condemn him to death' by analogy from θανάτῳ ζημιοῦν (and *capite damnare*?).—Mayser 11 2, 282ff., 357; Regard, Prép. 349–76; Smyth §§1506ff.; Rob. 532ff.

In MGr, where the dat. proper is rendered by εἰς and the acc., the instr. is expressed by μέ (= μετά; ἐν has disappeared). Ἐν for the instr. is particularly frequent in Rev, infrequent, on the other hand, in the first part of Acts, and in the second part, apart from δικαιοῦσθαι ἐν (*infra* (e)), the single example is καὶ ἐν ὀλίγῳ καὶ ἐν μεγάλῳ 26: 29 (answer of Paul) 'by little, much', i.e., either 'easily, with difficulty' or 'concerning both small and great' i.e. persons with and without rank—a play on Agrippa's words v. 28 (Fridrichsen, Con. Neot. 3 [1939] 15; ἐν ὀλίγῳ 28 in Agrippa's exclamation is different [§405(1)]; ἐν ὀλίγῳ E 3: 3 = διὰ βραχέων acc. to Chrys., s. Haupt, Meyer, Kom. *in loc.*). On the corresponding Lat. *in*, which is only partially influenced by Greek ἐν, cf. Stolz-Schmalz, Lat. Gr.⁵ 438, 537.

(1) (a) Ἐν μαχαίρῃ, ἐν ῥομφαίᾳ Mt 26: 52, Lk 22: 49, Rev 2: 16, 6: 8, 13: 10, 19: 21, ἐν φόνῳ μαχαίρης H 11: 37, but Rev 1: 23 ἀποκτενῶ ἐν θανάτῳ; without ἐν: μαχαίρῃ A 12: 2, στόματι μαχαίρης Lk 21: 24. LXX also with and without ἐν: Johannessohn 1 55, 11 353. Exx. of ἐν μαχαίρῃ (-ραις) in the pap. are analogous to ἐν ὅπλοις and mean 'to supply with weapons' (cf. ἠμφιεσμένος ἐν §159(1)), but are not combined with 'to kill' and the like (Mlt. 11f. [15f.]; Kuhring 43f.; Rossberg 28; Mayser 11 2, 358, 393).

S. also §198(2). Ἀκοντίῳ φονεύειν and the like in Lucian (Jannaris §1562) can be a Semitism (Humbert 109).—(b) Ἅλατι C 4: 6, ἁλίζειν πυρί Mk 9: 49 (ἁλί in the same place OT), but ἐν τίνι ἁλισθήσεται (τὸ ἅλας) Mt 5: 13, similarly Mk 9: 50, Lk 14: 31.—(c) Πυρὶ ἀσβέστῳ Mt 3: 12 = Lk 3: 17, ἐν πυρί Rev 14: 10, 16: 8, 17: 16 (without ἐν SP 046), 18: 8; only 'to burn with fire' is πυρὶ καίεσθαι even in Rev (8: 8, 21: 8). LXX with and without ἐν (Johannessohn I 52).—(d) Usually ἐν ὕδατι, ἐν πνεύματι, yet Lk ὕδατι: 3: 16 (D with ἐν, but in the same place all MSS have ἐν πνεύματι by contrast), A 1: 5 (in same verse: ἐν πν.), 11: 16 (ditto), χρίειν πνεύματι 10: 38.—(e) Δικαιοῦν (-οῦσθαι) with dat. e.g. R 3: 28 πίστει, with ἐν G 5: 4 (ἐν νόμῳ), A 13: 39, R 5: 9 (ἐν τῷ αἵματι τοῦ Χρ.); ἐκ πίστεως 5: 1 etc.— (f) Μειγνύναι with dat. Rev 15: 2, with ἐν 8: 7, with μετά Mt 27: 34, Lk 13: 1 (exx. from the poets in K.-G. II 431). Helb., Kas. 250f.—(g) Μετρεῖν 'to measure by something' with dat. Lk 6: 38, with ἐν Mt 7: 2, Mk 4: 24, 2 C 10: 12 (ἐν ἑαυτοῖς; class. also would not use the dat., nor ἐν either, but πρός τινα); 'to measure with something' with dat. Rev 21: 16 (ἐν P), with ἐν 11: 1.

(2) Class. also μεθύειν ἔρωτι; Lucian, Syr. D. 22 οἴνῳ ἑωυτὴν μεθύσασα; Rev has ἐκ: 17: 2, 6. The Hell. dat. with 'to fill' is usually limited to the pass. (M. Wellmann, Die Schrift des Diosk. π. ἁπλ. φαρμ. [Berlin, 1914] 69), but even there does not predominate; dat. with act. LXX Jer 13: 13 (Helb., Kas. 145), after a repeated gen. with pass. 13: 12, Herm Man 11.3, not in the NT. Class. dat. with πλήρης Eur., Ba. 18, with πληροῦν Eur., HF 372, Aeschyl., Th. 464. Cf. also ὑπερπερισσεύομαι τῇ χαρᾷ (ἐν τ. χ. B) 2 C 7: 4.—Κεκριμένοι τῷ θανάτῳ Barn 10.5; this dat. with 'to condemn' is Hell. (Lob. Phryn. 475; Ursing 42; Büchsel, TW III 953 n.1). Thus also 2 P 2: 6 καταστροφῇ (om. BC*) κατέκρινεν 'to extinction'; σταυρῷ Ps.-Clem., Epit. 1.145.

196. Dative of cause. R 11: 20 τῇ ἀπιστίᾳ ἐξεκλάσθησαν 'on account of their unbelief', 30 ἠλεήθητε τῇ τούτων ἀπειθείᾳ, 31 ἠπείθησαν τῷ ὑμετέρῳ ἐλέει 'because God desired to show you mercy', 4: 20 οὐ διεκρίθη τῇ ἀπιστίᾳ, ἀλλ' ἐνεδυναμώθη τῇ πίστει, G 6: 12 ἵνα τῷ σταυρῷ τοῦ Χρ. μὴ διώκωνται, 1 C 8: 7, etc. Also A 15: 1 περιτέμνεσθαι τῷ ἔθει τῷ Μωυσέως 'according to' (D has something different); cf. τῇτε (read τῇδε) τάξει 'according to this prescription' PHolm 2.18. The reason can also be indicated by a preposition (so by ἐν in ἐν τούτῳ 'for this reason' Jn 16: 30, A 24: 16, s. §219(2)); it is the rule with verbs of emotion (classical besides dative and accusative), where the dative appears only in a more refined style: H 13: 16 τοιαύταις θυσίαις εὐαρεστεῖται

(Diodor. Sic. 3.55 [1.354.18 Vogel] etc.); 1 P 4: 12 μὴ ξενίζεσθε τῇ . . . (with ἐν 4); otherwise ἐν, ἐπί τινι etc. Helb., Kas. 255ff.; Mayser II 2, 284f.— Smyth §§1517ff.; Rob. 532.

Χαίρειν ἐπί τινι Mt 18: 13 etc. (cf. 2 C 7: 4) ἐν τούτῳ Lk 10: 20 (cf. Vett. Val. 64.19 Kroll? R 12: 12 is different τῇ ἐλπίδι 'by virtue of hope, in hope', not 'over hope'); ἀγαλλιᾶσθαι and εὐφραίνεσθαι with ἐν and ἐπί.—Εὐδοκεῖν with ἐν (Hebr. בְּ), with εἰς 2 P 1: 17, Mt 12: 18 OT (ἐν D, acc. S*B, s. §148(2)); with dat. e.g. 2 Th 2: 12 v.l., cf. pap. [Helb., Kas. 263; Preisigke]). In the LXX εὐδοκεῖν ἐν is the most frequent form and is used even where the Hebr. text does not have בְּ, e.g. Ps 43: 11. Θαυμάζειν ἐπί τινι Lk 4: 22 etc., περί τινος 2: 18 (for θ. τινά, τι s. §148(2)); ἐθαύμασεν ὀπίσω τοῦ θηρίου Rev 13: 3 is altogether peculiar, a pregnant construction for ἐθ. ἐπὶ τῷ θ. καὶ ἐπορεύθη ὀπ. αὐτοῦ). Ἐκπλήσσεσθαι ἐπί τινι, καυχᾶσθαι ἐν and ἐπί (acc. §148(2)), συλλυπεῖσθαι ἐπί Mk 3: 5. Μακροθυμεῖν Mt 18: 26 etc. indicates the cause of the emotion with ἐπί, εἰς, πρός, ὀργίζεσθαι Rev 12: 17 with ἐπί. R 12: 12 τῇ θλίψει ὑπομένοντες assimilation (scribal corruption?) to the neighboring parallel datives (Marcion τὴν θλῖψιν).—For ἐν outside the NT cf. Helb., Kas. 267f. and supra §195.

197. The dative of respect in the NT is far more frequent than the accusative of respect (§160) (Oldenburger 29f.; F. Völker, Papyrorum graecarum syntaxis specimen [Diss. Bonn, 1900] 12; Mayser II 2, 149f., 285; influence of the Latin ablative of limitation?), while in classical usage the ratio is reversed. 1 C 14: 20 μὴ παιδία γίνεσθε ταῖς φρεσίν, ἀλλὰ τῇ κακίᾳ νηπιάζετε, ταῖς δὲ φρεσὶν τέλειοι γίνεσθε; A 16: 5 ἐστερεοῦντο τῇ πίστει καὶ ἐπερίσσευον τῷ ἀριθμῷ. Often with adjectives: A 7: 51 ἀπερίτμητοι καρδίαις καὶ τοῖς ὠσίν, 14: 8 ἀδύνατος τοῖς ποσίν. Φύσει 'by nature' G 2: 15 etc., τῷ γένει 'by birth' A 4: 36 etc., ὀνόματι 'by name' (§160). A 18: 25 ζέων τῷ πνεύματι, R 12: 10–12 several datives of respect (mixed with others), 1 C 7: 34 ἁγία καὶ τῷ σώματι καὶ τῷ πνεύματι.—Smyth §1516.

Ph 2: 7 σχήματι εὑρεθεὶς ὡς ἄνθρωπος (Philo Byz., s. Arnim 83); 3: 5 περιτομῇ ὀκταήμερος 'with respect to circumcision an eighth-day one' = 'circumcised on the eighth day'. Καθαρὸς τῇ καρδίᾳ Mt 5: 8, πτωχὸς τῷ πνεύματι 3. Ἐν appears to be used instead of this dative in Lk 1: 7 προβεβηκότες ἐν ταῖς ἡμέραις αὐτῶν (similarly 18, 2: 36) compared with προβεβηκὼς (ταῖς) ἡμέραις LXX, προβεβηκότας τῇ ἡλικίᾳ Lysias 24.16 etc. Προβεβηκὼς τῇ ἡλικίᾳ (ταῖς -ίαις) also Diodor. Sic. 12.18, 13.89, τοῖς ἔτεσι(ν) UPZ II 161.61 (119 BC), 162.7.29 (117 BC). LXX προβεβηκώς with (τῶν) ἡμερῶν Gen 18: 11, 24: 1, Josh 13: 1, with (ταῖς) ἡμέραις 23: 1 (2 προβέβηκα), 3 Km 1: 1; Atticistic with τὴν ἡλικίαν 2 Macc 4: 40, 6: 18 as in Ps.-Herodian in Lob. Phryn. 469; s. Pierson, Moeris p. 351. Xen., HG 6.1.5 τοὺς προεληλυθότας ἤδη ταῖς ἡλικίαις, Dit., Syll.³ 647.17 (ii BC, Phocis) τοὺς ἐνικομένους (= εἰσήκοντας) ταῖς ἀλικίαις. Cf. *iam gravis in annis* Apuleius, Metamorphoses 2.2 = *aetate provectus.*—Hermas: Humbert 131.—Dat. of measure πολλῷ s. §246. Humbert 131; C. Mohrmann, Vig. Christ. 3 (1949) 76 (Latinism). 2 C 7: 11 συνεστήσατε ἑαυτοὺς ἁγνοὺς εἶναι τῷ πράγματι is harsh; perhaps εἶναι is corrupted from ἐν (εἶναι ἐν DᵇEKLP), cf. ἁ. ἐν τῇ σαρκί 1 Clem 38.2 and on the double acc. §157(4). Τῷ μήκει ποδῶν ἑκατόν Herm Vis 4.1.6; γένει also in pap. (Mlt. 75 [116]), ἀριθμῷ πέντε οὔσας BGU II 388 III 8 (ii/iii AD). LXX dat. and acc. s. Johannessohn I 69–71; 2 Macc 5: 11 τεθηριωμένος τῇ ψυχῇ, which the Lucianic recension Atticizes into τὴν ψυχήν. The dat. is appropriate when contrast is involved either in the text or in the mind: φύσει–νόμῳ, λόγῳ μὲν–ἔργῳ δέ, Xen., Mem. 2.1.31 τοῖς σώμασιν ἀδύνατοι–ταῖς ψυχαῖς ἀνόητοι (K.-G. I 317, 19); on the other hand in An. 1.4.11 in place of (πόλις Θάψακος) ὀνόματι, ὄνομα is correctly restored from the MSS (but Σάμιος ὀνόματι Ἱππεύς HG 1.6.29 in all MSS; cf. Krüger §46, 4.3). The NT has a predilection for placing ὀνόματι first (Johannessohn, KZ 67 [1940] 69ff.).

198. The associative dative is used more loosely to designate accompanying circumstances and manner (*modi*). (1) Classical puts accompanying military forces in the dative, but the NT always uses ἐν (= Hebrew בְּ): Lk 14: 31 ἐν δέκα χιλιάσιν ὑπαντῆσαι τῷ μετὰ εἴκοσι χιλιάδων ἐρχομένῳ. (2) Ἐν ῥάβδῳ ἔλθω 1 C 4: 21 (cf. the meaning of ἐν μαχαίρῃ in pap., §195(1 a)) is similar. (3) Dative of manner: χάριτι μετέχω 'with thankfulness' 1 C 10: 30, προσευχομένη ἀκατακαλύπτῳ τῇ κεφαλῇ 11: 5; for which also μετά τινος (cf. MGr, Thumb² §162, 3, 4): ἠρνήσατο μετὰ ὅρκου Mt 26: 72; cf. 14: 7, but also ἐμεσίτευσεν ὅρκῳ H 6: 17. Ῥαπίσμασιν αὐτὸν ἔλαβον Mk 14: 65 is completely vulgar (Latinism?). (4) Dative of manner in formulaic usages: παντὶ τρόπῳ, εἴτε προφάσει εἴτε ἀληθείᾳ Ph 1: 18 (otherwise ὃν τρόπον etc. §160), but μετὰ φόβου 2 C 7: 15 etc., μετὰ βίας A 5: 26, 24: 7 (LXX Ex 1: 14; classical βίᾳ, πρὸς βίαν), μετὰ σπουδῆς Mk 6: 25, Lk 1: 39 (Thieme 25; πάσῃ σπουδῇ 2 C 8: 7) and ἐν τάχει, ἐν ἐκτενείᾳ etc. (s. §219(4)). (5) The dative ὁδῷ etc. with πορεύεσθαι, περιπατεῖν, στοιχεῖν in the NT (and LXX, Johannessohn I 57f.; also Hellenistic inscriptions and authors: Rouffiac 34) is note-

worthy, used in the NT only with figurative meaning, in the LXX also with literal meaning (cf. however Ja 2: 25 ἑτέρᾳ ὁδῷ ἐκβαλοῦσα; Lk 10: 31 B): A 14: 16 πορεύεσθαι ταῖς ὁδοῖς αὐτῶν, and then τοῖς ἔθεσιν περιπατεῖν 21: 21, πορεύεσθαι τῷ φόβῳ τοῦ κυρίου 9: 31. Classical in a different way: ἐπορεύετο τῇ ὁδῷ ἣν αὐτὸς ἐποιήσατο Thuc. 2.98.1, but figurative ἄδικον ὁδὸν ἰόντων 3.64.4. (6) The dative of the verbal substantives used with cognate verbs is a translation (imitation) of the Hebrew infinitive absolute like מוֹת יָמוּת, already employed in the LXX (Thack. 48f., Johannessohn I 56f.); analogous classical idioms like γάμῳ γαμεῖν 'in true marriage', φυγῇ φεύγειν 'in utmost haste' (K.-G. I 308; Fraenkel, WkP 1909, 177; Schwyzer II 166; later examples in Trunk 11; Wolf II 43; Ursing 41) furnished a connecting link. Ἐπιθυμίᾳ ἐπεθύμησα Lk 22: 15, παραγγελίᾳ παρηγγείλαμεν A 5: 28. If an attribute is added, the NT almost always substitutes the accusative of content (§153): χαρᾷ χαίρει Jn 3: 29, but ἐχάρησαν χαρὰν μεγάλην Mt 2: 10; on the other hand ἐξέστησαν ἐκστάσει μεγάλῃ Mk 5: 42 (ἐκστάσει ἐκστήσονται LXX Ezk 26: 16), Herm Sim 9.18.3 πονηρευομένους ποικίλαις πονηρίαις, 1.2 ἴσχυσας τῇ ἰσχύι σου. Jn 18: 32 ποίῳ θανάτῳ ἤμελλεν ἀποθνήσκειν is classical (cf. 21: 19 and Homer, Od. 11.412, Xen., Hiero 4.3) and not to be compared with θανάτῳ τελευτάτω Mt 15: 4 = Mk 7: 10 OT. (7) A 28: 11 is difficult (ἐν πλοίῳ...) παρασήμῳ Διοσκούροις: hardly 'marked by the Dioscuri' (Plut., Mor. 823 B ἐπιφθόνοις παράσημος), but either dative absolute 'with the Dioscuri as ship's insignia' (Ramsay, Luke 36f. considers this correct according to inscriptional usage) or better a mechanical declension of a registry-like (πλοῖον) παράσημον Διόσκουροι 'a ship, insignia the Dioscuri'.—Mayser II 2, 280f.; Smyth §§1513, 1526–7.

(1) Jd 14, A 7: 14, cf. LXX (Johannessohn I 58f.).
(2) Mt 16: 28, 2 C 10: 14 etc.; also εἰσέρχεσθαι ἐν αἵματι 'with blood' H 9: 25, cf. 1 Jn 5: 6. For LXX s. Johannessohn II 203f. Thus probably also Lk 23: 42 ὅταν ἔλθῃς ἐν τῇ βασιλείᾳ σου (εἰς τὴν βασιλείαν BL, correction or interchange of ἐν and εἰς acc. to §§205, 206, 218? D is different), Mt 16: 28. The type ἠμφιεσμένος ἐν (§159(1)) is established by examples like A 1: 10 παρειστήκεισαν ἐν ἐσθήσεσι λευκαῖς, Lk 24: 4, LXX 3 Macc 1: 16; cf. also Lk 4: 32 ἐν ἐξουσίᾳ ἦν ὁ λόγος αὐτοῦ, with εἶναι ἐν πορφύρᾳ 1 Macc 11: 58 (Johannessohn II 328f.).—Mk 1: 23 ἄνθρωπος ἐν πνεύματι ἀκαθάρτῳ = Lk 4: 33 ἁ. ἔχων πνεῦμα δαιμονίου ἀκαθάρτου, Mk 7: 25 𝔓⁴⁵ θυγάτριον ἐν πν. ἀκ. (§203).

(3) Herm Sim 9.20.3 γυμνοῖς ποσίν, Vis 5.1 εἰσῆλθεν ἀνὴρ σχήματι ποιμενικῷ; cf. καθεζόμενον σχήματι βασιλικῷ Callinicus, Vita S. Hypatii 97.6 (Teubner). Η 7: 21 μετὰ ὀρκωμοσίας, cf. Xen., Cyr. 2.3.12 σὺν θεῶν ὅρκω λέγω, PRev. Laws 42.17 (259/8 bc) μεθ' ὅρκου. Μετὰ φωνῆς μεγάλης Lk 17: 15, cf. μετὰ σπουδῆς καὶ κραυγῆς πολλῆς Aeschin. 2.10. Mayser II 2, 443.—Acta Joh. 90 (II 1 195.27 f. L.-B.) τί εἰ ῥαπίσμασίν με ἔλαβες; (αὐτὸν) κονδύλοις ἔλαβεν Pap. Hypothesis on Demosth. Midiana (Blass, N. Jahrb. 1892, 29, 33; c. 100 ad), verberibus accipere Cicero, Tusc. 2.34.

(4) In NT παρρησία, ἐν παρρησίᾳ and μετὰ παρρησίας. Ποίοις τρόποις Herm Man 12.3.1, ἐν παντὶ τρόπω (inferior v.l. τόπω) 2 Th 3: 16. Μετὰ βίας and the like in pap. s. Mayser II 2, 358.39ff. Μετά in LXX s. Johannessohn II 209ff.

(5) R 4: 12 στοιχεῖν τοῖς ἴχνεσιν, Cf. Homil Clem 10.15 τῷ ὑμῶν στοιχεῖτε παραδείγματι; Jd 11, περιπατεῖν κώμοις καὶ μέθαις R 13: 13, πνεύματι G 5: 16. Acc. in literal sense A 8: 39 τὴν ὁδὸν αὐτοῦ; figurative with ἐν Mt 21: 32 (ἐν ὁδῷ δικαιοσύνης), 1 P 4: 3, περιπατεῖν ἐν 2 C 4: 2 etc., περιπατεῖν κατὰ σάρκα R 8: 4.

(6) Ἐνυπνίοις ἐνυπνιάζεσθαι A 2: 17 OT, ἀπειλῇ (om. SABD al.) ἀπειλησώμεθα 4: 17; 23: 14, Ja 5: 17; ὅρκω ὤμοσεν A 2: 30, ἀναθέματι ἀνεθεματίσαμεν ἑαυτούς 23: 14, προσευχῇ προσηύξατο Ja 5: 17 (of Elijah; is there a comparable construction in the LXX?) and ἀκοῇ ἀκούειν Mt 13: 14 etc. OT are different. E. Hoffmann, Ausdrucksverstärkung 89f. (Semitism); non-Semitic parallels to an inf. used to strengthen the verb, ibid. 62–82; Havers, IF 43 (1925) 218ff. Contesting Semitism Nachmanson, Gnomon 8 (1932) 551; M.-H. 443f.; Rob. 531f. On Lk 22: 15 cf. Dalman, Worte I 21 [Words 34], Jesus-Jeschua 116 [Jesus-Jeshua 126f.]. Hermas: Humbert 131.

(7) Παράσημον subst. 'a figurehead, heraldic device on the bow' at times in the pap., also Plut.; s. M.-M., Preisigke, Bauer, e.g. PGrenf I 49.16 =Wilcken, Chr. 248.16 (220/1 ad) πλοῖον...οὗ παράσημον παντόμορφος ('Proteus'); class. likewise ἐπίσημον, s. Diels, Hermes 53 (1918) 81 n. 1; inscrip. from Cos Herzog-Klaffenbach, ABA 1952, 1, p. 20 (242 bc) ἔχον ἐπίσαμον γρῦπα; cf. p. 21 (two references). For the mechanical declension as used in commercial language, cf. Longus, Past. 2.33 ᾖσεν ἐπὶ μισθῷ τράγῳ καὶ σύριγγι 'he sang for goat and pipe as reward'.

(C) The Locative Dative

199. The dative of place, which is already extremely limited in the classical period, is missing from the NT (apart from stereotyped κύκλω and χαμαί; on πάντη and πανταχῇ s. §103; τῇ δεξιᾷ A 2: 33, 5: 31 is also local rather than instrumental). Ποίω τόπω ἀπῆλθεν Herm Vis 4.3.7 probably as a consequence of equating the dative

with εἰς (s. introduction to dative, §187); cf. ἰδίω τόπω Vett. Val. 181.22 Kroll, ἰδίω οἴκω 83.17, 18 Kroll, ἑτέρω τόπω and the like in the pap. (Mayser II 2, 295f.): e.g. PHolm 15.41 τόπω κϛ 'at point 26'.—Smyth §§1531ff.; Rob. 526f.

200. The temporal dative in answer to the question 'when?' is still quite common in the NT, in addition, of course, to the use of ἐν for clarification; the latter was already widespread in the classical language. Since the dative is used only to designate point of time, but ἐν for both point and duration of time, ἐν (τῇ) ἡμέρᾳ, ἐν (τῇ) νυκτί (Jn 11: 9, 10, A 18: 9, 1 Th 5: 2) are certainly possible for 'by day, by night' (period within which); however, without ἐν the dative is impossible. Only the genitive can be so used (§186(2)). Exceptions: τῷ θέρει Herm Sim 4.3 A (τῇ θερείᾳ PMich) 'in summer' (or instrumental?), but 5 ἐν τῷ θέρει ἐκείνω A (ἐν ἐκείνη τῇ [θερείᾳ]); ἡμέρᾳ R 13: 13 𝔓46 (the others ἐν ἡ.). (1) The simple dative, however, is appropriate to designate a specific day or night as well as the phrase with ἐν. Thus always τῇ τρίτῃ ἡμέρᾳ Mt 16: 21 (D is different), 17: 23 (likewise), Lk 9: 22 (likewise), 24: 7, 46, A 10: 40; but ἐν τῇ ἐσχάτη ἡμέρᾳ Jn 7: 37, 11: 24 besides τ. ἐ. ἡ. 12: 48 (6: 39, 40, 44, 54 vacillate). Ἡμέρᾳ καὶ ἡμέρᾳ 'every day' (יוֹם וָיוֹם) 2 C 4: 16, Protev Ja 12.3 (=καθ' ἑκάστην ἡμέραν [the correct Greek equivalent] H 3: 13) is a Hebraism. (2) Φυλακή 'night watch' and ὥρα are used like ἡμέρα. (3) The dative is still employed as in Attic with the names of festivals: Mk 6: 21 (ἐν 𝔓45) τοῖς γενεσίοις (γενεθλίοις D) αὐτοῦ; often τοῖς σάββασιν 'on the sabbath' Mt 12: 1 etc. (4) Other instances are infrequent: ἑτέραις γενεαῖς E 3: 5, ἰδίᾳ γενεᾷ A 13: 36, with ἐν 14: 16; καιροῖς ἰδίοις 1 T 6: 15.—Mayser II 2, 296f.; Smyth §§1539ff.; Rob. 522f., 527.

(1) With τῇ ἡμέρᾳ ἐκείνη or ταύτη, ἐν is usually prefixed except at Jn 20: 19; νυκτί without ἐν: Lk 12: 20, 17: 34, A 12: 6, 27: 23. Always dat.: τῇ ἐπιούσῃ (ἐχομένη) ἡμ. (νυκτί), but only A (7: 26, 21: 26, etc.); likewise τῇ ἐπιφωσκούσῃ Mt 28: 1 and usually τῇ ἑξῆς (A 21: 1 etc., with ἐν only Lk 7: 11 [om. ἐν D, strong v.l. ἐν τῷ ἑξῆς], vacillating 9: 37). Ἡμέρᾳ Mk 14: 12, A 7: 8 (τῇ ὀγδόη, with ἐν Lk 1: 59, yet DL without ἐν), A 12: 21, Mt 24: 42 (v.l. ὥρᾳ); ᾗ ἡμ. Lk 17: 29, 30 (30 D is different); τῇ ἡμ. τοῦ σαββάτου (τῶν -των) Lk 13: 14, 16, A 13: 14, 16: 13 (cf. τοῖς σάββασιν under (3)), with ἐν Lk 4: 16, vacillating 14: 5; (τῇ) μιᾷ τῶν σαββάτων Mk 16: 2 (ACE al. τῆς μιᾶς, D μιᾶς, which can be explained as partitive), Jn 20: 1, 19, with ἐν A 20: 7; πρώτη σαββάτου Mk 16: 9.

(2) Φυλακῇ Mt 14: 25 (-κῆς D), Lk 12: 38 D (elsewhere in the same verse even D has ἐν), Mt 24: 43. Ὥρᾳ Mt 24: 44, Lk 12: 39, 1: 10, Mk 15: 34; αὐτῇ τῇ ὥρᾳ Lk 2: 38 etc. (αὐτῇ τῇ νυκτί Herm Vis 3.1.2; 10: 7) besides ἐν 12: 12 etc.; ἐν with ἐκείνῃ τῇ ὥρᾳ Mt 26: 55 etc. (v.l. Jn 4: 53); μιᾷ ὥρᾳ Rev 18: 10, 16, 19; cf. § 161(3) for a competing use of the acc. Ἔτει with ἐν only Lk 3: 1; Jn 2: 20 τεσσεράκοντα ἔτεσιν ᾠκοδομήθη (but cf. also ἐν τρισὶν ἡμέραις 19 [om. ἐν B], 20 [om. ἐν S]) in answer to the question 'in how long a time?', is different; here ἐν is customary in class. (ἐν τρ. ἡμ. also Mt 27: 40, διὰ τριῶν ἡμ. 26: 61, Mk 14: 58).

(3) Ἐν τοῖς σάββασιν Lk 4: 31 etc.; τῷ σαββάτῳ Lk 6: 9, σαββάτῳ Mt 24: 40 (ἐν σ. EF al.; D σαββάτου, § 186(2)), Jn 5: 16 D, 7: 22 B (al. ἐν σ., as all MSS have twice in 23), τῷ ἐχομένῳ σ. A 13: 44; ἐν ἑτέρῳ σ. Lk 6: 6 (v. l ἐν σ. δευτεροπρώτῳ?); κατὰ πᾶν σάββατον A 13: 27 etc. Τῇ ἑορτῇ τοῦ πάσχα Lk 2: 41 (with ἐν D), otherwise ἐν τῇ ἑ. (κατὰ ἑορτήν 'at each feast' Mt 27: 15 etc.). Γενεσίοις BGU I 1.9, 24 (iii AD), cf. Mlt. 75 [116]; (τοῖς) γενεθλίοις ZenP Cairo III 59332.1 (248 BC), BGU I 149.15 (ii/iii AD), POxy I 112.4 (iii/iv AD), τῇ γενεθλίᾳ μου III 494.24 (156 AD); but ἐν τοῖς γενεθλίοις Xen., Cyr. 1.3.10, PSI IV 347.5, 11 (255 BC).—Mt 14: 6 γενεσίοις δὲ γενομένοις SBDL al., -σίων δὲ -μένων CK (cf. Mk 6: 2, 21; -σίων δὲ ἀγομένων EGW al.); the dat., if correct, would be a mixture of the ptcp. absolute and the temporal dat., the responsibility for which probably rests with copyists who were interpolating from Mk.

(4) Τῇ θλίψει ὑπομένοντες R 12: 12 is suspect, s. § 196. E 2: 12 τῷ καιρῷ ἐκείνῳ 𝔓⁴⁶ (second hand) SABD*FG, with ἐν 𝔓⁴⁶ (first hand) DᶜEKLP. Ἐκείνοις τοῖς χρόνοις [Dem.] 21.93. R. Koch, Observ. gramm. in decreta...(Diss. Münster, 1909) 24f.

201. The temporal dative in answer to the question 'how long?' is used instead of the accusative, contrary to classical usage. Its position is secure, however, only with transitive verbs along with scattered examples with the passive, while the accusative is retained with intransitives: Lk 8: 29 πολλοῖς χρόνοις συνηρπάκει αὐτόν, R 16: 25 χρόνοις αἰωνίοις σεσιγημένου (but ἀπεδήμησεν χρόνους ἱκανούς Lk 20: 9 and correspondingly elsewhere with intransitives). Homil Clem 13.5.5 τοσούτοις ἔτεσιν ἀφανής ἐστιν 'he disappeared so many years ago'. Cf. frequent ἐρρῶσθαί σε εὔχομαι πολλοῖς χρόνοις in the papyri, τετραετεῖ ἤδη χρόνῳ (cf. PFay 106.13 [140 AD])... ἐπιτηροῦντος PAmh I 77.7 (139 AD) and the like (Mlt. 75 [116]; Deissmann, LO⁴ 185 [LAE 218]). Examples from Hellenistic inscriptions, papyri and authors may be found in Schulze, Graeca Latina 14; Schmid III 56, IV 615f.; Hauser 140; Jannaris § 1394; Trunk 24; Schekira 147. Schmidt

382 f. finds no difference in Josephus between the dative and the accusative of the duration of time. The rationale for the dative seems to be that the accusative case was felt to be primarily the object, and hence there was some reluctance to put a second accusative alongside the direct object. The Latin temporal ablative (*vixit annis...* 'lived...years') might have helped to establish this construction (cf. Hering 38ff.).—Rob. 527f.

A 13: 20 ὡς ἔτεσιν τετρακοσίοις καὶ πεντήκοντα ἔδωκεν κριτάς 'for 450 years' (acc. 18, 21, s. *infra*, τοσούτοις ἔτεσιν Homil Clem 13.5, 15.4); the passage is badly corrupted in most MSS in that the temporal phrase is taken with the preceding clause in which a trans. verb also appears.—The acc., however, is used also with the pass. (Rev. 20: 3), and with transitives: Mk 2: 19 ὅσον χρόνον, A 13: 18 ὡς τεσσερακονταετῆ χρόνον, 21, Lk 13: 8. Textual variations: Lk 8: 27 χρόνῳ ἱκανῷ or ἐκ (ἀπὸ) χρόνων ἱκανῶν (οὐκ ἐνεδύσατο ἱμάτιον); 1: 75 λατρεύειν αὐτῷ...πάσαις ταῖς ἡμέραις (ἡμῶν) B pc. (πάσας τὰς ἡμέρας ℌℜDΘ pl.); Jn 14: 9 τοσούτῳ χρόνῳ SDLQW or τοσοῦτον χρόνον AB al. (μεθ' ὑμῶν εἰμι.); A 28: 12 ἡμέραι τρεῖς (§ 144), ἡμέραις τρισίν (B), ἡμέρας τρεῖς (Δ 1 69), ἡμέραι τρεῖς εἰσιν ἀπὸ πότε ὧδέ εἰσιν (D lat).—Ἐρρῶσθαί σε εὔχομαι πολλοῖς χρόνοις (ἔτεσιν) (acc. to Humbert 96 'for many years' not 'during many years') in pap. only in iii/iv AD (Ziemann, De epistularum Graec. formulis sollemnibus [Diss. phil. Hal. XVII 4, 1910] 342; Exler, The Form of the Ancient Greek Letter [Diss. Washington, 1923] 76). Χρόνος in late and MGr means 'year' (so also Lk 8: 29?).—Hippoc., Epid. 4 (5.148 Littré) μετὰ δὲ ὀλίγον νότια ἦν ἐφ' ἡμέρας πεντεκαίδεκα, μετὰ δὲ ταῦτα νιφετὸς τεσσαρεσκαίδεκα ἡμέρῃσιν.

(D) The Dative with Compound Verbs and Their Derivatives

202. The dative with compounds is very common; it may be supplemented, moreover, by a preposition. The division between the two is often that the older constructions with the dative are reserved for the figurative meaning, while the more recent with prepositions are used to denote the literal meaning. With ἀνα- only ἀνατίθεσθαί (προσανατίθ.) τινι 'to lay before someone for consideration' A 25: 14 etc. The dative dominates with ἀντι-. Compounds with εἰσ- nearly always take prepositions, those with ἐν- either prepositions only or dative only. Ἐπι- varies; παρα- nearly always dative. The dative predominates with περι-, likewise with προσ-; συν- with dative (seldom with μετά or πρός), ὑπο- nearly always dative. The dative is mostly local, with συν-associative. But many compounds were subsequently associated with simple forms which take the dative proper, e.g. προσφωνεῖν τινι with λέγειν τινί.—Once a compound verbal substantive (cf. §194(2)) is used with the dative: 2 C 11: 28 ἡ ἐπίστασίς μοι ἡ καθ' ἡμέραν 𝔓46 S*BFG, but ScD al. with μου are perhaps more correct (*in me* Lat.); cf. however ἐπανάστασις with the dative in Plato (K.-G. ɪ 426).—Helb., Kas. 268–319, 220 (ἀνατίθεσθαι); Mayser ɪɪ 2, 285ff.; Smyth §§1544ff.; Rob. 542f.

'Αντι-: ἀνθιστάναι, ἀντιλέγειν, ἀντικεῖσθαι, ἀντιπίπτειν etc.; seldom πρός τινα, e.g. ἀνταγωνίζεσθαι H 12: 4.

Εἰσ-: εἰσέρχεσθαι εἰς etc.; for which ἐν (§218) Lk 9: 46 εἰσῆλθεν διαλογισμὸς ἐν αὐτοῖς (minusc. 700 without ἐν).

'Εν-: always with prep. in literal sense: ἐμβαίνειν, -βιβάζειν, -βάλλειν, -βάπτειν, -πίπτειν; always dat. in metaphorical sense: ἐγκαλεῖν (§187(5)), ἐμμαίνεσθαι (A 26: 11), ἐμπαίζειν, ἐνέχειν, ἐντυγχάνειν 'appeal, petition', cf. LXX Wsd 8: 21 etc., BGU ɪ 246.12 (ii/iii AD) νυκτὸς καὶ ἡμέρας ἐντυγχάνω τῷ θεῷ ὑπὲρ ὑμῶν (Helb., Kas. 142; with πρός Herm Sim 2.8). But also ἐμβλέπειν τινί (person) = βλ. εἴς τινα, ἐγκρίνειν (2 C 10: 12) = κρίνειν ἔν τισιν. Varying: ἐγκεντρίζειν R 11: 24 εἰς καλλιέλαιον, τῇ ἰδίᾳ ἐλαίᾳ; ἐμμένειν dat. A 14: 22, G 3: 10 OT 𝔓46S*B (al. and LXX with ἐν), with ἐν H 8: 9 OT, Herm both; ἐμπτύειν. Παρενοχλεῖν A 15: 19 with dat. (Hell. more often acc.; Mayser ɪɪ 2, 299f.).

'Επι-: ἐπιβάλλειν ἐπὶ ἱματίῳ (-ιον) Mt 9: 16, Lk 5: 36; ἐπιβάλλειν τὰς χεῖρας ἐπί, only A 4: 3 dat. (D is different). Ἐπιτιθέναι τὴν χεῖρά τινι and ἐπί τινα; otherwise the prep. preponderates with this verb in the literal sense, as in ἐπὶ τοὺς ὤμους Mt 23: 4 (Jn 19: 2 τῇ κεφαλῇ, A ἐπὶ τὴν κεφαλήν; Lk 23: 26 αὐτῷ τὸν σταυρόν), the dat. in the figurative sense: thus ὄνομα Mk 3: 16, 17 (cf. ἐπικαλεῖν τινι ὄνομα Mt 10: 25 B*, Buttmann 132; class. and LXX καλεῖν τινι ὄν. s. Helb., Kas. 51; Katz, Philo's Bible 52f.), βάρος A 15: 28, πληγάς 16: 23; ἐπιτίθεσθαι 'attack' 18: 10, 'to provision' 28: 10 (sy adds *in navi*). Rev 22: 18 ἐάν τις ἐπιθῇ ἐπ' αὐτά ('adds'), ἐπιθήσει ὁ θεὸς ἐπ' αὐτὸν τὰς πληγάς. Ἐφίστασθαι dat. and ἐπί; ἐπέρχεσθαι ἐπί, dat. Lk 21: 26; ἐπιπίπτειν mostly ἐπί, with dat. Mk 3: 10, A 20: 10 (in literal sense) etc. Ἐπισκιάζειν with dat. and acc.

Παρα-: παρατιθέναι τινί 'place before', παρατίθεσθαί τινι 'commend'; παρεδρεύειν (v.l. προσ-) τῷ θυσιαστηρίῳ (figurative) 1 C 9: 13 and accordingly τὸ εὐπάρεδρον (v.l. εὐπρόσ-) τῷ κυρίῳ 7: 35 (more peculiar because the adj. is used instead of the subst.). Also with dat. παρέχειν, παριστάναι, παρίστασθαι (also in a literal sense like A 1: 10, 9: 39); παρεῖναι usually prep. (πρὸς ὑμᾶς 2 C 11: 8), dat. in

metaphorical sense 2 P 1: 9 (8 acc. to A); παραμένειν τινί (Dc al. συμπ.) Ph 1: 25 and accordingly παράμονός τινι (thing); Herm Sim 9.23.3.

Περι-: -τιθέναι dat., -βάλλειν Lk 19: 43 (figurative with τινά τι s. §155(5)); -κείμενον ἡμῖν νέφος μαρτύρων H 12: 1, in literal sense περὶ τὸν τράχηλον Mk 9: 42, Lk 17: 2, -πίπτειν εἰς τόπον A 27: 41, but λῃσταῖς Lk 10: 30, πειρασμοῖς Ja 1: 2; -πείρειν ἑαυτὸν ὀδύναις 1 T 6: 10 (τινὰ κακοῖς Philo, Flacc. 1 [6.120.7 Cohn-Wendland]; literally 'to pierce oneself with many pangs', cf. e.g. κεφαλὴ περιπεπαρμένη δόρατι Plut., C. Gracch. 17).

Προσ-: -τιθέναι ἐπί τι in literal sense Mt 6: 27, Lk 12: 25, ἐπί τινι 'to add to' Lk 3: 20 ('to the congregation' A 2: 47 τῇ ἐκκλησίᾳ EP, ἐν τῇ ἐ. D, al. absolutely like 41, 5: 14; 11: 24 in the same sense τῷ κυρίῳ, which, however, B* probably correctly omits; 'to be gathered to one's fathers' with πρός 13: 36), but the person for whom in the dat. Mt 6: 33 etc., H 12: 19. -έρχεσθαι always takes the dat. of person, also θρόνῳ, ὄρει H 4: 16, 12: 18, 22. Furthermore, with dat. προσέχειν (e.g. ἑαυτῷ), προσκαρτερεῖν, προσκλίνεσθαι (figurative); also in literal sense προσπίπτειν Mt 7: 25 (Lachmann's προσέπαισαν for -πεσαν is not certain, cf. ὑψηλὸν ἐς Δίκας βάθρον προσέπεσες Soph., Ant. 854f. and Buttmann 34f.) etc. (only Mk 7: 25 πρὸς τοὺς πόδας αὐτοῦ) and προσφέρειν (with πρός H 5: 7 precisely in a nonliteral sense). Προσκυλίειν λίθον τῇ θύρᾳ Mt 27: 60 (with ἐπί A, thus all MSS ἐπὶ τὴν θ. Mk 15: 46). Προσφωνεῖν τινι Mk 11: 16, Lk 7: 32, A 22: 2 (without αὐτοῖς D), trans. τινα 'to call here' Lk 6: 13 (D ἐφώνησεν), A 11: 2 D, Lk 23: 20 D (SB αὐτοῖς, absolutely A al.). Προσβλέπειν τινί Gospel frag. POxy v 840.29, τινά IEph 6.1.

Συν-: e.g. συγκαθῆσθαί τινι A 26: 30 (μετά Mk 14: 54, however D καθήμενος), -κακοπαθεῖν 2 T 1: 8, -κακουχεῖσθαι H 11: 25, -κατατίθεσθαι Lk 23: 51, συν-αναβαίνειν Mk 15: 41, A 13: 31 (μετά Herm Sim 9.16.7; cf. LXX, Johannessohn ɪ 64f.), -αντιλαμβάνεσθαι R 8: 26 (v.l. gen., §170(3)), Lk 10: 40 (συνλ. 𝔓45; D ἀντιλ. with gen.), etc. Οὐκ ὠφέλησεν ὁ λόγος ἐκείνους μὴ συγκεκερασμένους τῇ πίστει (instr.) τοῖς ἀκούσασιν (thus S; many variants) H 4: 2. With prep.: συλλαλεῖν μετά Mt 17: 3, A 25: 12 (dat. Mk 9: 4 etc.), πρὸς ἀλλήλους Lk 4: 36; συμφωνεῖν μετά Mt 20: 2 (dat. 13 etc.; peculiar συνεφωνήθη ὑμῖν *convenit inter vos* A 5: 9; this pass. is used with τινί and various prep. in the pap. [Preisigke s.v. 2]; with ὥστε and inf. Preisigke, Sammelbuch 6000.7 [vi AD] like A 5: 9 with inf.). Συνέρχεσθαί τινι 'to accompany somebody' is not classical A 1: 21 etc. (BGU ɪɪ 596.4 [84 AD]); Homil Clem 5.30.1 συνῆλθόν μοι 'they accompanied me'; s. Bauer s.v. 2.

'Υπο-: -τάσσειν with dat., not dative only in the quotation ὑπὸ τοὺς πόδας or ὑποκάτω τῶν ποδῶν 1 C 15: 27, H 2: 8; -τίθεσθαι 1 T 4: 6 'enjoin'; ὑπάρχειν, ὑπακούειν.

5. SYNTAX OF PREPOSITIONS

(1) INTRODUCTION

203. The NT has in general retained the old proper prepositions. On the one hand, however, ἀμφί and ὡς have been dropped (as in Arist., LXX and pap.: Schmidt 393; Rossberg 11; Regard, Prép. 683f.; Mayser II 2, 338), ἀνά and ἀντί have been greatly reduced; and, on the other, the use of prepositions like ἐν, εἰς, ἐκ has been much more widely extended. The dative is in the process of waning with all prepositions except ἐν (cf. introduction to the dative case preceding §187) and has disappeared entirely with μετά, περί, ὑπό, ἀνά, in which a development already present in the classical language is brought to a close. The improper prepositions, moreover, have begun to gain ground, i.e. adverbs or nouns in various cases which attained the character of prepositions only at a later period, but which from now on are never or hardly ever used without their case (gen.) like the proper prepositions. The line of demarcation between adverb and preposition is naturally difficult to draw (cf. §§184 and 214–16). The combination of preposition with adverb is common in the NT (Schmid IV 625; Hatzid. 213; Mlt. 99f. [159]; also MGr, Thumb² §158); in the NT for example, ἀπὸ τότε (quite vulgar Mk 8: 2 D ἀπὸ πότε for ἀφ' οὖ; §201), Herm ἀφ' ὅτε §241(2), ἀπὸ πέρυσι, ἐφάπαξ etc. (cf. also §§12 and 216(3)); μέχρι ὅτε §455(3).

In the LXX the dat. is used with περί only four times, with ὑπό only Job 12: 5 v.l. (Abel 227 n., 233).—The original adverbial meaning of the 'prepositions' (K.-G. I 526f.: Homer, Ion., less often in Attic prose) is weakly represented in Hellenistic: NT only ὑπέρ for certain (§230), ἐν is improbable (Mk 1: 23 ἐν πνεύματι ἀκαθάρτῳ [§§198(2); 219(4)] acc. to Lagercrantz, Glotta 21 [1933] 11 'with an unclean spirit in *him*' [opposed by G. Björck, Con. Neot. 7 (1942) 1ff.]. Ph 3: 13 ἐν δέ 'and thereby' Fridrichsen, Symb. Osl. 13 [1934] 38ff. instead of ἐν δέ [s. §481]); Ptol. pap. παρά only once (Mayser II 2, 339), ἐπὶ δέ 'moreover' in a pap., in Arrian etc. (Radermacher, RhM 57 [1902] 150), ἐξ καὶ πρός '6 and more' POxy I 68.24 (131 AD). LXX Greek has nothing comparable, but Aquila-like SSol 1: 16 has adverbial πρός 'moreover' = אַף; Aqu. Dt 33: 3 the same. Aqu. Eccl 1: 17, 7: 23 (22) πρός = גַּם. Classical usage requires a supporting particle such as is found in Symm. Eccl 9: 2 πρός τε = גַּם. These late translators take to classical modes of speech where these are closer to the Hebr. (Katz, ZAW 69 [1957] 83f.).

Literature: Schwyzer II 417f.; P. F. Regard, Contribution à l'étude des prépositions dans la langue du NT (Paris, 1919) 695 pp.; pp. 325–76 La réduction du datif et les faits qui s'y rattachent); Johannessohn II; Mayser II 2, 337–543.

(2) PREPOSITIONS WITH ONE CASE

(A) With Accusative

204. Ἀνά, which appears infrequently already in Attic prose, is retained only in ἀνὰ μέσον (w. gen.) 'between' Mt 13: 25 etc., and ἀνὰ μέρος 'in turn' 1 C 14: 27 (Polyb.) and distributive = 'each, apiece': ἔλαβον ἀνὰ δηνάριον Mt 20: 9 etc. (fixed as an adverb Rev 21: 21 ἀνὰ εἷς ἕκαστος τῶν πυλώνων, s. §§248(1) and 305).—Mayser II 2, 401ff.

Ἀνὰ μέσον Hell. in general: Schmid IV 626; Jannaris §1498; Nägeli 30; Rossberg 34; Raderm.² 138; Johannessohn II 170ff.; E. Lohmeyer, Diatheke (Leipzig, 1913) 86 n. 1. MGr ἀνάμεσα; ἀνὰ μέσον· ἀντὶ τοῦ ἐν μέσῳ (§215(3)), Ἀντιφάνης Ἀδώνιδι Antiatt., Bekker (Anec. Gr. I 80.24).—Distributive: ἀνὰ πτέρυγας ἓξ Rev 4: 8; ἀνὰ ἑκατὸν καὶ ἀνὰ πεντήκοντα Mk 6: 40 AL al. (as in Lk 9: 14 all witnesses), but SBD have the equivalent κατά (W ἄνδρες for ἀνά; the whole is missing in 𝔓⁴⁵). Hell. examples in K.-G. I 474; Raderm.² 20; Schmid *ibid.*—S. Bauer s.v. for special bibliography; s. also §139.

205. Εἰς instead of ἐν in a local sense. In MGr εἰς has absorbed the related preposition ἐν (in conjunction with the disappearance of the dative); in the NT ἐν appears almost twice as frequently as εἰς, but the confusion of the two has begun in that εἰς often appears for ἐν (ἐν for εἰς more rarely, §218). Cf. Hatzid. 210f.; Regard, Prép. 330–49. No NT writer except Mt is entirely free from the replacement of ἐν by εἰς in a local sense, not even Lk in Acts where most of the examples are found (Jn has the fewest); Mk 1: 9 ἐβαπτίσθη εἰς τὸν Ἰορδάνην (cf. Homil Clem 11. 36.2 εἰς τὰς...πηγάς; ἐν Mk 1: 5, Mt 3: 6), Lk 11: 7 εἰς τὴν κοίτην εἰσίν (ἐν D), A 8: 40 εὑρέθη εἰς Ἄζωτον, Jn 1: 18 ὁ ὢν εἰς τὸν κόλπον (ἐκ τοῦ -ου syᶜ) τοῦ πατρός. The Epistles and, still more surprisingly, Rev exhibit a correct differentiation between εἰς and ἐν in the local sense except 1 P 5:

12 (postscript in the author's own hand) τὴν χάριν... εἰς ἣν ἑστήκατε (KLP; στῆτε 'stand fast in it' found in the other MSS would suit εἰς, but according to the sense is very unlikely). For 1 Jn 5: 8 s. *infra*. Εἰς for ἐν is frequent in Hermas (Humbert 74–6): Vis 1.2.2 ἔχουσα βιβλίον εἰς τὰς χεῖρας, 2.4.3, Sim 1.2 etc.; s. also 2 Clem 8.2 (19.4?), Homil Clem 12.10. This εἰς appears therefore to have been still a provincialism at the time; however, the fact that some authors do not share the confusion is also surprising. Examples from the LXX, Diodor. etc. in Jannaris § 1548; Vogeser 26 ff.; Johannessohn II 331 f.; Mayser II 2, 373; Humbert *passim*; Oepke, TW II 418f. n.

Mk 1: 39 κηρύσσων εἰς τὰς συναγωγάς (ἐν ταῖς συναγωγαῖς EF al.), 2: 1 εἰς οἶκόν ἐστιν AC al. (ἐν οἴκῳ SBDL), 10: 10 (ἐν AC al.), 13: 3 καθημένου εἰς τὸ ὄρος (cf. Herm Sim 5.1.1; Musonius 43.18 Hense καθῆσθαι εἰς Σινώπην; correctly class. καθίζειν εἰς 2 Th 2: 4), 13: 9 εἰς συναγωγὰς δαρήσεσθε (= Mt 10: 17 ἐν ταῖς συναγωγαῖς [D εἰς τὰς σ.] αὐτῶν μαστιγώσουσιν ὑμᾶς), 13: 16 ὁ εἰς τὸν ἀγρόν (ἐν Mt 24: 18, Lk 17: 31). —Lk 4: 23 γενόμενα ('happened') εἰς τὴν (SB, εἰς DL, ἐν τῇ al.) Καφαρναούμ, 9: 61, 21: 37? A 2: 5 εἰς Ἱερ. κατοικοῦντες (ἐν SᶜBCDE; like class. H 11: 9 παρῴκησεν εἰς γῆν, Mt 2: 23, 4: 13; cf. Thuc. 2.102.6 κατοικισθεὶς ἐς τοὺς... τόπους), 2: 27 OT (cf. 31) ἐγκαταλείψεις τὴν ψυχήν μου εἰς ᾅδην, 39 τοῖς εἰς μακράν (class. τοῖς μακρὰν [scil. ὁδόν] ἀποικοῦσιν), 7: 4, 12, 8: (20,) 23 (v.l.), 9: 21 (ἐν all witnesses but SA), 11: 25 D, 14: 25 (ἐν BCD), 17: 13 D, 18: 21 D, 19: 22 (ἐν D), 21: 23, 23: 11 twice, 25: 4, 26: 20. The following are also unclass.: Lk 1: 44 ἐγένετο ἡ φωνὴ εἰς τὰ ὦτά μου and γενέσθαι εἰς Ἱερ. A 20: 16, 21: 17, 25: 15 (ἐν correctly 13: 5). Homil Clem 12.10.2 εἰς Ῥώμην καταλείψας, 25.1 γενομένων ἡμῶν 'since we had arrived (there)'.—Jn 17: 23 ἵνα ὦσιν τετελειωμένοι εἰς (τὸ) ἕν in which εἰς denotes rather the purpose, the result; 1 Jn 5: 8 οἱ τρεῖς εἰς τὸ ἕν εἰσιν belongs in § 145(1). Kilpatrick (by letter): A 4: 5 συναχθῆναι... εἰς (S, ἐν al.) Ἰ. 'in Jerusalem'; 12: 25 εἰς (BSℜ) Ἱερ. is to be taken with πληρώσαντες τὴν διακονίαν (conjecture of Wescott-Hort; also K. Grobel by letter): 'after they had delivered the relief offering in Jerusalem' (Debrunner prefers 'after they had [brought the relief offering] to Jerusalem and delivered it [there]; cf. R 15: 31 ἡ διακονία ἡ εἰς Ἰ. For a discussion of the literary problems involved here, s. Funk, JBL 75 (1956) 130–6; Dupont, NT 1 (1956) 275–303. —The corresponding class. usage is ἔστη εἰς τὸ μέσον Jn 20: 19, 26 (Xen., Cyr. 4. 1. 1); cf. 21: 4 (v.l. ἐπί). With ὕπαγε νίψαι εἰς τὴν κολυμβήθραν 9: 7 cf. ἵν' αὐτὸ λούσῃ εἰς σκάφην Epict. 3.22.71, yet νίψαι appears to be spurious (Lachmann; on A al., cf. 11). 1 P 3: 20 εἰς ἣν (κιβωτὸν) ὀλίγοι διεσώθησαν 'within which a few were saved'; cf. 2 T 4: 18 (LXX Gen 19: 19).—

Εἰς for ἐν is encountered also in the LXX (s. *supra*), on Egyptian private documents, e.g. PTebt I 38.14 (113 BC) εἰς ὃν ἐνοικεῖ... οἶκον, BGU II 385.5 (ii/iii AD) (ε)ἰς Ἀλεξάνδρειαν ἐσσι (= ἐστι? or εἶσι??), 423.7 (ii AD) κινδυνεύσαντος εἰς θάλασσαν, Epigr. Kaibel 134 (Imperial period) εἰς τύνβον κεῖμαι.—Cf. Bauer s.v. 1 d β, 9.

206. Interchange of εἰς and ἐν in a metaphorical sense. (1) Temporal: Lk 1: 20 πληρωθήσονται εἰς τὸν καιρὸν αὐτῶν, but correct with ἐν Mt 21: 41, 2 Th 2: 6. Instrumental: A 7: 53 ἐλάβετε τὸν νόμον εἰς διαταγὰς ἀγγέλων = ἐν διαταγαῖς (cf. Mt 9: 34 *et al.*). Similarly the Hebrew לֵךְ לְשָׁלוֹם is rendered in Mk 5: 34 and Lk 7: 50, 8: 48 by ὕπαγε (πορεύου) εἰς εἰρήνην (so also the LXX, 1 Km 1: 17 etc.), and in Ja 2: 16 by ὑπάγετε ἐν εἰρήνῃ (as D does in both references in Lk; Judg 18: 6 B); the notion behind ἐν was probably the loose associative dative (§ 198(2)). (2) The variation is understandable where a Hebrew בְּ is translated, to which the dative would correspond in classical Greek: thus with πιστεύειν, ὀμνύναι, εὐδοκεῖν and especially with the rendering of Hebrew בְּשֵׁם. (3) 'To do something to someone' is expressed by ποιεῖν (ἐργάζεσθαί) τι ἔν τινι, εἴς τινα, τινι (Attic τινα); s. § 157(1). (4) With verbs of preaching, etc. both εἰς and ἐν are permissible also in Attic if the message is directed to several (εἰπεῖν εἰς τὸν δῆμον, ἐν τῷ δήμῳ); so also the NT κηρύσσειν εἰς Mk 13: 10 (ἐν D), Lk 24: 47, 1 Th 2: 9 (ὑμῖν S*), and ἐν 2 C 1: 19, G 2: 2, εὐαγγελίζεσθαι εἰς 1 P 1: 25, ἐν G 1: 16.

(1) Lk 13: 9 κἂν ποιήσῃ καρπὸν εἰς τὸ μέλλον has class. pars., e.g. ἐς ὕστερον Hdt. 5. 74; also class. are A 13: 42 εἰς τὸ μεταξὺ σάββατον, 2 C 13: 2 εἰς τὸ πάλιν (cf. class. εἰσαῦθις). The temporal use of εἰς elsewhere accords fully with class. usage.

(2) For πιστεύειν (εἰς, ἐν, ἐπί, dat.) s. § 187(6); also for πεποιθέναι and ἐλπίζειν. Corresponding πίστις: ἡ ἐν Χρ. and ἡ εἰς Χρ. besides obj. gen. Θαρρῶ ἐν 'have confidence in' 2 C 7: 16, but εἰς 10: 1 = θρασύς εἰμι, 'towards you'. Ὀμνύναι Mt 5: 35 with ἐν and εἰς side by side (class. acc., § 149). Εὐδοκεῖν 'be well pleased' often with ἐν; with εἰς Mt 12: 18 OT (only ὃν S*B, ἐν ᾧ D), 2 P 1: 17. Διστάζειν εἰς τὸν θεόν Herm Man 9.5 = οὐ πιστεύειν.—Τῷ σῷ ὀνόματι (instr. dat.) is good Greek Mt 7: 22 (12: 21, s. § 187(6)), Mk 9: 38 AX al. (otherwise ἐν), Ja 5: 10 AKL (otherwise ἐν); cf. τῷ τῆς πόλεως ὀνόματι in an inscrip. from Asia Minor of 37 AD (Deissmann, NBS 26 [BS 198]). Εἰς τὸ ὄνομά τινος 'on somebody's account' is generally vulgar Hell. (Deissmann, LO⁴ 97f. [LAE 121 f.]; Rossberg 33, Mayser II 2, 415), but in the NT, if at all in this sense, only εἰς ὄνομα προφήτου etc. Mt 10: 41 f., εἰς τὸ ἐμὸν

ὄνομα 18: 20, (28: 19,) with which the Hebraism ἐν ὀνόματι κυρίου Mt 21: 9 has fused (LXX always ἐν ὀν. for בְּשֵׁם Psichari 202f.; Corssen, WkP 1919, 167f.). Once ἐπὶ τῷ ὀνόματί μου Mt 18: 5. With βαπτίζειν, εἰς τὸ ὄν. (A 8: 16, 19: 8) may be used as well as ἐν τῷ ὀν. (10: 48; 2: 38 ἐν or ἐπί). On the whole subject cf. also Witkowski, Bericht 74f.; Bietenhard, TW s.v. ὄνομα.

(3) Ποιεῖν (τὸ) ἔλεος μετά (Hebr. עַם) τινος Lk 1: 72, 10: 37 (§ 227(3)) besides ποιεῖν ἐλεημοσύνας εἰς A 24: 17. To express the destination or use ('for') εἰς is good class. (δαπανᾶν εἰς), thus e.g. Mk 8: 19, 20 and λογεία, διακονία εἰς τοὺς ἁγίους 1 C 16: 1, 2 C 8: 4 etc.

(4) Mk 14: 9 ὅπου ἐὰν κηρυχθῇ τὸ εὐαγγέλιον εἰς ὅλον τὸν κόσμον, λαληθήσεται...could be a case of εἰς for ἐν.

207. Other usages of εἰς. For εἰς in place of a predicate nominative s. § 145, in place of a predicate accusative § 157(5). But in G 3: 14 ἵνα εἰς τὰ ἔθνη ἡ εὐλογία τοῦ Ἀβραὰμ γένηται the simple case would be the dative (§ 189) or, more in accordance with classical usage, the genitive (yet rather 'in order that...might come among the Gentiles'); cf. A 24: 17, R 8: 18, Herm Sim 8.3.2 and ἐγγίζειν εἰς instead of τινί § 193(2). In MGr εἰς is the periphrasis for the missing dative. With γίνεσθαι εἰς cf. ἐλήλυθεν εἴς τινα 'to come to somebody (as a possession)' in two papyri (Mayser II 2, 406). (1) Εἰς is also used for ἐπί and πρός: Jn 4: 5 ἔρχεται εἰς πόλιν 'come to', not 'into', Mt 12: 41 μετενόησαν εἰς τὸ κήρυγμα Ἰωνᾶ (cf. Hdt. 3.52 πρὸς τοῦτο τὸ κήρυγμα 'at[; because of', s. Bauer s.v. 6 a]). Causal εἰς: J. R. Mantey, JBL 70 (1951) 45-8, 309-12; R. Marcus, op. cit. 129f.; 71 (1952) 43f. (2) With numbers εἰς is distributive = '-fold': Mk 4: 8 εἰς τριάκοντα etc. (v.l. ἕν; W τὸ ἕν [likewise 20 three times] or ἐν; s. §§ 248(3), 220(2)). (3) Εἰς τέλος 'fully'; εἰς κενόν 'in vain' Paul (classical διὰ κενῆς).

(1) Unclass. Lk 15: 22 δότε δακτύλιον εἰς τὴν χεῖρα, class. for which is περί; s. Plato, Rep. 2.359 E. Likewise Lk 15: 22 ὑποδήματα εἰς τοὺς πόδας (dat. Hom., Od. 15.369); Ljungvik 32. Acc. to Jeremias, ThZ 5 (1949) 230 an Aramaism. Εἰς of the recipients of a message (Semitism): Mk 14: 9 (for which Mt 26: 13 has ἐν), Lk 24: 47, 1 Th 2: 9, A 17: 15 D = Aram. לְ (cf. Black, Aramaic Approach 71 on Lk 4: 43 D); Jeremias, ZNW 44 (1952/3) 100. Εἰς for 'to, toward': Jn 11: 31, 38 ὑπάγει (ἔρχεται) εἰς (D 38 ἐπὶ) τὸ μνημεῖον, 20: 3 (6 and 8 εἰς 'into'); accordingly the v.l. of DHP Mk 3: 7 ἀνεχώρησεν εἰς (instead of πρὸς) τὴν θάλασσαν is acceptable, likewise in 2: 13 Tdf. ἐξῆλθεν εἰς τὴν θ. with S* instead of παρά, 7: 31 with SBDW al.; cf. εἰς τὸν ποταμόν 'to the river' and the

like in the LXX, Polyb. etc. (Kallenberg, RhM 66 [1911] 473ff.) and as early as Hdt. 4.200 ἀπίκατο εἰς τὴν πόλιν (which they afterwards besieged).

(2) MGr τἄφερε στὰ τριάντα acc. to Psichari 184; otherwise ἐπὶ διηκόσια, τριηκόσια 'up to...' Hdt. 1. 193. Barale, Didaskaleion 2 (1913) 436ff. (PTebt I 39.33 [114 BC], 49.11 [113 BC] βλάβος εἰς 'to derogate in value from...').

(3) Εἰς τέλος 1 Th 2: 16 'in full', Lk 18: 5 ἵνα μὴ εἰς τέλος ἐρχομένη ὑπωπιάζῃ με 'in order that she may not gradually (pres. ὑπωπιάζῃ!) wear me out completely by her continued coming (pres.!)' (cf. Klostermann, Hdb. in loc.; Oepke, TW II 424.35f. 'finally'), Jn 13: 1 εἰς τέλος ἠγάπησεν αὐτούς 'he gave them the perfect love-token' (Pernot, Études 207), LXX several times, Barn, Herm; εἰς τέλος τουτέστι παντελῶς Diodorus Tars. on Ps 51: 7 (MPG 33, 1589B). Cf. Debrunner, Gnomon 4 (1928) 444, Bauer s.v. εἰς 3. Pap. 'ultimately' and 'fully, completely'; Preisigke s.v. τέλος 4, Mayser II 2, 419, 570. Εἰς τέλος = יֶתֶר (עַל) 'remainder, exceedingly'. —Εἰς κενόν Diodor. and Hell. elsewhere, also LXX (with Is 65: 23 οὐ κοπιάσουσιν εἰς κ. cf. 1 Th 3: 5 μήπως...εἰς κ. γένηται ὁ κόπος ἡμῶν; the Prophets have εἰς κενόν, Job and Ps prefer διὰ κενῆς; side by side in Lev: διὰ κ. 26: 16, εἰς κ. 26: 20); Bauer s.v. κενός 2aβ. Following εἰς κ. the old equivalent μάτην (also Mt 15: 9, Mk 7: 7, Herm Sim 5.4.2) is then expanded to εἰς μάτην Herm Sim 5.4.2, 6.1.3, 9.4.8, 13.2 (LXX Ps 62: 10, 126: 1a, b, 2, Lucian, Trag. 28.241).

(B) With Genitive

208. Ἀντί is represented by only 22 examples. (1) Continuing in Hellenistic is first of all the classical ἀνθ' ὧν 'in return for which' = 'because' Lk 1: 20, 19: 44, A 12: 23, 2 Th 2: 10, 'for this' = 'therefore' Lk 12: 3. Also in the papyri (Rossberg 18; Mayser II 2, 375) and LXX. In the latter for the causal conjunctions תַּחַת אֲשֶׁר, יַעַן וּבְיַעַן, יַעַן, עַל- אֲשֶׁר עֵקֶב אֲשֶׁר, יַעַן כִּי, עֵקֶב, alternating with ὅτι, διότι, and at times combined ἀνθ' ὧν ὅτι 4 Km 22: 19 = יַעַן, 2 Km 12: 6 = עֵקֶב אֲשֶׁר, 12: 10 = עֵקֶב כִּי (Johannessohn II 200f.); ἀντὶ τούτου E 5: 31 = Gen 2: 24 ἕνεκεν τούτου = עַל-כֵּן, thus Mt 19: 5, Mk 10: 7, cf. ἀντὶ τούτου = לָכֵן Ezk 28: 7, 34: 9. See Bauer s.v. ἀντί 3. (2) Like the gen. of price (similarly classical, K.-G. I 454) H 12: 16 ἀντὶ βρώσεως μιᾶς ἀπέδοτο τὰ πρωτοτόκεια; cf. Epict. 1.29.21 ἀντὶ λύχνου κλέπτης ἐγένετο. With χάριν ἀντὶ χάριτος ἐλάβομεν Jn 1: 16 cf. Philo, Post. Caini 145 (II 33. 13 Cohn-Wendland): τὰς πρώτας χάριτας... ἑτέρας ἀντ' ἐκείνων...καὶ ἀεὶ νέας ἀντὶ παλαιοτέρων etc. With the meaning 'to follow without ceasing' cf. Ph 2: 27 λύπην ἐπὶ λύπην (εἷς καθ' εἷς § 305) and classical γῆν πρὸ γῆς ἐλαύνεσθαι 'from one land to another', ἐλπίσιν ἐξ ἐλπίδων and the like. Also cf. 2 C 2: 16, 3: 18, LXX Ps 83: 8, Jer 9: 2. For Plutarch s. Almqvist 83, 93. On Jn 1: 16 s. J. M. Bover, χάριν ἀντὶ χάριτος (Biblica 6 [1925] 454–60); Mart. Petri et Pauli 20 (L.-B I 136.13ff.) (Acta Petri et Pauli 41 [L.-B. I 197.1ff.]) ἄλλα ἀντὶ ἄλλων ψευσάμενοι. M. Black, JTS 42 (1941) 69f. = Aramaic חסדא חלף חסודה '(even) grace instead of disgrace'.—Mt 20: 28 λύτρον ἀντὶ πολ- λῶν = Mk 20: 45 (but 1 T 2: 6 ἀντίλυτρον ὑπέρ), cf. Mt 17: 27 δὸς αὐτοῖς ἀντὶ ἐμοῦ καὶ σοῦ. Mayser II 2, 374f.

209. Ἀπό for ἐκ. Ἀπό has absorbed ἐκ in MGr; the coalescence has begun in the NT, yet the instances of ἐκ still considerably outnumber those of ἀπό. Cf. ἐν and εἰς §205. (1) In a local sense ἀπό and ἐκ are still distinguished for the most part; only e.g. ἀπελθεῖν (ἐξ- EHLP) ἀπό (om. HLP; ἐκ E) τῆς πόλεως A 16: 39 'to leave the city', not 'to set out from the vicinity of the city'. On ἀπό for partitive ἐκ s. §164, on ἀπό and ἐκ with 'to take, eat of' etc. §169. (2) The ἐκ in οἱ ἐκ in Acts and Paul is classical (Crönert, Gnomon 4 [1928] 82), but τινὰς τῶν ἀπὸ τῆς ἐκκλησίας 'some of those belonging to the church' A 12: 1 is unclassical. (3) Ἀπό for ἐκ for the place of origin (so also MGr): ἦν ὁ Φίλιππος ἀπὸ Βηθσαϊδά, ἐκ τῆς πόλεως Ἀνδρέου Jn 1: 44. (4) 'After, from out of': ἐδυναμώθησαν ἀπὸ ἀσθενείας H 11: 34 in contrast with classical λευκὸν ἦμαρ εἰσιδεῖν ἐκ χείματος. Material: ἔνδυμα ἀπὸ τριχῶν Mt 3: 4 in contrast with classical ἔκπωμα ἐκ ξύλου (K.-G. I 461), but cf. εἵματα ἀπὸ ξύλων πεποιημένα Hdt. 7.65. Wittmann 15; Wolf II 38; MGr ἀπὸ μάρμαρο 'of marble'.

(1) [Mk] 16: 9 ἀφ' (παρ' C*DLW) ἧς ἐκβεβλήκει ἑπτὰ δαιμόνια, H 11: 15 ἀφ' ἧς (πατρίδος) ἐξέβησαν, A 13: 50. Melcher 69.

(2) Οἱ ἀπό also A 6: 9, 15: 5. Οἱ ἀπὸ βουλῆς Plut., Caesar 35 (cf. Jannaris §1512), pap. s. Rossberg 20, especially Ῥωμαῖος τῶν ἀπὸ συγκλήτου PTebt I 33.3 (112 BC). Class. οἱ ἐκ e.g. Aeschin. 1.54 οἱ ἐκ τῆς διατριβῆς ταύτης, but also pap. (Rossberg 12). Mayser II 1 14, 15f.

(3) Ἀπό also Jn 1: 45 (but 46 ἐκ Ναζ. δύναταί τι ἀγαθὸν εἶναι; cf. 4: 22 ἡ σωτηρία ἐκ τῶν Ἰουδαίων ἐστίν), Mt 21: 11, A 10: 38 and always where πόλις is not included unlike Lk 2: 4 (ἐκ πόλεως Ναζ.). Ἀπό also with the country (except in Jn): A 6: 9, 21: 27, 23: 34, 24: 18; cf. further 2: 5. Class. τοὺς ἐκ τῆς Ἀσίας Isocr. 4.82, cf. 83, but ἀπό as early as Hdt. and the poets (ἀπὸ Σπάρτης Hdt. 8.114, Soph., El. 701); pap. (ἀπό and ἐκ) s. Mayser II 1, 14, 15f.; II 2, 377,

383; Rouffiac 28. Οἱ ἀπὸ τῆς Ἀσίας Ἰουδαῖοι A 21: 27, cf. 24: 18 and τῶν ἀπὸ τῆς Ἀ. αἰχμαλώτων PPetr III 104.1 (pp. 249f.) (244/3 BC).—Ἀπό with acc. as in late (Vogeser 26, Wolf II 49) and MGr as early as Herm Vis 4.1.5 A.

(4) Pregnant ἀπ' ἀγορᾶς Mk 7: 4 'after the return from market'; cf. μετὰ τὴν κάμινον 'after baking in the oven' PHolm 20.26 and §234(8).

210. Ἀπό for ὑπό and παρά. (1) In a causal sense = 'because of, for' (MGr, Thumb² §161, 5): κοιμωμένους ἀπὸ τῆς λύπης Lk 22: 45, classical ὑπὸ λύπης. Heb 5: 7 εἰσακουσθεὶς ἀπὸ τῆς εὐλα- βείας 'heard because of his piety' Jeremias, ZNW 44 (1952/3) 119f. (2) Ὑπό with the agent with the passive or verbs with a passive meaning is also often (MGr always) replaced by ἀπό (the MSS normally vary greatly at this point): A 2: 22 ἀποδεδειγμένον ἀπὸ τοῦ θεοῦ. (3) Ἀπό is used for παρά with the genitive (as in MGr) in ἀκούειν ἀπό (§173(1)) and with 'to come from a person' (ἀπὸ Ἰακώβου G 2: 12).

(1) Ἀπὸ τῆς χαρᾶς Mt 13: 44 etc.; Herm Vis 3.11. 2; φοβεῖται ἀπὸ ἐνυπνίου τινός Theophr., Char. 25. Exx. from post-Christian pap. in Kuhring 35; others in Trunk 21; Huber 60; Johannessohn II 281f. On ἀπό for gen. of cause with interjections s. §176(1). Cf. ἐκ §212.

(2) Lk 6: 18, 8: 43, 17: 25, A 10: 33, 15: 4, 2 C 7: 13, Ja 1: 13, 5: 4, Rev 12: 6. A 4: 36 ἐπικληθεὶς Β. ἀπὸ (D ὑπό) τῶν ἀποστόλων; 4: 9 ἀνακρινόμεθα, D + ἀφ' ὑμῶν; Mt 11: 19 (in the event ἀπὸ τῶν τέκνων B²CDEF [al. ἔργων] is correct); 16: 21 πολλὰ παθεῖν ἀπὸ (D ὑπὸ) τῶν...(in the pars. Mk 8: 31 ἀπὸ only AX al., otherwise ὑπό; W has ἀπό corrected by the first hand to ὑπό; Lk 9: 22 all witnesses ἀπό); 1 P 2: 4 C; Herm Sim 2.9 ὑπὸ τοῦ θεοῦ in POxy IX 1172.43, PBer, PMich (A ἀπό). Cf. Kuhring 36 (only intransitives in pass. sense); Hatzid. 211; Jannaris §1507; Trunk 19, 20. Examples from Lev in Huber 60 introduce the agent in the passive with ἀπό instead of ὑπό; Johannessohn's examples (II 174f.) all have ἀπό (= partitive) after (ἐγ)καταλείπεσθαι (e.g. Lev 26: 43 'the land shall be left [= purged] of them'; Dt 3: 11 'the remnant of giants') and later revisers, without regard to the Hebrew and misled by the pass., replaced it with ὑπό, perhaps in a superficial attempt to 'improve' the style (Katz). Isolated instances also in class. (K.-G. I 457f.); cf. E. Schwyzer, ABA 10 (1943) 42.

(3) Μανθάνειν ἀπό G 3: 2, C 1: 7, παραλαμβάνειν ἀπό 1 C 11: 23 (παρά DE; Herm Vis 5.7 ἀπολαμβ. ἀπό, then παρά), etc. Ἀπὸ θεοῦ Jn 3: 2, 13: 3, 16: 30 (ἐκ 8: 42, παρά 16: 27, cf. 28 ἐκ τοῦ πατρός and §237(1)). Herm Sim 2.7 ἔλαβεν παρὰ τοῦ κυρίου POxy IX 1172.23, PBer (A ἀπό). Seldom in class. (K.-G. I 458). Meuwese 75–7; Zilliacus, Familienbriefe 41.

211. Ἀπό used to designate separation, alienation. On ἀπό for genitive of separation s. §180, on ἀπό for the accusative with verbs of 'fearing, fleeing', etc. §149. Ἀπό denotes alienation in some expressions, especially in Paul, which cannot be directly paralleled from the classical language: ἀνάθεμα εἶναι ἀπὸ τοῦ Χριστοῦ R 9: 3, ἀπεθάνετε ἀπὸ τῶν στοιχείων τοῦ κόσμου C 2: 20 (ἀποθνήσκειν τινί s. §188(2)); δικαιοῦν, θεραπεύειν, λούειν ἀπό approach still more closely to λύειν etc.

2 C 11: 3 μὴ φθαρῇ τὰ νοήματα ὑμῶν ἀπὸ τῆς ἁπλότητος; 2 Th 2: 2; with καταργεῖσθαι R 7: 6, G 5: 4; μετανοεῖν ἀπό A 8: 22 (μετάνοια ἀπό H 6: 1), ἐκ Rev (2: 21 etc.); H 10: 22 ῥεραντισμένοι ἀπὸ συνειδήσεως πονηρᾶς; Lk 24: 31 ἄφαντος ἐγένετο ἀπ' αὐτῶν (Hebraism acc. to Psichari 204–6). Herm and Clem: διαφθαρῆναι ἀπό Herm Sim 4.7, ἀποτυφλοῦσθαι ἀπό Man 5.2.7, κολοβὸς ἀπό Sim 9.26.8, κενὸς ἀπό §182(1); λιποτακτεῖν ἀπό 1 Clem 21.4, ἀργεῖν ἀπό 33. 1, ἔρημος ἀπό 2 Clem 2.3. H 5: 7 εἰσακουσθεὶς ἀπὸ τῆς εὐλαβείας cannot possibly be taken as 'heard (and released) from fear' (εὐλάβεια also in 12: 28 of the fear of (objective) God [cf. -βεῖσθαι 11: 7, -βής A 2: 5 etc.]), nor hardly either as 'on account of his piety' (cf. §210(1)); but either as καὶ εἰσακ., ἀπὸ τῆς εὐλαβείας...ἔμαθεν ἀφ' ὧν (τ') ἔπαθεν τὴν ὑπακοήν (τὴν ὑπ. obj. of ἔμαθεν; on the word order cf. §473(2)), or as (οὐκ) εἰσακ. ἀπὸ τ. ε. 'he was not heard apart from his fear (anxiety)' (Harnack, SAB 1929, 71). For Harnack against the objections of Jeremias (s. §210(1)): F. Scheidweiler, Hermes 83 (1955) 224–6. Παρελθεῖν ἀπό Mt 26: 39 = Mk 14: 35, παρενεγκεῖν ἀπό Mk 14: 36 = Lk 22: 42 '(let)...pass by (and hence depart from)'; cf. Ljungvik 83f. and LXX 2 Chr 9: 2 (παρῆλθεν ἀπό = נֶעְלַם מִן, 'remained hidden').

For ἀπό in expressions of distance s. §161(1). For ἀπὸ προσώπου τινός §217(1).

212. Regarding the extensive usage of ἐκ, ἐξ there is little to note. For the subjective genitive 2 C 9: 2 τὸ ἐξ ὑμῶν ζῆλος (without ἐξ 𝔓⁴⁶SBCP), 8: 7 τῇ ἐξ ὑμῶν ἐν ἡμῖν(?) ἀγάπῃ. For partitive ἐκ s. §§164, 169; for ἐκ with verbs of filling §172, ἐκ for genitive of price §179. Peculiar τοὺς νικῶντας ἐκ τοῦ θηρίου Rev 15: 2 probably = τηρήσαντας ἑαυτοὺς ἐκ τ. θ. (§149); however s. Bonaccorsi p. clxii. Causal = 'because of' (like ὑπό and ἀπό §210(1)): Rev 16: 10 ἐμασῶντο τὰς γλώσσας αὐτῶν ἐκ τοῦ πόνου 'from anguish'; cf. 11, 12. Rev and also the Gospel and 1 John make the greatest use of ἐκ comparatively. Ἐκ by attraction instead of ἐν s. §437. Ἐκ μέρους 'in part' 1 C 13: 9, 10, 12 as in Hellenistic (Bauer s.v. μέρος 1 c; s.v. ἐκ 6 c; Preisigke s.v. μέρος 3), but 1 C 12: 27 '(each) for his part'; cf. ἐκ δραχμῶν ϛ 'each 6 dr.' PHolm 1.7 (Riesenfeld, Con. Neot. 3 [1936] 23), ἐγ μέρους 'alternating, in turn' UPZ I 110.182 (164 BC).

213. Πρό provides but few examples, most of which illustrate the temporal idea 'before'. Local 'before' only in A (5: 23 v.l.,) 12: 6 (v.l. πρός with the dative), 14, 14: 13, Ja 5: 9 (otherwise ἔμπροσθεν s. §214(1)). Preference: πρὸ πάντων Ja 5: 12, 1 P 4: 8. On πρὸ προσώπου τινός s. §217(1), πρὸ τοῦ with an infinitive §403. The peculiar construction πρὸ ἐξ ἡμερῶν τοῦ πάσχα '6 days before the passover' is Hellenistic (properly '6 days ago, reckoned from the passover') Jn 12: 1, πρὸ ἐτῶν δεκατεσσάρων 2 C 12: 2 (πρὸ μιᾶς Herm Sim 6.5.3, Homil Clem 9.1.1 'the day before', 13.11.4, 17.6. 2, πρὸ μ. ἢ δύο Did 7.4, πρὸ δύο ἐτῶν τοῦ σεισμοῦ LXX Am 1: 1). Cf. §247(2).—Mayser II 2, 390ff.

There are many exx. of this (temporal) usage in Jannaris §1651; W. Schulze, Graeca Latina 14ff.; Schmidt 513; Schmid III 287f., IV 629; Kühner, Ausf. Gramm. der Griech. Sprache II² 287f.; W. Bauer, Hdb. on Jn 12: 1; K.-G. I 391; A. Gagnér, Strena Philol. Ups. (1922) 213f.; Per Persson, Eranos 20 (1923) 58–73; Wackernagel, Syntax II² 195f.; Johannessohn II 188f. For the same πρό in a local sense s. Schwyzer, RhM 77 (1928) 255ff.; Wolf II 47; Käser 12; Dionys. Hal., Ant. 9.35.5 (πρὸ πολλοῦ τῆς πόλεως). Cf. the corresponding construction with ἀπό §161(1) and μετά §226. Latin *ante diem tertium Kalendas* can only have had a supplementary influence (cf. Hering 69f.), for the earliest Gr. exx. are pre-Roman (in MSS as early as Hippoc. πρὸ τριῶν ἡμερῶν τῆς τελευτῆς [W. Schulze, Graeca Latina 15], without a second gen. after 'days' already in an inscrip. of the will of Epicteta [IG XII 3, 330.160; Thera, c. 200 BC] πρὸ τοῦ τὰν σύνοδον ἦμεν [= εἶναι] πρὸ ἀμερᾶν δέκα). On the whole question s. Mlt. 100ff. [161f.] and Günther, IF 20 (1906/7) 149: gen. in the sense of 'reckoned from' as early as Hdt. 6.46 δευτέρῳ ἔτει τούτων 'in the second year *after* these events', Xen., HG 1.1.2 μετ' ὀλίγον τούτων. Πρὸ ἀμερᾶν δέκα τῶν μυστηρίων '10 days before the mysteries' Dit., Syll.³ 736.70 (91 BC); πρὸ ἐννέα καλανδῶν Σεπτεμβρίων IRom 10.3, πρὸ ἑπτὰ καλ. Μαρτίων MPol 21 = *ante diem nonum (septimum) Kalendas*.

214. Improper prepositions for 'before' as alternatives to πρό which is seldom used in a local sense (§213): (1) Ἔμπροσθεν is the proper word in the NT for 'before' in a strictly spatial sense (as ἐμπρός 'ς or μπροστά 'ς, which arose therefrom, is in MGr): it is used more frequently in the classical language and in the Ptolemaic papyri (Mayser II 2, 539) as an adverb than with the genitive. (2) In the case of ἐναντίον the construction with the genitive is already the predominating one in classical; the meaning in the NT, however, has been weakened from 'opposite' to 'before'. Mayser II 2, 529f. (3) Ἀντικρύς 'opposite' (MGr ἀντίκρυ ('ς), Thumb² §171) only A 20: 15 (s. §21); ἀπ- and κατ-αντικρύ(ς) do not appear. (4) Ἔναντι, ἀπέναντι, κατέναντι are Hellenistic (Doricisms, s. Wackernagel, Hell. 3–6 [= Kl. Schr. 1034–7]); in the NT they mean 'opposite' or 'in the sight of' (Mt 27: 24 κατέναντι τοῦ ὄχλου). Mayser II 2, 538, 541. (5) Ἐνώπιον also is Hellenistic (Mayser I² 3, 120; II 2, 531; Mlt. 99 [159]. Also MGr; cf. τὰ ἐνώπια in Homer); in addition E 1: 4, C 1: 22 and Jd 24 κατενώπιον (cf. Homer κατενῶπα or κατ' ἐνῶπα). (6) Almost all of these words, but especially ἐνώπιον, serve to render Hebrew לִפְנֵי, בְּעֵינֵי, also נֶגֶד, for which, in classical, the simple case would often have sufficed.

Z. Frankel, Vorstudien zu der Sept. (Leipzig, 1841) 159; J. Waldis, Die Präpositionsadverbien mit der Bedeutung 'vor' in der Sept. (Beilage zum Jahresb. d. Kantonsschule in Luzern 1921/2); Johannessohn II 189–98.
(1) Ἔμπροσθεν A 18: 17, Rev 19: 10 (046 ἐνώπιον), 22: 8 (A πρό); 'before, ahead of someone' Jn 3: 28, 10: 4; temporal = πρό (class. also) perhaps Jn 1: 15, 30 (or = 'has precedence of me, ranks before me') [LXX Gen 48: 20], or [γέγονεν, cf. Plut., Per. 11.1 πρόσθεν...γεγονότα τῶν πολιτῶν 'has outrun [outstripped] me', Bauer, Hdb. ad loc. and Bauer⁵ s.v.); adverbial only Lk 19: 4, 28, Ph 3: 13, Rev 4: 6. Mt uses ἔμπρ. most frequently; it is missing in Peter, Ja, Jd, Heb.
(2) Ἐναντίον Mk 2: 12 ACD (al. ἔμπρ.), Lk 1: 8 SAC al., 20: 26, 24: 19 (ἐνώπιον D), A 7: 10, 8: 32 OT.
(4) Ἔναντι Lk 1: 8 BDE al., A 7: 10 S, 8: 21 (ἐνώπιον EHLP). The reading often varies between κατέναντι and ἀπέν. Ἀπ. τῶν δογμάτων A 17: 7 is peculiar 'contrary to' = class. ἐναντία τοῖς δ. or τῶν δ.); adv. Lk 19: 30.
(5) Ἐνώπιον frequently in Lk (Acts in first part, second part only 19: 9, 19, 27: 35) and Rev; Jn only 20: 30, 1 Jn 3: 22, 3 Jn 6; never in Mt, Mk. Also in a spatial sense proper: ἐνώπιον τοῦ θρόνου Rev; 'before, ahead of someone' Lk 1: 17 (76 SBW). A. Wikenhauser, BZ 8 (1910) 263–70. Above all in the OT formulae ἐν. τοῦ θεοῦ, τοῦ κυρίου (Johannessohn II 359ff.). Κατενώπιον LXX, Pol Ph 5.2 (related in substance to three NT references), Christian amulet BGU III 954.6 (c. vi AD), apparently attested nowhere else; Johannessohn II 361 n. 2.

(6) Ἔμπροσθεν, ἐναντίον, ἐνώπιον 'before somebody = in the eyes of someone' (alternating with ἐν ὀφθαλμοῖς in the LXX); thus 'pleasing in the eyes of someone' = 'to someone' A 6: 5, 1 Jn 3: 22, H 13: 21 (all with pars. in the LXX); ἁμαρτάνειν ἐνώπιόν τινος = εἰς τινα (both in Lk 15: 18, 21) or τινί (LXX εἰς, ἔναντι, ἐναντίον, ἐνώπιον [Helb., Kas. 215ff.], τινί). Προσκυνεῖν ἐνώπιον s. §187(2). Mt 18: 14 οὐκ ἔστιν θέλημα ἔμπροσθεν τοῦ πατρὸς ὑμῶν (for the simple gen.), 11: 26; Lk 15: 10 (for gen. or dat.), 24: 11 (for αὐτοῖς), Mt 7: 6 μηδὲ βάλητε τοὺς μαργαρίτας ὑμῶν ἔμπροσθεν τῶν χοίρων (= class. μὴ προβάλητε τοῖς χοίροις), etc. Similarly also H 4: 13 οὐκ ἀφανὴς ἐνώπιον αὐτοῦ. In the second part of Acts ἐνώπιον is merely the equivalent of class. ἐναντίον. R 3: 18 OT ἀπέναντι τῶν ὀφθαλμῶν αὐτῶν; cf. 1 Clem 8.4 OT.

215. Improper prepositions for 'behind', 'upon', 'under', 'between'. (1) Ὄπισθεν 'behind' is the spatial contrast to ἔμπροσθεν, but appears only in Mt 15: 23, Lk 23: 26 with the genitive, and also rarely as an adverb. Ὀπίσω, on the other hand, is found rather often, mostly as a preposition, less often as an adverb. The prepositional usage, foreign to profane authors, derives from the LXX (Hebr. אַחֲרֵי): ἔρχεσθαι ὀπίσω τινός 'to follow'. (2) The compounds ἐπ-άνω 'on top of' (for which Hellenistic also employs ὑπεράνω E 1: 21, 4: 10, H 9: 5) and ὑπο-κάτω 'underneath', already found in Attic, are weakened in the NT to 'above, under' (Attic also with genitive). Ἄνω and κάτω are always adverbial. (3) The following mean 'between': μεταξύ (Attic) Mt 18: 15 etc. (rare), ἀνὰ μέσον (§204), ἐν μέσῳ (ἐμμέσῳ) 'among, between' = Hebr. בְּתוֹךְ (classical ἐν or εἰς), μέσος as an adjective (Jn 1: 26; Lk 22: 55 BL, v.l. ἐν μέσῳ, μετ') or μέσον as an adverb (Jannaris §1525; cf. MGr μέσα); in addition ἐκ μέσου = מִתּוֹךְ Mt 13: 49 etc. (classical simple ἐκ) and διὰ μέσου = בְּתוֹךְ (Lk 4: 30 διελθὼν διὰ μέσου αὐτῶν = classical διά; s. also §222). All take the genitive.

(1) Ἔρχεσθαι ὀπ. τινός Mt 3: 11 etc. 'to come after someone (behind; later than)' in John's words about the Christ is different. Ἀκολουθεῖν ὀπίσω s. §193(1); ἀπέστησε λαὸν ὀπίσω αὐτοῦ A 5: 37, cf. 20: 30; even θαυμάζειν ὀπ. Rev 13: 3 (§196). The only secular exx.: ταύτης δ' ὀπίσω 'after this' Dit., Or. 56.62 (237 BC), ὀπίσω Καπιτολείου POxy 43 B IV 3 (iii AD), ὀπ. τοῦ Κορείου Dialekt-Inschr. 3246.10, 12 (Dor.-Sicilian; date?).
(2) E.g. Mt 5: 14 ἐπάνω ὄρους (= Att. ἐπ' ὄρους), Lk 8: 16 ὑποκάτω κλίνης (= Att. ὑπὸ κλίνην, cf. Mk 4: 21 and Mt 5: 15). Adverbial only ἐπάνω, not ὑποκάτω; the former also used with numbers =

'over', without affecting the case (§ 185(4)); before an adverb, Mt 2: 9 ἐπάνω οὗ ἦν τὸ παιδίον (D however ἐπ. τοῦ παιδίου). MGr (ἀ)πάνω 's 'upon', ἀποκάτω ἀπό 'under'. Mayser II 2, 539f., 541, 542.

(3) Μεταξύ also as an adv.: Jn 4: 31 ἐν τῷ μεταξύ 'meanwhile', but vulgar = 'later' (Plut., Mor. 240 B, Jos., Mitteis, Chr. 57.11 [40/1 AD], 64.5 [312 AD]): A 13: 42 εἰς τὸ μεταξὺ σάββατον; cf. 23: 24 add. 𝔓⁴⁸ (614, 2147) gig p, Barn 13.5, 1 Clem 44.2.—Ἐν μέσῳ Mt 10: 16, Lk 8: 7, 10: 3, 21: 21 etc.; 'where?' and 'whither?' are not distinguished (§ 103), therefore never εἰς μέσον except Mt 10: 16 B, 14: 24 D (v.l. μέσον; with ἦν); but without dependent case εἰς (τὸ) μέσον Mk 3: 3 etc.—Μέσον as prep. Ph 2: 15, Lk 10: 3 D, 17: 11 (§ 222); adj. Homil Clem 6.1; adj. or prep. Mt 14: 24 SCE al., Lk 8: 7 D. Johannessohn II 325f. Μέσον as prep. (ibid. n. 1): LXX 1 Km 11: 11, doubtful Dit., Syll.³ 888.18 (238 AD) μέσον (μέσην?) δύο στρατοπέδων, Plut., Publ. 8 τοῦτο νῦν νῆσός ἐστιν..., καλεῖται δὲ φωνῇ τῇ Λατίνων Μέσον (in reference to τοῦτο? v.l. μέση) δυεῖν γεφυρῶν (= Lat. inter duos pontes). From the LXX (ibid. 170, 174) it emerges that ἀνὰ μέσον is vulgar, μεταξύ, three times in Wsd, literary (Debrunner, ByzZ 28 [1929] 397), or clearly Atticizing, only in three insertions from Aqu. Judg 5: 27 (ἀνὰ μέσον earlier in the verse), 3 Km 15: 6, 32 (Katz, VT 8 [1958] 267).—Class. seldom with gen., e.g. κατὰ μέσον Hom., Il. 9.87, Plato, Critias 121 c, ἐν μέσῳ Symp. 222 E ('in the midst of, among'), Rep. 4.427 c ('in the middle').

216. Improper prepositions for 'on account of', 'without', 'until'. (1) 'On account of': ἕνεκεν (also ἕνεκα § 35(3) and εἵνεκεν § 30(3)) numbers only some 20 examples (including quotations). Χάριν is still less frequent (almost always in postposition, always in τούτου χ., οὗ χ., but 1 Jn 3: 12 χ. τίνος). (2) 'Apart from, without': the proper Hellenistic word is χωρίς (Solmsen 115; Mayser II 2, 537; MGr also); ἄνευ (likewise Attic) only Mt 10: 29 (ἄνευ τοῦ πατρὸς ὑμῶν insciente, invito patre, cf. ἄνευ θεῶν etc. in papyri in Kuhring 47, Mayser II 2, 519f., ἄνευ θεοῦ etc. as early as Homer), 1 P 3: 1, 4: 9. Ἄτερ (Inschr. v. Priene 109.106 [120 BC], otherwise in prose only in the imperial period) only Lk 22: 6, 35 (more often Herm, e.g. Sim 5.4.5; Barn 2.6 C [ἄνευ S]; LXX only 2 Macc 12: 15). Πλήν 'except' (Attic) Mk 12: 32 OT, [Jn] 8: 10 EGHK al., A 8: 1, 15: 28, 27: 22. Ἐκτός 'except' (post-classical) A 26: 22, 1 C 15: 27 (papyri s. Kuhring 51; Mayser II 2, 529), likewise παρεκτός Mt 5: 32, 19: 9 BD, A 26: 29 (s. Bauer s.v., Homil Clem 13.16.4 π. τοῦ ἀπειθεῖν τῷ θεῷ). (3) 'Until': ἄχρι(ς), μέχρι(ς) as in Attic (on the -ς s. § 21). In addition ἕως (LXX) which

was originally entirely a conjunction and became a preposition only in the Hellenistic period (Schwyzer II 533, 550 f.; MGr ὡς 'up to'); cf. πρίν § 395.—Mayser II 2, 518–26, 534, 535–8.

(1) The meaning of ἕνεκεν is almost always propter (hardly distinguished from διά with acc.), less frequently causa; cf. both in 2 C 7: 12 οὐχ ἕνεκεν τοῦ ἀδικήσαντος...ἀλλ' ἕνεκεν τοῦ φανερωθῆναι. The position (in Attic very free) is always before the gen. (s. also § 403) except with an interrog., whose proper place is at the beginning of the sentence (τίνος ἕνεκα A 19: 32; cf. Homil Clem 9.14, 17; 20.12), likewise with a relative (οὗ εἵνεκεν Lk 4: 18 OT; often in Homil Clem, e.g. 1.5; 2.51, ὧν ἕνεκεν 18.7). Position of ἕνεκ- in pap.: Ghedini, Aegyptus 15 (1935) 238; Mayser II 2, 521 (always in postposition with οὗ, ὧν, otherwise often placed before); N. Turner, VT 5 (1955) 210f.: in the LXX and NT always before the gen., except for the instances mentioned above (following the Semitic model, Debrunner by letter), postposition in Ptol. pap. and Polybius more than twice as frequent as pre-position. The preposition of χάριν is Hell. (Witkowski, Epistulae 87 with n.; Milligan p. 23.17 with n.; Deissmann, LO⁴ 154 n. 7 [LAE 188 n. 9]; Mayser II 2, 535, 536; but Plato, Phdr. 241 c χάριν πλησμονῆς); however the pap. almost always have οὗ χ. (Mitteis, Chr. 368.9 [i/ii AD]), ὧν χ., τούτου χ., τίνος χ.; yet χ. οὗ PTebt II 410.4 [16 AD]). Homil Clem 11.35.6 οὗ χάριν.

(2) The position is before the gen. except οὗ χωρίς H 12: 14, ITr 9.2; χωρίς as adv. (Att. often) only Jn 20: 7. Ὧν ἄνευ Xen., HG 7.1.3, Cyr. 6.1.14, Arist., Philo, Vita Cont. 37 (VI 56.2 Cohn-Wendland), οὗ (ἧς) ἄνευ Arist., Diamart. 2.1 (p. 3.12 Rehm), 4.1 (p. 4.8), ἧς ἄνευ Homil Clem 2.5.1.

(3) Ἄχρι(ς) Lk, Acts, Paul, Heb, Rev, and Mt 24: 38; μέχρι(ς) Mt 11: 23, 13: 30 (ἕως BD), 28: 15 (S*D ἕως), scattered instances Lk, Acts, Paul, Heb, Rev 14: 20 𝔓⁴⁷. Both are also conj. (ἄχρις οὗ, μ. οὗ are subordinating: Herm Vis 4.1.9 μ. ὅτε S*, μ. ὅτου SᶜA), s. § 383(1). Ἕως as prep. often in Mt, also Mk, Lk, Acts, seldom Paul, Ja, Heb only in quotation; Jn has none of the three (only [Jn] 8: 9 SUΛ). On ἕως (οὗ, ὅτου) as conj. s. §§ 383(1); 455(3). Ἕως is readily combined with an adv. (cf. § 203): ἕως πότε, ἀπὸ ἄνωθεν ἕως κάτω, ἕως ἄρτι, ἕως σήμερον (besides ἕως τῆς σ. and ἕως τοῦ νῦν), on the other hand ἄχρι (μέχρι) τοῦ νῦν Ph 1: 5 (Mayser II 2, 523.13ff.), τῆς σήμερον Mt 11: 23, 28: 15, 2 C 3: 14 (but Thuc. 7.83.2 μέχρι ὀψέ). The meaning 'within' (derived from 'as far as') appears in A 19: 26 D ἕως Ἐφέσου (cf. § 186(1)). Herm Man 4.1.5 ἄχρι τῆς ἀγνοίας οὐχ ἁμαρτάνει 'as long as he knows nothing'. Ἕως as a prep. is an imitation of the older double usage of ἄχρι, μέχρι; first in Hdt. 2.143 ἕως οὗ (dubious) following μέχρι (ἄχρι) οὗ, doubtful Thuc. 3.108.3 v.l. ἕως ὀψέ, Xen., Cyr. 5.1.25 ἕως ὅτε (only cod. D; al. εἰς ὅτε or ἔστε), besides

Arist.—For the distribution of ἄχρι, μέχρι and ὡς among the physicians (ἄχρι more often first in i AD) s. M. Wellmann, Die Schrift des Dioskur. π. ἁπλ. φαρμ. (Berlin, 1914) 70–4.—Ἕως 'during a period (up to its close)' Gesta Pil. A 15.5 (p. 255 Tdf.[1]), Acta Pil. B 15.5 (299 Tdf.[1]; acc. !), Ev. Thom. A 18.2 (148 Tdf.).

217. Hebraistic circumlocutions of prepositional concepts (cf. μέσος §215(3)) by means of certain substantives with the gen.: (1) Πρόσωπον: ἀπὸ προσώπου τινός = ἀπό or παρά with gen. = מִפְּנֵי, πρὸ προσώπου = πρό. Κατὰ πρόσωπον = coram is also known in secular language and thus in A 25: 16, 2 C 10: 1, Barn 15.1 (without gen.) is correctly used (Thieme 19; Rouffiac 33). Elsewhere it corresponds to Hebrew בִּפְנֵי; similarly εἰς πρ. τινός 2 C 8: 24. In Aquila εἰς πρόσωπον = לִפְנֵי: Katz, JTS 47 (1946) 31. (2) Χείρ: εἰς χεῖράς (בְּיַד) τινος (παραδιδόναι etc.) 'in someone's power, to someone' Mt 26: 45 etc., Lk 23: 46, Jn 13: 3, for which δέδωκεν ἐν τῇ χειρί (ἐν = εἰς §218) Jn 3: 35. Ἐν (σὺν ABCDE) χειρὶ ἀγγέλου A 7: 35 (cf. G 3: 19) = בְּיַד 'through, by means of'. Ἐκ χειρός τινος 'from the power of someone' (מִיַּד) Lk 1: 71. Διὰ χειρός, διὰ τῶν χειρῶν = διά Mk 6: 2 and often A (2: 23, 5: 12 etc.), of deeds. (3) Στόμα: διὰ στόματος Lk 1: 70, A 1: 16 etc. of speech which God utters through someone; for the pronouncements of someone (to hear, etc.) ἐκ (τοῦ) στόματός τινος; ἐπὶ στόματος 'upon the statement' §234(4) and others. Στόμα however is employed in many similar usages in classical.—On ὁδόν as a preposition s. §161(1).—Johannessohn II 383 (index) and especially 350–2 (LXX), 352–62 (NT), κατά πρ. 248; Helb., Kas. 240 n. 1.

(1) Ἀπὸ πρ. A 3: 20, 5: 41 with 'to go, come', A 7: 45, Rev 6: 16, 12: 14, 20: 11 with 'to drive away, hide, flee' (for NT ἀπό §211). Πρὸ πρ. Mt 11: 10 OT (לְפָנֶי), Lk 1: 76 (SB ἐνώπιον), 9: 52, even πρὸ προσώπου τῆς εἰσόδου αὐτοῦ 'before his coming' A 13: 24 (synagogue sermon of Paul). Κατὰ πρ. Πιλάτου A 3: 13, κατὰ πρ. πάντων τῶν λαῶν Lk 2: 31. Εἰς πρ.: the reference to Herm Vis 3.6.3 (Bauer, Bauer[5]) is based on the reconstruction (from Lat.) of Hilgenfeld (cf. the edition of M. Whittaker [GCS]); POxy VI 903.21f. (iv AD) εἰς πρ. μου.

(2) Η 10: 31 ἐμπεσεῖν εἰς χεῖρας θεοῦ; cf. Polyb. 8. 20.8 ὑπὸ τὰς τῶν ἐχθρῶν χ. πίπτειν (further also ὑποχείριος). A 12: 11 ἐξείλατό με ἐκ χειρὸς Ἡρῴδου; cf. Aeschin. 3.256 ἐκ τῶν χειρῶν ἐξελέσθαι τῶν Φιλίππου (here as a vivid, strong expression).

(3) Οἱ λόγοι οἱ ἐκπορευόμενοι ἐκ (διὰ) στόματός τινος and the like Mt 4: 4 OT (= LXX Dt 8: 3), Lk 4: 22 etc. = οἱ λ. τινός; ἀκούειν ἐκ (ἀπὸ, διὰ) τοῦ στ.

τινος Lk 22: 71, A 1: 4 D, E 4: 29 etc.; θηρεῦσαί τι ἐκ τ. στ. αὐτοῦ Lk 11: 54. Ἐκ στ. means also 'out of the jaws': 2 T 4: 17.

(C) With Dative

218. Statistics for ἐν and the interchange of ἐν and εἰς. Ἐν is the preposition most often used in the NT in spite of the fact that some authors occasionally substitute εἰς (§§ 205f.). The reverse, the hyper-correct use of ἐν for εἰς, is to be claimed for only a few scattered instances in the NT, the most obvious and certain of which are Lk 9: 46 εἰσῆλθεν διαλογισμὸς ἐν αὐτοῖς 'came into them, into their hearts' (cf. v. 47); cf. Humbert 58–63 and ἐν μέσῳ in response to the question 'whither?' (§215(3)).—Mayser II 2, 371 ff.

The 2698 NT exx. of ἐν (Mlt. 62, 98 [94, n. 2]) constitute 26·5% of all NT exx. of (proper) prep. overall, as can be reckoned from Mlt. 62f., 98 [158]. Heilmann, Reform. Kirchenztg. 1896, 413 calculates that ἐν in C constitutes 48% of the total no. of prep., in 2 P even somewhat more, in 1 Jn 45%, in E 44·5%. Rossberg 8 has counted 2245 cases in the Ptol. pap. and finds they equal c. 18%, making ἐν the most frequent prep.—Ἐν for εἰς: Lk 4: 1 ἤγετο... ἐν τῇ ἐρήμῳ SBDLW (al. εἰς) for Mt 4: 1 ἀνήχθη εἰς τὴν ἔρημον, Mk 1: 12 ἐκβάλλει εἰς τ. ἔ.; κατέβαινεν ἐν τῇ κολυμβήθρᾳ Jn 5: 4 (spurious verse), εἰσῆλθεν ἐν αὐτοῖς Rev 11: 11 only A (αὐτοῖς CP, εἰς αὐτούς 𝔓47S 046); Herm Sim 1.6 ἀπέλθῃς ἐν τῇ πόλει σου, Homil Clem 1.7; 14.6. But ἐξῆλθεν ὁ λόγος ἐν τῇ Ἰουδαίᾳ Lk 7: 17 (cf. 1 Th 1: 8) means it 'spread in'. The classical writers could also use ἐν with τιθέναι and ἱστάναι (cf. ἐμβάπτειν ἐν Mt 26: 23, εἰς Mk 14: 20), with which may be compared διδόναι ('place') ἐν τῇ χειρί τινος Jn 3: 35 (§217(2)); 1 Clem 55.5 παρέδωκεν Ὀλοφέρνην ἐν χειρὶ θηλείας), ἐν τῇ καρδίᾳ 2 C 1: 22, 8: 16. Cf. τὰς Ἑλένας ἐν ἀντωποῖς βλεφάροισιν ἔρωτα δέδωκας Eur., IA 584, Medea 425 and Porson on Medea 629. The metaphorical use, moreover, proves absolutely nothing: Lk 1: 17 ἐν φρονήσει δικαίων 'with the thought, so that they have the thought', καλεῖν ἐν εἰρήνῃ etc. The LXX often has ἐν for εἰς (Johannessohn II 330ff.), e.g. Tob 5: 5 πορευθῆναι ἐν Ῥάγοις. Also in the later pap. (Mayser II 2, 372f.; but not UPZ I 121.2 [156 BC] ἀνακεχώρηκεν ἐν Ἀλεξανδρείᾳ), e.g. [πέμψαι ἐν Β]αβυλῶνι PLond IV 1334.8 (709 AD); ἐπέμφθη (ἀπερχομένοις) ἐν Ἀλεξανδρείᾳ POxy I 127.4, 10 (vi AD), 151.2 (612 AD); Epict. 1.11.32 ἀνέρχῃ ἐν Ῥώμῃ, 2.30.33 ἀπελθεῖν ἐν βαλανείῳ; τῇ ἀνόδῳ τῇ ἐν τῷ ἱερῷ BCH 15 (1891) 181 no. 130A 15 (Roman period). Further Jannaris §1565; Humbert 58f.; Ghedini, Vang. ap. 453.

219. Instrumental ἐν. The use of ἐν owes its extension especially to the imitation of Hebrew constructions with בְּ. It is used for the simple instr. (§195), but (1) also to designate a personal agent: ἐν τῷ ἄρχοντι ('by means of') τῶν δαιμονίων ἐκβάλλει τὰ δαιμόνια Mt 9: 34 (,12: 24); (2) probably also the reason: Mt 6: 7 ἐν τῇ πολυλογίᾳ αὐτῶν εἰσακουσθήσονται. Johannessohn II 334; Ghedini, Vang. ap. 452. (3) The ἐν representing the gen. of price (§179) is also instr., and often appears in the phrase ἐν τῷ αἵματι (τοῦ Χρ.) common to Paul and others; it also appears in other, not always clear, combinations. On ἠμφιεσμένος ἐν and the like s. §159(1); on ἐν of accompaniment §198(1, 2), of the dat. of respect §197. (4) Manner (§198(4)): ἐν τάχει (classical) Lk 18: 8 etc.; κρίνειν ἐν δικαιοσύνῃ = δικαίως A 17: 31, Rev 19: 11.—Oepke, TW II 534ff.

(1) C 1: 16 ἐν αὐτῷ ἐκτίσθη...δι' αὐτοῦ ἔκτισται. Originally not instrumental: A 17: 31 κρίνειν τὴν οἰκουμένην ἐν ἀνδρί, 1 C 6: 2 ἐν ὑμῖν (as in 1 ἐπὶ τῶν ἀδίκων) as several times in Delphic inscrip. beginning c. 200 BC κριθέντω(ν) ἐν 'they should be judged by' (properly 'before the forum of'); cf. Mlt. 107 add. notes [168]. ʼEv is local also in quotation formulae (R 9: 25 ἐν τῷ Ὡσηέ 'in the book of Hosea', 11: 2 ἐν Ἠλίᾳ 'in the story of Elijah' [cf. ἐπί § 234(3, 8)], H 4: 7 ἐν Δαυίδ, Barn 6.14 ἐν ἑτέρῳ προφήτῃ) as in ἐν τῷ νόμῳ 'in the book of the law'. The class. exx. in K.-G. I 465 are somewhat different.

(2) A 7: 29 ἔφυγεν Μωυσῆς ἐν τῷ λόγῳ τούτῳ 'because of, at' (DE is different ἐφυγάδευσεν Μωυσῆν ἐν 'with'); ἐν τούτῳ 'for that reason' A 24: 16, Jn 16: 30, ἐν ᾧ 'while, because' R 2: 1, 8: 3, H 2: 18, 'wherefore' 6: 17; ἐν with χαίρειν etc. (§196) also belongs here.

(3) Rev 5: 9 ἠγόρασας ἐν τῷ αἵματί σου; cf. A 20: 28 ἣν περιεποιήσατο διὰ τοῦ αἵματος τοῦ ἰδίου. R 3: 25 (ἱλαστήριον...ἐν τῷ αὐτοῦ αἵματι [to be taken together?] 'at the price of his blood'), 5: 9 etc.; cf. εἶναι ἐν 'to amount to' PGrenf II 77.6 (iii AD end), also ἱμάτια ἐν 'valued at' BGU IV 1050.8 (c. the time of the birth of Christ).

(4) ʼEν πάσῃ ἀσφαλείᾳ = ἀσφαλέστατα A 5: 23, ἐν (πάσῃ) παρρησίᾳ 'freely, openly', etc.; cf. K.-G. I 466. The phrase ἐν Χριστῷ (κυρίῳ), which is copiously appended by Paul to the most varied concepts, utterly defies definite interpretation; cf. Deissmann, Die nt. Formel 'in Christo Jesu', Marburg, 1892; Oepke, TW II 534 n.; Bauer s.v. ἐν I 5 d. Ἄνθρωπος ἐν πνεύματι ἀκαθάρτῳ Mk 1: 23, 5: 2 (cf. 5: 25 = Lk 8: 43 οὖσα ἐν ῥύσει αἵματος) evidently means 'with an unclean s.' = ἔχων πνεῦμα ἀκ. (Mk 3: 30 etc.); yet e.g. R 8: 9 (ἐστὲ...ἐν πνεύματι,...πνεῦμα θεοῦ οἰκεῖ ἐν ὑμῖν....πνεῦμα Χριστοῦ οὐκ ἔχει) exhibits the fluctuation between the local and instr. meaning of ἐν. S. also §203. Percy 288–98.

220. Various other uses of ἐν. (1) Occasionally ἐν appears also to stand for the customary dat. proper, e.g. G 1: 16 ἀποκαλύψαι τὸν υἱὸν αὐτοῦ ἐν ἐμοί 'to me' (cf. 12) or 'in my case' ('in me' i.e. 'in my spirit' would be unnatural). (2) ʼEν also means 'in the case of, from someone's example' (Rob. 587) with μανθάνειν 1 C 4: 6, γινώσκειν Lk 24: 35 etc. (classical similarly). Ὀμνύναι ἐν s. §149. Ὁμολογεῖν ἔν τινι 'to acknowledge someone' Mt 10: 32, Lk 12: 8, for which the dat. (§187(4)), simple acc. (1 Jn 2: 23 etc.) or double acc. (§157(2)) may be used, is an Aramaism (Mlt. 104 [169] and Bauer s.v. ὁμ. 4). ʼEν μυστηρίῳ λαλοῦμεν σοφίαν 1 C 2: 7 'in the form of a mystery' (classical similarly). For temporal ἐν s. §200.—Oepke, TW II 534ff.

(1) 2 C 4: 3 ἐν τοῖς ἀπολλυμένοις ἐστὶν κεκαλυμμένον ('for' or 'to' is better than 'among'); probably also R 1: 19 φανερόν ἐστιν ἐν αὐτοῖς (cf. §263(2)). Further 2 C 8: 1 τὴν χάριν τὴν δεδομένην ἐν ταῖς ἐκκλησίαις τῆς Μακ.; cf. A 4: 12, where D omits ἐν, but 1 Jn 4: 9 ἐν τούτῳ ἐφανερώθη ἡ ἀγάπη τοῦ θεοῦ ἐν ἡμῖν 'in our case' like ποιεῖν ἔν τινι, γίνεσθαι ἔν τινι, for which certainly the dat. (or acc.) may also be used (§157(1)). 1 C 14: 11 ἔσομαι τῷ λαλοῦντι ('for the...') βάρβαρος καὶ ὁ λαλῶν ἐν (SAB al., without ἐν P46DFG Cl Chr) ἐμοὶ βάρβαρος 'in my eyes, judgment' (ἐν probably to prevent taking ἐμοὶ with λαλῶν). ʼEν is used thus several times in Att. poetry (K.-G. I 466); cf. Jd 1? For this ἐν Mt 21: 42 OT has the Hebraizing ἐν ὀφθαλμοῖς ἡμῶν (cf. §214(6)).—R 10: 20 εὑρέθην ἐν (P47BDFG, without ἐν [following the LXX] SAC) τοῖς ἐμὲ μὴ ζητοῦσιν, ἐμφανὴς ἐγενόμην ἐν (BD only) τοῖς ἐμὲ μὴ ἐπερωτῶσιν.—Aesop. τὸ φανερὸν ἐν πᾶσι 15c.11 Chambry, δόξει ἐν αὐτῇ 19. 8 v.l. (Ursing 44f.); exx. from the apocryphal lit. in Oepke, TW II 535.36ff.—Cf. Bauer s.v. IV 4a; Rob. 588.

(2) Γινώσκειν also takes ἐκ Lk 6: 44 etc., κατὰ τί 1: 18. A 7: 14 ἐν ψυχαῖς ἑβδομήκοντα πέντε '75 in number' from LXX Dt 10: 22; so perhaps also ἐν τριάκοντα etc. (cf. §248(3)).

221. Σύν is limited in classical Attic to the meanings 'including' and 'with the aid of', while μετά means 'with'. At the same time Ionic and accordingly Hellenistic (Mayser II 2, 398ff.) retain σύν in the sense of 'with' alongside μετά, and so it appears in the NT also. MGr however has only μετά (μέ). There is little to note regarding its use. Σὺν πᾶσι τούτοις 'besides all this' (LXX, Jos., s. Bauer s.v. 5) Lk 24: 21, σὺν τῷ καύσωνι 'together with its scorching heat' Ja 1: 11. Σύν sometimes approaches the meaning of καί 'and, (together) with': 1 C 1: 2, Lk 20: 1, 14: 5, 15: 22,

16: 32, etc.; s. Bauer s.v. 4 b. For ἅμα σύν s. §194.

NT authors differ considerably with regard to their use of σύν: it is frequent only in Lk (Gospel and Acts) and Paul, while it does not appear at all in Rev and the Johannine Epistles, and hardly ever in Jn (12: 2, 18: 1; without v.l. only 21: 3; μετά is very frequent); it is missing in 2 Th, 1 T, 2 T, T, Phm among Paul's Epistles; likewise in Heb and 1 P. Brief statistics for σύν and μετά in the NT are to be found in Tycho Mommsen, Beitr. zu der Lehre von den gr. Präp. (Berlin, 1895) 395. Johannessohn i 202ff.; Wackernagel, Syntax ii 154. J. Dupont, σὺν Χριστῷ, Bruges–Liège–Paris, 1952 (on which J. Schneider, ThLZ 1954, 99–101). G. Otto, Die mit syn verbundenen Formulierungen im paulin. Schrifttum (Diss. Berlin, unpublished): ThLZ 1954, 125.

(3) PREPOSITIONS WITH TWO CASES

222. Διά with accusative. In a local sense 'through' (classical only in poetry, Hellenistic in prose since Dionys. Hal. [Käser 54]) only Lk 17: 11 διήρχετο διὰ μέσον (SBL, A al. διὰ μέσου, D μέσον without διά [§215(3)]) Σαμαρείας καὶ Γαλιλαίας, hardly correct. J. Blinzler, Festschr. A. Wikenhauser (Munich, 1954) 50ff. holds that μέσον Σαμαρείας καί is to be struck out as a gloss; on the impossible geography s. H. Conzelmann, Die Mitte der Zeit 60–6[68–73]. Otherwise 'because of, for the sake of', for the reason (propter) as well as for the purpose (= classical ἕνεκα; cf. §216(1)), so that the MGr meaning 'for' also arises (Hatzid. 212f.): Mk 2: 27 τὸ σάββατον διὰ τὸν ἄνθρωπον ἐγένετο καὶ οὐχ ὁ ἄνθρ. διὰ τὸ σάββατον, Jn 11: 42, 12: 30, 1 C 11: 9 etc. (already in some books of the LXX the only use of διά with acc. [Johannessohn ii 240f.]). 'By someone's merit' (as in classical) Jn 6: 57, R 8: 20, therefore also 'by force of' Rev 12: 11, 13: 14.—Mayser ii 2, 368f., 426; Humbert 144ff.; Ljungvik, Syntax 33ff.; Ghedini, Vang. ap. 452; Rob. 583f.; Moule 54f.

223. Διά with genitive. 'Through' of space, time, agent. (1) Temporal also for a past interval = 'after' (Mayser ii 2, 420): δι' ἐτῶν πλειόνων 'after several years' A 24: 17; classical δι' ἐτέων εἴκοσι 'after 20 years' (Hdt. 6. 118) and often διὰ πολλοῦ (χρόνου) 'after a long time' etc. (K.-G. i 482). Unclassically for a period within which something takes place (Olsson 138; Ljungvik, Syntax 25f.; Mayser ii 2, 420): διὰ τριῶν ἡμερῶν 'within three days' Mt 26: 61 = Mk 14: 58 ([ἐν]

τρισὶν ἡμέραις Jn 2: 19 [§200(2)]), διὰ νυκτός per noctem 'at night' (classical νυκτός, νύκτωρ) A 5: 19 (v.l. διὰ τῆς ν.), 16: 9, 17: 10, 23: 31 (δι' ἡμέρας 'throughout the day' Inschr. v. Priene 112.61, 99 [after 84 BC]). (2) The originator is probably also denoted by διά instead of the agent (Johannessohn ii 237; Mayser ii 2, 421ff.; Ljungvik, Syntax 29ff.): R 11: 36 ἐξ αὐτοῦ (origin) καὶ δι' αὐτοῦ (the creator) καὶ εἰς αὐτὸν τὰ πάντα (on this formula, Norden 240ff.), Aeschyl., Agam. 1486 διαὶ Διὸς παναιτίου πανεργέτα. (3) To denote manner (classical): διὰ λόγου 'by way of speech, by word of mouth' A 15: 27; also the circumstances in which one finds oneself because of something: 2 C 2: 4 διὰ πολλῶν δακρύων, or the medium: δι' ἐπιστολῶν 2 C 10: 9. Mayser ii 2, 354ff., 425f.; Humbert 118, 120–4 etc. (4) Idiomatically with urgent questions = 'by' (Attic πρός τινος): R 12: 1 παρακαλῶ ὑμᾶς διὰ τῶν οἰκτιρμῶν τοῦ θεοῦ (Latinism = per?). (5) In a spatial sense also 'along' (?), e.g. A 9: 25 (s. L.-S. s.v. A i 4).

(1) 'After': G 2: 1, A 27: 5 614 pc. (h) syh; δι' ἡμερῶν 'after some days' Mk 2: 1 like class. διὰ χρόνου 'after some (long) time'. This meaning is denied by C. Bruston, Rev. Ét. gr. 33 (1920) 51ff. (cf. Indog. Jahrb. 9 [1924] 107), and for Paul by S. Giet, RSR 41 (1953) 323–4 (cf. R 11: 10, 2 Th 3: 16). —'During': A 1: 3 δι' ἡμερῶν τεσσεράκοντα ὀπτανόμενος αὐτοῖς 'during 40 days' (not continuously, but now and then, as the scholiast, acc. to Chrys., already observed); Lk 9: 37 D διὰ τῆς ἡμέρας 'in the course of the day'; G 2: 1 (? s. supra).

(2) H 2: 10, 1 C 1: 9, G 1: 1, Herm Vis 3.13.3, Sim 9.14.5; but separated 1 C 8: 6 εἷς θεὸς ὁ πατήρ, ἐξ οὗ τὰ πάντα καὶ ἡμεῖς εἰς αὐτόν, καὶ εἷς κύριος Ἰ. Χρ., δι' οὗ (ὃν B) τὰ πάντα καὶ ἡμεῖς δι' αὐτοῦ; cf. Jn 1: 3, Mt 1: 22 τὸ ῥηθὲν ὑπὸ κυρίου διὰ τοῦ προφήτου, etc. etc. Cf. Schettler, Die paulinische Formel 'Durch Christus', Tübingen, 1907; Jonker, De paulin. formule 'Door Christus' (ThStudiën 26 [1909] 173–208).

(3) R 14: 20 διὰ προσκόμματος ἐσθίειν 'with offense'. R 2: 27 τὸν διὰ γράμματος καὶ περιτομῆς παραβάτην νόμου 'you who, because (or while?) you have the writings and circumcision, . . .' (cf. Schrenk, TW i 765).—G 4: 13 δι' ἀσθένειαν τῆς σαρκὸς εὐηγγελισάμην ὑμῖν 'on account of an infirmity' is advocated by Mlt. 106 [172]; the widely held interpretation, suggested also by per (not propter) infirmitatem (vg) 'suffering from an infirmity, in weakness', requires δι' ἀσθενείας.

(4) R 15: 30, 1 C 1: 10 and elsewhere in Paul (cf. κατά τινος §225); however R 12: 3 λέγω διὰ τῆς χάριτος = 'by virtue of' (15: 15 διὰ τὴν χάριν 'for the sake of').

(5) A 9: 25, 2 C 11: 33 διὰ τοῦ τείχους 'along the wall'; cf. Hdt. 4.39 παρήκει διὰ τῆσδε τῆς θαλάσσης ἡ ἀκτὴ αὕτη and further in Ljungvik 81 f.; contrast Bauer A ı 2 and cf. A 9: 25 with 2 C 11: 33 in RSV!

224. Κατά with accusative appears frequently and in a great variety of constructions, but conforms on the whole to classical usage. (1) The use of κατά as a circumlocution for the possessive or subjective gen. is generally Hellenistic (Raderm.[2] 139; Mayser ıı 1, 11; ıı 2, 343): ἡ κατὰ τὸν ἥλιον ἀνατολή Polyb.; it is virtually limited to pronouns in the NT: E 1: 15 τὴν καθ᾽ ὑμᾶς πίστιν. (2) In the superscriptions to the Gospels κατά Ματθαῖον etc., the author of this form of the Gospel is designated by κατά (cf. §163). (3) Distributive κατά (κ. ἑορτήν 'at each feast' Mt 27: 15, Mk 15: 6) has been frozen as an adverb (cf. ἀνά §204) in καθ᾽ εἷς, s. §305.—Mayser ıı 2, 430 ff.

(1) A 18: 15 νόμου τοῦ καθ᾽ ὑμᾶς 'your own law', cf. 26: 3, 17: 28; the forerunner of this usage is found already in the class. period, e.g. τὰ καθ᾽ ὑμᾶς ἐλλείμματα 'shortcomings which are common with you' Dem. 2.27. Homil Clem 9.3.2 ἐκείνων τὸ ἁμάρτημα πολὺ ἧττον ἦν τοῦ καθ᾽ ὑμᾶς, 2.36.1 ἀπὸ τῆς κατὰ τὴν ζήτησιν ἀναβολῆς 'from the delay of the inquiry' (avoiding a second gen.); cf. 2.36.4 ἡ τῆς ζητήσεως ὑπέρθεσιν, 37.2 ἐπὶ τῇ τῆς ʒ. ὑπερθέσει. A 16: 39 D τὰ καθ᾽ ὑμᾶς = τὸ ὑμέτερον πρᾶγμα. R 1: 15 τὸ κατ᾽ ἐμὲ πρόθυμον = ἡ ἐμὴ προθυμία (τὸ πρόθυμον = ἡ προθυμία s. Lietzmann, Hdb.[2] in loc.; in addition Eur., Med. 173 τό γ᾽ ἐμὸν πρόθυμον [nom.], IT 1023 τὸ δὲ πρόθυμον ᾔνεσα, Plato, Lg. 9.859B τό γε πρόθυμον παρεχόμενον; cf. τὸ κατ᾽ ἐκείνους γενναῖον = ἡ ἐκείνων γενναιότης and similar constructions in Jos.; Schmidt 361 f.), but perhaps it could be taken as τὸ κατ᾽ ἐμέ 'quod in me est' (cf. τὸ κατὰ σάρκα 9: 5 etc., §160) πρόθυμος (cf. lat and Or) scil. εἰμί (§128(2); Plato, Rep. 499 D ἕτοιμοί scil. ἐσμεν). Cf. Bauer s.v. ıı 7b, c.—G. Rudberg, Ad usum circumscribentem praepositionum Graecarum adnotationes (Eranos 19 [1919/20] 173–206).
(2) Cf. ἡ παλαιὰ διαθήκη κατὰ τοὺς ἑβδομήκοντα, 2 Macc 2: 13 ἐν τοῖς ὑπομνηματισμοῖς τοῖς κατὰ Νεεμίαν 'those which bear the name of N.' Jos., c. Ap. 1.3.18 τὴν καθ᾽ αὑτὸν ἱστορίαν 'his history'.—A 11: 1 s. §225.
(3) S. Bauer s.v. ıı 1 d, ıı 2 c, ıı 3.

225. Κατά with genitive is far less strongly attested; it most often means 'against someone' (in a hostile sense). It does not appear often in a local sense: κατὰ τοῦ κρημνοῦ 'over and down' Mt 8: 32, also = 'throughout' (only Lk, Acts and always with ὅλος): A 9: 31 καθ᾽ ὅλης τῆς Ἰουδαίας,

9: 42, 10: 37, Lk 4: 14, 23: 5. Ἡ κατὰ βάθους (𝔓[46]D βάθος) πτωχεία 2 C 8: 2 'extreme, radical poverty'; cf. Strabo 9.419 ἄντρον κοῖλον κατὰ βάθους. Ὀμνύναι, (ἐξ)ορκίζειν κατά τινος s. §149. Stereotyped καθόλου (classical and Hellenistic; Mayser ı[2] 3, 206; ıı 2, 430) A 4: 18.—Mayser ıı 2, 428 ff.

Also for Att. ἐπί τινα (ἐστίν and similar verbs): Mt 12: 30 ὁ μὴ ὢν μετ᾽ ἐμοῦ κατ᾽ ἐμοῦ ἐστιν, Mk 9: 40, Lk 11: 23, R 8: 31; cf. Dem. 19.339 ἐπὶ τὴν πόλιν ἐστίν in contrast with Polyb. 10.8.5 κατὰ τῆς πόλεως ὑπελάμβανεν εἶναι (Att. κατά with 'to speak, witness', etc.). Κατὰ κεφαλῆς ἔχων 1 C 11: 4 'hanging down from the head, on the head' (contrast ἀκατακαλύπτῳ τῇ κεφαλῇ). 'Throughout' is Hell., cf. Polyb. 3.19.7 κατὰ τῆς νήσου διεσπάρησαν, Schmidt 390. With acc. οἱ ὄντες κατὰ τὴν Ἰουδαίαν A 11: 1, simply 'in'.— Ἠρώτησα ('entreated, requested') κατὰ τοῦ κυρίου ('by the Lord') Herm Vis 3.2.3, cf. 'to swear by' §149.

226. Μετά with accusative only in a temporal sense 'after'; also H 9: 3 μετὰ τὸ δεύτερον καταπέτασμα is probably not purely local 'behind', but 'after the second curtain one comes to...'. Οὐ μετὰ πολλὰς ταύτας ἡμέρας A 1: 5 'not many days after today'; cf. Herm Vis 4.1.1 μετὰ ἡμέρας εἴκοσι τῆς προτέρας ὁράσεως, LXX Gen 16: 3, further §164(4) and πρό §213.—Bauer s.v. B ıı; Mayser ıı 2, 444 f.

Cf. with the predicate οὗτος in A 1: 5 πρὸ πολλῶν τούτων ἡμερῶν in Acta S. Theogni ch. 119 p. 102.15 (Schulze, Graeca Latina 15), πρὸ ὀλίγων τούτων ἡμερῶν POxy vııı 1121.12 (295 AD), πρὸ τούτων τεττάρων ἐτῶν Alciphro 1.14.2 (Schepers); s. also Lk 24: 21 (§129). Μετὰ τὴν τρίτην and the like s. Kallenberg, RhM 69 (1914) 677 ff.

227. Μετά with genitive. (1) 'Among, with' (classical in the poets): μετὰ τῶν νεκρῶν Lk 24: 5, ἦν μετὰ τῶν θηρίων Mk 1: 13. (2) Meaning 'with', it is interchangeable with σύν (§221). (3) Hebraizing = 'to, for, on': ποιεῖν (τὸ) ἔλεος μετά τινος (§206(3)). On the whole μετά outnumbers σύν by far (almost three times the number of examples); in individual books, however, σύν is represented equally well or is even more numerous (Acts).— Mayser ıı 2, 440 ff.

(1) Μετὰ ἀνόμων ἐλογίσθη (Mk 15: 28,) Lk 22: 37 OT (Hebr. אֶת, LXX ἐν); ἔλεγον μετ᾽ ἀλλήλων Jn 11: 56, cf. 6: 43, 16: 19, τιθέναι μετά Herm Sim 9.8.2, 4, (5).
(2) With expressions of association like πολεμεῖν, εἰρηνεύειν, συμφωνεῖν, φίλος, λαλεῖν (Mk 6: 50 etc.)

etc. (§§ 193, 202), not σύν τινι, but μετά τινος (Hebr. **םﬠ**; class. dat. or πρός) is used for and beside the dat.; likewise for accompanying circumstances: μετὰ φόβου etc. (§ 198(4); class.).

(3) Herm Sim 5.1.1 περὶ πάντων ὧν ἐποίησεν μετ' ἐμοῦ 'to me' (A 14: 27 is different, = 'with'); LXX 1 Macc 10: 27 ἀνθ' ὧν ποιεῖτε μεθ' ἡμῶν; an ex. from a Byz. pap. may be found in Kuhring 35.—H 12: 14, 2 T 2: 22 εἰρήνην διώκειν μετά 'in company with', not 'peace with' (Foerster, TW II 412, 415).

228. Περί with accusative (not very frequent) local and temporal 'around, about, near'; then to designate the object of activity or effort like classical (not of speech or thought, for which περί τινος is used). Paul, who uses περί τινα only in Ph (and the Pastorals), uses it generally for 'concerning, regarding' (perhaps like Plato πονηρὸν περὶ τὸ σῶμα 'injurious with regard to...'): Ph 2: 23 τὰ περὶ ἐμέ.—Mayser II 2, 454 ff.

Οἱ περὶ αὐτόν 'his disciples' Mk 4: 10, Lk 22: 49; οἱ περὶ Παῦλον A 13: 13 including Paul as in the literary language. With ἐπιθυμίαι Mk 4: 19 (om. D); with περισπᾶσθαι, θορυβάζεσθαι Lk 10: 40, 41; with ἐργάται A 19: 25. 1 T 1: 19 περὶ τὴν πίστιν ἐναυάγησαν, 6: 4, 21, 2 T 2: 18, 3: 8, T 2: 7; τὰ περὶ τὸν πύργον Herm Vis 3.3.1. Jn 11: 19 πρὸς τὰς περὶ Μάρθαν καὶ Μαρίαν 𝔓⁴⁵AC²ΓΘ al. even to designate the two sisters alone (as often in later writers, s. Bauer s.v. 2 δ), but hardly genuine (πρὸς τὴν Μ. καὶ [τὴν W] Μ. SBC*LW al., likewise D without τήν; sy⁸ is still different).

229. Περί with genitive (quite common) most frequently with 'to speak, know, care etc. about, concerning'; at the beginning of a sentence = 'concerning, with reference to' 1 C 7: 1 etc. (classical). (1) Also 'on account of, because of' (classical and Hellenistic; Mayser II 2, 448 f.) with κρίνεσθαι, ἐγκαλεῖν, εὐχαριστεῖν, ἐρωτᾶν 'to request', δεῖσθαι, προσεύχεσθαι, πρόφασιν ('excuse') ἔχειν, αἰνεῖν etc., in which it often means 'for' and overlaps with ὑπέρ: Jn 17: 9 οὐ περὶ τοῦ κόσμου ἐρωτῶ, ἀλλὰ περὶ ὧν δέδωκάς μοι. (2) With verbs of emotion (rare in classical): ἀγανακτεῖν περί τινος 'at someone' Mt 20: 24, Mk 10: 41; cf. περὶ τῶν πραχθέντων Plato, Ep. 7.349 D. Ποιῆσαι περὶ αὐτοῦ 'with him' Lk 2: 27 (classical would be π. αὐτόν, NT αὐτῷ, ἐν αὐτῷ or μετ' αὐτοῦ; cf. § 206(3) and 227(3)). Λαγχάνειν ('to cast lots') περί τινος Jn 19: 24 can be compared with classical μάχεσθαι περί τινος.—Mayser II 2, 446 ff.

(1) Περί actually for ὑπέρ (Mayser II 2, 450 ff.; Bauer s.v. περί 1 f): Mt 26: 28 τὸ περί (D ὑπέρ)

πολλῶν ἐκχυννόμενον (in Mk 14: 24 only AP al. περί), 1 C 1: 13 ἐσταυρώθη περὶ ἡμῶν only 𝔓⁴⁶BD* (al. ὑπέρ); H 10: 6, 8 OT, 18, 26, 13: 11, 1 P 3: 18, Mk 1: 44, Lk 5: 14. A 26: 1 περί (SAC al., ὑπέρ BLP) σεαυτοῦ λέγειν, G 1: 4 (ὑπέρ ScB), H 5: 3 περί (ὑπέρ CcDc al. as in 1) ἁμαρτιῶν.

(2) Mt 9: 36 ἐσπλαγχνίσθη περὶ αὐτῶν (i.e. τῶν ὄχλων). Otherwise verbs of emotion take ἐπί τινα or ἐπί τινι (§§ 176(1); 233(2); 235(2)). Lk 2: 18 θαυμάζειν περί τινος ('over a thing'), cf. § 196. 3 Jn 2 περὶ πάντων εὔχομαί σε εὐοδοῦσθαι καὶ ὑγιαίνειν corresponds to the frequent salutation in letters in the pap. πρὸ μὲν πάντων ('above all') εὔχομαί σε ὑγιαίνειν, although περί with the gen. in this sense does not appear to be attested otherwise.

230. Ὑπέρ with accusative (Mt 10: 24 etc., not frequent) 'over, above', to designate that which excels or surpasses, therefore also with the comparative (§ 185(3)). No longer anywhere in a local sense except H 9:5 according to D*E* ὑπὲρ δ' αὐτήν 'over, above' (al. ὑπεράνω δὲ αὐτῆς; § 215(2)) as similarly in the papyri (Mayser II 2, 461). Adverbial in Paul (combined with adverbs):

Ὑπὲρ λίαν (or rather ὑπερλίαν, s. §§ 12; 116(3)) 2 C 11: 5, 12: 11, ὑπερεκπερισσοῦ 1 Th 3: 10, 5: 13 (-σσῶς BD*FG), E 3: 20, cf. class. ὑπέρλαμπρος, ὑπερεξακισχίλιοι ([Dem.] 59.89). Even 2 C 11: 23 διάκονοι Χριστοῦ εἰσιν; ὑπέρ ('to a higher degree, better') ἐγώ (scil. διακ. Χρ. εἰμι), cf. § 203. Phm 16 ὑπὲρ δοῦλον 'as one who is more than a slave' (cf. Aelian, VH 12.45?). A. T. Robertson, The Use of ὑπέρ in Business Documents in the Papyri (Exp. VIII 19 [1920] 321–7).

231. Ὑπέρ with genitive 'for, on behalf of' (its opposite is κατά τινος Mk 9: 40 etc.) is greatly limited by περί (§ 229(1)). Mayser II 2, 457 ff. (1) The reverse exchange of ὑπέρ for περί (e.g. λέγειν ὑπέρ 'to speak about'; Johannessohn II 217 f.; Mayser II 2, 453 f.), common in Attic and Hellenistic (LXX also), is less frequent and is virtually confined to Paul: 2 C 8: 23 εἴτε ὑπὲρ Τίτου 'regarding Titus'. (2) Also that which one wants to attain can be introduced by ὑπέρ (as in classical): 2 C 1: 6 ὑπὲρ τῆς ὑμῶν παρακλήσεως 'on behalf of' = 'for'.

(1) Jn 1: 30 ὑπὲρ οὗ (περὶ οὗ ScAC³L al.; ὃν without prep. Non Chr, which Blass took to be correct, is misplaced from 15) ἐγὼ εἶπον, 2 C 12: 8 ὑπὲρ τούτου 'because of that' (cf. περί § 229(1)), 2 Th 1: 1. Paul at times with καυχᾶσθαι, also φυσιοῦσθαι, φρονεῖν (Ph 1: 7 'to think about', 4: 10 'to care for').

(2) Ph 2: 13 ὑπὲρ τῆς εὐδοκίας (+ αὐτοῦ C) πάντα ποιεῖτε 'for the sake of his good will' (Schrenk, TW II 744).

232. Ὑπό. (1) With accusative (not very frequent) 'under' in response to the questions 'where?' and 'whither?' (the old local ὑπό τινος and ὑπό τινι have been absorbed in ὑπό τι; Mayser II 2, 371) in both literal and metaphorical sense; in a temporal sense only A 5: 21 ὑπὸ τὸν ὄρθρον *sub, circa* (classical). (2) With genitive 'by' to denote the agent with passive verbs and expressions passive in sense like πληγὰς λαμβάνειν 2 C 11: 24; in some instances it is supplanted by ἀπό (§ 210). S. also διά § 223(2).—Mayser II 2, 510 ff.

(1) In Johannine literature only Jn 1: 48 (ὑπὸ τὴν συκῆν εἶδόν σε); never Rev, which employs ὑποκάτω instead (§ 215(2)) as in Jn 1: 50 (εἶδόν σε ὑποκάτω τῆς συκῆς). Ὑπὸ χεῖρα properly 'under the hand', in pap. (Preisigke s.v. χείρ col. 727, Mayser II 2, 515) 'on occasion, immediately, just now', i.e. 'at hand', Herm Vis 3.10.7, 5.5, Man 4.3.6 'on every occasion' = 'continually' (Dibelius, Hdb. on Vis 3.10.7).

(2) Loosely used Herm Sim 9.1.2 ὑπὸ παρθένου ἑώρακας and ὑπὸ ἀγγέλου βλέπεις 'taught by'; cf. Rev 6: 8 ἀποκτεῖναι … ὑπὸ τῶν θηρίων = ποιῆσαι ἀποθανεῖν ὑπό.

(4) PREPOSITIONS WITH THREE CASES

233. Ἐπί with accusative. Ἐπί is the only preposition which is *extensively* used with all three cases. The acc. is by far the most frequent, however, and, as in classical Greek, is used not only in response to the question 'whither?' (including such instances as with στῆναι, with which εἰς can also be used, § 205), but often also (1) in response to the question 'where?' instead of classical gen. or dat. (on this case blending, cf. Jannaris § 1583; Mlt. 107 [174]; Mayser II 2, 369): Mk 4: 38 ἐπὶ τὸ προσκεφάλαιον (DW ἐπὶ προσκεφαλαίου) καθεύδων. (2) In a metaphorical sense, too, the acc. extends beyond its proper sphere: not only καθιστάναι δικαστὴν ἐφ' ὑμᾶς (direction 'whither?') Lk 12: 14, but also βασιλεύσει ἐπὶ τὸν οἶκον Ἰακώβ 1: 33 etc. (s. § 177; Hebraism or Hellenistic generalization of the acc. in place of the gen., cf. § 234(5)). (3) Temporally to designate the time when an act takes place: A 3: 1 ἐπὶ τὴν ὥραν τῆς προσευχῆς; in addition, like classical, of extension over a period of time: A 13: 31 ἐπὶ ἡμέρας πλείους, etc., also ἐφ' ὅσον (χρόνον) 'as long as' R 7: 1, Mt 9: 15 etc.—Mayser II 2, 476 ff.

(1) Mt 9: 9 (Mk 2: 14, Lk 5: 27); Lk 2: 25, cf. 40 where D has ἐν αὐτῷ; Jn 1: 32, 33; 2 C 3: 15; A 21:

35 ἐγένετο ἐπὶ τοὺς ἀναβαθμούς, cf. γίνεσθαι εἰς § 205 (but ἐπί τινος Lk 22: 40). Ἐπὶ τὸ αὐτό 'at the same place, together' also with εἶναι etc. rather often in Acts, also in Paul and others, LXX, Jos.; Dit., Syll.³ 736.66 (92 BC) (in contrast to κατὰ μέρος), often in pap. = 'in all, total' (Mayser II 2, 418 n. 2). Mt 14: 25 περιπατῶν ἐπὶ τὴν θάλασσαν SBW al., gen. CD al.; 26 gen. SBCD al., acc. EFGW al.; 28 f. all witnesses ἐπὶ τὰ ὕδατα. In Mk 6: 48 f. and Jn 6: 19 gen., which in some instances in Jn, like 21: 1, should be understood as 'by the sea'. Similar interchange of gen. and acc. without distinction in meaning: Rev 13: 1, 16, 14: 9 (but distinct 7: 1 ἐπὶ τῆς γῆς [θαλάσσης] 'on the face of the earth [sea]', ἐπὶ πᾶν δένδρον 'upon every tree'), Herm Man 11.1; the MSS also vary between gen. and acc. in Rev 10: 1, 13: 16, 14: 9 (𝔓⁴⁷ τῆς χειρός), 14. S. also Bonaccorsi 562 f. Καθῆσθαι ἐπί in Rev with acc. 4: 2, with dat. 21: 5, with gen. 14: 16. LXX: Johannessohn II 319 f., 323.

(2) Ἐπὶ ὀλίγα ἦς πιστός, ἐπὶ πολλῶν σε καταστήσω Mt 25: 21; σπλαγχνίζομαι ἐπὶ τὸν ὄχλον 15: 32, Mk 8: 2; cf. Herm Man 4.3.5, Sim 9.24.2 (Att. would have at least required ἐπὶ τῷ … [§ 235(2)]). Μὴ κλαίετε ἐπ' ἐμέ Lk 23: 28; ἐλπίζειν (Johannessohn II 314 f.), πιστεύειν, πίστις, πεποιθέναι ἐπί τινα or ἐπί τινι (§ 187(6)) in addition to εἰς τινα (ἔν τινι); ἐπίστευσαν ἐπὶ τὸν κύριον A 9: 42 (cf. 11: 17 etc.) can be compared with ἐπέστρεψεν ἐπὶ τὸν κ. 9: 35, 11: 21 etc. (direction 'whither?'), but this explanation will hardly do for τοὺς πιστεύοντας ἐπὶ σέ 22: 19 etc. Mk 9: 12 (,13) γέγραπται ἐπὶ τὸν υἱὸν τοῦ ἀνθρώπου 'concerning' (Att. rather ἐπί τινι), cf. H 7: 13. A 4: 22 ὁ ἄνθρωπος ἐφ' ὃν ἐγεγόνει τὸ σημεῖον 'on' (class. εἰς ὅν [Hdt 1.114] or περὶ ὅν; cf. also ἐπί τινος § 234(6)); 10: 25 πεσὼν ἐπὶ τοὺς πόδας προσεκύνησεν = Att. προσπεσὼν αὐτῷ (Jn 11: 32 πρός, v.l. εἰς, Mk 5: 22 πρός).

(3) Ἐπὶ τὴν αὔριον 'on the following day' A 4: 5 (Lk 10: 35 'for the morrow'?), more frequently τῇ ἐπαύριον. Ostracon, Preisigke, Sammelbuch III 6011.14 (i BC) ἐπὶ τὴν ἐφαῦριν, PRyl 441 (iii AD) ἐπὶ τὴν ἐπαύριον, but PLille I 15.2 (242/1 BC) τῇ ἐπαύριον ἡμέρα.

234. Ἐπί with genitive. (1) Most frequently, 'on, upon' in response to the question 'where?' (2) Also answering the question 'whither?' (for the reverse blending s. § 233(1)): Mk 4: 26 βάλῃ τὸν σπόρον ἐπὶ τῆς γῆς. (3) Further 'at, near, by': Mt 21: 19 ἐπὶ τῆς ὁδοῦ. (4) With persons 'before': Mk 13: 9 ἐπὶ ἡγεμόνων σταθήσεσθε. (5) Metaphorically 'over' of authority, control (Attic). (6) 'To do something to someone, to say something about someone' (as in Plato, Charm. 155 D): Jn 6: 2 ἃ ἐποίει ἐπὶ τῶν ἀσθενούντων. (7) Ἐπ' ἀληθείας 'in accordance with the truth' Mk 12:

14 etc. (8) Temporally more frequently of contemporaneity (classical): ἐπὶ Ἀβιάθαρ ἀρχιερέως Mk 2: 26 (om. D al.); Paul ἐπὶ τῶν προσευχῶν μου 'in' E 1: 16 etc.—Mayser II 2, 462 ff.

(1) Ἐπὶ τῆς γῆς, ἐπὶ κλίνης, καθήμενος ἐπὶ τοῦ ἅρματος, ἐπὶ τοῦ ἵππου etc.

(2) Mk 9: 20 πεσὼν ἐπὶ τῆς γῆς (acc. Mt 10: 29, 34), Mt 26: 12 etc.; Rev 14: 19 ἔβαλεν ἐπὶ τῆς γῆς S (ἐπὶ τὴν γῆν 𝔓⁴⁷, εἰς τ. γ. ACP); also H 8: 10 and 10: 16 OT ἐπὶ καρδίας (according to the original gen. sing., not acc. plur.). Rev 21: 16 s. § 165.

(3) Ἐπὶ τῆς θαλάσσης Jn 21: 1 etc.; also ἐπὶ τῆς (τοῦ) βάτου Mk 12: 26, Lk 20: 37 (if ἐπί here does not = 'on the occasion of', s. infra (8); but certainly local 1 Clem 17.5). Strengthened ἐπάνω § 215(2).

(4) A 25: 9 κρίνεσθαι ἐπ' ἐμοῦ (10 ἐπὶ τοῦ βήματος Καίσαρος ἐστώς 'before', but 17 καθίσας ἐπὶ τ. β. 'upon'), Mt 28: 14 with ἀκουσθῇ (BD ὑπό), 1 T 5: 19 ἐπὶ... μαρτύρων (Mt 18: 16, 2 C 13: 1 OT ἐπὶ στόματος μαρτ. = Hebr. עַל־פִּי), cf. § 235(2). 2 C 7: 14 ἐπὶ Τίτου (v.l. πρὸς Τίτον); Homil Clem 12.24 ἐπὶ παντὸς τοῦ ὄχλου. Att. precedent in ἐπὶ μαρτύρων πράσσεται, τὰ ὡμολογημένα ἐπὶ τοῦ δικαστηρίου and the like (K.-G. I 497); pap. also (Rossberg 45; Mayser II 2, 466 f.) and inscrip. (Viereck 64; Johannessohn II 309).

(5) With εἶναι, yet also with καθιστάναι (§ 233(2)) A 8: 27, R 9: 5, Mt 24: 45 etc., also with βασιλεύειν (§§ 233(2); 177) Mt 2: 22 CD al. (SB gen. alone).

(6) G 3: 16 οὐ λέγει... ὡς ἐπὶ πολλῶν....

(7) Cf. Dem. 18.17 etc.; pap. Mayser II 2, 471.

(8) Mt 1: 11 etc.; Hebraizing ἐπ' ἐσχάτου τῶν ἡμερῶν H 1: 2, cf. 1 P 1: 20, 2 P 3: 3, Jd 18; § 264(5). H 7: 11 ἐπ' αὐτῆς is not temporal, but 'on the basis of it' (the Lev. priesthood) like § 234(6) (Riggenbach in loc.).—A 11: 19 τῆς θλίψεως τῆς γενομένης ἐπὶ Στεφάνου 'at the time of the death of S.' acc. to AE, lat sub Stephano, however an early v.l. has ἐπὶ Στεφάνῳ 'on account of' (§ 235(2)). Ἐπί 'in the passage where' and the like s. P. Persson, Eranos 20 (1921/2) 61, 62 f. e.g. Thuc. 3.68 μετὰ τὸν Μῆδον 'after what happened to the Mede' (cf. §§ 209(4); 219(1)); so perhaps ἐπὶ τῆς βάτου (s. supra (3)).

235. Ἐπὶ **with dative.** (1) The gen. and acc. predominate in the local sense, but a sharp division between them and the dat. cannot be carried through. The dat. is also involved in the metaphorical meaning 'to set over': Mt 24: 47; similarly in classical and the papyri (Mayser II 2, 471 f.). (2) Ἐπί τινι most frequently denotes the basis for a state of being, action, or result, especially with verbs of emotion like θαυμάζειν, χαίρειν, λυπεῖσθαι, μετανοεῖν, s. § 196 (ἐπί with acc. § 233(2)). Ἐφ' ᾧ 'for the reason that, because' R 5: 12?, 2 C 5: 4, Ph 3: 12, 'for' 4: 10 (S. Lyonnet, Le sens de ἐφ' ᾧ en Rom 5: 12 et l'exégèse des pères grecs [Biblica

36 (1955) 436–56]: it does not = διότι). (3) 'In addition to' (classical): ἐπὶ πᾶσιν (τούτοις) Lk 3: 20, 16: 26 (ἐν SBL, E 6: 16 (ἐν 𝔓⁴⁶SBP), C 3: 14, ἐπὶ τοῖς λεγομένοις H 8: 1. (4) Purpose, result (classical ἐπὶ βλάβῃ 'at, to the damage' and the like): ἐπὶ ἔργοις ἀγαθοῖς E 2: 10; ἐπὶ καταστροφῇ 2 T 2: 14 (besides acc., however with v.l.). (5) 'At, in' (predominantly temporal): Ph 1: 3 ἐπὶ πάσῃ τῇ μνείᾳ ὑμῶν.—Mayser II 2, 471 ff.

(1) Question 'where?': ἐπὶ θύραις, ἐπὶ τῇ θύρᾳ (class.) 'before the door' Mt 24: 33, A 5: 9 etc. (however acc. Rev 3: 20), ἐπὶ πίνακι 'on' Mt 14: 8, 11, Mk 6: 25, 28. For 'on something' class. prefers ἐπί τινος (A 27: 44 gen. and dat. vary; Rev 14: 9 S dat. for gen.). 'At, by, near' Jn 4: 6, 5: 2; 'on' Mt 16: 18 (acc. D Eus; 7: 24ff. all witnesses acc.); with ἐπιβάλλειν, -κεῖσθαι, -πίπτειν Mt 9: 16, Jn 11: 38 (without ἐπ' S*, cf. § 202), A 8: 16 (D* acc., which is generally far more frequent). Ἐφ' ἵπποις Rev 19: 14, otherwise always gen.

(2) Πεποιθέναι, πιστεύειν, ἐλπίζειν ἐπί τινι (besides ἐπί τινα, § 233(2)) παρρησιάζεσθαι ἐπὶ τῷ κυρίῳ A 14: 3, also ἐπὶ (τῷ) ὀνόματί τινος (properly 'based on the name'; cf. § 206(2) and Bauer s.v. II 3). Ἐπ' ἐλπίδι 'on the basis of hope' A 2: 26 etc. (so also R 8: 20, 1 C 9:10, T 1: 2). Ἐπὶ δυσὶν μάρτυσιν ἀποθνήσκει H 10: 28 'on the basis of the testimony' (§ 234(4)). 'On the basis of = by virtue of, in accordance with' H 8: 6, 9: 10, 15, 17. Εὐχαριστεῖν (as in PLond I 42. 10f. p. 30 [168 BC], Jos., Ant. 1.193), δοξάζειν τὸν θεόν, κρίνεσθαι (A 26: 6), σπλαγχνίζεσθαι Mt 14: 14 etc. (cf. §§ 233(2); 176(1)), καλεῖν 'to name after' Lk 1: 59, ζῆν 'to live by' Mt 4: 4 OT, ἀρκεῖσθαι 3 Jn 10 (pap.: Mayser II 1, 120, 329; II 2, 475).

(3) Also acc. Ph 2: 27 λύπην ἐπὶ λύπην (cf. § 208(2)).

(4) G 5: 13 ἐπ' ἐλευθερίᾳ ἐκλήθητε 'to freedom', 1 Th 4: 7 οὐκ ἐπὶ ἀκαθαρσίᾳ ἀλλ' ἐν ἁγιασμῷ (= εἰς ἁγιασμόν?). With persons 'against' (cf. acc. § 232(2)) Lk 12: 52f. (along with the acc.); class. similarly (K.-G. I 503).

(5) 1 C 14: 16, E 4: 26, Ph 2: 17, 1 Th 3: 7, H 11: 4; ἐπὶ τούτῳ (ἐν S*D is better) Jn 4: 27; ἐπὶ συντελείᾳ τῶν αἰώνων H 9: 26. With persons 'about' Rev 10: 11 (cf. gen. § 234(6)), likewise with γεγραμμένα Jn 12: 16 (D περὶ αὐτοῦ; om. b e Non); 'with' A 5: 35.

236. Παρά **with accusative.** (1) Mostly local 'by, along'; never used with persons (frequent in classical), for which πρός τινα is used § 239(1) (but often παρὰ τοὺς πόδας τινός). (2) Metaphorically as in classical 'against, contrary to' (contrast κατά 'in accordance with'): παρὰ φύσιν R 1: 26, 11: 24 (contrast κατὰ φύσιν). (3) 'Other than' G 1: 8, 9, also with ἄλλος 1 C 3: 11 (classical); often 'more than' with (§ 185(3)) or without comparative; classical 'in comparison with' leads into this usage. (4) 'In contradistinction to, about' (classical): 2 C 11: 24 τεσσεράκοντα παρὰ μίαν '40 less one'. (5) Παρὰ τοῦτο 'for this reason' (classical) 1 C 12: 15, 16.—Mayser II 2, 489 ff.; Riesenfeld, TW v 724–33.

Only local in Mt, Mk; in Jn and the Catholic Epistles it does not appear at all.
(1) The distinction between 'where?' (properly παρά τινι; cf. §238) and 'whither?' has been lost in the NT just as it had already become indistinct in class. owing to the extension of παρά with acc.
(2) Κατὰ δύναμιν...παρὰ δύν. ('beyond') old) 2 C 8: 3 (v.l. ὑπέρ).
(3) 'More than': R 1: 25 ἐλάτρευσαν τῇ κτίσει παρά (virtually = 'instead of') τὸν κτίσαντα, 12: 3, 14: 5, Barn 11.9, Herm Man 10.1.2; παρὰ πάντας 'more than all (others)' Lk 13: 2, 4, PSI IV 317.6 f. (95 AD).
(4) Παρά τι 'nearly, almost' (literally 'with the omission of') Lk 5: 7 D, Herm Sim 9.19.3 (for which 8.1.14 παρὰ μικρόν).
(5) Οὐ παρὰ τοῦτο οὐκ ἔστιν ἐκ τοῦ σώματος 'it is not for that reason any the less...', 'nevertheless it still belongs...' 1 C 12: 15 f.

237. Παρά with genitive. (1) 'From the side of' only with persons (classical), with 'to come, hear, receive' etc. (for which ἀπό is occasionally used, §210(3)). (2) Without verb: Mk 5: 26 δαπανήσασα τὰ παρ' ἑαυτῆς (παρ' om. DW) is also correct in classical; cf. Lk 10: 7, Ph 4: 18 etc.—Mayser II 2, 483 ff.

(1) Also correct τοῖς λελαλημένοις παρὰ κυρίου Lk 1: 45, since it is not God himself who had spoken, but an angel by his command. But A 22: 30 παρά with κατηγορεῖσθαι only HLP (al. ὑπό).
(2) Mk 3: 21 οἱ παρ' αὐτοῦ 'his own people, family' (LXX [and Theod.] Sus 33, 1 Macc 9: 44 v.l., 58; pap. Rossberg 52, Mlt. 106 f. [173], Olsson 201 f.; in class. it could be the envoys of someone). S. Bauer s.v. I 4 β for biblio.

238. Παρά with dative. The dat. is least used with παρά (on account of the competition of πρός §239). Nevertheless, it is found in all NT books except Hebrews and Jude. The meaning 'by, near, beside' answering the question 'where?' only with persons (predominantly also in classical; Hellenistic, s. Wifstrand, K. Hum. Vet.-samf. i Lund, Årsber. 1933–4 IV 60 ff.) with the exception of Jn 19: 25 παρὰ τῷ σταυρῷ (Homil Clem 11.15.2 παρὰ τῇ θεοῦ θρησκείᾳ κηρύσσεται νήφειν..., παρὰ δὲ τοῖς λεγομένοις θεοῖς τὰ ἐναντία γίνεται). And not just of immediate proximity (Lk 9: 47 ἔστησεν αὐτὸ παρ' ἑαυτῷ, D ἑαυτόν): not καθῆσθαι

παρά, but μετά Rev 3: 21, σύν A 8: 31, πρός Mt 26: 55 CD. On the other hand, 'in someone's house' (Lk 19: 7, Jn 1: 40, A 10: 6) or with a group of people (Rev 2: 13). Moreover in a figurative sense:

Lk 1: 30 εὗρες χάριν παρὰ τῷ θεῷ, R 2: 11 οὐκ ἔστιν προσωπολημψία παρὰ τῷ θεῷ, Mt 19: 26 δυνατόν, ἀδύνατον παρά τινι. Especially 'in the judgment of someone' (class.): R 12: 16 φρόνιμοι παρ' ἑαυτοῖς (11: 25 s. §188(2)), 1 C 3: 19 μωρία παρὰ τῷ θεῷ, also A 26: 8 ἄπιστον κρίνεται παρ' ὑμῖν (Mt 21: 25 διελογίζοντο παρ' ἑαυτοῖς, however ἐν BL al. as in 16: 8 etc.). C 3: 19 πρὸς αὐταῖς 𝔓⁴⁶ is an error for πρὸς αὐτάς.—Mayser II 2, 487 ff.

239. Πρός with accusative is used very extensively with 'to come, send, bring, say etc. to, toward(s)' (a person). (1) It appears often also with 'to be' and the like instead of παρά τινι 'with, in the company of': Mt 13: 56 πρὸς ἡμᾶς εἰσιν. Mk 14: 4 ἦσαν...ἀγανακτοῦντες πρὸς ἑαυτούς (DΘ read differently) = Aramaic *dativus ethicus* (Black, Aramaic Approach 77); 'they were greatly agitated' (J. Jeremias, ZNW 44 [1952/3] 103). (2) Also instead of παρά τινα (§236(1)): A 5: 10 ἔθαψαν πρὸς τὸν ἄνδρα αὐτῆς. (3) Also of places and things: πρὸς τὸ ὄρος Mt 21: 1 (v.l. εἰς), Mk 11: 1, Lk 19: 29. (4) Temporally to denote the approach toward (classical): πρὸς ἑσπέραν ἐστίν Lk 24: 29 (πρὸς ἑ. κέκλικεν ἡ ἡμέρα D); also 'for a period' (no longer): πρὸς καιρόν, ὥραν, ὀλίγας ἡμέρας, τὸ παρόν Lk 8: 13, Jn 5: 35, H 12: 10, 11 etc. (5) Hostile and friendly relationships: μάχεσθαι, εἰρήνην ἔχειν, ἀσύμφωνος (A 28: 25), ἤπιος etc. (6) With reference to: τί πρὸς ἡμᾶς; 'what is that to us?' Mt 27: 4, Jn 21: 22, 23 (classical similarly; §127(3)). (7) Purpose, result, destiny: ἀγαθός, ὠφέλιμος, δυνατός *et al.* ('for, to') E 4: 29, 1 T 4: 8, 2 C 10: 4 etc.; ὁ πρὸς τὴν ἐλεημοσύνην καθήμενος A 3: 10. (8) 'In accordance with' (classical): πρὸς τὸ συμφέρον 1 C 12: 7. Πρὸς τὴν σκληροκαρδίαν ὑμῶν Mt 19: 8, Mk 10: 5 'in view of' = 'because of'. 'In comparison with' (classical): ἄξια πρός R 8: 18.—Mayser II 2, 497 ff.

(1) Mt 26: 18 πρὸς σὲ ποιῶ τὸ πάσχα, 55 v.l., Mk 6: 3, Jn 1: 1 etc.; Herm Man 11.9 etc.; also Mk 11: 31 (Lk 20: 5) διελογίζοντο πρὸς ἑαυτούς (cf. Mt 21: 25, §238). Mk 9: 10 πρὸς ἑαυτούς with ἐκράτησαν or rather with συνζητοῦντες (as in Lk 22: 23).
(2) A 11: 3 εἰσῆλθες πρὸς ἄνδρας, i.e. in the house of, therefore Att. παρά.
(3) Πρὸς τὴν θύραν Mk 1: 33, 2: 2, 11: 4 (, Lk 16: 20) answering the question 'whither?' and 'where?'; to

the latter πρὸς τῇ θύρᾳ is correct Jn 18: 16, as are πρὸ (v.l. ἐπὶ) τῶν θυρῶν A 5: 23, ἐπὶ θύραις Mt 24: 33. Πρὸς τὸ οὖς λαλεῖν Lk 12: 3. Also θερμαίνεσθαι πρὸς τὸ φῶς (turning toward) Mk 14: 54 (Lk 22: 56) are like class. Πρὸς τὴν θάλασσαν Mk 3: 7, v.l. εἰς; cf. § 207(1). Lk 24: 50 ἐξήγαγεν αὐτοὺς ἕως (om. D) πρὸς (εἰς AW²X al.) Βηθανίαν 'as far as Bethany, to within sight of B.', since an actual entry is out of the question; on εἰς cf. § 207(1). Pap. τὸ πρὸς Μέμφιν or Μέμφει μέγα Σαραπιεῖον (Mayser II 2, 371).

(4) Πρὸς τὸ παρόν class.: Thuc 2.22.1, 3.40.7, Plato, Lg. 5.736 A. Homil Clem 20.15 πρὸς μίαν ἡμέραν, BGU III 850.7f. (76 AD) πρὸς ἡμ. μίαν.

(5) Πρᾶγμα ἔχειν πρός τινα 1 C 6: 1 as BGU I 22.8 (114 AD). H 4: 13 πρὸς ὃν ἡμῖν ὁ λόγος, cf. ὡς πρὸς σὲ (ὑμᾶς) τοῦ λόγου ἐσομένου PHib I 53.3 (246 BC), 75.8 (232 BC), POxy IX 1188.17 (13 AD) 'since you will have to give account'.

(6) Mk 12: 12 and Lk 20: 19 πρὸς αὐτοὺς τὴν παραβολὴν εἶπεν 'with reference to them, meant for them', cf. Lk 12: 41, 18: 1 etc.

(7) Τὰ πρὸς εἰρήνην Lk 14: 32 (§155(2)), 19: 42; λευκαὶ πρὸς θερισμόν Jn 4: 35; πρὸς θάνατον 11: 4

(1 Jn 5: 16, 17); πρὸς τί εἶπεν 'with respect to what' Jn 13: 28.

(8) 'In accordance with': πρὸς ἃ ἔπραξεν 2 C 5: 10 Lk 12: 47, Herm Man 11.3.

240. Πρός with genitive and dative. (1) With gen. only A 27: 34 (literary language) τοῦτο πρὸς τῆς ὑμετέρας σωτηρίας ὑπάρχει 'on the side of' = 'is in the interest of, to the advantage of' as in Thuc. 3.59.1 οὐ πρὸς τῆς ὑμετέρας δόξης τάδε.— Rob. 623. (2) With dat. only six times, always local 'near, at, by' (classical): Mk 5: 11 πρὸς τῷ ὄρει, Lk 19: 37 (D acc.), Jn 18: 16, 20: 11 (v.l. acc.), 12, Rev 1: 13 (LXX 104 times according to Mlt. 106 [173]). Otherwise acc. (§239(1)). Classical πρὸς τούτοις 'in addition to' 1 Clem 17.1 (masc. or neut.?).—Mayser II 2, 493ff.

(1) Also Arist., Polyb.; rarely in inscrip. (Schmidt 389) and Ptol. pap. (Mayser II 2, 493f.), 23 times in LXX (Mlt. 106 [173]; Merlier, Rev. Ét. gr. 47 [1934] 198).

6. SYNTAX OF ADJECTIVES
Rob. 650–71

(1) ATTRIBUTIVE

241. Ellipsis with adjectival (and other) attributives. The substantive is often omitted, if it can be easily supplied from the sense and the context, with attributives, especially adjectival, but also pronominal, participial and adverbial attributives; in this case the attributive usually takes on the value of a substantive. Ellipsis is most common with (1) γῆ: ἡ ξηρά (Xen., Arist., LXX) Mt 23: 15 (τὴν θάλασσαν καὶ τὴν ξ.), H 11: 29 DᶜKLP (with γῆς 𝔓¹³𝔓⁴⁶SAD*E), ἡ περίχωρος (LXX, Plut.) Mt 3: 5 etc., ἡ ὀρεινή (scil. γῆ or χώρα; Arist., Philo, LXX) Lk 1: 39, 65, ἡ ἔρημος (LXX, pap.), ἡ οἰκουμένη (Hdt., Arist., etc., LXX); (2) ἡμέρα, e.g. τῇ ἐπιούσῃ A 16: 11, 20: 15, 21: 18 (with ἡμ. 7: 26), ἡ ἑβδόμη 'sabbath' H 4: 4 (same vs. also with ἡμ.; Hdt., Arist., Philo, LXX), μέχρι τῆς σήμερον (LXX, Jos., pap.) Mt 11: 23 etc. (elsewhere with ἡμ.); (3) ὥρα, e.g. (ἡ) πρωΐα, ὀψία Mt, Mk, Jn, Herm (not classical); (4) ὁδός, e.g. εἰς εὐθείας Lk 3: 5 OT (ὁδούς follows shortly however). Other substantives are omitted less frequently, including (5) masculines, e.g. πρόϊμον καὶ ὄψιμον scil. ὑετόν Ja 5: 7 according to (S)B; (6) feminines, e.g. τῇ πνεούσῃ scil. αὔρᾳ

A 27: 40 (Lucian, Herm. 28, ταῖς αὔραις ταῖς... πνεούσαις Arrian, ep. ad Trai. 5, p. 87.21 Hercher, τῷ πνέοντι Lucian, Charon 3); ἡ δεξιά, ἀριστερά, scil. χείρ Mt 6: 3 etc., ἡ ἀγριέλαιος, καλλιέλαιος (§120(3)); (7) neuters, e.g. τὸ διοπετές scil. ἄγαλμα A 19: 35.

Substantivized adjs. like ὁ πονηρός 'the evil one', τὸ πονηρόν 'evil' are common in the NT as generally.

(1) With ἐκ τῆς ὑπὸ τὸν οὐρανὸν εἰς τὴν ὑπ' οὐρανόν Lk 17: 24 (cf. Test Levi 18: 4) μερίδος is rather to be supplied. The ellipsis with ἐξ ἐναντίας (class.) Mk 15: 39 (om. W; ἐκεῖ D), T 2: 8 has been completely obliterated. Jn 11: 54 shows that χώρα cannot always be supplied with ἔρημος; the sing. with art. has more probably become fully substantivized (as in the LXX), e.g. A 7: 36, 38, 42, etc.: Funk, JBL 78 (1959) 205–14. Cf. § 263.

(2) Τῇ ἑτέρᾳ A 20: 15, τῇ ἐχομένῃ 20: 15, Lk 13: 33 (with ἡμ. A 21: 26), elsewhere Acts (Lk) τῇ ἑξῆς; ἡ (ἐπ-)αύριον also Mt, Mk, Lk, Jn, Acts Ja; σήμερον καὶ αὔριον καὶ τῇ τρίτῃ Lk 13: 32 (cf. A 27: 19; otherwise τῇ τρ. ἡμ.); εἰς τὴν αὔριον... πρὸ μιᾶς Herm Sim 6.5.3 (Homil Clem 9.1); (ἐν) τῇ μιᾷ τῶν σαββάτων A 20: 7 etc.; ἡ προθεσμία G 4: 2. Ἀφ' ἧς (with ἡμέρας C 1: 6, 9, Herm Man 4.4.3) 2 P 3: 4, A 24: 11, LXX 1 Macc 1: 11, Herm Sim 8.1.4 ἀφ' ἧς (A; ἄφες PMich is better; s.

§364(2)) πάντα ἴδῃς 'as soon as, after', 6.6 A (POxy XIII 1599.9 [iv AD] and PMich ἀφότε). But in Lk 7: 45 only ὥρας can be supplied with ἀφ' ἧς.

(3) Ἐξαυτῆς 'at once' s. §12(3). Mk 11: 11 ὀψίας οὔσης τῆς ὥρας v.l., but B without τῆς ὥρας; others have ὀψέ (§434(1)); ὀψ(ε)ίας τῆς ὥρας BGU II 380.3 [iii AD], ὀψίας POxy III 475.16 [182 AD]). With ἡ -μηνος, περίοδος is to be supplied (Mayser I² 2, 19.33; II 1, 23 with exx. from the pap.): ἡ τετράμηνος Jn 4: 35 (HW al. -νον nom.), Dit., Syll.³ 410.4, 24 (Erythrae, c. 274 BC), 442.3, 17 (same, c. 250 BC) (acc. τετράμηνον without art. LXX Judg 19: 2 A, 20: 47 A), ἡ τρίμηνος H 11: 23 (acc. -νον without art.; 𝔓⁴⁶ is different, s. §243), LXX (only acc. -ον without art.), Hdt. 2.124. Cf. ἡ δίμηνος Polyb. 6.34.3, ἡ ἔκμηνος *ibid.* and 27.7.2; τὴν ἐπτάμηνον LXX Ezk 39: 14, ἑπτὰ δεκάμηνοι 4 Macc 16: 7. So also with ἡ νυχθήμερος §121.

(4) Stereotyped ἐκείνης Lk 19: 4, ποίας 5: 19 (§186(1)), μακράν §161(1).

(5) Τῷ πνέοντι (spurious v.l. πλέοντι) scil. ἀνέμῳ A 27: 15 add. 614 pc. syʰ.

(6) Ἐπὶ τῇ προβατικῇ scil. πύλῃ Jn 5: 2 (s. Bauer). Ἐν δεξιᾷ R 8: 34 etc. 'on the right hand' unless it is to be written ἐνδέξια (§ 141(2)) (class.; NT otherwise ἐκ δεξιῶν, εἰς τὰ δεξιὰ μέρη Jn 21: 6, ἐν τοῖς δεξιοῖς Mk 16: 5, Herm also δεξιά, εὐώνυμα 'right, left' Sim 9.12.8). Δαρήσεται πολλάς...ὀλίγας scil. πληγάς Lk 12: 47f. (§154; class.), cf. 2 C 11: 24. Κατὰ μόνας 'alone' (Thuc. 1.32.5 etc.; vulgar Koine acc. to W. Schmid, PhW 1934, 933; MGr καταμόναχο) Mk 4: 10, Lk 9: 18 (LXX; Herm Man 11.8); often κατ' ἰδίαν (Hell.), ἰδίᾳ 1 C 12: 11, δημοσίᾳ 'publicly' *in publico* (Att. is different) A 16: 37 etc. With ἐν τῇ Ἑλληνικῇ (S -νίδι) Rev 9: 11 διαλέκτῳ (cf. A 21: 40, 22: 2, 26: 14), γλώσσῃ (class. Ἑλληνὶς γλ. and the like), or φωνῇ (LXX 4 Macc 12: 7, 16: 15) can be supplied. A 19: 19 ἀργυρίου μυριάδας πέντε scil. δραχμῶν. Ἱκετηρία scil. ῥάβδος or ἐλαία 'olive-branch of the suppliant', then since Isocr. 'earnest supplication', and so H 5: 7 (Büchsel, TW III 297f.). What is to be supplied with the stereotyped ἀπὸ μιᾶς is not clear: Lk 14: 18 'unanimously, with one accord', PSI II 286.22 (iii/iv AD; acc. to Preisigke s.v. εἷς col. 426 'once for all', but rather 'at once'), MGr ὅλοι ἀπὸ μνιὰ 'all at once' Thumb² 228 [240] l.14 from the bottom (two lines earlier ἀπὸ μνιὰ τεσκουριά 'with *one* blow'); ἐπὶ μιᾶς ἀπολεῖσθε 'all together' Enoch Sim. 45 p. 4.13 (99.9) Bonner (Lucian, D. Mar. 11.2 ἐπὶ μιᾶς ἡμέρας). MGr μὲ μιᾶς 'at once' (Thumb² §162 n. 2); cf. Aristoph., Lys. 1000 ἀπὸ μιᾶς ὑσπλαγίδος (properly of the runners who dashed off together at the drop of *one* rope [a contrivance for starting races ὕσπληγξ, ὑσπλαγίς, s. L.-S. s.v.]), Philo, Spec. Leg. 3.73 (v 170.8 Cohn-Wendland) ἀπὸ μιᾶς καὶ τῆς αὐτῆς γνώμης (Bauer s.v. ἀπό VI). Kapsomenakis 50 supplies φορᾶς; acc. to Wellhausen, Einl.² 26 Aramaism = מִן חֲדָא 'at once' (cf. Black, Aramaic Approach 82f.).

(7) Τὸ τρίτον, τέταρτον, δέκατον scil. μέρος Rev (not class.), ποτήριον ψυχροῦ scil. ὕδατος Mt 10: 42; cf. Ja 3: 11. Ἐν λευκοῖς scil. ἱματίοις Jn 20: 12, Herm Vis 4.2.1; cf. Mt 11: 8, Rev 18: 12, 16; Artem. 2.3 (p. 86.17 Hercher), 4.2 (p. 205.9); s. also Mayser II 1, 26.

242. **The adjectival use of substantives** which designate persons—adapted by means of ἀνήρ—is found in Lk (following the classical model): ἀνὴρ προφήτης Lk 24: 19, ἄνδρα φονέα A 3: 14, ἀνὴρ Ἰουδαῖος 22: 3 (cf. 10: 28) and in addresses ἄνδρες Γαλιλαῖοι, Ἀθηναῖοι, ἀδελφοί etc. A 1: 16 etc. Semitizing ἄνθρωπος is used in the same way, e.g. Mt 18: 23 (cf. §301(2)). A 16: 16 πνεῦμα πύθωνα SABC*D* (-νος 𝔓⁴⁵C³D²E al.).

(2) PREDICATE ADJECTIVE CORRESPONDING TO AN ADVERB (OR PREPOSITIONAL PHRASE)

243. In classical Greek a predicate adjective appears in certain expressions added to the predicate which correspond to an adverb or prepositional phrase in English. This idiom is rare in the NT, most of the instances being in Lk. The adjective μόνος and the adverb μόνον, which have already grown close in classical, are occasionally confused.—Mayser II 2, 173f., 174f.

Adj. of time: δευτεραῖοι ἤλθομεν 'on the second day' A 28: 13, πεμπταῖοι 20: 6 D (al. ἄχρι ἡμερῶν πέντε); ἐκρύβη τρίμηνος H 11: 23 𝔓⁴⁶ (s. §241(3)); γενόμεναι ὀρθριναὶ ἐπὶ τὸ μνημεῖον Lk 24: 22, ὀρθρινὸς ἐλήλυθας Herm Sim 5.1.1; ἐπιστῇ αἰφνίδιος Lk 21: 34. 'Willingly': ἑκών, ἄκων 1 C 9: 17, R 8: 20; αὐτομάτῃ ἠνοίγη A 12: 10, cf. Mk 4: 28. Sequence: πρῶτος 'as the first', e.g. R 10: 19. Further ἀνάστηθι ὀρθός A 14: 10. Τοῦτο ἀληθὲς (ἀληθῶς SE) εἴρηκας Jn 4: 18, cf. τοῦτό γ' ἀληθῆ λέγουσι [Dem.] 7.43; less class. λέγω ὑμῖν ἀληθῶς Lk 9: 27, 12: 44, 21: 3 = ἀμήν (as in 12: 44 D, 21: 3 Cypr). Μόνος: Mk 6: 8 μηδὲν εἰ μὴ ῥάβδον μόνον (μόνην D), A 11: 19 μηδενὶ εἰ μὴ μόνον (μόνοις D) Ἰουδαίοις, 1 Jn 5: 6 οὐκ ἐν τῷ ὕδατι μόνον (μόνῳ B). If 'alone, only' is plainly connected with a verb (or a pred. noun like ἀκροαταί Ja 1: 22, ἀργαί 1 T 5: 13), only μόνον is possible; but also H 12: 26 OT σείσω οὐ μόνον τὴν γῆν, ἀλλὰ καὶ τὸν οὐρανόν 'I am not content with shaking the earth alone' is not un-Greek; likewise οὐ μόνον δὲ ἐμοί, ἀλλὰ καὶ πᾶσιν 2 T 4: 8 (an award to one would be too little).—Adv. for an adj. s. §434.

(3) COMPARISON

244. **Meaning of the comparative.** With the leveling of the comparative and superlative (§60), the remaining common form was almost

always that of the comparative; only πρῶτος and ἔσχατος are exceptions (§62). The two degrees are not distinguished as in MGr, French, etc., by the addition of the article to the superlative, but are indistinguishable in form; e.g.: 1 C 13: 13 πίστις ἐλπὶς ἀγάπη, τὰ τρία ταῦτα· μείζων δὲ τούτων ἡ ἀγάπη; likewise Barnabas, e.g. 12.2 ὑψηλότερος πάντων. Since, however, in classical Greek the superlative can also be used absolutely = 'very...' (the elative), and the comparative is also used with a slight elative nuance, almost the equivalent of an English positive (θᾶττον 'quite quickly'), so the comparative in the NT is often ambiguous. (1) Jn 13: 27 ὃ ποιεῖς ποίησον τάχιον (Luther 'bald' [RSV 'quickly'], but it can also mean 'as quickly as possible'; cf. 1 T 3: 14, with v.l. ἐν τάχει), H 13: 19 τάχιον probably 'more quickly, sooner', 23 ἐὰν τάχιον ἔρχηται 'if he comes very soon', 2 T 4: 9 ταχέως (I τάχειον [itacistic]) (A 17: 15 ὡς τάχιστα from literary language, but D ἐν τάχει). (2) Also ἆσσον, μᾶλλον, ἄμεινον et al.; furthermore νεώτερος, -ον (καινότερον) of the classical language can sometimes be rendered by the positive, although we too in a similar way say 'come closer', 'it is better to...' and the like. Thus in the NT, e.g. A 17: 21 λέγειν τι ἢ ἀκούειν τι καινότερον (Atticism, s. Norden 333ff.); cf. K.-G. II 306 f. (3) Οἱ πλείονες can mean 'the majority': 1 C 15: 6 ἐξ ὧν οἱ πλείονες μένουσιν, 10: 5, A 19: 32, 27: 12, H 7: 23, but also 'others, even more': (1 C 9: 19 ἵνα τοὺς πλείονας κερδήσω? Origen τοὺς πλ. αὐτῶν), 2 C 2: 6, 4: 15, 9: 2, Ph 1: 14, in contrast to 'those (him) previously mentioned'. —On remnants of the superlative s. §60; for the manner of expressing comparison (gen., ἤ, παρά, ὑπέρ) §185.—Mayser II 1, 46ff.; Rob. 659–71; Smyth §§1063–93; Moule 97f.

(1) Homil Clem 1.14 τάχιόν σε καταλήψομαι 'as quickly as possible', 11.13 τάχιον ἐπιλανθάνεσθε and -νόμενοι 'immediately'; 9.23 ὡς τάχιον εἶπον = φθάσας modo 'just, quite recently' is quite different. Superl. or elative also e.g. BGU II 417.28 (ii/iii AD), 451.11 (i/ii AD), ταχύτερον 615.9, 28 (ii AD). Πυκνότερον A 24: 26 is ambiguous ('very often' or 'all the more frequently'), 2 Clem 17.3 probably 'as often as possible', Ep. Clem. ad Jac. 9.2 (p. 12.11f. Rehm) πυκνότερον...ὡς δύνασθε (weaker Homil Clem 4.2, 8.7); cf. Witkowski, Epistulae on no. 69.4; similarly συνεχέστερον Homil Clem 3.69 (UPZ I 110.186 [164 BC]). The elative comparative in the Koine is mostly colloquial (Mayser II 1, 50).
(2) Besides πρεσβύτερος as a Jewish or Christian designation for a dignitary, cf. further: ἆσσον παρελέγοντο τὴν Κρήτην A 27: 13 (if θᾶσσον is not

correct) 'as near as possible'; ἀκριβέστερον εἰδώς 24: 22 = ἀκριβέστατα (cf. 18: 26, 23: 15, 20, BGU II 388 II 41 [ii/iii AD]; Mayser II 1, 49; Bauer s.v. ἀκριβῶς); κάλλιον ἐπιγινώσκεις 25: 10 = ἄριστα. Βέλτιον σὺ γινώσκεις 2 T 1: 18 (not 'you know better than I', which does not fit here at all; the reference from Lucian compared by Winer is different: Pisc. 20 ἄμεινον σὺ ταῦτα οἶσθα, ὦ Φιλοσοφία: the goddess really does know it better); cf. A 10: 28 D; φανερώτερον A 4: 16 D (al. φανερόν); 1 C 11: 17 εἰς τὸ κρεῖσσον—εἰς τὸ ἦσσον 'in a good, bad way' A. Fridrichsen, Horae Soederblomianae I 1 (1944) 30–2 (with pars. from Plut.). Ambiguous A 17: 22 ὡς δεισιδαιμονεστέρους ὑμᾶς θεωρῶ 'unusually (too) religious' (class.) or 'very religious'; but σπουδαιότερος 2 C 8: 17 simply 'very zealous'. Frequently there is a corresponding use of the English comparative, the standard of comparison being readily supplied: 7: 7 ὥστε με μᾶλλον χαρῆναι 'still more'. Hermas constantly uses the superl. in an elative sense (ἀγαθώτατος, σεμνότατος etc.), while he elsewhere confuses the comp. and superl. (Man 8.4 πάντων πονηρότατα needs correction, i.e. to -τέρα, cf. 10.1.2). Sim 9.10.7 ἦσαν δὲ ἱλαρώτεραι appears elative, therefore perhaps to be corrected to the superl. (however Lat. hilares satis). The comp. is also used for the positive: Vis 3.10.3 λίαν πρεσβυτέρα 'very old' (cf. POxy XIV 1672.6f. [c. 40 AD] καλλιότεραι...λείαν), 5 ὅλη νεωτέρα 'quite youthful', Sim 9.11.5.
(3) Ταῦτα εἰπὼν καὶ τὰ τούτων πλείονα Ep. Clem. ad Jac. 17 (p. 19.6 Rehm) (so A 2: 40 ἑτέροις τε λόγοις πλείοσιν?). Class. has comparable usages: τριάκοντ' ἄνθρωποι πλείους '30 men more' Dem. 20.22, τὸν πλείονα χρόνον 'more time', πλείονες λόγοι 'further speeches' (τὸν πλείω λόγον Soph., Tr. 731). Cf. Tournier, Revue Phil. 1877, 253; Schwab II 178; K.-G. I 637.

245. Positive for comparative. The positive can also be used in the sense of a comparative (superlative), as sometimes also in classical, but more so after the Semitic pattern which does not provide for degree at all. (1) Οἱ πολλοί 'the many' as opposed to the few, therefore 'the majority' (classical). (2) Positive for superlative: Mt 22: 36 ποία ἐντολὴ μεγάλη ἐν τῷ νόμῳ 'the greatest' (Heikel, StKr 106 [1934/5] 314 changes to ἡ μεγ.), cf. 5: 19, Mk 12: 28, Buttmann 73; τὰ ἅγια τῶν ἁγίων H 9: (2,)3 (LXX). (3) Positive for comparative, if the comparison (on the analogy of Semitic usage) is introduced by παρά (§185(3)): Lk 13: 2 (,4) ἁμαρτωλοὶ (ὀφειλέται) παρὰ πάντας (the comparative of ὀφ. was lacking; cf. δεδικαιωμένος παρά 18: 14 SBL), but also by ἤ: καλόν ἐστιν...ἤ Mt 18: 8, 9, Mk 9: 43, 45, 47 (42 is different: the apodosis refers to the offense mentioned in the preceding clause), 1 Clem 51. 3, and even without an adjective (with μᾶλλον missing): Lk 15: 7 χαρὰ ἔσται...ἤ. Also with ἐν: Lk 1: 42 εὐλογημένη σὺ ἐν γυναιξίν; cf. LXX SSol 1: 8 (Zerwick, Graec. bibl. 34).—For comparison by means of τῷ θεῷ s. §192.

(1) Πλεῖστος is also used in this way: Mt 21: 8 ὁ πλεῖστος ὄχλος (Plato, Lg. 3.700c) = ὁ πολὺς ὄ. Mk 12: 37, αἱ πλεῖσται δυνάμεις αὐτοῦ Mt 11: 20 'numerous', cf. τὰ πολλὰ γράμματα A 26: 24. Οἱ πολλοί Mt 24: 12, Mk frequently (Gregory 128): 6: 2 BL (v.l. without οἱ), 9: 26 SABLΔ (similarly), cf. 12: 37 (s. *supra*); in Paul 1 C 10: 33 τῶν πολλῶν opp. to ἐμαυτοῦ, therefore similar to οἱ πλείονες elsewhere (§244(3)). Οἱ πολλοί = πάντες (Semitism) J. Jeremias, TW vi 540.36–545.25.

(2) Cf. κακὰ κακῶν and the like in class. poetry (K.-G. i 21, 339). Ursing 50f.; E. Hofmann, Ausdrucksverstärkung 55ff.; Poutsma, Curme Volume of Ling. Stud. (1930) 126–8 (Eng. parallels acc. to Leopold, *op. cit.* 127 n. 1 from biblical language). Pap. and MGr s. M.-H. 443.

(3) LXX often: μέγας παρά Ex 18: 11, πραΰς παρά Num 12: 3; λευκοὶ ἤ Gen 49: 12, μακάριος ἤπερ Constit. Apost. 4.3. Positive with παρά and the like MGr also, s. Pernot, Études 75, who sees in this a 'Greco-Hebraism' of MGr. Ἤ without adj. also 1 C 14: 19 θέλω...ἤ (Epict. 3.22.53, Justin, Apol. 15.8 [Agraphon], BGU iii 846.15 [ii AD], θ. ἤπερ LXX 2 Macc 14: 42, βούλομαι...ἤ Homer), λυσιτελεῖ...ἤ Lk 17: 2 (Tob 3: 6 B-text, μᾶλλον ἤ S-text), ἔξεστιν ἤ Mk 3: 4; δεδικαίωται ἤ LXX Gen 38: 26, ἀπαγγέλλειν ...ἤ Sir 37: 14, καταλείψει ἤ 39: 11; class. pars. in K.-G. ii 303 (e.g. Hdt. 9.26 fin. δίκαιον scil. ἐστι... ἤπερ, Andocides 1.125 λυσιτελεῖν ἤ); s. also Wellhausen, Einl.² 21.

245a. Comparative expressing exclusion.

In addition to the comparative proper, which is wanting in Hebrew, the positive or a verb followed by a preposition (παρά, ὑπέρ; in the LXX even ἀπό, ἐκ) or a particle (ἤ, ἤπερ) can be used to express comparison (§185; for other less common constructions, s. §§245, 192); the latter have parallels in secular Greek, but their frequency is due to the Semitic model. מִן, which is the normal means of expressing comparison in Hebrew, denotes separation (comparison is with something outside or seen from a distance) and hence may indicate either comparison 'compared with', or exclusion 'in contrast to' (cf. §185(2) on 1 T 1: 4). In biblical Greek the choice can be made only on the basis of the context. Expressions of com-

parison meaning exclusion include: (1) μᾶλλον ἤ, e.g. Jn 3: 19 μᾶλλον τὸ σκότος ἤ τὸ φῶς, 12: 43 τὴν δόξαν τῶν ἀνθρώπων μᾶλλον ἤπερ (ὑπέρ SL al.) τὴν δόξαν τοῦ θεοῦ, 1 T 1: 4; (2) παρά, ὑπέρ, ἤ (ἤπερ), e.g. Lk 18: 14...οὗτος δεδικαιωμένος... παρ' ἐκεῖνον (ἤ vg sysc, ἤ -νος WΘ al., μᾶλλον π. -νον... D it syp) 'rather than the other' = 'and not the other', cf. Gen 38: 26 δεδικαίωται Θαμαρ ἤ ἐγώ 'Tamar is in the right, not I'. (3) Comparison = exclusion may be contained in the verb, or rather its preposition, Mt 21: 31 προάγουσιν ὑμᾶς '...go into the Kingdom, but you do not' (J. Jeremias, Die Gleichnisse Jesu [3rd ed., 1954] 104 n. 2 [The Parables of Jesus (1955) 101 n. 54]; adopted by G. Bornkamm, Jesus von Nazareth [2nd ed., 1957] 72 and n. 29 p. 185). There seems to be nothing comparable to ἀπό or ἐκ = מִן in the NT.

(1) Bauer⁵ (s.v. μᾶλλον 3c), quoting Appian, Hisp. 26.101, accepts the exclusive meaning for most of the NT passages (excepting A 20: 35, 1 C 9: 15, G 4: 27): 2 T 3: 4, A 27: 11, H 11: 25, in addition to those cited above. Bauer also accepts this meaning for A 4: 19, 5: 29, which is contested by Haenchen¹⁰ *ad loc.* and especially n. 4 pp. 532f. (¹² 526f.); Lk knew and used secular proverbs and current sayings (e.g. 20: 35, 26: 14, and the quotation 17: 28f.) the meaning of which he is unlikely to have changed; they occur in contexts very different from those exhibiting Septuagintisms. The μᾶλλον...ἤ of A 20: 35 is comparative rather than exclusive: the saying is quoted as a Persian νόμος by Thuc. 2.97.4, and in this or similar form had long been known by the Greeks; it also appears in 1 Clem 2.1, but is not attributed to Jesus (Haenchen¹⁰ n. 4 pp. 532f. [¹² 526f.] against J. Jeremias, Unbekannte Herrenworte [1951] 73ff. [Unknown Sayings of Jesus (1958) 77ff.]; on the other hand, the reading μακάριός ἐστιν [D it syp] ὁ διδοὺς μᾶλλον ἤ ὁ λαμβάνων [syp] comes closer to the form of the beatitudes and is to be given the Hebraizing exclusive sense).

(2) Cf. §§185(3); 245(3). Also with an adj.: 1 Km 24: 18 δίκαιος σὺ ὑπέρ ἐμέ 'You are in the right, not I'. At times there seems to be a mixture of comparison and exclusion: in Ezk 16: 52 ἐδικαίωσας αὐτὰς ὑπέρ σεαυτήν, ὑπέρ at least comes close to expressing contrast; cf. Lk 13: 2 ἁμαρτωλοὶ παρὰ πάντας τοὺς Γαλιλαίους, 4 ὀφειλέται...παρὰ πάντας....

(3) Cf. E. Klostermann, Hdb. *ad loc.* 'in this context nothing is said about whether the ὑμεῖς will succeed them at all'.—Ἀπό = מִן Ex 19: 5 ἔσεσθέ μοι λαὸς περιούσιος ἀπὸ πάντων τῶν ἐθνῶν 'among', i.e. 'in contrast to', Dt 14: 2, cf. 7: 6 παρὰ πάντα τὰ ἔθνη. Ἐκ = מִן Gen 37: 4 αὐτὸν ἐφίλει ὁ πατὴρ

αὐτοῦ ἐκ πάντων τῶν υἱῶν αὐτοῦ. Cf. Johannessohn I 44.

246. The comparative is heightened as in classical by the addition of πολύ, πολλῷ: e.g. 2 C 8: 22, Jn 4: 41, also occasionally by the accumulation of several comparatives: Ph 1: 23 πολλῷ γὰρ μᾶλλον κρεῖσσον, similarly μᾶλλον διαφέρετε αὐτῶν Mt 6: 26 (Lk 12: 24, but D is different) and περισσεύσῃ πλεῖον τῶν... Mt 5:

20. The same accumulation appears in classical (Schwab III 59 ff., K.-G. I 26).

2 C 7: 13 περισσοτέρως μᾶλλον ἐχάρημεν, Mk 7: 36 μᾶλλον περισσότερον (-τέρως D) ἐκήρυσσον, cf. § 60 (3). It is more pleonastic in the Ap. Frs.: Herm Sim 9.28.4 μᾶλλον ἐνδοξότεροι, 1 Clem 48.6 ὅσῳ δοκεῖ μᾶλλον μείζων εἶναι, and the like (Reinhold 61). Ἥδιστα μᾶλλον 2 C 12: 9 do not go together: 'gladly (stereotyped elative superl.) will I boast rather...'.

7. SYNTAX OF NUMERALS

(Rob. 671–5)

247. Εἷς. (1) The first day of the month or week is designated in the NT as in the LXX, not by πρώτη, but by μία, e.g. εἰς μίαν σαββάτων 'on Sunday' Mt 28: 1. Above one, however, δευτέρα etc. are used because a *single* day cannot be expressed by a plural (δύο etc.). The model was Hebraic where all the days of the month are designated by cardinals (Nöldeke, Ztschr. f. deutsche Wortf. I [1901] 162; also Aramaic, s. Dalman 247). (2) Εἷς passes now and again from the force of a numeral (*one* as opposed to several) to that of τις (indefinite article). This development, paralleled in English (Rob. 674), German, and the Romance languages, has reached its climax in MGr. The model for the NT was also Hebrew אֶחָד and Aramaic חַד. (3) Εἷς in the sense of ἕτερος appears in ὁ εἷς...ὁ ἕτερος or ὁ εἷς...ὁ εἷς and the like instead of ὁ μὲν (ἕτερος)...ὁ δὲ (ἕτερος). (4) Εἷς τὸν ἕνα (= ἀλλήλους) depends upon a Semitic, especially Aramaic, model, 1 Th 5: 11. MGr ὁ ἕνας τὸν ἄλλον is similar.

(1) Μία = πρώτη also e.g. A 20: 7, 1 C 16: 2, Mk 16: 2, Lk 24: 1; πρώτῃ σαββάτου only [Mk] 16: 9 for which, however, Eus. quotes τῇ μιᾷ. Rev 6: 1 μίαν ἐκ τῶν ἑπτὰ σφραγίδων 'the first'. Jos. already sensed the Hebraism: Ant. 1.1.1 (I 29) αὕτη μὲν ἂν εἴη πρώτη ἡμέρα, Μωυσῆς δ' αὐτὴν μίαν εἶπεν; MGr ἡ πρώτη τοῦ μηνός. Rev 9: 12 ἡ οὐαὶ ἡ μία 'the first woe' is also a Hebraism. LXX: the days of the week occur only in some uncials in the titles of Psalms which are not in the Hebr. text: τῇ μιᾷ σαββάτου (or -των) 23 (24) (this probably means on the first day reckoned from the sabbath; cf. § 213. Is there such a thing as אֶחָד־לַחֹדֶשׁ? אֶחָד־לַשַׁבָּת is attested), δευτέρᾳ σαββάτου 47 (48), τετράδι σαββάτων 93 (94), moreover in a cursive πέμπτῃ σαββάτου 131; cf. Swete, Introduction 251. The days of the month, on the other hand, which are not found in the NT,

appear frequently in the LXX: μιᾷ τοῦ μηνός Gen 8: 13 etc., ἐν ἡμέρᾳ μιᾷ τ. μ. Ex 40: 2, ἐν μιᾷ τ. μ. Num 1: 1, 18 (but τῇ πρώτῃ τ. μ. Gen. 8: 5 is better Greek), ἀπὸ ἐνάτης τ. μ. Lev 23: 32, (ἐν) τῇ πεντεκαιδεκάτῃ (ἡμέρᾳ) τ. μ. Lev 23: 6, 34, 39, Num 29: 12 etc. On the question of Semitism, Debrunner, GGA 1926, 141f. The MGr form for dates (στὴν) πρώτη, (στὶς) δέκα (τοῦ) Ἀπρίλι 'on the first, tenth of April' (Thumb[2] § 131) uses the ordinal just for 1 and copies Italian *ai primi, ai dieci di aprile*. Cf. further L. Spitzer, Urtümliches bei rom. Zahlwörtern (Ztschr. f. rom. Phil. 45, 1925) 1ff., especially 14f. Class. εἷς καὶ εἰκοστός etc. is not comparable (so Att. inscrip. regularly); it merely betrays an incomplete development of ordinals (from the cardinal εἷς καὶ εἴκοσι taken as one word) like Lat. *unus et vicesimus*, German *der ein-und-zwanzigste* etc.

(2) Mt 8: 19 προσελθὼν εἷς γραμματεύς, 21: 19 συκῆν μίαν (Mk 11: 13 v.l.), 26: 29 μία παιδίσκη, Mk 11: 29 ἕνα λόγον (Mt 21: 24 λ. ἕ., but Lk 20: 3 only λόγον), Rev 8: 13 ἤκουσα ἑνὸς ἀετοῦ, etc. = class. τις. Moreover, like the latter, εἷς occurs with gen. or ἐκ: Lk 15: 15 ἑνὶ τῶν πολιτῶν, 15: 19 ὡς ἕνα τῶν μισθίων σου, 12: 6 ἐν ἐξ αὐτῶν, 15: 26 ἕνα τῶν παίδων, Rev 7: 13 εἷς ἐκ (S om. ἐκ) τῶν πρεσβυτέρων. Εἷς for τις without addition: Mt 19: 16, Mk 10: 17 (but Lk 18: 18 has τις ἄρχων, v.l. τις). The combination of εἷς τις is class. (Schwyzer II 215b1): Lk 22: 50 εἷς τις ἐξ αὐτῶν, Jn 11: 49, as v.l. also Mk 14: 47, 51; in that case εἷς forms the contrast to the rest of the group. Εἷς = τις in LXX 1 Esdr 3: 5, 4: 18, 2 Macc 8: 33 (Katz, ZNW 51 [1960] 11). The instances sometimes adduced from Plato and Xen. for the weakening of εἷς are not to the point, since there εἷς is still a genuine numeral (thus e.g. Plato, Lg. 9.855D); also in ἑνὶ τῶν πολιτῶν Hyperid., Lyc. 13, in τῶν ἑταίρων εἷς Aeschin. 3.89 εἷς still carries a certain emphasis ('belonging to this definite number [class]'); Aristoph., Aves 1292 εἷς κάπηλος 'one, namely a dealer' therefore belongs to (3). Br.-Th. 489; Schwyzer II 27; L.-S. s.v.; Mayser

II 2, 85f.; Johannessohn, KZ 67 (1940) 68f.; on MGr Anagnostopulos 222–4.—Ὁ εἷς also appears in this sense: Mk 14: 10 ὁ εἷς (εἷς only C²Wᵇ al., without ὁ εἷς A) τῶν δώδεκα; cf. pap. (Mayser II 2, 86; Mlt. 97 n. 2 [155.2]).—The (infrequent) postposition of εἷς is Semitic (Johannessohn, KZ 67 [1940] 36, 66f.): Mt 5: 18 ἰῶτα ἕν, 6: 27 πῆχυν ἕνα, 9: 18 ἄρχων εἷς B lat, Mt 21: 19 συκῆν μίαν, Jn 6: 9 παιδάριον ἕν AΓ al.

(3) Ὁ εἷς... ὁ ἕτερος Mt 6: 24, Lk 7: 41, 16: 13, 17: 34, 35 (36), A 23: 6; (ὁ) εἷς... καὶ εἷς Mt 20: 21, 24: 40, 41, 27: 38, Mk 15: 27, Jn 20: 12, G 4: 22 (24), Lk 18: 10 D ([ὁ]εἷς... καὶ ὁ ἕτερος al.), Rev 21: 19 ὁ εἷς S (pm. ὁ πρῶτος)... ὁ δεύτερος etc., Herm Man 6.2.1, after Hebr. אֶחָד like LXX Ex 17: 12; on Mk 4: 8, 20 s. § 248(3); ὁ μὲν εἷς... ὁ δὲ εἷς Barn 7.6–9 (following the LXX). Even classical writers employ εἷς (repeatedly) in the division of a duality or quantity: Arist., Ath. 37.1 δύο, ὧν ὁ μὲν εἷς... ὁ δ᾽ ἕτερος, Rh. 2.20 p. 1393a 27 δύο, ἓν μὲν... ἓν δέ, Hyperid., Ath. 14f. ὁ εἷς νόμος ... ἕτερος ν., Dem. 18.215 τρία... ἓν μὲν... ἕτερον δὲ ... τρίτον δέ; cf. Rev 17: 10 ἑπτά... οἱ πέντε... ὁ εἷς... ὁ ἄλλος. Cf. § 250. Corresponding usage in the pap.; cf. Mlt. 97 [155]; ClR 15 (1901) 440; Mayser II 1, 57. Philo, Decal. 51 (Cohn-Wendland IV 280) of the two tables of the law: ἡ μία γραφή... ἡ δ᾽ ἑτέρα πεντάς. Parallels from other languages in Niedermann, Gnomon 3 (1927) 353.

(4) 1 C 4: 6 is different: εἷς ὑπὲρ τοῦ ἑνὸς κατὰ τοῦ ἑτέρου 'each one on behalf of one against the other' ('none... in favor of one against the other' RSV) (perhaps in full εἷς ὑπὲρ τοῦ ἑνὸς κ. τ. ἑτ. καὶ ἕτερος ὑπ. τ. ἑνὸς [with reverse relationship] κ. τ. ἑτ.). Cf. Almqvist 95.

248. Numeral adverbs and the like. (1) Ἀνά and κατά are used with cardinals in a distributive sense as in classical: Mk 6: 40 κατά (v.l. ἀνά as in Lk 9: 14) ἑκατὸν καὶ κατὰ πεντήκοντα. In a way known to vulgar Greek, but due to the translation of a Semitic idiom in this case, the cardinal is doubled: Mk 6: 7 δύο δύο (D ἀνὰ δύο as in Lk 10: 1). (2) Multiplicatives: ἕως ἑβδομηκοντάκις ἑπτά Mt 18: 22 is peculiar (D* ἑβδ. ἑπτάκις) 'seventy-seven times' (not 'seventy times seven') as in LXX Gen 4: 24. Ἐπὶ τρίς 'three times' or 'yet a third time' A 10: 16, 11: 10, PHolm 1.18, s. also Bauer s.v. τρίς. (3) Ἐν τριάκοντα etc. is an Aramaism Mk 4: 8, 20 (inferior reading ἐν) 'thirty-fold'; s.

§ 207(2). (4) 'The third time (τὸ) τρίτον Mk 14: 41 etc., ἐκ τρίτου Mt 26: 44; 'now for the third time' τρίτον τοῦτο (§ 154). (5) Ὄγδοον Νῶε ἐφύλαξεν 'Noah with seven others' (cf. German selbacht 'he being the eighth') 2 P 2: 5 is good classical. K.-G. I 653.

(1) Herm Sim 9.2.3 ἀνὰ δύο παρθένοι cf. § 204; on ἀνὰ εἷς ἕκαστος, εἷς καθ᾽ εἷς and the like s. § 305. On δύο δύο: Aeschyl., Pers. 981 μυρία μυρία πεμπαστάν = τὸν κατὰ μυρίους ἀριθμοῦντα, Soph., Frag. 191 Nauck² μίαν μίαν = κατὰ μίαν. Since anti-Atticistic grammarians adduce these references to Soph., Atticists must have censured the same thing in Koine as vulgar; also pap. and MGr (Mlt. 97 [156]; Dieterich 188; Jannaris § 666; Kapsomenakis 49f.). Cf. also § 493(2) and Brugmann, Grundriss II² 2, 74; Ljungvik, Aegyptus 13 (1933) 163f. On Semitic influence E. Hofmann, Ausdrucksverstärkung 38; LXX: Johannessohn II 253 n. 2.—Mixed ἀνὰ δύο δύο Lk 10: 1 BΚΠ; cf. Reinhold 62; W. Schulze, Graeca Latina 13; δίδει αὐτῇ ἀνὰ ἓν ἕν 'give her one each' PColumb no. 318 (c. 100 AD; Class. Phil. 30 [1935] 145.31), κατὰ δύο δύο POxy VI 886.19 (iii AD).

(2) Cf. Mlt. 98 [158].

(3) The fluctuation between the multiplicative on the one hand and the cardinal (ἑπτά = ἑπτάκις) or the ordinal (ἐπὶ τρίς for τὸ τρίτον) on the other is due largely to the Semitic ambiguity with regard to numerals (§ 247(1)). Late Greek and Latin, however, concur in this ambiguity. In Rev 22: 2 ποιοῦν καρποὺς δώδεκα, as interpreted by the following clause κατὰ μῆνα ἕκαστον ἀποδιδοῦν τὸν καρπὸν αὐτοῦ, δώδεκα = δωδεκάκις; cf. Ezk 47: 12 (Hebrew) and Lohmeyer, Hdb. ad loc. who quotes Shemot r. 15: 'trees which bear fruit every month' (with an identical reference to its healing properties following). Rev 9: 12 ἔρχεται ἔτι δύο οὐαί: Lohmeyer, Hdb. ad loc. takes δύο = δίς 'twice, two more times' (taking οὐαί as sing. here as in the preceding ἡ οὐαί ἡ μία); Katz now concurs (cf. §§ 58; 136(5)). For later Greek and Latin δεύτερον, τρίτον instead of δίς, τρίς, etc., s. Schulze, Graeca Latina 13f. Cf. Kautzsch § 66, 2. For Mt 13: 8, 23 s. § 250.

(4) Cf. e.g. τέταρτον τοῦτο Hdt. 5.76. Ἐκ δευτέρου (Mk 14: 72?) Jn 9: 24, A 10: 15 etc.; ἐκ τετάρτου PHolm 1.32. Τὸ τρίτον etc. scil. μέρος s. § 241(7). Kapsomenakis 50.

(5) Ὄγδοον αὐτόν would be still more customary. MPol 19.1 σὺν τοῖς ἀπὸ Φιλαδελφείας δωδέκατος.

8. THE ARTICLE

(1) Ὁ ἡ τό AS A PRONOUN

249. Introduction. The original use of ὁ ἡ τό as a demonstrative pronoun is retained in classical usage in certain fixed phrases; the forms of the old relative pronoun ὅς ἥ ὅ replace it occasionally in classical and more frequently in Hellenistic times. The origin of this confusion was, on the one hand, the old sigmatic alternative form of ὁ: ὅς which in Greek had become identical with the relative in form; and, on the other, the Epic and dialectal use of ὁ ἡ τό as a relative pronoun (cf. the article *der* in German which serves as article, relative and demonstrative; in English *that* is both demonstrative and relative and is related to the article). Cf. K.-G. II 227. In the NT (except the Epic quotation from Aratus in A 17: 28 where τοῦ = τούτου) there are preserved only ὁ μὲν...ὁ δέ (ὅς μὲν...ὅς δέ) 'the one...the other' and ὁ δέ 'but he', ὁ μὲν οὖν 'now he'. Other expressions like καὶ ὅς (Homil Clem 6.2.13 καὶ ὃς ἔφη), καὶ τόν 'and he, him', τὸν καὶ τόν 'such and such', or 'so and so', πρὸ τοῦ 'formerly' have completely disappeared.

250. Ὁ μὲν...ὁ δέ (ὃς μὲν...ὃς δέ) 'the one... the other' is no longer very frequent in the NT, but the relative forms are more common (neuter ὃ μὲν...ὃ δέ, plural ἃ μέν, οἷς μέν, οὓς μέν, etc.; barely attested in Attic prose, K.-G. II 228). It refers either to what is already known ('*the* one...*the* other', 'this...that') or is wholly indefinite ('one...another'). Εἷς serves instead to differentiate among a newly introduced *number* of individuals (§247(3)): Lk 23: 33 τοὺς κακούργους, ὃν μὲν...ὃν δέ, but Mt 27: 38 δύο λῃσταί, εἷς...καὶ εἷς.

Ὁ μὲν...ὁ δέ occurs only as follows: Mt 22: 5 C²X al.; Mk 4: 4 τὸ μέν W; 1 C 7: 7 ὁ μὲν οὕτως, ὁ δὲ οὕτως (ὅς...ὅς...𝔓⁴⁷ScKL); E 4:11 τοὺς μέν...τοὺς δέ (all MSS); also H 7: 20, 21, 23, 24; 12: 10 οἱ μέν...ὁ δέ with reference to *definitely* designated persons (7: 20, 21 the priests of former times...Jesus) instead of repeating the nouns, a case in which ὅς is not usual (cf. §251). Further, Lk 8: 5, ὃ μὲν (scil. σπόρος)... καὶ ἕτερος (so Blass with minusc. 700); in the parallel Mt 13: 23 ὃς δή (D more correctly reads τότε for ὃς δή) καρποφορεῖ καὶ ποιεῖ ὃ μὲν ἑκατόν, ὃ δὲ ἑξήκοντα, ὃ δὲ τριάκοντα (ὅ as neut., not ὅ; cf. v. 8; also 19ff. is to be read with Old Lat. k τοῦτό ἐστι τὸ...σπαρέν, τὸ

δέ...σπαρὲν τοῦτό ἐστιν, lest parable and interpretation be confused in a most awkward way; neut. likewise in Mk 4: 20 ἒν τριάκοντα etc., s. §248(3)). Ὃς μὲν...ὃς δέ (inclusive of οἵ...which can also be written οἱ): Mt 13: 4 (ἃ μὲν...ἄλλα δέ [ἃ δέ D]; such looser correspondence is at times found elsewhere also: K.-G. I 585 n., II 228), 13: 8, 16: 14 (οἱ μέν... ἄλλοι δὲ...ἕτεροι δέ, cf. Jn 7: 12), 21: 35, 22: 5 (ὃς SBC*LW, οἳ D), 25: 15, 26: 67 (only οἱ δέ 'but others', 28: 17 (ditto; in these two places no differentiation is indicated at the beginning of the sentence, but with the appearance of οἱ δέ it becomes evident that what was said first did not apply to all; cf. K.-G. I 585, Gild. 219f.), Mk 4: 4, 12: 5, Lk 8: 5, Jn 7: 12, A 14: 4, 17: 18 (τινὲς...οἱ δέ), 32, 27:44, 28: 24, R 9: 21, 14: 2 (ὃς μὲν...ὁ [ὃς FG] δὲ ἀσθενῶν), 5, 1 C 11: 21, 12: 8, 28, 2 C 2: 16 ('the latter...the former'), Ph 1: 16, 17 (ditto), 2 T 2: 20, Jd 22, 23.— Ptol. pap. ὃς μέν etc. only PTebt I 61.b 29 (118/7 bc) τὴν μέν...ἣν δέ (cf. τοὺς μέν...οὓς δέ Aristeas 12). Mayser II 1, 57. POxy IX 1189.7 (c. 117 ad) ἣν μέν... ἣν δέ. S. also ὁτὲ μέν...ὁτὲ δέ §436.

251. Ὁ δέ 'but he', ἡ δέ, οἱ δέ (only in nominative) to mark the continuation of a narrative are common in all the historical books, though least frequent in John; ὁ μὲν οὖν 'he then', without a δέ corresponding strictly to the μέν, is limited to Acts.

There is a tendency for a ptcp. to follow ὁ δέ, ὁ μὲν οὖν (as in the pap.; Mayser II 1, 57f.), through which ambiguity occasionally arises (cf. §293(3)): e.g. A 8: 4 οἱ μὲν οὖν διασπαρέντες 'now those who were scattered' (taken up by 9: 1 ὁ δὲ Σαῦλος; Joachim Jeremias, ZNW 36 [1937] 216) where the separation of οἱ and διασπ. would presuppose the proximity of the antecedent, while here it is quite remote; in 1: 6, however, οἱ μὲν οὖν συνελθόντες is ambiguous: 'now they who had come together' or 'now they, when they had come together'. Ὁ δέ in Jn 5: 11 ὁ δὲ ἀπεκρίθη (ἀπεκρίνατο S*W) SC*GKLW al., merely ἀπεκρίθη C³DEF al. (cf. §462(1)), striking ὃς δὲ ἀπ. AB (so also Mk 15: 23 SD ὃς δέ for ὁ δέ; ὃς δέ PRyl II 144.14 [38 ad], PSI IV 313.8 [iii/iv ad]).

(2) THE ARTICLE WITH A SUBSTANTIVE

(A) With Appellatives

252. Introduction. Ὁ ἡ τό as article with appellatives has double meaning as in classical usage, individual and generic: ὁ ἄνθρωπος (1) 'the known, particular, previously mentioned man' or also 'man κατ' ἐξοχήν (*par excellence*)' (ἡ ἀγάπη 'Christian Love', ὁ προφήτης Jn 1: 21, 7: 40 'the expected prophetic forerunner of the Messiah', cf. §273(1, 2)); (2) 'man as a class' (e.g. οἱ ἄνθρωποι in contrast to τὰ ἄλλα ϡῷα or ὁ θεός). (1) is also known as the 'anaphoric' use (since Apollonius Dyscolus ii AD) because there is reference back (ἀναφορά) to what is known or assumed to be known: ὁ δοῦλός σου 'your slave', i.e. 'he whom you know I mean' or 'the only one you have', but δοῦλός σου 'a slave of yours'. Accordingly, the article is not used with the introduction of a hitherto unknown individual if the whole class is not subsumed under this individual (generic use); therefore, e.g. not with a predicate noun, since in ὑμεῖς μάρτυρες τούτων there is neither anaphora nor is the class taken as a whole; cf. Jn 4: 34 ἐμὸν βρῶμά ἐστιν, 13: 35 ἐμοὶ μαθηταί ἐστε, and so usually with predicates (exceptions §273). Contrary to the above rules, omission of the article in some instances is to be understood as a survival from earlier anarthrous usage, especially in formulae or set phrases (§255; to which belong also titles, salutations, etc.), in definitions (e.g. R 1: 16f., 8: 24) and in lists (e.g. R 8: 35, 38f. and in the catalogues of vices) (v. Dobschütz, ZNW 33 [1934] 64), in closely related pairs of substantives (W.-S. §19, 7; Mayser II 2, 23), and in a generic ('qualitative') sense particularly when the class is represented only by a *single* individual. For the Semitizing omission of the article with nouns followed by a genitive, s. §259. D often omits the article in a way foreign to Greek: Scrivener, Codex Bezae Cant. p. xlviii (Latinism). For a detailed discussion of the use and non-use of the article s. Funk 34–71.

Formulae with generic article: οὐχ ὁ τυχών 'not the first that happens along, not a chance person', s. §430(2); the corresponding class. usage ὁ βουλόμενος 'everyone who wants' does not appear in the NT.—Distributive article (K.-G. I 593f.; Mayser II 2, 42ff.): Lk 17: 4 ἑπτάκις τῆς ἡμέρας, H 9: 7 ἅπαξ τοῦ ἐνιαυτοῦ; but Mt 20: 2 ἐκ δηναρίου τὴν ἡμέραν 'for the day in question' and distributive without article Rev 6: 6 χοῖνιξ σίτου δηναρίου etc. Mt 10: 29 δύο στρουθία τοῦ (D only) ἀσσαρίου. Individual-indefinite article (ἔστιν ὁ σῴζων 'the needed or expected one, who, however, is not known or mentioned') is not certainly attested in the NT except in the fut. in 1 P 3: 13 (§351(2)): 1 C 14: 5 εἰ μὴ ᾖ ὁ διερμηνεύων FG, 28 ἐὰν δὲ μὴ ᾖ ὁ ἑρμηνευτής D*FG (ὁ διερμηνεύων minusc. 73). LXX: Ps 17: 42 οὐκ ἦν ὁ σῴζων, 49: 22, 70: 11, Is 59: 20, Da Theod. 11: 45 ὁ ῥυόμενος;

2 Chr 20: 24 οὐκ ἦν σῳζόμενος (without art.) = Hebr. וְאֵין פְּלֵיטָה. K.-G. I 594, 5; Krüger §50, 4 n. 3, 4; §56, 3 n. 4; Mayser II 2, 41f. S. also §§412(4); 413.

253. The article with ἥλιος, γῆ and the like.

(1) Usually ὁ ἥλιος, ἡ σελήνη (cf. Mayser II 2, 18f.), but also without the article, e.g. Lk 21: 25 ἔσονται σημεῖα ἐν ἡλίῳ καὶ σελήνῃ καὶ ἄστροις (followed by contrasting καὶ ἐπὶ τῆς γῆς 'here on earth'). (2) Also θάλασσα sometimes without the article: Lk 21: 25 ἤχους θαλάσσης, Ja 1: 6 κλύδωνι θαλάσσης. (3) The article is omitted with γῆ especially after prepositions (formulaic expressions), but even here the arthrous form preponderates; οὐρανός (-οί) is frequently anarthrous after prepositions (the MSS often vary): ἐπὶ γῆς Mt 28: 18 (with τῆς BD), Lk 2: 14, 1 C 8: 5, E 3: 15, H 12: 25, 8: 4 (except for the last, it always appears in conjunction with ἐν οὐρανοῖς (-ῷ) or ἀπ' οὐρανῶν or ἐν ὑψίστοις). (4) Κόσμος: ἐν κόσμῳ 1 C 8: 4, 14: 10, Ph 2: 15 etc. (v.l. 2 P 1: 4). (5) The points of the compass, found only with prepositions, never take the article; cf. Mayser II 2, 18.

(1) Mt 13: 6 ἡλίου δὲ (τοῦ δὲ ἡ. D) ἀνατείλαντος; A 27: 20 μήτε δὲ ἡλίου μήτε ἄστρων ἐπιφαινόντων 'when neither sun nor stars shone'; 1 C 15: 41 ἄλλη δόξα ἡλίου, καὶ ἄλλη δόξα σελήνης, καὶ ἄλλη δόξα ἀστέρων; Rev 7: 2 and 16: 12 ἀπὸ ἀνατολῆς ἡλίου; 22: 5 οὐκ ἔχουσιν χρείαν φωτὸς λύχνου καὶ φωτὸς ἡλίου (cf. the arthrous form 21: 23). In some of these instances the use or non-use of the article was evidently a matter of preference; but in A 27: 20 the meaning appears to be strengthened by the anarthrous form: 'neither any sun...', and 1 C 15: 41 is to be compared with 39: ἄλλη μὲν (σὰρξ) ἀνθρώπων, ἄλλη δὲ σὰρξ κτηνῶν etc. (this is a reference not to the whole class nor to the uniquely existing sun, but to a characteristic of the class, or, in the sun's case, of the single thing); cf. (2).

(2) 2 C 11: 26 κινδύνοις ἐκ γένους (my kindred, i.e. Jews), κ. ἐξ ἐθνῶν (s. §254(3)), κ. ἐν θαλάσσῃ where the article would be incorrect. Θάλασσα after preps.: Mt 4: 15 OT ὁδὸν θαλάσσης (§161(1)) in spite of Hebr. דֶּרֶךְ הַיָּם, A 10: 6, 32 παρὰ θάλασσαν. Jd 13 κύματα ἄγρια θαλάσσης (part of the predicate; also the thing being emphasized is this particular characteristic of the sea).

(3) Ἐκ γῆς 1 C 15: 47 ('earthly'; the essential thing is the earth's specific quality; in contrast to ἐξ οὐρανοῦ), cf. also ἀπὸ ἄκρου γῆς ἕως ἄκρου οὐρανοῦ Mk 13: 27. Mt 21: 25, 26 (pars.) ἐξ οὐρανοῦ–ἐξ ἀνθρώπων 'of heavenly–human origin'. Without prep.: A 17: 24 οὐρανοῦ καὶ γῆς κύριος; 2 P 3: 10 οὐρανοί (with οἱ ABC)...στοιχεῖα...γῆ (with ἡ CP),

cf. *v.* 12 (5 οὐρανοὶ…καὶ γῆ '*one* [different] heaven', similarly *v.* 13); A 3: 21 ὃν δεῖ οὐρανὸν δέξασθαι. On οὐρανός s. Mayser II 2, 29.

(4) *One* world in contrast to another 2 P 2: 5 (cf. γῆ *supra* (3)); κόσμου as a part of an anarthrous predicate R 4: 13, 11: 12, 15; in all authors regularly anarthrous in the formula ἀπὸ καταβολῆς (ἀρχῆς, κτίσεως) κόσμου Mt 25: 34 etc., cf. ἀπ’ ἀρχῆς κτίσεως Mk 10: 6, 13: 19, 2 P 3: 4. Otherwise κόσμος without art.: 2 C 5: 19, G 6: 14.

(5) Κατὰ μεσημβρίαν A 8: 26, ἀπὸ ἀνατολῆς ἡλίου Rev 7: 2, 16: 12, ἀπὸ ἀνατολῶν (καὶ δυσμῶν) Mt 2: 1, 8: 11 etc., ἀπὸ δυσμῶν Lk 12: 54 etc., ἕως δ. Mt 24: 27, ἀπὸ βορρᾶ καὶ νότου Lk 13: 29 (so also other authors); also βασίλισσα νότου Mt 12: 42 of a more definite *land* in the south (νότου borders here on a proper name; s. §259(2)), but in this sense ἐν τῇ ἀνατολῇ Mt 2: 2, 9. Also νότος 'south wind' (Lk 12: 55, A 27: 13, 28: 13) always without art. (pap. with and without; Mayser II 2, 18). For Paul cf. Funk 72–6.

254. The article with nouns designating persons like θεός, κύριος, νεκροί, ἔθνη. (1) Θεός and κύριος (= יהוה but also Christ) designate beings of which there is only one of a kind, and these words (especially κύριος) frequently come very close to being proper names; the article appears when the specific Jewish or Christian God or Lord is meant (not 'a being of divine nature' or 'a Lord'), but it is sometimes missing, especially after prepositions (ἀπὸ θεοῦ Jn 3: 2 [but subsequently ὁ θεός], frequently ἐν κυρίῳ) and with a genitive which depends on an anarthrous noun (especially a predicate noun): Mt 27: 43 ὅτι θεοῦ εἰμι υἱός, Lk 3: 2 ἐγένετο ῥῆμα (subject) θεοῦ. Cf. papyri (Mayser II 2, 25ff.). So also υἱὲ διαβόλου A 13: 10. (2) The generic article is sometimes omitted with νεκροί, especially after prepositions and in other formulae: ἐκ νεκρῶν ἐγείρεσθαι (ἀναστῆναι) Mt 17: 9 and regularly except in E 5: 14 OT, C 2: 12 BDEFG, 1 Th 1: 10 (ACK omit τῶν), but ἠγέρθη ἀπὸ τῶν ν. Mt 14: 2 etc. (3). Ἔθνη 'the Gentiles' appears frequently without article.

(1) Also however εἰ υἱὸς εἶ τοῦ θεοῦ Mt 4: 3, 27: 40, υἱὲ τοῦ θεοῦ 8: 29; the absence of the art. depends more on formal assimilation than on inner reasons. Θεὸς πατήρ is often an actual name for God (2 P 1: 17, Jd 1). Διάβολος otherwise with art., likewise σατανᾶς except at Lk 22: 3 (Mk 3: 23 *a* satan). Καῖσαρ is still partly a proper name and has the art. only in Jn 19: 12, cf. Att. βασιλεύς 'the Persian King'. For Χριστός s. §260(1). On the art. with θεός and κύριος s. B. Weiss, StKr 84 (1911) 319–92; 503–38 and Debrunner's review, ThLZ 1912, 488f.; Debrunner, Festschr. K. Marti (Beihefte zur ZAW 41 [1925] 69–78) (in the LXX literalistic translators

like to render anarthrous יהוה with anarthrous κύριος, but ל, אֶל and אֵת with τῷ κ., τὸν κ.; hence ἄγγελος κυρίου, ἐν κυρίῳ etc. are naturally found in the NT; the less literalistic translators of the OT and the NT prefer a general conformity to the Greek usage of the art.; cf. Bauer s.v. κύριος II 2 γ; κύριος ὁ θεός with and without gen. Lk 1: 68 OT, Rev 1: 8 etc. as in LXX); W. W. Graf Baudissin, Kyrios als Gottesnamen im Judentum, I. Teil (Giessen, 1929): Der Gebrauch des Gottesnamens Kyrios in Sept. (detailed examination of the art. with κ. and θ.); Ghedini, Atti del IV. Congr. Intern. di Papirologia (Milan, 1936) 338ff. (pagan and Chr. pap. ὁ κύριος θεός [s. also Ghedini, Lett. crist. 37 n. 6; 352]; pagan χάρις τῷ θεῷ, μετὰ τὸν θεόν etc., Christian usually ὁ θεός). For Paul (including Χριστός) Funk 144–98.

(2) Cf. also κρείττων γενόμενος ἀγγέλων H 1: 4 (𝔓46B Chr). Ἀνάστασις (ἐκ) νεκρῶν A 17: 32, 23: 6 etc. (*with* art. Mt 22: 31, 1 C 15: 42); in 1 C 15: 15, 16, 29, 32 the art. has to be omitted because the concept, not the collective dead, is under discussion (otherwise 52); 1 P 4: 5 κρῖναι ζῶντας καὶ νεκρούς 'all, whether living or dead', cf. *v.* 6.

(3) Translating Hebrew גּוֹיִם A 4: 25 OT, R 15: 12 OT; after preps.: ἐξ ἐθνῶν A 15: 14, G 2: 15, ἐν ἔθνεσιν 1 T 3: 16, σὺν ἔ. A 4: 27; gen. depending on predicate noun R 11: 12, 13 πλοῦτος ἐθνῶν, ἐ. ἀπόστολος. R 3: 29, 30 ἢ Ἰουδαίων (as such) ὁ θεὸς μόνον; οὐχὶ καὶ ἐθνῶν; ναὶ καὶ ἐθνῶν, εἴπερ εἷς ὁ θεός, ὃς δικαιώσει περιτομὴν (as such, or in an indefinite individual case 'a circumcised man') ἐκ πίστεως καὶ ἀκροβυστίαν διὰ τῆς (anaphoric) πίστεως. 2 C 11: 26 s. §253(2). For art. with both nouns τὰ ἔθνη τοῦ κόσμου Lk 12: 30, s. §259(1).

255. The article can be omitted in **prepositional phrases** (formulae from the earlier anarthrous stage of the language): (1) ἀπ’ ἀγροῦ, ἐν ἀγρῷ, εἰς ἀγρόν, but also ἐν τῷ ἀγρῷ etc. (without reference to a particular field) with generic article (as in τὰ κρίνα τοῦ ἀγροῦ Mt 6: 28). (2) Ἀπ’ ἀγορᾶς Mk 7: 4; ἐπὶ θύραις Mt 24: 33. (3) Often in designations of time (also classical): πρὸς ἑσπέραν Lk 24: 29; ἐν καιρῷ = ὅταν καιρὸς ᾖ Mt 24: 25; ἀπ’ (ἐξ) ἀρχῆς, ἐν ἀρχῇ. (4) Ἐπὶ πρόσωπον πίπτειν Lk 5: 12 etc., κατὰ πρ. 2 C 10: 7.—Cf. also §§253f., 256ff. Mayser II 2, 14f., 35ff.; Eakin 333.

(1) Ἐν τῷ ἀγρῷ αὐτοῦ Mt 13: 24 is self-explanatory. Ἀγρός combines the meanings *ager* and *rus*; the art. in Mt 13: 44 is incorrect (D and Chr omit) where 'a field' is to be understood.

(2) Ἐν ἀγορᾷ Lk 7: 32 = ἐν ταῖς ἀγοραῖς Mt 11: 16 (ταῖς om. CEFW al.) etc.

(3) Ἕως ἑσπέρας A 28: 23, μέχρι μεσονυκτίου 20: 7 (κατὰ τὸ μεσονύκτιον 16: 25), διὰ νυκτός v.l. διὰ τῆς ν.

A 5: 19, 16: 9, etc. (the art. designates that specific night); πρὸ καιροῦ = πρὶν καιρὸν εἶναι Mt 8: 29, ἄχρι καιροῦ Lk 4: 13, A 13: 11, πρὸς καιρόν Lk 8: 13, κατὰ κ. R 5: 6 ('at the right time, in his own good time'? or is it to be attached to the preceding clause, i.e. 'while we were yet in the period of weakness'?), παρὰ καιρὸν ἡλικίας H 11: 11.

(4) Also in secular authors like Polyb.; similarly class. κατ' ὀφθαλμούς, ἐν ὀφθαλμοῖς etc. Cf. also § 259(1).

256. The article is still sometimes omitted with **ordinals** (mostly in designations of time) following an earlier usage (K.-G. I 639; Gild. 261; H. Kallenberg, RhM 69 [1914] 665 ff., esp. 669, 675, 676 f.): ἀπὸ πρώτης ἡμέρας A 20: 18, Ph 1: 5 (𝔓⁴⁶SABP with τῆς), ἀπὸ ἕκτης ὥρας Mt 27: 45; ἕως τρίτου οὐρανοῦ 2 C 12: 2; πρώτην φυλακὴν καὶ δευτέραν A 12: 10; here belong also ἐν καιρῷ ἐσχάτῳ 1 P 1: 5, ἐν ἐσχάταις ἡμέραις 2 T 3: 1, Ja 5: 3 (besides ἐπ' ἐσχάτου or -των τῶν ἡμερῶν; s. § 264(5)).

In designations of the hour only the anaphoric art. is used (Mt 27: 46, cf. 45) or when there is an ellipsis of ὥρα (Mt 20: 6; in v. 9 it is anaphoric) or where a further limiting word is added (A 3: 1 τὴν ὥραν τῆς προσευχῆς τὴν ἐνάτην). It is missing, on the other hand, with ἡμέρα only in more or less indefinite expressions, but is used in specific designations (always τῇ τρίτῃ ἡμέρᾳ) and in the phrase ἐν τῇ ἐσχάτῃ ἡμέρᾳ Jn 6: 39, 40, 44. Ἕως ὥρας ἐνάτης Mk 15: 33, cf. Herm Vis 3.1.2, Sim 9.11. 7; πρώτης (MSS, -τη corrupt) μερίδος τῆς Μακεδονίας πόλις A 16: 12; 1 Jn 2: 18 ἐσχάτη ὥρα (predicate) is understandable (§ 273).

257. The article with θάνατος, πνεῦμα, πατήρ and the like. (1) Θάνατος very frequently without article (where German but not English would use the arthrous form): ἕως θανάτου Mt 26: 38, ἔνοχος θανάτου, ἄξιον θ., παραδιδόναι εἰς θάνατον, γεύεσθαι θανάτου; Iambl., VP 191. (2) Τὸ ἅγιον πνεῦμα sometimes with article as more or less a person; sometimes without article as a divine spirit entering into man. Occasional anarthrous ἐκκλησία in Paul also has the character of a proper name (K. L. Schmidt, TW III 508.18 ff.). (3) Πατήρ, γυνή and the like may be anarthrous not only in formulae (ἀπὸ θεοῦ πατρὸς ἡμῶν R 1: 7 etc., σὺν γυναιξίν A 1: 14, σὺν γ. καὶ τέκνοις 'with wife and children' 21: 5 [classical similarly]), but also when anaphora is ignored (§ 260): H 12: 7 τίς γὰρ υἱός, ὃν οὐ παιδεύει πατήρ ('a father', not 'his father'; cf. T 2: 9 § 286(2)). For Paul, Funk 85–94. For πενθερά s. § 260(2).—Mayser II 2, 22.

(1) Θάνατος with art. either of the death of a definite person (1 C 11: 26) or of death in the abstract (virtually limited to Jn, Paul, Rev; e.g. Jn 5: 24 μεταβέβηκεν ἐκ τοῦ θανάτου εἰς τὴν ζωήν; cf. § 258) or of death half personified (Rev 13: 3, 12, but it may be more anaphoric) or through assimilation to an arthrous noun (τὸ ἀπόκριμα τοῦ θανάτου 2 C 1: 9). Paul: Funk 116–20.

(2) Omission of the art. also with preps. (ἐν πν. ἁγίῳ) and by assimilation to an anarthrous noun (ἐν δυνάμει πνεύματος ἁγίου). In Lk τὸ πνεῦμα τὸ ἅγιον is rather the Pentecostal Spirit, ἅγ. πν. rather an unknown power (Procksch in TW I 105). With art. of course by anaphora: A 2: 4, 8: 18 (cf. 17); 10: 44 with reference to the known fact of the outpouring of the Spirit, but also bordering on personification. Cf. Funk 83 f. for Paul.—2 T 3: 15 ἱερὰ γράμματα SCᵇD*FG is an OT formula; s. Schrenk, TW I 765. 11 ff.

(3) Formulae: πιστῷ κτίστῃ 1 P 4: 19 (v.l. ὡς π. κτ. in any case makes sense). Jn 1: 14 δόξαν ὡς μονογενοῦς παρὰ πατρός shows a kind of assimilation to μονογενοῦς. 1 T 2: 12 γυναικί...ἀνδρός (instead of: 'over her husband'), Herm Sim 9.28.4 ἵνα δοῦλος κύριον ἴδιον ἀρνήσηται; contrast κεφαλὴ γυναικὸς ὁ ἀνήρ 1 C 11: 3 and ἀνήρ ἐστιν κεφαλὴ τῆς γυναικός E 3: 23. Iambl., VP 148 ἑαυτοῦ πατέρα, 192 γυνὴ αὐτοῦ.

(B) The Article with Abstract Nouns

258. The article is often lacking with abstracts (where German but not English would use one). The more abstract the sense in which the noun is used, the less likely it is to take any other than the generic article; hence in some instances the problem is rather to account for the presence of the article than its absence. (1) C 3: 5 πορνείαν ἀκαθαρσίαν πάθος ἐπιθυμίαν...καὶ τὴν πλεονεξίαν, ἥτις ἐστὶν εἰδωλολατρία 'and that chief vice, covetousness' (the addition of the relative clause ἥτις etc. occasions the use of the article by making the preceding noun definite; this use may be called kataphora, i.e. reference forward to a subsequent adjunct; cf. A 19: 3, 26: 27, 2 C 8: 18). (2) Paul tends to omit the article with ἁμαρτία and νόμος and sometimes also with θάνατος (R 6: 9, 8: 38; cf. § 257(1)), but the reason is recognizable: R 5: 13 ἄχρι γὰρ νόμου ἁμαρτία ἦν ἐν κόσμῳ ('before there was a law, there was sin'), ἁμαρτία δὲ οὐκ ἐλλογεῖται μὴ ὄντος νόμου. Σάρξ, too, is strongly inclined to an abstract sense (the natural state of man); hence often ἐν σαρκί and nearly always κατὰ σάρκα (2 C 11: 18 v.l. with τήν; nearly all MSS have τήν Jn 8: 15). E 2: 5 χάριτί ἐστε σεσωσμένοι 'it is grace which has saved you', but in 2: 8 τῇ γὰρ χάριτί ἐστε σεσ.

διὰ πίστεως 'the grace previously mentioned (or well known?) has delivered you to faith's way'. Cf. Zerwick, Graec. bibl. 40.

(1) 1 C 14: 20 (τῇ κακίᾳ on account of ταῖς φρεσίν). H 1: 14 εἰς διακονίαν...κληρονομεῖν σωτηρίαν (2: 3, 5: 9, 6: 9, 9: 28, 11: 7; with art. only 2: 10 τὸν ἀρχηγὸν τῆς σωτηρίας αὐτῶ ν). The art. is anaphoric in 1 C 13: 13 νυνὶ δὲ μένει πίστις ἐλπὶς ἀγάπη...μείζων δὲ τούτων ἡ ἀγάπη (similarly in German; cf. 4 and 3, R 13: 10 and 9), R 12: 7 εἴτε διακονίαν, ἐν τ ῇ διακονίᾳ· εἴτε ὁ διδάσκων, ἐν τῇ διδασκαλίᾳ etc., but 9ff. ἡ ἀγάπη ἀνυπόκριτος etc. as virtues assumed to be well known.

(2) R 3: 20 διὰ γὰρ νόμου ἐπίγνωσις ἁμαρτίας (a general assertion). Anarthrous νόμος also in Ja 4: 11, 2: 11, 12 (νόμου ἐλευθερίας not of the Mosaic law), but 10 ὅλον τὸν νόμον, 1: 25 εἰς νόμον τέλειον τὸν τῆς ἐλευθερίας. Cf. ἐν γραφῇ 1 P 2: 6 SAB (§ 308) (usually ἡ γραφή, αἱ γραφαί) 'in a scriptural passage'. R 6: 14 ἁμαρτία (not 'no sin', but 'sin as power' as usual in Paul; s. Lohmeyer, ZNW 29 (1930) 2ff.; Jeremias, Die Abendmahlsworte Jesu (1935) 72f. [The Eucharistic Words of Jesus (1955) 129f.]; cf. v. 9 θάνατος)...ὑπὸ νόμου...ὑπὸ χάριν (the same). 2: 13 οἱ ἀκροαταὶ νόμου (τοῦ ν. KLP al.) 'the hearers of a law' is difficult and also the phrase introduced for the sake of the parallelism (E. Tengblad, Syntakt.-stil. Beiträge zur Kritik und Exegese des Clem. v. Alex. [Diss. Lund, 1932] 2) οἱ ποιηταὶ νόμου (τοῦ ν. DcEKL al.) 'the doers of the (Mosaic) Law' (acc. to Origen in ep. ad Rom. III 7 [on R 3: 21 = MPG 14, 941f.] Paul uses ὁ νόμος for the Mosaic Law).—On the article with abstracts in Paul cf. Funk 106–35.

(C) The Article with Nouns Governing a Genitive

259. While up to this point no difference between the classical and NT use of the article has appeared, such a difference emerges in the case of a noun which governs a genitive. In Hebrew the *nomen regens* would appear in the construct or with a suffix and hence would be anarthrous. In the NT this Semitic construction makes its influence felt especially where a Semitic original lies behind the Greek (hence 'translation-Semitisms'), but occasionally also elsewhere in Semitizing formulae ('Septuagintisms'). Cf. Mlt. 81f. [130]; Raderm.² 116; Wolf II 16; Trunk 30. (1) This omission of the article takes place most frequently in fixed prepositional phrases (cf. § 255) like ἀπὸ ὀφθαλμῶν σου Lk 19: 42, ἐν ἡμέραις Ἡρῴδου Mt 2: 1, ἐν δακτύλῳ θεοῦ Lk 11: 20. Pure Greek offers good parallels for these. The article is also omitted with the *nomen rectum* in such cases (which was not required by Hebrew, but

rather by Greek; cf. § 257(2, 3) and Völker 16ff.), or the article appears with both *nomen rectum* and *regens*. (2) No preposition is needed for the article to be omitted in formulae with the genitive of a proper name: γῆ Ἰσραήλ, Σοδόμων, Αἰγύπτου, Χαλδαίων, etc. (3) Only in passages with strong Semitic coloring is such omission carried still further, e.g. in Mary's song of praise Lk 1: 46ff.: ἐν βραχίονι αὐτοῦ, διανοίᾳ καρδίας αὐτῶν, Ἰσραὴλ παιδὸς αὐτοῦ.—Cf. Funk 203–10; for Paul 227–34.

(1) Ἀπὸ (πρὸ) προσώπου τινός, διὰ χειρός τινος, διὰ στόματός τινος, ἐν ὀφθαλμοῖς ἡμῶν Mt 21: 42 OT, πρὸ ὀφθαλμῶν ὑμῶν 1 Clem 2.1. Authors writing pure Greek do not add a gen. to expressions of this kind; cf. § 255(4). Εἰς οἶκον αὐτῶν Mk 8: 3, cf. 26; otherwise the arthrous form largely preponderates; Lk 14: 1 εἰς οἶκόν (τὸν οἶκόν A) τινος τῶν ἀρχόντων is understandable, cf. with οἰκία A 10: 32, 18: 7; τὴν κατ' οἶκον αὐτῶν (αὐτοῦ) ἐκκλησίαν R 16: 5, 1 C 16: 19, C 4: 15 (cf. Phm 2) is a standard phrase and perhaps not a Hebraism. Ἐν ἡμέρᾳ ὀργῆς R 2: 5, ἄχρις ἡμέρας Ἰησοῦ Χριστοῦ Ph 1: 6, cf. 10; 2: 16; in addition ἐν τῇ ἡμέρᾳ τοῦ κυρίου 1 C 5: 5, 2 C 1: 14 (cf. 2 Th 2: 2); but even with the nom. ἡμέρα κ. 1 Th 5: 2 (AKL add ἡ), 2 P 3: 10 BC (SAKLP add ἡ). Ἐκ κοιλίας μητρὸς (αὐτοῦ) Mt 19: 12, Lk 1: 15, A 3: 2, 14: 8; ἐν βίβλῳ ζωῆς Ph 4: 3 (but Rev has the art. with both), ἐν β. λόγων Ἠσαΐου Lk 3: 4, cf. 20: 42, A 1: 20, 7: 42 (ἐν τῇ β. Μωυσέως Mk 12: 26); ἐν τῷ Βεελζεβοὺλ ἄρχοντι τῶν δαιμονίων Mt 12: 24 (and v.l. in Lk 11: 15), and elsewhere.

(2) Βασιλέως Αἰγύπτου A 7: 10 (βασίλισσα νότου is comparable Mt 12: 42 [§ 253(5)]; Wellhausen, Einl.² 11), εἰς πόλιν Δαυίδ Lk 2: 4, cf. 11 (*the* city of David), οἶκος Ἰσραήλ Mt 10: 6 etc., ἐξ οἴκου καὶ πατριᾶς Δαυίδ Lk 2: 4 (but Lk 1: 35, H 8: 8 OT, 10 OT with art. as also in the LXX), ἐξ ἐφημερίας Ἀβία Lk 1: 5.

(3) Zechariah's song of praise Lk 1: 68ff.: ἐν οἴκῳ Δαυὶδ παιδὸς αὐτοῦ, ἐξ ἐχθρῶν ἡμῶν, διαθήκης ἁγίας αὐτοῦ, ὁδοὺς αὐτοῦ, διὰ σπλάγχνα ἐλέους θεοῦ ἡμῶν; Simeon's song of praise Lk 2: 32; also Ja 1: 26, 5: 20. Exceedingly frequent in the LXX, hence also in quotations: 1 C 2: 16 τίς γὰρ ἔγνω νοῦν κυρίου, 1 P 3: 12 ὀφθαλμοὶ κυρίου, ὦτα αὐτοῦ. But in ἁγίων πόδας 1 T 5: 10 πόδας is assimilated to ἁγίων; in τραπέζης κυρίου...τρ. δαιμονίων 1 C 10: 21 the emphasis lies on the characteristic quality (the one is a table of the Lord, the other a table of the devil), cf. § 252.

(D) The Article with Proper Names

B. Weiss, Der Gebrauch des Art. bei den Eigennamen [in the NT], StKr 86 (1913) 349–89.

260. In the case of personal names, the final development of the language has been that in MGr they take the article as such. In classical, on the contrary, as also in the NT, they do not as such take the article. They can, however, be used with the article as the result of anaphora, e.g. A 9: 1 ὁ δὲ Σαῦλος with reference to the earlier mention of him (Σαῦλος δέ 8: 3; likewise immediately thereafter in 9: 3 τῇ Δαμασκῷ with anaphora to v. 2 ἐπιστολὰς εἰς Δαμασκόν) in the same way perhaps as κλάσας τὸν ἄρτον 20: 11 with reference to κλάσαι ἄρτον v. 7. An untranslatable nuance of the language is often involved. However, it obviously depends to a large measure on the preference of the author whether he desires to express the relation between frequent references to the same person or not (cf. Mayser II 2, 9ff.) and the MSS, too, often dissent. The use of the article with proper names was colloquial (Deissmann, BPhW 1902, 1467f.; Meltzer, BPhW 1916, 1393f.; Gild. 229; Mayser II 2, 6f.). Papyri: Eakin 340; MGr: Anagnostopulos 244; Paul: Funk 136–9. (1) Ἰησοῦς takes the article as a rule in the Gospels, excluding perhaps John, except where an arthrous appositional phrase is added (where either the article with the name or the appositional phrase would be superfluous), e.g. Mt 26: 69, 71 μετὰ Ἰ. τοῦ Γαλιλαίου (Ναζωραίου). On the other hand, the article is omitted as a rule in the Epistles and Rev (in part also in Acts) because, lacking a narrative context, anaphora in narrative does not come into view (perhaps in the way in which the Greek orators handle the name of the defendant; Gild. 229). Χριστός is properly an appellative = the Messiah, which comes to expression in the Gospels and Acts in the frequent appearance of the article; the Epistles usually (but not always) omit the article. (2) In the case of *indeclinable* names the article is occasionally called for, though without its proper meaning, to assist in indicating the case (as in German but not English; cf. O. Erdmann, Grundzüge der d. Syntax §36).

(1) Mt 27: 17, 22 Ἰ. τὸν λεγόμενον Χριστόν, Lk 2: 43 Ἰ. ὁ παῖς (27 τὸ παιδίον Ἰησοῦν); cf. A 1: 14 Μαρία τῇ μητρὶ τοῦ Ἰ., etc. The art. is omitted with Ἰησοῦς, besides the first mention generally, also in the case of the first appearance after the resurrection: Mt 28: 9 (ὁ Ἰ. DL al.), Lk 24: 15 (ὁ Ἰ. DNPX al.); in Jn, however, the anaphoric art. is possible in view of the context: 20: 14 θεωρεῖ τὸν Ἰησοῦν ἑστῶτα following 12 τὸ σῶμα τοῦ Ἰησοῦ. (Jeremias follows similar lines: ThBl 20 (1941) 45 on Jn 21: 4a.) On the other hand, Jn frequently omits the art. with Ἰησοῦς elsewhere (e.g. 1: 48, 50 ἀπεκρίθη

Ἰησοῦς is a set phrase; Abbott 57), a phenomenon which is common in the other Gospels with other names like Ἰωάνης and Πέτρος which are to be less strongly emphasized. Ἰησοῦς with art. in the Epistles: 2 C 4: 10, 11 (but not acc. to D*FG) (attraction to the art. with the governing subst.), E 4: 21 (anaphora to ἐν αὐτῷ), 1 Th 4: 14 (anaphora), 1 Jn 4: 3 (anaphora to v. 2; but S without art.). A 1: 1 ὁ Ἰ. (without ὁ BD) calls to mind the content of the Gospel although such a reminiscence was not necessary. Χριστὸς Ἰησοῦς is a proper name and is rarely used therefore with art.; Ἰησοῦς Χριστός even more rarely. Mk 16: 1 ἡ (only B*L, missing elsewhere) Μαρία ἡ Μαγδαληνή. Ἡρῴδης in Mt 2 is noteworthy in that it never has the art. (although no attributive is added), except τοῦ Ἡρ. in 2: 19; but in ch. 14 it has the art. throughout except with a phrase in apposition: Ἡρ. ὁ τετραάρχης 1 (but ὁ Ἡρ. X al.). Lk 3: 19 ὁ δὲ Ἡρῴδης ὁ τετραάρχης (but without ὁ τ. e, cf. 1; yet 'the Herod mentioned above [1], that is, the tetrarch' would be a possible though pedantic expression).

(2) Mt 1: 2ff. Ἀβραὰμ ἐγέννησεν τὸν Ἰσαάκ...τὸν Ἰακώβ etc. and thereafter with declinable names too: 2 τὸν Ἰούδαν, 6 τοῦ Οὐρίου, but probably not with those having appositives: 6 τὸν Δαυὶδ (but without τὸν minusc. 700) τὸν βασιλέα, 16 τὸν Ἰωσὴφ (POxy 12B6 correctly without τὸν) τὸν ἄνδρα Μαρίας, cf. Jn 4: 5 where only SB add τῷ before Ἰωσὴφ τῷ υἱῷ αὐτοῦ. Is the peculiar anarthrous use of πενθερὰ δὲ τοῦ Σίμωνος Lk 4: 38 treated as a proper name? Or: 'a mother-in-law was there, namely Simon's'? Mk 1: 30 ἡ δὲ π. Σ., Mt 8: 14 τὴν πενθερὰν αὐτοῦ. Cf. πατήρ §257(3) (?). Inflection of Ἀβραάμ in the NT: nom. Ἀ. (18 times); gen. after a subst. Ἀ. (19 times, Lk 3: 34 τοῦ [υἱοῦ] Ἀ., Jn 8: 53 and R 4: 12 τοῦ πατρὸς ἡμῶν Ἀ.), less often anaphoric (better Greek) τοῦ Ἀ. Jn 8: 39 (twice), G 3: 14, 29; dat. τῷ Ἀ. (11 times), without τῷ only H 7: 1 (A 7: 2 τῷ πατρὶ ἡμῶν Ἀ.), acc. τὸν Ἀ. Mt 3: 9, Lk 3: 8, H 7: 6, without τὸν Lk 13: 28, 16: 23, Jn 8: 57 (R 4: 1 Ἀ. τὸν πατέρα ἡμῶν, Jn 8: 58 Ἀ. as acc. subj. with inf.); voc. πάτερ Ἀ. Lk 6: 24, 30; always anarthrous after prepositions (5 times) except σὺν τῷ πιστῷ Ἀ. G 3: 9. Therefore in agreement with κύριος; s. §254(1).

261. Geographical names. (1) The same rule applies in general to place-names as to personal names, i.e. the article is used only for special reasons. (2) The use of the article in Acts with the stations on the journeys is peculiar: 17: 1 τὴν Ἀμφίπολιν καὶ τὴν Ἀπολλωνίαν (places which lie on the well-known road from Philippi to Thessalonica). (3) Ἱεροσόλυμα Ἱερουσαλήμ hardly ever takes the article. (4) Many names of countries regularly take the article as a result of their original use as adjectives (scil. γῆ, χώρα): ἡ Ἰουδαία, ἡ Γαλιλαία, ἡ Μεσοποταμία, ἡ Μυσία, ἡ Ἑλλάς (A 20: 2). (5) ἡ Ἀσία and ἡ Εὐρώπη (but not ἡ Λιβύη) as opposite divisions of the world take the article in accordance with established usage (K.-G. I 599; Gild. 239 ff.), and ἡ Ἀσία also retains the article as a designation of the Roman province. (6) The article is more frequently used with other names of countries than it would be with names of cities: thus always with Ἰταλία, usually with Ἀχαΐα (without article R 15: 26, 2 C 9: 2). (7) Αἴγυπτος hardly ever takes the article (Hebraism). (8) Names of rivers: ὁ Ἰορδάνης ποταμός Mk 1: 5, otherwise ὁ Ἰορδάνης. Ὁ Ἀδρίας (scil. κόλπος) as the name of a sea A 27: 27 as in classical.

(1) Anaphoric art. A 9: 3 (§260), τῇ Ἰόππῃ 38, τῆς Ἰόππης 42, cf. 36; τῆς Ῥώμης 18: 2 on account of τῆς Ἰταλίας in the same vs.; τὴν Ῥώμην 28: 14 denotes Rome as the goal of the entire journey. Τρῳάς, which should have the art. (Ἀλεξάνδρεια ἡ Τρῳάς), takes only the anaphoric art.: A 16: 11, 20: 6, 2 C 2: 12 (with reference to 1: 23 where Troas was probably in the back of his mind; or 'to the Troas where we had agreed to meet'); without art. A 16: 8, 20: 5, 2 T 4: 13.
(2) A 20: 13, 21: 1, 3, 23: 31, but 20: 14 ff. without art.
(3) Anaphoric Jn 2: 23, 5: 2 in addition to 10: 22 (only ABLW), 11: 18, A 5: 28. In Jos. εἰς Ἱερ. etc. usually without art. (Schmidt 359 f.).
(4) Hebraizing γῆ Ἰούδα Mt 2: 6 (ἡ Ἰουδαία γῆ Jn 3: 22 and 4: 3 D); anarthrous Ἰουδαίαν A 2: 9 is certainly corrupt. In Lk 17: 11 μέσον Σαμαρείας καὶ Γαλιλαίας, the omission of the art. with Σ. has prompted the omission with Γ.
(5) In A 2: 9, 10 only ἡ Μεσοποταμία, ἡ Ἀσία and ἡ Λιβύη ἡ κατὰ Κυρήνην have the art.; A 6: 9 ἀπὸ Κιλικίας καὶ Ἀσίας without art. In the address of 1 P (1: 1) the art. is missing not only with the names of all countries but with all substs. (ἐκλεκτοῖς παρεπιδήμοις διασπορᾶς Πόντου etc.); cf. §§268(2); 272 and W.-S. §18, 14). Here the addressee is characterized and the omission of the art. perhaps becomes understandable from the parallel 1 T 1: 2 Τιμοθέῳ γνησίῳ τέκνῳ = ὃς εἶ γνήσιον τέκνον; epistolary introductions, moreover, are stereotyped.
(6) Συρία, Κιλικία, Φρυγία, Ἀραβία are properly adjs. and so usually take the art.; however εἰς Σ. A 21: 3, ἀπὸ Κ. 6: 9 (supra (5)), 23: 34, Φρυγίαν καὶ Παμφυλίαν 2: 10, εἰς Ἀραβίαν G 1: 17. Although Παμφυλία was also originally an adj. (τὸ Παμφύλιον πέλαγος Jos., Ant. 2.348), it is usually anarthrous; with art. A (27: 5 τὴν Κιλ. καὶ Παμφ.), 13: 13 εἰς Πέργην τῆς Παμφυλίας in a chorographic gen. (§164(3)) which requires the art. (Gild.

242 f.; A 13: 14 DEHLP, 22: 3, 27: 5, cf. 16: 12, 21: 39).
(7) With art. on account of ὅλος (§275(2)) A 7: 11 𝔓⁴⁵SABCD; inferior v.l. 36 BC. Strongly Hebraizing γῆ Αἴγυπτος A 7: 36 OT, 40 OT, 13: 17 OT (v.l.), still more strongly τὴν γῆν Αἰγύπτου 7: 11 EHP; ἐκ γῆς Αἰγύπτου H 8: 9 (D τῆς Α.), Jd 5 as in LXX Ex 20: 1. Ptol. pap. have anarthrous Αἴγ. only after prep. and in dependent gen., otherwise with art. (Mayser II 2, 13 f.).
(8) Τοῦ χειμάρρου τοῦ Κεδρών Jn 18: 1 (§56(2)); τὸν ποταμὸν τὸν Τίβεριν Herm Vis 1.1.2; seldom thus in class. Katz, ThLZ 1957, 115; Krüger 50, 7.1; K.-G. I 610 (Thuc. 7.80, cf. 82).

262. Names for peoples, if they denote the group as a collective whole, do not require the article any more than do personal names. (1) For example, in Paul's speeches of defense against the Jews in Acts (25: 10, 26: 2, 3, 4, 7, 21) the article is missing in almost every instance with Ἰουδαῖοι (as with names of the defendants in Attic lawsuits; §260(1)); in the Epistles of Paul, moreover, Ἰουδ. does not have the article except in 1 C 9: 20 ἐγενόμην τοῖς Ἰουδαίοις ὡς Ἰουδαῖος (individual use 'those with whom I had to deal on each occasion', corresponding to τοῖς ἀνόμοις etc. below). (2) Nor does Ἕλληνες take the article in Paul because the emphasis is always on the distinctive quality ('people like the Greeks', cf. §252) and not on the existing group as a collective whole, while in classical the arthrous form is the rule (in contrast to οἱ βάρβαροι, cf. K.-G. I 599; Gild. 230 and on ἡ Ἀσία §261(5)). (3) On the other hand, the article is seldom omitted in the Gospel narratives (and in part in Acts) with Ἰουδαῖοι and other designations of nations or peoples. Ὁ Ἰσραήλ is a collective, but the article is omitted in Hebraizing formulae like γῆ Ἰ., ὁ λαὸς Ἰ. (υἱοὶ Ἰ.), but frequently elsewhere too.—The Ptolemaic papyri do not exhibit uniformity in the use of the article (Mayser II 2, 12 f.).

(1) With art. A 25: 8 τὸν νόμον τῶν Ἰουδαίων because τὸν ν. Ἰ. could not well be used and τὸν ν. τὸν Ἰ. (Attic, s. §271) would have been contrary to customary NT usage (or assimilation to the art. with νόμον, s. §259(1)?).
(2) R 1: 14 Ἕλλησίν τε καὶ βαρβάροις is no less class. than Dem. 8.67 πᾶσιν Ἕλλησι καὶ βαρβάροις ('all, be they Greek or barbarian') nor than σοφοῖς τε καὶ ἀνοήτοις which follows in Paul; s. §264(1).
(3) Correct class. phrases also are found in Acts: Ἀθηναῖοι πάντες 17: 21, cf. §275(1); πάντες Ἰουδαῖοι 26: 4 BC*E* (with οἱ SAC² al.). Mt 28: 15 παρὰ

'Ιουδαίοις (D with τοῖς); εἰς πόλιν (κώμην) Σαμαριτῶν 10: 5 and Lk 9: 52 are easily explained; 'Ιουδαῖοι Jn 4: 9 in the spurious addition.

(3) THE ARTICLE WITH ADJECTIVES USED AS SUBSTANTIVES

263. Substantivized adjectives with article (cf. § 241). As in the case of substantives (§ 252), the article is used with non-predicate adjectives, principally substantivized adjectives, in (*a*) an individual sense, with the quality κατ' ἐξοχήν (*par excellence*): ὁ ἀληθινός 1 Jn 5: 20 (God), ὁ μόνος 'the only One' (God) Jn 5: 44 BW (al. with θεός, cf. 17: 3), ὁ πονηρός (the devil), ὁ ἅγιος τοῦ θεοῦ Lk 4: 34 (Christ), ὁ δίκαιος A 22: 14 (Christ); likewise ἡ ἔρημος (in contrast to the inhabited land; or is the art. anaphoric? It is clearly so in Mt 3: 1, 3 [OT = Is 40: 3], Mt 24: 26, 1 C 10: 5 etc. In Lk 15: 4 it may be generic. Cf. § 241(1) and W. Schmauch, Orte der Offenbarung und der Offenbarungsort im Neuen Testament [Göttingen, 1956], 28 ff. Lk's use of the feminine plur. [e.g. 1: 80] may be a 'Septuagintism'). Also in an anaphoric sense: Ja 2: 6 τὸν πτωχόν 'that beggar' (with reference to v. 2, cf. § 139). (*b*) A generic sense: 1 P 4: 18 ὁ δίκαιος–ὁ ἀσεβής 'the righteous–the godless as (representing) their classes', very often in the plur.: οἱ πλούσιοι 'the rich', οἱ ἅγιοι 'the holy ones' (= Christians), and also with a substantive: ὁ ἀγαθὸς ἄνθρωπος Mt 12: 35, Lk 6: 45 (§ 139). The substantivized *neuter* of adjectives calls for special remarks: (1) The neuter sing. is used in an individual sense of a particular definite thing or act: τὸ ἀγαθόν σου 'your good deed' Phm 14, τὸ πολὺ...τὸ ὀλίγον 2 C 8: 15 OT; but frequently in a more generic sense: ἐργαζώμεθα τὸ ἀγαθόν G 6: 10. Mayser II 1, 3 ff. (2) Peculiar to Paul (Heb) is the use of a neuter sing. adjective like an abstract, mostly with a dependent gen.: R 2: 4 τὸ χρηστὸν τοῦ θεοῦ εἰς μετάνοιάν σε ἄγει (goodness in a concrete instance; χρηστότης is used in the same vs. in a different sense), 2 C 8: 8 τὸ τῆς ὑμετέρας ἀγάπης γνήσιον ('what is genuine with respect to your love'). This usage is often attested in earlier classical authors (Hdt., Thuc.), but is also 'completely familiar in higher κοινή' (Schmid IV 608). Mayser II 1, 1 ff. (not with a gen.). (3) The neuter sing. is occasionally used as a collective to denote persons: τὸ ἔλαττον...τοῦ κρείττονος = οἱ ἐλάττονες...τῶν κρειττόνων (§ 138(1)); τὸ δωδεκάφυλον

ἡμῶν 'our 12 tribes' A 26: 7 (Paul before Agrippa) is peculiar. (4) The neuter plur. is also used in this way with a gen.: of persons 1 C 1: 27, 28 τὰ μωρὰ τοῦ κόσμου etc. (§ 138(1)); and abstractly of things: τὰ κρυπτὰ τῶν ἀνθρώπων, τοῦ σκότους, τῆς καρδίας, τῆς αἰσχύνης R 2: 16, 1 C 4: 5, 14: 25, 2 C 4: 2, in a way related to the use of the sing. (*supra* (2)) but referring to a plurality of phenomena.—For the use of the article with names of festivals s. § 141(3) and Mayser II 2, 19.

(1) Generic: Lk 6: 45 ὁ ἀγαθὸς ἄνθρωπος ἐκ τοῦ ἀγαθοῦ θησαυροῦ τῆς καρδίας προφέρει τὸ ἀγαθόν (corresponding to ὁ ἀγ. ἄνθρ., s. *supra*); R 13: 3 τὸ ἀγαθὸν ποίει, cf. τῷ ἀγαθῷ ἔργῳ = (τοῖς) ἀγαθοῖς ἔργοις just preceding, as in Mt 12: 35 (par. to Lk 6: 45) τὰ (om. B al.) ἀγαθά...πονηρά (LUΔ with τά); also cf. R 3: 8 τὰ κακά...τὰ ἀγαθά. Mt 6: 13 ἀπὸ τοῦ πονηροῦ masc. or neut.?

(2) 1 C 1: 25 τὸ μωρὸν τοῦ θεοῦ σοφώτερον τῶν ἀνθρώπων ἐστίν (cf. μωρία 21, 23) 'the (ostensible) foolishness of God'. As Deissmann shows (NBS 86 ff. [BS 259 ff.]) τὸ δοκίμιον ὑμῶν τῆς πίστεως Ja 1: 3 = 1 P 1: 7 also belongs here, since δοκίμιος = δόκιμος is found in the pap. Chantraine, La formation des noms en grec (1933) 53, shows that the form -εῖος is correct; cf. μεγαλεῖος, καθάρειος (accent?). L.-S., Katz, ThLZ 1958, 341 f., accepted by Debrunner; s. § 23. 2 C 4: 17 τὸ παραυτίκα ἐλαφρὸν τῆς θλίψεως ἡμῶν (contrasted with βάρος); Ph 3: 8 διὰ τὸ ὑπερέχον τῆς γνώσεως Χριστοῦ (more concrete and graphic than ὑπεροχή); 4: 5 τὸ ἐπιεικὲς ὑμῶν; 1 C 7: 35 τὸ εὔσχημον καὶ εὐπάρεδρον τῷ κυρίῳ (§ 202) ἀπερισπάστως; R 9: 22, H 6: 17, 7: 18. R 8: 3 τὸ ἀδύνατον τοῦ νόμου 'the one thing the law could not do', not abstract.—1: 19 τὸ γνωστὸν τοῦ θεοῦ φανερόν ἐστιν ἐν αὐτοῖς is interpreted by Origen as 'what is known (knowable) of (or about) God is manifest to them' (§ 220(1)), for which the continuation ὁ θεὸς γὰρ ἐφανέρωσεν is suitable; therefore comparable to τὰ ἀόρατα αὐτοῦ 20 (s. *infra* (4)). Chrys.'s explanation is: ἡ γνῶσις ἡ περὶ τοῦ θεοῦ δήλη ἦν αὐτοῖς which therefore, with the abstract, means the same thing. Bultmann, TW I 719 also considers the conception 'God in his knowableness' (like 1 C 4: 5 τὰ κρυπτὰ τοῦ σκότους, R 2: 4 τὸ χρηστὸν τοῦ θεοῦ, 1: 20 τὰ ἀόρατα αὐτοῦ 'He, the invisible').—Cf. e.g. τὸ βιαζόμενον τῆς ἀρρωστίας Jos., Ant. 15.246, τὸ εὐμεταχείριστον τῆς θήρας Strabo 3, p. 168, τὸ πρὸς τὴν πατρίδα γνήσιον inscription of Sestos (c. 120 BC; Deissmann, NBS 78 [BS 250]; further exx. in Schmidt 364 ff.; Winer § 34, 2 [Winer-M.³ 294 f.]; Ljungvik 24 f. Also s. 1 Clem 19.1, 47.5. For the LXX Johannessohn I 23.

(3) Cf. 1 Clem 55.6 τὸ δωδεκάφυλον τοῦ 'Ισραήλ and synonymous τὸ δωδεκάσκηπτρον τ. 'Ι. 31.4.

(4) Other instances, like τὰ ὁρατὰ καὶ τὰ ἀόρατα C 1: 16 (without gen.), need only be mentioned; τὰ

καλά–τὰ σαπρά of the catch in the net ('*what* is good or bad') Mt 13: 48. For R 1: 20 s. *supra* (2). In the Gospels such neuters are not common because they belong to cultured language.

264. Anarthrous substantivized adjectives

can be used as readily as substantives in analogous constructions (cf. §253(1) on 1 C 15: 39): (1) R 1: 14 Ἕλλησίν τε καὶ βαρβάροις (§262(2)) and then σοφοῖς τε καὶ ἀνοήτοις, 1 C 1: 20 ποῦ σοφός; ποῦ γραμματεύς; (2) The article is sometimes missing even with neuters: Ja 4: 17 καλὸν ποιεῖν ('something good'). (3) Besides ἐν τῷ φανερῷ (Mt 6: 4 etc.), εἰς φανερὸν ἐλθεῖν (Mt 4: 22, Lk 8: 17) also appears, always without article, denoting something not yet actual; usually ἐν τῷ κρυπτῷ (e.g. Mt 6: 4, R 2: 29). (4) Εἰς τὸ μέσον, ἐν τῷ μέσῳ, ἐκ τοῦ μέσου if a gen. does not follow; otherwise the article is omitted, not so much because of Hebrew usage (§259), as because ἐν μέσῳ etc. had become more or less frozen (as a kind of preposition; cf. German *inmitten* and English *amidst*). (5) Similarly ἐπ' ἐσχάτου τῶν ἡμερῶν H 1: 2, 2 P 3: 3 (v.l. ἐσχάτων from τὰ ἔσχατα; so also Barn 16. 5, Herm Sim 9.12.3); ἀπ' ἄκρου γῆς ἕως ἄκρου οὐρανοῦ Mk 13: 27 (Mt 24: 31 s. §270(2)). (6) When participles used adjectivally are substantivized, the use of the article closely corresponds to that of substantivized adjectives; in the great majority of instances they take the article, but occasionally, as in classical, the article is omitted, even with the participle as subject: Mt 2: 6 OT ἡγούμενος.

(1) Mt 23: 34 προφήτας καὶ σοφούς; 11: 25 = Lk 10: 21 ἀπὸ σοφῶν καὶ συνετῶν...νηπίοις; Mt 5: 45 ἐπὶ πονηροὺς καὶ ἀγαθούς.

(2) Herm Man 10.2.3 πονηρὸν ἠργάσατο, but then 4 τὸ πονηρόν anaphorically. 2 C 8: 21 προνοούμενοι καλὰ οὐ μόνον ἐνώπιον κυρίου, ἀλλὰ καὶ ἐνώπιον ἀνθρώπων; here the art. would have broken the connection with what follows.

(3) In Jn ἐν κρυπτῷ 7: 4, 10, 18: 20 (εἰς κρυπτήν Lk 11: 33 is a subst.) in contrast to (ἐν) παρρησίᾳ or φανερῶς, not ἐν τῷ φανερῷ.

(4) Without gen. and without art. (class. also often) Mk 14: 60 (with τὸ DM), Lk 4: 25 DΓΔ al., [Jn] 8: 3, 9, A 4: 7 DEP, 2 Th 2: 7.

(5) Ἐπ' ἐσχάτου τῶν χρόνων 1 P 1: 20 (τοῦ χρόνου S, cf. Jd 18) = בְּאַחֲרִית הַיָּמִים (LXX); ἕως ἐσχάτου τῆς γῆς A 13: 47 OT; but τὰ ἔσχατα τοῦ ἀνθρώπου ἐκείνου Mt 12: 45 = Lk 11: 26, in contrast to τὰ πρῶτα. Ἐπ' ἄκρον ὄρους ὑψηλοῦ(ς?) logion POxy I 1 recto 16.

(6) Cf. Bauer s.v. ἡγεῖσθαι 1. For further exx. s. §413(1).

(4) THE SUBSTANTIVIZING ARTICLE WITH NUMERALS, ADVERBS, ETC.

265. The article with numerals denotes, as in classical, that a part of a previously stated number is being introduced: οἱ ἐννέα Lk 17: 17 following δέκα ('the nine [of the ten]'), cf. 15: 4, Mt 8: 12, 13 and probably also Mt 25: 2 (following δέκα) αἱ (Z) πέντε...αἱ (EUX al.) πέντε 'the first five... the remaining five'; Rev 17: 10 ἑπτά...οἱ πέντε...ὁ εἷς...ὁ ἄλλος. Cf. H. Kallenberg, RhM 69 (1914) 662 ff.

In Mk 10: 41 = Mt 20: 24 the ten who were moved with indignation against the two brothers are the *remaining* ten disciples, i.e. the twelve minus the sons of Zebedee. Οἱ δέκα do not form a fixed group of disciples as do οἱ δώδεκα (Wackernagel, Syntax II² 318). Cf. οἱ ἕνδεκα (less Judas) Mt 28: 16, A 1: 26, 2: 14.

266. With substantivized adverbs and prepositional expressions and where it governs a genitive (where the article stands for an understood *nomen regens*) the article is in general indispensable (only πλησίον 'neighbor' as a predicate appears without ὁ Lk 10: 29, 36). This usage is not frequent, however, in the NT. Mayser II 1, 9–20, 7 f. (1) Οἱ (om. S*BD) ἐκεῖθεν Lk 16: 26, τὰ κάτω, τὰ ἄνω Jn 8: 23, C 3: 1, 2; οἱ περὶ αὐτόν Mk 4: 10, Lk 22: 49, τὰ περί τινος often in Lk and Paul (also Mk 5: 27, but without τὰ SᶜAC²DLW al.). (2) Adverbial accusatives (§160) like τὸ ἐξ ὑμῶν R 12: 18 are especially noteworthy. Lk 17: 4 D is quite peculiar: ἐὰν ἑπτάκις ἁμαρτήσῃ καὶ τὸ ἑπτάκις ἐπιστρέψῃ 'these seven times' (anaphoric; cf. syˢ); to be compared is Mt 20: 10 τὸ ἀνὰ δηνάριον SCLNZ which is likewise anaphoric: 'a denarius to each man *as to the others who preceded*.' (3) With a gen. following: οἱ τοῦ Ζεβεδαίου Jn 21: 2 (§162(1)), τὰ Καίσαρος and τὰ τοῦ θεοῦ Lk 20: 25.

(1) Πέτρος καὶ οἱ σὺν αὐτῷ Lk 9: 32; τὸ ναί and τὸ οὔ 2 C 1: 17, Ja 5: 12, τὸ ναί...τὸ ἀμήν 2 C 1: 20, τὸ ἀμήν 1 C 14: 16, ὁ Ἀμήν Rev 3: 14; ἕως τοῦ νῦν Mt 24: 21.

(2) Τὸ κατὰ σάρκα R 9: 5 where the addition of the art. strongly emphasizes the limitation ('insofar as the physical is concerned'). Τὸ κατ' ἐμέ R 1: 15 s. §224(1); τὰ κατ' ἐμέ as subj. Ph 1: 12, as obj. C 4: 7. With τὸ καθ' ἡμέραν and τὸ πρωΐ the art. could just as well be omitted (§160).

(3) Οἱ τοῦ Χριστοῦ 1 C 15: 23. Ja 4: 14 is more peculiar: τὸ (A τὰ) τῆς αὔριον 'the things of the morrow, what happens tomorrow' (B without τό or τά, therefore τῆς αὔριον is to be taken with ἡ ζωή);

similarly Mt 21: 21 τὸ τῆς συκῆς; 2 P 2: 22 τὸ τῆς ἀληθοῦς παροιμίας 'that which is found in the true proverb'; R 14: 19 τὰ τῆς εἰρήνης 'what makes for peace'. A 16: 33 οἱ αὐτοῦ πάντες (ἅπαντες), but A οἱ οἶκ(ε)ῖοι αὐ. ἅπαντες, 𝔓⁴⁵ (probably correct) ὁ οἶκος αὐτοῦ ὅλος (cf. ὁ οἶκος αὐ. ἅπαντες minusc. 40).

267. The article with quotations and indirect questions.
(1) The article τό is used as in classical before quoted words, sentences and sentence fragments: τὸ ᾿Ανέβη E 4: 9, ἐν τῷ ᾿Αγαπήσεις (smoothed in 𝔓⁴⁶ to ἀγαπῆσαι) etc. G 5: 14.
(2) Even indirect questions are occasionally substantivized by τό (already in classical), but seldom outside the Lukan corpus: R 8: 26 τὸ γὰρ τί προσευξώμεθα οὐκ οἴδαμεν.

(1) Τὸ ῎Αγαρ G 4: 25 (ABD al.); τὸ Οὐ φονεύσεις etc. Mt 19: 18 (om. τὸ DMW), R 13: 9; H 12: 27. On ὁ ἦν in Rev s. § 143. Mk 9: 23 SAB al. τὸ εἰ δύνῃ (δύνασαι) 'so far as the εἰ δύνῃ is concerned [I tell you]' (without τό DKNUΠ, τοῦτο [as obj. of εἶπεν] W) or (acc. to Blass) τί τὸ εἰ δύνῃ following a (quid est si quid potes?). Περὶ τοῦ ἐξένηψε Νωε Philo, Sob. title (Cohn-Wendland II 215; cod. H), referring to the initial lemma of the treatise (Katz, Philo's Bible 108 f. n. 1).

(2) In Lk: 1: 62, 9: 46 (εἰσῆλθεν διαλογισμός, τὸ τίς ἂν εἴη etc.), 19: 48, 22: 4, 23, 24, A 4: 21, 22: 30. There appears to be no difference in meaning between the arthrous and anarthrous forms. 1 Th 4: 1 παρελάβετε...τὸ πῶς (FG ὅπως without τό) δεῖ..., Herm Sim 8.1.4 (PMich ὅ τι for τὸ τί), Homil Clem 1.6, Acta Thom. (Reinhold 25), cf. Jannaris § 2041. UPZ I 6.29 (163 BC) πυνθανομένων τοῦ with indirect question (B. Olsson, DLZ 1934, 1693; Mayser II 1, 80; II 3, 52 f. Also MGr (Thumb² § 269).

For the articular infinitive s. §§ 398 ff.

(5) THE ARTICLE WITH APPOSITIVES

268.
(1) **Appositives with proper names** take the article if a well-known person is to be distinguished from others with the same name: ᾿Ιωάνης ὁ βαπτιστής, A 21: 8 Φιλίππου τοῦ εὐαγγελιστοῦ, but 10: 6 παρά τινι Σίμωνι βυρσεῖ, 21: 16 Μνάσωνί τινι Κυπρίῳ. The person need not be well known in the case of ὁ (ἐπι-)καλούμενος with a surname following, or the equivalent ὁ καί (A 13: 9), or the designation by father, etc. with the article and gen. (with or without υἱός etc.; § 162). (2) Appositives with anarthrous θεός (§ 254(1)) can dispense with the article, but only in formal and solemn contexts such as the introduction to an epistle (§ 261(5)): R 1: 7 ἀπὸ θεοῦ πατρὸς ἡμῶν καὶ κυρίου ᾿Ι. Χρ. This applies also to κύριος (§ 254(1)) in apposition to ᾿Ιησ. Χρ., although it too is not common outside epistolary introductions (Ph 3: 20). Κύριος ὁ θεός s. § 254(1).—Mayser II 2, 103 ff.

(1) ῾Ο βασιλεὺς ῾Ηρῴδης (v.l. ῾Ηρ. ὁ β.) A 12: 1, ᾿Αγρίππας ὁ β. 25: 13; in this case the proper name itself must be anarthrous (§ 260), therefore not τῆς (SABD) Μαρίας τῆς μητρὸς 12: 12; cf. 25 D* τὸν ᾿Ιωάνην τὸν ἐπικληθέντα Μᾶρκον. Lk 24: 10 ἡ Μαγδαληνὴ Μαρία (D Μαρία ἡ Μαγδ.). Μαναὴν ῾Ηρῴδου τοῦ τετραάρχου σύντροφος A 13: 1; in the same vs. Λούκιος ὁ Κυρηναῖος is incorrect (all except D*) unless the author perhaps wants to distinguish between this Luke and himself (Λουκᾶς = Λούκιος § 125(2)). A 13: 20 ἕως Σαμουὴλ προφήτου. R 16: 21 Τιμόθεος ὁ συνεργός μου 'my well-known co-laborer'. On Φαραὼ βασιλέως Αἰγύπτου A 7: 10 s. § 259(2); on Mt 12: 24 § 259(1).—On ὁ καί cf. Mayser I² 2, 69; II 1, 60 ff., II 3, 56 (ὁ καί in nom. seldom in pre-Christian papyri; ὃς καί is earlier); further Herzog, Philol. 56 (1897) 35; Ramsay, ClR 19 (1905) 429; Lambertz, Glotta 4 (1912) 78 ff.; 5 (1913) 99 ff.; Hélène Wuilleumier, Mém. prés. à l'Ac. des Inscr. XIII 11 (1932); Rita Caldrini, Ricerche sul doppio nome personale nell'Egitto greco-romano (Aegyptus 21 [1941] 221–60).

(2) 1 Th 1: 1 ἐν θεῷ πατρὶ καὶ κυρίῳ ᾿Ι. Χρ., 1 T 1: 1 ἀπόστολος...κατ᾽ ἐπιταγὴν θεοῦ σωτῆρος ἡμῶν.—In ὁ ἀντίδικος ὑμῶν διάβολος 1 P 5: 8 ἀντίδ. is treated as an adj.—Jn 8: 44 ὑμεῖς ἐκ τοῦ πατρὸς τοῦ διαβόλου ἐστέ would be, acc. to strict grammatical analysis, 'of the father of the devil'; but it is certainly meant as 'of your father (cf. 38) the devil' (the omission of τοῦ before πατρός is thus correct in several minusc.); perhaps τοῦ π. with K and Or or ἐκ τοῦ π. with sy⁵ (Chr) is to be deleted (accordingly τοῦ δ. ἐστέ following § 162(7)).—Appositives with a personal pron. require the article (K.-G. I 602; Gild. § 606; Thumb² 39); thus Lk 6: 24 ὑμῖν τοῖς πλουσίοις, Mk 7: 6; 1 C 15: 8 τῷ ἐκτρώματι ἐμοί, A 13: 33 (32) τοῖς τέκνοις αὐτῶν ἡμῖν C²EHLP; G. Björck, Con. Neot. 3 (1939) 8.

(6) THE ARTICLE WITH TWO OR MORE ATTRIBUTIVES

269.
(1) If a substantive has two or more qualifying adjuncts, the intermediate position (i.e. between article and substantive) of all of them often becomes cumbersome and clumsy so that there is a tendency to distribute them, i.e. some before and some after the substantive (but not e.g. 1 P 3: 3). The repetition of the article with those in postposition is not generally required (especially after a substantive with verbal power), but only in those cases where the attributive in post-

position receives emphasis (implies contrast) or where ambiguity is to be avoided. (2) The second article is likewise unnecessary if a substantive is directly followed by a gen. which does not require the article (§271) and then by an attributive prepositional phrase: E 3: 4 τὴν σύνεσίν μου ἐν τῷ μυστηρίῳ τοῦ Χρ. (τὴν ἐν...would place this σύνεσις in contrast with another); but 1 Th 1: 8 ἡ πίστις ὑμῶν ἡ πρὸς τὸν θεὸν ἐξελήλυθεν (to avoid ambiguity). (3) An adjective (participle) following a gen. must have the article (ὁ υἱός μου ὁ ἀγαπητός Mt 3: 17), otherwise it is predicate: T 2: 11 ἐπεφάνη ἡ χάρις τοῦ θεοῦ (ἡ add. Cᶜ al.) σωτήριος πᾶσιν ἀνθρώποις. (4) A numeral in intermediate position never makes a second article dispensable: Ja 1: 1 ταῖς δώδεκα φυλαῖς ταῖς ἐν.... (5) On the other hand, an adjective (participle) in intermediate position can do so: 1 P 1: 18 τῆς ματαίας ὑμῶν ἀναστροφῆς πατροπαραδότου (but C Clem Or πατρ. ἀναστρ.). (6) The repetition of the article *before* the substantive is rare (more often in classical): 1 P 4: 14 τὸ τῆς δόξης καὶ τὸ τοῦ θεοῦ πνεῦμα; but ὁ ἄλλος and οἱ λοιποί require the second article as in classical if they are not (or not immediately) followed by a substantive but an adjectival adjunct: Jn 19: 32 τοῦ ἄλλου τοῦ συνσταυρωθέντος, Rev 2: 24 τοῖς λοιποῖς τοῖς ἐν Θυατίροις (ἄλλος and λοιποί do not unite with other attributive adjuncts to form a unit).—Mayser II 2, 59 ff.

(1) G 1: 13 τὴν ἐμὴν ἀναστροφήν ποτε ἐν τῷ Ἰουδαϊσμῷ, 1 C 16: 21 τῇ ἐμῇ χειρὶ Παύλου, C 1: 8 τὴν ὑμῶν ἀγάπην ἐν πνεύματι.
(2) With art. repeated for emphasis R 8: 39, to avoid misunderstanding 7: 5, 2 C 9: 3. 2 Th 3: 14 τῷ λόγῳ ἡμῶν διὰ τῆς ἐπιστολῆς (v.l. without τῆς in which case δι' ἐπ. goes with the following, which does not appear to be correct), Ph 1: 5, C 1: 4. 1 C 8: 7 τῇ συνηθείᾳ (v.l. συνειδήσει) ἕως ἄρτι τοῦ εἰδώλου with the position of the gen. reversed.
(3) With art. 2 C 6: 7, H 13: 20, E 6: 16 (τὰ om. BD*FG).
(4) Jn 6: 13, Rev 21: 9; the numeral is nothing but a closer definition of the plural.
(5) But τὸ λογικὸν ἄδολον γάλα 1 P 2: 2 because ἄδ. γάλα was probably an everyday expression (Moulton, Exp. VI 8 [1903] 107 f.; cf. πυροῦ καθαροῦ ἀδόλου κεκοσκινευμένου pap. 49/8 BC [Zilliacus, Aegyptus 19 (1939) 62] lines 10 f., 29 'pure, unadulterated, winnowed wheat'). Mt 24: 45 ὁ πιστὸς δοῦλος καὶ φρόνιμος is not offensive because καί carries over the art. also. Necessary repetition Rev 2: 12 τὴν ῥομφαίαν τὴν δίστομον τὴν ὀξεῖαν and H 11:

12 ἡ ἄμμος ἡ παρὰ τὸ χεῖλος τῆς θαλάσσης ἡ ἀναρίθμητος. Cf. Mayser II 2, 60.18ff.; further PTebt I 53.5 (110 BC) τῶν ὑπαρχόντων τοῖς ἐκ τῆς κώμης προβάτων ἱερῶν, POxy I 99.5 (55 AD) τῆς ὑπαρχούσης αὐτῷ μητρικῆς οἰκίας τριστέγου, cf. 15 (Witkowski, Bericht 218). Strong variants 1 C 10: 3, 4 τὸ αὐτὸ πνευματικὸν βρῶμα (πόμα) or τὸ αὐτὸ βρ. (π.) πνευμ. (𝔓⁴⁶A without αὐτό); G 1: 4 τοῦ ἐνεστῶτος αἰῶνος πονηροῦ, which is harsher in 𝔓⁴⁶S*AB τοῦ αἰ. τοῦ ἐν. πον. like Herm Man 10.3.2 τὸ πνεῦμα τὸ δοθὲν τῷ ἀνθρώπῳ ἱλαρόν; cf. K.-G. I 615f.
(6) Lk 1: 70 τῶν ἁγίων τῶν (only AC al.) ἀπ' αἰῶνος...προφητῶν, cf. A 3: 21. MGr τὰ πολλὰ τὰ δάκρυα etc. (Thumb² §57). Mayser II 2, 56, 60.

(7) THE ARTICLE AND THE POSITION OF THE ATTRIBUTIVE

270. Attributive and predicate adjective. An attributive adjective (participle) when used with an arthrous substantive must, as in classical, participate in the force of the article by taking an intermediate position (ὁ ἀγαθὸς ἄνθρωπος); or, if placed in postposition (to which the participle with additional adjuncts is especially susceptible), it must have its own article (ὁ ἄνθρωπος ὁ ἀγαθός). In the first instance the emphasis is rather on the adjective (ὁ ἀγαθὸς ἄνθρωπος Mt 12: 35), in the second more on the substantive (εἰς τὴν γῆν τὴν ἀγαθήν Lk 8: 8, in contrast to πέτραν etc.) or on the participle together with its adjuncts (A 21: 28 ὁ ἄνθρωπος ὁ...διδάσκων). Cf. §474(1). (1) However, if the adjective does not take intermediate position and has no article of its own, it is predicate: Jn 5: 36 ἔχω τὴν μαρτυρίαν μείζω = ἡ μαρ. ἣν ἔχω μείζων ἐστίν. (2) The (classical) 'partitive' usage also belongs here. It appears in the NT with μέσος (Lk 23: 45, Mt 25: 6, Jn 19: 18, A 26: 13; cf. §186(2)), while τὸ ἄκρον with the gen. is usually used for ἄκρος just as τὸ μέσον usually appears for μέσος (cf. §264(4,5), also for ἔσχατον ἔσχατα); elsewhere only with πᾶς and ὅλος (§275), where they stand in contrast to a part. (3) It is also possible for an attributive adjective used in postposition with an anarthrous substantive to take the article, by means of which the definiteness of the substantive is supplied only as an afterthought through the additional phrase (clause). This construction is used especially in the case of a participle which is the equivalent of a relative clause (§412(3, 4)): A 7: 35 σὺν χειρὶ ἀγγέλου τοῦ ὀφθέντος αὐτῷ 'an angel, *viz.* that one who' etc.—Mayser II 2, 51 ff.; for a summary of the frequency of these usages in classical writers s. Gild. §609, in Paul, Funk 219–26 (add 1 C 11: 5 to col. 6 p. 220).

(1) 1 C 11: 5 ἀκατακαλύπτῳ τῇ κεφαλῇ = ἀκατακάλυπτον ἔχουσα τὴν κ. (§198(3)); A 14: 10 εἶπεν μεγάλῃ τῇ φωνῇ (26: 24) = ἡ φ. ἥ εἶπεν... μεγάλη ἦν (also with anarthrous adj. in postposition φωνῇ μεγάλῃ 8: 7 etc.). Mk 7: 5 κοιναῖς ταῖς χερσίν only DW (the others without art.); 8: 17, E 1: 18, H 7: 24. Predicate adj. with a pron.: Jn 4: 18 (§292). Ὁ ὄχλος πολύς Jn 12: 9, 12 (9 om. ὁ AB³D al.; ὁ ὄ. ὁ π. W; 12 ὁ only BL) (= ὁ π. ὄ. Mk 12: 37) is probably by analogy to πᾶς and ὅλος (§275; Rob. 774; cf. πολλῇ τῇ ἐμφερείᾳ Plut. *et al.* in Raderm.² 112; ὁ φόνος πολύς Arrian, An. 1.9.6).

(2) A 27: 27 κατὰ μέσον τῆς νυκτός, for which 16: 25 κατὰ τὸ μεσονύκτιον, never περὶ μέσας νύκτας as in class. Τὸ μέσον is also old (Xen. *et al.*), Lob. Phryn. 53f. Partitive μέσος also Herm Sim 9.7.5, 8.2, 4, 6. Τὸ ἄκρον τοῦ δακτύλου αὐτοῦ Lk 16: 24 = τὸν δ. ἄκρον; H 11: 21, Mk 13: 27; Mt 24: 31 ἀπ' ἄκρων οὐρανῶν ἕως (τῶν add. B) ἄκρων αὐτῶν is class. in appearance only: the pl. ἄκρα is occasioned by the pl. οὐρανοί (cf. ἔσχατα §264(5)). LXX and pap. s. Bonaccorsi 582; Katz, Philo's Bible 143.

(3) Lk 23: 49 γυναῖκες αἱ συνακολουθοῦσαι 'women, *viz.* those who' etc. Jn 14: 27 εἰρήνην ἀφίημι ὑμῖν, εἰρήνην τὴν ἐμὴν δίδωμι ὑμῖν; 2 T 1: 13. A 9: 22 Ἰουδαίους τοὺς κατοικοῦντας S*B. K.-G. I 613f.; Gild. 283, 287, 291; Raderm.² 115. Mayser II 2, 57 sees in this construction a literary mannerism of the Hell. period.

271. The article with an attributive genitive is subject in classical Greek to the same rules as apply to adjectives: ὁ Ἀθηναίων δῆμος or ὁ δῆμος ὁ Ἀθ., but ὁ ἵππος τοῦ στρατηγοῦ is also possible (always ὁ πατήρ μου). An attributive gen. in intermediate position is frequent in the NT (e.g. Jn 18: 10 ABC, 2 C 8: 8, 19, 1 P 3: 1, 4: 17, 5: 1 [twice], 2 P 1: 8, 2: 7, 3: 2, ten occurrences in Paul [s. Funk 234]), still more frequent in postposition without the repeated article; postposition with the repeated article is not common. The *partitive gen.* as in classical must stand outside without the article repeated.—Funk 210–12.

A 15: 1 τῷ ἔθει τῷ (om. DEHLP) Μωυσέως, on the other hand Μωυσέως in postposition without the art. (13: 39,) 15: 5, 28: 23, Mk 12: 26, Lk 2: 22, 24: 44, 2 C 3: 7; Jn 7: 23 ὁ νόμος ὁ Μ. S, like 6: 33 ὁ ἄρτος ὁ τοῦ θεοῦ SD. 1 C 1: 18 ὁ λόγος ὁ τοῦ σταυροῦ appears to be a kind of anaphora to 17 ὁ σταυρὸς τοῦ Χριστοῦ. T 2: 10 τὴν διδασκαλίαν τὴν τοῦ σωτῆρος ἡμῶν θεοῦ. Cf. §262(1). 2 C 4: 11 ἡ ζωὴ ἡ (only 𝔓⁴⁶) τοῦ, but 10 also 𝔓⁴⁶ ἡ ζ. τοῦ. Appositives like Μαρία ἡ τοῦ Ἰακώβου scil. μήτηρ do not belong to this category. Partitive e.g. οἱ πρῶτοι τῶν Ἰουδαίων;

A 28: 17 τοὺς ὄντας τῶν Ἰουδ. πρώτους is different. Art. only with the attributive (cf. §270(3)): Ja 1: 25 εἰς νόμον τέλειον τὸν τῆς ἐλευθερίας, A 1: 12, 26: 12. With A 14: 13 ὁ ἱερεὺς τοῦ Διός cf. οἱ ἱερεῖς τοῦ Διός Dit., Or. 65.11 (247–221 BC) and the like in the Ptol. pap. (Mayser II 2, 3.30ff.). For the types Περικλῆς (ὁ) Ξανθίππου s. §162(2). The pre-position of the gen. is less common in Att. and Hell. (K.-G. I 617f.; Mayser II 2, 145); thus e.g. Mt 1: 18 τοῦ Ἰησοῦ Χριστοῦ ἡ γένεσις.

272. With prepositional attributives, if in postposition, the repetition of the article appears to be especially necessary for the sake of clarity. The omission of the article is by no means well-attested in classical authors. There are a number of examples of the omission of the article in the NT which are generally accepted, even apart from those cases where the substantive has other attributives (§269): R 6: 4 συνετάφημεν αὐτῷ διὰ τοῦ βαπτίσματος εἰς τὸν θάνατον, cf. 3 εἰς τὸν θ. αὐτοῦ ἐβαπτίσθημεν. Cf. Raderm.² 117; Johannessohn I 365 (*supra* and *infra*); Mayser II 2, 161f., 166f. In some instances the repetition of the article would not even be possible because the predicate sense is intended: Lk 16: 10 ὁ πιστὸς ἐν ἐλαχίστῳ = ὁ ὢν πιστὸς ἐν ἐλ., in which case πιστός is anarthrous as a predicate. In the case of a participle, it goes without saying that the article is not repeated: R 15: 31 τῶν ἀπειθούντων ἐν τῇ Ἰουδαίᾳ.—Article only with the attributive (cf. §270(3); Gild. 287; Mayser II 2, 161f., 164ff.): R 9: 30 δικαιοσύνην δὲ τὴν ἐκ πίστεως, Ph 3: 9 (§285(2)), 1 T 1: 4, 2 T 1: 13.—Detailed treatment: Percy 54–61, 209–11; Funk 212–14, 235–9 (Paul).

1 C 11: 24 μου τὸ σῶμα (+ τὸ S*ABC*) ὑπὲρ ὑμῶν 𝔓⁴⁶. Lk 5: 36 ἐπίβλημα τὸ ἀπὸ τοῦ καινοῦ (Stephanus, Lachmann) is not based on MS evidence. A 15: 23 ἀδελφοῖς (the correct reading; s. the edition of Blass) τοῖς κατὰ τὴν Ἀντιόχειαν is an address, s. §261(5). Doubtful are 1 Th 4: 16 οἱ νεκροὶ (+ οἱ FG, cf. lat *mortui qui in Chr. sunt*) ἐν Χριστῷ; R 10: 1 ἡ δέησις (+ ἡ KL) πρὸς τὸν θεόν; 2 C 9: 13 (τῇ) ἁπλότητι τῆς κοινωνίας εἰς αὐτούς (Chrys. has τῆς εἰς α. in three places); 1 C 12: 12 πάντα τὰ μέλη ἐκ (D, om. pm.) τοῦ σώματος; Rev 2: 9 τὴν βλασφημίαν (+ τὴν S) ἐκ τῶν λεγόντων ABC (om. ἐκ P 1 al.). Also predicative: ὁ δέσμιος ἐν κυρίῳ E 4: 1, τοῖς πλουσίοις ἐν τῷ νῦν αἰῶνι 1 T 6: 17. Likewise 1 C 10: 18 βλέπετε τὸν Ἰσραὴλ κατὰ σάρκα, cf. τοῖς κατὰ σάρκα κυρίοις E 6: 5 SAB (τοῖς κ. κατὰ σ. 𝔓⁴⁶DEFG al.), C 3: 22 𝔓⁴⁶S al. (τοῖς κ. κατὰ σ. FG), τὰ ἔθνη ἐν σαρκί E 2: 11, therefore R 9: 3 DEFG τῶν ἀδελφῶν μου τῶν συγγενῶν (μου) τῶν (om. pm.) κατὰ σάρκα is incorrect.—Pre-

positional attributives going with anarthrous substantives are usually avoided for the sake of clarity. In 1 C 12: 31 acc. to 𝔓⁴⁶D*F (Klostermann, Hdb.) εἴ τι is to be read instead of ἔτι whereby καθ' ὑπερβολήν (scil. ζηλοῦτε) is separated from ὁδόν. The conjecture of Heikel, StKr 106 (1934/5) 315 ἔτι καθ' ὑπερβολὴν [καλὴν] ὁδόν is superfluous. But Mk 1: 23 ἄνθρωπος ἐν πνεύματι ἀκαθάρτῳ, R 14: 17. Mayser II 2, 167f.; Schwyzer, Emerita (Madrid) 8 (1940) 37ff.

(8) THE ARTICLE WITH PREDICATE NOUNS

273. Predicate nouns as a rule are anarthrous. Nevertheless the article is inserted if the predicate noun is presented as something well known or as that which alone merits the designation (the only thing to be considered). Thus (1) with a substantive: Mk 6: 3 οὐχ οὗτός ἐστιν ὁ τέκτων (who is known by this designation); Mk 15: 2 σὺ εἶ ὁ βασιλεὺς τῶν Ἰουδαίων, 12 ὃν λέγετε τὸν βασιλέα τῶν Ἰουδ. (ADW without ὃν λέγετε); Jn 5: 35 ἐκεῖνος (John) ἦν ὁ λύχνος ὁ καιόμενος καὶ φαίνων (he who alone really deserves the designation 'light' [cf. Sir 48: 1 (with ὡς) of Elijah]). (2) With an adjective: Rev 3: 17 σὺ εἶ ὁ ταλαίπωρος etc. (3) And very often with a participle: Jn 5: 39 ἐκεῖναί εἰσιν αἱ μαρτυροῦσαι περὶ ἐμοῦ ('they who...', without the article it would be merely a periphrasis of the verbal idea with εἶναι, cf. §65(4)).

E. C. Colwell, JBL 52 (1933) 12–21 has sought to ascertain rules for the use of the article with pred. nouns (cf. Bonaccorsi 615): definite predicate nouns regularly take the art. in sentences in which the verb appears; exceptions are occasioned by a change in word-order: definite predicate nouns preceding the verb are anarthrous; proper names are regularly anarthrous in the predicate; predicate nouns in relative clauses regularly follow the verb whether they have the article or not (he deals only with sentences in which the verb appears and only with nouns which are unambiguously definite).

(1) Jn 3: 10 σὺ εἶ ὁ διδάσκαλος τοῦ Ἰσραήλ 'the great (true) teacher'; Mt 24: 45 τίς ἄρα ἐστὶν ὁ πιστὸς δοῦλος καὶ φρόνιμος; Ja 3: 6 ὁ κόσμος is pred. acc. to Sasse, TW III 883.11ff. Mt 5: 13 ὑμεῖς ἐστε τὸ ἅλας τῆς γῆς, cf. 14; 6: 22 (ὁ λύχνος pred.), 16: 16 ὁ Χριστός, A 21: 38, 1 Jn 3: 4, Jn 1: 4, 8 etc. Coordinated with an anarthrous subst.: Jn 8: 44 ψεύστης ἐστὶν καὶ ὁ πατὴρ αὐτοῦ (cf. §§268(2); 282).

(2) Mt 19: 17 εἷς ἐστιν ὁ ἀγαθός, cf. §263. With a pron.: Herm Sim 9.19.3 αἱ αὐταὶ αἱ πράξεις αὐτῶν εἰσι 'their deeds are the same deeds'.

(3) Mk 7: 15 ἐκεῖνά ἐστιν τὰ κοινοῦντα τὸν ἄνθρωπον, etc.; the idea which runs through the whole discourse is that there is really something

which produces this effect, and this given category is now referred to a particular subject. S. also §413(1). Björck, Die periphr. Konstruktionen 90f.

(9) THE ARTICLE WITH PRONOUNS AND PRONOMINAL ADJECTIVES

274. With pronouns. For the possessive pronouns, αὐτός 'self', οὗτος, ἐκεῖνος with an article with a substantive s. §§285; 288; 292. Τοιοῦτος occasionally takes the article (when pointing to individuals or embracing a class): e.g. Mt 19: 14 τῶν τοιούτων (referring to τὰ παιδία above); but rarely with a substantive following: 2 C 12: 3, Mk 9: 37 ABDLNW al. The article is used with τοσοῦτος only in Rev 18: 17 ὁ τοσοῦτος πλοῦτος; cf. Herm Vis 4.1.9 τὸ τηλικοῦτο κῆτος. Τοιούτους before τούς in Jn 4: 23 is predicate.

275. With πᾶς, ὅλος, etc. Ἕκαστος is never followed by the article (usage in Attic and the papyri [Mayser II 2, 90ff.] is different). With ὅλος and πᾶς (cf. §270(2); ἅπας is found only in Lk with any frequency; σύμπας does not appear in the NT [1 Clem 19.12]) the situation is more complicated: (1) In the case of πάντες 'all', the substantive to which it belongs, being defined as embracing the whole in a plurality of cases, retains the (generic) article; πάντες, however, no more requires the article than does οὗτος: πάντες ἄνθρωποι = 'everything to which the term man is applicable' (plur. to πᾶς ἄνθρωπος infra 3). Likewise ἐν πᾶσιν ἀγαθοῖς (neuter) G 6: 6. The omission of the article is unclassical in Lk 4: 20 πάντων ἐν τῇ συναγωγῇ ('those who were in the synagogue'), cf. 28. Ἀμφότεροι, like πάντες, is also followed by the article but only in Lk 5: 7 (elsewhere without a substantive; similarly in the papyri: Mayser II 2, 94). (2) Πᾶς 'whole' is used in Attic only of individual determinate concepts, ὅλος also with indeterminate: thus Jn 7: 23 ὅλον ἄνθρωπον 'a whole man' and with anarthrous names of cities A 21: 31 ὅλη Ἰερουσαλήμ. (3) Πᾶς before an anarthrous substantive means 'everyone' (not 'each one' like ἕκαστος, but 'anyone'); Mt 3: 10 πᾶν δένδρον, 19: 3 κατὰ πᾶσαν αἰτίαν, etc. Also belonging here is πᾶσαν χαράν Ja 1: 2 'all that joy means = pure joy', μετὰ παρρησίας πάσης A 4: 29 'with complete candor'. (4) Hebraizing: πᾶς Ἰσραήλ R 11: 26 'the whole of Israel' (cf. §262(3)). Similarly but not incorrectly πᾶσα σάρξ כָּל־בָּשָׂר Mt 24: 22, Lk 3: 6, R 3: 20, 1 C 1: 29 (never otherwise) = πάντες ἄνθρωποι (supra (1)). (5) If πᾶς follows an arthrous substantive, emphasis is placed on the substantive (papyri often: Mayser II 2, 99f.; but rare in the LXX because it is non-Semitic: N. Turner, VT 5 [1955] 211f.). (6) Πᾶς ὁ appears very frequently with a participle (§413 (2)); without the article Mt 13: 19 παντὸς ἀκούοντος, Lk 11: 4, and always without article when a substantive intervenes: Mt 3: 10 πᾶν δένδρον μὴ ποιοῦν etc. (7) Ὁ πᾶς, οἱ πάντες contrasts the whole or the totality with the part: A 19: 7 ἦσαν οἱ πάντες ἄνδρες ('as a whole, together') ὡσεὶ δώδεκα (cf. classical; K.-G. I 632f.; Gild. 311), 27: 37. G 5: 14 ὁ πᾶς νόμος ἐν ἑνὶ λόγῳ πεπλήρωται (in contrast to the several laws) (cf. Mayser II 2, 100f.). Οἱ πάντες and τὰ πάντα are often used by Paul without a substantive (cf. Mayser II 2, 101f.). The usage in 1 T 1: 16 is unusual: τὴν ἅπασαν (πᾶσαν) μακροθυμίαν 'the utmost ("perfect", cf. supra (3)) patience of which he is capable', cf. Herm Sim 9.24.3 τὴν ἁπλότητα αὐτῶν καὶ πᾶσαν νηπιότητα. (8) Οἱ ἀμφότεροι, τὰ ἀμφότερα are used like οἱ πάντες, τὰ πάντα E 2: 14, 16, 18; τοὺς δύο E 2: 15 utrumque ('each of the two'), while 16, 18 οἱ ἀμφότεροι is correctly used like utrique ('both together').—Mayser II 2, 90ff.

῞Απας apart from Lk only Mt 6: 32, 24: 39 (πάντας D), 28: 11 (πάντα A), Mk 8: 25 (πάντα DW), 11: 32 v.l., [Mk] 16: 15 (om. D), G 3: 28 SAB³, E 6: 13 (all), Ja 3: 2. The Att. distinction that πᾶς follows vowels and ἅπας consonants (Diels, GGA 1894, 298ff.) cannot be applied consistently even to Lk (cf. 1: 3 ἄνωθεν πᾶσιν), although ἅπας is found prevailingly after a consonant. Likewise in the pap., s. Mayser I¹ 161f., II 2, 96 n. 3.
  (1) Πάντες ἄνθρωποι in Lk (A 22: 15) and Paul (R 5: 12, 18, 12: 17, 18 etc.), Herm Man 3.3, often weakened to the sense of 'all the world, everyone' as in Att. (e.g. Dem. 8.5, 42; K.-G. I 632). Πάντες ἄγγελοι H 1: 6 OT. Ἀθηναῖοι πάντες A 17: 21 as in Att. because the names of peoples do not require the art.; cf. 26: 4 and §262(3). Πάσας καταλαλιάς (πᾶσαν καταλαλιάν S*) 1 P 2: 1, πᾶσιν ὑστερουμένοις Herm Man 2.4. But in 2 P 3: 16 πάσαις ταῖς (om. ταῖς ABC) ἐπιστολαῖς, E 3: 8 πάντων τῶν (P only) ἁγίων (without τῶν ἁγ. 𝔓⁴⁶!) the art., acc. to class. usage, can by no means be omitted.
  (2) A 11: 26 ἐνιαυτὸν ὅλον, Mt 2: 3 πᾶσα (om. D) Ἱεροσόλυμα (§261(3)), Lk 5: 5 δι' ὅλης νυκτὸς SABLW (τῆς ν. CD al.); otherwise with the art. (but s. infra (4)). Only the predicate position for ὅλος is used in the NT (e.g. ἐν ὅλῳ τῷ κόσμῳ Mt 26: 13, τὸν κόσμον ὅλον 16: 26) and not the attributive position which is also possible in class. and the pap. (K.-G. I 632; Mayser II 2, 95, 568); the same is true of the Ap.

Frs. except for the substantival use in τὸ ὅλον ISm 6.1, τῶν ὅλων Diogn 7.2, 8.7.
  (3) Πᾶσα δικαιοσύνη Mt 3: 15 = πᾶν ὃ ἂν ᾖ δίκαιον (Bauer s.v. δικαιοσύνη 2a); πάσῃ συνειδήσει ἀγαθῇ A 23: 1 (in every respect). Πᾶσα ἡ κτίσις 'the whole creation' R 8: 22, but πᾶσα κτ. 'every created thing' 1 P 2: 13, C 1: 23 (with τῇ ScDc al.), 15 (πρωτότοκος πάσης κτίσεως); Ph 1: 3 ἐπὶ πάσῃ τῇ μνείᾳ 'in the whole of…' or without the art. with DE; E 2: 21 read πᾶσα ἡ οἰκοδομή with SᵃACP, cf. 4: 16 πᾶν τὸ σῶμα. 2 C 1: 4 ἐπὶ πάσῃ τῇ θλίψει ἡμῶν (all tribulation actually encountered)… τοὺς ἐν πάσῃ θλ. (in any which may be encountered); so also A 12: 11 πάσης τῆς προσδοκίας (the whole actually entertained), 1 C 13: 2 πᾶσαν τὴν γνῶσιν (πίστιν) (all that there is in its entirety). Πᾶς can come very close to the meaning 'anyone, someone' (cf. §302); thus Mk 4: 13 πάσας τὰς παραβολάς 'any parables' (O. Lagercrantz in Ljungvik, Syntax 22 and in Riesenfeld, Con. Neot. 3 [1939] 24f.).
  (4) Πᾶς οἶκος Ἰσραήλ A 2: 36. Οὐ… πᾶς s. §302(1). Also Semitic Herm Sim 7.4 ἐξ ὅλης καρδίας αὐτῶν and often similarly; likewise as a weak variant Mk 12: 30, 33, Lk 10: 27, and a stronger variant Mt 22: 37.
  (5) 1 C 15: 7 ἔπειτα Ἰακώβῳ, ἔπειτα τοῖς ἀποστόλοις πᾶσιν 'to the apostles, indeed to all the ap.', because James, who never left Jerusalem, was not an 'emissary' (Holsten). Further exx. in Cuendet 123.
  (6) Cf. the ptcp. with art. without πᾶς e.g. ὁ κλέπτων 'he who used to steal' E 4: 28.
  (7) A 20: 18 τὸν πάντα χρόνον (ἀπὸ πρώτης ἡμέρας just before) as often in class. (Gild. 309ff.). Οἱ πάντες 1 C 9: 22 (the individual groups named in 20ff. are treated as a whole; moreover, πᾶσιν has preceded in v. 19), 10: 17, R 11: 32, E 4: 13. 2 C 5: 10 τοὺς πάντας ἡμᾶς (not just he of whom Paul had previously spoken [cf. 1st pers. plur. in v. 9]); 14 is somewhat different οἱ πάντες 'they all' (ὑπὲρ πάντων preceding), cf. Ph 2: 21; similarly τὰ πάντα 1 C 12: 6 (in contrast with the individual thing), 19, R 8: 32, 11: 36 ('the universe'), 1 C 15: 27f. (similarly 'the universe' and with reference to πάντας preceding, v. 25), etc.; also A 17: 25 (Mk 4: 11 v.l.).
  (8) Τὰ ἀμφότερα also A 23: 8 where, however, there is no contrast with individual things so that ἀμφότερα ταῦτα would be more correct. Plato, Theae. 203c τὰ ἀμφότερα στοιχεῖα; late Greek. S. K.-G. I 634; Passow-Crönert 445.22ff.; Psaltes 199; Wolf II 14; Anagnostopulos 239f.

(10) THE ARTICLE WITH TWO OR MORE SUBSTANTIVES CONNECTED BY καί

276. (1) With two or more substantives connected by καί the article can be carried over from the first to the others especially if the gender and number are the same, but also occasionally when the gender is different: C 2: 22 κατὰ τὰ ἐντάλματα καὶ διδασκαλίας τῶν ἀνθρώπων (allusion to LXX Is 29: 13 where κατὰ τὰ is missing; κατὰ [τὰ] could be dittography). (2) On the other hand, there are cases where the repetition of the article with the same gender or number is necessary or more appropriate: A 26: 30 ὁ βασιλεὺς καὶ ὁ ἡγεμών (different persons). With τε καί the article is usually repeated, though in A 14: 5 τῶν ἐθνῶν τε καὶ (τῶν add. D) Ἰουδαίων it is not. There are frequent variants but mostly of no consequence. (3) The article is (naturally) omitted with the second of two phrases in apposition connected by καί: T 2: 13 (τὴν) ἐπιφάνειαν τῆς δόξης τοῦ μεγάλου θεοῦ καὶ σωτῆρος ἡμῶν Ἰ. Χρ. In the case of two connected substantival expressions, e.g. R 4: 12 τοῖς (om. Beza cj.) στοιχοῦσιν, the article is not good Greek and is superfluous.—Paul: Funk 239–43.

(1) Lk 14: 23 εἰς τὰς ὁδοὺς καὶ φραγμούς, 1: 6, Mk 12: 33 v.l. Cf. e.g. PTebt I 14.10 (114 BC) τά τε μέτρα καὶ γειτνίας καὶ ἀξίας.

(2) 1 C 3: 8 ὁ φυτεύων καὶ ὁ ποτίζων ἕν εἰσιν, cf. Jn 4: 36. Jn 19: 6 οἱ ἀρχιερεῖς καὶ οἱ ὑπηρέται, whereas ἀρχ., πρεσβύτεροι, γραμματεῖς *can* be subsumed under a *single* art. (Mt 16: 21 etc.; Thieme 21f.), cf. οἱ Φαρισαῖοι καὶ Σαδδουκαῖοι and Schmidt 357–9; μεταξὺ τοῦ θυσιαστηρίου καὶ τοῦ οἴκου Lk 11: 51 (Mt 23: 35).

(3) Cf. 2 P 1: 1 (but here S has κυρίου for θεοῦ, probably correctly; cf. 11, 2: 20, 3: 2, 18); however σωτῆρος ἡμ. Ἰ. Χρ. may be taken by itself and separated from the preceding (cf. § 268(2) for the omission of the art. elsewhere). Cf. W.-S. § 18, 7d(!); Mlt. 84 [134f.]; A. T. Robertson, The Greek Article and the Deity of Christ (Exp. VIII 21 [1921] 182–8).—1 Th 1: 7 ἐν τῇ Μακεδονίᾳ καὶ ἐν τῇ Ἀχαΐᾳ, A 19: 21 τὴν Μακεδονίαν καὶ Ἀχαΐαν; s. Stauffer, TW III 105–7.

9. SYNTAX OF PRONOUNS

(1) PERSONAL PRONOUNS

277. The use of the nominative of pronouns, αὐτός as a personal pronoun. (1) The nominatives ἐγώ, σύ, ἡμεῖς, ὑμεῖς are employed according to the standards of good style as in classical Greek for contrast or other emphasis: Jn 4: 10 σὺ ἂν ᾔτησας αὐτόν (and not the reverse 'he–you'); 18: 33, Mt 27: 11 etc. σὺ εἶ ὁ βασιλεὺς τῶν Ἰουδαίων (a man like you), Jn 1: 30 ὑπὲρ οὗ ἐγώ (om. syᶜ al.) εἶπον (I myself), E 5: 32 τὸ μυστήριον τοῦτο μέγα ἐστίν· ἐγὼ δὲ λέγω εἰς Χριστὸν καὶ εἰς τὴν ἐκκλησίαν (contrast of subject and speaker); thus with imperative ὑμεῖς Mt 6: 9, σύ 17. Ἐγώ εἰμι Stauffer, TW II 341 ff. (2) However, where the MSS of the Gospels supply this nom. it is by no means everywhere a question of contrast or in general of emphasis; in that case it is a question of a Hebraism or a scribal addition. (3) As an equivalent for the 3rd person, αὐτός is used for emphasis = 'he' (besides ὁ in ὁ δέ, ὁ μὲν οὖν § 251) especially in Lk (Mt, Mk, also LXX): Lk 2: 28 (the parents bring the child Jesus in) καὶ αὐτός (Simeon) ἐδέξατο αὐτό etc. (in the actual narrative of Simeon it would run: καὶ ἐγὼ ἐδεξάμην), Mk 14: 44 ὃν ἂν φιλήσω, αὐτός ἐστιν ('*he* it is'); also αὐτὸς δέ: Mk 5: 40 (ὁ δέ AMW), Lk 4: 30, 8: 37 etc. Classical sometimes used οὗτος, sometimes ἐκεῖνος (also ὁ), s. §§ 290(1); 291(6). In MGr αὐτός is a personal pronoun of the 3rd person (Thumb² §§ 144, 147; cf. also § 288) and

has been replaced by ὁ ἴδιος in the intensive sense. (4) Among the oblique cases only αὐτός in the gen. is used for emphasis (classical ἐκείνου etc.): Lk 24: 31 αὐτῶν δὲ διηνοίχθησαν οἱ ὀφθαλμοί.—Attic ἔγωγε, σύγε do not appear in the NT.—Mayser II 1, 62f.

(1) A 4: 7 ('have people like *you* done *this* [miracle]?'), Jn 5: 44 ὑμεῖς (om. L Chr al.) (people like you), 39 ὑμεῖς (om. Chr) (you yourselves), 38 ὑμεῖς (om. L Chr) (ἐκεῖνος–ὑμεῖς contrasted), 1: 42 σὺ εἶ Σίμων...σὺ κληθήσῃ Κηφᾶς (cf. 49; this particular person in contrast to others); accordingly σὺ εἶπας (λέγεις) Mt 26: 64, 27: 11 etc. = 'you yourself...'. For ἐγώ εἰμι also s. Bauer s.v. ἐγώ.

(2) Mt 10: 16 etc. ἰδοὺ ἐγὼ ἀποστέλλω = LXX Mal 3: 1 for Hebr. הִנְנִי שֹׁלֵחַ, but Mt 11: 10, 23: 34, Lk 7: 27, 10: 3 are more or less good authority for the omission of ἐγώ (as also in Mal 3: 1), Lk 24: 49 for the omission of ἰδού (ἐγώ in contrast); in A 20: 25 ἰδοὺ ἐγὼ οἶδα one minusc. and Ir omit ἐγώ.—Aramaic אֲנָה is also readily used without emphasis, especially with a ptcp. Nevertheless, ἐγώ can be emphatic, particularly in a messianic sense: K. L. Schmidt, Le problème du christianisme primitif (Paris, 1938) 41 ff. Unemphatic ἐγώ seldom appears in the pap. (Mayser II 1, 63).—Jn 18: 37 σὺ λέγεις = 'you, not I' acc. to Merlier, Rev. Ét. gr. 46 (1933) 204–9.

(3) Αὐτὸς δέ (γάρ) even with a name added: Mt 3: 4 αὐτὸς δὲ ὁ (om. ὁ D) Ἰωάνης 'now he, namely John', Mk 6: 17 αὐτὸς γὰρ ὁ (om. ὁ D) Ἡρ. ('For he, the aforementioned H.', cf. 22 αὐτῆς τῆς Ἡρῳδιάδος;

O. Lagercrantz in Riesenfeld, Con. Neot. 3 [1939] 24 with exx. from PHolm); cf. Lk 3: 23 (not D), Jn 2: 24, 4: 44. This is an Aramaism acc. to Wellhausen, Einl.² 19. The fem. is not so used: αὕτη is to be written in Lk 2: 37, καὶ αὕτη in 7: 12, 8: 42; καὶ αὐτός (BDR καὶ οὗτος) 8: 41, 19: 2 (D οὗτος without καὶ) are also spurious; καὶ γὰρ αὐτή R 16: 2 is 'also she herself'. Lk 1: 22 (καὶ αὐτός), 2: 50 (καὶ αὐτοί), 9: 36 (same), 11: 14 (καὶ αὐτό); 24: 21 αὐτός ἐστιν ὁ μέλλων (here ἐγώ would also be used in the 1st pers.), A 3: 10 αὐτὸς (BDEP οὗτος, cf. Jn 9: 8, 9) ἦν ὁ...καθήμενος (likewise ἐγώ in 1st pers., cf. Jn 9: 9); cf. Herm Man 6.2.5 γίνωσκε ὅτι αὐτός ἐστιν ἐν σοί; Mt 12: 50 (with οὗτος Mk 3: 35), Mt 5: 4ff. The emphasis with αὐτός is occasionally very weak (W.-S. §22, 2b): Lk 4: 15 καὶ αὐτὸς ἐδίδασκεν, thereby eliminating the preceding φήμη as continuing subj.; αὐτός, however, can be omitted with A e. Elsewhere the reading is often uncertain (e.g. 5: 17, 19: 2). Καὶ αὐτός is a strong Semitism acc. to E. Schweizer, ThZ 6 (1950) 163; to the contrary W. Michaelis, 'Das unbetonte καὶ αὐτός bei Lukas', Studia Theol. 4 (1950) 86–93 (several things converge in Lk's case: genuine late Gr. αὐτός 'he', emphasis on the person of Jesus, Septuagintisms; unemphatic καὶ αὐτός is a secondary matter). Cf. Bonaccorsi 5. Cf. Buttmann 93ff.; W.-S. §22 n. 2; Wolf I 46; Psaltes 194f.; Mayser II 1, 64. The usage is an old one, although foreign to Attic: Hom., Il. 3, 282f. αὐτὸς ἔπειθ' Ἑλένην ἐχέτω—ἡμεῖς δέ 'he-we'.

(4) Mt 5: 3, 10, cf. §283(4); Herm Sim 5.7.3 αὐτοῦ γάρ ἐστι πᾶσα ἐξουσία A, similarly PMich 8.7.1 ἄκουε καὶ περὶ αὐτῶν.

278. The frequency of oblique cases of the personal pronouns used without emphasis is a conspicuous feature of NT Greek (still more of the LXX, Johannessohn II 369ff.). The reason for this frequency is not so much the dependence upon a Semitic language, where the pronouns are used with facility as suffixes to nominal and verbal forms and generally where they complete the thought, as the dependence on vernacular Greek, which, like all vulgar tongues, does not shun redundancy. The classical language, on the other hand, only used these pronouns where they were necessary for clarity and was often satisfied with the article as the only means of determination. There is a strong tendency in the NT, for example, to supplement each verb in a complex sentence with a pronoun even where classical Greek would have left it to be supplied from the previous instance. So the possessive gen. μου σου αὐτοῦ etc. appear with great frequency (even in a reflexive sense, §283). However, a rule cannot be formulated since usage varies according to the degree of

dependence on the vernacular or possibly even on a Semitic original (§§3f.), and according to the preference of the author at the moment. It is to be concluded from the numerous MS variants, moreover, that the copyists frequently made alterations (§277(3)).

As in class., the favored ὁ πατήρ μου (ὁ ἐμὸς πατήρ) or ὁ πατήρ, means 'my father'; so Christ speaks of God in Jn as ὁ πατήρ μου and more frequently ὁ πατήρ: 8: 38 παρὰ τῷ πατρὶ (μου add. SD al.)...παρὰ τοῦ πατρός (thus without ὑμῶν BLTW). Like class. ἀπενίψατο τὰς χεῖρας Mt 27: 24, cf. 15: 2 (αὐτῶν add. CDEF al.); A 7: 58 (Hatzid. 197). For the acc. with the inf. instead of the simple inf. s. §406; for αὐτοῦ etc. after the relative §297. S. also §466(4).—Vulgar language: Mlt. 85 [135]; M.-H. 431f.; Psichari 186; Wolf II 13; Helbing, BPhW 1917, 1072; Ljungvik 27; Mayser II 1, 63f.—A 16: 15 παρεκάλεσεν (scil. ἡμᾶς) λέγουσα (without ἡμῖν), 19 ἐπιλαβόμενοι τὸν Παῦλον καὶ τὸν Σιλᾶν εἵλκυσαν...instead of the fuller ἐπ. τοῦ Π....εἵλκ. αὐτούς; but contrast 22: 17 ἐγένετο δέ μοι ὑποστρέψαντι...καὶ προσευχομένου μου... γενέσθαι με (§423(2, 5); did Lk really write this?), 7: 21 αὐτοῦ...αὐτὸν...αὐτόν (none of the pronouns was necessary and only the first is generally transmitted; cf. §423(3)).

279. In oblique cases the accented forms of the 1st person singular ἐμοῦ, ἐμοί, ἐμέ are used as in classical to denote emphasis and contrast. They are generally used with proper prepositions (also ἕνεκεν) except πρός. Accordingly, the 2nd person σοῦ etc. after prepositions (except πρός) is to be accented. For the 3rd person s. §277(4). Ἔμοιγε, like ἔγωγε (§277), does not appear.

K.-Bl. I 347; Mayser I² 2, 62f.; II 1, 63; B. Laum, Das Alexandrin. Akzentuationssystem (Paderborn, 1928) 262f.—Πρός με Mt 25: 36 (S ἐμέ), Mk 9: 19 (𝔓⁴⁵S ἐμέ), A 22: 10 (8 ἐμέ S*AB); even in contrasts: Mt 3: 14 σὺ ἔρχῃ πρός με (where Tdf. puts an impossible, accented μέ), Jn 6: 37 the first time almost all MSS πρὸς ἐμέ, then πρὸς ἐμέ SE al., πρός με ABD al. Cf. Inschr. v. Magn. 22.5 πρός με (letter of Attalus I), 19.10 πρὸς ἐμέ (letter of the son of Antiochus III).

280. The literary plural (*pluralis sociativus*), i.e. the use of ἡμεῖς instead of ἐγώ and the 1st person plur. of the verb instead of the 1st sing., is a widespread tendency among Greek authors as well as in vulgar texts and other languages. The writer (or speaker) thereby brings the reader (or hearer) into association with his own action. This plur. is frequently sought in Paul; however, as the salutations to his Epistles show, he is usually

REFLEXIVE PRONOUNS

writing in the name of two or more persons and where this is not the case ([Pastorals,] R, [E]), no such plurals are found: cf. e.g. C 1: 3 εὐχαριστοῦμεν with E 1: 15f. κἀγώ...οὐ παύομαι εὐχαριστῶν. It is admittedly not always possible in letters written in the name of two or more persons to refer a plur. to that plurality without some compelling reason (thus 2 C 10: 11 ff.). The author of Hebrews, who admittedly does not name the sender(s), certainly appears to use sing. and plur. without distinction: 5: 11, 6: 1, 3, 9, 11 etc., 13: 18f. (plur.–sing.), 22f. (ἐπέστειλα, ἡμῶν); in 1 Jn 1: 4 γράφομεν ἡμεῖς appears to be equivalent of γράφω in 2: 1 etc.

R 1: 5 δι' οὗ ἐλάβομεν χάριν καὶ ἀποστολήν etc.: ἀποστολήν evidently applies to Paul himself, but the addressees and all Christians (4 τοῦ κυρίου ἡμῶν) are included in χάρις, so that he could not have written ἔλαβον χάριν.—Lit.: K. Dick, Der schriftst. Pl. bei Paulus (Halle, 1900), and Deissmann's review ThR 5 (1902) 65. Harnack, SAB 1923, 96–113 ('we' in the Johannine writings either the conspicuous authoritative 'I' of the author or the author in community with the readers or the congregation of believers; on which Behm, ThLZ 1924, 252–5). Stauffer, TW II 341 n., 354f.; Slotty, IF 44 (1927) 155–90; 45 (1927) 348–63. Further s. Bauer s.v. ἐγώ; Moule 118f. On the pap. Mayser II 1, 40ff. (pl. above all in the style of the chancellery). Sg. and pl. interchange in the diatribe (Epict. 2.4) without distinction.—The inclusion of the hearers is especially evident in cases like Mk 4: 30 πῶς ὁμοιώσωμεν....

281. The 1st and 2nd person sing., used to represent any third person in order to illustrate something universal in a vivid manner by reference to a single individual, as though present, does not appear in Greek as frequently as in other languages; it apparently occurs in Greek literature for the first time in the late classical period (as a peculiarity of animated colloquial language). Paul furnishes several examples, especially R 7: 7ff., where Origen et al. so understand it, particularly in 9f. The words ἐγὼ δὲ ἔζων χωρὶς νόμου ποτέ etc. are with difficulty referred to the person of the apostle. In αὐτὸς ἐγώ 25, as Origen emphasizes, Paul certainly applies the words to himself (gloss and/or misplaced?); later, in 8: 2 ἠλευθέρωσέν σε (SBFG, others με) the 2nd person is again used in a universal sense. Cf. Stauffer, TW II 355ff.; Rob. 678; Bauer s.v. ἐγώ (end) for bibliography.

1 C 10: 30 (cf. 29), G 2: 18 (put as a real case [εἰ, not ἐάν], which, however, by no means applies to Paul; from 19 on a genuine 1st person is used, but in such

a way that the words are meant to be universally valid for all true Christians). 2nd pers.: R 2: 17, 11: 17, 14: 4 etc., also occasionally combined with a direct address to the persons in mind as in 2: 1 ὦ ἄνθρωπε, which fits well with the vivid and quite frequent conversational character of the Pauline epistolary style. Cf. K.-G. I 557; Dem. 9.17 ὁ γὰρ οἷς ἂν ἐγὼ ληφθείην, ταῦτα πράττων..., οὗτος ἐμοὶ πολεμεῖ (anyone, even any state).

282. *Constructio ad sensum* with αὐτοῦ etc.
(cf. §134). The 3rd person pronoun αὐτοῦ etc. is often used without formal agreement, i.e. without a noun present in the same gender and number to which it would refer. (1) Thus the name of a place is sufficient to introduce the inhabitants subsequently with αὐτῶν etc.: A 8: 5 Φίλιππος κατελθὼν εἰς τὴν πόλιν τῆς Σαμαρείας ἐκήρυσσεν αὐτοῖς τὸν Χριστόν. (2) A concrete pronoun may refer to an abstract noun: R 2: 26 ἐὰν ἡ ἀκροβυστία τὰ δικαιώματα τοῦ νόμου φυλάσσῃ, i.e. ὁ ἀκροβυστίαν ἔχων, with αὐτοῦ subsequently of this man. (3) A plur. may refer to a collective sing.: πᾶν...αὐτοῖς (S*W αὐτῷ) Jn 17: 2 (§138(1)). Similar instances in classical. (4) A diminutive (= neuter) designating a person can be resumed by αὐτοῦ, αὐτῆς etc. as in classical (the physical gender replacing the grammatical), e.g. Mt 14: 11 = Mk 6: 28 αὐτῆς refers to κοράσιον, Mk 5: 23 αὐτῇ (𝔓45AK al. αὐτῷ) to θυγάτριον, 41 (L al. αὐτῷ) to παιδίον, Lk 2: 21, 22 αὐτόν to 17 παιδίου (but αὐτό 1: 59; in 1: 62, 2: 28 the reading varies). Cf. §134(3).

(1) A 16: 10, 20: 2, 2 C 2: 12f., G 2: 1f. etc.

(2) E 5: 12 ὑπ' αὐτῶν = of those who belong to the σκότος (11).

(3) Κόσμος...αὐτοῖς 2 C 5: 19.—Other exx.: Lk 23: 50f. βουλευτής...αὐτῶν, i.e. the member of the high council (easily understood from the preceding narrative). 1 P 3: 14 τὸν φόβον αὐτῶν, i.e. the persecutor (to be supplied from the context). There are further exx. like Jn 20: 15 αὐτόν, 1 Jn 2: 12 αὐτοῦ, where what is meant suggests itself without further reference. Jn 8: 44 (ὁ πατὴρ) αὐτοῦ (§273(1)) is to be referred through ψεύστης to ὅταν λαλῇ τὸ ψεῦδος, provided the text is sound; 'and his father' has also frequently been understood (as part of the subj.; ὡς καί 'as also' is an interpolated reading); cf. §268(2).—On the whole cf. Buttmann 92f.; W.-S. §22, 9.

(2) REFLEXIVE PRONOUNS

283. The reflexive pronouns ἐμαυτοῦ, σεαυτοῦ, ἑαυτοῦ, and ἑαυτῶν (1st, 2nd, 3rd person plur., §64(1)) have surrendered some of their original function to the simple personal pronoun in the NT (as in Hellenistic). What is more obvious is that the reflexives have no share at all in the increased use of the personal pronouns (§278). (1) In all authors we find the reflexive used almost exclusively as the direct complement of the verb referring to the subject; (2) but if the pronoun is governed by a preposition, Mt at least provides numerous examples of the simple pronoun. (3) Furthermore, if a substantive as a governing word is interposed and the pronoun receives no emphasis at all (so that it would be omitted in classical, §278), then the reflexive customarily does not appear. In general, the greater the number and the more independent the interposed words, the more rarely is the reflexive used. As a possessive gen. with a substantive (cf. §284(2)) ἐμαυτοῦ is found only in 1 C 10: 33 τὸ ἐμαυτοῦ σύμφερον, σεαυτοῦ not at all, ἑαυτῶν as 1st person H 10: 25 τὴν ἐπισυναγωγὴν ἑαυτῶν. In the third person the text tradition often varies between ἑαυτ- and αὐτ- (cf. papyri: Mayser II 2, 71ff.). (4) The strengthening of the reflexive with αὐτός, frequent in Attic, appears only in scattered instances (literary language): 2 C 10: 12 αὐτοὶ ἐν ἑαυτοῖς ἑαυτοὺς μετροῦντες.—Ἑαυτῶν for ἀλλήλων s. §287.

(1) Also ἔδοξα ἐμαυτῷ occurs with inf. A 26: 9, while class. Greek would use δοκῶ μοι, provided no emphasis was placed on the reflexive as it is here. On the other hand Mt 6: 19, 20 θησαυρίζετε ὑμῖν (instead of ἑαυτοῖς) θησαυρούς. For ἑαυτόν as acc. subj. with inf. s. §406 and Buttmann 236 (αὐτόν for σαυτόν only A 25: 21).

(2) Mt 5: 29, 30, 18: 8, 9, 6: 2, 11: 29, 18: 16 παράλαβε μετὰ σοῦ BDIW (σεαυτοῦ SKLM); moreover with two pronouns combined: 18: 15 ἔλεγξον... μεταξὺ σοῦ καὶ αὐτοῦ, 17: 27 δὸς ἀντὶ ἐμοῦ καὶ σοῦ (Aramaism acc. to Wellhausen, Einl.² 26). However also in Mt εἶπον ἐν ἑαυτοῖς (9: 3, cf. 21), μερισθεῖσα καθ' ἑαυτῆς (12: 25), ἔχοντες μεθ' ἑαυτῶν (15: 30) etc.

(3) For several exx. of the same type in class. writers K.-G. I 563f., 569, in pap. Mayser II 1, 68ff., II 2, 68ff., 568. Λέγω οὐχὶ τὴν ἑαυτοῦ 'your own' 1 C 10: 29 is easy to understand. Ἑαυτοῦ, -τῆς, -τῶν in an intermediate position (§284(2)): Mk 8: 35 v.l., Lk 11: 21 (𝔓⁴⁵D τὴν αὐλὴν αὐτοῦ), 13: 34 (D τὰ νοσσία αὐτῆς), 14: 26 (αὐτοῦ W; ἑαυτοῦ in postposition SB), 33 (αὐτοῦ DW al.), in addition 16: 8 εἰς τὴν γενεὰν τὴν ἑαυτῶν; Paul more often, e.g. R 4: 19, 5: 8, 16: 4, 18. A simple personal pronoun, on the other hand, e.g. also A 28: 19 τοῦ ἔθνους μου, same vs. τὴν ψυχήν μου add. 614 pc. gig p syʰ; G 1: 14 μου twice, 16 τὸν υἱὸν αὐτοῦ, etc. For ἐμός and σός s. §285(1). Other exx. of a reflexive not directly

dependent on the verb: Mt 12: 45 πονηρότερα ἑαυτοῦ (DE*W αυτου), Mk 5: 26 τὰ παρ' ἑαυτῆς (αυτης ABL), Lk 24: 27 τὰ περὶ ἑαυτοῦ (αυτου DEL al.), Jn 11: 20 ἐν τῷ οἴκῳ+ἑαυτῆς 𝔓⁶⁶; conversely Ph 2: 23 τὰ περὶ ἐμέ, R 1: 15 τὸ κατ' ἐμὲ πρόθυμος (§224(1)).

(4) 2 C 1: 9; A 5: 36 D κατελύθη αὐτὸς δι' ἑαυτοῦ; Jn 9: 21 is different: αὐτός ('he himself') περὶ ἑαυτοῦ λαλήσει (αὐτός is emphasized, not περὶ ἑ.; cf. R 8: 23).—Semitic idiom provides for the reflexive relationship by means of נֶפֶשׁ 'soul'; occasionally, therefore, in translation from Semitic τὴν ψυχὴν αὐτοῦ appears: Lk 9: 24 ἀπολέσῃ τὴν ψ. αὐτοῦ alongside 25 ἑαυτὸν δὲ ἀπολέσας ἢ ζημιωθείς; also cf. Mt 20: 28 (=Mk 10: 45) with 1 T 2: 6. Cf. W.-S. §22, 18b; Mlt. 87 [139]; Huber 67; Mayser II 1, 65–72; II 2, 65–74.

(3) POSSESSIVE PRONOUNS

284. The possessive genitives. (1) Μου, σου, ἡμῶν, ὑμῶν, and the corresponding forms for the 3rd person αὐτοῦ, -ῆς, -ῶν, are placed as in classical (K.-G. I 619) either after an arthrous substantive without repetition of the article or before the article: Mt 8: 8 ἵνα μου ὑπὸ τὴν στέγην (cf. §473(1)); or finally, if an attributive precedes the substantive, after the former: 2 C 4: 16 ὁ ἔξω ἡμῶν ἄνθρωπος. A. Wifstrand, A Problem Concerning Word Order in the NT, Studia Theol. (Lund, 1951) 172 pp. (regarding enclitic personal pronouns; s. IZBG 1951/2, Heft 1, 180f. [no. 1282] for a summary); Funk 216f., 243–8 (Paul). (2) The emphatic forms of the gen. ἐμαυτοῦ, σεαυτοῦ, ἑαυτοῦ, τούτου, ἐκείνου ('his') take the classical attributive position (statistical summary for Paul: Funk 247); in the NT ὑμῶν when emphasized takes this position in Paul: 1 C 16: 18 τὸ ἐμὸν πνεῦμα καὶ τὸ ὑμῶν; but other positions also: ἡμῶν γὰρ τὸ πολίτευμα Ph 3: 20 (strong emphasis for which τὸ γὰρ ἡμ. πολ. was not sufficient) as does the reflexive proper: τὴν ἐπισυναγωγὴν ἑαυτῶν H 10: 25 (=ἡμῶν αὐτῶν), δήσας ἑαυτοῦ τοὺς πόδας A 21: 11 (αὐτοῦ is a spurious variant which would refer to Paul). Emphatic ἐμοῦ does not appear in the NT except in combination with another gen. (R 16: 13 αὐτοῦ καὶ ἐμοῦ, 1: 12 ὑμῶν τε καὶ ἐμοῦ), emphatic σοῦ not at all. (3) Emphatic αὐτοῦ in attributive position = 'his' (weakening of the classical meaning ipsius; Hdt. already in a similar way 2.133 ὁ αὐτοῦ πατήρ, cf. K.-G. I 564) is frequent: T 3: 5 κατὰ τὸ αὐτοῦ ἔλεος (contrast ἡμεῖς above; τὸ ἔλ. αὐτοῦ D*EFG).

(1) 1 Th 3: 10 ἰδεῖν ὑμῶν τὸ πρόσωπον, 13 στηρίξαι ὑμῶν τὰς καρδίας, Jn 1: 27 ἵνα λύσω αὐτοῦ

τὸν ἱμάντα. Mt 27: 60 ἐν τῷ καινῷ αὐτοῦ μνημείῳ, 1 P 1: 3, 2: 9, 5: 10 etc. LXX: Helb., Kas. 178 (with exx. from the pap.). The position of μου before the art. and noun is to be explained by the absence of emphasis (cf. §473(1) and Cuendet 41). Μου sometimes also appears in a contrast (probably not intended at first): Lk 22: 42 μὴ τὸ θέλημά μου, ἀλλὰ τὸ σὸν γενέσθω (the emphasis is on the 'not' above all), Jn 15: 20 τὸν λόγον μου–τὸν ὑμέτερον (in spite of a preceding ἐμέ–ὑμᾶς).

(2) 2 C 1: 6 ὑπὲρ τῆς ὑμῶν παρακλήσεως (objective gen. which, however, can also be expressed by a possessive adj.: R 11: 31 τῷ ὑμετέρῳ ἐλέει, 1 C 11: 24 τὴν ἐμὴν ἀνάμνησιν; cf. class. K.-G. ι 560). 2 C 9: 2 τὸ ὑμῶν (v.l. ἐξ ὑμῶν) ζῆλος, 1 C 16: 17 τὸ ὑμῶν (ὑμέτερον BCD al.) ὑστέρημα, 2 C 12: 19, 1 Th 3: 7; Homil Clem 10.15 τῷ ὑμῶν (reflex.) παραδείγματι. Cf. Soph., OT 1458 ἡ μὲν ἡμῶν μοῖρα, PGM ι 4.763; Mayser ιι 2, 65.33ff.—G 6: 4 τὸ ἔργον ἑαυτοῦ, 8 εἰς τὴν σάρκα ἑαυτοῦ (αὐτοῦ D*FG, cf. v.l. E 4: 16, Mt 21: 8, 23: 37; Herm Vis 3.11.3 ἑαυτοῦ [2nd pers.] τὰς μερίμνας, Sim 2.5 τὸν πλοῦτον ἑαυτοῦ POxy ιx 1172.6 [iv AD] [A αὐτοῦ], 4.5 τῷ κυρίῳ ἑαυτῶν A [αὐτῶν PMich] [3rd pers.], 5.4.3 A [αὐτοῦ PMich]; in general αὐτοῦ deserves preference acc. to §283.) Cf. Dieterich 194; Trunk 33; Mayser ιι 2, 70.19f.

(3) H 2: 4 κατὰ τὴν αὐτοῦ θέλησιν, R 11: 11 τῷ αὐτῶν παραπτώματι ἡ σωτηρία τοῖς ἔθνεσιν, 3: 24, 1 Th 2: 19, Ja 1: 18 (v.l. ἑαυτοῦ); cf. §277(3, 4). In R 3: 25 ἐν τῷ αὐτοῦ αἵματι, αὐτοῦ is the gen. of αὐτός 'self'. Class. uses ἐκείνου for emphatic 'his' (even reflexive, K.-G. ι 649); this is found in the correct (attributive) position also in the NT: Jn 5: 47, 2 C 8: 9, 14, 2 T 2: 26 etc. (exception R 6: 21 τὸ τέλος ἐκείνων); cf. with τούτου etc. R 11: 30, 2 P 1: 15 (but contrary to the rule A 13: 23 τούτου ὁ θεὸς ἀπὸ τοῦ σπέρματος, cf. Ph 3: 20 supra (2); Rev 18: 15 οἱ ἔμποροι τούτων, H 13: 11). Without emphasis H 7: 18 διὰ τὸ αὐτῆς ἀσθενὲς καὶ ἀνωφελές (adj., not substantive; the author could hardly have said τὴν αὐτῆς ἀσθένειαν; cf. however the unstressed τὰς αὐτῶν ἐνεργείας Herm Man 6.2.2, and Homil Clem 1.7, 11; 3.8 and very often, LXX 2 Macc 7: 9, but not MGr). Αὐτοῦ in attributive position with and without emphasis in the pap.: Mayser ιι 2, 66.3ff.

285. The possessive adjectives, which classical Greek employed for the emphatic possessive gen. of the person pronoun, have to a great extent disappeared in the Hellenistic period and so also in the NT (in MGr they are retained only in dialect, Thumb² §143, 3) and were replaced by the personal pronoun (§284(2)), ἴδιος (μου) (§286), ὑπάρχων μοι and the like; this applies also to the papyri (Kuhring 12f.; Mayser ιι 2, 67f., 68, 71ff.). (1) Ἡμέτερος and ὑμέτερος appear only about nine times each and are not found in all books, not at

all e.g. in Mt and Mk. Ἐμός is quite frequent in Jn (Koine of Asia Minor? s. Thumb, ThLZ 1903, 421; Mlt. 40 [59]), but otherwise not very frequent (1 C ten times), σός outside of the Gospels and Acts only three times in Paul; both are also used as reflexives for ἐμαυτοῦ, σεαυτοῦ (classical also here and there, K.-G. ι 568f.). Detailed statistics may be found in G. D. Kilpatrick, 'The Possessive Pronouns in the NT', JTS 42 (1941), 184–6. (2) The possessive adjectives are also used predicatively (without article).

(1) Reflexives ἐμός, σός: 2 C 1: 23, Phm 19, Mt 7: 3, (3 Jn 4), Herm Sim 1.11 τὸ σὸν ἔργον ἐργάζου. On the other hand non-reflexive ἐμός often has little emphasis so that it is not easy to distinguish from μου: R 10: 1 ἡ εὐδοκία τῆς ἐμῆς καρδίας = τῆς κ. μου, G 1: 13, Ph 1: 26. Ὑμέτερος 1 C 15: 31 = objective gen.—Position of the possessive adj. (Cuendet 40): in Jn 31 times in postposition (e.g. 17: 27 ὁ λόγος ὁ σός), placed before with emphasis (6 times, e.g. 7: 16 ἡ ἐμὴ διδαχὴ οὐκ ἔστιν ἐμή); only emphatic in the other Gospels, therefore placed before (e.g. Mt 7: 22 τῷ σῷ ὀνόματι twice).

(2) Mt 20: 23 = Mk 10: 40 οὐκ ἔστιν ἐμὸν τοῦτο δοῦναι (cf. ἐμὸν ἂν εἴη λέγειν Plato, Lg. 2.664β; for which in the pl. ὑμῶν ἐστιν 1 C 3: 21, 22, cf. §284(2) on Ph 3: 20 and §162(7)). With subst. (predicate): Jn 4: 34 ἐμὸν βρῶμά ἐστιν ἵνα etc., 13: 35. The art. can also be omitted in certain cases: Ph 3: 9 μὴ ἔχων ἐμὴν δικαιοσύνην ('a righteousness of my own') τὴν ἐκ νόμου (cf. §272), just as with ἴδιος (§286); with ἑαυτοῦ: Lk 19: 13 δέκα δούλους ἑαυτοῦ ('of his'). Homil Clem 13.20.6 σῶμα σόν (as object) is probably a Latinism; cf. Schekira 157.7, 158. Jn 17: 6 σοὶ ἦσαν s. §162(7).

286. Ἴδιος in classical is opposed to κοινός, δημόσιος; in MGr the new possessive ὁ (ἐ)δικός μου, σου etc. 'mine' etc. has developed from it by the addition of the suffix -ικός. (1) It is still used occasionally in the NT in contrast to κοινός: A 4: 32 (H 7: 27), or = 'peculiar to, according to a particular condition' 1 C 3: 8, 7: 7 etc. (classical also), but for the most part simply = 'own' = ἑαυτοῦ etc. (like classical οἰκεῖος): Jn 1: 11 εἰς τὰ ἴδια ἦλθεν, καὶ οἱ ἴδιοι αὐτὸν οὐ παρέλαβον. M. Ant. 8.50.3 χώρᾳ τῇ ἑαυτῆς καὶ ὕλη τῇ ἑαυτῆς καὶ τέχνῃ τῇ ἰδίᾳ. It is then readily combined with the gen. αὐτοῦ etc. (cf. MGr; this is also classical in form). Frequently κατ' ἰδίαν = classical καθ' ἑαυτόν 'privately, by oneself': Mt 14: 13 etc.; classical ἰδίᾳ ἑκάστῳ 1 C 12: 11. (2) The occasional omission of the article is not surprising (cf. §285(2)).

(1) Jn 1: 41 εὑρίσκει...τὸν ἀδελφὸν τὸν ἴδιον Σίμωνα (unemphatic in spite of its position), Mt 22: 5 εἰς τὸν ἴδιον ἀγρόν (likewise unemphatic = εἰς τὸν ἀγ. αὐτοῦ), 25: 14, Lk 2: 3 (v.l. ἑαυτοῦ). With gen. (before or after the subst.): Mk 15: 20 (v.l. without αὐτοῦ, D also without ἴδια), A 1: 19, 2: 8, 24: 23, 24, T 1: 12, 2 P 3: 3, 16. Jn usually puts ἴδιος in post-position (also πατέρα ἴδιον 5: 18), the other Gospels place it with emphasis before (e.g. Lk 6: 41 ἐν τῷ ὀφθαλμῷ τοῦ ἀδελφοῦ σου...ἐν τῷ ἰδίῳ ὀ.). Cuendet 41.—Corrupt τὰ ἴδια (𝔓⁴⁶ lat, pm. διὰ) τοῦ σώματος 2 C 5: 10.

(2) 1 C 15: 38 (v.l. with τό), T 1: 12 (cf. Homil Clem 17.1); δούλους δεσπόταις ἰδίοις ὑποτάσσεσθαι T 2: 9 with a kind of assimilation to anarthrous δούλους (possibly like H 12: 7, § 257(3)); ἔλεγξιν ἰδίας παρανομίας 2 P 2: 16 is Hebraizing, as παραν. αὐτοῦ would be (§ 259); ἰδίᾳ γενεᾷ (for τῇ ἰ. γ.) A 13: 36 is also Semitic —Cf. Schmidt 369; Kuhring 13; Thieme 28f.; Mayser ɪ² 2, 65; ɪɪ 2, 73f.; Mlt. 87–91 [140–5]; Psaltes 197; Wittmann 17; Schekira 158f.; Waldis 47.

On periphrasis with κατά for the possessive gen. s. § 224(1).

(4) RECIPROCAL PRONOUNS

287. Ἑαυτῶν may be used for ἀλλήλων (as already in classical, K.-G. ɪ 573; for the papyri s. Mayser ɪ² 2, 64; ɪɪ 1, 73): 1 C 6: 7, C 3: 13, 16, etc.; often one alongside the other for variety: Lk 23: 12 μετ᾽ ἀλλήλων...πρὸς ἑαυτούς (SBLT πρὸς αὐτούς; the simple pronoun, however, does not appear to be admissible here). In ἄλλος πρὸς ἄλλον A 2: 12 the elements remain separate = πρὸς ἀλλήλους; cf. εἶς τὸν ἕνα for ἀλλήλους § 247(4). 1 Th 5: 13 εἰρηνεύετε ἐν ἑαυτοῖς (SD*FGP αὐτοῖς) = Mk 9: 50 εἰρ. ἐν ἀλλήλοις (Foerster, TW ɪɪ 416f.). Mk 9: 16 πρὸς ἑαυτούς S*AW (ἀλλήλους Θ, ἐν ὑμῖν D, αὐτούς al.).

(5) Αὐτός AS INTENSIVE AND IDENTICAL

(Rob. 685–7)

288. The NT uses of αὐτός are the classical: e.g. αὐτὸ τὸ πνεῦμα 'the Spirit himself' R 8: 26, τὸ αὐτὸ πνεῦμα 'the same spirit' 2 C 4: 13. The article is sometimes omitted: e.g. αὐτὸς Ἰησοῦς Jn 2: 24 (§ 260(1)). (1) Combined with the personal pronoun αὐτὸς ἐγώ, αὐτοὶ ὑμεῖς etc. (naturally not with the 3rd person: ἵνα αὐτοὺς ζηλοῦτε 'themselves' G 4: 17); thus ἐξ ὑμῶν αὐτῶν A 20: 30 (coinciding with the reflexive in

appearance only). (2) Simple αὐτός in Lk stands for αὐτὸς οὗτος (ἐκεῖνος) in several phrases, e.g. ἐν αὐτῷ τῷ καιρῷ Lk 13: 1 (ἐν ἐκείνῳ τῷ κ. Mt 11: 25). —Mayser ɪɪ 2, 75ff.

(1) Only in 1 C 5: 13 ἐξάρατε τὸν πονηρὸν ἐξ ὑμῶν αὐτῶν is ὑμ. αὐτ. reflexive in the usual way; the passage is a quotation, however, from Dt 17: 7 ἐξαρεῖς τὸν π. ἐξ ὑμῶν αὐτῶν, where ὑμ. αὐτ. has been inserted because ἑαυτῶν could not correctly be used due to the sg. ἐξαρεῖς (W.-S. 204; cf. Thack. 191).

(2) Ἐν αὐτῇ τῇ ὥρᾳ, ἡμέρᾳ Lk 10: 21, 12: 12 (with ἐκεῖνος Mk 13: 11), 20: 19, 13: 31, A 22: 13 etc.; Theod. Da 3: 6, 3: 15, 4: 30 αὐτῇ τῇ ὥρᾳ; LXX, Theod. 5: 5 ἐν α. τ. ὤ.=בַּהּ־שַׁעֲתָא 'forthwith'. Cf. ἐξαυτῆς § 241(3); also ἐν αὐτῇ τῇ οἰκίᾳ Lk 10: 7; αὐτῇ τῇ νυκτί Herm Vis 3.1.2 S, 10.7. With ἐν LXX Tob 2: 9, ἐν αὐτῷ τῷ καιρῷ 3: 17; αὐτῆς ἡμέρας (ἑσπέρας, ὥρας), αὐτῇ νυκτί and the like 'on that day' etc. Homil Clem 12.1, 13.13, (16.1,) 20.16, 21. Αὐτός in the pap. (Mlt. 91 [145f.]) is anaphoric ('the aforementioned') (therefore = οὗτος or ἐκεῖνος), peculiar especially to the style of the chancellery (Mayser ɪɪ 2, 76f.); cf. in particular αὐτῇ ὥρᾳ PTebt ɪ 411.3 (ii AD), αὐτῇ τῇ ὥρᾳ POxy ɪɪɪ 528.14 (ii AD), αὐτῆς ὥρας Class. Phil. 22 (1927) 255.14, κατ᾽ αὐτὴν τὴν ὥραν Preisigke, Sammelbuch ɪ 5298.5 (Byz.); inscrip. αὐταῖς ταῖς ἡμέραις Dit., Syll.² 1173.1 (ii AD), τὴν αὐτήν (the aforementioned εὐσέβεια, therefore = ταύτην) Dit., Or. 383.14 (i BC). Ljungvik, Syntax 8f. MGr αὐτός 'he'. Cf. also § 277(3, 4).

(6) DEMONSTRATIVE PRONOUNS

On the remnants of the demonstratives ὁ, ἡ, τό s. §§ 249–51; on the beginning of a demonstrative αὐτός §§ 277(3, 4); 288; on τούτου, ἐκείνου § 284(2).

289. Ὅδε is almost never used in the NT outside the formula τάδε λέγει (introductory as in classical) A 21: 11, Rev 2: 1 etc. and, because it belongs to the literary and no longer to the living idiom, it is not always used correctly at that. Ja 4: 13 stems from the vernacular: πορευσόμεθα εἰς τήνδε τὴν πόλιν 'into such and such a town' = Attic τὴν καὶ τήν; it is followed in 15 by ποιήσομεν τοῦτο ἢ ἐκεῖνο in a similar sense.—On ὧδε s. § 103.

Lk 10: 39 καὶ τῇδε ἦν ἀδελφή (instead of class. ταύτῃ) appears to be dependent on the LXX, which renders Hebr. זֶה by τῇδε, e.g. Gen 25: 24, 38: 27 (W.-S. § 23, 1b); cf. however PHolm 2.18 τῇδε τάξει 'acc. to the foregoing prescription'. Lk 16: 25 ὧδε, λ pc. Marcion ὅδε: the latter is accepted by Moule 123 and Katz, ThLZ 1954, 241; the sense requires it (the contrast is between 'he' and 'you', not 'here' and 'there') and the confusion is a common one in

DEMONSTRATIVE PRONOUNS §§ 289–291

the LXX (ὅδε = הַזֶּה was no longer understood and accordingly replaced by ὧδε [and ἥδε by ἴδε], ἰδού is a translation, ὧδε a corruption of הַזֶּה = ὅδε: Katz, Philo's Bible 75ff., 153f., Moule 203; J. Ziegler, Beiträge zur Jeremias-Septuaginta 38f.: Jer 3: 22 οἶδε = הֵנּוּ). Τοιᾶσδε for τοιαύτης only 2 P 1: 17 (in the class. way introducing the following). On τάδε λέγει s. Thieme 23; Thack. 11; Rudberg, Eranos 11 (1911) 177f.; Mayser II 1, 74.—Ὅδε 'such and such' is colloquial Att. and Hell.: Plato, Phdr. 270 D ff. (τάδε, τήνδε, τοιάδε, τόσα καὶ τόσα etc. several times), Arist. τόδε = τὸ αἰσθητόν 'this and that perceptible thing', τόδε τι = οὐσία τις 'this or that actuality', Theophr., Char. 8, Diog. Oen. 45.3. 11f., LXX Ruth 1: 17, τήνδε τὴν ἡμέραν Plut., Mor. 623 E (= IV p. 28.11 Hubert); s. Bauer s.v. 3; MGr ὁ τάδε(ς) = ὁ δεῖνα. K.-G. I 585f.; Brugmann, Dem. 132f.; Sonny, Glotta 6 (1915) 66ff.; Trunk 35; Wendland, BPhW 1905, 7; Von der Mühll, Hermes 68 (1933) 116ff.—1 Clem 50.3, 63.2 has ὅδε correctly, but ἡ δέ is to be written rather than ἥδε in 12.4 (anacoluthon following a gen. absol.; cf. § 468(3)).—Ὅδε is rare also in the pap. (it is not found in i BC): Mayser I² 2, 66; II 1, 73f.—Rob. 696f.

290. Οὗτος is used (1) to point to someone present (deictic): Mt 3: 17 οὗτός ἐστιν ὁ υἱός μου, etc.; to someone previously mentioned = the subject which is *continued* in the discussion (continuative): Mt 3: 3 οὗτος (John 1 f.) γάρ ἐστιν ὁ ῥηθείς... etc.; and especially to introduce what is to be narrated about a person after an introduction and description: Mt 27: 57 f. ἄνθρωπος πλούσιος ἀπὸ Ἀριμαθαίας...οὗτος προσελθών.... (2) Οὗτος is very common in the main clause with reference to the preceding subordinate clause: Mt 10: 22 ὁ δὲ ὑπομείνας εἰς τέλος, οὗτος σωθήσεται. (3) On the other hand, οὗτος (τοιοῦτος likewise) is seldom used to point to a following clause (οὗτος ὅς... Lk 5: 21, τούτους ὅσοι H 2: 15); only τοῦτο is somewhat more frequently used as preparation for a subordinate clause with ὅτι, ἵνα etc. or for an infinitive or substantive (examples in Pernot, Études 50f., 62, 119, 144f.). (4) Paul frequently has αὐτὸ τοῦτο 'just this (and nothing else)'; he also uses it adverbially (§160) = 'for this very reason' (2 C 2: 3) (Bauer s.v. αὐτός 1 h). (5) Τοῦτο μέν...τοῦτο δέ... 'on the one hand...on the other, not only...but also' is also adverbial H 10: 33 (Attic; literary language), further καὶ τοῦτο like Latin *idque* 'and at that, and especially' (Attic καὶ ταῦτα, K.-G. I 647). (6) Οὗτος appears to be used in a contemptuous sense (like *iste*) of a person present: Lk 15: 30 ὁ υἱός σου οὗτος.

(1) Introducing what is to be related: Lk 23: 50ff., Jn 3: 2, 4: 47, A 1: 18 (οὗτος μὲν οὖν ..) etc.; καὶ οὗτος in Lk in the continuation of a description is somewhat different: Lk 2: 25f. καὶ ἰδοὺ ἄνθρωπος ἦν...ᾧ ὄνομα Συμεών, καὶ ὁ ἄ. οὗτος δίκαιος etc.; cf. 17, 7: 12, 8: 41 (αὐτός is a spurious variant, s. § 277(3)), 19: 2 (likewise; D simply οὗτος); cf. also καὶ τῇδε 10: 39 (§ 289). Possible ambiguities in the antecedent of οὗτος may be resolved by the context: A 8: 26 αὕτη ἐστὶν ἔρημος (to ἡ ὁδός, not ἡ Γάζα), Lk 16: 1 καὶ οὗτος (to οἰκονόμον) διεβλήθη αὐτῷ (to ὁ ἄνθρωπος πλούσιος).

(2) R 7: 15 οὐ γὰρ ὃ θέλω, τοῦτο (missing in DFG) πράσσω, ἀλλ' ὃ μισῶ, τοῦτο ποιῶ.

(3) 1 T 1: 9 εἰδὼς τοῦτο, ὅτι, 1 Jn 2: 3 ἐν τούτῳ..., ἐάν, Jn 8: 47 (and Jn elsewhere) διὰ τοῦτο..., ὅτι, 2 C 2: 1 τοῦτο, τὸ μή...ἐλθεῖν, 2 C 13: 9 τοῦτο..., τὴν ὑμῶν κατάρτισιν. Τοῦτο δέ φημι 1 C 7: 29, 15: 50. Mayser II 1, 75; Rob. 698ff.

(4) Ph 1: 6 πεποιθὼς αὐτὸ τοῦτο with reference to the constancy emphasized in 5 (or to the following ὅτι?); R 9: 17 OT (to the following ὅπως), 13: 6 (anaphoric). 2 P 1: 5 καὶ αὐτὸ δὲ τοῦτο (v.l. κ. α. τοῦτο δέ) may be corrupted from κατ' α. δὲ τ.

(5) Καὶ τοῦτο 1 C 6: 6 (καὶ ταῦτα CDᵇ), 8 (καὶ ταῦτα L), R 13: 11, E 2: 8. On καὶ ταῦτα with ptcp. 'although' H 11: 12 s. § 425(1).

(6) Lk 18: 11 οὗτος ὁ τελώνης, A 17: 18; cf. a similar usage in English.—For οὐ μετὰ πολλὰς ταύτας ἡμέρας A 1: 5 s. § 226.—On the whole Rob. 697–706.

291. Ἐκεῖνος is used much less frequently than οὗτος, but comparatively most often in Jn. It is used to designate (1) absent persons as such; they must have been mentioned previously, of course, for the pronoun to be understood at all. Without special mention: ἐκείνη ἡ ἡμέρα = 'the last day' (often, e.g. Mt 7: 22, 2 Th 1: 10). (2) It is almost never used in combination with, or in contrast to, οὗτος (Lk 18: 14, Ja 4: 15 [§289]). (3) It is used especially in narrative, even imaginary narrative, to designate something previously mentioned together with things associated therewith. Here it is distinguished from οὗτος, in that the latter is used of that which is under immediate consideration, so that confusion rarely arises: Mt 7: 25, 27 τῇ οἰκίᾳ ἐκείνῃ (with reference to 24, 26; in between the narrative has dealt with other subjects, rain, floods, etc.). (4) In a subordinate clause (cf. οὗτος): Mk 7: 20 τὸ ἐκ τοῦ ἀνθρώπου ἐκπορευόμενον, ἐκεῖνο (that *other* thing) κοινοῖ τὸν ἄνθρωπον. (5) Infrequently *preceding* the word or clause referred to: Mt 24: 43 ἐκεῖνο (that other thing, s. 42) δὲ γινώσκετε ὅτι. (6) Weakened to 'he' Jn 10: 6 ταύτην τὴν παροιμίαν εἶπεν αὐτοῖς ὁ Ἰησοῦς, ἐκεῖνοι δέ (for which οἱ δέ, §251, or αὐτοὶ δέ, §277(3), can also be used; however according to S* simply καὶ οὐκ here), and so Jn frequently with reference to the immediately preceding subject: 9: 9, 11, 25, 36, likewise [Mk] 16: 10, 13, 20.

Independent ἐκεῖνος predominates in the pap. and in Jn (Paul, Wsd), while attributive ἐκ. seems to be a characteristic of the LXX and the rest of the NT: N. Turner, VT 5 (1955) 208ff.

(1) Ὑμεῖς–ἐκεῖνοι contrasted Mt 13: 11, Jn 5: 39, A 3: 13, 2 C 8: 14; ἡμεῖς (ἐγώ)–ἐκεῖνοι Jn 3: 28, 30, 1 C 9: 25, 10: 11, 15: 11. Contemptuously or invidiously of a person absent Jn 9: 28; cf. οὗτος §290(6); A 5: 28 D τοῦ ἀνθρ. ἐκείνου for τ. ἀ. τούτου of the other MSS (caused by ἐπὶ τῷ ὀνόματι τούτῳ in the same vs.).

(2) Herm Man 3.5 ἐκεῖνα (the earlier)–ταῦτα (the present).

(3) Mt 3: 1 ἐν δὲ ταῖς ἡμέραις ἐκείναις in the transition to a new narrative; cf. Mk 1: 9, 8: 1, Lk 2: 1. But Lk also with ταύταις: 1: 39, 6: 12 (D ἐκείναις), A 1: 15, 6: 1 (v.l. ἐκείν.), 11: 27 (B αὐταῖς, cf. §277(3)); Mt 8: 28 διὰ τῆς ὁδοῦ ἐκείνης (where the demoniacs dwelt; the road itself had not yet been mentioned), 9: 22 ἀπὸ τῆς ὥρας ἐκείνης (when these words were spoken), 26, 31; 13: 44 τὸν ἀγρὸν ἐκεῖνον (referring to ἐν τῷ ἀγρῷ in the same vs., but again with intervening narrative). Jn 1: 6ff. ἐγένετο ἄνθρωπος... Ἰωάνης· οὗτος (§290(1)) ἦλθεν εἰς μαρτυρίαν...ἵνα πάντες πιστεύσωσιν δι᾽ αὐτοῦ. Οὐκ ἦν ἐκεῖνος τὸ φῶς (Jesus has now been introduced so that John is the remote person). 7: 45 ἦλθον οὖν οἱ ὑπηρέται πρὸς τοὺς ἀρχιερεῖς, καὶ εἶπον αὐτοῖς ἐκεῖνοι (those mentioned before [32], remote from the scene; however the reading is once again doubtful).

(4) Jn 10: 1 (ἐκ. in contrast to the speaker), R 14: 14. Weakened and indefinite = 'he': Jn 14: 21 ὁ ἔχων τὰς ἐντολάς μου..., ἐκεῖνός ἐστιν ὁ ἀγαπῶν με; cf. 6: 57, 2 C 10: 18, Herm Man 7.5 etc.; even with reference to the speaker: Jn 9: 37.

(5) R 14: 15 ἐκεῖνον... ὑπὲρ οὗ (in contrast to σύ); Jn 13: 26 'he' (cf. supra (4)).

(6) Steitz and A. Buttmann (StKr 1859, 497ff.; 1860, 505ff.; 1861, 267ff.; ZWTh 1862, 204ff.) discuss Johannine ἐκεῖνος in detail with reference to 19: 35 καὶ ἐκεῖνος (of the narrator) οἶδεν etc.; everything, however, is critically uncertain in this verse: the whole is omitted in e and the Fuldensis Vulgate, while Nonnus read ἐκεῖνον οἴδαμεν etc. Cf. Blass, StKr 1902, 128–33; Zahn, Einl.[3] II 489f. and his commentary on Jn 19: 35. It is only due to a total neglect of textual criticism that so many scholars have erected their theories of the origin of the Fourth Gospel upon this verse and its customary interpretation (Blass).—On ἐκεῖνος in the Gospels s. Havers, IF 19 (1906) 83ff. (Synoptics) and 86f. (Jn).—On the whole Rob. 706–9.

292. The article is used with substantives (adjectives) when combined with οὗτος and ἐκεῖνος as in classical. The only point that must be noted is whether the words are really to be connected or whether the substantive or pronoun forms part of the predicate: Jn 2: 11 ταύτην (object) ἐποίησεν ἀρχὴν τῶν σημείων, Lk 2: 2 αὕτη (subject) ἀπογραφὴ πρώτη ἐγένετο (on the agreement in gender s. §132(1)), A 24: 21 περὶ μιᾶς ταύτης φωνῆς = ἡ φωνὴ ἣν μία αὕτη (predicate). Likewise with adjectives: Jn 4: 18 τοῦτο (object) ἀληθὲς (predicate) εἴρηκας. For anarthrous οὗτος used predicatively s. also §§129, 226, for τρίτον τοῦτο §248(4).

The position of the pronoun before the article or after the substantive is entirely a matter of choice (cf. the papyri, Mayser II 2, 80, 82): οὗτος (ἐκεῖνος) ὁ ἄνθρωπος or ὁ ἄ. οὗτος (ἐκεῖνος). Hebrew, however, supports the postposition in ἡ γενεὰ αὕτη, ὁ κόσμος οὗτος and the like.

Ἡ γενεὰ αὕτη as a rule in Mt, Mk, Lk, H 3: 10 as in LXX Gen 7: 1 הַדּוֹר הַזֶּה; ὁ κόσμος οὗτος Jn, Paul; cf. Cuendet 67f.; ὁ αἰὼν οὗτος Mt, Mk, Lk, Paul, ὁ αἰὼν ἐκεῖνος Lk 20: 35 (but οὔτε ἐν τούτῳ τῷ αἰῶνι οὔτε ἐν τῷ μέλλοντι Mt 12: 32, μέλλοντος αἰῶνος H 6: 5), ὁ νῦν αἰών 1 T 6: 17, T 2: 12 is better Greek; ὁ καιρὸς οὗτος 'this present age' Mk 10: 30 = Lk 18: 30, 12: 56, ὁ νῦν καιρός in Paul is better, but in the sense 'at that time, then' both a position before the article (Mt 11: 25, 12: 1, 14: 1, A 12: 1, cf. Lk 13: 1 [§288(2)]) and after the substantive (A 19: 23, R 9: 9 OT, E 2: 12) is possible. Late Jewish עוֹלָם הַזֶּה 'this present age', עוֹלָם הַבָּא 'the coming age' (Billerbeck IV 815), so that οὗτος (ἐκεῖνος) in this sense is almost without exception in postposition (R without exception: v. Dobschütz, ZNW 33 [1934] 59).—Various positions are possible in combination with πᾶς: πάντα ταῦτα τὰ πονηρά Mk 7: 23 (all of that, the evil), τὴν ἐξουσίαν ταύτην ἅπασαν Lk 4: 6 (this authority and indeed all of it), πάντα τὰ ῥήματα ταῦτα Lk 1: 65 (all these events); Cuendet 131f. Lk has ταῦτα πάντα only in this position, but usually reversed after prep.; s. Debrunner, Gnomon 4 (1928) 443. Always τὰ ῥήματα ταῦτα etc. outside of Jn 8: 20, 10: 21: Debrunner, ThLZ 1955, 537.—On the whole, Rob. 700ff., 708.

(7) RELATIVE PRONOUNS

293. Ὅς and ὅστις (ὅσπερ). The definite relative ὅς and the indefinite relative ὅστις are no longer clearly distinguished in the NT. With this is connected the fact that ὅστις is virtually limited to the nom. (§64(3)); nearly all authors use it in this case (Jn least of all; ὅσος except in Hebrews is also limited to the nom. and acc.). (1) Mt uses ὅστις correctly in sentences of general reference: 5: 39, 41, 10: 33 etc., but also ὅς 10: 14, 23: 16, 18, and especially πᾶς ὅστις 7: 24, 10: 32, 19: 29. (2) Ὅστις is correctly used in connection with a substantive of indefinite reference: Mt 7: 15 τῶν ψευδοπροφητῶν οἵτινες (description follows), also with reference to a definite person where the relative clause expresses the general quality: Jn 8: 53 Ἀβραάμ, ὅστις ἀπέθανεν ('who nevertheless was a man who died'). (3) These limitations are overridden, especially by Lk, and οἵτινες, ἥτις are used as the equivalents of οἵ, ἥ: Πέτρον καὶ Ἰωάνην, οἵτινες A 8: 14f., τὴν πύλην, ἥτις 12: 10. (4) This usage cannot be established for Paul since ὅς and ὅστις vary in R 16: 3ff. according to whether a simple assertion is made (ὅς) or a characteristic (ὅστις) given.—Furthermore, for ὅς instead of ὅστις, note οὐδεὶς (οὐ)…ὅς οὐ § 431(1). Ὅσπερ has been abandoned (§ 64(3)), for which ὅστις is perhaps used (Mlt. 92 [146]). (5) Not only an interrogative clause, but also a relative clause, may follow verbs of knowing as in the classical period (K.-G. II 438f.), e.g. Mt 20: 22 οὐκ οἴδατε, τί αἰτεῖσθε, but 6: 8 οἶδεν…, ὧν χρείαν ἔχετε (cf. Bauer s.v. οἶδα 1f, g), Jn 13: 18 οἶδα τίνας (WΨ οὓς) ἐξελεξάμην. Thus also alternately: 1 T 1: 7 μήτε ἅ…μήτε περὶ τίνων, 2 Clem 1. 2 πόθεν…ὑπὸ τίνος…εἰς ὃν τόπον…ὅσα. For corresponding οἷος or ποῖος etc. s. § 304. Cf. also Rob. 725f., 733f.; Mayser II 1, 79. For ἔχω with interrogative and relative clauses s. § 368, for ὅς in alleged direct questions § 300(2). On τίς as a relative s. § 298(4).

On ὅς and ὅστις: Pernot, Études 150–80; Mayser I² 2, 68 n. 1; II 1, 76f.—Acc. to Cadbury, JBL 42 (1923) 150–7 the normal inflection in Lk is ὅς ἥτις ὅ, οὗ ἧς etc., οἵτινες αἵτινες ἅ, ὧν etc.; cf. the interchange in H 9: 2 ἐν ᾗ–ἥτις, 9 ἥτις–καθ' ἥν, 13: 7 οἵτινες–ὧν, E 5: 5 ὅς (v.l. ὅ) ἐστιν εἰδωλολάτρης = C 3: 5 ἥτις ἐστὶν εἰδωλολατρία, R 4: 16 ὅς ἐστιν πατὴρ πάντων ἡμῶν–G 4: 26 f. ἥτις ἐστὶν μήτηρ ἡμῶν. Exceptions (in Acts only 4 among more than 200 exx.) are explicable for the most part on the basis of doubtful readings, the sources of Lk (e.g. Lk 8: 13 = Mk 4: 16), and euphonic consideration with regard to a foregoing τινες (e.g. Lk 8: 2 γυναῖκές τινες αἳ ἦσαν…); the sole exception to the rule in Heb is οἵ in 11: 33; the rule also applies to Paul except in that he almost always uses ἅτινα. Moule 123f.—Ὅστις in Jn only in 8: 53 (otherwise ὅ τι and ἅτινα) where Pernot, Études 52f. would read ὅτι with D.—Nom. sg. ὅστις (in a generalizing sense) in Mk only 8: 34 AC², εἴ τις SBC*DLW is more correct. Pernot, Études 174.—

Οὗ 'where' has also retreated before ὅπου: Mt, Mk, Jn do not use οὗ, Lk only in passages original with him, while in pars. to Mt and Mk he has ὅπου. Pernot, Études 153, 156, 161.

(1) Πᾶς ὅς Lk 14: 33, A 2: 21 OT, G 3: 10 OT, παντὶ ᾧ Lk 12: 48; Mt with a subst. in addition: πᾶν ῥῆμα ἀργὸν ὅ 12: 36, πᾶσα φυτεία ἣν 15: 13 (πᾶσα ψυχὴ ἥτις A 3: 23 OT). Cf. Hebr. כָּל־אֲשֶׁר, Aram. כָּל־דִי 'everyone who, everything which'.

(2) Mt 7: 24 ἀνδρὶ φρονίμῳ ὅστις, etc., but ὅς in Lk: 6: 48 ἀνθρώπῳ ὅς, 49 οἰκίαν ᾗ. A 7: 53 οἵτινες ἐλάβετε (people who).

(3) Πόλιν Δαυὶδ ἥτις Lk 2: 4; Rev 12: 13 τὴν γυναῖκα ἥτις ἔτεκεν τὸν ἄρσενα; especially with a ptcp. following, in which case οἵ, ἥ could be confused with the art.: A 8: 15, οἵτινες παραγενόμενοι 17: 10. The use of ὅστις for ὅς is very old in Ion., e.g. Hdt. 2.99 πόλιν ἥτις νῦν Μέμφις καλέεται (K.-G. II 400), and very common in Koine (Trunk 35; Psaltes 198; Schwyzer II 643; Mayser II 3, 57; e.g. POxy I 110.3 [ii AD] αὔριον ἥτις ἐστὶν ιε [the 15th], cf. 111.3 [iii AD], VI 927.2 [iii AD] and Mt 27: 62; ἥτις is a gloss on ᾗ in PBerlin 5014 in Erman-Krebs, Aus den Pap. d. kgl. Mus. 232 [= Ziebarth, Kleine Texte 65, no. 23.4]; cf. further Mlt 91f. [146]; Moule 123f.; Rob. 67, 726ff.). Cf. also Dieterich 199f.; exx. from Cretan inscrip. of ii BC in Kieckers, IF 27, 105.2.

(4) R 16: 7 οἵτινές εἰσιν ἐπίσημοι ἐν τοῖς ἀποστόλοις, οἳ καὶ πρὸ ἐμοῦ γέγοναν ἐν Χριστῷ, yet with v.l. ἀποστ. τοῖς πρὸ ἐμοῦ ἐν Χρ.; also in G 4: 24, 26 ἥτις = ἡ τοιαύτη; cf. 1 C 3: 17, Ph 1: 28, 1 T 3: 15.

294. Attraction of the relative. The simple relative ὅς, ἥ, ὅ (not ὅστις) is assimilated to the case of its antecedent even though it should take another case, usually the acc., in conformity with its use in the relative clause (attraction or assimilation). The NT, especially Lk, like the LXX (also the papyri, Radermacher, WSt 31, 7f.), conforms fully with classical usage in this peculiarity of the Greek language. (1) Exceptions are permissible, as in classical (Thuc. 2.70.5), if the relative clause is more clearly separated from its antecedent by additional nominal modifiers and the importance of its own content: H 8: 2 τῆς σκηνῆς τῆς ἀληθινῆς, ἣν ἔπηξεν ὁ κύριος, οὐκ ἄνθρωπος. (2) In addition to the acc. object, attraction can take place not only in the case of the so-called acc. of content (§§ 153f.), but also occasionally in the case of the dat.: A 1: 22 ἄχρι τῆς ἡμέρας ἧς ἀνελήμφθη (cf. Lk 1: 20 D, LXX Lev 23: 15, 25: 50, Bar 1: 19). Lk 5: 9 ἐπὶ τῇ ἄγρᾳ τῶν ἰχθύων ὧν (BDX, ἣν Θ, ᾗ SC ℜ pl.) συνέλαβον. (3) The repetition of a preposition before the relative can be dispensed with (classical): A 1: 21 ἐν παντὶ χρόνῳ (scil. ἐν) ᾧ.

(4) Also corresponding to classical usage is the relative, which includes the demonstrative (unlike German and English), assimilated to the case of the omitted demonstrative: Lk 9: 36 οὐδὲν ὧν = οὐδὲν τούτων ἅ. (5) The occasional incorporation of the antecedent in the relative clause, in which case the article going with the noun must be omitted and the noun itself then attracted to the case of the relative, stems from literary usage; the noun does not immediately follow the relative: Lk 19: 37 πασῶν ὧν εἶδον δυνάμεων, except in (ἐφ’) ὅσον χρόνον (§455(3)) and with ἡμέρα: Lk 1: 20 ἄχρι ἧς ἡμέρας γένηται ταῦτα = ἅ. τῆς ἡμ. (ἐν) ᾗ (cf. *supra* (2)); also in scattered instances otherwise. Mayser II 3, 98ff.—For attraction with the relative adverb s. §437.—Mayser II 3, 101ff.; Moule 130f.; Rob. 714–17, 719–21.

(1) Non-attraction elsewhere only as v.l.: Mk 13: 19 κτίσεως ἣν (ἧς AC²W al., ἣν ἔ. ὁ θ. om. D) ἔκτισεν ὁ θεός, Jn 2: 22 and 4: 50 τῷ λόγῳ ὃν (ᾧ AW al., DW al.; the relative clause is absent in other witnesses), 4: 5 χωρίου ὃ (οὗ C*DW al.), 7: 39 (οὗ SDGHLTW al.), Rev 1: 20 (ὧν 046); v.l. with separation by additional modifiers T 3: 5 οὐκ ἐξ ἔργων τῶν ἐν δικαιοσύνῃ ἃ (ὧν CᵇDᶜ al.). On A 8: 32 s. Blass *in loc.*

(2) Attraction of an acc. of content: E 4: 1 τῆς κλήσεως ἧς ἐκλήθητε, A 24: 21, 26: 16, Jd 15; of a dat.: R 4: 17 κατέναντι οὗ ἐπίστευσεν θεοῦ, i.e. κ. τοῦ θ. ᾧ ἐπ. (for the incorporation of the subst. s. (5)) and probably also 2 C 1: 4, E 1: 6. Of a nom.: IPol 3.2 πλέον σπουδαῖος γίνου οὗ (= τούτου ὃ) εἶ 'than what you already are'.

(3) A 13: 2 εἰς τὸ ἔργον (scil. εἰς) ὅ, 38 ἀπὸ πάντων (scil. ἀφ’) ὧν; Herm Sim 9.7.3 μετὰ πάντων (scil. μεθ’) ὧν; when there is a stricter separation of the relative clause the prep. is repeated: A 7: 4 εἰς τὴν γῆν ταύτην, εἰς ἥν, 20: 18 ἀπὸ πρώτης ἡμέρας, ἀφ’ ἧς, Jn 4: 53 (ἐν) ἐκείνῃ τῇ ὥρᾳ, ἐν ᾗ.

(4) Jn 7: 31 πλείονα ὧν = τούτων ἅ, 17: 9 περὶ ὧν = περὶ τούτων οὕς; there are in addition fixed phrases like ἀνθ’ ὧν = ἀντὶ τούτων ὅτι, ἐφ’ ᾧ = ἐπὶ τούτῳ ὅτι, διότι = διὰ τοῦτο ὅτι, further ἐν ᾧ, ἐν οἷς, ἀφ’ οὗ, μέχρις οὗ etc., ἐφ’ ὅσον Mt 25: 40, Barn 4.11, 17.1.

(5) Without the attraction of the relative, the same incorporation of the noun into the relative clause can, of course, take place with the noun in the same case as the relative (class. likewise, K.-G. II 416ff.): Lk 24: 1 φέρουσαι ἃ ἡτοίμασαν ἀρώματα, Jn 6: 14 ὃ ἐποίησεν σημεῖον; with the relative clause preceding: Mk 6: 16 ὃν ἐγὼ ἀπεκεφάλισα Ἰωάνην, οὗτος ἠγέρθη. On (ἐν) ᾧ μέτρῳ Mt 7: 2, Mk 4: 24, Lk 6: 38 s. W.-S. §24, 3b (similar to ὃν τρόπον, δι’ ἣν αἰτίαν). Cf. Lindhamer (*passim*) who derives the splitting of elements syntactically belonging closely together from rhetoric; however, cf. e.g. ᾗ εἶχεν ῥάβδῳ PGrenf I 38.12 (ii/i BC), PTebt I 44.20

(114 BC). Bo Reicke, The Disobedient Spirits 149–72 (NT 165–9). Also belonging here: Jn 17: 3 τὸν... θεὸν καὶ ὃν ἀπέστειλας Ἰησοῦν Χριστόν, Phm 10ff., Jn 16: 8, R 7: 19, H 7: 14, A 7: 20, 26: 6, H 10: 10, 1 P 1: 12, R 9: 23ff., G 2: 10. Lk 3: 19 περὶ πάντων ὧν ἐποίησεν πονηρῶν (τῶν π. ὧν ἐπ. S*W), cf. A 25: 18.—*Antecedent immediately following the relative*: ἡμέρα also A 1: 2, Mt 24: 38 etc.; but always ἐν ἡμέρᾳ ᾗ (Mt 24: 50, Lk 1: 25 pl., 12: 46; without art. like Hebr. sometimes before אֲשֶׁר, §295; but without ἐν Lk 17: 29, 30 ᾗ ἡμέρα [30 D ἐν τῇ ἡμ....ᾗ]; ἡμ. separated Herm Man 4.4.3 ἀφ’ ἧς μοι παρεδόθης ἡμέρας. Ὥρα Lk 12: 40 (the whole vs. however appears to be spurious); with loose connection to the preceding A 7: 20 ἐν ᾧ καιρῷ, 26: 7 περὶ ἧς ἐλπίδος, 1 P 1: 10 περὶ ἧς σωτηρίας, a kind of 'relative connection' that is particularly Latin, but also Greek (K.-G. II 434ff.; Mayser II 1, 77f.; Werner, ByzZ 31 [1931] 175; Tabachovitz, Eranos 30 [1932] 99); cf. Jannaris§ 1437b; Meuwese 109f.—*Resolution doubtful*: Lk 1: 4 περὶ ὧν κατηχήθης λόγων = περὶ τῶν λ. οὕς or τῶν λόγων περὶ ὧν (acc. to passages like A 18: 25, 21: 24, 25: 26 the former is more correct); R 6: 17 ὑπηκούσατε εἰς ὃν παρεδόθητε τύπον διδαχῆς = τῷ τύπῳ εἰς ὅν or εἰς τὸν τ. ὃν παρ. (Büchsel, TW II 173) (= ὃς παρεδόθη ἡμῖν; cf. ὃ ἐπιστεύθην ἐγώ 1 T 1: 11, T 1: 3 and §159(4)). A. Fridrichsen, Con. Neot. 7 (1942) 8 'You became obedient to the form of teaching, for the learning of which you were given over'. A 26: 16 s. §444(1). *With the omission of a preposition*: A 21: 16 (D is different) ἄγοντες παρ’ ᾧ ξενισθῶμεν Μνάσωνι = πρὸς Μνάσωνα ἵνα ξ. παρ’ αὐτῷ (§378). 2 C 10: 13 κατὰ τὸ μέτρον τοῦ κανόνος οὗ ἐμέρισεν ἡμῖν ὁ θεὸς μέτρου is difficult; οὗ is probably attracted from ὅ (referring to μέτρον) to κανόνος and then μέτρου repeated, lest οὗ be referred to κανόνος.—Intertwining of a relative clause with a clause dependent upon it: Jn 21: 25 ἅτινα (referring to the preceding ἄλλα πολλά) ἐὰν γράφηται καθ’ ἕν (ἅτινα cannot be construed with the following clause which governs the ἐάν-clause). K.-G. II 420f.; Mayser II 3, 107.9ff.

295. Inverse attraction. Even though the antecedent is not incorporated into the relative clause, but precedes, it is still occasionally assimilated to the case of the relative (classical also, K.-G. II 413, Blaydes on Aristoph., Lys. 408): 1 C 10: 16 τὸν ἄρτον ὃν κλῶμεν οὐχὶ κοινωνία... ἐστίν; Cf. §466(1).—Mayser II 3, 107f., 198.37ff.; Rob. 717f.

Lk 12: 48 παντὶ ᾧ ἐδόθη πολύ, πολὺ ζητηθήσεται παρ’ αὐτοῦ (the nom. is used in such sentences elsewhere with anacoluthon, s. §466(2, 4)). Mt 21: 42 λίθον ὃν etc. OT; Herm Sim 9.13.3; cf. LXX Gen 31: 16, Num 19: 22. Lk 1: 73 ὅρκον ὃν ὤμοσεν instead of τοῦ ὅρκου οὗ is peculiar (here the phrase does not precede the main clause, but follows as an appositive; the whole passage is strongly colored by Hebr.; s. § 259(3). There is a close connection of the antecedent with the relative also in Hebr. מָקוֹם אֲשֶׁר and the like, Gesenius-Kautzsch § 130, 3).

296. Constructio ad sensum with the relative (cf. § 282): G 4: 19 τεκνία μου οὕς; Jn 6: 9 παιδάριον ὅς (v.l. ὅ) ἔχει; Ph 2: 15 γενεᾶς σκολιᾶς ἐν οἷς. Also A·15: 36 κατὰ πᾶσαν πόλιν ἐν αἷς; 2 P 3: 1 ἤδη δευτέραν ἐπιστολὴν ἐν αἷς (i.e. ἐν ταῖς δυσὶν ἐπιστ.); Mk 3: 28 αἱ βλασφημίαι ὅσα, etc. Adverb of place instead of a relative in the loc.: 1 Clem 23.3 ἡ γραφὴ αὕτη ὅπου (= ἐν ᾗ) λέγει; s. Debrunner, Gnomon 4 (1928) 443.

297. The pleonastic personal pronoun incorporated into the relative clause is a phenomenon especially suggested by Semitic usage (Hebrew אֲשֶׁר...לוֹ; similarly דִּי, דְּ in Aramaic; s. also Schulthess 223 f.), but it is a slip not unknown in classical and later Greek: Mk 7: 25 γυνὴ ἧς εἶχεν τὸ θυγάτριον αὐτῆς (om. αὐτῆς SDW) πνεῦμα ἀκάθαρτον. Also corresponding to this redundancy: Rev 12: 6, 14 ὅπου...ἐκεῖ (אֲשֶׁר...שָׁם), Mk 13: 19 οἵα οὐ γέγονεν τοιαύτη.—Something entirely different and unobjectionable in classical usage is the linking of a clause logically parallel to a relative clause by means of καί...αὐτοῦ: 1 C 8: 6 ἐξ οὗ τὰ πάντα καὶ ἡμεῖς εἰς αὐτόν (a second example in the same vs.), Rev 17: 2, 2 P 2: 3 (K.-G. II 432f.); cf. § 469.—Ljungvik 27f., Rob. 722f.

Mk 1: 7 = Lk 3: 16, Rev 7: 2, 9, 3: 8, 13: 8, 20: 8, A 15: 17 OT, 1 Clem 21.9 οὗ ἡ πνοὴ αὐτοῦ; Rev 17: 9 ὅπου...ἐπ᾽ αὐτῶν, Mk 9: 3 οἷα...οὕτως, Rev 16: 18 οἷος...τηλικοῦτος; cf. LXX Gen 41: 19 βόες οἵας οὐκ εἶδον τοιαύτας...αἰσχροτέρας. Lk 12: 43 D ὅν... εὑρήσει αὐτόν. Black, Aramaic Approach 75: Mt 3: 12 = Lk 3: 17, Mt 10: 11 D, 18: 20 D, Mk 1: 7, 7: 25, Lk 8: 12 D, 12: 43 D, Jn 1: 27, 33, 9: 36, 13: 26, 18: 9. The personal pron. is closely connected with the relative in 1 P 2: 24 οὗ τῷ μώλωπι αὐτοῦ S*LP. G 3: 1 ἐν ὑμῖν after οἷς only DEFG al.; 2: 10 ὅ καὶ ἐσπούδασα αὐτὸ τοῦτο ποιῆσαι is justified since αὐτό in this sense ('very') cannot be joined to the relative and so must be supported by τοῦτο (thus Hdt. 4.44 ὅς...δεύτερος οὗτος, K.-G. II 433).—Often in the LXX (W.-S. § 22, 7; Thack. 46; οὗ...ἐκεῖ e.g. Gen 20: 13, 1 Km 9: 10; also ὅθεν...ἐκεῖθεν Gen 10: 14 etc.). Classical e.g. Hyperid., Eux. 3 ὧν... τούτων, cf. K.-G. II 433f. Pap. e.g. ἐξ ὧν δώσεις...ἐν ἐξ αὐτῶν POxy I 117.15 (ii/iii AD), ὅπερ φανερὸν τοῦτο ἐγένετο PAmh II 77.26 (139 AD) (on which cf. Wilcken, Chr. notes on no. 277.26); cf. Jannaris

§ 1439; Mlt. 94, 237 [149 ff.]; M.-H. 434 f.; Helb. p. iv; Psichari 182 f. (MGr ποῦ with demonstrative pron. following = rel. pron.). Parallels outside of Greek in Abel 134; Pernot, Études 152; W. Süss, Studien zur lat. Bibel I (1933) 52 ff.; M. Niedermann, Emerita 14 (1946) 400 (where the exx. are, in part, not parallels). —The pleonastic personal pron. after a ptcp., which is the equivalent of a relative clause, is related to this usage. The ptcp. (a) can be construed: gen. Herm Man 7.5 τῶν φοβουμένων..., ἐκείνων ἡ ζωή ἐστι, Vis 3.9.3; dat. 2.2.8 S τοῖς δὲ πρότερον ἀρνησαμένοις..., ἐγένετο ἵλεως αὐτοῖς, Rev 2: 7, 17 τῷ νικῶντι, δώσω αὐτῷ (§ 466(4)), PTebt I 26.11 (114 BC) ὄντι μοι ἐν Πτολεμαΐδι, προσέπεσεν ἡμῖν; (b) is without formal relationship to the sentence (in nom. or acc.), s. § 466(4). The pleonastic pronoun after a relative clause *incorporating its antecedent* can be construed not only as anacoluthon (§ 466(1)), but also as correct Greek, i.e. the antecedent is resumed in the original case: IEph 6.1 πάντα γὰρ ὅν πέμπει..., οὕτως δεῖ ἡμᾶς αὐτὸν δέχεσθαι; Lk 13: 4 ἐκεῖνοι...ἐφ᾽ οὕς ἔπεσεν...καὶ ἀπέκτεινεν αὐτούς, δοκεῖτε ὅτι αὐτοί....For the relative as connective s. § 458.

For τίς as a relative s. § 298(4).

(8) INTERROGATIVE PRONOUNS

298. Τίς (in direct and indirect questions). (1) Τίς is used also for πότερος 'which of two?' (§ 64). Stereotyped πότερον...ἤ (*utrum...an*) appears in an indirect double question Jn 7: 17 (likewise Barn 19.5, Did 4.4, Herm Sim 9.28.4), for which τί...ἤ also appears Mt 9: 5, but not in the sense of a particle. (2) Τίς and ποῖος: τίς is used substantivally for the most part; ποῖος, too, is used adjectivally with little distinction (as already in classical; MGr ποιός 'who?'), but never in questions about persons. With adjectives it is always τί: τί ἀγαθόν; τί κακόν; τί περισσόν; Both may be combined (tautology for emphasis?): εἰς τίνα ἤ ποῖον καιρόν 1 P 1: 11. Ποῖα is used independently Lk 24: 19 with reference to 18 τὰ γενόμενα. (3) Besides ποῖος, Hellenistic ποταπός appears (MGr also; from ποδαπός [thus D Cantabrig. always] 'from what country?', like ἀλλοδαπός, ἡμεδαπός; τ for δ probably by assimilation to the two π's), also of persons: ποταπός ἐστιν οὗτος ὅτι...; Mt 8: 27 = τίς ἄρα Mk 4: 41, Lk 8: 25. (4) The use of τίς *as a relative* (usually instead of ὅστις, § 293) is Hellenistic (and dialectal; cf. K.-G. II 517 f.; Buresch, RhM 46 [1891] 231; Dindorf on Soph., El. 316; Schwyzer II 644; Mayser II 1, 80): τίνα με (𝔓[45]? CD al., τί ἐμέ SAB) ὑπονοεῖτε εἶναι, οὐκ εἰμὶ ἐγώ A 13: 25. (5) Τίς as predicate: ἐγὼ τίς ἤμην; A 11: 17; cf. LXX 2 Km 8: 13 and §131. Double interrogative without conjunction (distributive): τίς τί ἄρη 'what each one...' Mk 15: 24.

(1) Mt 27: 21 (§164(1)), 21: 31 τίς ἐκ τῶν δύο;, Lk 7: 42 etc.

(2) Τίς adjectivally, e.g. τίς βασιλεύς Lk 14: 31, τί σημεῖον Jn 2: 18, τίς μετοχή etc. 2 C 6: 14ff. Ἐν ποίᾳ ἐξουσίᾳ, ἐν ποίῳ ὀνόματι (A 4: 7), ποίᾳ ὥρα, ποίαν ὥραν, ἐκ ποίας ἐπαρχίας (A 23: 34), διὰ ποίου νόμου (R 3: 27); in the proper sense 'of what kind?' 1 C 15: 35 ἐν ποίῳ σώματι, Ja 4: 14 ποία γὰρ ἡ (ἡ om. B) ζωὴ ὑμῶν ('how miserable is your life'; otherwise τίς not ποῖος with art.: Mk 6: 2 τίς ἡ σοφία ['where does it come from?'], A 10: 21 τίς ἡ αἰτία, 17: 19 etc.). In Herm Vis 3.1.3 the question runs εἰς ποῖον τόπον, the answer ὅπου θέλεις. Correctly distinguished 2 Clem 6.9 ποίᾳ πεποιθήσει–τίς παράκλητος. Ποῖος = τίς in pap. s. Mayser II 1, 78; ἐκ ποίας (= τίνος) πόλεως Dit., Syll.³ 344.59 (c. 303 BC). Τίς and ποῖος together also e.g. PTebt I 25.18 (117 BC), BGU II 619.8 (155 AD); also cf. ποῖον οἶκον...ἢ τίς τόπος; A 7: 49 OT. Ποῖος as v.l. to τίς Mk 4: 30 ἐν τίνι (ποίᾳ AC²DW al.) παραβολῇ;

(3) Lk 7: 39 τίς καὶ ποταπὴ ἡ γυνή, 2 P 3: 11; of things Mk 13: 1, Lk 1: 29, 1 Jn 3: 1 ('what kind of', also 'how great, mighty'; Herm Man 8.3 ποταπαί εἰσιν αἱ πονηρίαι = τίνες [like ποῖαι]). Ποταπός = qualis also Herm Vis 3.4.3; Sim 4.3, 6.3.4, 8.6.3, ApocP 5; LXX Sus 54 ὑπὸ τί δένδρον καὶ ποταπῷ ...τόπῳ; POxy III 413.155 (Mimus); γράψον μοι ποταπὸν (quodcumque) θέλεις XIV 1678.16 (iii AD). Cf. Schmidt 530; Schweizer 107f.; Jannaris §591; Trunk; Psaltes 73f.; Mlt. 95 [152]. The Atticists also permit ποταπός in the sense of qualis: Phryn. 56 Lob., Thom. Mag. 289, Schmid III 253, IV 371, 684. Ποδαπός = qualis since Soph., Frag. 415 Nauck² and Dem.

(4) On A 13: 25 s. Moule 124. Mk 14: 36 οὐ τί ἐγὼ θέλω, ἀλλὰ τί σύ (οὐχ ὅ...ἀλλ' ὅ D), Lk 17: 8 ἑτοίμασον τί δειπνήσω (11: 6 is different). Ja 3: 13 τίς σοφὸς καὶ ἐπιστήμων ἐν ὑμῖν, δειξάτω (or τίς... ὑμῖν; as interrogative sentence cf. 5: 13 κακοπαθεῖ τις; προσευχέσθω [§494]). Mk 14: 60 οὐκ ἀποκρίνῃ οὐδὲν ὅ τι (BW pc. Weiss; τί rell.) οὗτοί σου καταμαρτυροῦσιν; and the par. Mt 26: 62 οὐδὲν ἀποκρίνῃ τί are difficult to resolve. Blass regarded it as impossible to construe the whole as a single sentence because ἀποκρίνεσθαι would require πρός (Mt 27: 14); Chrys. quotes οὐκ ἀκούεις τί...; as in 27: 13. Taylor, The Gospel of St Mark (1953) 567 regards the double question as more in line with Mark's style (cf. 8: 17f.). However, Buttmann 218 proposes to supply 'hearing' (cf. Mt 27: 13) so as to avoid the awkward dependence of ὅ τι/τί on ἀποκρίνῃ; if so, ὅ τι/τί would introduce a relative clause, quod dicunt rather than quid dicant. Lohmeyer-Schmauch (Das Evangelium des Matthäus

[Meyer Kom.] 1958) 369 n. 1 and Katz follow Buttmann in construing the whole as one question: the High Priest does not inquire whether Jesus knows the charges brought against him but why he does not answer (Katz); πρός is not to be expected in subordinate clauses (Lohmeyer). For the intrusion of Matthean τί into Mk s. §300(2a). I Rom 5.3 τί μοι συμφέρει, ἐγὼ γινώσκω. Cf. e.g. Ptolem. Euerg. in Athen. 10.438 E τίνι ἡ τύχη δίδωσι, λαβέτω, BGU III 822.4 (iii AD) εὗρον γεωργόν (sic), τίς αὐτὰ ἑλκύσῃ, pap. (Aevum 3 [1929] 329f., cf. PhW 1931, 1334) ὅτι τί θέλ(ε)ις πράξω 'that I will do what you want', Dialekt-Inschr. 3542.2, 8 and 3547.3 (Cnidus, ii/i BC). LXX Lev 21: 17 s. §376. Certain usages have disappeared: first that like οὐκ ἔχω τί σοι πάθω ἢ τί χαρίσωμαι (graffito iii BC; Lamer, ZDPV 1931, 61), οὐδὲν ἔχω τί ποιήσω σοι BGU III 948.13 (iv/v AD), where the dubitative question approximates the relative clause (§368); cf. Mt 15: 32, Lk 9: 58 and τόπον δὲ αὐτοῖς παράσχες ποῦ μ(ε)ίνωσιν PGenève 75.13 (iii/iv AD). Secondly, that like LXX 1 Esdr 4: 54 ἔγραψε τὴν ἱερατικὴν στολὴν ἐν τίνι λατρεύουσιν ἐν αὐτῇ with prolepsis = ἔγρ. ἐν τίνι στολῇ. Thirdly, that like Ja 3: 13 (s. supra). On the close association of relative and interrogative clauses cf. further Mk 2: 25 οὐδέποτε ἀνέγνωτε τί ἐποίησεν Δαυίδ; = Lk 6: 3 οὐδὲ τοῦτο ἀνέγνωτε ὃ ἐπ. Δ.; Mt 10: 19 δοθήσεται τί λαλήσητε = Lk 12: 12 διδάξει ὑμᾶς ἃ δεῖ εἰπεῖν (Abel 143).

(5) Τίς τί διεπραγματεύσατο Lk 19: 15 AR al.; Herm Vis 3.8.6, Man 6.1.1; τίς τίνος ἐστὶν ἐργάτης Homil Clem 2.33.5; class. likewise (K.-G. II 521f.). UPZ I 42.45 (162 BC) τίνα πρὸς τίνας χρόνους προσωφείληται καὶ ὑπὸ τίνων.—On the whole Rob. 735–40.

299. Τί.
(1) Τί can be used predicatively with ταῦτα: τί (ἂν) εἴη ταῦτα Lk 15: 26 (τί θέλει τοῦτο εἶναι D); ἄνδρες, τί ταῦτα ποιεῖτε; 'what are you doing?' A 14: 15 (or, better, 'why?', s. infra (4)). (2) Τί is also used as predicate (also with personal subjects) in instances like τί ἄρα ὁ Πέτρος ἐγένετο; 'what has become of Peter?' A 12: 18 (§131); abbreviated οὗτος δὲ τί; 'what will become of him?' Jn 21: 21. (3) Other elliptical usages with τί: τί πρὸς ἡμᾶς; (scil. ἐστιν) 'what is that to us?' Mt 27: 4, τί πρὸς σέ; Jn 21: 22, cf. §127(3). In Paul τί γάρ; 'what does it matter?' or 'what difference does it make?' R 3: 3, Ph 1: 18, τί οὖν; R 6: 15 (scil. ἐροῦμεν; cf. 6: 1 and n. 4 on p. 2). (4) Adverbial τί either 'why?' (classical) Mt 6: 28, Lk 2: 48 etc. (for which also διὰ τί, ἵνα τί [scil. γένηται; according to A. Kuenzi, Festschr. Tièche (Bern, 1947) 61 ff., ἵνα τί is not elliptical but an interrogative word instead of a phrase in affected style] and τί ὅτι), or 'how!' Mt 7: 14 τί στενή (v.l. ὅτι, s. §492),

Lk 12: 49 τί θέλω (translation of Hebrew מָה, W.-S. §21, 4, Black, Aramaic Approach 87 ff.; LXX; but also cf. Basil the Great τί καλή [Trunk 36], MGr τί καλά 'how beautiful' Thumb[2] §256, further Jannaris §591).—Bauer s.v. τίς 3.

(1) A 17: 20 DEHL (v.l. τίνα), Herm Vis 4.3.1; it is essential in Jn 6: 9 ἀλλὰ ταῦτα τί ἐστιν ('what good are they?') εἰς τοσούτους; Cf. class. (Krüger §61, 8. 2). With A 14: 15 cf. Dem. 55.5 Τεισία, τί ταῦτα ποιεῖς; and with sg. Lk 16: 2 τί τοῦτο ἀκούω περὶ σοῦ; further τί οὗτοί σου καταμαρτυροῦσιν Mt 26: 62 = Mk 14: 60 is sometimes resolved into τί (pred.) ἐστιν ὃ οὗτοί σ. κ. (but cf. §298(4)). Cf. further Mk 11: 3 where however punctuation and reading are doubtful.

(2) Lk 1: 66 τί ἄρα τὸ παιδίον τοῦτο ἔσται; 1 Jn 3: 2 τί ἐσόμεθα; A 13: 25 (§298(4)); A 5: 24 τί ἂν γένοιτο τοῦτο 'what would happen, how it would turn out'. Cf. ποιεῖν τινά τι §157(1). Cf. Att. τί γένωμαι; 'what will become of me?' Xen., HG 2.3.17 τί ἔσοιτο ἡ πολιτεία; Jos., Vit. 296 οἱ εἴκοσι χρυσοῖ τί γεγόνασιν;

(3) Also with dat.: τί ἐμοὶ (ἡμῖν) καὶ σοί; (scil. ἐστιν, K.-G. I 417; also Hebr. like LXX 4 Km 3: 13 Mt 8: 29 etc. (§127(3)); with inf. 1 C 5: 12 (τί γάρ μοι τοὺς ἔξω κρίνειν;) as in Epict. 2.17.14, 3.22.66, Maximus Tyr. 2.10 (p. 29.7 Hobein). Att. also τί ταῦτ᾽ ἐμοί; (K.-G. I 417); also Jn 2: 4 acc. to Nonnus' paraphrase τί ἐμοὶ ἢ σοί, γύναι; 'of what concern is that to you or me?'

(4) A 4: 25 OT ἵνα τί (ἱνατί) ἐφρύαξαν ἔθνη; etc. (already in Att.; indirect question Did 1.5); τί ὅτι (LXX also) A 5: 4, 9, Lk 2: 49, v.l. Mk 2: 16 (§300(2)), more fully Jn 14: 22 τί γέγονεν ὅτι ἡμῖν μέλλεις ἐμφανίζειν σεαυτόν; (ὅτι = δι᾽ ὅ τι, as one can use τί for διὰ τί [but cf. §300(2)]; however D τί ἐστιν ὅτι, syᶜ syˢ Chr simply τί ὅτι). Cf. §456(2) and Ghedini, Vang. ap. 463. K. van Leeuwen-Boomkamp, Τί et διὰ τί dans les Évangiles (Rev. Ét. gr. 39 [1926] 327–31): the Gospels prefer τί; διὰ τί is used only in negative sentences (only thus in Jn) and in the sense of 'for what reason?'—ἵνα τί in LXX: Johannessohn II 241 n. 7.

300. Ὅστις. (1) Ὅστις, ὁποῖος, etc., which also serve as relatives, were frequently used in classical Greek in indirect questions besides the direct interrogative pronouns τίς, ποῖος, etc. This use of ὅστις is confined in the NT to the neuter ὅ τι in addition to ὁποῖος (besides ποῖος) and once (Lk 24: 20) ὅπως. (2) Ὅ τι is used more frequently, however, to introduce a *direct* question with the meaning 'why'. Blass found this incredible, except that he regarded ὅ τι as an abbreviation for τί ὅ τι (s. *infra*): (a) In the NT, variants for ὅ τι,

viz. τί ὅτι, διὰ τί, (διότι), mean 'why'; they were introduced because OTI was ambiguous in *scriptio continua*, as the spelling device ὅ τι (earlier ὅ, τι) was not feasible. In Mk, where most of the examples are found, variants are corrections introduced from parallel passages (thus bringing the Greek of Mk closer to classical standards). (b) In the LXX this ὅ τι always renders interrogative pronouns meaning 'why' such as מָה, לָמָה, מַדּוּעַ. This usage represents the same obliteration of the distinction between direct and indirect questions as the use of εἰ = הֲ in direct questions (§440(3)). It is characteristic of popular speech in general and of Semitic usage in particular, both of which tend to avoid indirect speech as much as complex periods.

(1) Ὅ τι introducing an indirect question: ὅ τι σε δεῖ ποιεῖν A 9: 6 (τι ℜ E pm.; Blass rejected ὅ τι on the basis of general usage). Rob. 731: a mark of the literary language in Lk. For Mk 14: 60 = Mt 26: 62 s. §298(4). Herm Sim 8.1.4 s. §267(2). Ὅστις in indirect questions is infrequent in the pap.; Mayser II 1, 79.—Ὁποῖος 1 C 3: 13, G 2: 6 (ὁποῖοί ποτε), 1 Th 1: 9, Ja 1: 24; οἵου πνεύματος Lk 9: 55 is a spurious reading (ποίου D minusc. 700 Chr; the best MSS [even 𝔓⁴⁵W] leave the saying out entirely; cf. also §304).

(2) Ὅ τι introducing a direct question is especially Markan: 2: 16 (διὰ τί SDW, τί Θ, τί ὅτι AC al.); 9: 11 (τί οὖν WΘ lat); 9: 28 (διὰ τί D 33 al.); to these should be added Mk 2: 7 (with BΘ, WH margin; cf. Black, Aramaic Approach² 47, 88) and possibly 8: 12 (with C Or; C. H. Turner, JTS 27 [1926] 58; Taylor, The Gospel of St Mark (1953) 61, 362, Black, Aramaic Approach² 89 and Katz take it as exclamatory מָה here). It is also possible in A 11: 3 'Why did you go...' (RSV; s. Beginnings III 102f., IV 124; Moule 159; Haenchen¹² 299 takes it as ὅτι *recitativum*). In Jn 8: 25 ὅ τι may be taken in the sense of מָה 'that I speak with you at all!' (τὴν ἀρχήν = ὅλως), or interrogatively 'why do I speak with you at all?' Blass interprets acc. to class. usage (not attested in the NT): '(You ask,) why (an indefinite relative is commonly used when a question is repeated by the respondent before his reply; scil. ἐρωτᾷς [Smyth §2670]) do I speak to you at all?' (but they have not asked this question). Or '(You reproach me,) that (ὅτι) I speak with you at all?' Cf. the direct question in Homil Clem 6.11.4 τί καὶ τὴν ἀρχὴν διαλέγομαι; 19.6.6 ἐπεὶ τί καὶ τὴν ἀρχὴν ζητεῖ; R. W. Funk, HTR 51 (1958) 95–100 and E. R. Smothers, HTR 51 (1958) 111–22 independently adopt the reading of 𝔓⁶⁶ (from the margin): ειπον υμιν την αρχην...'I told you at the beginning', which gives good grammar and sense; rejected by C. K. Barrett, ET 66 (1957) 176. Cf.

Bultmann (Das Evangelium des Johannes [Meyer Kom.] 1941) 267f. for full discussion. Barn 7.9 has the sequence τί...; καὶ ὅ τι...; In 8.5 ὅ τι δέ is parallel to διὰ τί δέ in 8.4 and 8.6, but in the latter SH read καὶ ὅ τι as do all MSS in 7.9 (gap in H), the διότι of the acephali being corrupt as everywhere in the LXX (Ziegler, Beiträge zur Jeremias-Septuaginta 15). All known examples in the LXX are in direct questions. Representing לָמָּה: 2 Km 7: 7 ὅ τι B, τί ὅτι L(ucian), τί O(rigen), with the par. 1 Chr 17: 6; Job 27: 12 (Katz, ThLZ 1957, 114 n. 4). מַדּוּעַ: 2 Km 12: 9 ὅ τι BO^{-A}, τί A, τί ὅτι pc.; Jer 22: 28; 33(26): 9. מָה: 4 Km 8: 14; Jer 2: 36; in 30 (49): 4 ὅ τι is a variant of τί, just as in 22: 23 Lucian adds ὅ τι and Origen τί (Katz in Ziegler, op. cit. 15). In Gen 18: 13 A alone has ὅ τι, the remainder τί ὅτι for לָמָּה זֶּה (= τί τοῦτο in 25: 22); this τί ὅτι is frequently used to render כִּי...מָה (§ 299(4)) and is not therefore to be read as τί ὅ τι. W.-S. § 24, 18a observes that to explain ὅτι as an abbreviation of τί ὅτι is odd because it leaves out what is essential; moreover, in τί ὅτι the second word is ὅτι, not ὅ τι. מַדּוּעַ in Judg 5: 28 twice introduces questions which are answered; A correctly has διὰ τί in both cases, while διότι B is corrupt, for it is not to be interpreted as δι' ὅ τι since this διότι is always a poor variant in the LXX. Interrogative ὅ τι was postulated for Jn 8: 25 by Lachmann in his edition of 1832 I, praef. xliii, then by Buttmann 218 (for the LXX also); it is accepted by Mlt. 94; Rob. 729f.; C. H. Turner, JTS 27 (1926) 58–62 (who finds in it a characteristic of Markan usage); Katz, ThLZ 1957, 114; 1958, 318. As the parallels in the LXX and early Christian literature indicate, ὅ τι with direct questions is a piece of 'biblical Greek'.—Controversial Mt 26: 50 ἑταῖρε ἐφ' ὅ (inferior v.l. ἐφ' ᾧ) πάρει: hardly a direct question 'For what?'; the easiest solution is to take it as a painful, ironic reminiscence of a toast like the one attested on a goblet from Syria: εὐφραίνου ἐφ' ὅ (ᾧ) πάρει 'Enjoy yourself! for that's why you are here' (on the aposiopesis cf. Iambl., VP 145 ὅσα βούλει, παρὰ τῶν θεῶν [scil. γένοιτό σοι], cf. ibid. βουλοίμην μᾶλλον, ὅσ' ἄν μοι παρὰ τῶν θεῶν γένηται). Biblio.: Debrunner, Jahresb. Altertumsw. 236 (1932) 220; 261 (1938) 189; Deissmann, LO⁴ 104 [LAE 125–31]; Schwartz, ByzZ 25 (1925) 154f.; Crönert, Gnomon 4 (1928) 90 n. 3 (who sees in it an expression of eastern colloquial speech without sufficient reason); Klostermann, ZNW 29 (1930) 311 (he compares Acta Carpi 44 ἐγὼ δὲ ἐφ' ὅ πάρειμι scil. ποιήσω); Sedgwick, ClR 46 (1932) 12 (he also compares ὅσον ζῆς φαίνου [error for εὐφραίνου?] on an epitaph [Musici scriptores ed. Jan p. 452]). Abbott § 2231e is against interrogative ἐφ' ὅ; but ἀνθ' ὅτου and the like appear in direct questions in the Church Fathers (Jannaris § 2038; Usener, Der heilige Tychon 50). ῟Ων ἕνεκα

Eus., Praep. Ev. 6.7 p. 257D (I 316.10 Mras) is probably not interrogative, but 'why did I come to speak about it—the reason is that...' (Abbott, loc. cit.). Also cf. Ljungvik 4; Deissmann, LO⁴ 101 n. 4 [LAE 126 n. 4]; Bauer s.v. ὅς 2a, 2b β, and 9b with references cited there; Zerwick, Graec. bibl. 51.

(9) INDEFINITE PRONOUNS

301. Τις, τι. As an enclitic τις τι, even when used adjectivally, can stand second in the sentence instead of following its noun (cf. § 473(1)): καί τις ἀνήρ A 3: 2, ἵνα τι μεταδῶ χάρισμα R 1: 11. At the beginning of a sentence we find only τινές, in contrasts: τινὲς (μὲν)...τινὲς δέ 1 T 5: 24, Ph 1: 15 (Dem. 9.56), though also where there is no contrasting clause: τινὲς δέ A 17: 18, 19: 31, Jn 7: 44 etc. (Dem. 18.44).—Special usages: (1) in the sense of quidam 'a certain one'; (2) = 'each' Herm Sim 8.2.5 καθώς τις ἄξιός ἐστιν κατοικεῖν. On τις to be supplied with a participle s. § 164(2); on ἄνθρωπος for τις (Mt 12: 10?, 13: 28, 45, 52 etc., Mk 1: 23 etc.) like Aramaic נַשׁ cf. Wellhausen, Einl.² 20, M.-H. 433 (with a pertinent reference to Epict. 3.23.15). Classical ἀνήρ (ἄνθρωπος) = τις only with a substantive (s. § 242).—A. Svensson, Artikel in der nachkl. Epik (1937): ὁ ἀνήρ (ὁ ἄνθρωπος) = τις is an emotionally conditioned use of the appellative supplied with an article; it is also ironic, contemptuous (excursus I, 136–40). Black, Aramaic Approach² 248–52.—Mayser II 2, 84ff.; Rob. 741–4.

(1) Ja 1: 18 ἀπαρχήν τινα τῶν αὐτοῦ κτισμάτων to soften the metaphorical expression ('so to say, a kind of'). With adj. in the literary language (class. often) φοβερά τις ἐκδοχή H 10: 27 (intensifying like quidam, K.-G. I 663), ὑπερηφανία πολλή τις Herm Man 6.2.5; but in A 8: 9 εἶναί τινα ἑαυτὸν μέγαν, μέγαν appears to be an interpolation and τινα to be used emphatically = 'somebody extraordinary', cf. 5: 36 A²DE al. and § 131; thus εἶναί τι 'something special' G 2: 6 (exactly like δοκούντων εἶναί τι Plato, Gorg. 472A), 6: 3. With numerals τινας δύο 'a certain two' A 23: 23; cf. Lk 7: 18, Herm Vis 1.4.3 (corresponding to εἷς τις Lk 22: 50, Jn 11: 49. Cf. § 247(2); in class. τινές with numerals means 'about', K.-G. I 664).

(2) 'Each' Herm Sim 8.4.2, A 15: 2 acc. to sy. On ἄνθρωπος = אִישׁ 'someone, every one' Thack. 45, Huber 70; however Homer and class. already show a similar usage (K.-G. I 272). Also ἀνήρ for τις in Lk, e.g. 9: 38; Johannessohn, KZ 67 (1940) 48. M. Vock, ἀνήρ und ἄνθρωπος (Diss. Freib. i. d. Schweiz, 1928).

302. 'Nobody, no one'. (1) Besides the customary οὐδείς μηδείς (or -θείς, §33), Hebraizing οὐ (μή)...πᾶς (the negative goes with the verb) = Hebrew כֹּל...לֹא: Mt 24: 22 = Mk 13: 20 οὐκ ἂν ἐσώθη πᾶσα σάρξ, cf. R 3: 20, 1 C 1: 29 (with μή), LXX Ps 142 (143): 2 etc. (Huber 70). The reverse order is synonymous but less harsh: πᾶς...οὐ (Hebrew also לֹא...כֹּל). (2) Εἷς...οὐ is stronger than οὐδείς: Mt 10: 29 ἕν...οὐ πεσεῖται ('unadulterated Semitism' Wellhausen, Einl.² 24, but also classical), likewise divided οὐδὲ εἷς (classical and Hellenistic).

(1) Lk 1: 37 οὐκ...πᾶν ῥῆμα (= 'nothing'), Rev (7: 1, 16, 9: 4,) 21: 27; A 10: 14 οὐδέποτε ἔφαγον πᾶν κοινόν; on the other hand οὐ πᾶς combined = 'not everyone' is class.: Mt 7: 21. Πᾶς...οὐ (μή) Rev 18: 22, 22: 3, E 4: 29, 5: 3, 5, 2 P 1: 20, 1 Jn 2: 21, 3: 15; this is excusable if a positive clause with ἀλλά follows as the main point: Jn 3: 16 ἵνα πᾶς ὁ πιστεύων μὴ ἀπόληται, ἀλλ᾽ ἔχῃ etc., 6: 39, or where it is clearly to be supplied: 12: 46. For 1 C 15: 51 πάντες οὐ as for οὐ πάντως, πάντως οὐ s. §433(2). Radermacher, WSt 31, 7; Debrunner, GGA 1926, 142f.; Wackernagel, Syntax II² 273f.; Benni (s. Indog. Jahrb. 14 [1930] 321); Ljungvik, Syntax 18ff.; Tabachovitz, Eranos 31 (1933) 118ff. Extra-biblical exx. are not numerous: PRyl II 113.12f. (133 AD) μὴ ἔχοντας πᾶν πρᾶγμα πρὸς ἐμέ 'without having anything against me', Apollonius Dysc., Synt. 1.14 (16.13 Uhlig) πᾶς λόγος ἄνευ τούτων οὐ συγκλείεται (where however οὐ can be more closely connected with συγκλ.: 'is not concluded').

(2) Εἷς...οὐ also Mt 5: 18, Lk 11: 46 etc.; οὐδὲ εἷς A 4: 32, Mt 27: 14 (πρὸς οὐδὲ ἕν, but Xen., Mem. 2.6.3 μηδὲ πρὸς ἕν), Mk 5: 37 D, Jn 1: 3 (S*D οὐδέν), 3: 27 B, 10: 41 𝔓⁴⁵WΘ, R 3: 10 OT (οὐκ...οὐδὲ εἷς, cf. §431(2); R 3: 12 OT οὐκ ἔστιν ἕως ἑνός), 1 C 6: 5 DᶜFGLP. Dem. 30.33 ἡ γυνὴ μίαν ἡμέραν οὐκ ἐχήρευσεν ('not a single day'), Xen., An. 5.6.12 ἀριθμῷ ἕνα μή ('not a single one in number'), Hdt. 3.6 ἕν...ἀριθμῷ...οὐκ; BGU IV 1141.18 (13 BC, where, Olsson 50 notwithstanding, on account of 23 ἡ σὴ ψυχή = σύ [cf. §283(4)] a Semitism must be considered). Schäfer on Dionys. Hal., De Comp. Verb. p. 247.

303. Generalizing relatives as indefinite pronouns. Ὁστισοῦν, ὅστις δήποτε, etc. appear neither as relatives nor (with the verb to be supplied) as indefinite pronouns ('anyone') apart from G 2: 6 ὁποῖοί ποτε ἦσαν 'what kind of people they were' (relative; ποτε is not to be taken separately here, but ποτε 'once' G 1: 13, 23 [twice, once ἤν ποτε], E 2: 2 ἐν αἷς ποτε, 2: 13 οἵ ποτε).

Att. for 'whoever it may be' ὅστις ἐστίν, ὅστις ἂν ᾖ (Eur., Ba. 247, Dem. 4.27); thus Paul in G 5: 10 ὅστις ἂν ᾖ. Οἵῳ δηποτοῦν, v.l. ᾧ δήποτε (relative) Jn 5: 4 comes in an interpolation. On Hell. δηποτοῦν s. Arnim 106. So also ὅπως ποτέ 'somehow' Homil Clem 2.22.7, ὅποι ποτέ [Plato], Ax. 365ᴄ (Meister 31f.), Musonius p. 45.4 Hense. Further on indefinite pronouns from relatives s. Mayser I² 2, 70; II 2, 86f.; Raderm.² 77; Wackernagel, Syntax II² 116, 317.—In A 19: 26 D adds τις τοτε after Παῦλος which is to be corrected to τίς ποτε (with indef. τις) 'nescio quis'; cf. Homil Clem 5.27 τίς ποτε Ἰουδαῖος 'some Jew or other', τί ποτε 11.28, 17.8, POxy XIV 1680.15 (iii/iv AD), BGU III 948.11 (iv/v AD), τινί ποτε POxy IV 745.7 (c. 1 AD), τινά ποτ᾽ ἀκούω Πολέμωνα 'a certain P.' Epict. 3.1.14, πού ποτε 'somewhere, somehow' 2.1.31, 3.10.5, 16.10, 4.11.16, πώς ποτε 'somehow' 4.13.1 (further Melcher 73f. and the indices to the edition of Schweighäuser [III 458] and Schenkl); s. also Wolf I 50, Trunk 37. MGr τίποτε 'something' (and 'nothing'); similarly τινοσοῦν for ἡστινοσοῦν Homil Clem 10.20 acc. to PO. Homil Clem 12.25.3 ἡ πρὸς οἰονδήποτε στοργή 'amor erga qualemcumque', 10.5. 4 ᾧδήτινι τρόπῳ 'in any way', 11.1 εἰς ὑπόνοιαν ὡνδήποτε, 16.1.2 ὁπώσποτε, 17.15.7 ᾧδήποτε τρόπῳ. Ὁσδήποτε (scil. ἐστιν etc.), ὅπως ποτέ etc., originally relative, but having become indefinite, became synonymous with those combinations τίς ποτε etc. which were indefinite from the beginning; thus the first position in the sentence, possible only for the first type, was carried over to τίς ποτε etc. (e.g. Epict. 3.1.14, s. supra).—D. F. Georgacas, Class. Phil. 51 (1956) 249–51 οἷος for ὅς is Medieval and MGr; also οἴων = οἵων as early as a Locrian inscrip.: Buck, Greek Dialects² no. 59.

(10) DERIVATIVE CORRELATIVES

304. In exclamations (direct or indirect) classical Greek employed οἷος, ὅσος, ἡλίκος etc. to point to some definite thing at hand (ὁποῖος etc. is therefore excluded). In the NT, however, the interrogatives are in part employed as in indirect questions: Mk 15: 4 ἴδε πόσα etc. (cf. τί §299(4)).— Τοιούτους ὁποῖος in correlation A 26: 29, cf. qualiscumque; τοσούτῳ...ὅσῳ H 1: 4.—Ὁ τοιοῦτος (§274) is weakened here and there to a less definite designation for οὗτος: 1 C 5: 5, 2 C 2: 6, 7, 12: 2, 3, 5.

Interrogatives in exclamations: Mt 27: 13 (B* ὅσα), A 21: 20, 2 C 7: 11 (direct), G 6: 11 (ἴδετε πηλίκοις, 𝔓⁴⁶B ἡλίκοις), H 7: 4; cf. Ljungvik 28f. Οἷος is used correctly in 1 Th 1: 5, 2 T 3: 11 (Lk 9: 55 D correctly ποίου, §300(1)); ἡλίκος C 2: 1; cf. πῶς §436.—Since ὅσοι = πάντες οἵ, οὗτοι at times has to follow, as e.g. R 8: 14; τὸν αὐτόν...οἷος Ph 1: 30 is peculiar.—R 9: 6 οὐχ οἷον δὲ ὅτι ἐκπέπτωκεν is a mixture of οὐχ οἷον (Hell. = οὐ δήπου Phryn. 372, Buttmann 319) and οὐχ ὅτι (§ 480(5)).—Ὅσον doubled in exclamations 'how much! how little!' has gone over to the meaning 'very little': Lk 5: 3 D ἐπαναγαγεῖν ὅσον ὅσον (rell. ὀλίγον); also strengthened by the synonym μικρόν H 10: 37 ἔτι μικρὸν ὅσον ὅσον 'only for a very little while' (from LXX Is 26: 20; likewise 1 Clem 50.4). Passages like A 9: 16 ὑποδείξω αὐτῷ ὅσα δεῖ αὐτὸν παθεῖν can also be understood as exclamations, although the interpretation = πάντα ἅ seems more obvious (likewise 14: 27 etc.). O. Lagercrantz, Eranos 18 (1918) 26–113 attempts to demonstrate that the interrog. in exclamations is pre-Hell.—Exclamatory ὅσον Theoc. 25.73, Pallad., Hist. Laus. 17.8 (τὸ ὅσον), Hesychius (ὅσον· ὀλίγον), doubled Philetas 7 D, Paulus Silentiarius, Anth. Pal. v 254 (255).5, Arrian, Ind. 29, Hesychius (= ὀλίγον ὀλίγον); combined with words meaning 'small, little', therefore = 'very' Aristoph., Pl. 750 ὄχλος ὑπερφυὴς ὅσος, Hdt. 4.194 ἄφθονοι ὅσοι, Xen., Cyr. 2.4.22 ὅσον μέτριον 'a little bit', Theoc. 1.45 τυτθὸν ὅσον, Lucian, Prom. 12 ὀλίγον ὅσον, and Peregr. 25 οὐδ' ὅσον ὀλίγον (on the equivalency of pron. and adj. of quantity cf. Eur., Supp. 899 πολλοὺς δ' ἐραστὰς κἀπὸ θηλειῶν ὅσας ἔχων). Combined with a substantive in an adverbial phrase in the sense of 'only just as much as' Philemo, Frag. 98.3 (II 509 Kock) ὅσον ὀσμήν, fragment of comedy POxy VI 855.8 (Menander?) ὅσον γε φορτίον, also with double ὅσον Aristoph., Vespae 213, Leonidas, Anth. Pal. VII 472.3. Cf. K.-G. II 415; Wackernagel, Glotta 4 (1913) 244f. (= Kl. Schr. 1201f.); Lagercrantz, *op. cit.* 53–7; Crönert, Gnomon 4 (1928) 85.

(11) PRONOMINAL ADJECTIVES

305. 'Each'. Ἕκαστος, intensified εἷς ἕκαστος. From the distributive use of κατά (ἀνά, § 248(1)), καθ' (ἀνά) εἷς developed, since καθ' ἕνα ἕκαστον became fixed as καθένα ἕκ. and a corresponding nom. was created: thus MGr καθείς καθένας 'each'; cf. Jannaris § 664; W.-S. p. 247 n.; Psaltes 192. Yet not many examples of this vulgarism are found in the NT.

Rev 21: 21 ἀνὰ εἷς ἕκαστος, R 12: 5 τὸ (v.l. ὁ) δὲ καθ' εἷς (τὸ καθ' ἕν in pap. 'detailed proof, list' Mayser I² 3, 205.38ff.) 'individually, with relation to each individual' (cf. ὁ καθεὶς τῶν φίλων LXX 3 Macc 5: 34), Herm Sim 9.3.5 and 6.3 κατὰ (καθ') ἕνα λίθον as object = ἕκαστον λ., Homil Clem 4.15.2 τῶν καθ' ἕνα ἕκαστον 'of the particulars' (cf. Hauser 102), 1.19. 6 τὸ καθ' ἓν ἕκαστον τῶν ὑπ' αὐτοῦ λεγομένων ἀνακρίνειν, 1.20.3 τὰς καθ' ἕκαστον ἐνιαυτὸν ὁμιλίας τε καὶ πράξεις. Moreover εἷς καθ' εἷς [Jn] 8: 9, Mk 14: 19 (v.l. κατά; C εἷς ἕκαστος as in Mt 26: 22).—On ἕκαστος without art. and its distinction from πᾶς s. § 275; on τις 'each' § 301(2). Ἕκαστος can also be used with a

plur. subj. as in class. (Winer § 58, 4 [Winer-M.³ 648]; K.-G. I 286ff.): Jn 16: 32 ἵνα σκορπισθῆτε ἕκαστος... κἀμὲ μόνον ἀφῆτε etc.; likewise εἷς 'each': 1 C 4: 6 ἵνα μὴ εἷς ὑπὲρ τοῦ ἑνὸς φυσιοῦσθε. Cf. § 134(1); Mayser II 2, 115; II 3, 37.37ff. Καθ' ἕν with the original meaning 'in detail' in the addition to Jn (21: 25). LXX 4 Macc 8: 5 καθενὸς ἑκάστου, 15: 12 καθένα παῖδα καὶ ὁμοῦ πάντας, 14 καθένα...ὁρῶσα; Johannessohn II 254. As early as Hdt. 1.9 τῶν ἱματίων κατὰ ἓν ἕκαστον...θήσει (κ. ἓν ἕκ. is the object). Εἷς καθ' εἷς is a conflation of εἷς (ἕκαστος) and καθ' εἷς due to the association with examples like μίαν ἐκ μιᾶς 'one (day) after the other' POxy I 86.15 (338 AD) (cf. § 208(2)); cf. εἷς ἕκαστος LXX Lev 25: 10, where the reading of A alone εἰς κατ εκαστος cannot be genuine (Katz, renouncing ThLZ 1936, 284), ἓν καθ' ἕν PLeid II x 1.22. Deissmann, BS 135–7 [BS 138–40]; Rob. 745f., 675.

306. Ἕτερος and ἄλλος. (1) Ἕτερος is the sole surviving dual pronominal adjective besides ἀμφότεροι (§ 64). It, too, has disappeared in MGr and is no longer attested in all NT authors. (2) Its use is also no longer always entirely correct, e.g. Mt 16: 14 οἱ μὲν...ἄλλοι δὲ...ἕτεροι δέ (for which ἄλλος is used twice in Mk 8: 28, Lk 9: 19, ἕτεροι could have been used correctly in the *second* place = a second division). Cf. Homil Clem 9.3; Lk 4: 43 ταῖς ἑτέραις πόλεσιν (ὁ ἕτερος is limited in Attic to definite bipartition); Lk 19: 20 ὁ ἕτερος, i.e. the third (but A al. without ὁ). Homil Clem 19.1.1 τῆς ἄλλης ἡμέρας 'on the following day'. (3) The encroachment of ἄλλος upon the province of ἕτερος is most obvious in that ὁ ἄλλος is used of the second of two parts: Mt 5: 39 (Lk 6: 29) στρέψον αὐτῷ καὶ τὴν ἄλλην (σιαγόνα). (4) Ἄλλος and ἕτερος are sometimes combined, it seems, only for the sake of variety: 2 C 11: 4 ἄλλον Ἰησοῦν...πνεῦμα ἕτερον...εὐαγγέλιον ἕτερον, 1 C 12: 9f. (s. under (2)). (5) Ἕτεροι is used pleonastically (by our standards) like classical ἄλλος and ἕτερος (K.-G. I 275 n. 1, Gild. 275f.), Lk 23: 32 καὶ ἕτεροι δύο κακοῦργοι = 'and, besides, two malefactors' (Smyth § 1272 with a substantive regarded as appositive). On the other hand, ἄλλος is sometimes omitted where we would add 'other' (§ 480(1)): A 5: 29 Πέτρος καὶ οἱ ἀπόστολοι (D is different) 'Peter and the other apostles'. But cf. Jn 14: 16 ἄλλον παράκλητον 'another, namely a counselor' (Michaelis, Con. Neot. 11 [1947] 153). —Juxtaposed: ἄλλοι ἄλλο (τι) 'some this—the others that' (classical) A 19: 32, 21: 34.—On the position of ἄλλος and ἕτερος Cuendet 112f.— Mayser II 2, 87ff.; Rob. 746–50.

(1) Never in Mk (spurious 16: 12), Rev, Peter, almost never Jn (19: 37), principally in Lk and to a certain extent in Mt and Paul.

(2) Lk 8: 6 ff. καὶ ἕτερον three times (D ἄλλο like Mt 13: 5 ff., Mk 4: 5 ff.); of the second and third parts Lk 9: 59, 61; third and seventh in a list of eight 1 C 12: 8 ff. (ᾧ μὲν...ἄλλῳ δὲ...ἑτέρῳ...ἄλλῳ δὲ...ἄλλῳ δὲ...ἄλλῳ [δὲ]...ἄλλῳ δὲ...ἑτέρῳ...ἄλλῳ δέ); second H 11: 36; Homil Clem 19.9 (πολλοὺς... ἄλλους δὲ...ἑτέρους δὲ...ἄλλους δέ). At the conclusion of an enumeration καὶ ἑτέρους πολλούς Mt 15: 30 (cf. Lk 3: 18, R 8: 39, 13: 9, 1 T 1: 10), which is also attested in Att. (Dem. 18.208, 219, 19.297): 'others, different from those named' (the latter taken collectively); Ph 2: 4 τὰ τῶν (add. D*FG) ἑτέρων also correctly in contrast to τὰ ἑαυτῶν. Cf. 1 C 10: 24 etc. On ὁ εἷς...ὁ ἄλλος (ἕτερος) s. § 247(3). Mt 10: 23 ἐν τῇ πόλει ταύτῃ...εἰς τὴν ἑτέραν (SBW CDE al., where the art. is still more surprising; it probably means 'the next') is peculiar; the fuller version of D al. continues: κἂν ἐν τῇ ἑτέρᾳ (ἄλλῃ) διώκωσιν ὑμᾶς, φεύγετε εἰς τὴν ἄλλην ('again to the next'; cf. τῆς ἄλλης ἡμέρας 'on the following day' Homil Clem 15.4, 19.1, cf. 20.21, 22); abbreviated (or original?) ὅταν δὲ διώκωσιν ὑμᾶς, φεύγετε ἐκ πόλεως εἰς πόλιν Tertullian et al.

(3) Mt 12: 13, Jn 18: 16, 19: 32, 20: 3f. etc. Aeschyl., Supp. 230f. κἀκεῖ δικάζει...Ζεὺς ἄλλος can be compared with ἄλλος ἐστὶν ὁ μαρτυρῶν Jn 5: 32 (in contrast to ἐγώ), moreover Mt 25: 16, 17, 20, 22

ἄλλα πέντε (δύο) τάλαντα is attested in classical authors: Plato, Lg. 5.745 A ἄλλο τοσοῦτον μέρος. Ὁ ἄλλος 'the other' appears in isolated cases in Attic writers: Eur., IT 962f. θάτερον...τὸ δ' ἄλλο, Plato, Lg. 1.629 D τὸ μὲν...τὸ δ' ἄλλο; and pap. (Mayser II 1, 57; also τὸ ἄλλο ἥμισυ PRainer 22.15 [ii AD]).

(4) G 1: 6f. εἰς ἕτερον εὐαγγέλιον ὃ οὐκ ἔστιν ἄλλο, εἰ μή τινές εἰσιν οἱ etc. likewise appears to be used without distinction (cf. Mlt. 79f., 80 n. 1, 246 [126 n.]; and Rob. 747 who insists on a difference here and in 2 C 11: 4), but ἄλλο is used pleonastically to a certain extent in order to introduce εἰ μή...(cf. nihil aliud nisi) 'not that there is any other, except that...'. Thus Epict. 1.25.4 τίς κωλύσει χρῆσθαι αὐτοῖς ἄλλος εἰ μὴ σύ, 1.16.20 τί γὰρ ἄλλο...εἰ μή. Soph., El. 739 τότ' ἄλλος, ἄλλοθ' ἅτερος, UPZ I 42.32, 33 (162 BC) καὶ ἄλλοι...καὶ ἕτεροι. Homil Clem 18.3 ὅτι δὲ τὸ δίκαιον ἄλλο ἐστὶν καὶ τὸ ἀγαθὸν ἕτερον.

(5) A 2: 14 (§ 480(1)); Mk 6: 15 προφήτης ὡς εἷς τῶν προφητῶν (Semitizing [cf. LXX Judg 16: 7] = 'one prophet like another' acc. to Wellhausen, Einl.² 23; Lk 9: 8 προφήτης τις τῶν ἀρχαίων 'one of the other old prophets' is better); class. Ἕκτορι καὶ Τρώεσσι Hom., Il. 17.291. Hermas has ἕτερος nearly always for 'other' (cf. Sim 8.1.7–18), also with art. as e.g. Vis 3.7.1, 3 τοὺς δὲ ἑτέρους (λίθους); yet ἄλλος καὶ ἄλλος 'each different' Sim 9.1.4, 10; cf. Xen., Cyr. 4.1.15 ἄλλην καὶ ἄλλην (ἡδονήν) 'always new pleasures'. Tabachovitz, Museum Helveticum 3 (1946) 161 f., 162 f.

10. SYNTAX OF THE VERB

(1) VOICE

307. Introduction. The system of voices in general remained the same in the Hellenistic period (including the NT) as in the classical period of the language. Modifications have arisen mainly because of the tendency to merge the middle and passive into a single voice. In MGr only an active and a passive-deponent are left. This trend explains, for example, the following phenomena: the future and aorist middle, which alone were formally distinguished from the passive in classical Greek, are declining in that future middle forms belonging to present actives are often replaced by the active (§ 77) and deponents in the future and aorist prefer passive forms (§§ 78 and 79). The active is also used in instances where classical Greek was fond of expressing a more or less loose participation of the subject in the action of the verb by means of the middle (§ 310; cf. Mlt. 159f. [249] for the mixture of active and middle in the papyri). Still to be mentioned is the occasional transition of intransive actives to the category of deponent (§ 148(3)); verbs of emotion are involved for the most part as e.g. θαυμάζεσθαι etc. (§ 78), further ἀγαλλιᾶσθαι, ἀπορεῖσθαι (§ 101) and χαιρόμενος A 3: 8 D (cf. Mlt. 161 [253.1]; Byzantine [Psaltes 247] and MGr χαίρομαι).

On the whole: Schwyzer II 217–42; Wackernagel, Syntax I 119–49. Transition to the category of deponent: A. Prévot, L'aoriste grec en -θην (Paris, 1935) 130ff. (Hom.), 153ff. (class.). Ἀκαιρεῖσθαι Ph 4: 10, Herm Sim 9.10.5; there is fluctuation between act. and depon. in the case of προνοεῖν: -εῖ or -εῖται 1 T 5: 8, -οῦμεν 2 C 8: 21 (-ούμενοι C), -ούμενοι R 12: 17 (from LXX Pr 3: 4 προνοοῦ), -οῦντες Pol Ph 5.3, 6.1, -ήσατε Did 12.4—Rob. 797ff.

(A) Active

308. Intransitive (reflexive) use of transitive active verbs of motion. This occurs most frequently with ἄγειν and βάλλειν together with their compounds, and with compounds of στρέφειν; also less often with αἴρειν, (ἀνα-) κάμπτειν, κλίνειν, (ἀνα-)λύειν, ῥίπτειν and in imitation of verbs of motion also with ἔχειν 'to be, be disposed'. Papyri: Mayser II 1, 82–7.

"Αγειν apart from stereotyped ἄγε (class.) also in ἄγωμεν 'let us go' Mt 26: 46 etc. More frequently in the compound ὑπάγειν, the word in the vernacular for 'to go' (§101), for which the rudiments are found already in class.: ὑπάγεθ' ὑμεῖς τῆς ὁδοῦ Aristoph., Ra. 174, ὑπάγοιμι τἄρ' ἄν Aves 1017, but still with a more clearly defined meaning; Bonaccorsi 521f. Παράγειν 'to pass by' Mt 20: 30, Mk 15: 21 etc. (Hell.); figuratively 'to pass away' 1 C 7: 31, for which 1 J 2: 8, 17 has παράγεται (the interpretation discedere arises from Mt 9: 27 παράγοντι ἐκεῖθεν, where however ἐκ. is to be deleted with sy^s; likewise in 9: 9 with S*L Chr). Περιάγειν 'to go about' Mt 4: 23, A 13: 11 etc., with acc. of the district traversed (§150; not so in class.: περιαγαγὼν τὴν ἐσχατιάν Dem. 42.5 means 'to lead about', and in Cebes, Tab. 6.3 περιάγονται is the reading now adopted). Ἐπανάγειν 'to return' Mt 21: 18 like Xen. et al., 'to put out (to sea)' Lk 5: 3, 4. Προάγειν also has in addition to the meaning 'to bring before' that of 'to go before someone (τινα)' (§150) Mt 2: 9 and often, and 'to forge ahead' (Hell.) 2 Jn 9 (v.l. παραβαίνων); ὁ προάγων 'the earlier, preceding' (Hell.) 1 T 1: 18, H 7: 18; the meaning 'to precede' is found in Plato, Phdr. 227 D and Hell.; Phaedo 90 B σοῦ προάγοντος ἐγὼ ἐφεσπόμην is somewhat different; class. otherwise προηγεῖσθαί τινι which is used in the NT in this sense as little as ἡγ. is. Προσάγειν 'to come near' A 27: 27 (Xen. and Hell.). (Συνάγειν intr. 'to advance' only in the spurious addition to Mt 20: 28.) On the other hand always ἀνάγεσθαι ἀνήχθην. Judg 19: 6 only the early A-text ἀρξάμενος αὐλίσθητι = the late B recension ἄγε δὴ αὐλ. Katz, ThLZ 1952, 157. Βάλλειν 'to rush' A 27: 14 (which is otherwise hardly paralleled, but cf. Raderm.² 23 and infra ῥίπτειν). Ἐπιβάλλειν 'to beat upon' (as already in class.) Mk 4: 37; τὸ ἐπιβάλλον μέρος 'the part that falls to someone' Lk 15: 12 (from Dem. onward; a fixed formula in the pap.; s. Deissmann, NBS 57 [BS 230]; Preisigke s.v. 12, 13; Mayser II 1, 84); ἡ ἐπιβάλλουσα μερίς PGrenf I 33.33 (103 BC); Hdt. has a parallel usage. Ἐπιβαλὼν (ἔκλαιεν) Mk 14: 72 is correctly glossed by Theophylactus and Euthymius as ἀρξάμενος (ἤρξατο κλαίειν DΘ minusc. 565 and many versions), therefore 'he began to weep'. 'To set about, to begin': ἐπέβαλε τερετίζειν 'he began to hum' Diog. Cyn. in Diog. L. 6.27, pap. (Mayser II 1, 84), Epict. 1.4.14 (cod. S -εις; Epict. elsewhere ἐπιβάλλεσθαι with acc. as in Herm Man 10.2.2, Sim 6.3.5); cf. Aristeas 78 ἐπιβαλούσης (intr.) τῆς διανοίας ἐπὶ..., LXX 1 Esdr 9: 20 ἐπέβαλον τὰς χεῖρας ἐκβαλεῖν τὰς γυναῖκας αὐτῶν; ἐπιβάλλων τούτῳ

(scil. τὸν νοῦν or something similar) M. Ant. 10.30 'to reflect on this'. Later βάλλειν 'to begin' s. Ljungvik 77, Leont. Neap. (MPG 93, 1708). For the inversion of the construction cf. A 11: 4 ἀρξάμενος ἐξετίθετο as against the customary ἤρξατο with inf.; Lucian, Ver. Hist. 2.1 ἀρξάμενοι διεκόπτομεν, Xen. Eph. 5.7 ἐκεῖθεν ἀρξαμένη κατέχομαι and §435; PTebt I 50.12 (112/1 BC) ἐπιβαλὼν συνέχωσεν 'he went to work and dammed up' (Mlt. 131f. [213]).—Στρέφειν (Mayser II 1, 87) simple form A 7: 42? Always ὑποστρέφειν, never pass. (although it is found in class. in addition to the active). Ἐπιστρέφειν 'to turn around, be converted' (for which 1 P 2: 25 has -εστράφητε, however C -εστρέψατε) as often especially in Polyb.; pass. 'to turn, look around' (Att.). Ἐπιστρέψωσιν Jn 12: 40 WKLMX (al. (ἐπι-)στραφῶσιν) from the LXX. Ἀναστρέφειν 'return', also often trans. (intrans. as a military expression already in Att.), pass. 'to behave, conduct oneself' (Att. 'to stay'). Ἀποστρέφειν A 3: 26 intr. (usually pass. in Att.), more often trans., pass. τινά 'to turn away from' (Att.).—Αἴρειν as terminus technicus 'to weigh anchor' ancoras tollere A 27: 13. Μεταίρειν 'to go away' Mt 13: 53, 19: 1 (not class.; but ἀπαίρειν and καταίρειν are also intr. in class.).—Ἀνακάμπτειν 'to bend back, return' as in class. (Ionic, Mayser I¹ 20). —Κλίνειν 'to decline' (of the day) Lk 9: 12, 24: 29 (Hell., MGr κλίν' ἡμέρα [Hatzid. 202]). Ἐκκλίνειν 'to turn away, aside' R 16: 17 etc. (class.).—Προκόπτειν 'to advance, progress' as in Hell., R 13: 12 'to be advanced' (of time).—Ἀναλύειν 'to return' Lk 12: 36, 'to depart' (from life, i.e. die) Ph 1: 23 (Hell., Nägeli 34, Bonhöffer 112, Bauer s.v., Büchsel, TW IV 338).—Ῥίπτειν: ἀπο(ρ)ρίπτειν 'to throw oneself down' A 27: 43 (ῥίπτειν thus in the poets and later authors).—Ἔχειν 'to be, be disposed' as in class., frequently with adverb of manner; also ὑπερέχειν 'to excel' (also with τινά Ph 4: 7), ἀπέχειν 'to be distant' (with acc. of distance); for impersonal ἀπέχει s. §129. Ἐνέχειν τινί 'to have a grudge against someone, hate someone, persecute' Mk 6: 19, Lk 11: 53. LXX Gen 49: 23 = Hebr. שׂטם which in Gen 27: 41 is rendered by ἐγκοτεῖν; it has perhaps arisen from ἐνέχειν χόλον τινί (Hdt.).—Ἐπέχειν 'to pay attention to something' Lk 14: 7 etc. (class. similarly), also 'to stop, stay' A 19: 22 (also class.). Προσέχειν τινί 'to pay attention to, give heed to' (as in the pap. [Mayser II 1, 85] never with the original τὸν νοῦν supplied which is often found in Att.); also with and without ἑαυτῷ = cavere Mt 6: 1, Lk 17: 3 etc. Περιέχειν 'to contain' (of a reference, cf. περιοχή) is primarily trans.: περιέχουσαν τάδε A 15: 23 D, π. (ἔχουσαν SB) τὸν τύπον τοῦτον 23: 25, cf. Pol Ph 13.2; intr. 1 P 2: 6 περιέχει ('it is written') ἐν (τῇ) γραφῇ (ἡ γραφή C, in which case the direct quotation would be the object). Περιέχειν τι often in Hell., with inf. as obj. Usener, Legenden der Pelagia 9.17 οἱ κανόνες περιέχουσιν, cf. Kos. and Dam., Arab.

Mart. 2.1.6 Deubner; intr. 'to run, read' with ὡς, οὕτως and the like, LXX, inscrip., pap., καθὼς ἐν αὐτῇ (in the letter) περιέχει Jos., Ant. 11.104, τὰ περιέχοντα 'the content' Proclus, Chrest. (Metrici script. p. 234. 1). Cf. Preisigke, Bauer, Johannessohn I 69. Homil Clem 19.18.4 ὅσα τοιαῦτα τυγχάνει, τοῦτον περιέχει τὸν τρόπον. Further on intr. περιέχει E. Fraenkel, Gnomon 1951, 374: MGr ἔτσι γράφει 'thus it is written', Cretan, Gortyn XI 19 f. ἅι τάδε τὰ γράμματ' ἔγραπσε = IX 15; VI 15 ἅι τάδε τὰ γράμματα ἔγρατται; cf. H. Jacobsthal, IF 21 Beiheft 117 f.—Intrans. φαίνω s. Bauer s.v. (and ἐπιφαίνω §101).—For ἐγείρειν and καθίζειν s. §101.—'To turn aside, withdraw' Jn 5: 13 ἐκνεύειν (νεύειν S*D*), UGosp 1.31 ἀπονεύειν; both class. and Hell.—Rob. 799-801.

309. Other variations between transitive and intransitive use of the active.

(1) Factitives (causatives) sometimes arise from intransitive verbs (often in MGr, Psichari 185), thus in the NT μαθητεύειν 'to make a disciple of' (§148(3)), θριαμβεύειν 'cause to triumph' (?§148 (1)) and κατακληρονομεῖν 'cause to inherit, give over as an inheritance' A 13: 19 OT. (2) An active which is used only transitively in Attic can appropriate an intransitive function from the middle-passive voice: thus, in addition to αὐξάνειν, φύειν and δύειν (cf. §101), also καταπαύειν, ἐπιφαίνειν, βρέχειν.

(1) The factitive (causative) meaning with ἀνατέλλειν 'cause to rise' Mt 5: 45 (in parallelism with βρέχειν 'cause to rain', s. infra; intrans. Mt 13: 6 and often) is old: as early as Homer and other poets (therefore probably Ion.), then also LXX Gen 3: 18 etc. (Helb., Kas. 78), 1 Clem 20.4, Diogn 12.1, GNaass 2. However, εὐαγγελίζειν (A 16: 17 D*) Rev 10: 7, 14: 6 (mid. 𝔓47S) does not = 'cause the good news to be preached', but as elsewhere in Hell. (Friedrich, TW II 708.9 f.; 710.16) = εὐαγγελίζεσθαι (Att., NT commonly, even Rev). Ἀναφάναντες τὴν Κύπρον A 21: 3 SB* only appears to belong here; it means 'we made it visible to ourselves' (therefore with the customary meaning of φαίνειν), i.e. by drawing near; cf. Lucian, D. Mar. 10.1 ἀνάφηνον 'make (the island) visible' (by causing it to appear on the horizon); on the v.l. ἀναφανέντες cf. Theophanes, Chron. 1.721 ἀναφανέντων αὐτῶν τὴν γῆν 'as they came in sight of land'; both are probably nautical expressions like ἀποκρύπτειν (abscondere) expressing the opposite.—Factitives (causatives) in -εύειν: εἰρηνεύειν 'to work for reconciliation' Did 4.3 (Barn 19.12?), βασιλεύειν et al. in the LXX (Helb., Kas. 75 ff.; Psichari 185; Hebraism acc. to W. Schmid, PhW 49 [1929] 468; some translators, especially in Lamentations, go very far in using intrans. actives as causatives [Katz in Ziegler, Beiträge zur Jeremias-Septuaginta 53]).

(2) Καταπαύειν 'to rest' H 4: 4, 10 OT (LXX Gen 2: 2, Ex 31: 18 etc.); intr. Eur., Hec. 918(?), Com. Att. Frag. III, no. 110.8, p. 425 Kock; further in Helb., Kas. 169 f. Ἐπιφαίνειν 'to appear, rise (of stars)' Lk 1: 79, A 27: 20; Hell. (s. Bauer); cf. Hatzid. 202 (ex. from a hymn). Βρέχειν trans. (class.) 'to wet', intr. and impersonal (§129) for class. ὕειν (which does not appear) as in MGr.— Rob. 801 f.

310. Active for (classical) middle.

(1) A reflexive relationship indicated by the context can be left unexpressed, e.g. in (κατα-)δουλοῦν (Att. also along with -οῦσθαι): 2 C 11: 20 εἴ τις ὑμᾶς καταδουλοῖ (cf. G 2: 4; so also ἀναφάναντες §309 (1)), and especially in the case of ποιεῖν with a verbal substantive where the active frequently represents a classical middle; this is the case if those ποιοῦντες are the same persons who carry out the action expressed by the verbal substantive. (2) On the other hand, if there is emphasis on the reflexive relationship, then the middle is required, although the active can be used with a reflexive pronoun (Attic also, K.-G. I 110 f.; papyri: Mayser II 1, 104 f.): ἀπέκτεινεν ἑαυτόν 'he killed himself' (but ἀπήγξατο, because ἀπάγχειν τινά 'to hang someone else' is not common whereas the reflexive action is the usual one). The middle, however, can be used even where the reflexive relationship is emphasized by means of a reflexive pronoun (cf. §316(3); classical similarly, K.-G. I 111; Stahl 66.2).

(1) In the NT also ποιεῖσθαι λόγον, ἀναβολήν, μνείαν (Hell. epistolary formula), πορείαν, σπουδήν etc. Ποιεῖν τὴν ἐκδίκησιν Lk 18: 7, 8, (τὸ) ἔλεος μετ' αὐτοῦ is Hebraizing (LXX Gen 24: 12; §206(3)) Lk 1: 72, 10: 37, ἐνέδραν A 25: 3(?), κοπετόν 8: 2 (mid. EHP), κρίσιν Jn 5: 27, Jd 15, πόλεμον Rev 11: 7 etc., συμβούλιον Mk 3: 6 (mid. W, ἐδίδουν BL), 15: 1 (v.l. ἑτοιμασάντων), συστροφήν A 23: 12, μονήν Jn 14: 23 AEG al. (v.l. mid.), ὁδόν Mk 2: 23 (BGH ὁδοποιεῖν, om. W), συνωμοσίαν A 23: 13 HP. Mlt. 159 f. [250]; Mayser II 1, 124-7 (ποιεῖσθαι); 128 (seldom ποιεῖν thus); Hatzid. 197; Trunk 38 n. 2; Thieme 23; Rouffiac 51. Εὑρίσκειν 'to obtain' is the usual form except for H 9: 12 (mid. in Att., act. also in poets); καθῆψεν τῆς χειρὸς αὐτοῦ A 28: 3 (C καθήψατο), cf. the quotation τόξου καθάψαι in Pollux 1.164; λῦσον τὸ ὑπόδημα τῶν ποδῶν σου A 7: 33 OT (LXX λῦσαι); συναίρειν λόγον Mt 18: 23 (24), 25: 19 (pap. act. and mid., Mlt.160 [250]); for γαμεῖν = γαμεῖσθαι and πειράζειν = πειρᾶσθαι s. §101, for παρέχειν §316(3); ψηφίζειν 'to reckon' Lk 14: 28, Rev 13: 18 (Polyb., Plut. etc., MGr ψηφῶ, ψηφίζω 'heed') is not the equivalent of class. ψηφίζεσθαι 'to vote, resolve'.

Σπασάμενος τὴν μάχαιραν Mk 14: 47 and A 16: 27 in Att. style, but Mt 26: 51 ἀπέσπασεν τ. μ. αὐτοῦ; similarly 26: 25 διέρρηξεν τὰ ἱμάτια αὐτοῦ (cf. A 14: 14), but here class. also uses act. (Aeschyl., Pers. 199 πέπλους ῥήγνυσιν, cf. 1030). Mayser II 1, 115f.

(2) Herm Sim 9.9.3 βασανίζεις σεαυτόν. Pap. e.g. ἑαυτὸν ἐντείνειν (258 BC) for ἐντείνεσθαι 'to strain, exert oneself', σκῆψιν αὐτῷ ζητησάμενος (218 BC); Mayser II 1, 104f. Further Raderm.² 147; W. Schmid, PhW 45 (1925) 1070f. Doubly reflexive: διεμερίσαντο ἑαυτοῖς Jn 19: 24 OT (Mt 27: 35 is different), cf. A 7: 21, 58.—On the whole, Rob. 802.

(B) Passive

311. Passive forms of transitive deponents appear in the NT as in classical. (1) Examples of the present, in which case the passive forms are identical with the middle, are infrequent in the NT as in classical: e.g. λογίζεται 'is reckoned' R 4: 4, 5 (middle in v. 6), 9: 8, infinitive 4: 24; cf. λογιζόμενον Hdt. 3.95. In the perfect ἴαται Mk 5: 29, ἐσμὲν εὐηγγελισμένοι H 4: 2 (more common in classical). (2) Examples of the aorist, which is also formally distinguished from the middle, are numerous.—A. Prévot, L'aoriste grec en -θην (Paris, 1935) 148–53; Mayser II 1, 121f.

(1) Εὐαγγελίζεται, -ονται Mt 11: 5, Lk 7: 22, 16: 16 (but cf. § 309(1)); βιάζεται Mt 11: 12 (Lk 16: 16 is different), cf. Stahl 73.3, Schekira 162, 194; ἐργαζομένη Herm Sim 5.3.8; ἰῶντο A 5: 16 D, Barn 8.6 ἰᾶται; Herm Vis 3.9.3 λυμαίνονται trans. and -νεται pass., 6.7 χρᾶσαι. Pf. ἐπήγγελται G 3: 19 (ἐπαγγέλλεσθαι in the NT is deponent only), cf. 1 Clem 35.4, LXX 2 Macc 4: 27; ἐπιλελησμένον Lk 12: 6.

(2) Ἐλογίσθην, ἰάθην, ἐχαρίσθην, ἐρρύσθην, ἐμνήσθην (A 10: 31, Rev 16: 19; LXX also, not class.) etc. Likewise in the fut.: λογισθήσεται R 2: 26 (s. however § 145(2)), ἰαθήσεται Mt 8: 8, ἀπαρνηθήσεται (§ 78) Lk 12: 9, Phm 22 χαρισθήσομαι 'I will be given'. ISm 5.1 ὃν...ἀρνοῦνται, μᾶλλον δὲ ἠρνήθησαν ὑπ' αὐτοῦ.

312. The passive of intransitive verbs. (1) As in Attic the passive may have a person as subject which in the active would stand in the gen. or dat.; an acc. of the thing in the active remains the same in the passive. Examples from the NT cannot be directly paralleled in classical, but they are perfectly analogous: ἐγκαλεῖσθαι 'be accused' A 19: 40 etc. (ἐγκαλεῖν τινι), κατηγορεῖσθαι Mt 27: 12, A 25: 16, with an acc. of the thing 22: 30 (active τινός τι). Mayser II 1, 118ff. (2) The passive with a thing as subject is quite distinct, as are the passive of which an infinitive or a ὅτι-clause may

be considered subject, and also the impersonal passive (§ 130(1)).

(1) Διακονηθῆναι 'to let oneself be served' Mt 20: 28 = Mk 10: 45 (act. τινι). Κατεγνωσμένος G 2: 11 (Diodor., M. Ant.; act. τινός). Μαρτυρεῖσθαι 'be (well) spoken of, of (good) repute' A 6: 3, 1 T 5: 10; H 7: 8 'be witnessed', etc. (late; cf. Deissmann, NBS 93 [BS 265], Windisch, Hdb. on 3 Jn 12; act. τινι), but with 3 Jn 12 Δημητρίῳ μεμαρτύρηται cf. Dionys. Hal., Thuc. 8. Πιστεύεσθαί τι 'to receive something in trust' R 3: 2 etc. (Polyb. etc., Deissmann, LO⁴ 320 [LAE 379]; πιστεύειν τινί τι), also (without obj.) 'be believed in' (Att. also; act. in NT τινί or εἴς τινα) 1 T 3: 16 ἐπιστεύθη (Χριστὸς) ἐν κόσμῳ, cf. § 488(3) and 2 Th 1: 10. Χρηματίζεσθαι 'to receive a direction (from God)' Mt 2: 12 etc. (act. τινί); only Lk 2: 26 ἦν αὐτῷ κεχρηματισμένον (-ος ἦν D). Εὐαρεστεῖσθαι 'be satisfied' H 13: 16 (Diodor., Diog. L.) is the pass. to εὐαρεστεῖν τινι 'please someone' H 11: 5 (allusion to Gen 5: 24; here and elsewhere in the LXX εὐαρεστεῖν renders הלך Hithp., which is unfortunate because an action is transformed into a quality [Aqu. and 4 Km 20: 3 have περιπατεῖν]; understood in the Hebrew sense, the point in H 11: 6 would be much more forceful: Katz, JTS 47 [1946] 31; cf. Philo's Bible 19f.), Ap. Frs., Hell.; the older ἀρέσκεσθαι (class.), pass. to ἀρέσκειν τινί (older τινά; Foerster, TW I 455.17ff.), is synonymous, and so is ἀρκεῖσθαι 'be satisfied with' Lk 3: 14, 1 T 6: 8, H 13: 5, 1 Clem 2.1, IPol 5.1 (seldom in class.) as pass. of ἀρκεῖν τινι 'suffice one'. Cf. δυσαρεστεῖσθαι Hippoc., Arist., Polyb., Aquila and Symm. But with a thing as subj. (s. (2)) Diodor. 17.113 ἀποκρίσεις εὐαρεστουμένας 'which are pleasing', Plut., Mor. 94D (I 189.22 Paton) δυσαρεστουμένην φιλίαν.

(2) 2 C 1: 11 ἵνα τὸ χάρισμα εὐχαριστηθῇ pass. to εὐχαριστεῖν τι Herm (§ 148(2); NT with ἐπί, περί etc.); ἐπιτρέπεταί σοι...λέγειν A 26: 1 (1 C 14: 34).

313. Passives with intransitive meaning. The passives of ὁρᾶν, γι(γ)νώσκειν and εὑρίσκειν have a certain independence from the active voice in that they retain the earlier intransitive-deponent meaning (E. Wistrand, Über das Passivum [Göteborg, 1941] 33; cf. φαίνεσθαί τινι) and the person concerned takes the dat. instead of ὑπό; cf. § 191.

Frequently ὀφθῆναί τινι (long in use) *apparere, supervenire*, with the new present ὀπτάνεσθαι A 1: 3 (§ 101 under ὁρᾶν). Ὀπτάνεσθαι, ὀφθῆναι with dat., s. Mayser II 1, 222, Ljungvik 34. Acc. to Joachim Jeremias, Die Abendmahlsworte Jesu (Göttingen, 1935) 73 [The Eucharistic Words of Jesus (1955) 130] ὤφθη = ἐφάνην in Aram.; *idem*, ZNW 44 (1952/3) 103: Aram. generally uses the pass. for actions of a celestial being. Γνωσθῆναι 'become known' A 9: 24

etc., cf. γιγνώσκεσθαί τινι 'be known' Eur., Cyc. 567, Xen., Cyr. 7.1.44; but ἔγνωσται 'is known' pass. with ὑπό 1 C 8: 3. Εὑρεθῆναι R 10: 20 OT (v.l. with ἐν) besides ἐμφανῆ γενέσθαι; on 2 P 3: 14 s. § 192. A 8: 40 εὑρέθη εἰς Ἄζωτον 'came to Azotus, appeared suddenly in Azotus', cf. LXX (esp. Esth 1: 5 τοῖς εὑρεθεῖσιν εἰς τὴν πόλιν), Herm Sim 9.13.2, Ljungvik 39 ff. Θεαθῆναι Mt 6: 1, 23: 5 = ὀφθῆναι. Σταθῆναι = στῆναι s. § 97(1).

314. The passive in the sense of 'to allow oneself to be ...' (cf. German *sich lassen*) was common from earliest times: ἀδικεῖσθε 1 C 6: 7 'let yourselves be wronged' (in the sense of allowing it), likewise ἀποστερεῖσθε in the same vs. Βαπτίζεσθαι 'get oneself baptized' (in the sense of to cause it; aorist ἐβαπτίσθην, cf. however § 317). For a similar use of the middle s. § 317.—For the passive as a circumlocution for the divine name s. §§ 130(1); 313.

Permissive: δογματίζεσθαι 'submit to regulations (lit. let yourself be regulated)' C 2: 20, γαμίζεσθαι (§ 101), συσχηματίζεσθαι and μεταμορφοῦσθαι R 12: 2, ἱλάσθητι 'let yourself be disposed to grace' Lk 18: 13. Causative: ἁγνισθῆναι A 21: 24, 26, διακονηθῆναι Mt 20: 28 = Mk 10: 45, often περιτέμνεσθαι (also in the sense of allow).—Cf. Rob. 808 f.

315. The substitution of the active of another verb for the passive is the rule with certain verbs in Attic. Thus the passive to ἀποκτείνειν is ἀποθνῄσκειν, to εὖ (κακῶς) ποιεῖν (λέγειν) is εὖ (κακῶς) πάσχειν (ἀκούειν) (ὑπό is used for the agent as with real passives). There are only a few traces of this usage in the NT, but neither are there many examples of the passives of these verbs (ἀποκτανθῆναι Mk 9: 31 etc.).

Ἐκπίπτειν A 27: 17, 26, 29 = ἐκβάλλεσθαι, but not with ὑπό; on the other hand ἐκβάλλεσθαι Mt 8: 12 etc. which, however, is also found in Att. Πάσχειν ὑπό Mt 17: 12 (where ἐποίησαν has preceded), Mk 5: 26, 1 Th 2: 14. Herm Vis 2.2.2 ἤκουσαν προδόται 'they had to allow themselves to be called betrayers'. The pass. of ποιεῖν appears hardly at all (H 12: 27). On Aramaisms in the Gospels like Lk 8: 2 ἐξεληλύθει = ἐξεβέβλητο (cf. 4: 41, Mk 4: 21) or Mt 17: 27 τὸν ἀναβάντα ('drawn up') πρῶτον ἰχθύν, s. Wellhausen, Einl.[2] 19. For the 3rd pers. plur. act. for the pass. s. § 130(2). Στῆναι = σταθῆναι s. § 97(1).

(C) Middle

316. Middle instead of active. NT authors in general preserve well the distinction between middle and passive. The middle is occasionally used, however, where an active is expected (cf. the reverse §§ 307 and 310). (1) *Examples*: ἀμύνεσθαι 'to aid' (? s. Bauer) = Attic ἀμύνειν A 7: 24 (*hapax legomenon*); πληροῦσθαι E 1: 23 'to fill' = active 4: 10; προβλέπεσθαι H 11: 40 formed on the model of προορᾶσθαι (βλέπειν for ὁρᾶν § 101); always περιβλέπεσθαι (Polyb. etc.; active in Attic); συγκαλεῖν and -εῖσθαι ('call together; summon') is correctly distinguished everywhere if συγκαλεῖται instead of -εῖ is read in Lk 15: 6 with DF and in *v.* 9 with ADEGW al. (2) Some older grammarians make the distinction between αἰτεῖν and -εῖσθαι that 'to ask as a loan' requires αἰτεῖσθαι. In general, however, αἰτεῖσθαι is used of requests in commerce and so as a rule in the NT; the active is usually used for requests addressed to God. (3) Παρεχόμενος σεαυτὸν τύπον T 2: 7 = παρέχων is contrary to classical usage.—Rob. 803–14, Moule 24–6.

(1) Ἀπειλεῖσθαι mid. depon. A 4: 17, 21 (LXX also) for Att. ἀπειλεῖν (1 P 2: 23); διαπειλ- Att. also as depon. Ἀπεκδυσάμενος τὰς ἀρχάς C 2: 15, while ἀποδύσασθαι 'to undress oneself' is Att. Ἡρμοσάμην ὑμᾶς ἀνδρί 2 C 11: 2 'betrothed' for ἥρμοσα (Philo ἡρμόσατο LA 2.67 [ɪ 103.18 Cohn-Wendland]). Μνηστεύεσθαί τινά τινι or ὑπέρ τινος 'to be a suitor to a maiden for someone' PFlor 36.4 (iv AD), PMasp 6 ɪɪ 8 (vi AD). Ἐκδίδοσθαι 'lease' (class. act.) Mt 21: 33, 41, Mk 12: 1, Lk 20: 9. Καταλαμβάνεσθαι 'become aware of' A 4: 13 etc. (Att. -ειν, mid. also Dionys. Hal. *et al.*). Παρατηρεῖσθαι Lk 14: 1 etc. (besides act.; simple form only in act.). Θέσθαι 'appoint, install' 1 C 12: 28 ἀποστόλους, 1 Th 5: 9 εἰς ὀργήν = Att. ποιῆσαι, καταστῆσαι, Ion. θεῖναι (H 1: 2 ὃν ἔθηκεν κληρονόμον); but θέσθαι ἐν φυλακῇ and the like 'to put in custody' A 4: 3 etc. has class. parallels, cf. Dem. 56.4 καταθησόμενος εἰς τὸ οἴκημα. Ταῦτα πάντα ἐφυλαξάμην Mk 10: 20 over against τ. π. ἐφύλαξα in the pars. (Mt 19: 20, Lk 18: 21). Ἐκλέγεσθαι always mid. 'choose'; only in A 6: 5, 15: 22, 25 is the force of the mid. ('for oneself') not absolutely necessary. Ἐπιδείκνυσθαι A 9: 39 (act. elsewhere in the NT) can be 'to show on oneself'. Ἀπορεῖσθαι (εὐπορεῖσθαι) and ὑστερεῖσθαι s. § 101. Ἐνεργεῖσθαι does not belong here (only Paul and Ja 5: 16): it is intr. generally 'to prove effective' and is used only non-personally; only the act. is used of God; also the δυνάμεις, which are the subj. of the act. in Mt 14: 2, Mk 6: 14, are thought of as divine.

(2) Αἰτεῖσθαι in commerce: Mt 27: 20, 58 etc.; Mk 6: 22 αἴτησον (SW -σαι), 23 αἰτήσῃς, but then *v.* 24 αἰτήσωμαι, 25 ᾐτήσατο (D εἶπεν) is quite subtle, since the daughter of Herodias, after the King's pronouncement, stands in a sort of business relationship to him; cf. Mt 20: 20, 22, Mk 10: 35, 38. Mid. of requests addressed to God: Mt 18: 19 etc. (in A 13:

21 ἠτήσαντο βασιλέα, καὶ ἔδωκεν αὐτοῖς ὁ θεός etc. the request is probably not directed to God, cf. LXX 1 Km 8: 5); mid. alternating with act. (arbitrarily) Ja 4: 2f., 1 Jn 5: 14f. etc.; the request of the beggar, son, etc. is naturally αἰτεῖν A 3: 2, Mt 7: 9f. (cf. A 16: 29, 1 C 1: 22). G. Kittel, ZNW 41 (1942) 85, 89 (αἰτεῖν and mid.). Ἀπαιτεῖν, παραιτεῖσθαι as in Att.; ἐξητήσατο Lk 22: 31 (Att. -εῖν and -εῖσθαι). In the pap. the mid. preponderates in business style (Mayser II 1, 109f.).

(3) C 4: 1 τὴν ἰσότητα τοῖς δούλοις παρέχεσθε (-ετε C) is not unclass., nor is παρέξῃ Lk 7: 4, but the act. παρεῖχον φιλανθρωπίαν A 28: 2 probably is (cf. however φιλότητα παρασχεῖν in Hom.), also -χεν ἐργασίαν 16: 16 (-ετο C), 19: 24 A*DE (-χετο al.; the passage appears to be corrupt). For the mid. in spite of a refl. pron. s. also §310(2). Hell. exx. of ἑαυτὸν παρέχεσθαι and the like may be found in Hatzid. 197 (also from Xen. etc.); Deissmann, NBS 81f. [BS 254]; Thieme 24; Rouffiac 52; Witkowski, Bericht 232; Mayser II 1, 105; W. Schmid, PhW 45 (1925) 1071; Hering 54f.

317. The middle in the sense of 'to let oneself be . . . ' (cf. German *sich lassen*) (causative; cf. §314) also occurs in scattered passages in the NT:

Κείρασθαι and ξύρασθαι 1 C 11: 6; ὄφελον καὶ ἀποκόψονται G 5: 12 'get themselves emasculated' (cf. ἀποκεκομμένος LXX Dt 23: 1; περιτέμνεσθαι on the other hand is treated as a pass.). Ἐβαπτισάμην: A 22: 16 βάπτισαι καὶ ἀπόλουσαι (1 C 6: 11 ἀπελούσασθε) can be explained as causal; but in 1 C 10: 2 -ίσαντο appears to be spurious (BKLP; in 𝔓⁴⁶ corrected from ἐβαπτίζοντο) and -ίσθησαν alone to be correct; ἐβαπτίσθη in Lk 11: 38 in an entirely different sense 'to dip his hands' is incorrect (ἐβαπτίσατο is correct with 𝔓⁴⁵ minusc. 700). Ἀπογράφεσθαι Lk 2: 1, 3 also belongs here 'have oneself enrolled' on account of the aor. -γράψασθαι in v. 5.—Mayser II 1, 89; 109, Rob. 808f.

(2) TENSE

318. Introduction. The original function of the so-called tense stems of the verb in Indo-European languages was not that of levels of time (present, past, future) but that of *Aktionsarten* (kinds of action) or aspects (points of view). Cf. Hebrew. *Past time* (past from the standpoint of the speaker or narrator) was designated within the several tense stems by a prefixed, originally independent (but not obligatory) particle, the so-called augment. The old and common temporal significance (contemporary time) assigned to the unaugmented indicative (present, perfect) grew out of the contrast to augmented forms. In Greek the temporal significance of the corresponding indicatives has been carried over to a much smaller degree to the moods (subjunctive and optative, also to the infinitive and participle), and then it is, of course, so-called *relative time*, i.e. the temporal relationship is determined by something else appearing in the speech or narrative. The Greek *future* occupies a special place: formally it is probably a mixture of the Indo-European future, which denoted future time, and the subjunctive of the sigmatic aorist (with which in Greek it always had certain forms in common, e.g. λύσω, middle λύσῃ). In meaning, time is practically the only significance of the future (even in the optative, infinitive and participle); *Aktionsart* is expressed only occasionally at most and then only in a secondary way (Wackernagel, Verhandl. der 49. Versamml. deutscher Philol. und Schulmänner in Basel, 1907, pp. 157f.). Periphrases provide further possibilities in expressing levels of time (s. §§352ff.).

The most important kinds of action (*Aktionsarten*) retained in Greek (including the NT) are the following: (1) The *punctiliar* (*momentary*) in the aorist stem: the action is conceived as a point with either the beginning or the end of the action emphasized (ingressive and effective aorist: ἐβασίλευσεν 'became king', ἔβαλεν 'hit'), or the action is conceived as a whole irrespective of its duration (constative or complexive aorist: ἐποίησεν 'he made it'). (2) The *durative* (*linear* or *progressive*) in the present stem: the action is represented as durative (in progress) and either as timeless (ἔστιν ὁ θεός) or as taking place in present time (including, of course, duration on one side or the other of the present moment: γράφω 'I am writing [now]'; the periphrastic construction τυγχάνω ὤν designates only the present moment but it does not appear in the NT [s. §414(1)]). (3) The present stem may also be *iterative*: ἔβαλλεν 'threw repeatedly (or each time)'. (4) The *perfective* in the perfect stem: a condition or state as the result of a past action is designated (ἕστηκεν 'he placed himself there and stands there now'). Cf. Mt 18: 12 πλανηθῇ . . . τὸ πλανώμενον, 13 τοῖς μὴ πεπλανημένοις. (5) 'Perfectivizing' by means of prepositions (especially ἐξ, ἀπό, κατά, διά) can be introduced at this point: the action is conceived as having reached its consummation (aorist, e.g. κατέφαγον 'devoured' Mt 13: 4) or as continuing to its completion or as repeatedly achieved (present stem, e.g. κατεσθίειν G 5: 15,

Mk 12: 40). The distinction between repeated or durative and point action is still preserved in MGr (Thumb² §180).

On the whole cf. Schwyzer II 246–69; Wackernagel, Syntax I 149–210; Mlt. 108–19 [176–80]; Rob. 821–30.

(1) Rob. 830–79. C. U. Broach, The Meaning of the Aorist Passive in the NT (Diss. Southern Baptist Sem. 1942).

(2) Rob. 879–92.

(3) Rob. 892–910.

(5) Wackernagel, Kl. Schr. 127–47; 1000–21; Mlt. 111–18 (with notes) [180–93]; A. Rapaport, Novi Testamenti Graeci verba recipiantne praepositione praefixa vim perfectivae actionis necne (Studia Leopolitana, ed. St. Witkowski II.), Lemberg, 1924. Stiebitz, Studie o slovesném vidu...(1929; s. Debrunner, Jahresb. Altertumsw. 236 [1932] 207 f.). J. Brunel, L'aspect verbal et l'emploi des préverbes en grec, particulièrement en attique (Paris, 1939) and Debrunner's comments in IF 58 (1942) 284 ff. J. P. Allen, The Force of Prepositions in Compound Verbs in the Perfect Tense in John's Gospel and Epistles (Diss. Southern Baptist Sem. 1941).

(A) The Present Indicative

319. Conative present. Inasmuch as the description of the occurrence in the durative present is bound up with the notion of incompleteness, the present itself can denote an attempted but incomplete action (universal in Greek): Jn 10: 32 διὰ ποῖον αὐτῶν ἔργον ἐμὲ λιθάζετε; ('*want* to stone me?'), G 5: 4 οἵτινες ἐν νόμῳ δικαιοῦσθε ('want [are attempting] to be justified'), Jn 13: 6 νίπτεις, G 6: 12 ἀναγκάζουσιν. The imperfect more frequently has this nuance (§326).—Rob. 880; Burton 8.

320. Aoristic present. In those few cases where a punctiliar act taking place at the moment of speaking is to be denoted, the present is usually used since the punctiliar aorist stems form no present (Burton 9; Debrunner, Glotta 11 [1920] 18 n. and IF 48 [1930] 12–16, 18, 91 f.). Thus A 9: 34 (Peter to Aeneas) ἰᾶταί σε Ἰησοῦς Χριστός 'he heals you in this moment in which I proclaim it to you', or more briefly 'he herewith heals you' (ἰᾶται otherwise = 'he treats the sickness').—Rob. 864 ff.

Likewise παραγγέλλω σοι...A 16: 18 (exorcism of a demon) 'I herewith command you...' (punctiliar action; from the standpoint of the narrator it would have to be παρήγγειλεν; cf. εἶπεν before

παραγγ.). Further ἀσπάζεται '...herewith sends his greetings' (but ἀσπάσασθε). Burton 9 correctly adds (in addition to A 26: 1 ἐπιτρέπεται *et al.*) ἀφίενταί σου αἱ ἁμαρτίαι Mk 2: 5, Mt 9: 5 etc., insofar as the reading is certain (cf. §97(3)).

321. The historical present can replace the aorist indicative in a vivid narrative at the events of which the narrator imagines himself to be present; the *Aktionsart* usually remains punctiliar in spite of the present tense form. This usage is common among NT authors, especially Mk (the Aramaic participial sentence may have contributed to its frequency; s. M.-H. 456 f.), as it is among classical writers; only Lk uses it less frequently, probably because he regarded it as a vulgarism (papyri, LXX and Jos. often, also MGr). Cf. Hawkins, Horae Synopt. pp. 143 ff., 213 ff. Mayser II 1, 131. H. St John Thackeray, The Septuagint and Jewish Worship 1920 (²1923) pp. 20 ff. and App. 1.—Rob. 866–9.

Jn 1: 29 τῇ ἐπαύριον βλέπει...καὶ λέγει..., 35 τῇ ἐπαύριον εἱστήκει (pluperf. = imperf. 'was standing')..., 36 καὶ...λέγει..., 43 τῇ ἐπαύριον ἠθέλησεν ἐξελθεῖν (Chr ἐξῆλθεν)...καὶ εὑρίσκει; thus the circumstances, or all that is secondary, are given in a past tense; on the other hand the main action is likely to be represented by the present, while the concluding events are again put into the aor. because here a historical present would not be natural: 39 ἦλθον καὶ εἶδον...καὶ...ἔμειναν. The present is used in a similar way even outside a narrative: 15 Ἰωάνης μαρτυρεῖ περὶ αὐτοῦ καὶ κέκραγεν (= κράζει; κέκραγα is pres. in Att., also LXX; also cf. μαρτυρόμενος καὶ κεκραγώς Plut., Cato Min. 58, βοᾷ καὶ κέκραγεν Hippoc., Morb. Sacr. 15 [VI 388 Littré]). Λέγει, φησίν and the like appear to be especially vernacular (occasionally in Plut.) in the reporting of a conversation (λέγει chiefly in Mt, Mk, Jn, φησίν especially in Lk); cf. LXX (Thack. 10, 24). Rodemeyer (Das Präs. histor. bei Herodot und Thukyd., Diss. Basel, 1889) attempts to show that the historical present indicates that an event took place at the same time as, or immediately after, a point of time already given; this is valid to a certain degree: Mt 2: 13 ἀναχωρησάντων αὐτῶν ἰδοὺ ἄγγελος κυρίου φαίνεται (B ἐφάνη); Herm Vis 1.1.3 διαβὰς ἦλθον...καὶ τιθῶ τὰ γόνατα; cf. Svensson 102; there is a corresponding usage in MGr (Mlt. 121 n. 2 [197 n. 1]; Thumb² §186).—Svensson 99 takes Mk 6: 1 ἀκολουθοῦσιν and 11: 1 ὅτε ἐγγίζουσιν as a *descriptive* present (under Aramaic influence, but it is more probably a Latinism; cf. Svensson 95 f.); Pallis, Notes 38 holds that a pres. after ὅτε is impossible and conjectures ἐγγίζοσαν (cf. ἤγγιζεν D al., M ἤγγισαν).

322. The perfective present appears only with a very limited number of special verbs. In the NT in addition to the well-known ἥκω ('am here' Lk 15: 27 etc.) there is ἀκούω 'I hear = have heard' Lk 9: 9, 1 C 11: 18, 2 Th 3: 11 (also in classical), ἀδικῶ 'be in the wrong, an offender' (as in Attic) appears only in A 25: 11 (Mt 20: 13 is the usual present); also ὁ νικῶν Rev 2: 7 etc. calls to mind the Attic use of νικῶ 'I am the victor'.— Mayser II 1, 132f.; Rob. 881.

Πάρεισιν 'have come' A 17: 6 is a pres. for the perf. of another verb (Burton 10) like ἀπέχω Mt 6: 2 etc. (often in receipts, Deissmann, LO⁴ 88 [LAE 110f.]) for ἀπείληφα (differently Br.-Th. 549f.; cf. Schwyzer II 268). Λέγεται would be the equivalent (in meaning) of ἀκούω, so that ἀκούεται in 1 C 5: 1 is not surprising. Ἀδικῶ in A 25: 11 stands alongside ἄξιον θανάτου πέπραχά τι (cf. v. 10 οὐδὲν ἠδίκηκα); thus the perf. is used for individual trespasses, the pres. only for the general result. H 13: 18 πειθόμεθα 'we are convinced' (or 'we keep hopefully persuading ourselves...'?), hence SᶜCᶜDᵇˑᶜ IK al. πεποίθαμεν. The pres. is not perfective in those cases where the duration or repetition of an act *up to and including the present* is to be designated (a temporal expression indicates the intended period of the past): Lk 15: 29 τοσαῦτα ἔτη δουλεύω σοι, 13: 7 ἰδοὺ τρία ἔτη ἀφ' οὗ ἔρχομαι, Jn 5: 58 εἰμί, 15: 27 ἐστέ, 2 C 12: 19 πάλαι δοκεῖτε, and others; A 26: 31 πράσσει without temporal designation (referring to Paul's whole way of life, especially his Christianity).

323. The futuristic use of the present. In confident assertions regarding the future, a vivid, realistic present may be used for the future (in the vernacular; a counterpart to the historical present §321). Ordinarily a temporal indication of the future is included (cf. §322). (1) In prophecies this usage is not unknown in classical Greek; cf. the oracle in Hdt. 7.140f. In prophecies it is very frequent in the NT. It is hardly entirely accidental that the verb ἔρχομαι figures strongly in this usage (cf. especially ὁ ἐρχόμενος 'the one who *is to come* [the Messiah]' Mt 11: 3; cf. v. 14 Ἠλίας ὁ μέλλων ἔρχεσθαι, 17: 11 Ἠλ. ἔρχεται). (2) Without the predictive sense so that μέλλει (ἔρχεσθαι) could have been used: e.g. Mt 24: 43 ποίᾳ φυλακῇ ὁ κλέπτης ἔρχεται. (3) Verbs of going (coming) however also have the meaning of 'to be in the process of going (coming)' for which reaching the destination still lies in the future: e.g. Jn 8: 14 πόθεν ἦλθον καὶ ποῦ ὑπάγω...πόθεν ἔρχομαι ἢ ποῦ ὑπάγω. (4) The imperfect is sometimes used analogously = ἤ\ελλεν with an

infinitive: e.g. Mk 14: 1 ἦν τὸ πάσχα μετὰ δύο ἡμέρας ('was to take place').—For εἶμι, which in classical Greek has a futuristic meaning by virtue of its punctiliar *Aktionsart* (Br.-Th. 544; cf. Schwyzer II 265), s. §99(1).—Mayser II 1, 133f.; Rob. 869f., 881f.; Burton 9f.; Moule 7.

(1) Ἔρχομαι: Jn 14: 3 ἔρχομαι καὶ παραλήμψομαι (but with only the first verb in the pres., not the second, which expresses a further consequence; cf. the following exx. and §369(3)); Lk 12: 54f. ἔρχεται...ἔσται; 1 C 16: 5f. ἐλεύσομαι...διέρχομαι...καταμενῶ; Jn 11: 48 ἐλεύσονται καὶ αἴρουσιν 𝔓⁴⁵ (ἐροῦσιν Θ, ἀροῦσιν pm.). Other verbs: Mk 9: 31 παραδίδοται (= μέλει παραδίδοσθαι Mt 17: 22)...καὶ ἀποκτενοῦσιν; Mt 27: 63 ἐγείρομαι; 1 C 15: 32 OT ἀποθνήσκομεν; Jn 20: 23 ἀφίονται (-ενται) futuristic-eschatological (Joachim Jeremias, TW III 753); Herm Vis 2.2.4 ἀφίενται. For the futuristic present of verbs of going in other languages s. Wackernagel, Syntax I² 161; Koschmieder, KZ 56 (1929) 99f.

(2) Jn 4: 35 ἔτι τετράμηνός ἐστιν καὶ ὁ θερισμὸς ἔρχεται and repeatedly ἕως ἔρχομαι (-εται), s. §383(1) (in other instances ἐλεύσομαι is necessary: Mt 24: 5, Mk 12: 9, 13: 6 etc.). Other verbs: γίνεται Mt 26: 2, γεννᾶται 2: 4 ('where...*is* to be born').

(3) Jn 3: 8 πόθεν ἔρχεται ἢ ποῦ ὑπάγει (approximately = 'will go', or rather 'goes each time'). Thus ποῦ ὑπάγω -εις Jn 14: 4f., πορεύομαι 14: 2, 12, Lk 14: 19, A 20: 22, ἀναβαίνομεν Mt 20: 18, Jn 20: 17. But Jn 7: 8 οὐκ ἀναβαίνω εἰς τὴν ἑορτὴν ταύτην, provided neither οὔπω (𝔓⁶⁶BL al., οὐδέπω W) nor the omission of εἰς τ. ἑ. τ. (minusc. 69, Lat. q, Chr; Blass) is to be preferred, is futuristic.

(4) Lk 23: 54 σάββατον ἐπέφωσκεν ('was about to dawn').

324. The present used to express relative time. In indirect discourse from past time classical can use either the present or the past depending on whether the temporal point of view of the original speaker or that of the reporter is adopted. In the NT the latter (*oratio obliqua*) is not popular and the former, which conforms to direct speech (*oratio recta*), prevails. This relative use of the present appears not only with verbs of saying, but even with verbs of perception and belief:

E.g. Mt 2: 22 ἀκούσας ὅτι Ἀρχέλαος βασιλεύει; Jn 6: 24 εἶδεν ὁ ὄχλος ὅτι Ἰησοῦς οὐκ ἔστιν ἐκεῖ; likewise Mt 18: 25 πάντα ὅσα ἔχει (B Or for εἶχεν) after ἐκέλευσε πραθῆναι. This pres. also appears in class. for the imperf., but not as the rule; while in the NT the imperf. in such sentences is to be rendered usually by the pluperf. (§330). Mk 8: 16, for example, shows the relation to direct speech: διελογίζοντο, ὅτι ἄρτους οὐκ ἔχουσιν 𝔓⁴⁵BW (εἶχαν D), but pm. have ἔχομεν. But Jn 16: 19 ἔγνω ὅτι ἤθελον (v.l. ἤμελλον) αὐτὸν ἐρωτᾶν (A 22: 2 ἀκούσαντες ὅτι προσεφώνει, but προσφωνεῖ DEH is better); cf. §345 (pluperf. for perf.). The aorist can also be used of relative time: Mk 12: 12 ἔγνωσαν ὅτι τὴν παραβολὴν εἶπεν 'that he had told the parable' (but Mt 21: 45 ὅτι περὶ αὐτῶν λέγει 'that he was speaking of them'); cf. Jn 9: 18 (§330). S. also fut. (§349(2)). For Jn 2: 25, 6: 6 s. §330.—Burton 11.

(B) The Imperfect and Aorist Indicatives

The distinction between linear and punctiliar *Aktionsart* (§318) stands out most sharply in the imperfect and the indicative aorist and does so in the NT just as much as in the classical language. Of course, there remained a certain interplay between the two tenses in many individual cases; whether it was especially great among the non-Greek authors of the NT (F. Hartmann, NJklA 43 [1919] 327f.) is questionable. C. L. Vice, The Aoristic Use of ἦν in the NT (Diss. Southern Baptist Sem. 1941).

325. Iterative imperfect (§318(3)): A 2: 45 τὰ κτήματα ἐπίπρασκον καὶ διεμέριζον αὐτὰ πᾶσιν (the aorist would have implied: it happened often but was neither universal nor completely carried out), cf. 4: 34, 18: 8, Mk 12: 41.—Rob. 884; Burton 12f.

326. Conative imperfect (cf. §319): A 7: 26 συνήλλασσεν αὐτοὺς εἰς εἰρήνην 'tried to reconcile' ('would have reconciled' RSV).

A 26: 11 ἠνάγκαζον βλασφημεῖν, expressing repetition at the same time like ἐδίωκον in the same vs. (Haenchen¹² 610: both may be descriptive [§327]; Nestle, Septuaginta-Studien IV [1903] 20: cf. 2 Macc 6: 18 ἠναγκάζετο φαγεῖν for the same impf.); Lk 1: 59 ἐκάλουν αὐτὸ Ζαχαρίαν 'wanted to name'; Mt 3: 14 διεκώλυεν 'wanted to prevent, tried to prevent' ('would have prevented' RSV), cf. Mk 9: 38 ἐκωλύομεν (v.l. aor.), Lk 9: 49 𝔓⁴⁵SBL (pm. aor.). A 27: 41 ἐλύετο 'began to break loose' or 'broke up more and more'. On H 11: 17 s. §327; on the imperf. = ἔμελλεν with inf. §323(4).—Rob. 885; Burton 12; Moule 9.

327. Imperfect used to portray the manner of the action, i.e. a past action is represented as being in *progress* (with further qualification): A 5: 26 ἦγεν αὐτοὺς οὐ μετὰ βίας, but 27 ἀγαγόντες δὲ (concluded) αὐτοὺς ἔστησαν. Contrast with a following verb which denotes completion is occasionally expressed by the imperfect alone (with-

out further qualification): A 21: 20 ἐδόξαζον τὸν θεόν, εἶπόν τε (they praised God for some time and in various ways until they finally said...). Cf. in Paul 1 C 10: 4 ἔπιον (a fact)-ἔπινον γὰρ ἐκ πνευματικῆς πέτρας (manner); 11 ταῦτα τυπικῶς συνέβαινεν (manner, each individually)-6 ταῦτα τύποι ἡμῶν ἐγενήθησαν (result, altogether).—Rob. 883f.

A 5: 41 ἐπορεύοντο χαίροντες ἀπὸ προσώπου τοῦ συνεδρίου (it was not necessary here to indicate the conclusion); 15: 3 διήρχοντο...ἐκδιηγούμενοι...καὶ ἐποίουν (everywhere, every time) χαρὰν μεγάλην (conclusion to the matter v. 4 παραγενόμενοι δέ), v. 41 is similar; on the other hand 16: 6 διῆλθον δὲ τὴν Φρυγίαν without description. 21: 3 ἐπλέομεν εἰς Συρίαν, καὶ κατήλθομεν εἰς Τύρον: here the description lies in the indication of the direction (εἰς), as in 15; v. 30 is comparable εἷλκον ἔξω τοῦ ἱεροῦ, καὶ εὐθέως ἐκλείσθησαν αἱ θύραι (indirect indication of the completion of the first action: εὐθέως scil. ἑλκυσθέντων αὐτῶν), while in 14: 19 the v.l. ἔσυραν (instead of ἔσυρον) ἔξω τῆς πόλεως is to be preferred, for otherwise the completion of action, which certainly took place, would nowhere be indicated. H 11: 17 πίστει προσενήνοχεν Ἀβραὰμ τὸν Ἰσαάκ..., καὶ τὸν μονογενῆ προσέφερεν...(a supplementary descriptive characterization of what was peculiar to this case; cf. v. 4 προσήνεγκεν...μαρτυροῦντος; or conative imperf.).—The imperf. is also descriptive (durative) if the past is placed in sharp contrast to the present (like the Lat. perf. in *fuimus Troes*): R 6: 17 ἦτε δοῦλοι τῆς ἁμαρτίας 'were then, but no longer', cf. class. e.g. Aristoph., Vespae 1063 πρίν ποτ' ἦν, πρὶν ταῦτα, νῦν δ' οἴχεται. A 18: 19 without further qualification διελέγετο (D, other MSS have spurious -λέξατο or -λέχθη) τοῖς Ἰουδαίοις—conclusion in 20 f.; but in 17: 2f. first a constative (complexive) aor. διελέξατο, and only then a supplementary description; there is also an anticipatory aor. in 28: 14 ἤλθαμεν (cf. vv. 15, 16); still more striking is Jn 4: 3 ἀπῆλθεν εἰς τὴν Γαλιλαίαν, yet in 4ff. what happened on the way is related, and the arrival in Galilee does not take place until 45. But A 27: 1f. is the most striking: παρεδίδουν (Old Lat. *tradidit* is probably better)...ἐπιβάντες δέ.—The aor. is the rule with negatives because usually the action as a whole is negated (e.g. Mt 26: 55 οὐκ ἐκρατήσατε in spite of καθ' ἡμέραν); but the imperf. also makes sense (cf. Br.-Th. 558f.; Schwyzer II 279; Svensson 103ff.), thus e.g. Mk 14: 55 οὐχ εὕρισκον 'they could find none' (in spite of repeated attempts), Mt 18: 30 οὐκ ἤθελεν, cf. 22: 3.

328. The imperfect with verbs of commanding, asking etc. Certain verbs by virtue of their special meaning prefer to some extent a form which denotes incomplete action. If an action is complete in itself, but the achievement of a second action, towards which the first points, is to be represented as unaccomplished or still outside the scope of the assertion, then the first takes the imperfect; in this case the first without the complement of the second remains unfulfilled (therefore a sort of conative imperfect; at times the idea of duration is uppermost). Such verbs include κελεύειν, ἀξιοῦν, παρακελεύεσθαι, ἐρωτᾶν, πέμπειν, ἀποστέλλειν, and others. Cf. Blass, RhM 44 (1889) 414–16; Svensson also puts the linear present in this category (§ 322); Mayser II 1, 135. In the NT κελεύειν, προστάττειν, παραγγέλλειν always denote a valid command whose execution is taken for granted. Consequently (as in Attic with such commands) ἐκέλευσεν, προσέταξεν, παρήγγειλεν, likewise only ἔπεμψεν, ἀπέστειλεν; on the other hand (ἐπ-)ἠρώτα 'asked' and 'besought' along with (ἐπ-)ἠρώτησεν, παρεκάλει (instead of Attic παρεκελεύετο, which does not appear) and παρεκάλεσεν 'besought' (παρήνει A 27: 9 literary language, ἠξίου 15: 38 likewise). These are used in such a way, however, that a satisfactory account may usually be given for the choice in each case:

In A 10: 48 ἠρώτησαν is necessary because the fulfilment of the request, which did take place, is indicated only by this aor. (likewise 23: 18), while ἠρώτα 'requested' in 3: 3 is used quite in the way outlined above. 'Asked' is usually ἠρώτησεν (Att. thus or ἤρετο), but Mk 8: 5 ἠρώτα; 8: 23, 27, 29 ἐπηρώτα, which could be used elsewhere where the aor. is found, as in 9: 16. Παρεκάλεσαν Mt 8: 34 of the Gadarenes who are requesting Jesus to leave (for which Lk 8: 37 has ἠρώτησαν, Mk 5: 17 ἤρξαντο παρακαλεῖν, yet D παρεκάλουν), where the fulfilment of the request necessarily followed. Mt 18: 32 ἀφῆκά σοι, ἐπειδὴ παρεκάλεσάς με (the simple request sufficed), 26: 53 παρακαλέσαι τὸν πατέρα (likewise), A 8: 31 παρεκάλεσεν ἀναβάντα καθίσαι (the fulfilment, being self-evident, is not mentioned). In A 16: 15 παρεκάλει is what one would expect since the conclusion is expressly indicated by καὶ παρεβιάσατο; the imperf. could also be used in 16: 39 (like ἠρώτων in the same vs.). Ἐπύθετο is incorrect in Jn 4: 52 (the imperf. is weakly attested); but ἐπυνθάνετο (-οντο) is correct in Mt 2: 4, Lk 15: 26, 18: 36, A 4: 7, 10: 18 (BC ἐπύθοντο), 21: 33, 23: 19f. (Jn 13: 24 πυθέσθαι, which is incorrect, only ADW al.; the other witnesses read quite differently). Προσκυνεῖν in the sense of 'beseech' is as regularly used in the imperfect (Mt 8: 2, 9: 18, 15: 25 S*BDM), as it is in the aor. in the sense of 'to pay homage, reverence' (Mt 2: 11, 14: 33 etc.). Ἐκέλευον (ῥαβδίζειν) only

A 16: 22 (of magistrates), and probably corrupt: vg *iusserunt* = -σαν (ῥαβδίζειν expressing the duration, cf. § 338(2); the conclusion: πολλὰς δὲ ἐπιθέντες πληγάς v. 23). Παρήγγελλεν Lk 8: 29, cf. § 329.

329. The interchange of ἔλεγεν (-ον) and εἶπεν (-αν, -ον). A double view is possible with verbs of saying: the aorist serves for a simple reference to an utterance previously made (especially for a specific pronouncement of an individual); the imperfect for the delineation of the content of a speech. Statements of an unspecified number of individuals are also usually indicated by the imperfect, whereupon the mention of a concluding statement can follow in the aorist (A 2: 13, 14; Jn 11: 37 τινὲς δὲ ἐξ αὐτῶν εἶπον following 36 ἔλεγον οἱ Ἰουδαῖοι [ΑΚΠ read ἔλεγον also in v. 37]).—Mayser II 1, 135; Svensson 50–60, 108–10, 120–3.

Ἔλεγεν is thus used to introduce longer discourses, as in Lk 6: 20 before the Sermon on the Plain, following a description in the imperf. (vv. 18, 19; Mt 5: 2 introduces the Sermon with ἐδίδασκεν λέγων). Furthermore, additional statements are likely to be connected to the preceding with καὶ ἔλεγεν or ἔλεγεν δέ: Mk 4: 21, 24, 26, 30, 7: 9, 20, Lk 5: 36, 6: 5, 9: 23 and often, while elsewhere εἶπεν is used: Lk 6: 39, 15: 11 etc. Thuc. sometimes also introduces his speeches with ἔλεγε, sometimes with ἔλεξε. Also cf. λέγων (not εἰπών) which is often appended to another verb of saying (§ 420). In narration ἔλεγε(ν) and εἶπε(ν) vary similarly also in MGr: Thumb, ThLZ 1903, 422f.; Schwyzer II 277f.

330. The imperfect used to express relative time. The imperfect after verbs of perception (and belief) is not in itself temporally relative. Since, however, the present expressed time contemporary with that of the verb of perception (§ 324), the imperfect was virtually limited to those cases where a time previous to the time of perception was to be indicated (exceptions below and in § 324; the imperfect would be rendered here by the German and English pluperfect). It is self-evident that the imperfect thereby retains its implication of linear action. For the papyri s. Mayser II 1, 137.

Mk 11: 32 εἶχον τὸν Ἰωάνην ὅτι προφήτης ἦν ('had been'; RSV 'was', but John had been beheaded in chap. 6); A 3: 10 ἐπεγίνωσκον ὅτι ἦν ὁ καθήμενος; 16: 3 ᾔδεισαν τὸν πατέρα αὐτοῦ (who had died) ὅτι Ἕλλην ὑπῆρχεν; Jn 5: 13 οὐκ ᾔδει τίς ἦν (D for ἐστιν) 'had been'; 6: 22 ἰδὼν (v.l. εἶδον; εἰδὼς following e is better) ὅτι οὐκ ἦν; 9: 18 οὐκ ἐπίστευσαν ὅτι ἦν ('had been') τυφλὸς καὶ ἀνέβλεψεν ('had received his sight', cf. §324 end). In the case of οἱ θεωροῦντες αὐτὸν τὸ πρότερον (τὸ πρ. is missing 1 sy^s Chr) ὅτι προσαίτης ἦν Jn 9: 8, θεωρεῖν refers to the same pre-past (pluperf.) time that is expressed in the dependent clause by προσαίτης ἦν; since past time is not expressed by the ptcp. at all, it had to be indicated by the imperf. in the ὅτι-clause. The reading in Mk 9: 6 is uncertain: οὐ γὰρ ᾔδει τί λαλεῖ 𝔓^{45}W, ἐλάλει Θ, λαλήσει (-ση) AC^{3}D al., ἀποκριθῇ SBC*L.—Indirect questions behave somewhat differently: Jn 6: 6 ᾔδει τί ἔμελλεν ποιεῖν (contemporary time) and even 2: 25 ἐγίνωσκεν τί ἦν ἐν τῷ ἀνθρώπῳ (assimilation of tense instead of ἐστιν, which would apply universally, or ἦν referring to that particular time; cf. v. 24 αὐτοῖς and πάντας). G 2: 6 ὁποῖοί τινες ἦσαν 'assimilation of the tense' B. Häsler, ThLZ 1957, 393f.

331. The ingressive (inceptive) aorist (§318 (1)):

e.g. ἐσίγησεν 'became silent' A 15: 12, ἐπτώχευσεν 'became poor' 2 C 8: 9, ἔζησεν 'came to life' R 14: 9 (Rev 13: 14, 20: 4). (The inchoative presents in -σκω do not denote the beginning point, but duratively denote a *gradual* becoming: γηράσκω 'am growing older and older'.)—Rob. 834.

332. The complexive (constative) aorist (cf. §318(1))

is used (1) for linear actions which (having been completed) are regarded as a whole. The external indication that the action is conceived as a whole is usually a temporal adjunct: ἐβίω ἔτη πολλά (then he died), ἔτη δύο ἦρξε (but then he was deposed); on the other hand κακῶς ἔζη (manner emphasized; conclusion left out of account), δικαίως ἦρχε (δικ. ἦρξε would be ingressive 'he rightly took office'). NT, e.g. A 28: 30 ἐνέμεινεν διετίαν ὅλην ἐν ἰδίῳ μισθώματι (then this situation ceased). (2) Repeated actions may also take the aorist provided the repetition is summed up and has a terminus: τρὶς ἐραβδίσθην 2 C 11: 25.—Rob. 831–4.

(1) A 14: 3 ἱκανὸν χρόνον διέτριψαν (until the end of their stay related in *vv.* 5, 6 where the limit is indicated); on the other hand v. 28 διέτριβον χρόνον οὐκ ὀλίγον without reference to a definite period (cf. 16: 12, 25: 14); 18: 11 ἐκάθισεν (Paul in Corinth; 'sat' = 'stayed') ἐνιαυτὸν καὶ μῆνας ἕξ (until his departure). If the aor. of a verb like μένειν is used without a time limit, it indicates merely the fact of a stay in contrast to departure: Jn 7: 9 ἔμεινεν ἐν τῇ Γαλιλαίᾳ = οὐκ ἀνέβη εἰς Ἱεροσόλυμα (the negative here denies the act as a whole; cf. Gild. 106); 10: 40 ἔμεινεν ἐκεῖ 'he settled down there (therefore somewhat ingressive), without returning (for the time being) to Judea' (B ἔμενεν). R 15: 2 ἀρεσκέτω-

ἤρεσεν (in his whole earthly life). A 10: 38 διῆλθεν (with pres. ptcp.) 'always went about' (or 'time after time') until his death in Jerusalem (v. 39).

(2) A 11: 26 ἐγένετο αὐτοῖς καὶ ἐνιαυτὸν ὅλον συναχθῆναι (ἐγέν. συν. = συνήχθησαν) ἐν τῇ ἐκκλησίᾳ. Mk 12: 44 ἔβαλον (separate acts of various people treated as a whole, hence without regard for the iterative factor), but above in v. 41 ἔβαλλον is either descriptive or iterative.

333. The gnomic and futuristic aorist.

(1) An act which is valid for all time can be expressed by the aorist, either because the aorist indicative serves for a non-existent perfective present (for which the imperfective present can also be used, §320), or because (originally at least) the author had a specific case in mind in which the act had been realized (cf. the parabolic *narratives* in Mk 4: 3–9, Lk 10: 30–5 and Aesop's Fables; Abel 256). This gnomic aorist appears infrequently in the NT and is found nearly always in comparisons or in conjunction with them (K.-G. ɪ 161; for the perfect with a similar meaning s. §344). This use has survived however in MGr (Jannaris §1852). (2) An aorist after a future condition is, to a certain extent, futuristic: Jn 15: 8 ἐν τούτῳ ἐδοξάσθη ὁ πατήρ μου, ἵνα καρπὸν πολὺν φέρητε = ἐὰν φέρητε, δοξασθήσεται. Mt 18: 15 ἐὰν σου ἀκούσῃ, ἐκέρδησας τὸν ἀδελφόν σου (= vg *lucratus eris*); G 5: 4 (Zerwick, Graec. bibl. 59).—Rob. 836f., 846f.

(1) Jn 15: 6 ἐὰν μή τις μείνῃ ἐν ἐμοί, ἐβλήθη ἔξω ὡς τὸ κλῆμα καὶ ἐξηράνθη, καὶ συνάγουσιν αὐτὰ καὶ εἰς τὸ πῦρ βάλλουσιν καὶ καίεται; likewise in the parable in Herm Vis 3.12.2 the pres. follows the aor.: κατελείφθη ...ἐξηγέρθη...ἐνεδύσατο...οὐκέτι ἀνάκειται, ἀλλ' ἕστηκεν etc.; also 13.2 ἐπελάθετο...προσδέχεται etc. Also in parables (without a present following) in Mt 13: 44, 46, 48, Ja 1: 11, 24, 1 P 1: 24 (from the LXX Is 40: 7).

(2) Herm Man 3.2 (ἐὰν ἀποδώσωσιν, ἐμίαναν 'they have thereby already defiled', therefore a complexive aor. from the viewpoint of the futuristic conditional clause), 5.1.7, Sim 9.26.2. Mk 11: 24 πιστεύετε ὅτι ἐλάβετε SBCLW (if you asked for it 'you received it'; λαμβάνετε AN al., λήμψεσθε D). Exx. from Homer on in K.-G. ɪ 166, Br.-Th. 562f. Also cf. Mt 5: 28 πᾶς ὁ βλέπων γυναῖκα...ἤδη ἐμοίχευσεν = ἐὰν βλέπῃ; but hardly Jn 1: 5 καὶ ἡ σκοτία αὐτὸ οὐ κατέλαβεν. There is one MGr ex. apiece in Jannaris §1855, Thumb^2 §189, 2 n. 2 and Trunk 44 n. 2; s. also Jensen, IF 47 (1929) 292f. Cf. Epict. 4.10.27 ὅταν θέλῃς, ἐξῆλθες ('you will be outside in a second') καὶ οὐ καπνίζῃ (cf. Svensson 116). Since the Hebr. 'perf.' serves not only as a

narrative tense, but also to denote a timeless act, the Greek aor. also appears for this second kind of perfect in lyrical passages in the LXX, and hence also in the Magnificat Lk 1: 46 ff.

334. The epistolary aorist can denote time contemporary with the writing and sending of the letter, since the letter is written from the standpoint of an orally delivered message. In the NT only ἔπεμψα A 23: 30, Ph 2: 28, C 4: 8, Phm 12, 19 (also 21?) etc. is used in this way; on the other hand, always ἀσπάζεται and γράφω.

1 C 5: 9 ἔγραψα refers to an earlier epistle if the phrase ἐν τῇ ἐπιστολῇ, omitted by Chrys., is genuine; if not, then to an earlier reference in the same letter as in R 15: 15 and elsewhere. Ἔγραψα G 6: 11 is disputed. Ἔπεμψα first in Thuc. 1.129.3 and Isocr. S. Gild. 127 f. (who sees in it a Latinism without justification); Witkowski, Bericht 110; Schwyzer II 281; Rob. 845 f.; Mayser II 1, 143 f. (likewise imperf. 138 f., perf. 183 f., 204, pluperf. 209 f.); Debrunner, IF 48 (1930) 16–18; Burton 21; Moule 12. Cf. the beginning of the oldest Greek autograph letter (iv BC, a lead tablet, Witkowski, Epistulae, Appendix no. 1, Deissmann, LO⁴ 119 f. [LAE 151]): Μνησίεργος ἐπέστειλε ('has asked [the bearer]') τοῖς οἴκοι χαίρε(ι)ν ('to bring greetings to his family')... καὶ ἔφασκε... 'and said...' or 'asks...says...'.

For the aorist used to denote relative time cf. § 324.

(C) The Present and Aorist Imperatives and the Prohibitive and Adhortative Subjunctives

335. Introduction. The present and aorist imperatives differ in the same way as the imperfect and aorist indicatives: the present imperative is durative or iterative, the aorist imperative punctiliar (the distinction holds completely good for MGr, Thumb² § 196). The result of this distinction is that in general precepts (also to an individual) concerning attitudes and conduct there is a preference for the present, in commands related to conduct in specific cases (much less frequent in the NT) for the aorist. The same thing is true e.g. in the Cretan inscriptions (Jacobsthal, IF 21 [1907] Beiheft pp. 22 ff., 43 ff.). The subjunctive of prohibition in the 2nd person sing., which in the aorist replaces the imperative in negative commands, is included here because the same principles apply to it; likewise the hortatory subjunctive in the 1st person plur.—Rob. 890, 851–4, 855 f.; Moule 20–3.

Schwyzer II 339–43; Mayser II 1, 145 ff.; F. Hartmann, KZ 49 (1920) 44 ff.; G. Cuendet, L'impératif dans le texte grec...des Évangiles (Geneva Diss., Paris, 1924); A. Poutsma, Over de tempora van de imperativus en de conjunctivus hortativus-prohibitivus in het Grieks (Verhandelingen Ak. Wet. Amsterdam, Afd. Letterk. 27, 2, 1928).

336. Present imperative (subjunctive). The durative force manifests itself in the following ways: (1) The action hangs in the balance; no definite goal is envisaged: Mt 26: 38 = Mk 14: 34 μείνατε ὧδε ('don't go away', § 332(1)) καὶ γρηγορεῖτε ('be on guard constantly') μετ' ἐμοῦ; Lk 22: 40, 46 προσεύχεσθε μὴ εἰσελθεῖν εἰς πειρασμόν. Often ὕπαγε and πορεύου. (2) The manner or the character of the action may be denoted (cf. § 327): 1 P 4: 15 μή τις ὑμῶν πασχέτω ὡς φονεύς etc. (3) Something already existing is to continue (in prohibitions: is to stop): H 13: 18 προσεύχεσθε περὶ ἡμῶν ('continue to pray')· πειθόμεθα γὰρ ('we persuade ourselves, we may tell ourselves confidently' [πεποίθαμεν only SᶜCᶜDᵇᐟᶜK al.]) ὅτι ('that...'); then v. 19 περισσοτέρως δὲ παρακαλῶ τοῦτο ποιῆσαι = ποιήσατε περισσοτέρως, i.e. this (more intense praying) is something which had not been taking place. Lk 8: 52 ἔκλαιον...ὁ δὲ εἶπεν· μὴ κλαίετε. It is, of course, also iterative (examples in § 337).

(1) Πορεύου is used at times even where the destination is stated: A 22: 10 ἀναστὰς πορεύου ('go on your way') εἰς Δαμασκόν ('to Damascus'), κἀκεῖ etc.; cf. 8: 26, 10: 20. Mt 25: 9 πορεύεσθε πρὸς τοὺς πωλοῦντας ('here and there, wherever you may find one') καὶ ἀγοράσατε (goal) ἑαυταῖς; cf. 25: 41 (a punctuation mark is to be placed after κατηραμένοι). Cf. Epict. 1.25.10 πορεύου πρὸς τὸν Ἀχιλλέα καὶ ἀπόσπασον τὴν Βρισηΐδα. Lk 5: 24 πορεύου εἰς τὸν οἶκόν σου (more direction than goal; whether he arrives or not is beside the point); Jn 20: 17. On the other hand πορεύθητι A 9: 11, 28: 26 OT, Mt 8: 9 = Lk 7: 8 (πορεύου DX in Lk. Command of the centurion to his soldier; it is a question of coming or going in itself. Ἔρχου in the same vs. could mean 'come with me' [cf. Jn 1: 46 ἔρχου καὶ ἴδε, v. 39, 11: 34] or 'come back' [as the passage from Epict. referred to above continues: πορεύομαι. 'ἔρχου'. ἔρχομαι]. Ἐλθέ Mt 14: 29 means 'come [back] *here*'; also Jn 4: 16 and Homil Clem 9.21 in quoting Mt 8: 9).

(2) 1 C 7: 36 ὃ θέλει ποιείτω...γαμείτωσαν (cf. 37 f.): it is a question of the quality of his behavior: improper—sinful or not—good, better.

(3) Jn 20: 17 μή μου ἅπτου (which therefore has already happened or has been attempted). Lk 8: 50 πίστευσον BL (-ευε rell.) = Mk 5: 36 πίστευε. Often

μὴ φοβοῦ, φοβεῖσθε ('don't be so afraid [as you just were]') Lk 5: 10, 8: 50, Mk 5: 36, 6: 50 etc. Mt 1: 20 μὴ φοβηθῇς is different: 'do not forbear out of fear'. Ja 1: 7 μὴ οἰέσθω 'let him stop thinking', Jn 5: 45 μὴ δοκεῖτε 'stop thinking'; but 2 C 11: 16 μή τίς με δόξῃ 'let no one get the idea...', where the notion cannot yet have been entertained; cf. Mt 3: 9, 5: 17, 10: 34 'don't get the notion'. Φέρε, φέρετε 'bring' is a special case (always pres. impera. in the simple verb except for Jn 21: 10 ἐνέγκατε); pres. impera. is used for the aor. as in class., since this verb has no aor. stem (ἔφερα is the aor. in MGr). The two imperatives are, however, distinguished in compounds: Mt 8: 4 προσένεγκε τὸ δῶρον (a direction as to *what* is to be done), 5: 24 διαλλάγηθι...καὶ τότε ἐλθὼν πρόσφερε τὸ δῶρόν σου (a direction as to *how* and under what circumstances it may be carried out; 'then you *may* bring'; at the same time also 'resume bringing').—Rob. 890; Moule 20f.

337. The aorist imperative (subjunctive) can (1) express the coming about of conduct which contrasts with prior conduct; in this case it is ingressive: Ja 4: 9 ταλαιπωρήσατε καὶ πενθήσατε· καὶ κλαύσατε...μεταστραφήτω...(10) ταπεινώθητε '*become* wretched' etc. (2) It is difficult to distinguish in individual cases the effective use from the complexive (commandment in the strict sense, *infra* (3)): Ja 5: 7 μακροθυμήσατε ἕως τῆς παρουσίας τοῦ κυρίου (the command applies categorically until the end without reference to the interval; however it can also be referred to (1), cf. *v.* 8 μακροθυμήσατε καὶ ὑμεῖς, στηρίξατε τὰς καρδίας ὑμῶν). (3) Categorical prohibitions readily take the aorist (complexive): Mt 7: 6 μὴ δῶτε τὸ ἅγιον τοῖς κυσίν, μηδὲ βάλητε etc. (4) The regular use of the aorist imperative in prayers and greetings is also complexive. All petitions in the Lord's Prayer are in the aorist except Lk 11: 3 τὸν ἄρτον...δίδου (SD δός, as in Mt, is spurious) ἡμῖν τὸ καθ' ἡμέραν (i.e. iterative; D σήμερον as in Mt). It is always ἀσπάσασθε; also 3 Jn 15 ἄσπασαι according to S (ἀσπάζου also occasionally in the papyri).

(1) Thus R 13: 13 περιπατήσωμεν with reference to the commencement of this way of life; cf. *vv.* 12, 14. Περιπατεῖν (and στοιχεῖν) appears in admonitions usually in the pres. (1 C 7: 17, G 5: 16, E 4: 17, 5: 2, 8, C 2: 6, 4: 5, 1 Th 4: 12; G 5: 25, Ph 3: 16); but where the *new* life of the Christian, corresponding to the divine call which creates a new beginning, is meant, the aor. is used: R 6: 4 ἵνα ἐν καινότητι ζωῆς περιπατήσωμεν (cf. in the same passage *v.* 13 παραστήσατε, whereas before that μηδὲ παριστάνετε and in *v.* 12 μὴ βασιλευέτω 'let not sin reign *any more*'),

E 2: 10, 4: 1, C 1: 10 (in a similar passage in 1 Th 2: 12 v.l. περιπατεῖν and -τῆσαι).—Κρατεῖν 'hold fast' with this meaning one of the characteristic marks of Hellenistic speech (Wackernagel, Homer 192) (apart from κρατοῦσιν Mk 14: 51, which is a historical pres. for an ingressive aor.), κρατῆσαι 'seize'. Thus e.g. κρατεῖτε 2 Th 2: 15, but κρατήσατε Mt 26: 48; only in Rev 2: 25 is (ὃ ἔχετε) κρατήσατε not ingressive, but perhaps complexive-terminative. Obviously φοβηθῶμεν οὖν τὸν θεόν (which we have not done until now: ὁρῶ γάρ τινας ἀτελεῖς τοῦ πρὸς αὐτὸν φόβου πλεῖστα ἁμαρτάνοντας precedes [17.4]; therefore 'let us begin to fear') Homil Clem 17.12.5 is ingressive (for which elsewhere φοβεῖσθαι is nearly always used, as in 11.2ff.). Cf. in the NT H 4: 1 φοβηθῶμεν οὖν etc. (to be translated in the same way), Rev 14: 7. In Hermas Man 7.1ff. φοβήθητι τὸν κύριον καὶ φύλασσε τὰς ἐντολὰς αὐτοῦ...τὸν δὲ διάβολον μὴ φοβηθῇς...φοβήθητι δὲ τὰ ἔργα τοῦ διαβόλου, everywhere concerning the adoption of a basic viewpoint; but then 4: ἐὰν ('as often') θέλῃς τὸ πονηρὸν ἐργάσασθαι, φοβοῦ τὸν κύριον, and again: φοβήθητι οὖν τὸν κύριον καὶ ζήσῃ αὐτῷ, καὶ ὅσοι ἂν φοβηθῶσιν αὐτόν...ζήσονται. Man 1.2 πίστευσον αὐτῷ καὶ φοβήθητι αὐτόν...φοβηθεὶς δὲ ἐγκράτευσαι.

(2) Mt 5: 39 ὅστις σε ῥαπίσει...στρέψον, likewise *v.* 40, then 42 τῷ αἰτοῦντί σε δός, καί...μὴ ἀποστραφῇς, however a pres. iterative is also possible: Lk 6: 29f. τῷ τύπτοντί σε ἐπὶ τὴν σιαγόνα πάρεχε καὶ τὴν ἄλλην...παντὶ αἰτοῦντί σε δίδου, καί...μὴ ἀπαίτει; cf. Mt 5: 12 with Lk 6: 23. 1 T 6: 20 (2 T 1: 14) τὴν παραθήκην φύλαξον (cf. 1 T 5: 21 ἵνα ταῦτα φυλάξῃς, 2 T 1: 12 φυλάξαι, 1 Jn 5: 21 φυλάξατε ἑαυτά, 1 T 6: 14 τηρῆσαι...μέχρι..., 1 Th 5: 23) 'until the end', definitively; but 1 T 5: 22 σεαυτὸν ἁγνὸν τήρει ('henceforth, in all things'), cf. Ja 1: 27 ἄσπιλον ἑαυτὸν τηρεῖν of the way of pure religion. Further, 2 T 4: 2, 5 κήρυξον ἐπίστηθι ἔλεγξον etc., κακοπάθησον ποίησον πληροφόρησον (until the end, i.e. until the appearance of Christ, cf. 1, 5, 6). So the striking aorists in 1 P are to be interpreted acc. to (1) and (2): 1: 13 τελείως ἐλπίσατε 'set your hope', 22 ἀγαπήσατε 'direct your love'; 17 ἀναστράφητε (until the end), 5: 2 ποιμάνατε (until the appearance of Christ); 2: 17 πάντας τιμήσατε 'give to each his honor', completed in the pres. τὴν ἀδελφότητα ἀγαπᾶτε etc. 2 Clem 8.6 τηρήσατε τὴν σάρκα ἁγνήν..., ἵνα τὴν ζωὴν ἀπολάβωμεν, cf. 4 τηρήσαντες...λημψόμεθα ζωήν. Herm Man 8.2 first τὸ πονηρὸν ἐγκρατεύου, then taken as a whole ἐγκράτευσαι ἀπὸ πονηρίας πάσης; 3ff. again the pres. until 6 ἐγκράτευσαι ἀπὸ πάντων τούτων (recapitulation), cf. 12 ἐὰν τὸ πονηρὸν μὴ ποιῇς καὶ ἐγκρατεύσῃ ἀπ' αὐτοῦ. So also 9.12 δούλευε τῇ πίστει καὶ ἀπὸ τῆς διψυχίας ἀπόσχου. - In Vis 5.7 the corresponding usage in the hypothetical subj. is found: ἐάν...φυλάξητε καί...πορευθῆτε (cf. *supra* (1) περιπατεῖν καὶ ἐργάσησθε..., ἀπολήμψεσθε....

(3) Mt 6: 34 μὴ μεριμνήσητε εἰς τὴν αὔριον, cf. v. 31, 10: 19, but 6: 25 μὴ μεριμνᾶτε 'do not have such cares'; cf. Lk 12: 22 μὴ 3ητεῖτε, 29. Jn 3: 7 μὴ θαυμάσῃς 'don't marvel at all' (which he had done in v. 4). Cf. Mlt. 129f. [202, 204]. Lk 14: 8 μὴ κατακλιθῇς, but 𝔓⁴⁵ -κλ(ε)ίνου.

(4) The aor. impera. is used almost exclusively in early liturgies (Mlt. 173 [273]), and preponderates in class. (Schwyzer II 341). The Ptol. pap. on the whole as in the NT; the aor. is regularly used in prayers (specific petitions). The aor. is more definite, therefore used especially in official edicts and among equals. In formulae of greeting only the pres. is used: Mayser II 1, 145f., 148. W. Beschewliew, Der Gebrauch des Imp. aor. and praes. im altgr. Gebet (Annuaire de l'Univ. de Sofia, Fac. hist.-philol. XXIII 4, Sofia, 1927) shows that the pres. impera. in prayers (petitions for extended favor or repeated response) is more frequent than was supposed.

The distinction in other uses between the present subjunctive (durative, iterative) and aorist subjunctive (punctiliar, ingressive, complexive) requires no special remarks. The optative is too rare in the NT to permit an investigation of the use of the tenses.

(D) The Present and Aorist Infinitives

338. (1) The distinction between the two forms is the same as in the imperative (§335) and on the whole easy to grasp. (2) Some verbs by virtue of their nature prefer an aorist dependent infinitive: thus θέλειν (Attic likewise with the corresponding βούλεσθαι; the volition is usually directed toward the action itself or to its consummation), δύνασθαι, δυνατός, κελεύειν etc. (3) Μέλλω most often takes a future infinitive in classical. This future infinitive after μέλλω is confined in the NT, however, to Acts (§350); elsewhere as in the vernacular (Witkowski, Bericht 119) it is replaced by the present (less often by the aorist with punctiliar action). 'Ελπίζειν also takes the aorist infinitive in the NT (instead of future), correctly so far as the action is concerned.—Mayser II 1, 150–68.

(1) Also in R 14: 21 καλὸν τὸ μὴ φαγεῖν κρέα μηδὲ πιεῖν οἶνον μηδὲ ἐν ᾧ ὁ ἀδελφός σου προσκόπτει the aor. is to be taken strictly: 'it is good not to eat meat *for once* (in a specific instance) if it might cause offense'; it is not a question of continuous abstention. Lk 5: 7 ὥστε βυθίζεσθαι αὐτά 'so that they were in danger of sinking' (Zerwick, Graec. bibl. 64).

(2) Exceptions such as θέλω εἶναι, τί πάλιν θέλετε ἀκούειν (-οῦσαι D) Jn 9: 27 ('to hear the same thing endlessly'), ἐκέλευον ῥαβδίζειν A 16: 22 (linear; §328)

are easily explained. Hesseling, ByzZ 20 (1911) 147–64: verbs of 'beginning, stopping, being accustomed, continuing' take a dependent inf. in the pres. in Greek ('to begin, with a continuing activity'); but the translators of the OT have a preference for the aor. inf.; but ἄρχεσθαι takes only the pres. inf. in the NT. Cf. Lat. and Germ. (Stolz-Schmalz, Lat. Gr.⁵ 551 §143c).

(3) Pres. (often also in class.) e.g. μέλλει παραδίδοσθαι Mt 17: 22, for which simply παραδίδοται is also used (§323(1)). Aor. (class. also infrequently) only R 8: 18 and G 3: 23 μέλλουσαν ἀποκαλυφθῆναι (on the other hand ἀποκαλύπτεσθαι 1 P 5: 1), Rev 3: 2, 16, 12: 4 (A 12: 6 AB, Lk 20: 36 D Marcion). In the pap. the aor. inf. is used most often with μέλλειν, the pres. inf. belongs to the vulgar idiom, and the future inf. is found only occasionally in official documents; Mayser II 1, 166. Similarly in the LXX: Job 24: 23 ἐλπιζέτω ὑγιασθῆναι; 2 Macc 6: 20 τοὺς ὑπομένοντας ἀμύνασθαι (v.l. -εσθαι); 11: 14 ἔπεισε συλλύεσθαι (v.l. -σεσθαι). In 2 Macc 15: 7 πεποιθὼς μετὰ πάσης ἐλπίδος... τεύξασθαι (v.l. -εσθαι) the aor. has been questioned by Wackernagel, ThLZ 1908, 636, because this sigmatic aor. would be unique in Greek. 9: 22 ἔχων... ἐλπίδα ἐκφεύξεσθαι (v.l. -ασθαι) is an exact parallel in that the sigmatic aor. is almost wanting in Greek. In 3 Macc 2: 33 Rahlfs and Hanhart, LXX 3 Macc follow the minority in reading εὐελπίδες... τεύξασθαι (A pc., -ξεσθαι rell.) in conformity with 2 Macc 5: 17. Katz, ZNW 51 (1960) 22 sees in these aorists late scribal blunders comparable with επελευσασθαι 2 Macc 9: 17 A 347 (Mayser I 2², 164.15ff., II 1, 220 gives exx. of the same confusion in the pap. beginning ii BC end) and exx. in Thack. 287 εσασθαι, παρεξασθαι.—Rob. 856ff., 890f.

(E) The Present and Aorist Participles

339. Participles originally had no temporal function, but denoted only the *Aktionsart*; their temporal relation to the finite verb was derived from the context. Since, however, a participle expressing the notion of completion often preceded the finite verb (Kieckers, IF 35 [1915] 49ff.) so that the sequence normally was: the completion of the action denoted by the participle, then the action of the finite verb, the idea of relative past time became associated to a certain degree with the aorist participle: ταῦτ' εἰπὼν ἀπῆλθεν = ταῦτα εἶπε καὶ ('and after that') ἀπῆλθεν. The same applies to the participle coming after the verb: Mk 1: 31 ἤγειρεν αὐτὴν κρατήσας τῆς χειρός. Η 6: 10 διακονήσαντες τοῖς ἁγίοις καὶ διακονοῦντες: the present and aorist participles could the more readily be used with temporal nuances because the future participle (like the future infinitive and optative) always expressed relatively future time. The notion of relative past time, however, is not at all necessarily inherent in the aorist participle. (1) The element of past time is absent from the aorist participle especially if its action is identical with that of an aorist finite verb: A 1: 24 προσευξάμενοι εἶπαν = προσεύξαντο καὶ εἶπαν = προσεύξαντο εἰπόντες (cf. Mk 14: 39). (2) The present participle can also denote a relatively future action with various nuances: (a) a complexive aorist may be supplemented by a present participle *describing the same action*: A 18: 23 ἐξῆλθεν (from Antioch) διερχόμενος τὴν Γαλατικὴν χώραν (= καὶ διήρχετο, 'that is to say he traversed...'); (b) 21: 3 ἐκεῖσε τὸ πλοῖον ἦν ἀποφορτιζόμενον τὸν γόμον (= ἔμελλεν ἀποφορτίζεσθαι: literally 'the ship had the characteristic of...'?); Jn 17: 20, Lk 1: 35, 2: 34, 14: 31, A 21: 2, 3, 26: 17, Lk 22: 19f.; (c) instead of a future participle of purpose: A 15: 27 ἀπεστάλκαμεν ἀπαγγέλλοντας 'we have sent them (they have already departed) and they are bringing the message with them'. (3) Furthermore, the present participle is occasionally used, as in classical, for something which happened previously (representing the imperfect): πωλοῦντες ἔφερον A 4: 34 (= ἐπώλουν καὶ ἔφερον), ὁ πλανῶν Rev 20: 10 (= ὃς ἐπλάνα), 14: 4 οἱ ἀκολουθοῦντες 'who (always) followed' (but οὐκ ἐμολύνθησαν and ἠγοράσθησαν in the same verse).

(1) Mt 27: 4 ἥμαρτον παραδοὺς ('in that I') αἷμα ἀθῷον, A 10: 33 καλῶς ἐποίησας παραγενόμενος; so also ἀποκριθεὶς εἶπεν and the like (§§ 419(3, 4); 420(1, 3)). The aor. ptcp. is frequent in the pap. with καλῶς ποιήσεις and the like; UPZ ι 6.30 (163 BC) ἀπεκρίθησαν φήσαντες; Mayser II 1, 173ff. A future meaning of the aor. ptcp. is often assumed for A 25: 13 κατήντησαν...ἀσπασάμενοι (since the v.l. ἀσπασόμενοι is found in Ψ et al.) (Chambers, JTS 24 [1923] 183–7 [for two references in the LXX and three in the NT]; Howard, JTS 24 [1923] 403–6; Rob., JTS 25 [1924] 286–9; Harding, Trans. Am. Phil. Ass. 57 [1926] p. xxxix [only for A 25: 13]); yet the meaning could perhaps be: 'in connection with which they greeted him'; ἀσπασάμενοι = καὶ ἠσπάσαντο. Zerwick, Graec. bibl. 61 n. 3: Philostr., VA 1.222 οἱ στρουθοί...οὓς ὁ δράκων μὲν...ἐδαίσατο ὀκτὼ ὄντας, ἐννάτην ἐπ᾽ αὐτοῖς τὴν μητέρα ἑλών 'whereby it seized...' (cf. Hom., Il. 2. 305ff.: the mother last); which leads Moule 202 to suggest: 'thus (thereby) making a complimentary visit'. Jos., Ant. 6.377 πένθος...ἦγον κοπτόμενοι καὶ θρηνοῦντες...μήτε τροφῆς μήτε πότου γευσάμενοι 'whereby they tasted

neither food nor drink' (Katz). Cf. Mlt. 132 [214]; Rob. 863 'by way of salutation [coincident action]'. An aor. for a future ptcp. is found also occasionally elsewhere; thus Wilcken, Chr. 26 II 32 (156 AD), ἀπέστειλε...κοινολογησάμενον (Lucianic v.l.; the majority have -σόμ-) LXX 1 Macc 15: 28. Jn 11: 2 ἦν δὲ Μαριὰμ ἡ ἀλείψασα τὸν κύριον μύρῳ is understandable: 'M. was ("is" would be more exact) the one who is *known* (cf. Mt 26: 13) to have anointed him'; for that which in the past was still future ('who later [12: 1ff.] anointed, who was to anoint'), the future tense was not common in Greek, so the author makes his parenthetical statement from his own point in time. Likewise Mt 10: 4 Ἰούδας ὁ καὶ παραδοὺς αὐτόν = ὃς καὶ παρέδωκεν αὐτόν Mk 3: 19.— The aor. ptcp. (after the main verb) in the continuation of the narrative: A. Wifstrand, Eranos 54 (1956) 123–37 (mostly extra-biblical and in part new exx.).

(2) (a) A 14: 21f. ὑπέστρεψαν...ἐπιστηρίζοντες. (b) 21: 2 εὑρόντες πλοῖον διαπερῶν (cf. §323(3)) εἰς Φοινίκην. Cf. ὁ ἐρχόμενος = ὁ μέλλων ἔρχεσθαι and παραδίδοται = μέλλει παραδίδοσθαι (§323(1)). Jn 5: 45 ἔστιν ὁ κατηγορῶν (like κατηγορήσω just before, therefore the end of the age is meant), from which UGosp 1.13 (but with νῦν κατηγορεῖται in 18 referring to the present). The timelessness of the Semitic ptcp. facilitated such use of the pres. ptcp. (Joachim Jeremias, TW IV 871 n. 216). POxy II 275.10 (*A* hands over his son to *B*) διακονοῦντα καὶ ποιοῦντα πάντα τὰ ἐπιτασσόμενα. (c) A 21: 16 συνῆλθον...ἄγοντες; cf. also Thuc. e.g. 7.25.9 ἔπεμψαν ἀγγέλλοντας. Mayser II 1, 170f. E.g. Preisigke, Sammelbuch 3776 (i BC) παρεγενήθην προσκυνῶν, PSI IV 406.23 (iii BC) ἀπάγεται εἰς φυλακὴν ἡμέρας ζ ἐν πέδαις ὤν, POxy I 120.11 (iv AD) ἀπόστιλόν μοί τινα...παραμένοντά μοι.

(3) E 4: 28 ὁ κλέπτων ('who stole up to now') μηκέτι κλεπτέτω; also τυφλὸς ὢν ἄρτι βλέπω Jn 9: 25. The conative impf. also can be represented by the pres. ptcp.: Mt 27: 40 ὁ καταλύων...καὶ οἰκοδομῶν = ὃς κατέλυες...ᾠκοδόμει...('who would destroy... build...'); 23: 13 τοὺς εἰσερχομένους. Mayser II 1, 170.—On the whole Rob. 858–64; 891f.; Moule 99–103; Burton 53–70.

(F) The Perfect

340. Introduction. The perfect combines in itself, so to speak, the present and the aorist in that it denotes the *continuance* of *completed action*: before the form καθέστᾰκα 'I have placed' arose, the same idea was expressed by ἔχω (present) καταστήσας (aorist) (Dem. 19.288), and a perfect like πεπληρώκατε A 5: 28 may be resolved into ἐπληρώσατε καὶ νῦν πλήρης ἐστίν. The form is still in full use in the NT and conforms almost entirely to late classical (somewhat expanded from earlier use) and Hellenistic usage. The perfect was dropped in later Greek (MGr retains only εὕρηκα but as an aorist) after it had earlier competed in vain with the aorist as a narrative tense.—J. C. Trotter, The Use of the Perfect Tense in the Pauline Epistles (Diss. Southern Baptist Sem. 1951).

Chantraine 214–52 (Le parfait à l'époque hellénistique). Hesseling (Mededeel. Akad. Amsterdam, Afd. Letterk. 65 A 6, 1928): the perf. is more subjective than the aor., therefore used more by rhetoricians than by historians, more by John than by the Synoptics (Chantraine 229–32: on account of the solemn and emphatic style of John). Mayser II 1, 176–207.

341. The present perfect. The perfect with certain verbs has wholly the sense of a present (as in classical). This is the case with ἕστηκα (§ 342(3)), πέποιθα, μέμνημαι (μιμνήσκομαι only H 2: 6 OT, 13: 3); similarly when the verb expresses a state or condition: τέθνηκα 'am dead', πέπεισμαι 'am convinced' R 8: 38 etc.; and πεπλήρωται in Lk 4: 21 (Debrunner with Horst in TW v 554 n. 108).

Ἤλπικα εἰς τινας Jn 5: 45 etc. 'have set my hope on = I hope' (cf. πέποιθα), but stronger than ἐλπίζω by virtue of the continuing character of the hope formed. Ἥγημαι 'consider, regard' (class.) A 26: 2 (Paul before Agrippa), but with the usual meaning in Ph 3: 7 'have considered, counted'. Κέκραγεν Jn 1: 15 perhaps from literary idiom instead of Hell. κράζει, cf. §§ 321 and 101, where κεκράξομαι ἐκέκραξα are also noted. Κέκτημαι does not appear in the NT, only κτήσασθαι and κτᾶσθαι.—Rob. 894f.

342. The perfect used to denote a continuing effect on subject or object (extensive perfect, Rob. 895f.). (1) On the subject: 2 T 4: 7 τὸν καλὸν ἀγῶνα ἠγώνισμαι, τὸν δρόμον τετέλεκα, τὴν πίστιν τετήρηκα, that is, up to now, from which the lasting result mentioned in v. 8 is derived: λοιπὸν ἀπόκειταί μοι ὁ τῆς δικαιοσύνης στέφανος. Aorist and perfect are clearly distinguished in 1 C 15: 3f. ὅτι Χριστὸς ἀπέθανεν...καὶ ὅτι ἐτάφη καὶ ὅτι ἐγήγερται τῇ ἡμέρᾳ τῇ τρίτῃ. J. Jeremias, Die Abendmahlsworte Jesu 73 [The Eucharistic Words of Jesus 130]: ἐγήγερται passive to avoid the divine name (Aramaic). (2) The effect on the subject is also emphasized in ἑώρακα: A 22: 15 ἔσῃ μάρτυς...ὧν ἑώρακας καὶ ἤκουσας: that Paul had seen the Lord is what establishes him permanently as an apostle (that is why Paul himself says in 1 C 9: 1 οὐκ εἰμὶ ἀπόστολος; οὐχὶ Ἰησοῦν... ἑώρακα;), whereas hearing the voice (A 22: 7 ff.) is

far less essential. (3) 'He is risen' is almost always ἐγήγερται: Mk 6: 14, Paul often in 1 C 15, 2 T 2: 8, never ἀνέστηκεν (in spite of ἀνάστασις) because ἕστηκα had acquired too much of a present meaning (cf. the new form στήκω § 73). (4) Continuing effect on the object: A 21: 28 Ἕλληνας εἰσήγαγεν εἰς τὸ ἱερὸν καὶ κεκοινώνηκεν τὸν ἅγιον τόπον: their entrance *in the past* produced defilement as a *lasting effect*. (5) The perfect with reference to an OT event can mean that this event still retains its (exemplary) meaning: G 4: 23 ὁ ἐκ τῆς παιδίσκης κατὰ σάρκα γεγέννηται approximately = γέγραπται ὅτι ἐγεννήθη.

(1) The effect need not always be expressed even though it is present: C 1: 16 ἐκτίσθη–ἔκτισται, Mt 25: 20 ὁ τὰ πέντε τάλαντα λαβών–24 ὁ τὸ ἓν τάλαντον εἰληφώς ('the possessor'). Lk 12: 58 ἀπηλλάχθαι (mid.) '(to become) and remain free', cf. POxy VI 889.26, 31 (iii BC) ἀξιοῖ (δύναται) ἀπηλλάχθαι; Büchsel, TW I 253. Jn 1: 3 χωρὶς αὐτοῦ ἐγένετο οὐδὲ ἓν ὃ γέγονεν ('of the things created = existing'; however, Schwartz, NGG 1908, 534f. puts a full stop before ὃ like cod. W, the old versions and Greek Fathers). Effect not expressed: Mt 23: 2 ἐκάθισαν (they are still sitting there; cf. H 1: 3, 8: 1, 10: 12 ἐκάθισεν; κεκάθικεν only 12: 2; Rev 3: 21 POxy VIII 1080 (iv AD) νενείκηκα καὶ κεκάθικα but corrected by a later hand to the aor. of the other MSS); cf. § 333 and class. exx. like the saying of Eur. (Frag. 638 Nauck²) τίς οἶδεν εἰ τὸ ζῆν μέν ἐστι κατθανεῖν (= τεθνάναι), τὸ κατθανεῖν δὲ ζῆν κάτω νομίζεται; Mk 3: 21 ἐξέστη 'he has become mad' (acc. to the sense 'he *is* out of his mind' would also be possible; D* ἐξέστᾱται αὐτούς 'he has made them mad', W ἐξήρτηνται αὐτοῦ 'they are attached to him'). Cf. 2 C 5: 13 ἐξέστημεν 'we yielded to ecstasy'. Mt 1: 15 etc. ἤγγικεν 'is near'. Mk 11: 21 ἐξήρανται (ἐξηράνθη DNΣΨ), 12: 43 βέβληκεν (ἔβαλεν SB al.).

(2) Also Jn 3: 32 ὃ ἑώρακεν καὶ ἤκουσεν puts the chief emphasis on seeing (the text is less certain however), but 5: 37, 1 Jn 1: 1, 3 ἑώρακα and ἀκήκοα co-ordinated, where hearing is equally essential. Ἑώρακα also Lk 24: 23, Jn 19: 35, 20: 18 and often; seldom ἀκήκοα, not at all in Mt, Mk, Lk. Also cf. ἅ τε ἤκουσεν καὶ ἑώρακεν Homil Clem 1.9. Perf. 'I have seen' in reports of dreams (Mayser II 1, 141); Plato, Crito 44A ἐνυπνίου, ὃ ἑώρακα.

(3) Ἠγέρθη (effect not expressed) Mk 6: 16 and v.l. 6: 14.

(4) Jn 19: 22 ἃ γέγραφα γέγραφα (the 1st perf. is more aoristic; cf. ἐγράψαμεν–γεγράφαμεν LXX 1 Macc 11: 31). H 11: 28 πίστει πεποίηκεν τὸ πάσχα (permanent institution, cf. v. 3 and ἐγκεκαίνισται 9: 18, but s. also *infra* (5)). Homil Clem 12.11.1 ταῦτα εἴ τις πεπόνθει (*passus esset*)..., οἷα ὁ τούτου πέπονθεν πατήρ (who is forgotten; *passus est*).

(5) G 3: 18 κεχάρισται (and believers still possess it); H 11: 17 προσενήνοχεν (an abiding example); likewise 12: 3 ἀναλογίσασθε τὸν τοιαύτην ὑπομεμενηκότα...ἀντιλογίαν (an abiding ex. from the life of Jesus; in v. 2 ὑπέμεινεν σταυρόν). Cf. Mlt. 142, 143f., 248 [223].

343. Perfect for the aorist. There are scattered traces of the late use of the perfect in narrative (§340): (1) unquestionable examples in Rev: 5: 7 ἦλθεν καὶ εἴληφεν, cf. 8: 5. (2) In Paul: 2 C 2: 13 ἔσχηκα in historical narration, 12: 17 ἀπέσταλκα among nothing but aorists (ἔπεμψα DE, ἀπέστειλα several minusc.), 11: 25 νυχθήμερον ἐν τῷ βυθῷ πεποίηκα alongside aorists only and without adequate reason. J 12: 29 𝔓[66] ἐλάλησεν; pm. λελάληκεν. (3) Γέγονεν for ἐγένετο (Burton 43) Mt 25: 6 (B ἐγένετο), 17: 2 (according to Chr), γεγόναμεν ApocP 11 (for papyri s. Mlt. 146 [229f.] and an example from an inscrip. 239 n. on 168 [263]).

Hatzid. 204; Dieterich 235; Mlt. 141–7 [222–31]; Psaltes 229f.; Eakin, Aorists and Perfects in First Century Papyri (AJTh 20 [1916] 266–73; aoristic use in pap. of i AD only in the cases of εἴρηκα and εἴληφα); Mayser II 1, 140f.; Chantraine 233–45; Meuwese 87ff.; Rob. 898–901. Εἴληφα and ἔσχηκα in pap. and LXX: Thack. 24; Huber 74.
(1) Rev 7: 14 εἴρηκα (046 εἶπον), cf. 19: 3, i.e. in forms in which reduplication is not clearly indicated. Mk 11: 2 κεκάθικεν 'has sat' (ἐκάθισεν SBCZΨΘ). Certain aoristic use likewise in Herm Vis 1.1.1 πέπρακεν (cf. Mt 13: 46 πέπρακεν καὶ ἠγόρασεν), 3.1.2 ὦπται S (A ὤφθη), Homil Clem 2.53 ἐγήγερται, GP 23 δεδώκασιν, cf. 31.
(2) Ἔσχηκεν 2 C 7: 5 (ἔσχεν 𝔓[46]BFGK) and ἐσχήκαμεν 1: 9, R 5: 2 can be taken as correct perfects, but not Mk 5: 15 τὸν ἐσχηκότα τὸν λεγιῶνα. Ἀπέσταλκα (often in Koine) also A 7: 35 -κεν, where it may well be incorrect for -στειλεν CHP al.
(3) Mt 1: 22 = 21: 4 can be interpreted as perfective, although Jn (19:36) uses ἐγένετο analogously; cf. Lightfoot, A Fresh Revision of the English NT 100f.; γέγονεν Mt 25: 56 is quite correct. Mt 24: 21 οὐκ ἐγένετο SDΘ (οὐ γέγονεν BLWZ) = Mk 13: 19 οὐ γέγονεν (D οὐκ ἐγένοντο) from Da 12: 1, where the LXX has οὐκ ἐγενήθη ἀφ' οὗ ἐγενήθησαν, Theod. οὐ γέγονεν ἀφ' οὗ γεγένηται. Acc. to Chantraine 235f. this aor. is a purism in Mt. However cf. ἡλίκος οὐδεὶς πω γέγονεν Dem. 1.9, likewise Isocr. 15.30 (Oguse, Rev. crit. 64 [1930] 203).—Lk ἑωράκασιν 9: 36 (cf. Jn 3: 32? §342(2)).

344. The perfect in general assertions or imaginary examples is rarely used, as in classical: futuristic e.g. 1 Jn 2: 5 ὃς ἂν τηρῇ...

τετελείωται, Ja 2: 10 ὅστις τηρήσῃ...γέγονεν (cf. 11), R 14: 23 etc. These are entirely in conformity with classical usage (Aristoph., Lys. 595 ὁ μὲν ἥκων γάρ, κἂν ᾖ πολιός, ταχὺ...γεγάμηκεν). The aorist may also be so used (§333(2)).

Gnomic: Mt 13: 46 πέπρακεν (ἐπώλησεν D) πάντα καὶ ἠγόρασεν αὐτόν, in which case there is a strong suspicion that the aor. (which for πιπράσκω does not exist) and the perf. are incorrectly mixed; cf. §343(1). Likewise Ja 1: 24 κατενόησεν καὶ ἀπελήλυθεν καὶ εὐθέως ἐπελάθετο.—Rob. 897.

345. The perfect used to express relative time. Verbs of perception take a following perfect for a pluperfect in the same way as they do a present for an imperfect (§324): Mk 5: 33 εἰδυῖα ὃ γέγονεν αὐτῇ, Lk 20: 19 D ἔγνωσαν ὅτι εἴρηκεν (al. εἶπεν = Mk 12: 12); likewise after a verb of emotion: A 10: 45 ἐξέστησαν ὅτι ἐκκέχυται.

The plupf., on the other hand: Mk 15: 10 ἐγίνωσκεν ὅτι παραδεδώκεισαν (but DHSW παρέδωκαν as in Mt 27: 18; AE al. παρέδωκαν). A 19: 32 οὐκ ᾔδεισαν τίνος ἕνεκεν συνεληλύθεισαν (attraction of the tense, cf. §330 end). Acc. to D also A 14: 23 παρέθεντο τῷ κυρίῳ, εἰς ὃν πεπιστεύκασιν (vg crediderunt); Lk 9: 36 οὐδενὶ ἀπήγγειλαν οὐδὲν ὧν ἑωράκασιν (D ἐθεάσαντο) by analogy with the equivalent phrase οὐδενὶ ἀπ., ὅτι ταῦτα ἑωράκασιν. Jn 12: 1 Λάζαρος ὁ τεθνηκώς AD 'who had been dead'.

346. Concerning the moods of the perfect (cf. §352) it is only necessary to remark that the imperative, apart from ἔρρωσο ἔρρωσθε (formulae; A 15: 29, 23: 30, but not in all witnesses; often in the papyri), and periphrasis with εἶναι (§352), appears only in the emphatic command πεφίμωσο Mk 4: 39 (φιμώθητι 1: 25, Lk 4: 35). Πεφίμωσο as a solemn adjuration (Meillet, Bull. Soc. Ling. 27 [1927] c.-r. 41; Bauer). In Ptolemaic papyri imperative only 3rd person sing. in official decrees (Mayser II 1, 185).—For ἴστε s. §99(2).

(G) The Pluperfect

347. The pluperfect, which naturally did not outlive the perfect, is still a familiar form to the NT writers, although it is not used abundantly. It was used much less often in classical Greek than in Latin, German or English just because it was not used to express relative time. (1) The pluperfect equals the aorist plus the imperfect (cf. the perfect §340): Lk 16: 20 Λάζαρος ἐβέβλητο πρὸς τὸν πυλῶνα αὐτοῦ '(had been prostrated and) lay' (ἐβέβλητο 'he lay ill' Fable of Aesop 284

Halm [ɪ 1, 166 Hausrath]). (2) If an action takes place without a lasting consequence in the subsequent past, the aorist must be employed. (3) The pluperfect has the same range as the perfect (§§341 ff.) between a more or less aoristic meaning. The aoristic meaning predominates e.g. in A 4: 22 ἄνθρωπος ἐφ᾽ ὃν γεγόνει τὸ σημεῖον, but the element of lasting result is also contained therein, and generally there is no encroachment upon the territory of the aorist in the NT.—Mayser ɪɪ 1, 207 ff.; Rob. 903–6.

(1) Jn 11: 44 ἡ ὄψις αὐτοῦ σουδαρίῳ περιεδέδετο, 9: 22 ἤδη γὰρ συνετέθειντο οἱ 'Ιουδαῖοι ('the agreement already existed at that time'), A 14: 26 ἀπέπλευσαν εἰς 'Αντιόχειαν, ὅθεν ἦσαν παραδεδομένοι (which had the effect of causing them to return there).
(2) The plupfs. of the Vulgate in A 14: 27 *venissent–congregasset–fecisset–aperuisset* rest as a rule on the aor.; although there is a durative result, it was unnecessary to emphasize it (cf. §342(1)). Mk 5: 8 ἔλεγεν, Lk 2: 50 (*non intellexerant verbum, quod locutus erat eis*): Zerwick, Graec. bibl. 67.
(3) A 9: 21 ὧδε εἰς τοῦτο ἐληλύθει (Paul to Damascus, words of the Jews) is explained in that this purpose is now a thing of the past so that the perf. was no longer admissible.—For the attraction of tense in συνεληλύθεισαν A 19: 32 s. §345.—Hermas uses the plupf. often for that which is doubly past in imitation of Latin: e.g. Vis 2.1.3 βλέπω... τὴν πρεσβυτέραν, ἣν καὶ πέρυσιν ἑωράκειν (*videram*), likewise ἑωράκειν 3.1.6, Sim 6.1.1; 7.1; 8.1.3; s. also §360(3) on Sim 9.15.6.

(H) The Future

348. Introduction. As remarked above (§318) the future is the only tense which expresses only a level of time and not an *Aktionsart* so that completed and durative action are not distinguished. In MGr the future has been replaced by periphrasis. In the NT the future indicative is still in full use and is not seriously curtailed either by periphrasis (§§352f., 356) or by the present (§323).—Mayser ɪɪ 1, 211–33; Bănescu; Rob. 353–7, 870–6, 888f.; V. W. Searns, The Use of the Future Tense in the NT (Diss. Southern Baptist Sem. 1950).

349. The future indicative is used (1) occasionally as a *gnomic future* in order to express that which is to be expected under certain circumstances (as in classical): R 5: 7 μόλις ὑπὲρ δικαίου τις ἀποθανεῖται; (2) *relatively* in declarative sentences after verbs of believing to denote a time subsequent to the acquisition of belief: Mt 20: 10 ἐνόμισαν ὅτι λήμψονται.

(1) Cf. R 7: 3 χρηματίσει ἐὰν γένηται; ὑπὲρ δικαίου 5: 7 is also = ἐὰν δίκαιος ᾖ.
(2) Cf. the pres. §324, imperf. §330, perf. §345. However, another mode of expression is hardly possible in this case and class. differs only in that after νομίζειν the always relative fut. inf. is used (instead of ὅτι and the indic.).—Jn 21: 19 σημαίνων ποίῳ θανάτῳ δοξάσει τὸν θεόν = ἤμελλεν δοξάζειν, s. 18: 32; class. likewise (or δοξάσοι).—For the modal functions of the fut. indic. s. §§362f.; 365f.; 368f.; 373(2); 375; 378f.; 380(3); 382(4); 383(2).

350. The future infinitive, which expresses *relative* time with reference to the principal action (as do the participle and future optative), has disappeared from the vernacular and is found only in Acts and Hebrews: after μέλλειν A 11: 28, 24: 15, 27: 10 (ἔσεσθαι each time; 3: 3 εἰσιέναι, 20: 7 ἐξιέναι); after ἐλπίζειν 26: 7 B (the others aorist), after ὀμνύναι H 3: 18 (οἶμαι χωρήσειν according to SBC* in the conclusion of the supplementary chapter Jn 21: 25, χωρῆσαι AC²D al. On the Hellenistic confusion of the future and the aorist active infinitives s. Mayser ɪ² 2, 163f.; ɪɪ 1, 219f.; Ursing 55f.; Ghedini, Lett. crist. 308), after μηνύειν A 23: 30 (ἔσεσθαι).

Elsewhere the pres. inf. appears after μέλλειν, less often the aor. (§338(3)), and after ἐλπίζειν (often), προκαταγγέλλειν (A 3: 18), ὀμνύναι (2: 30), προσδοκᾶν (3: 5), ὁμολογεῖν 'to promise' (Mt 14: 7) the aor. inf., which preserves the *Aktionsart* but abandons the future time level. 'Ελπίζω πεφανερῶσθαι 2 C 5: 11 shows a deviation of the conception 'hope' in the direction of 'think', with which both German and English are familiar (likewise class. and pap., Mayser ɪɪ 1, 217f.).

351. The future participle is used (1) equally rarely as a supplement to the main verb (to express purpose) and is virtually limited to Acts; the present infinitive is occasionally used in its place (§339(2c)), and elsewhere the infinitive (1 C 16: 3), a relative clause (4: 17), or some other phrase. (2) The use of the future participle in a more nearly independent position as in 1 C 15: 37 τὸ σῶμα τὸ γενησόμενον is scarcely more extensive (cf. §356).

(1) A 8: 27 ἐληλύθει προσκυνήσων, 22: 5, 24: 11, 17, H 13: 17 ἀγρυπνοῦσιν, ὡς λόγον ἀποδώσοντες, Mk 11: 13 v.l. ὡς εὑρήσων (§425(3)), Mt 27: 49 ἔρχεται σώσων (W σῷζων, S* σῶσαι, D καὶ σώσει). Mayser ɪɪ 1, 220; ɪɪ 3, 57.

(2) A 20: 22 τὰ συναντήσοντα, 1 P 3: 13 τίς ὁ κακώσων ὑμᾶς (= ὅς κακώσει) (cf. § 252 and Mayser II 1, 221), Lk 22: 49 τὸ ἐσόμενον (τὸ γενόμενον D; other witnesses leave the whole out), H 3: 5 τῶν λαληθησομένων (the sole ex. of the fut. pass. ptcp. in the NT); probably also R 8: 34 ὁ κατακρινῶν. Jn 6: 64 παραδώσων, but D παραδιδούς, S μέλλων παραδιδόναι as in 12: 4; Nonnus omits the whole addition καὶ τίς etc. 2 P 2: 13 κομιούμενοι (S*BP ἀδικούμενοι may well be more correct) μισθὸν ἀδικίας 'wronged by the reward which is paid for wrongdoing' (Schrenk, TW I 157). Γενησομένων for γενομένων (v.l. -ναμ-, μελλόντων) H 9: 11 conjectured by Nissen, Philol. 92 (1937) 247.

For the supposed future subjunctive s. § 28. The simple future perfect (third future) does not appear in the NT; cf. § 352.

(I) Periphrastic Conjugations

Raderm.[2] 102; Regard 111–85; Bauer εἰμί 4; Mayser II 1, 223 ff.; Moule 16 ff.; Rob. 826, 878 f., 887 f., 889, 906; Björck, Die periphr. Konstruktionen.

352. In the perfect system. The classical language had already made use of εἶναι with the perfect participle as periphrasis for the perfect, pluperfect and future perfect active and passive, which under certain circumstances was necessary, but which was extended far beyond these limits. The cases in the NT where periphrasis is necessary include the future perfect and (as already in classical in the passive) the perfect subjunctive (optative), except of course for εἰδῶ (subjunctive of οἶδα); in the other forms it matters little whether one writes ἐπεγέγραπτο (A 17: 23) or ἦν γεγραμμένον (Jn 19: 19 f.), γέγραπται (very often) or γεγραμμένον (-α) ἐστίν (Jn 6: 31, 20: 30; ταῦτα δὲ γέγραπται follows in v. 31). Cf. Herm Sim 9.4.1 ὑποδεδυκυῖαι ἦσαν–ὑποδεδύκεισαν. Periphrasis occasionally provides a rhetorically more forceful expression: A 25: 10 (S*B) ἑστὼς ἐπὶ τοῦ βήματος Καίσαρός εἰμι is better than ἕστηκα ἐπὶ... or ἐπὶ... ἕστηκα.

Periphrasis is less frequently used for the active, e.g. ἦσαν προεωρακότες A 21: 29. Even where the notion of a continuing condition recedes into the background, the periphrastic form can be used: οὐ γάρ ἐστιν ἐν γωνίᾳ πεπραγμένον τοῦτο A 26: 26.— Further exx.: pluperf. Lk 2: 26 ἦν αὐτῷ κεχρηματισμένον; fut. perf. 12: 52 ἔσονται διαμεμερισμένοι, H 2: 13 OT ἔσομαι πεποιθώς, Mt 16: 19, 18: 18, subjunctive Jn 16: 24 ᾖ πεπληρωμένη; impera. Lk 12: 35 (§ 65(4)) ἔστωσαν περιεζωσμέναι. Periphrasis may

even be used for the ptcp. itself: E 4: 18 and C 1: 21 ὄντες (-ας) ἀπηλλοτριωμένοι (-ους), obviously to express still more forcibly the persistence of the new state of things (in C καὶ ἐχθρούς is added; cf. Aristoph., Ra. 721 οὖσιν οὐ κεκιβδηλευμένοις, ἀλλὰ καλλίστοις...); similarly ἦν κείμενος Lk 23: 53 = ἦν τεθειμένος (§ 97(2)). Hell. exx. are collected by J. E. Harry, Trans. Am. Phil. Ass. 37 (1906) 60 (subj.), 61 f. (opt.), 65 (impera.). Periphrasis of the fut. perf. is also the rule in the pap. (Mayser II 1, 215, 225). Impera. e.g. ἴσθι πεφυλακτηριασμένος PGM I 4.2626 f. 'be furnished with an amulet (phylactery)'.— Πεποιθότες ὦμεν 2 C 1: 9 (LXX Is 10: 20, 17: 8 π. ὦσιν, 20: 6 ἦμεν, 5 ἦσαν, 8: 14 πεποιθὼς ᾖς). Periphrasis for ptcp. also Xen., HG 2.1.28 διασκεδασμένων τῶν ἀνθρώπων ὄντων (cod. C).

353. Forms of εἶναι with a present participle are widely employed in the NT as periphrases: ἦν for the imperfect; ἔσομαι for the future; εἰμί rarely for the present indicative; and sometimes εἶναι for the infinitive and ἴσθι for the present imperative. (1) Some parallels can be cited from the classical language (K.-G. I 38 ff. n. 3; Rosenkranz IF 48 [1930] 162 f.); it can also be maintained that this mode of expression is analogous to the use of periphrasis in the perfect system (§ 352; cf. φλεγόμενοι ἦσαν...καὶ βεβλημένοι ApocP 27) and that its use in the future makes it possible to express linear action. Since, however, the Hellenistic language (even the more vernacular of the papyri) is familiar with this development only to a very limited degree (Schmid III 112 ff.; Mlt. 226 f. [358 f.]; Mayser II 1, 223 f.; Widmann 135) and since, on the other hand, the frequency of NT examples is highest in Lk (Gospel and first half of Acts) then Mark (less in Mt), this idiom, which is just possible in Greek, was at least strongly supported by the extensive Semitic use of such periphrases, especially in the imperfect (Debrunner, IF 58 [1942] 313). A certain emphasis in periphrasis, which is the rule in classical examples, is also often unmistakable in the NT. (2) Instances like R 3: 12 OT οὐκ ἔστιν ('there is no one') ποιῶν χρηστότητα do not belong here. (3) Nevertheless, even in Acts the number of examples remains quite large even after making allowance for all instances where periphrasis differs sharply in sense from the simple form. (4) Examples of periphrasis of the present indicative: 2 C 9: 12 ἡ διακονία οὐ μόνον ἐστὶν προσαναπληροῦσα..., ἀλλὰ καὶ περισσεύουσα. (5) Periphrasis of impersonal verbs by means of the adjectival participle is not only general in

Hellenistic (Schmid III 114), but is found already in Attic (K.-G. I 39; ἐστὶ προσῆκον Dem. 3. 24): δέον ἐστίν A 19: 36, 1 Clem 34.2 (1 P 1: 6) alongside the very frequent δεῖ. (6) Examples for the infinitive: Lk 9: 18 = 11: 1 ἐν τῷ εἶναι αὐτὸν προσευχόμενον. For the imperative: Mt 5: 25 ἴσθι εὐνοῶν (this verb does not appear elsewhere in the NT). There are no examples for the subjunctive. (7) For the future: Mt 10: 22 and pars. ἔσεσθε μισούμενοι. The reason for periphrasis is the emphasis on duration (cf. the periphrastic future perfect §352; Buttmann 266f.).

G. Björck, Ἦν διδάσκων. Die periphr. Konstruktionen im Griech. (Skrifter K. Hum. Vet.-samf. i Uppsala 32, 2; 1940).

(1) Ἦν exhibits a certain independence in all references in Jn (1: 9, 28, 2: 6, 3: 23), e.g. 1: 28 ὅπου ἦν... βαπτίζων 'where he was staying and baptizing'; for that reason 18: 30 ἦν κακὸν ποιῶν is probably a spurious variant for ἦν κακοποιός (cf. §355). From Mt cf. 7: 29, 19: 22 etc. In Paul, G 1: 22f. ἤμην ἀγνοούμενος... ἀκούοντες ἦσαν. The narrative style of Mk and Lk also exhibits the most examples of periphrasis with the perf. ptcp. (Buttmann 268). Periphrasis readily denotes 'the frame of reference' (Björck, op. cit. 44ff.). Björck, op. cit. 68f. opposes translation Semitism; acc. to Björck, op. cit. 37f., 60 n. 1 emphasis can be observed only occasionally. The instances in which the ptcp. is adjectival are only seemingly periphrastic (also class.); e.g. A 9: 9 ἦν... μὴ βλέπων (= τυφλός, cf. 13: 11), Mt 5: 25 ἴσθι εὐνοῶν, Lk 1: 20 (Björck, op. cit. 53f.). Since the ptcp. also elsewhere in periphrasis approximates the function of an adjective, the two can interchange: Herm Vis 3.2.8 (pf. ptcp. and pres. with adj.), Man 5.2.3, Sim 6.1.1; cf. infra 7 end.— Lk 24: 13 καὶ ἰδοὺ δύο... ἦσαν πορευόμενοι = Hebr. וַיֵּלֶךְ with ptcp. (§128(7)), but improved by the addition of ἦσαν (Johannessohn, KZ 67 [1940] 54f.). Lk 9: 53 τὸ πρόσωπον αὐτοῦ ἦν πορευόμενον, but 𝔓⁴⁵ lat τὸ πρ. αὐτοῦ ἦν πορευομένου.

(2) A 21: 23 εἰσὶν ἄνδρες ('there are men here') εὐχὴν ἔχοντες ('who have taken...'); likewise Lk 2: 8 καὶ ποιμένες ἦσαν... ἀγραυλοῦντες καὶ φυλάσσοντες (first their presence, then their activity; cf. A 19: 14, 24).

(3) A 1: 10 ἀτενίζοντες ἦσαν, 13 ἦσαν καταμένοντες, 14 ἦσαν προσκαρτεροῦντες, 2: 2 ἦσαν καθήμενοι, etc., fut. 6: 4 D ἐσόμεθα προσκαρτεροῦντες. From A 13 on only 16: 12 ἦμεν... διατρίβοντες (cf. 14: 7 and supra 1 [main §] on Jn), 18: 7 ἡ οἰκία ἦν συνομοροῦσα (easily understood), 21: 3 ἦν ἀποφορτιζόμενον (s. §339(2b); ἀπεφορτίζετο could not very well have been said), 22: 19 ἤμην φυλακίζων (in the speech delivered τῇ Ἑβραΐδι διαλέκτῳ!).

(4) G 4: 24, Ja 1: 17, 3: 15. C 2: 23 ἅτινά ἐστιν

λόγον μὲν ἔχοντα σοφίας, cf. Dem. 31.11 οὐδὲ λόγον τὸ πρᾶγμ' ἔχον ἐστί and similar passages with ἔχων (Rehdantz, Index Dem. II Partic.); Herm Vis 1.2.4 ἔστιν μὲν... ἡ τοιαύτη βουλή... ἐπιφέρουσα (emphasis, somewhat like Dem. 20.18 ἔστι δὲ... ἔχον). Mt 27: 33 s. §132(2). The phrase ὅ ἐστιν ('which means') μεθερμηνευόμενον does not belong to this category; cf. §132(2) and Polyb. 2.15.9 τὸ γὰρ τράνς ἐξερμηνευόμενόν ἐστι πέραν.

(5) Björck, op. cit. 35f., 106f.; Mayser II 1, 223. Ἐξόν (scil. ἐστι) A 2: 29, 2 C 12: 4, s. §127(2); also with imperf.: ἐξὸν ἦν Mt 12: 4 (ἐξῆν is not found, but ἔξεστιν is very common); with inf. MPol 12.2. 2 C 12: 1 συμφέρον (scil. ἐστίν; or acc. absol. [§424]?) 𝔓⁴⁶SBFGP (συμφέρει DEKL). Ὄφελον s. §67(2).

(6) Lk 19: 17 ἴσθι ἐξουσίαν ἔχων, Ep. Clem. ad Jac. 3 (p. 8. 6 Rehm) εὖ ἴσθι εἰδώς. Mart. Pelag. 26.15 Usener (Legenden der Pelagia) ἔσο γινώσκων 'know'. E 5: 5 is doubtful: τοῦτο γάρ ἐστε (DᶜKL al. for ἴστε, s. §422) γινώσκοντες (s. §98; it is probably better to take γάρ ἐστε as imperatival rather than indic.; ἴστε would also not be indic., s. §99(2)).

(7) Mk 13: 25 ἔσονται πίπτοντες (for LXX Is 34: 4 πεσεῖται; cf. Mt 24: 29 πεσοῦνται), Lk 5: 10 ἀνθρώπους ἔσῃ ζωγρῶν, 1 C 14: 9 ἔσεσθε εἰς ἀέρα λαλοῦντες, Herm Man 5.2.8 ἔσῃ εὑρισκόμενος, Sim 9.13.2 ἔσῃ φορῶν. Lk 21: 24 ἔσται πατουμένη, A 6: 4 D ἐσόμεθα προσκαρτεροῦντες for προσκαρτερήσομεν. Xen., Hiero 11.7 (MS) ἔσῃ νικῶν. Björck, op. cit. 86f. Ptcp. interchanging with adj.: Barn 19.4 (with ἔσῃ) = Did 3.8 (with γίνου).

354. Γίνεσθαι (in various tenses) with a present or perfect participle is sometimes also used in an analogous way to denote the beginning of a state or condition: 2 C 6: 14 μὴ γίνεσθε ἑτεροζυγοῦντες ἀπίστοις ('do not lend yourselves to...'), cf. §98. Further, e.g. C 1: 18, H 5: 12, Rev 3: 2, 16: 10, Mk 9: 3 (7). Ὑπάρχειν only with the perfect participle; s. §414(1). Arnim 92; Regard 217ff. Did 3.8 s. §353(7).—LXX Is 30: 12 πεποιθὼς ἐγένου.

355. Εἶναι with the aorist participle, used to emphasize the verbal idea, was not unknown in classical (K.-G. I 38f.; Gild. 125f.); later it serves to express the pluperfect. The earliest example (if original) is Lk 23: 19 BLT: ὅστις ἦν... βληθείς (βλ. om. S*; the others have βεβλημένος) ἐν τῇ φυλακῇ.

Jn 18: 30 εἰ μὴ ἦν οὗτος κακὸν ποιήσας S* (κακὸν ποιῶν SᶜBLW, κακοποιῶν C*, κακοποιός AC²Dˢᵘᵖᵖˡ.; cf. §353(1)). Alleviated by co-ordination with a perf. ptcp.: Herm Sim 8.9.1 οὗτοί εἰσιν πιστοὶ μὲν γεγονότες, πλουτήσαντες δὲ καὶ γενόμενοι ἔνδοξοι (A, ἐνδοξότεροι PMich) ('such who', therefore similar to

§ 353(2); however πλουτ. καὶ γεν. as circumstantial ptcps. probably go with the following ἐνεδύσαντο with anacoluthon); GP 23 θεασάμενος ἦν, 51 ἦν τεθείς, POxy xiv 1682.9 (iv AD) εἰ ἧς ἐπιδημήσασα *si adveneris* (fut. ex.). Raderm.[2] 102; Vogeser 14; Wittmann 20; Wolf i 66f.; ii 55f.; Psaltes 230; Kapsomenakis 44 n. 2; Björck, *op. cit.* 74ff., 128ff. (77f.: influenced in part by Lat.).

356. Μέλλειν with the infinitive expresses imminence (like the future). This form of periphrasis, which was not foreign to classical Greek, has the advantage of being able to express imminence in past time: Lk 7: 2 ἤμελλε τελευτᾶν and frequently. Furthermore, a subjunctive can be formed in this way: Mk 13: 4 ὅταν μέλλῃ συντελεῖσθαι; and it is a replacement for the disappearing non-finite future forms (infinitive and participle), which is the reason why periphrasis is most often used for them: μέλλειν πίμπρασθαι A 28: 6, ὁ τοῦτο μέλλων πράσσειν Lk 22: 23. The future participle cannot be used to indicate relative time in a genitive absolute and is always confined to combinations with a finite verb, while μέλλειν with the participle is capable of wider application; the latter is necessary for instance in μέλλοντος ἀνοίγειν (genitive absolute) A 18: 4, αὐτῷ μέλλοντι ἀνάγεσθαι 20: 3, Ἰούδας ὁ μέλλων αὐτὸν παραδιδόναι Jn 12: 4 (but 6: 64 τίς ἐστιν ὁ παραδώσων; § 351(2)).

(3) THE MOODS

357. Introduction. The difference between the language of the NT, as of the Hellenistic in general, and the classical is generally considerably greater in the use of the moods than in the use of tenses. The main feature is, of course, the strong retreat of the optative (§§ 65(2); 384–6). The infinitive has in part been weakened (through the advance of ἵνα and ὅτι), and in part strengthened (e.g. the infinitive with τοῦ § 400). The aorist subjunctive is intermingling with the future (§ 363).

(A) The Indicative of Secondary Tenses in Main Clauses

358. The imperfect (without ἄν) in expressions of necessity, obligation, duty, possibility etc. denotes in classical something which is or was actually necessary, etc., but which does not or did not take place (cf. Latin). In this case German uses the unreal subjunctive, which corresponds to 'should, could' or 'should have, could have' in

English. (1) This usage is retained in the NT: e.g. Mt 23: 23 ταῦτα ἔδει ποιῆσαι κἀκεῖνα μὴ ἀφεῖναι, Mt 26: 9 ἐδύνατο τοῦτο πραθῆναι πολλοῦ. (2) This usage is expanded in some cases in the NT where classical would more likely have used the present indicative for an assertion about present time (so that χρή, προσήκει etc. contain an injunction): E 5: 4 may be so understood ἃ οὐκ ἀνῆκεν (DE al. τὰ οὐκ ἀνήκοντα) 'what is (really) not proper' (but yet happens), cf. *v.* 3 καθὼς πρέπει.

(1) 2 C 12: 11 ἐγὼ γὰρ ὤφειλον ὑφ᾽ ὑμῶν συνίστασθαι; 1 C 5: 10 ἐπεὶ ὠφείλετε ἐκ τοῦ κόσμου ἐξελθεῖν 'you would have in that case to go...' (but do not go) is somewhat different, where class. *might* have inserted ἄν; so also H 9: 26 ἐπεὶ ἔδει αὐτὸν πολλάκις παθεῖν. Impersonal expressions with εἶναι: καλὸν ἦν αὐτῷ, εἰ οὐκ ἐγεννήθη Mt 26: 24 (καλόν ἐστιν 18: 8 is different), κρεῖττον ἦν 2 P 2: 21. With δύνασθαι apparently rare in class. (K.-G. i 205 only Thuc. 1.37 ἐξῆν). Ἔδει elsewhere now and then; of course also simply to report a past necessity: οὐχὶ ταῦτα ἔδει ('had to') παθεῖν τὸν Χριστόν Lk 24: 26; A 26: 32 ἀπολελύσθαι ἐδύνατο ('could be free'), Jn 9: 33. (2) C 3: 18 ὡς ἀνῆκεν 'as is fitting'; A 22: 22 οὐ γὰρ καθῆκεν αὐτὸν ζῆν (they are requesting his death; καθῆκον D², καθήκει Ψ; cf. § 353(5)). Οἷς καθῆκεν PMagd 36.5 (iii BC) is a scribal error for the common οἷς καθήκει (Mayser ii 1, 227). Οὐκ ἄτοπον ἦν (it happens, however, at once) Plut., C. Gracch. 15.1, therefore like ἐβουλόμην § 359(2). Att. προσήκει does not appear in the NT. Χρή (NT only Ja 3: 10; LXX only Pr 25: 27, 4 Macc 8: 25 [corruption of A alone; the others ζῆν]; Schmid iv 592) and the verbal adj. in -τέος with ἦν etc. are not Hell. Ἐξῆν 'it would be possible' is also not found in the NT; on the other hand ἔξεστιν is common (also cf. ἐξόν § 353(5)).—The Att. use of the aor. indic. for something which *nearly* happened (ὀλίγου ἐπελαθόμην, ὀλίγου ἐδέησα with inf.) is unattested in the NT; Homil Clem 13.6.4 ὀλίγου διεφώνει 'she was nearly dead'.—Rob. 885f., 919ff.

359. The indicative of secondary tenses in wishes. A wish impossible of fulfilment (unfulfilled) is one in which the thought is present that 'this is (was) unfortunately not so'; others are called capable of fulfilment even though, strictly speaking, fulfilment is inconceivable and this impossibility is forgotten only for the moment. (1) Only ὤφελον or ὄφελον (§ 67(2)), which has become a particle (= εἴθε), with the imperfect or aorist indicative is used to express an unattainable wish, not the hybrid classical idiom εἴθε (εἰ γὰρ) ὤφελον with the infinitive: e.g. 1 C 4: 8 ὄφελον (ὤφ.

DᶜEL) ἐβασιλεύσατε. (2) If the notion of wishing is expressed by a particular verb, then ἐβουλόμην (without ἄν; Attic orators also omitted it, s. Stahl 358) or the more popular ἤθελον (perhaps by analogy to ὤφελον; cf. also καθῆκεν §358(2)) with an infinitive is used without distinction. In Attic a (modestly expressed) attainable wish was expressed by βουλοίμην ἄν, while an unattainable wish was expressed by ἐβουλόμην ἄν. E.g. A 25: 22 ἐβουλόμην ἀκοῦσαι (perfectly attainable), G 4: 20 ἤθελον (unreal); classical optative is found only in A 26: 29 (SᶜAB) εὐξαίμην ἄν (s. §385(1)).

(1) The NT has no trace of Att. εἴθε and εἰ γάρ nor of their use with the indic. without ὤφελον. The NT has ὄφελον even with the fut. for an attainable wish (§384). 2 C 11: 1 ὄφελον (ὤφ. DᶜEFGHKLΨ) ἀνείχεσθέ μου, Rev 3: 15 (ὤφ. P 046); ISm 12.1. Ὤφελον ὤφελον with the indic. also appears in the LXX, Epict. (2.18.15 cod. S ὄφελον) etc.; s. Sophocles, Lexicon s.v. ὀφείλω; for which Callim. ὤφελε. Ὄφελον with the subj. in Greek Enoch 10: 6–10 Bonner.—An εἰ-clause can become a wish by the omission of the apodosis (§482).

(2) R 9: 3 ηὐχόμην ἀνάθεμα εἶναι (hardly thought of as attainable). Herm (e.g. Vis 3.8.6; 11.4), Homil Clem 1.9 ἤθελον = βουλοίμην ἄν. Ἠβουλόμην in two pap. of ii BC (Mayser II 1, 227). Phm 13 ἐβουλόμην 'I should have liked, but I do not, or did not, do it', cf. v. 14. Thus also Aristoph., Ra. 866, PFlor I 6.7 (210 AD), and thus ἤθελον Soph., Aj. 1400 (cf. Passow-Crönert 451.56ff.), BGU IV 1078.8 (39 AD), PLond III 897.20 (p. 207) (84 AD). Ἤθελον 'I should like' often also in Epict.; MGr likewise ἤθελα (Thumb² §195).—Rob. 886f., 919; Moule 9.

360. The unreal (contrary-to-fact) indicative in conditional sentences

(protasis and apodosis) has been retained according to classical norms. (1) But the addition of ἄν to the apodosis is no longer obligatory: Jn 15: 24 (cf. 22) εἰ τὰ ἔργα μὴ ἐποίησα ἐν αὐτοῖς..., ἁμαρτίαν οὐκ εἴχοσαν. (2) The position of ἄν is as near the beginning of the clause as possible (often οὐκ ἄν). (3) The tense (imperfect, aorist; pluperfect A 26: 32, 1 Jn 2: 19) retains its *Aktionsart*; the imperfect is temporally ambiguous. (4) An unreal subordinate clause going with a present indicative which according to the sense was felt to be unreal: Mk 14: 21 BLW καλὸν (+ἦν SACD al. as all witnesses Mt 26: 24) αὐτῷ, εἰ οὐκ ἐγεννήθη, Mk 9: 42 DW καλόν ἐστιν αὐτῷ μᾶλλον, εἰ περιέκειτο... καὶ ἐβλήθη (s. §372(3)).—Unreal periods are remarkably scarce in Paul (1 C 2: 8, 11: 31, 12: 19, G 1:10, 3: 21, 4: 15), while the single Epistle to the

Hebrews has four (five) examples (4: 8, 8: 4, 7, 11: 15; 7: 11?); in Acts only 18: 14.

(1) Jn 19: 11 (SA al. have an inferior reading ἔχεις instead of εἶχες B al.); (8: 39 SB²DLTW ἐποιεῖτε, al. ἐποιεῖτε ἄν or ποιεῖτε); R 7: 7, G 4: 15 (add. ἄν SᶜDᶜEKLP); Mt 26: 24 = Mk 14: 21 (καλὸν [ἦν] αὐτῷ); Jn 9: 33 and A 26: 32 s. §358(1). On the other hand with ἄν Jn 18: 30 εἰ μὴ ἦν..., οὐκ (οὐδ' following sy⁸ is better) ἄν σοι παρεδώκαμεν, and so in the great majority of examples. Mt 15: 5 = Mk 7: 11 also belongs here ὃ ἐὰν (D is better with ἄν; on ἐάν for ἄν s. §107; ἐάν for ἄν with the unreal indic. nowhere else, but here because ὃ ἄν resembled a generalizing relative clause or really was one) ἐξ ἐμοῦ ὠφελήθης 'you would have gained (if it were not δῶρον)' (cf. Lk 19: 23 *infra* (2); the customary orthography ὠφεληθῇς is impossible). Without ἄν also e.g. 2 Clem 20.4, GP 2.5, LXX 2 Macc 5: 18, 3 Macc 5: 32 (ἄν added by the Atticizing Lucian in both instances); pap. (Mlt. 200 n. 1 [315 n.]; Mayser II 1, 228; Frisk, Gnomon 5 [1929] 39), Epict. (Melcher 75). On Mt 15: 5 cf. Debrunner, Glotta 11 (1921) 6 on Xen., Ages. 2.24 and Dem. 19.29.

(2) Lk 19: 23 κἀγὼ ἐλθὼν σὺν τόκῳ ἄν αὐτὸ ἔπραξα (cf. Mt 25: 27) contains in ἐλθὼν an unreal-temporal protasis as it were. Ἄν when negated cannot precede its οὐ: G 1: 10 Χριστοῦ δοῦλος οὐκ ἄν ἤμην. Jn 18: 36 οἱ ὑπηρέται ἄν οἱ ἐμοὶ ἠγωνίζοντο (ἄν is missing in B*, in SBᵐᵍ LWX it stands after ἠγων. [a similar variation in 8: 19 ἄν ᾔδειτε BLW, ᾔδ. ἄν SΓΔ al.]; perhaps ἄν is to be deleted with D just as it is omitted in v. 39 on the weight of overwhelming evidence).—Ἐπεί can also represent a conditional clause ('if it were otherwise'): H 10: 2 ἐπεὶ οὐκ ἄν ἐπαύσαντο; 'for otherwise would they not have ceased?' as in UPZ I 110.204ff. (164 BC) ἐπεὶ οὐκ ἄν οὕτως παντάπασιν ἀλόγητοι ⟨εἴ⟩ητε (Mayser II 1, 228), ZenP Cairo I 59016.4 (259 BC) ἐπεὶ μετ' ἐκείνου ἄν αὐτὸν ἐπέστειλα (Mayser II 3, 91 f.).

(3) Jn 18: 36 ἠγωνίζοντο ἄν (s. *supra* (2)) 'would have fought and continued to fight' (the outcome and result being uncertain).

(4) So also Lk 12: 49 τί θέλω, εἰ ἤδη ἀνήφθη 'how I wish = I would be glad if it were already kindled!' H. Riesenfeld, Arbeiten und Mitteilungen I (1936) 8–11; for τί = מָה s. §299. Class. similarly (K.-G. II 370.5ff.).—Unreal plupf. for Lat. plupf. subj. (Latinism): Herm Sim 9.15.6 εἰ μὴ ἐσχήκεισαν, οὐκ ἄν γεγόνεισαν (therefore in 28.6 εἰ μὴ πεπόνθατε, τεθνήκειτε, probably πεπόνθειτο is to be read rather than πεπόνθατε), Homil Clem 7.3 εἰ μὴ ἐγεγόνειτε = *nisi facti essetis*.—Potentiality in past time only Homil Clem 3.3 πῶς οὐκ ἄν ἠθύμησα; 'How could I not have become despondent?', Diogn 8.11 ἢ τίς ἄν πώποτε προσεδόκησεν ἡμῶν (in a rel. clause; very refined language); cf. 2 exx. from Basil the Great in Trunk 46.—On the whole cf. Rob. 921ff.

361. The indicative of unreality in final (purpose) clauses which depend on an indicative of the same type in the main clause is not found in the NT. The subjunctive is used in its place: Jn 18: 36 οἱ ὑπηρέται ἂν οἱ ἐμοὶ ἠγωνίζοντο, ἵνα μὴ παραδοθῶ [τοῖς Ἰουδαίοις] (τοῖς Ἰουδ. which is contrary to the sense is not in Chr); 1 C 4: 8. (Μήπως ἔδραμον G 2: 2 is not unreal, s. §370(2).)

(B) The Future Indicative for Volitive Expressions in Main Clauses (instead of the Imperative and Subjunctive)

362. The future indicative is employed to render the categorical injunctions and prohibitions (negative οὐ) in the legal language of the OT (not entirely so in classical: K.-G. I 174, 176; Stahl 359 f.), without thereby greatly influencing the rest of NT usage. Thus Mt 5: 43 OT ἀγαπήσεις τὸν πλησίον σου, but the injunction of Jesus in v. 44 is ἀγαπᾶτε; 5: 21 OT οὐ φονεύσεις, etc., but the future is nowhere used in this chapter in independent injunctions of Jesus, for ἔσεσθε (γίνεσθε Chr) τέλειοι in v. 48 also goes back to the OT (Dt 18: 13, Lev 19: 2, cf. ἅγιοι ἔσεσθε 1 P 1: 16 OT).

The fut. is used elsewhere only in scattered references (2nd and 3rd pers.): Mt 6: 5 οὐκ ἔσεσθε, 21: 3 ἐρεῖτε (= εἴπατε Mk 11: 3), Herm Vis 2.2.6 ἐρεῖς. Mt 20: 26 (cf. Mk 9: 35) οὐχ οὕτως ἔσται ἐν ὑμῖν, then ἔσται twice more in 26f. with v.l. ἔστω. 1 Clem 60.2 καθαρεῖς. Mt 10: 13 the impera. however (ἐλθάτω ἡ εἰρήνη ὑμῶν ἐπ’ αὐτήν [D however ἔσται]...ἐπιστραφήτω), where the fut. would be more natural as it actually stands in Lk 10: 6. For ὄφελον with the fut. indic. s. §384. Mt 27: 4 σὺ ὄψῃ, 24 ὑμεῖς ὄψεσθε, A 18: 15 ὄψεσθε αὐτοί (cf. Epict., M. Ant.) are Latinisms = videris etc. ‘see to it yourself’. Volitive fut. in the Ap. Frs.: Barn 19.2ff. several times (OT style), Herm Man 12.3.1, Did 11.7. For the MS fluctuation between fut. and impera. s. Cuendet, L’impératif (s. §335) 124 (e.g. Lk 17: 4, Mt 20: 27); Mt employs this fut. more frequently than the other Evangelists (Cuendet, op. cit. 131). The fut. appears often in specific individual enjoinders in the Ptol. pap. (Mayser II 1, 212).— Passio Perpet. et Felic. 1.3 (5.13 van Beek) ὄψωνται = viderint of the Lat. translation; read ὄψονται (van Beek, Neophilologus 20 [1934/5] 55); Corp. Gloss. Lat. II 208.25 viderit ὄψεται. Latinism (already recognized by Korais): Hesseling, Mededeel. Akad. Amsterdam, Afd. Letterk. 65 A 4, 1928. MGr ἃς ὄψεται, ὄψονται Hesseling, op. cit. 11.

For the future with οὐ μή in denials with respect to the future s. §365; in questions of doubt and deliberation §366.

(C) The Subjunctive in Main Clauses

363. Introduction. Corresponding to the formal affinities of the subjunctive and future mentioned in §318, the two were also logically connected from the beginning so that the former can occasionally be replaced by the latter. This is true of a subjunctive which expresses volition or obligation (the future λέξω can also be the equivalent of βούλομαι λέγειν), a subjunctive which has close ties with the imperative. It also applies not only to the deliberative (dubitative) subjunctive, but also to the subjunctive denoting that which may be the outcome of the present situation under certain circumstances (futuristic or prospective subjunctive; attested elsewhere in main clauses only in Homer), which naturally can refer only to the future. In late Greek the future was driven out by θέλω ἵνα (becoming θά in MGr) with the present or aorist subjunctive, and thus made a distinction in the Aktionsarten of this tense also possible. The NT, however, is still a long way from this stage, whereas the intermixture of the future indicative and the aorist subjunctive has progressed considerably in comparison with the classical language.

For this mixture in late Greek, growing out of the futuristic subj. and favored by the phonetic leveling of -σει with -σῃ, -σεις with -σῃς, -σομεν with -σωμεν etc., which led e.g. to a purely futuristic use of the aor. subj. (e.g. εἴπω σοι = ἐρῶ σοι), s. Sophocles, Lexicon p. 45; Hatzid. 218; Reinhold 101ff.; Mlt. 240 [292]; Psaltes 217f.; Slotty 34, 60; Debrunner, Glotta 11 (1920) 22ff.; Bănescu 72ff.; Horn 124; Mayser II 1, 234f.; Ghedini, Aegyptus 15 (1935) 235; Bezdechi 44ff.; Ljungvik, Syntax 69. There are already instances throughout the LXX, thus Ex 3: 10 ἀποστείλω σε...καὶ ἐξάξεις, Da Theod. 12: 10 ἀνομήσωσιν ἄνομοι καὶ οὐ συνήσουσιν ἄνομοι, Homil Clem 11.3.2 δυνηθῇ (main clause) = δυνήσεται. The subj. for the positive impera. is older (§364(3)).

364. The hortatory and prohibitive subjunctive. The subjunctive supplements the imperative (as in Latin, etc.) in the 1st person plur. as in classical, e.g. Jn 14: 31 ἄγωμεν, G 5: 26 μὴ γινώμεθα. (1) Also in 1st person sing. but in a slightly different way in that an invitation is extended to another to permit the speaker to do something. This is introduced in classical with ἄγε, φέρε, also δεῦρο; in the NT the 1st sing. only with ἄφες (Hellenistic; from which the MGr usage ἃς with 1st and 3rd person subjunctive = imperative is derived; s. Psaltes 88f.) and δεῦρο (plur. δεῦτε): Mt 7: 4 = Lk 6: 42 ἄφες ἐκβάλω τὸ κάρφος,

A 7: 34 OT δεῦρο ἀποστείλω σε. (2) The same words can also introduce the 1st plur. subjunctive and 2nd person imperative: δεῦτε ἴδετε Mt 28: 6, ἄφες ἴδωμεν Mt 27: 49 = Mk 15: 36 SDV (ἄφετε ABC al.) = 'let us see'. (3) The use of the aorist subjunctive with μή (§335) for the *negative* aorist imperative corresponds to classical usage; ὅρα, ὁρᾶτε, βλέπετε appear at times before such sentences (Mt 8: 4, 18: 10, Mk 1: 44, 1 Th 5: 15), and like ἄφες etc. do not influence the construction; s. §461(1).—For μή expressing apprehension in independent clauses s. §370 end.

(1) Δεῦρο δείξω σοι Rev 17: 1 and 21: 9. Eur., Ba. 341 δεῦρό σου στέψω κάρα, Mimus, POxy III 413.184 (ii AD) ἄφες ἐγὼ αὐτὸν θρηνήσω, Epict. ἄφες ἴδω, ἅ. σκέψωμαι (Melcher 91), Homil Clem 13.3.6 ἐάσατέ με προαγάγω ὑμᾶς (Rehm: προσαγωγῶς acc. to Syr. ['ἠρέμα'; cf. 13.4.1 προσαγωγῶς]); Herm Sim 8.2.7 πειράσω παραχέω PMich (-σωμεν -χέειν A). 1 C 11: 34 διατάξωμαι ADEFG is mistaken (-ξομαι 𝔓⁴⁶SBC al. is correct).

(2) Δεῦτε ἀποκτείνωμεν Mk 12: 7 (Lk 21: 14 v.l.), Epict. 1.9.15 ἄφες δείξωμεν, Jannaris § 1914. With the stereotyped singular form ἄφες, cf. ἄγε, φέρε etc. before the plur. (§144; K.-G. I 84f.), likewise MGr ἄς. With the 3rd pers. Epict. 1.15.7 ἄφες ἀνθήσῃ. 2nd pers. Herm Sim 8.1.4 ἄφες ἴδῃς s. §241(2).

(3) The subj. of prohibition is infrequent in the NT in the 3rd pers., where also in class. the subj. or impera. can be used: 1 C 16: 11 μή τις αὐτὸν ἐξουθενήσῃ, 2 C 11: 16, 2 Th 2: 3. Aor. subj. for the positive impera. (a transfer from the subj. of prohibition): IPol 8.3 διαμείνητε, Barn 19.1 σπεύσῃς; cf. Reinhold 104; Mayser II 1, 229f. (seldom in the pap.; earlier only in dialect inscriptions), POxy VII 1061. 10, 16 (22 BC) συμπροσέσῃ... συντύχῃ καὶ σπουδάσει. Γαμηθῇ 1 C 7: 39 FG is erroneous (pm. -θῆναι), ἀπέχου... καὶ οὐδὲν (οὐδὲ ἕν) (οὐ, not μή!) διαμάρτῃς Herm Sim 4.5 A PMich (-τήσεις pap. Berl. Klassikertexte VI p. 15.53f.). Also incorrect is the pres. subj.: μὴ ψεύδησθε C 3: 9 𝔓⁴⁶ (pm. -δεσθε), ἐκδέχησθε 1 C 11: 33 𝔓⁴⁶ (pm. -χεσθε). Μὴ δόξῃ *et al.* in Vett. Val. (J. Wikström, Eranos 47 [1949] 22).—For the replacement of the aor. subj. by the fut. cf. Mlt. 184f. [278f.] (Dem. and pap.; in μηδένα μισήσετε [P μισήσητε] Homil Clem 3.69.1 it is not the fut. but the μή that is surprising; s. §427(1)).

365. Οὐ μή with the aorist subjunctive or future indicative, both of which are classical, is the most definite form of negation regarding the future. This mode of expression is more common in the NT and for the most part less emphatic than in the classical language, but it is virtually limited to quotations from the LXX and sayings of Jesus (Mlt. 187–92 [297–303]). (1) The only certain example of the future is Mt 16: 22 οὐ μὴ ἔσται σοι τοῦτο. (2) Otherwise the future forms are very similar to the aorist subjunctive and the text varies between the two, e.g. οὐ μή σε ἀπαρνήσομαι Mt 26: 35 (-σωμαι AEGK al.), Mk 14: 31 (-σωμαι SEFGK al.). (3) However, in numerous places the subjunctive is absolutely certain due to its distinctive form, e.g. Rev 2: 11 οὐ μὴ ἀδικηθῇ. (4) The same subjunctive *as a question* can denote an affirmation (the two uses have, therefore, the same relationship as that between οὐ πράξω and οὐ πράξω;): Jn 18: 11 οὐ μὴ πίω αὐτό;—The subjunctive is that of the aorist throughout, whereas in classical the present subjunctive also appears.

(1) Herm Man 9.2 οὐ μή σε ἐγκαταλείψει POxy XV 1783.2 (iv AD beg.) (-λίπῃ A), 9.5 οὐδὲν οὐ μὴ λήψῃ (for which the same pap. 1783.18 has οὐ μὴ λάβεις [= λάβῃς]), Sim 1.5 οὐ μὴ παραδεχθήσῃ. Lk 21: 33 οὐ μὴ παρελεύσονται is perhaps merely attraction to the preceding positive παρελεύσονται or a combination from the pars. Mt 24: 35 οὐ μὴ παρέλθωσιν and Mk 13: 31 οὐ παρελεύσονται (BD*, οὐ μὴ π. SL, οὐ μὴ παρελεύσετε [= -ται] W, οὐ μὴ παρέλθωσαν ACDᶜ al. with assimilation to Mt).

(2) Mt 15: 6 οὐ μὴ τιμήσει (τιμήσῃ E*FGK al.) τὸν πατέρα (quotation of a saying of the rabbis: 'need not honor'. Οὐ μή in the LXX is also prohibitive, e.g. Gen 3: 1; so also Mt 21: 19 ? s. Slotty 43f.). Rev 9: 6 οὐ μὴ εὑρήσουσιν (εὕρωσιν AP), Jn 13: 8 οὐ μὴ νίψῃς (-εις D), G 4: 30 οὐ μή (om. 𝔓⁴⁶ FG) κληρονομήσει (-σῃ ACFG al.). Οὐ μή with the (aor.) subj. is vulgar Koine: LXX, NT, private documents of the Ptol. period; Mayser II 1, 233; II 2, 564; Horn 92f.; POxy I 119.4, 7, 14, 15 (ii/iii AD) οὐ μὴ γράψω, οὐ μὴ λάβω... οὔτε πάλι χαίρω σε, οὐ μὴ φάγω, οὐ μὴ π(ε)ίνω; Witkowski, Epistulae, Index s.v. μή.

(3) Lk 12: 59 οὐ μὴ ἐξέλθῃς, 13: 35 οὐ μὴ ἴδητέ με, 1: 15 οὐ μὴ πίῃ (from LXX Num 6: 3 and 1 Km 1: 11 where οὐ πίεται is found). Lk 8: 17 ὃ οὐ μὴ γνωσθῇ καὶ εἰς φανερὸν ἔλθῃ is parallel to ὃ οὐ φανερὸν γενήσεται, 18: 29f. οὐδείς ἐστιν... ὃς οὐχὶ μὴ ἀπολάβῃ = ὃς οὐκ ἀπολήψεται (the emphasis of the saying rests on the positive content of the whole 'everyone will certainly...'; cf. R 4: 8 OT οὗ οὐ μὴ λογίσηται κύριος ἁμαρτίαν = a simple negation), H 13: 5 οὐ μή σε ἀνῶ οὐδὲ (𝔓⁴⁶; pm. οὐδ' οὐ) μή σε ἐγκαταλίπω (D; the rest incorrectly have -λείπω), Herm Man 9.2 οὐ μή σε ἐγκαταλίπῃ (s. (1)), Sim 4.7 οὐ μὴ διαφθαρῇ PMich (οὐ διαφθαρήσεται A).

(4) Rev 15: 4 τίς οὐ μὴ φοβηθῇ; Lk 18: 7. The 2nd pers. οὐ μὴ λαλήσεις and the like in class. mean something different (negative in sense, therefore prohibitive, not interrogative; s. K.-G. II 222f.; Slotty 43). Epict. 3.22.33 οὐ μὴ ἀποθάνωσιν; 'will they *not* die, then?'

366. In doubtful or deliberative questions about what is to take place classical employs the subjunctive (deliberative, dubitative) or (less often) the future indicative (e.g. Eur., Ion 758 εἴπωμεν ἢ σιγῶμεν; ἢ τί δράσομεν; K.-G. ι 174, 223; Gild. 116; Slotty 51). It is found mostly with the 1st person, rarely with the 3rd person. The question can be introduced with βούλει βούλεσθε (without conjunctions). The negative is μή. (1) The NT nearly always has the subjunctive (usually aorist; present subjunctive perhaps in Mt 11: 3; the future appears at times as v.l.), and, in addition to the 1st person, occasionally also the 2nd and 3rd. Unlike classical it is not found in questions which are repeated nor with τίς = 'I, we' (Slotty 46 f.). The subjunctive has more of a futuristic or potential meaning in the NT: Lk 23: 31 ἐν τῷ ξηρῷ τί γένηται; ('what will happen then?', DK al. γενήσεται; Epict. 4.1.97 τί οὖν γένηται; 100 πῶς οὖν τοῦτο γένηται; Timo Phliasius 66.2 Diels τί πάθω; τί . . . γένηται; also cf. class. τί γένωμαι; 'what will happen to me?', K.-G. ι 222 f.; Slotty 56 ff. Ep. Clem. ad Jac. 10.5 [p. 13.14 Rehm] τίς γὰρ ἂν ἁμαρτήσῃ; 'who would commit a sin?'; M. Ant. 10.30.2 τί γὰρ ποιήσῃ; [deliberative]; 12.16 A3 τί γὰρ πάθῃ; 'what shall be his fate?'), Mt 23: 33 πῶς φύγητε; ('how shall [can] you escape?'). (2) The 1st person future in R 3: 5, 4: 1 etc. τί ἐροῦμεν; (cf. Plato, Crito 50 B) at least approaches the deliberative meaning. (3) Introduced with θέλεις, βούλεσθε etc. (also often in classical, K.-G. ι 221 f.): Mt 13: 28 θέλεις συλλέξωμεν; Jn 18: 39 βούλεσθε ἀπολύσω; (4) The present indicative is used very rarely in a deliberative sense in place of the future (§ 323): Jn 11: 47 (Herm Sim 9.9.1) τί ποιοῦμεν; for which there are parallels in colloquial Latin.—Δεῖ can be used analytically for the deliberative subjunctive (χρή is unusual in the NT, § 358(2)): τί με δεῖ ποιεῖν A 16: 30, as can δύνασθαι in the 2nd and 3rd persons (Viteau 32): Mt 12: 34 πῶς δύνασθε λαλεῖν;

(1) Mt 26: 54 πῶς οὖν πληρωθῶσιν αἱ γραφαί; 12: 26 in Homil Clem 19.2 πῶς οὖν αὐτοῦ στήκῃ ἡ βασιλεία; (classical would have to use the fut. here, and thus Lk 16: 11 f. τίς πιστεύσει; . . . τίς δώσει, cf. 11: 11). Mt 16: 26 τί δώσει = Mk 8: 37 τί δοῖ (δώσει 𝔓45ACDW al.); Epict. 1.17.2 ὑπὸ τίνος διαρθρωθῇ = 3 τίς διαρθρώσει. M. Ant. 5.36.3 διὰ τοῦτ' οὖν καὶ σὺ μωρὸς γένῃ; 'should you on that account also become a fool?' R 10: 14 f. ἐπικαλέσωνται (-σονται 𝔓46KLP), πιστεύσωσιν (v.l. -σουσιν), ἀκούσωσιν (SᶜA²B; -σουσιν L, -σονται S*D al., -σωνται 𝔓46), κηρύξωσιν (-ουσιν is weakly attested) 'how should they, can

they . . .?', πῶς γνωσθῇ 1 C 14: 7 D*FG (pm. -θήσεται), Herm Sim 5.7.3 πῶς σωθῇ (A; -θήσεται PMich) ὁ ἄνθρωπος, LXX 2 Km 23: 3 πῶς κραταιώσητε, Is 1: 5 τί ἔτι πληγῆτε, Passio Perpet. et Felic. 1.1 διὰ τί μή . . . γραφῇ παραδοθῇ (Harris-Gifford; cod. -θεῖς); Raderm.² 167 f. Lk 11: 5 is peculiar: τίς ἐξ ὑμῶν ἕξει φίλον, καὶ πορεύσεται . . . καὶ εἴπῃ (ἐρεῖ AD al.) . . . 7 κἀκεῖνος εἴπῃ (ἐρεῖ D); this is an awkwardly expressed thought (§ 442(3); Viteau 10), for which the conditional form (ἐὰν φίλος πορευθῇ etc.) with a fut. in the apodosis would have been more appropriate; cf. vv. 11 f.

(2) Definitely deliberative Lk 22: 49 εἰ (direct question, § 440(3)) πατάξομεν ἐν μαχαίρῃ (-ωμεν GH al.); Mk 6: 37 ἀγοράσωμεν . . . καὶ δώσομεν (-σωμεν), cf. § 369(3).

(3) Mk 10: 51 = Lk 18: 41; 9: 54.

(4) Πῶς ποιοῦμεν; Plato, Symp. 214 A is not deliberative as is τί ποιῶμεν; in 214 B, but gently finds fault with a present situation; so also perhaps Jn 11: 47 (Abbot 358 f.). In 1 Jn 3: 17 μενεῖ is to be read instead of μένει.

(D) Indicative and Subjunctive in Subordinate Clauses

(i) *The augmented tenses of the indicative with ἄν in an iterative sense*

367. Repetition in past time is expressed in Hellenistic (not classical) in relative and temporal clauses by an augmented tense of the indicative with ἄν; i.e. the type ὃς ἂν (ὅταν) βούληται, δύναται is transferred to past time by means of an augmented tense: ὃς ἂν (ὅταν) ἐβούλετο, ἐδύνατο. The classical iterative optative is thereby avoided (§ 386). The classical iterative past tense with ἄν in *main clauses* is only incidentally similar, and is found neither in the NT nor in ordinary Koine. Debrunner, Glotta 11 (1920) 1 ff. Ἄν (or ἐάν, § 107) stands, like the subjunctive of repeated action in present time, as near the conjunction or relative as possible; in certain cases ἄν is compounded with the conjunction: Mk 6: 56 ὅπου ἐὰν (ἄν) εἰσεπορεύετο . . ., ἐν ταῖς ἀγοραῖς ἐτίθεσαν τοὺς ἀσθενοῦντας, 3: 11 τὰ πνεύματα, ὅταν αὐτὸν ἐθεώρουν, προσέπιπτον. The aorist is by no means excluded: Mk 6: 56 b καὶ ὅσοι ἂν ἥψαντο (SBDW, ἥπτοντο AN al.) αὐτοῦ, ἐσῴζοντο.

Mk 15: 6 DG ὃν ἂν ᾐτοῦντο correctly (cf. § 64(3)); A 2: 45 and 4: 35 (καθότι ἄν); 1 C 12: 2 (ὡς ἄν); Mk 11: 19 ὅταν (ὅτε AD al.) ὀψὲ ἐγένετο, ἐξεπορεύετο ἔξω τῆς πόλεως, here, too, probably denoting a habit, cf. Lk 21: 37 (but s. Mlt. 168, 248 [263] and on Rev 8: 1

infra §382(4)). For other Hell. exx. s. Glotta 11 (1920) 4 and 10 ff.: imperf. e.g. Polyb. 4.32.5, LXX Num 21: 9 (A aor.), 1 Macc. 13: 20, Herm Sim 9.6.4; aor. e.g. Polyb. 4.32.6, 13.7.8, 10, LXX Gen 30: 42 best reading, Ezk 10: 11, Herm Sim 9.4.5 and 17.3 ὅταν ἐτέθησαν; Barn 12.2 ὁπόταν καθεῖλεν; pluperf.: Herm Sim 9.1.6 ὅταν ἐπικεκαύκει. For ὅταν with the indic. in a non-iterative sense s. §382(4).

(ii) *Indirect questions*

368. The subjunctive is employed in delibera-tive questions in dependent clauses as it is in main clauses (§366). A normal example is Mt 6: 25 μὴ μεριμνᾶτε τί φάγητε. An extension of the sub-junctive beyond its classical limits is illustrated by Lk 12: 36 προσδεχομένοις τὸν κύριον, πότε ἀναλύσῃ (-σει GKX al.); cf. Ph 3: 12 with εἰ 'whether' διώκω εἰ καταλάβω (§375), whereas elsewhere the future indicative follows this εἰ. The future indicative, which is also possible in a deliberative sense in classical (cf. §366(2)), is probably not found in Ph 1: 22 τί αἱρήσομαι οὐ γνωρίζω (𝔓⁴⁶B αἱρήσωμαι), where τί αἱρήσομαι; would be a better punctuation (cf. §442(8)).

In the sphere of past time, where class. used the opt. for the subj. as a rule, the NT here as in other cases retained the subj.: A 4: 21 μηδὲν εὑρίσκοντες τὸ πῶς κολάσωνται αὐτούς. After ἔχω 'I have on hand, I know' may follow (*a*) a question with the subj. (§298(4)): e.g. Lk 12: 17 ποῦ συνάξω, Mk 8: 1f. (6: 36 ΑΓ al.) τί φάγωσιν; or (*b*) a relative clause with the future: Lk 11: 6 ὃ παραθήσω; or (*c*) a relative clause with the deliberative subj. (mixture of relative and interrogative clause): H 8: 3 ὃ προσενέγκῃ (§379); or (*d*) an inf. (§392(2)) or (*e*) an indirect question with an inf. (s. *infra* for exx.).—Subj. used in an unclass. manner: Epict., Ench. 7 δεῖ . . . ἐπιστρέφεσθαι, μή ποτε ὁ κυβερνήτης καλέσῃ 'one must pay attention whether perchance the steersman calls'. M. Ant. 9.3.7. More loosely deliberative: Mt 10: 19 δοθήσεται ὑμῖν (i.e. 'to know'), τί λαλήσητε, Mk 6: 36 ἵνα ἀγοράσωσιν ἑαυτοῖς (arising from the anxious ques-tion:) τί φάγωσιν 𝔓⁴⁵SBLWΘ.—1 P 5: 8 ζητῶν τίνα καταπιεῖν SKLP is a combination (cf. §397(6)) of ζ., τίνα καταπίῃ (A al.) and ζ. τινα καταπιεῖν (BΨ𝔓²⁵ only ζητῶν καταπιεῖν). There is a corresponding construction in Lk 9: 58 Λ* and Mt 8: 20 Γ al. οὐκ ἔχει ποῦ . . . κλῖναι, Mt 15: 32 οὐκ ἔχουσιν τί φαγεῖν W (pm. φάγωσιν), Herm Man 2.6 μὴ διακρίναντος τίνι δῶσιν ἢ μὴ δῶσιν PMich (ii AD) (if δώσειν is meant [Bonner 133]; S τίνι δῷ ἢ μὴ δῷ, A τί δῷ), Xen., HG 1.6.5 cod. V οὐκ ἔχω τί ἄλλο ποιεῖν (the others correctly have ποιῶ), Ps.-Callisth. 104.16 Kroll τί γὰρ [παρ'] ἡμῶν βαστάσαι οὐκ ἔχεις (Kroll τὶ in-correctly), PSI IV 368.25 (250 BC) ἕως συντάσσῃς τί ποιῆσαι, POxy XVII 2153.14 (iii AD) φρόντισον πῶς

ἀνελθεῖν ἡμᾶς, Dionys. Hal., Ant. 6.26 p. 1099 τίνας εἶναι δυνάμεις . . . σκοπούσης (all MSS), M. Ant. 7.58.2 περὶ τὸ πῶς χρῆσθαι αὐτοῖς (v.l. χρήσει), Test Jos 7.1 περιεβλέπετο, ποίῳ τρόπῳ με παγιδεῦσαι; further in K.-G. II 23 n. 1; Lob. Phryn. 772; Raderm.² 181; Vogeser 37f.; Ursing 60; Ghedini, Vang. ap. 460; Mayser II 3, 54.20ff.; Ljungvik 40f. Parallels from Latin J. Svennung, Untersuchungen zu Palladius (Uppsala, 1936) 439f.; from other languages W. Havers, Erkl. Synt. 84, 232f.; Norberg, Glotta 27 (1939) 261ff.—Ἔχω with an indirect question (subj. and fut.) in pap. s. Mayser II 1, 214, 235f.; mixture of relative and interrogative clauses II 1, 79f.; II 3, 52.—Ἔχω with pron. and inf.: Lk 12: 17 οὐκ ἔχω ποῦ συνάξω WΛ (pm. -ξω), Vita Phocae (Anal. Boll.) 30.278.21, Schol. Aeschin. 2.161 μὴ ἔχοντας πόθεν ζῆσαι (L. Radermacher, Wien. Sitzb. 224, 5 [1947] 63); further in G. Björck 'I don't know what to do' in Greek (Eranos 47 [1949] 13–19).—With ἐάν in-stead of εἰ (cf. §372(1*a*)) Mk 11: 13 D ἰδεῖν ἐάν τί ἐστιν.—Rob. 1043–5.

(iii) *Final (purpose) clauses and* μή *after ex-pressions of apprehension*

369. Final (purpose) clauses introduced by ἵνα, ὅπως (no longer with ὡς except in A 20: 24 S* [§391(1)]), μή ·have greatly extended their sphere in the NT because a ἵνα-clause so often serves as periphrasis for the infinitive. We are concerned here with mood only, upon which the character of ἵνα (i.e. whether it indicates purpose or not) exerted no influence. (1) The mood in the NT is generally the subjunctive. The classical 'oblique optative' is never used even after a secondary tense in the NT nor elsewhere in the lower Koine vernacular; cf. Knuenz 15ff. (2) The future indicative has also been introduced to a very limited degree in the very places where it would *not* have been permissible in classical, i.e. after ἵνα and final μή, most frequently in Rev and usually with the aorist subjunctive as variant. (3) A special case is that in which a future con-nected by καί follows upon ἵνα or μή with the subjunctive to designate some further conse-quence: Jn 15: 8 ἵνα καρπὸν . . . φέρητε καὶ γενήσεσθε (γένησθε BDL al.) ἐμοὶ μαθηταί, where the consequence has a kind of independence: 'and then you will become . . .'. It is still more easily understood when it follows an independent subjunctive: Mk 6: 37 ἀγοράσωμεν καὶ δώσομεν (𝔓⁴⁵ΑΛΔ, -σωμεν SBD, al. δῶμεν). (4) The old Attic (Meisterhans 255) combination of ὅπως and ὅπως μή with the future indicative after verbs of reflection, striving, guarding is not found in the

NT. Ἵνα (negated ἵνα μή, μή) is used throughout with these verbs, and ὅπως, in so far as it appears at all (never in Rev, once in Jn, not often in Paul), is confined to the purely final sense and to combinations with verbs of asking (παρακαλεῖν etc.). (5) Furthermore, ὅπως, with the exception of a few places in Lk and a quotation from the LXX, has lost the ἄν often appended in Attic (Hermann 267f.; Knuenz 13ff., 26ff.; Rosenkranz, IF 48 [1930] 166), especially in the older inscriptions (Meisterhans 254). Ἄν could not be joined to ἵνα and μή even in Attic. (6) The present indicative after ἵνα is, of course, only a corruption of the text.—For μή (μήποτε, μήπως) expressing apprehension s. §370.

Pap. ὡς (ὡς ἄν) iii BC 4 times, ii–i BC 18 times; Mayser II 1, 258–61. Cf. Rob. 982. D. Buzy, Les sentences finales des paraboles évangéliques (RB 40 [1931] 321–44). On ὅπως- and ἵνα-clauses in the Apocr. Gospels Ghedini, Vang. ap. 474–8. Kalinka, WSt 55 (1937) 91–4 (compendium of the results of the work of Knuenz).

(1) The alleged opt. δώῃ E 1: 17 is subj. (§95(2); B correctly δῷ). Τίς δώῃ = מִי יִתֵּן is frequent in the LXX and is an unmistakable subj. The subj. with ὅπως is aor. except ὅπως ᾖ Mt 6: 4 and ὅπως μή δύνωνται Lk 16: 26. Mayser II 1, 240ff. (subj.), 295 (opt.).

(2) Fut.: Rev 22: 14 ἵνα ἔσται...καὶ εἰσέλθωσιν (ἵνα here = 'because' ὅτι, as in 14: 13), therefore both forms thought of as equivalent (? s. infra). In Paul: 1 C 9: 15 ἵνα τις (οὐδείς is incorrect) κενώσει, 18 ἵνα θήσω, 13: 3 παραδῶ ἵνα καυθήσομαι (incorrect -σωμαι CK, καυχήσωμαι 𝔓⁴⁶SAB), G 2: 4 καταδουλώσουσιν (SAB*CDE), Ph 2: 11 ACD al. Further: 1 P 3: 1 κερδηθήσονται; Jn 7: 3 θεωρήσουσιν (-σωσι B³X al.), 17: 2 δώσει (-ῃ SᶜACG al., δώσω S*, δῷς W, ἔχῃ D); Lk 14: 10 ἐρεῖ (ADW al. εἴπῃ), 20: 10 δώσουσιν (CDW al. δῶσιν); Mt 12: 10 κατηγορήσουσιν DWX. After μή: C 2: 8 βλέπετε μή...ἔσται, H 3: 12 βλέπετε μήποτε ἔσται, Mt 7: 6 μήποτε καταπατήσουσιν (-σωσιν SEG al.)...καὶ ῥήξωσιν. Cf. also Gregory 124. Rev 3: 9 ἵνα ἥξουσιν (-ωσι 046) καὶ προσκυνή-σουσιν (-σωσιν 046)...καὶ γνῶσιν (S γνώσῃ is not good); 8: 3 δώσει (-ῃ P 046), 13: 16 (written ΔΩΣΙ from which the wrong reading δωσι(ν) in all majuscules arose); 6: 4, 11, 9: 4, 5, 20, 13: 12, 14: 13 (ὅτι 𝔓⁴⁷). 1 Th 5: 10 ἵνα ζήσωμεν (A; ζῶμεν D*E; the aor. is correct S etc. 'live again', i.e. at the parousia); ἄν is also omitted in the intervening clause εἴτε γρηγορῶμεν εἴτε καθεύδωμεν (cf. Ph 1: 27 ἵνα εἴτε... ἀκού(σ)ω [subj.], Homil Clem 9: 2 ἵν'....ὅτε θελήσωσιν, ἀνέλωσιν). Interchange of fut. indic. and aor. subj. (cf. §363): Reinhold 106; Raderm.² 173f.; Melcher 90; Vogeser 34f.; Knuenz 23ff., 39.—On 'causal' ἵνα (Rev 22: 14) s. Jannaris §1741; Hesseling

and Pernot, Neophilologus 12 (1927) 41–6; Pernot, Études 90–5; Windisch, ZNW 26 (1927) 203–9; Robertson, Studies in Early Christianity, ed. by S. J. Case (N.Y. and London, 1928) 51–7. Of the NT exx. adduced by Hesseling and Pernot, Rev 22: 14 at the best stands the test if μακάριοι...ἵνα = μακάριοι...ὅτι of Mt 5: 3ff.; but 'in order that' (dependent on πλύοντες) is also possible; likewise Rev 16: 15. 14: 13 ἵνα (𝔓⁴⁷ ὅτι!) ἀναπαήσονται is a main clause 'they shall rest' (§387(3)). Mk 4: 12 = Lk 8: 10 ἵνα is final (theory that some are incapable of repentance), softened by Mt 13: 13 to causal ὅτι (διὰ τοῦτο in answer to διὰ τί 10). Ed. Schweizer, ThZ 8 (1952) 153f. accepts ἵνα in 1 P 4: 6 as causal. Literature on causal ἵνα also in Zerwick, Graec. bibl. 95n. The LXX is also ruled out: Gen 22: 14 ἵνα 'so that' (§391(5)), likewise Epict.: 3.4.10 ἵνα is final, cf. θέλω in 11. But still there remain the grammarians (e.g. Apollonius Dysc., Synt. 3.28 [Gramm. Gr. II 2, 382.2] explains ἵνα φιλολογήσω παρεγενήθη Τρύφων as identical with διότι ἐφιλολόγησα π. Τ.), the Church Fathers and late papyri (e.g. BGU IV 1081.3 [ii/iii AD] ἐχάρην ἵνα σε ἀσπάζομαι [however cf. §392(1a)]; Ghedini, Aegyptus 15 [1935] 236).

(3) A 21: 24 ἵνα ξυρήσωνται (-σονται SB*D*E al.)...καὶ γνώσονται, E 6: 3 OT ἵνα...γένηται καὶ ἔσῃ, R 3: 4 OT ὅπως ἄν δικαιωθῇς...καὶ νικήσεις (SADE), Lk 22: 30 (many vv.ll.), 12: 58 (μήποτε), Mt 5: 25 (likewise), Mk 5: 23 (acc. to A), Mt 13: 5 = Jn 12: 40 = A 28: 27 (μήποτε or ἵνα μή) OT (Is 6: 10); Mt 20: 28 add. D μήποτε...ἐπέλθῃ...καὶ καταισχυνθήσῃ; Barn 4.3 ἵνα ταχύνῃ καὶ ἥξει (S for -ῃ), Herm Man 6.2.10, Sim 9.7.6, 28.5; Raderm.² 216. Following an impera.: Herm Vis 2.1.3 λάβε καὶ ἀποδώσεις μοι, Man 2.1 ἄκακος γίνου καὶ ἔσῃ (Lat. esto) ὡς...(Lk 22: 10 ἀκολουθήσατε...καὶ ἐρεῖτε); Raderm.² 216f.

(4) The one instance in Jn is 11: 57 where ὅπως is evidently used for the sake of variety since ἵνα has just preceded; the same thing applies to Paul in 1 C 1: 29, 2 C 8: 14, 2 Th 1: 12 (not 2 C 8: 11, G 1: 4, Phm 6; ἵνα...ἵνα G 4: 5, 1 C 4: 6). Further Epict. 4.5.5, Tatian 41.8 Schwartz. For the expression of purpose Jn uses hardly anything but ἵνα and does not care for the final inf. at all. On the retreat of ὅπως in the Hell. period cf. Reinhold 106; Knuenz 9ff., 28, 34ff.; Schwyzer II 673. However, in the Ptol. pap. ὅπως is almost as frequent as ἵνα but four-fifths of the exx. are in official documents (Mayser II 1, 247–52, 256, 257, 261). Ἵνα in final object clauses: ibid. 242ff.; II 3, 51. Ὅπως and ἵνα often interchange (ibid. II 1, 245; cf. Diog. Oen. 60.1.8 οὐχ ἵνα...ἀλλ' ὅπως, 1 Clem 65.1 ὅπως...εἰς τό with inf.). The fut. also appears infrequently with ὅπως in the pap. (ibid. 251).

(5) Ὅπως ἄν: Lk 2: 35, A 3: 20, 15: 17 OT (from Amos 9: 12, where our text does not have ἄν [Ziegler except in A as a back-reading]); in quotation also R 3: 4 = Ps 50 (51): 6 (R 9: 17 OT acc.

to FG; from Ex 9: 16, where our text is without ἄν). Mayser II 1, 254–7 (ὅπως ἄν very often in the pap., predominantly in official texts); II 3, 50. An uncertain ex. of ἵνα ἄν may be found in Mayser II 1, 246.

(6) Jn 5: 20 SL, G 6: 12 𝔓⁴⁶ACF al., T 2: 4 S*AF al., E 1: 18 FG ἵνα οἴδατε, etc. Cf. Gregory 125; Reinhold 106. Φυσιοῦσθε 1 C 4: 6 and ζηλοῦτε G 4: 17 are subjunctives, s. §91. Jn 17: 24 θεωροῦσιν W, -ῶσιν W², Rev 16: 15 βλέπουσιν 𝔓⁴⁷ minusc. IEph 4.2 ἵνα... ᾄδετε and ἵνα... μετέχετε (Reinhold 107). Only inferior orthography in the Ptol. pap. (Mayser II 1, 244d 1).—On the whole Rob. 980–7; Moule 138f.

370. Μή in an expression of apprehension is combined in classical with the subjunctive if the anxiety is directed towards warding off something still dependent on the will, with the indicative of all tenses if directed towards something which has already taken place or is entirely independent of the will. (1) This μή appears in the NT, usually strengthened by ποτε or πως (cf. MGr φοβοῦμαι μήπως), after φοβεῖσθαι only in Lk and Paul (Hebrews), and then always with the aorist subjunctive except H 4: 1 (μήποτε δοκῇ) and G 4: 11 (μήπως κεκοπίακα with reference to what has taken place). This construction is evidently literary and not a part of the vernacular (Viteau 83). Βλέπετε μή s. §364(3). (2) Dependent clauses with μήποτε (μήπως), which may be made to depend on any verb in order to express the accompanying and determining feeling of apprehension (moods and tenses as after φοβοῦμαι), are more common: G 2: 2 ἀνεθέμην αὐτοῖς τὸ εὐαγγέλιον..., μήπως εἰς κενὸν τρέχω (subjunctive) ἢ ἔδραμον. (3) The notion of negation is sometimes so weakened that something surmised is introduced without any thought of averting it: consequently Hellenistic μήποτε = 'whether perhaps, if possibly' (in main clauses = 'perhaps'). (4) Μή οὐ is used as in classical if the thing feared (or conjectured) is something negative.

(1) With aor. subj. A 23: 10 φοβηθεὶς (HLP εὐλαβηθεὶς) μὴ διασπασθῇ, 27: 17, 29 (μήπως), 2 C 11: 3 (ditto), 12: 20 (ditto). With pres. subj. cf. the related ἐπισκοποῦντες μή τις ἐνοχλῇ H 12: 15 (but cf. §165). R 11: 21 μήπως (𝔓⁴⁶DFG al.; om. SABCP) οὐδὲ σοῦ φείσεται (-σηται only minusc.) loosely dependent on v. 20 φοβοῦ (therefore fut.). Ἀγωνιᾶν with μήποτε following GP 5: 15 (Da LXX 1: 10 ἀγωνιῶ τὸν βασιλέα ἵνα μὴ ἴδῃ = Theod. φοβοῦμαι τ. β. μήποτε ἴδῃ, with μήποτε PGiess 19.3, with μή Polyb. 3.9.2 ἀγωνιῶν μὴ πιστευθῇ). (2) 1 Th 3: 5 ἔπεμψα..., μήπως ἐπείρασεν ὑμᾶς ὁ σατανᾶς καὶ εἰς κενὸν γένηται (feared result) ὁ κόπος ἡμῶν, A 5: 39 (Lk 3: 15 opt., s. §386(2)). With transi-

tion to final μή: Lk 14: 8f. μὴ κατακλιθῇς..., μήποτε... ᾖ κεκλημένος (ἥξει D; perf. subj. also after ἵνα: Jn 17: 19, 23, 1 C 1: 10, 2 C 1: 9, in all cases easily understandable)..., καὶ ἐρεῖ (cf. §369(3)). As in D in the above passage the fut. = the aor. subj., so elsewhere the fut. occasionally after final μή: Mk 14: 2 μήποτε ἔσται (Mt 7: 6 v.l.), Herm Sim 9.28.7, Man 10.2.5 (to be corrected to ἐντεύξεται instead of -ηται); cf. Reinhold 106 and βλέπετε μή (μήποτε) ἔσται C 2: 8, H 3: 12 (§369(2)). Mt 20: 28 s. §369(3).

(3) 2 T 2: 25 μήποτε δῷ (not δώῃ opt., cf. §§95(2) and 369(1)) αὐτοῖς ὁ θεός etc. (Lk 3: 15 [§386(2)] indirect question, likewise 11: 35 σκόπει μή... ἐστίν).

(4) Mt 25: 9 μήποτε οὐκ ἀρκέσῃ SALΣ, for which BCDW al. have μ. οὐ μὴ ἀρκ. (not impossible) (ἀρκέσει D).—Independent clauses with μή and the subj. are usually imperative (§363(3)); 1 Th 5: 15 ὁρᾶτε, μή τις ἀποδοῖ, ἀλλά... διώκετε belongs here (on ὁρᾶτε before impera. and subj. s. §364(3) and 461(1)). Mt 25: 9 is an exception: μήποτε οὐκ ἀρκέσῃ (supra), cf. Plato's μὴ ἀγροικότερον ᾖ 'it might be too rude', also UPZ I 61.16 (162 BC) μὴ οὐκ ἀποδῶ σοι (only ex. in Ptol. pap.; Mayser II 1, 234).—On the whole Rob. 987ff.

(iv) Conditional sentences

371. Introduction. The following five forms of conditional sentence are represented in classical Greek: (1) Εἰ with the indicative of all tenses denotes a simple conditional assumption with emphasis on the reality of the assumption (not of what is being assumed): the condition is considered 'a real case'. (2) Εἰ with the optative presents something as thought of, without regard for reality or unreality, and emphasizes the hypothetical character of the assumption: 'a potential case'. (3) Εἰ with an augmented tense of the indicative marks the assumption as contrary to fact: 'an unreal case'. (4) Ἐάν with the subjunctive denotes that which under certain circumstances is expected from an existing general or concrete standpoint in the present: 'case of expectation' and 'iterative case in present time'. (5) Εἰ with the optative also specifies repetition in past time. A great amount of shifting has taken place in the later language: (2) is barely represented in the NT (§385(2)); (5) has disappeared (s. §367); (1) has lost ground in that it is predominantly used with reference to a present or alleged reality (probably as a result of its contrast to the unreal case). Furthermore, the contrary to fact condition (3) persists (§360), but otherwise ἐάν with subjunctive prevails. It goes without saying that these categories are also sometimes mixed. MGr uses only ἄν (= ἐάν) with the real and unreal indicative and with a futuristic and generalizing subjunctive (Thumb² §277).—Debrunner, GGA 1926, 149f.; Mayser ɪɪ 1, 275ff.

ʼΕάν–ἄν: disyllabic ἐάν is always used for 'if', never ἄν, while inversely ἐάν frequently appears for ἄν in relative clauses; s. §107. On the other hand, κἄν also appears along with καὶ ἐάν for 'and if' and 'even if', s. §18. *Negatives*: class. employs μή in all conditional sentences; in the NT often εἰ οὐ, but always ἐὰν μή, cf. §428 (1 and 2). On the relationship of εἰ and ἐάν also s. Mayser ɪɪ 1, 277f.; ɪɪ 3, 86f., 91; Wahrmann, IF 54 [1936] 65f.—S. Rob. 1004–27 whose organization is especially lucid (adapted from Hermann *et al.*): the two major types yield four basic forms (with variations; classified acc. to function): (1) determined as fulfilled (*supra* (1)); (2) determined as unfulfilled (*supra* (3)); (3) undetermined, with prospect of determination (*supra* (4)); (4) undetermined, with remote prospect of determination (*supra* (2)). The lack of any generally accepted terminology makes easy reference difficult. The classical grammars are also hopelessly at variance.

372. Εἰ with the indicative of reality. (1) With reference to a present reality = 'if...really' (as you say, as is believed, as you see, etc.) or = 'if therefore' (resulting from what has been said), often closely bordering on causal 'since' (Stahl 513; Hermann 276): (*a*) with the present e.g. A 5: 38f. ἐὰν ᾖ ἐξ ἀνθρώπων ἡ βουλὴ αὕτη..., but then εἰ δὲ ἐκ θεοῦ ἐστιν 'if, as one may suppose, it be..., but if (as these persons claim) it really is'. Mt 6: 30 εἰ τὸν χόρτον...ὁ θεὸς οὕτως ἀμφιέννυσιν 'if therefore (according to what has been said in *vv.* 28f.) God so clothes (even)...', οὐ πολλῷ μᾶλλον ὑμᾶς; (*b*) with the past, e.g. Mk 3: 26 εἰ ὁ σατανᾶς ἀνέστη ἐφ᾽ ἑαυτόν (which according to his opponents' words must now have taken place), but in the fictive examples of 24f.: ἐὰν βασιλεία (οἰκία) ἐφ᾽ ἑαυτὴν μερισθῇ; (*c*) with the future, e.g. Mt 26: 33 = Mk 14: 29 εἰ (καὶ) πάντες σκανδαλισθήσονται (as you have just predicted); 1 C 9: 11 εἰ ἡμεῖς ὑμῖν τὰ πνευματικὰ ἐσπείραμεν ('since we, as everyone admits...'), μέγα εἰ ἡμεῖς ὑμῶν τὰ σαρκικὰ θερίσομεν; ('if subsequently, as actually happened, we...' = 'that we...'). (2) Without this causal or restrictive implication, εἰ with the indicative of reality is nearly limited (*a*) to disjunctive deductions (predominantly in Paul), e.g. 1 C 3: 14f. εἴ τινος τὸ ἔργον μενεῖ..., εἴ τινος τὸ ἔργον κατακαήσεται, and (*b*) to other kinds of logical reasoning in Paul, e.g. 1 C 15: 13ff. above all; (*c*) other cases are very rare. (3) Encroachment of εἰ on the sphere of ἐάν appears to have

taken place sporadically, e.g. Mt 5: 29 εἰ ὁ ὀφθαλμός σου σκανδαλίζει σε, cf. 30, 18: 8f., but ἐὰν σκανδαλίζῃ Mk 9: 43, 45, 47. (4) Εἰ in oaths and asseverations is a strong Hebraism = 'certainly not' (Hebr. **אִם**; aposiopesis): Mk 8: 12 εἰ δοθήσεται. The complete sentence implied by this kind of aposiopesis appears e.g. LXX Ps 7: 4ff. εἰ ἐποίησα τοῦτο, εἰ..., καταδιώξαι ἄρα ὁ ἐχθρὸς τὴν ψυχήν μου (the most frequent type of self-execration is τάδε ποιήσαι μοι κύριος καὶ τάδε προσθείη).

(1) (*a*) Jn 11: 12 εἰ κοιμᾶται (D thus for κεκοίμηται) (as Jesus has just said); Mt 17: 4 εἰ θέλεις (if, as appears to be the case...); 8: 2 ἐὰν θέλῃς 'if you wish (but in modesty I leave that open)...': Zerwick, Graec. bibl. 71; but without such a nuance Lk 22: 42 (Mt 26: 39; cf. Mk 14: 36?), Zerwick, *op. cit.* 72. Mt 19: 10, R 8: 11, G 1: 9 (8 is different). Jn 7: 4 εἰ ταῦτα ποιεῖς ('if, as you say, you want to do that...'). H 7: 15 ('as said before' [11]). 1 C 7: 36 εἰ δέ τις ἀσχημονεῖν ἐπὶ τὴν παρθένον αὐτοῦ νομίζει ('as you tell me'), ἐὰν ᾖ ὑπέρακμος (referring to the future). Also belonging here are the references from §281: R 7: 16, 20 and G 2: 18 (= 'by the fact that...') for the 1st pers. and R 2: 17ff. and 11: 17 for the 2nd pers. Εἰ οὖν = 'if therefore' e.g. Lk 11: 13, Jn 13: 14 (aor.). 'Inasmuch as': Jn 13: 17 εἰ ταῦτα (what I just said) οἴδατε (ταῦτα εἰδότες *em*), μακάριοί ἐστε ἐὰν ποιῆτε (referring to the future) αὐτά. Lk 17: 6 is pregnant: εἰ ἔχετε πίστιν..., ἐλέγετε ἄν...'if you really (*v.* 5) have—(but you do not; yet if you had), then...'. There is a construction somewhat different from Lk 17: 6 in an imperfect letter UPZ ɪ 70.3 (c. 152 ʙᴄ) (ε)ἰ μὴ μικρόν τι ἐντρέπομαι, οὐκ ἄν με (ε)ἶδες (mixture of 'If I were not ashamed' and 'I am ashamed' (cf. Mayser ɪɪ 1, 228); BGU ɪɪ 595.13f. (70–80 ᴀᴅ) εἰ μὴ ὅτι ὁ υἱός μου ἀσθεν(ε)ῖ δ(ε)ινῶς, τούτου εἵνεκα ἀνηρχόμην (mixture of εἰ μὴ ἠσθένει, ἀνηρχόμην (ἄν) and ὅτι ἀσθενεῖ, οὐκ ἀνέρχομαι; cf. Olsson p. 136). ʼΕάν can express indefinite relation to a present reality: 1 C 4: 15 ἐὰν γὰρ μυρίους παιδαγωγοὺς ἔχητε 'even if you should have' (class. potential or unreal). 13: 2 ἐὰν ἔχω προφητείαν καὶ οὐδα (error for οἶδα) FG (pm. εἰδῶ)...οὐθέν εἰμι, cf. *vv.* 1, 3. Jn 5: 31 ἐὰν ἐγὼ μαρτυρῶ περὶ ἐμαυτοῦ, ἡ μαρτυρία μου οὐκ ἔστιν ἀληθής; μαρτυρῶ could also be meant as an indic. ('as I said before', cf. 8: 14 κἂν ἐγὼ μαρτυρῶ 'even if I do...'). Sporadically ἐάν appears for εἰ (= ἐπεί) with such causal pres. (perf.) indicatives (vulgarism; Debrunner, Glotta 11 [1920] 25): 1 Jn 5: 15 ἐὰν οἴδαμεν (Sᶜ ἴδωμεν is not good; in a similar sense 2: 29 ἐὰν εἰδῆτε 'just as, as soon as..., you also know', where the transition to the other, here less appropriate, ἐάν-construction is complete); 1 Th 3: 8 ἐὰν ὑμεῖς στήκετε (-ητε S*DE); cf. Ghedini, Vang. ap. 466. ʼΕὰν ἦν (also 𝔓⁴⁶ 1 C 7: 36, 14: 28), ἦσθα or

ἦσαν in the pap. (Mayser I² 2, 86; II 1, 285; Mlt. 187 [264]; Harsing 47f.; Horn 27–31) and in the LXX is different; these forms of εἶναι are meant as subj. (confusion of subj. and imperf. of εἶναι; cf. ἦι for imperf. ἦν Mayser I² 2, 86), s. Debrunner, *op. cit.* 25f. Ἐάν with indic. elsewhere in the pap. (Mayser II 1, 284f.): ἐὰν δεῖ PTebt I 58.56 (111 BC) (Dit., Syll.² 344.7 [*c.* 303 BC]; acc. to the editor δεῖ = δῇ = δέῃ; cf. ὅσων ἂν προσδεῖ 973.32 [338–322 BC]; but ἐὰν δῇ 972.62 [175–2 BC], Aristoph., Ra. 565, Plut. 216 [where the best MSS have δεῖ]) for the common ἐὰν δέῃ; ἐὰν φαίνεται in pap. of 141 BC, 116 BC, 181 AD (PSI v 501.2 [257 BC] corrected to φαίνηται) for the common ἐὰν φαίνηται. Otherwise ἐάν with indic. from ii AD on. Mk 11: 13 D s. § 368; ὅπου ἐάν with pres. indic. § 380(3). Only ἐάν in MGr, not εἰ; s. § 371. (*b*) H 12: 25 εἰ γὰρ ἐκεῖνοι οὐκ ἐξέφυγον..., πολὺ μᾶλλον ἡμεῖς; cf. *supra* (*a*) Jn 13: 14, Mt 6: 30 and Lk 11: 13. (*c*) 1 P 2: 20 εἰ ὑπομενεῖτε twice ('that...') as above v. 19 εἰ ὑποφέρει τις. Εἰ with the fut. in pap. is frequently employed for veiled threats and the like: Mayser II 1, 283.

(2) (*a*) 2 T 2: 11f. εἰ συναπεθάνομεν..., εἰ ὑπομένομεν..., εἰ ἀρνησόμεθα; R 8: 13, 1 C 11: 6; Rev 13: 10 v.l. ἀποκτείνει (and ἀπάγει), Lk 6: 4 add. in D. (*b*) R 8: 10, 11, 1 C 7: 9. (*c*) 1 C 10: 30 εἰ ἐγὼ χάριτι μετέχω (§ 281; or 'if, as of course I do, I...' = 'inasmuch as'?). Hell. εἰ θέλεις corresponds to French *s'il vous plaît*: Herodas 7.70, 8.6 etc.; similar request Mt 17: 4 εἰ θέλεις ποιήσω 'please, shall I make...?'

(3) Lk 6: 32 εἰ ἀγαπᾶτε, but 33 ἐὰν ἀγαθοποιῆτε (Mt 5: 46 ἐὰν ἀγαπήσητε); Lk 11: 8 εἰ καὶ οὐ δώσει (= Att. ἐὰν καὶ μὴ δῷ; Lk has in mind 'though he will not give'), cf. the mixture of the fut. and aor. subj. in vv. 5ff. Mk 9: 42 is an encroachment on the domain of the unreal: καλόν ἐστιν αὐτῷ μᾶλλον, εἰ περίκειται..., καὶ βέβληται (DW correctly περιέκειτο... ἐβλήθη) = Lk 17: 2 (D περιέκειτο...ἔρ(ρ)ιπτο); cf. § 360(4). Zerwick, Graec. bibl. 72 takes it differently: '*talis homo lapide aggravatus in mare projectus bene stat*' (Ital. *sta bene!*); vivid presentation; likewise G 5: 11 εἰ ἔτι κηρύσσω 'assuming that I preach'. On 1 Th 5: 10 εἴτε...εἴτε with subj. inserted within a final clause s. § 369(2). Εἰ is found with the subj. in early poets and Hdt. (K.-G. II 474), but also in Aristoph., Eq. 698, etc. and in various dialects (Hermann 277ff.), then again in later prose (Reinhold 107; Jannaris § 1988f.; Mlt. 239 n. on p. 169 [295]; Raderm.² 199; O. Schulthess, Festgabe Kaegi [Frauenfeld, 1919] 161f.; Debrunner, *op. cit.* 25; Ghedini, Vang. ap. 465; Bezdechi 44), in the pap. beg. i AD (Olsson 146; Ghedini, Aegyptus 15 [1935] 235); Rev 11: 5 καὶ εἰ...θελήσῃ SA (θέλει CP, 𝔓⁴⁷ probably correct θελήσει; or is κἄν to be written in view of ΚΑΙΗ in S*??); εἰ...μερισθῇ Lk 11: 18 𝔓⁴⁵Γ (pm. (δι)ἐμερίσθη). On 1 C 14: 5 s. § 376.

(4) Εἰ εἰσελεύσονται εἰς τὴν κατάπαυσίν μου H 3: 11, 4: 3, 5 stems from the LXX Ps 94 (95): 11; further references from the LXX in Riggenbach on H 3: 11. S. § 454(5).

For εἰ with the unreal indicative s. § 360, with the optative §§ 385(2); 386(2).

373. Ἐάν. (1) Ἐάν with the present subjunctive refers to the future: ἐὰν θέλῃς δύνασαι Mt 8: 2 etc. (εἰ θέλεις s. § 372(2c)). (2) There is no certain example of ἐάν with the future indicative (cf. § 363) in the NT: Mt 18: 19 ἐὰν συμφωνήσουσιν (-ωσιν FGKMW al.; general condition). (3) The aorist subjunctive appears in the great majority of cases, both in general conditions and in those referring to something impending, and occasionally also in those referring to something which was impending in past time (ἐὰν εὕρῃ A 9: 2; province of the optative, s. § 385(2)).—For ἐάν instead of εἰ with the present indicative s. § 372(1a).

(1) Mk 14: 31 ἐάν με δέῃ; 1 Jn 2: 3 ἐὰν τηρῶμεν (φυλάξωμεν S*), cf. 2: 1 ἵνα μὴ ἁμάρτητε and ἐάν τις ἁμάρτῃ. Ἐάν in the sense of the class. 'real' εἰ: Jn 21: 22 ἐὰν αὐτὸν θέλω μένειν is safeguarded by the author in *v.* 23 against the interpretation 'if, as is to be expected' which is the only possible one in Att., and is also a conceivable one in Koine.

(2) Lk 19: 40 ἐὰν σιωπήσουσιν SABLRW al., -σωσιν ΓΔ al., σιγήσουσιν D (of an imminent possibility), A 8: 31 ἐὰν μή τις ὁδηγήσει με SB*CE (ditto), 2 C 10: 8 καυχήσομαι SLP (-σωμαι al., both side by side 𝔓⁴⁶), Rev 2: 22 SA (ditto, but *v.* 5 ἐὰν μὴ μετανοήσῃς). Herm Man 5.1.2 ἐὰν ἔσῃ (A for ᾖς), 4.3.7 ἐὰν μηκέτι προσθήσω, Vis 1.3.2 v.l.—Pap. (Mayser II 1, 285; II 3, 91): γράψεις ZenP Cairo III 59 496.4 (iii BC), κυριεύουσι Mitteis, Chr. 153.23 (108 BC), ἐρεῖ Preisigke, Sammelbuch 5627.11 (vulgar; Ptol.?). Aesop.: Ursing 71.

(3) Now impending, e.g. Mt 21: 25f. ἐὰν εἴπωμεν, Jn 16: 7 ἐὰν μὴ ἀπέλθω...ἐὰν δὲ πορευθῶ. In the pap. almost as many pres. subjunctives (mostly futuristic) as aor. subj. (Mayser II 1, 288).

374. Concessive clauses, introduced by εἰ καί or ἐὰν καί 'although', require no special remarks since they merely form a subspecies of the conditional clause as in the classical period.

Κἄν combines in itself the meanings 'and if' (purely conditional) and 'if only, even if' (*etsi*, i.e. concessive in itself), cf. § 457; it has also become a particle = 'at least, (even) if only' (cf. § 18), thus Mk 5: 28, 6: 56, A 5: 15, 2 C 11: 16, H 10: 2 𝔓⁴⁶ (SACD correctly οὐκ ἄν), 2 Clem 7.3, 18.2 (Att.). Κἄν also in the pap. (Harsing 46; Ghedini, Lett. crist. 70), Hell. and later authors (Jannaris § 598; Scham 57; W. Schmid, PhW 1934, 923) and MGr; s. Passow-Crönert 477f.

375. Εἰ is used in expressions of expectation which accompany the action like classical εἰ and ἐάν = Latin *si (forte)*. It exhibits its relationship to the εἰ in indirect questions in that it may also be strengthened by the addition of ἄρα or ἄραγε (also with πως A 27: 12, R 1: 10, 11: 14, Ph 3: 11, which appears in the NT only after εἰ and μή), and in that it does not exclude the subjunctive (Mayser II 3, 54): διώκω εἰ καταλάβω Ph 3: 12 (cf. § 368 and for the related μή, μήποτε, μήπως 'whether perhaps' § 370). With Ph 3: 12 cf. UPZ I 78.16 (159 BC) ἐπορευόμην, ἕως καταλάβω αὐτάς (Mayser II 1, 270) in the light of § 383(2). ISm 4.1 προσεύχεσθαι..., ἐάν πως μετανοήσωσιν. Also with the future indicative: A 8: 22 εἰ ἄρα ἀφεθήσεται; with the optative s. § 386(2).

376. (᾿Εκτὸς) εἰ [ἐάν] μή (τι) 'unless, except (that)' and εἰ δὲ μή 'otherwise'. Εἰ μή (classical) usually without a finite verb following. Εἰ μή (τι) with a verb e.g. G 1: 7 εἰ μή τινές εἰσιν = πλὴν ὅτι (A 20: 23) τ. ε. 'except that', 2 C 13: 5 εἰ μή τι ἀδόκιμοί ἐστε 'unless it were so', Mk 6: 5. ᾿Εκτὸς εἰ μή (Hellenistic, Nägeli 33; mixture of εἰ μή and ἐκτὸς εἰ) with aorist indicative 1 C 15: 2, with subjunctive 14: 5 ἐκτὸς εἰ μή διερμηνεύῃ (-νεύων D*), cf. § 372(3), Homil Clem 11.6.6, 17.16.4; without verb 1 T 5: 19, Homil Clem 17.8.6 (*ibid.* with the optative; 18.6.4, 14.2 with present indicative, 10.9.3 ἐκτὸς εἰ μή τις οὐ βλέπει 'unless...not'). ᾿Εκτὸς εἰ μή is pleonastic: J. Vendryes, Bull. Soc. Ling. 46 (1950) 16f. Just as εἰ has driven out ἐάν for the most part in these constructions, εἰ often appears for the ἐάν of the sentence in its full form in the elliptical formula εἰ δὲ μή(γε) 'otherwise' (§ 439(1)), while ἐάν δὲ μή does not appear at all. The situation is comparable in Attic (§ 480(6)); MGr εἰδεμή(ς) 'otherwise'.

1 C 7: 17 εἰ μή...περιπατείτω with εἰ μή = πλήν 'but', s. § 448(8). Εἰ μή with the subj. Lk 9: 13 εἰ μή τι πορευθέντες ἀγοράσωμεν (all uncials) 'if we do not perhaps buy'; Viteau 114 interprets the subj. as deliberative, scil. βούλει 'if we should not buy', but cf. ἐκτὸς εἰ μή...κατασκευάσωσιν in Vett. Val. p. 37. 20 Kroll (Raderm.² 199) and the inscr. χωρὶς εἰ μή τι πάθῃ CIG 3902 m 6 (ἐκτὸς εἰ μή ἐάν with subj. on an inscr., s. Deissmann, BS 115 [BS 118]). Frequently οὐκ...εἰ μή in the Synoptics (also εἰ μή...οὐκ, e.g. Mk 8: 14) in imitation of Aram. (Wellhausen, Einl.² 16). ᾿Εάν μή is seldom used for 'but, save' (Att. likewise) and always without verb: G 2: 16, Mk 4: 22 SB (s. § 448(8)). Homil Clem 18.9.2 οὐκ εἴ τις δὲ συλλογισθείη. 1 C 7: 5 εἰ μή τι ἄν (om. ἄν 𝔓⁴⁶B) ἐκ συμφώνου 'except by agreement' is a hypo-

thetical modification of εἰ μή τι which was felt to be a unit (this was popular especially with Coptic scribes and even penetrated Coptic; Kapsomenakis 110 n. 1) after the analogy of ὅστις ἄν etc. (cf. οὐκ ἄλλως..., εἰ μήτι ἄν ὅτι...'for no other reason than that...' Homil Clem 16.4. So in Hellenistic εἰ τι(ς) which was felt to be the equivalent of ὅστις, ὅ τι (e.g. Mt 18: 28 ἀπόδος, εἰ τι ὀφείλεις for ὅ τι ἄν ὀφείλῃς; also cf. § 475(2) and Tabachovitz, Eranos 30 [1932] 122ff.) was often supplemented with ἄν (ἐάν) (pap. and inscrip. from 99 AD on: Deissmann, NBS 32.1 [BS 204.1]; Reinhold 35; Trunk 56; Mlt. 169, 239 [264f.]; Raderm.² 199; Wackernagel, Anredeformen 27f. [= Kl. Schr. 994f.]; Hermann 273; Debrunner, Glotta 11 [1920] 14 n. 2; Ursing 72): Ljungvik, Syntax 9ff. (who rightly rejects Wackernagel's assumption of the adoption into Koine of Dor. αἴ τί(ς) κα, although εἰ τι(ς) ἄν was probably facilitated by it).

(v) Relative clauses

377. Introduction. The subjunctive may be employed in three ways in relative clauses: (1) with ἄν in the sense of a conditional clause: ὅστις ἄν θέλῃ = ἐάν τις θέλῃ. (2) Without ἄν in a final sense, in which case the subjunctive has driven out the Attic future, though not entirely. (3) As a hortatory subjunctive (as in Attic): H 12: 28 δι' ἧς λατρεύωμεν (-ομεν SKMP, -σωμεν 𝔓⁴⁶) 'through which let us worship', corresponding to the 2nd person imperative (1 P 5: 9 ᾧ ἀντίστητε, 12 εἰς ἣν στῆτε).—Rob. 953–62.

᾿Εάν–ἄν: ἐάν also appears for ἄν following the popular custom of the period, with prodigious variation, of course, in the MSS (s. § 107); as in Att., the position of the particle is immediately after the relative, unless δέ or γάρ intervenes.—*Negatives*: μή is always the negative with the subj., οὐ usually after the indic. even in the instances where Att. required μή (cf. § 428(4)), hence similar to εἰ οὐ § 371.

378. Final relative clauses in the NT also occasionally exhibit the future as in Attic, but otherwise the subjunctive; the latter is to be explained as an accommodation to the equivalent ἵνα-clause (and to Latin?).

Future: Mk 1: 2 = Mt 11: 10 = Lk 7: 27 ἀποστέλλω τὸν ἄγγελόν μου...ὃς κατασκευάσει (from Mal 3: 1, where the LXX as we know it reads differently), 1 C 4: 17 (RSV correctly 'to remind'). Subj. Mk 14: 14 = Lk 22: 11 ποῦ ἐστιν τὸ κατάλυμα ὅπου φάγω; (D in Mk φάγομαι) = ἵνα φάγω (accommodation to the indirect question οὐκ ἔχω, ὅπου φάγω or something similar); A 21: 16 ἄγοντες παρ' ᾧ ξενισθῶμεν Μνάσωνι = πρὸς Μνάσωνα, ἵνα ξεν. παρ' αὐτῷ. On the other hand ἵνα 2 C 12: 7 ἐδόθη μοι σκόλοψ…ἄγγελος σατανᾶ, ἵνα με κολαφίζῃ (Viteau 135). The LXX varies in Jer 17: 5 ἐπικατάρατος ὁ ἄνθρωπος, ὅς… ἔχει…καὶ στηρίσει…καὶ…ἀποστῇ (with secondary variants, cf. Ziegler). Only the fut., not the subj., in the Ptol. pap. (Mayser II 1, 214, 267). Hell. exx. of the subj. in Raderm.² 170.

379. Qualitative-consecutive relative clauses.
Related to final relative clauses are those which designate a sort of consequence resulting from some quality ('such that'); in Latin such clauses, like those of §378, take the subjunctive. The few NT examples have either future (classical) or aorist subjunctive; οὐδείς (ἐστιν) ὅστις (ὅς) is used as in classical with any indicative (e.g. aorist Mk 10: 29).

Fut.: in Lk 7: 4 ἄξιός ἐστιν ᾧ παρέξῃ (mid.) τοῦτο the relative instead of ἵνα is a Latinism: *dignus qui* with the subj.; Senatorial decree, Thisbe, Dit., Syll.³ 646.8f. (170 BC) ὅπως αὐτοῖς δοθῶσιν, οἷς τὰ καθ' αὐτοὺς πράγματα ἐξηγήσωνται = *ut sibi darentur, quibus suas res exponerent* (or something similar). On the other hand ἵνα Jn 1: 27 ἄξιος ἵνα λύσω (synonymous with ἱκανός λῦσαι; the inf. after ἄξιος, Mk 1: 7 etc., is also customary in class.). The fut. in Lk 11: 6 οὐκ ἔχω ὃ παραθήσω is classical, but ὅ is not; ὅ τι would have been required (§293). In ἔχειν τι ὃ προσενέγκῃ H 8: 3 (cf. 1 Clem 38.2 ἔδωκεν δι' οὗ ἀναπληρωθῇ, s. Reinhold 108; Raderm.² 170f.) classical would have used either ὅ τι (indirect question) or the fut. as in Ph 2: 20 οὐδένα ἔχω… ὅστις μεριμνήσει (cf. §368); Isocr. 4.44 ἔχειν ἐφ' οἷς φιλοτιμηθῶσιν. Here, too, the inf. ἔχει τι προσενέγκαι would have been possible (§392(2)); for ἵνα as a NT substitute, s. Jn 5: 7.

380. Conditional relative clauses.
(1) Relative clauses which can be converted into conditional clauses usually make no assertions about concrete realities, but rather general assertions or suppositions, so that ὅς (ὅστις §293) ἄν, corresponding to the ἐάν of the conditional clause proper, appears as a rule. The present indicative in conditional relative clauses, which also appears in classical, expresses the definite supposition or the fact derived from preceding statements that such people exist; cf. εἰ §372(1a) and Mayser II 1, 266f. (2) The distinction between the aorist subjunctive with ἄν and the future indicative without ἄν is often obliterated: Mt 10: 32 ὅστις ὁμολογήσει, which corresponds to 33 ὅστις δ' ἂν ἀρνήσηται (cf. Lk 12: 8). The future, of course, can also be equal to the present with ἄν (Lk 17: 31 ὃς ἔσται ἐπὶ τοῦ δώματος), and the latter can replace the former in a durative *Aktionsart* (Mk 8: 35 ὃς ἐὰν θέλῃ…, ἀπολέσει, s. (3); Lk 8: 18, s. (1)). (3) The future indicative is just as permissible after ὃς ἄν as after ἐάν; unambiguous examples are wanting however (cf. ἐάν §373(1)); but cf. LXX Lev 27: 12 καθότι ἂν τιμήσεται, Barn 11: 8 SC ὃ ἐὰν ἐξελεύσεται. (4) It is claimed that the subjunctive without ἄν occurs with ὅστις, but nowhere do all the witnesses agree.—For ὃς ἄν with the imperfect and aorist indicative s. §367.

(1) Lk 8: 18 ὃς γὰρ ἂν (ἂν γάρ SBLX; om. ἂν W) ἔχῃ, δοθήσεται αὐτῷ, καὶ ὃς ἂν μὴ ἔχῃ, καὶ ὃ δοκεῖ ἔχειν (no longer hypothetical, for the supposition made in ὃς ἂν μὴ ἔχῃ has already been adopted; i.e. 'what, in view of what has just been said [*viz.* ὃς ἂν μὴ ἔχῃ], he in reality only thinks [δοκεῖ] he has') ἀρθήσεται ἀπ' αὐτοῦ; the form of the same gnomic saying in Mt 13: 12 and Mk 4: 25 is ὃς (ὅστις) γὰρ ἔχει (ἂν ἔχῃ in Mk AE²G al., ἂν ἔχει DE*F al.)…ὃς (ὅστις) οὐκ ἔχει (in Mk E*G al. οὐκ ἔχῃ). Lk 9: 50 (= Mk 9: 40) ὃς γὰρ οὐκ ἔστιν καθ' ὑμῶν (as follows from your report [*v.* 49]), ὑπὲρ ὑμῶν ἐστιν.

(2) Mt 18: 4 ὅστις ταπεινώσει ἑαυτόν instead of ὅ. ἄν with the subj., while in a similar sense the fut. in 23: 12 can be occasioned by the reference to the future of the disciples; 5: 39 (ῥαπίζει SBW is not good), 41 (D pres.).

(3) Ἀπολέσει Mk 8: 35 SBCD² al. (-σῃ ALW al.), Lk 17: 33 SAL al. (-σῃ BDEW al.); ὁμολογήσει 12: 8 AB*DR al.; δουλεύσουσιν A 7: 7 ACD. Cf. an inscr. ὃς ἂν συντελέσουσιν in a translation from Lat. (Viereck 38.48; 67 §8). Ἄν with the fut. Radermacher, Wien. Sitzb. 224, 5 (1947) 37 n. 1; Schwyzer II 352, 2; in Lucian and in the Sol.: M. D. Macleod, ClQ n.s. 6 (1956) 102–11. The pres. indic. after ἄν (ὅπου ἂν ὑπάγει Rev 14: 4, ᾧ ἐὰν βούληται Mt 11: 27 WL al.) is only late (Mlt. 166f. [262f.]) and is to be rejected in the NT. Cf. ἐάν and ὅταν with the pres. indic. §§372(1a); 382(4).

(4) Mt 10: 33 (om. ἄν BLW), Ja 2: 10 ὅστις… τηρήσῃ (SBC, -σει AKLP), πταίσῃ (SABC, -σει KLP) δὲ ἐν ἑνί; ὅσοι without ἄν G 6: 16 𝔓⁴⁶ στοιχήσουσιν (pm. -χήσουσιν, -χοῦσιν), twice in Herm Sim 8.11.3 (cf. Reinhold 108 above). Similar fluctuation in Mk 4: 26 ὡς ἄνθρωπος βάλῃ 'as if a man throws' (SBD al.; the other MSS add the indispensable ἐάν or ὅταν); cf. the analogous cases in LXX Is 7: 2, 17: 11, 31: 4. S. also Raderm.² 177.1; Mlt. 168f. [264]; Trunk 61; Hermann 278 n.; Mayser II 1, 264, 265.— Rob. 956f., 961f.

(vi) *Temporal clauses*

381. Introduction.
Temporal clauses in general are only a special class of relative clause and exhibit the same constructions. They are introduced by ὅτε, ὅταν, ὡς etc. (ὁπόταν only Barn 12.

2; ὁπότε and temporal ἐπεί and ἐπειδή only once each as v.l.), s. § 455. For temporal ὡς s. § 455(2).— Rob. 970–9.

382. Ὅτε and ὅταν. (1) Ὅτε is very frequently followed by the aorist indicative, but also takes the imperfect, perfect, present, and future according to the circumstances. The last usually occurs in constructions like ἔρχεται ὥρα, ὅτε προσκυνήσετε Jn 4: 21, to which relative constructions like οὐδέν ἐστιν κεκαλυμμένον, ὃ οὐκ ἀποκαλυφθήσεται Mt 10: 26 are closely related. (2) Consequently, in accordance with § 379 the subjunctive (without ἄν) for this future is also possible: Lk 13: 35 ἕως ἥξει ὅτε ('the time when') εἴπητε AD al. (3) Otherwise 'the day when' is expressed by ἡμέρα ὅταν with the subjunctive: Mt 9: 15 (= Mk 2: 20) ἐλεύσονται ἡμέραι ὅταν ἀπαρθῇ. (4) Ὅταν with the indicative denotes in the first place indefinite repetition in past time (§ 367); further, it is used with the future (§ 363) and present indicative (Debrunner, Glotta 11 [1920] 26 f.) like ἐάν (§§ 373(2); 372(1 a)): Lk 13: 28 ὅταν ὄψεσθε B*DX (-ησθε ACᶜᵒʳʳW al., ἴδητε S); Mk 11: 25 ὅταν στήκετε ACD al. (-ητε BGW al., στῆτε S), Barn 4.14 ὅταν βλέπετε 'when you see' (Reinhold 108 f.). With perfect indicative IEph 8.1 ὅταν…ἐνήρεισται (MSS ἐνείρισται). Finally in a quite vulgar way in narration of the past = 'when': Rev 8: 1 ὅταν ἤνοιξεν AC (ὅτε SP, as elsewhere in Rev, e.g. 6: 1, 3), cf. Reinhold 109; Debrunner, Glotta 11 (1920) 23 f. and MGr ὅταν with the indicative 'when' (correspondingly MGr ἄν 'if' with the indicative; § 371).

(1) Perf. 1 C 13: 11 ὅτε γέγονα, however B ἐγενόμην. Pres. H 9: 17, Jn 9: 4. Fut. on the pattern of ἔρχεται ὥρα ὅτε and the like also Jn 4: 23, 5: 25 (cf. 28), 16: 25, Lk 17: 22 (ὅτε ἐπιθυμήσετε, D τοῦ ἐπιθυμῆσαι ὑμᾶς), 2 T 4: 3; in such cases as in relative clauses (§ 379) the inf. can take the place of the fut., which in turn can be replaced by ἵνα with the subj.: Jn 16: 2 ἔρχεται ὥρα ἵνα δόξῃ; Mk 4: 22 (par. to Mt 10: 26, s. *supra*) ἐὰν μὴ ἵνα φανερωθῇ approximately = ὥστε φανερωθῆναι or, in better Att., οἷον φανερωθῆναι.

(2) V.l. ἕως (ἄν) εἴπητε as it reads in Mt 23: 39. Ὅτε with the subj. otherwise appears only in late Greek (Jannaris § 1988).

(3) Lk 5: 35 in the par. to Mt 9: 15 uses a clumsy but more correct construction: ἐλεύσονται ἡμέραι καί (§ 442(4)) ὅταν ἀπαρθῇ…, τότε νηστεύσουσιν (om. καί SC al.). Ὅταν Mt 26: 29 (Mk 14: 25) is more legitimate in the construction ἕως τῆς ἡμέρας ἐκείνης ὅταν πίνω, since this phrase is a periphrasis for Att. πρὶν ἄν. With ὅτε and the future in this

phrase R 2: 16 ἐν ἡμέρᾳ ὅτε κρινεῖ, but v.l. ἐν ᾗ ἡμ. κρινεῖ; Marcion by all appearances read neither the former nor the latter, but read it with asyndeton: ἀπολογουμένων. κρινεῖ etc., whereby the passage becomes correct.

(4) Ὅταν with the fut. also Rev 4: 9 ὅταν δώσουσιν (-σωσιν SQ; cf. § 95(1)); 2 Clem 12.2 ὅταν ἔσται (quotation), 17.6, Barn 15.5 (Reinhold 108). With Mk 11: 25 cf. ἐὰν στήκετε 1 Th 3: 8, for which, however, there is a reason (§ 372(1 a)). The pres. after ὅταν elsewhere is not sufficiently attested: Lk 11: 2 προσεύχεσθε ACHW al., Jn 7: 27 ἔρχεται SHXΔ*; entirely insufficiently Mk 13: 7 ἀκούετε. In the pap. only in the post-Christian period, e.g. BGU II 424.6 (ii/iii AD) ἐπὰν ἐπυθόμην (not pre-Christian: PPar 26. 14 = UPZ I 42.14 [162 BC] ὅτ' ἀνέβημεν, not ὅταν ἔβημεν, is to be read); Mlt. 168 [263]; Debrunner, Glotta 11 (1920) 24; Mayser II 1, 211 n. 1. Several places in the LXX; s. Debrunner, *loc. cit.*; Swete, Introduction 306.—Rob. 971–3.

383. 'Until, while, before'. (1) The particles and composite phrases meaning 'until' and 'while' (ἕως, ἕως οὖ [following μέχρι οὖ, ἄχρι οὖ; Ionic, s. Arnim 96 f.], ἕως ὅτου, ἐν ᾧ, ἄχρι(ς), ἄχρις οὖ, μέχρι(ς), μέχρις οὖ s. § 455(3)) take the indicative after the classical pattern. (2) Where the subjunctive appears ἄν is at times omitted with ἕως and probably always with ἕως οὖ (ὅτου), ἄχρις (οὖ), μέχρις (οὖ). The reason for this usage, which may be traced back a long way, probably lies in the fact that the old prospective subjunctive (Schwyzer II 310) survived in these clauses due to a certain affinity with the final clause. (3) Πρίν with the simple subjunctive, a favorite phrase of the classical authors (though Attic prose nearly always has ἄν; Hermann 309 f.; Rosenkranz, IF 48 [1930] 164), has the same affinity; NT authors have, so to speak, completely replaced such clauses by ἕως etc.

(1) Rarely the fut. indic.: Lk 13: 35 v.l. (§ 382(2)). The pres. in a fut. sense may be used for it: ἕως ἔρχομαι (cf. § 323) Jn 21: 22, 1 T 4: 13 'until I come' (cf. Mk 6: 45 SBL ἕως αὐτὸς ἀπολύει, v.l. ἀπολύσῃ -σει, D αὐτὸς δὲ ἀπολύει) = ἐν ᾧ ἔρχομαι Lk 19: 13; Viteau 129 f. interprets the references in Lk and Jn as 'while I go, while I depart', without being able to carry through this interpretation for 1 T. All contrary interpretations are utterly wrecked by Herm Sim 9.11.1: ἐὰν δὲ μὴ ἔλθῃ, μενεῖς μεθ' ἡμῶν ὧδε ἕως ἔρχεται 'until he comes' (his coming is *certain*, § 323(1)), 5.2.2, 9.10.5, 6. The meaning 'until' = ἐς ὅ (Hdt.) must therefore also be attributed to ἐν ᾧ Lk 19: 13 with *this* pres. (cf. ἐν ὅσῳ 'until' Thuc. 4.52. 3 [Stahl 454 f.], also ἕως etc. 'so long as' and 'until').

(2) *With* ἄν: Mt 5: 26 ἕως ἂν ἀποδῷς, and elsewhere

the fut. with ἄν (cf. ὅταν §382(4)): Rev 2: 25 ἄχρι
οὗ ἄν ἥξω. *Without* ἄν: Rev 17: 17 (however 046
τελεσθῶσιν as in 15: 8, 20: 3, 5). Cf. Reinhold 109.
Mk 13: 30 μέχρις οὗ (μ. ὅτου B, μέχρι S, ἕως W, ἕως οὗ
D) ταῦτα πάντα γένηται, 1 C 11: 26 ἄχρι οὗ (+ ἄν
ScDc al.) ἔλθῃ, E 4: 13 μέχρι καταντήσωμεν, Lk 21: 24
ἄχρι οὗ (om. οὗ A al.) πληρωθῶσιν, Lk 17: 8 ἕως
(+ ἄν AK al.) φάγω, Mk 14: 32 ἕως προσεύξωμαι
(D al. -ξομαι). Further e.g. 2 Th 2: 7 (ἕως ἄν FG),
Mt 14: 22 (ἀπολύσει ΚΓ al.), Lk 13: 8, 2 P 1: 19, even
ἄχρι ἧς ἡμέρας γένηται Lk 1: 20. Class. (Hdt., Thuc.
et al.; K.-G. II 449f.; Rosenkranz, IF 48 [1930]
164f.). Ptol. pap. ἕως with the subj., usually aor.
(Mayser II 1, 268, 270, 274; II 3, 79).

(3) Πρίν with the subj. Lk 2: 26 πρὶν ἤ (om. ἤ BW)
ἄν (om. ἄν ADW al.) ἴδῃ, however S* here, too, has
ἕως ἄν ἴδῃ; 22: 34 πρὶν ἤ ἀπαρνήσῃ AWΓ al., yet SBL
ἕως, K al. ἕως οὗ, D ἕως ὅτου; πρὶν ἀκουσθῶσι Herm
Sim 5.7.3 A (-θῆναι PMich). With the opt. A 25: 16,
s. §386(4). Elsewhere always with the inf. (§395).
Ptol. pap. never πρίν or πρὶν ἄν with a finite verb
(Mayser II 1, 275, 310).—Rob. 974–8.

(E) The Optative

384. The optative proper used to denote an
attainable wish (s. §359) is still in use in the NT as
it is in the LXX and papyri (negative μή). There
is, however, a strong tendency to use the imperative instead of the optative, not only in requests,
for which the imperative has a place in classical
too, but also in imprecations which in classical
take the optative: ἀνάθεμα ἔστω G 1: 8f., cf. 1 C
16: 22. The single example of the present optative
in a wish is A 8: 20 τὸ ἀργύριόν σου εἴη εἰς
ἀπώλειαν. Attic εἴθε and εἰ γάρ, used to introduce
a wish (§359(1)), do not occur; ὄφελον (s. §359(1))
is used with the future indicative for an attainable
wish: G 5: 12 ὄφελον καὶ ἀποκόψονται (-ψωνται
𝔓46DEFG) οἱ ἀναστατοῦντες ὑμᾶς 'would that
they would go ahead and castrate themselves'.
Cf. Lucian, Sol. 1 end, where ὄφελον...δυνήσῃ is
meant to be a solecism.

Altogether Mlt. 194f. [307f.] now counts 38 exx.
of the opt. in wishes, of which 15 are μὴ γένοιτο (Lk
20: 16, otherwise only in Paul, to express strong
rejection [always in response to a question, §440(2)];
likewise in the LXX [חָלִילָה] and elsewhere in Hell.
[p. 3 n. 2; §128(5)]; the only remnant of the
optative in MGr [and that not in the vernacular;
Mlt. p. 240 n. on p. 194 and p. 249 n. on p. 240 (307)];
exx. from the pap. in Mlt. 195f. [308 n.]); of the
remaining 23, 15 belong to Paul. Except Phm 20
ἐγώ σου ὀναίμην, used always in the 3rd pers. sing.
(Burton 79). Ὀναίμην (with gen.) 6 times in Ign;
βίου μὴ ὄναιντο on an imprecatory tablet iii BC

(Audollent, Defix. Tab. 92.3). 1 Th 5: 23 ἁγιάσαι
...καὶ...τηρηθείη, H 13: 21 καταρτίσαι (the only
ex. of the opt. in the literary Greek of the Epistle to
the Hebrews!), 1 P 5: 10 καταρτίσαι KLP (s. §74(1);
στηρίξαι, σθενώσαι only in minusc.), Mk 11: 14 μηκέτι
μηδεὶς φάγοι (DU. φάγῃ) (Mt 21: 19 is different). Opt.
in an adverse wish only Mk 11: 14, A 8: 20; in the quotation from Ps 108 (109): 8, A 1: 20 has λαβέτω for
LXX λάβοι. In such cases the opt., impera. and fut.
indic. are used in the pap. (Harsing 25). R 16: 20
συντρίψαι A, -ψει al.; 1 C 4: 6 λάμψαι ScCDc (opt.,
but vg *splendescere*), -ψει 𝔓46S*ABD*; Ph 4: 19
πληρώσαι D*FGΨ; 2 Th 2: 8 ἀνέλοι DG (al. ἀνελεῖ,
ἀναλώσει, ἀναλοῖ).—Rob. 939f.

385. The potential optative. (1) The optative
with ἄν in a main clause denoting what is merely
thought has disappeared from the vernacular.
The few examples are literary language befitting
the occasion; they are all in Lk: A 26: 29 (Paul
before Agrippa!) εὐξαίμην ἄν (with v.l. εὐξάμην
S*HLP al.; cf. Aeschin. 1.159); also the rhetorical
direct questions: πῶς γὰρ ἄν δυναίμην A 8: 31
and (as an utterance of the Athenians!) τί ἄν
θέλοι...οὗτος λέγειν 17: 18 (17: 20 DEHLΨ τί ἄν
θέλοι ταῦτα εἶναι; cf. §386(1)). The future indicative is often used in the NT where in Attic a
potential optative could have been used: R 3: 6
ἐπεὶ πῶς κρινεῖ ὁ θεὸς τὸν κόσμον; The deliberative
subjunctive also may substitute for the potential
optative (§366(1)), also τάχα with the indicative
(R 5: 7, cf. Arnim 86; Scham 83). (2) For the
potential optative in hypothetical protases (without ἄν) there are, in addition to the formulaic εἰ
τύχοι 'it may be, for example' in Paul (1 C 14:10,
15: 37), only a few examples in Acts and 1 P
(literary language), but it is never combined with
a potential optative in the apodosis.

(1) Fut. for potential (not unclass., §349(1),
Buttmann 188) also 1 C 15: 35 ἐρεῖ τις. Ἐβουλόμην
is used for βουλοίμην ἄν (§359(2)). On the infre-
quency of the potential in the pap., LXX and Ap.
Frs. s. Harsing 28; Reinhold 111; Mayser II 1,
290ff.; R. R. Ottley, A Handbook to the Sept.
(London, 1920) 199f. (LXX opt. with ἄν virtually
only in Gen and Job and nearly always in questions).
The potential opt. can also be replaced by a pres.
indic. with the meaning 'would' or 'could': πῶς
ὑμεῖς παιδεύειν θέλετε; Herm Vis 3.9.10, τί ἔχω
διψυχῆσαι; 'how (what) could I doubt?' 4.1.4. Τάχα:
Homil Clem 13.21.2 'if it were not a law that no
unbaptized person can enter the kingdom of God',
τάχα που τῶν ἐθνῶν οἱ πεπλανημένοι διὰ σωφροσύνης
μόνον σωθῆναι ἐδύναντο.

(2) A 24: 19 οὓς ἔδει...κατηγορεῖν, εἴ τι ἔχοιεν πρὸς

ἐμέ, for which εἴ τι ἔχουσιν or ἐάν τι ἔχωσιν might be more correct; 20: 16 ἔσπευδεν γάρ, εἰ δυνατὸν εἴη (ἦν LP al.; for the ἐστίν of direct discourse, due to the shift in tense; cf. K.-G. II 553f.) αὐτῷ, ... γενέσθαι εἰς Ἰερουσαλήμ (indirect; moreover εἰ may easily be understood in the sense of 'whether'; cf. 27: 12, 39, §386(2)); 1 P 3: 14 εἰ καὶ πάσχοιτε διὰ δικαιοσύνην, μακάριοι, 17 κρεῖττον ἀγαθοποιοῦντας, εἰ θέλοι τὸ θέλημα τοῦ θεοῦ, πάσχειν ἢ κακοποιοῦντες ('if perchance' as in Att.). For ἐάν with the subj. instead of the potential opt. s. §372(1a). Herm Sim 9.12.4 οὐδεὶς εἰσελεύσεται, εἰ μὴ λάβοι is the only ex. of the opt. in Hermas; Harnack reads λάβῃ on account of 8 ὃς ἂν μὴ λάβῃ, οὐκ εἰσελεύσεται; Reinhold 113. Εἰ with the potential opt. is infrequent also in the LXX, pap. (pap. almost never with potential opt. also in the apodosis): Mlt. 196 [309f.]; Harsing 38f.; Reinhold 112f.; Mayser II 1, 293; II 3, 91. Εἰ τύχοι also appears in Philo (Reik, Der Opt. bei Polyb. und Philo von Alex., Leipzig, 1907, p. 154).

386. The oblique optative. (1) The optative in indirect discourse (in subordinate clauses after secondary tenses), corresponding to the indicative or subjunctive of the direct, would be little used in the NT even without further reason simply because of the very strong overall preference for direct discourse. Only Lk occasionally employs the optative and even he never after ὅτι and ὡς, and rarely in indirect questions proper. Rather, his examples usually have ἄν with the optative and accordingly correspond to the potential optative of the direct question (§385(1)). (2) Isolated examples of the optative in indirect discourse after εἰ 'whether' (§§368 and 375): A 17: 27 ζητεῖν τὸν θεόν, εἰ ἄραγε ψηλαφήσειαν αὐτὸν καὶ εὕροιεν, cf. εἰ (πως) δύναιντο 27: 12, 39 and §385(2) and after μήποτε 'whether perhaps' (§370): Lk 3: 15 μήποτε εἴη. (3) No examples of the optative in final clauses occur (Mk 12: 2 ἵνα λάβοι only S). (4) In temporal clauses a single example: A 25: 16 (words of Festus) ἀπεκρίθην ὅτι οὐκ ἔστιν ἔθος χαρίζεσθαι..., πρὶν ἢ ὁ κατηγορούμενος ἔχοι...λάβοι τε, correctly used in indirect discourse for the subjunctive (with ἄν) of the direct. There are no instances of the optative in relative clauses.

(1) Lk 22: 23 τίς (ἄρα) εἴη all uncials (ἐστίν or ἦν only minusc.), A 21: 33 τίς εἴη (ἂν εἴη EHLP) καὶ τί ἐστιν πεποιηκώς; Lk 1: 29 ποταπὸς εἴη (ἂν εἴη D), 1: 62 τί ἂν θέλοι καλεῖσθαι, 6: 11 τί ἂν ποιήσαιεν (D is different), 8: 9 τίς εἴη (LΓΖ̄ without εἴη), 9: 46 τίς ἂν εἴη, 15: 26 (om. ἂν SAW al., D τί θέλει τοῦτο εἶναι), 18: 36 (om. ἂν SABPW al.), A 5: 24 τί ἂν γένοιτο τοῦτο, 10: 17 τί ἂν εἴη (2: 12 τί θέλει τοῦτο εἶναι as a direct question; E ἂν θέλοι; S θέλοι, i.e. as an indirect

question, which after λέγοντες is hardly admissible). Class. can retain every form of the direct question in the indirect, consequently the potential opt. also (Krüger §54, 6.6). Exx. of the oblique opt. in declarative and interrogative sentences are also scarce in the pap. and virtually limited to the pre-Christian period (Harsing 29ff.; Mayser II 1, 293f.).

(2) Cf. εἴπως δύναιντο in a pap. Wilcken, PTheb. Bank 12.12 (ii BC end).

(3) On E 1: 17 s. §§369(1) and 370(3). The opt. in final clauses is also exceedingly rare in the pap. etc. (it emerges to some extent again only under the influence of Atticism); Harsing 32f.; Reinhold 112; Mlt. 196f. [311]; Mayser II 1, 238, 252f.

(4) There are no examples of the oblique opt. in temporal clauses in the pap. (Harsing 36). 2 Clem 12.3 ὅταν λαλῶμεν...καὶ...εἴη is probably wrong (Reinhold 113).—Rob. 1030f., 1043f.

The iterative optative in subordinate clauses (§371) has been supplanted by ἄν with the imperfect or aorist indicative; s. §367.

(F) The Imperative

387. (1) The imperative in the NT keeps for the most part within the same limits as in classical usage. As in the latter it is by no means confined to commands, but also expresses a request or a concession: Mt 8: 32 ὑπάγετε, 2 C 12: 16 ἔστω δέ; cf. §384. (2) In the latter case the imperative can simply be the equivalent of a concessive clause: Jn 2: 19 λύσατε τὸν ναὸν τοῦτον (=ἐὰν καὶ λύσητε) καὶ ἐν τρισὶν ἡμέραις ἐγερῶ αὐτόν. (3) As a substitute for the imperative, in addition to the subjunctive (§364), the future indicative (§362) and the infinitive (§389), ἵνα with the subjunctive is also occasionally employed (vernacular, s. Slotty 35), and then either independently (like classical ὅπως with the future, French *que*) or with θέλω: E 5: 33 (after ἀγαπάτω) ἡ δὲ γυνὴ ἵνα φοβῆται τὸν ἄνδρα (cf. 1 C 7: 29, 2 C 8: 7 [ἵνα περισσεύητε; περισσεύετε would have been ambiguous]; §389), Mk 6: 25 θέλω ἵνα δῷς (δός Mt 14: 8).

(1) E 4: 26 OT also belongs here: ὀργίζεσθε καὶ μὴ ἁμαρτάνετε which most probably means 'you may be angry as far as I am concerned (if you can't help it), but do not sin thereby'.

(2) Cf. Soph., Ant. 1168ff. πλούτει K.-G. I 236f.

(3) Questions with οὐ and the fut. can also have an impera. sense (class. often): A 13: 10 οὐ παύσῃ διαστρέφων; (perhaps more of a reproach than a command); cf. Viteau 37. Ἵνα=impera. perhaps also in 1 T 1: 3; but in Mk 5: 23 παρεκάλει...ἵνα... ἐπιθῇς should probably be joined in thought (mixture

of ἵνα ἐπιθῇ and direct ἐπίθες). Ἵνα-clause as impera.:
C. F. Cadoux, JTS 42 (1941) 165–73; H. G. Meecham,
JTS 43 (1942) 179f. (180: 'certain in a few NT passages and probable in others'); A. R. George, JTS 45
(1944) 55–60. Pap. 41/2 AD (Aegyptus 33 [1953]
317) μὴ ἵνα σκύλῃς με ἐλθεῖν ἐπὶ σέ 'do not force me'.
T. Kalén, Selbständige Finalsätze...(Skrifter K.
Hum. Vet.-samf. i Uppsala 34, 2 [1914]), explains
the independent ἵνα-clause on the basis of the
imperatival inf. (pp. 22f.); NT exx. pp. 53–65, LXX
65–8. Pap. Mlt. 178f. [281]; Horn 120ff.; Mayser II
1, 231f. (ἵνα), 230f. (ὅπως). LXX e.g. 2 Macc 1: 9
καὶ νῦν ἵνα ἄγητε τὰς ἡμέρας τῆς σκηνοπηγίας.
Further (Epict. etc.) in Raderm.² 170; Windisch,
ZNW 26 (1927) 205 n. 5; Pernot, Études 63, 97ff.,
123, 148f.; Ghedini, Vang. ap. 477 and Aegyptus 15
(1935) 236; Ljungvik 38f. M. Ant. 11.3 τὸ δὲ ἕτοιμον
τοῦτο ἵνα ἀπὸ ἰδικῆς κρίσεως ἔρχηται, 4 τοῦτο ἵνα ἀεὶ
πρόχειρον ἀπαντᾷ, καὶ μηδαμοῦ παύου. In MGr νά
with the subj. serves as the impera. of the 2nd and
3rd person.—Rob. 941–50.

(G) The Infinitive

388. Introduction. The use of the infinitive in
the NT has shifted greatly when compared with
the classical Attic language. Some categories have
become more familiar (probably under Ionic influence), as, for example, the infinitive of purpose
with verbs of motion (§390(1)) and certain forms
of the substantival infinitive with and without
preposition, which enable the infinitive to replace
temporal clauses, causal clauses, etc. Especially
the infinitive with τοῦ is used in a lavish way. On
the other hand, analytical constructions with ἵνα
and ὅτι have developed into serious rivals of the
infinitive. The following picture obtains for the
NT: what can be interpreted as intended or
probable result is expressed to a great extent by
ἵνα and the subjunctive; ἵνα in other words has a
subjunctive (imperatival) sense. Even before
early Hellenistic Greek, this development can be
recognized in the classical language, except that
in the latter it is ὅπως and not ἵνα that is used in
such expressions (e.g. πειρᾶσθαι ὅπως σῳζώμεθα
Xen.=π. σῴζεσθαι). Later ὅπως retreats (§369
(4)) and finally disappears. Cf. ut in Latin which
often interchanges with the infinitive. On the
other hand, ὅτι (ὡς) with the indicative had been
used for a very long time for the infinitive to
denote actual facts, particularly those belonging
to past time; cf. Latin quod, quia (e.g. Vulg. Mt
26: 21 dico vobis, quia unus vestrum me traditurus
est). The remaining province belonging exclusively to the infinitive is not large in the NT.

E.g. δύνασθαι and μέλλειν are combined only with
infinitives.

Nevertheless, the infinitive is still used abundantly
by all authors and the choice between the inf. and ἵνα
appears to be a matter of preference in each case.
John exhibits a marked preference for ἵνα instead of
the inf., and Mt and Mk use the former very prolific-
ally, Lk much less so, especially in Acts which
exhibits very little of an unclassical use of ἵνα. In Ja,
Peter and Heb it also occurs only as a proper final
conjunction.

On the inf., ὅτι, and ἵνα in the Gospels s. Pernot,
Études 31–149: the inf. is used in Lk more frequently
and in a wider variety of constructions than in the
other Gospels (140); Jn, Mk, and Lk have a tendency
to employ the inf. where the subj. is identical and
ὅτι or ἵνα where the subj. is different (48, 84, 144),
but not so Mt (123), nor Lk in the case of ἵνα (146);
Jn 12: 18 avoids ὅτι by using the acc. and inf.
because of the preceding ὅτι ἤκουσαν (48).—MGr
has in general abandoned the inf. and replaced it by
νά (=ἵνα) and πῶς (=ὅτι) respectively; only the
Pontic dialect has retained the inf. after verbs of
motion (Mlt. 40f., 205 [323f.]). In the LXX ἵνα
instead of the infinitive is rare because Hebr.
favored the latter (Thack. 24). Latin has probably
encouraged the substitution of ἵνα or ὅπως for the
inf. (J. B. Ullrich, Über die Latinismen des Dio
Cassius [Progr. Nürnberg, 1912] 26–33; Hering
46f.).—P. Aalto, Studien zur Geschichte des Inf. im
Gr. (Annales Acad. Sc. Fennicae B 80, 2, Helsinki,
1953) (especially detailed statistics for the inf. with
art. in the LXX and NT). C. W. Votaw, The Use of
the Infinitive in Biblical Greek (1896); Rob. 1051–
95.

*(i) The infinitive and analytical constructions
with ἵνα*

389. The imperatival infinitive is extremely
old and is especially common in Homer, while in
Attic it has become less frequent (Schwyzer II
380; subject in nom.). It is limited in the NT to
two passages in Paul, both *without subject*; when
the subject is to be expressed, even Paul uses ἵνα:
E 5: 33 (§387(3)).

R 12: 15 χαίρειν μετὰ χαιρόντων, κλαίειν μετὰ
κλαιόντων, Ph 3: 16 πλὴν εἰς ὃ ἐφθάσαμεν, τῷ αὐτῷ
στοιχεῖν; but cf. also Lk 9: 3 μηδὲν αἴρετε...μήτε
ἀνὰ δύο χιτῶνας ἔχειν. A governing verb (of saying,
or χρή, δεῖ) can readily be supplied everywhere in the
NT passages (which was not the case with the old
imperatival inf.); cf. the accusatives with inf. in
T 2: 2–10 with a single occurrence of παρακάλει in
v. 6. The salutatory inf. χαίρειν in epistolary style
(A 15: 23, 23: 26, Ja 1: 1 [§480(5)]) is likewise clearly
elliptical. The independent inf. (with any modifiers

belonging to the subj. in the acc.) or acc. with inf. in legal phraseology (λέγειν 'one must say' = λεκτέον, κεῖνον ἀπόλλυσθαι 'he must die') is also the result of a subsequent detachment of a governing δοκεῖ etc.; cf. Schwyzer II 383; Bonitz, Index Aristotelicus s.v. Infinitiv. The better reading in 2 T 2: 14 is μὴ λογομάχει AC* latt (pm. -χεῖν, conceived as dependent upon διαμαρτυρόμενος). Is IEph 11.1 μόνον ἐν Χριστῷ Ἰησοῦ εὑρεθῆναι imperatival or a loose addition (§391(4)) to ἤ...φοβηθῶμεν ἤ...ἀγαπήσωμεν? Imperatival inf. in the pap. Mayser II 1, 150f., 303–5 (primarily in official orders and the like). Interchange of impera. and inf. (Lk 9: 3) e.g. PEleph 1.4 (311 BC) παρεχέτω Ἡρακλείδης πάντα, εἶναι δὲ ἡμᾶς....—Rob. 1092f.; Moule 126f.

390. The infinitive of purpose likewise dates very far back and it certainly has a much wider range of usage in Homer than in Attic authors, who use it mostly after verbs meaning 'to give, appoint, present, send', etc. (1) In the NT it has become common again in a wide sphere (probably under Ionic influence) with a variety of verbs of motion (cf. LXX, Thack. 24; Huber 80), and is the equivalent of a final clause: Mt 5: 17 οὐκ ἦλθον καταλῦσαι, ἀλλὰ πληρῶσαι. (2) Also, of course, with διδόναι, ἀποστέλλειν, etc. as in Attic: Mk 3: 14 ἀποστέλλῃ κηρύσσειν. (3) Ἵνα can again represent this infinitive (also final ὥστε: Lk 9: 52 εἰσῆλθον ὥστε ἑτοιμάσαι, 4: 29, s. §391(3)); an analytical construction with ἵνα is the natural one, especially when the subordinate clause is loosely connected or is of considerable extent, while the especially close connection of the infinitive to the main verb in certain fixed idioms does not permit the replacement of the infinitive. (4) As to the differences among NT authors, what has been outlined in §388 applies here also.

(1) Mt 4: 1 ἀνήχθη πειρασθῆναι, Lk 18: 10 ἀνέβησαν προσεύξασθαι (cf. UPZ I 62.33 [c. 160 BC] ἐὰν ἀναβῶ κἀγὼ προσκυνῆσαι), A 10: 33 πάρεσμεν ἀκοῦσαι; Mt 11: 7, 2: 2, Jn 21: 3 etc. Mt 27: 55 ἠκολούθησαν διακονῆσαι W (pm. -νοῦσαι). Ἦλθον with inf. not in Jn but UGosp 1.11 (Joachim Jeremias, ThBl 15 [1936] 40). Pap.: Mayser II 1, 296f.; otherwise in Hell.: Jannaris 575; Hatzid. 226f.; Raderm.² 186f. In such cases Att. would use the fut. ptcp. which is almost unknown in the NT (§351(1); cf. A 24: 11 ἀνέβην προσκυνήσων with Lk 18: 10 above). Yet the inf. is found sporadically in the earliest Att. prose: Thuc. 6.50.4 πλεῦσαί τε σκέψασθαι, Gorg., Frag. 8 τόλμης (δεῖται)...ὑπομεῖναι, σοφίας...γνῶναι (Rosenkranz, IF 48 [1930] 167f., who denies Ionicism without cause).

(2) Mt 25: 35 ἐδώκατέ μοι φαγεῖν (cf. MGr τὸ φαγί = φαγεῖν as a subst.). A 5: 21 is different ἀπέστειλαν ἀχθῆναι αὐτούς, with a pass. construction and therefore acc. with inf. (§392(4)).

(3) Mt 27: 26 = Mk 15: 15 = Jn 19: 16 παρέδωκεν ἵνα σταυρωθῇ. In close connection and in fixed phrases: παραδιδόναι φυλάσσειν A 12: 4, 16: 4, παρέλαβον κρατεῖν Mk 7: 4; often διδόναι (αἰτεῖν) φαγεῖν (s. supra (2)) or πιεῖν. The inf. is also possible in looser combinations: A 20: 28 ἔθετο ἐπισκόπους, ποιμαίνειν τὴν ἐκκλησίαν etc., 1: 24f. ἐξελέξω... λαβεῖν, Mt 5: 13 etc. Mt 10: 1 ἔδωκεν ἐξουσίαν ὥστε s. §393(5); [Dem.] 21.22 ἐκδόντος δέ μοι Δημοσθένους στέφανον χρυσοῦν ὥστε κατασκευάσαι. UPZ I 18.22 (163 BC) δέξασθαι τὸν υἱὸν αὐτῆς εἶνα διεκονεῖ (= ἵνα διακονῇ) ὑμῖν = 19.25 (163 BC) προσλαβέσθαι τὸν ἐκείνης υἱὸν διακονεῖν ἡμῖν. In 1 Esdr 4 sequences of infinitives are twice interrupted by ἵνα-clauses, both in regal decrees which are reported in indirect speech: 47 ἵνα προπέμψωσιν αὐτὸν καὶ τοὺς... ἀναβαίνοντας οἰκοδομῆσαι τὴν Ἰερουσαλήμ; 50f.... ὑπάρχειν, καὶ ἵνα...ἀφιῶσι...καὶ...δοθῆναι. This passage belongs to the tale of the 'three youths' which has no counterpart in Hebrew.

(4) Acc. to Blass ἵνα in the Gospels has perhaps often been introduced only by the commentators: e.g. Jn 5: 36 he would read τελειῶσαι following Tert, 11: 31 κλαῦσαι (without ἐκεῖ) following syˢ Chr, 11: 55 ἁγνίσαι following Chr, 12: 20 προσκυνῆσαι following syˢ Chr; however the infinitives are more likely puristic corrections. Purpose is also represented in the NT by the ptcp. (§418(4)) and frequently by τοῦ and the inf. (§400). With παραδιδόναι etc. εἰς τό with the inf. is still a rival of the simple inf. (§402(2)).— Rob. 1087–9.

391. The infinitive of result is related to the infinitive of purpose, yet is distinguished from it as ἵνα is distinguished from ὅτι according to §388; i.e. if actual result is to be denoted, an analytical construction with ἵνα cannot, or should not, be substituted (s. infra (5)). (1) The introductory particle for the infinitive of result is ὥστε as in classical, in addition to which simple ὡς is no more certainly established than it is in customary Attic usage. (2) Ὥστε is used in the NT to introduce independent sentences, too (as in classical), and may take the indicative, imperative, or hortatory subjunctive ('therefore'). The use of the indicative after ὥστε in really dependent clauses, possible in Attic, is not genuine NT idiom. The construction with the infinitive (usually with the subject present in the accusative if it cannot be easily supplied from the context; cf. 405ff.) accordingly has a wider reach in the NT than in Attic. (3) But as in Attic, ὥστε is by no means used in the NT only to introduce real or possible result, but also intended result (which is an even earlier usage), so that the line dividing it from purpose clauses is hardly distinguishable: thus Lk 20: 20 ἵνα ἐπιλάβωνται αὐτοῦ λόγου, ὥστε παραδοῦναι αὐτὸν τῇ ἀρχῇ τοῦ ἡγεμόνος 'so that they might' (the v.l. εἰς τό for ὥστε in AWΓ al. is quite appropriate to the meaning, cf. §390 end). Cf. Moule 143 f. (4) The infinitive *without* ὥστε (also with any expressed subject in the acc.) is used in a comparable free way to express result, e.g. A 5: 3 διὰ τί ἐπλήρωσεν ὁ σατανᾶς τὴν καρδίαν σου ψεύσασθαί σε etc. (5) ἵνα can be substituted for the infinitive of result (probably also for other kinds, too, in later writers), but hardly for actual result, e.g. 1 Jn 1: 9 πιστός ἐστιν καὶ δίκαιος, ἵνα ἀφῇ τὰς ἁμαρτίας (cf. H 6: 10 *infra* (4)), Rev 13: 13 ποιεῖ σημεῖα μεγάλα, ἵνα καὶ πῦρ ποιῇ καταβαίνειν (cf. Mt 24: 24 with ὥστε). The classical boundaries of ἵνα are here overstepped; cf. Latin *ut* (Hering 48 f.). Moule 142 f.

(1) Homil Clem use consecutive ὡς with inf. (8.11, 20.13), with unreal indic. (2.25) and with subj. (12.17), final ὡς with inf. 12.1. Lk 9: 52 ὡς only 𝔓⁴⁵SB. A 20: 24 ὡς τελειώσω S* (ἕως τ. Sᶜ) B, ὡς τελειῶσαι AHLP; τε appears to have dropped out before τελ. (thus ὥστε E, ὡς τό C). On Att. s. Rosenkranz, IF 48 [1930] 165. Only one certain and one uncertain ex. of ὡς in the Ptol. pap. (Mayser II 1, 297; II 3, 96.31 ff.); later pap. Mlt. [334]. Jos. ὡς often (Raab, De Flavii Josephi elocutione [Erlangen, 1890] 37 f.). Later exx. in Jannaris §1757ᵇ; Wolf II 70; Trunk 53; Schekira 169; Brockmeier 29.

(2) G 2: 13 ὥστε συναπήχθη (συναπαχθῆναι is a very weak variant). In a sentence like A 15: 39 ἐγένετο παροξυσμός, ὥστε ἀποχωρισθῆναι αὐτοὺς ἀπ' ἀλλήλων an Attic writer would more likely have used the indic. on account of the lack of close connection of the two clauses and the importance attached to the ensuing result. Pap.: Mayser II 1, 300; II 3, 97. In Jn 3: 16 a variant ὅτι for ὥστε is doubly attested, by Chrys. (in many passages) and by Nonnus (Blass; cf. §456(2); late pars. in Jannaris §1758b; Raderm.² 197, Mlt. p. 249 n. on p. 209 [332 n.]; Trunk 53 f.; Ursing 58; οὕτως could be taken as an exclamation = 'so great a love for men' and ὅτι as '[as one sees by the fact] that' [cf. §480 end]).

(3) Lk 4: 29 ὥστε ('in order to'; v.l. εἰς τό AC al.) κατακρημνίσαι αὐτόν, 9: 52 ὥστε ('in order to'; v.l. ὡς s. *supra* (1)) ἑτοιμάσαι αὐτῷ, Mt 27: 1 συμβούλιον ἔλαβον ὥστε θανατῶσαι αὐτόν (D, correctly interpreting, ἵνα θανατώσουσιν αὐτόν). A 20: 24 also belongs here (s. *supra* (1)) 'in order to accomplish', if ὥστε τελειῶσαι is the correct reading. There are many exx. of this ὥστε in Jos. (Schmidt 418 ff.); further Jannaris 571; Raderm.² 197; Mlt. 207 [328]; Trunk 52 f.; Mayser II 1, 298 f.; Ghedini, Vang.

ap. 464. For the contiguity of purpose and result cf. Callim., Hymn. in Art. 27 ἐτανύσσατο χεῖρας, μέχρις (result) ἵνα (purpose) ψαύσειε. Ὥστε (ἐφ' ᾧτε) 'on the condition that' does not appear in the NT (for which ἵνα G 2: 9), nor does ἢ ὥστε after a comparative (νεώτερος ἢ ὥστε εἰδέναι), s. Burton 150. On ἵνα Mk 4: 22 s. §382(1).

(4) Rev 5: 5 ἐνίκησεν ὁ λέων...ἀνοῖξαι (046 ὁ ἀνοίγων) etc., 16: 9 οὐ μετενόησαν δοῦναι αὐτῷ δόξαν, H 6: 10 οὐ γὰρ ἄδικος ὁ θεός (scil. ὥστε) ἐπιλαθέσθαι. Still more freely used Lk 1: 54 (the Magnificat of Mary [or Elizabeth: Harnack, SAB 1900, 538 ff.; Blass]) ἀντελάβετο Ἰσραὴλ παιδὸς αὐτοῦ, μνησθῆναι ἐλέους etc. and 72 (the Benedictus of Zechariah) ποιῆσαι ἔλεος etc. (a very loose construction as is often the case with Hebr. לְ; the par. in the preceding *v.* 71 is an acc. of a noun: σωτηρίαν ἐξ ἐχθρῶν etc.); cf. 78 f. after ἐπεσκέψατο. Cf. POxy III 526.3 (ii AD) οὐκ ἤμην ἀπαθὴς ἀλόγως σε καταλείπ(ε)ιν (Mlt. 210 [333]), Epict. 4.1.50 οὐδεὶς οὕτως ἐστὶν ἀναίσθητος μὴ ἀποδύρασθαι, Herm Man 8.2 ἐὰν ἐγκρατεύσῃ τὸ πονηρὸν μὴ ποιεῖν, Did 4.3 οὐ λήψῃ πρόσωπον ἐλέγξαι ἐπὶ παραπτώμασιν 'you shall not be partial, so that you (rather) may call (the guilty) to account for their trespasses'. Xen., HG 5.1.14 ἥ γε μὴν θύρα ἡ ἐμὴ ἀνέῳκτο...εἰσιέναι, Hdt. 5.76 οὐ γὰρ ἐκαλλιέρεε οὐδαμῶς διαβαίνειν νιν (9.38 οὐκ ἐκ. ὥστε μάχεσθαι).

(5) Rev 9: 20 (cf. 16: 9, *supra* (4)) οὐδὲ μετενόησαν, ἵνα μὴ προσκυνήσουσιν, Lk 9: 45 ἦν παρακεκαλυμμένον ἀπ' αὐτῶν, ἵνα μὴ αἴσθωνται αὐτό; 2 C 1: 17, 1 Th 5: 4, Herm Sim 7.1, 3 (ὥστε 2), 9.1.10. Cf. Epict. 2.2.16 οὕτω μωρὸς ἦν, ἵνα μὴ ἴδῃ. The possibility of a purely final conception is certainly not to be denied in several of the NT exx. cited, e.g. Lk 9: 45, 2 C 1: 17; it is still more probable in the frequently recurring ἵνα πληρωθῇ ('in order that [by divine decree] it might be fulfilled'); indeed Jewish teleology in general has contributed to the blurring of the distinction between purpose and result (Mlt. 210, 219 [333, 348]; Moule 142); also cf. Epict. 1.19.13, 4.1.148. Jn 9.2 τίς ἥμαρτεν..., ἵνα τυφλὸς γεννηθῇ; 'with the result that' (cf. Zahn³ *ad loc.* 433 n. 61); the weakly attested reading ὅτι...ἐγεννήθη (cf. §456(2)), preferred by Blass, is unnecessary; cf. Epict. 3.1.12 τί εἶδεν ἐν ἐμοὶ ὁ Ἐπίκτητος, ἵνα...περιίδῃ; R 5: 20 ἵνα πλεονάσῃ τὸ παράπτωμα: ἵνα acc. to Chrys. (MPG 60.878; cf. 59.307): οὐκ αἰτιολογίας (final) ἀλλ' ἐκβάσεως (consecutive) ἐστιν: Zerwick, Graec. bibl. 81. Homil Clem 2.29.6 οὐ γὰρ ἐσμεν οὕτως νήπιοι, ἵνα πανοῦργον ἐνσπείρῃς ἐν ἡμῖν ὑποψίαν. For exx. of consecutive ἵνα in Jos., where however the result is still only conceived and not actual, s. Schmidt 420 f. Much in Jannaris §§1758, 1951; further Raderm.² 191 f.; Trunk 53. For 'teleological' ἵνα in Paul s. Stauffer, StKr 102 (1930) 232–57, in the NT generally Stauffer, TW III 327 ff. Comparable features are found also in other languages: E. Lerch, Hauptprobleme der franz.

Syntax ɪ (Berlin, 1930) 52; Spitzer, Germ.-Rom. Monatsschrift 7 (1915) 222ff. = Stilstudien ɪ (München, 1928) 19–25; Harder, Germ.-Rom. Monatsschrift 9 (1921) 188f.; Nisbet, AJPh 44 (1923) 30ff. There is a similar construction in German in imitation of French, e.g. *er schlief ein, um nicht wieder aufzuwachen* ('he fell asleep, never to waken again', lit. 'in order not to waken again').—On the whole Rob. 1089–91.

391a. The so-called infinitive absolute after ὡς, which is fairly common in Attic in certain formulae, appears only in ὡς ἔπος εἰπεῖν 'so to speak' H 7:9 (literary language). Τὸ δοκεῖν 'only in appearance, *pro forma*' ITr 10 = ISm 2, cf. 4.2, ἁπλῶς εἰπεῖν Diogn 6.1. Only twice in the Ptolemaic papyri σὺν θεῷ (θεοῖς) εἰπεῖν (Mayser ɪɪ 1, 302).

392. The infinitive as complement of a verb borders closely on the infinitive of purpose and result. (1) It is used with verbs meaning 'to wish, strive, avoid, ask, summon, make, allow, permit, hinder, be able, have power', etc. In classical many of these verbs can take ὥστε in addition to the infinitive, and with several a rival construction in Attic is ὅπως with the future indicative, yet the latter is not used to the extent that *ut* is after such verbs in Latin. Ἵνα later came to occupy the place of ὅπως (in the NT only retained with verbs of asking) and its sphere was expanded more and more until in the NT it alternates with the infinitive after a large number of these verbs, and, especially if Lk, Paul, and Hebrews are left out of account, even encroaches upon it. The subject of the infinitive is often necessarily (δύνασθαι) or as a rule (θέλειν) identical with that of the governing verb; with other verbs identical with the object (ἐᾶν) or the dative supplement to the main verb (προστάσσειν). If the subject is expressly stated, it stands in the accusative. (2) Verbs meaning 'to be able, know how to', etc. are used only with the infinitive, as are those expressing obligation, custom, and the like. (3) The construction with the infinitive in particular cases has been greatly extended in the NT and is used with greater freedom than in Attic, partly due to the influence of Hebrew (in such cases ἵνα is therefore rarely used; cf. §388). (4) Regarding voice it is to be noted that with verbs of commanding the passive infinitive is used instead of the active, in a way which is more Latin than classical Greek, if it is to be stated that something is to happen to a person without mentioning the

one who is to effect it: e.g. Mt 18: 25 ἐκέλευσεν αὐτὸν πραθῆναι, but A 23: 10 ἐκέλευσε τὸ στράτευμα ἁρπάσαι αὐτόν.

(1) (a) 'To wish, desire, strive': Θέλειν mostly (acc. and) inf.; ἵνα Mt 7: 12, 1 C 14: 5 (θέλω ὑμᾶς λαλεῖν..., μᾶλλον δὲ ἵνα προφητεύητε) etc. Cf. MGr θά, θενά = θέλω ἵνα.—Βούλεσθαι (no longer generally used) only with (acc. and) inf. (βούλεσθε ἵνα ἀπολύσω Jn 18: 39 SDKUW [without ἵνα AB al.]); the following likewise only with inf.: τολμᾶν, λογίζεσθαι 'intend' (2 C 10: 2), ἀρνεῖσθαι 'refuse' (H 11: 24), δοκεῖν (in μὴ δόξητε λέγειν 'don't get the idea of saying' [RSV 'do not presume'] Mt 3: 9; cf. 1 C 11: 16; ἔδοξέ μοι Lk, e.g. 1: 3).—Βουλεύεσθαι inf. and ἵνα (Jn 11: 53, v.l. συνεβουλ.; 12: 10; class. inf. and ὅπως); συμβουλεύεσθαι ἵνα Mt 26: 4, inf. A 9: 23; συμβουλεύειν τινί 'advise' inf. Rev 3: 18.—Κρίνειν 'to decide' s. §397(2).—Ὁρίζειν inf. A 11: 29.—Συντίθεσθαι inf. (with τοῦ §400(7)) and ἵνα (Jn 9: 22). —Προστίθεσθαι inf. R 1: 13.—Ἐπιθυμεῖν and ἐπιποθεῖν only inf. (acc. with inf. H 6: 11).—Κρέμασθαι 'be eagerly attentive' also belongs here: Lk 19: 48 acc. to D ἐκρέματο ἀκούειν αὐτοῦ (the other reading ἐξεκρ. αὐτοῦ ἀκούων).—Ζητεῖν (ἐπιζ.) with inf.; ἵνα 1 C 4: 2, 14: 12.—Ζηλοῦν 'strive earnestly' ἵνα 1 C 14: 1.—Σπουδάζειν only (acc. and) inf.; nom. with inf. IEph 10: 3; σπεύδειν inf. A 20: 16, 1 Clem 33. 1, acc. with inf. Herm Sim 9.3.2; σπουδὴν ποιεῖσθαι with inf. Jd 3; ἀγωνίζεσθαι inf. Lk 13: 24, 1 Clem 35.4, Barn 4.11, ἵνα Jn 18: 36; φιλοτιμεῖσθαι with inf. Paul.—Ἐπιχειρεῖν (Lk only) inf., likewise ἀσκεῖν 'take pains' (only A 24: 16).—Πειρᾶσθαι (Att.) 'attempt' inf. (only A 26: 21, Paul before Agrippa; as v.l. 9: 26; 2 Clem 17.3, MPol 13.2; Att. also πειρᾶν act.) likewise πειράζεσθαι inf. IMag 7.1, Herm Sim 8.2.7 A παραχέειν (PMich -χέω); A 15: 10 τί πειράζετε τὸν θεόν, ἐπιθεῖναι ζυγὸν must be explained similarly, even if τὸν θεόν, missing in certain Lat. witnesses, is not an interpolation.—Ἠγαλλιάσατο (impf. Nonnus [ἠγάλλετο] and 2 Lat. MSS) ἵνα ἴδῃ Jn 8: 56 'he longed with desire, rejoiced that he was to...'; cf. ἐχάρην ἵνα σε ἀσπάζομαι BGU ɪν 1081.5 (ii/iii AD), ἠγωνίασα...ἵνα ἀκούσω PGiess 17.5 (ii AD); with τοῦ and inf. (§400) Herm Vis 3.8.1 περιχαρὴς ἐγενόμην τοῦ ἰδεῖν, 10.6.

(b) 'To take care, be ashamed, afraid': Βλέπετε ἵνα 'see to it that' 1 C 16: 10 (Att. ὁρᾶτε ὅπως).—Φυλάσσεσθαι ἵνα μή 2 P 3: 17 (Att. μή and ὅπως μή).—Αἰσχύνεσθαι (ἐπ-), φοβεῖσθαι 'be ashamed to do, shun doing something' only inf. (Mt 1: 20, Lk 16: 3 etc.), likewise ὀκνεῖν A 9: 38.—Προσέχειν μὴ ποιεῖν Mt 6: 1 (Att. not thus), with ἵνα Barn 16.8; the opposite ἐπιλανθάνεσθαι with inf. (as Att.) Mt 16: 5 = Mk 8: 14.

(c) 'To ask, request': Δεῖσθαι 'ask' with ἵνα and ὅπως; inf. Lk 9: 38 v.l., A 26: 3, Lk 8: 38 (εἶναι 'to be allowed to be', cf. 2 C 10: 2 §399(3)), 2 C 5: 20

D*FG (Att. inf. and ὅπως).—Ἐρωτᾶν ἵνα 'ask' (Hell.) Mk 7: 26 etc., ὅπως Lk 7: 3, 11: 37, A 23: 20; otherwise inf. (and acc. of the object going with ἐρωτᾶν; likewise ἐπερωτᾶν Mt 16: 1).—Παρακαλεῖν 'beg, exhort' ἵνα Mt 14: 36 etc., ὅπως Mt 8: 34 (B ἵνα), A 25: 2, inf. Mk 5: 17 etc., inf. with τοῦ §400(7); cf. Att. παρακελεύεσθαι with inf. and ὅπως.—Αἰτεῖσθαι (-εῖν) (acc. and) inf.; ἵνα C 1: 9 (καὶ αἰτούμενοι om. B); class. inf. and ὅπως.—Προσεύχεσθαι ἵνα Mk 14: 35 etc., ὅπως A 8: 15, inf. Lk 22: 40, cf. τοῦ with inf. Ja 5: 17; εὔχεσθαι (more literary) with (acc. and) inf. A 26: 29 etc. (εὔχομαί σε ὑγιαίνειν 3 Jn 2, as often in pap. letters), ἵνα IPhld 6.3, and the ἵνα after εὐχαριστεῖν E 1: 16f. is similar.—Ἀξιοῦν 'demand, request' (Lk, Diogn, 1 Clem; literary language) only (acc. and) inf.: A 15: 38, 28: 22, ἵνα Herm Vis 4.1.3 (class. also ὅπως; ἵνα in the forged document in Dem. 18.155); 'deem worthy' likewise with inf. (cf. ἄξιος §393(4)) Lk 7: 7; καταξιοῦν with inf. Lk 20: 35, A 5: 41, IRom 2.2, with ἵνα ISm 11.1, IPol 7.2.

(d) 'To enjoin, encourage, command': Παραινεῖν with acc. of the object and inf. (only A 27: 22, literary language).—Κελεύειν only (acc. and) inf. (only Mt, Lk, 1 Clem); likewise τάσσειν A 15: 2, δια- (mid. A 24: 23), προσ- (rare), ἐπι- (rare), ἀναμιμνήσκειν 2 T 1: 6, ἀπειλεῖσθαι (mid.) A 4: 17, νεύειν A 24: 10 (κατα- with τοῦ and inf. §400(7)); others may also take ἵνα: thus παραγγέλλειν ἵνα Mk 6: 8 (ἀπαγγέλλειν in the same sense with ἵνα Mt 28: 10, with inf. A 26: 20), διαμαρτύρεσθαι ἵνα 1 T 5: 21, ἐντέλλεσθαι ἵνα Mk 13: 34; κηρύσσειν ἵνα Mk 6: 12; with ἵνα only: διαστέλλεσθαι Mt 16: 20 (v.l. ἐπετίμησεν), Mk 7: 36, 9: 9 and ἐπιτιμᾶν 'urge threateningly' Mt 20: 31. In class. such verbs (except κελεύειν) have a strong inclination to the construction with ὅπως.—Χρηματίζεσθαι pass. 'receive a divine command' inf. Mt 2: 12, A 10: 22 (Lk 2: 26 the inf. expresses an assertion); cf. §405(2).—Ἐξορκίζειν ἵνα Mt 26: 63, ὁρκίζειν or ἐνορκίζειν with acc. and inf. 1 Th 5: 27, ἵνα Herm Sim 9.10.5.—Λέγειν (εἰπεῖν) often with ἵνα as with (acc. and) inf. when it denotes a command (thus ἵνα Mt 20: 21, Rev 14: 13, Herm Vis 2.2.6); γράφειν likewise: γέγραπται ἵνα Mk 9: 12, (12: 19); ἀποστέλλειν ἵνα A 16: 36, cf. §390(2).—In PPetr II 13 (18a) 12 (258–253 BC) σύνταξον ἵνα is corrected to σ. χορηγεῖν ὅπως (Mayser II 1, 243 n. 1). Ἔγραψαν, ὅπως ἀποδέξωνται is an addition in D to A 18: 27.

(e) 'To cause, effect': Πείθειν ἵνα Mt 27: 20, otherwise acc. of object and inf.—Ποιεῖν ἵνα Jn 11: 37, C 4: 16, Rev 3: 9 (ποιήσω αὐτοὺς ἵνα ἥξουσιν, cf. 13: 12, 15f. [15 lacks ἵνα in 𝔓47S 046]); with a more nearly purposive ἵνα Mk 3: 14, cf. ἔθηκα ἵνα Jn 15: 16; with acc. with inf. Mk 1: 17 (but Mt 4: 19 with double acc.), Lk 5: 34 etc. and thus also Hebraizing διδόναι A 10: 40 (sermon), 14: 3, 2: 27 OT; also ποιεῖν ὅπως 'cause, bring about, that' occasionally in class.; ποιεῖν τοῦ with inf. s. §400(7).—Ἀγγαρεύειν ἵνα Mt 27: 32; no ex. of the inf.; ὅστις σε ἀγγαρεύσει μίλιον ἕν Mt 5: 41.

(f) 'To allow, permit': Ἐᾶν τινα only inf.; ἀφιέναι 'allow', which is more common, also with ἵνα (Mk 11: 16); καταλείπειν τινά with inf. Lk 10: 40 (inf. of result, not of purpose, cf. Hom., Il. 17.151).—Ἐπιτρέπειν τινί only inf., likewise κωλύειν τινά (with which Att. μή is not added to the simple inf.; §§400(4); 429).

(2) 'To be able, understand' only with inf.: δύνασθαι (Paul δυνατεῖν), ἰσχύειν (κατ- Lk 21: 36 SB al., v.l. καταξιωθῆτε; ἐξ- E 3: 18), ἔχειν e.g. Mt 18: 25 (in the NT also with the meaning 'have to, be obliged to': e.g. Lk 12: 50 βάπτισμα ἔχω βαπτισθῆναι, cf. Homil Clem 1.17, 2. 28, 3.61, 12.8 etc.), Herm Sim 9.10.5 ἔχω ἀκαιρεθῆναι, Paradosis Pilati (pp. 430f. Tischendorf) 9 εἶχες σταυρῷ προσηλωθῆναι, 10 ὀφθῆναι ἔχεις, Homil Clem 1.4.3 μήτι γε...ἐκεῖ χεῖρον παθεῖν ἔχω; also εἰδέναι Mt 7: 11 etc., γινώσκειν [Mt] 16: 3; in addition μανθάνειν 1 T 5: 4 etc. (§416(2)), παιδεύεσθαι (pass.) 1: 20; προμελετᾶν Lk 21: 14, διδάσκειν 11: 1, παραλαμβάνειν Mk 7: 4, δεικνύειν A 10: 28, ὑπο- Mt 3: 7 = Lk 3: 7. Likewise only with inf.: ὀφείλειν, μέλλειν, εἰωθέναι, φιλεῖν Mt 6: 5 (,23: 6f.), ἄρχεσθαι (never takes the ptcp. in the NT, cf. §414(2); ἄρχεσθαι in Mt, Mk, Lk is often used in an almost redundant way, as e.g. Mk 1: 45 where ἤρξατο κηρύσσειν is hardly distinguishable from ἐκήρυσσεν [on pleonastic ἄρχεσθαι in the NT s. Hunkin, JTS 25 (1924) 390–402; M.-H. 455f.; as an Aramaism: J. Jeremias, ThZ 5 (1949) 229 (Lk appears to have an antipathy for it); in other languages J. B. Hofmann, IF 43 (1926) 95 (Lat.); Havers, IF 45 (1927) 238–40; as an Aramaism in Jos. acc. to Thackeray, JTS 30 (1929) 361–70]; προέλαβεν μυρίσαι Mt 14: 8 also belongs here, cf. φθάνειν in Att. with ptcp. and inf., προφθάσῃ βαλεῖν Clem 8.2; ἐκβαίνειν ἔφθασας 'you departed early' Homil Clem 18.32.4, ὡς φθάσας εἶπον ut supra dixi 20.4.3; Jannaris §2121), προστίθεσθαι 'continue to do, do again' (LXX also act., προσθήσω τοῦ ἐπερωτῆσαι Herm Man 4.3.1), cf. §435a and Schmidt 516, κινδυνεύειν A 19: 27, 40, προσποιεῖσθαι Lk 24: 28.

(3) Διαβλέψεις ἐκβαλεῖν Mt 7: 5, Lk 6: 42; δοκιμάζειν 'approve', οὐ δοκ. 'disdain' R 1: 28, 1 Th 2: 4 (in Att. with inf. of opinion); εὐδοκεῖν with (acc. and) inf. R 15: 26, C 1: 19 (Polyb. 1.8.4), συν- inf. 1 C 7: 12 (acc. with inf. Herm Sim 5.2.11, ἵνα 8). Η 5: 5 οὐχ ἑαυτὸν ἐδόξασεν γενηθῆναι ἀρχιερέα (like ἀξιοῦν). A 25: 21 τοῦ Παύλου ἐπικαλεσαμένου τηρηθῆναι αὐτόν (like verbs of asking). A 15: 14 ἐπεσκέψατο λαβεῖν, cf. Lk 1: 25 ἐπεῖδεν ἀφελεῖν. A 14: 15 εὐαγγελιζόμενοι ὑμᾶς (+ἀποστῆναι...καὶ 𝔓45) ἐπιστρέφειν (D is different with ὅπως). 17: 21 εἰς οὐδὲν ἕτερον ηὐκαίρουν ἢ λέγειν τι...καινότερον (there is no need to supply εἰς τό before the inf. since εὐκαιρεῖν takes the inf. in Lucian, Amor. 33 and Plut., Mor. 223 DE) and R 1: 10

εὐοδωθήσομαι ἐλθεῖν after δύνασθαι (εὐοδοῦν with inf. in the LXX: W. Michaelis, TW v 116 n. 16). 1 Th 2: 2 (E 6: 20) παρρησιάζεσθαι (on the model of τολμᾶν). Mk 5: 32 περιεβλέπετο ἰδεῖν. A 16: 10 προσκέκληται ἡμᾶς εὐαγγελίσασθαι αὐτούς. Η 11: 8 ὑπήκουσεν ἐξελθεῖν. Τ 3: 8 φροντίζωσιν προΐστασθαι (not class., s. K.-G. ΙΙ 73). Lk 12: 45 χρονίζει ἔρχεσθαι. So also in idiomatic expressions: τιθέναι (τίθεσθαι) ἐν τῇ καρδίᾳ (τῷ πνεύματι) 'to intend to..., to think of...' (Hebraism) Lk 21: 14, A 19: 21, ἧς διήνοιξεν τὴν καρδίαν (Hebraism) προσέχειν A 16: 14 (cf. with τοῦ and the inf. Lk 24: 45); so also with ἵνα: βουλὴ ἐγένετο A 27: 42, θέλημά ἐστιν Mt 18: 14 etc., with inf. ἐγένετο ὁρμή A 14: 5; cf. Lk 2: 1, Jn 13: 2, 34, A 17: 15, E 3: 8 etc.

(4) A 23: 3 κελεύεις με τύπτεσθαι, 14: 19 (cf. *infra*), and often with κελεύειν in Mt and Lk (who so use this word only, s. *supra* (1 *d*)). Contrary to the above rule only A 16: 22 ἐκέλευον ῥαβδίζειν. A 22: 24 εἴπας μάστιξιν ἀνετάζεσθαι αὐτόν. A 24: 23 (διαταξάμενος), Lk 8: 55 (διέταξεν), Lk 19: 15 (εἴπεν), A 25: 21 (ἐπικαλεσαμένου), 1 Th 5: 27 ([ἐν-]ὁρκίζω), A 13: 28 (ᾐτήσαντο, cf. 1 Clem 55.4). Pass. *with* mention of the one to execute the order Herm Sim 9.8.3 ἐκέλευσε διὰ τῶν παρθένων ἀπενεχθῆναι. A 5: 21 ἀπέστειλαν ἀχθῆναι αὐτούς; cf. ἀξιῶ ἀχθῆναι αὐτούς PTebt ΙΙ 331.16 (*c.* 131 AD), cf. BGU I 22.34 (114 AD), ἐκέλευσεν αὐτὸν ἀπαχθῆναι POxy I 33 col. ΙΙ 14 (cf. col. ΙΙΙ 3) (ii BC end). Mk 6: 27 ἐπέταξεν ἐνεχθῆναι (SBCΔ ἐνέγκαι) τὴν κεφαλὴν αὐτοῦ, but 39 ἐπέταξεν αὐτοῖς ἀνακλῖναι πάντας (ἀνακλιθῆναι is an inferior reading from Mt 14: 19 where the executors are not expressed). Cf. Buttmann 236 f. who rightly rejects the v.l. δοῦναι (D) instead of δοθῆναι Mk 5: 43, ἐνέγκαι (s. *supra*) 6: 27, ἀνετάζειν (D*) A 22: 24 instead of -ζεσθαι and who also gives preference to εἶπεν αὐτὸν φωνηθῆναι (ADWX al.) above εἶπεν· φωνήσατε αὐτόν (SBCLΔ) Mk 10: 49. In Mk 8: 7 there is fluctuation in the MSS between εἶπεν (ἐκέλευσεν D is spurious) παραθεῖναι (-θῆναι)–παρατίθεναι–παρατεθῆναι (A, cf. it vg *apponi*)–παρέθηκεν (S* without εἶπεν); -τεθῆναι is recommended by usage (Buttmann). Cf. LXX and Theod. (Bonaccorsi 553), Aristeas 11, 33, Apocr. Gos. and Acts (Ghedini, Vang. ap. 458; Ljungvik 42 f.); pap. (Abel 309), e.g. PGM I 4.2454 f. διπλᾶ ὀψώνια αὐτῷ ἐκέλευσεν δίδοσθαι, PAmh ΙΙ 65.6 (ii AD beg.), 66.48 (124 AD), 70.2 (*c.* 115 AD), 78.23 (184 AD), 108.11 (185/6 AD), PTebt ΙΙ 327.21 (ii AD), BGU ΙΙ 388. ΙΙ 32 (ii AD end), 448.20 (ii AD); often in Appian (Hering 49 ff.) and Dio Cassius (Ullrich [s. § 388] 24 f.).—On the whole Rob. 1058–62; 1077 f.

393. The infinitive in impersonal expressions and with nouns and adjectives. A relationship between the infinitive and ἵνα similar to that which exists between them with verbs exists with a series of impersonal expressions, whether they be (1) simple verbs like δεῖ, συμφέρει, ἔξεστιν, ἐγένετο, or (2) combinations of ἐστίν and an adjective like δυνατόν ἐστιν, ἀρεστόν ἐστιν. (3) This applies also to combinations of ἐστίν with a substantive like ὥρα ἐστίν, καιρός ἐστιν, and (4) to adjectives like δυνατός, ἄξιος, ἱκανός, ἕτοιμος (used as predicates with εἶναι or as attributives). (5) Equivalent to these are combinations like ἐξουσίαν ἔχειν, χρείαν ἔχειν (Mayser ΙΙ 1, 318). The infinitive may be thought of as expressing here also the direction or goal. In Attic ὅπως is excluded from such expressions, but ὥστε is not entirely precluded (ἔστιν ὥστε 'it is possible that' Soph.). ἵνα can be used in all these cases in the NT, except when an event is represented as having occurred, as in the common ἐγένετο (§ 442(5); ἐὰν γένηται Mt 18: 13, ὅπως μὴ γ. A 20: 16, μὴ γένοιτο G 6: 14) and the classical word συνέβη (only A 21: 35) which has been driven out by it (s. further *infra*); and in cases where the combination with the infinitive has become firmly established, as with δεῖ (however Barn 5.13 ἔδει ἵνα πάθῃ) and ἔξεστιν (cf. ἐλευθέρα ἐστιν γαμηθῆναι 1 C 7: 39). (6) Freer usages with a comparable sense also appear with the infinitive and with ἵνα: ἐμοὶ εἰς ἐλάχιστόν ἐστιν ἵνα 1 C 4: 3, ὀφειλέτης ἐστιν (= ὀφείλει) ποιῆσαι G 5: 3 (cf. Soph., Aj. 590).

(1) Συμφέρει ἵνα Mt 5: 29 f., 18: 6, etc., also with (acc. and) inf. Likewise ἵνα after a comparative with ἤ: Lk 17: 2 λυσιτελεῖ αὐτῷ εἰ περίκειται...ἢ ἵνα σκανδαλίσῃ.

(2) Ἀρκετόν (scil. ἐστιν) ἵνα γένηται Mt 10: 25 (different from ἀρκοῦσιν ἵνα Jn 6: 7 where the result is stated = ὥστε); contrast the inf. in 1 P 4: 3 ἀρκετός. Δυνατόν ἐστιν (A 2: 24 acc. with inf.) and δυνατός εἰμι (somewhat more frequent) with inf. only like δύναμαι. Here belongs also 1 C 9: 15 καλόν μοι μᾶλλον ἀποθανεῖν ἢ τὸ καύχημά μου ἵνα τις κενώσει (𝔓⁴⁶S*BD* οὐδείς [anacoluthon] for ἵνα τις), cf. Lk 17: 2 *supra* (1).

(3) Συνήθειά ἐστιν ἵνα Jn 18: 39. Ἔρχεται (ἡ) ὥρα ἵνα Jn 12: 23, 13: 1, 16: 2, 32; acc. with inf. as in Att. R 13: 11. ('Ο καιρός (scil. ἐστιν) τοῦ ἄρξασθαι τὸ κρίμα 1 P 4: 17, cf. § 400(1); otherwise with ὅτε or ἐν ᾗ: ἔσται καιρὸς ὅτε...ἀνέξονται 2 T 4: 3, ἔρχεται ὥρα ὅτε Jn 4: 21, 23, 5: 25, 16: 2, 25, ἔρχεται ὥρα ἐν ᾗ... ἀκούσουσιν Jn 5: 28 where the prediction is definite, while ἵνα or the inf. is used to denote the general direction of the impending event. Cf. εἶχον ἂν καιρὸν ἀνακάμψαι Η 11: 15. Rev 11: 18 is peculiar: ἦλθεν ὁ καιρὸς τῶν νεκρῶν κριθῆναι καὶ δοῦναι etc. = ἵνα κριθῶσιν οἱ νεκροὶ καὶ δῷς etc.; cf. R 9: 21 ἔχει ἐξουσίαν τοῦ πηλοῦ, ποιῆσαι etc.

(4) Οὐκ εἰμὶ ἱκανὸς ἵνα Mt 8: 8 = Lk 7: 6, otherwise

inf.; cf. πολλά, μικρὸν λείπει ('fail, fall short in') with ἵνα and with inf. Herm Vis 3.1.9, Sim 9.9.4; πρὸ ἱκανῶν ἡμερῶν ἵνα PHolm 4.23. Οὐκ εἰμὶ ἄξιος ἵνα Jn 1: 27, cf. Herm Sim 9.28.5; often with the inf.; with τοῦ and the inf. 1 C 16: 4 (§400(3)), with relative clause Lk 7: 4 (§379). Ἕτοιμος, also ἑτοίμως (ἐν ἑτοίμῳ) ἔχειν with inf. A 21: 13, 2 C 10: 6, 12: 14, 1 P 4: 5.

(5) Χρείαν ἔχειν ἵνα Jn 2: 25, 16: 30, 1 Jn 2: 27; elsewhere with inf. Mt 3: 14 etc. (with τοῦ and acc. with inf. H 5: 12; §400(1)). Jn 13: 10 ἔχει χρείαν νίψασθαι with the same subject, while in the references with ἵνα a new subject is introduced. Accordingly Jn 16: 30 οὐ χρείαν ἔχεις, ἵνα τίς σε ἐρωτᾷ, where, among the very interesting vv.ll., that of sy^s ἵνα τινὰ ἐρωτᾷς is to be preferred. 1 Th 4: 9 οὐ χρείαν ἔχομεν γράφειν ὑμῖν S^cD* al.; ἔχετε γράφειν S*AD^c al. is incorrect, but ἔχετε γράφεσθαι (= 5: 1) H al. is correct. Cf. Mayser II 1, 318; with ὥστε Plato, Ep. 6.322 c. Ἐξουσίαν ἔχειν with inf. Jn 10: 18, 1 C 9: 4ff., H 13: 10, Rev 11: 6 (R 9: 21 s. supra (3)); διδόναι ἐξουσίαν with inf. Jn 1: 12, Rev 13: 5 (with ὥστε Mt 10: 1, cf. §391(3)); δότε κἀμοὶ τὴν ἐξουσίαν ταύτην A 8: 19.—Also γίνεται Mk 2: 15 SBLW (pm. ἐγένετο); cf. UPZ I 62.28f. (c. 160 BC) γίνεται γὰρ ἐντραπῆναι 'for it appears that one feels ashamed', PAmh II 135.10 (ii AD) ἐὰν γένηται ἡμᾶς μὴ... ἀναπλεῖν; further exx. from the pap. in Witkowski, Epistulae² 38.29 and Mayser II 1, 307; the earliest ex. is in Theognis 639; also cf. Att. ἔστι with inf. 'it appears, is possible'. Epict., Ench. 12 οὐχ...ἐστὶν αὐτῷ καλῶς, ἵνα..., Plut., Mor. 179 B μὴ γένοιτό σοι...καλῶς οὕτως, ἵνα....

(6) Ἐμὸν βρῶμά ἐστιν ἵνα Jn 4: 34; cf. §394. Ἐγένετο ὁρμὴ τῶν ἐθνῶν...ὑβρίσαι (= 'they resolved, intended') A 14: 5, καταλειπομένης ἐπαγγελίας εἰσελθεῖν H 4: 1 (cf. ἀπολείπεται, ἀπόκειται with inf. 4: 6, 9: 27); 5: 11 λόγος δυσερμήνευτος λέγειν sounds class. (like class. λευκὸς ἰδεῖν etc.; otherwise this type is not common in the NT), 9: 5 οὐκ ἔστιν νῦν λέγειν (Viteau 151). Ὁ ἔχων ὦτα ἀκούειν ἀκουέτω Mk 4: 9, Lk 14: 35 etc. ('for hearing', δυνάμενα ἀκούειν) is a peculiar use of the inf., cf. ὦτα τοῦ μὴ ἀκούειν 'such ears that they...' R 11: 8 (§400(2)).—Rob. 1058f., 1075–7.

394. The explanatory (epexegetical) infinitive

(acc. with infinitive) preceded by a demonstrative is closely related to the infinitive in some of the constructions cited in §§392f. The demonstrative can also be omitted without thereby making the construction with the infinitive impossible. Ἵνα can also take the place of the infinitive (Raderm.² 190, 192), especially in Jn, e.g. 1 Jn 5: 3 αὕτη γάρ ἐστιν ἡ ἀγάπη τοῦ θεοῦ, ἵνα τὰς ἐντολὰς αὐτοῦ τηρῶμεν. If, however, the epexegetical phrase refers to an actual fact, Jn

uses ὅτι rather than ἵνα (§397(3) end): 1 Jn 3: 16 ἐν τούτῳ ἐγνώκαμεν τὴν ἀγάπην, ὅτι ἐκεῖνος...τὴν ψυχὴν αὐτοῦ ἔθηκεν; and if the fact is only assumed, ἐάν or ὅταν: 2: 3 ἐν τούτῳ γινώσκομεν ὅτι..., ἐὰν τηρῶμεν, 5: 2 ὅταν ἀγαπῶμεν (at the same time double ὅτι is thus avoided).

Inf.: Ja 1: 27 θρησκεία καθαρὰ αὕτη ἐστίν, ἐπισκέπτεσθαι ὀρφανούς, A 15: 28 πλὴν τούτων τῶν ἐπάναγκες, ἀπέχεσθαι, 1 Th 4: 3 τοῦτο γάρ ἐστιν θέλημα τοῦ θεοῦ, ὁ ἁγιασμὸς ὑμῶν, ἀπέχεσθαι ὑμᾶς (cf. with ἵνα without demonstrative 1 C 16: 12), E 3: 8. With ἵνα: Lk 1: 43 τοῦτο, ἵνα ἔλθῃ (here not quite correct since the action introduced by ἵνα is already a fact; cf. Epict. 2.5.16). Jn 15: 8 ἐν τούτῳ ἐδοξάσθη ὁ πατήρ μου, ἵνα καρπὸν πολὺν φέρητε = ἐν τῷ φέρειν ὑμᾶς (conception and intention, not actuality), unless ἐν τούτῳ is to be referred to the preceding (cf. 14: 13); further, 6: 39, 17: 3, 1 Jn 3: 11, 23, 4: 21, 2 Jn 6 (without demonstrative Jn 4: 34, §393(6)). 1 Jn 3: 1 is related: ποταπὴν ἀγάπην...ἵνα, and 1 C 9: 18 τίς οὖν μού ἐστιν ὁ μισθός; ἵνα....Another noteworthy instance is Jn 15: 13 μείζονα ταύτης ἀγάπην οὐδεὶς ἔχει, ἵνα τὴν ψυχὴν αὐτοῦ θῇ (= τοῦ θεῖναι), cf. 3 Jn 4; Herm Sim 9.28.4 ἡ βουλὴ αὕτη, ἵνα.... Cf. Moule 145f. who adduces also Ph 2: 2. An inf. corrected into a ὅτι-clause: Herm Vis 3.5.5 μόνον τοῦτο ἔχουσιν, παρὰ τῷ πύργῳ κεῖσθαι S, ὅτι...κεῖνται A.—Without demonstrative pron.: R 5: 8 (ὅτι 'in that'), Barn 6.18 τὸ ἄρχειν ἐξουσίας ἐστίν, ἵνα τις ἐπιτάξας κυριεύσῃ 'sovereignty depends upon the power of command', i.e. literally, 'the power that one, commanding, rules'. With 1 C 9: 18 cf. Epict. 4.1.99 πῶς...; ἵνα..., Περὶ ὕψους 10.1 ποῦ...; ὅτι...(so Wifstrand, K. Hum. Vet.-samf. i Lund, Årsber. 1933–4 [1934] 70 for ὅτε).—Rob. 1078f., 1086f.

395. The infinitive with πρίν

(Ionic πρὶν ἤ is more popular in Koine [Stahl 446; Meltzer, Jahresb. Altertumsw. 159 (1912) 380, 382; Tschuschke 31, 33], which is a mixture of πρίν and πρότερον ἤ, cf. Homil Clem 8.2 πρότερον...πρὶν ἤ) also belongs in general to this series of infinitives which correspond to a subjunctive rather than to an indicative (Mayser II 1, 319), although ἵνα cannot be substituted here and the subjunctive is sharply distinguished from the indicative. Both moods can be used only after negative principal clauses (the NT like the rest of Koine is not, however, familiar with the indicative: Meltzer, op. cit. 382), while the infinitive is used after positive clauses (as in Attic). Πρὸ τοῦ with the infinitive can be used in a way similar to this πρίν (§403; also classical), especially in the case of events which are thought of as having actually taken place (subsequently); but πρίν is not excluded in such cases (A 7: 2, Jn 8: 58; Attic likewise).

Mt 1: 18 πρὶν ἢ συνελθεῖν αὐτοὺς εὑρέθη etc., 26: 34, 75 πρὶν (ἤ add. A 75; Lk 22: 61 ἤ add. B; Mk 14: 30 ἤ om. SD, 72 all witnesses without ἤ) ἀλέκτορα φωνῆσαι τρὶς ἀπαρνήσῃ με, Jn 4: 49, 14: 29, A 2: 20 OT, 7: 2; never in the Epistles.—Only Lk with the subj. after a negative principal clause (§ 383(3)), likewise with the opt. in indirect discourse (§ 386(4)). Subj. (without ἄν) after a *positive* principal clause, and hence incorrect, in Herm Sim 5.7.3. Jn 8: 58 in D (and it) πρὶν Ἀβραάμ without γενέσθαι so that πρίν is used as a prep. like ἕως (§ 216(3)); cf. with the gen. πρὶν ὥρας Pind., Pyth. 4.43, often in Jos., Arrian etc. (Stephanus-Dindorf s.v. πρίν, Schmidt 395); but in D with the acc.: Jn 11: 55 πρὶν τὸ πάσχα for πρὸ τοῦ π., Mk 15: 42 πρὶν σάββατον (J. Wellhausen, Das Ev. Marci², 134); more important is the v.l. in Mt 26: 34 πρὶν ἀλεκτοροφωνίας attested by 𝔓³⁷,⁴⁵ L a (supported by Or, who has πρό, not πρίν; L has πρὶν ἤ) in place of πρὶν ἀλέκτορα φωνῆσαι (cf. § 123(1)). Philo quotes πρὸ τοῦ with inf. from the LXX accurately, but paraphrases with πρίν and inf. when composing freely (Katz, Philo's Bible 8).—Diogn 2.3 πρὶν ἤ with inf. dependent on a negative interrogative clause which anticipates an affirmative answer.

(ii) *The infinitive and analytical constructions with ὅτι*

396. Introduction. In classical Greek the complement of verbs of (perceiving,) believing, (showing,) and saying which indicate the content of the conception or communication, is formed to a great extent by the infinitive. If the subject of the infinitive is the same as that of the governing verb, it is not expressed (modifiers, however, are in the nom.); otherwise it is in the acc. The participle is an alternative construction (§ 416). In addition, the complement of verbs of perception, showing, saying, but not of believing, is often formed by means of an indirect question, from which there developed even before Homer the construction with ὅτι 'that' (strictly ὅ τι, an indirect interrogative particle); this construction is possible with these same verbs—i.e. excepting the verbs of believing. Finally, with verbs of saying, hearing etc. ὡς with a finite verb is also used as a less definite expression (Riemann, Rev. Phil. 1882, 73 ff.; Kallenberg, RhM 68 [1913] 467).

Among these constructions in the NT the infinitive has not been driven out of use, but it has been sharply curtailed and only among the literary authors, so to speak (Lk, Paul, Heb), is it still common, while the construction with ὅτι predominates and has also drawn in the verbs of believing. The indirect question remains within its proper limits. Ὡς is found almost exclusively in Lk and Paul and more or less clearly retains its proper meaning 'how', but the confusion with πῶς has already begun; in late Greek πῶς takes on more and more the meaning of ὅτι until in MGr it has nearly driven the latter out. The unclassical combination ὡς ὅτι = ὅτι is apparently found three times in Paul; the Vulg. in two instances, however, translates the phrase in question with *quasi*. Indirect discourse with (acc. and) infinitive, so strongly developed in classical Greek, is almost entirely wanting in the NT; Lk is probably the only one who retains it to any considerable degree, and even he quickly slides over into the direct form (s. A 25: 4f., 1: 4, on Mk s. Zerwick 24 ff.). The very common use of ἄν with the infinitive in classical (where the direct form had had ἄν with the optative or with the unreal indicative) is missing in the NT (ὡσάν with the infinitive does not belong here, § 453(3)), but in Diogn 1 there is a potential infinitive with ἄν in a consecutive clause.

Ὅτι for the inf. is not vulgar but vivid style: Préaux, Chronique d'Égypte 6 (1931) 414f. (ByzZ 32 [1932] 171).—Ὡς Mk 12: 26 after ἀναγινώσκειν (v.l. πῶς), Lk 6: 4 (ἀναγ.; v.l. πῶς, om. BD), 8: 47 (ἀπαγγέλλειν; D ὅτι), 23: 55 (θεάσασθαι), 24: 6 (μνησθῆναι; D ὅσα), 35 (ἐξηγεῖσθαι; D ὅτι), A 10: 28 (ἐπίστασθε, ὡς ἀθέμιτον), 38 (εἰδέναι; D is different), 20: 20 (ἐπιστ.; πῶς precedes in v. 18); R 1: 9, Ph 1: 8 and 1 Th 2: 10 after μάρτυς; and only a few other passages.—Πῶς (Raderm.² 196; Ghedini, Vang. ap. 463; Ljungvik 66f.): Mt 12: 4 and Mk 2: 26, 12: 26 after ἀνέγνωτε, 41 after ἐθεώρει, Lk 14: 7 after ἐπέχων, A 11: 13 and 1 Th 1: 9 after ἀπαγγέλλειν; Barn 11.1, 14.6, 1 Clem 19.3, 21.3, 34.5, 37.2, 50.1. Πῶς = ὅτι perhaps also in Mk 10: 23 (Pallis, Notes 35, who also takes 10: 24 λέγει αὐτοῖς· Τέκνα, πῶς δύσκολόν ἐστιν as hyperbaton for λέγει, πῶς ['that'] δ. ἐ., τέκνα).—Ὡς ὅτι: 2 C 11: 21 κατὰ ἀτιμίαν λέγω, ὡς ὅτι ἡμεῖς ἠσθενήσαμεν, cf. 17 οὐ κατὰ κύριον λαλῶ, ἀλλ' ὡς ἐν ἀφροσύνῃ (vg also has *quasi* here), therefore ὡς ὅτι ἡμεῖς ἠσθ. = ὡς ἡμῶν ἀσθενησάντων. Likewise 2 Th 2: 2 ὡς ὅτι ἐνέστηκεν ἡ ἡμέρα = ὡς ἐνεστώσης τῆς ἡμέρας. In the third passage, 2 C 5: 19, vg has *quoniam quidem*; nevertheless the explanation is no different: ὡς ὅτι θεὸς ἦν ἐν Χριστῷ κόσμον καταλλάσσων ἑαυτῷ = ὡς θεοῦ ὄντος etc. (in which case the ptcps. would have piled up and the imperf. ἦν gotten lost), and this very construction immediately appears in v. 20: ὡς τοῦ θεοῦ παρακαλοῦντος (§ 425(3)). Here the origin of the later ὡς ὅτι is perhaps most evident, except that a verb of saying does not yet precede. On late ὡς ὅτι = ὅτι s. Jannaris §1754; Sophocles, Lexicon s.v. ὡς; Wolf II 68; Trunk 50; Mlt. 212 [336f.]; Wessely, Stud. Pal. 20 (1921) no. 86.3; Tabachovitz 21 f.; Mayser II 3, 45 n. 1. Cf. Homil Clem 1.7 ('that is, ...'), 16.6 (likewise), 11.28 (οὐχ ὡς ὅτι ..., ἀλλ' ὡς ὅτι 'not as though..., but that, so to speak'), 14.7 (ὡς ὅτι = ὅτι *recitativum*), 16.7 (ὥσπερ ὅτι 'whereby it has supposedly been said that'); ὡς ὅτιπερ POxy XVI 1831.1 (v AD), 1833.1 (v AD).—Inf. with potential ἄν in a declarative sentence PLille 1 recto 9 (259/8 BC); Mayser II 1, 313.

397. The infinitive and ὅτι with verbs of perception (recognizing, knowing), believing, saying, showing, etc.:

(1) **Perception**: Ἀκούειν with acc. and inf. Jn 12: 18, 1 C 11: 18, i.e. 'to receive a communication' (also class.); otherwise the ptcp. and usually ὅτι. Θεωρεῖν, βλέπειν, ἰδών etc. with ὅτι Mk 16: 4 etc. (especially with the meaning 'to recognize' as in the LXX; Johannessohn, KZ 64 [1937] 171ff., 217ff., 242ff., 248f.); but elsewhere with the ptcp. §416(1), not inf. Γινώσκειν with acc. and inf. H 10: 34 (in class. only with the meaning 'to pass judgment', which can also be accepted for this passage); ὅτι predominates, cf. ptcp. §416(2). Μανθάνειν 'to find out' ὅτι A 23: 27, Barn 9.8 (the inf. is differently used, s. §392(2)). Εἰδέναι Lk 4: 41, 1 P 5: 9, 1 Clem 43.6, 62.3 with acc. and inf. (class. occasionally also), otherwise ptcp. and usually ὅτι (ὡς), which is also the construction with ἐπίστασθαι. Καταλαμβάνεσθαι 'perceive, find' (post-classical; cf. Att. -νειν) with acc. and inf. A 25: 25; elsewhere ὅτι (4: 13, 10: 34).

(2) **Verbs of believing**, contrary to Att. usage, very commonly take ὅτι (Hell., Raderm.² 190): Δοκεῖν 'believe' with (acc. and) inf. Lk 8: 18 etc., with ὅτι Mt 6: 7 and almost always except in Lk and Paul (in Mk 6: 49 the reading is doubtful); δοκεῖν 'to seem', however, only inf. (Lk, Paul, Heb; Herm Sim 9.5.1 impersonal ἐδόκει μοι with acc. and inf.), likewise ἔδοξέ μοι 'it seems best to me' (only Lk, literary language, §392(1a)). Ἐλπίζειν inf. Lk 6: 34, R 15: 24 etc. in Lk and Paul (fut. inf. A 26: 7 B, otherwise aor., §350), 2 Jn 12, 3 Jn 14; ὅτι A 24: 26, 2 C 1: 13 etc. in Lk and Paul. Ἔχειν τινὰ ὅτι 'hold, think' (*habere*, Latinism? cf. §157(3)) Mk 11: 32 (D ᾔδεισαν). Ἡγεῖσθαι acc. and inf. Ph 3: 8 (double acc. §157(3)). Κρίνειν 'decide that something is' acc. and inf. A 16: 15, τοῦτο ὅτι 2 C 5: 14; 'decide that something shall be; choose, determine' inf. A 15: 19, 1 C 2: 2, acc. and inf. A 25: 25, τοῦ with inf. 27: 1, and belongs like ἔδοξέ μοι in the same category with βούλεσθαι, κελεύειν etc. (§392(1)). Λογίζεσθαι 'be of the opinion' R 3: 28, 14: 14, 2 C 11: 5, Ph 3: 13 with

(acc. and) inf.; ὅτι R 8: 18, Jn 11: 50, H 11: 19 (Jn and Heb 'consider, tell oneself' as in 2 C 10: 11; ὅτι is not unclass. with such a meaning). Νοεῖν acc. and inf. H 11: 3, ὅτι Mt 15: 17 etc. (neither is class.). Νομίζειν (acc. and) inf. Lk 2: 44 etc. in Lk and Paul (ἐνόμιζον [*solebant*] ἐν προσευχῇ εἶναι A 16: 13? s. Blass *ad loc.*), ὅτι Mt 5: 17 etc., A 21: 29 (acc. and inf. would have been ambiguous; Thuc. 3.88 is quite wrongly cited as an instance of νομίζειν ὅτι). Οἴεσθαι (acc. and) inf. Jn 21: 25 (last verse of the Gos.), Ph 1: 17, 1 Clem 30.4 OT, 2 Clem 14.2, Diogn, ὅτι Ja 1: 7 (Lucian, e.g. Lex. 24), 2 Clem 6.6, 15.1. Πείθεσθαι acc. and inf. A 26: 26, apparently with ὅτι H 13: 18 (πεποίθαμεν is a better v.l., s. §336(3)), certain in Herm Sim 8.11.2; πεποιθέναι and πεπεῖσθαι likewise with (acc. and) inf. Lk 20: 6, R 2: 19, 2 C 10: 7, ITr 3.2, with ὅτι R 8: 38, Ph 2: 24 etc. Πιστεύειν inf. A 15: 11, R 14: 2 (πιστεύει φαγεῖν πάντα, i.e. it does not mean 'believe' here, but 'to have the confidence to risk, to feel equal to...' [s. Bauer s.v. πιστεύω 4]), often ὅτι. Προσδοκᾶν (acc. and) inf. A 3: 5 (aor. inf.), 28: 6 (with μέλλειν πίμπρασθαι), Diogn 4.6 (δύνασθαι), Herm Sim 1.2 (aor. inf.). Ὑποκρίνεσθαι acc. and inf. Lk 20: 20 (cf. §157(2)). Ὑπολαμβάνειν ὅτι Lk 7: 43, 1 Clem 35.9 OT, GP 30 (Att. also, Plato, Ap. 35A). Ὑπονοεῖν acc. and inf. A 13: 25, 27: 27, Herm Vis 4.1.6. On the whole, therefore, the inf. with verbs of believing is limited with rare exceptions to Lk and Paul (Heb) as a 'remnant of the literary language' (Viteau 52). —Mayser II 1, 312.

(3) **Verbs of saying** etc. take ὅτι to a very large extent: Φάναι ὅτι 1 C 10: 19, 15: 50 (acc. and inf. R 3: 8), while in class. this verb hardly ever takes ὅτι (any more than it takes an indirect question). Λαλεῖν seldom ὅτι H 11: 18, never with acc. and inf.; the common construction rather is ἐλάλησεν λέγων like ἔκραξεν λέγων, ἀπεκρίθη λ. etc., formed on the model of Hebr. יְדַבֵּר לֵאמֹר (§420). Κράζειν, (ἀπο-) φθέγγεσθαι, φωνεῖν never take ὅτι or the acc. and inf. Ἀποκρίνεσθαι only in Lk: Lk 20: 7 inf., A 25: 4 acc. and inf., 16 and IPhld 8.2 ὅτι. Βοᾶν only A 25: 24 (inf.). Ὀμνύειν ὅτι Mt 26: 74 = Mk 14: 71, Rev 10: 6 (unclass.; aor. inf. A 2: 30, Barn 14.1, fut. inf. as in class. H 3: 18); so also in other expressions of asseveration: ἔστιν ἀλήθεια τοῦ Χριστοῦ ἐν ἐμοί, ὅτι 2 C 11: 10, cf. G 1: 20, R 14: 11 (cf. 1 Clem 58.2), 2 C 1: 23 (s. *infra*). In contrast to ὅτι, the (acc. with) inf. has strongly retreated in NT authors outside of Lk and Paul: acc. and inf. λέγειν Mt 16: 13, 15, 22: 23 (= Mk 8: 27, 29, 12: 18), Jn 12: 29 etc., κατακρίνειν Mk 14: 64, ἐπιμαρτυρεῖν 1 P 5: 12, ἐπαγγέλλεσθαι inf. Mk 14: 11, A 7: 5, 2 Clem 11.6, Herm Vis 3.1.2; in Lk and Paul also ἀπαγγέλλειν A 12: 14, προκαταγγέλλειν 3: 18, ἀπαρνεῖσθαι Lk 22: 34, διισχυρίζεσθαι A 12: 15, μαρτυρεῖν 10: 43, προαιτιᾶσθαι R 3: 9, σημαίνειν A 11: 28, χρηματίζειν 'prophesy' Lk 2: 26; but ὅτι with παραγγέλλειν 'to command' 2 Th 3: 10

is ὅτι *recitativum* (*infra* (5)).—Also taking ὅτι are equivalent expressions like μάρτυρα τὸν θεὸν ἐπικαλοῦμαι 2 C 1: 23, αὕτη ἐστὶν ἡ μαρτυρία 1 Jn 5: 11, ἔστιν αὕτη ἡ ἀγγελία 1: 5, ἵνα πληρωθῇ ὁ λόγος Jn 15: 25, ἀνέβη φάσις A 21: 31, ἐν ὀνόματι Mk 9: 41 'on the claim, on the basis that' (Heitmüller, Im Namen Jesu [Göttingen, 1903] 63 f.).

(4) **Verbs of showing, indicating** (which may be regarded as causatives of verbs of perception) in Att. form the complement for the most part with the ptcp. (δεικνύναι, δηλοῦν, also φανερός εἰμι etc.; occasionally ἀπαγγέλλειν and the like) if ὅτι is not used. The acc. with inf. is found in the NT with διασαφεῖν (an add. in D to A 10: 25), ἐπιδεικνύναι A 18: 28 (ὅτι Barn 5.7) and δηλοῦν H 9: 8 (not contrary to Att. usage; on συνιστάναι with doubtful acc. and inf. 2 C 7: 11 s. §197); ὅτι is found with ὑποδεικνύναι A 20: 35 and φανεροῦσθαι pass. 2 C 3: 3 and 1 Jn 2: 19 (Diogn 9.2, act. Barn 2.4) (but φανεροῦν with acc. and inf. in Barn 5.9); also δῆλον (πρόδηλον) ὅτι 1 C 15: 27, G 3: 11, H 7: 14 (δῆλός εἰμι ὅτι and the like are also class., Xen., An. 5.2.26, K.-G. II 367). There are no exx. of the ptcp. (§416 end).

(5) By far the most common form of complement with verbs of saying is *direct* discourse which can be introduced by ὅτι (*recitativum*); s. §470(1). The indirect form after verbs of perception and believing often has its tenses assimilated to those of the direct; s. §§324; 330; 345; 347(3).

(6) Ὅτι with the acc. and inf. is used irregularly after θεωρεῖν in A 27: 10 (class. and Hell.; mixture of the inf.- and ὅτι-construction; ὅτι was required to avoid ambiguity and the inf. is due to a lapse of memory [a long phrase intervenes]). Ὅτι with acc. and inf. [Xen.], Ath. 1.2, Xen., HG 2.2.2, Polyb. etc.; UPZ II 162 7.3 f. (117 BC), POxy II 237.5.8 (2 AD), PSI III 168.6 ff. (118 BC; διότι); K.-G. II 357 f.; Rosenkranz, IF 48 (1930) 164; Raderm.² 195 f.; Arnim 88; Trunk 49 n. 4, 50; M. Wellmann, Die Schrift des Dioskur. π. ἁπλ. φαρμ. (Berlin, 1914) 69 f.; Ursing 60; Ljungvik, ZNW 32 (1933) 210; Préaux, Chronique d'Égypte 6 (1931) 414 f.; Mlt. 213 [338]; Mayser II 1, 314 n. 6; II 3, 204.26 ff. For mixture of indirect question and inf. s. §368. Καὶ ὅτι (= λέγοντες ὅτι) with a finite verb after παρακαλοῦντες with an inf. in A 14: 22 is more easily tolerated.—On the whole Rob. 1032–40.

(iii) *The articular infinitive*

398. Introduction. The article with an infinitive, strictly speaking, has the same (anaphoric) significance as it has with nouns. The infinitive, however, has no case endings so that wherever it is necessary to express the case of the infinitive, especially in the gen. and dat. and after prepositions, the article is used with no other significance than to make the case and substantivization clear.

Starting from literary Attic the use of the articular infinitive spread farther and farther and the NT (as the higher levels of all Koine) consequently exhibits a great wealth of usages; yet most of the usages are not represented by many examples, least of all outside the more literary authors (Lk, Paul, Heb, Ja, Peter; they are nearly wanting in Jn). S. Viteau 173; Mlt. 213, 216 [343]; Mayser II 1, 320 ff.; II 3, 59 ff. The rarest of these constructions is the addition of an attributive in the same case (possible in classical only with pronouns): only H 2: 15 διὰ παντὸς τοῦ ζῆν (τὸ ζῆν from the Tragedians on = ὁ βίος).

The articular inf. is especially characteristic of the official style in the Ptol. pap., but is also well represented in the lower levels of the language (Mayser II 1, 321).—Attributive added: δι' ὅλου τοῦ ζῆν Aristeas 130, 141, 168; ἐκ τοῦ παρόντος ζῆν LXX 2 Macc 7: 9, ἐκ τοῦ προκειμένου ζῆν IEph 17.1, cf. 3.2, 11.1, ISm 4.1, τὸ ζῆν αὐτοῦ IMag 5.2, τοῦ διὰ παντὸς ἡμῶν (v.l. ἡμᾶς) ζῆν 1.2, τὸ τῶν ἀνθρώπων ζῆν Aristeas 27, αὐτοῦ τοῦ ζῆν Homil Clem 15.8; cf. Dem. and Xen. (Wackernagel, Syntax I² 272 f.), as well as Plato, Parm. 152 E διὰ παντὸς τοῦ εἶναι.

399. The nominative and accusative of the substantivized infinitive (without preposition) are found sporadically in Mt and Mk, somewhat more frequently in Paul, and almost never elsewhere. In general the anaphoric significance of the article, i.e. its reference to something previously mentioned or otherwise well known, is more or less evident. Without this anaphoric reference, an infinitive as subject or object is usually anarthrous. (S. *infra*.) (1) Anaphoric, e.g. Mt 15: 20 τὸ ἀνίπτοις χερσὶν φαγεῖν (subject), cf. *v.* 2; 20: 23 τὸ καθίσαι (object), cf. καθίσωσιν *v.* 21. R 13: 8 τὸ ἀλλήλους ἀγαπᾶν (the well-known command). (2) Less clearly anaphoric: 2 C 9: 1 περισσόν ἐστιν τὸ γράφειν, cf. Dem. 2.3 τὸ διεξιέναι . . . οὐχὶ καλῶς ἔχειν ἡγοῦμαι (the article denotes something obvious which could take place). (3) Loosely with μή: 2 C 10: 2 δέομαι τὸ μὴ παρὼν θαρρῆσαι: here τὸ μή (like τοῦ μή §400) is the equivalent of a ἵνα μή-clause and is to be compared with classical τὸ μή after verbs of hindering (κατέχειν τὸ μὴ δακρύειν Plato, Phaedo 117 C); δέομαι τὸ θαρρῆσαι without μή would obviously be impossible even in Paul.

In the Ptol. pap. only in the more cultured style of the officials (Mayser II 1, 321).
(1) Mk 9: 10 τὸ ἀναστῆναι (9 ἀναστῇ; D also in 10 τί ἐστιν 'ὅταν ἐκ νεκρῶν ἀναστῇ'), 12: 33 τὸ ἀγαπᾶν

(cf. 30), A 25: 11 θανάτου... τὸ ἀποθανεῖν, R 4: 13 ἡ ἐπαγγελία... τὸ κληρονόμον αὐτὸν εἶναι (epexegetical to ἐπαγγ.; the art. both times designates what is well known); 7: 18 τὸ θέλειν... τὸ κατεργάζεσθαι concepts already discussed, cf. 2 C 8: 10f. (τὸ θέλειν added as a contrast), Ph 2: 13 (similar), 1: 29 (likewise), 1: 21f., 24; 1 C 11: 6 κειράσθω (ἢ ξυράσθω add. B)... τὸ κείρασθαι ἢ ξυράσθαι, 14: 39, Ph 2: 6, 4: 10 τὸ ὑπὲρ ἐμοῦ φρονεῖν (which you have previously done; however FG τοῦ, cf. §101 under θάλλειν), H 10: 31, G 4: 18 (SABC without τό); in 1 C 7: 26 and 2 C 7: 11 (R 14: 13, 2 C 2: 1) τοῦτο precedes, but this by no means calls for the art., cf. (without art.) 1 C 7: 37 etc. (§394, Buttmann 225).

(2) Herm Vis 4.2.6 αἱρετώτερον ἦν αὐτοῖς τὸ μὴ γεννηθῆναι.

(3) R 14: 13, 21, 2 C 2: 1; 1 Th 3: 3 τὸ μηδένα σαίνεσθαι, 4: 6 τὸ μὴ ὑπερβαίνειν (but 3 f. no art. with ἀπέχεσθαι and εἰδέναι). A 4: 18 παρήγγειλαν τὸ (om. S*B) καθόλου μὴ φθέγγεσθαι: the art., if correct, is to be taken with καθόλου, cf. §160, Diodor. 1.77 (ι 130. 17 Vogel). One may compare from the LXX (Viteau 164) 2 Esdr 6: 8 τὸ μὴ καταργηθῆναι 'that it may not be hindered'.

400. **The genitive of the articular infinitive** (not dependent on a preposition) has a wide range of usage in Paul and especially in Lk. Mt and Mk use it to a limited extent, but in the remaining books it appears either rarely or not at all. It belongs, in other words, to a higher stratum of Koine (often in the LXX, rare in the papyri, s. Mlt. 219f. [348f.]; M.-H. 448ff.; Mayser II 1, 321ff. Examples from Polyb., Diodor. etc. in Allen 32f.; Jannaris p. 578). In classical usage it is used either with a noun or a verb which governs the gen., or it is employed (from Thuc. on, but not very frequently; Rosenkranz, IF 48 [1930] 167) to denote purpose (equivalent to a final clause or an infinitive with ἕνεκα). Both constructions are found in the NT, but the usage has been extended to approximately the same degree as that of ἵνα. (1) With *substantives* like χρόνος, καιρός, ἐξουσία, ἐλπίς, χρεία. (2) Certain passages exhibit a very loose relationship between the substantive and infinitive and tend toward the consecutive sense: Lk 2: 21 ἐπλήσθησαν ἡμέραι ὀκτὼ τοῦ περιτεμεῖν αὐτόν (approximately = ὥστε περιτεμεῖν, ἵνα περιτέμωσιν); the transition is complete in 1 C 10: 13 τὴν ἔκβασιν, τοῦ δύνασθαι ὑπενεγκεῖν. (3) With an *adjective*, as in classical: ἄξιον τοῦ πορεύεσθαι 1 C 16: 4; rarely also with *verbs* which in classical govern the gen.: ἐξαπορηθῆναι τοῦ ζῆν 2 C 1: 8 (ἀπορεῖν τινος, also ἐξαπορεῖσθαί τινος [Dionys. Hal.]; on τὸ ζῆν s. §398). (4) The construction

with *verbs of hindering, ceasing* etc. with τοῦ μή and the infinitive (Lk, but also the LXX) has classical precedent (Xen., An. 3.5.11 πᾶς ἀσκὸς δύ' ἄνδρας ἕξει τοῦ μὴ καταδῦναι), but the usage is carried further and τοῦ μή clearly becomes 'so that... not' (cf. *supra* (2)). (5) The use of τοῦ and τοῦ μή in a *final* (or *consecutive*) sense without connection with a noun or verb governing the gen. is the commonest in the NT (but not in Paul), e.g. Mt 13: 3 ἐξῆλθεν ὁ σπείρων τοῦ σπείρειν. (6) The simple infinitive itself has the same final meaning (§390(1, 2)). There is a tendency to prefix the τοῦ to the second of two infinitives for the sake of clarity (only in passages with an OT cast), e.g. A 26: 17f. ἀποστέλλω σε, ἀνοῖξαι..., τοῦ ἐπιστρέψαι..., τοῦ λαβεῖν. (7) Elsewhere τοῦ is pleonastically prefixed to any sort of infinitive after the pattern of LXX (= Hebr. לְ), at least by Lk (especially in Acts) and sporadically by Ja. Thus after ἐγένετο A 10: 25 (D not here, but in 2: 1; cf. ἵνα Lk 1: 43 §394), προσεύχεσθαι Ja 5: 17, ἕτοιμος A 23: 15, Herm Sim 8.4.2 A (τῷ PMich), LXX. An infinitive which is the equivalent of a ὅτι-clause, however, cannot take τοῦ; the choice is limited in this case to a ἵνα- or ὥστε-construction. (8) Often very little of the consecutive sense is left with τοῦ and the infinitive and its relationship to other elements in the sentence is very loose (epexegetical usage, cf. §394), e.g. A 7: 19 ἐκάκωσεν τοὺς πατέρας, τοῦ ποιεῖν ('so that, in that he made', = ποιῶν or καὶ ἐποίει).

(1) Lk 1: 57, 2: 6, 1 P 4: 17, Lk 10: 19, 22: 6 (εὐκαιρία), A 27: 20, 1 C 9: 10, R 15: 23 (ἐπιποθίαν), H 5: 12. The anarthrous inf. and periphrasis with ἵνα can also be used here (§393(3, 5)) without distinction in meaning, whereas in Att. a τοῦ after such substantives usually retained its meaning.

(2) R 8: 12 ὀφειλέται... τοῦ κατὰ σάρκα ζῆν. 1: 24 ἀκαθαρσίαν, τοῦ ἀτιμάζεσθαι (=ὥστε ἀτ.); 11: 8 OT ὀφθαλμοὺς τοῦ μὴ βλέπειν καὶ ὦτα τοῦ μὴ ἀκούειν 'such eyes that they' (10 OT σκοτισθήτωσαν οἱ ὀφθ. τοῦ μὴ βλ.). Also A 14: 9 ὅτι ἔχει πίστιν τοῦ σωθῆναι 'necessary faith for salvation' = π. ὥστε σωθῆναι; Ph 3: 21 τὴν ἐνέργειαν τοῦ δύνασθαι 'the power so that he can'; 2 C 8: 11 ἡ προθυμία τοῦ θέλειν 'zeal in willing so that one really wills'.

(3) Lk 1: 9 ἔλαχε τοῦ θυμιᾶσαι (so also LXX 1 Km 14: 47 ἔλαχεν τοῦ βασιλεύειν, a doublet in B, hexaplaric correction for κατακληροῦται ἔργον, i.e. following Lk 1: 9 rather than the reverse, if the two instances are related at all [Katz, ThLZ 1957, 112; earlier in the Dodd Festschrift 195]); but in class. in spite of λαγχάνειν τινός this verb takes only the

simple inf., and τοῦ with the inf. corresponds rather to its free use in the exx. cited below (*infra* (5 ff.)).

(4) Lk 4: 42 (after κατέχειν), 24: 16 (κρατεῖσθαι), A 10: 47 (κωλύειν), 14: 18 (καταπαύειν), 20: 20, 27 (ὑποστέλλεσθαι; D rather badly omits the μή), also Lk 17: 1 ἀνένδεκτόν ἐστιν τοῦ μὴ.... LXX Gen 16: 2 συνέκλεισεν τοῦ μὴ..., 20: 6 ἐφεισάμην σε τοῦ μὴ..., Ps 38: 2 φυλάξω τὰς ὁδούς μου τοῦ μὴ..., 68: 24 (= R 11: 10); s. Viteau 172. PGenève 16.23 (207 AD) κωλύοντες τοῦ μὴ σπείρειν. Paul, however, omits μή after 'to hinder' so that the dependence on the verb is clear: R 15: 22 ἐνεκοπτόμην τοῦ ἐλθεῖν. Cf. Philo, Cong. 1 (III 72.3 Cohn-Wendland) quoting Gen 16: 2 τοῦ μὴ τίκτειν (s. *supra*) = LXX, but the inferior group of MSS (*c.* iv AD) reads τοῦ τεκεῖν (Katz, Philo's Bible 36). Cf. τὸ μή §399(3).

(5) Mt 2: 13 ζητεῖν τοῦ ἀπολέσαι, 21: 32 μετεμελήθητε τοῦ πιστεῦσαι ('so that'), 3: 13, 11: 1, 24: 45 (D om. τοῦ), H 10: 7 OT, 11: 5, Homil Clem 9.22 ('so that'). Cf. Jos. etc. (Schmidt 428), Ps.-Callisth. 2.39 (ὀμνύναι), 3.23 (θέλειν); equally free final clause Men., Epit. 307, 310, Perik. 56 (Körte³). Pap. (cf. Mayser II 1, 321 n. 1, 322 f.; Olsson 198) e.g. πεῖσαι τοῦ γράψαι PSI IV 340.18 (257 BC), π. τοῦ ἐλθεῖν BGU I 164.26 (ii/iii AD). On 2 C 2: 13 s. §401.

(6) Also Lk 1: 76 f., 78 f., 2: 22, 24.

(7) Ἐκρίθη τοῦ... A 27: 1, cf. ἐγένετο γνώμης τοῦ 20: 3 (ἀνέβη ἐπὶ τὴν καρδίαν Herm Vis 3.7.2); ἐπιστεῖλαι A 15: 20, παρακαλεῖν 21: 12, ἐντέλλεσθαι Lk 4: 10 OT (Ps 90 [91]: 11), κατανεύειν Lk 5: 7, στηρίζειν τὸ πρόσωπον 9: 51, συντίθεσθαι A 23: 20, ποιεῖν 3: 12 (cf. πᾶν ποιεῖν τοῦ BGU II 625.28 [ii/iii AD]). LXX e.g. 3 Km 1: 35 ἐνετειλάμην, Ezk 21: 11 and 1 Macc 5: 39 ἕτοιμος; s. Viteau 170. In Hermas even in the sense of a ὅτι-clause: Man 12.3.6 σεαυτῷ κέκρικας τοῦ μὴ δύνασθαι = ὅτι οὐ δύνασαι. Aesop. often, even as subj. (Ursing 59).

(8) LXX 3 Km 17: 20 σὺ κεκάκωκας τοῦ θανατῶσαι τὸν υἱὸν αὐτῆς is quite similar to A 7: 19. Further, Lk 24: 25 βραδεῖς τῇ καρδίᾳ, τοῦ πιστεῦσαι 'in believing' (τοῦ π. om. D), cf. βρ. εἰς τὸ §402(2); Lk 1: 73, A 18: 10, R 6: 6, 7: 3, Ph 3: 10 (R 1: 24, 1 C 10: 13, s. *supra* (2)). Cf. Ghedini, Vang. ap. 469. Rev 12: 7 ὁ Μιχαὴλ καὶ οἱ ἄγγελοι αὐτοῦ τοῦ (ACP; τοῦ om. 𝔓⁴⁷S 046) πολεμῆσαι represents the Semitic imperatival לְ with inf. (M.-H. 448 f.), cf. LXX Hos 9: 13 Ἐφραῒμ τοῦ ἐξαγαγεῖν 'E. must lead forth', Eccl 3: 15, 1 Chr 9: 25. Τοῦ with the inf. is nowhere else firmly established in Rev (9: 10 om. τοῦ 𝔓⁴⁷SAP, very weakly attested in 14: 15); perhaps the author is following his tendency in other respects to use the nom. instead of other cases (§136(1)), i.e. here nom. instead of the gen. or dat. (Buttmann 231 gives a slightly different explanation; also s. Viteau 168).

401. The articular infinitive in the dative

(not dependent on a preposition) is found only

once; that one occurrence is in Paul, and denotes cause (Polyb. e.g. 5.48.14 [Allen 42]): 2 C 2: 13 οὐκ ἔσχηκα ἄνεσιν τῷ πνεύματί μου, τῷ μὴ εὑρεῖν με Τίτον (LP τὸ μή, S*C² τοῦ μή, neither one correct in all probability; DE ἐν τῷ μή is perhaps correct, cf. §404(3)).

Dat. in the pap.: Mayser II 1, 323 f.; II 3, 61.10. In Atticists: Schmid III 82, IV 618; Brockmeier 27. Causal τοῦ with inf. also in BGU II 595.5 (70–80 AD) τοῦ δέ σε μὴ εὑρεθῆναι (Olsson 135), Aesop. 58 λέαινα ὀνειδιζομένη... τοῦ (v.l. ἐπὶ τῷ)...ἕνα τίκτειν (Ursing 59).

402. Prepositions with the accusative of the articular infinitive.

(1) Διὰ τό used to denote cause is frequent in Lk: 2: 4, 8: 6 etc., A 4: 2, 8: 11 etc.; also Mt 13: 5, 6, 24: 12, Mk 4: 5, 6, 5: 4 (D differs), Ja 4: 2, Ph 1: 7 (the only example in Paul), H 7: 23 f., 10: 2. (2) Εἰς τό is used to denote purpose or result, apparently not differing from τοῦ and the infinitive (§400); the former predominates in Paul (and Heb), the latter in Lk. Also cf. freer uses like τὴν ἐπιθυμίαν ἔχων εἰς τὸ ἀναλῦσαι Ph 1: 23 (𝔓⁴⁶DEFG without εἰς, which is impossible) with ζητεῖν τοῦ ἀπολέσαι Mt 2: 13 and similar non-Pauline examples in §400(5). It is used in still another way in Ja 1: 19 ταχὺς εἰς τὸ ἀκοῦσαι, βραδὺς εἰς τὸ λαλῆσαι, βραδὺς εἰς ὀργήν, where the infinitive is treated entirely like a substantive. (3) Μετὰ τό serves as a temporal designation. (4) Παρὰ τό 1 Clem 39.5, 6 = LXX Job 4: 20, 21 'because'. (5) Πρὸς τό likewise denotes purpose (or result), but it is nowhere frequent: Mt 5: 28 ὁ βλέπων γυναῖκα πρὸς τὸ ἐπιθυμῆσαι 'with respect to'.—It is not found with ἐπί, κατά, περί.

(1) Blass preferred to strike out διὰ τὸ αὐτὸν γινώσκειν πάντας Jn 2: 24 (om. syˢ Non) and continue in *v.* 25 with καὶ οὐ χρείαν εἶχεν with ATᵇ sy or οὐ γὰρ χρ. εἶχεν with Non al. Except after πρὸ τοῦ (§403) Jn does not use the inf. after prep. and art. Mayser II 1, 330; Rob. 1070.

(2) Mt 20: 19 παραδώσουσιν εἰς τὸ ἐμπαῖξαι, cf. 26: 2, 27: 31, Mk 14: 55 (ἵνα θανατώσουσιν D), Lk 5: 17 (D differs), A 7: 19, Ja 1: 18, 3: 3 (v.l. πρός), 1 P 3: 7, 4: 2; Paul e.g. R 1: 11, 20, 3: 26 (parallel to *v.* 25 εἰς ἔνδειξιν), 4: 11 (twice), 16, 18. Freer usage: 2 C 8: 6 εἰς τὸ παρακαλέσαι 'in such a manner that we have urged'; 1 Th 3: 10 δεόμενοι εἰς τὸ ἰδεῖν = ἵνα ἴδωμεν (§392(1 c)); cf. 2: 12, 4: 9. Εἰς τό is wanting in the Johannine writings; on the other hand it is found in 1 Clem, e.g. 65.1 where it is parallel to ὅπως. With Ja 1: 19 cf. Herm Man 1.1 ὁ ποιήσας ἐκ τοῦ μὴ ὄντος εἰς τὸ εἶναι τὰ πάντα, like ποιεῖν εἰς ὕψος 1 Clem 59.3. Mayser II 1, 331; Rob. 1071 f.

(3) Mt 26: 32, Mk 1: 14, 14: 28, [16: 19,] Lk 12: 5, 22: 20, A 1: 3, 7: 4, 10: 41, 15: 13, 19: 21, 20: 1, 1 C 11: 25, H 10: 15, 26. Rob. 1074.

(4) Pap., Dit., Syll.³ 495.132 (*c.* 230 BC), Polyb. *et al.* (Thuc. differs); Mayser II 1, 331; Johannessohn II 234f.

(5) Mt 6: 1 πρὸς τὸ θεαθῆναι αὐτοῖς, 13: 30, 23: 5, 26: 12, Mk 13: 22, Lk 18: 1 (πρὸς τὸ δεῖν προσεύχεσθαι 'with reference to'), A 3: 19 SB (the others εἰς), 2 C 3: 13, E 6: 11 (DEFG εἰς), 1 Th 2: 9, 2 Th 3: 8. The weakened participle-like Hebr. inf. preceded by לְ (cf. § 400(7, 8)) also contributed to this construction; cf. Bonaccorsi 32f., 522f. to the contrary. Rob. 1075.

403. Prepositions with the genitive of the articular infinitive.

'Αντὶ τοῦ 'instead of' Ja 4: 15. Διὰ παντὸς τοῦ ζῆν H 2: 15 'throughout life' (cf. § 398). 'Εκ τοῦ ἔχειν 2 C 8: 11 probably = καθὸ ἂν ἔχῃ 12 (*pro facultatibus*, Grimm). Ἕνεκεν τοῦ φανερωθῆναι 2 C 7: 12. Ἕως τοῦ ἐλθεῖν A 8: 40 (post-classical; LXX Gen 24: 33, 28: 15, 33: 3 [also with other verbs and occasionally without article, Johannessohn II 304], Polyb., Jos. etc.; s. Viteau 173; Schmidt 428f.; Allen 35); μέχρι (ἄχρι) τοῦ and the infinitive (Attic) does not appear. Πρὸ τοῦ with the aorist Mt 6: 8, Lk 2: 21, 22: 15, A 23: 15, Jn 1: 49, 13: 19, G 2: 12, 3: 23; with the present only Jn 17: 5 (εἶναι, but D γενέσθαι). 'Από, ἐπί, μετά, περί, ὑπέρ and ἄνευ, χωρίς, χάριν etc. nowhere appear with the gen.

In 2 C 7: 12 ἕνεκεν τοῦ is formed on the model of the preceding ἕνεκεν τοῦ ἀδικήσαντος etc.; otherwise ἕν. would be superfluous; cf. ἕνεκεν *before* τοῦ and the inf. in Jos. etc. (Schmidt 426; Allen 35), in the pap. (Mayser II 1, 325), in the LXX 1 Esdr 8: 21 ἕνεκεν τοῦ μὴ γενέσθαι ὀργήν, Am 1: 6 etc. Ἕως τοῦ in the pap. beg. iii BC (Mayser II 1, 325f.), in the LXX (Johannessohn II 304). Πρὸ τοῦ in the Ptol. pap. only with the aor. (Mayser II 1, 327). Cf. Rob. 1070–5 *passim*.

404. A preposition with the dative of the articular infinitive.

Only ἐν τῷ is involved (chiefly in Lk). (1) Mostly temporal = 'while': Mt 13: 4 ἐν τῷ σπείρειν αὐτόν = classical σπείροντος αὐτοῦ. Attic does not use ἐν τῷ in this way, but Hebrew does so use בְּ with the infinitive (Gesenius-Kautzsch § 114, 2), for which the LXX has ἐν τῷ (Johannessohn II 335); this construction is not found in Aramaic (Dalman, Worte Jesu 26f. [The Words of Jesus 33]). (2) The present infinitive is normally used, but Lk also has the aorist, whereby the translation usually shifts from 'while' to 'after that' (therefore = aorist participle or ὅτε with the aorist [but contrast

Bauer s.v. ἐν II 3; Rob. 1073]): Lk 2: 27 ἐν τῷ εἰσαγαγεῖν = εἰσαγαγόντων or ὅτε εἰσήγαγον. Cf. the LXX (Huber 83; Johannessohn II 335f.). (3) It occasionally appears in a sense not purely temporal: H 8: 13 ἐν τῷ λέγειν 'in speaking, in that he says'; cf. LXX (Huber 84; Johannessohn II 335).—'Επί and πρός do not appear with the dat.

(1) Mt 13: 25, 27: 12, Mk 4: 4, Lk 1: 8, 2: 6, 43, 5: 1 etc. (especially often ἐγένετο ἐν τῷ = בְּ וַיְהִי, e.g. 1: 8, 2: 6), A 2: 1, 9: 3, 19: 1 (ἐγένετο), R 3: 4 OT, 15: 13 (ἐν τῷ πιστεύειν om. DEFG, probably dittography on εἰς τὸ περισσεύειν), G 4: 18. Cf. PSI IV 354.12 (254 BC) ἐν τῷ παραπορεύεσθαι τὸν βασιλέα 'on the occasion of'.

(2) With aor. inf. also Lk 3: 21 ἐν τῷ βαπτισθῆναι (= ὅτε ἐβαπτίσθη) ἅπαντα τὸν λαὸν καὶ 'Ιησοῦ βαπτισθέντος (both simultaneously), 8: 40 (ὑποστρέφειν SB), 9: 34 (simultaneous), 36, 11: 37, 14: 1, 19: 15, 24: 30, A 11: 15. Lk 10: 35 ἐν τῷ ἐπανέρχεσθαί με ἀποδώσω 'on my return journey', but 19: 15 ἐν τῷ ἀπανελθεῖν αὐτόν 'after his return'.

(3) Mk 6: 48 βασανιζομένους ἐν τῷ ἐλαύνειν 'in (by) rowing'; Lk 1: 21 ἐθαύμαζον ἐν τῷ 'when' and 'that'; A 3: 26 ἐν τῷ ἀποστρέφειν 'in turning' = 'in that you turned'; similarly 4: 30, Herm Vis 1.1.8. The aor. inf. likewise H 2: 8 ἐν τῷ ὑποτάξαι = ὑποτάξας, 3: 12 ἐν τῷ ἀποστῆναι 'in the form of an (accomplished) apostasy'. 1 Clem 10.1 πιστὸς εὑρέθη ἐν τῷ αὐτὸν ὑπήκοον γενέσθαι ('in that'). POxy IV 734.35 (2 BC) ἐν τῷ δέ με περισπᾶσθαι ('because') οὐκ ἐδυνάσθην συντυχεῖν; cf. 2 C 2: 13 (§ 401). Inscrip. Preisigke, Sammelbuch I 620.6f. (97/6 BC) λείπεσθαι ἐν τῷ μὴ εἶναι ἄσυλον '(the sanctuary) falls short in not being a place of refuge' (Mayser II 1, 329).—Rob. 1072f.

(iv) *Cases with the infinitive*

405. The nominative with the infinitive.

Classical Greek has only a few exceptions to the rule that the subject of the infinitive, if it is identical with the subject of the governing verb, is not expressed, but supplied in the nom. from the governing verb (§ 396). The few exceptions are prompted by the need of laying greater emphasis on the subject or by assimilation to an additional contrasting subject which must necessarily stand in the acc. Dependence of the infinitive on a preposition causes no change in the rule, nor does the insertion of δεῖ, χρή (NT not with the nom., except perhaps A 26: 9 [s. *infra* (2)] in the speech of Paul before Agrippa; otherwise with the acc. and infinitive). (1) In the majority of cases in the NT too, a subject already given in or with the main verb is not repeated with the infinitive, and if the infinitive is accompanied by a nominal predicate or a modifying word or phrase agreeing with its subject, the latter is never and the former not always a basis for altering the construction to the acc. with the infinitive. In other words, the modifiers must, and the predicate can, be in the nom. as in classical: R 9: 3 ηὐχόμην ἀνάθεμα εἶναι αὐτὸς ἐγώ, 1: 22 φάσκοντες εἶναι σοφοί, H 11: 4 ἐμαρτυρήθη εἶναι δίκαιος. (2) In those cases, however, in which, in addition to the personal construction preferred in Attic, an impersonal construction is also possible, the NT prefers the impersonal. The personal construction with the nom. is not at all common, especially with the passive (λέγομαι εἶναι and the like; H 11: 4, s. *supra*), though it is a little more likely in the case of an infinitive denoting what is to happen (δεδοκι-μάσμεθα πιστευθῆναι 1 Th 2: 4) and with adjectives like δυνατός, ἱκανός (§393(4)); thus we have ἔδοξα ἐμαυτῷ δεῖν πρᾶξαι A 26: 9 along with ἔδοξέ μοι Lk 1: 3 etc.

(1) In Ph 4: 11 ἔμαθον αὐτάρκης εἶναι the nom. is necessary since here μανθάνειν is related in meaning to 'be able', with which the acc. and inf. is impossible. 2 C 10: 2 δέομαι τὸ μὴ παρὼν θαρρῆσαι. Jn 7: 4 acc. to BDW αὐτό (acc.) for αὐτός; αὐτός can also be omitted with *b e* sy^c. Without additional modifiers or predicate noun: Lk 24: 23 λέγουσαι ἑωρακέναι, Ja 2: 14, 1 Jn 2: 6, 9, T 1: 16 (after λέγειν, ὁμολογεῖν; exx. of θέλειν, ζητεῖν etc. are abundant). Also, the *object* of the inf., if it is the same as that of the governing verb, does not need to be repeated: A 26: 28 ἐν ὀλίγῳ με πείθεις χριστιανὸν ποιῆσαι 'you will make me believe that you, in the turn of a hand, have made me a Christian' (Fridrichsen, Con. Neot. 3 [1939] 14f.); cf. Xen., Mem. 1.2.49 πείθων τοὺς συνόντας αὐτῷ σοφωτέρους ποιεῖν τῶν πατέρων 'that he makes *them* wiser' (K.-G. II 32). Haenchen[12] 615 n. 1 takes με as the subject, not the object, of the infinitive: 'to play the Christian', cf. 3 Km 20 (21): 7 οὕτως ποιεῖς βασιλέα; (B only, -είαν Origen and Lucian, -εύς multi)=תַּעֲשֶׂה מְלוּכָה; cf. Beginnings IV 323.

(2) As regards the personal pass. cf. Χριστὸς κηρύσσεται ὅτι 1 C 15: 12, ὁ ῥηθεὶς Mt 3: 3, ἠκούσθη ὅτι (personal?) Mk 2: 1, φανεροῦσθαι ὅτι 2 C 3: 3, 1 Jn 2: 19; χρηματίζεσθαι with nom. and inf. of intention s. §392(1*d*), with nom. and inf. of assertion Lk 2: 26 only D. Ἀρκετός 1 P 4: 3 is without influence on the inf. which has its own subj. ('you'). Herm Sim 4.4 φανεροὶ (PMich ἀφάνεροι, probably wrong) ἔσονται, ὅτι ἡ πρᾶξις αὐτῶν πονηρὰ ἐγένετο (with a harsh change in subj.). Impersonal δοκεῖ with acc. and inf. Herm Man 4.2.2 S, Sim 9.5.1, Homil Clem 10.2.1 πολλή μοι δοκεῖ εἶναι διαφορά, 2 οὕτως οὖν μοι

δοκεῖ πολλὴν διαφορὰν εἶναι (Latinism: *multum mihi videtur interesse* [Debrunner]).

406. The infinitive with a subject accusative identical with that of the governing verb is frequent in the NT, especially when a nominal predicate is introduced. In the way well known from Latin (faithfully imitated in Greek inscriptional translations from Latin; Viereck 68.12), the reflexive pronoun going with the infinitive takes the acc. and the predicate follows suit. (This construction is customary in classical only in contrasts; thus A 25: 4 τηρεῖσθαι τὸν Παῦλον, ἑαυτὸν δὲ μέλλειν etc., in which case αὐτὸς δέ would also be possible in classical.) (1) E.g. A 5: 36 Θευδᾶς λέγων εἶναί τινα ἑαυτόν, R 2: 19 πέποιθας σεαυτὸν ὁδηγὸν εἶναι. (2) It is rarely found without a nominal predicate: e.g. Ph 3: 13 ἐγὼ ἐμαυτὸν οὔπω λογίζομαι κατειληφέναι. (3) The construction is more striking in the case of an articular infinitive, where it is not the reflexive, but the simple personal pronoun that is inserted. The only example in the NT of such an acc. with an articular infinitive *without* preposition is 2 C 2: 13 (dat., s. §401; but 𝔓^46 without με!), cf. 1 Clem 25. 2 (gen.). On the other hand, the addition of the pronoun is quite common in those cases where the infinitive with a preposition occupies a more independent position in the sentence (therefore not a reflexive pronoun): thus Mt 26: 32=Mk 14: 28 μετὰ τὸ ἐγερθῆναί με προάξω, Ja 4: 2 οὐκ ἔχετε διὰ τὸ μὴ αἰτεῖσθαι ὑμᾶς.

(1) A 8: 9, Lk 23: 2; 20: 20 ὑποκρινομένους ἑαυτοὺς δικαίους εἶναι (om. εἶναι D; §157(2)), R 6: 11 λογίζεσθε ἑαυτοὺς εἶναι νεκρούς, Rev 2: 2 (most MSS without εἶναι). There would not be sufficient grounds, by class. usage, to add the reflexive pron. in any of these cases. Rev 2: 9 and 3: 9 τῶν λεγόντων Ἰουδαίους (2: 9 Ἰουδαίων S*A) εἶναι ἑαυτούς would have to be τῶν λ. Ἰουδαίων εἶναι in classical (s. §410 on this assimilation which is not common in the NT); 2 C 7: 11 συνεστήσατε ('have demonstrated') ἑαυτοὺς ἁγνοὺς εἶναι would be ὑμᾶς αὐτοὺς ὄντας in class. (cf. §397(4)). Herm Man 11.16 τὸν λέγοντα ἑαυτὸν πνευματοφόρον εἶναι.

(2) Otherwise only H 10: 34 γινώσκοντες ἔχειν ἑαυτοὺς κρείσσονα ὕπαρξιν (cf. §397(1)). Further 1 Clem 39.1 ἑαυτοὺς βουλόμενοι ἐπαίρεσθαι = class. αὐτοί, cf. Herm Sim 6.3.5. With a non-reflexive pronoun only A 25: 21 τοῦ Παύλου ἐπικαλεσαμένου τηρηθῆναι αὐτόν (cf. §392(3)), Lk 20: 7 CD μὴ εἰδέναι αὐτούς, E 4: 22 (ὑμᾶς, but the structure of the sentence is not at all clear). Herm Man 12.6.4 ἐλπίζω δύνασθαί με, 1 Clem 62.3 ᾔδειμεν γράφειν ἡμᾶς; in vulgar pap. (Mayser II 1, 335f.), e.g.

PPetr II 11 (1).4 (iii BC) πέπεισμαι ῥᾳδίως με συσταθήσεσθαι.

(3) A 1: 3 παρέστησεν ἑαυτὸν ζῶντα μετὰ τὸ παθεῖν αὐτόν (19: 21 μετὰ τὸ γενέσθαι, D with με). Lk 2: 4 ἀνέβη...διὰ τὸ εἶναι αὐτόν, 19: 11, H 7: 24. Ἕως A 8: 40. Πρό Lk 22: 15. Ἐν Mt 27: 12, Lk 9: 34, 10: 35, A 4: 30, R 3: 4 OT, 1 Clem 10.1. Never in the NT with εἰς τό and πρὸς τό used to denote purpose (but with εἰς τό 1 Clem 34.7); and not always with μετά etc. Often in Herm: Vis 2.1.3, Man 4.1.7 (ἐὰν μετὰ τὸ ἀπολυθῆναι τὴν γυναῖκα μετανοήσῃ ἡ γυνή), Sim 6.1.5, 8.2.5 (μετὰ τὸ ταῦτα τελέσαι τὸν ἄγγελον λέγει [scil. ὁ ἄγγελος]), 6.1 (similar), 2.9, 9.6.8, 18.3. On Jn 2: 24 s. §402(1). With ὥστε 1 Clem 11.2, 46.7, Herm Sim 9.6.3, 12.2; with πρίν 16.3 πρὶν φορέσαι τὸν ἄνθρωπον τὸ ὄνομα τοῦ θεοῦ, νεκρός ἐστιν. Apocr. Acts s. Ljungvik 42 f.; pap. (Mayser II 1, 336), e.g. PEleph 13.3 (223 BC) ἐχάρην ἐπὶ τῷ με αἰσθέσθαι; POxy IV 734.35 s. §404(3).

407. The simple infinitive with a different subject. In spite of the unmistakable tendency to use the fuller construction of acc. and infinitive, the acc. need not be inserted at every point at which it could be according to classical practice (§396): οὕτως ἔχειν A 12: 15, whereas 24: 9 ταῦτα οὕτως ἔχειν. So also with ἀνάγκη and δεῖ: Mt 23: 23 ἔδει ποιῆσαι (scil. ὑμᾶς; however the generalizing subject 'one' would also fit), R 13: 5 ἀνάγκη ὑποτάσσεσθαι (but cf. §127(2)); or in instances where the subject of the infinitive has already appeared in some other case with the main verb: Lk 2: 26 ἦν αὐτῷ κεχρηματισμένον μὴ ἰδεῖν (scil. αὐτόν) θάνατον; or where the subject can be easily supplied from an adjunct such as a vocative: 1 P 2: 11 ἀγαπητοί, παρακαλῶ (scil. ὑμᾶς) ὡς παροίκους...ἀπέχεσθαι, cf. 15, H 13: 6 ὥστε θαρροῦντας λέγειν 𝔓⁴⁶M (pm. + ἡμᾶς). Viteau 149 f.; Mayser II 1, 336 f.

The indefinite 'you' as subject omitted with an inf. of obligation (or is ἀγαθοποιοῦντας substantivized and subject? K. Grobel): 1 P 2: 15 φιμοῦν 'should put to silence'; cf. ἐρρῶσθαι εὔχομαι often in the pap.; Aristoph., Ra. 1220 ὑφέσθαι μοι δοκεῖ 'that one (= you) must let down'; further in Wifstrand, K. Hum. Vet.-samf. i Lund, Årsber. 1932–3 ı 18 ff.

408. The proper sphere of the accusative and infinitive (cf. §§391–404). In comparison with the classical language the acc. with the infinitive is greatly reduced owing to the increase of direct discourse and of ἵνα and ὅτι. Also, examples of τό (nom. or acc.) with acc. and infinitive, for example, are almost entirely wanting (R 4: 13).

On the other hand, it has made some gains at the expense of the simple infinitive (§§406, 397 etc.), and a certain inclination for the more complete construction is unmistakable. The sphere of the acc. and infinitive: with verbs of perception, cognition, believing, assertion, showing, whose subject is usually different from the subject of the infinitive, which in this case is identical with the object of the main verb; with verbs of making and allowing and some verbs of commanding and bidding like κελεύειν, where the difference in subject always obtains; with verbs of volition where a difference in subject is the exception (hence usually with simple infinitive); and with verbs of wishing etc. Then with impersonal expressions such as δεῖ, ἐνδέχεται, ἀνάγκη, δυνατόν, ἀρεστόν (ἐστιν), ὥρα (ἐστίν) etc., and further with ἐγένετο and συνέβη. (In some expressions in the last category the subject of the infinitive, however, stands in the dat. outside the infinitive clause [§409], and in others it is left unexpressed, either because it is to be supplied according to §407 or for the sake of greater indefiniteness in a general statement.) To these must be added the articular infinitives with a preposition as well as the infinitive with πρίν, τό, τοῦ, ὥστε, if the subject is stated and not merely implied.

The customary pass. construction with verbs of commanding is to be noted in particular (§392(4)). The acc. is retained at times (as in class.) with verbs of perception, knowing etc., also with 'to make', even though the inf. has been replaced by ὅτι or ἵνα with a finite verb (prolepsis): A 16: 3 (𝔓⁴⁵DEH al.) ᾔδεισαν τὸν πατέρα αὐτοῦ ὅτι Ἕλλην ὑπῆρχεν; 3: 10, 4: 13; Mk 11: 32 εἶχον τὸν Ἰωάννην ὅτι προφήτης ἦν; Rev 3: 9 ποιήσω αὐτοὺς ἵνα ἥξουσιν. Cf. §405(2) for the corresponding personal (pass.) construction with the nom. and ὅτι; s. also §476 and Debrunner, Gnomon 4 (1928) 441 f. on the origin of prolepsis. The acc. with inf. is infrequent in the Gospels; e.g. Lk 11: 18 ἐκβάλλειν με rather than ὅτι probably due to the preceding ὅτι λέγετε.

409. The infinitive with an accusative which substitutes for a dative (or genitive). (1) Verbs of commanding prefer the dat. of the person addressed with the infinitive, but the acc. is also possible, not only when the subject of the infinitive is different from the person addressed (A 15: 2 ἔταξαν ἀναβαίνειν Παῦλον, and especially with the passive: 10: 48 προσέταξεν αὐτοὺς βαπτισθῆναι), but also when they are identical (1 T 6: 13 f. παραγγέλλω...τηρῆσαί σε). (2) Λέγειν in the sense of command exhibits the same variation:

A 21: 21 λέγων (om. D) μὴ περιτέμνειν αὐτοὺς τὰ τέκνα. (3) Impersonal and adjectival or substantival expressions like συμφέρει, ἔθος ἐστίν, ἀθέμιτον, αἰσχρόν, καλόν ἐστιν usually take the dat. (cf. § 190). The infinitive, however, can have its own different subject in the acc. to distinguish it from the person(s) concerned (Jn 18: 14 συμφέρει ἕνα ἄνθρωπον ἀποθανεῖν). It is even more striking that καλόν ἐστιν 'it is good' can take an acc. of the person concerned with the infinitive (Mt 17: 4 = Mk 9: 5 = Lk 9: 33 καλόν ἐστιν ἡμᾶς ὧδε εἶναι, which one can justify as being equivalent to 'it pleases me that we...'; R 13: 11 ὥρα ἡμᾶς [or ὑμᾶς] ἐγερθῆναι, where ἡμῖν [or ὑμῖν] would be just as good). (4) Ἐγένετο is often used with acc. and infinitive; with the dat. 'it befell him that he...' A 20: 16 (ὅπως μὴ γένηται), G 6: 14 (μὴ γένοιτο); but even after such a dat. the acc. with infinitive is possible or even necessary: A 22: 6 ἐγένετο δέ μοι... περιαστράψαι φῶς. (5) Δεῖσθαι takes the gen. of the person addressed. Verbs with a cognate sense like ἐρωτᾶν, παρακαλεῖν, αἰτεῖσθαι and ἀξιοῦν, παραινεῖν take the acc. of the person asked.

(1) With the dat.: διατάσσειν (-εσθαι A 24: 23, Herm Vis 3.1.4), ἐπιτάσσειν (Mk 6: 39 etc.; also τάσσειν A 22: 10), παραγγέλλειν, ἐντέλλεσθαι; in addition ἐπιτρέπειν 'permit'. Also with the acc. Mk 6: 27 ἐπέταξεν ἐνεχθῆναι (ἐνέγκαι is less appropriate to NT usage) τὴν κεφαλὴν αὐτοῦ; s. § 392(4). PRev. Laws 44.8 (258 BC) τοὺς δὲ ἐλαιουργοὺς μὴ ἐπιτρεπέτωσαν... μεταπορεύεσθαι. Cf. προαγορεύειν with acc. and inf. Thuc. 4.97.4 and the like in K.-G. II 26.

(2) With the dat.: Mt 5: 34, 39, Lk 12: 13, A 21: 4. With acc.: A 22: 24 (pass.), Lk 19: 15 (pass.), also Mk 5: 43 δοθῆναι (δοῦναι D) αὐτῇ φαγεῖν (φαγεῖν is the equivalent of a substantive, § 390(2)). The ambiguity (command or assertion) must be resolved by the context. UPZ I 78.21 (159 BC, vulgar) εἶπα Ἀρμάεις... ἐλθ(ε)ῖν αὐτόν. Mayser II 1, 338. Examples from poets of the classical period in K.-G. II 26.

(3) Cf. the impersonal pass. συνεφωνήθη ὑμῖν πειράσαι A 5: 9 (§ 202 σύν). Καλόν ἐστιν with acc. and inf.: Mk 9: 45 καλόν ἐστίν σε εἰσελθεῖν... χωλόν (cf. vv. 43, 47 where the reading varies between σοι and σε; σοι Mt 18: 8, 9). Πρέπον ἐστὶν ἡμῖν (S* ἡμᾶς) πληρῶσαι Mt 3: 15 against πρ. ἐ. γυναῖκα... προσεύχεσθαι 1 C 11: 13; Lk 6: 4 οὓς οὐκ ἔξεστιν φαγεῖν εἰ μὴ μόνους τοὺς ἱερεῖς (D dat. like Mt 12: 4; Mk 2: 26 acc. SBL, dat. ACDW al.); Lk 20: 22 ἔξεστιν ἡμᾶς (ἡμῖν CDW al.)... δοῦναι. PLille 26.6 (iii BC) ἐξέσται ἡμᾶς λαβεῖν, PPetr III 1 = I 21 col. II 4 (237 BC) εἴη μέν μοι ὑγιαίνοντα ἐμὲ... κύριον εἶναι. Mayser II 1, 338. Exx. from class. prose and poetry in K.-G. II 27.

Dat. *and* acc. of the same person also 1 Clem 57.2 ἄμεινον γάρ ἐστιν ὑμῖν... μικρούς... ὑμᾶς εὑρεθῆναι.

(4) Acc. even when the subject of the inf. is identical with the dat. of the person: A 22: 17 ἐγένετό μοι... γενέσθαι με (a very clumsy sentence), G 6: 14 ἐμοὶ δὲ μὴ γένοιτο (+ με 𝔓⁴⁶) καυχᾶσθαι. For the indic. after ἐγένετο s. § 442(5).

(5) The simple inf. may also be used if the one petitioned is also the subject of the inf. (A 26: 3; add σου CHLP al.). With δεῖσθαι the nom. is used if the subject of the inf. is the one making the request (Lk 8: 38, 2 C 10: 2); this appears unusual but it is found elsewhere; ἠρώτα λαβεῖν A 3: 3, ᾐτήσατο εὑρεῖν 7: 46 (28: 20?), class. αἰτῶν λαβεῖν Aristoph., Pl. 240. In the case of ἐρωτᾶν, παρακαλεῖν etc. the inf. is still more independent than in the ordinary construction with the acc. and inf. and consequently can take a second acc. as subj. in spite of the acc. object, especially in pass. constructions (cf. *supra* (1)): A 13: 28 ᾐτήσαντο Πιλᾶτον ἀναιρεθῆναι αὐτόν, 1 Th 5: 27 ὁρκίζω ὑμᾶς ἀναγνωσθῆναι τὴν ἐπιστολήν (there is a reason for the choice of the pass. here, while the v.l. of D τοῦτον μὲν σταυρῶσαι in A 13: 28 is also possible); cf. A 21: 12 παρεκαλοῦμεν τοῦ μὴ ἀναβαίνειν αὐτόν. Cf. Ljungvik 43.

410. The case of adjuncts and predicates to the subject of the infinitive.
Since the subject of the infinitive generally is, or is thought of as being, in the acc., it is natural that adjuncts and predicates going with the subject follow suit. This is the case not only when the subject actually takes, or would take, the acc., but also when it has appeared in the gen. or dat. with the governing verb. Classical has the free choice between συμβουλεύω σοι προθύμως εἶναι and πρόθυμον εἶναι; with verbs that can take the gen., the gen. predominates as in δέομαί σου προθύμου εἶναι (adjective), but προστάτην γενέσθαι (substantive; K.-G. II 24f.); participles as adjuncts may be in the dat. (or acc.) but not in the gen., for which the acc. is used. Examples of a predicate in the gen. or dat. are completely lacking in the NT and participial adjuncts are usually in the acc.—For the papyri s. Mayser II 1, 338f.

Acc.: Lk 1: 73f. τοῦ δοῦναι ἡμῖν... ῥυσθέντας λατρεύειν; G 6: 14 𝔓⁴⁶ (§ 409(4)), H 2: 10, A 15: 22, 25 (25 𝔓⁴⁵ABL ἐκλεξαμένοις) etc. Dat. only infrequently: 2 P 2: 21 κρεῖττον ἦν αὐτοῖς μὴ ἐπεγνωκέναι... ἢ ἐπιγνοῦσιν ὑποστρέψαι (where however the ptcp. belongs more to κρεῖττον ἦν αὐτοῖς than to the inf.; this is decidedly the case in A 16: 21 where Ῥωμαίοις οὖσιν goes with ἔξεστιν ἡμῖν; so also in Lk 1: 3). Lk 9: 59 ἐπίτρεψόν μοι πρῶτον ἀπελθόντι (but -τα DΘ, ἀπελθεῖν καί AKP) θάψαι..., A 27: 3 ἐπέτρεψεν (scil. τῷ Παύλῳ)...πορευθέντι (SAB, -τα HLP) ἐπιμελείας τυχεῖν.—Nom. for the dat. by anacoluthon after ἔδοξε A 15: 22f. (§468(3)). Also s. §406(1).

(H) The Participle

411. Introduction. The fullness of form and usage of the participle exhibited by classical Greek is not greatly reduced in the NT. As regards form, the loss is confined to the less frequent appearance of the future participle (§351); of the three major categories of usage, the *supplementary* participle (predicative completion of the idea of the main verb: παύομαι λέγων etc.) is disappearing, while the *attributive* participle (attributive or substantival use) and the *adverbial* (circumstantial) participle (conjunctive and absolute) are still in full bloom. The situation in MGr vernacular is thus anticipated, in which only the (present and) perfect passive participle plus an indeclinable present active participle used as a gerund (§136) are left; the predicative usage is no longer found.

Nomenclature for participial usage varies: Rob. (1103f.) employs the terms supplementary (complementary), attributive, circumstantial for the three categories; Burton (163f.) substantive, adjective, adverbial. In Debrunner's terminology, circumstantial designates both the conjunctive and absolute adverbial ptcp.

(i) *The attributive participle*

412. The participle as attributive with or without the article, equivalent to a relative clause. (1) Mt 25: 34 τὴν ἡτοιμασμένην ὑμῖν βασιλείαν = τὴν β. ἣ ὑμῖν ἡτοίμασται. Lk 6: 48 ὅμοιός ἐστιν ἀνθρώπῳ οἰκοδομοῦντι οἰκίαν, cf. Mt 7: 24 ἀνδρὶ ὅστις ᾠκοδόμησεν αὐτοῦ τὴν οἰκίαν. (2) Ὁ λεγόμενος, καλούμενος is frequently found followed by a proper name; it is always used with the article and placed after the original name or term that is being re-designated: Mt 1: 16 Ἰησοῦς ὁ λεγόμενος Χριστός. (3) The participle often takes the article even when the preceding substantive to which it belongs is anarthrous; definiteness or anaphora is often thus provided as an afterthought by the participial clause: 1 P 1: 7 χρυσίου τοῦ ἀπολλυμένου. (4) The articular participle is striking in some instances where Attic usage would have preferred to express the attributive relationship by means of a relative clause: A 4: 12 οὐδὲ γὰρ ὄνομά ἐστιν ἕτερον τὸ δεδομένον, Lk 18: 9 πρός τινας τοὺς πεποιθότας ἐφ᾽

ἑαυτοῖς. Evidently the identification of the relative clause with the attributive participle has given rise to this construction; the article is not absolutely necessary (cf. §353(2)), but desirable (Björck, Die periphr. Konstruktionen 92), because, e.g. Mk 14: 4 ἦσάν τινες ἀγανακτοῦντες without article is merely periphrasis for ἠγανάκτουν τινές. (5) The arthrous participle is used with a personal pronoun as in Attic: σὺ τίς εἶ ὁ κρίνων Ja 4: 12 (ὃς κρίνεις KL), R 14: 4 (cf. 2: 1); A 13: 16 ἄνδρες Ἰσραηλῖται καὶ (scil. ὑμεῖς) οἱ φοβούμενοι τὸν θεόν, cf. 2: 14.—For the position of the other adjuncts of the participle, s. §474(5).

(1) Mk 3: 22 οἱ γραμματεῖς οἱ ἀπὸ Ἱεροσολύμων καταβάντες, 5: 25 γυνὴ οὖσα ἐν ῥύσει αἵματος etc. (many ptcps. follow; cf. Lk 8: 43, where a relative clause follows the first ptcp.).

(2) A 1: 12 ὄρους τοῦ καλουμένου ἐλαιῶνος. Lk also uses ὁ ἐπικαλούμενος with bynames: A 10: 18, cf. ὃς ἐπικαλεῖται 10: 5, 32. Jn 5: 2 ἔστιν...[ἐπὶ τῇ προβατικῇ] κολυμβήθρα ἡ ἐπιλεγομένη...Βηθεσδά (λέγ. without ἡ D, τὸ λεγόμενον S*, τῇ ἐπιλεγομένῃ W) the art. would be omitted acc. to Att. usage, but acc. to NT usage it may appear (cf. (4)); the reading with art. arose perhaps from taking κολυμβήθρα as a dat. (Blass). Constructions such as Thuc. 2.29.3 τῆς Φωκίδος νῦν καλουμένης γῆς are never found, nor anything like 4.8.6 ἡ νῆσος ἡ Σφακτηρία καλουμένη.

(3) Lk 7: 32 παιδίοις τοῖς ἐν ἀγορᾷ καθημένοις, 1 C 2: 7 θεοῦ σοφίαν...τὴν κεκρυμμένην. Cf. §270(3). Jn 12: 12 ὄχλος πολὺς (ὁ ὄ. π. BL; cf. §270(1)) ὁ ἐλθών.

(4) Further references Mk 15: 41, A 11: 21 (DE al. without art.), Jd 4, 2 Jn 7, cf. Jn 5: 2 (s. *supra* (2)). With τινες: G 1: 7 εἰ μή τινές εἰσιν οἱ ταράσσοντες ὑμᾶς, C 2: 8. Τινὲς οἱ λέγοντες and the like is classical and later: Raderm.[2] 115; Stahl 691, 694; Trunk 29; cf. with a relative clause from Isocrates: εἰσί τινες, οἳ μέγα φρονοῦσιν 10.1, ε. τ. οἵ...ἔχουσι 15.46; in Lysias 19.57 for εἰσί τινες οἱ προαναλίσκοντες, οἳ προαναλίσκουσι has been proposed for good reasons. Οὐδείς ἐστιν ὁ with a fut. ptcp. is good class. Greek (Dem. 15.26 οὐδείς ἐσθ᾽ ὁ διδάξων, Xen., An. 2.4.5 ὁ ἡγησόμενος οὐδεὶς ἔσται); cf. also §252 for ἔστιν ὁ with a ptcp.

(5) 1 C 8: 10 σὲ (𝔓[46]B al. om.) τὸν ἔχοντα, R 9: 20, Jn 1: 12 etc.; with the addition of the pronoun: H 4: 3 εἰσερχόμεθα...οἱ πιστεύσαντες, 6: 18, especially with impera.: Mt 7: 23, 27: 40; also οὐαὶ ὑμῖν, οἱ ἐμπεπλησμένοι Lk 6: 25 (voc.), but οὐαὶ ὑμῖν τοῖς πλουσίοις 24; cf. §147(2).

413. The participle used as a substantive. (1) As a rule the article is used as in classical. (2) When the participle has a generic meaning, πᾶς may be inserted, and even then the article is usually used, although elsewhere, when πᾶς means 'everyone', the article should be omitted (§ 275(3, 6)). (3) The neuter singular and plural participles appear as substantives with the article, though in general not very frequently in comparison with classical usage; like the masculine it may refer to some individual thing, or it may generalize.

(1) With individualizing art. e.g. Mt 26: 46 ὁ παραδιδούς με (cf. 48; Ἰούδας ὁ παρ. αὐτόν 25); generic art. e.g. E 4: 28 ὁ κλέπτων 'one who hitherto stole'; also as pred. (cf. § 273(3)) Jn 8: 18 ἐγώ εἰμι ὁ μαρτυρῶν, 6: 63, ἔστιν ὁ ζητῶν καὶ κρίνων 8: 50 etc. Without art. (sometimes also class., K.-G. ι 608f.): ἡγούμενος Mt 2: 6 OT (s. § 264(6)), στρατευόμενοι Lk 3: 14, φωνὴ βοῶντος Mk 1: 3 OT, ἔχεις ἐκεῖ κρατοῦντας Rev 2: 14, οὐκ ἔστιν συνίων etc. R 3: 11f. OT [BG(A], others have the art.; LXX Ps 13: 1ff. mostly without art.), i.e. 'one who', 'people who', although with οὐκ ἔστιν, ἔχειν and the like, Attic did not normally omit the art. Ὁ βαπτίζων Mk (1: 4), 6: 14 (,24) has become the equivalent of ὁ βαπτιστής Mt 3: 1 etc., στρατευόμενοι 'soldiers' Lk 3: 14. Cf. Pallis, Notes 1. G. Mayeda, Das Leben-Jesu-Fragment Papyrus Egerton 2...(Bern, 1946) 24; 1 C 14: 5 FG εἰ μὴ ᾖ ὁ διερμηνεύων (Cf. § 252).

(2) A 1: 19 πᾶσι τοῖς κατοικοῦσιν, Mt 5: 22 πᾶς ὁ ὀργιζόμενος, 5: 28, 7: 8 etc., Lk 6: 30 (ADPR al.), 47 etc., A 10: 43, 13: 39 (otherwise not in Acts), R 1: 16, 2: 1 etc. Without art. Mt 13: 19 παντὸς ἀκούοντος, Lk 11: 4 παντὶ ὀφείλοντι (LX with art.; D reads differently), 6: 30 SBW, 2 Th 2: 4, Rev 22: 15; and always where a substantive is inserted, e.g. Mt 12: 25. Πᾶς ὁ is also the equivalent of a relative clause: πᾶς ὅστις ἀκούει Mt 7: 24 = πᾶς ὁ ἀκούων 26. Cf. e.g. Soph., Aj. 152 πᾶς ὁ κλύων, Dem. 23.97 πᾶς ὁ θέμενος (Krüger § 50, 4.1; 11.11; Gild. 308f.).

(3) Mt 1: 20 τὸ ἐν αὐτῇ γεννηθέν, 2: 15 and often τὸ ῥηθέν, Lk 2: 27 κατὰ τὸ εἰθισμένον (ἔθος D) τοῦ νόμου (cf. § 263(2)), 3: 13 παρὰ τὸ διατεταγμένον ὑμῖν, 4: 16 κατὰ τὸ εἰωθὸς αὐτῷ, 8: 56 τὸ γεγονός, 9: 7 τὰ γινόμενα, Jn 16: 13 τὰ ἐρχόμενα, 1 C 1: 28 τὰ ἐξουθενημένα...τὰ μὴ ὄντα...τὰ ὄντα, 10: 27 πᾶν τὸ παρατιθέμενον (cf. supra (2)), 14: 7, 9 τὸ αὐλούμενον etc.; 2 C 3: 10f. τὸ δεδοξασμένον, τὸ καταργούμενον etc.; H 12: 10 κατὰ τὸ δοκοῦν αὐτοῖς...ἐπὶ τὸ συμφέρον, 11 πρὸς τὸ παρόν, etc. Completely substantivized: τὰ ὑπάρχοντα 'the possessions' with gen. e.g. Lk 12: 33, 44 (with dat. 8: 3 etc.); also τὸ συμφέρον (as in Att.) if in 1 C 7: 35, 10: 33 τὸ ὑμῶν αὐτῶν (ἐμαυτοῦ) συμφέρον (Sᶜ al.) is the correct reading instead of σύμφορον.—The fut. ptcp., too, occurs with art. without a substantive, s. § 351(2).—The ptcp. ὤν can only be used when there are other adjuncts to the predicate: Λ 22: 17 τοὺς ὄντας τῶν Ἰουδαίων πρώτους, R 8: 28 τοῖς κατὰ·πρόθεσιν κλητοῖς οὖσιν, 2 C 11: 31 ὁ ὢν εὐλογητὸς εἰς..., 1 T 1:

13 τὸν πρότερον ὄντα βλάσφημον; otherwise it must be omitted (§§ 263, 264; it can be omitted even with further adjuncts: §§ 271, 272); therefore E 1: 1 τοῖς ἁγίοις οὖσιν καὶ πιστοῖς (𝔓⁴⁶; D adds ἐν Ἐφέσῳ which satisfies the rule) is impossible (ὁ ὤν 'the existing one or thing' is different § 474(5c)).

(ii) *The supplementary participle*

For the use of the supplementary participle in the formation of the periphrastic conjugations, s. §§ 352–5.

414. The supplementary participle with verbs denoting a modified sense of to be or to do is severely curtailed in the NT and is confined almost entirely to Lk and Paul (Heb). If the complement is formed by an adjective or prepositional phrase, ὤν should be inserted; however, in the NT, it is usually omitted with verbs of this type. Phryn. 277 designates φίλος σοι τυγχάνω without ὤν as Hellenistic, but examples are not lacking in Attic; cf. also § 418(6).

The supplementary ptcp. is still very strong in the Ptol. pap. even though it has receded when compared with the class. language (Mayser ΙΙ 1, 352f.).

(1) Verbs which express a modified sense of to be: ὑπάρχειν (properly 'to be already in existence, to exist originally'; weakened in the later language to the sense of εἶναι; it nowhere has the meaning of 'to take the lead in an action' in the NT) A 8: 16 with the perf. pass. ptcp. = perf. pass. inf., likewise 19: 36 where the ptcp. is really an adjective; Ja 2: 15 γυμνοὶ ὑπάρχωσιν καὶ λειπόμενοι (ὦσιν add. ALP) τῆς...τροφῆς; ὅπως...ὑπάρχῃ καθιδρυμένος Dit., Or. 383.48 (ι BC). **Προϋπάρχειν** (already in class.), which clearly includes the sense of 'before', is used with a ptcp. in Lk 23: 12 (D has a different reading); the ptcp. in A 8: 9 προϋπῆρχεν ἐν τῇ πόλει, μαγεύων etc. is circumstantial (cf. the text of D). **Διατελεῖν** 'to be continuously' (class.) with adj. without ὤν A 27: 33, unless we should construe προσδοκῶντες διατελεῖτε together: 'you have been waiting uninterruptedly'; Homil Clem 14.8 πενθοῦντες διατελέσητε; for the same idea **ἐπιμένειν** [Jn] 8: 7 ἐπέμενον ἐρωτῶντες, A 12: 16, 2 Clem 10.5. Ἐπιμένειν with ptcp.: λέγων Mart. Paul. 4 (L.-B. ι 112.13), POxy ι 128.7 (vi/vii AD), ἑστηκώς Plato, Meno 93D, τὸ χρέος ἀπεργαζόμενος Men., Her. 35 Körte³, ἐνυβρίζων POxy ΙΙ 237.6.17 (186 AD); cf. likewise διαμένειν Dem. 8.71, ἐμμένειν Dit., Syll.³ 780.25 (letter of Augustus, 6 BC), μένειν (Ljungvik 48f.). Like Att. οὐ διέλιπεν καταφιλοῦσα Lk 7: 45; cf. A 8: 24 D, 17: 13 D, Herm Vis 1.3.2, 4.3.6, Man 9.8. With ptcp. also in LXX Jer 17: 8, 51 (44): 18 (without negative), Aristeas 274, Jos., Ant. 11.119, pap.

(Mayser II 1, 353; Preisigke); s. also Ljungvik 48. **Τυγχάνειν** 'happen to be' does not appear with ptcp. in NT, except as v.l. in Lk 10: 30 ACW (the other MSS without τυγχ.); with designation of place without ptcp. Diogn 5.8 ἐν σαρκί, 10.7 ἐπὶ γῆς; with subj. or adj. without ὤν Homil Clem 10.7, 15.7, 16.21; pap. often with and (apparently for the first time ii AD) without ὤν (Preisigke; Mayser II 1, 352f.). Classical examples of the omission of ὤν in Lorimer, ClQ 20 (1926) 195ff., later examples in Ljungvik 45. In the LXX this usage is confined to the Apocr.: Tob 5: 14 S σὺ τυγχάνεις ἀδελφὸς ὤν (om. B, which is a secondary abbreviation reducing two clauses to one); without ὤν Wsd 15: 19 καλὰ τυγχάνει; 2 Macc 6: 18 ἀνήρ... κάλλιστος τυγχάνων (v.l. ἀναχανών erroneous) (Katz, ZNW 51 [1960] 14 and a forthcoming paper to appear in TU 1961).

(2) 'To begin' and 'to stop': **Ἄρχεσθαι** took the ptcp. in Attic if the incipient action was contrasted with its continuation or end, otherwise the inf.; in the NT always the inf., though there are no instances where, acc. to the Att. rule, the ptcp. should have been used; also in Lk 14: 30 ἤρξατο οἰκοδομεῖν... ἐκτελέσαι, where ἐκτελ. is to be contrasted with οἰκ. rather than ἤρξατο. K.-G. II 75 (and 56); Stahl 744ff.; Bauer s.v. 2a. Ἄρχεσθαι with ptcp. also does not appear in the Ptol. pap. (Mayser II 1, 353). **Παύεσθαι** with ptcp. Lk 5: 4, A 5: 42, 6: 13 etc., E 1: 16, C 1: 9, H 10: 12 (with pass. ptcp. οὐκ ἂν ἐπαύσαντο προσφερόμεναι); for the same idea (unclass.) **τελεῖν** Mt 11: 1 ἐτέλεσεν διατάσσων, Lk 7: 1 D; ἐτέλεσεν ἀναγινώσκουσα Herm Vis 1.4.1, συντελεσθῇ οἰκοδομούμενος 3.8.9; cf. Ljungvik 48. To this group also belongs **ἐγκακεῖν** 'to be remiss, lax' with ptcp., G 6: 9, 2 Th 3: 13; Att. κάμνειν and ἀπαγορεύειν are lacking, ἀνέχεσθαι, καρτερεῖν, ὑπομένειν do not appear with supplementary ptcp.

(3) 'To be hidden' and 'to be manifest, evident': **Λανθάνειν** only in H 13: 2 ἔλαθον (scil. ἑαυτούς) ξενίσαντες ἀγγέλους (literary language), otherwise λάθρᾳ (§ 435). **Φαίνεσθαι**: Mt 6: 18 ὅπως μὴ φανῇς τοῖς ἀνθρώποις νηστεύων where νηστεύων is an addition to the subject as in 17 σὺ δὲ νηστεύων ἄλειψαι, and φανῇς τοῖς ἀνθρ. is an independent clause as in vv. 5, 16. Nowhere φαίνομαι or φανερός εἰμι, δῆλός εἰμι with a ptcp. in Attic fashion 'it is evident that I'; on φανεροῦσθαι ὅτι s. § 397(4).

(4) 'To come before': προέφθασεν αὐτὸν λέγων Mt 17: 25 as in class. (the simple verb has almost lost the meaning 'before'); with inf. 2 Clem 8.2, s. § 392(2).

(5) Other expressions of a modified sense of 'to do': **καλῶς ποιεῖν** as in Att.: καλῶς ἐποίησας παραγενόμενος A 10: 33, cf. Ph 4: 14, 2 P 1: 19, 3 Jn 6 (καλῶς ποιήσεις with aor. ptcp. as frequently in the pap.) (for which A 15: 29 has διατηροῦντες... εὖ πράξετε incorrectly?); in the pap. εὖ ποιεῖς and the like appear with aor. and (more rarely) pres. ptcp.

(Mayser II 1, 173f.). To this category belongs also τί ποιεῖτε λύοντες Mk 11: 5, cf. A 21: 13; further ἥμαρτον παραδούς Mt 27: 4; ἀκούσας αὐτοῦ πολλὰ ἐποίει Mk 6: 20 ACD al. is a translation Semitism (= πολλάκις ἤκουεν).—Οἴχεσθαι and the like do not appear with ptcp. in the NT.

415. The supplementary participle with verbs of emotion

such as χαίρειν, ὀργίζεσθαι, αἰσχύνεσθαι has almost disappeared in the NT; A 16: 34 ἠγαλλιᾶτο πεπιστευκώς is an unquestionable example.

But Jn 20: 20 ἐχάρησαν ἰδόντες (ἰδ. τὸν κύριον om. a) may well mean 'when they saw' (the ptcp. as an independent adjunct) as in Ph 2: 28 ἵνα ἰδόντες αὐτὸν χαρῆτε, Mt 2: 10. Compare 2 P 2: 10 δόξας οὐ τρέμουσιν βλασφημοῦντες 'are not afraid to blaspheme'; the variant in 1 C 14: 18 is incorrect εὐχαριστῶ... λαλῶν (KL; λαλεῖν 𝔓46, om. A; λαλῶ SBD al. is correct).

416. The supplementary participle with verbs of perception and cognition

is better preserved in the NT. In classical Greek the participle takes the nominative case if it refers to the subject of the verb (ὁρῶ ἡμαρτηκώς); the accusative (or genitive) if it refers to the object. Except with passive verbs the nominative does not appear in the NT referring to the subject (ὅτι is substituted Mk 5: 29, 1 Jn 3: 14).

(1) Verbs of perception: *to see* (βλέπειν, θεωρεῖν, [ὁρᾶν,] ἰδεῖν, θεάσασθαι, ἑωρακέναι, τεθεᾶσθαι, ὄψεσθαι, κατανοεῖν): Mt 24: 30 ὄψονται τὸν υἱὸν τοῦ ἀνθρώπου ἐρχόμενον, cf. 15: 31, Mk 5: 31, Jn 1: 32, 38, H 3: 1f., etc.; with ὄντα A 8: 23, 17: 16, with ellipsis of this ptcp. (cf. § 414; also class., Krüger § 56, 7.4): Jn 1: 50 εἶδόν σε ὑποκάτω τῆς συκῆς, Mt 25: 38f. σε εἴδομεν ξένον, ἀσθενῆ (ἀσθενοῦντα is preferable, BD), ἐν φυλακῇ etc., cf. 44; A 17: 22 ὡς δεισιδαιμονεστέρους ὑμᾶς θεωρῶ (no further examples of this ὡς are found with verbs of seeing; but cf. *infra* (3) ὡς ἐχθρὸν ἡγεῖσθε 2 Th 3: 15 'as if he were an enemy' [s. also § 157(3)]; the meaning of A 17: 22 must therefore be: 'as far as I see, it appears as if' [softening of the reproach]). Occasionally with the verb 'to see' and other verbs of this type the ptcp. is more independent of the object and constitutes an additional clause, while the obj. and verb are fairly complete in themselves: Mt 22: 11 εἶδεν ἄνθρωπον οὐκ ἐνδεδυμένον etc. = ὃς οὐκ ἐνεδέδυτο, Mk 11: 13 ἰδὼν συκῆν ἀπὸ μακρόθεν ἔχουσαν φύλλα ('which had...'). For ὅτι after 'to see' s. § 397(1).—**Ἀκούειν** is no longer frequent with ptcp.; when the content of what is heard is stated, its rivals are the acc. with inf. and especially ὅτι (§ 397(1)). Examples of the acc. with ptcp.: Lk 4: 23 ὅσα ἠκούσαμεν γενόμενα, A 7: 12,

3 Jn 4, 2 Th 3: 11 (Mk 5: 36? however B τὸν λόγον τὸν λαλούμενον, D has yet another reading); a distinction between the inf. and ptcp. as in class. (the ptcp. denoting more the actual fact, the inf. hearsay, K.-G. II 68) probably cannot be claimed for the NT. The acc. construction appears also (A 9: 4, 26: 14) for the class. gen. construction which is not frequent outside of Acts: Mk 12: 28 ἀκούσας αὐτῶν συνζητούντων, 14: 58; Lk 18: 36 ὄχλου διαπορευομένου, Jn 1: 37, A 2: 6, 6: 11, etc.; 11: 7 and 22: 7 ἤκουσα φωνῆς λεγούσης μοι, for which 9: 4 and 26: 14 (E has gen.) have φωνὴν λέγουσαν, although φωνή refers to the speaker and not to what was said; cf. §173(2).

(2) Verbs of cognition: **Γινώσκειν** Lk 8: 46 ἔγνων δύναμιν ἐξεληλυθυῖαν ἀπ' ἐμοῦ, A 19: 35, H 13: 23; but ἐπιγιν. Mk 5: 30 (cf. Lk 8: 46) with object and *attrib.* ptcp.: ἐπιγνοὺς τὴν ἐξ αὐτοῦ δύναμιν ἐξελθοῦσαν; inf. and ὅτι s. §397(1). **Εἰδέναι** only in 2 C 12: 2 οἶδα... ἁρπαγέντα τὸν τοιοῦτον (for which 3 f. has οἶδα..., ὅτι ἡρπάγη); with adj. without ὄντα Mk 6: 20 εἰδὼς αὐτὸν ἄνδρα δίκαιον, where D inserts εἶναι; elsewhere the inf. and most frequently ὅτι (§397(1)). **Ἐπίστασθαι** A 24: 10 ὄντα σε κριτὴν ἐπιστάμενος, cf. 26: 3 where S*BEH omit ἐπιστ.; 1 Clem 55.2 ἐπιστάμεθα πολλοὺς παραδεδωκότας ἑαυτούς; with ὅτι A 15: 7 etc. **Εὑρίσκειν** usually with ptcp. (also class., Thuc. 2.6.3): Mt 12: 44 εὑρίσκει (scil. τὸν οἶκον, which D inserts) σχολάζοντα, 24: 46 ὄν... εὑρήσει οὕτως ποιοῦντα, etc.; sometimes, as with verbs of seeing, the ptcp. is more independent of the object: A 9: 2 τινας εὕρῃ τῆς ὁδοῦ ὄντας ('who might be'). Passive εὑρίσκεσθαι with nom. ptcp. (=Att. φαίνεσθαι, Viteau): εὑρέθη ἐν γαστρὶ ἔχουσα Mt 1: 18. **Δοκιμάζειν**: 2 C 8: 22 ὃν ἐδοκιμάσαμεν ('have proved') σπουδαῖον ὄντα; in another construction it takes the inf. (§392(3)).—This construction with ptcp. is wanting with αἰσθάνεσθαι, μεμνῆσθαι and others; μανθάνειν (class. μανθάνω διαβεβλημένον 'that I am...') only appears to be so used in 1 T 5: 13 ἅμα δὲ καὶ ἀργαὶ μανθάνουσιν περιερχόμεναι, where (Winer 325f. [Winer-M.³ 436f.]) περιερχ. introduces, in any case, a subordinate clause and ἀργαί is predicate to the ellipsed (through textual corruption? S. however Winer, *loc. cit.* and Mlt. 229 [362]) εἶναι (μανθ. with inf. as in class. 1 T 5: 4, Ph 4: 11, T 3: 14, 1 Clem 8.4 OT, 57.2; συνιέναι is interpolated in 2 C 10: 12: read without οὐ συνιοῦσιν ἡμεῖς δέ, so that αὐτοί etc. [§283(4)] connects with 13 οὐκ εἰς etc., cf. G 6: 4 [so Griesbach following D*FG]).

(3) Verbs of *opinion* only appear to take the construction with ptcp. since they can take (either the inf. or) the double acc. (§157(3)), in which the pred. acc. may be a ptcp.: Lk 14: 18 ἔχε με παρῃτημένον, Ph 2: 3 ἀλλήλους ἡγούμενοι ὑπερέχοντας. The ptcp. with ὡς may also be used with verbs of this class in class. (Hdt. 2.1 ὡς δούλους πατρωΐους ἐόντας ἐνόμιζε); thus 2 C 10: 2 τοὺς λογιζομένους ἡμᾶς ὡς... περι-

πατοῦντας, but equally well εὑρεθεὶς ὡς ἄνθρωπος Ph 2: 7, ὡς ἐχθρὸν ἡγεῖσθε 2 Th 3: 15, so that it can be seen that the ptcp. has no peculiar function of its own in the first instance. Cf. §425(3). Likewise **ὁμολογεῖν**: with double acc. (§ 157(2)) Jn 9: 22 (D has εἶναι), R 10: 9 ἐὰν ὁμολογήσῃς κύριον Ἰησοῦν 'confess Jesus as Lord'; accordingly also 1 Jn 4: 2 Ἰησ. Χρ. ἐν σαρκὶ ἐληλυθότα unless ἐληλυθέναι B (and Pol Ph 7.1) is correct; cf. *v.* 3 Ἰ. κύριον ἐν σ. ἐληλυθότα acc. to S and 2 Jn 7.—Mayser II 1, 312ff., 356.

Verbs meaning 'show, indicate' never take the ptcp. in the NT., s. §397(4); but Ignatius has: δηλώσατε ἐγγύς με ὄντα IRom 10.2.

(iii) *The circumstantial (adverbial) participle*

417. Introduction. The circumstantial participle as an additional clause in the sentence is still very much in use (especially in short narratives [parables], Black, Aramaic Approach² 45f.), either referring to a noun (pronoun) in the same sentence and in agreement with it (conjunctive participle), or used absolutely; in the latter the subject and participle are in the genitive (genitive absolute; for accusative absolute, s. §424, nominative absolute, §466(4)). The logical relation of the circumstantial participle to the rest of the sentence is not expressed by the participle itself (apart from the future participle), but is to be deduced from the context; it can be made clear, however, by the addition of certain particles. Other more extended but more precise constructions are available for the same purpose: prepositional phrases, conditional, causal, temporal clauses, etc., and finally the grammatical co-ordination of two or more verbs.

For the possibilities of these alternatives, cf. e.g. 1 T 1: 13 ἀγνοῶν ἐποίησα with A 3: 17 κατὰ ἄγνοιαν ἐπράξατε '*per inscitiam*'; Mt 6: 27 (Lk 12: 25) τίς μεριμνῶν (without μερ. D in Lk, it in Mt) δύναται προσθεῖναι etc. 'by being anxious' or =ἐὰν καὶ μεριμνᾷ.

418. The conjunctive participle as the equivalent of an adverbial clause. (1) Causal as in classical, only never with ἅτε, οἷον, οἷα (for ὡς s. §425(3)). (2) Conditional. (3) Concessive; for καίπερ and the like s. §425(1). (4) Final: in classical the future participle is used, but in the NT, except for Lk, it is found only in Mt 27: 49 ἔρχεται σώσων (σώζων W, σῶσαι S*, καὶ σώσει D); more commonly the present participle is used (§339 (2c)), or an entirely different construction related in meaning. (5) The conjunctive participle is used most frequently to indicate the manner in which an action takes place, what precedes it and what accompanies it (modal and temporal). In some instances a temporal clause may be substituted (e.g. A 17: 1); in others not, namely when the assertion is of too little importance. (6) The occasional omission of the participle ὤν is to be noted (cf. §414): Lk 4: 1 Ἰησοῦς δὲ πλήρης πνεύματος ἁγίου ὑπέστρεψεν.

(1) E.g. Mt 1: 19 Ἰωσήφ..., δίκαιος ὢν καὶ μὴ θέλων αὐτὴν δειγματίσαι, ἐβουλήθη... =ὅτι δίκαιος ἦν or διὰ τὸ δίκαιος εἶναι.

(2) E.g. Lk 9: 25 τί ὠφελεῖται ἄνθρωπος κερδήσας τὸν κόσμον ὅλον = Mt 16: 26 ἐὰν κερδήσῃ. Mt 24: 41 δύο ἀλήθουσαι... μία παραλαμβάνεται καὶ μία ἀφίεται: Nyberg, Arbeiten und Mitteilungen 4 (1936) 28 (the ptcp. is not good Greek; Lk 17: 35 ἔσονται δύο ἀλ. is better), *ibid.* 35 (Aram.) = Con. Neot. 13 (1949) 6, 10. H. Riesenfeld, Con. Neot. 13 (1949) 12 ff.: this is the special participial form of μετάβασις ἀπὸ ὅλου εἰς μέρη (or μέρος), cf. Homer, Od. 12.73 (without ptcp.), Il. 7.306 (with ptcp.) etc., also class. and Hell. (related to nom. absol.).

(3) E.g. Mt 7: 11 (cf. Lk 11: 13) εἰ ὑμεῖς πονηροὶ ὄντες οἴδατε...'although you are evil'.

(4) Fut. ptcp.: A 8: 27 ἐληλύθει προσκυνήσων, 22: 5, 24: 17; A 25: 13 ἀσπασόμενοι? (§339(1)). Pres. ptcp. e.g. Lk 7: 6 ἔπεμψεν φίλους ὁ ἑκατοντάρχης λέγων αὐτῷ. Other constructions (Viteau 186): Mt 11: 2 πέμψας εἶπεν, 1 C 4: 17 ἔπεμψα Τιμόθεον, ὃς ἀναμνήσει. The inf. is the most common (§390(1, 2)).

(5) E.g. for Mk 1: 7 οὗ οὐκ εἰμὶ ἱκανὸς κύψας λῦσαι τὸν ἱμάντα one would not have said ἐπειδὰν κύψω nor for A 21: 32 ὃς παραλαβὼν στρατιώτας κατέδραμεν ἐπ' αὐτούς something like ἐπειδὴ παρέλαβεν; here the ptcp. corresponds to English 'with' as λαβών often does in class. S. also λαβών Jn 18: 3, which Viteau 190 compares with Mt 26: 47, where μετ' αὐτοῦ is the equivalent; Mt 25: 1. Cf. §419(1).

(6) A 6: 8 (also πλήρης), H 7: 2f., A 19: 37 οὔτε ἱεροσύλους οὔτε βλασφημοῦντας (cf. K.-G. II 102f.). Mk 1: 23 s. §272. The omission of ὤν also in Monum. Ancyr. (Meuwese 104ff.), Strabo (Raderm.² 208), Appian (G. Kratt, De Appiani elocutione [Baden-Baden, 1886] 35), Philostr. (Schmid IV 109).

419. Idiomatic (pleonastic) ἔχων, λαβών, ἀρξάμενος **and the like.** (1) The following occur with the meaning 'with' (accompanying): φέρων Jn 19: 39, ἔχων Lk 2: 42 D, παραλαβών, λαβών Mt 25: 1, Jn 18: 3 (cf. §418(5)), never ἄγων. (2) Λαβών and other descriptive participles are common in pleonastic usage following the Hebrew pattern (Viteau 191; Dalman, Worte Jesu 16ff. [The Words of Jesus 17ff.]; Wellhausen, Einl.² 14); Mt 13: 31 κόκκῳ σινάπεως, ὃν λαβὼν ἄνθρωπος ἔσπειρεν. Similarly ἀναστάς (after Hebr. קוּם)

and the like. (3) The classical ἀρχόμενος 'at the beginning' and τελευτῶν 'in conclusion' are not used; however ἀρξάμενος with the meaning 'beginning with' (classical) and the pleonastic use appear. (4) Προσθεὶς ἔφη 'he said further (again)' ApocP 4. (5) Besides the use of the pleonastic participle, it is just as possible to use co-ordination with καί, which corresponds exactly to the Hebrew model, but which in extended use would have been felt cumbersome in Greek: so LXX Gen 32: 22 ἀναστὰς δὲ τὴν νύκτα ἐκείνην ἔλαβε τὰς δύο γυναῖκας...καὶ διέβη..., 23 καὶ ἔλαβεν αὐτοὺς καὶ διέβη, slavishly following the original except that exact reproduction would also have required καὶ ἀνέστη...καὶ ἔλαβε at the beginning, something which even this translator did not tolerate. The NT authors have usually adhered to the participle.

(1) Mt 15: 30 ἔχοντες μεθ' ἑαυτῶν.
(2) Mt 13: 33 ζύμη ἣν λαβοῦσα γυνὴ ἐνέκρυψεν, 14: 19 λαβὼν τοὺς ἄρτους εὐλόγησεν, 21: 35, 39 etc.; Lk 15: 18 ἀναστὰς πορεύσομαι, 20, A 5: 17, 8: 27 etc.; Mt 13: 46 ἀπελθὼν πέπρακεν (cf. 25: 18, 25), πορευθεὶς 25: 16 (both verbs after the Hebr. הָלַךְ).
(3) Lk 24: 47 ἀρξάμενοι (SBC*, -μενος ΘΨ, -μένων D, -μενον AC³F) ἀπὸ Ἰερουσαλήμ 'beginning with'. [Jn] 8: 9 ἀρξάμενοι ἀπὸ τῶν πρεσβυτέρων with the unclassical addition ἕως τῶν ἐσχάτων (D reads differently), cf. A 1: 22 ἀρξάμενος...ἄχρι..., Lk 23: 5, Mt 20: 8. Pleonastic A 11: 4 ἀρξάμενος Πέτρος ἐξετίθετο αὐτοῖς καθεξῆς, accounted for by καθεξῆς to which it has a certain relation; cf. LXX Job 6: 9 εἰς τέλος (an instructive mistranslation acc. to Katz, ThLZ 1952, 157). On pleonastic ἄρχομαι s. Hunkin, JTS 25 (1923/4) 390–402; Delling, TW I 477. Cf. ἤρξατο with inf. §392(2). For ἐπιβαλὼν ἔκλαιεν Mk 14: 72 s. §308.
(4) Lk 19: 11 is different; s. §435b.
(5) Examples of co-ordination: A 8: 26 ἀνάστηθι καὶ πορεύου (ἀναστὰς πορεύθητι here also D; the MSS also provide ἀνάστα without καί [asyndeton] as v.l. to ἀναστάς: A 9: 11 B, 10: 13 vg, 20 D*vg, likewise 11: 7; cf. §461(1)). Lk 22: 17 λάβετε τοῦτο καὶ διαμερίσατε. Προσέθηκε καί and the like are not found in the NT, but in LXX, e.g. 1 Km 3: 6 προσέθετο κύριος καὶ ἐκάλεσεν, 1 Chr 14: 13 προσέθεντο ἔτι...καὶ συνέπεσαν ἔτι; the active is vulgar: Judg 11: 14 B καὶ προσέθηκεν ἔτι Ἰεφθάε καὶ ἀπέστειλεν. LXX parallels to προσθεὶς Thack. 52f. On the primitive resolution of an event into its parts cf. E. Cassirer, Die Sprache (Berlin, 1923) 174; Havers, IF 45 (1927) 229ff. ('enumerative Redeweise').

420. Λέγων, εἰπών, ἀποκριθείς and the like and their relation to co-ordination. After a finite verb like 'asked, answered' direct discourse is usually introduced in Hebrew with לֵאמֹר (LXX λέγων); λέγων appears thus in the NT after ἀποκρίνεσθαι, λαλεῖν, κράζειν, παρακαλεῖν, etc. in numerous examples. Herodotus has a comparable usage ἔφη λέγων, εἰρώτα λέγων, ἔλεγε φάς and the like (Kieckers, IF 35 (1915) 34ff.). (1) 'Answered' in Hebrew is also readily followed by וַיֹּאמֶר (LXX καὶ εἶπεν); thus in the NT besides ἀπεκρίθη λέγων we find ἀπ. καὶ εἶπεν (often in Jn, never in Mt, seldom in Mk, Lk; Kieckers, op. cit. 48) and the formula predominant by far (except for Jn; but UGosp 1.17f.). ἀποκριθεὶς εἶπεν. (2) These same combinations also appear in Jn (and elsewhere) with other verbs, e.g. Jn 13: 21 ἐμαρτύρησεν καὶ εἶπεν, A 13: 22 εἶπεν μαρτυρήσας, Jn 1: 32 ἐμαρτύρησεν λέγων (without λ. S*e). Lk 1: 63 ἔγραψεν λέγων 'he wrote as follows' is entirely Semitic (Kieckers, op. cit. 41); cf. LXX 2 Km 11: 15 καὶ ἔγραψεν ἐν βιβλίῳ λέγων, 4 Km 10: 6, 1 Macc 11: 57. (3) The aorist participle in such cases does not indicate sequence of time (§339) any more than does the equivalent coordination with καί: cf. Lk 15: 23 φαγόντες εὐφρανθῶμεν = D φάγωμεν καὶ εὐφρ. (4) Coordinated verbs of this sort, of course, may both be participles: ἀποταξάμενος καὶ εἰπών A 18: 21 (cf. ℵΨ gig which have one or both as finite verbs) = ἐπειδὴ ἀπετάξατο καὶ εἶπεν.

PSI IV 340.5 (257 BC) ἀποκέκριται...τοιαῦτα λέγων, 8 ἀντιλέγω ταῦτα λέγων(?) (Mayser II 1, 349), both times the ptcp. has an object, therefore λέγων is a somewhat independent conj. ptcp.; without object UPZ I 6.30 (163 BC) ἀπεκρίθησαν ἡμῖν φήσαντες, PGiess 36.10 (135 BC) τάδε λέγει 'Ἀμμωνία καὶ 'Ἀπολλωνία καὶ..., αἱ τέτταρες λέγουσαι ἐξ ἑνὸς στόματος ('the four women speaking...'; 'demotic'!) (Mayser II 3, 63.14).

(1) Neither ἀποκρινόμενος εἶπεν nor ἀπεκρίθη εἰπών ever occurs. The act of answering is reported as simple fact, therefore aor.; the added ptcp. 'saying', however, denotes manner (already mentioned as mere fact), therefore the pres. ptcp. is used. 'Ἀπεκρίθη καὶ εἶπεν: Jn 14: 23, 18: 30, 20: 28 etc. (Jn almost always so unless ἀπ. stands alone), Lk 17: 20; ἀπ. λέγων Mk 15: 9 (D ἀποκριθεὶς λέγει), A 15: 13 (D differs), cf. Jn 12: 23, ἀπεκρίθησαν λέγουσαι Mt 25: 9, ἀποκριθήσονται λέγοντες 37, 44, (45), ἀπεκρίθη καὶ λέγει Mk 7: 28; ἀποκριθεὶς εἶπεν twice also in the second half of Acts (19: 15, 25: 9). Acc. to M.-H. 454 ἀποκριθεὶς εἶπεν stems from the LXX, ἀπεκρίθη (in Jn always with asyndeton) λέγων from the Aram. עָנָה וְאָמַר. P. Joüon, 'Respondit et dixit' (Biblica 13 [1932] 309–14). Plato, Protag. 314D ἀποκρινόμενος εἶπεν.

(2) Jn 9: 28 ἐλοιδόρησαν αὐτὸν καὶ εἶπαν, R 10: 20 ἀποτολμᾷ καὶ λέγει. Jn 18: 25 ἠρνήσατο καὶ εἶπεν, Mt 26: 70 etc. ἠρν. λέγων, but A 7: 35 ὃν ἠρνήσαντε εἰπόντες (the aor. ptcp. here is due to the fact that ἠρν. is not here a verb of saying and that the ptcp. is the first word that introduces the fact of speech; the following examples are to be appraised similarly: Jn 11: 28 ἐφώνησεν ['called'] τὴν ἀδελφὴν εἰποῦσα ['with the words'] = καὶ εἶπεν 18: 33, A 22: 24 ἐκέλευσεν εἰσάγεσθαι...εἴπας, and still clearer 21: 14 ἡσυχάσαμεν εἰπόντες, Lk 5: 13 ἥψατο εἰπών, 22: 8 ἀπέστειλεν εἰπών [Mt 2: 8 reverses the ptcp. and verb πέμψας εἶπεν 'sent with the words', 11: 2f. is different πέμψας διὰ τῶν μαθητῶν εἶπεν 'he sent word...']); also ἔγραψεν λέγων Lk 1: 63 (s. supra and infra). Jn 1: 25 καὶ ἠρώτησαν αὐτὸν καὶ εἶπαν αὐτῷ (? the text is doubtful), Mt 15: 23 ἠρώτουν λέγοντες and Jn even ἠρώτων (-τησαν) λέγοντες 4: 31, 9: 2 (λεγ. om. D) etc. Ἔκραξεν καὶ εἶπεν Jn 12: 44 (D ἔκραξεν καὶ ἔλεγεν), cf. Lk 8: 28 D, ἔκραξαν (-εν) λέγοντες (λέγων) Mt 8: 29, 14: 30 etc., κράξας λέγει Mk 5: 7 (εἶπε D), κράξας ἔλεγεν 9: 24 (λέγει DΘ is better; εἶπεν 𝔓45W); ἐκραύγαζον (v.l. ἔκραζον) λέγοντες Jn 19: 12 (S* ἔλεγον instead of ἐκρ. λ.), cf. 18: 40 (without λέγ. b c e Chr). Regarding Lk 1: 63, the rule was perhaps that one spoke at the same time as one wrote (Klostermann, Hdb. in loc.). Lk 5: 21 is certainly pleonastic ἤρξαντο διαλογίζεσθαι ('to reflect')...λέγοντες, cf. 12: 17; likewise the passages cited from the LXX.

(3) Λέγων is occasionally found with εἶπεν as a finite verb (Lk 12: 16, 20: 2; s. §101 under λέγειν), but other ptcps., expressing more than mere saying, are always found in the aor. (as in the examples given above): παρρησιασάμενοι εἶπαν A 13: 46, προσευξάμενοι ε. 1: 24; what happens is that the two verbs, both denoting the same action (§339(1)), assimilate to each other in tense.

(4) Mt 9: 27 κράζοντες καὶ λέγοντες. On C 2: 5 s. §471.

421. Conjunctive participles combined. The participles are asyndetic if they do not have equal value in the sentence: A 18: 23 ἐξῆλθεν, διερχόμενος τὴν Γαλατικὴν χώραν, στηρίζων τοὺς μαθητὰς = ἐξῆλθεν καὶ διήρχετο (§339(2a)) στηρίζων. Such accumulations of participles, not infrequent in Acts, reveal a certain feeling for style which is lacking in the more or less strung-together accumulations of Paul's epistolary style. Cf. F. Dölger, ByzZ 41 (1941) 464; for a detailed study, s. G. Rudberg, Zu den Partizipen im NT (Con. Neot. 12 [1948] 1–38).

A 19: 16 ἐφαλόμενος ὁ ἄνθρωπος ἐπ' αὐτούς..., κατακυριεύσας ἀμφοτέρων ἴσχυσεν κατ' αὐτῶν = ἐφήλετο καὶ...; the v.l. καὶ κατακυριεύσας (S*HLP) provides κατακυριεύειν with a poorer connection (with ἐφαλέσθαι). 18: 22 κατελθὼν εἰς Καισάρειαν, ἀναβὰς καὶ ἀσπασάμενος τὴν ἐκκλησίαν, κατέβη εἰς Ἀντιόχειαν; a second καί before ἀναβάς would be possible but inept. The sentence may be resolved: κατῆλθεν εἰς Κ., ἀναβὰς δὲ καί.... Constructions such as this are found only occasionally in the simpler style of the Gospels: Mt 14: 19 κελεύσας (SZ ἐκέλευσεν)...λαβών...ἀναβλέψας, 27: 48 δραμών... καὶ λαβών...πλήσας τε (τε om. D)...καὶ περιθείς.

422. The addition of a cognate (or related) participle to a finite verb in order to strengthen the verbal idea is the customary translation of the Hebrew infinitive absolute in the LXX (Thack. 48f.; Johannessohn I 57; Huber 89); in pure Greek only very remotely related examples are to be found. The NT has this usage only in quotations from the LXX: Mt 13: 14 βλέποντες βλέψετε, A 7: 34 ἰδὼν εἶδον, H 6: 14 εὐλογῶν εὐλογήσω σε καὶ πληθύνων πληθυνῶ σε.

Examples in pure Greek: Mlt. 75f. [118f.]; K.-G. II 99f.; Kieckers, Festschrift Kretschmer 107ff.; E. Hofmann, Ausdrucksverstärkung 86.—Not certainly attested ἴστε γινώσκοντες E 5: 5 (§353(6)), exactly as in the Hexapla Jer 49 (42): 22; cf. γινώσκουσα γινώσκω 1 Clem 12.5, further LXX 1 Km 20: 3 γινώσκων οἶδεν. Homil Clem 16.13.3 γινώσκων γνώσῃ 'you will certainly know'. (Fritzsche [III 1 p. 95] does not recognize as original the variant ἰδὼν εἶδον in Lucian, DMar. 4.3.) PTebt II 421.12 (iii AD) ἐρχόμενος δὲ ἔρχου (ε)ἰς Θεογονίδα ('come by all means to Th.' or 'if you come, come to Th.'? M.-H. 444).—It is better Greek to render the inf. absol. by the dat. of the cognate noun; s. §198(6).

423. The genitive absolute is limited in normal classical usage to the sentence where the noun or pronoun to which the participle refers does not appear either as subject or in any other capacity; otherwise the circumstantial (conjunctive) participle is employed. Just as the NT authors are inclined to detach the infinitive from the closely structured sentence and give it a special subject of its own (in the accusative), even when it is identical with the subject of the main verb (§406), so they tend to make the participial clause independent and to prefer the absolute construction in numerous instances where a classical author would not have admitted it even as a special license. (1) Thus the genitive absolute is used while referring to a following dative: Mt 9: 18 ταῦτα αὐτοῦ λαλοῦντος αὐτοῖς, ἰδοὺ ἄρχων...προσεκύνει αὐτῷ. (2) To a following accusative with and without preposition: Mt 18: 25 μὴ ἔχοντος

αὐτοῦ ἀποδοῦναι, ἐκέλευσεν αὐτὸν πραθῆναι, Jn 8: 30 (εἰς αὐτόν). (3) To a following genitive so that the pronoun becomes pleonastic: Mt 6: 3 σοῦ ποιοῦντος ἐλεημοσύνην μὴ γνώτω ἡ ἀριστερά σου. (4) The harshest and at the same time rarest case is where the 'antecedent' follows as subject: Mt 1: 18 μνηστευθείσης τῆς μητρὸς αὐτοῦ Μαρίας τῷ Ἰωσήφ, πρὶν ἢ συνελθεῖν αὐτοὺς εὑρέθη, but here the inserted infinitive with πρίν (with another subject) mitigates the ensuing anacolouthon, for which classical parallels may be found (K.-G. II 110). (5) The genitive absolute with reference to a *preceding* word is even more striking: 2 C 4: 18 ἡμῖν, μὴ σκοπούντων ἡμῶν (but D*FG anacolouthon μὴ σκοποῦντες, perhaps rightly). (6) The omission of the noun or pronoun to which the participle refers is admissible in the NT as in classical, if it is implicit: Lk 12: 36 ἐλθόντος καὶ κρούσαντος (αὐτῷ following).— Mayser II 3, 74ff.

This same popular independence of the gen. absol. is known also to the LXX (Viteau 199f.; Johannessohn I 46) and pap. (Moulton, ClR 18 [1904] 153; PFay 108.8 [c. 171 AD]), likewise to Hell. and class. authors (Schmidt 435; Raderm., WSt 31, 3; Jannaris §2145; Trunk 66; K.-G. II 110f.). Diversity of the NT authors in the use of the gen. absol.: in Mk only temporal and, except for 4: 35, 16: 2, it is always in postposition; Acts much freer and more diverse (Crönert, Gnomon 4 [1928] 87f.).

(1) Mt 1: 20, 9: 10 (easily excused), 17: 9, 18: 24, 24: 3 (Chr without αὐτῷ), 26: 6, 27: 17 (αὐτοῖς om. a), 5: 1 (αὐτῷ om. B), 8: 1 (S*KL al. καταβάντι δὲ αὐτῷ...ἠκολούθησαν αὐτῷ, likewise incorrect, cf. *infra* (3); the first αὐτῷ can be omitted; similarly v.l. 8: 5, 28, 21: 23, however 8: 28 S* correctly has ἐλθόντων αὐτῶν); Mk 13: 1, Lk 12: 36, 14: 29 (without αὐτῷ 𝔓⁴⁵, D reads quite differently), 17: 12 (BL om. αὐτῷ; D differs), 22: 10, Jn 4: 51 (many vv.ll.), A 4: 1 (D om. αὐτοῖς); Barn 2.3, Herm Vis 3.1.9, Sim 2.1. Pap. s. Mayser II 3, 67f.

(2) If the ptcp. construction precedes an acc. dependent on a prep., the circumstantial (conj.) ptcp. construction is not possible at all. Mk 5: 18, 9: 28 (v.l. εἰσελθόντα αὐτόν...ἐπηρώτων αὐτόν, 𝔓⁴⁵ εἰσελθόντι αὐτῷ προσῆλθον...καὶ ἠρώτησαν αὐτόν), 10: 17, 11: 27 (πρὸς αὐτόν), 13: 3, Lk 9: 42, 15: 20, 18: 40, 22: 53 (ἐπ' ἐμέ), A 7: 21, 19: 30 (αὐτόν om. D), 21: 17 (D syʰ ᵐᵍ differ), 25: 7, 28: 17 (πρὸς αὐτούς), 2 C 12: 21 (v.l. ἐλθόντα με and without the second με).

(3) Herm Sim 9.14.3 κατεφθαρμένων ἡμῶν...τὴν ζωὴν ἡμῶν. The same pleonasm in the dat. (Mt 8: 1 v.l., *supra* (1)) and acc. (Mk 9: 28 v.l., *supra* (2)). Cf. Mt 5: 1 with the omission of αὐτῷ (B, s. *supra* (1)). Mayser II 3, 67.

MOOD

§§ 423–425

(4) A 21: 34. Very clumsy A 22: 17 ἐγένετο δέ μοι ὑποστρέψαντι εἰς Ἰερουσ., [καὶ] προσευχομένου μου ἐν τῷ ἱερῷ, γενέσθαι με ἐν ἐκστάσει (it appears that καί must be omitted, because with it the relation of the dat. and gen. remains inexplicable). Mk 6: 22 εἰσελθούσης τῆς θυγατρὸς...καὶ ὀρχησαμένης, ἤρεσεν...ὁ δὲ βασιλεὺς εἶπεν SBC*, smoothed in...καὶ ἀρεσάσης...εἶπεν (plus δέ A) ὁ βασ. 𝔓⁴⁵C³DWΘ. Herm Vis 1.1.3, 2.2, 2.1.1; Sim 5.1.1 νηστεύοντός μου καὶ καθημένου...εὐχαριστῶν...βλέπω (H, a vellum fragment now in Hamburg, s. LCL Ap. Frs. II, 4; PMich and A smooth to νηστεύων καὶ καθημενος...καὶ εὐχ.). Cf. LXX Ex 4: 21 πορευομένου σου... ὅρα...ποιήσεις. Often in pap. (Mayser II 3, 68ff.; Ghedini, Aegyptus 15 [1935] 231ff.). Further in Ursing 62; Ghedini, Vang. ap. 479f.

(5) Herm Vis 3.1.5 φρίκη μοι προσῆλθεν, μόνου μου ὄντος, 2.9 μὴ δυναμένους κυλισθῆναι...καίπερ θελόντων κυλισθῆναι, Sim 9.6.8, 1 Clem 60.4. LXX e.g. Gen 18: 1, Ex 5: 20. Pap.: Mayser II 3, 67.20ff., 68.9f., 13ff., 70.6ff. (2 examples ii BC); Ghedini, Aegyptus loc. cit.; BGU IV 1040.19 (ii AD) χαίρω, ὅτι μοι ταῦτα ἐποίησας, ἐμοῦ μεταμελομένου περὶ μηδενός. Further in Ursing 62; Ghedini, Vang. ap. 480. Peculiar H 8: 9 OT (gen. absol. dependent on ἐν ἡμέρᾳ: 'on the day when I took'; cf. LXX Bar 2: 28 ἐν ἡμέρᾳ ἐντειλαμένου σου αὐτῷ [Viteau 210]; similar examples from three pap. in Olsson, Glotta 23 (1935) 111).

(6) Mt 17: 9 καταβαινόντων W (-ντες D, plus αὐτῶν rell.), 14 SBZ (C al. with αὐτῶν), 26 (strong v.l.), Mk 14: 22 W, A 21: 31 ζητούντων (10 has an inserted ἡμῶν as v.l.), etc. Cf. pap., Polyb., Jos., etc. (Mlt. 74, 235f. [114 n. 1]; ClR 18 [1904] 153; Mayser II 3, 71f.; Schmidt 435; Wolf II 78).

424. The only example, rather obscured, of an **accusative absolute** (classical δέον 'when, although it is, was, might be necessary'; perhaps the nominative absolute in part lies at the base of it [Mayser II 3, 66]) is τυχόν 'perhaps, possibly' (from Xen. on, often in Hellenistic, s. Lautensach 56): 1 C 16: 6, Lk 20: 13 D, A 12: 15 D (MGr τυχόν 'by chance'). It is notable that Lk A 23: 30 says μηνυθείσης δέ μοι ἐπιβουλῆς εἰς τὸν ἄνδρα ἔσεσθαι (presupposing the nom. with infinitive, ἐμηνύθη ἐπιβουλή ἔσ., which would have been just as possible in Attic) rather than μηνυθὲν ἐπιβουλὴν ἔσ. (Buttmann 237). Possibly 2 C 3: 14 μὴ ἀνακαλυπτόμενον ὅτι...'because it has not been revealed (to them) that...' or does ἀνακ. refer to κάλυμμα?

Ἐξόν, ὑπάρχον, προστεταγμένον, etc. are not found; ἐξόν appears in the NT only as a pred. with ἐστιν to be supplied: §353(5). On A 26: 3 s. §137(3). The Hell. substitution of the gen. for acc. is also missing in the NT, e.g. δόξαντος (e.g. Polyb. 2.26.7; Schmidt 436), οὐκ ἐξόντος (pap. e.g. POxy II 275.22 [66 AD], III 496.6, 13 [127 AD], IV 724.12 [155 AD], μηδενὶ ἐξόντος BGU IV 1137.18 [6 BC]), ἐπισταλέντος and the like (Mayser II 1, 309; II 3, 66).—Συμφέρον s. §353(5).

425. Particles used with a participial construction (cf. §417). (1) Καίπερ used to clarify the concessive sense of the participle is rare in the NT; καὶ ταῦτα (K.-G. II 85) is only apparently synonymous H 11: 12 (rather = 'and that even'); less classical is καίτοι (K.-G. II 85; Meister 31.5) used with participle (only H 4: 3, before a genitive absolute). (2) Genuine examples of ἅμα and εὐθύς after the classical pattern τρίβων ἅμα ἔφη 'while rubbing', εὐθὺς παῖδες ὄντες 'even from childhood' are lacking in the NT except perhaps for διδάσκων ἅμα ἔλεγεν Mk 12: 38D. (3) Only ὡς is rather frequent with the participle (ὥσπερ A 2: 2, denoting comparison; ὡσεί 'as if' R 6: 13). For the most part, however, the participle with ὡς (as also with ὡσεί in the instance cited above) is used as any noun would be (cf. §§157(5); 416(3); 453), and many of the special participial constructions with ὡς are almost or entirely lacking in the NT; only of the ὡς which gives the subjective motivation of the subject of the discourse or action (= 'with the assertion that, on the pretext that, with the thought that') is there a number of examples (one with a future participle). (4) This same ὡς occurs also in elliptical constructions from which the participle is dropped: e.g. C 3: 23 ὃ ἐὰν ποιῆτε, ἐκ ψυχῆς ἐργάζεσθε, ὡς τῷ κυρίῳ (scil. ἐργαζόμενοι αὐτό) καὶ οὐκ ἀνθρώποις. Similar examples in classical. (5) Ἄν is no longer used with participle (nor with infinitive). (6) The classical liberty to use οὕτως to summarize the content of a preceding participial construction is found only in Acts: 20: 11 ὁμιλήσας...οὕτως ἐξῆλθεν, 27: 17; cf. papyri (Mayser II 3, 73f.).

(1) Ph 3: 4 καίπερ ἐγὼ ἔχων πεποίθησιν; H 5: 8, 7: 5, 12: 17 (καίτοι 𝔓⁴⁶); 2 P 1: 12; 1 Clem 7.7, 16.2, ISm 3.3, MPol 17.1, Herm Vis 3.2.9, Sim 8.6.4, 11.1. Καίτοιγε (in class. γε is separated and joined to the word to be emphasized) mostly with a finite verb, therefore in a kind of parataxis (cf. Trunk 58): Jn 4: 2 (καίτοι C), A 14: 17 (καί γε 𝔓⁴⁵DE, καίτοι SᶜABC*); with ptcp. only in A 17: 27 (cf. Homil Clem 10.3), where however καίγε (BD²HLP*, καίτε D*) 'inasmuch as' (= class. ἅτε, missing in the NT; Norden 18 n. 2) appears to be better (καίτοιγε SP², καίτοι AE); cf. §§439(2); 450(3). Καίτοι(γε) with gen. absol.

219

also in inscrip. and pap. (Mayser II 3, 169; POxy VI 898.26 [123 AD]; XIV 1763.7 [iii AD]). Καίτοιγε ὑπολαμβάνω ZenP Cairo IV 59628.11 (iii BC).

(2) A 24: 26 ἅμα καὶ ἐλπίζων 'at the same time also in the expectation', 27: 40 ἅμα ἀνέντες 'while they at the same time also', C 4: 3 προσευχόμενοι ἅμα καὶ περὶ ἡμῶν 'at the same time also for us', 1: 12 καὶ εὐχαριστοῦντες ἅμα 𝔓⁴⁶B; cf. ἅμα δὲ καί with impera. Phm 22. Mk 6: 25 εἰσελθοῦσα εὐθύς 'she came in immediately'.

(3) With fut. ptcp. H 13: 17 ἀγρυπνοῦσιν ὡς λόγον ἀποδώσοντες 'as men who', 'with the thought that'; Mk 11: 13 ὡς εὑρήσων 0188 Θ pc. (cf. *quasi paraturi* Lk 9: 52 instead of ὥστε [ὡς SB] ἑτοιμάσαι), probably only an Atticistic correction. With pres. ptcp.: Lk 16: 1, 23: 14, A 23: 15, 20, 27: 30 (with προφάσει preceding); 3: 12 ἡμῖν τί ἀτενίζετε ὡς…πεποιηκόσιν 'as though we had done this', 1 C 7: 25 γνώμην δίδωμι ὡς ἠλεημένος 'as one who', 'with the conviction that I'; 2 C 5: 20 (gen. absol., for which 5: 19, 11: 21, 2 Th 2: 2 have ὡς ὅτι with

indic., § 396); H 12: 27; A 20: 13 D ὡς μέλλων…'since he said that…', Herm Sim 9.6.8 ὡς μελλόντων αὐτῶν…'with the intention that they should…'. Negated οὐχ ὡς 'not as if' A 28: 19, 2 Jn 5. Never ὡς with acc. absol. like the class. ὡς τοὺς θεοὺς κάλλιστα εἰδότας 'in the belief that'. Ἄτε not in the NT; in Ptol. pap. only once (Mayser II 1, 350).

(4) 1 C 9: 26, 2 C 2: 17, E 6: 7, 1 P 4: 11; R 13: 13 ὡς ἐν ἡμέρα = ὡς ἡμέρας οὔσης. 2 Th 2: 2 δι' ἐπιστολῆς, ὡς δι' ἡμῶν, scil. γεγραμμένης or rather = ὡς ἡμῶν γεγραφότων αὐτήν. G 3: 16 etc.

(5) In Barn 6.11 and Diogn 2.1 ὡς ἄν does not go with the ptcp. but with what is to be supplied, either a potential opt. or what grew out of it, a potential indic. (past tense); cf. K.-G. I 243 f. (e.g. Dem. 49.27); also MGr (ὡ)σάν 'as' and § 453(3). Ἄν with ptcp. is seldom found in Ptol. pap. (Mayser II 1, 356).

(6) But A 20: 35 ὅτι οὕτως κοπιῶντας δεῖ ἀντιλαμβάνεσθαι not 'thus—namely by toiling' but with a forceful gesture 'look, thus must one work and…'.

11. ADVERBS AND PARTICLES

(1) NEGATIVES

426. Introduction. The distinction between the two negatives, objective οὐ and subjective μή, is in part fairly complicated in classical Greek. On the other hand, essentially everything can be subsumed under one rule for the Koine of the NT: οὐ negates the indicative, μή the remaining moods including the infinitive and participle. Individual words or phrases are always negated by οὐ (likewise classical, e.g. Lysias 13.62 εἰ μὲν οὐ πολλοί [= ὀλίγοι] ἦσαν, K.-G. II 182); connected with this is the preference for οὐ in contrasting statements (e.g. R 15: 20, 1 P 3: 3, also καὶ οὐ, cf. § 430 and H 7: 11 [§ 429]).—Mayser II 2, 543–67; Rob. 1155–75.

H 11: 1 οὐ βλεπομένων: here οὐ is almost the equivalent of ἀ- privative; cf. § 430(3). R 9: 25 τὸν οὐ λαόν μου etc. (cf. § 430(3)) is a quotation from the LXX Hos 2: 23 (cf. 1 P 2: 10), where οὐ λαός μου serves as a proper name; cf. class. ἐν οὐ καιρῷ 'inopportunely' and the like K.-G. II 197. Also cf. LXX 2 Macc 4: 13 τοῦ ἀσεβοῦς καὶ οὐκ ἀρχιερέως Ἰάσονος, Eccl 10: 11 ἐν οὐ ψιθυρισμῷ; Aqu. Ps 43: 13 ἐν οὐχ ὑπάρξει. Homil Clem 2.10 is different τῷ μὴ προφήτῃ 'the non-prophet' (= ὃς ἂν μὴ προφήτης ᾖ or τῷ μὴ πρ. ὄντι; class. [K.-G. II 197]), also ὁ μὴ πατήρ 4.21, 11.12, τὰ μὴ σεμνά 6.18.—S. Wackernagel, Syntax II² 263–6.

427. Negatives in main clauses. (1) Οὐ is used with the indicative, even with the future of prohibition: οὐ φονεύσεις Mt 5: 21 OT (§ 362). (2) Both οὐ and μή are still used in questions as in classical: οὐ (οὐ μή, § 365(4); often οὐχί) when an affirmative answer is expected, μή (cf. K.-G. II 524; Witkowski, Bericht 242; μήτι is very common) when a negative one is expected. Thus Lk 6: 39 μήτι δύναται τυφλὸς τυφλὸν ὁδηγεῖν; ('A blind man can't lead a blind man, can he?' Answer: 'Certainly not'); οὐχὶ ἀμφότεροι εἰς βόθυνον ἐμπεσοῦνται; (Answer: 'Of course'); cf. 1 C 9: 8. Homil Clem 18.8.2 διὰ τί μὴ πᾶσιν ἀποκαλύπτει; is entirely abnormal. (3) Elliptical μήτιγε 1 C 6: 3 = πόσῳ γε μᾶλλον 'not to speak of'. (4) Μή is used with the subjunctive, optative (negation appears in the NT only with the optative of wish), and imperative.

(1) In Homil Clem 3.69.1 μηδένα μισήσετε follows several positive futures of assertion and shows that the impera., which actually appears two clauses later, is already in the mind of the author. S. § 364(3).—R 4: 19 μὴ ἀσθενήσας τῇ πίστει (+ οὐ DEFG pm.) κατενόησεν: μή belongs to the ptcp. (where it is correct) and to the finite verb (where οὐ should have been used) 'Did he become weak in the faith and did he not consider…?'

(2) In questions with μή the verb itself can already be negated (class. also), producing μή…οὐ with an

affirmative answer implied: R 10: 18 μὴ οὐκ ἤκουσαν; 'have they not heard?' (Answer: 'Indeed they have'), 1 C 11: 22 etc. (Paul only). It does not depend of course on the *actual* answer: Mt 26: 25 Judas asks with the others (22) μήτι ἐγώ εἰμι; 'it is not I, is it?' and receives the unexpected answer σὺ εἶπας. The meaning of μή is slightly modified in some passages: Jn 4: 33 μή τις ἤνεγκεν αὐτῷ φαγεῖν; 'surely no one can have brought him food' (yet it appears as if someone had; cf. μή 'whether...not' after interrogative verbs in Plut. etc., K.-G. II 394); 4: 29 μήτι οὗτός ἐστιν ὁ Χριστός; 'that must be the Messiah at last, perhaps this is the Messiah'. Cf. Mt 12: 23, Jn 7: 26. Nor does this conception seem to suit Jn 21: 5: μή τι προσφάγιον ἔχετε; ('it seems that you have...unexpectedly'; Chrys. interprets it as ὡς μέλλων τι ὠνεῖσθαι παρ' αὐτῶν; cf. Mlt. 170 n. [267 n.] and Rob. 1168.). J. E. Harry, Rev. Phil. 14 (66) (1940) 5 ff.: Soph., Ant. 632 ἆρα μή...πάρει; 'you will perhaps not be present...(but apparently you will!)'; cf. Studies Gildersleeve (Baltimore, 1902) 427–34. On later μήτι 'perhaps' (Clem. Alex. etc.) s. Abbott 2702 b. 1. The answer of the speaker is added in Lk 17: 9 οὐ δοκῶ acc. to ADW al. ITr 5.1 μὴ οὐ δύναμαι τὰ ἐπουράνια γράψαι; (certainly), ἀλλὰ φοβοῦμαι...; Epict. 3.22.80 μήποτε οὐκ αἰσθανόμεθα; 'for do we not perceive?' Jn 5: 28 μὴ θαυμάζετε, ὅτι...'do you perhaps marvel at this, that (as the Rabbis say)...? No! You do not wonder, although it is just as astonishing as what I said earlier.' Μή 'Yes, perhaps': Theophr., Char. 8.2 μὴ λέγεταί τι καινότερον; 'is there perhaps anything new?' Polyb. 5.50.12 διηρώτα..., μή τινας ἐπιστολὰς κεκόμισται 'whether he has perhaps after all received...'.— A. T. Robertson, The NT Use of μή with Hesitant Questions in the Indic. Mood (Exp. VIII no. 152, 1923); J. Konopásek, Les 'questions rhétoriques' dans le NT (RHPR 12 [1932] 47–66, 141–61, esp. 149); Bonaccorsi 585.

(3) Cf. μή τί γε δὴ θεοῖς Dem. 2.23. Μήτιγε 'perhaps' with aor. ind. Homil Clem 20.9.7; μήτι γε τοῖς υἱοῖς Plut., Mor. 14A. Since Plato: Wettstein II 121.

(4) In R 3: 8 καὶ μὴ καθὼς βλασφημούμεθα καὶ φασίν τινες ἡμᾶς λέγειν ὅτι ποιήσωμεν τὰ κακά the parenthetical clause (καθώς) is mixed up with the indirect discourse somehow: perhaps from μὴ λέγομεν (λέγωμεν) ὅτι 'do we say perhaps (should we perhaps say)' (with ὅτι *recitativum*), or from τί (7) οὐ ποιοῦμεν or μὴ ποιήσωμεν 'we surely do not want to do evil?' (G vg Or etc. thus with omission of ὅτι, smoothing the construction); class. and vulgar Hell. are comparable, e.g. Xen., An. 6.4.18 ὡς ἐγὼ ἤκουσα, ὅτι Κλέανδρος μέλλει ἥξειν from ὡς ἐγὼ ἤκουσα, Κλ. μ. ἥ. + ἐγὼ ἤκουσα ὅτι Κλ. μ. ἥ. Lietzmann, Hdb.³ *in loc.*; Fridrichsen, Serta Rudbergiana (Oslo, 1931) 24 f.; Ljungvik, ZNW 32 (1933) 207 ff.; s. also the reference to Plutarch §482.—Rob. οὐ: 1157 f., 1160 ff.; μή: 1168 ff. and *passim*.

428. Negatives in subordinate clauses.

(1) The 'real' indicative with εἰ takes οὐ (Hom., Hdt.; MGr δέν = οὐδέν), rarely μή which is normal in classical. Οὐ is always used when εἰ = ἐπεί or = 'if, as you maintain' (§372(1)); in such cases οὐ is not unknown in Attic writers (K.-G. II 189 f.). (2) Οὐ is used once even with the 'unreal' indicative (always in MGr δέν = οὐδέν): Mt 26: 24 = Mk 14: 21 καλὸν (ἦν) αὐτῷ, εἰ οὐκ (*si non*) ἐγεννήθη ὁ ἄνθρωπος ἐκεῖνος. Otherwise μή is used in contrary to fact protases, not only in the sense of 'apart from the case that' (*nisi*; *infra* (3)), but also in that of 'suppose that...not' (Jn 15: 22, 24; *si non*). (3) For *nisi* 'except' (without verb as is usually the case), 'unless' (with verb, usually the present indicative) εἰ μή is always used. (4) Relative clauses with the indicative have οὐ except in two instances. (5) The use of οὐ is more firmly established in declarative clauses with ὅτι (ὡς), likewise in temporal and causal clauses with the indicative. But in Koine μή is also very common. (6) After μή (πως) expressing apprehension (§370) οὐ must be used even before a subjunctive if the verb itself is to be negated.

(1) Also Lk 11: 8 εἰ καὶ οὐ δώσει = ἐὰν καὶ μὴ δῷ (§372(3)); Homil Clem 18.7.2 εἰ οὐ συνῆκας...εἰ δὲ οὐκ ἐπίστασαι; 10.21.4 ἐπεὶ μὴ ἔστιν ('since it actually...'); 13.19.2 ἐπεὶ μὴ ἀνθρώποις βλέπεται. Remnants of class. μή: 1 T 6: 3 εἴ τις ἑτεροδιδασκαλεῖ καὶ μὴ προσέχεται...(literary; εἰ...οὐ 3: 5, 5: 8); addition in D to Lk 6: 4 εἰ δὲ μὴ οἶδας. Εἰ οὐ Barn 6.19 ('since...not'), Did 12.4, 5 (alternatives).

(2) Μή with the unreal indic.: Jn 15: 22 εἰ μὴ ἦλθον...ἁμαρτίαν οὐκ εἴχοσαν, 24, 9: 33, 18: 30, 19: 11; Mt 24: 22 = Mk 13: 20; A 26: 32; R 7: 7.

(3) Without finite verb: Mt 5: 13 εἰς οὐδὲν εἰ μὴ βληθῆναι. Here also εἰ δὲ μή (γε) §439(1). With finite verb: εἰ μή τινές εἰσιν G 1: 7 (§376).

(4) T 1: 11 διδάσκοντες ἃ μὴ δεῖ (cf. Homil Clem 10.12.3; ἃ μή is neither conditional nor generalizing-iterative, therefore unclass.; ἃ μὴ δεῖ is probably merely a mixture of τὰ μὴ δέοντα [1 T 5: 13] and ἃ οὐ δεῖ; cf. the reverse in τὰ οὐκ ἀνήκοντα §430(3)). 2 P 1: 9 ᾧ μὴ πάρεστιν ταῦτα, τυφλός ἐστιν (literary; the reference is not to definite persons or things: K.-G. II 185 f.). A 15: 29 only D (likewise class.). 1 Jn 4: 3 ὃ μὴ ὁμολογεῖ is a spurious reading for ὃ λύει; cf. Rahlfs, ThLZ 1915, 525, Katz: originating from dittography? C 2: 18 is textually entirely uncertain: ἃ μὴ ἑώρακεν C vg syᵖ (without μή 𝔓⁴⁶S*ABD*). Post-class. ἃ μὴ δεῖ and the like: Lucian, Jud. Voc. 2 ἔνθα μὴ δεῖ, 4 εἰς ἃ μὴ χρή; sometimes ὃ (ἃ) μὴ θέμις (LXX 2 Macc 12: 14, Philo, Abr. 44 [IV 10.23 Cohn-Wendland], Lucian, DDeor. 13.1,

PGM ɪ 4.2653; ὅσα μὴ θέμις...παθεῖν Dionys. Hal., Ant. 4.82.1). Also cf. ἃ μὴ συνεφώνησα CPR 19.17 (330 AD), ᾧ μηθὲν ὑπάρχει 'who possesses no property' PHib ɪ 113.15 (c. 260 BC). In class. only after a purpose clause with μή, i.e. the second μή is by assimilation for οὐ (but at the same time 'it must not be' itself includes a warding-off of something): Aeschyl., Agam. 342 (354) ἃ μὴ χρή, Hdt. 1.11 τὰ μή σε δεῖ, Xen., Oec. 9.5 ὅ τι μὴ δεῖ; cf. Solmsen, Inscr. Graecae...selectae (Leipzig, 1930) 39 A 26 (iv BC, Cyrene) ἱαρήιον ὅ τι μὴ νόμος θύεν in a conditional clause (αἴ κα...θύσηι). Rev 14: 4 𝔓⁴⁷ οἳ μὴ μετὰ γυναικῶν ἐμολύνθησαν (pm. οἱ μετὰ γ. οὐκ ἐμ.). Conditional: LXX Sir 13: 24 ἀγαθὸς ὁ πλοῦτος, ᾧ μή ἐστιν ἁμαρτία.

(5) Jn 3: 18 ὁ μὴ πιστεύων ἤδη κέκριται, ὅτι μὴ πεπίστευκεν; 1 Jn 5: 10 is similar but with ὅτι οὐ. In Jn 3: 18 ὅτι μή is hardly an indication that the tautological subordinate clause, omitted by Chr, is not genuine (Blass; Rahlfs, ThLZ 1915, 525 takes a different view). The use of μήποτε speaks against taking H 9: 17 in the same way: ἐπεὶ μήποτε (S*D* μὴ τότε) ἰσχύει, ὅτε ζῇ ὁ διαθέμενος is clearly interrogative (Theophylactus; 'never' would be μηδέποτε, οὐδέποτε). Homil Clem ὅτι μή 'since...not' 8.14, 11.8, 32 etc.; 'that...not' 3.55, 6.1 etc., 'so that not' 13.9; ὅτι μὴ χρή...ἀμελεῖν ('since') 9.22.3; ἐπεὶ μή 8.11, 9.14 etc.; ἐ. μήπω 2.31. Ὅτι μή, ἐπεὶ μή etc. in Jos., c. Ap. 1.217, Philostr. (Schmid ɪᴠ 92f.), Epict. (2.1.32, 4.4.8 etc.), etc., cf. K.-G. ɪɪ 188; Jannaris § 1818; Mlt. 239 n. on 171 [271 n.]; Raderm.² 211; O. Birke, De particularum μή et οὐ usu Polybiano (Diss. Leipzig, 1897) 25ff.; Wackernagel, Syntax ɪɪ² 281; Mayser ɪɪ 2, 545 n. 1; Brockmeier 26f. (to avoid the hiatus of ὅτι οὐ, or ἐπεὶ οὐ?). Apollonius Dysc., Pron. p. 70.24 Schneider-Uhlig; in pap. not before the post-Ptol. period (Mayser ɪɪ 2, 551; ἐπεὶ μή BGU ɪɪ 530.35 [i AD]). MGr does not use μή in this way.

(6) Mt 25: 9 μήποτε οὐκ ἀρκέσῃ 'it will hardly be enough' (cf. § 431); 2 C 12: 20 φοβοῦμαι μή...οὐ. UPZ ɪ 61.17 (162 BC) μὴ οὐκ ἀποδῶ σοι 'I will hardly return (it) to you' (Mayser ɪɪ 2, 548). For R 11: 21 s. § 370(1).—Rob. οὐ: 1158–60; μή: 1169, 1170, 1170ff. and *passim*.

429. Negatives with the infinitive.
Μή is used throughout (also after verbs of thinking: A 25: 25, 2 C 11: 5; cf. Jannaris § 1815, Mlt. 239 n. on 171 [271 n.]). In H 7: 11 it is not the infinitive but the concept κατὰ τὴν τάξιν Ἀαρών that is negated by καὶ οὐ (cf. § 426). In Mk 7: 24 οὐδένα ἤθελεν γνῶναι, the negative goes with ἤθελεν; in Jn 21: 25 οὐδέ goes with οἶμαι; A 26: 26 οὐ with πείθομαι (and accordingly οὐθέν instead of μηθέν). Μή is used also in certain instances after verbs denoting a negative idea (as in classical, s. K.-G. ɪɪ 207 ff.;

papyri s. Mayser ɪɪ 2, 564f.), a redundant usage by the canons of English, German etc.

Lk 20: 27 οἱ ἀντιλέγοντες (APW al.; SBCDL λέγοντες as in Mt and Mk) ἀνάστασιν μὴ εἶναι (ἀντιλέγειν with the inf. here only). 22: 34 ἕως τρὶς ἀπαρνήσῃ μὴ εἰδέναι με (με ἀπ. εἰδ. SBLT; ἀπαρν. not with inf. elsewhere); cf. Homil Clem 9.22 ἀρνούμενοι τὸ μὴ δεῖν, 1 Jn 2: 22 ὁ ἀρνούμενος ὅτι Ἰησοῦς οὐκ ἔστιν ὁ Χριστός (like Dem. 9.54 ἀρν. ὡς οὐκ εἰσὶ τοιοῦτοι). H 12: 19 παρῃτήσαντο μή (om. S*P) προστεθῆναι. G 5: 7 τίς ὑμᾶς ἐνέκοψεν ἀληθείᾳ μὴ πείθεσθαι; (s. however § 488(1b); ἐγκόπτεσθαι with τοῦ ἐλθεῖν R 15: 22; cf. K.-G. ɪɪ 215). But H 11: 24 ἠρνήσατο ('disdained') λέγεσθαι. Κωλύειν regularly without μή (admissible also in class.: K.-G. ɪɪ 214f.; but cf. §§ 399(3); 400(4)).—Mayser ɪɪ 2, 552ff.; Rob. 1093ff., 1162.

430. Negatives with the participle.
The drift in late Greek towards μή in this connection is noticeable even in authors like Plutarch (Jannaris §§ 1815f.; MGr only μή). In Attic the choice was made according to the meaning of the participle in the individual case. Cf. the papyri (Mayser ɪɪ 2, 556ff.). Μή is used as a rule in the NT, especially when the article is present. (1) Hardly any instances of οὐ appear in Mt and Jn. (2) Lk, on the other hand, has some examples of classical οὐ. (3) There are various reasons for the few examples of οὐ in Paul (Hebrews, Peter).

(1) Mt 22: 11 εἶδεν ἄνθρωπον οὐκ ἐνδεδυμένον ἔνδυμα γάμου = ὃς οὐκ ἐνεδέδυτο (i.e. the οὐ with the ptcp. here is Att., yet C³D have μή, perhaps correctly; cf. 12). Jn 10: 12 ὁ μισθωτὸς καὶ οὐκ ὢν ποιμήν (not a definite person, hence μή would have been used in Att.): the οὐ is no doubt due to the preference for καὶ οὐ instead of καὶ μή (s. § 426 and *infra* (3)) and to the emphasis on the negation so that recourse to the Hebraism mentioned *infra* (3) is hardly necessary.

(2) Lk 6: 42 αὐτός...οὐ βλέπων (D is different), A 7: 5 οὐκ ὄντος αὐτῷ τέκνου, 26: 22 οὐδὲν ἐκτὸς λέγων, 28: 17 οὐδέν...ποιήσας. Οὐχ ὁ τυχών 'not any chance person' (§ 252) is readily understood (the single idea is negated) A 19: 11, 28: 2, 1 Clem 14.2, οὐ τὴν τυχοῦσαν ἰσχύν Homil Clem 18.11.2; in the pap. beginning in iii BC (Preisigke s.v. τυγχάνω 4, Mayser ɪɪ 2, 518), Com. Att. Frag. ɪɪɪ 442 frag. 178 Kock (οὐδὲ τοῖς τυχοῦσι), Theophr., Hist. Pl. 8.7.2; Περὶ ὕψους 9.9 οὐχ ὁ τυχὼν ἀνήρ; on which H. Lebègue, Mél. Desrousseaux (Paris, 1937) 273f., M. Ant. (Schekira 229), inscrip. (Bauer s.v. τυγχάνω 2 d). Οὐ is used for a different reason in A 28: 19 οὐχ ὡς ἔχων...('I did not do this as one who...'); likewise 1 Th 2: 4.

(3) G 4: 8 οὐκ εἰδότες θεόν is like class. 4: 27 OT is

a Hebraism: ἡ οὐ (DEFG μή) τίκτουσα... ἡ οὐκ (all witnesses) ὠδίνουσα; also 1 P 2: 10 OT οἱ οὐκ ἠλεημένοι, R 9: 25 OT τὴν οὐκ ἠγαπημένην (the LXX translates לֹא with οὐ with an articular ptcp.; Viteau 217f.; on R 9: 25 OT τὸν οὐ λαόν s. §426). 1 Th 2: 4 s. *supra* (2). Καὶ οὐ twice (cf. *supra* (1)): Ph 3: 3 καὶ οὐκ ἐν σαρκὶ πεποιθότες, C 2: 19 καὶ οὐ κρατῶν... (elsewhere καὶ μή, e.g. Lk 1: 20 ἔσῃ σιωπῶν καὶ μὴ δυνάμενος λαλῆσαι). E 5: 4 τὰ οὐκ ἀνήκοντα is probably a mixture of τὰ μὴ ἀνήκοντα and the v.l. ἃ οὐκ ἀνῆκεν (§358(2)); cf. §428(4) on T 1: 11 ἃ μὴ δεῖ. H 11: 1 πραγμάτων οὐ βλεπομένων (= Att. ὧν ἄν τις μὴ ὁρᾷ), because = ἀοράτων? (§426). 11: 35 οὐ προσδεξάμενοι (class.). 1 P 1: 8 ὃν οὐκ ἰδόντες ἀγαπᾶτε correctly, but in the continuation εἰς ὃν ἄρτι μὴ ὁρῶντες πιστεύοντες δὲ ἀγαλλιᾶσθε (in the first instance the inactuality is emphasized more). Οὐ after ὡς where it is also preferred in Att. (K.-G. II 200): 1 C 9: 26 ὡς οὐκ ἀδήλως... ὡς οὐκ ἀέρα δέρων; cf. C 3: 23 (§425(4)). 2 C 4: 8f. θλιβόμενοι ἀλλ' οὐ στενοχωρούμενοι etc. (again it is the single idea which is negated; 𝔓⁴⁶ has καὶ μή incorrectly for the first ἀλλ' οὐ). 5: 12 πρὸς τοὺς ἐν προσώπῳ καυχωμένους καὶ μή (𝔓⁴⁶SB, οὐ(κ) CDEFG al.) (ἐν) καρδίᾳ. In 1 C 11: 17 read τοῦτο δὲ παραγγέλλω· οὐκ ἐπαινῶ with Dᵍʳ*; A. Fridrichsen, Horae Soederblomianae I 1 (1944) 28f. prefers παραγγέλλω ὑμῖν οὐκ ἐπαινῶν (AC sy lat) (οὐκ ἐπ. 'very censorious'). R 1: 28 τὰ μὴ καθήκοντα (τὸ μὴ καθῆκον is a common Stoic expression), but Herm Man 6.2.5 ποικίλων τρυφῶν καὶ οὐ δεόντων 'improper things'. Cf. A. G. Laird, 'When is Generic μή Particular?' (AJPh 43 [1922] 124–45), on the class. distinction between ὁ μὴ εἰδώς and ὁ οὐκ εἰδώς.—On the whole Rob. 1136–9, 1162f.

431. The combination of negatives.
(1) The only examples of οὐ...οὐ cancelling each other (classical) are: 1 C 12: 15 οὐ παρὰ τοῦτο οὐκ ἔστιν ἐκ τοῦ σώματος (cf. Homil Clem 10.12 οὐ γάρ, εἴ τις..., οὐκ ἀποθνήσκει), A 4: 20 οὐ δυνάμεθα... μὴ λαλεῖν, 1 C 9: 6 οὐκ ἔχομεν ἐξουσίαν μὴ ἐργάζεσθαι; (2) The classical way of strengthening the negative by combinations like οὐ (μή)... οὐδείς (μηδείς) is not unduly common: e.g. Mk 15: 4 οὐκ ἀποκρίνῃ οὐδέν; 5 οὐκέτι οὐδὲν ἀπεκρίθη; but contrary to the classical rule (K.-G. II 203, but cf. 206.4; Mayser II 2, 567; Meuwese 107f.), e.g. Jn 10: 28 οὐχ ἀρπάσει τις, 1 Th 1: 8 μή...τι. (3) The mixture of οὐδέ and οὐ μή to produce οὐδ' οὐ μή instead of οὐδὲ μή is unclassical: e.g. Mt 24: 21 οὐδ' οὐ μὴ γένηται (D Chr al. οὐδὲ μή).—For μὴ οὐ s. §§427(2); 428(6). On frequent οὐ μή with the subjunctive and future indicative s. §365; μήποτε οὐ μή once as v.l. Mt 25: 9 BCD al. (§428(6)); cf. μήποτε οὐ μὴ φοβηθήσονται Did 4.10.

(1) The negatives also neutralize each other in οὐδείς...ὅς (class. ὅστις) οὐ; however this form in the NT is to be taken as two separate clauses since οὐδείς does not appear to be so directly connected with, and assimilated to, the relative as in class. (K.-G. II 414f.); e.g. Mt 10: 26, Lk 12: 2; οὐ...ὃς οὐ Mt 24: 2 etc. The interrogative form of the main clause without negation is equivalent (Buttmann 305): τίς ἐστιν...ὃς οὐ A 19: 35. Herm Sim 5.5.4 is incorrect: οὐδὲ ἕτερος...οὐ δύναται 'and no other' (οὐ on account of the τις in the intervening clause).

(2) Mk 11: 2 οὐδείς...οὔπω (but v.l.), Lk 4: 2 οὐκ...οὐδέν, 23: 53 οὐκ ἦν οὐδεὶς οὐδέπω, Jn 19: 41 οὐδέπω οὐδείς, A 8: 39 οὐκ...οὐκέτι, 1 T 1: 7 μή...μήτε...μήτε, Mk 11: 14 μηκέτι...μηδείς, R 13: 8 μηδενὶ μηδέν, Herm Man 3.3 οὐδέποτέ μοι οὐδείς; etc. But 1 C 6: 12 οὐκ...ὑπό τινος, Mt 11: 27 οὐδὲ τὸν πατέρα τις ἐπιγινώσκει. 12: 19 οὐδὲ ἀκούσει τις. A 28: 21 οὔτε τις. Lk 16: 2 οὐ δυνήσῃ ἔτι οἰκονομεῖν, 2 P 1: 21 οὐ...ποτέ.

(3) Lk 10: 19 οὐδέν...οὐ μὴ ἀδικήσει (-σῃ) instead of οὐδέν...μή...or simply οὐδέν (thus S*D), Herm Man 9.5. Mk 14: 25 οὐκέτι οὐ μὴ πίω (avoided by the Hebraizing οὐ μὴ προσθῶ πεῖν of D al., s. Jeremias, Die Abendmahlsworte Jesu 93 n. 6 [The Eucharistic Words of Jesus 125 n. 4]) is 'barbaric' (P. Benoit, RB 48 [1939] 379). Katz: the redundant οὐδ' οὐ μή in the last of several οὐ- (οὐ μή-) clauses seems to be due to the desire to retain the οὐ (οὐ μή) of the preceding clauses. Mt 24: 21 οὐ...οὐδ' οὐ μή (οὐδὲ μή D al.) = Mk 13: 19 οὐ...καὶ οὐ μή (οὐδὲ μή D); cf. Am 2: 15 οὐ μή...οὐ μή...οὐδέ...οὐ μή (the later recensions of Origen, Lucian, and the Catenae group have καὶ [= MT]...οὐ μή), Job 32: 21 οὐ μή...οὐδέ...οὐ μή. H 13: 5 οὐ μή σε ἀνῶ, οὐδ' οὐ μή σε ἐγκαταλίπω (= Philo, Conf. 166 [II 261.8f. Cohn-Wendland]) is from Gen 28: 15, enlarged from Dt 31: 6, as found in the recension of the LXX used by Philo and Hebrews (Katz, Philo's Bible 72 n. 2 and Biblica 33 [1952] 523–5). Here, too, οὐδ' οὐ μή is due to the preceding οὐ μή. In Dt 31: 6 οὐδ' οὐ μή is found also in the secondary A group; οὐδὲ μή (H 13: 5 𝔓⁴⁶) is the Lucianic reading, while B has οὔτε μή...οὔτε μή. ISm 10.1 οὐδέν...οὐ μή; but 1 Clem 27.5 οὐδὲν μὴ παρέλθῃ is correct. Pap.: οὐδ' οὐ μὴ γένηται Wilcken, Chr. no. 122.4 (6 AD).—Rob. 1164.

432. Οὐ (οὐχί) and ναί.
(1) 'Yes' and 'No' are ναί (Attic ναίχι does not appear) and οὐ or οὐχί: οὐχί Lk 1: 60, οὔ Mt 13: 29 etc.; οὔ οὔ, ναὶ ναί 2 C 1: 17. (2) Οὐχί also appears in questions (§427(2)) and occasionally elsewhere.

(1) Lk 12: 51, 13: 3, 5 οὐχί, λέγω ὑμῖν (cf. the opposite ναί, λέγω ὑμῖν 7: 26; οὐ λέγω ὑ. would not have been clear). In Mt 5: 37 ἔστω δὲ ὁ λόγος ὑμῶν ναὶ ναί, οὔ οὔ is a corrupt variant for the well-attested

and correct reading ἔστω δὲ ὑμῶν τὸ ναὶ ναὶ καὶ τὸ οὐ οὔ (Θ al.); s. the ed. of Blass and cf. Ja 5: 12 ἤτω δὲ ὑμῶν τὸ ναὶ ναὶ καὶ τὸ οὐ οὔ.

(2) Jn 13: 10f. οὐχὶ πάντες, 14: 22, 1 C 10: 29; πῶς οὐχί R 8: 32; οὐχὶ μᾶλλον 1 C 5: 2, 6: 7, 2 C 3: 8.— Rob. 1164f.

433. The position of the negative.

The negative stands as a rule before that which is to be negated. (1) Especially a negated verb attracts the negative to itself: ἑνὸς οὐκ ἔστιν G 3: 20. The verb and negative frequently coalesce into a single idea: οὐκ ἐῶ, more colloquial οὐκ ἀφίω, 'hinder' A 19: 30 etc. (2) Several uncertain passages in R and 1 C exhibit an unusual position of οὐ with πᾶς. (3) The negative with a participle or adjective governed by a preposition usually precedes the preposition in classical (as do other adverbial adjuncts in general); this is occasionally the case in the NT.

(1) The separation of the negative from the verb to which it belongs can be ambiguous: A 7: 48 ἀλλ' οὐχ ὁ ὕψιστος ἐν χειροποιήτοις κατοικεῖ (the author probably does not mean to imply that somebody else dwells there). Ja 3: 1 μὴ πολλοὶ διδάσκαλοι γίνεσθε (but s. §115(1)).

(2) At R 3: 9 οὐ πάντως would have to mean 'not at all' (cf. 1 C 16: 12 πάντως οὐκ ἦν θέλημα) as in Diogn 9.1, Epict., Ench. 1.5 (or is 'not in every case' possible?); but D*GP sy Or Chr simply omit οὐ πάντως, and the best text appears to be τί οὖν προκατέχομεν; πάντως ἡτιασάμεθα Ἰουδαίους etc. On the other hand the meaning of οὐ πάντως in 1 C 5: 10 appears to be 'not meaning the immoral in general' (Winer 515ff. [Winer-M.³ 693ff.]; cf. Homil Clem 4.8.3, 19.9.4 [20.5.3 μὴ πάντως]). 1 C 15: 51 is uncertain on text-critical grounds: πάντες (μὲν) οὐ κοιμηθησόμεθα, (+ οὐ 𝔓⁴⁶) πάντες δὲ ἀλλαγησόμεθα 𝔓⁴⁶B al. is understandable only if πάντες οὐ is taken in the sense of οὐ πάντες (as in Xen., An. 2.5.35 πάντες μὲν οὐκ ἦλθον, Ἀριαῖος δὲ..., Herm Sim 8.6.2 πάντες οὐ μετενόησαν 'not all'); but several other readings are to be found in MSS and the Fathers.

(3) H 11: 3 εἰς τὸ μὴ ἐκ φαινομένων (= ἐκ μὴ φ.) τὸ βλεπόμενον γεγονέναι, cf. LXX 2 Macc 7: 28 A pm. ὅτι οὐκ ἐξ ὄντων ἐποίησεν αὐτὰ ὁ θεός (ἐξ οὐκ ὄντων Lucian, Origen's quotations, Syriac, and the majority of the Latin witnesses), but ἐξ οὐκ ὄντων Homil Clem 19.4.2, 9.1, 16.1, 18.2. Οὐ μετὰ πολλὰς ἡμέρας A 1: 5, Lk 15: 13 D (al. μετ' οὐ πολλάς in A 27: 14 μετ' οὐ πολύ), Homil Clem 3.58.3 (μετ' οὐ π. ἡμ. 11.35.2, 14.7.7, μετ' οὐ πολύ 6.1.2, 12.18.2 etc.; μετ' οὐ πολύ M. Ant. 12.21). Οὐ μετὰ πολλόν Hdt. 5.64, 6.69, πολὺ σὺν φρονήματι μείζονι Xen., An. 3.1. 22; Dem. ὡς εἰς ἐλάχιστα, οὕτω μέχρι πόρρω et al. Cf. Schwyzer II 666, 9; Deissmann, KZ 45 (1913) 60; Radermacher, PhW 44 (1924) 306; Wifstrand, K.

Hum. Vet.-samf. i Lund, Årsber. 1930/1 III 142f. Further, Havers, Erkl. Synt. 91, 234; Stolz-Schmalz, Lat. Gr.⁵ 615; Hofmann, Gnomon 9 (1933) 519. ὡς is treated as a preposition in 2 C 10: 14 μὴ ὡς (𝔓⁴⁶P; the others have the normal order ὡς μή) ἐφικνούμενοι εἰς ὑμᾶς 'as not (actually) reaching you'; likewise in 1 C 15: 8 ὡσπερεὶ τῷ ἐκτρώματι = τῷ ὡ. ἐκτρώματι ὄντι 'to me who am, so to speak, one untimely born'; cf. Björck, Con. Neot. 3 (1939) 8.

(2) ADVERBS

434. Adverbs could be used as adjectives

already in the classical language, not only as attributive (R 3: 26 ἐν τῷ νῦν καιρῷ), but also as predicate (just as prepositional phrases were abundantly used: ἦν ἐν τῇ πόλει). (1) With εἶναι present or to be supplied: with ἐγγύς, πόρρω and the like (e.g. ὁ κύριος ἐγγύς Ph 4: 5) as in classical, but the usage with οὕτως is less classical. Τὸ εἶναι ἴσα (adverbial neuter plur.) θεῷ corresponds to an old usage: Ph 2: 6; cf. Thuc. 3.14 ἴσα καὶ ('as good as') ἱκέται ἐσμέν (Winer 167 [Winer-M.³ 221]). (2) An adverb with γίνεσθαι ('act, behave') is readily understandable (cf. K.-G. I 143). An adverb in place of a predicate acc. is found only in R 9: 20 τί με ἐποίησας οὕτως (= τοιοῦτον), instead of an acc. object in Mk 2: 12 οὕτως οὐδέποτε εἴδαμεν.

(1) Οὕτως: Mt 1: 18 ἡ γένεσις οὕτως ἦν (= τοιαύτη ἦν or οὕτως ἔσχεν), 19: 10 εἰ οὕτως ἐστὶν ἡ αἰτία τοῦ ἀνθρώπου, R 4: 18 OT, 1 P 2: 15. In addition, οὕτως ἔχει A 7: 1 etc. For ὀψέ and πρωΐ as predicate s. §129 (ὀψέ ἐστι is of course also class.). Herm Sim 5.5.4 μεγάλως καὶ θαυμαστῶς πάντα ἐστὶν καὶ ἐνδόξως (πάντα) ἔχει. In ἔσεται οὕτως, i.e. ὡς λέγεις, and in the answer ἔστιν οὕτως the adv. is good class. idiom. Cf. Lat. aliter est etc. from aliud est and aliter se habet (Stolz-Schmalz, Lat. Gr.⁵ 467). PSI IV 442.14f. (iii BC) οὐ δίκαιον οὖν ἐστιν οὕτως εἶναι 'so to conduct oneself'.

(2) 1 Th 2: 10 ὡς ὁσίως καὶ δικαίως καὶ ἀμέμπτως ὑμῖν τοῖς πιστεύουσιν ἐγενήθημεν (but adjective ἐγενήθημεν ἤπιοι 2: 7); cf. A 20: 18 πῶς...ἐγενόμην (D ποταπῶς ἦν).—Rob. 547f.

435. The use of special verbs to express an adverbial idea:

'secretly, unconsciously' can be expressed by λανθάνειν with a participle as in H 13: 2 (§414(3)), otherwise by the adverb λάθρᾳ as also in classical (Mt 1: 19 etc.). 'Continuously, further, incessantly' by διατελεῖν, ἐπιμένειν, οὐ διαλείπειν (§414(1)). 'Again, further' by various constructions: (a) προστίθεσθαι with the infinitive (Hebraism), (b) προσθεὶς εἶπεν Lk 19: 11; s. also §419(5).

(a) Προσέθετο πέμψαι Lk 20: 11 f. (not D) = πάλιν ἀπέστειλεν Mk 12: 4, 5, although (acc. to A 12: 3 προσέθετο συλλαβεῖν καὶ Πέτρον) it should more likely be translated 'he proceeded to...' (Hebr. וַיֹּסֶף לְ with inf.); οὐ μὴ προσθῶ πεῖν Mk 14: 25 D; cf. §392(2). 1 Clem 12.7 καὶ προσέθεντο αὐτῇ δοῦναι σημεῖα 'in addition they gave her a sign'. But Ps.-Callisth. 2.41 end (Meusel, N. Jahrbücher Suppl. v [1864-72]) οὐκέτι οὖν προσεθέμην ἀδύνατα ἐπιχειρεῖν = C. Müller, appendix to Dübner's Arrian p. 91 b under οὐκέτι οὖν προσέθετο ἀδυνάτοις ἐπιχειρεῖν 'proceeded to...'; the influence of the LXX is also possible here (R. Helbing, Auswahl aus gr. Inschr. [Berlin-Leipzig, 1915] 87). PGrenf I 53.29 (iv AD) is uncertain, s. M.-H. 445. Jos., Ant. 6.287, 19.48 is different ('to follow, acquiesce'); cf. Thackeray, JTS 30 (1929) 361-70.

(b) Lk 19: 11 'he continued and told a parable' (something he had not just done), i.e. like Polyb. 31.7.4 προσθέμενος ἐξηγεῖτο 'he appended the narrative'. 'To continue the preceding activity' is Semitic idiom in the LXX references cited below; further ApocP 4 προσθεὶς ἔφη 'he said further (again)', Acta Phil. 10 (II 2, 5.27 L.-B.) ἔτι δὲ προσθέντες λέγουσιν αὐτῷ. The denial of all Hebrew influence by Crönert in Wessely, Stud. Pal. IV (1904) 85, and by Helb. p. iv is unjustified. Cf. LXX Job 27: 1, 29: 1, 36: 1 προσθεὶς εἶπεν (λέγει), Gen 38: 5 προσθεῖσα ἔτι ἔτεκεν (Thack. 52 f.).—Cf. the same change of construction in the case of ἄρχεσθαι and ἐπιβάλλειν §§308, 419(3); further, e.g. ἐκπέμψειε λαθών Hom., Il. 24.681 = λάθοι ἐκπέμψας; ἀπενέγκατο οἰχόμενος BGU I 22.30 (114 AD) = ᾤχετο ἀπενεγκάμενος; K.-G. II 66; Raderm.² 207.—Rob. 551 f.

436. The use of correlative adverbs. In exclamations the interrogative adverb is used in addition to the classical relative adverb.

Πῶς δύσκολόν ἐστιν Mk 10: 24, cf. 23 = Lk 18: 24, πῶς συνέχομαι Lk 12: 50, πῶς ἐφίλει αὐτόν (Att. ὅσον) Jn 11: 36. Herm Man 11.20, 12.4.2. Cf. the analogous phenomenon with the pron. (§304). But relative adverb: R 10: 15 OT ὡς ὡραῖοι..., 11: 33 ὡς ἀνεξεραύνητα....—Ὅπως in an indirect question for πῶς only Lk 24: 20 (D ὡς), cf. §300(1). On πῶς = ὡς = ὅτι s. §396.—Ὁτὲ μὲν...ὀτὲ δὲ...Barn 2.4, 5 'now... now' for τοτὲ μὲν...τοτὲ δὲ...is Hell. (Mayser II 1, 58; cf. ὃς μὲν...ὃς δὲ...§250). But also class. ποτὲ μὲν...ποτὲ δὲ...Barn 10.7. Neither of these is attested for the NT.

437. 'Whence?' instead of 'where?' in the case of adverbs of place. The classical attraction ὁ ἐκεῖθεν πόλεμος (for ὁ ἐκεῖ ὤν) δεῦρο ἥξει (Dem. 1.15, K.-G. I 546 f.) is attested in the NT only in one place: Lk 16: 26 μηδὲ οἱ (οἱ om. S*BD)

ἐκεῖθεν πρὸς ἡμᾶς (ὑμᾶς) διαπερῶσιν, where, however, θέλοντες διαβῆναι could perfectly well be supplied from the preceding. However, the corresponding ἐκ for ἐν is found several times. The attraction of οὗ to ὅθεν, which is analogous to the attraction of the relative pronoun (§294), is found in Mt 25: 24, 26 συνάγω(ν) ὅθεν (= ἐκεῖθεν οὗ) οὐ διεσκόρπισα(ς); cf. K.-G. II 410.—Mayser II 2, 179 f.; Rob. 548.

Ἐκ for ἐν: Lk 11: 13 ὁ πατὴρ ὁ (ὁ om. SLX) ἐξ οὐρανοῦ ($\mathfrak{P}^{45}$ smooths to ὁ οὐράνιος) δώσει πνεῦμα ἅγιον, Mt 24: 17 μὴ καταβάτω ἆραι τὰ (DΘ ἆραί τι = Mk 13: 15) ἐκ τῆς οἰκίας αὐτοῦ, C 4: 16 τὴν ἐκ (= the one that is at) Λαοδικείας (ἐπιστολὴν) ἵνα καὶ ὑμεῖς ἀναγνῶτε. But in οἱ ἐκ τῆς Καίσαρος οἰκίας Ph 4: 22 the ἐκ denotes membership as in οἱ ἐκ περιτομῆς R 4: 12 (cf. §209(2)); ἀσπάζονται ὑμᾶς οἱ ἀπὸ τῆς Ἰταλίας H 13: 24 is ambiguous and obscure, since the place of origin of the letter is unknown.

(3) PARTICLES AND CONJUNCTIONS

438. Introduction. Part of the function of the particles is to give greater prominence to the modal character of a clause or sentence (ἄν and the interrogative particles), but more often to express the interrelation of sentences and clauses (the conjunctions). The number of particles used in the NT is considerably smaller than in the classical language (s. §107); yet in comparison with the poverty of the Semitic languages in this regard it appears exceedingly large. The conjunctions may be divided into co-ordinating, i.e. those which connect elements in sentence structure which are on a par with each other, and subordinating, i.e. those which subordinate and give a dependent character to the elements introduced by them. Co-ordinating conjunctions have the most diverse origins, while subordinating conjunctions are derived for the most part from the stem of the relative pronoun. They may be divided according to the relationships they imply (membership in a series, antithesis, a relation of cause or effect, or one of condition or result, etc.) into: (1) copulative, (2) disjunctive, (3) adversative, (4) comparative, (5) conditional, (6) temporal, (7) final, (8) conjunctions introducing (dependent) declarative and interrogative clauses, (9) consecutive, (10) causal, (11) concessive. In groups (1)-(3) there are only co-ordinating conjunctions, in (4)-(8) only subordinating, and in (9)-(11) both types.—J. D. Denniston, The Greek

Particles (Oxford, 1934) gives a very detailed treatment. Rob.: particles 1142–55, 1175–7; conjunctions 1177–93.

(A) Modal Particles

For ἄν s. the Greek index; statistics and discussion Mlt. 165ff. [260].

439. The emphatic or intensive particle γε is used in the NT nearly always in connection with other conjunctions and thereby often becomes no more than a meaningless appendage. (1) This is the case in ἄρά γε, ἆρα γε (§§ 440(2); 451(2c)) and the like; at times in εἰ δὲ μή γε 'otherwise' with a verb to be supplied (§ 376; classical). (2) The emphatic meaning 'at least' is preserved only in a few combinations: e.g. καί γε ἐπὶ τοὺς δούλους A 2: 18 OT 'and even' (the classical order would be καὶ ἐπί γε; K.-G. II 173, 176); s. also § 425(1). (3) Without another particle: Lk 11: 8 διά γε τὴν ἀναίδειαν αὐτοῦ, cf. 18: 5; ὅς γε *qui quidem* 'he who' R 8: 32 (DFG only ὅς).—Mayser II 3, 123ff.; Rob. 1147ff.

(1) Καίτοιγε and μενοῦνγε §§ 425(1), 450(3, 4); μήτιγε § 427(3). Εἰ δὲ μή γε Mt 6: 1, 9: 17 (B without γε), Lk 5: 36 etc., 2 C 11: 16; Mk, Jn, Rev do not use γε.
(2) 1 C 9: 2 ἀλλά γε ὑμῖν εἰμι '*at least* to you' (class. ἀλλ' ὑμῖν γε, K.-G. II 177). Lk 24: 21 ἀλλά γε καὶ σὺν πᾶσιν τούτοις 'but even' is somewhat different. With separation from καί 1 C 4: 8 καὶ ὄφελόν γε ἐβασιλεύσατε 'and I even wish that you...' (without γε D*FG). Εἴ γε *siquidem* (class.) 2 C 5: 3 (εἴ γε καί), G 3: 4, E 3: 2, 4: 21, C 1: 23 (R 5: 6 v.l.). Καί γε 'and also (even)' Herm Man 8.5 καί γε πολλά, 9.9 καί γε λίαν πιστούς; LXX for גַּם, וְגַם (consistently so in Aqu.), e.g. Ruth 1: 5 καὶ ἀπέθανον καί γε ἀμφότεροι; Hell. (Raderm.² 35f.). Passages involving difficulties: Lk 19: 42 εἰ ἔγνως καὶ σὺ καί γε ἐν τῇ ἡμέρᾳ σου ταύτῃ τὸ πρὸς εἰρήνην σου (Eus καί γε σὺ ἐν, D καὶ σὺ ἐν; καίγε must mean 'at least', i.e. = class. ἔν γε τῇ...); A 17: 27 (cf. § 425(1)).
(3) Herm Vis 1.1.8 ἁμαρτία γέ ἐστιν ('indeed it is'), καὶ μεγάλη.

For -περ and -τοι s. § 107.

440. Interrogative particles. Direct questions not introduced by an interrogative pronoun or adverb but which expect a yes or no answer do not require a distinguishing particle any more than in classical Greek. In the spoken language the inflection of the voice makes their nature clear, but in the written language only the context, which can sometimes be ambiguous, can yield the necessary clue (§ 16; thus in Jn 16: 31, 1 C 1: 13 there is ambiguity: Viteau § 50). Οὐ is employed to suggest an affirmative answer, μή (μήτι) a negative reply; in the latter, μή with the indicative is an external indication that it is a question, since independent μή can be used in no other way than interrogatively (cf. § 427(2)). (1) The double question indicated by πότερον...ἤ is found only once in the NT; s. § 298(1). Otherwise the first member is left undesignated: G 1: 10 ἄρτι γὰρ ἀνθρώπους πείθω ἢ τὸν θεόν; (2) However, there are the interrogative particles ἆρα and ἆρά γε, but they are rarely used and then only in Lk and Paul (i.e. in rather literary language); they are not to be confused with inferential ἄρα (ἄρα γε), which tends to follow interrogative words (as in classical). MGr however uses ἄραγε (= ἆρά γε) as an interrogative particle (Thumb² § 255 n. 2). (3) Εἰ, which normally introduces an indirect question (§ 368; cf. § 375), may precede a direct question: Mt 12: 10 εἰ ἔξεστιν τοῖς σάββασιν θεραπεῦσαι; But interrogative ἦ does not appear at all in the NT (nor does the affirmative). In the LXX it is found only in Job 25: 5 B (rell. correctly εἰ); ἦ, e.g. in Job, is an incorrect spelling, introduced by Swete (9: 14) and Rahlfs (9: 14, 17: 15f.): Katz, JTS 47 (1946) 168 n. 1.—Rob. 1175ff.

(1) Simple interrogative ἦ = *an* 'or': Mt 20: 15, 26: 53, 1 C 9: 8, 2 C 11: 7 (where FG ἢ μή 'or perhaps', a combination not elsewhere attested).
(2) Lk 18: 8 ἆρα εὑρήσει τὴν πίστιν ἐπὶ τῆς γῆς; A 8: 30 ἆρά γε γινώσκεις ἃ ἀναγινώσκεις; G 2: 17 ἆρα Χριστὸς ἁμαρτίας διάκονος; μὴ γένοιτο (μὴ γέν. in Paul is always the answer to a question [§ 384], so this is not ἆρα in a declarative sentence; however αρα = 'then, consequently' as ἄρα elsewhere [§ 451 (2d)] so that it is perhaps to be accented ἄρα). In addition, Herm Man 4.1.4 (ἄρα), Diogn 7.3 (ἆρά γε). Ἆρ' οὐ and ἆρα μή do not appear in the NT. Τίς ἄρα Mt 18: 1, Lk 1: 66 etc. (indirect 22: 23), εἰ ἄρα (direct and indirect) Mk 11: 13, A 7: 1, 8: 22 (εἰ ἄρα γε 17: 27), μήτι ἄρα 2 C 1: 17. Οὐκ ἄρα denotes astonishment in A 21: 38 οὐκ ἄρα σὺ εἶ ὁ Αἰγύπτιος; ('*why*, are you not...'), elsewhere it corresponds to 'well' or 'then'. Τί(ς) ἄρα Mt 19: 25, 27 inferential 'now, then'. It is often incapable of direct translation. Rob. 1176, cf. 1189f.
(3) This usage is unclass., but it is found in the LXX also (Gen 17: 17 etc., Winer 474 [Winer-M.³ 638ff.]), and is therefore probably a Hebraism (Viteau 22) as a translation (along with μή) of Hebr. הֲ and אִם, which in an indirect question correspond to Greek εἰ, but which also introduce direct questions. Mt 19: 3 λέγοντες· εἰ (indirect with the same words Mk 10: 2, Viteau 22 n.), A 1: 6, 7: 1 etc. (most

frequently in Lk). Homil Clem 15.9, 16.16, 17.19; Ev. Thom. B 8.3 (p. 153 Tdf.); cf. Ghedini, Vang. ap. 464 f.

441. Particles of asseveration and corroboration.

(1) Asseverative sentences in classical, direct and indirect (the infinitive is used in the latter), are introduced by ἦ μήν which in the Hellenistic-Roman period was written εἶ (accent?) μήν (§ 24). This is the case in the LXX, from which H 6: 14 εἶ (ἦ KL*, εἰ μή v.l.; s. § 454(5)) μήν εὐλογῶν εὐλογήσω σε is taken. Ναί 'yes' is another corroborative particle, the opposite being οὔ, οὐχί 'no' (§ 432). Ναί is also used in emphatic repetition of something already stated: 'yes, indeed'; it is also used in a repeated request. (2) The question may also be repeated in a positive form as an affirmative answer (classical likewise). (3) Another form is σὺ λέγεις (εἶπας) i.e. 'you say it yourself, not I' (§ 277(1)) in which there is always something of an implication that the statement would not have been made had the question not been asked.—Δήπου 'of course, certainly' (an appeal to information shared by the reader) somewhat softens an assertion, but it does assert: only H 2: 16 (classical, literary).—Καὶ μήν s. § 450(4).—Rob. 1150.

(1) Ναί 'yes, indeed': Lk 12: 5 ναί, λέγω ὑμῖν, τοῦτον φοβήθητε, 11: 51, Rev 1: 7, 14: 13, 16: 7; Mt 11: 25 f. = Lk 10: 21 πάτερ...ναί, ὁ πατήρ (Norden 50 n. 4). In a repeated request: Mt 15: 27, Ph 4: 3, Phm 20 (preferred in class. in formulae of adjuration and asseveration as in ναὶ πρὸς τῶν γονάτων Aristoph., Pax 1113).

(2) Mk 14: 61 f. σὺ εἶ...; ...ἐγώ εἰμι, cf. A 22: 27 D gig read εἰμί for ναί; with abbreviation ἐγὼ κύριε scil. ὑπάγω (which D adds) Mt 21: 29.

(3) Σὺ λέγεις (εἶπας) Mt 27: 11, 26: 25, Mk 15: 2, Lk 23: 3; in Jn 18: 37 σὺ λέγεις, ὅτι (not 'that', but 'because, for', § 456(1)) βασιλεύς εἰμι, cf. Lk 22: 70 ὑμεῖς λέγετε, ὅτι ἐγώ εἰμι.

(B) Co-ordinating (Paratactic) Conjunctions

(i) *Copulative conjunctions* (καί, τε, οὔτε μήτε, οὐδέ μηδέ)

442. Καί.

The properly copulative meaning of καί 'and' is to be distinguished from the adjunctive 'also'. The excessive and monotonous use of καί to string sentences together makes the narrative style of some NT authors, especially Mk (Zerwick 1 ff.), but also Lk (e.g. A 13: 17 ff.), unpleasing and colloquial (cf. § 458). Elsewhere

in Lk as well as in Jn the other particles τε, δέ, οὖν and asyndeton provide more variety, even apart from the use of participial and subordinate constructions. (1) Καί can be used even where there is actual contrast (at times = 'and yet', e.g. Mt 6: 26 οὐ σπείρουσιν...καὶ ὁ πατὴρ ὑμῶν ὁ οὐράνιος τρέφει αὐτά). (2) 'Consecutive' καί = 'and so, so': Mt 5: 15 ἀλλ' ἐπὶ τὴν λυχνίαν (τιθέασιν), καὶ λάμπει... (= ὥστε λάμπειν, Lk 8: 16 = 11: 33 with ἵνα). It is especially frequent after imperatives (also classical; for the papyri s. Mayser II 3, 145.9): Ja 4: 7 ἀντίστητε τῷ διαβόλῳ, καὶ φεύξεται ἀφ' ὑμῶν (= φεύξεται γάρ, εὐθὺς γὰρ φ.). Καί with a connotation of purpose is related: Rev 14: 15 πέμψον τὸ δρέπανόν σου καὶ θέρισον, and after an interrogative clause Mt 26: 15 τί θέλετέ μοι δοῦναι κἀγὼ ὑμῖν παραδώσω αὐτόν; (3) Καί with the future even after final clauses with the subjunctive is used to denote a further result; s. § 369(3). (4) Co-ordination instead of subordination (cf. § 471) with temporal designations: Mk 15: 25 καὶ ἦν ὥρα τρίτη καὶ ('when') ἐσταύρωσαν αὐτόν (the crucifixion was narrated earlier in v. 24), unless D καὶ ἐφύλασσον αὐτόν is correct (for which Tischendorf compares Mt 27: 36); Lk 23: 44. (5) Καί with a finite verb after καὶ ἐγένετο or ἐγένετο δέ instead of the accusative and infinitive (which is better Greek; § 393(1, 5)) is Hebraizing (but not Aramaizing; Dalman, Worte Jesu 25 f. [Words of Jesus 32 f.]; but cf. A. J. Wensinck, Bull. of the Bezan Club 12 [Leiden, 1937] 38; on καὶ ἐγένετο and καί, δέ, τε generally in Lk. s. Ed. Schweizer, ThZ 6 [1950] 165 f.). However the καί is for the most part omitted in this construction. The purely pleonastic ἐγένετο, of which Lk is especially fond, owes its origin to an aversion to beginning a sentence with a temporal designation (§ 472(3)). (6) The use of καί to co-ordinate words with independent clauses is Hebraizing (and slovenly vernacular): Lk 1: 49 (Magnificat) ὁ δυνατός, καὶ ἅγιον τὸ ὄνομα αὐτοῦ = οὗ τὸ ὄν. ἅγιόν ἐστιν. (7) The use of καί to introduce an apodosis is also due primarily to Hebrew, although it appears as early as Homer (e.g. Il. 1.478): Lk 2: 21 καὶ ὅτε ἐπλήσθησαν..., καὶ (om. D) ἐκλήθη...,Homil Clem 2.43.1 εἰ γὰρ ψεύδεται (God), καὶ τίς ἀληθεύει and twenty-four times through 44.5. Καὶ ἰδού is even more Semitic. (8) Καί is to be understood differently when the apodosis is a question: 2 C 2: 2 εἰ γὰρ ἐγὼ λυπῶ ὑμᾶς, καὶ τίς ὁ εὐφραίνων με; = 'who then' (under the circumstances set forth in the protasis); without a protasis cf. Mk

10: 26 καὶ τίς δύναται σωθῆναι; Jn 9: 36, 14: 22 SGW al. (9) Καί 'that is to say...' (epexegetical καί), e.g. Jn 1: 16 καὶ χάριν ἀντὶ χάριτος. (10) Καί 'and likewise': A 16: 15 ὡς δὲ ἐβαπτίσθη καὶ ὁ οἶκος αὐτῆς ('together with'). (11) Καί after πολύς before a second adjective (classical) is pleonastic by English usage A 25: 7 πολλὰ καὶ βαρέα αἰτιώματα (literary); T 1: 10 v.l. (12) Καί 'also' (thus even at H 7: 26 τοιοῦτος γὰρ ἡμῖν καὶ ἔπρεπεν ἀρχιερεύς, cf. καὶ γάρ §452(3)), and ascensive καί 'even' (Mt 5: 46 etc., before a comparative 11: 9). (13) Μετὰ καὶ Κλήμεντος (pleonastic) Ph 4: 3. It is also pleonastic with 'as': ὁποῖος καὶ ἐγώ A 26: 29 (good classical). (14) After an interrogative (as in classical): τί καὶ βαπτίζονται; 1 C 15: 29 'why at all, still?' (15) Καὶ νῦν (as a translation of Hebrew וְעַתָּה) 'come now, come' (with commands and questions), 'now then' (with assertions): A 10: 5 (πέμψον), 22: 16 (τί μέλλεις; ...βάπτισαι), 3: 17 (οἶδα). (16) The co-ordination of two ideas, one of which is dependent on the other (hendiadys), serves in the NT to avoid a series of dependent genitives (cf. §162(2)): A 23: 6 περὶ ἐλπίδος καὶ ἀναστάσεως νεκρῶν 'on account of the hope *of* the resurrection of the dead'; 14: 17 ἐμπιπλῶν τροφῆς καὶ εὐφροσύνης 'with joy *for* food' (likewise ὑετοὺς καὶ καιροὺς καρποφόρους 'fruitful seasons *through* rains' [literally 'rains of fruitful seasons']?); A 1: 25, 1 P 4: 14, Ja 5: 10 ὑπόδειγμα...τῆς κακοπαθίας καὶ τῆς μακροθυμίας 'of perseverance in suffering'. Also e.g. Lk 2: 47 ἐπὶ τῇ συνέσει καὶ ταῖς ἀποκρίσεσιν αὐτοῦ 'at his intelligent answers', 21: 15, R 1: 5, 2 T 4: 1, T 2: 13, 2 P 1: 16. Wilke, Rhetorik 149.—Καί...δὲ...s. §447(9).— S. Trenkner, Le style καί dans le récit attique oral (Cahiers de l'Inst. d'Études polonaises en Belgique I [Brussels, 1948] 153 pp. [mimeographed]). Rob. 1179–83.

NT: Gonzaga, Class. Journ. 21 (1925/6) 580–6; Apocr. Gos.: Ghedini, Vang. ap. 471ff.; pap.: Mayser II 3, 140ff.
(1) 'And yet' (καὶ ὅμως and ὅμως δέ are not used): Mt 10: 29, Jn 1: 10, 3: 11, 32 etc. It is less surprising with a negative: Mt 11: 17, A 12: 19 etc. Mk 12: 12 καὶ ἐζήτουν αὐτὸν κρατῆσαι, καὶ ἐφοβήθησαν τὸν ὄχλον; cf. Lk 20: 19 (D has ἐφοβ. δέ), Jn 1: 5. Καί defines the relationship between clauses very inexactly, so that rather laborious interpretation is required, e.g. Jn 7: 28 κἀμὲ οἴδατε καὶ οἴδατε πόθεν εἰμί (as you have said), καὶ ἀπ' ἐμαυτοῦ οὐκ ἐλήλυθα, ἀλλ'...' 'and yet I did not really...' (= class. καὶ μήν, καίτοι, or καὶ ταῦτ' ἀπ' ἐμαυτοῦ οὐκ ἐληλυθότα with

a ptcp.). Ljungvik, Syntax 55. Mt 5: 29 ἵνα ἀπόληται...καὶ μή ('rather than that')...βληθῇ; cf. Ljungvik, Syntax 57.
(2) Η 3: 19 καὶ βλέπομεν 'and so we see' (ὁρῶμεν οὖν). After an impera.: Mt 8: 8 εἰπὲ λόγῳ καί ('then') ἰαθήσεται; cf. Lk 7: 7 where BL gives a closer connection by reading ἰαθήτω. Class. θέσθε...καὶ... οἴσει Soph., OC 1410ff., πείθου λέγοντι, κοὐχ ἁμαρτήσῃ ποτέ El. 1207 (K.-G. II 248). A conditional clause could have been substituted in such cases (Mt 8: 8 'If you say the word, he will be healed'); e.g. Mk 4: 13, Jn 2: 19, 7: 34, 36, 8: 21, 10: 12, 13: 33. Fridrichsen, Arbeiten und Mitteilungen IV (1936) 44f.—Final καί after ἔρχομαι Jn 14: 3. Ljungvik, Syntax 59f., 60f., 61ff., 67f., 72ff.
(3) Cf. further Mt 26: 53, H 12: 9. Lk 11: 5ff. τίς ἐξ ὑμῶν ἕξει φίλον, καὶ πορεύσεται πρὸς αὐτόν...καὶ εἴπῃ αὐτῷ...κἀκεῖνος εἴπῃ (§366(1)) instead of subordination with ἐάν or a gen. absol., just as the first καί might have been avoided by ἔχων φίλον.
(4) Lk 19: 43 ἥξουσιν ἡμέραι...καί ('when')...is unclass., as is Mt 26: 45, H 8: 8 OT. There are class. pars. for the use of καί with temporal designations, e.g. Hom., Od. 5.362, Plato, Symp. 220 c, Aeschin. 3.71 νὺξ ἐν μέσῳ καὶ παρῆμεν; cf. Winer 406 [Winer-M.³ 543f.]; K.-G. II 231; Br.-Th. 640. There is a corresponding usage in Romance languages (Jensen, Arch. Stud. n. Sprachen 155 [1929] 61). Pallis, Notes 6; Ljungvik, Syntax 84f. On καί in constructions with hendiadys s. *infra* (16).
(5) Lk 19: 15 καὶ ἐγένετο ἐν τῷ ἐπανελθεῖν αὐτόν... καί (om. sy and lat witnesses) εἶπεν; 9: 28 ἐγ. δὲ μετὰ τοὺς λόγους τούτους, ὡσεὶ ἡμέραι ὀκτώ (§144), καί (om. 𝔓⁴⁵S*BH lat and sy)...ἀνέβη; 5: 1 ἐγ. δὲ ἐν τῷ...ἀκούειν..., καὶ αὐτὸς ἦν ἑστώς (D ἑστῶτος αὐτοῦ)...2 καὶ εἶδεν. Cf. A 5: 7 (καί all witnesses); without καί (Mt, Mk infrequently, Lk often) e.g. Mk 4: 4 καὶ ἐγένετο ἐν τῷ σπείρειν, ὃ μὲν ἔπεσεν etc.; Mt 7: 28 etc. For καὶ ἐγένετο and the like in the NT and LXX s. Thack. 50ff.; Viteau, Sujet 82ff.; Pernot, Études 189–99 (=RHPR 4 [1924] 553–8; on which s. Debrunner, Gnomon 4 [1928] 443f.); Johannessohn, KZ 53 (1925) 161–212 (on which s. Dibelius, Gnomon 3 [1927] 646–50). Data with reference to Lk: (1) with finite verb without καί the Gos. often, esp. Lk 1–2; (2) with finite verb and καί the Gos. rather often, but only A 5: 7; (3) five times with an inf. in the Gos., often in A. Viteau, *op. cit.* rightly compares καὶ ἔσται in similar references to the future (LXX; in the NT only in quotations like A 2: 17; the two exx. from the pap. in Mlt. [371] are different: ἔσται with the inf. 'it will be possible').
(6) Also cf. (with ptcp. preceding) 2 Jn 2 τὴν μένουσαν ἐν ἡμῖν (=ἥ...μένει), καὶ μεθ' ἡμῶν ἔσται, and esp. in Rev (§468(3)) much of this sort of thing.
(7) Lk 7: 12 ὡς δὲ ἤγγισεν...καὶ ἰδοὺ ἐξεκομίζετο etc., where the v.l. of D shows that this usage was scarcely distinguished from that with ἐγένετο:

ἐγένετο δὲ ὡς ἤγγιζεν...ἐξεκομίζετο. A 1: 10 (καὶ ἰδού), 10: 17 (καὶ ἰδού CD al., without καὶ 𝔓⁴⁵SAB), Rev 3: 20 after an ἐάν-clause (without καί AP). But in Ja 4: 15 the second clause can be considered to begin with καί ('both...and') ζήσομεν rather than with καὶ ποιήσομεν (Buttmann 311 n.). On καὶ ἰδού in the LXX and NT s. Johannessohn, KZ 64 (1937) 179–215; 66 (1939) 145–95; 67 (1940) 30–84. For the use of 'and' to introduce apodoses in Germanic and Romance languages, s. Jensen, *op. cit.* 59 f.; M. Niedermann, Emerita 14 (1946) 400.

(8) E. C. Colwell, The Greek of the Fourth Gospel (1931) 87 f.; Almqvist 74. Ph 1: 22 should be punctuated: εἰ δὲ (𝔓⁴⁶ ἐπεί) τὸ ζῆν ἐν σαρκί, τοῦτό μοι καρπὸς ἔργου, καὶ τί αἱρήσομαι; οὐ γνωρίζω, συνέχομαι δὲ.... R 3: 7 τί ἔτι καί 'why then...still?' Cf. the class. exx. in K.-G. II 247 f. (also Xen., Cyr. 5.4.13); there are many exx. in Homil Clem 2.43 f. Mk 9: 12 D: εἰ Ἠλίας ἐλθὼν ἀποκαθιστάνει πάντα, καὶ πῶς γέγραπται 'how is it that it is written (how is this to be reconciled with...)?'

(9) 1 C 3: 5 and 15: 38 καὶ ἑκάστῳ. Emphatic with demonstrative καὶ τοῦτον ἐσταυρωμένον 1 C 2: 2; καὶ τοῦτο *idque* (R 13: 11?), 1 C 6: 6, 8 (8 v.l. καὶ ταῦτα as in H 11: 12 and class. [K.-G. II 247]. For pap. s. Mayser II 3, 141). Mk 1: 19 καὶ αὐτούς (Mt 4: 21 without κ. α.); cf. LXX 1 Km 16: 18 ἑόρακα υἱόν... καὶ αὐτὸν εἰδότα ψαλμόν. Ljungvik, Syntax 57 ff. G. Schrenk, Judaica 5 (1949) 85 n. 9: explicative καί 1 C 8: 12, 15: 38, 12: 27 f., 14: 27, 2 C 5: 15, always used to particularize; conditionally also 1 C 3: 5. Καὶ τοῦτο and the like 1 C 2: 2, 5: 1, 6: 6, 8, 10 f., R 13: 11, E 2: 8, (H 11: 12).

(10) Cf. A 18: 2 and Aristoph., Ra. 697 f.: οἱ μεθ' ὑμῶν πολλὰ δὴ χοῖ πατέρες ἐναυμάχησαν.

(11) There is no ex. of class. καί 'as' after ὁ αὐτός, ὁμοίως and the like (K.-G. I 413). A corresponding use of καί is found after *definite* numbers: Barn 11.2 = LXX Jer 2: 13 (where of the Gr. witnesses S* alone omits καί) δύο καὶ πονηρά 'two evils'.

(12) Καί 'also': often after διό, διὰ τοῦτο to introduce the result: Lk 1: 35, 11: 49. Also in and after comparative clauses; s. § 453(1). Διὰ τοῦτο καί is so fixed a phrase that καί can even be separated from the verb which it emphasizes: 1 Th 2: 13 διὰ τ. καὶ ἡμεῖς εὐχαριστοῦμεν, 3: 5 διὰ τ. κἀγὼ μηκέτι στέγων ἔπεμψα. Καὶ τὸ πρότερον 'earlier, before' Herm Vis 3.3.5.

(13) 1 Clem 65.1 σὺν καὶ Φορτουνάτῳ. Σὺν καί in the pap.: Deissmann, NBS 93 [BS 265 f.]; Mayser II 1, 60 f.; further W. Schulze, KZ 33 (1894) 240 = Kl. Schr. 389 f. Ὁ καί s. § 268(1).

(14) Lk 13: 7; K.-G. II 255. R 8: 24 ὃ γὰρ βλέπει, τίς καὶ ὑπομένει S 'for who needs to wait patiently for that which he sees' (after Paul soon misunderstood and much emended; om. καὶ 𝔓⁴⁶B*DFG).

(15) Further A 7: 34 OT (δεῦρο ἀποστείλω σε), 13: 11, 20: 22, 25, 1 Jn 2: 28 (μένετε), so also perhaps

Jn 14: 29 (εἴρηκα ὑμῖν), 2 Th 2: 6 (καὶ νῦν τὸ κατέχον οἴδατε; however s. § 474(5 c)). Joachim Jeremias, ZNW 38 (1939) 119 f.

(16) Lagercrantz, ZNW 31 (1932) 86 f.; Riesenfeld, Con. Neot. 3 (1939) 26; Björck, *ibid.* 4 (1940) 1–4. Cf. e.g. Aristoph., Eq. 1310 ἐκ πεύκης...καὶ ξύλων 'made of pine'. So also Mk 6: 26 = Mt 14: 9 διὰ τοὺς ὅρκους καὶ τοὺς (συν)ανακειμένους 'because of the oath taken before his guests'?

443. Τε. (1) Τε appears in by no means all the books of the NT, and would not be strongly represented at all were it not for Acts, which alone has twice as many examples as the rest of the NT put together. (2) Simple τε, which is foreign on the whole to Attic proper but is abundantly used in more sophisticated poetry, is used infrequently in the NT to combine single ideas (in classical limited virtually to poetry, K.-G. II 241). (3) In the connection of clauses, τε indicates rather close connection and relationship, e.g. A 2: 40 ἑτέροις τε (δέ D is inferior) λόγοις πλείοσιν διεμαρτύρατο ('and likewise').—Mayser II 3, 155 ff.; Rob. 1178 f.

(1) Τε is evenly distributed in all sections of Acts; after Acts come Hebrews and Romans. There are only 8 exx. in Lk; simple τε only 21: 11 (twice), and even then not without a following καί: σεισμοί τε ('and', om. τε AL) μεγάλοι καὶ...λιμοὶ ἔσονται, φόβητρά τε ('and') καὶ...σημεῖα...ἔσται (unless perhaps asyndeton is to be assumed [s. § 444(4)] since τε is not very suitable as a connective particle). In 24: 20 the correct reading may be ὅπως (ὡς) τοῦτον (D) for ὅπως (ὡς D) τε αὐτόν. Only in D: ἀνακραυγάσαν τε 4: 35, ὄξος τε προσέφερον αὐτῷ λέγοντες 23: 36. Τε in Jn only 2: 15, 4: 32, 6: 18, and always textually contestable. It is not surprising that τε was often confused with δέ in the course of transmission; it is not admissible in parentheses as in A 1: 15 ἦν τε (SAB for ἦν δέ); s. § 447(7).

(2) Η 6: 5 θεοῦ ῥῆμα δυνάμεις τε μέλλοντος αἰῶνος, 9: 1, 1 C 4: 21; also cf. § 444.

(3) A 2: 37 κατενύγησαν τὴν καρδίαν, εἶπόν τε ('and so they said'), 27: 4 f. ὑπεπλεύσαμεν τὴν Κύπρον...τό τε πέλαγος τὸ κατὰ τὴν Κιλικίαν... διαπλεύσαντες...(in accordance with this course). Similarly 1 Clem 20.10 twice, 1.3–2.1 four times. Occasionally a τε γάρ appears to be the equivalent of γάρ or καὶ γάρ (cf. Bonitz, Index Aristotelicus, p. 750 a; Lietzmann, Hdb.² on 2 C 10: 8): 2 C 10: 8 ἐάν τε (om. τε 𝔓⁴⁶BFG) γὰρ περισσότερόν τι καυχήσωμαι (or is a second ἐάν τε suppressed, as often in Aristotle [s. Bonitz, *ibid.*]? Cf. ἐάν τε γάρ...ἐάν τε, ἐάν τε οὖν...ἐάν τε R 14: 8), R 7: 7 τήν τε (om. τε FG lat) γὰρ ἐπιθυμίαν οὐκ ᾔδειν (supply: 'as well as the ἁμαρτία mentioned above'). s. also § 452(3)). Other

Hell. exx. of superfluous τε may be found in Raderm.[2] 5; τε γάρ=γάρ in the class. and Hell. period, s. K.-G. II 245; Franz Zimmermann, PhW 44 (1924) 609.

444. Καί...καί..., τε...καί...(τε καί...), τε... τε 'both...and, not only...but also'. (1) Τε... τε places the elements connected in a parallel relationship (often = 'as...so'). In addition to οὔτε...οὔτε etc. (§445), it is found in εἴτε...εἴτε and ἐάν τε...ἐάν τε (§454(3)). Otherwise only A 26: 16 ὧν τε εἶδες ὧν τε ὀφθήσομαί σοι (Paul before Agrippa). (2) Τε...καί provides a closer connection than simple καί. Consequently it is used in the NT to connect words but not whole clauses. Τε καί which is not infrequent in classical without an intervening word is also common in the NT: Mt 22: 10 πονηρούς τε καὶ ἀγαθούς. Ἰουδαῖοι and Ἕλληνες are nearly always connected by τε καί or τε...καί. (3) Καί...καί...e.g. Lk 5: 36 καὶ τὸ καινὸν σχίσει, καὶ τῷ παλαιῷ οὐ συμφωνήσει etc. ('on the one hand...on the other', i.e. a double loss). It is somewhat more frequent in Jn, e.g. 4: 36 ἵνα καὶ ὁ σπείρων ὁμοῦ χαίρῃ καὶ ὁ θερίζων (the first καί is omitted in BCW al.), here to sharpen the distinction between the two persons. (4) In longer enumerations a further τε may be added to τε (...) καί, but other combinations of τε and καί also occur. (5) Correlative τε comes as a rule after the first word of the pair that is to be correlated. Exception: it follows a preposition which precedes and governs both of the words to be connected (classical also, K.-G. II 245): A 25: 23 σύν τε χιλιάρχοις καὶ ἀνδράσιν, 28: 23, 10: 39 (v.l. with repeated ἐν). Contrast τῶν ἐθνῶν τε καὶ Ἰουδαίων A 14: 5 (τῶν ἐ. καὶ τῶν Ἰ. D).—Rob. 1179, 1182f.

(1) In R 1: 26f. the mild anacoluthon with ὁμοίως δὲ καί (APD*G 1739 pm.) is better than τε... ὁμοίως τε καί (BSℜ). In A 2: 46 the first τε connects the whole new clause, the second connects κλῶντες with προσκαρτεροῦντες. In class. τε...τε in prose is far more frequent than simple τε, but less frequent than in poetry (K.-G. II 243).

(2) A 1: 1 ποιεῖν τε καὶ διδάσκειν, 2: 9f., 4: 27; R 1: 12 ὑμῶν τε καὶ ἐμοῦ. 1 C 10: 32 ἀπρόσκοποι καὶ Ἰουδαίοις γίνεσθε καὶ Ἕλλησιν καὶ τῇ ἐκκλησίᾳ τοῦ θεοῦ, where the distinction between the members is retained, whereas with τε καί the distinction is rather set aside. Ἰουδαῖοί τε (...) καὶ Ἕλληνες A 14: 1, 19: 10 (D without τε), 17 (DE without τε), 20: 21, R 1: 16 (S* without τε), 2: 9, 10, 3: 9, 10: 12 (DE without τε), 1 C 1: 24 (FG without τε). A 18: 4 ἔπειθέν τε Ἰ. καὶ Ἕλληνας is different for an obvious reason. Τε καί is

also rarely used in the pap. to connect clauses (Mayser II 3, 160, 163f., 165). On the whole, Mayser II 3, 159ff.

(3) Jn 7: 28 (§442(1)), 11: 48 (with a less definite meaning in both of these passages), 12: 28; 15: 24 νῦν δὲ ἑωράκασιν καί ('and yet') μεμισήκασιν καὶ ἐμὲ καὶ τὸν πατέρα μου (who appear to them to be different persons). In Paul: R 14: 9 twice, 1 C 1: 22 etc. Ph 4: 12 is peculiar: οἶδα καὶ ταπεινοῦσθαι, οἶδα καὶ περισσεύειν, where the first καί also has more the sense of 'even'. Mt 10: 28 καί (not in all witnesses) ψυχὴν καὶ σῶμα can also mean 'even body and soul' (this is still more evident in 8: 27 = Mk 4: 41 = Lk 8: 25 καὶ οἱ ἄνεμοι καὶ ἡ θάλασσα αὐτῷ ὑπακούουσιν). Mayser II 3, 142f.

(4) A 9: 15 ἐθνῶν τε (om. τε HLP) καὶ βασιλέων υἱῶν τε Ἰσραήλ, 26: 10f., 1 Clem 20.3. On the other hand, Lk 22: 66 τὸ πρεσβυτέριον τοῦ λαοῦ, ἀρχιερεῖς τε καὶ γραμματεῖς; the latter is an explanatory phrase in apposition since otherwise the art. would necessarily have been used. (D καὶ ἀρχ. καὶ γρ.). H 6: 2 τε...τε...καί...(ἀναστάσεως and κρίματος are closely connected by καί) and 11: 32 Γεδεών, Βαράκ τε καί...καί...τε καί...καί...(enumeration of names; however the first three conjunctions are omitted in 𝔓[13]𝔓[46]SA); in the latter τε is merely a connective and not correlated with καί. Likewise A 13: 1, 1 C 1: 30. On the other hand, in the long enumerations in A 1: 13 and 2: 9ff. τε καί, or simple καί, form pairs which are asyndetic among themselves; cf. Mt 10: 3f., 24: 38, R 1: 14, 1 T 1: 9, 1 Clem 3.2, 35.5, Herm Man 12.3.1. In Lk 6: 14ff. SBD(W) al. have καί throughout (against A al.) as in Mk 3: 16ff. (all witnesses).

(5) PTebt I 39.19 (114 BC) τήν τε τοῦ ἱεροῦ καὶ τῆς οἰκίας θύραν.

445. Negative correlatives: οὔτε...οὔτε... (μήτε...μήτε...); the connective after a negative clause is οὐδέ (μηδέ), after a positive καὶ οὐ (καὶ μή). All of this remains the same as in classical. (1) Thus οὐ..., οὔτε...οὔτε...is 'not...,neither (either)...nor (or)...' (Mt 12: 32 etc.). (2) If οὐδέ (μηδέ) stands at the beginning of the whole sentence or follows an οὐ (μή) within the same clause, it means 'not even': Mk 8: 26 μηδὲ (μὴ S*W) εἰς τὴν κώμην εἰσέλθῃς (many vv.ll.; the sense requires εἴπῃς instead of εἰσέλθῃς), Mt 6: 15, etc. Mk 3: 20 ὥστε μὴ δύνασθαι αὐτοὺς μηδὲ (μήτε SCDE al. is inferior) ἄρτον φαγεῖν. (3) The correlation of negative and positive members is, of course, admissible, though it is not common in the NT. E.g. Jn 4: 11 οὔτε ἄντλημα ἔχεις, καὶ φρέαρ ἐστὶν βαθύ (οὐδέ D sy[s], which seems to be better Greek). (4) Καὶ οὐ after negative clauses does not indicate correlation but an independent continuation (Buttmann 316), e.g. Mt 15: 32, or a kind of parallelism, e.g. Lk 18: 2 τὸν θεὸν μὴ φοβούμενος καὶ ἄνθρωπον μὴ ἐντρεπόμενος (likewise 4 καὶ οὐκ ADW al., οὐδὲ SBLX).—Mayser II 3, 171 ff.; Rob. 1166, 1182, 1189, etc.

(1) Cf. Lk 9: 3 μηδὲν..., μήτε...μήτε etc. with Mt 10: 9f. In 1 C 6: 9f. a very long enumeration begun with οὔτε...οὔτε etc. reverts finally to asyndeton with οὐ...οὐ; in Mt 10: 10 μή also occurs once among a number of instances of μηδέ. Οὔτε and οὐδέ, μήτε and μηδέ are sometimes confused in the MSS as they are in secular authors (which is also the case with δέ and τε: §443(1)): Lk 20: 36 οὔτε γὰρ SQRW al. is corrupt for οὐδὲ γάρ (§452(3)); Rev 9: 21 all MSS have οὔτε several times after οὐ, as also in 21: 4, in 5: 4 almost all have οὐδείς...οὔτε, but in 3 they are divided; οὐδέ preponderates in 12: 8 and 20: 4 (as in Jn 1: 25); in 7: 16, 9: 4 and 21: 23 all have οὐδέ; Ja 3: 12 is completely corrupt. Acc. to Billerbeck I 328 Mt 5: 34ff. μὴ ὁμόσαι ὅλως μήτε...μήτε... can not mean 'not..., either...or', but 'at all—(in particular) not...'; i.e. μήτε = μηδέ.

(2) The positive term corresponding to this οὐδέ 'not even' is καί 'even', as the positive equivalent of (οὐ...,) οὐδέ etc. is a series connected by καί, but the equivalent for οὔτε...οὔτε is καί...καί, τε...καί, (τε...τε). Thus οὔτε οἶδα οὔτε ἐπίσταμαι in Mk 14: 68 SBDLW appears to be inadmissible; since full synonyms cannot be connected by καί...καί, τε καί, so AKM οὐκ...οὐδέ (οὐκ...οὔτε CE al., which is apparently the source of the confusion) is correct. A disjunctive expression following a negative can be equivalent to οὐ...οὐδέ, οὐ...οὔτε...οὔτε: Mt 5: 17 μὴ νομίσητε ὅτι ἦλθον καταλῦσαι τὸν νόμον ἢ τοὺς προφήτας = οὐκ ἦ. κατ. οὔτε τ. ν. οὔτε τ. πρ., A 17: 29, etc.; cf. §446 (in English this is a bit confusing since the negative is omitted either from the preceding clause or from the correlated members: 'I have come to destroy neither...nor'; or 'I have not come to destroy either...or'; thus the two possible forms in Greek have only one counterpart in English). The sequence οὔτε...οὔτε...οὔτε...οὐδὲ...is perfectly admissible ('not at all', as if a single οὐ or οὐδαμοῦ had preceded): A 24: 12f. (Buttmann 315n.); likewise μή...μηδὲ (μήτε SABCE)...μήτε A 23: 8 because the second member is subdivided (cf. class., K.-G. II 289c); G 1: 12 οὐδὲ γάρ ('for...not')... παρέλαβον οὔτε ἐδιδάχθην (B al.) is also possible, although οὐδὲ ἐδιδ., which is better attested, is more in accordance with the rule.

(3) 3 Jn 10 οὔτε αὐτὸς ἐπιδέχεται...καὶ τοὺς βουλομένους κωλύει. In A 27: 20 the τε after μήτε... μήτε is hardly correlative but connective. With οὐ instead of οὔτε Mt 10: 38 (cf. Lk 14: 27) ὃς οὐ λαμβάνει τὸν σταυρὸν αὐτοῦ καὶ ἀκολουθεῖ μοι ('and yet follows me'; καί is not used for οὐδέ here); so L. Zatočil (s. PhW 1935, 584). Οὔτε...καί is very

rare in class. (K.-G. II 291, 3a), but becomes rather frequent later (W. Bauer, Hdb. on Jn 4: 11); in the Ptol. pap. only one questionable ex., and οὔτε (μήτε)...τε is rare (Mayser II 3, 174).

(4) Jn 5: 37f. οὔτε...οὔτε...καὶ...οὐ, but Chrys. has οὐδέ for καὶ...οὐ.

(ii) Disjunctive conjunctions

446. Ἤ, or ἢ καί = 'or even' (Lk 18: 11 etc.); with a correlative ἤ...ἤ... 'either...or' (for which ἤτοι... ἤ is found in R 6: 16; classical [K.-G. II 298] and Hellenistic [Raderm.² 33]). Εἴτε...εἴτε sive... sive is properly used to introduce subordinate clauses, but by virtue of an ellipsis is used also without a finite verb (as in classical): 2 C 5: 10 ἵνα κομίσηται ἕκαστος...εἴτε ἀγαθὸν εἴτε κακόν, E 6: 8, Ph 1: 18 (𝔓⁴⁶ εἰ...εἴτε), etc. It is never strictly disjunctive, but is just as much copulative (τε is a component of it); cf. §454(3). Ἤ also comes close to the force of a copulative conjunction, especially in negative clauses: A 1: 7 οὐ... χρόνους ἢ καιρούς (synonyms), Jn 8: 14 οἶδα πόθεν ἦλθον καὶ ποῦ ὑπάγω· ὑμεῖς δὲ οὐκ οἴδατε πόθεν ἔρχομαι ἢ ποῦ ὑπάγω (the reading καί for ἤ S al. is inferior, but Chr Non omit ἢ ποῦ ὑπ.). Likewise in interrogative sentences which are equivalent in sense to a negative sentence: 1 Th 2: 19 τίς γὰρ ἡμῶν ἐλπὶς ἢ χαρὰ ἢ στέφανος; (20 ἡ δόξα καὶ ἡ χαρά is an assertion).—Rob. 1188f.

A 11: 8 κοινὸν ἢ ἀκάθαρτον οὐδέποτε etc., cf. 10: 28 οὐδέποτε ἔφαγον πᾶν κοινὸν καὶ (ἢ CD al.) ἀκάθαρτον. 1 C 11: 27 ὃς ἂν ἐσθίῃ...ἢ πίνῃ...ἀναξίως.—Ἤ an in interrogative sentences (s. §440(1)) is sharply disjunctive ('otherwise this would have to be the case'). R 9: 11 μήπω γὰρ γεννηθέντων μηδὲ (ἢ FG vg) πραξάντων..., G 3: 28 οὐκ ἔνι (𝔓⁴⁶ οὐκέτι) Ἰουδαῖος οὐδὲ Ἕλλην, οὐκ ἔνι (𝔓⁴⁶ οὐκέτι?) δοῦλος οὐδὲ (ἢ D*) ἐλεύθερος, οὐκ ἔνι (lacuna 𝔓⁴⁶) ἄρσεν καὶ (ἢ Chr) θῆλυ. 1 Th 2: 19 is unusual ἤ (om. S*) οὐχὶ καὶ ὑμεῖς; (ἤ has probably crept into the text on account of τίς ['who else but']; cf. Jn 13: 10 v.l. and ἀλλ' ἤ §448(8)). R 12: 7 ἤτοι 𝔓⁴⁶ for εἴτε is spurious. Ἤ in the LXX, Margolis, AJSL 25 (1908/9) 257–75; in the pap. Mayser II 3, 138ff.; εἴτε...εἴτε in the pap. ibid. 159.

(iii) Adversative conjunctions

447. Δέ, μέν, μὲν...δὲ.... (1) Δέ has μέν as its correlative, while ἀλλά usually refers to a preceding negative ('but'). This latter relationship can also be expressed, though more weakly, by δέ. A distinction is to be observed between general contrast (δέ) and that which is directly contrary (ἀλλά), which is roughly comparable to German *aber* and *sondern*: H 2: 8 οὐδὲν ἀφῆκεν αὐτῷ ἀνυπότακτον· νῦν δὲ οὔπω ὁρῶμεν αὐτῷ τὰ πάντα ὑποτεταγμένα ('but, however'). (2) The correlative use of μέν and δέ, so basically characteristic of classical style, is greatly reduced in the NT; the result is that μέν is not found at all in Rev, 2 P, 1–3 Jn, 2 Th, 1 T, T (the μέν in 1: 15 is not genuine), Phm, and is practically unrepresented in Ja, E, C, 1 Th. It is comparatively rare in the Gospels as a whole and is somewhat more frequent only in Acts, Heb (1 P) and in some Pauline Epistles. For ὁ μέν ... ὁ δέ s. §250. (3) A large part of the Lukan examples, however, consists of resumptive μὲν οὖν (§451(1)), in which the μέν only in rare cases indicates real contrast, and of anacoluthic μέν (without correlative δέ) with a more or less serious breach of good sentence structure. (4) To be sure, the omission of δέ in some instances (in Lk and elsewhere) is excusable or even good classical usage: πρῶτον μέν R 1: 8 and 1 C 11: 18 (perhaps 'from the very outset'; Herm Man 4.2.3 'first of all, above all'), R 10: 1 ἡ μὲν εὐδοκία etc. (so far as it depends on my desire). (5) It is to be noted in cases of an uncertain reading involving μέν that the inclusion of μέν throws the emphasis on the second member (indicated by δέ); therefore, where the emphasis is on the first part and the second is only an appendage, μέν is not to be read. (6) Μέν is less often correlated with ἀλλά, πλήν, and asyndeton. (7) Δέ may introduce a parenthesis: A 12: 3 ἦσαν δὲ ἡμέραι τῶν ἀζύμων; (8) also an explanation or an intensification ('but', 'and...at that'): R 3: 22 δικαιοσύνη δὲ θεοῦ. (9) There is also the combination καί...δέ: A 3: 24 (2: 44) καὶ πάντες δέ 'and also all'; δὲ καί 'but also' A 22: 28 etc.— Mayser II 3, 125 ff.; Rob. 1150–3.

(1) Δέ 'but' (in the sense of ἀλλά): A 12: 9 οὐκ ᾔδει...ἐδόκει δέ ('rather'), 14, H 4: 13, 6: 12 etc.

(2) Ja 3: 17 πρῶτον μέν...ἔπειτα (without δέ as also in class. in this contrast; Jn 11: 6 [not without v.l.], 1 C 12: 28]. E 4: 11 τοὺς μέν...τοὺς δέ. C 2: 23 anacoluthon (s. *infra* (3) and (4)), likewise 1 Th 2: 18 ἐγὼ μὲν Παῦλος. Μέν is not infrequently interpolated in inferior MSS (Buttmann 313). It is less common in the Ptol. pap. than in the class. period (Mayser II 3, 128). Μέν in the Ap. Frs.: 1 Clem 3 times in 34½ pages in the *ed. quinta minor* of Gebhardt-Harnack-Zahn, therefore 0·087 to the page; 2 Clem 4 (0·4), Barn 18 (0·82), Diogn 27 (3·3), Ign 9 (0·33), MPol 13 (1·62), Herm 71 (0·87), Did 6 (0·92).

(3) Μέν without correlative δέ: Lk 8: 5f. ὁ μέν... καὶ ἕτερον (occasioned by an intervening development of the story; likewise Mk 4: 4f.), A 1: 1, 3: 13, 21, 17: 30, 27: 21; also cf. 2 C 11: 4, H 7: 11.

(4) A 28: 22 ('this much we do know'), R 11: 13. Origen, as the cod. Athous and his extant Lat. commentary show, and Eusebius read the better form πρῶτοι γὰρ ἐπιστεύθησαν instead of πρῶτον μὲν γὰρ ὅτι ἐπ. in R 3: 2. Class. exx. of contrast which is adequately implied by μέν but not actually stated may be found in K.-G. II 273, e.g. Hdt. 3.3 ἐμοὶ μέν ('at least') οὐ πιθανός. For the pap. s. Mayser II 3, 129 f.

(5) S. Godet on R 16: 19 σοφοὺς [μέν], G 2: 9 ἡμεῖς [μέν]. A 5: 23 μέν EP, om. SABD.

(6) Μέν...ἀλλά A 4: 16, R 14: 20, 1 C 14: 17. Μέν...πλήν Lk 22: 22 (cf. K.-G. II 271); Mt 17: 11f. Ἠλίας μὲν ἔρχεται...λέγω δὲ ὑμῖν is also related, cf. Mk 9: 12f. μέν (om. DLW)...ἀλλά..., where μέν means 'certainly, of course', and δέ (ἀλλά) an emphatic 'but'. In Jn 7: 12 οἱ μέν is followed by ἄλλοι (ἄ. δέ BTWX, οἱ δέ without ἔλεγον Chr) with the asyndeton of which Jn is so fond (§462(1)). H 12: 9 οὐ πολλῷ (πολύ) δέ (ScD*, the rest without δέ) is probably correct or nearly so.

(7) A 1: 15 ἦν δέ...(τε SAB al. is incorrect), 4: 13 ἐπεγίνωσκον δέ...(so D instead of τε).

(8) R 9: 30, 1 C 2: 6, Ph 2: 8.

(9) A 22: 29 καὶ ὁ χιλίαρχος δέ, Mt 16: 18 κἀγὼ δὲ σοὶ λέγω, Jn 8: 16 etc. (Tischendorf on 6: 51), etc. Καὶ πάντες δέ also Herm Vis 3.2.2, Man 4.4.4, 5.1.7, 12.6.5; καὶ μετὰ πάντων δέ Sim 5.3.4; καὶ ἀπὸ π. δέ 7.7, always with the meaning 'but (and) also all *others*' (§480(1)), except in A 2: 44 where the omission of καί (BEP) is accordingly to be preferred. On the position of δέ s. also §475(2). Cf. further καὶ οἱ λοιποὶ δέ Herm Sim 9.22.4, 23.2. Καί...δέ is common in the pap., especially in κἀγὼ δὲ ὑγίαινον (Mayser II 3, 131f.); δὲ καί...is likewise frequent (*ibid.* 132).

448. Ἀλλά. (1) It appears most frequently as the contrary to a preceding οὐ. The construction οὐ μόνον...ἀλλὰ καί also belongs here. (2) With an οὐ also used as the contrary to a preceding positive clause ('but not'): 1 C 10: 23 πάντα ἔξεστιν, ἀλλ' οὐ πάντα συμφέρει, also 5, Mt 24: 6. Moreover, without a negative preceding or following: 1 C 6: 11 καὶ ταῦτά τινες ἦτε, ἀλλὰ ἀπελούσασθε, ἀλλὰ ἡγιάσθητε, where 'but you are so no longer' may be easily supplied, followed by 'on the contrary...'. (3) At the beginning of a sentence with or without a negative: R 10: 16 ἀλλ' οὐ πάντες ὑπήκουσαν, with a stronger reference to the difference than δέ would have provided. Jn 8: 26 ἀλλ' ὁ πέμψας με...('but, yet'), 15: 21 ἀλλὰ ταῦτα ποιήσουσιν.... Cf. πλήν §449(1). (4) Ἀλλά may be used after a question to one's self as in classical: Jn 12: 27 τί εἴπω; πάτερ, σῶσόν με...; ἀλλὰ διὰ τοῦτο ἦλθον.... (5) Ἀλλά in an apodosis after εἰ, ἐάν, εἴπερ means 'yet, certainly, at least' (classical): 1 C 4: 15 ἐὰν μυρίους παιδαγωγοὺς ἔχητε ἐν Χριστῷ, ἀλλ᾽ οὐ πολλοὺς πατέρας. (6) Ἀλλά (ἀλλὰ καί, ἀλλά γε καί, ἀλλ᾽ οὐδέ) = 'not only this, but also', used to introduce an additional point in an emphatic way: 2 C 7: 11 πόσην κατηργάσατο ὑμῖν σπουδήν, ἀλλὰ ἀπολογίαν, ἀλλὰ ἀγανάκτησιν, ἀλλὰ φόβον... (six times), cf. Jn 16: 2. Ph 1: 18 χαίρω, ἀλλὰ καὶ χαρήσομαι, 1 C 3: 2 οὔπω γὰρ ἐδύνασθε, ἀλλ᾽ οὐδὲ ἔτι νῦν δύνασθε. (7) Elliptically ἀλλ᾽ ἵνα 'on the contrary (but) this happened (or a similar verb), in order that' = 'rather they were to be...'. (8) Ἀλλά (ἀλλ᾽ ἤ) = εἰ μή 'except'.—Mayser II 3, 116ff.; Rob. 1185f., 1186f.

(1) Οὐ...ἀλλά also means 'not so much...as' in which the first element is not entirely negated, but only toned down: Mk 9: 37 οὐκ ἐμὲ δέχεται, ἀλλὰ τὸν ἀποστείλαντά με, Mt 10: 20, Jn 12: 44, A 5: 4 etc. Οὐ μόνον...ἀλλά without καί if the second member includes the first: A 19: 26, 1 Jn 5: 6, or as in Ph 2: 12 ἀλλὰ νῦν πολλῷ μᾶλλον.... For elliptical οὐ μόνον δέ, ἀλλὰ καί s. §479(1).—A. Kuschke, ZNW 43 (1950/1) 262: 'relative negation' in the NT: Mt 9: 13, 15: 24, 18: 21f., Jn 7: 16 ('not...but').

(2) 1 C 3: 6 ἐγὼ ἐφύτευσα, Ἀπολλῶς ἐπότισεν, ἀλλὰ ὁ θεὸς ηὔξανεν ('but he who caused it to grow was not Apollos or I, but God'); 7: 7.

(3) R 10: 18f. ἀλλὰ λέγω..., 11: 4, 1 C 12: 24, 15: 35. Also before commands or requests: A 10: 20, 26: 16, Mt 9: 18, Mk 9: 22 etc. In Jn 16 the ἀλλά appears to belong in v. 3 (lat) not in 4 (where D* lat Chr omit it); on 16: 2 s. supra (6).

(4) A simpler form is found in Jn 7: 49, 1 C 10: 20. In multiple questions (with the answer in each case given or suppressed) Mk 11: 8f. = Lk 7: 24ff. τί ἐξήλθατε...; ...ἀλλὰ τί ἐξήλθατε...; etc. (class.). H 3: 16 is peculiar: τίνες...παρεπίκραναν; ἀλλ᾽ οὐ πάντες οἱ ἐξελθόντες ἐξ Αἰγύπτου..., where however ἀλλ᾽ (cf. sy) is probably due to a misunderstanding of the first τίνες as though it were τινές. Lk 17: 7f. is a different matter: τίς...ὃς...ἐρεῖ αὐτῷ...ἀλλ᾽ οὐχὶ ἐρεῖ αὐτῷ; 'and not rather' (D omits οὐχί, in which case the second part would not be interrogative).

(5) Mk 14: 29, 2 C 4: 16, 11: 6, (13: 4 v.l.), C 2: 5 etc.; cf. ἀλλά γε ὑμῖν εἰμι 1 C 9: 2 (§439(2)).

(6) Ἀλλὰ καί: 2 C 11: 1 ὄφελον ἀνείχεσθε...ἀλλὰ καὶ ἀνέχεσθε ('I will not only express the wish, but I forthwith entreat you' [ἀνέχεσθε taken as impera.], or 'but you have already done it' [ἀνέχ. taken as indic.]); Lk 12: 7, 16: 21, 24: 22, ἀλλά γε καί 24: 21 (§439(2)). Ἀλλ᾽ οὐδέ: Lk 23: 15, A 19: 2, 1 C 4: 3. G 2: 3 ἀλλ᾽ οὐδὲ Τίτος...ἠναγκάσθη περιτμηθῆναι is probably an afterthought ('moreover, even Titus was not'); acc. to Blass v. 3 fits better between vv. 6 and 7. Further ἀλλὰ μενοῦν γε (without γε BDF

al.) καὶ (om. S* [𝔓⁴⁶?]) ἡγοῦμαι Ph 3: 8; cf. § 450 (4).

(7) Mk 14: 49 ἀλλ᾽ ἵνα πληρωθῶσιν αἱ γραφαί = Mt 26: 56 τοῦτο δὲ ὅλον γέγονεν ἵνα πλ. αἱ γρ.; Jn 1: 8, 9: 3, 13: 18, 15: 25, 1 Jn 2: 19, Epict. 1.12.17; §480(5).

(8) Ἀλλ᾽ ἤ = εἰ μή: Lk 12: 51 οὐχί, λέγω ὑμῖν, ἀλλ᾽ ἤ (𝔓⁴⁵DΘ ἀλλά) διαμερισμόν ('nothing but'), 2 C 1: 15 οὐ γὰρ ἄλλα...ἀλλ᾽ (ἀλλ᾽ om. BFG) ἤ (om. 𝔓⁴⁶A) ἃ (om. AD*) ἀναγινώσκετε (ἀλλ᾽ ἤ is interpolated in 1 C 3: 5 DLP). 1 Clem 41.2 is somewhat different: οὐ πανταχοῦ...ἀλλ᾽ ἤ ἐν Ἱερουσαλὴμ μόνῃ ('but only'); Barn 2.7f. OT μὴ ἐγὼ ἐνετειλάμην...; ἀλλ᾽ ἤ ('no; rather') τοῦτο ἐνετειλάμην (from Jer 7: 22f. where the LXX has οὐκ ἐνετ...., ἀλλ᾽ ἤ τὸ ῥῆμα τοῦτο ἐνετ.); Barn 11.7 = LXX Ps 1: 4 (cf. 2); Dt 4: 12.— Ἀλλά = εἰ μή: Mk 4: 22 οὐ γάρ ἐστίν τι κρυπτόν, ἐὰν μὴ ἵνα (ὃ ἐὰν μή EFGH, ἀλλ᾽ ἵνα W) φανερωθῇ· οὐδὲ ἐγένετο ἀπόκρυφον, ἀλλ᾽ ἵνα ἔλθῃ εἰς φανερόν; so also Mt 20: 23. Also cf. Lk 8: 17 ὃ οὐ φανερὸν γενήσεται; ἵνα and ὅ = Aram. יִ (Zerwick, Graec. bibl. 99; Black, Aramaic Approach² 57f.). The reverse, εἰ μή for ἀλλά: Lk 4: 26, 27, cf. G 1: 7, 1 C 7: 17 (§376) and οὐκ εἴασεν ἡμᾶς εἰσελθεῖν..., εἰ μὴ γυνή τις...ἐδέξατο ἡμᾶς Acta Barn. 20 (L.-B. II 2, 299.22). The interchange of εἰ μή and ἀλλά is abetted by Aram., in the Gospels at any rate, since both are represented by אֶלָּא (Wellhausen, Einl.² 16f.; M.-H. 468). An important article is that of G. Harder, ThLZ 1954, 367–72.—Οὐκ (ἄλλος) ἀλλ᾽ ἤ, which is not uncommon in class. (K.-G. II 284f.; Denniston 24ff.), is a mixture of οὐκ ἄλλος..., ἀλλά (cf. 1 Clem 51.5 οὐ δι᾽ ἄλλην τινὰ αἰτίαν..., ἀλλὰ διὰ τό..., PTebt I 104.19 [92 BC]; without ἄλλος Mk 9: 8 οὐδένα εἶδον, ἀλλὰ τὸν Ἰησοῦν μόνον, LXX Gen 21: 26, Did 9.5. Both types have class. pars., K.-G. II 284 above) and οὐκ ἄλλος ἤ...(Homil Clem 16.20 οὐκ ἄλλου τινὸς ἤ τοῦ κτίσαντος τὸν κόσμον; the neut. οὐκ ἀλλ᾽ [= ἄλλο, ἄλλα] ἤ can easily be taken as οὐκ ἀλλὰ ἤ). Cf. a similar mixture οὐ...μᾶλλον ἀλλά 2 Clem 4.4 from οὐ...μᾶλλον ἤ and οὐ...ἀλλά. Interrogative: ἐπὶ τίνα (the answer ἐπ᾽ οὐδένα is expected)...ἀλλ᾽ ἤ 1 Clem 13.4.—Εἰ μή = ἀλλά also in the inscrip. of Silko (Dit., Or. 201.20f. [vi AD]) οὐκ ἀφῶ αὐτοὺς καθεσθῆναι εἰς τὴν σκιάν, εἰ μὴ ὑπὸ ἡλίου ἔξω; Raderm.² 13f. notwithstanding, there is no connection with the humorous Att. idiom μὰ τοὺς θεούς (or something similar), εἰ μή...γε (the references to Aristoph. in Dit., op. cit. n. 33) 'certainly—unless (on the contrary)'. Cf. Mayser II 3, 118f.; Ljungvik, Syntax 32f.; E. Fraenkel, KZ 54 (1927) 298f.; ἀλλ᾽ ἤ in Arist., Cook Wilson, ClQ 3 (1909) 121–4; ἀλλ᾽ εἰ μή = εἰ μή Wifstrand, K. Hum. Vet.-samf. i Lund, Årsber. 1932/3 I 24; Lat. nisi = sed Löfstedt, Skrifter K. Hum. Vet.-samf. i Lund 23 (1936) 29–35. Further exx. of the same type of confusion: 2 Clem 7.1 οὐ πάντες στεφανοῦνται εἰ μή...from οὐ πάντες... ἀλλά and οὐ...εἰ μή; ἄλλως οὐ...εἰ (ἐὰν) μή Herm

Sim 7.3, 9.12.5 (οὐ...εἰ μή just previously), 6, Epict., Ench. 31.2 from οὐ...εἰ (ἐὰν) μή and ἄλλως οὐ...ἤ (ἤ ἐὰν...). Cf. Passow-Crönert 302.39 (but in Xen., An. 6.6.10 ἄλλως = 'otherwise than had previously been said').

449. Πλήν. (1) Πλήν means 'nevertheless, however' in Mt and Lk (but not Acts): Mt 26: 39 (Lk 22: 42) πλὴν οὐχ ὡς ἐγὼ θέλω, ἀλλ' ὡς σύ = Mk 14: 36 ἀλλ' οὐχ etc. Πλήν rather than ἀλλά (§ 448(3)) was evidently the really colloquial word for this idea (Schmid I 133). (2) Πλήν means more nearly 'only, in any case' in Paul, used to conclude a discussion and emphasize what is essential.—Rob. 1187.

(1) Mt 11: 22, 24, 26: 64 πλὴν λέγω ὑμῖν, but Mk 9: 13 ἀλλὰ λέγω ὑμῖν; cf. Mt 17: 12 λέγω δὲ ὑμῖν. Mt 18: 7 πλὴν οὐαί = Lk 17: 1 οὐαὶ δέ (πλὴν οὐαί SBDL). Lk 12: 56 πλήν 𝔓⁴⁵D, pm. δέ. Cf. Homil Clem 9.18.4, 11.28.1, 18.6.3. Πλήν is even used for ἀλλά correlated with a negative: Lk 23: 28 μὴ κλαίετε ἐπ' ἐμέ, πλὴν ἐφ' ἑαυτὰς κλαίετε (ἀλλ' D), 12: 31 (D ζητεῖτε δέ). Mk and Acts use πλήν only as a prep. 'except' as in class. (§ 216(2)); πλὴν ὅτι 'except that' (class.) A 20: 23. For Lk 22: 22 s. § 447(6). Πλήν 'nevertheless' ZenP Cairo III 59454.10 (iii BC), IV 59647.45 (iii BC), UPZ I 110.207 (164 BC), PTebt I 27.42 (113 BC); for Polyb., Plut. s. L.-S. πλήν B III 2. 'Except' without governing a case, Homil Clem 6.3.1 οὐδὲν πλὴν χάος καὶ...μεῖξις.

(2) 1 C 11: 11, E 5: 33, Ph 3: 16, 4: 14; cf. Arist. (Bonitz, Index Aristotelicus s.v. πλήν). Rev 2: 25, likewise (?)Ph 1: 18 τί γάρ; πλήν (om. B) ὅτι (om. DEKL) παντὶ τρόπῳ...Χριστὸς καταγγέλλεται, (+ ἀλλά 𝔓⁴⁶) καὶ ἐν τούτῳ χαίρω, where τί γάρ (like R 3: 3) = 'what of it?' and πλήν (with or without ὅτι) appears to mean 'in any case' and is unnecessary anyway (for ὅτι...καὶ ἐν τούτῳ cf. R 11: 7 τί οὖν; ὅ...τοῦτο). Homil Clem 16.11.2 πλὴν οὐχ ἕνα 'everything else,) only not a single one', 10.17.2 πλήν...γελᾶτε 'but you just laugh'. Πλήν 'only' in the LXX (Johannessohn II 343 n. 2), Preisigke, Sammelbuch III 6994.28 (ii BC mid.).

450. Less common adversative conjunctions. (1) Μέντοι 'however': οὐ(-δεὶς) μέντοι Jn 4: 27, 7: 13, 20: 5, 21: 4 (Herm Sim 6.1.6 A, om. PMich), ὅμως μέντοι Jn 12: 42. (2) Ὅμως, in addition to the instance cited above, appears only twice more, used both times in a peculiar way: 1 C 14: 7 ὅμως τὰ ἄψυχα φωνὴν διδόντα... ἐὰν διαστολὴν φθόγγου μὴ δῷ, πῶς γνωσθήσεται...; G 3: 15 ὅμως ἀνθρώπου κεκυρωμένην διαθήκην οὐδεὶς ἀθετεῖ. (3) Καίτοι class. 'and yet' (so LXX 4 Macc 2: 6, καίτοιγε Diogn 8. 3), rarely with a participle 'although' (§ 425(1)). In the NT καίτοιγε (§ 439(1)) appears in parenthesis: Jn 4: 2

καίτοιγε Ἰησοῦς οὐκ ἐβάπτιζεν 'although John did not baptize'. (4) Μὲν οὖν is used in classical in replies either to heighten or correct (with compound force, s. Smyth § 2901a, b), and always in such a way that another word precedes the μέν (as elsewhere). In this position in the NT only 1 C 6: 4 βιωτικὰ μὲν οὖν κριτήρια; cf. 7 (οὖν om. 𝔓⁴⁶ S*D*). Μενοῦν (γε) is used elsewhere in the same sense but stands at the beginning of the sentence.

(1) It appears only in scattered passages outside of Jn: 2 T 2: 19 ὁ μέντοι στερεὸς θεμέλιος; in Ja 2: 8 and Jd 8 it is weakened to 'but'. Mayser II 3, 169f.

(2) 1 C 14: 7 and G 3: 15 are usually explained as cases of displaced ὅμως (Fritzsche), thus G 3: 15 = καίπερ ἀνθρώπου, ὅμως οὐδεὶς ἀθετεῖ 'even though only a man's will, nevertheless...', perhaps like Xen., Cyr. 6.1.26 σὺν σοὶ ὅμως καὶ ἐν τῇ πολεμίᾳ ὄντες θαρροῦμεν (K.-G. II 95f.; Ed. Fraenkel, NGG 1933, 324f. n.). Since both times, however, a comparison is introduced and in 1 C 14: 7 οὕτως also follows, we have to do rather with the earlier ὁμῶς 'equally', and it is therefore to be translated 'also, likewise' (Wilke, Rhetorik 225 writes ὁμῶς in 1 C). Cf. Homil Clem 1.15.4 (= Ps.-Clem., Epit. 1.14) καὶ ὁμῶς (= ἅμα 'at the same time'; Recognitions: ὡς ἔμαθον καὶ τῷ πυλῶνι ἐπέστην, 19.23.1 καὶ ὁμῶς (= ὁμοίως) τοιαῦτά τινα μυρία..., cf. 3.15.3; 13.1.1, 2, 13.8.2, 16.5.1 ὁμῶς 'at once', 16.7.9 ὁμῶς 'likewise', 15.5.4 καὶ ὁμῶς ταῦτα εἰπών.

(3) Καίτοιγε is independent in A 14: 17 (cf. § 425(1)), although it can also be translated 'although' here. On A 17: 27f. s. § 425(1); καίτοι with ptcp. H 4: 3 (§ 425(1)).

(4) At the beginning (Phryn. 342): Lk 11: 28 μενοῦν (with γε B³CD al.) μακάριοι οἱ...('rather'), R 9: 20 (without μενοῦν γε 𝔓⁴⁶, without γε only B), 10: 18 μενοῦν γε (om. FG); ἀλλὰ μενοῦν (γε) Ph 3: 8 (§ 448(6)). For inferential or continuative μὲν οὖν s. § 451(1). Diogn 7.4 οὐμενοῦν 'not at all' (reply); 5.3 οὐ μήν 'indeed not' (class.). Class. καὶ μήν 'and yet' does not appear in the NT, but in Barn 9.6. Herm Man 4.1.8, 5.1.7 to heighten the reply, approximately = immo (class., K.-G. II 137).

(iv) *Consecutive (inferential) co-ordinating conjunctions*

451. (1) **Οὖν,** one of the more frequent particles in the NT, is the most common of these. It is fairly well distributed in all books, although it is far commoner in the narrative books and commonest by far in Jn (of the Johannine Epistles only 3 Jn 8; it is interpolated in 1 Jn 2: 24, 4: 19). It does not always furnish a strictly causal connection, but may be used more loosely as a temporal connective in the continuation or resumption of a narrative. In Acts, Lk is in the habit of emphasizing οὖν in a narrative sentence beginning with a noun or pronoun (or articular participle) with μέν, which need not be followed by a contrasting clause with δέ. After parenthetical remarks οὖν indicates a return to the main theme (resumptive). Interrogative οὐκοῦν 'so, then' (K.-G. II 163ff.) is found only in Jn 18: 37 οὐκοῦν βασιλεὺς εἶ σύ; (probably *ipsissima verba*). For μὲν οὖν, μενοῦν 'rather' s. §450(4). (2) Ἄρα 'so, therefore, consequently' is used, especially by Paul, as the second word in the sentence, as in classical (e.g. R 7: 21 εὑρίσκω ἄρα); but he also places it first, contrary to classical usage, as (a) the only conjunction, (b) strengthened by οὖν. (c) The strengthened form ἄρα γε is also placed first in the NT, (d) and ἄρα (always simple) may be used in an apodosis after a protasis with εἰ. (3) Τοιγαροῦν (class.) rarely begins a sentence; τοίνυν is not much more frequent. (4) Δή, though rare, is used in accordance with classical usage in sentences containing a command or exhortation; it is used differently only in Mt 13: 23 ὃς δὴ καρποφορεῖ 'he is just the man who' (good classical usage; D has τότε for ὃς δή, it *et*). UGosp 1.37 ὁ δὴ κ̄ς̄. (5) Διό (διόπερ) is properly used to introduce a subordinate relative clause (from δι' ὅ), but this limitation has been lost. (6) Ὅθεν is similar, expressing a consecutive relationship like our 'whence'.

(1) Μὲν οὖν in Acts: 1: 6 οἱ μὲν οὖν συνελθόντες..., 18 οὗτος μὲν οὖν..., 2: 41 οἱ μὲν οὖν ἀποδεξάμενοι, 9: 31 αἱ μὲν οὖν ἐκκλησίαι..., etc. It is sometimes used here to state further events, sometimes to summarize what has been previously narrated in order to form a transition to a new subject. Cf. class. K.-G. II 157f., Mayser II 3, 152f. It is used in this way in Lk 3: 18 πολλὰ μὲν οὖν καὶ ἕτερα παρακαλῶν εὐηγγελίζετο τὸν λαόν (the only ex. of μὲν οὖν in the Gosp. of Lk). Simple οὖν after a ptcp. A 10: 23, (15: 2 v.l.), 16: 11, 25: 17 (cf. 26: 22 etc.), in Lk only 23: 16 = 22, D also 5: 7. Resumptive οὖν after parenthetical remarks: Jn 4: 45, 6: 24, 1 C 8: 4, 11: 20 (also class.; class. resumptive δὲ οὖν does not appear). Οὐκοῦν 'therefore' (self-evident deduction) Barn 5.3, 11, 12 etc., Diogn 2.9. Merlier, Rev. Ét. gr. 46 (1933) 204ff. regards Jn 18: 37a (with οὐκοῦν) as an addition. J. R. Mantey, Newly Discovered Meanings for οὖν (Exp. VIII 22 [1921] 205–14), needlessly finds the meaning 'however' for οὖν in Jn 20: 30, Lk 14: 34, A 8: 25 (and pap.).—Rob. 1191f. (2) (a) R 10: 17 ἄρα (ἄ. οὖν FG) ἡ πίστις ἐξ ἀκοῆς, 1 C 15: 18, 2 C 7: 12 etc. (H 4: 9). (b) R 5: 18, 7: 3, 25, 8: 12, 9: 16, 18 etc., G 6: 10, E 2: 19 (om. οὖν

FG), 1 Th 5: 6, 2 Th 2: 15. (c) Mt 7: 20, 17: 26, A 11: 18 EHLP (al. ἄρα as in Lk 11: 48, for which Mt 23: 31 has ὥστε with the indic.). (d) Mt 12: 28 = Lk 11: 20; 2 C 5: 14 (S𝖼C* al.; most witnesses omit εἰ, but it could easily drop out before εἰς), G 2: 21 (17 is interrogative, therefore ἄρα, §440(2)), 3: 29, H 12: 8. For εἴπερ ἄρα s. §454(2); ἐπεὶ ἄρα §456(3); ἄρα (ἆρα) in interrogative clauses §440(2). Ἄρα in the Ptol. pap. only Eudoxos (literary); Mayser II 3, 119.—Rob. 1189f.

(3) Τοιγαροῦν 1 Th 4: 8, H 12: 1 (𝔓⁴⁶ τοίγαρ). Τοίνυν as the second word (as in class.) Lk 20: 25 ACPW al., 1 C 9: 26 (not genuine in Ja 2: 24); as the first word (unclass.; later authors also use it correctly, s. Lob. Phryn. 342f.) Lk 20: 25 SBL (D omits as do all witnesses in Mk 12: 17; οὖν Mt 22: 21), H 13: 13, 1 Clem 15. 1.

(4) 1 C 6: 20 δοξάσατε δή ('so') τὸν θεόν (asyndeton without δή S* d Ir), 15: 49 𝔓⁴⁶ φορέσωμεν δή (om. δή pm.); at the beginning of a statement ('come now') Lk 2: 15, A 13: 2, 15: 36. For δήπου s. §441. For ᾧ (οἵῳ) δήποτε [Jn] 5: 4 s. §303. Mayser II 3, 134; Rob. 1149.

(5) Διό: Mt 27: 8; Lk 1: 35 (A*W διότι is incorrect; it interchanges at times with διό), where the combination διὸ καί appears, one which is common e.g. in Arist., Ath. and the pap. (Mayser II 3, 135); διὸ οὐδέ Lk 7: 7 is a corresponding negative form. Διό (διὸ καί) is more common in Acts and the Epistles. Διόπερ 1 C 8: 13, 10: 14 (14: 13 most witnesses have διό). Molland, Serta Rudbergiana (Oslo, 1931) 43–52 (syntactical observations on 'illogical' διό in connection with R 2: 1; cf. PhW 1932, 657).

(6) Ὅθεν Mt 14: 7, A 26: 19, now and then in Heb, e.g. 2: 17, 3: 1; also in Arist., Ath. (3.2 etc.) and pap. (Mayser II 3, 148). Homil Clem e.g. 19.19.4, 20.8; 20.4.2, 6.1, 7.6, 13.3. Out of the λοιπόν used with asyndeton to begin a sentence 'further, as far as the rest is concerned, now' (cf. §160) there developed an inferential 'therefore' in Hell. (MGr): Polyb., IEph 11.1, Epict. (cf. M.-M.), pap. (Mayser II 3, 146.5ff.). A. Cavallin, Eranos 39 (1941) 121–44; A. Fridrichsen, K. Hum. Vet.-samf. i Uppsala, Årsbok 1943, 24–8: Mk 14: 41 = Mt 26: 45 'So you are still sleeping!', 1 C 4: 2 ὧδε λοιπόν 'in this connection, then; furthermore', 2 C 13: 11 'finally', H 10: 13 'by now'.

(v) *Causal co-ordinating conjunctions*

452. Γάρ is one of the most common particles in the NT, being used relatively least often in Jn, especially in the Johannine Epistles; it is also rare in Rev. Its use in the NT conforms to classical. (1) Γάρ is frequently used in questions where English must often leave it untranslated and add 'then, pray' or a prefix (s. Bauer s.v.): Mt 27: 23

τί γὰρ κακὸν ἐποίησεν; 'Why, what evil has he done?' (RSV). (2) In replies it affirms what was asked (giving the reason for a tacit 'yes'): 'to be sure, just so' (K.-G. II 330 f.): 1 C 9: 10 ἢ δι' ἡμᾶς πάντως λέγει (rhetorical question); δι' ἡμᾶς γὰρ ἐγράφη. (3) Καὶ γάρ 'for even', '—yes, even', in which each particle retains its own force (= ἐπειδὴ καί).—Rob. 1190 f.

(1) A 8: 31 πῶς γὰρ ἂν δυναίμην; It is here the reason for an unexpressed denial or refusal; or it may indicate the reason for a reproach (expressed or unexpressed) as in Mt 9: 5 τί γάρ ἐστιν εὐκοπώτερον..., 23: 17 μωροὶ καὶ τυφλοί, τίς γάρ..., A 19: 35 etc., unless it should be rendered literally by 'for which' as in Lk 22: 27. C. H. Bird, Some γάρ-clauses in St Mark's Gospel, JTS n.s. 4 (1953) 171–87.

(2) 1 Th 2: 20; cf. an analogous use in the repeated assertion R 15: 26 f. ηὐδόκησαν γάρ...ηὐδόκησαν γάρ, καὶ.... It is used somewhat differently after an indignant question in A 16: 37 οὐ γάρ non profecto (class.; s. Blass ad loc.), and again differently in the retort of the man born blind Jn 9: 30: ἐν τούτῳ γάρ (οὖν D) τὸ θαυμαστόν ἐστιν, ὅτι..., which is the equivalent of an interrogative οὐ γὰρ ἐν τούτῳ...; (cf. supra (1)).

(3) The well-known use of καὶ γάρ for etenim 'for' (K.-G. II 338), in which καί has completely lost its force, is sometimes suggested for passages like 1 C 5: 7, 11: 9, 12: 13 (where οὕτως καὶ ὁ Χρ. precedes); but here, too, καί = 'also', although it refers to the whole sentence and not to a single idea. The meaning etenim is more easily conceded for H 5: 12 and 12: 29. Herm Sim 9.8.2 καὶ γάρ (etenim) καὶ ('also') οὗτοι.... On 2 C 13: 4 s. §457. The corresponding negative form is οὐδὲ γάρ R 8: 7 'for it can not either', but in Jn 8: 42 (where D has οὐ γάρ) it rather = neque enim, to which etenim is the corresponding positive form (acc. to Chr sy^s καὶ ἀπ' ἐμαυτοῦ οὐκ). In τε γάρ R 7: 7, there is no close relationship between the two; if τε and γάρ really are genuine, anacoluthon is to be assumed (§443(3)). Mayser II 3, 122 f. F. W. Grosheide, Καὶ γάρ in het NT (ThStudiën 33 [1915] 108–10).

For co-ordinating concessive conjunctions (ὅμως, καίτοι) s. §450.

(C) Subordinating (Hypotactic) Conjunctions

453. Comparative conjunctions. They are ὡς, ὥσπερ (καθώσπερ H 5: 4, 2 C 3: 18 B) and καθώς, a Hellenistic and MGr word common to virtually every author. Phryn. 425 strongly objects to καθώς and recommends either καθό (R 8: 26, 2 C 8: 12, 1 P 4: 13) or καθά (only Mt 27: 10 OT; also in Lk 1: 2 according to D Eus, surely rightly, cf.

§95(1) on παρέδοσαν in the same verse; IMag 10.1) instead. Καθάπερ, which is also Attic, is found only in Paul and Hebrews. Also cf. §456(4) and Hermann 321 ff. The uses of ὡς are so diverse and in part so well known and commonplace that some of them are omitted here. (1) Correlative ὡς (ὥσπερ, καθώς, καθάπερ)...οὕτως (or καί [e.g. Mt 6: 10] or οὕτως καί). (2) 'Ως and especially καθώς used to introduce a sentence may have something of the meaning 'because'. (3) When used to introduce single words or phrases, ὡς may be replaced by ὡσεί, with much variation between them in the MSS; ὡσπερεί and ὡσάν likewise, though less often. (4) The use of ὡς with a predicate is very extensive.—Rob. 1192 f., 966–9.

Καθώς appears sporadically beginning with Hdt. 9.82 (Aly, Glotta 15 [1927] 95 f.); pap. (more often beginning ii BC) s. Mayser I¹ 485; II 2, 440; II 3, 92 n. 4. Καθάπερ R 10: 15 B, 11: 8 SB (the rest have καθώς both times), 12: 4 𝔓⁴⁶SAB (ὥσπερ D*EFG), but all have καθάπερ e.g. 2 C 1: 14, 3: 13, 18 (not B).

(1) Καί can be added to ὡς and can even stand in both members of the comparison: R 1: 13 ἵνα τινὰ καρπὸν σχῶ καὶ ἐν ὑμῖν, καθὼς καὶ ἐν τοῖς λοιποῖς ἔθνεσιν, Mt 18: 33 etc. (class., K.-G. II 256). 'Ως...καί (for οὕτως καί) Plut., Mor. 39 E as in Mt 6: 10.

(2) R 1: 28 ('just as' = 'since', quandoquidem), 1 C 1: 6, 5: 7, E 1: 4, Ph 1: 7 (Mt 6: 12 ὡς καὶ ἡμεῖς ἀφήκαμεν = Lk 11: 4 καὶ γὰρ αὐτοὶ ἀφίομεν). Cf. ὡς with a ptcp. §425(3, 4). Acc. to Bonaccorsi 597 καθώς in A 15: 14 and 3 Jn 3 is used to introduce indirect discourse (?).

(3) Ὡσπερεί (comparative) only 1 C 15: 8 (ὥσπερ D*) and v.l. 4: 13; ὡσάν (ὡς ἄν) only 2 C 10: 9 ὡσὰν ('so to speak') ἐκφοβεῖν, cf. §§396 and 425(5). Herm Sim 9.9.7 οὕτω...ὡσὰν ἐξ ἑνὸς λίθου ('as if'; subsequently ὡς also). Ὡσεί esp. in the Gospels and Acts, also Hermas (e.g. Sim 6.2.5, 9.11.5); also before numerical expressions = 'approximately' Mt 14: 21 (D ὡς, om. W), Jn 4: 6 (the evidence favors ὡς) etc. (class.; pap. s. Mayser II 3, 167). With ὡς ἐτῶν δώδεκα Lk 8: 42 (ὡσεὶ ἐτῶν τριάκοντα 3: 23) cf. the common ὡς ἐτῶν...in the pap. (§165). 'Ωσάν = ὡς in the pap. (Mlt. 167 n. 3 [261 n. 2]), Diodor. etc. (Raderm.² 203; Ljungvik, Syntax 98); MGr (ὡ)σάν = ὡς. Herm Vis 4.1.4 is not clear: ὡς ἦχος φωνῆς μοι ἀπεκρίθη 'something like an echoing voice answered me' or 'he answered me like an echoing voice'.

(4) With a predicate nom.: Mt 22: 30 ὡς ἄγγελοι θεοῦ εἰσιν, 18: 3 ἐὰν μὴ γένησθε ὡς τὰ παιδία, 1 C 7: 8 ἐὰν μείνωσιν ὡς κἀγώ. With a predicate acc.: Lk 15: 19 ποίησόν με ὡς ἕνα τῶν μισθίων σου, and esp. with λογίζεσθαι, ἡγεῖσθαι etc., s. §157(3). All these are unclass.; cf. on the other hand LXX Gen 3: 5 ἔσεσθε ὡς θεοί = class. ἰσόθεοι (or ἴσα καὶ θεοί acc. to Thuc. 3.14; cf. εἶναι ἴσα θεῷ Ph 2: 6 and §434(1)).—Τὴν ἴσην ὡς

καὶ ἡμῖν A 11: 17; cf. class. K.-G. I 413 n. 11.—Ὡς in Mk 13: 34, and ὥσπερ γάρ (om. γάρ D) in Mt 25: 14 are used to introduce a parable with neither a following correlative nor any close connection to what precedes; cf. §482. Ὥσπερ γάρ 'it is indeed so that...' Plut., Mor. 7c (Almqvist 46).—Ὡς τάχιστα A 17: 15 class. (literary; §244(1)).—Πορεύεσθαι ὡς (ἕως SABE) ἐπὶ τὴν θάλασσαν A 17: 14 with the Hell. ὡς ἐπί = versus (Polyb. 1.29.1 etc.; ὡς ἐπὶ Ἀντιόχειαν Homil Clem 12.1.1. S. Wettstein on A 17: 14; Radermacher, Philol. 60 [1901] 495f. Ὡς πρὸς ἀνατολάς = ad solis orientis regionem Monum. Ancyr. c. 26; but ἕως ἐπὶ τὴν κοινὴν ἡμῶν ὁδόν PMagd 29.10 [218 BC], ἕως [ὡς V] ἐπὶ τὸ ὀχύρωμα LXX 1 Macc 5:29, ἕως εἰς Βηθλεέμ 1 Km 16: 1, 20: 28, ἕως εἰς τὸν αἰῶνα 2 Km 7: 13, ἕως ἐπὶ [A, εἰς V] τὴν ἰδίαν οἰκίαν 3 Macc 7: 18, ἕως εἰς βορρᾶ(ν) BGU III 1002.6 [55 BC]); on the interchange of ὡς and ἕως also s. §455(2, 3).—For ὡς with a ptcp. and in abbreviated clauses s. §425(3, 4); in exclamations §436; ὡς (ὡς ὅτι) in assertions §396; temporal §455(2); with the inf. §391(1). Ὡσαύτως s. §12(1).

454. Conditional conjunctions (cf. §§370ff.). (1) Εἰ is often interrogative, 'whether'. (2) Εἴπερ 'if indeed, if after all' in Paul (ἐάνπερ Hebrews) with reference to a further condition (or fact). (3) The correlatives εἴτε...εἴτε (ἐάν τε...ἐάν τε twice R 14: 8) appear only in Paul and 1 P, either with a finite verb or more frequently in abbreviated expressions without a verb (§446; class. K.-G. II 300, 2d). (4) Εἰ μέν... εἰ δέ, e.g. A 18: 14f. At Lk 13: 9 the thoroughly classical suppression of the first apodosis is to be noted (cf. Mayser II 3, 8f.): κἂν μὲν ποιήσῃ καρπόν (scil. 'so much the better)· εἰ δὲ μήγε, ἐκκόψεις αὐτήν. (5) Εἰ after formulae used to introduce oaths is Hebraizing = 'not' (אִם, §372(4)).

(1) So also after θαυμάζειν Mk 15: 44 (class.) instead of ὅτι which is used elsewhere (cf. §372(3)). But in 1 Jn 3: 13 εἰ = 'if' and has no closer connection with θαυμάζειν than with any other verb. For εἰ in direct and indirect questions as well as εἰ to express expectation (also εἴ πως si forte) s. §§368; 375; 386(2); 440(3).
(2) Εἴπερ R 3: 30 (v.l. ἐπείπερ), 8: 9, 17, 2 Th 1: 6; also 1 P 2: 3. Ἐάνπερ H 3: 14, (3: 6 v.l.), 6: 3. In 1 C 8: 5f. καὶ γὰρ εἴπερ εἰσὶν λεγόμενοι θεοί..., ἀλλ' ἡμῖν εἷς θεός is concessive 'however much', as in class. Hom. (K.-G. II 489f.). Εἴγε is used similarly, but implies a more definite assumption (G. Hermann), s. §439(2). 1 C 15: 15 ὃν οὐκ ἤγειρεν, εἴπερ ἄρα ('if, as they say, it is true that...') νεκροὶ οὐκ ἐγείρονται (the not indispensable clause εἴπερ... ἐγείρ. is missing in DE and in other witnesses: is the omission original or due to homoioteleuton [cf. 16]?

The class. use of ἄρα 'as they say' is striking). G 6: 3 𝔓46 εἴπερ (pm. εἰ γάρ).
(3) 1 C 10: 31 'whether...or'. With the subj. s. §372(3). Without verb: 3: 21f. πάντα γὰρ ὑμῶν ἐστιν, εἴτε Παῦλος εἴτε Ἀπολλῶς εἴτε Κηφᾶς etc.: 'whether one mentions, whether it be, whether it concerns' (cf. 2 C 8: 23 εἴτε ὑπὲρ Τίτου, κοινωνὸς ἐμός etc., but then the continuation is in the nom.). 1 C 13: 8, R 12: 6ff. ἔχοντες δὲ χαρίσματα...εἴτε προφητείαν (scil. ἔχοντες), κατὰ τὴν...etc. The sense of εἴτε...εἴτε comes very close to that of καὶ...καί in such passages and the two constructions are in accord. This passage concludes with asyndeton in 12: 8 as do enumerations elsewhere (R 2: 17–20; §460(3)): ὁ μεταδιδοὺς ἐν ἁπλότητι etc.; cf. Ljungvik 68. In Ph 1: 18 εἰ (pm. εἴτε)...εἴτε 𝔓46 is incorrect.
(4) For εἰ δὲ μή (γε) (abbreviation of the second protasis) s. §439(1); on εἰ (ἐὰν) μή (τι) 'except, except that' §§376; 428(3). Εἰ μή H 6: 14 CDᵇLᶜᵒʳʳ lat for εἰ (ἦ) μήν (§441(1)). On Lk 13: 9 cf. K.-G. II 484f., PHib I 47.28 (256 BC) εἰ μὲν ἀπέσταλκας εἰς Δικωμίαν. εἰ δὲ μή...; Epict. 1.24.14, Ench. 29.7.
(5) Mk 8: 12 ἀμὴν λέγω ὑμῖν, εἰ δοθήσεται τῇ γενεᾷ ταύτῃ σημεῖον (cf. Mt 16: 4, main clause with οὐ; H 3: 11 = 4: 3, 5 OT. Εἰ μή 'it will certainly' R 14: 11 OT acc. to D*FG is comparable (v.l. ὅτι = LXX Is 45: 23 where εἰ μή also appears [S*B] for ἦ [εἰ] μήν Ziegler, but only before ἐξελεύσεται earlier in the verse [nothing corresponding in Hebrew]). N. D. Coleman, Some Noteworthy Uses of εἰ or εἶ in Hellenistic Greek, with a Note on St Mark 8: 12 (JTS 28 [1927] 159–67). Björck, Arbeiten und Mitteilungen 2 (1936) 6f., gives pars. for this εἰ in class., Swedish and English (which, however, do not contain a definite prediction). Cf. Rob. 1023f. and Bauer s.v. εἰ IV and §482 for the aposiopesis involved in the suppression of the apodosis.—On concessive εἰ καί, ἐὰν καί s. §374.

455. Temporal conjunctions. (1) Those denoting 'when' are ὅτε, ὅταν and less frequently ἐπάν. Paul employs ἡνίκα as an exception in 2 C 3: 15f. (1 Clem 57.4 OT), which strictly refers to an hour or season of the year, but already in Attic is used interchangeably with ὅτε. Ὁπότε is also rare, if correct at all. (2) Moreover, ὡς is not infrequently used in the narrative of Lk (Gospel and Acts) and Jn. Paul uses ὡς ἄν with the subjunctive as the equivalent of ὅταν with the subjunctive (MGr σάν 'if, as'). (3) 'While, as long as': ἕως (class.) is rare, otherwise ἕως ὅτου Mt 5: 25 (ἕως having become a preposition, §216(3); ἕως οὗ only means 'until' as in classical), ἄχρις οὗ (A 27: 33, H 3: 13), ἐν ᾧ (Mk 2: 19, Lk 5: 34, Jn 5: 7), and ἐφ' ὅσον χρόνον (also without ἐφ' or χρόνον) R 7: 1, Mt 9: 15, Mk 2: 19, etc. Μέχρι μὲν ὅτε οὐκ ᾔδειν 'as

long as I did not know' Homil Clem 18.21.2.—
Rob. 970–8.

(1) Ἐπεί and ἐπειδή are causal, as is ἐπειδήπερ;
temporal ἐπειδή only Lk 7: 1 (v.l. ἐπεί and ὅτε).
Ἐπάν Mt 2: 8 (ὅταν D), Lk 11: 22 (ἐάν D) and in 11: 34
par. to ὅταν (D ὅταν for ἐπάν). Ἡνίκα is literary, but
also LXX (e.g. Ex 1: 10, Dt 7: 12); 2 C 3: 16 from
Ex 34: 34 and accordingly in 3: 15. Ὁπότε ἐπείνασεν
Lk 6: 3 AEHK al. (ὅτε SBCDLW al. as in Mt, Mk),
ὁπότε ἔπεμψεν Barn 12.9 (ὁπόταν 2). Ἐπεί and
ὁπότε are not found in MGr.

(2) Ὡς, e.g. Lk 1: 23 ὡς ἐπλήσθησαν αἱ ἡμέραι,
Jn 2: 9 ὡς δὲ ἐγεύσατο. Class. also (Hermann 263f.);
LXX, esp. 1 Macc (Wilke-Grimm). Ὡς ἄν R 15: 24
'on my imminent journey to Spain', 1 C 11: 34
'when I come (shall come)', Ph 2: 23. Ὡς ἂν δέ μέ
τις παρυβρίσει..., μήτε ἐγ γῆς καρπὸν λάβοιτο Inscr.
Ponti Eux. IV 342.9ff. (Panticapaeum iii AD). With
pres. indic. Lk 12: 58 ὡς ('when') ὑπάγεις...ἐπ' ἄρχοντα, ἐν τῇ ὁδῷ (Mt 5: 25 differs, having ἕως ὅτου; in
Lk's case ἕως ὑπάγεις with ἐν τῇ ὁδῷ would have been
tautological); G 6: 10 (2 Clem 9.7, ISm 9.1) ὡς καιρὸν
ἔχομεν (-ωμεν SB*) cum 'now while' (but ὡς is more
likely = ἕως, s. infra (3); s. §383(2) on ἕως with the
subj.). With ὡς ἄν cf. LXX (e.g. Josh 2: 14), pap.
(e.g. ὡς ἂν λάβῃς PHib I 59.2 [247 BC], ὡς ἂν εὐκαιρήσω
UPZ I 71.18 [152 BC], s. Witkowski, Epistulae on
no. 47.18; Horn 133; Mayser II 1, 271f., 274, 275).
Ὡς ἐάν Herm Vis 3.8.9, 13.2, ὡς ἐὰν βλέπῃς PFay I
111.16 (95/6 AD). Temporal ὡς with the subj. has
only weak class. pars.: Hdt. 4.172 τῶν δὲ ὡς ἕκαστος
οἱ μειχθῇ (without ἄν), διδοῖ δῶρον. Points of contact
between temporal ὡς 'now that', causal ὡς 'since
(while)' and ἕως 'while still': 2 Clem 9.7 ὡς ἔχομεν
καιρὸν τοῦ ἰαθῆναι (s. supra), 8.1 ὡς ἐσμὲν ἐπὶ γῆς,
I Rom 2.2 ὡς ἔτι θυσιαστήριον ἕτοιμόν ἐστιν. Also cf.
Lat. dum 'while, as long as', and then 'because'.
Ὡς ἐπί is another confusion of ἕως and ὡς; §453(4).

(3) Jn 9: 4 ἕως ἡμέρα ἐστίν (ὡς C*W), cf. 12: 35f.
(the pres. also appears with ἕως 'until': Mk 6: 45,
Jn 21: 22, 23, 1 T 4: 13; §383(1)), where ABD al. have
ὡς in v. 35 (S also in 36), which does not appear to be
impossible in light of the two exx. cited above;
nevertheless the sense 'as long as' appears to suit
better, at least in 35. Exx. of ὡς instead of ἕως in
Radermacher, Philol. 60 (1901) 495f.; also cf.
2 Clem 8.1 (2 with ἕως), Anacreontea 30.13 Hiller-
Crusius (date uncertain) ὡς ἔτι ζῶ = ἕως, Soph., Aj.
1117, OC 1361, Ph 1330 acc. to some MSS, ὡς ἐπί
§453(4) and finally MGr ὡς 'until'. The two are
hardly confused elsewhere in the NT (ὥστε with inf.
'until' [Jn] 8: 9 D?), so that in Jn 12: 35 we probably
ought to read ἕως (S) 'as long as', but in 36 ὡς
'quando, now while'. There are strong variants in
Mk 9: 21 ὡς τοῦτο γέγονεν S*A al. (ἕως 𝔓⁴⁵B, ἐξ οὗ
ScW, ἀφ' οὗ N; Pallis, Notes 32 compares Soph.,
OT 115 ὡς ἀπεστάλη 'since then', Thuc. 4.90.3

ὡς οἴκοθεν ὥρμησαν). On G 6: 10 s. supra (2).—
On ἕως (οὗ, ὅτου), ἄχρι(ς οὗ), μέχρι(ς οὗ) 'until' with
the indic. or subj. s. §§382(2); 383(1, 2). Πρίν (πρὶν ἤ,
πρὸ τοῦ) 'before' is used mostly with the inf., §395.

Final ἵνα, ὅπως, μή §369; on the enlarged use of
ἵνα §§388ff.; μή, μήπως, μήποτε after φοβεῖσθαι
etc. §370.

Declarative clauses with ὅτι (ὡς, πῶς) §§396f.

Indirect questions with εἰ (πότερον...ἤ Jn 7:
17) §§368; 440(2, 3).

Consecutive (subordinating) ὥστε, also ἵνα,
§391.

456. Causal conjunctions. (1) The principal
conjunction is ὅτι 'because', for which Lk and
Paul (Heb, Ja, 1 P, Diogn, Herm) also use διότι
(classical). Subordination with ὅτι and διότι is
often very loose (cf. διό, ὅθεν §451(5, 6)), so that it
must be translated 'for'. (2) A special use of ὅτι
in the NT as in the OT is one which corresponds
to Hebrew כִּי (§480(6)), e.g. H 2: 6 OT τί ἐστιν
ἄνθρωπος, ὅτι μιμνήσκῃ αὐτοῦ, ἢ υἱὸς ἀνθρώπου,
ὅτι ἐπισκέπτῃ αὐτόν; כִּי is consecutive here, but
ὅτι seems more likely to have been felt as meaning
'for what reason, why' (§§299(4); 480(6); or as
meaning '(I ask) because' and is found already
in pre-classical Greek: Hom., Od. 5.339f. τίπτε
τοι ὧδε Ποσειδάων...ὠδύσατ' ἐκπάγλως, ὅτι τοι
κακὰ πολλὰ φυτεύει; (with an obvious reference to
τίπτε); for which ἵνα may also be used §391(5).
(3) Ἐπεί is used in a way similar to ὅτι (διότι). In
the NT it is regularly causal (often = 'for, for
otherwise', e.g. Homil Clem 20.3.8 [with the
'unreal' indicative], 19.5 [with the future]), as is
also ἐπείπερ which appears once as a variant
(R 3: 30, s. §454(2)). Ἐπειδή is purely causal, but
is also only loosely subordinating. Ἐπειδήπερ
appears only in Lk 1: 1 'inasmuch as' with
reference to a fact already well known (cf. εἴπερ
§454(2)). Ὅπου 'insofar as' quando 1 C 3: 3, 2 P
2: 11 is not far removed. It is used by Hdt. et al.
in a similar way, as is ποῦ in MGr (Hesseling,
Neophilologus 12 [1927] 219, 221). (4) Καθότι
(only Lk) strictly means 'to the degree that,
according as' and is so used in A 2: 45, 4: 35. In
Hellenistic, however, it also passes over to the
meaning of διότι (Mayser II 2, 440; II 3, 83f.).—
Rob. 963–6.

(1) Ὅτι = 'for': 1 C 1: 25, 4: 9, 10: 17, 2 C 4: 6, 7: 8,
14; with διότι: R 1: 19, 21, 3: 20, 8: 7 (ὅτι FG) etc.

(2) Mt 8: 27 ποταπός ἐστιν οὗτος, ὅτι καὶ οἱ ἄνεμοι
καὶ ἡ θάλασσα ὑπακούουσιν αὐτῷ; Mk (1: 27 v.l.),
4: 41, Lk 4: 36, 8: 25, Jn 2: 18, (14: 22). On Jn 9: 2 s.

§ 391(5). Pernot, Études 51, 85, 119, 145; W. Bauer, Hdb. on Jn 2: 18. Cf. LXX Ex 3: 11, 16: 7, Judg 9: 28, 38 etc. (Gesenius-Kautzsch § 107, 4*b* 3). 1 Km 11: 5 τί ὅτι (§ 300(2)) κλαίει ὁ λαός = מַה־לָּעָם כִּי יִבְכּוּ; Jannaris § 1758*b*; Schol. Aeschyl., Ch. 214 τίνος γὰρ ἤδη ἐπέτυχον ὑπὸ θεῶν, ὅτι εἶπες τὰ λοιπά; Cf. on the abbreviated clause τί (scil. γέγονεν) ὅτι § 299(4). Ὅτι appears even for ὥστε acc. to one variant (§ 391(2)).

(3) Ἐπεί 'for otherwise': R 3: 6, 11: 6, 22. Likewise ἐπεὶ ἄρα 1 C 5: 10, 7: 14. Ἐπειδή: 1 C 14: 16 (B ἐπεί), 1: 22 (FG ἐπεί), A 13: 46 (S*BD*, ἐπειδὴ δέ S^cAD³, ἐπεὶ δέ 𝔓⁴⁵C), Mt 21: 46 v.l. Ἐπεί 'for otherwise' is class. (Xen., Cyr. 2.2.31 etc.) and Hell. (e.g. Plut., Agis 2.5, M. Ant. 8.56.2, UPZ I 110.204 [164 BC], BGU II 530.30 [I AD]; Brinkmann, RhM 54 [1899] 94; Ljungvik 62 n. 1). Ἐπειδή gradually retreats in the Ptol. pap. in favor of ἐπεί (Mayser II 3, 82).

(4) Lk 1: 7 καθότι ἦν ἡ Ἐλισαβὲτ στεῖρα, 19: 9, A 2: 24, 17: 31 (διότι HLP), ITr 5.2, Homil Clem 16.2. Cf. καθό and καθά 'much as, in so far as' Herm Sim 1.8.8, Homil Clem 12.26, 30, but καθό 'because' 12.27.—Also causal are: ἐφ᾽ ᾧ § 235(2); ἀνθ᾽ ὧν § 208(1); ὡς and καθώς § 453(2); οὗ χάριν § 216(1) (Lk 7: 47); δι᾽ ἣν αἰτίαν 2 T 1: 6, 12 etc.

457. Concessive conjunctions. Εἰ καί, ἐὰν καί § 374. Also κἄν 'even if' Mt 21: 21, 26: 35, Jn 8: 14, 10: 38. Καὶ εἰ, on the other hand, appears in textually certain readings only as 'and if'. For καίπερ, καίτοι with a participle, καίτοι(γε) with a finite verb (paratactic) s. § 425(1); καίτοι vacillates between an adversative and a concessive sense, § 450(3).

Mk 14: 29 εἰ καί SBCW al., καὶ ἐάν or κἄν D, καὶ εἰ AE al. 2 C 13: 4 καὶ γὰρ εἰ S^cA al. is more nearly correct than καὶ γάρ without εἰ (𝔓⁴⁶S*BD*F al.; εἰ γὰρ καί Or, s. Tdf.).

12. SENTENCE STRUCTURE

458. Introduction. Aristotle distinguishes two opposed types of style in Greek (Rh. 3.9 p. 1409 a 24 ff.), the running or continuous (εἰρομένη) and the compact (κατεστραμμένη) or periodic (ἐν περιόδοις). In the latter the whole discourse is composed of articulated units; in the former the elements are strung loosely together one after the other without leading up to an anticipated conclusion. The periodic style is characteristic of artistically developed prose, while the running style is characteristic of plain and unsophisticated language in all periods, and thus of the earliest Greek prose as well as of the narrative sections of the NT on the whole. The latter conform at this point to Semitic style: to a first idea complete in itself is added a second similar one, usually connected by καί (Hebr. וְ), then a third, and so on in a continuous series. This produces a monotonous style which has left its imprint on the narrative of Mark, but is not infrequently found in Mt, Lk and Jn. Another form of the running style is that in which the first sentence is extended by means of a participial phrase, a clause introduced by ὅτι, a relative clause, or similar construction. This manner of writing, which (Paul) uses in large portions of Ephesians and Colossians, does not admit any prospect of conclusion and is even more tedious and especially less lucid than the simple linking together of sentences by καί. In addition to the connection of elements by conjunctions, relatives, subordinate participles, etc., there remains the unconnected (asyndetic) paratactic style; this is repugnant by and large to the spirit of the Greek language, whether the parallel members joined by asyndeton are whole sentences or parts of sentences or merely words. Its use is accordingly limited in the NT, yet it is found there in greater abundance than earlier (Schwyzer II 633f.).

Normal sentence structure may be interrupted in two ways: parenthesis, i.e. a grammatically independent thought thrown into the midst of the sentence; and anacoluthon, i.e. the failure to carry through the structure of the sentence as originally conceived. Anacoluthon must in general be considered incorrect in artistic prose, although it is not entirely absent even in the prose of Isocrates. On the other hand, when a natural conversational tone is imitated, as in Plato, it is quite inoffensive and can even be allowed in epistolary style provided that it does not impair understanding. The latter is a limit which Paul, it seems, quite often violated. Finally, sentence structure in the NT can be distinguished from that of the classicist composing in the rhetorical style, in that the former employs co-ordination—which is popular in folk language in all periods—even where the latter would employ only subordination.

'Relative connective' (= a loosening of the connection of the relative clause to the preceding complex sentence; something intermediate between a relative clause and a demonstrative clause: ὅς = and this, but this, this very thing): more Lat. than Greek (K.-G. II 434 ff.). Exx.: A 3: 15 (twice), 13: 31, 43; speech of Festus 25: 16, 18, 26: 7 (περὶ ἧς ἐλπίδος), 19 (ὅθεν), 12 (ἐν οἷς 'among others'), 10 (ὃ καὶ ἐποίησα); 2 T 4: 15, H 13: 7, Phm 13; ἦ γάρ epigram of Thuc. (Anth. Pal. VII 45). Br.-Th. 639; Schwyzer II 644, 13; Bo Reicke, The Disobedient Spirits, Chap. 6 (on 1 P 3: 21). S. also §294(5).— P. Fiebig, Der Erzählungsstil der Evangelien im Lichte des rabbinischen Erzählungsstils untersucht (Leipzig, 1925; Untersuchungen zum NT 11), Der Erzählungsstil der Ev. (Ἄγγελος 2 [1926] 39–43). 'The heathen found fault with the language of Christians as συνδέσμων ἐλλείπουσαν': Isid. Pelus. 4.28 (MPG 78, 1080f.) Mayser II 3, 114 n. 2.— Rob. 427–45, esp. 432 ff.

(1) ASYNDETON

459. The demonstrative as connective, with and without conjunction. Those instances in which a new sentence is begun with a demonstrative pronoun or adverb referring to something preceding are not, strictly speaking, to be considered asyndeton. (1) As in classical, e.g. A 16: 3 τοῦτον (Timothy) ἠθέλησεν ὁ Παῦλος σὺν αὐτῷ ἐξελθεῖν, after a preceding introduction and description of him. (2) On the other hand, the use of τότε as a connective particle to introduce a subsequent event, but not one taking place at a definite time ('thereupon', not 'at that time'), is unclassical; it is particularly characteristic of Mt, but is also found in Lk (especially Acts). (3) Some equivalent circumstantial formulae likewise would not have served in classical as full conjunctions: ἐν ἐκείνῳ τῷ καιρῷ and the like, also ἀπὸ τότε, μετὰ τοῦτο (ταῦτα). (4) Ἔπειτα and εἶτα are used preferably without δέ even in Attic (Krüger §69, 24.1); this is true also of the NT, in which ἔτι and πάλιν (Mt) are also likely to be used without δέ.

(1) Jn 5: 6 τοῦτον ἰδών etc. (21: 21 AWX al., SBCD τοῦτον οὖν; e Chr are different and greatly abbreviated); a nice parallel, e.g. Dem. 21.58 Σαννίων ἐστὶν δήπου τις. . . . Οὗτος ἀστρατείας ἥλω. . . . Τοῦτον μετά etc.

(2) Jn uses τότε οὖν in 11: 14 (οὖν om. AW sy), 19: 1, 16, 20: 8 with a fuller sense = 'now' (in contrast to the preceding time). Mt 2: 7, 16, 17, 3: 5, 13, 15, 4: 1, 5, 10, 11 etc. (A. H. McNeile, Τότε in St Matthew, JTS 12 [1911] 127f.), Lk 14: 21 (D καί), 21: 10 τότε ἔλεγεν αὐτοῖς (om. D), 24: 45, A 1: 12, 4: 8 etc. (especially often in D, e.g. 2: 14 [with δέ], 37). Acc. to Lagrange (s. Abel 356f.) this τότε is an Aramaism.

(3) Ἐν ἐκείνῳ τῷ καιρῷ Mt 11: 25, 12: 1, (14: 1, where D has ἐν ἐκ. δέ), ἐν ἐκείνῃ τῇ ὥρᾳ 18: 1 (ἐν ἐκ. δέ BM), ἐν ἐκείναις (δέ add. DW) ταῖς ἡμέραις Mk 8: 1 (ἐν δὲ ταῖς ἡμ. ἐκ. Mt 3: 1, but DE al. without δέ), ἐν αὐτῇ (δέ add. D) τῇ ὥρᾳ Lk 10: 21 (7: 21 v.l. ἐν ἐκείνῃ τῇ ὥ.; with δέ AD al.). Ἀπὸ τότε Mt 4: 17 (with γάρ D), 16: 21, Lk 16: 16 (καὶ ἀ. τ. Mt 26: 16). Μετὰ τοῦτο (ταῦτα) without conjunction A 18: 1 (SAB al.; Lk 10: 1, 18: 4 the Greek witnesses with δέ), more frequently in Jn (cf. §462(1)), e.g. 2: 12, 3: 22, 5: 1, 14, 6: 1 (19: 38 μετὰ δὲ τ., but without δέ EGK al.) and Rev (4: 1, 7: 9, 18: 1, 19: 1, 20: 3; with καί 7: 1 [om. καί AC], 15: 5).

(4) Ἔπειτα (εἶτα) Mk 4: 17, Lk 16: 7, Jn 11: 7 etc. (Ja 4: 14 SABK, ἔπ. δὲ καί LP only; H 7: 27 without δέ; 7: 2 ἔπ. 𝔓⁴⁵, ἔπ. δέ K, ἔπ. καί Theo, ἔπ. δὲ καί al.). Ἔτι Mt 17: 5 = Mk 5: 35 = Lk 8: 49 ἔτι αὐτοῦ λαλοῦντος, A 10: 44, Mt 12: 46 (with δέ CE al.), cf. 26: 47 (lat without conj.; v.l. καὶ ἔτι and ἔτι δέ); ἔτι 'in addition, further' several times in the pap. (Mayser II 3, 137). Πάλιν: Mt 4: 8, 20: 5, 21: 36, 22: 4, 26: 42, Mk 14: 61.

460. Asyndeton (and polysyndeton) between individual words and concepts. (1) Asyndeton is regularly avoided in the case of only two words or ideas (as in classical), except in contrasting pairs: 2 T 4: 2 ἐπίστηθι εὐκαίρως ἀκαίρως, and with numerals (§63(2)). (2) Asyndeton appears naturally in lengthy enumerations, if only for the sake of convenience; there is an inclination, however, to combine pairs in the interests of clarity (§444(4)) up to the point where this becomes burdensome (1 T 1: 10). If a series is not strictly a summary but merely an enumeration, asyndeton may even be necessary: 1 P 4: 3 πεπορευμένοις ἐν ἀσελγείαις, ἐπιθυμίαις, οἰνοφλυγίαις, κώμοις, πότοις, καὶ ἀθεμίτοις εἰδωλολατρίαις (καί is necessary because of the adjective); the insertion of καί each time would make the separate items too important. This asyndeton is moderate compared with Philo who relishes the huge vocabulary at his disposal. (3) The use of a particle repeatedly in longer enumerations produces polysyndeton. Asyndeton and polysyndeton often, though by no means always, lend rhetorical emphasis: polysyndeton produces the impression of extensiveness and abundance by means of an exhausting summary; asyndeton, by breaking up the series and introducing the items staccato fashion, produces a vivid and impassioned effect.—Mayser II 3, 175 ff.; Rob. 427 f.

(1) If the opposite term is added with a negative (οὐ), καί may or may not be used: 1 C 10: 20 δαι-

μονίοις καὶ οὐ θεῷ, 3: 2 γάλα..., οὐ βρῶμα (DEFG with καί), 7: 12 etc. Cf. ἄνω κάτω, *sursum deorsum*; K.-G. II 346*d*. PLeipz 28.10 (381 AD) ὡς (ἐτῶν) ῑ πλείω ἐλάττον(α?), similarly APF 3 (1906) 419.26f. and elsewhere (vi AD). T 3: 1 ἀρχαῖς ἐξουσίαις is dubious; if this is correct, then because of the following asyndeton; but καὶ ἐξ. DᶜKLP al. Also in a mixed number: Rev 11: 11 μετὰ (τὰς) τρεῖς ἡμέρας ἥμισυ 𝔓⁴⁷ (pm. καὶ ἥμ.).

(2) 2 T 3: 2 (asyndeton because the same men are not all of these things).

(3) Polysyndeton in R 9: 4 (cf. 2: 17ff.) is rhetorically effective, as in Rev 5: 12; the same applies to asyndeton in 1 C 3: 12, which is to be read with animation emphasizing the studied scale of descending value. Not rhetorical: Lk 18: 29 (= Mt 19: 29, Mk 10: 29) οὐδείς ἐστιν ὃς ἀφῆκεν οἰκίαν ἢ γυναῖκα ἢ ἀδελφούς etc. cannot very well be otherwise expressed; Lk 14: 21 τοὺς πτωχοὺς καὶ ἀναπείρους etc. is also a simple expression as is Jn 5: 3 πλῆθος τῶν ἀσθενούντων, τυφλῶν χωλῶν ξηρῶν (here καί is superfluous, but not in the Lukan passage because it is a summary).

461. Asyndeton instead of subordination with finite verbs. (1) With certain imperatives: Mt 5: 24 ὕπαγε πρῶτον διαλλάγηθι (cf. classical ἄγε, ἴθι), ἔγειρε ἆρον Mk 2: 11 (in 9 most witnesses have καί); ἐγείρεσθε ἄγωμεν Mt 26: 46 = Mk 14: 42. Ὅρα, ὁρᾶτε, βλέπετε = *cave(te)*: Mt 9: 30 ὁρᾶτε μηδεὶς γινωσκέτω, 24: 6 ὁρᾶτε μὴ θροεῖσθε (imperative, Buttmann 209). Ἄφες with subjunctive s. §364(1, 2); θέλεις with subjunctive §366(3). Σιώπα πεφίμωσο Mk 4: 39 (σ. καὶ φιμώθητι D) is not unrelated. (2) The corresponding phenomenon with the indicative, apart from ἐγένετο with a finite verb (§442(5)), is confined to uncertain examples.—See also §471.

(1) Ὁρᾶτε (βλέπετε) μή with the subj. is probably also to be considered a case of asyndeton in Mt, Mk, Lk: Mt 24: 4 βλέπετε μή τις ὑμᾶς πλανήσῃ, although in passages like C 2: 8 βλ. μή τις ἔσται, A 13: 40, H 12: 25, the μη-clause is subordinate as in βλεπέτω μὴ πέσῃ 1 C 10: 12. Cf. §370(4) and e.g. ὅρα μηδενὶ... προσκρούσῃς POxy III 531.10 (ii AD). Also ὕπαγε Mt 8: 4 etc.; 18: 15 ὕπαγε ἔλεγξον SBD, with καί W al.; Mk 6: 38 is similar (but in Rev 16: 1 all uncials have καί). Ἔρχου is not used in the NT in this way, but ἔ. καὶ ἴδε Jn 1: 47, 11: 34, Rev 6: 1, 3, 5, 7 (in Rev the correct v.l. is ἔρχου without κ. ἴ.). Ἔγειρε στῆθι Lk 6: 8 only A, the witnesses with καί predominating; Mt 9: 6 SC al. ἐγερθεὶς ἆρον, B as in Mk 2: 11 ἔγειρε ἆρον, D ἔγ. καὶ ἆ.; ἀνάστα in the same way, at least as v.l. (§419(5)); σπεῦσον κατάβηθι Lk 19: 5 only D (pm. σπεύσας). Asyndetic imperatives are also found in Hebr. (e.g. LXX 3 Km 19: 7

ἀνάστα φάγε) and in Lat. (Stolz-Schmalz, Lat. Gr.⁵ 824).

(2) 1 C 4: 9 δοκῶ γάρ (add. ὅτι SᶜDᶜ al.) ὁ θεὸς ἀπέδειξεν, cf. K.-G. II 351 and a parenthetic δοκεῖτε, μαρτυρῶ (§465(2)). Lk 3: 20 is good classical (K.-G. II 344) προσέθηκεν καὶ τοῦτο..., κατέκλεισεν (S*BDW, others have καὶ κατέκλ., Eus, it appears, προσθείς). Λέγω with a finite verb can also be included here, e.g. Lk 17: 34 λέγω ὑμῖν, ταύτῃ τῇ νυκτὶ ἔσονται δύο.... Also cf. Raderm., WSt 31, 8f., where νομίζω ἡττήθημεν and the like are adduced.

462. Asyndeton between clauses and sentences. (1) The connective is retained on the whole in narrative, at least by Mt, Mk, Lk. Jn, to be sure, exhibits a striking difference at this point; the textual witnesses are at constant variance between asyndeton, οὖν, δέ, and καί. The asyndeta give the impression of ease rather than vividness or haste on the part of the narrator. (2) Asyndeton between individual axioms and sayings is very common in the didactic style of the Gospels. Although asyndeton lends solemnity and weight to the words, it is not a conscious rhetorical device. The hortatory and paraenetic style of the Epistles is comparable. There are, however, many and, in part, brilliant examples of rhetorical asyndeton in the Epistles, particularly Paul's (§494).—Mayser II 3, 179ff.; Rob. 428–32, 443.

(1) Asyndeton in Jn (cf. §420): 1: 23 ἔφη, 26 ἀπεκρίθη, 29 τῇ ἐπαύριον βλέπει (cf. 35), 37 ἤκουσαν (καὶ ἤκ. SᶜABC al.), 38 στραφεὶς (+ δέ SᵃABCW al.), 39 λέγει, ἦλθον (acc. to many witnesses; v.l. ἦ. οὖν, ἦ. δέ, καὶ ἦ.), ὥρα ἦν, 40 ἦν (A ἦν δέ), 41 εὑρίσκει, 42 ἤγαγεν (καὶ ἤγ. AX al.), ἐμβλέψας (+ δέ in late MSS), etc. 65 times altogether in Jn, otherwise only Mk 12: 29 ἀπεκρίθη ὁ Ἰ. SBL (ὁ δὲ Ἰ. ἀπ. AC, ὁ δὲ εἶπεν W). With ἔφη and λέγει (good Greek, s. Kieckers, IF 35 [1915] 7f.) also Mt 4: 7, 19: 20, 21, 25: 21, 23, 26: 34, 35, 27: 65 (also Mk 9: 38 SBΔ); in the parable in Mt 25: 22 also with προσελθών. On Mk s. Zerwick 22f. For πάλιν and the like s. §459(4). Similarly in Hermas, e.g. Vis 3.10.2 ἀποκριθείσά μοι λέγει, 9 ἀποκριθεὶς αὐτῷ λέγω...ἀπ. μοι λέγει, again in 10. Therefore we find it used precisely in those formulae of narrated dialogue which in John are usually asyndetic, and it is here that there is a common tendency to use the historical pres. (Winer §61, 1 [Winer-M.³ 673f.]); it is found moreover with μετὰ πολλὰ ἔτη, μ. χρόνον τινά and the like Vis 1.1.1ff.; cf. §459(3). Elsewhere, too, Hermas is inclined to asyndeton in narrative, probably under Lat. influence, e.g. Vis 1.4.3 λαλούσης αὐτῆς...ἐφάνησαν, 2.1.4 ἔλαβον ἐγώ. A 13: 46 ἐπειδή (ἐπεὶ δέ 𝔓⁴⁵C 33 pc. Or, ἐπειδή δέ AℜE pl., only ἐπειδή BS*D* pc.).

(2) There is asyndeton e.g. almost throughout Mt 5: 3–17, not only where there is no connection in thought, but also in spite of such connection: 17 οὐκ ἦλθον (instead of οὐ γάρ), Lk 6: 27f. (from here on it is more connected). Also frequently in Jn: 3: 6, 7, 8 etc. Asyndeton in an explanation, e.g. UPZ ι 69.4 (152 BC) τοῖς θεοῖς τὴν ἐπιτροπὴν δίδομει (= δίδωμι)· ἄνευ τῶν θεῶν οὐδὲν γίνεται. The Atticists also employ asyndeton in paraenetic discourse where there is insufficient continuity: Isocr. 1; 2; 3; cf. his remark on this subject 15.67f.—Asyndeton in the catalogue of hardships 2 C 11: 23ff.: A. Fridrichsen, K. Hum. Vet.-samf. i Uppsala, Årsbok 1943, 32f. (in the novel, Mysteries: hieratic).

463. Asyndeton between paragraphs. New paragraphs or sections in didactic writings are in general joined to the preceding as in classical works, a practice which more polished workmanship demands. On the other hand, there is a greater tendency towards asyndeton in the transition from one subject to another in the less careful epistolary style. There are plenty of examples in Paul and others of fresh starts (ἐξ ἀποστάσεως, i.e. with a break), quite apart from James, which has the character of a collection of aphorisms, and 1 John, which is no less loosely composed.

Connectives predominate in Romans as far as 8: 16 αὐτὸ τὸ πνεῦμα συμμαρτυρεῖ etc. where one may well speak of the figure ἐξ ἀποστάσεως; by its use the idea can spring all the more directly out of the emotion (as in 10: 1). The lack of connection between the two major divisions of the letter (9: 1), which are so different, may appear odd, but a mere conjunction here would still be a far cry from a real connection. Ἐξ ἀποστάσεως is profusely and effectively employed in 1 Corinthians, but new subjects are sometimes also introduced without a conjunction: 5: 9, 6: 1, 12, but 7: 1, 25, 8: 1, 12: 1, 16: 1 περὶ δέ, 15: 1 γνωρίζω δέ etc. The sections in Hebrews are regularly connected except within the hortatory passages.

(2) THE PERIOD

464. The period, i.e. the organization of a considerable number of clauses and phrases into a well-rounded unity, is rare in the NT. Since the period belongs to the more elegant style, it is most frequently met in Hebrews, which certainly is to be regarded as artistic prose by reason of the composition of its words and sentences (§§ 486f.). Paul, the ἰδιώτης τῷ λόγῳ (2 C 11: 6), does not generally make the effort required by so careful a style; artistic periods, therefore, in spite of all his eloquence, are not to be found in his writings, while harsh parentheses and anacolutha abound.

The prologue to the Gospel of Luke is a beautiful period; Lk elsewhere forsakes this device, it is true, and the introduction to Acts is not a period but a series of clauses strung together; only the introduction of the apostolic decree in A 15: 24–6 forms a genuine period.

H 1: 1–2a (by ancient standards this is a complete, two-member period, to which other loose elements are appended), 2b (with rhetorical anaphoric use of the relative with asyndeton [§ 489] as in the following clauses), 3 (a period with four clauses), 4 (an appended two-member period connected by τοσούτῳ...ὅσῳ); the rest of the Epistle is composed in a similar flowing style. Lk 1: 1–4 exhibits moderate length of the members and a beautiful relationship between the protasis with its three members and the corresponding structure of the apodosis. Πολλοί corresponds to κἀμοί, ἀνατ. διήγησιν το γράψαι, καθώς etc. to the ἵνα ἐπιγνῷς etc., so that the last clause, though appended to an idea already completely expressed, is called forth at least by the stylistic correspondence. Cf. Jn 13: 1–5. The following types, for example, are to be attributed to periodic sentence structure in the broader sense: the introduction of a period by a lengthy temporal or conditional expression, or by a subject with long modifying phrases; a weaker but still effective connection is produced if the first member of an antithesis, an alternative, or a parallelism points to the second by means of μέν, ἤ, τε, or καί. The particle is not absolutely necessary for the connection even in the second member, so that one can even speak of asyndetic periods as in 1 C 7: 27 δέδεσαι γυναικί· μὴ ζήτει λύσιν / λέλυσαι ἀπὸ γυναικός· μὴ ζήτει γυναῖκα = εἰ μὲν δέδεσαι... / εἰ δὲ λέλυσαι (cf. § 494).— On rhythm and style in the NT s. M. Jousse, Études de psychologie linguistique. Le style oral, rythmique et mnémotechnique chez les verbo-moteurs (Paris, 1921; acc. to A. Loisy, Rev. crit. 1925, 264ff., claims to demonstrate the genuineness of biblical writings by the rhythm); A. Loisy, Journ. de Psychol. 20 (1923) 405–39 (the style of the NT s. not Greek but OT; it corresponds to the Babylonian inscriptions and liturgies, to the magical-religious narratives of primitive peoples; cf. Rev. crit. 1925, 266). S. also § 487.—Cf. Rob. 432f.

(3) THE PARENTHESIS

465. (1) The parenthesis (cf. § 458) usually originates in a need which suddenly crops up to enlarge upon a concept or thought where it appears in the sentence; or it may be due to the difficulty of adapting an afterthought which suddenly comes to mind to the structure of the sentence as it was begun. The NT, especially the Epistles of Paul, contains a variety of harsher parentheses, harsher than a careful stylist would allow. Since Paul's train of thought in general includes many and long digressions (Winer §62, 4 [Winer-M.³ 706f.]), it is not surprising that his sentence structure even in narrower contexts is not uninterrupted: e.g. R 1:13 ὅτι πολλάκις προεθέμην ἐλθεῖν πρὸς ὑμᾶς (καὶ ἐκωλύθην ἄχρι τοῦ δεῦρο) ἵνα τινὰ καρπὸν σχῶ καὶ ἐν ὑμῖν, where the ἵνα-clause goes with προεθέμην. G. Rudberg, Parentesen i Nya Testamentet (Svensk Exeg. Årsbok 5 [1940] 126–38). (2) A short finite verb is occasionally thrown into the construction (as in classical) forming a slight parenthesis (a type of popular co-ordination, §471): e.g. 2 C 8:3 ὅτι κατὰ δύναμιν, μαρτυρῶ, καὶ παρὰ δύναμιν etc., Lk 18: 41 τί σοι θέλεις ποιήσω; (cf. PCairo 10448.6 [i AD; Wilcken, Chr. no. 14 III] καὶ σοὶ [= σὺ] λέγε τίνος θέλεις [κα]τηγορήσω).—Mayser II 3, 186ff.; Rob. 433–5.

(1) Mt 24: 15f. (ὁ ἀναγινώσκων νοείτω), A 12: 3f. Πέτρον (ἦσαν δὲ ἡμέραι τῶν ἀζύμων) ὅν, in which case perhaps περὶ αὐτὰς τὰς ἡμέρας τὰς τῶν ἀζύμων καὶ Πέτρον συλλαβὼν εἰς φυλακὴν ἔθετο could have been used to tie the phrase in with the construction. Cf. 1: 15, 4: 13 (§447(7)). The parenthesis in A 5: 14 is harsh, though the connection with 13 is smooth enough; but the resumption in 15 is awkward and ὥστε καὶ εἰς τὰς πλατείας etc. is in reality a consequence of 13, not of 14 as seems to be the case (cf. Rob. 435); Cf. *supra* R 1: 13. In R 2: 15f. there appears to be a gap in thought between ἀπολογουμένων and ἐν ᾗ ἡμέρᾳ, so that a parenthesis may be supposed; but a logical connection for ἐν ᾗ ἡμ. is to be found only some distance back, so that the simplest solution would be the deletion of ἐν ᾗ ἡμ. (Marcion [Zahn, Geschichte des nt. Kanons II 516]) or ἐν ἡμ. ᾗ (A) or ἐν ἡμ. ὅτε (SD al.). Thus we have asyndeton … ἢ καὶ ἀπολογουμένων. Κρινεῖ ὁ θεός . . . .

(2) Lk 13: 24 λέγω ὑμῖν ('I tell you'); H 10: 29 πόσῳ δοκεῖτε χείρονος ἀξιωθήσεται τιμωρίας; (Herm Sim 9.28.8 τί δοκεῖτε ποιήσει;). Somewhat longer parentheses: R 3: 5 κατὰ ἄνθρωπον λέγω, 2 C 11: 21 ἐν ἀφροσύνῃ λέγω, 6: 13 ὡς τέκνοις λέγω, cases of epidiorthosis and prodiorthosis (s. §495(3)) expressed in the briefest possible way. The insertion of ἔφη (only A 23: 35), φησίν etc. does not belong here since it is only a question of a shift in word order: 2 C 10: 10 ὅτι αἱ ἐπιστολαὶ μέν φησιν (φασιν B) βαρεῖαι = ὅτι φησίν· 'Αἱ μέν . . .', Mt 14: 8, A 23: 35 etc.; it is the same problem in 2 C 6: 2 acc. to 𝔓⁴⁶D*FG: 'καιρῷ' γὰρ λέγει 'δεκτῷ . . .' (on the position of γάρ cf. Kieckers, IF 35 [1915] 70f.); the customary reading alleviates the order: λέγει γάρ· 'καιρῷ δεκτῷ . . .'; H 8: 5 ὅρα γάρ φησιν. Cf. the numerous class.

references with parenthetical οἶδα, ὁρᾷς, οἶμαι etc. (K.-G. II 353f.; e.g. Aristoph., Ach. 12 πῶς τοῦτ' ἔσεισέ μου δοκεῖς τὴν καρδίαν;). E. Howind, De ratione citandi in Ciceronis Plutarchi Senecae Novi Testamenti scriptis obvia (Diss. Marburg, 1921). Parentheses in Mk: Zerwick 130–8.—On nominative absolutes introducing proper names or as temporal designations which form an essential part of the thought and occupy the proper place in the sentence, and therefore not strictly parenthetic, s. §144.—If an insertion disturbs the structure of the sentence as a whole, then the parenthesis becomes anacoluthon. Parenthetical remarks can also be given in the form of a relative clause without interrupting the structure of the sentence: Mt 27: 33 εἰς . . . Γολγοθᾶ, ὅ ἐστιν κρανίου τόπος; but if the same construction is inserted in direct discourse of which it can form no part, then it becomes a parenthesis in spite of the grammatical unity of the sentence: Mk 7: 11 ἐὰν εἴπῃ . . . κορβᾶν (ὅ ἐστιν δῶρον); Jn 1: 38. It is again a different matter if such a scholion is appended to direct discourse: Jn 9: 7, 1: 41 etc.; Winer 524.1 [Winer-M.³ 705 n. 1].

(4) ANACOLUTHON

466. The resumption of a suspended case by a pronoun in another case (the suspended subject [or object] Rob. 436; Abbot 32) is a construction belonging to the popular idiom (cf. Raderm.² 219; also MGr, Thumb² §42). (1) The simplest form of anacoluthon is where a preceding case is assimilated by attraction to a following relative clause which required an antecedent (§295; classical, s. K.-G. II 591, 7): A 7: 40 ὁ Μωυσῆς οὗτος, ὅς . . . , οὐκ οἴδαμεν, τί ἐγένετο αὐτῷ (from the LXX Ex 32: 1), 2 C 12: 17 μή τινα ὧν (ὧν = τούτων οὕς) ἀπέσταλκα πρὸς ὑμᾶς, δι' αὐτοῦ ἐπλεονέκτησα ὑμᾶς; (2) The nom. without such attraction is rare (*nom. pendens*: the psychological subject precedes the clause as if it were the grammatical subject): Mt 10: 11 D ἡ πόλις εἰς ἣν ἂν εἰσέλθητε εἰς αὐτήν, ἐξετάσατε τίς ἐν αὐτῇ etc. (3) Anacoluthon after πᾶς is a peculiarity in which a Semitic convention left a definite mark on a tendency of the vernacular to anacoluthon (the πᾶς is usually subject to attraction): Mt 12: 36 πᾶν ῥῆμα ἀργὸν (nom. or acc. by attraction?), ὃ λαλήσουσιν οἱ ἄνθρωποι, ἀποδώσουσιν περὶ αὐτοῦ λόγον; cf. Jn 17: 2. Lk 12: 48 παντὶ δὲ ᾧ ἐδόθη πολύ, πολὺ ζητηθήσεται παρ' αὐτοῦ (Lk elsewhere removes the anacolutha of Mt and Mk; Hawkins, Horae Synopt. 135ff.). (4) Anacoluthon (without a relative clause) following an introductory participle (nearly always in the nom.) is common: Jn 7: 38 ὁ πιστεύων εἰς ἐμὲ..., ποταμοὶ ἐκ τῆς κοιλίας αὐτοῦ ῥεύσουσιν. This construction is Semitic, but a comparable usage is found in classical; cf. K.-G. II 106f.; Mlt. 225 [356].— Mayser II 3, 189ff.; Ursing 65ff.; M.-H. 423ff.; Rob. 435–7.

(1) Ταῦτα is not resumed in Lk 21: 6 (ἅ is probably to be deleted with DL, unless the reference lies in ὧδε SB(D)LX). In imitation of the well-known Hebr. *parallelismus membrorum* there occasionally appear two ideas set over against each other with a pause between and a reference in the second to the first; they are given more weight individually because of the loose grammatical connection between them. 1 Jn 2: 27 καὶ ὑμεῖς (emphasis on the exceptional position of the reader; cf. *v.* 20); similarly in 24 ὑμεῖς (in contrast to those ἀρνούμενοι 22f. or πλανῶντες 26), taken up again by μένει (μενέτω): μένει and μενέτω are not in themselves sufficient to constitute a member of the period and the author wanted to express strongly the contrast between the beginning and the continuation. This is not to be taken therefore merely as the anticipation of the subject before the relative (§475(1)), while 1 C 11: 14 ἀνὴρ μὲν ἐὰν κομᾷ, ἀτιμία αὐτῷ ἐστιν...can be so interpreted (= ἐὰν μὲν ἀνήρ...). For exx. with πᾶς s. *infra* (3). An anticipatory acc. is found also, e.g. Hom., Il.10.416, Hdt. 2.106 τὰς δὲ στήλας, τὰς ἴστα..., αἱ μὲν πλεῦνες, 9.88, Paus. 3.13.7, Appian p. 158.7 Mendelssohn; s. Havers, IF 43 (1926) 252. MGr πρῶτον ἄθρωπο ποῦ (here = ὃν) βρίσκω (= εὑρίσκω) μου λέει (= μοι λέγει) Mitsotakis, Chrestom. (Berlin, 1895) p. 160.

(2) A substantive placed at the head of a clause without regard for the construction (*casus pendens*) is a common Semitic construction (Gesenius-Kautzsch §143). It is more common in Jn than in the Synoptics (Burney, Aramaic Origin 64f.). Of the 28 exx. in Jn, 22 are found in words of Jesus, 2 in the prologue (1: 12, 18), 2 in words of the Baptist (1: 33, 3: 32), 1 in the discussion of John's disciples (3: 26), 1 in the mouth of the paralytic (5: 11): Black, Aramaic Approach[2] 35 (where exx. like ὁ ποιήσας... ἐκεῖνος are also counted). The situation is similar in the Synoptics and Acts (Black, *op. cit.* 35f.). From the LXX cf. e.g. Gen 28: 13 ἡ γῆ, ἐφ' ἧς σὺ καθεύδεις ἐπ' αὐτῆς, σοὶ δώσω αὐτήν. On this 'thematic' nom. s. Havers, *op. cit.* 212–39, esp. 213f., 226–8, 233–7, with many exx. from Greek and other languages. On Att. also s. Rosenkranz, IF 48 (1930) 163f. It is a sign of unadorned speech (Aristid., Ars rhet. 545 Spengel ἀφελῆ ποιεῖ τὸν λόγον), therefore especially frequent in the post-classical period and often without the emphasis originally connected with it. It is also common in MGr; e.g. ἕνας χωριάτης ἀπέθανε τὸ παιδί του 'a peasant, his child died' = 'the child of a peasant died' (Schwyzer, Jahrb. 500).

(3) Mt 7: 24 (ὁμοιώσω αὐτόν CEGW al.), 10: 32. Jn 6: 39 ἵνα πᾶν ὃ δέδωκέν μοι, μὴ (πᾶς... μή = μηδείς §302(1)) ἀπολέσω ἐξ αὐτοῦ, ἀλλὰ ἀναστήσω αὐτό...: when writing πᾶν, the second, positive clause was probably in the author's mind here as in Jn 3: 16 (Buttmann 106; cf. Mt 13: 19 where παντὸς ἀκούοντος is resumed by ἐν τῇ καρδίᾳ αὐτοῦ). Acc. to Buttmann 325 πᾶν in these and similar exx. is nom. (cf. *supra* (2) *nom. pendens*), so that, acc. to him, Jn 15: 2 is to be included: πᾶν κλῆμα ἐν ἐμοὶ μὴ φέρον καρπόν, αἴρει (ἀρεῖ is better, following it vg, and subsequently καθαριεῖ [s. §101 under καθαίρειν]) αὐτό; but cf. *infra* (4).

(4) A 19: 34 ἐπιγνόντες... φωνὴ ἐγένετο μία ἐκ πάντων (instead of ἐβόησαν ὁμοῦ πάντες, which would not suit the following words well); Mk 9: 20 καὶ ἰδὼν αὐτόν, τὸ πνεῦμα συνεσπάραξεν αὐτόν (instead of συνεσπαράχθη ὑπὸ τοῦ πν.); in D also Mt 4: 16, 5: 40, 17: 2, 9, 14. Rev 2: 26, 3: 12, 21 ὁ νικῶν, δώσω αὐτῷ is more awkward, but 2: 7, 17 τῷ νικῶντι, δώσω αὐτῷ, cf. 6: 4, Mt 4: 16 OT, 5: 40, with the pronoun everywhere referring back to something preceding (§278; cf. POxy II 299.2 [i AD] Λάμπωνι μυοθηρευτῇ ἔδωκα αὐτῷ..., Epict. 3.1.22 οὐδὲ γὰρ λέοντι... τολμᾷ ἀντιστῆναί αὐτῷ). With a hanging acc. Mk 1: 34 D καὶ τοὺς δαιμόνια ἔχοντας (acc. following the preceding καὶ ἐθεράπευσεν αὐτούς) ἐξέβαλεν αὐτὰ ἀπ' αὐτῶν. Exx. in Havers, *op. cit.* 227, 234–6; Ljungvik 26; Ljungvik, Synt. 6ff.; Mayser II 1, 63f., 343f.; II 3, 65, 197; Ghedini, Vang. ap. 478f.; further Fr. Horn, Zur Gesch. der absol. Partizipialkonstruktionen im Lat. (Lund and Leipzig, 1918), esp. p. 55 n. 1, 56, 56f., 60f., 65f., 67 n. 2. With Rev 2: 26 etc. in particular cf. e.g. BGU II 385.7 (ii/iii AD) ὁ ἐνιγὼν (= ἐνεγκών) σοι τὴν ἐπιστολήν, δὸς αὐτῷ ἄλλην. With Mk 1: 34 D cf. Plato, Phdr. 233в εὐτυχοῦντας (assimilated to the preceding δυστυχοῦντας)... παρ' ἐκείνων, Xen., An. 5.5.19 etc. (Havers, *op. cit.* 248f.). Typical exx. from the LXX: Ex 9: 7 ἰδὼν δὲ Φαραώ (nom.)... ἐβαρύνθη ἡ καρδία Φαραώ (gen). Something like a nom. absolute (instead of a gen. absol.) acc. to the class. type (e.g. Hdt. 7.157 ἁλὴς γινομένη πᾶσα ἡ Ἑλλάς, χεὶρ μεγάλη συνάγεται; K.-G. II 108f.) is found only in Herm Man 5.1.4 ἀμφότερα τὰ πνεύματα ἐπὶ τὸ αὐτὸ κατοικοῦντα, ἀσύμφορόν ἐστιν (instead of ἀσύμφορά ἐστιν, which the author was unaccustomed to use)... ἐκείνῳ ἐν ᾧ κατοικοῦσιν. 7.5 τῶν δὲ μὴ φυλασσόντων... οὐδὲ ζωὴ ἐν αὐτοῖς (the gen. is due to assimilation to the preceding antithetical clause).—For the gen. absol. instead of the conjunctive ptcp. s. §423.

467. Anacoluthon after an intervening clause or sentence.
In more complicated sentences an interrupting clause or sentence sometimes causes the author to forget the original construction and substitute another for it in resuming: A 24: 5f.

(speech of Tertullus which is reported by Lk with less care than any other) εὑρόντες γὰρ τὸν ἄνδρα τοῦτον λοιμόν..., ὃς καὶ..., ὃν καὶ ἐκρατήσαμεν etc.; something like εὕρομεν was in the mind of the author when he introduced the third clause. In order to correct the mistake, ὃν καί which was occasioned by the ὃς καί preceding, would have to be dropped. The narrative parts of the NT do not contain many anacolutha of this type. They are more numerous and flagrant in the Pauline Epistles, although the Epistles are uneven in this respect since the care with which they were composed varies considerably: G 2: 6 ἀπὸ δὲ τῶν δοκούντων εἶναί τι—ὁποῖοί ποτε ἦσαν, οὐδέν μοι διαφέρει· πρόσωπον θεὸς ἀνθρώπου οὐ λαμβάνει—ἐμοὶ γὰρ οἱ δοκοῦντες οὐδὲν προσανέθεντο (instead of ἐμοὶ οὐδὲν προσανετέθη; the author has either forgotten the opening clause, or deemed it convenient to replace it with a new form).—Rob. 437–9.

Belser (Die Selbstverteidigung des P. im Gal.-br. [Freiburg i. Br., 1896] 69) says with regard to the attempt (of Spitta and others) to give a uniform construction to this sentence: 'A philologist who proceeds to expound this verse with a sane mind cannot doubt οὐδὲ πρὸς ὥραν that these attempts have to be rejected.' It is more difficult to determine what Paul was driving at in the opening clause in G 2: 4f. διὰ δὲ τοὺς παρεισάκτους ψευδαδέλφους..., οἷς οὐδὲ πρὸς ὥραν εἴξαμεν etc., unless οἷς, which is missing in D* and Irenaeus, be spurious. The construction in 1 T 1: 3ff. is reduced to utter chaos by interminable insertions and appended clauses. In any case, ᾧ is to be deleted with B in R 16: 27, not only because of anacoluthon, but especially in order to connect διὰ 'I. Χρ. In other cases, too, the defective transmission of the text is perhaps to blame: in R 2: 17ff. it is possible to transform what appear to be protases without a correct apodosis (21?) into independent clauses by adopting the reading ἴδε instead of εἰ δέ (ΕΙΔΕ–ΙΔΕ both = ide [§ 23] and is hardly therefore a variant!); cf. G 5: 2 ἴδε ἐγὼ Π. λέγω etc. (Wilke, Rhetorik 215f., who admittedly decides in the end for εἰ δέ). Likewise ide (not εἰ δέ) τῶν ἵππων τοὺς χαλινούς...Ja 3: 3, cf. 4 ἰδοὺ καὶ τὰ πλοῖα.... R 9: 22 is different; here εἰ δέ is universally acknowledged and anacoluthon is not involved if καί in v. 23 is dropped with B Or vg etc. (cf. § 482). The textual tradition in Jn 6: 22–4 is too diverse to enable us to discern the hand of the author; acc. to the customary reading τῇ ἐπαύριον ὁ ὄχλος at the beginning is resumed by ὅτε οὖν εἶδεν ὁ ὄχλος in v. 24, in a way which is not unknown among classical writers and where there is no question of a lapse of memory; cf. 1 Jn 1: 1–3.

468. Participle and finite verb. (1) Paul is fond of continuing a construction begun with a finite verb by means of co-ordinated participles, sometimes in a long series. E.g. 2 C 7: 5 οὐδεμίαν ἔσχηκεν ἄνεσιν ἡ σὰρξ ἡμῶν, ἀλλ᾽ ἐν παντὶ θλιβόμενοι, ἔξωθεν μάχαι, ἔσωθεν φόβοι (short exclamations: 'always plagued!' etc.; Frisk, Glotta 17 [1928] 62). (2) Related to this type of anacoluthon and probably arising from it is the peculiar use of a participle in place of a finite verb and without any connection to one, usually in a long series and in an imperatival sense; it is common in Paul and even more so in Peter (Mlt. 222ff. [285ff.]): 1 P 3: 7 οἱ ἄνδρες ὁμοίως, συνοικοῦντες..., ἀπονέμοντες, 9 μὴ ἀποδιδόντες..., τοὐναντίον δὲ εὐλογοῦντες... with several parallel adjectives intervening (8 τὸ δὲ τέλος πάντες ὁμόφρονες etc.) so that ἐστέ may be supplied throughout.—The case throughout the examples in (1) and (2) is nom. (because forms of εἶναι were mentally supplied originally or because the nom. is the absolute case); cf. λέγων, λέγοντες § 136(4). (3) The reverse of (1) is sometimes also encountered, i.e. a participle is continued by a finite verb: C 1: 26 τὸ μυστήριον τὸ ἀποκεκρυμμένον—νῦν δὲ ἐφανερώθη (D φανερωθέν), Jn 15: 5 ὁ μένων ἐν ἐμοί, κἀγώ (scil. μένω because ὁ μένων was felt to be the equivalent of ἐάν τις μένῃ) ἐν αὐτῷ, οὗτος φέρει καρπόν.—Rob. 439f.

(1) 2 C 5: 12 οὐ...συνιστάνομεν..., ἀλλ᾽ ἀφορμὴν διδόντες (scil. γράφομεν ταῦτα). 2 C 8: 18ff. χειροτονηθείς has roughly the same function as οὗ ὁ ἔπαινος (Frisk, op. cit. 61f.), then στελλόμενοι τοῦτο is definitely anacoluthon in relation to συνέκδημος ἡμῶν (not to συνεπέμψαμεν).

(2) R 12: 9ff. is a very free construction: after the construction has become very loose in 6ff. (cf. § 454(3)), ptcps. alternating with adjs. are continuously appended to each other in the exhortation without any possibility of construing them; although he interrupts his participial enjoinders to the Romans with ἡ ἀγάπη ἀνυπόκριτος (v. 9), he continues with ἀποστυγοῦντες...φιλόστοργοι etc. until διώκοντες v. 13; then clauses with impera. (inf.; 14f.), ptcp. (φρονοῦντες etc.; 16), impera. (γίνεσθε 16), and ptcp. again (17ff.) follow alternately. It appears as if Paul considered the descriptive ptcp. to be the equivalent of the impera. Further exx.: E 4: 1ff. παρακαλῶ ὑμᾶς περιπατῆσαι...ἀνεχόμενοι ἀλλήλων...σπουδάζοντες, 3: 17 (ὑποτασσόμενοι in 5: 21 is smoother, yet greatly detached from the finite verb and already approaching the imperatival usage; cf. 1 P 2: 18, 3: 1), Ph 1: 29f., C 3: 16f. ὁ λόγος ἐνοικείτω...διδάσκοντες etc. (as in the passage from Romans cited above,

after and therefore equivalent to the impera.). 2 C 9: 11 πλουτιζόμενοι after a declarative clause in the fut.; 13 δοξάζοντες etc. is an elaboration of the preceding διὰ πολλῶν εὐχαριστιῶν τῷ θεῷ (the subj. of the ptcp. is the recipients of the benefit), cf. 1: 7. 1 P 4: 8ff., 2 P 3: 3, H 13: 5. Ptcps. without anacoluthon, but in a very long series, 2 C 6: 3–10. Frisk, *op. cit.* 65f. explains all the cited cases of 'imperatival' ptcps. as correctly subordinated (in part with the nom. instead of another case acc. to §136f.). In several instances, however, the ptcp. is more or less independent, so that it receives the meaning of an independent statement or exhortation acc. to the situation. The ptcp., accordingly, is on a par with other nouns (subst. and adj.), which also, without a verb, can have the value of a sentence in the popular, energetic, cliché-laden style. A ptcp. can thus be co-ordinated with other nouns: Did 5.1 (and similarly Barn 20) ἡ δὲ τοῦ θανάτου ὁδός ἐστιν αὕτη· πρῶτον πάντων πονηρά ἐστι καὶ κατάρας μεστή (a normal sentence), then follow 22 substs. of action as sentence equivalents: φόνοι, μοιχεῖαι etc.; in 5.2 there is a *nomen agentis* διῶκται ἀγαθῶν, followed by 5 ptcps.: μισοῦντες ἀλήθειαν etc. All are used in a descriptive sense. 1 P 2: 13–3: 9 first imperatives, then (2: 18) οἱ οἰκέται ὑποτασσόμενοι, (3: 1) γυναῖκες ὑποτασσόμεναι, (3: 7) οἱ ἄνδρες... συνοικοῦντες...ἀπονέμοντες, followed by (3: 8) τὸ δὲ τέλος πάντες ὁμόφρονες, συμπαθεῖς..., μὴ ἀποδιδόντες..., (9) εὐλογοῦντες (cf. Frisk, *op. cit.*); R 12: 9ff. (s. *supra*). Mlt. 223f. [352f.] collects exx. from the pap. of the ptcp. without finite verb; Mayser II 1, 196 n. 3; 340–6; II 3, 72 explains them all as anacolutha or as a failure to project the construction or a weakness in style (but the gen. absol. is common in headings: Mayser II 3, 72f.); also cf. Frisk, *op. cit.* 56–60, Björck, Die periphr. Konstruktionen 116f. Further Ursing 68f. Vett. Val. (also in subordinate clauses): T. Wikström, Eranos 47 (1949) 35–8. For Latin s. E. Löfstedt, Komm. zur Peregr. Aeth. (1911) 249.

(3) 2 Jn 2 τὴν μένουσαν ἐν ἡμῖν, καὶ μεθ᾽ ἡμῶν ἔσται. Mt 13: 22, 23, Lk 8: 12, 14, 2 C 6: 9; Rev 1: 5f., 2: 2, 9, 3: 7, 9; less harsh 1 C 7: 37 ὃς ἕστηκεν...μὴ ἔχων...ἐξουσίαν δὲ ἔχει; cf. Jn 5: 44 (v.l. ζητοῦντες, correct), 1: 32, Herm Vis 3.6.3, 4, 7.1, 2, 3, Sim 6.2.5, §442(6). Similar exx. of anacoluthon in the exchange of finite verb and ptcp. may be cited from class. authors (K.-G. II 105ff., especially 109; M.-H. 428f. [also pap. 429]); the non-class. element in the NT consists in the frequency of the cases and the extension of the freedom with which they are used. The mildest form is like that in A 15: 22f. ἔδοξε τοῖς ἀποστόλοις (as if=οἱ ἀπόστολοι ἐβουλεύσαντο)... πέμψαι...γράψαν τες; cf. Thuc. 3.36.2 ἔδοξεν αὐτοῖς... ἀποκτεῖναι, ἐπικαλοῦντες (K.-G. II 105). On the whole subject, cf. further R. Koch, Observ. gramm. in decreta...(Diss. Münster, 1909) 25f.; Regard

186–216 ('Les tournures sans copule', therefore taken as elliptical); Ursing 68f. 1 Clem 11.1 is strange: Λὼτ ἐσώθη ἐκ Σοδόμων, τῆς περιχώρου κριθείσης..., πρόδηλον ποιήσας ὁ δεσπότης...(as if ἔσωσεν τὸν Λὼτ had preceded). IEph and ISm begin with a ptcp. without a finite verb (ἀποδεξάμενος 'I bid welcome', δοξάζων 'I give praise'; or is the ptcp. to be taken with χαίρειν [scil. λέγω]?). LXX Ps 17: 33 ὁ θεὸς ὁ περιζωννύων με δύναμιν, καὶ ἔθετο..., 34 ὁ καταρτιζόμενος...καὶ...ἱστῶν με, 35 διδάσκων...καὶ ἔθου....

469. Anacoluthon following a relative clause.

Another clause in which the relative cannot take the same form is sometimes joined to a relative clause by a co-ordinating particle (καί etc.) (classical, K.-G. II 432ff.): T 1: 2f. ζωῆς, ἣν ἐπηγγείλατο..., ἐφανέρωσεν δέ...τὸν λόγον αὐτοῦ, Mk 6: 11 ὃς ἂν τόπος (v.l. ὅσοι ἄν) μὴ δέξηται (-ωνται) ὑμᾶς μηδὲ ἀκούσωσιν ὑμῶν; cf. §297.—Rob. 440ff.

Rev 17: 2, Lk 17: 31; also 1 C 7: 13 if the reading ἥτις is followed, but εἴ τις 𝔓[46]SD* al. is better. The following are rather *oratio variata* than anacolutha: R 2: 6ff. ὃς ἀποδώσει...τοῖς μέν...ζωήν· τοῖς δέ... ὀργὴ καὶ θυμός, which is followed by the same construction but with a new contrast: θλῖψις καὶ στενοχωρία ἐπὶ πᾶσαν ψυχήν..., δόξα δέ etc. (scil. ἔσται [it would be impossible to supply δώσει]; cf. 11: 22 ἴδε οὖν χρηστότητα καὶ ἀποτομίαν θεοῦ· ἐπὶ μὲν τοὺς πεσόντας ἀποτομία etc.). Mt 7: 9f. has an interrogative clause instead of a relative clause, construed entirely in the Semitic manner: τίς ἐστιν ἐξ ὑμῶν, ὃν αἰτήσει ὁ υἱὸς αὐτοῦ ἄρτον, μὴ λίθον ἐπιδώσει αὐτῷ; ἢ καὶ ἰχθὺν αἰτήσει, μὴ ὄφιν ἐπιδώσει αὐτῷ; (the correct form would be: τίς ἐξ ὑ. τῷ υἱῷ ἄρτον αἰτοῦντι λίθον ἐπιδώσει; ἢ ἰ. αἰτοῦντι ὄ. ἐπιδώσει;). Lk 11: 11 (Marcion 𝔓[45]ABCWΘ) gives the saying in not much better Greek: τίνα...τὸν (om. 𝔓[45]M) πατέρα... 'of whom...as his father' (cf. Zahn *in loc.* [p. 453 n. 24]). There is little of this sort of thing in the Ptol. pap. (Mayser II 3, 112). MGr: Jensen, IF 47 (1929) 296.

470. Mixture of direct and indirect discourse.

(1) Since indirect discourse, whether it be with ὅτι and the optative or with the acc. (nom.) and infinitive, is not at all congenial to the NT narrators any more than it is to folk-narrators in general (§§ 386(1); 396), ὅτι is usually followed not only by the indicative instead of the optative (a tendency also in classical), but also by an exact representation of direct discourse, so that ὅτι serves the function of our quotation marks (good classical: K.-G. II 367; Br.-Th. 648). Ὅτι *recitativum* is most common in Mk (Zerwick 39–48) and

Jn, less in Lk, and still less in Mt. Jn 10: 36 is a characteristic example (Buttmann 234): . . . ὑμεῖς λέγετε ὅτι 'βλασφημεῖς', ὅτι εἶπον etc., instead of βλασφημεῖν which would connect up much better with the preceding ὅν etc. Also Jn 20: 17 εἰπὲ αὐτοῖς· (my Master says to tell you,) ἀναβαίνω. (2) It is quite impossible for a NT author to do what is so common in classical Greek (still more so in Latin), namely, to maintain indirect discourse in an extended passage. Instead he reverts without fail to the direct, a tendency which is not at all unusual in classical authors (K.-G. II 556f.): A 1: 4 παρήγγειλεν . . . μὴ χωρίζεσθαι, ἀλλὰ περιμένειν . . . ἣν ἠκούσατε. (3) Inversely, the direct form is occasionally abandoned in favor of the indirect or narrative form: A 23: 23 εἶπεν· ἑτοιμάσατε . . . 24 κτήνη τε παραστῆσαι etc.—Rob. 442f.

(1) Cf. Hebr. כִּי and Aram. דְּ 'that' before direct speech (Kautzsch 130, but cf. Dalman 239 n. 4), but likewise MGr πῶς. Kieckers, IF 35 (1915) 21ff., esp. 26f.; Mayser II 3, 46f., 112f.; Abel 361; Crönert, Gnomon 4 (1928) 88 n. 1; Ljungvik, Eranos 27 (1929) 175; Préaux, Chronique d'Égypte 6 (1931) 414f. The frequency in Mk is due to the fact that it is non-literary (Sundwall, Eranos 31 [1934] 73–84); comparison of Mt and Lk with Mk by C. H. Turner, JTS 28 (1927) 9–15. Hyperbaton in Mk 1: 40 is to be doubted (in spite of Pallis, Notes 35) λέγων αὐτῷ· κύριε, ὅτι . . . (only B; SΑΓ al. om. κύριε, CL om. ὅτι, DW om. κ. ὅτι; κύριε stems from the parallels). Ὅτι *recitativum* may also precede direct questions: R 10: 15 𝔓⁴⁶ γέγραπται ὅτι πῶς ὡραῖοι . . . (all others omit ὅτι), Herm Man 9.1 λέγων ὅτι πῶς δύναμαι . . . . Post-Christian exx. may be found in Ghedini, Vang. ap. 462f.; Ljungvik 67; Ljungvik, Synt. 54. Moreover, before a hortatory subj. R 3: 8 (s. §427(4)), before an imperatival ἵνα-clause Mk 12: 19 ἔγραψεν ἡμῖν ὅτι, ἐάν . . . , ἵνα λάβῃ (cf. ὅτι *rec.* with impera. POxy XIV 1683.20 [iv AD]). Jn 3: 28 is peculiar: ὅτι εἶπον· οὐκ εἰμὶ ὁ Χριστός, ἀλλ' ὅτι ἀπεσταλμένος εἰμί . . . (ὅτι is omitted before οὐκ because ὅτι already comes before εἶπον; the omission is rectified after ἀλλ').

(2) Mk 6: 8f. παρήγγειλεν ἵνα . . . , ἀλλ' ὑποδεδεμένους . . . (as if an inf. had preceded), καὶ μὴ ἐνδύσησθε etc. Lk 5: 14, A 23: 22, 25: 4f. Mayser II 3, 112f.; Kieckers, IF 36 (1916) 52f.

(3) Mk 2: 10 is different: ἵνα δὲ εἰδῆτε (addressed to the Pharisees as is the preceding) . . . , λέγει τῷ παραλυτικῷ· 'Σοὶ λέγω' etc. (Lk 5: 24 is similar, but Mt 9: 6 τότε λέγει): the direct form is given and the apostrophe directed to the paralytic is prepared for by the insertion of λέγει τῷ π.; this use of ἵνα with 'I will say this' to be supplied is also class. (Krüger §54, 8.14); also cf. Xen., An. 1.6.6.—Mk 7: 11 ὑμεῖς δὲ λέγετε· ἐὰν εἴπῃ ἄνθρωπος . . . , οὐκέτι ἀφίετε αὐτὸν

οὐδὲν ποιῆσαι is a mixture of ἐὰν εἴπῃ, οὐκέτι ἀφ. α. οὐδὲν π. and ὑμεῖς λέγετε· ἐὰν εἴπῃ, οὐκέτι οὐδὲν ποιήσει. Transition from direct speech to indirect: K.-G. II 557; Mayser II 3, 113 (only one ex.); Kieckers, IF 36 (1916) 65; Xen., An. 8.1.39. Mk 11: 31f. ἐὰν εἴπωμεν . . . , ἐρεῖ . . .· ἀλλὰ εἴπωμεν . . . ; ἐφοβοῦντο τὸν ὄχλον . . . ; for which φοβούμεθα Mt 21: 26 (from which D²W al. in Mk) is an awkward improvement; Pernot, Études 19. Like Mk 2: 10 but in reverse order, Barn 7.5 ἵνα δείξῃ '(He said this) in order to show'; cf. Philostr., VA 6.10 'ὅτι ('as proof that') οὐκ ἀδυνατοῦμεν σοφίζεσθαι' ('to work tricks'), (he turned to a tree and) 'τὸ δεῖνα', ἔφη, 'δένδρον (voc.) . . . , πρόσειπε τὸν σοφὸν Ἀπολλώνιον', καὶ προσεῖπε . . . (Fridrichsen, Arbeiten und Mitteilungen 2 [1936] 8–10).

On 1 C 9: 15 s. §393(2); on A 27: 10 §397(6). For μέν without a corresponding δέ §447(3–5).

(5) THE USE OF PARATAXIS IN THE VERNACULAR

471. (1) Parataxis in place of subordination with the infinitive or ἵνα (§392(1 c)), especially in those cases which go together with the preference for direct speech (§470(1)): Lk 14: 18 (19) ἐρωτῶ σε, ἔχε με παρῃτημένον. (2) Parataxis in interrogative sentences under the influence of Semitic usage is repeatedly attested in the Synoptics: Mt 18: 21 ποσάκις ἁμαρτήσει εἰς ἐμὲ ὁ ἀδελφός μου καὶ ἀφήσω αὐτῷ; (3) Parataxis in place of conditional subordination (cf. §494): R 13: 3 θέλεις δὲ μὴ φοβεῖσθαι τὴν ἐξουσίαν· τὸ ἀγαθὸν ποίει. (4) Parataxis instead of a supplementary or circumstantial participle: Rev 15: 5 εἶδον καὶ ἠνοίγη ὁ ναός for εἶδον τὸν ναὸν ἀνοιγέντα (§416(1)); Mk 2: 15 ἦσαν γὰρ πολλοὶ καὶ (οἳ καί D, *multi qui* lat) ἠκολούθουν (-θησαν, W -θει). (5) The awkward coordination of participles: C 2: 5 χαίρων καὶ βλέπων 'viewing with joy' or 'rejoicing to see'.—Rob. 426f.

(1) Cf. A 21: 39, 1 C 4: 16, Ph 4: 3. Ἐρωτῶ σε, γράψον μοι BGU II 423.11 (ii AD); cf. Raderm.² 221; Ghedini, Lett. crist. 326. Somewhat freer 1 C 14: 18 εὐχαριστῶ τῷ θεῷ, πάντων ὑμῶν μᾶλλον γλώσσαις λαλῶ. Cf. §461(2). 1 C 7: 40 δοκῶ . . . ἔχω FG (pm. ἔχειν). Mayser II 3, 184ff.; Ljungvik, Synt. 87ff. (esp. 94f.); Kapsomenakis 108 n. 1. Herm Sim 8.2.7 πειράσω καὶ . . . παραχέω (s. §73), cf. Plato, Phil. 13c πειρασόμεθα καὶ ἐροῦμεν. Rev 11: 3 δώσω . . . καὶ προφητεύσουσιν in place of the acc. and inf. (§392(1e)).

(2) Mt 26: 53, Lk 14: 5 (Wellhausen, Einl.² 13). Also cf. §469 on Mt 7: 9f.

(3) Cf. PTebt II 421.8 (iii AD) θέλ(ε)ις αὐτὸ πωλῆσα(ι), πώλησον. θέλ(ε)ις αὐτὸ ἀφεῖναι τῇ θυγατρί σ(ου), ἄφες. Kieckers, Acta et comm. Univ. Tartuensis B xxxiii 5 (1935) 6–14. More temporal than conditional: Jn 10: 12 θεωρεῖ...καὶ ἀφίησιν, 7: 34 ζητήσετέ με καὶ οὐχ εὑρήσετε, cf. 36, 8: 21, (13: 33); Mt 12: 44f. εὑρίσκει...τότε πορεύεται; Nyberg, Arbeiten und Mitteilungen 4 (1936) 22ff. (=Con. Neot. 13 [1949] 1ff.); Fridrichsen, ibid. 44f. Subordinate clauses are also co-ordinated with each other: 2 C 9: 4 μήπως (BD^b; + ἄν or ἐάν pm.) ἔλθωσιν... καὶ εὕρωσιν...καὶ (D*D^bE*L) καταισχυνθῶμεν; Mk 4: 12 (cf. Lk 8: 10) ἵνα βλέποντες βλέπωσιν ('although they look with perceptive eyes') καὶ ('yet') μὴ ἴδωσιν καὶ ἀκ.ἀκ. καὶ μὴ συνιῶσιν, μήποτε ἐπιστρέψωσιν ('in case they repent') καὶ ἀφεθῇ αὐτοῖς. Cf. UPZ I 64.10 (156 BC) ἐὰν τολμήσωσι καὶ καταβῶσι.—Also cf. §§442(4) (co-ordination with temporal designations); 442(5) (co-ordination with ἐγένετο); 461(2) (with προσέθηκε); 336(3) (with θέλεις συλλέξωμεν etc.); 461(1) (with ὅρα, ὕπαγε, ἄφες etc.); 465(2) (with interpolated clauses).—Co-ordination has gone still farther in MGr (Thumb² §§261, 265; Schwyzer, Jahrb. 500).—On the whole subject Schwyzer II 703–6; Raderm., WSt 31, 8f.; non-Greek parallels in E. Fraenkel, IF 43 (1926) 306; W. Meyer-Lübke, Gramm. d. Rom. Sprachen III (1899) 588.

(4) Mk 6: 14 ἤκουσεν...καὶ ἔλεγον (BDW, ἔλεγεν pm.); 9: 4 ὤφθη αὐτοῖς Ἠλίας σὺν Μωυσεῖ καὶ ἦσαν συλλαλοῦντες (Mt 17: 3 omits καὶ ἦσαν); Lk 6: 48 ἔσκαψεν καὶ ἐβάθυνεν 'dug deep' (βαθύνας would consequently be smoother; but καί can be taken as 'and indeed'; also cf. LXX Judg 13: 10 [following the Hebr.] ἐτάχυνε καὶ ἐξέδραμεν); Jn 8: 59 ἐκρύβη καὶ ἐξῆλθεν (= ἐκρύβη ἐξελθών 'he eluded them'? or rather 'he hid himself among the people and so escaped'); 2 C 9: 10 χορηγήσει καὶ πληθυνεῖ καὶ αὐξήσαι 𝔓⁴⁶ could be the correct reading (Debrunner, Festschr. Fridrichsen [= Con. Neot. 11 (1947)] 42). Ljungvik, Synt. 76ff. and ZNW 33 (1934) 90f.

(5) Mt 8: 14 βεβλημένην καὶ πυρέσσουσαν = Mk 1: 30 κατέκειτο πυρέσσουσα.

13. WORD AND CLAUSE ORDER

(1) WORD ORDER

472. Normal word order in the simple sentence. Word order in Greek and so in the NT is freer by far than in modern languages. There are, nevertheless, certain tendencies and habits (in the NT especially in narrative) which have created something like a normal word order. (1) The verb or nominal predicate with its copula stands immediately after the conjunction (the usual beginning of a sentence); then follow in order the subject, object, supplementary participle, etc. Thus (a) a sentence with a verb: Lk 1: 12 καὶ ἐταράχθη Ζαχαρίας ἰδών...13 εἶπεν δὲ πρὸς αὐτὸν ὁ ἄγγελος...18 καὶ εἶπεν Ζ. πρὸς τὸν ἄγγελον...; (b) with a nominal predicate: Mt 13: 31 (33) ὁμοία ἐστὶν ἡ βασιλεία τ. οὐρ. κόκκῳ... = 24 ὡμοιώθη etc. (c) The predicative participle, on the other hand, stands after the subject: Lk 2: 33 ἦν ὁ πατὴρ αὐτοῦ καὶ ἡ μήτηρ θαυμάζοντες. (d) Unemphatic pronouns tend to follow immediately on the verb, as do other parts of the sentence governed by the verb, especially when the subject is expanded: Lk 1: 11 ὤφθη δὲ αὐτῷ ἄγγελος κυρίου ἑστὼς ἐκ δεξιῶν. (2) These positions, however, are by no means mandatory. Any emphasis on an element in the sentence causes that element to be moved forward; thus Lk 1: 67 καὶ Ζαχαρίας ὁ πατὴρ αὐτοῦ...(in contrast with the neighbors who were the preceding subject of the narrative), 57 τῇ δὲ Ἐλισάβετ ἐπλήσθη ὁ χρόνος τοῦ τεκεῖν αὐτήν. (3) Transitional temporal phrases tend to stand at the beginning; but sometimes as a result of the tendency to begin the sentence with a verb, a meaningless ἐγένετο, which does not even always influence the construction, may precede: Lk 2: 1 ἐγένετο δὲ ἐν ταῖς ἡμέραις ἐκείναις ἐξῆλθεν δόγμα etc. Cf. §442(5).

(1) The verb can certainly occupy the initial position in the sentence in the continuation of a narrative in non-biblical Greek as well, but it is very common only with verbs of saying. In Semitic languages, on the other hand, this order is the rule with all verbs and consequently very popular in the NT, especially in Mk (on account of Aramaic); cf. Kieckers, Stellung des Verbs 3ff.; Schwyzer II 693ff.; Fischer, Glotta 13 (1924) 202. On word order in subordinate clauses, especially relative clauses, in the NT etc. s. Frisk, Wortstellung: relative clauses: 16, 23, 28–30 (in the NT and Polyb. the verb comes early in the sentence more frequently than in the older language; cf. MGr), 39f. (the pronominal subj. usually comes first, especially if a personal pron.), 56 (preference for putting a nom. proper name after the verb in the NT and in the language of the chancellery), 133 (so also θεός, κύριος, πατήρ, σατανᾶς, as if proper names), 134 (ἐστιν and ἦν usually precede the subject); temporal clauses 136–8; conditional clauses 138–

41. (*a*) The same rule applies for inf. and ptcp. clauses (and for the ptcp. coming at the beginning of the sentence) as for sentences with a finite verb: Lk 1: 19 καὶ ἀποκριθεὶς ὁ ἄγγελος εἶπεν αὐτῷ. For details s. Gersdorf 90f., 502ff. (*b*) Mk 2: 28 ὥστε κύριός ἐστιν ὁ υἱὸς τοῦ ἀνθρώπου καὶ τοῦ σαββάτου (cf. Lk 6: 5), for which Mt 12: 8 has κύριος γάρ ἐστιν τοῦ σαββ. ὁ υἱὸς τοῦ ἀνθρ., in which the expanded subj. was treated as more weighty than the gen. (not emphasized by καί). (*c*) A 12: 6 ἦν ὁ Πέτρος κοιμώμενος, Mk 1: 6, 14: 4, 40. (*d*) Lk 2: 13 καὶ ἐξαίφνης ἐγένετο σὺν τῷ ἀγγέλῳ πλῆθος στρατιᾶς οὐρανίου αἰνούντων etc., A 27: 2 ὄντος σὺν ἡμῖν Ἀριστάρχου Μακεδόνος Θεσσαλονικέως.

(2) Lk 1: 12b καὶ φόβος ἐπέπεσεν ἐπ' αὐτόν, evidently because φόβος rather than ἐπέπεσεν stands in parallelism with ἐταράχθη 12a (*supra* (1*a*)); contrast A 19: 17 καὶ ἐπέπεσεν φόβος ἐπὶ πάντας αὐτούς, Lk 1: 65 καὶ ἐγένετο ἐπὶ πάντας φόβος (D φόβος μέγας ἐπὶ π.) τοὺς περιοικοῦντας αὐτούς, the reason for moving πάντας forward in the usual reading being to give it stress and preserve the parallelism; for there follows: καὶ ἐν ὅλῃ τῇ ὀρεινῇ... διελαλεῖτο πάντα τὰ ῥήματα ταῦτα, καὶ ἔθεντο πάντες οἱ ἀκούσαντες ἐν τῇ καρδίᾳ αὐτῶν.

(3) Lk 1: 8 ἐγένετο δὲ ἐν τῷ ἱερατεύειν αὐτὸν... ἔλαχε etc., 23 καὶ ἐγένετο ὡς ἐπλήσθησαν..., ἀπῆλθεν etc. The initial position of ἐγένετο in the continuation of a narrative is also class. (Kieckers, Stellung des Verbs 74).

473. Separation of elements in the sentence belonging together. Closely related elements in the sentence, e.g. noun and attributive, noun and dependent gen., several subjects or objects connected by καί, etc., are usually placed together in simple speech. Poetic language and that rhetorically stylized in any way frequently pulls them apart in order to give greater effect to the separated elements by their isolation (cf. §294(5)). Such a word, torn out of its natural context and made more independent, is emphatic even when placed at the end of the sentence (whereas an early position in the sentence carries emphasis with it in any case). The connection with the following clause may also be decisive for a final position: 1 P 2: 7 ὑμῖν οὖν ἡ τιμὴ τοῖς πιστεύουσιν· ἀπειθοῦσιν δέ etc. (1) The old rule, observable in Greek and cognate languages, that unemphatic (enclitic) pronouns and the like are placed as near the beginning of the sentence as possible (Schwyzer II 690, 691), applies also to the NT (they are not, however, placed first). Elements belonging together are often thereby separated, e.g. in the epistolary formula χάρις ὑμῖν καὶ εἰρήνη, or A 26: 24 τὰ πολλά σε γράμματα εἰς

μανίαν περιτρέπει. This rule, however, is not absolutely mandatory: 2 C 11: 16 κἂν ὡς ἄφρονα δέξασθέ με, where the important thing probably was to place δέξασθε earlier for emphasis. (2) Hebrews often exhibits elegant, genuinely oratorical word order. Many such instances may also be adduced from Paul and 1 Peter. Because of the flexibility of the Greek language, vivid, impassioned speech easily gives rise to these dislocations. Notice even Rev 3: 8 μικρὰν ἔχεις δύναμιν (cf. 4, with v.l.) (not artificial: Kieckers, Stellung des Verbs 3; Schwyzer II 696ff.; J. Palm 131f.).

(1) Mt 8: 8 ἵνα μου ὑπὸ τὴν στέγην εἰσέλθῃς (Lk 7: 6 differs), Lk 18: 18 καὶ ἐπηρώτησέν τις αὐτὸν ἄρχων λέγων; R 1: 11 ἵνα τι μεταδῶ χάρισμα ὑμῖν πνευματικόν, 1 C 5: 1 ὥστε γυναῖκά τινα τοῦ πατρὸς ἔχειν (also to emphasize γυν. as well as πατρός), H 4: 11 ἵνα μὴ ἐν τῷ αὐτῷ τις ὑποδείγματι πέσῃ etc. Also cf. A 22: 1 ἀκούσατέ μου τῆς πρὸς ὑμᾶς ἀπολογίας and the like (§173(1)). The forward position of the gen. of the pron. often corresponds to the unemphatic Indo-European *dativus sympatheticus* (Havers 165f.), e.g. Jn 9: 6 ἐπέχρισεν αὐτοῦ (SABL, αὐτῷ D, om. C*WX al.) τὸν πηλὸν ἐπὶ τοὺς ὀφθαλμοὺς (αὐτοῦ), 11: 48 ἀροῦσιν ἡμῶν ('for us') καὶ τὸν τόπον καὶ τὸ ἔθνος, 13: 6 σύ μου νίπτεις τοὺς πόδας, 20: 23 ἄν τινων ἀφῆτε τὰς ἁμαρτίας, ἀφέωνται αὐτοῖς. Cf. §284(1) and Merlier, BCH 55 (1931) 216ff. The adnominal gen. can also have this position: Lk 12: 16 ἀνθρώπου τινὸς πλουσίου εὐφόρησεν ἡ χώρα.

(2) From Heb: 1: 4 τοσούτῳ κρείττων γενόμενος τῶν ἀγγέλων, ὅσῳ διαφορώτερον παρ' αὐτοὺς κεκληρονόμηκεν ὄνομα (ἀγγ. and ὄνομα were to be emphasized; ὄν. also forms a link with the following clause). 1: 5 τίνι γὰρ εἶπέν ποτε τῶν ἀγγέλων (likewise). Cf. Lindhamer *passim* and §294(5). H 11: 32 ἐπιλείψει με γάρ (v.l. γάρ με §475(2)) διηγούμενον ὁ χρόνος περὶ Γεδεών etc. (strongly reminiscent of Dem. 18.296 ἐπιλείψει με λέγονθ' ἡ ἡμέρα τὰ τῶν προδοτῶν ὀνόματα, a passage also utilized by Dionys. Hal. 2.21.5 Usener-Rademacher and by Philo [Riggenbach on H 11: 32 and p. xvii n. 23], most accurately at Sacr. Abel. 27 [I 213.1 Cohn-Wendland]; also s. Wendland, Die urchrist. Lit.-formen [Tübingen, 1912] 373 n. 2 and Bauer s.v. ἐπιλείπω), 12: 1 (τοσοῦτον and ὄγκον are emphatic), 8 εἰ δὲ χωρίς ἐστε παιδείας. The regular word order is sometimes abandoned because it would be too cumbersome and ungraceful: A 4: 33 ΑΕ μεγάλῃ δυνάμει ἀπεδίδουν οἱ ἀπόστολοι τὸ μαρτύριον τῆς ἀναστάσεως Ἰησοῦ Χρ. τοῦ κυρίου, but 𝔓⁴⁶SB etc. τὸ μαρτ. οἱ ἀπ. is better, B also has τοῦ κ. Ἰ. τῆς ἀναστάσεως.

474. The position of nouns and adverbs. (1) The rule is that an anarthrous adjectival attributive usually *follows* its substantive. (2) An adverb which further defines an adjective (or verb) also takes second position. (3) Mt particularly has the habit of placing adverbs after imperatives while he places them before indicatives. (4) Any case of an anarthrous noun which depends on a preposition is usually placed before a case governed by it, but not always (Mt 13: 33 εἰς ἀλεύρου σάτα τρία). Even the rule that an anarthrous gen. dependent on a preposition, if it governs another gen., must stand first (to avoid misunderstanding) is not without exception (Buttmann 294f. notwithstanding). (5) The participle is often separated from its adjuncts (classical) in one of three ways: (*a*) 1 C 12: 22 τὰ δοκοῦντα μέλη...ὑπάρχειν, (*b*) Mk 5: 30 τὴν ἐξ αὐτοῦ δύναμιν ἐξελθοῦσαν (D differs here and in Lk 8: 45), (*c*) C 2: 8 μή τις ὑμᾶς ἔσται ὁ συλαγωγῶν. The 'normal' inclusion of all the elements between article and noun is illustrated by H 6: 7 τὸν ἐπ' αὐτῆς ἐρχόμενον πολλάκις ὑετόν; transitional examples: Plato, Crat. 414c τὰ πρῶτα ὀνόματα τεθέντα κατακέχωσται ἤδη ('the original words, after they were given, were already buried', but more appropriately 'the words given at first'), Dem. 18. 82 οἱ γὰρ παρὰ τοῦ Κλειτάρχου καὶ τοῦ Φιλιστίδου τότε πρέσβεις δεῦρ' ἀφικνούμενοι παρὰ σοὶ κατέλυον. With a substantivized participle: Rev 19: 9 οἱ... κεκλημένοι. (6) The normal position of the vocative: at the beginning (Mt 8: 2 and often) or near the beginning of the clause (H 3: 1 ὅθεν, ἀδελφοὶ ἅγιοι, etc.), after the 2nd person pronoun (1 C 1: 10 παρακαλῶ δὲ ὑμᾶς, ἀδελφοί), after a verbal form in the 2nd person (Ja 1: 2 πᾶσαν χαρὰν ἡγήσασθε, ἀδελφοί μου), and also after a 1st person plur. which includes the persons addressed (H 10: 19 ἔχοντες οὖν, ἀδελφοί, etc.). (7) A habitual order is observable in the sequence of words in certain established pairs of nouns connected by καί (Winer 513f. [Winer-M.³ 690f.]), e.g. ἄνδρες καὶ γυναῖκες, γυν. καὶ παιδία (τέκνα), but παιδία first Mt 14: 21 D, likewise in 15: 38 SD. (8) Separation of the preposition from its case: A 5: 16 τῶν πέριξ πόλεων Ἰερουσαλήμ (SAB; it was first conceived as 'the surrounding cities', then the additional qualification was added). For πρὸ ἐξ ἡμερῶν τοῦ πάσχα and the like s. § 213.

(1) Adj. before the subst.: Mt 12: 43 δι' ἀνύδρων τόπων (ἀν. is the main idea), 13: 27 καλὸν σπέρμα (καλόν likewise), 28 ἐχθρὸς ἄνθρωπος, 45 καλοὺς μαργαρίτας, etc. The rule only applies to adjs. of quality; those of quantity can always stand before,

thus μικρός. Cf. Gersdorf 334ff., Cuendet 26–30. A rule for an adj. with an articular subst. cannot be formulated: πνεῦμα ἅγιον without art., but with art. τὸ πν. τὸ ἅγ. or τὸ ἅγ. πν. (Mt 28: 19, A 1: 8), the latter having the character of a unified concept (cf. § 270). Ἡ ἁγία πόλις (Jerusalem) Mt 4: 5, 27: 53, but ἡ πόλις ἡ ἁγία Rev 11: 2, 21: 2, 22: 19. Hebr. favored the postposition of the adj.; cf. § 292. Numerals (Cuendet 139–42) are more often placed first in the Gospels, but in lists, statements of date and distance, with ὡς and ὡσεί, they usually come after; cf. Jn 2: 6, Lk 1: 26, Mt 5: 41, Lk 8: 42, 22: 59. Uncertainty often prevails, e.g. Lk 8: 43 ἔτη δώδεκα = Mt 9: 20 and Mk 5: 25 δ. ἔτη; Mt 5: 18 ἰῶτα (emphatic) ἓν ἢ μία (the emphasis lies on the number due to the repetition) κεραία, cf. 4: 2 (acc. to SD) ἡμέρας τεσσεράκοντα καὶ τεσσ. νύκτας.

(2) Mt 4: 8 ὑψηλὸν λίαν, 2: 16 ἐθυμώθη λίαν, cf. μέλας δεινῶς Aelian, NA 1.19, ἔρημος δεινῶς 4.27. But also λίαν (om. D) πρωΐ Mk 16: 2, λίαν γὰρ ἀντέστη 2 T 4: 15.

(3) After an impera.: Mt 27: 42 καταβάτω νῦν, 43 ῥυσάσθω νῦν, 3: 15 ἄφες ἄρτι, 18: 16 (ἔτι); before an indic.: 19: 20 ἔτι ὑστερῶ, 26: 65 (5: 13 ἰσχύει ἔτι, but om. ἔτι DW), 9: 18 (ἄρτι); 26: 53 ἄρτι before παρακαλέσαι acc. to ACDW al., but it is missing in lat and syˢ), 26: 65 (νῦν); s. Gersdorf 106. Cf. Mayser II 2, 181f.

(4) An attributive gen. coming first (cf. § 271): ἐπὶ πλούτου ἀδηλότητι 1 T 6: 17, ὡς θεοῦ οἰκονόμον Jn 1: 7, ἐθνῶν ἀπόστολος R 11: 13, πάσης ἀντιλογίας πέρας H 6: 16, κατάρας τέκνα 2 P 2: 14, θεοῦ συνεργοί 1 C 3: 9. Winer § 30, 3 n. 4 [Winer-M.³ 239f.]; Rob. 502f. 2 C 3: 18 ἀπὸ κυρίου πνεύματος 'from the spirit of the Lord' (cf. 17): vg *a domini spiritu* (Marcion acc. to Tertullian *a domino spirituum* = κυρίου πνευμάτων); the variant of Origen on 1 C 2: 4 also appears to be an irregularity in word order (in Matt. tom. xiv c. 14 = x 316.9 Klostermann): οὐκ ἐν πειθοῖ σοφίας λόγων, ἀλλ' ἐν ἀποδείξει πνεύματος δυνάμεως, but cf. 2 C 4: 13 πνεῦμα τῆς πίστεως, E 1: 17 πν. σοφίας καὶ ἀποκαλύψεως, etc. Βαπτισμῶν διδαχῆς H 6: 2 can only be 'teaching of baptism' (𝔓⁴⁶B διδαχήν correctly [cf. § 168(2)]). Cf. LXX Wsd 17: 13 ἐξ ἀδυνάτου ᾅδου μυχῶν. Gersdorff 295ff. Mt 24: 31 μετὰ σάλπιγγος φωνῆς μεγάλης means 'with loud trumpet call' (cf. H 12: 19, Rev 1: 10, 4: 1, 8: 13), if the reading is correct; SLW al. omit φωνῆς, σ. καὶ φ. μ. D al., Blass takes σαλπ. to be an interpolation from references like Rev 1: 10 (cf. 1 Th 4: 16).

(5) Gild. 289f.; Stahl 691; K.-G. ι 616f., 623f.; H. Schöne, RhM 73 (1920) 151–3 and Hermes 60 (1925) 144–73; Fr. P. Jones, The *ab urbe condita* construction in Greek (Language VI 1 Suppl.; Baltimore, 1939) 83–6; A. Wifstrand, EIKOTA v 12 (K. Hum. Vet.-samf. i Lund, Årsber. 1944–5); Palm 138f.; E. Percy, Skrifter K. Hum. Vet.-samf. i Lund 39 (1946) 185f., 191f., 213. (*a*) R 8: 18 τὴν

μέλλουσαν δόξαν ἀποκαλυφθῆναι (cf. G 3: 23; but 1 P 5: 1 τῆς μελλούσης ἀποκαλύπτεσθαι δόξης), R 3: 25 τῶν προγεγονότων ἁμαρτημάτων ἐν τῇ ἀνοχῇ τοῦ θεοῦ, Ja 1: 5 παρὰ τοῦ διδόντος θεοῦ πᾶσιν ἁπλῶς, Lk 23: 48, A 10: 37, 2 P 3: 2. Mayser II 2, 62 f. ('by far the most frequent position in the pap.'), 63. A 14: 13 τοῦ ὄντος Διὸς πρὸ πόλεως acc. to D (Προπόλεως Ramsay, The Church in the Roman Empire before AD 170, pp. 51 f.; but cf. τοῦ ὄντος ἀνδρισμοῦ ἐν αὐτῷ 'the male population dwelling in it' PLond IV 1338.21 [709 AD], τῶν οὐσῶν πόλεων συμμαχίδων 'the communities presently allied' Dit., Syll.[3] 147.70 [378/7 BC], αἱ νῦν οὖσαι πόλεις ξύμμαχοι Thuc. 7.14.2, τῶν παρεόντων Ἑλλήνων ἐς Ἐρυθρὰς Hdt. 9.22; s. also infra (c)). Homil Clem 16.5.3 τὰς πεπιστευμένας γραφὰς παρὰ Ἰουδαίοις. (b) A 13: 32 τὴν πρὸς τοὺς πατέρας ἐπαγγελίαν γενομένην, cf. Homil Clem 11.2.2 τὰ ἐκ μακρῶν χρόνων ἀτοπήματα πληθυνθέντα (6.26.3 is somewhat different: τὰς τερατώδεις φαντασίας ὑπ᾽ αὐτοῦ γεγενημένας). Mk 6: 2 αἱ δυνάμεις...γενόμεναι (v.l. γίνονται). Dem. 20.84 τὸ τῷ Χαβρίᾳ ψήφισμα ψηφισθέν, Dit., Or. 736.20 (i BC) ἐν τῇ ὑπ᾽ ἐμοῦ στήλῃ ἀνατεθείσῃ, PPetr III 6 (a) 26 (237 BC) τὴν ἐν Ἀλεξανδρείᾳ οἰκίαν μοι ὑπάρχουσαν. Mayser II 2, 63.49. (c) R 10: 5 ὅτι τὴν δικαιοσύνην...ὁ ποιήσας ἄνθρωπος ζήσεται ἐν αὐτῇ S*AD* (𝔓[46]BSᶜDᶜEF al. ὅτι before ὁ ποιήσας), 1 Clem 35.6 ταῦτα γὰρ οἱ πράσσοντες, cf. 54.3, 4, Herm Sim 9.15.2, 3, Homil Clem 11.26.4 τοῦτο ὁ μήπω προσελθεῖν θέλων. H 12: 25 ἐπὶ γῆς παραιτησάμενοι τὸν χρηματίζοντα... οἱ τὸν ἀπ᾽ οὐρανῶν ἀποστρεφόμενον.—Herm Sim 9. 19.1 = 29.1 ten times ἐκ τοῦ ὄρους...οἱ πιστεύσαντες = 23.1 οἱ ἐκ τ. ὄ.... π. Uncertain Mk 9: 1 εἰσίν τινες ὧδε τῶν ἑστηκότων BD* (τῶν ἑστ. ὧδε 𝔓[45] minusc. 1; τῶν ὧδε ἑστ. al., cf. the par.), A 13: 1 ἐν Ἀντιοχείᾳ κατὰ τὴν οὖσαν ἐκκλησίαν (here rather 'in Antioch in the local church' [Mlt. 228 [360]]; cf. supra (a)) and on ὁ ὤν 'the existing one or thing, the respective thing or thing in question' s. Debrunner, Glotta 4 [1914] 250; 13 [1924] 169; Mayser II 1, 347 f.; Bauer s.v. εἰμί v), 2 Th 2: 6 καὶ νῦν τὸ κατέχον (cf. καὶ νῦν ὃν ἔχεις Jn 4: 18 [§ 475(1)], but also § 442(15)), Lk 12: 28 ἐν ἀγρῷ σήμερον τὸν χόρτον ὄντα 𝔓[45] (SBL ἐν ἀ. τὸν χ. ὄντα σήμ., AWΘ τὸν χ. σήμ. ἐν ἀ. ὄντα). Cf. Plato, Crat. 411 E τὸ ὄνομα ὁ θέμενος, Thuc. 6.64.3 ταῦτα τοὺς συνδράσοντας, Plut., C. Gracch. 14 τοῦτο πολλοῖς τῶν ἰδόντων 'many of those who saw that', Plut., Mor. 4 A (I 7.27 Bernardakis) νῦν γε τὸ γινόμενον 'as it now happens', ἕκαστα ὁ διατάσσων Epict. 3.22.4, μεταξὺ ἀλλήλων τῶν λογισμῶν κατηγορούντων R 2: 15. A. Wifstrand, K. Hum. Vet.-samf. i Lund, Årsber. 1930–1 III 143–5.

(6) The voc. elsewhere infrequently comes at the end: Lk 5: 8, A (2: 37), 26: 7 (speech of Paul before Agrippa, in which the direct address has still other choice positions: 2, 13). The position of the voc. with the 2nd pers. sing. of the verb: the voc. may be compared with the usual sequence of verb–subj.;

thus Jn 14: 9 τοσοῦτον...καὶ οὐκ ἔγνωκάς με, Φίλιππε, where Φ. could not well have stood earlier.

(7) Ἐσθίειν καὶ πίνειν, οἱ πόδες καὶ χεῖρες (reversed in Lk 24: 39, but not in S), etc.

(8) Xen., An. 7.8.12 τὰ μὲν πέριξ ὄντα ἀνδράποδα τῆς τύρσιος, Hdt. 7.124 τὰς μεταξὺ πόλις τούτων (Schöne, Hermes 60 [1925] 167 f.).

475. The position of conjunctions. (1) As in classical Greek, there are some exceptions (especially in Paul) to the obvious rule that the *subordinating* conjunctions stand at the beginning of the dependent clause. In such cases elements belonging to the subordinate clause which are to be emphasized precede the conjunction: 2 C 2: 4 τὴν ἀγάπην ἵνα γνῶτε. Such elements sometimes precede the relative also: Jn 4: 18 νῦν ὃν ἔχεις, 1 C 15: 36 σὺ ὃ σπείρεις, and at times the interrogative: Jn 1: 19 (= 8: 25, 21: 12, R 9: 20, 14: 4, Ja 4: 12) σὺ τίς εἶ; (2) Some co-ordinating conjunctions take first position, e.g. καί, ἤ, ἀλλά, others second; the latter sometimes come third, fourth or fifth in the clause (like classical: K.-G. II 267 f.), partly because of necessity, as in 1 Jn 2: 2 οὐ περὶ τῶν ἡμετέρων δὲ μόνον, Jn 8: 16 καὶ ἐὰν κρίνω δὲ ἐγώ ('Even if I however'), and partly by the choice of the author, as for example when a preposition with its object or a noun with an attributive gen. precede the conjunction.

(1) The effort not to separate conj. and verb has aided this order (cf. MGr νά, Thumb, ThLZ 1903, 423). Ἵνα in postposition: 1 C 9: 15, (2 C 12: 7,) G 2: 10, C 4: 16, A 19: 4. Ἐάν: 1 C 6: 4, 11: 14 (§ 466(1)), 14: 9, Mt 15: 14, Jn 10: 9. Ὡς: R 12: 3, 1 C 3: 5, 7: 17 (twice). Ἕως 2 Th 2: 7, ὅταν Jn 7: 27. An emphatic element before the interrogative: Jn 9: 17, 8: 25 (ὅ τι § 300(2)), Lk 9: 20, 16: 11 f.; Jn 21: 21 οὗτος δὲ τί; etc. (Buttmann 333 c; Dem. is also familiar with the final position of τί: 9.39 etc. ταῦτα δ᾽ ἐστὶ τί; also cf. Mt 6: 23 τὸ σκότος πόσον, Lk 17: 17 οἱ δὲ ἐννέα ποῦ; Wilke, Rhetorik 375).

(2) 2 C 1: 19 ὁ τοῦ θεοῦ γὰρ υἱός SAB al. (which gives more emphasis to θεοῦ than ὁ γὰρ τ. θ. υἱός DF al.; 𝔓[46] ὁ τοῦ γὰρ θ. υἱός is impossible), 1 C 8: 4 περὶ τῆς βρώσεως οὖν τῶν εἰδωλοθύτων (DE δέ after περί instead of οὖν), H 11: 32 (§ 473(2)) ἐπιλείψει με γάρ (γάρ με 𝔓[46]DᶜIKLP), R 9: 19 ἐρεῖς μοι οὖν (οὖν μοι DFG al.). Οὖν often stands third: ὃς ἐὰν οὖν..., ...μὲν οὖν, and εἴ τις οὖν Ph 2: 1 (because εἴ τις is felt to be one word; Reinhold 35; Deissmann, LO⁴ 75.6; Ljungvik, Syntax 11; cf. § 376 and ὃν τρόπον δέ 2 T 3: 8, because ὃν τρ. = ὡς is felt to be one word, s. Wackernagel, Anredeformen 30 [= Kl. Schr. 997]). On the position of τε s. § 444, on καὶ πάντες δέ and the like § 447(9), on parenthetical γάρ *before* its verb

(ὅρα γάρ φησιν 'for he said, 'look'") § 465(2). 1 C 16: 7 etc. οὐ θέλω δέ (γάρ) (= Lat. *nolo*?). R 11: 22 ἐπὶ τοὺς μέν 𝔓⁴⁶ (ἐπὶ μ. τ. pm.), POxy XIII 1599 41, 43, 44 (iv AD), Herm Sim 8.7.6 καὶ τὰς ἐντολὰς δέ...ἐν τοῖς δὲ τοιούτοις...ἐν δὲ τοῖς διχοστάτοις (A ἐν ταῖς ἐντολαῖς δέ, PMich om. δέ; A [PMich] ἐν τοῖς τοιούτοις οὖν; A ἐν τοῖς διχ. δέ). Herm Sim 9.21.1 ἐπὶ τὴν καρδίαν δέ; Man 9.3 οὐκ ἔστι γάρ, Vis 3.13.2 ὡς ἐὰν γάρ; Sim 2.8 παρὰ τοῖς οὖν ἀνθρώποις PBer (π. τ. ἀ. οὖν A). Homil Clem 3.53.3 ὃς ἂν δὲ μὴ ἀκούσῃ. Pap.: Mayser II 2, 517; II 3, 125.

For the position of negatives s. § 433; for the improper prepositions § 216.

476. Prolepsis, i.e. the anticipation of the subject (object) of the subordinate clause by making it the object of the main clause. (1) Anticipation of the subject with verbs which can take the acc. and infinitive (acc. and participle) as well as a clause with ὅτι or ἵνα (mixture of both constructions: § 408): Mk 12: 34 ἰδὼν αὐτὸν ὅτι νουνεχῶς ἀπεκρίθη, Rev 3: 9 ποιήσω αὐτοὺς ἵνα ἥξουσιν. (2) With the same verbs also often with an interrogative clause: Mt 6: 28 καταμάθετε τὰ κρίνα πῶς αὐξάνουσιν (or οὐ ξαίνουσιν Skeat, ZNW 39 [1938] 211–14; Katz, JTS 5 [1954] 207–10). (3) The anticipation of the object is infrequent (as in classical, K.-G. II 579 n. 3): G 5: 21 ἃ προλέγω ὑμῖν..., ὅτι οἱ τὰ τοιαῦτα πράσσοντες... (therefore with resumption of the object).

(1) Mk 7: 2 ἰδόντες αὐτὸν ὅτι...etc.; thus also Mk 11: 32 εἶχον (= ἐνόμιζον) τὸν Ἰωάνην ὅτι προφήτης ἦν. Anticipation of the subj. in a gen. absol. R 5: 6 ἔτι γὰρ (SACD* pl., εἴ γε B, still differently al.) Χριστὸς ὄντων ἡμῶν ἀσθενῶν ἔτι (om. DᶜEKLP pm.). Class. and Hebr. also (Johannessohn, KZ 64 [1937] 161f.), pap. (Mayser II 3, 111) and MGr (δὲ θὰ κάμετε τὸν κόσμον, νὰ σᾶς πιστέψῃ = Hell. οὐ ποιήσετε τὸν κόσμον, ἵνα ὑμῖν πιστεύσῃ [Thumb² § 266(3)], θαυμάζομαι τὸν οὐρανό, πῶς στέκει χωρὶς στύλο 'I wonder how the heavens stand without supports' [*ibid.* p. 180 n. [189]]).

(2) Οἶδά σε τίς εἶ Mk 1: 24; Jn 7: 27 τοῦτον οἴδαμεν πόθεν ἐστίν, Lk 13: 25 οὐκ οἶδα ὑμᾶς πόθεν ἐστέ (Mt 25: 12 without πόθεν ἐστίν; cf. Norden 77.1), etc. Mayser II 3, 111. UGosp 1.16 σὲ δὲ οὐκ οἴδαμεν [πόθεν εἶ], cf. Jn 9: 29.

(3) Lk 24: 7 τὸν υἱὸν..., ὅτι δεῖ παραδοθῆναι (scil. αὐτόν), A 13: 32 τὴν ἐπαγγελίαν, ὅτι ταύτην etc. (cf. § 152(2)). G 4: 11 is doubly noteworthy: φοβοῦμαι ὑμᾶς ('*for* you'; φοβ. cannot take an acc. with inf.), μήπως εἰκῇ κεκοπίακα εἰς ὑμᾶς, with which Winer 582 (Winer-M.³ 782) compares Soph., OT 767; MGr

φοβοῦμαι σε μήν (= μή) ἀποθάνῃς acc. to Jannaris § 1937.—Rob. 423.

477. (1) To assume *hyperbaton,* i.e. an artificial misplacement of a word (or words) as opposed to natural word order, is a very old exegetical expedient. Plato has Socrates use it (Protag. 343 E) in order to force Simonides the poet to express what Socrates regards as correct. It has been employed in the same way and with scarcely more warrant by NT exegetes. (2) *Chiasmus,* i.e. the literary pattern a b/b a, is not common in the NT, e.g. Phm 5 τὴν ἀγάπην καὶ τὴν πίστιν...πρὸς τὸν κύριον Ἰ. καὶ εἰς πάντας τοὺς ἁγίους, 1 C 8: 5 𝔓⁴⁶ πολλοί εἰσιν θεοί (pm. εἰσὶν θεοὶ π.) καὶ κύριοι πολλοί. Debrunner's judgment is contested by J. Jeremias, ZNW 49 (1958) 145–56: Chiasmus plays a considerable role in Paul; he arranges words, parts of sentences, and even whole sentences according to the schema a b/b a, e.g. C 3: 11 οὐκ ἔνι Ἕλλην καὶ Ἰουδαῖος / περιτομὴ καὶ ἀκροβυστία, 1 C 4: 10, etc., sometimes for purely rhetorical reasons, but sometimes also due to the course of his argument. Paul also articulates a stated theme with two or more elements in a chiastic pattern in larger contexts (even a whole Epistle—Gal.!), e.g. 1 C 1: 24f.: Χριστὸν θεοῦ δύναμιν καὶ θεοῦ σοφίαν / ὅτι τὸ μωρὸν τοῦ θεοῦ σοφώτερον τῶν ἀνθρώπων ἐστίν / καὶ τὸ ἀσθενὲς τοῦ θεοῦ ἰσχυρότερον τῶν ἀνθρώπων; cf. R 11: 22, 9: 24–9. Galatians: two criticisms leveled at Paul are indicated in 1: 10–12, that his gospel is κατὰ ἄνθρωπον (*vv.* 10f.) and that it stems παρὰ ἀνθρώπου (*v.* 12); his replies are articulated in a chiastic pattern, i.e. in reverse order: παρὰ ἀνθ. (1: 13–2: 21), κατὰ ἄνθ. (3: 1–6: 10). Cf. § 474(1) on Mt 5: 18 and 4: 2.

(1) S. also §§ 396; 470(1); Winer § 61, 5 [Winer-M.³ 692ff.]; Rob. 423.—On irregular word order: in Mk s. Zerwick 126–9, 129f.; in Jn s. E. Schweizer, EGO EIMI (Göttingen, 1939) 94ff.; in Attic orators J. de Vries, Diss. Freib. i. B., 1938 (PhW 1939, 291ff.); A. Loepfe, Die Wortstellung im gr. Sprechsatz (Diss. Freib. i. d. Schweiz, 1940) 138ff. Literature: Bo Reicke, The Disobedient Spirits 149 n.

(2) Wilke, Rhetorik 372; Winer 383 [Winer-M.³ 511, 658]. Chiasmus is in greater favor in Lat. than in Greek (K.-G. II 603); it is common in Hebrew: Gesenius-Kautzsch § 114 r, n., Brockelmann, GVG II § 317 d; cf. Hebräische Syntax § 138. Jeremias, *op. cit.* 151f., sees in it Semitic influence (Greek and Latin forms of chiasmus are different), since chiasmus is common in *parallelismus membrorum,*

e.g. Ps 1: 6. N. W. Lund, Chiasmus in the NT, A Study in Formgeschichte (Chapel Hill and London, 1942; cf. ThR 17 [1948] 146 and for an adverse review Jeremias, *op. cit.* 145); Palm 142f. Chiasmus in Mk: Zerwick 124f.; in Lk: R. Morgenthaler, Die lukanische Geschichtsschreibung als Zeugnis ɪ (Zürich, 1948) 42.

(2) CLAUSE ORDER

478. It is to be noted that there is the possibility of shifting a final clause forward: Jn 19: 28 μετὰ τοῦτο 'I. εἰδὼς..., ἵνα τελειωθῇ ἡ γραφή, λέγει 'Διψῶ', 19: 31, R 9: 11. Jn 10: 36 has the appearance of a rhetorical period in that the subordinate clause ὃν ὁ πατὴρ ἡγίασεν etc. has been placed

before the main clause ὑμεῖς λέγετε ὅτι βλασφημεῖς (= βλασφημεῖν, §470(1)); in fact, however, the sentence with its defective structure (ὅν refers to βλασφημεῖς) is one of the examples of loose sentence structure (where two clauses are involved) found elsewhere in Jn (§466 (1)).

It would be forced to make τίνι λόγῳ εὐηγγελισάμην ὑμῖν 1 C 15: 2 dependent on the following εἰ κατέχετε; it is more likely that εἰ as well as the reading of D*FG ὀφείλετε κατέχειν (for εἰ κατέχετε) is an explanatory gloss ($\mathfrak{P}^{46}$ has a dash, then κατέχειν deleted by dots, then εἰ κατέχετε) so that it is only a question of a subordinate clause preceding a main clause (κατέχετε) (therefore a full stop after σῴζεσθε and a new, independent sentence following, §463).

14. ELLIPSIS, BRACHYLOGY, PLEONASM

(1) ELLIPSIS AND BRACHYLOGY

479. Ellipsis (brachylogy) in the broad sense applies to any idea which is not fully expressed grammatically and leaves it to the hearer or reader to supply the omission because it is self-evident. (1) First of all, the figure ἀπὸ κοινοῦ (K.-G. ɪɪ 560f.) belongs to this category, i.e. the repetition of a grammatical element is left to be supplied. For example, the repetition of a preposition with the second of two nouns or pronouns connected by καί is a matter of preference (Winer §50, 7 [Winer-M.³ 522ff.]): ἀπὸ πάντων (ἀφ') ὧν A 13: 38. The same is true of a verb in the protasis: 2 C 5: 13 εἴτε γὰρ ἐξέστημεν, θεῷ (scil. ἐξέστ.)· εἴτε σωφρονοῦμεν, ὑμῖν (scil. σωφρ.). Some adjustment is permissible in this figure (cf. in the case of the article §276(1)): Mk 14: 29 εἰ καὶ πάντες σκανδαλισθήσονται, ἀλλ' οὐκ ἐγώ, scil. σκανδαλισθήσομαι, which in D and in Mt 26: 33 is actually added. (2) *Zeugma* is a special type of ellipsis requiring a different verb to be supplied (K.-G. ɪɪ 570f.), i.e. *one* verb is used with two objects (subjects) but suits only one: 1 C 3: 2 γάλα ὑμᾶς ἐπότισα, οὐ βρῶμα (scil. ἐψώμισα or the like, §155(7)).

(1) Exx. of harsher adjustments: G 3: 5 ἐξ ἔργων νόμου scil. ἐπιχορηγεῖ τὸ πνεῦμα καὶ ἐνεργεῖ etc. (to be deduced from the ptcps.). Combination of positive and negative: 1 C 10: 24 μηδεὶς τὸ ἑαυτοῦ ζητείτω, ἀλλὰ τὸ τοῦ ἑτέρου, scil. ἕκαστος (to be deduced from μηδείς; this is good class., K.-G. ɪɪ

566f.). Also Mt 4: 25 ἀπὸ τῆς Γαλιλαίας...καὶ 'Ιουδαίας καὶ (ἀπὸ) πέραν τοῦ 'Ιορδάνου. Verb not repeated: Herm Vis 2.1.4 ἡρπάγη..., ὑπὸ τίνος δέ (scil. ἡρπάγη), οὐκ εἶδον; cf. POsl ɪɪ 23.10 (214 AD) οὐκ ὀλίγη μοι βλάβη ἐπηκολούθησεν, ὑπὸ τίνων, ἀγνοῶ (Olsson, IF 52 [1934] 155). Pap. (prep.): Mayser ɪɪ 2, 515f. The formula οὐ μόνον, ἀλλὰ καί = 'not only, but also; also, in addition' (R 5: 3, 11, 8: 23, 9: 10, 2 C 8: 19) with something to be supplied from what immediately precedes also belongs to the ἀπὸ κοινοῦ construction. In 2 C 7: 7 it is actually supplied; only in R 9: 10 are the words to be supplied not definitely given in the context. Cf. Winer 543 [Winer-M.³ 729] and Wifstrand, K. Hum. Vet.-samf. i Lund, Årsber. 1930–1 ɪɪɪ 134f.; 1932–3 ɪ 26 with exx. from Plato (οὐ μόνον ἀλλὰ γε) and the Hell. period; Mitteis, Chr. 26.9 = 27.9 (108 BC).

(2) 1 T 4: 3 κωλυόντων γαμεῖν, ἀπέχεσθαι βρωμάτων scil. κελευόντων. Moulton puts Lucian, Charon 2 in the same class: σὲ δὲ κωλύσει ἐνεργεῖν τὰ τοῦ Θανάτου ἔργα καὶ (scil. ποιήσει) τὴν Πλούτωνος ἀρχὴν ζημιοῦν μὴ νεκραγωγοῦντα. This passage however is corrupt: ⟨ὡς⟩ καὶ τὴν... is a good emendation by Fritzsche following Jensius. Further exx. of zeugma in Wilke, Rhetorik 130: 1 C 14: 34 with ἐπιτρέπεται (if ὑποτάσσεσθαι is read with DFG al.), A 14: 22 with παρακαλοῦντες. A 1: 21 is also related: εἰσῆλθεν καὶ ἐξῆλθεν ἐφ' ἡμᾶς for εἰσ. ἐφ' ἡμᾶς καὶ ἐξ. παρ' ἡμῶν (cf. 9: 28).—Cf. Rob. 1200f., 1202f.

480. Ellipses proper of the formulaic (conventional) type. By ellipsis in the strict sense is understood a case in which a term neither is present nor can be supplied from some related term. The following can be omitted in this category: whatever is obvious from the structure of the sentence, like the copula (§§ 127 f.); the subject if it is very general ('thing' or 'men') or is required by the assertion (§§ 129 f.); the substantive if it is made sufficiently evident by an attributive, especially feminines like ἡμέρα, ὥρα etc. (§ 241), or by the article with certain attributive genitives (§ 162). Such ellipses are conventional and partially corresponding usages are found in other languages. Further ellipses: (1) The omission of the notion 'other, whatever' (§ 306(5)) is specifically Greek: 1 C 10: 31 εἴτε ἐσθίετε εἴτε πίνετε εἴτε τι (scil. ἄλλο 'whatever else') ποιεῖτε. (2) Verbs may become intransitive by the omission of objects, e.g. τελευτᾶν (scil. τὸν βίον) 'to die'. (3) Ellipsis of adjectives: γλώσσαις λαλεῖν is properly ἑτέραις γλ. λαλεῖν, as it is designated in the narrative where the phenomenon first appears (A 2: 4). (4) Ellipsis of the adverb μᾶλλον: 1 C 14: 19 θέλω...λαλῆσαι...ἢ... (§ 245(3)). (5) Ellipsis of the verb in various usages: the repetition of 'he said' can be omitted as superfluous and cumbersome in reports of conversations, e.g. A 25: 22 Ἀγρίππας δὲ πρὸς τὸν Φῆστον (CEHLP with ἔφη; in 9: 5, 11 the verb can be supplied from the foregoing: ἀπὸ κοινοῦ). Cf. Xen. and Hellenistic authors (Kieckers, IF 36 [1916] 23 ff.); for the papyri s. Mayser II 3, 4. In letters χαίρειν is always used without λέγει (§ 389) or ἐπέστειλεν (Mayser, op. cit. 5 f.), if indeed χαίρειν itself is not omitted (Mayser, op cit. 6), as for example Rev 1: 4 and in Paul; in the latter, however, the Christian greeting χάρις ὑμῖν is substituted. All sorts of verbs are omitted in formulae and proverbs which tend to be expressed in a laconic form: Mt 5: 38 ὀφθαλμὸν ἀντὶ ὀφθαλμοῦ etc. (δώσει according to LXX Ex 21: 23 f.), Rev 6: 6 χοῖνιξ σίτου δηναρίου (scil. πωλεῖται 'costs'). Ὅρα μή (scil. ποιήσῃς) must also have been common: Rev 19: 10, 22: 9. (6) Εἰ δὲ μή (γε) (§ 439(1)) 'otherwise' has become frozen so that it can be used after a negative clause (instead of εἰ δέ), e.g. Lk 5: 36 (classical, K.-G. II 486; papyri, Mayser, op. cit. 7 ff.).—On the whole, D. Tabachovitz, Museum Helveticum 3 (1946) 162–79; Rob. 1201 ff., 1203 f.

(1) A 2: 14 Πέτρος σὺν τοῖς ἕνδεκα = σὺν τοῖς λοιποῖς ἑνδ. (ἀποστόλοις), cf. v. 37 where S pm. have τὸν Πέτρον καὶ τοὺς λοιποὺς ἀποστόλους, D al. without λοιπούς; 5: 29 (§ 306(5)). R 14: 21 μηδέ scil. 'or to do anything else'. Mt 16: 14. Mt 20: 24 = Mk 10: 41 οἱ δέκα 'the other ten'; s. also § 265 and Wackernagel, Syntax II² 136 f., 318. Καὶ πάντες 'and all others'

Herm Man 4.3.7, 5.2.8, 8.12; s. also καὶ πάντες δέ § 447(9).

(2) Διάγειν (scil. τὸν βίον) 'spend life' T 3: 3 (with βίον 1 T 2: 2), s. Bauer s.v. διάγω; διατελεῖν and διατρίβειν are used similarly; further προσέχειν (scil. τὸν νοῦν), cf. § 308 etc.

(3) In similar narratives in A (10: 46, 19: 6) ἑτέραις has only weak versional support, and is always omitted by Paul (but s. 1 C 14: 21). Γλώσσαις καιναῖς [Mk] 16: 17.

(4) Consequently θέλω = 'prefer, want rather' like βούλομαι Hom., Il. 1.117.

(5) There is ellipsis of λέγω also in the formula οὐχ ὅτι = οὐ λέγω ὅτι (as we say 'not that'): Jn 6: 46 οὐχ ὅτι τὸν πατέρα ἑώρακέν τις, 7: 22, 2 C 1: 24, 3: 5, Ph 4: 17, 2 Th 3: 9. The origin is so obscure that Paul can say Ph 4: 11 οὐχ ὅτι καθ' ὑστέρησιν λέγω (Winer 555 [Winer-M.³ 746]; or it is to be understood as οὐχ ὅτι κ. ὑ., λέγω 'so I say'?); cf. class. (K.-G. II 257 ff.) and ZenP Cairo III 59362.11 (242 BC). A comparison, however, is involved in class. (with a following ἀλλά; also Homil Clem 7.11 οὐ λέγω ὅτι...ἀλλά) which is absent from the NT. Paul uses οὐχ οἷον ὅτι ('it is not so that') once in a similar sense: R 9: 6 οὐχ οἷον δὲ ὅτι ἐκπέπτωκεν ὁ λόγος τοῦ θεοῦ (like Polyb. 3.82.5 οὐχ οἷον...ἀλλά used with comparison = class. οὐχ ὅτι). Cf. elliptical μήτιγε, § 427(3). Καὶ (ἰδοὺ) φωνή scil. ἐγένετο Mt 3: 17, 17: 5, A 10: 15 (cf. 13), s. § 128(7). Ὑμεῖς δὲ οὐχ οὕτως ('should not act') Lk 22: 26, cf. R 13: 11 καὶ τοῦτο. On elliptical ἀλλ' ἵνα s. § 448(7). On ἵνα τί, τί πρὸς σέ etc. s. § 299(3, 4). Formulae and proverbs: A 18: 6 τὸ αἷμα ὑμῶν ἐπὶ τὴν κεφαλὴν ὑμῶν, cf. Mt 27: 25 (scil. ἐλθάτω following Mt 23: 35; Hebr., s. LXX 2 Km 1: 16). 2 P 2: 22 ὗς λουσαμένη εἰς κυλισμὸν βορβόρου (cf. class. γλαῦκ' Ἀθήναζε etc.; however in 1 P ἐπιστρέψασα can be supplied from the preceding proverbial saying, Winer 547 [Winer-M.³ 735]). Epict. 4.8.34 εὐθὺς ἐπὶ τὸ σκῆπτρον, ἐπὶ τὴν βασιλείαν ('go at once to...'). R 4: 1 τί οὖν ἐροῦμεν Ἀβραάμ (εὑρηκέναι, which B correctly omits, is interpolated; an indefinite 'has done' or 'has experienced' is to be supplied); cf. G 3: 19 τί οὖν ὁ νόμος 'Why then the law?'

(6) Εἰ δὲ μή is also used for ἐὰν δὲ μή after ἐὰν μέν...: Lk 10: 6, 13: 9 (in Rev 2: 5 an explanatory clause with ἐὰν μή is added at the end); s. class. (Krüger § 65, 5.12) and pap. (Mayser II 3, 8). Also εἰ μή, ἐὰν μή (Mk 4: 22, G 2: 16) 'except' were originally elliptical.

2 Th 1: 5 ἔνδειγμα τῆς δικαίας κρίσεως...(after ταῖς θλίψεσιν αἷς ἀνέχεσθε) stands for ὅ ἐστιν ἔνδ. (cf. E 3: 13, Ph 1: 28), but it can be taken as a loose 'acc. in apposition to a clause' (K.-G. I 284; Buttmann 134) as in R 12: 1 τὴν λογικὴν λατρείαν ὑμῶν ('which is...') and with reverse order in 8: 3 τὸ γὰρ ἀδύνατον τοῦ νόμου (= ὃ τῷ νόμῳ ἀδ. ἦν; on the gen. s. § 263(2))...ὁ θεὸς τὸν ἑαυτοῦ υἱόν.... Jn 7: 35 ποῦ οὗτος μέλλει πορεύεσθαι, ὅτι ἡμεῖς οὐχ

εὑρήσομεν αὐτόν; is not elliptical, but ὅτι = δι' ὅ τι is, as in 14: 22 (§ 299(4)), 9: 17, Mt 8: 27, Mk 4: 41 (cf. the Semitic sequence of interrogative plus 'that'). Cf. § 456(2) on these constructions. Mt 16: 7 is different: ὅτι ἄρτους οὐκ ἐλάβομεν = τοῦτ' ἐκεῖνο, ὅτι 'with reference to the fact that'; cf. class. ellipses with ὅτι (K.-G. II 371 f.).—Cf. Rob. 1201 f., 391 ff., 395 f.

481. Freer individual ellipses. Ellipses dependent on individual style and choice go much farther, especially in letters, where the writer can count on the knowledge which the recipient shares with himself and where he imitates ordinary speech. In the latter there is likewise an abundance of elliptical expressions, both conventional and those more dependent on individual preference.

Exx.: 1 C 1: 31 ἵνα καθὼς γέγραπται· 'Ο καυχώμενος... = 'in order that it may come to pass, work out just as...', or else (Winer 557 [Winer-M.³ 749]) the literal quotation is adopted (cf. § 470) in place of a paraphrase which would have required the subjunctive.—4: 6 ἵνα ἐν ἡμῖν μάθητε τὸ μὴ ὑπὲρ ἃ γέγραπται (S^cD^c al. add φρονεῖν).—2 C 8: 15 OT ὁ τὸ πολὺ οὐκ ἐπλεόνασεν, καὶ ὁ τὸ ὀλίγον οὐκ ἠλαττόνησεν = LXX Ex 16: 18, where on the basis of v. 17 (καὶ συνέλεξαν ὁ τὸ πολὺ καὶ ὁ τὸ ἔλαττον) something like συλλέξας is to be supplied (cf. Num 11: 32); Winer 548 [Winer-M.³ 737; cf. n. 4] supplies ἔχων, comparing Lucianic expressions like ὁ τὸ ξύλον scil. ἔχων 'the one with the rod' (Cat. 4). Further exx. relative to this passage in A. Wifstrand, Beiträge zur gr. Syntax (Vet.-Soc. i Lund, Årsbok 1934) 8 ff. (animated dialogistic style).—R 13: 7 ἀπόδοτε πᾶσιν τὰς ὀφειλάς, τῷ τὸν φόρον (scil. something like ὀφειλόμενον ἔχοντι) τὸν φόρον, τῷ τὸ τέλος τὸ τέλος etc.— G 5: 13 μόνον μὴ τὴν ἐλευθερίαν εἰς ἀφορμὴν τῇ σαρκί, perhaps scil. ἔχετε; we also are inclined to an ellipsis with this admonitory '(only) not'. Cf. further Mt 26: 5 = Mk 14: 2 μὴ ἐν τῇ ἑορτῇ, where however it is possible and necessary to supply something from the preceding. With G 5: 13 cf. Epict., Ench. 29.7 μὴ ὡς τὰ παιδία νῦν φιλόσοφος, ὕστερον δὲ τελώνης...(scil. ἴσθι). Ph 3: 13 ἐν δέ (scil. 'I do'. Fridrichsen, Symb. Osl. 13 [1934] 44–6 interprets it as ἐν δέ 'but thereby'[?]; Heikel, StKr 106 [1934/5] 316 ἐμ' αὐτὸν [scil. μὲν] οὔπω λογίζομαι κατειληφέναι, ἐν δέ 'still not made him my own, but at least one thing'. Fridrichsen, Con. Neot. 9 [1944] 32: ἐν δέ, τοῦτο δέ, τοσοῦτο δέ are abbreviated interjectional clauses; cf. K.-G. I 285. Thus 'but one thing I do do', cf. Xen. Eph. 5.3 τοσοῦτο δέ· ἐστέναξεν ἂν ποτε 'Αβροκόμης).—2 C 9: 6 τοῦτο δέ (scil. φημι following 1 C 7: 29, 15: 50). 2 C 9: 7 ἕκαστος scil. 'let him give'. G 2: 9 δεξιὰς ἔδωκαν κοινωνίας, ἵνα ἡμεῖς εἰς τὰ ἔθνη (Winer 546 [Winer-M.³ 735] supplies εὐαγγελιζώμεθα

following 2 C 10: 16). R 4: 9 ὁ μακαρισμὸς...; (λέγεται). 5: 18 ὡς δι' ἑνὸς παραπτώματος εἰς πάντας ἀνθρώπους εἰς κατάκριμα, οὕτως...which would be unintelligible without the long exposition preceding and even so hardly admits of being supplemented with a definite word such as ἀπέβη, ἀποβήσεται: Paul again emphasizes the correspondence between the two contrasting causes (διά) and ultimate ends (εἰς) and in between their equivalent extension (εἰς). Herm Vis 4.1.9 οὐδὲν (scil. ἐποίει) εἰ μὴ τὴν γλῶσσαν προέβαλλεν.

482. Aposiopesis in the strict sense, i.e. a breaking-off of speech due to strong emotion or to modesty, is unknown in the NT (but cf. Rob. 1203). On the other hand, aposiopesis takes the form of the omission of the apodosis to a conditional subordinate clause (protasis), which is also classical.

Jn 6: 62 ἐὰν οὖν θεωρῆτε..., scil. 'would you then still take offense?' A 23: 9 εἰ δὲ πνεῦμα ἐλάλησεν αὐτῷ, scil. 'what opposition could we make?' (HLP interpolate μὴ θεομαχῶμεν). R 9: 22 s. § 467. For the omission of the first apodosis of a hypothetical alternative, s. § 454(4); cf. Lk 19: 42 εἰ ἔγνως καὶ σὺ τὰ πρὸς εἰρήνην (scil. 'it would be pleasing to me'), νῦν δὲ ἐκρύβη, likewise 22: 42 if εἰ βούλει παρενέγκαι τοῦτο τὸ ποτήριον ἀπ' ἐμοῦ, πλήν...is to be read (v.l. παρενεγκεῖν and παρένεγκε).—Abbreviation is probably also to be assumed for the main clause in comparisons: 2 C 3: 13 καὶ οὐ ('we do not do...') καθάπερ Μωυσῆς etc., Mt 25: 14, Mk 13: 34; cf. § 453(4). On Mt 26: 50 s. § 300(2). With 2 C 3: 13 cf. Plut., Mor. 470 B (III 221.21 Bernardakis) ἀποθεωρεῖν καὶ μὴ καθάπερ οἱ πολλοὶ πρὸς τοὺς ὑπερέχοντας ἀντιπαρεξάγουσιν (instead of -άγειν) (Ljungvik, ZNW 32 [1933] 207 f.). Jd 22 f. οὓς μὲν...οὓς δέ... relative clause with the second main clause missing? (Tabachovitz, Eranos 33 [1935] 90).

483. Brachylogy is the omission, for the sake of brevity, of an element which is not necessary for the grammatical structure but for the thought. The abbreviated form of a train of thought is conventional in the ἵνα-clauses which are put ahead of the main clauses and state the purpose of the subsequent clause: Mt 9: 6 ἵνα δὲ εἰδῆτε... (§ 470(3); probably to be included here are 2 C 10: 9 ἵνα δὲ [δέ add. H vg al.] μὴ δόξω...[10 is parenthetical]; a final clause after a question [scil. 'answer'] Jn 1: 22, 9: 36). R 11: 18 εἰ δὲ κατακαυχᾶσαι, ('you should know that, remember that') οὐ σὺ τὴν ῥίζαν βαστάζεις, ἀλλ' ἡ ῥίζα σέ, 1 C 11: 16 (Winer 575 [Winer-M.³ 773f.]) are examples of a more individualistic type. Herm

Vis 3.1.8 ὅ σοι λέγω, φησίν (scil. 'that do:'), κάθισον; Sim 8.6.1 ἵνα ἴδῃς '(it happened) in order that ...'.—Cf. Rob. 1203f.

(2) PLEONASM

484. Pleonasm consists in the repetition of an idea which has already been expressed in the sentence, not for any rhetorical purpose (as is the case, for example, with epanadiplosis, §493(1)) nor because of mere carelessness, but as a consequence of certain habits of speech: e.g. A 18:21 πάλιν ἀνακάμψω, Lk 22:11 τῷ οἰκοδεσπότῃ τῆς οἰκίας (Mk 14:14 without τῆς οἰκ.; the Atticists postulated οἰκίας δεσπότης). With these may be classed classical αἰπόλια αἰγῶν and the like (K.-G. II 582). For pleonastic ἕτερος and ἄλλος s. §306(4, 5).

Πάλιν ὑποστρέφειν G 1:17 (π. ἐπιστρ. 4:9); π. ἐκ δευτέρου, δεύτερον, ἐκ τρίτου, ἄνωθεν Mt 26:42, 44, A 10:15, Jn 4:54 (πάλιν δεύτ. om. e, πάλιν om. sy^c), G 4:9; Winer 562 [Winer-M.³ 755], however, rightly emphasizes that ἐκ δευτέρου *after* πάλιν is not superfluous but a closer specification. A 14:10 εὐθέως παραχρῆμα D is class.; εὐθὺς καὶ π. PStrassb 35.17 (iv/v AD). Ἔπειτα (D al. εἶτα) μετὰ τοῦτο Jn 11:7 (Chr without μ. τ.); a similar phrase is found in class. (K.-G. II 584).—For ἀπὸ μακρόθεν and the like s. §104(2); προδραμὼν (εἰς τὸ) ἔμπροσθεν (προλαβὼν ἔμπρ. D) Lk 19:4 is similar. In Jn 20:4 προέδραμεν τάχιον τοῦ Πέτρου, ἔδραμον τάχιον or προέδραμεν τοῦ Π. would be sufficient, especially since καὶ ἦλθεν πρῶτος εἰς τὸ μνημεῖον follows. The text, as so often in Jn, is not unanimously attested: Blass adopted προέφθασεν τὸν Π. (following sy^s etc.). Lk 1:76 προπορεύσῃ πρὸ προσώπου (=πρὸ) κυρίου is somewhat different, for it is a common feature of the language that a prep. compounded with a verb in its literal, local sense is repeated with the complement (εἰσβάλλειν εἰς) (§202).—Cf. μᾶλλον with the comparative §246; αὐτοῦ after ὅς (Hebr.) §297; pleonastic negation §§429; 431(2, 3); ἐκτὸς εἰ μὴ = εἰ μή §376. Εἶπεν λέγων (§420), ἰδὼν εἶδον (§422), θανάτῳ τελευτάτω (§198(6)) and other Hebraizing redundancies can also be counted among pleonasms. On ἄρξασθαι, ἀρξάμενος s. §§392(2); 419(3); on ἐγένετο §442(5).—Cf. Rob. 1205.

15. THE ARRANGEMENT OF WORDS: FIGURES OF SPEECH

485. Introduction. The sophists and rhetoricians who created Attic *Kunstprosa* towards the end of the v and the beginning of the iv centuries BC, did so with a certain amount of emulation of the only artistic form then in existence, the poetic, and so they sought in the arrangement of words (composition, σύνθεσις) and what is connected therewith—we are not speaking here of the choice of words—partly to take over the external charms of poetic diction and partly to supplant them with equivalents for prose. Since versification was excluded, Gorgias of Sicily, the first master of artistic rhetoric, employed certain figures as equivalents to the devices of poetry; in rhetoric these bear his name (Γοργίεια σχήματα). They consist in the artificially arranged and calculated combination of contrasts (antithesis) or parallels (parison, isocolon), the appeal of which was frequently enhanced by the use of assonance at the end of a member (rhyme) as also at the beginning and within members (παρόμοια, parechesis, etc.). These devices have obvious affinities with that which elsewhere constitutes the characteristic distinction of poetry from prose and have special affinities with the old Hebrew *parallelismus membrorum*. The affected and wooden style of Gorgias subsequently went out of fashion. The Attic orators of the iv century created an entirely new, flexible style for practical oratory, for which the figures of Gorgias were least suited; the new style depended on an imitation of the living language with its forms and figures springing directly from the feelings. In place of excessive rhyme and the use of assonance in general, the prose style of the iv century adopted from the poets the practice of joining words smoothly together (which had already begun with Gorgias) by avoiding so-called hiatus, i.e. the unpleasing succession of vowels in the final and initial sounds of adjoining words. Hellenistic and Atticistic authors in the following centuries likewise avoided hiatus more or less strictly.

The rhetoricians distinguished and named, in addition to the figures of expression (σχήματα λέξεως), an equally large number of figures of thought (σχήματα διανοίας). In the latter the replacement of a word by a synonym, the deletion of a word or an alteration in word order does not obliterate the figure as it does in the former. Figures of thought belong in general more to the later than to the earlier epoch of Attic oratory, since their development presupposes a certain advance in cunning and *raffinement*.

The relation of NT authors to artistic prose: 'As artistic prose, in my opinion, none of the Pauline Epistles can be considered the equal of Hebrews; however Romans and 1 Corinthians, with which the author has taken special pains in conformity with the type of persons he is addressing, approach it. In all the others there is at most only occasionally such an approximation to artistic prose. Among the other books of the NT the Gospel of Matthew is the only one which exhibits any approximation to it (cf. §492). Acts is indeed excellent in structure and arrangement, but in presentation strongly "amateurish" (ἰδιωτικὴ φράσις in contrast to τεχνική). Lest *Kunstprosa* be left undefined, I must remark that I apply this label to all writings which are intended by an author technically trained in this regard, not only to instruct, nor merely to make an impression, but also to please. This applies to Hebrews in my opinion, but nowhere else in the NT, at least not fully' (Blass in the 2nd ed. of the present work, 1902, 312 n.).

J. Weiss, Beiträge zur paulinischen Rhetorik (ThStudien, presented to B. Weiss, Göttingen, 1897) on which s. Deissmann, ThR 5 (1902) 65 f. C. Starcke, Die Rhetorik des Ap. Paulus im Galaterbrief und die 'πηλίκα γράμματα' Gal. 6: 11 (Programm, Stargard in Pommern, Ostern 1911). Also cf. Ed. König, Stilistik, Rhetorik, Poetik in Bezug auf die biblische Litteratur, Leipzig, 1900 (deals almost exclusively with the OT). Black, Aramaic Approach, 105–42. For misc. comments, Moule 193–201.

(1) FIGURES OF EXPRESSION
(A) Avoidance of Hiatus (in Hebrews)

486. Writers and speakers are not aware of hiatus under all circumstances: it becomes inaudible in pause, i.e. at a break in thought (end of a sentence or clause). Hiatus can be avoided by elision of the first vowel (ἀλλ᾽, δ᾽) or crasis (κἄν). In the case of small 'form-words' like καί, εἰ, μή, τοῦ, ὁ, τό (forms of the article; also ὅ, οὗ etc.), it offers a prose writer an almost necessary liberty; in such words a final long vowel or diphthong is shortened and since the same shortening is equally possible in any other words ending in a vowel, even polysyllabic words, a way is opened for the negotiation of several harsher forms of hiatus. Hiatus is of course permitted with τί, τι, ὅτι, περί, πρό, as was the case even in the poets. On the other hand, both hiatus and the need for elision were preferably avoided in the case of -ᾰ, -ε, -ο in other than 'form-words' (§17). However, the αι of the verbal endings, which was reckoned short for the purpose of accent, was sometimes elided (e.g. in the Herculanean rolls of Philodemus, K.-Bl. I 238). If the question of hiatus is examined in detail and the data grouped for *Hebrews*, setting aside all quotations and the final chapter (closing admonitions, etc.), the result is that, in proportion to the length of the Epistle, there is a strikingly small number of instances; this suggests that the author paid attention to such matters as the avoidance of hiatus.

Hiatus in Hebrews: in pause it is a matter of indifference as is more or less the case with καί. With μή 7 exx., with ὁ only 5 (6: 16, 9: 7, 25, 10: 23, 11: 28), τό 15, τά 4, οἱ 6, ἡ 1, τοῦ 8, τῷ 5, τῇ 1, ὅ 1, διό 2 (10: 5, 11: 16; in 2: 11 it is avoided by δι᾽ ἣν αἰτίαν), οὗ 2, ᾧ 1, ᾗ 1. The article and relative together come to 52 instances [in Romans this number is already exceeded at 4: 18, quotations excluded; in 1 C at 7: 4]. With -ᾰ, -ε, -ο (ἀλλά, δέ, τε, ἵνα and prep. not counted) 20 (αἰῶνα / ἀπαράβατον 7: 24 pause; κῶλα ἔπεσεν 3: 17, quotation; ἄρα 4: 9 and πατρίδα ἐπιζητοῦσι 11: 14 [D* al. ζητοῦσι] are counted), 7 and 0 respectively. With -αι in verbal endings 18 (εἶναι / ἀλλά 12: 11 in pause) [in the 20 vss. of 1 C 6 there is found: Hiatus with -α 10, with -ε 3, with -ο 2, with -αι 4, eliminating everything which in any way can be taken as a pause, e.g. οὐκ οἴδατε / ὅτι]. The harsher forms of hiatus are also found less often in Hebrews than elsewhere, but they are not very rare and cannot be eliminated. The author, therefore, had not learned the avoidance of hiatus as an absolute rule, but regarded ἀδελφοὶ ἅγιοι, ἔνοχοι ἦσαν, πίστει Ἐνώχ and the like, with a shortening of the vowel at any rate, as permissible.

(B) Verses and Verse Fragments

487. The search for verses and fragments of verses (apart from quotations: A 17: 28, 1 C 15: 33, T 1: 12), i.e. for rhythm, is a needless waste of time and those that are found are of such quality that they are better left unmentioned (Ja 1: 17 πᾶσα δόσις etc. is a hexameter but contains a tribrach in the second foot; the preceding μὴ πλανᾶσθε gives some indication that this verse is a quotation; cf. Braun, TW VI 245.30 ff.). The Epistle to the Hebrews is probably no exception, although it is a strange coincidence that after the faultless hexameter in 12: 13 there soon follow two equally flawless trimeters in succession:

12: 13 καὶ τροχιὰς ὀρθὰς ποιήσατε τοῖς ποσὶν ὑμῶν (𝔓⁴⁶S*P have ποιεῖτε as the model LXX Pr 4: 26 has ποίει; as a matter of fact ποιεῖτε should probably be chosen and the hexameter thereby abandoned), 14 οὖ χωρὶς (χωρίς takes postposition only here, §216(2); but a hiatus is also thereby avoided) οὐδεὶς ὄψεται τὸν κύριον / 15 ἐπισκοποῦντες μή τις ὑστερῶν ἀπό.... The question of rhythm in Hebrews was treated particularly by Delitzsch in his commentary; s. the review by J. Köstlin in GGA 1858, 827ff., who is unreceptive of the idea. Delitzsch emphasized the verse in 12: 14 and Köstlin adds the one following.— Rob. 422 points to the trimeter in Jn 4: 35 τετρά- μηνός ἐστιν καὶ ὁ θερισμὸς ἔρχεται (καὶ ὁ = χώ) and A 23: 5 OT ἄρχοντα τοῦ λαοῦ σου οὐκ ἐρεῖς κακῶς (σου = ◡). The hexameter suggested by Oepke, TW III 991.10f. for Ja 4: 5 πρὸς φθόνον ἐπιποθεῖ(!) τὸ πνεῦμ'(α) ὃ κατῴκισ'(εν) ἐν ὑμῖν (quoted from 'ἡ γραφή') would be a poor one. Pentameter: 2 Clem 2.7 καὶ καλέσας ἡμᾶς ἤδη ἀπολλυμένους (Knopf, Hdb. in loc.). Verse in late Greek prose: U. v. Wilamowitz, Griech. Verskunst (Berlin, 1921) 50 n. 2.—On rhythm in prose, colometry, strophe and Schall- analyse s. reviews of the literature: Debrunner, Jahresb. Altertumsw. 236 (1932) 208–13; 261 (1938) 182–4; Karg, Indog. Jahrb. from Band 22 (1938) on (Abteilung IB13). In addition: Innitzer, Der Hymnus im Epheserbrief (1: 3–14) (ZkTh 28 [1904] 612f.; following Blass' example); A. Thumb in Fortschr. der Psychol. 1 (1913) 139ff. (144f. opposed to Blass); Jülicher, Prot. Monatshefte 1920, March/ April pp. 41ff.; E. Grupe, PhW 1922, 1045–7; H. Lietzmann, Schallanalyse und Textkritik (1922); Altwegg, IF 48 (1930) 82–4; Bonaccorsi p. xcix n. 1, cxv n. 1, cxxxiff. n. 3; H. J. Rose, The Clausulae of the Pauline Corpus (JTS 24 [1923] 12–43; 25 [1924] 17–72); P. Gächter, Der formale Aufbau der Ab- schiedsrede Jesu, Die Form der eucharist. Rede Jesu, Strophen im Joh.-Ev. (Innsbruck, 1936; re- prints from ZkTh 1934–6; rev. by Seesemann, ThLZ 63 [1938] 118); A. Olivier (s. Behm, ThLZ 1941, 25f.). Augustine observed the absence of clausal rhythm in the NT (De doctr. Christ. 4.41). Colometry: E. Lohmeyer, Die Offenbarung des Joh., 2nd ed. (Tübingen, 1953) (have the objections expressed by Debrunner and others [Bursians Jahresb. Altertumsw. 236, 211] been considered?). Further s. §§16, 464 and the preface to the 4th ed.—Cf. Moule 198f.

(C) Gorgian Figures Based on Assonance

488. Gorgian assonances used in an affected style are all the more foreign to the NT since they

were relatively unknown in the whole period. Chance, of course, produced some things of this sort and an author did not avoid any that the com- mon language offered or that the train of thought or the mood of his discourse suggested. The Paul- ine examples correspond to the style of the dia- tribe (Bultmann 20ff., 74ff.). (1) *Paronomasia* is the name given to the recurrence of the same word or word stem in close proximity: (*a*) Mt 21: 41 κακοὺς κακῶς ἀπολέσει αὐτούς (popular itera- tion; also good classical, cf. Dem. 21.204 εἰ κακὸς κακῶς ἀπολῇ, Winer 592 [Winer-M.³ 794]). See also χάριν ἀντὶ χάριτος *et al.* §208. (*b*) In con- trasts, so that a certain subtlety and occasionally a sort of humor is present: 2 C 4: 8 ἀπορούμενοι, ἀλλ' οὐκ ἐξαπορούμενοι. Most caustically in Ph 3: 2f. βλέπετε τὴν κατατομήν (Jewish circumcision)· ἡμεῖς γάρ ἐσμεν ἡ περιτομή, where Paul seizes up- on the word in which his opponents take pride and in a rhetorical manner uses it to their discredit (Winer 592 [Winer-M.³ 795] compares Diog. L. 6.24 who says of Diogenes the Cynic: τὴν μὲν Εὐ- κλείδου σχολὴν ἔλεγε χολήν, τὴν δὲ Πλάτωνος διατριβὴν κατατριβήν). (*c*) A word in the preceding conversation may be taken up and its meaning turned to a metaphorical sense. Thus Paul retorts in A 23: 3 to Ananias who has com- manded τύπτειν αὐτοῦ τὸ στόμα: τύπτειν σε μέλλει ὁ θεός; cf. Rev 22: 18f. and with parechesis ὑπὸ σχῖνον...σχίσει, ὑπὸ πρῖνον...καταπρίσῃ LXX Sus 54f., 58f. (Winer 593 [Winer-M.³ 796]). (*d*) Paul loves to dwell on an idea or word without giving it different meanings and without re- introducing it too quickly, yet with some artistry and reflection (known as *traductio* to the Latin rhetoricians). (2) *Parechesis*, i.e. the assonance of different words, appears in old combinations from the folk-speech: Lk 21: 11 λιμοὶ καὶ λοιμοὶ ἔσονται (Hesiod, Opera 243 λιμὸν ὁμοῦ καὶ λοιμόν), Η 5: 8 ἔμαθεν ἀφ' ὧν ἔπαθεν (cf. the proverb πάθει μάθος, Aeschyl., Agam. 164). (3) Ὁμοιοτέλευτον (to be distinguished from a type of scribal error): R 12: 15 χαίρειν μετὰ χαιρόντων, κλαίειν μετὰ κλαιόντων (there is also assonance in the initial words, therefore ὁμοιοκάταρκτον) arose of itself without affectation. 1 T 3: 16 is strongly stylized (aorist passive in -θη six times); cf. Dibelius, Hdb. *in loc.* and Norden 255.3.

(1) (*a*) Mk 5: 26, 2 C 9: 8, 8: 22, A 21: 28, 24: 3, cf. Plato, Menex. 247A (Gorgian) διὰ παντὸς πᾶσαν πάντως προθυμίαν πειρᾶσθε ἔχειν. S. the numerous NT exx. in Wilke, Rhetorik 342ff., 402–15. Herm

Man 11.3 αὐτὸς γὰρ κενὸς ὢν κενῶς (MSS κενὸς) καὶ ἀποκρίνεται κενοῖς.—R. Morgenthaler, Die lukanische Geschichtsschreibung als Zeugnis I, 18f. —Repeated σύν, Almqvist 112.—Active-passive: ἀνακρίνει...ἀνακρίνεται 1 C 2: 15 (Almqvist 93). *Figura etymologica* (cf. §153): accumulation of σπερ- Lk 8: 5, LXX Gen 1: 29 (secondary acc. to Katz, Philo's Bible 150f.); less repetition Mt 13: 24, 27, 37, Mk 4: 14, Aqu., Symm., Theod. Gen 1: 29, Plut., Mor. 1109c (E. Schwentner, KZ 71 [1953] 16). (*b*) 2 Th 3: 11 μηδὲν ἐργαζομένους ἀλλὰ περιεργαζομένους, A 8: 30 ἄρα γινώσκεις ἃ ἀναγινώσκεις; (cf. 2 C 3: 2), R 12: 3 μὴ ὑπερφρονεῖν παρ' ὃ δεῖ φρονεῖν, ἀλλὰ φρονεῖν εἰς τὸ σωφρονεῖν (which might almost be called flowery), 1 C 11: 29ff. κρίμα...διακρίνων...διεκρίνομεν...ἐκρινόμεθα...κρινόμενοι...κατακριθῶμεν (likewise), 2 C 10: 2f. κατὰ σάρκα...ἐν σαρκὶ...κατὰ σάρκα. Paul is not playing upon the name of the slave Onesimus, although he uses ὀναίμην only here (Phm 20); at most the recipient could make the obvious word-play himself from 'Ονήσιμον...ἄχρηστον 10f. In G 5: 7f. first of all ἐτρέχετε καλῶς· τίς ὑμᾶς ἐνέκοψεν; is to be accepted as it stands (with Tert Chr), then μηδενὶ πείθεσθαι (read -σθε, Lat. *consenseritis*) taken up from FG latt (dropped out by homoioteleuton) after πείθεσθαι; thus we have: ἀληθείᾳ μὴ πείθεσθαι μηδενὶ πείθεσθε· ἡ πεισμονὴ οὐκ ἐκ τοῦ καλοῦντος ὑμᾶς 'obey no one in such a way as to disobey the truth; *that* (sort of) obedience is not from him who calls you' (cf. Stählin, TW III 855 n. 6); πεισμονή here means 'obedience, acquiescence' (cf. Collitz, Curme Volume of Linguistic Studies [Baltimore, 1930] 62–8; cf. NT ἐπιλησμονή 'forgetfulness'), otherwise 'persuasion' (Apollonius Dysc., Synt. 299.17 = 429.9 Uhlig; '*fiducia*' Uhlig, Schneider correctly '*persuasio*' in the Register to Grammatici Graeci II 3, 243; Justin et al., IRom 3.3; cf. Bauer s.v.), which the Vulg. (*persuasio*) and more recent interpreters assume for G 5: 8. Chrys. entirely overlooks ἀληθείᾳ μὴ πείθεσθαι (-σθε) in his exposition. Bultmann, TW VI 9: if the reading of FG latt is adopted (cf. 4 n. 11), then πεισμονή means obedience and takes up πείθεσθαι again 'which would correspond well to the Pauline style'; Bauer s.v. opposes because of the textual tradition and the attestation for the meaning 'persuasion'; cf. Schlier, Der Brief an die Galater (Meyer Kom., 1951) *ad loc.* (*c*) Lk 9: 60 (Mt 8: 22) ἄφες τοὺς νεκροὺς θάψαι τοὺς ἑαυτῶν νεκρούς, Mt 5: 19 (ἐλάχιστος), 2 C 3: 1ff. (ἐπιστολή). (*d*) 2 C 3: 5ff. first ἱκανοί...ἱκανότης...ἱκάνωσεν, then γράμμα three times (after ἐγγεγραμμένη in 2f.), likewise πνεῦμα (also mentioned in 3); διάκονος once in 6, διακονία four times 7ff.; δόξα eight times 7–11 and in addition οὐ δεδόξασται τὸ δεδοξασμένον 10 (a type of oxymoron, with apparent contradiction).

(2) In the enumeration in R 1: 29 (G 5: 21?) Paul combines φθόνου φόνου, 31 ἀσυνέτους ἀσυνθέτους.

But κλάδων (-οι) ἐξεκλάσθησαν 11: 17, 19 can be due either to accident or a type of etymological figure (like φόβον φοβεῖσθαι).

(3) In R 5: 16 (as previously in 14f.) Paul is playing on nouns in -μα (therefore ἁμαρτήματος DFG is probably better than -τήσαντος), which belong to the dainties of the Hell. artists of style—Epicurus, for example, from whom Cleomedes, Meteor. II 1 (Usener, Epicurea p. 89) gives excerpts offering κατάστημα, ἔλπισμα, λίπασμα, ἀνακραύγασμα, λήκημα.—On the whole cf. Rob. 1200f.

(D) Parallelism (Antithesis)

489. Introduction. Antithetic and other forms of parallelism are strongly developed in the NT, not only in the Epistles of Paul but also in the Gospels, especially in Mt and Lk. In the latter the pattern is that of the ancient Hebraic gnomic poetry (§485), in the former it is the result of dialectic and oratory, especially that of the then current style of heathen preaching. (For the distinction between Greek and Semitic parallelism s. Norden 355ff.) In this connection there come to mind other 'figures' (σχήματα) which were noted by the Greek and Latin rhetoricians and supported by examples from Demosthenes, Cicero, etc. Antithesis and parison (§485) as such belong to this group. Parallelism, however, was often heightened by the identity of the initial words in each member (anaphora), or of the last words (antistrophe), or of both together (symploce); words in the middle of the phrase could also be entirely alike or alike in termination. Moreover, each member of the parallelism can again be split into sub-parallelisms, and finally the number of repetitions is not limited to two (on double and triple parallelism of ideas and clauses s. Norden 348ff., 357.3). R. Schütz, Der parallele Bau der Satzglieder im NT (Göttingen, 1920) 8, distinguishes between Semitic lyric-poetic and Hellenistic recitative-prosaic parallelism.—Cf. Rob. 1199f.

490. A model example of parallelism in Paul: 1 C 1: 25 ὅτι τὸ μωρὸν τοῦ θεοῦ / σοφώτερόν ἐστιν τῶν ἀνθρώπων // καὶ τὸ ἀσθενὲς τοῦ θεοῦ / ἰσχυρότερόν ἐστιν τῶν ἀνθρώπων (ἐστιν both times before τῶν ἀνθρ. DEFG; σοφώτ. τ. ἀ. ἐστίν SABC al.; then SᶜAC al. have corresponding ἰσχ. τ. ἀ. ἐστίν, but S*B here omit ἐστίν. The likeness in termination must be preserved in any case [but the scribe of 𝔓⁴⁶ read τῶν ἀ. ἐστίν...ἐστιν τῶν ἀ. yet jumped inadvertently from the first τῶν ἀ. to the second]; cf. 10: 16 where B is incorrect). 26 βλέπετε γὰρ τὴν κλῆσιν ὑμῶν, ἀδελφοί / ὅτι οὐ πολλοὶ σοφοὶ κατὰ σάρκα / οὐ πολλοὶ δυνατοί / οὐ πολλοὶ εὐγενεῖς // 27 ἀλλὰ τὰ μωρὰ τοῦ κόσμου ἐξελέξατο ὁ θεός / ἵνα καταισχύνῃ τοὺς σοφούς (τὰ σοφά Marcion) // καὶ τὰ ἀσθενῆ τοῦ κόσμου ἐξελέξατο ὁ θεός (Chr without ὁ θεός) / ἵνα καταισχύνῃ τὰ ἰσχυρά // 28 καὶ τὰ ἀγενῆ τοῦ κόσμου καὶ τὰ ἐξουθενημένα ἐξελέξατο ὁ θεός / τὰ μὴ ὄντα (καὶ τὰ μὴ ὄντα S^{c}B al., also Chr and TheoMops; καί is certainly an interpolation) / ἵνα τὰ ὄντα καταργήσῃ / 29 ὅπως μὴ καυχήσηται πᾶσα σὰρξ ἐνώπιον τοῦ θεοῦ. The text of Marcion and in part also that of the Fathers shows many divergencies in the closing section: καὶ τὰ ἀγενῆ καὶ τὰ ἐλάχιστα (Tert *minima*) καὶ τὰ ἐξουθενημένα (Marcion Chr TheoMops without ἐξελ. ὁ θεός [in the quotation on R 7: 5]) / τὰ μὴ ὄντα / ἵνα καταισχύνῃ τὰ ὄντα. Of these, καὶ τὰ ἐλάχιστα is certainly far better than the repeated τοῦ κόσμου, and we could readily do without ἐξελέξατο ὁ θεός repeated for the third time (Norden 356 thinks differently and lets it stand precisely because of the Semitic type of parallelism) as without ὁ θεός for the second time.—The parallelism is carried out in the entire passage as exactly as the thought permits without sacrificing the clarity of thought to the form. The rhetoricians say to the credit of Demosthenes that his antitheses are *not* painfully exact throughout; perhaps for this reason Paul also did not write τὰ σοφά in spite of τὰ μωρά, just as he did not say ἵνα τὰ εὐγενῆ καταργήσῃ in spite of τὰ ἀγενῆ, but the expansion of the final section gives rise to τὰ μὴ ὄντα which, together with the contrasting τὰ ὄντα, expresses the thought better and much more forcefully. From any Greek orator the artistry of this passage—it must, of course, be compared with speeches as actually delivered and not with the smooth artistic oratory of literature in which everything that can be termed δὶς ταὐτὸν λέγειν is scorned —would have called forth the utmost admiration (so Blass; Norden 356 changes it to: 'would have been called the utmost monstrosity'!). Also the fact that the third and concluding parallel section exceeds the first two in the length and number of its members corresponds to what the rhetoricians required: Cicero, Orat. 3.48.186 (apparently following Theophrastus): *quae* (scil. *membra*) *si in extremo breviora sunt, infringitur ille quasi verborum ambitus* ('period')...*quare aut paria esse debent posteriora superioribus et extrema primis, aut, quod etiam est melius et iucundius, longiora*; Demetrius, Eloc. 18: ἐν ταῖς συνθέτοις περιόδοις τὸ τελευταῖον κῶλον μακρότερον χρὴ εἶναι καὶ ὥσπερ περιέχον καὶ περιειληφὸς τἆλλα. Cf. 1 C 15: 42ff. σπείρεται ἐν φθορᾷ / ἐγείρεται ἐν ἀφθαρσίᾳ // σπείρεται ἐν ἀτιμίᾳ / ἐγείρεται ἐν δόξῃ // σπ. ἐν ἀσθενείᾳ / ἐγ. ἐν δυνάμει // σπ. σῶμα ψυχικόν / ἐγ. σῶμα πνευματικόν (ten syllables, the longest of all these cola); 48f., three parallel periods, the last being by far the longest in both its members; R 8: 33ff., 2: 21ff. On this so-called 'law of expanding members' s. Behaghel, IF 25 (1909) 111ff.; Havers, Erkl. Synt. 178. On possible strophic arrangement in the NT s. §§ 16 and 487. Cf. 1 P 4: 3 (§460(2)).—Cf. Moule 194ff.

491. Simple anaphora and antistrophe (Gospels excepted).

For antistrophe cf. H 2: 16 οὐ γὰρ δήπου ἀγγέλων ἐπιλαμβάνεται, ἀλλὰ σπέρματος Ἀβραὰμ ἐπιλαμβάνεται (more emphatic than if the second ἐπιλ. had been left to be supplied). For anaphora cf. the exceedingly long example in 11: 3–31 (eighteen times), which, together with the stirring summary in 32–40, to a certain extent conforms to the peroration of a speech following the main argument. Before (and after) this point the Epistle is by no means so rich in figures as some of the Pauline Epistles, but in this respect discloses a certain classical restraint. With H 11 cf. the description of hope in Philo, Praem. et Poen. 11 (= v 338.11ff. Cohn-Wendland).

On the other hand, Paul has, for example, ἐν 19 times in 2 C 6: 4ff., immediately thereafter διά 3 times, ὡς 7; further s. Wilke, Rhetorik 396f. For anaphora with members beginning in ἐν (especially in Eph) s. Percy 215–40. 1 Clem 36.2 anaphora with διὰ τούτου (5 times), 49.4 with ἀγάπη (following 1 C 13). The speeches in Acts, which are only ostensible excerpts from speeches, for that very reason can scarcely contain much adornment: anaphora ὑμεῖς...ὑμῖν 3: 25f., τούτῳ...οὗτος 4: 10f., τοῦτον (twice)...οὗτος (3 times) 7: 35ff.; s. further 10: 42f., 13: 38f.

492. Parallelism in the Gospels.

The absence of rhetorical art in the Johannine discourses is quite clear. In Mk there is little discourse, and Lk has not so elaborated his speeches nor made them so long as did Mt, nor does he seem particularly to have stylized them. But there are actually some traces of artistic style to be found in Mt, more Semitic than Greek of course, since we are probably dealing with the work of a translator-reviser rather than with a Greek original (Blass). Yet the presentation even in Greek is effective and in good taste.

For this reason Blass prefers whichever variant readings produce the most exact parallelism, e.g. in the Sermon on the Mount: Mt 5: 45 ὅτι τὸν ἥλιον αὐτοῦ ἀνατέλλει ἐπὶ ἀγαθοὺς καὶ πονηρούς (it sy Or al., which is better than πονηροὺς καὶ ἀγ. with respect to the following parallel [SB etc.; the latter in itself is an unnatural order]) καὶ τὸν ὑετὸν αὐτοῦ (added in quotations in Homil Clem etc.) βρέχει ἐπὶ δικαίους καὶ ἀδίκους. Further, 7: 13f. τί (it instead of ὅτι) πλατεῖα καὶ εὐρύχωρος ἡ ὁδὸς ἡ...· τί (ὅτι here only S*B*X) στενὴ καὶ τεθλιμμένη ἡ ὁδὸς ἡ.... Also in other discourses: 25: 35 ἐπείνασα γὰρ καὶ ἐδώκατέ μοι φαγεῖν· ἐδίψησα καὶ ἐδώκατέ μοι πιεῖν: following it Cl^pt, not ἐποτίσατέ με, whereas ποτίσαι is correct in 37: πότε σε εἴδομεν πεινῶντα καὶ ἐθρέψαμεν ἢ διψῶντα καὶ ἐποτίσαμεν; The conclusion of the Sermon on the Mount especially is slightly marred in its conventional form; the conjunctions are to be omitted following the unanimous testimony of six Lat. MSS and Cypr Chr Eus, since asyndeton suits well and is particularly effective: 7: 25 κατέβη ἡ βροχή, ἦλθον οἱ ποταμοί, ἔπνευσαν οἱ ἄνεμοι καὶ προσέπεσαν (προσέπαισαν Lachmann, προσέρρηξαν Eus) τῇ οἰκίᾳ ἐκείνῃ, καὶ οὐκ ἔπεσεν· τεθεμελίωτο γὰρ ἐπὶ τὴν πέτραν, then 27 κατέβη ἡ βροχή, ἦλθον οἱ ποταμοί, ἔπνευσαν οἱ ἄνεμοι καὶ προσέκοψαν τῇ οἰκίᾳ ἐκείνῃ, καὶ ἔπεσεν, καὶ ἦν ἡ πτῶσις αὐτῆς μεγάλη.—Further, s. Black, Aramaic Approach 105–17; C. F. Burney, The Poetry of Our Lord (Oxford, 1925).

(E) Figures Involving Repetition

493. (1) *Epanadiplosis*, i.e. the repetition of an important word for emphasis, is not unknown in the NT, but it can nowhere be considered rhetorical. It is rather a direct report of words actually spoken, which is best seen in A 19: 34: μεγάλη ἡ Ἄρτεμις Ἐφεσίων, μεγάλη ἡ Ἄ. Ἐ. (thus B), which was shouted for two hours. (2) *Distributive doubling* is not rhetorical, but vulgar. It appears not only with numerals (s. §248(1)) but occasionally also elsewhere (Hebrew, but also MGr, cf. Dieterich 188; Psichari 183f.): Mk 6: 39 συμπόσια συμπόσια, 40 πρασιαὶ πρασιαί = κατὰ συμπόσια, κ. πρασιάς; cf. §158. (3) *Climax* consists in taking up the key word of the preceding member in the following one: R 5: 3ff. ἡ θλῖψις ὑπομονὴν κατεργάζεται, ἡ δὲ ὑπομονὴ δοκιμήν, ἡ δὲ δοκιμὴ ἐλπίδα, ἡ δὲ ἐλπὶς οὐ καταισχύνει; cf. 8: 29f.

(1) Rev 14: 8 = 18: 2 ἔπεσεν ἔπεσεν Βαβυλὼν ἡ μεγάλη, Mt 25: 11 κύριε κύριε, Lk 8: 24 ἐπιστάτα ἐπιστάτα, Mt 23: 7 (DΓ etc.) and Mk 14: 45 (AEFG etc.) ῥαββὶ ῥαββί, Mk 5: 41 acc. to e τὸ κοράσιον τὸ κοράσιον, Jn 19: 6 σταύρωσον σταύρωσον, Lk 10: 41 Μάρθα Μάρθα, Rev 4: 8 ἅγιος ἅγιος ἅγιος (LXX Is 6: 3). Dyadic word combination and composition: Morgenthaler, Die lukanische Geschichtsschreibung als Zeugnis (I 17f.: Lk 7 times, A 9: 4 = 22: 7 = 26: 14 Σαοὺλ Σαούλ). Rhetorical: 1 Clem 47.6 αἰσχρά, ἀγαπητοί, καὶ λίαν αἰσχρὰ καὶ

ἀνάξια etc. Cf. LXX (e.g. Jdth 4: 2 σφόδρα σφόδρα) and pap. (e.g. the magic formula ἤδη ἤδη ταχὺ ταχύ PGM II 7.373 (iii AD), BGU III 956 (c. iii AD). Cf. Jannaris §§ 513, 521; Raderm.² 68f., 225 and IF Anz. 31 (1913) 8; Bonaccorsi 140, 562; Norden 169, and on Virgil's Aeneid VI 46 (2nd ed.); E. Hofmann, Ausdrucksverstärkung, especially 16f. (adj.), 24 (address), 24f. (impera.), 38 (adv.), 44f. (stylistic usage); W. Schulze, BPhW 1895, 8 = Kl. Schr. 680. Hebr. J. Muilenburg, VT Supplement I (1953) 101f., Brockelmann, Hebräische Syntax §129b. MGr e.g. Thumb² 264.4 [276] κλαίει κλαίει, 263 [275] ἔκλαιε ἔκλαιε twice, 263 σφιχτὰ σφιχτά 'very tight', 257 [269] γύμναζε γύμναζε 'he exercised untiringly'; Ljungvik, Aegyptus 13 (1933) 162 ἐπερίμενα ὥρες ὥρες 'I waited for hours'. With καί: μείζων καὶ μείζων Herm Vis 4.1.6, ἔτι καὶ ἔτι 'again and again' Barn 21.4. Cf. Ἑρμῆς ὁ μέγας καὶ μέγας Dit., Or. 90.65 (196 BC; decree from Rosetta), similarly in the pap. (Mayser II 1, 54; with and without καί).

(2) In Mt 13: 30 δεσμὰς δεσμάς (Epiph Or) also appears to be the correct reading. Cf. §158. Hofmann, *op. cit.* (*supra* (1)) 21 (subst.), 37f. (numbers). LXX e.g. ἄνθρωπος ἄνθρωπος 'everyone' Num 9: 10, ἔθνη ἔθνη 'every nation' 4 Km 17: 29, συνήγαγον αὐτοὺς θημωνιὰς θημωνιάς 'in heaps' Ex 8: 14 (10) (all in Hebr. as well; cf. Brockelmann, Hebräische Syntax §129a). With καί: ἡμέρα καὶ ἡμέρα §200(1); Brockelmann, *op. cit.* §129d (syndetic pairs of this type are rare in Hebr.). On the other hand ἐν γενεᾷ καὶ γενεᾷ 1 Clem 7.5, εἰς γενεὰς καὶ γενεάς (v.l. εἰς γενεὰν καὶ γενεάν like LXX Ps 48: 12 etc., γενεὰς γενεῶν *et al.*) Lk 1: 50 more nearly means 'on many generations to come' than 'for every generation'; M.-H. 439f. Also with distributive κατά (cf. §248(1)): LXX 1 Km 7: 16 κατ' ἐνιαυτὸν ἐνιαυτόν and the like (M.-H. 439), κατὰ πρᾶγμα πρᾶγμα 'for every thing'(?) PLond V 1732.7 (586 AD?).

(3) R 10: 14 is decidedly rhetorical: πῶς οὖν ἐπικαλέσωνται εἰς ὃν οὐκ ἐπίστευσαν; πῶς δὲ πιστεύσωσιν οὗ οὐκ ἤκουσαν; πῶς δὲ ἀκούσωσιν χωρὶς κηρύσσοντος; πῶς δὲ κηρύξωσιν, ἐὰν μὴ ἀποσταλῶσιν; 2 P 1: 5ff. likewise: ἐπιχορηγήσατε ἐν τῇ πίστει ὑμῶν τὴν ἀρετήν, ἐν δὲ τῇ ἀρετῇ τὴν γνῶσιν, ἐν δέ etc. (7 members in all; but the purpose of the figure here is difficult to understand). Herm Man 5.2.4 ἐκ τῆς ἀφροσύνης γίνεται πικρία, ἐκ δὲ τῆς πικρίας θυμός, ἐκ δὲ τοῦ θυμοῦ ὀργή, ἐκ δὲ τῆς ὀργῆς μῆνις· εἶτα ἡ μῆνις.... There is a similar figure in a fragment of the comedian Epicharmus (Frag. 148 Kaibel) ἐκ μὲν θυσίας θοίνα, ἐκ δὲ θοίνας πόσις ἐγένετο...ἐκ δὲ πόσιος κῶμος, ἐκ κώμου δ' ἐγένεθ' ὑανία ('swinish behavior'), ἐκ δ' ὑανίας δίκα.... The rhetoricians found the climax as early as Hom., Il. 2. 102ff. (Ἥφαιστος μὲν δῶκε Διὶ..., αὐτὰρ ἄρα Ζεὺς δῶκε διακτόρῳ ἀργεϊφόντῃ, Ἑρμείας δὲ....)—Cf. Wilke, Rhetorik 398, who adduces Ja 1: 14f. and (incorrectly) 1 C 11: 3 in addition.

(F) Asyndeton in Periods

Polarity in style (antitheses): H. Riesenfeld, Con. Neot. 9 (1949) 1–21 (literature 19–21).

494. The resolution of a sentence into unconnected components produces a more powerful effect than would the periodic form proper: 1 C 7: 27 δέδεσαι γυναικί / μὴ ζήτει λύσιν // λέλυσαι ἀπὸ γυναικός / μὴ ζήτει γυναῖκα (§ 464) = εἰ μὲν δέδεσαι γυν., μὴ ζ. λ., εἰ δέ... (§ 471(3). At the same time there is strong antistrophe (§ 489), while in λύσιν / λέλυσαι the term which ends one member is used to begin the next (anastrophe). The point of the sentence, moreover, is heightened by the brevity of the components. Much of the same type of thing appears among practical Greek orators and in Attic comedy, both of which were produced in the lively style of colloquial speech: cf. Teles 6.14 Hense γέρων γέγονας / μὴ ζήτει τὰ τοῦ νέου // ἀσθενὴς πάλιν / μὴ ζήτει τὰ τοῦ ἰσχυροῦ etc. (Bultmann 15, 69); Dem. 18. 274. Also in MGr (Thumb² § 277 n. 3). In the NT and elsewhere the parts of such resolved sentences which correspond to a conditional protasis are usually written as a question—unnecessarily. Cf. § 298(4); K.-G. II 234 n.; Br.-Th. 640f.

Cf. 1 C 7: 18, 21, Ja 5: 13f.; also Ja 4: 2 if it is punctuated thus: ἐπιθυμεῖτε καὶ οὐκ ἔχετε· φονεύετε. καὶ ζηλοῦτε καὶ οὐ δύνασθε ἐπιτυχεῖν· μάχεσθε καὶ πολεμεῖτε. οὐκ ἔχετε etc. Paul occasionally makes an almost too profuse use of the commoner forms of asyndeton (§§ 460ff.) so that the figure as a rhetorical medium loses its power and his discourse disintegrates into a series of short fragments. In this regard Hebrews is more temperate, even in the brilliant passage where πίστει appears 18 times with asyndeton (§ 491); here the separate parts, which are often of considerable length, are not themselves composed with asyndeton; and even though in the concluding summary 11: 32ff. there twice appear ten mostly short elements joined with asyndeton, a piece of connected speech is interposed between them (35f.) and a period rounds off the whole (39f.).—Nyberg, Arbeiten und Mitteilungen 4 (1936) 24–6, 28–35 (Semitic also; 32: west Aramaic); also Fridrichsen, *ibid.* 44f.; Rob. 427–33.

(2) FIGURES OF THOUGHT (§ 485)

495. (1) *Paralipsis (praeteritio)*: The orator pretends to pass over something which he in fact mentions: ὅτι μέν..., παραλείπω. If one insists, Paul's remark in Phm 19 may be such a case

(following the customary punctuation): ἵνα μὴ λέγω σοι ὅτι καὶ σεαυτόν μοι προσοφείλεις (but s. *infra*). (2) Paul also occasionally makes use of *irony* (εἰρωνεία) of the sharpest kind: 2 C 11: 19f. ἡδέως ἀνέχεσθε τῶν ἀφρόνων, φρόνιμοι ὄντες· ἀνέχεσθε γάρ etc. (3) Paul also knows how to change his tone in an astonishing way and uses *prodiorthosis* (an anticipatory correction) when he feels that he is about to give offense (e.g. 2 C 11: 1ff., 16ff., 21 ἐν ἀφροσύνῃ λέγω, 23), or *epidiorthosis* (a subsequent correction of a previous impression) when he feels that he has offended (e.g. 12: 11 γέγονα ἄφρων etc., 7: 3; R 3: 5 κατὰ ἄνθρωπον λέγω), always maintaining the most sensitive contact with his readers.

(1) Phm 19 is, rather, a case of epidiorthosis: ἐμοὶ ἐλλόγα...ἵνα μὴ λέγω· σοί, ὅτι (because)... (Joachim Jeremias by letter). Also 2 C 9: 4 μήπως... καταισχυνθῶμεν ἡμεῖς, ἵνα μὴ λέγωμεν ὑμεῖς is far from a simple and straightforward statement; the simple expression of the thought would be ἵνα μὴ καταισχυνθῆτε, but since that would be painful to his readers, he turns the reproach ostensibly against himself while making it clear that he is doing so. The rhetoricians call this the σχῆμα ἐπιεικές. Wilke, Rhetorik 365 also cites passages like 1 Th 4: 9 where no mere figure, however, is recognizable (οὐ χρείαν ἔχετε), any more than in H 11: 32 where the expression corresponds exactly to the thing.

(2) 1 C 4: 8 ἤδη κεκορεσμένοι ἐστέ; ἤδη ἐπλουτήσατε; χωρὶς ἡμῶν ἐβασιλεύσατε; Wilke, Rhetorik 356. From the Gospels Lk 13: 33, Mk 7: 9 καλῶς, likewise ἑταῖρε Mt 20: 13, 22: 12, 26: 50 (cf. § 300(2)).

(3) Wilke, Rhetorik 292ff. In another sense a correction which intensifies what has been said is also epidiorthosis: R 8: 34 ὁ ἀποθανών, μᾶλλον δὲ ἐγερθείς, G 4: 9.—Cf. Rob. 1198f.

496. The rhetorical question can be employed in a variety of ways: (1) It sometimes serves vivacity and lucidity in dialectic (real or fictitious), e.g. R 3: 1 τί οὖν τὸ περισσὸν τοῦ Ἰουδαίου; with the answer πολὺ κατὰ πάντα τρόπον. (2) It is sometimes used to express vivid emotion such as astonishment or indignation, but also joyous elation as in R 8: 31 τί οὖν ἐροῦμεν πρὸς ταῦτα; εἰ ὁ θεὸς ὑπὲρ ἡμῶν, τίς καθ᾽ ἡμῶν; to which are subjoined pairs of questions with their pretended answers (ὑποφορά, *subjectio* = the fictitious answer supplied by an orator to his fictitious opponent), also in interrogative form: τίς ἐγκαλέσει κατὰ ἐκλεκτῶν θεοῦ; θεὸς ὁ δικαιῶν; τίς ὁ κατακρινῶν; Χριστὸς Ἰησοῦς ὁ... etc.

J. Konopásek, Les 'questions rhétoriques' dans le NT (RHPR 12 [1932] 47–66, 141–61).

(1) R 4: 10 πῶς οὖν ἐλογίσθη; ἐν περιτομῇ ὄντι ἢ ἐν ἀκροβυστίᾳ; οὐκ ἐν περιτομῇ etc. Especially often in Romans; but cf. also Jn 12: 27.

(2) There is a detailed analysis of many passages in J. Weiss (s. § 485), on which s. Heinrici, Der Zweite Korintherbrief (Meyer Kom., 8th ed., [1900]) 457 f. Augustine and most recent commentators take R 8: 31 θεὸς ὁ δικ. and Χριστός... as questions; Tischendorf (following Wettstein) and Wilke, Rhetorik 396 oppose this view. But the third instance is undoubtedly interrogative, and θεὸς ὁ δικ. cannot mean 'God is here who...' (Luther). The passage is not so much strictly logical as it is more rhetorical, like much else in Romans and 1, 2 Corinthians (§ 485). Cf. further e.g. 2 C 11: 22 Ἑβραῖοί εἰσιν; κἀγώ. Ἰσραηλῖταί εἰσιν; κἀγώ etc.—In this connection s. Moule 196 f. for notes on implied dialogue in the diatribe style with further references.

INDICES

All references in these Indices are to the SECTIONS *of the Grammar, except for occasional reference to the notes in the Introduction, in which case the page is cited.*

I. INDEX OF SUBJECTS

Ablative (not distinguished from gen.), s. Genitive
Accent: 13; in amalgamated words 12(2); in Sem. words 37
Accusative: third decl. masc.-fem. sg. 46(1), plur. 46(2); mixture of dental and vocalic stems acc. sg. and plur. (third decl.) 47(3)

 Syntax 148–61: acc. of obj. 148–56, w. original intransitives 148, w. vbs. of fearing etc. 149, w. transitives dependent on a prep. in compounds 150, alternating w. dat. 151f., of content (cognate acc.) 153f., 294(2), double acc. (both external obj.) 155f., acc. of obj. and pred. acc. 157, acc. of obj. and result 158, acc. w. the pass. 159, acc. of respect and adverbial acc. 160, 266(2), acc. of extent (space and time) 161, 201; in apposition to a clause 480(6); w. prep. 204–39; of inf. w. art. 399, 408, dependent on prep. 402; of adjuncts and predicates to the subj. of the inf. 410; of supplementary ptcp. 416; incongruence w. (anacoluthon) 136(2), 466(4); attraction of the acc. of the relative 294(1, 2); s. also Accusative with infinitive and Accusative absolute.
Accusative absolute: 137(3), 424, 425(3)
Accusative with infinitive: 391(2, 4), 392–7, 405f., 408f.; f. which acc. w. ὅτι, ἵνα 408, 476(1)
Action, kinds of: 318
Active (voice): 307–10; f. pass. 315; mid. f. act. 316; fut. act. instead of mid. 77; transformation of intr. actives into causatives 148(3)
Acts: 1st and 2nd halves (distinguished) 353(1, 3); instrumental ἐν 195; ἐνώπιον 214(5, 6); periphrasis f. the impf. 353(3); ἀποκριθεὶς εἶπεν 420(1)

 Speeches: of Tertullus (24: 2–8) 467; of Paul before Agrippa (26) 3 (w. p. 2f. n. 4), 474(6); ἕνεκα 35(3); ἀκριβέστατος 60(1); ἴσασιν 92(2); τὸ δωδεκάφυλον 263(3); ἥγημαι instead of ἡγοῦμαι 341; εὐξαίμην ἄν 385(1); χρή w. nom. 405; τε... τε 444(1); s. also Reference Index
 S. further s.v. Luke
Adjectives: formation of new feminines and comparison 59–62; syntax 241–6; fem. (masc., neut.) w. ellipsis of a subst. 241; substantivized (w. and without art.) 263f.; substantivized neut. (sg. and plur.) of persons 138, 263(3, 4); neut. w. gen. 263; for adv. 243; attrib. w. art., predicative (and partitive) without art. 269(3), 270; the separation

of two attrib. adj. 269(5); gen. of quality for adj. 162 intro., 165; ellipsis of 480(3); position 474(1)
Adverbs: dependent on prep. 12, 203, 216(3); of manner 102, derived from ptcp. 102(6); of place 103f., 437; of time 105; correlative 106; interrog. 436; comparison of 62; compound 116(3); adverbial compounds 122; w. art. 266; adj. instead of adv. 243; as pred. 434; ellipsis of 480(4); position of 474(2, 3)
Adversative conjunctions: 447–50
Aeolicisms: 2, χύν(ν)ειν 73; Aeolic forms of aor. opt. 85
Agent: prep. w. gen. f. 210(2), 223(2), 232(2); dat. of, w. pass. 191, 313
Agreement (congruence): 131–7: of gender in adjectival or pronominal pred. 131, in pronominal subj. 132, in formulaic phrases 132(2); of number w. neut. plur. subj. 133, in *constructio ad sensum* 134, 282, 296, w. two or more co-ordinate words 135; incongruencies (solecisms) in gender, number and case: Rev 136, other NT books 137
Aktionsarten: 318
Alexandrian dialect: p. 1 n. 2
Alpha privative: 117(1), 120(2); before o 124
Anacoluthon: 423(4, 5), 447(2–4), 452(3), 458, 465(2), 466–70
Anaphora: 464, 489, 491; also s. Article
Anastrophe (figure): 494
Antistrophe (figure): 489, 491, 494
Antithesis: 485, 489–92
Aorist: first and second act.-mid. 75, pass. 76; endings 80–3; of depon. vbs. 78; kinds of action 318

 Syntax: 328f., 331–4, 347(2), 360, 363–6, 368–83; moods: impera. 335, 337; subj. 318, 363–6, 368–83; opt. 384; inf. s. Infinitive; ptcp. s. Participle; indic. w. ἄν 360, 367; indic. in wishes 359(1); indic. w. ὀλίγου 358(2); s. also Indicative
Apocalypse, s. Revelation
Aposiopesis: 482, 300(2)
Apposition: w. and without art. 260(2), 268, 271, 276(3), 412(2) (ptcp.); nom. instead of oblique case 136(1), 137(3); appositive gen. 167; apposition to a clause 480(6)
Aramaic: 4; s. also Semitisms

INDEX OF SUBJECTS

Article: ὁ ἡ τό: crasis 18

Syntax: 252–76; as pronoun 249–51; individual and generic 252, 263; anaphoric 252, 256, 257(1, 2), 258(1), 260, 261(1, 3), 263, 264(2), 266(2), 271, w. the inf. 398f.; w. personal names 162(2) (in the gen.), 260, 268(1); w. geographical names 261; w. names of peoples 262, 275(1); w. adj. 263f., 270; w. ptcp. 264(6), 270, 273(3), 412f.; w. numerals 265; w. adv. 266; w. prepositional expressions 160, 209(2), 266, 272; used only w. the attrib. 270(3), 272; 'governing' the gen. 162, 266(3); w. several qualifying adjuncts 269; repeated w. ἄλλος, λοιποί 269(6); w. τοιοῦτος and τοσοῦτος 274, 304; not w. ἕκαστος 275; w. ὅλος, πᾶς (ἅπας), ἀμφότεροι 275; w. possessive pron. and ἴδιος 284–6; w. αὐτός 288; w. οὗτος, ἐκεῖνος 292; w. ἕτερος and ἄλλος 306(2, 3, 5); w. several substantives connected together 276; w. appositives s. Apposition; w. the attraction of the relative 294(5); w. inf. 398–404, 406(3); τό before quoted words and sentences and before indirect interrog. sentences 267; in connection w. an arthrous noun (assimilation) 162(2), 257(1), 261(4); omission: in connection w. an anarthrous noun (assimilation) 253(4), 254(1, 3), 257(2, 3), 259, 286(2), w. pred. 252, 273, 285(2), 292, in formulae and following prep. 252, 255, 257(2, 3), 259(1, 2), 261(5), w. ordinals 256, w. abstracts 258, w. qualitative sense 252, in introductions (salutations) to epistles 261(5), 268(2), 272

Article, indefinite: (εἷς) 247(2)

Articular infinitive, s. Infinitive

Aspects: 318

Aspirates: doubling 40

Aspiration, s. Breathing

Asseverative particles: 441

Assimilation: of consonants 19; remote assimilation of vowels 32(1); of the pron. subj. to the pred. in gender 132(1); of ἥμισυς to the dependent gen. 164(5); of the rel. and of tense, s. Attraction; w. art., s. Article

Asyndeton: 442, 445(1), 447(6), 454(3), 458–64, 465(1), 494, 421 (ptcp.)

Athematic inflection: 92–100

Attic declension: 44(1)

Attic future: 74(1)

Attic reduplication: 68; without augm. 67(2)

Atticisms: in the Koine of the NT 2, 3, p. 2 f. n. 4; α for αι 30(1); ε for ει 30(2); οὐθείς and μόγις 33; ττ 34(1); ρρ 34(2); βορρᾶς 34(3), 45; ἀλυκός 35(3); ἕνεκα 35(3); γῆ, μνᾶ, Ἑρμῆς, συκῆ 45; κεκράξομαι 65(1b), 77; Attic redupl. 68; δύνῃ 93; κάθῃ κάθου 100; ἡ παῖς 111(3); polite, unemotional ὦ 146(1a); πειθαρχεῖν τινι 187(6)

Attraction: of the rel. 294, 466(1, 3); of rel. adv. 437; inverse attraction 295; of tense 330, 345, 365(1)

Attributive: w. more than one subst. 135(3); ellipsis w. attributives 241; subst. w. ἀνήρ 242;

art. w. several attributives 269; position 269–72, 473, 474(1, 4); s. also Apposition; ptcp. as attrib., s. Participle

Augment: 66f., 69

Barnabas: comp. and superl. 60(1); particles 107; ptcp. co-ordinated w. nouns 468(2)

Biblicisms: 4

Brachylogy: 483

Breathing (*spiritus asper, lenis*): 14; in Sem. words 39(3)

Cardinals: 63(1, 2); syntax: instead of ordinal 247(1); 248

Case: syntax 143–202; incongruencies 136(1, 2, 4), 137(1, 3); s. further Nominative, Genitive, etc.

Catalogues of vices: 252

Causal clauses: 456, negation 428(5); w. ptcp. 417, 418(1), 425(3)

Causal conjunctions: co-ordinating 452; subordinating 456

Causative verbs: from intransitives 148(3); declaratory, forensic 148(4); in -εύειν 309(1); w. double acc. 155(7)

Chiasmus: 477

Circumstantial (adverbial) participle: syntax 417–24, particles w. 425; s. also Participle

Clause order: 478

Clausulae: 487

Clement of Rome, Epistle to the Corinthians: style 3, 34(1), 51(1), 61(1), 97(3), 176(1), 211

Clementine Homilies: particles 107; Atticizing (dat. of agent) 191; post-position of ἕνεκ- 216(1); comp. 244(1); unreal plupf. f. Lat. plupf. subj. 360(4); potentiality in past time 360(4); use of ὡς 391(1); καί introducing an apodosis 442(7)

Climax (figure): 493(3)

Colometry: 16, 487

Comparative: 60–2, 244–6; decl. in -ων 47(2); of adv. 62, 102(1, 4); instead of superl. 60(1), 244; positive f. 245; expressing exclusion 245a; heightened 61(2), 246; ἵνα following a comp. w. ἤ 393(1, 2)

Comparative conjunctions (clause): 454; abbreviation of the main clause in comparisons 482

Comparison of adjectives (adverbs): 60–2, 102(1, 4, 5), 244–6

Composition: 35(2), 59(1), also s. Word-formation

Composition, prose and verse: 485–96

Composition vowel: 35(2)

Compounds: 35(2), 59(1), 114–24; also s. Derivatives from compounds

Concessive clauses: 374, 425(1), 457; w. ptcp. 418(3); impera. as equivalent 387(2)

Concessive conjunctions: 457

Conditional clauses: 360, 371–6, 385(2), 454; w. ptcp. 417, 418(2); parataxis instead 471(3); negation 428(1–3)

Conditional conjunctions: 371, 454

INDEX OF SUBJECTS

Ellipsis: 479–83: in the broad sense 479, formulaic 480, dependent on style and circumstances 481, aposiopesis 300(2), 482, brachylogy 483; of εἶναι 127f., 190(4); of subj. 129f.; of a subst. (usually fem.) w. an adj. etc. 241; of a subst. w. the art. w. a gen. 162; of the subst. governing a gen. (υἱός, μήτηρ etc.) 162; of 'than' after πλείων, ἐλάσσων 185(4); of ἄλλος 306(5), 480(1); of the apodosis 454(4), 482; elliptical μήτιγε 427(3), εἴτε...εἴτε 446, 454(3), ἀλλ' ἵνα 448(7), ἵνα δέ 470(3), 483

Epanadiplosis: 493(1, 2)

Epexegetical use of: the inf. and of ἵνα, ἐάν, ὅταν 394; the inf. w. τοῦ 400(8); καί 442(9)

Epic: ῥήσσειν 'strike, stamp' 101 s.v. ῥηγνύναι

Epidiorthosis: 465(2), 495(3)

Euthalius: 13, 16

Exclamations: 304, 436, 468(1)

Factitive verbs: 108(1), 148(3), 309(1)

Feminine: (of pron.) f. neut. 138(2); masc. and fem., s. Masculine and ἡ Βάαλ

Festivals: names of 200(3)

Figures of speech: 485–96; Gorgian figures (assonances) 488; parallelism 489–92; involving repetition 493; asyndeton 494; paralipsis 495(1); irony 495(2); prodiorthosis and epidiorthosis 495(3); rhetorical question 496; figure ἐξ ἀποστάσεως 463; ἀπὸ κοινοῦ 479(1)

Final clauses: 361, 369, 386(3), 390, 392–4, 400, 402(2, 4), 403, 418(4) (ptcp.); position 478; also s. ἵνα

Final particles: ἵνα, ὅπως, μή 369; the enlarged uses of ἵνα 388ff.; μή, μήπως, μήποτε after expressions of apprehension 370

Future (tense): retreat of 65(1); formation of act. and mid. 74, 77; of pass. (depon.) 76(1), 78f.; no fut. subj. 28; third fut. replaced by periphrasis 65(1b, 4), 352; Att. fut. 74(1)

    Syntax of 318, 348–51; interchanging w. pres. 323; periphrasis f. 353 (εἶναι), 356 (μέλλειν); f. impera. 362, 427(1); f. potential opt. 385(1); interchanging w. subj. (aor.): 369(2), in main clauses 363, w. οὐ μή 365, in questions 366, in subordinate clauses 368–70, 373(2), 375, 378f., 380(2–4), 382f.; used to continue subj. (aor.) or impera. 366(2), 369(3), 370(2), 442(3); w. ὅτε 382(2); w. ὄφελον 384; fut. inf. s. Infinitive, fut. ptcp. s. Participle; relation to other moods and tenses 318, 357

Gemination (consonants): 11, 40; aspirates 40, 42(3)

Gender: peculiarities in use 138: neut. w. reference to persons 138(1), fem. f. neut. 138(2), masc. f. fem. and reverse 138(3); agreement 131f.: in adjectival or pronominal pred. 131, in pronominal subj. 132; gender in *constructio ad sensum* 134; incongruencies involving gender 136(3); s. also Masculine, Feminine, Neuter

Genitive: third decl. sg. 46(3), uncontracted plur. 48

    Syntax 162–86: adnominal 162–8, origin and relationship 162, objective 163, partitive 164, quality 165, direction and purpose 166, content and appositive 167, concatenation of 168; adverbial 169–80, price and value 179, separation (driven out by ἀπό or ἐκ) 180; dependent on a prep. in compounds 181; w. adj. and adv. 182ff.; comparison 185; time and place 186; hanging 136(2); art. w. attrib. gen. 271, w. partitive gen. of country 261(6), w. gen. of origin, relationship, etc. 162, 266(3); partitive gen. as subj. or obj. 164(2), position of 271, w. adj. and adv. 182, 194; w. prep. (proper and improper) 208–40; w. ἴδιος 286(1); possessive (objective) gen. and possessive adj. 284f.; circumlocution of w. ἔμπροσθεν, ἐνώπιον 214, w. ἐκ, ἀπό, ἐν, κατά s.v. the respective words; of the inf. 388, 400, of the articular inf. dependent on a prep. 403; w. the inf. 409(5), 410; w. a ptcp. w. vbs. of hearing 416(1)

Genitive absolute: 417, 423

Geographical names: 56f.; w. and without art. 261; the country in partitive gen. 164(3)

Gorgian assonances: 485, 488

Half-vowels: Sem., translit. 39(1)

Haplography: in word formation 40

Hebrew, influence on NT Greek (Hebraisms): 4 and *passim*; s. further Semitisms

Hebrews, Epistle to: style 3f., 463f., 485–7, 491, 494; πόρρω(θεν) 34(2), 104(3); ἰέναι 99(1); ἀποδίδοσθαι 101 s.v. πιπράσκειν; που 103; particles 107; partitive gen. w. vbs. 169(1); παρά in comparison 185(3); dat. w. vbs. of emotion 196; ἔως, ἄχρι, μέχρι 216(3); absence of σύν 221; absence of παρά w. dat. 238; neut. adj. w. dependent gen. 263(2); ἡμεῖς f. ἐγώ 280; fut. inf. 65(1c), 350; fut. pass. ptcp. 351(2); φοβεῖσθαι μή 370(1); ἵνα only in a final sense 388; inf. w. vbs. of believing etc. 396f.; articular inf. 398; εἰς τό w. inf. 402(2); supplementary ptcp. 414; δήπου 441(3); τε 443(1); μέν 447(2); ὅθεν 451(6); καθάπερ 453; ἐάνπερ 454(2); διότι 456(1); word order 473(2)

Hellenistic Greek, s. Vernacular

Hellenization of non-Greek personal names: 53f., 56

Hendiadys: 442(16)

Hermas: style p. 1 n. 2, §3, p. 5 n. 1, 60(1), 244(2); opt. does not appear 65(2); ἀεί in Sim. 9.30–10.4 105; particles 107; plur. vb. w. neut. plur. subj. 133; εἰς f. ἐν 205; ἀπό to denote alienation 211; ἕτερος and ἄλλος 306(5); plupf. in imitation of Lat. 347(3); unreal plupf. f. Lat. plupf. subj. 360(4); ὡσεί 454(3); διότι 456(1); asyndeton 462(1)

Hexameter in the NT: 487

Hiatus: avoided in *Kunstprosa* 485, in the NT (Heb) 486, by means of ν-movable 20; not avoided in composition 124

INDEX OF SUBJECTS

John (*cont.*)

of ἕως, ἄχρι, μέχρι 216(3); σύν and μετά 221; rarely ὑπό w. acc. 232(1); absence of παρά w. acc. 236; ὁ δέ infrequent 251; 'Ιησοῦς w. and without art. 260(1); ἐμός frequent 285(1); high frequency of ἐκεῖνος 291; ὅστις rare 293; ἕτερος virtually lacking 306(1); periphrasis f. the impf. 353(1); ὅπως virtually lacking 369(4); lavish use of ἵνα 369(4), 388, 394; articular inf. 398, after prep. 402(1, 2); λέγων, καὶ εἶπεν and the like 420(1, 2); use of τε infrequent and textually uncertain 443(1); μέν lacking in the Epistles 447(2); μέντοι 450(1); οὖν 451(1); γάρ rare 452; temporal ὡς 455(2); τότε οὖν 459(2); μετὰ τοῦτο (ταῦτα) 459(3); ὅτι *recitativum* 470(1)

Koine, s. Vernacular
Kunstprosa: 485

Latin: loanwords 5(1); translit. of 41; personal names 54, 55(1a)

Latinisms (influence of Lat. on the Koine of the NT): 5; κράτιστε 60(2), 146(3); ἱκανόν etc. 131; ὅ ἐστιν, τοῦτ' ἔστιν 132(2); γάμοι 141(3); voc. without ὦ 146; ἔχειν 'to regard as' 157(3), 397(2); ἀπὸ σταδίων δέκα 161(1); ὅμοιος w. gen. 182(4); 'Εφέσου 'in E.' 186(1); οὐαί 4(2a), w. dat. and acc. 190(2); θανάτῳ κατακρίνειν 195(2); dat. of respect 197; κονδύλοις λαμβάνειν 198(3); dat. of the duration of time 201; πρὸ ἓξ ἡμερῶν τοῦ πάσχα 213; σῶμα σόν 285(2); καὶ τοῦτο instead of καὶ ταῦτα 290(5); 'relative connection' 294(5), 458; epistolary aor. 334; εἰ w. plupf. 360(4); σὺ ὄψῃ etc. 362; subj. in rel. clauses 378f.; ἵνα, ὅπως instead of the inf. 388; pass. inf. instead of the act. 392(4); acc. reflex. pron. in acc. w. inf. construction 406; παρακαλεῖν διά 223(4); descriptive historical pres. 321; plupf. 347(3); asyndeton 462(1)

Literary language: 3 and *passim*

Loanwords: Coptic 6; Lat. 5(1); other 6

Locative, s. Dative

Luke: identification of 268(1); style (Gos. and Acts) 3, p. 1 n. 2, p. 2 n. 2, p. 2f. n. 4, p. 3 n. 3, 4, 5, 5(1), 126(3), 421 (Acts), 442, 458, 462, 464, 466(3), 485 (Acts), 489, 491 (Speeches in Acts), 492 (discourse in the Gos.); πόρρω(θεν) 34(2), 104(3); ἄρνας and ναῦν 47(4); ἡ παράλιος 59(1); ὡς τάχιστα 60(2); ἐτάχθην 76(1); ἀπεκρίνατο 78; κεῖσθαι 97(2); ἰέναι 99(1); ἀποδίδοσθαι 101 s.v. πιπράσκειν; ταχέως 102(2); ἐνθάδε 103; particles 107; ἐάν (Acts) 126(1a α); ὀνόματι (Acts) 128(3); polite, unemotional ὦ (Acts) 146(1a); gen. f. an adj. 162 intro.; partitive gen. w. vbs. 169(1); φείδεσθαι 180(5); πειθαρχεῖν τινι 187(6); ὑπάρχειν w. dat. 189; τὸ εἰωθὸς αὐτῷ etc. 189(1); εἰς f. ἐν (esp. Acts) p. 1 n. 2, 205; ἐνώπιον 214(5); ἕως, ἄχρι, μέχρι 216(3); σύν 221; κατά w. gen. 225; σύν and μετά (Acts) 227; ἀνὴρ 'Ιουδαῖος 242; ὁ μὲν οὖν (Acts)

251; art. w. place-names (Acts) 261(2); τό before indirect questions 267(2); ἅπας 275; πάντες ἄνθρωποι 275(1); αὐτός 277(3), 288(2); καὶ οὗτος 290(1); ὅς and ὅστις 293(2, 3); ἕτερος 306(1); historical pres. infrequent 321; fut. inf. (Acts) 65(1c), 338(3), 350; fut. ptcp. 65(1c), 351, 418(4); ἀκήκοα lacking 342(2); periphrasis f. the pres. etc. 353(1, 3); ὅπως ἄν 369(5); φοβεῖσθαι μή 370(1); opt. 65(2), 385(1, 2), 386(1); ἵνα 388; ἀξιοῦν 392(1c); κελεύειν 392(1d, 4); παραινεῖν 392(1d); ἄρχεσθαι 392(2); ὡς f. ὅτι 396; direct and indirect discourse 386, 396; inf. w. vbs. of believing and saying 396f.; articular inf. 398, 400, 402(1), 404; supplementary ptcp. 414; ἀκούειν w. gen. and ptcp. (Acts) 416(1); gen. absolute (Acts) 423; οὕτως after a ptcp. 425(6); οὐ w. ptcp. 430(2); γε 439; ἆρά (γε) 440(2); εἰ in direct questions 440(3); pleonastic ἐγένετο 442(5); τε 443(1); μέν, μὲν οὖν (Acts) 447(3, 4), 451(1); πλήν 449(1); διό 451(5); ὡσεί 453(3); temporal ὡς 455(2); διότι, καθότι 456(1, 4); τότε 459(2); ὅτι *recitativum* 470(1)

Prologue (Gos. 1: 1-4): 3, 95(1), 464; s. also Reference Index

Hymns (in Lk 1 and 2), s. Hymns of Praise

Acts: s. further s.v. Acts

Macedonian word: Βερ(ε)νίκη 42(1)

Mark, Gospel of: style p. 2 n. 2, 442, 458, 462, 472(1), 492; κοράσιον 126(3); ἐνώπιον lacking 214(5); ἕως 216(3); παρά w. acc. only in a local sense 236; αὐτός 277(3); ἕτερος not used 306(1); historical pres. 321; ἀκήκοα lacking 342(2); periphrasis f. the pres. etc. 353(1); lavish use of ἵνα 388; ἄρχεσθαι 392(2); articular inf. 399f.; gen. absolute 423; πλήν 449(1); ὅτι *recitativum* 470(1); initial position of vb. 472(1)

Martyrdom of Polycarp: p. 2 n. 3, 34(1), 61(1); particles 107; s. also Reference Index

Masculine: referring to fem. and/or neut. in *constructio ad sensum* 134; instead of fem. or neut. 136(3), 138(3); agreement w. a compound subj. (masc. and fem.) 135(2)

Matthew, Gospel of: style 458, 462, 485, 489, 492; κοράσιον 126(3); φαίνεσθαι f. φανεροῦσθαι 191; εἰς and ἐν correctly distinguished 205; ἐνώπιον lacking 214(5); ἕως, ἄχρι, μέχρι 216(3); παρά w. acc. only in local sense 236; αὐτός 277(3); ὅστις 293(1); ἕτερος 306(1); ἀκήκοα lacking 342(2); γέγονεν f. aor. 343(3); periphrasis f. the pres. etc. 353(1); lavish use of ἵνα 388; κελεύειν 392(1d, 4); ἄρχεσθαι 392(2); articular inf. 399f.; πλήν 449(1); τότε 459(2); πάλιν 459(4); ὅτι *recitativum* 470(1); word order 474(3)

Metaplasm (fluctuation of declension): 49–52

Metathesis of consonants: 32(2)

Middle (voice): 307, 316f.; fut. mid. going w. pres. act. 77; aor. (fut.) mid. and pass. 78f.; act. f. mid. 310

INDEX OF SUBJECTS

Pauline Corpus (*cont.*)

440(2); τε 443(1); μέν 447(2); πλήν 449(2); ἄρα 451(2); καθάπερ 453; εἴπερ 454(2); εἴτε...εἴτε 454(3); ἡνίκα 455(1); temporal ὡς ἄν 455(2); διότι 456(1); anacoluthon 458, 467 f.; χάρις ὑμῖν 480(5); οὐχ οἷον ὅτι 480(5); figures of speech 463 (ἐξ ἀποστάσεως), 488, 491; parallelism 489, 490(1c); hiatus 486 (Rom, 1 C)

Pentameter in 2 Clem: 487

Peoples, names of: w. art. 262

Perfect: periphrasis f. 65, 352, 354; endings 80, 83, 101 s.v. ἥκειν; *Aktionsart* 318(4); syntax 340–6; after ὅτε 382(1); moods 346; subj. 370(2)

Perfectivizing by means of prepositions: 318(5)

Period: 458, 464, 489 f.; asyndetic 464, 494

Periodic style: 458, 464

Periphrasis: of verbal forms 4, 65(4), 348, 352–6; f. the divine name 130(1)

Persian loanwords: 6, 42(2)

Person: indefinite 'one' 130; 1st plur. instead of 1st sg. 280; 1st and 2nd pers. sg. f. any third pers. 281

Personal construction: ἔμελεν 176(3); 405(2)

Personal names: formation of 125; decl. of foreign 53–5; from Asia Minor 42(3)

Personal pronouns: 277–82; instead of reflex. 283, 406(2, 3); variation in position of gen. of possessive pron. 284; pleonastic after rel. 297, 466; w. art. and ptcp. 412(5)

Peter, Epistles of (esp. 1 P): κοινωνεῖν 169(1); φείδεσθαι (in 2 P) 180(5); ὑπάρχειν w. dat. (2 P) 189; dat. w. vbs. of emotion 196; σύν lacking (1 P) 221; ἕτερος lacking 306(1); εἰ w. opt. 385(2); ἵνα only in a final sense 388; articular inf. 398; μέν frequent in 1 P, lacking in 2 P 447(2); εἴπερ 454(2); εἴτε...εἴτε 454(3); διότι 456(1); ptcp. f. finite vb. 468(2); word order 473(2)

Phonetics in composition: 17–21

Place-names, s. Geographical names

Pleonasm: 484; μᾶλλον w. the comp. 60(3), 246; ἀπ' ἄνωθεν and the like 104(2); personal pron. 278, 297, 423(3), 466; reflex. pron. w. mid. 310(2), 316(3); ἄλλος 306(4); ἕτεροι 306(5); ἄρχεσθαι 392(2); 419(3); τοῦ w. inf. 400(6, 7); λαβών, ἔχων and the like 419; μή 429; ἐγένετο 442(5); πολλὰ καί 442(11); μετὰ (σὺν) καί 442(13)

Pluperfect: usually without augm. 66(1); endings 86; syntax 347, unreal 360(3); periphrasis f. 352, 355; w. ὅταν 367

Plural: 141 f.; plur. and sg. vb. w. neut. plur. subj. 133; referring to a collective sg. 134(1); w. two or more subjs. 135(1, 2); f. one person (allusive plur.) 141; literary plur. (editorial 'we') esp. in Paul 280; ἴδε, ἄγε, ἄφες w. plur. 144, 364(2)

Polycarp, Martyrdom of: p. 2 n. 3

Polysyndeton: 460(3)

Position, s. Word order

Positive: f. comp. 245; comp. f. positive 244

Possessive pronouns: 284–6; without art. 285(2)

Potential optative: 385

Potentiality: pres. 372(1a), 385, 386(1); past 360(3); inf. 396

Predicate (nominal): agreement w. subj. 131 f.; pred. nom. 145; pred. acc. 157; pred. noun w. εἶναι and the dat. 190; case of the pred. w. the inf. 405 f., 410; ὡς w. the pred. 157(5), 453(4); without art. 252; w. art. 273, 413(1); pred. adj. without art. 270(1, 2), possessive adj. 285(2); ptcp. as part of the pred. 414–16 (352–5); position of the pred. adj. 270, of pred. prepositional phrases 272; pred. οὗτος 226; pred. τί 131, 157, 299(1, 2)

Predicate (verbal): made to agree w. the pred. noun 133(3)

Prepositions: 203–40; w. adv. s. Adverbs; omission w. the assimilation of the rel. 294(3); perfectivizing w. vbs. 318(5); w. inf. 402–4, 406(3); repetition or non-repetition w. two nouns connected by καί 459(1)

Present (tense): new formations 73; *Aktionsarten* 318; syntax 319–24: conative 319, aoristic 320, historical 321, 462(1), futuristic 323, used to express rel. time 324; periphrasis f. 353 f.; indic. s. Indicative; subj. 363 f., 365(4), 366(1), 369(1), 370, 373(1), 376, 382(4); opt. 384; impera. 335–7; inf. 338, also s. Infinitive; ptcp. 339, also s. Participle

Prodiorthosis: 465(2), 495(3)

Prolepsis: 476

Prologue to the Gospel of Luke, s. Luke and Reference Index

Pronouns: 64; syntax 277–306 (s. Personal, Possessive, Reflexive, Relative, Reciprocal, Demonstrative, Interrogative, Indefinite Pronouns); agreement w. subj. as pred. 131; agreement w. pred. as subj. 132; position 472(1d), 473(1); art. w., s. Article

Proper names: Sem. (declinable and indeclinable) 53, 55–7; Lat. 54, 55(1a); hypocoristic 125; w. and without art. 260–2, 268(1); cause of the omission of the art. w. *nomen regens* 259(2)

Proportionals: 63(3)

Prothetic vowel: 29(6), 39(3)

Punctuation: 16

Purpose clause, s. Final clause

Quantity: leveling of, in Koine 22, 28; disappearance of quantitative distinctions in MGr 22; diacritical mark (diaeresis) f. 15

Questions: Direct questions: 300(2) (w. ὅ τι), 366, 385(1), 386(1), 427(2, 4), 432(2), 440; w. οὐ and fut. = impera. 387(3); w. οὐ μή 365(4); doubtful and deliberative questions 366; w. ἤ 446; w. οὐκοῦν 451(1); w. γάρ 452(1); question instead of a subordinate clause 469, 471(2)

Indirect questions: 300(1), 368, 385(2), 386(2), 396, 454(1), 476(2); substantivized by means of the

INDEX OF SUBJECTS

art. τό 267(2); interchanged and/or mixed w. rel. clause 293(5), 298(4), 368; mixed w. exclamation 304; w. prolepsis 476(2)

Rhetorical questions: 448(4), 452(2 , 496
Double questions: 298(1), 440(1)

Reciprocal pronouns: 287; εἶς τὸν ἕνα 247(4)
Redundancy, s. Pleonasm
Reduplication: 68 f.
Reflexive pronouns: 64(1); syntax 283, ἐμός and σός 285(1); w. the mid. 310(2), 316(3); acc. w. inf. 406
Relative adverbs: 106; attraction 437
Relative clauses: incorporation of the antecedent 294(5); f. fut. ptcp. 351(1); equivalent to the ptcp. 412 f.; continued by main clauses 297, 469; interchanged and/or mixed w. interrog. clause 293(5), 298(4), 368, 379; in direct and indirect exclamations 304; mood w. 377–80, 386(4); negation 428(4); as parenthesis 465(2)
Relative pronouns: 64(3); syntax 293–7, ὅς and ὅστις (ὅσπερ) 293, attraction of rel. 294, inverse attraction 295, constructio ad sensum w. 296, pleonastic personal pron. in rel. clause 297; interchanged w. the interrog. 298(4); generalizing rel. as indefinite 303; in exclamations 304; position 475(1)
Repetition: ellipsis or repetition 479(1); epanadiplosis 493(1, 2); distributive doubling 158, 248(1), 493(2)
Result clause, s. Consecutive clause
Revelation: usage and style 3 f.; solecisms 136, 400(8); instr. ἐν frequent 195; εἰς not used f. ἐν p. 1 n. 2, 205; ἐκ frequent 212; ἐνώπιον 214(5); ἄχρι(ς) 216(3); σύν lacking 221; ὑπό w. acc. lacking 232(1); παρά w. acc. lacking 236; Ἰησοῦς without art. 260(1); ἕτερος lacking 306(1); perf. instead of aor. 343(1); ὅπως lacking 369(4); ἵνα w. fut. 369(2); τοῦ w. inf. 400(8); μέν lacking 447(2); γάρ 452; μετὰ τοῦτο (ταῦτα) 459(3)
Rhetoric, s. Figures of speech
Rhetorical questions, s. Questions
Rhythm in prose: 464, 487
Rivers, names of: 56; w. art. 261(8)
Running style: 458

Schallanalyse: 487
Semitic words: translit. 36–40; personal names 53, 55–7
Semitisms (influence of Semitic languages on the Koine of the NT): 4; ἡ Βάαλ 53(4); αὕτη = τοῦτο 138(2); αἰῶνες, οὐρανοί 141(1); εἰς instead of pred. nom. and acc. 145, 157(5); omission of ὦ w. the voc. 146; nom. instead of voc. 147(3); declaratory, forensic causative = hiphil 148(4); ὀμνύναι ἐν 149; κρύπτειν ἀπό 155(3); χρίειν w. double acc. 155(6); καλεῖν τὸ ὄνομα w. acc. of the name 157(2); λογίζεσθαι ὡς 157(5); distributive doubling 158, 248(1), 493(2); 'to fill' etc. w. acc. instead of gen.

159(1); ὁδόν as prep. 161(1); υἱός 162(1, 6); μυριάδες μυριάδων 164(1); partitive gen. as subj. and obj. 164(2); gen. instead of adj. 165; σπλαγχνίζεσθαι 176(1); βασιλεύειν ἐπί 177, 233(2); κωλύειν ἀπό 180(1); gen. w. verbal adj. 183; γίνεσθαι w. dat. 189(2); dat. of agent w. pass. 191; ethical dat. 192; ἐν (esp. instrumental) 195, 219 f.; dat. = Hebr. inf. absolute 198(6); ἡμέρᾳ καὶ ἡμέρᾳ 200(1); interchange of εἰς and ἐν 206; ἄφαντος ἐγένετο ἀπό 211; ἔμπροσθεν, ἐναντίον, ἐνώπιον 187(2), 214(6); ὀπίσω 215(1); ἐν μέσῳ and the like w. gen. 215(3); circumlocutions w. πρόσωπον, χείρ, στόμα 149, 217, 234(4); ποιεῖν μετά 'to, for, on' 227(3); ἐπ' ἐσχάτου τῶν ἡμερῶν 234(8); ἀπὸ μιᾶς 241(6); positive instead of comp. 245; comp. expressing exclusion 245a; εἷς 247, 306(5); ἐν τριάκοντα 248(3); art. 259, 261(4, 7), 262(3), 275(4), 286(2), 294(5); personal pron.: unemphatic nom. 277(2, 3), oblique cases frequent 278; δὸς ἀντὶ ἐμοῦ καὶ σοῦ 283(2); ψυχή = refl. pron. 283(4); ὅδε f. οὗτος 289; post-position of the adj. 292, 474(1); πᾶς ὅς 293(1); ὅρκον ὃν ὤμοσεν 295; pleonastic personal pron. following a rel. pron. 297; τί = 'how!' 299(4); ἄνθρωπος = τις 301(2); πᾶς...οὐ, εἷς...οὐ 302; factitives in -εύειν 309(1); ἐξέρχεσθαι = ἐκβάλλεσθαι and the like 315; historical pres. 321; aor. = Hebr. perf. 333(2); periphrasis supported by Sem. usage 353(1); fut. indic. instead of impera. 362; εἰ = οὐ in oaths 372(4), 454(5); οὐκ...εἰ μή 376; free use of the inf. to express result 391(4); διδόναι w. acc. and inf. 392(1 e); προστίθεσθαι 392(2), 435(a); pleonastic ἄρχεσθαι 392(2); free use of complementary inf. 392(3); τοῦ w. inf. 400(6, 7); ἐν τῷ w. inf. 404(1); πρὸς τό w. inf. 402(5); ἀκούσας πολλά ἐποίει 414(5); pleonastic λαβών, λέγων and the like 397(3), 419 f.; ἔγραψεν λέγων 420(2); ptcp. = Hebr. inf. absolute 422; οὐ w. ptcp. 430(3); εἰ before direct questions 440(3); καὶ ἐγένετο, ἐγένετο δέ 442(5), 472(3); καί used to co-ordinate words w. clauses 442(6); καί used to introduce an apodosis 442(7); interchange of εἰ μή and ἀλλά 448(8); ἵνα and ὅ = Aram. דִּי 448(8); 'consecutive' ὅτι 456(2); καί = וְ 458; τότε 'thereupon' 459(2); anacoluthon after a rel. clause or ptcp. 466; interrog. clause instead of a rel. clause 469; parataxis in interrog. sentences 471(2); vb. in initial position in the sentence 472(1); *parallelismus membrorum* 466, 485, 489, 492; prolepsis 476(1); chiasmus 477(2); ellipsis 480(5)

Sense-lines (στίχοι): 16
Sentence structure: 458–71
Septuagintisms: 4; ἵλεώς σοι 128(5); s. also Semitisms
Singular: vb. w. neut. plur. subj. 133, w. fem. plur. 136(5), w. collectives 134, w. compound subj. 135; neut. sg. 138(1), 263(1–3); collective 139; distributive 140; ἕκαστος w. plur. subj. 305; ἴδε, ἄγε, ἄφες w. plur. 144, 364(2)

INDEX OF SUBJECTS

II. INDEX OF GREEK WORDS AND FORMS

INDEX OF GREEK WORDS AND FORMS

ἄγγελοι: without art. 254(2)
ἄγε: 308; w. plur. 144, 364(2)
ἄγειν: 101 (s. also ἄγε); aor. 75; intr. 308; ἄγει τρίτην ταύτην ἡμέραν 129; ἀγοραῖοι ἄγονται 5(3b); never idiomatic ἄγων 419(1)
ἄγια, τά: 141(8); τὰ ἄγ. τῶν ἁγίων 141(8), 245(2); ἡ ἁγία πόλις 474(1)
ἅγιος: ἁγιώτατος 60(1); ὁ ἅγ. 263(a,b)
ἁγνίζειν: pass. 314
ἀγορά: without art. 255(2)
ἀγοράζειν: constr. w. 179(1)
ἀγοραιος: accent ?13; ἀγοραῖοι ἄγονται 5(3b)
Ἀγοῦστος, s. Αὐγ-
ἀγριέλαιος, ἡ: 120(3), 241(6)
Ἀγρίππας: 54, 55(1a)
ἀγρός: without art. 255(1)
ἀγωνιᾶν: w. μήποτε 370(1)
ἀγωνίζεσθαι: 392(1a)
Ἀδάμ: 53(1)
ᾄδειν: constr. w. 187(4)
ἀδελφός: ἄδελφε 13; to be supplied w. gen. 162(4)
ἀδελφότης: 110(1)
ᾄδης: ἐν τῷ ᾄδῃ, εἰς ᾄδην (not Ἅιδου) 162(8)
ἀδικεῖν: w. acc. 151(1); pass. 'let yourself be wronged' 314; perfective pres. 322
Ἀδραμυντηνός, -μυττ-: 42(3)
Ἀδρίας, ὁ: 261(8)
ἀδύνατόν (ἐστιν): 127(2)
ἀεί: not αἰεί 30(1); f. which πάντοτε 105
Ἀενδωρ: 39(3)
Ἀερμών: 39(3)
ἀετός: not αἰετός 30(1)
ἄζβεστον: 10
-άζειν: vbs. in 108(4); fut. 74(1)
ἄζυμα, τά: 141(3)
Ἄζωτος: 39(4), 56(1)
ἀήλι: 39(3)
ἀθέμιτόν ἐστιν: constr. w. 409(3)
Ἀθηναῖοι: art. 262(3)
ἀθῷος: 26; ἀπό 182(3)
αι: ᾱι loss of second element 26; αι–ε 22, 25; αι–α 30(1), 41(1); = Lat. ae 41(1); αι- unaugmented 67(1)
-ᾳ: subject to elision 486
-ᾳ, -αιεν: not -ειε(ν), -ειαν in the opt. 85
Αἴγυπτος: without art. 261(7)
αἰδώς: 47(4); αἰδεῖσθαι αἰδώς 126(1b α)
-αιεν: in opt. s. -ᾳ
Αἰλαμῖται: or Ἐλ-? 38
αἷμα: plur. 141(6); ἐν τῷ αἵματι 219(3)
αἱματεκχυσία: 119(3)
Αἰνέας: 30(2)
-αίνειν: aor. -ᾱνα 72; perf. pass. -αμμένος 72
αἰνεῖν: constr. w. 187(4), 229(1)
Αἰνών: 56(3)
-αῖος: 111(2)
-αίρειν: aor. -ᾱρα 72
αἴρειν: ἐκ (τοῦ) μέσου αἴρειν 5(3b); intr. 308; constr. w. 170(2)

αἱρεῖν: 101; fut. 74(3); aor. 80
αἰσθάνεσθαι: τι 173(3); not. w. ptcp. 416(2)
αἰσχρός: 61(2); -όν ἐστιν constr. w. 409(3)
αἰσχύνεσθαι: ἀπό 149; w. inf. 392(1b); w. supplementary ptcp. 415
Αἰσχύνη: 53(4)
αἰτεῖν: act. and mid. distinguished 316(2); constr. w. 155(2), 390(3), 392(1c, 4), 409(5)
αἰτία: causa 5(3b); δι' ἣν αἰτίαν 456(4)
αἰτίωμα: 109(2)
αἰχμαλωτεύειν and -τίζειν: 108(5)
αἰών: αἰῶνες 4(2), 141(1); ὁ αἰὼν οὗτος, ἐκεῖνος 292
αἰώνιος: two and three endings 59(2)
ἀκαθαρσία: w. τοῦ and inf. 400(2)
ἀκαιρεῖν: -ρεθῆναι 70(1), 307
ἀκατάπα(υ)στος: 65(3); τινός 182(3)
Ἀκελδαμάχ: 39(3)
ἄκκεπτα: p. 5 n. 1
ἀκμήν: 160
ἀκολουθεῖν: 126(1a β); constr. w. 193(1)
ἀκόλουθος: w. gen. 182(1)
-ακός: 113(2)
ἀκούειν: fut. 77; constr. w. 163, 173(1, 2), 198(6), 210(3), 397(1), 405(2), 416(1); perfective pres. 322; aor. and perf. 342(2)
ἀκριβῶς: ἀκριβέστερον 244(2); ἀκριβέστατος 60(1)
ἀκρο-: in composition 123(1)
ἀκροβυστία: 120(4); gen. 163
ἀκροθίνια: 123(1)
ἄκρος: τὸ ἄκρον w. gen. 270(2), without art. 264(5)
ἀκτίς: nom. ἀκτίν 46(4)
Ἀκύλας: 41(2), 54
ἀκύλων, s. εὐρακύλων
ἄκων: 243
ἀλάβαστρος: ὁ and ἡ (τὸ -ον) 49(1)
ἅλα(ς): τό f. οἱ ἅλες 47(4); ἅλατι instr. 195(1b)
ἀλεκτοροφωνία: 123(1); gen. of time when 186(2)
ἀλέκτωρ: Dor. 2
Ἀλεξανδρεύς, -ίνος: 5(2)
ἀλήθεια: ἐπ' ἀληθείας 234(7); ἔστιν ἀλ. τοῦ Χρ. ἐν ἐμοί, ὅτι 397(3)
ἀλήθειν: f. ἀλεῖν 101
ἀληθινός: ὁ 263(a)
ἀληθῶς λέγω ὑμῖν: 243
ἁλιεύς, ἁλεεῖς: 29(5)
ἀλλά: elision 17; adversative conj. 447(1, 6), 448; ἀλλά γε 439(2), 448(5, 6); ἀλλ' ἵνα 448(7), 480(5)
ἀλλάσσειν: τι ἐν 179(2)
ἀλλαχόθεν: 104(1); -χοῦ 103
-άλλειν: aor. -ᾱλα 72
ἄλλεσθαι: 101
ἀλληλουια: 39(3)
ἀλλήλων: 287
ἄλλος: 306, ἄλλος παρά 236(3); w. repeated art. 269(6); ἄλλος πρὸς ἄλλον 287; to be supplied 306(5), 480(1); οὐκ ἄλλος ἀλλά (ἤ, ἀλλ' ἤ) 448(8)
ἀλλοτρι(ο)επίσκοπος: 119(1), 124

275

ἀπαιτεῖν: 316(2)

ἀπαλλοτριοῦν: constr. w. 180(1)

ἀπαντᾶν: fut. 77

ἀπαρνεῖσθαι, s. ἀρνεῖσθαι

ἀπαρτί, ἀπ' ἄρτι: 12(3)

ἀπαρτίζειν: f. ἀνύειν 126(1 b α)

ἅπας: 275

ἀπειθεῖν: constr. w. 187(6)

ἀπειθής: constr. 187(8)

ἀπειλεῖν: and depon. 316(1); constr. w. 392(1 d)

ἀπείραστος κακῶν: 117(1), 182(3)

ἀπεκδύεσθαι: 316(1)

'Απελλῆς besides 'Απολλῶς, -ώνιος: 29(4), 125(1); decl. 55 (1 d)

ἀπέναντι: 12(3); w. gen. 214(4, 6)

ἀπέρχεσθαι: ἀπελθών pleonastic 419(2)

ἀπέχειν: intr. 308; ἀπέχει 129; constr. w. 180(3), 308; -εσθαι constr. w. 180(5); ἀπέχω = ἀπείληφα 322

ἀπιστεῖν: constr. w. 187(6)

ἄπιστος: used only absolutely 187(8)

ἁπλοῦς: 45; comparison 60(1), 61(2)

ἀπό: elision w. 17; w. gen. 209–11; f. partitive gen. 164, w. vbs. 169, 172; f. gen. of separation 180, 182, 211; f. παρά w. ἀκούειν 173(1), 210(3); w. gen. w. vbs. of emotion 176(1); w. φεύγειν, φυλάσσεσθαι etc. 149; w. κρύπτειν 155(3); f. 'how far away' 161(1); w. adj. 182; ἀπὸ προσώπου τινός 140, 217(1); ἀπὸ τοῦ στόματός τινος 217(3); ἀφ' ἧς 241(2, 3); ἀφ' οὗ 294(4); ἀπὸ μιᾶς 241(6); ἀπὸ πέρυσι 12(3), 203; ἀπὸ τότε (πότε) 203, 459(3); perfectivizing in compounds 318(5)

ἀπογράφεσθαι: 317

ἀπογραφή: 5(3 a)

ἀποδημεῖν: augm. 69(4)

ἀποδίδοσθαι: 101 s.v. πιπράσκειν

ἀποθνήσκειν, s. θνήσκειν

ἀποκαθιστάναι: augm. 69(3)

ἀποκαραδοκία: 119(1)

ἀπόκειται: w. inf. 393(6)

ἀποκόπτεσθαι: 317

ἀποκρίνεσθαι: aor., fut. 78; constr. w. 397(3), 420(1); ἀποκριθεὶς εἶπεν and the like p. 3 f. n. 5, 420(1), 462(1)

ἀποκρύπτειν: intr. 309(2)

ἀποκτείνειν: -έννειν, -ιννύναι and the like 73; aor. pass. 76(2); pass. 315

ἀποκυεῖν: 101 s.v. κυεῖν

ἀπολείπεται: w. inf. 393(6)

ἀπολλύναι: 92, 101 s.v. ὀλλύναι

'Απολλῶς: also -ώνιος 29(4), 125(1); decl. 55(1 g)

ἀπολογεῖσθαι: aor. 78; w. dat. 187(4)

ἀπολούειν: mid. 317

ἀπονεύειν: intr. 308

ἀποπέρυσι or ἀπὸ π.: 12, 203

ἀπορεῖσθαι: 101, 307; constr. w. 148(2), 400(3)

ἀπορίπτειν: 11(1); intr. 308

ἀποστάσιον: 111(4)

ἀποστέλλειν: 83(1); use of aor. 328, of perf. 343(2); constr. w. 390(2), 292(1 d, 4), 420(2)

ἀποστερεῖν, -σθαι: constr. w. 155(4), 180(1); pass. 'to allow oneself to be' 314

ἀποστρέφειν: intr. 308; -εσθαί τινα 149, 308

ἀποσυνάγωγος: 120(2)

ἀποτάσσεσθαι: τινί 187(4)

ἀποτολμᾶν: constr. w. 420(2)

ἀποφθέγγεσθαι: constr. w. 397(3)

ἀπροσωπολήμπτως: p. 3 n. 5

ἅπτεσθαι: w. gen. 170(1); w. ptcp. 420(2); pres. impera. 336(3)

'Απφία or 'Αφφία: 42(3)

ἆρα, ἄραγε: 439(1), 440(2), 451(2), 454(2); ἆρα οὖν 451(2 b); ἐπεὶ ἄρα 456(3); εἰ ἄρα(γε) 375, 440(2)

ἄρα, ἀρά γε: 439(1), 440(2)

'Αραβία: w. and without art. 261(6)

ἄραφος: 11(1)

ἀργός, -ή: 59(1)

ἀργύρια: 141(8)

ἀργυροῦς: 45

'Αρεοπαγίτης: 30(2)

ἀρέσκειν: constr. w. p. 3 n. 5, 187(2), 214(6); pass. 312(1)

ἀρεστός: constr. 187(2), 214(6); -όν ἐστιν 393(2), 408

ἀρήν: only ἄρνας 47(4)

-άριον: diminutives in 111(3); as new sg. from plur. -άρια = -aria p. 5 n. 1

'Αρίσταρχος, -άρχης: 50

ἀριστερά: (χείρ) 241(6); ἐξ -ῶν 141(2)

ἀρκεῖν: 101; constr. w. 393(2); -εῖσθαι (ἐπί w. dat.) 235(2), 312(1); ἀρκεῖ (class.) = ἀπέχει 129

ἀρκετόν: satis 131; constr. 393(2); ἀρκετός 187(8), 393(2), 405(2)

ἄρκος: f. ἄρκτος 34(4)

ἁρμόζειν: 71, 101; mid. instead of act. 316(1)

ἀρνεῖσθαι (ἀπ-): aor. 78; pass. 311(2); constr. w. 392(1 a), 397(3), 420(2), 429

ἀρνίον: 47(4), 111(3)

ἁρπάζειν: 71; fut. 77; aor., fut. pass. 76(1)

ἀρραβών: 40

ἄρρην and ἄρσην: 34(2)

ἄρρητος: 11(1)

ἄρρωστος: 11(1)

ἄρσην and ἄρρην, ἀρσενοκοίτης: 34(2), 119(2)

'Αρτεμᾶς: 125(1)

ἄρτι: position 474(3)

-αρτίζειν: f. ἀνύειν 126(1 b α)

ἀρχάγγελος: 118(2)

ἀρχε- s. ἀρχι-

ἄρχειν: compounds w. 50; w. gen. 177; -εσθαι only w. pres. inf. 338(2); constr. w. 180(6), 391(2), 414(2); ἀρξάμενος 308, 'beg. w.' 419(3)

ἀρχή: τὴν ἀρχήν 160, 300(2); ἀπ' ἀρχῆς etc. without art. 255(3)

-άρχης and -αρχος: 50, 119(2)

ἀρχι- (ἀρχε-): in compounds 118(2), 124

ἀρχ(ι)ιερεύς: 44(1), 118(2), 124

ἀρχιποίμην: 118(2)

ἀρχισυνάγωγος: 118(2)

ἀρχιτέκτων: 118(2)

ἀρχιτελώνης: 118(2)

ἀρχιτρίκλινος: 118(2)

-αρχος, s. -άρχης

-ᾶς (acc. plur.): f. -ς 46(2); replaced by -ες 46(2)

-ᾶς: neut. in 47(1)

-ᾶς (-ᾶς): names in: Sem. 53(1, 2), Lat. 54, decl. 55(1a, b, 2); 125

-ᾶσαι: second sg. f. -ᾷ 87

Ἀσάφ: 39(7)

ἀσεβής: ὁ 263(b)

-ασι: f. which -αν (perf. third plur.) 83(1)

Ἀσία: w. art. 261(5)

ἀσκεῖν: w. inf. 392(1a)

ἀσπάζεσθαι: pres. 320, 334; ἀσπάσασθε 320, 337(4)

ἄσπιλος: ἀπό 182(3)

ἀσσάριον: 5(1c), 111(3)

Ἀσσάρωνα: 56(2)

ἆσσον: 61(1), 244(2)

ἀστεῖος: τῷ θεῷ 192

ἀστήρ: plur. without art. 253(1)

ἀστοχεῖν: constr. w. 171(2), 180(2)

ἀστράπτειν: 129

ἄστρον: plur. without art. 253(1)

ἀσύνετος: 117(1)

ἀσφαλίζειν: f. κλείειν 126(1a α, 2)

ἄτερ: w. gen. 216(2)

Ἀτταλ-: 34(1)

αυ: αυ–ευ 30(4); αυ–α 41(1); augmented to ευ 67(1)

αὐγή: 44(1)

Αὔγουστος: 5(3a); Ἀγ- 41(1)

αὐθαδία: 23

αὐθεντεῖν: τινός 177

αὔξειν, -άνειν: augm. 67(1); 101; 309(2)

αὔρα: ellipsis of 241(6)

αὔριον, s. ἐπαύριον

αὐτο-: in compounds 117(2)

αὐτόματος: 117(2); -μάτη 59(1); adj. instead of adv. 243

αὐτός: intensive 283(4), 288; not written ταὐτό(ν) 64(4); αὐτὸ τοῦτο 154, 290(4); τὸ δ' αὐτό 12(1), constr. 154; ὁ αὐτός constr. 194(1), 304, 442(11); ἐπὶ τὸ αὐτό 233(1); ἐξ αὐτῆς, s. ἐξαυτῆς; 'he' emphatic 277(3, 4), 284(3) (αὐτοῦ 'his'), αὐτὸς δέ 277(3), καὶ αὐτός 277(3); αὐτοῦ etc. possessive gen. 284(1); αὐτοῦ etc. without formal agreement 282, high frequency and redundancy (pleonastic) 278, 423, 466, 297 (following rel.); καὶ...αὐτοῦ following a rel. clause 297; ἴδιος αὐτοῦ 286(1); confusion of αὐτοῦ and ἑαυτοῦ, s. ἑαυτοῦ

αὐτοῦ: adv. 103

ἀφαιρεῖν: constr. w. 155(4)

ἀφεδρών: 111(6)

ἀφελότης: 110(1)

ἄφες: w. subj. 364(1, 2)

ἀφιδεῖν: 14

ἀφιέναι (s. also ἄφες and ἱέναι): ἀφίειν 94(2); aor. 95(1); ἀφέθην 67(2); ἤφιεν 69(1); ἀφέωνται 97(3); f. ἐᾶν 126(1a α); ἀφίενται aoristic pres. 320; futuristic pres. 323(1); constr. w. 392(1f); οὐκ ἀφίω 433(1)

ἀφίστασθαι: 180(2)

ἀφορίζειν: fut. 74(1)

ἀφυπνοῦν: 108(1)

Ἀχάζ: 39(3)

Ἀχαΐα: Ἀχαΐα, Ἀχαϊκός w. -αϊ- 15, not -αιι- 30(1); w. and without art. 261(6)

ἀχρεῖος: accent 13; ἀχρεῖος, ἀχρεοῦν 30(2)

ἄχρι(ς): 21; w. gen. 216(3); conj. 383; ἄ. οὗ 216(3), 383, 455(3)

ἄψινθος: ὁ ?49(1)

Βάαλ: as fem. 53(4)

βαθμός: 34(5)

βάϊα: 6

βαίνειν: pres. -βέννειν 73; βήσομαι 77; ἔβην 95(1); -βηθι, -βα, -βατε 2, 95(3)

βαλ(λ)άντιον: 11(2)

βάλλειν: aor. 81(3); intr. 308; aor. and perf. 342(1)

βάπτειν: constr. w. 172

βαπτίζειν: 206(2); ptcp. 413(1); -εσθαι aor. 314, 317

βάπτισμα and -σμός: 109(2)

Βαραββᾶς: 55(1b)

βάρβαροι: οἱ 262(2)

βαρεῖν (-ύνειν): 101

Βαρναβᾶς: 55(1b), 125(2)

βασανίζω: reflexive 310(2)

βασιλεία: gen. 163

βασίλειον: = -λεία 50

βασιλεύειν: 309(1); constr. w. 177, 234(5)

βασιλεύς: acc. plur. 46(2); voc. 146(3), 147(3)

βασίλισσα: 34(1), 111(1)

βασκαίνειν: aor. 72; constr. w. 152(1)

βαστάζειν: 71

βάτος: ὁ and ἡ 49(1)

βατταλογεῖν (βαττο-): 40

βατταρίζειν: 40

βέβαιος, -αία: 59(2)

Βελίαρ: 39(6)

βελτίων: 61(1); βέλτιον adv. 61(1), 102(1), 244(2)

Βενιαμ(ε)ίν: 38

βέννειν: = βαίνειν 73

Βερ(ε)νίκη: 42(1)

Βηθανία: 56(2)

Βηθλεέμ: 56(3)

Βηθσαϊδά(ν): 37, 56(3)

Βηθφαγῆ: 56(3)

βιάζεσθαι: pass. 311(1)

βιβλαρίδιον: 111(3)

βιβλίον: from βυβλίον 32(1); art. 259(1)

βιοῦν: 101; aor. 75

βλάπτειν: 151(1)

βλαστάνειν: and -ᾶν 101; aor. 75

βλασφημεῖν: constr. w. 152(1)

βλασφημία: plur. 142

βλέπειν: instead of ὁρᾶν 101; fut. 77; constr. w. 149, 392(1*b*), 397(1), 416(1); βλέπετε 364(3), 369(2), 370(2), 461(1)

βλητέον: 65(3)

βοᾶν: constr. w. 397(3)

Βοες, Βοος, Βοοϛ: 39(4)

βορρᾶς: 2, 34(3), 45; without art. 253(5)

βότρῦς: 46(2)

βούλεσθαι: 101 s.v. θέλειν; βούλει 27; augm. 66(3); ὁ βουλόμενος 252; constr. w. 392(1*a*); ἐβουλόμην 359(2); βούλεσθε introducing deliberative questions 366(3)

βουλεύεσθαι: constr. w. 392(1*a*)

βουνός: 2, 126(1*b* α)

βοῦς: acc. plur. βόας 46(2)

βραδύνειν: τινός 180(5)

βραδύς: constr. 400(8), 402(2)

βρέχει: f. ὕει 126(1*a* α); impersonal and personal 129; trans. and intr. 309(2)

βροντὴ γέγονεν: 129

βροχή: 126(3)

βρώματα: 126(3)

βυρσεύς: 34(2)

βύσσος: p. 3 n. 1

γ: ν f. γ- nasal 19; γ–λ 33; γ = ע 39(3)

Γαβριήλ: 53(2*c*)

Γάϛα: 39(3)

γαϛοφυλάκιον (γάϛα): 6, 13, 115(1)

Γάϊος: 41(1)

Γαλϊλαία: 38, 56(2); -αῖος 38, 111(2); w. art. 261(4)

Γαμαλιήλου: 53(1)

γαμεῖν, -ίϛειν, -ίσκειν: 101; aor. pass. 78; -εῖσθαί τινι 188; act. f. mid. 310(1); -ίϛεσθαι 314

γάμος: plur. 141(3)

γάρ: 452; τε γάρ, καὶ γάρ 443(2); position 475(2)

γε: 439

γέεννα: 39(8)

Γεθσημανί (-σαμανί): 38

-γειος: in compounds 44(1)

γελᾶν: fut. 77

γέμειν, γεμίϛειν: w. ἀπό 169(2); constr. w. 172

γενεά: 34(3); ἡ γ. αὕτη 292

γενεαλογία: 34(3)

γενέσια (γενέθλια): 141(3); dat. 200(3)

γένημα and γέννημα: 11(2), 34(3)

γεννᾶν: 34(3); futuristic pres. 323(2)

Γεννησαρ: not -αρεθ, -αρετ 39(2)

γεννητός: w. gen. 183

γένος: τῷ γένει 197

γερμανε: p. 4 n. 2

γεύεσθαι: w. acc. and gen. 169(3)

γεώργιον: 111(4)

γῆ: 45; ellipsis of 241(1); art. w. 253(3), 259(2); γῆ Ἰούδα, ἡ Ἰουδαία γῆ 261(4); γῆ Ἰσραήλ 262(3)

γῆρας: γήρει 47(1)

γηράσκειν: 101, 331

γίνεσθαι: not γιγν- 34(4); 78, 79, 81(3), 83(1), 101; w. τί 299(2); w. gen. 162(7), 165; w. dat. 189; w. εἰς and ἐν 145(1), 157(1), 205, 207; w. ἐπί 233(1, 2); w. adv. 434(2); w. ptcp. in periphrasis 354; futuristic pres. 323(2); ἐγένετο w. inf. 130(1), 393 (1, 5), 400(7), 408, 409(4), w. finite vb. (w. and without καί) 144, 442(5), 461(2), 472(3); ἐγένετο ἐν τῷ w. inf. 404(1); γέγονεν instead of ἐγένετο 343(3); μὴ γένοιτο p. 2 n. 4, 128(5), 384, 440(2); ellipsis of ἐγένετο 128(7), 480(5); ellipsis of γένηται (ἵνα τί) 299(4)

γινώσκειν: not γιγν- 34(4); γνώσομαι 77; ἔγνωκαν 83(1); ἔγνων 95(1); γνῷ and γνοῖ 95(2); γνώην opt. 26; f. εἰδέναι 126(1*a* β); pass. (w. dat.) 191(2), 313; constr. w. 220(2), 392(2), 397(1), 406(2), 416(2)

γλῶσσα: -σσ-, -ττ- 34(1); ellipsis of 241(6); γλώσσαις (ἑτέραις) λαλεῖν 480(3)

γλωσσόκομον: 119(5)

γναφεύς: or κν- 34(5)

γνόφος: ὁ 51(2)

γνωρίϛειν: 74(1)

γογγύϛειν: impf. 82

Γολγοθᾶ: 39(6), 56(2)

Γόμορρα: 39(3); decl. 57

γόνυ: τιθέναι τὰ γόνατα 5(3*b*)

γονυπετεῖν: 119(4); constr. w. 151(2)

γοῦν: 107

γραπτός: 112

γράφειν: γέγραπται impersonal pass. 130(1); γράφω and ἔγραψα in epistles 334; constr. w. 392(1*d*); w. λέγων 420(2)

γρηγορεῖν: 68, 73; pres. impera. 336

γυμνητεύειν: or γυμνιτ- 24; 108(5)

γυναικάριον: 111(3)

γυνή: to be supplied w. gen. 162(4); art. w. 257(3); ἄνδρες καὶ γυναῖκες, γ. καὶ παιδία 474(7)

δ: δ–θ 33

δαιμόνια: w. sg. and plur. pred. 133(1)

δάκρυον: dat. plur. -υσιν 52

δάκτυλος: without art. 259(1)

Δαλματία: or Δελμ- 41(1)

δαμάϛεσθαι: pass. constr. 191(5)

Δαμασκός: 56(1)

δανείϛειν, -νίϛειν: 23

Δανιήλου: 53(2)

δανιστής: 23

Δαυίδ (-είδ): 38, 39(1), 53(1)

δέ: 442, 443(1), 447, 459(4), 462(1); elision 17; position 475(2); μέν...δέ s. μέν

δεδιέναι: does not appear 96

δεῖ: 130(1), 393(1, 5), 405, 407 f.; δέον (ἐστίν) 353(5), 424; ἔδει 358(1); f. deliberative subj. 366(4); to be supplied (w. inf.) 389; ἃ μὴ δεῖ, τὰ μὴ δέοντα 428(4)

δεικνύναι, -ύειν: 92; constr. w. 392(2), 397(4)

δειλινόν: τό time when 160, 161(3)

δεῖν ('to bind'): w. double acc. 158; pass. w. acc. 159(3); perf. pass. w. dat. 193(3)

δεῖνα: ὁ 64(5); f. which ὅδε 289

δειπνοκλήτωρ: 119(2)

δεῖπνος: instead of -ον 49(2)

δεῖσθαι: ἐδέετο 89; constr. w. 180(4), 229(1), 392(1c), 399(3), 405(1), 409(5)

δεισιδαίμων: comp. 244(2)

δέκα: οἱ 265

δεκαδύο, δεκατέσσαρες, etc.: 63(2)

δέκατον: τό (scil. μέρος) 241(7)

Δελματία, s. Δαλμ-

δεξιά: ἡ 241(6); ἐν δεξιᾷ (ἐνδέξια), ἐκ δεξιῶν etc. 141(2), 241(6); τῇ δεξιᾷ 199

δεξιολάβος: 119(1)

δεπόσιτα: p. 5 n. 1

δέρειν: 126(2); πολλάς, ὀλίγας 154

δέρρις: 34(2)

δεσέρτωρ: p. 5 n. 1, 109(8)

δεσμοί and -ά: 49(3)

δεσπότης: ὁ voc. 147(3)

δεῦρο, δεῦτε: w. subj. and impera. 364(1, 2)

δευτεραῖος: 243

δευτερόπρωτον σάββατον: 115(2)

δεύτερος: without art. 256

δή: 451(4)

δηλαυγής, s. τηλαυγής

δῆλος: δῆλον ὅτι 127(2), 397(4); never δῆλός εἰμι w. ptcp. 414(3)

δηλοῦν: constr. w. 397(4)

• Δημᾶς: 125(1)

δημοσίᾳ: 241(6)

δηνάριον: 5(1c), 111(3); τὸ ἀνὰ δ. 266(2)

-δήποτε: 107, 303

δήπου: 103, 107, 441(3)

διά: elision 17; w. acc. 222; διὰ τί 299(4), 300(2); διὰ τό w. inf. 402(1), 406(3); w. gen. 223; διὰ μέσου s. μέσος; διὰ χειρός (χειρῶν) τινος 140, 217(2), 259(1); διὰ στόματός τινος 140, 217(3), 259(1), 173(1); διὰ τοῦ w. inf. 403 (398); διά in compound vbs.: trans. 150, w. dat. 193(4), perfectivizing 318(5)

διαβάλλεσθαι: τινί 193(4)

διαβλέπειν: constr. w. 392(3)

διάβολος: without art. 254(1)

διάγειν: τὸν βίον 480(2)

διαθῆκαι: 141(8)

διακατελέγχεσθαι: constr. w. 193(4)

διακονεῖν: augm. 69(4); w. dat. 187(2); pass. 312(1), 314

διακρίνεσθαι: aor. 78; constr. w. 193(4)

διάκων: 52

διαλέγεσθαι: aor. 78; constr. w. 193(4)

διαλείπειν: w. ptcp. 414(1), 435

διαλλάσσεσθαι: constr. w. 193(4)

διαμαρτύρεσθαι: constr. w. 163, 392(1d)

διαμερίζεσθαι: mid. 310(2)

διανοίγειν: constr. w. 392(3)

διαπαρατριβή: 116(4)

διαρρηγνύναι: instead of mid. 310(1)

διασαφεῖν: constr. w. 397(4)

διαστέλλεσθαι: constr. w. 187(5), 392(1d)

διάστεμα: f. -στημα 109(3)

διατάσσειν, -εσθαι: constr. w. 392(1d, 4), 409(1)

διατελεῖν: w. ptcp. 414(1), 435; intr. 480(2)

διατηρεῖν: ἐκ, ἀπό 149

διατρίβειν: impf. and aor. 332(1); intr. 480(2)

διαφέρειν: w. gen. 180(3)

διαφθείρειν: pass. w. acc. 159(3)

διδακτός: w. gen. 183

διδάσκαλος: ὁ voc. 147(3)

-διδάσκαλος: in compounds 115(1, 2)

διδάσκειν: w. double acc. 155(1); pass. w. acc. 159(1); w. inf. 392(2); impf. 329

διδόναι: 94(1), 95(1), 97(2); subj. δῷ(ς), (δι)δοῖ(ς) (δώῃ) 95(2); opt. δῴη 26, 95(2), 369(1), 370(3); w. dat. (ἐν, εἰς) 187(1), 218; w. dat. and partitive gen. 169(2); aor. and pres. 337(2–4); w. inf. 390(2); w. acc. and inf. 392(1e), 410; ἐργασίαν διδόναι 5(3b) and p. 5 n. 9

διέρχομαι: complexive aor. 332

διετής: accent 13

διετία: 5(3a)

διηνεκής: 29(3)

διισχυρίζεσθαι: constr. w. 397(3)

δικαιοκρισία: 119(3)

δίκαιος: ὁ 263(a, b)

δικαιοσύνη: constr. 163; ἐν δικ. 219(3); πᾶσα δικ. 275(3)

δικαιοῦν: forensic 148(4); constr. w. 195(1e)

διό: 451(5); διὸ καί 442(12), 451(5); διὸ οὐδέ 451(5)

διόπερ: 107, 451(5)

διοπετές: τό 241(7)

Διόσκουροι: 30(3)

διότι: 208(1), 294(4), 451(5), 456(1)

διπλοκαρδία: 61(2)

διπλοῦς: 45; διπλότερον 61(2), 102(4)

δισμυριάδες: 63(3)

διστάζειν: 71, 206(2)

διψᾶν: pres. 88; fut., aor. 70(2); constr. w. 171(1)

δίψος: τό 51(1)

διώκειν: fut. 77

δογματίζειν: pass. 314

δοκεῖν: w. dat. 187(3); impf., pres. and aor. 336(3); constr. w. 392(1a), 397(2); τὸ δοκεῖν 391a; ἔδοξέ μοι 397(2), 405(2), 468(3); ἔδοξα ἐμαυτῷ 283(1), 405(2); δοκῶ w. finite vb. 461(2); parenthetical δοκεῖτε 465(2)

δοκιμάζειν: constr. w. 392(3), 405(2), 416(2)

δοκιμή: 110(2)

δοκίμιος: = δόκιμος 263(2); -εῖον, not -ιον 23

δοξάζειν: constr. w. 235(2), 392(3)

δουλεύειν: w. dat. 187(2)

δοῦλοι: to be supplied 162(5)

δουλοῦν: constr. w. 187(2), 191(4); act. 310(1)

δράπανον: 29(1)

δράσσεσθαι: 170(2)

INDEX OF GREEK WORDS AND FORMS

δραχμή: 5(1c); ellipsis of 241(6)

δύειν: also δύνειν, ἐνδιδύσκειν 101; aor. act., pass. 75, 76(2); intr. 309(2)

δύνασθαι: 101; augm. 66(3); fut. mid.-pass. 79; transition to ω-conjugation 93; constr. w. 338(2), 366(4), 388, 392(1, 2); ἐδύνατο 'could have' 358(1)

δυνατεῖν: 108(2); constr. w. 392(2)

δυνατόν ἐστιν, δυνατός: constr. 338(2), 393(2, 4), 405(2), 408; δυνατόν without ἐστίν or ἦν 127(2), 128(3)

δύο: decl. 63(1); δύο δύο 248(1); οἱ δύο 275(8)

δυσ-: 117(1)

δυσβάστακτα: 71

δυσεντέριον: 50

δυσμαί: 141(2); without art. 253(5)

δώδεκα and δεκαδύο: 63(2); οἱ δώδεκα 265

δωδεκάφυλον: τὸ δ. ἡμῶν 120(3), 138(1), 263(3)

δωρεά: 30(2); δωρεάν 160

δωροφορία: 119(1)

ε: ε–α 29(1, 2), 41(1), 42(2, 3) (ευ–αυ 30(4)); ε–ο 29(4); ε–ι 29(5), 41(1); ε–αι 25; ε–ει 30(2, 3); prothetic ε 29(6)

ἐάν: not ἄν or ἦν 31(1), 107, 360(1), 371; constr. 371(4), 372(1a), 373; instead of εἰ 368, 372(1a); ἐὰν καί 374; ἐὰν μή 'unless, except' 376, 480(6); εἰ...ἄν 376; ἐάν...ἀλλά 448(5); ἐάν τε...ἐάν τε 454(3); epexegetical 394; position 475(1)
  ἐάν f. ἄν 107, 371

ἐᾶν: f. which ἀφιέναι 126(1a); constr. w. 392(1, 1f); οὐκ ἐῶ 433(1)

ἐάνπερ: 107, 454(2)

ἑαυτοῦ: not αὑτοῦ 31(1); also f. ἐμαυτοῦ, σεαυτοῦ 64(1); ἑαυτῶν also f. ἡμῶν αὐτῶν, ὑμῶν αὐτῶν 64(1), f. ἀλλήλων 287; ἑαυτῷ (-οῖς) 188(2); εἰς, πρὸς ἑαυτόν (-ούς)=Hebr., Aram. ethical dat. 192; ἑαυτοῦ etc. and αὐτοῦ 283; αὐτὸς ἑαυτοῦ etc. 283(4); position 283(3), 284(2)

ἕβδομος: ἡ ἑβδόμη 241(2)

Ἑβραῖος: 39(3)

Ἑβραϊστί: 15

ἐγ-: f. ἐκ- 19(3)

ἐγγαρεύειν, s. ἀγγαρεύειν

ἐγγίζειν: 74(1); descriptive pres. 321; perf. 342(1); constr. w. 193(2)

ἔγγιστα, s. ἐγγύς

ἔγγονα:=ἔκγονα 19(3)

ἐγγύθεν: does not appear 104(3)

ἐγγύς: ἔγγιστα 60(2); ἐγγύτερον 62; w. gen. (dat.) 184; as pred. 434(1)

ἐγείρειν, -εσθαι: aor., fut. 78; 101; w. double acc. (εἰς) 157(5); futuristic pres. 323(1); ἠγέρθη, ἐγήγερται 'he is risen' 342(3), 343(1); ἔγειρε ἆρον, ἐγείρεσθε ἄγωμεν 461(1)

ἐγκαίνια: 123(1), 141(3)

ἐγκακεῖν: ἐκκ- 123(2); constr. w. 414(2)

ἐγκαλεῖν: constr. w. 178, 187(5), 229(1); pass. 312(1)

ἐγκεντρίζειν: constr. w. 202

ἐγκόπτειν: constr. w. 152(4), 400(4), 429

ἐγκρατεύεσθαι: 108(5); constr. w. 154; pres. and aor. 337(2)

ἐγκρίνειν: constr. w. 202

ἐγώ: use of nom. 277(1, 2), ἐγώ εἰμι 277(1), possessive gen. 278, emphatic oblique cases 279; literary plur. 280; to represent any third person 281; position of the possessive μου 284(1)

ἐδαφίζειν: fut. 74(1)

Ἐζεκίας: 38, 53(1)

ἐθελο-: in composition 118(2)

ἐθελοθρησκία: 118(2)

ἐθνάρχης: 50

ἔθνη: w. sg. and plur. pred. 133(1); without art. 254(1)

ἔθος ἐστίν: constr. 409(3)

ει: ει–ῑ(ῐ) 2, 22f., 38, 42(3), 113(3); ει–ε 30(2, 3); ει–η 27; ει rather than ε in plupf. 86

-ει (second sg. mid.-pass.): 27, 87

-εί (adv. in): 23, 122

ει-: augm. of 67(1); ει- and η- as augm. of ε- 67(3)

εἰ: 360, 371f., 374–6, 428 (οὐ and μή), 454; ='whether' 368, 375, 386(2); instead of ἐάν (w. subj.) 372(3), 376; εἰ...ἄν 376; εἰ...ἀλλά 448(5); introducing direct questions 440(3); εἰ καί 374; καὶ εἰ 457; εἰ μή (τι, γε) 376, 428(1–3), 448(8), 454(5), 480(6); ἄλλος εἰ μή 306(4); εἰ δὲ μή (γε) 376, 439(1), 454(4), 480(6); εἰ ἄρα (γε) 375, 440(2); εἴ γε 439(2), 454(2); εἴ πως, s. εἴπως

εἰ μήν: f. ἦ μήν 24, 107, 441(1)

-ειά and -ιᾶ: interchange 23; decl. of subst. in -εια; subst. in from adj. in -ής 110(2)

-είᾱ: subst. in 109(5); -είᾱ or -ίᾱ 23

-είας: proper names in 38, 53(1)

εἰδέναι: 99(2), 101, 126(1a β); ἴσασιν and οἴδασιν p. 2 n. 4; constr. w. 392(2), 396, 397(1), 408, 416(2)

εἶδον: 101 s.v. ὁρᾶν, confusion of endings 80, 81(3); s. also ὁρᾶν, ἰδεῖν, ἴδε, ἰδού

εἰδωλεῖον: not -ιον 13, 111(5)

εἰδωλόθυτον: 117(2)

εἰδωλολάτρης, -εῖν, -(ε)ία: 119(2)

εἴκειν: εἶξα 67(1)

εἰκῆ: 26

Εἰκόνιον, s. Ἰκόνιον

εἴκοσι: not -σιν 20

εἰλικριν-: 119(4)

-εῖν: vbs. in 89; formation 108(2), 119(1, 4) (from compound adj. in -ος); fut. 74(1, 2); impf. third plur. -οῦσαν 84(3); second sg. -ῇ and -εῖσαι 87; confused w. -ᾶν 90

-ειν-: not -ην first sg. plupf. 86

εἶναι: ἐστί(ν), εἰσί(ν) 20; 98; confusion of subj. and impf. 372(1a); ellipsis of 127f., inf. 157(2, 3), ptcp. 413(3), 414, 416, 418(6); in periphrasis 4(3), 65(4), 352f.; ὅ ἐστιν w. ptcp. 353(4), cf. 132(2); w. aor. ptcp. 355; w. gen. 162(7), 164(1), 165; w. dat. 189f.; w. εἰς 145, ἐπί 234(5), πρός 239(1, 4); w. adv. 434(1); καλὸν ἦν and the like 358(1); ἐστίν w.

INDEX OF GREEK WORDS AND FORMS

εἶναι (*cont.*)
  adj. or subst. and inf. 393(2, 3); ὁ ὢν καὶ ὁ ἦν (καὶ ὁ ἐρχόμενος) 143
εἵνεκεν, s. ἕνεκα
-εῖον or -ιον: subst. in 111(5)
εἴπερ: 107, 454(2); εἴπερ...ἀλλά 448(5)
εἶπον: -ον and -α 81(1); εἶπεν and ἔλεγεν 329; ὡς ἔπος εἰπεῖν 391(*a*); w. inf. 392(4); εἰπών, καὶ εἶπεν 420; εἶπεν λέγων etc. 101 s.v. λέγειν, 420; s. also λέγειν
εἴπως: 12, 106, 375, 386(2)
εἴρηκεν, s. λέγειν
εἰρηνεύειν: 309(1); μετά 227(2)
εἰρήνη: ε. ὑμῖν 128(5); ὕπαγε εἰς εἰρήνην, ἐν εἰρήνῃ 206(1), 218
-εῖς: f. -έας (acc. plur.) in subst. in -εύς 46(2)
εἰς: not ἐς 30(3); encroachment on the simple case 187 intro.; 203; w. acc. 205–7; interchanging w. dat. 187, 193(2), 194–end; confused w. ἐν, s. ἐν; f. ἐπί, πρός 207(1); w. γίνεσθαι, ἔσεσθαι (εἶναι) 145, 190(1); w. λογίζεσθαι (pass.) 145(2); w. ἐγείρειν, ἔχειν etc. 157(5); εἰς τό w. inf. 391(3), 402(2), 406(3); compounds w. εἰς, constr. w. 202; εἰς πρόσωπον 217(1); εἰς χεῖρας 217(2); εἰς ἐλάχιστόν ἐστιν 145(2), 393(6)
εἷς: μία μιᾶς 43(1); w. partitive gen. and ἐκ 164(1); μία f. πρώτη 247(1); (ἐν) τῇ μιᾷ 241(2); ἀπὸ μιᾶς 241(6); indefinite art. 247(2); εἷς τις 247(2), 301(1); ὁ εἷς...ὁ ἕτερος 247(3); εἷς...καὶ εἷς and the like 247(3), 250; εἷς τὸν ἕνα 247(4); ἐν τριάκοντα etc. 248(3); εἷς...οὐ (οὐδὲ εἷς) 302(2); εἷς ἕκαστος etc. 305; ἐν δέ elliptical 481
-εῖσαι: = -ῇ second sg. mid.-pass. of vbs. in -εῖν 87
εἰσακούειν: 173(3)
-εισαν: plupf. 86
εἰσέρχεσθαι: 83(1); w. εἰς, ἐν 218
εἴσω: 103
εἶτα, εἶτεν: 35(3), 459(4)
εἴτε...εἴτε: 369(2), 372(3), 446, 454(3)
εἰωθέναι: constr. w. 392(2); τὸ εἰωθός w. dat. 189(1)
ἕκαστος: 64(6), 305; w. partitive gen. 164(1); without art. 275; distinguished from πᾶς 275(3)
ἑκατονταετής: 13, 124
ἑκατονταπλασίων: 63(3)
ἑκατοντάρχης and -αρχος: 5(1, 3*a*), 50
ἐκβάλλειν: 126(2); pass. 315; constr. w. 181
ἐκδίδοσθαι: mid. 316(1)
ἐκ-διδύσκειν or -δύειν: ἐξέδυσα 101 s.v. δύειν; constr. w. 155(5)
ἐκεῖ: 103; redundant after ὅπου 297
ἐκεῖθεν: 104(1); οἱ ἐκ 266(1); instead of ἐκεῖ? 437
ἐκεῖνος: 64(2), 291; art. 292; ἐκείνης (scil. τῆς ὁδοῦ) 186(1), 241(4); ἐκείνου possessive 284(2, 3); αὐτός f. αὐτὸς ἐκεῖνος 288(2); as connective 459(3)
ἐκεῖσε: = ἐκεῖ 103
ἐκκαθαίρειν: 72
ἐκκλησία: without art. 257(2)
ἐκκλίνειν: intr. 308
ἐκλανθάνεσθαι: constr. w. 175

ἐκλέγειν: perf. pass. 101 s.v. λέγειν 'gather'; mid. 316(1)
ἐκλεκτός: w. gen. 183
ἐκνεύειν: intr. 308
ἔκπαλαι: 12(2), 116(3)
ἐκπερισσοῦ, -ῶς: 12(3), 116(3)
ἐκπίπτειν: constr. w. 181; = ἐκβάλλεσθαι 315
ἐκπλήσσεσθαι: -σσ-, -ττ-, 34(1); 101 s.v. τύπτειν; constr. w. 196
ἐκτός: without art. 256
ἐκτός: 103; w. gen. 184, 216(2); ἐκτὸς εἰ μή 376
ἔκτρομος: 120(2)
ἐκφεύγειν: 28
ἔκφοβος: 120(2)
ἐκχέω, s. χέω
ἐκχύν(ν)ειν, s. χύν(ν)ειν
ἑκών: 243
ἐλαία: not ἐλάα 30(1)
Ἐλαιῶν (or -ών) ὄρος: 143
Ἐλαμῖται, s. Αἰλαμῖται
ἐλάσσων: -σσ-, -ττ- 34(1) (and derivatives); decl. 47(2); meaning 61(1); before numbers without ἤ 185(4); τὸ ἔλαττον f. persons 263(3)
ἐλάχιστος: *perexiguus* 60(2); -ιστότερος 61(2); εἰς ἐλάχιστόν ἐστιν 145(2), 393(6)
Ἐλεάζαρ and Λάζαρος: 53(2)
ἐλεεῖν: -ᾷ -ᾶτε 90; trans. 148(2); = σπλαγχνίζεσθαι 176(1)
ἐλ(ε)εινός: 31(3)
ἐλεημοσύνη: 110(2)
ἔλεος: (ὁ and) τό 51(2)
ἐλεύθερος: ἀπό and ἐκ 182(3); ἐλ. εἰμι w. inf. 393(5)
ἐλευθεροῦν: ἀπό 180
Ἐλισάβετ, -εθ: 38, 39(2), 53(3)
Ἐλισαῖος: 38
ἕλκειν: 74(3), 101
ἑλκοῦν: redupl. 68
Ἑλλάς: w. art. 261(4)
Ἕλληνες: art. 262(2); Ἰουδαῖοί (τε) καὶ Ἕ. 444(2)
ἑλληνιστής: 109(8)
ἐλλογεῖν: -α, -ᾶται 90; 123(2)
ἐλπίζειν: ἐλπ- 14; fut. 74(1); ἤλπικα 341; aor. impera. 337(2); constr. w. 187(6), 233(2), 235(2), 338(3), 350, 397(2)
ἐλπίς: ἐλπίς 14; ἐπ' ἐλπίδι 235(2); constr. 400(1)
Ἐλυμαΐς (ἡ), -αία, οἱ Ἐλυμαῖοι: 38
ἐμαυτοῦ: 64(1), 283; position 284(2)
ἐμβάπτειν: ἐν and εἰς 218
ἐμβατεύειν: (Col 2: 18) 154
ἐμβλέπειν: constr. w. 202
ἐμβριμᾶσθαι, -οῦσθαι: 90; aor. 78; w. dat. 187(7)
ἐμμένειν: constr. w. 202; complexive aor. 332
ἐμός: 284(2), 285; ἐμόν ἐστιν 285(2)
ἐμπαίζειν, s. παίζειν
ἐμπερίτομος: 120(2), 123(1)
ἐμπι(μ)πλάναι: s. πιμπλάναι; constr. w. 172
ἐμπι(μ)πράναι, s. πίμπρασθαι
ἐμπνεῖν: w. gen. 174

INDEX OF GREEK WORDS AND FORMS

ἔτι: 459(4); position 474(3); ἔτι ἄνω, κάτω f. ἀνώτερον, κατώτερον 62; ἔτι μικρὸν καί 127(2)

-ετία: 5(3a)

ἑτοιμάζειν: =comparare p. 5 n. 1

ἕτοιμος: accent 13; two and three endings 59(2); constr. 393(4), 400(7)

ἔτος: not ἔτος 14; ἐτῶν 48; ὡς (ὡσεί) ἐτῶν as gen. of quality 165, 453(3); ἐν ἔτει, ἔτεσιν 200(2)

ευ: written εου 9; ευ–αυ 30(4); augm. 67(1); ευ- augmented to αυ- 67(1)

εὖ: f. which καλῶς 102(3), 126(1a α); εὖ ποιεῖν (πράσσειν) constr. 151(1), 414(5); compounds w. εὐ- 117(1), augm. of 69(4)

Εὖα: 39(1, 3)

εὐαγγελίζειν: augm. 69(4); -εῖν and -εσθαι 119(1), 309(1); -εσθαι pass. 311(1); constr. w. 152(2), 163, 206(4), 392(3)

εὐαγγέλιον: 119(1); w. gen. and w. κατά and acc. 163, 224(2)

εὐάγγελος: 119(1)

εὐαρεστεῖν: augm. 69(4); pass. w. dat. 196, 312(1)

εὐγενίς: 59(3)

εὐδοκεῖν: 67(1), 119(1); constr. w. 148(2), 196, 206(2), 392(3)

-εύειν, -εύεσθαι: vbs. in 108(5)

εὐεργεσία: constr. 163

εὐθύς, εὐθέως: 21, 102(2), 425(2); εὐθέως παραχρῆμα 484; εἰς εὐθείας (scil. ὁδούς) 241(4)

εὐκαιρεῖν: constr. w. 392(3)

εὐκαιρία: τοῦ w. inf. 400(1)

εὐλάβεια, -εῖσθαι, -ῆς: 211

εὐλογεῖν: τινά 151(1)

εὐλογητὸς ὁ θεός: 128(5)

εὐοδοῦσθαι: constr. w. 392(3)

εὐπάρεδρος: 117(1); constr. w. 202 s.v. παρα-

εὐπερίστατος: 117(1)

εὐποιία: 119(1)

εὐπορεῖσθαι: 101 s.v. ἀπορεῖν

εὐρακύλων: 5(1d), 41(2), 115(1)

εὑρίσκειν: augm. 67(1); aor. εὗρον and εὗρα 81(3); ἀνάπαυσιν etc. w. dat. 190(3); pass. w. dat. 191(3), 313; act. instead of mid. 310(1); constr. w. 416(2, 3)

Εὐρώπη: w. art. 261(5)

-εύς: acc. plur. -εῖς 46(2)

εὐσεβεῖν: trans. 148(1)

εὐφραίνεσθαι: fut. pass. 79; constr. w. 196

εὐχαριστεῖν: constr. w. 148(2), 187(8), 229(1), 235(2), 312(2), 415

εὐχαριστία: w. dat. 187(8)

εὔχεσθαι: augm. 67(1); constr. w. 180(4), 187(4), 392(1c); εὐξαίμην ἄν, ηὐχόμην 359(2)

εὐώνυμος: ἐξ -ων 141(2); -α 241(6)

ἐφάπαξ: or ἐφ᾽ ἅπαξ 12(3); 203

ἐφικνεῖσθαι: τινός 171(2)

ἐφιορκεῖν: 14

ἐφίστασθαι: constr. w. 202

ἐφορᾶν: constr. w. 392(3)

᾽Εφραίμ: 37

εφφαθα: 40

ἔχειν: 82, 101; 'have as, take to be' (w. double acc., ὡς, εἰς, ὅτι) 157(1, 3, 5), 397(2), 408, 416(3); 'be obliged to' 392(2); 'have to, know' w. inf., rel. and interrog. clause 298(4), 368, 379, 392(2); ἔχειν ἄνεσιν w. dat. 190(3); ἔχειν πρόφασιν 229(1); ἔχων 'with' 419(1); incongruent ἔχων 136(4); intr. (w. adv.) 308, 393(4), 407, 434(1); τὸ νῦν ἔχον 160; ἔχεσθαί τινος 170(3); τῇ ἐχομένῃ (ἡμέρᾳ) 241(2); ἔσχηκα instead of aor. 343(2); ellipsis of 481

ἐχθές: 29(6)

ἐχθρός: 61(2); subst. w. gen. 190(1)

-έως: gen. of adj. in -ύς 46(3)

ἕως, ἡ: not in use 44(1)

ἕως (prep. and conj.): w. gen. 216(3); w. gen. of the inf. 403, 406(3); ἕως οὗ, ὅτου 216(3), 383, 455(3); w. adv. 216(3); conj. 383, 455(3); interchanging w. ὡς 453(4), 455(3); ἕως ἄν (not ἐάν) 107; position 475(1)

ζ: =σδ 39(4); f. σ 10; =Hebr. ז 39(4)

Ζαχαρίας: 55(1a)

ζβ: f. σβ 10

ζβεννύναι: 10

ζευγνύναι: 92

ζευκτηρία: 113(1)

ζῆλος: ὁ and τό 51(2)

ζηλοῦν: constr. w. 163, 392(1a)

ζημιοῦν: pass. w. acc. 159(2)

ζῆν: 77, 88, 101; ἐπί τινι 235(2); ἔζησεν ingressive 331; τὸ ζῆν 398, 400(3)

Ζηνᾶς: 55(1b), 125(1)

ζητεῖν: pres. impera. 337(3); constr. w. 392(1a), 400(5)

ζμ: f. σμ 10

Ζμύρνα: 10

ζυγός: not -όν 49(2)

ζωννύναι: 92, 101

ζῷον: 26

η: η–ι 24, 41(1); η–ει 24; η–α 29(3); η–η 22, 26; η–ει 27

-ή: in compounds denoting action 109(7)

-η or -ῃ: adv. in 26, 103

-ῃ: second sg. mid.-pass. 27; -ῇ and -εῖσαι of vbs. in -εῖν 87

η-: augm. instead of ε- 66(3); augm. η- and ει- (of ε-) 67(3)

ἤ: 446; w. comp. 185(2), 245a(1, 2); w. positive 245(3); πότερον (τί)...ἤ 298(1); in questions (also ἤ μή) 440(1), 446; ἤ...ἤ 446; ἀλλ᾽ ἤ 448(8); in the period 464

ἦ: 440(3); ἦ μήν, s. εἶ μήν

ἡγεῖσθαι: w. double acc. 157(3); w. acc. and inf. 157(3), 397(2); w. ὡς and acc. 157(3), 416(3), 453(4); w. gen. 177; ἡγούμενος substantivized 264(6), 413(1); ἥγημαι pres. 341

ἡγεμών and -μονεύειν: 5(3a); -εύειν constr. w. 177

ἥδιστα: 'very gladly' 60(2), 246

ἡδύοσμον: 120(3)

ἡδύτερος: 61(1)

ἥκειν: inflection 95(1), 101; meaning of the perf. 322

Ἠλίας: 38, 39(3); decl. 55(1a)

ἡλίκος: 64(4), 304

ἥλιος: w. and without art. 253(1)

ἡμεῖς: use of the nom. 277(1, 2); f. ἐγώ 280; position of the possessive ἡμῶν 284(1, 2); ἡμεῖς–ἐκεῖνοι contrasted 291(1)

ἡμέρα: 'day appointed by a court' 5(3); temporal acc. 161(2, 3); ἡμέρας (μέσης) 186(2); (ἐν) (τῇ) ἡμέρᾳ 200, 294(5); ἡμέρᾳ καὶ ἡμέρᾳ 200(1); ἡμέραις temporal dat. 201; διὰ τῆς ἡμέρας 186(2), 223(1); δι᾽ ἡμερῶν τεσσεράκοντα (τεσσ. ἡμ.) 186(2), 223(1); πρὸ ἒξ ἡμερῶν τοῦ πάσχα 213; οὐ μετὰ πολλὰς (ταύτας) ἡμέρας 226, 433(3); (τὸ) καθ᾽ ἡμέραν 160, 266(2); ἐν αὐτῇ τῇ ἡμέρᾳ 288(2); ἐκείνη ἡ ἡμ. 'the last day' 291(1); ἐν ταῖς ἡμ. ἐκείναις (ταύταις) 291(3), 459(3); ἐν ἡμέρᾳ ᾗ 294(5); ἐπ᾽ ἐσχάτου (-ων) τῶν ἡμ. and the like, s. ἔσχατος; ellipsis of 241(2); art. 256, 259(1); ἡμ. ὅταν 382(3); ἡμ. τοῦ w. inf. 400(2); ἡμ. καί 144, 442(4); ἐν ἡμέρᾳ w. gen. absolute 423(5); w. gen. of quality 165; w. rel. clause (attraction) 294(5)

ἡμέτερος: 285(1)

ἡμιθανής: 119(4)

ἥμισυς: decl. 48; ἥμισυ indeclinable 48; ἥμισυ and τὰ ἡμίσεια w. gen. 164(5)

ἡμιώριον: 123(1)

-ην (-ῆν): instead of -η (-ῆ) acc. sg. third decl. 46(1)

ἤνεγκα, ἐνεγκεῖν etc.: 81(2)

ἡνίκα: 105, 455(1)

ἤπερ: 107, 185(3)

Ἡρῴδης: 26; art. w. 260(1)

Ἡρῳδιανοί: 5(2)

-ης: in compounds w. vbs. in -ᾶν, -εῖν 119(2, 3)

-ης, -εντος: in proper nouns = Lat. -ēns, -entis 41(2), 54

-ής, -ές: in compounds 119(4)

-ῆς: personal names in, decl. 55(1d)

Ἠσαΐας, Ἠσ.: 37, 39(1)

-ήσιοι: = Lat. -ē(n)ses 5(2)

ἥσσων, ἥττων, ἐσσοῦσθαι, ἡττᾶσθαι, etc.: 34(1); ἥσσων, ἧσσον meaning 61(1), 244(2)

ἡσυχάζειν: constr. w. 420(2)

ἤτοι: 107, 446

ἡττᾶν, s. ἥσσων; perf. pass. 191(5)

ηυ: 9, f. augmented ευ-, αυ- 67(1)

ἦχος: ὁ and τό 50, 51(2)

θ: doubled 40; θ–δ 33; = Hebr. ת 39(2)

θάλασσα: w. and without art. 253(2)

θάλλειν: 101

θαμβεῖν: and depon. 78; aor. 78

θάμβος: ὁ and τό 51(2)

θάνατος: p. 3 n. 4; without art. 257(1), 258(2); θάνατοι 142

θαρρεῖν: also θάρσος, θάρσει 34(2); intr. 148(2); constr. w. 206(2), 407

θᾶσσον (θᾶττον): 61(1)

θαυμάζειν: and depon. 78, 307; aor. 78, aor. impera. 337(2); constr. w. 148(2), 196, 215(1), 229(2), 235(2), 454(1)

θεά: along w. ἡ θεός 44(2)

θεᾶσθαι: defective 101; w. ὡς 396; w. ptcp. 416(1); ἐθεάθην w. dat. 191(1), 313; constr. w. 396, 416(1); s. also θεωρεῖν

θειότης–θεότης: 30(2)

θέλειν: 66(3), 101; constr. w. 148(2), 338(2), 387(3), 392(1, 1a); θέλεις w. subj. 366(3), 465(2); ἤθελον 'I would like' 359(2); εἰ θέλεις 372(2c); ἐὰν θέλῃς 373(1); θέλεις = εἰ θ. 471(3); θέλω ἤ 245(3), 480(4)

θεμέλιον and -ος: 49(3)

θεμελιότης: 110(1)

-θεν: adv. in 104; always w. ν 20

θεός: voc. ὁ θεός and θεέ 44(2), 147(3), 192; without art. 254(1), 268(2); θεοῦ 163; ἀστεῖος τῷ θεῷ 192; θεῷ as loose dat. of advantage 188(2); ἡ θεός 44(2)

θερίζειν: 74(1)

Θευδᾶς: 125(1, 2)

θεωρεῖν: supplemented by θεᾶσθαι 101; instead of ὁρᾶν 101 s.v. ὁρᾶν; constr. w. 396, 397(1, 6), 416(1)

θιγγάνειν: w. gen. 170(1)

θλῖψις: 13; πᾶσα (ἡ) θ. 275(3)

θνήσκειν (ἀπο-): 26, 27; fut. 77; aor. 81(3); perf. 96, 341; futuristic pres. 323(1)

θραύειν: 70(3)

θρῆσκος: 118(2)

θριαμβεύειν: 5(1); trans. 148(1), 309(1)

θρίαμβος: 5(1)

-θρον: 35(3)

Θυάτιρα: 23; decl. 57

θυγάτηρ: 147(3)

θυμομαχεῖν: 119(1)

θύρα: sg. and plur. 141(4); w. gen. of direction 166; ἐπὶ θύραις, πρὸς τῇ θύρᾳ and the like 235(1), 239(3), 255(2)

θυρουρός, θυρωρός: 119(1)

Θωμᾶς: 53(2d), 125(2)

ι: ι–ει 22f., 38, 42(3), 113(3); ῑ–η 22, 24, 41(1); ι–ε 29(5), 41(1); ι–υ 42(3), 73 (ἐνδιδύσκειν, -δυδισ-); shortened before ξ 13; = Hebr. ʼ 39(1); subscript, adscript (silent) 22, 26

-ί: adv. in 23

-ί: demonstrative (νυνί) 64(2)

-ια-: -ια-/-ιε- 29(2)

-ιᾶ: subst. in 110(2), 111(7), 119(1) (going w. adj. in -ος and vbs. in -εῖν); interchanging w. -ειᾰ and -είᾱ 23

-ιάζειν: vbs. in 108(3)

-ιακός, s. -ικός

Ἰακώβ and Ἰάκωβος: 53(1, 2)

Ἰαμβρῆς: 39(5), 53(1)

Ἰαννῆς: 53(1)

INDEX OF GREEK WORDS AND FORMS

-ιανός: Lat. suffix 5(2)

-ίας, gen. -ίου: personal names in 38, 53(1), 55(1a)

ἰᾶσθαι: pass. 311; aoristic 320

'Ιάσων: 53(2d)

ἴδε: not ἴδέ 13; ἴδε and εἰ δέ confused 467; s. also ἰδού

ἰδέα (not εἰδέα): 23

ἰδεῖν: ἰδεῖν 14; s. also εἶδον, ἴδε, ἰδού, ὁρᾶν

-ίδιον: diminutives in 111(3)

ἴδιος: ἴδιος 14; syntax 286; κατ' ἰδίαν, ἰδίᾳ 12, 241(6), 286(1)

ἰδού: 101 s.v. ὁρᾶν; ἰδού 14; without finite vb. 128(7); ἰδού, ἴδε w. nom. 144; ἴδε w. plur. 144; ἰδού ἐγώ ἀποστέλλω (οἶδα) 277(2); καὶ ἰδού 4(2), 127(7), 442(7)

-ιε-: -ιε-/-ια- 29(2)

-ιει-: contracted to -ει- 31(2), 94(2)

ἱέναι: remnants 99(1); syntax 99(1), 323(4)

ἱέναι: only in composition 94(2), 95(1), 97(3); ἀν-, ἀφ-έθην 67(2); s. also ἀφιέναι, συνιέναι, ἀνιέναι

'Ιεράπολις: dat. 'Ιερᾷ πόλει 115(2)

'Ιεριχώ: 38, 39(1)

ἱεροπρεπής: 119(4)

'Ιεροσόλυμα, 'Ιερουσαλήμ: 38, 56(1); breathing 39(1); both as fem. 56(4); nearly always without art. 261(3), 275(2)

ἱερουργεῖν: 31(1), 124; trans. 148(1)

ἱερωσύνη (ἱερεωσύνη): 31(2)

'Ιεσσαί: 37

-ίζειν: vbs. in 108(3); fut. 74(1)

'Ιησοῦς: 53(1, 2b); decl. 55(1f); w. and without art. 260(1), 288

ἱκανός: constr. 187(8), 379, 393(4), 405(2); ἱκανόν satis 5(3b) (τὸ ἱκ. ποιῆσαι, λαμβάνειν), 131

ἱκετηρία: 241(6)

'Ικόνιον, Εἰκόνιον: 42(3)

-ικός (-ιακός): adj. in 113(2); -τικός w. gen. barely represented 182(5)

ἱλάσκεσθαι: 101, 314; constr. w. 148(2)

ἵλεώς (σοι): p. 3 n. 2, 44(1), 128(5)

ἱμάς, -άντος: accent 13

ἱματίζειν: 108(3)

ἱμάτιον: plur. 141(8); ellipsis of 241(7)

-ίν, -ῖνος: instead of -ίς, -ῖνος 46(4)

ἵνα: 369, 379, 382(1), 386(3), 387(3), 388–94, 408; causal 369(2); ἀλλ' ἵνα 448(7), 480(5); ἵνα δέ w. ellipsis 470(3), 483; position 475(1); w. prolepsis 476(1)

ἱνατί or ἵνα τί: 12(3), 299(4)

-ῖνος: adj. in 113(3); proper names in -ῖνος 5(2)

-ιον: subst. in 111(3, 4)

'Ιόππη: 40, art. 261(1)

'Ιορδάνης: 56(1); ὁ 261(8)

-ιος: adj. in 113(1); compounds (hypostasis) in -ιος 123(1)

'Ιουδαία: ἡ 'Ι. (γῆ), γῆ 'Ιούδα 261(4)

'Ιουδαῖοι: w. and without art. 262(1, 3); 'Ι. (τε) καὶ Ἕλληνες 444(2)

'Ιούδας: 53(1, 2b), 55(1a)

'Ιούλιος: 41(1)

'Ιουνιᾶς or -νία: 125(2)

-ις: diminutives in 111(3); fem. w. masc. compounds in -ης 119(2)

ἴσα: adv. w. εἶναι 434(1), 453(4)

'Ισ(α)άκ: 39(3)

ἰσάγγελος: 118(1)

ἴσασιν, s. εἰδέναι

-ισκο-: diminutives in 111(3)

ἰσο- in compounds 118(1)

ἴσος: constr. 194(1), 453(4); s. also ἴσα

ἰσότιμος: 118(1)

ἰσόψυχος: 118(1)

'Ισραήλ: 'Ισδρ- and 'Ιστρ- 39(5); (ὁ) 262(3); πᾶς 'Ι., πᾶς οἶκος 'Ι. 275(4)

-ισσα: subst. in 111(1); cf. 34(1)

ἱστάναι: ἱστάνειν, ἱστᾶν, στάνειν 93; ἔστην 95(1); ἔστην and ἐστάθην 97(1), 313; ἡνέστη 69(2); second aor.-impf. 95(3); ἕστηκα 96, 97(1); other tenses 97(1); s. also ἑστακέναι and στήκειν

-ιστος: superl. in 60(2)

ἰσχύειν: constr. w. 392(2)

'Ιταλία: w. art. 261(6)

-ίτης, -ῖτις: 111(2)

ἰχθύδιον: 111(3)

ἰχθύς: accent 13; acc. plur. -ύας 46(2); 111(3)

'Ιωάν(ν)α: 40, 53(3)

'Ιωάν(ν)ης: 40, 53(2c), 55(1c); also 'Ιωανάν (-άμ), 'Ιωνᾶ 53(2)

-(ι)ων: comp. in 61(1)

'Ιωνάθας (-ης): 53(2)

'Ιωσήφ, -ῆ(ς): 53(2); gen. -ῆτος 55(2)

'Ιωσίας: 38

κ: κ–χ 33; = Hebr. ק, כ 39(2); κο-, κουα-= Lat. qua- 41(2); κυ= Lat. qui 41(2)

καθά: 453, 456(4)

καθαίρειν: 101; constr. w. 180(1)

καθάπερ: 107, 453

καθάπτειν: w. gen. 170(1); instead of mid. 310(1)

καθαρίζειν: also -ερ- 29(1); fut. 74(1); f. καθαίρειν 101; ἀπό 180

καθαρός: always -αρ- 29(1); w. ἀπό 182(3)

καθέζεσθαι: 101

καθ' εἷς: 305; τὸ καθ' εἷς 160; also s. εἷς

καθεύδειν: augm. 69(1)

καθῆκεν (-ον, -οντα): 358(2), 430(3)

καθημερινός: 113(3)

καθῆσθαι: 100, 101; constr. w. 205, 233(1), 238

καθιέναι: 94(2)

καθίζειν: 101; augm. 69(1); fut. 74(1); εἰς 205; aor. and perf. 342(1), 343(1)

καθιστάναι: constr. w. 157(1), 234(5)

καθό: 453, 456(4)

καθ' ὅλης: 225

καθόλου: 12(3), 225; τὸ κ. 399(3)

καθότι: 456(4); κ. ἄν 367

καθώς, καθώσπερ: 453

287

INDEX OF GREEK WORDS AND FORMS

καί: 107, 442, 458, 460, 462(1), (419(5), 420, 471); crasis 18; art. w. subst. connected by καί 276; used to introduce an apodosis 442(7); in comp. clauses 453(1); καὶ...καί, τε (...) καί etc. 444, 445(2); καὶ...δέ, δὲ καί 447(9); ἀλλὰ (ἀλλά γε) καί 448(6); διὸ καί and the like 442(12); καὶ γάρ 452(3); ἢ καί 446; καὶ οὐ, καὶ μή 426, 430(3), 445, 460(1); ὁ καί 268(1); καὶ οὗτος 290(1); καὶ τοῦτο 290(5), 442(9); καὶ ταῦτα w. ptcp. 290(5), 425(1), 442(9); epexegetical καί 442(9), 471(3); καὶ τίς 'who then...' 442(8); τί καί 442(14); καὶ νῦν 442(15); καὶ... αὐτοῦ following a rel. clause 297; καὶ εἰ 457; καί in the period 464; εἰ καί, s. εἰ; ἐὰν καί, s. ἐάν; καὶ ἄν, καὶ ἐάν, s. κἄν; also s. καίγε, καίπερ, καίτοι(γε)

Και(α)φας: 37, 55(1a)

καίγε: 425(1), 439(2)

καίειν: never κάειν 30(1); aor. and fut. 76(1), 28

Καϊν: 37

Καιναν: 37, 53(2)

καινότερος: f. positive 244(2)

καίπερ: 107; w. ptcp. 425(1)

καιρός: without art. 255(3); κ. (ἐστιν) constr. 393(3), 400(1); ἐν ἐκείνῳ τῷ καιρῷ 459(3); ὁ κ. οὗτος, ὁ νῦν καιρός 292

Καῖσαρ: 5(1b, 3a), 41(1); w. and without art. 254(1)

καίτοι(γε): 107, 425(1), 450(3), 457

κακολογεῖν: τινά 151(1)

κακοπαθία (-εια): 23

κακοποιός: 119(1)

κακός: comp. 61(1); κακοὺς κακῶς 488(1a)

κακοῦργος: 31(1), 119(1), 124

καλεῖν: fut. καλέσω 74(1), fut. perf. 65(1b); w. double acc. 157(2); w. ἐπί τινι 235(2); ὁ καλούμενος 268(1), 412(2)

καλλιέλαιος, ἡ: 120(3), 241(6)

καλοδιδάσκαλος: 115(2)

καλόν (ἐστιν): 358(1), 360(1); substantivized without art. 264(2); constr. 190(2), 393(2), 409(3)

καλῶς: instead of εὖ 102(3), 126(1a α); κάλλιον 61(1), 244(2); καλῶς (εὖ) ποιεῖν (λέγειν) constr. 151(1), 414(5); ironic 495(2)

κάμηλος and κάμιλος: 24

κάμινος: 49(1)

καμμύειν: 69(1)

κάμπτειν: intr. 308

κἄν: 18, 371, 374, 457

Καπερναούμ: 39(2)

καραδοκεῖν: 119(1)

καρδιογνώστης: 119(2)

καρτερεῖν: trans. 148(1)

κατά: elision 17; w. acc.: 224, circumlocution f. the possessive or subjective gen. 224(1), distributive, frozen as an adv. 224(3), 248(1), 305; κ. μόνας 241(6), κ. ἰδίαν 241(6), 286(1), κ. πρόσωπον 140, 217(1), τὸ (τὰ) κ. 266(2); w. gen.: 225, w. ἐγκαλεῖν 187(5); compounds w. κατά: constr. w. 150, 177, 181, perfectivizing 318(5)

καταβαίνω: κατάβα Atticism 2; 73

καταγινώσκεσθαι: pass. 312(1)

καταγνύναι: augm. 66(2), 101 s.v. ἀγνύναι

καταδικάζειν: constr. w. 181

καταδίκη: Dor. 2

καταδουλοῦν: act. 310(1)

καταδυναστεύειν: constr. w. 177

καταισχύνειν: 72

κατακληρονομεῖν: trans. and intr. 309(1)

κατακλίνειν: w. double acc. 158

κατακρίνειν: constr. w. 181, 397(3); θανάτῳ 195(2)

κατακυριεύειν: τινός 177

καταλαμβάνεσθαι: mid. 316(1); constr. w. 397(1)

καταλείπειν: constr. w. 392(1f.)

καταλλάσσειν and depon.: w. dat. 193(4)

κατάλυμα: 109(2)

καταναρκᾶν: τινός 181

κατανεύειν: constr. w. 400(7); s. also νεύειν

κατανύσσειν: aor. pass. 76(1)

καταξιοῦν: constr. w. 179(2), 392(1c, 2)

καταπαύειν: intr. 309(2); constr. w. 180(6), 400(4)

καταρᾶσθαι: τινά 152(1)

καταρτίζειν: 74(1); f. ἀνύειν 126(1a β)

κατατρώγειν: 101 s.v. ἐσθίειν

καταχεῖν: constr. w. 181

καταχθόνιος: 123(1)

κατείδωλος: 120(2)

κατέναντι: τινός 214(4)

κατενώπιον: w. gen. 214(5); as circumlocution f. dat. 192

κατεξουσιάζειν: constr. w. 177

κατεσθίειν and καταφαγεῖν: 318(5)

κατέχειν: constr. w. 400(4)

κατηγορεῖν: augm. 69(4); pass. 312(1)

κατήγωρ: f. -ορος 52

κατηχεῖσθαι: pass. w. acc. 159(1)

κατισχύειν: constr. w. 177, 392(2)

κατοικεῖν: augm. 67(1)

κατοπτρίζεσθαι: 30(3)

κάτοπτρον: 30(3)

κάτω: 103, 104(2), 215(2); τά 266(1)

κάτωθεν: does not appear 104(2)

κατώτερος, -έρω: 62; τὰ -ερα τῆς γῆς 167

καυ(σ)τηριάζειν: 70(3)

καυχᾶσθαι: intr. and trans. 148(2); constr. w. 187(4), 196, 231(1)

Καφαρναούμ: 39(2), 56(3)

Κεδρών: 56(3); ὁ 261(8)

κείρεσθαι: 'have one's hair cut' 317

κειρία or κηρία: 24

κεῖσθαι: 100; f. which τεθεῖσθαι 97(2); ἦν κείμενος 352

κεκραγέναι, s. κράζειν

κεκτῆσθαι: does not appear 341

κελεύειν: constr. w. 187(5), 338(2), 392(1d, 4), 408, 420(2); w. acc. and pass. inf. 5(3b), 392(4); impf. and aor. 328

κέλευσμα: 70(3)

λαμβάνειν (cont.)
  5(3b); λ. πρόσωπον p. 3 n. 5; λ. πληγὰς ὑπό τινος
  232(2); λαμβάνεσθαι constr. w. 170(2)
λανθάνειν: constr. w. 149, 414(3), 435
λᾱξευτός: 2
λαός: 44(1); w. constructio ad sensum 134(1); ὁ λαὸς
  Ἰσραήλ 262(3); ὁ λαός μου voc. 147(3)
λάρυ(γ)ξ: 46(4)
λᾱτομεῖν: 2
λατρεύειν: w. dat. 187(2)
λέγειν: 'to collect' 101
λέγειν (s. also ἐρρέθην): impf. 82; perf. 83(1); supplemented by εἶπον 101; λέγει etc. without subj.
  130(3); ἐροῦσιν impersonal third plur. 130(2);
  λέγει ἐν in quotation formulae 219(1); w. personal
  acc. 151(1); καλῶς, κακῶς λέγειν 151(1); w. double
  acc. 157(2); πρός 180(4); w. ἵνα and acc. w. inf.
  392(1d, 4); w. ὅτι and (acc. w.) inf. 397(3), 405(1,
  2), 406(1), 409(2); w. εἰ 440(3); τάδε λέγει 289;
  λέγει historical pres. 321; ἔλεγεν and εἶπεν 329;
  εἴρηκα aoristic 343(1); λέγων, λέγοντες 136(4),
  397(3), 420; σὺ λέγεις (εἶπας) 277(1), 441(3); ὁ
  λεγόμενος 412(2); λέγω ὑμῖν, κατὰ ἄνθρωπον λέγω
  and the like as parenthetical 465(2); asyndetic
  λέγω w. finite vb. 461(2); asyndetic λέγει 462(1);
  ellipsis of λέγω, λέγει 480(5)
λεγεών, λεγιών: 5(1a), 41(1), 138(3)
λείπειν: pres. also -λιμπάνειν 101; aor. 75; λείπει τινί
  189(3); πολλά, μικρὸν λείπει 393(4); λείπεσθαί
  τινος 180(4)
λειτουργός, -ία etc.: 27
λέντιον: linteum 5(1d), 41(1)
λεπτόν: 5(1)
Λευ(ε)ί(ς): 38, 39(1), 53(1, 2b); decl. 55(1e)
λευκαίνειν: aor. -ᾱνα 72
Λεωνίδας: 55(1a)
ληνός: ἡ (ὁ) 49(1)
λῃστής: 27
λίαν: usually in post-position 474(2)
λιβερτῖνος: 5(1b)
Λιβύη: w. art. 261(5)
λίθος: ὁ (not ἡ) 49(1)
λιμός: ὁ and ἡ 2, 49(1); λιμός and λοιμός combined
  488(2)
λινοῦς: 45
λιποτακτεῖν: 118(2)
λίτρα: 5(1c)
λογεία: 23
λογίζεσθαι: w. double acc. 145(2), 157(3); τινὰ ὡς
  and acc. 157(3), 416(3); w. (acc. w.) inf., ὅτι
  392(1a), 397(2), 406(1, 2); pass. 311, w. εἰς 145(2),
  w. τινί 145(2), w. μετά 227(1), w. ὡς and nom.
  157(5), 453(4)
λόγος: constr. 163; διὰ λόγου 223(3); ὅτι 397(3)
λοιδορεῖν: τινά 152(1); constr. w. 420(2)
λοιπός: ellipsis of 306(5), 480(1); art. repeated after
  λ. 269(6); (τὸ) λοιπόν 160, 451(6); τοῦ λοιποῦ 160,
  186(2)

λούειν: perf. pass. 70(3); pass. w. acc. 159(3);
  constr. w. 180
Λουκᾶς, Λούκιος: 41(1), 125(2), 268(1)
Λύδδα: 56(2); Λύνδα 39(7)
λύειν: instead of mid. 310(1); constr. w. 180
λυμαίνεσθαι (τινά): 152(1), 311(1)
λυπεῖσθαι: constr. w. 196, 235(2)
Λυσίας: 55(1a)
λυσιτελεῖν: constr. w. 151(1), 245(3), 393(1)
Λύστρα: decl. 57
λυτροῦν: constr. w. 180
Λωθ, Λωτ: 39(2)

μ: μ–ν 19
-μα: subst. in 109(2); w. short stem vowel 109(3);
  in affected word play 488(3)
μαζός, s. μαστός
μαθητεύειν: intr. and trans. 148(3), 309(1); pass.
  constr. 191(4)
Μαθθαῖος, Μαθθίας etc.: 40
μακαρίζειν: fut. 74(1)
μακάριος: without vb. 127(4)
μάκελλον: 5(1)
μακράν: 34(2); 161(1); w. gen. and ἀπό 184; f. πόρρω
  34(2)
μακρόθεν: ἀπὸ μ. 104(2, 3); f. πόρρω 34(2)
μακροθυμεῖν: constr. w. 196
μᾶλλον: μ., μάλιστα 60(3), 244(2); μάλα does not
  appear 102(3); ellipsis of 245(3), 480(4); pleonastic 246; expressing exclusion 245a(1)
μαμ(μ)ωνᾶς: 40
Μανασσῆς: 53(1), 55(1d)
μανθάνειν: constr. w. 210(3), 220(2), 392(2), 397(1),
  405(1), 416(2)
μάννα: 38, 58
μαραίνειν: 72
Μάρθα, -ας: 53(3), 55(1a)
Μαριάμ and -ία: 53(3); -ῐ- 38; art. 260(1)
Μᾶρκος: 41(3)
μαρτυρεῖν: constr. w. 188(1), 397(3); w. λέγων and
  the like 420(2); -ρῶ as parenthetical 465(2);
  -εῖσθαι pass. 312(1), 405(1)
μαρτυρία: ὅτι 397(3)
μάρτυς: w. ὡς 396; w. ὅτι 397(3)
μᾱρυκᾶσθαι: 2, 29(3)
Μαρώνεια, Μαρωνίτης: 38
μαστός, μασθός, μαζός: 34(5)
μάταιος: two and three endings 59(2)
μάτην: εἰς μ. 207(3)
μάχαιρα: decl. 43(1); ἐν μ. 195(1a)
μάχεσθαι: constr. w. 193(4)
μέγας: μέγιστος 60(2); μείζων 61(1), decl. 47(2);
  μειζότερος 61(2)
μεγιστᾶνες: 2
μεθιστάναι: constr. w. 180(1)
μεθοδεία: 23
μεθύσκεσθαι: οἴνῳ 195(2)
μεῖγμα or μίγμα: 13

INDEX OF GREEK WORDS AND FORMS

Ναθαναήλ: 39(3), 53(2)

ναί: 432(1), 441(1, 2); ναὶ ναί 432(1); ναί, λέγω ὑμῖν 432(1), 441(1); τὸ ναί 266(1)

Ναιμάν, Νεεμάν etc.: 37; Ναιμᾶς 53(2)

Ναΐν: 37

ναός: 44(1)

ναῦς: literary f. πλοῖον 47(4)

Νεάπολις: Νέαν πόλιν 115(2)

νεκροί: without art. 254(2)

νεομηνία, νουμηνία: 31(1)

νέος: comp. 244(2)

ν(ε)οσσός, ν(ε)οσσία etc.: 31(3)

νεύειν: w. inf. 392(1d); also s. κατα-, ἐκνεύειν

νεωκόρος: 44(1)

-νη, s. -να

νή: 107, 149

νήθειν: 101

νῆστις: plur. νήστεις 47(3)

νηφαλ-: 35(3), 59(2)

νικᾶν: ὁ νικῶν perfective 322

Νικάνωρ: 29(3)

νῖκος: τό f. ἡ νίκη 51(1)

Νινευή, -ῖται: 39(1)

νίπτειν: f. νίζειν 73

νοεῖν: constr. w. 397(2)

νομίζειν: not w. double acc. 157(3); w. inf. or ὅτι 349(2), 397(2)

νόμος: without art. 258(2)

νοσσ-, s. νεοσσ-

νότος: without art. 253(5)

νουμηνία, νεομηνία: 31(1)

νουνεχῶς: 52, 119(4)

νοῦς: gen. νοός 52

Νυμφᾶς or Νύμφα: 125(1)

νῦν: τὸ νῦν (ἔχον) 160, 266(1); position 474(3); καὶ νῦν 442(15)

-νύναι: vbs. in 92

νυνί: 64(2)

νύξ: νύκτα καὶ ἡμέραν 161(2); (διὰ) (τῆς) νυκτός, μέσης ν. 186(2), 223(1), 255(3); ἐν (τῇ) νυκτί 200; κατὰ μέσον τῆς νυκτός 270(2)

νύσσειν, s. κατανύσσειν

νυστάζειν: ἐνύσταξα 71

νυχθήμερος: 121

νῶτος: f. νῶτον 49(2)

ξενίζειν: 126(2); constr. w. 196

ξένος: w. gen. 182(3)

ξέστης: *sextarius* 5(1c)

ξηρά: ἡ 241(1)

ξηραίνειν: ἐξήρανα, ἐξηραμμένος 72; aor. and perf. 342(1)

ξυρεῖν (-ᾶν?): 101; ξύρασθαι 317

ο: ο–ε 29(4); ο–ου 30(3); ο–ω 28, 35(1, 2); ο–α 35(2), 42(3); κο-=Lat. *qua-* 41(2)

ὁ ἡ τό: as pron. 249–51; ὁ μὲν...ὁ δέ (ἄλλος δέ, ἕτερος δέ) 250, 306(2, 3); as art. 252–76; ὁ καί

268(1); τό (τά) as adv. acc. 160, 266(2); ὁ, οἱ, τό, τά w. gen. 266(3); οἱ ἐκ 209(2); τό, τοῦ, τῷ w. inf. 388, 398–404, 408

ὀδαγός, ὀδαγεῖν: =ὀδηγ- 29(3)

ὅδε: 64(2), 289

ὁδός: fem. 49(1); ellipsis of 186(1), 241(4); ὁδός w. gen. of direction (ὁδόν w. gen.=*versus*) 161(1), 166; ὁδῷ w. πορεύεσθαι etc. 198(5)

ὄζειν: constr. w. 174

’Οζίας: 38

ὅθεν: 104(1); w. attraction 437; as conj. 451(6)

οι: >ο 30(2); >υ 22

οἰ-: often unaugmented 67(1)

Οἰδίπους: 55(1a)

οἴεσθαι: 101; pres. impera. 336(3); constr. w. 397(2)

οἰκία: w. *constructio ad sensum* 134(1)

οἰκοδεσπότης: 115(1); οἰκ. τῆς οἰκίας 484

οἰκοδομεῖν: augm. 67(1)

οἰκοδομή: 109(7)

οἶκος: art. 259(1, 2, 3), 275(4); ὁ οἶκος voc. 147(3)

οἰκουμένη: ἡ (scil. γῆ) 241(1)

οἰκτίρειν: 23, 101; trans. 148(2)

οἰκτιρμός (-μων): 23; -μοί 142

-οῖν: instead of -οῦν inf. 91

οἷος: 64(4), 300(1), 304; οἷος δηποτοῦν 303; οὐχ οἷον ὅτι 304, 480(5)

οἷς: replaced by πρόβατον 126(1a α)

οἴχεσθαι: 101; not w. ptcp. 414(5)

ὀκνεῖν: constr. w. 392(1b)

ὀλίγος: οὐχ ὀλ. 14; ὀλίγως 102(6); ὀλίγας δέρεσθαι 154, 241(6); μετ’ ὀλίγον w. gen. 164(4); ἐν ὀλίγῳ 195; τὸ ὀλίγον 263(1); ὀλίγου w. aor. indic. lacking 358(2); also s. ἐλάσσων and ἐλάχιστος

ὀλιγωρεῖν: constr. w. 176(2)

ὀλλύναι: 92

ὀλοθρεύειν etc.: f. ὀλεθρ- 32(1)

ὅλος: art. 270(2), 275(2, 4); καθ’ ὅλης τῆς ’Ιουδαίας and the like 225; w. Αἴγυπτος 261(7)

’Ολυμπᾶς: 125(1)

ὁμείρεσθαι: f. ἱμ- 101; w. gen. 171(1)

ὁμιλεῖν: constr. w. 193(4)

ὀμνύναι: 92, 101; constr. w. 149, 198(6), 206(2), 350, 397(3)

ὁμοθυμαδόν: 122

ὁμοιάζειν: constr. w. 193(6)

ὅμοιος: accent 13; two endings? 59(2); w. gen. or dat. 5(3b), 182(4), 194(1)

ὁμοιοῦν: constr. w. 193(6)

ὁμολογεῖν: constr. w. 157(2), 187(4), 220(2), 350, 405(1), 416(3)

ὁμόσε: =ὁμοῦ 103

ὅμως: 450(1, 2)

ὄναρ: only κατ’ ὄναρ 47(4)

ὀνάριον: 111(3)

ὀνειδίζειν: τινά 152(1)

ὀνίνασθαι: 384, 488(1b); w. gen. 169(3)

ὄνομα: ᾧ ὄν., οὗ τὸ ὄν., καὶ τὸ ὄν. αὐτοῦ (-τῆς), ὄν. αὐτῷ ὀνόματι 128(3), 144, 197; τοὔνομα 18, 160; καλεῖν

INDEX OF GREEK WORDS AND FORMS

ὄνομα (*cont.*)

τὸ ὄνομά τινος w. acc. 143, 157(2); πιστεύειν εἰς τὸ ὄνομά τινος 187(6); ἐπιτιθέναι, ἐπικαλεῖν τινι ὄν. 202; ἐπὶ (ἐν) τῷ ὀνόματι (εἰς τὸ ὄνομά) τινος 206(2); ἐν ὀνόματι ὅτι 397(3)

ὄντως: 102(6)

-οος: contracted forms (second decl.) 45

ὄπισθεν: 104(2); w. gen. 215(1)

ὀπίσω: w. gen. 193(1), 215(1)

ὁποῖος: 64(4), 300(1), 304; ὁποῖός ποτε 303

ὁπόταν: 381

ὁπότε: 105–7, 381, 455(1)

ὅπου: 106, 293, 298(2); 'where' and 'whither' 103; ὅπου ἄν w. indic. 367, 380(3); causal 'insofar as, since' 456(3)

ὀπτάνεσθαι: 101 s.v. ὁρᾶν; w. dat. 191(1), 313

ὅπως: 106, 300(1), 369, 388, 392(1), 436; ὅπως ἄν 369(5)

ὁρᾶν: 101; impf. 66(2); ἑώρακα (ἑόρ-) 68, 83(1); fut. ὄψομαι 77; pass. ὀπτάνεσθαι, ὤφθην 101, 313; use of the perf. 342(2), plupf. 347(3); constr. 149, 191(1), 397(1), 416(1); ὅρα, ὁρᾶτε μή 364(3), 370(4), 461(1); elliptical ὅρα μή 480(5); σὺ ὄψῃ 362; also s. εἶδον, ἴδε, ἰδού, ἰδεῖν

ὀργίζεσθαι: augm. 67(2); constr. w. 196, 415

ὀρέγεσθαι: w. gen. 171(1)

ὀρεινή: ἡ 241(1)

ὀρθοποδεῖν: 120(4)

ὀρθός: adverbial 243

ὀρθοτομεῖν: 119(1)

ὀρθρινός: 113(3)

ὁρίζειν: constr. w. 392(1a)

ὁρκίζειν: 2; constr. w. 149, 155(7), 392(1d, 4), 409(5)

ὅρκος: plur. 142

ὁρκωμοσία: 2, 119(3)

ὄρνις, ὄρνεον: 45, ὄρνις and ὄρνιξ 47(4)

ὁροθεσία: ἡ or τὰ -έσια 119(3)

ὄρος: gen. ὀρέων 48; 126(1b α)

ὀρύσσειν: ὠρύγην 76(1)

-ος: neuters in: gen. plur. 48; metaplasm 51

ὅς ἥ ὅ: 64(3); syntax 293–7, 377–80; confused w. ὅστις 293; f. τίς 368; ὅτι introducing direct question 300(2); position 475(1); ὅ εἰμι 131; ὅ ἐστιν 132(2), 353(4); ὅς μὲν...ὅς δέ 249f.; ὅς δέ 251; ὅς δήποτε 303; ὅς γε 439(3); ἀνθ' ὧν s. ἀντί; ἀφ' ἧς 241(2); ἐν ᾧ 219(2), 383(1), 455(3); ἐφ' ᾧ s. ἐπί

ὅσιος: ὁ, ἡ 59(2)

ὁσίως: γίνεσθαι ὁσίως w. dat. 190(2)

ὀσμή: 34(5)

ὅσος: 64(4), 293, 304; ὅσον ὅσον, τοσούτῳ...ὅσῳ 304

ὅσπερ: 64(3), 107, 293(4)

ὀστέον, ὀστοῦν: 45

ὅστις: virtually limited to nom. 64(3); syntax 293, 300; only ὅ τι to introduce an indirect question 300(1); ὅ τι introducing direct questions 300(2); ὅ τι = δι' ὅ τι 299(4), 300(2); ὅστις ἄν ᾖ 303; w. subj. without ἄν? 380(4)

ὀσφῦς: accent 13

ὅταν: ὅταν δέ 12(1); 367, 382, 394, 455(1); position 475(1)

ὅτε: 105, 382, 393(3), 455(1); μέχρι ὅτε 455(3)

ὁτὲ μέν...ὁτὲ δέ: 436

-ότερος: new comp. in 61(2)

-ότης: subst. in 110(1)

ὅτι (s. also ὅστις): 386(1), 388, 394, 396f., 408, 416, 470(1); introducing direct discourse 397(5), 470(1); w. acc. and inf. p. 1 n. 2, 397(6); w. prolepsis 476(1); causal 208(1), 456(1, 2), 480(6); τί (γέγονεν) ὅτι 299(4); οὐχ (οἷον) ὅτι 304, 480(5); πλὴν ὅτι 449(1, 2); ὡς ὅτι s. ὡς; negation 428(5)

ὅτου: in ἕως ὅτου, ἀφ' ὅτου 64(3); also s. ἕως

ου: ου–ο 30(3); ου–υ 42(4); = Lat. u 41(1); κου–= Lat. qu- 41(2)

-οῦ: adv. in 103

οὐ: 371, 377, 426–33; τὸ οὔ 266(1); οὐ...πᾶς (πᾶς...οὐ) 302(1); εἷς...οὐ 302(2); οὐχ (οἷον) ὅτι 304, 480(5); οὐ μή w. subj. (fut.) 365; οὐκ...εἰ μή 376; οὐχ ὡς 425(3); οὐχ ὅτι 480(5); in questions 387(3), 427(2), 440; οὐ οὔ 432(1); οὐ πάντως and the like 433(2); οὐ..., οὔτε...οὔτε 445(1), οὐ...οὐ 445(1); οὐ (μή) w. οὐδέ (μηδέ) 445(2); καὶ οὐ after neg. clauses 445(4); οὐ...ἀλλά (δέ) 447(1), 448(1); οὐ μόνον...ἀλλά (καί) 448(1); ἀλλ' οὐ 448(2, 3); οὐ μόνον δὲ ἀλλὰ καί 479(1); οὐ γάρ 452(2)

οὗ: 'where' and 'whither' 103, 293

οὐαί: 4(2a), 136(5); ἡ 58; constr. 190(2), 412(5)

οὐδαμῶς: 33

οὐδέ: 445; elision 17; οὐδὲ εἷς 302(2); οὐδὲ μή 431(3); ἀλλ' οὐδέ 448(6); οὐδὲ γάρ 452(3)

οὐδείς: also οὐθείς 3, 33; 12(2); οὐδέν ('good for nothing') 131; οὐδεὶς ὅς οὐ 293(4), 431(1); οὐδείς and οὐδὲ εἷς 302(2); οὐδείς (ἐστιν) ὅστις (ὅς) 379

οὐθέτερος: 33

οὐκοῦν: 107, 451(1)

οὐμενοῦν: 450(4)

-οῦν: vbs. in, conjugation 91; impf. third plur. 84(3); second sg. mid.-pass. 87; formation 108(1)

οὖν: 442, 451(1), 462(1); εἰ οὖν 372(1a); ἄρα οὖν 451(2b); μὲν οὖν s. μέν; τότε οὖν 459(2); position 475(2)

οὐράνιος: ὁ, ἡ 59(2)

οὐρανόθεν: 104(1, 3)

οὐρανός: sg. and plur. 4(2), 141(1); without art. 253(3)

Οὐρίας: 38, 55(1a)

οὖς: 111(3); ὦτα (τοῦ) ἀκούειν 393(6), 400(2)

-οῦσαι: second sg. mid.-pass. w. vbs. in -οῦν 87

οὔτε...οὔτε (οὔτε...καί): 445

οὗτος: 64(2); αὕτη = τοῦτο 138(2); interchange of αὐτή and αὕτη 277(3); syntax 290, 291(2, 3); τούτου possessive 284(2, 3); αὐτός f. αὐτὸς οὗτος 288(2); αὐτὸ τοῦτο s. αὐτός; pointing to a following clause w. ὅτι, ἵνα or inf. 290(3), 394, 399(1); τοῦτο μέν...τ. δέ 290(5); καὶ οὗτος, καὶ τοῦτο *idque* 290(5), 442(9); καὶ ταῦτα (τοῦτο) w.

οὗτος (*cont.*)
 ptcp. 290(5), 425(1), 442(9); w. and without art.
 292; as connective (asyndetic) 459(1, 3); w.
 anaphora 491; ἐν τούτῳ 219(2); ἐπὶ τούτῳ 235(5);
 predicative 226; μετὰ τοῦτο (ταῦτα) (asyndetic)
 459(3); παρὰ τοῦτο 236(5); πρὸς τούτοις 240(2);
 τρίτον τοῦτο 248(4); elliptical τοῦτο δέ 481
οὕτω(ς): 21; following ptcp. 425(6); as pred. 434;
 ὡς...οὕτως (καί) 453(1)
οὐχί: 427(2), 432; οὐχί, λέγω ὑμῖν 432(1)
ὀφείλειν: ὤφειλον 358(1); constr. w. 392(2); ὄφελον
 particle introducing wishes 67(2), 359(1), 384
ὀφειλέτης (εἰμί): constr. 190(1), 393(6), 400(2)
ὄφελον, s. ὀφείλειν
ὀφθαλμοδουλία (-εία): 115(1)
ὀφθαλμός: without art. 259(1, 3); τοῦ μὴ βλέπειν
 400(2)
ὄχλος w. *constructio ad sensum* 134(1)
ὀχυρός, ὀχύρωμα: 32(1)
ὀψάριον: 111(3)
ὀψέ: ἐγένετο 129, 434(1); ὀψὲ σαββάτων 164(4)
ὀψία: ἡ 241(3)
ὄψιμον: scil. ὑετός 241(5)
ὀψώνιον: 111(4), 126(2); plur. 141(8)

π: = Hebr. פ 39(2)
παθητός: 65(3)
παιδεύεσθαι: 5(1*b*); constr. w. 392(2)
παιδιόθεν: ἐκ π. 104(2, 3)
παίειν: 71, 101 s.v. τύπτειν
παίζειν: 71, 77, 101
παῖς: ἡ 111(3), 126(3); as voc. 147(3)
παλαιός: 61(2)
πάλιν: not πάλι 20; asyndetic connective 459(4);
 pleonastic 484
παλιγγενεσία: 19
παμπληθεί: 23, 122
Παμφυλία: w. and without art. 261(6)
πανδοκεῖον, -χεῖον: 33
πανοικεί: 23, 122
πανταχῇ, πάντη: 26, 103
πανταχοῦ: 103
πάντοθεν, πανταχόθεν: 104(1)
πάντοτε: instead of ἀεί 105
πάντως οὐ, οὐ π.: 433(2)
πάνυ: does not appear 102(3)
παρά: elision 17; w. acc. 236, w. comp. 185(3),
 236(3), 245a(2), w. inf. 402(4), w. positive 245(3);
 w. gen. 237, w. gen. and vbs. of perception 173(1),
 f. which ἀπό 173(1), 210(3), 217(1); w. dat. 238;
 compounds w. παρά: trans. 150, w. dat. etc. 202;
 adverbial use 203
πάρα: = πάρεστιν 98
παραβολεύεσθαι: 108(5)
παραγγέλλειν: aoristic pres. 320; impf. and aor. 328;
 constr. w. 198(6), 392(1*d*), 397(3), 409(1)
παράγειν: intr. 308
παράδεισος: 6

παραδίδοσθαι: futuristic pres. 323(1); constr. w.
 187(1), 390(3), 402(2)
παραθαλάσσιος: 123(1); -ία 59(1)
παραινεῖν: παρήνει 328; constr. w. 152(3), 392(1*d*),
 409(5)
παραιτεῖσθαι: 316(2); w. μή and inf. 429
παρακαλεῖν: impf. and aor. 328; constr. w. 392(1*c*),
 397(6), 400(7), 407, 409(5), 420
παρακαλύπτειν: ἀπό 155(3)
παρακελεύεσθαι: impf. and aor. 328
παρακούειν: constr. w. 173(3)
παραλαμβάνειν: constr. w. 210(3), 390(3), 392(2);
 παραλαβών 418(5), 419(1)
παράλιος: ὁ, ἡ 59(1), 123(1)
παραμένειν, -μονος: w. dat. 202
παραμύθιον: 111(4)
παραπλήσιον: w. gen. or dat. 184
παράσημον: 198(7)
παρατηρεῖν, -εῖσθαι: 316(1)
παρατιθέναι, -εσθαι: constr. w. 202
παραυτίκα: 12(3)
παραχέω, s. χέω
παραχρῆμα: 12(3), 102(2); εὐθέως π. 484
παρεδρεύειν: constr. w. 202
παρεῖναι: ellipsis of 128(7); constr. w. 202; use 322
παρεκτός: 12(3), 216(2)
παρενοχλεῖν: constr. w. 202
παρέχειν, -εσθαι: 316(3); constr. w. 202
παριέναι (ἵημι): 97(3)
παρίστασθαι: constr. w. 202
Παρμενᾶς: 125(1)
παροικεῖν: augm. 67(1)
παροργίζειν: fut. 74(1)
παρρησία: 11(1); (ἐν) -ίᾳ, μετὰ -ίας 198(4), 264(3)
παρρησιάζεσθαι: augm. 69(4); constr. w. 235(2),
 392(3)
πᾶς: indecl. πᾶσα? 56(4); πάντων as frozen masc.-
 neut. w. πρώτη? 164(1); πᾶς ἐκ 164(1); w. art.
 270(2), 275; ὁ πᾶς, οἱ πάντες, τὰ πάντα 275(7);
 πᾶς ὁ w. ptcp. 413(2); πᾶν τό w. ptcp. 138(1),
 413(3); πᾶς ὅστις (ὅς) 293(1), 413(2); πᾶς...οὐ,
 οὐ...πᾶς = οὐδείς 275(4), 302(1), 466(3); πάντες
 οὐ 433(2); καὶ πάντες δέ 447(9); anacoluthon after
 πᾶς 466(3); repetition of (paronomasia) 488(1*a*);
 position 292
πάσχα (φάσκα): 39(2, 3), 58; τὰ πάσχα 141(3)
πάσχειν: fut. παθεῖται 74(3); εὖ (κακῶς) πάσχειν w.
 ὑπό 315; pres. impera. 336(2)
Πάταρα, -ερα: 42(3)
πατάσσειν: 101 s.v. τύπτειν
πατήρ: nom. and voc. 147(3); w. and without pron.
 192, 278; art. 257(3)
πατριάρχης: 50
Πατροβᾶς: 125(1)
πατρολῴας and μητρολῴας: 26, 35(2), 119(2)
πατρῷος: 26
παύειν: ἐπάην 76(1), 78; act., constr. w. 180(6),
 400(4); mid., constr. w. 180(6), 414(2)

πεʒῇ: 26
πειθαρχεῖν: constr. w. 187(6)
πείθειν: 101; -ειν and -εσθαι constr. w. 159(1), 187(6), 392(1e), 397(2); perfective pres. 322; πέπεισμαι 341, 397(2); also s. πεποιθέναι
πειθός or πειθώ: 47(4), 112, 474(4)
πεῖν f. πιεῖν, s. πίνειν
πεινᾶν: pres. 88; fut.-aor. 70(2); constr. w. 171(1)
πειράʒειν and πειρᾶσθαι: meaning 101, 310(1); constr. w. 171(2), 392(1a)
πεισμονή: 109(6), 488(1b)
πέμπειν: use of aor. 328, 334 (in epistolary style); πέμψας εἶπεν 418(4), 420(2)
πενθεῖν: intr. and trans. 148(2)
πεντεκαιδέκατος: 63(2)
πεποιθέναι: constr. w. 187(6), 233(2), 235(2), 397(2), 406(1); w. pres. sense 341
πεποίθησις: 68
-περ: 107
πέραν: w. gen. 184
πέρας γέ τοι: 107
περί: not w. dat. 203; w. acc. 228, οἱ περὶ αὐτόν, Παῦλον 228, 266(1); w. gen. 229; w. μνημονεύειν etc. 175, w. σπλαγχνίʒεσθαι, μεριμνᾶν, μέλει 176, w. ἐγκαλεῖσθαι 178, w. θαυμάʒειν 196; interchanging w. ὑπέρ 229(1), 231; τὰ περί τινος 266(1); compounds w. περί: trans. 150, w. dat. etc. 202
περιάγειν: intr. 150, 308
περιβάλλειν: constr. w. 155(5), 202; mid., constr. w. 159(1)
περιβλέπεσθαι: mid. 316(1); constr. w. 392(3)
περιέχειν: 308
περικεῖσθαι: w. acc. 159(4); w. dat. etc. 202
περιμένειν: 148(1)
περίοδος: ellipsis of 241(3)
περιούσιος: 113(1)
περιπατεῖν: w. dat. 198(5); pres. and aor. 337(1)
περιπείρειν: constr. w. 202
περιπίπτειν: constr. w. 202
περισσεύειν: augm. 69(4); constr. w. 172
περισσός, -ῶς, -ότερος, -οτέρως: 60(3) (instead of πλείων, μᾶλλον etc.), 102(1), 246; περισσός w. gen. 185(1)
περιτέμνεσθαι: pass. 314, 317
περιτιθέναι: τινί τι 155(5), 159(4), 202
περίχωρος: ἡ 241(1)
περπερεύεσθαι: p. 4 n. 1
πέρυσι, πέρσυ, πέρισυ, πέρυσιν, περυσινός, περ(ι)συνός: 20
πετ- 'to fly': 101
πετάννυναι: 92
Πέτρος: 53(2e)
πηγνύναι: 92, 101
πηλίκος: 64(4); in exclamations 304
πηνίκα etc.: do not appear 105
πῆχυς: -χῶν 48
πιάʒειν, πιέʒειν: 29(2), 101; constr. w. 170(2)
πίεσαι, s. πίνειν

πικρία: gen. of quality 165
πιμπλάναι, -ᾶν: 93, 101; constr. w. 172
πιμπράναι: 93, 101
πίνειν: fut. πίομαι, πίεσαι 74(2), 77, 87; aor. 81(3); πεῖν f. πιεῖν 31(2), 101; constr. w. 169(2), 390(3)
πιπράσκειν: 101; perf. 343(1)
πίπτειν: fut. 77; ἔπεσον, ἔπεσα 80, 81(3)
πιστεύειν: constr. w. 163, 187(6), 206(2), 233(2), 235(2), 397(2); pass. 159(4), 312(1)
πιστικός: 113(2)
πίστις: constr. 163, 206(2), 233(2), 400(2)
πιστός: constr. 187(8)
-πλασίων: f. -πλάσιος 63(3)
πλάτος: 51(2)
πλεῖστος: 60(2); τὸ πλεῖστον 'at most' 60(2), 160; ὁ πλεῖστος 245(1)
πλείων: neut. πλεῖον, πλέον 30(2); inflection 47(2); 60(1); (οἱ) πλείονες meaning 244(3); πλείων before numbers without ἤ 185(4), f. which ἐπάνω 185(4)
πλεονάʒειν, πλεονέκτης: 30(2)
πλεονεκτεῖν: trans. 148(1)
πληγή: ellipsis of 241(6)
πλῆθος: w. *constructio ad sensum* 134(1)
πλήμ(μ)υρα: 11(2); -ης 43(1)
πλήν: 216(2), 447(6), 449
πλήρης: 44(1); indecl., use 137(1); constr. 182(1); without ὤν 418(6)
πληροῦν: pass. w. acc. 159(1); constr. w. 172, 188(1), 195(2); act. and mid. 316(1); ἵνα πληρωθῇ 391(5), 397(3)
πληροφορεῖν, -ία: 119(1)
πλησίον: w. gen. 184; (ὁ) πλ. 184, 266
πλήσσειν: 101 s.v. τύπτειν
πλοιάριον: 111(3)
πλόϊμος, πλώϊμος: 35(1)
πλοῖον: f. ναῦς 47(4)
-πλοῦς: 45
πλοῦς, πλοός: 52
πλούσιος: οἱ 263(b)
πλοῦτος: ὁ and τό 51(2)
πνεῖν: πνέει 89; constr. w. 174; τῷ πνέοντι 241(5); τῇ πνεούσῃ 241(6)
πνεῦμα: plur. w. pred. in sg. and plur. 133(1); (ἐν) πνεύματι 195(1d); πν. ἅγιον w. and without art. 257(2), 474(1); w. gen. 474(4)
πνῖγος: accent 13
ποδαπός, s. ποταπός
ποθεῖν: tenses 70(1)
πόθεν: 104(1)
ποιεῖν and -εῖσθαι: ποεῖν 30(2); constr. w. 157(1, 3), 206(3), 227(3), 229(2), 234(6), 453(4); καλῶς (εὖ) ποιεῖν 151(1), w. ptcp. 414(5); εὖ (κακῶς) ποιεῖν pass. f. 315; ποιεῖν w. ἵνα, inf. 392(1e), 400(7), 408; ποιεῖσθαι σπουδήν w. inf. 392(1a); act. instead of mid. 310(1); pass. rarely used 315; use of perf. 343(2); ποιεῖν τὸ ἱκανόν 5(3b), συμβούλιον 5(3b), 310(1), (τὸ) ἔλεος μετά τινος 206(3), 227(3), 310(1); ellipsis of 480(5)

INDEX OF GREEK WORDS AND FORMS

ποιμαίνω: aor. impera. 337(2)

-ποιός, -ποιεῖν, -ποιία, -ποίησις: 119(1)

ποῖος: 64(4), 298(2), 300(1), 304; ποίας (scil. ὁδοῦ) 186(1), 241(4)

πολεμεῖν: constr. w. 193(4), 227(2)

πόλις: w. gen. of the name 167; ἡ ἁγία π. 474(1)

πολιτάρχης: 50

πολλαπλασίων: 63(3)

πολυδιδάσκαλοι: 115(1)

πολύς: πολλὰς δέρεσθαι 154, 241(6); πολλά acc. of content 155(1); τὰ πολλά adv. 160; οἱ πολλοί 245(1); τὸ πολύ 263(1); πολύ, πολλῷ w. comp. 246; ὁ ὄχλος πολύς 270(1); w. καί following 442(11)

πονηρός: ὁ 241, 263(a); substantivized without art. 264(2)

Πόπλιος: 41(2)

πορεύεσθαι: fut. 79; to supplement ὑπάγειν 101 s.v. ἄγειν, 126(1 b γ); ὁδῷ etc. 198(5); use of pres. 323(3); πορεύου, πορεύθητι 336(1), 419(5); πορευθείς 419(2)

πόρρω: -ρρ- (literary) 34(2); as pred. 434(1)

πόρρωθεν: 104(3); w. -ρρ- literary f. (ἀπὸ) μακρόθεν 34(2)

πορρωτέρω (-ον): 62

πόσος: 64(4), 304

ποταμοφόρητος: 117(2)

ποταπός: 298(3), 394

πότε: 105; ἀπὸ πότε 203

ποτέ: 105f.; τίς ποτε 303; ποτὲ μέν...ποτὲ δέ 436; also s. μήποτε

πότερος (πότερον...ἤ): 64(6), 298(1), 440(1)

ποτίζειν: w. double acc. 155(7); pass. w. acc. 159(1)

Ποτίολοι: 41(1)

ποῦ: 'where?' and 'whither?' 103

που: rare 103

Πούδης: 54

πούς: οἱ πόδες καὶ αἱ χεῖρες 474(7)

πραιτώριον: 5(1 a)

πρᾶος, πραΰς, πραότης: 26, 47(4)

πράσσειν: κακόν τινι 157(1); εὖ 414(5)

πραΰς, s. πρᾶος

πρέπει, πρέπον ἐστίν: 130(1), 409(3)

πρεσβύτερος: 244(2)

πρηνής: 29(3)

πρίν: constr. 383(3), 395, 406(3), 408; πρὶν ἤ 383(3), 395; prep. w. gen. or acc. 395

Πρίσκα, Πρίσκιλλα: 41(3)

πρό: w. gen. 213; πρὸ προσώπου τινός 217(1); πρὸ τοῦ w. inf. 395, 403, 406(3); compounds w. πρό, trans. or w. πρό 150, 484

προάγειν: trans. 150; intr. 308

προαιτιᾶσθαι: constr. w. 397(3)

προβάτιον: 111(3)

πρόβατον: f. οἶς and ἀρήν 47(4), 126(1 a α); πρόβατα w. sg. pred. 133(2)

προβεβηκώς: w. ἐν and dat. (acc.) of respect 197

προβλέπεσθαι: mid. 316(1)

πρόδηλον: ὅτι 397(4)

προε-: 18

προηγεῖσθαι: trans. 150, 308 s.v. ἄγειν

προθεσμία: ἡ (scil. ἡμέρα) 241(2)

προθυμία: τοῦ w. inf. 400(2)

πρόϊμος, πρώϊμος: 35(1), 241(5)

προκαταγγέλλειν: constr. w. 350, 397(3)

προκόπτειν: 308

προλαμβάνειν: w. inf. 392(2)

προμελετᾶν: w. inf. 392(2)

προνοεῖν and depon.: 307; -εῖσθαί τινος 176(2)

προορᾶν: προορώμην 66(2), 67(2); mid. 316(1)

πρός: w. acc. 180(4), 193(3, 4), 196, 239, instead of παρά τινι (τινα) 239(1, 2); τὰ πρὸς τὸν θεόν 160, τί πρὸς ἡμᾶς 239(6), πρὸς τί 239(7), πρός με 279, πρὸς τό w. inf. 402(5), 406(3); w. gen. and dat. 240; πρός w. acc. interchanging w. dat. 187(4, 8), 193(4), 202 s.v. προσ-; compounds w. πρός, constr. w. 202; adverbial use 203

προσάγειν: intr. 308

προσβλέπειν: constr. w. 202

προσδεῖσθαι: w. gen. 180(4)

προσδοκᾶν: constr. w. 350, 397(2)

προσέρχεσθαι: constr. w. 202; w. asyndeton 462(1)

προσεύχεσθαι: augm. 67(1); w. dat. 187(4); περί τινος 229(1); pres. impera. 336(1, 3); w. ἵνα etc. 392(1c), 400(7)

προσευχή: 109(7)

προσέχειν: intr. 308, 480(2); constr. w. 149, 202, 392(1b)

προσήκει: does not appear 358(2)

προσήλυτος: 117(2)

προσκαλεῖσθαι: constr. w. 392(3)

προσκαρτερεῖν: constr. w. 202

προσκλίνεσθαι: constr. w. 202

προσκολλᾶσθαι: constr. w. 193(3)

προσκυλίειν: constr. w. 202

προσκυνεῖν: constr. w. 151(2), 187(2); impf. and aor. 328

προσλαμβάνεσθαι: constr. w. 169(2)

προσπίπτειν: constr. w. 202

προσποιεῖσθαι: constr. w. 392(2)

προστάσσειν: constr. w. 187(5), 392(1, 1d), 409(1); use of aor. 328

προστάτις: 5(3a)

προστιθέναι: constr. w. 202; -εσθαι 'to continue' w. inf. 392(2), 435(a); προσθεὶς εἶπεν and the like 419(4, 5), 435(b), 461(2)

προσφάγιον: 123(1)

προσφέρειν: impersonal third plur. 130(2); constr. w. 202; pres. impera. 336(3)

προσφωνεῖν: constr. w. 202

πρόσωπον: without art. 255(4), 259(1); Hebraistic circumlocutions 217(1), p. 3 n. 5, 140, 149, 259(1); πρ. λαμβάνειν p. 3 n. 5; προσωπολήμπτης etc. p. 3 n. 5, 119(2)

πρότερος, -ον: 62; πρότερον τούτων 164(4)

προτίθεσθαι: constr. w. 392(1a)

INDEX OF GREEK WORDS AND FORMS

προϋπάρχειν: w. ptcp. 414(1)
προφητεύειν: augm. 69(4)
προφθάνειν: constr. w. 414(4)
πρύμνα: 43(2)
πρωί: τὸ πρ. of time when 160, 161(3), 266(2); ἦν πρ. 129, 434(1)
πρωία: ἡ 241(3)
πρώϊμος, s. πρόϊμος
πρῷρα: 26, 43(1)
πρῶτος: f. πρότερος 62; 'as the first' 243; πρῶτον μέν 447(4); without art. 256; πρώτως 102(5)
πρωτότοκος, τὰ πρωτοτοκεῖα (-ια): 120(1)
πρώτως: 102(5)
πτέρνα: 43(2)
Πτολεμαῖς: -αΐ- 15; not -αιι- 30(1); πτ- 34(6)
πτωχεύειν: ingressive aor. 331
πτωχός: ὁ 263(a)
πυκνότερον: 244(1)
πύλη: sg. and plur. 141(4); ellipsis of 241(6)
πυνθάνεσθαι: constr. w. 173(3); impf. and aor. 328
πῦρ: π. φλογός, φλὸξ πυρός 165; (ἐν) πυρὶ καίειν 195(1c)
πυρρός: 34(2)
πωλεῖν: 101 s.v. πιπράσκειν; constr. w. 179(1)
πῶς: 436; instead of ὡς, ὅτι 396
πως: 106, 375; also s. εἴπως, μήπως

ρ: ρ–ρρ 11(1); redupl. of ῥ- 11(1), 68; ρρ–ρσ 2, 34(2); ρρ from ρε 34(3)
-ρᾶ: first decl., gen. -ρης 43(1)
Ῥαάβ, Ῥαχάβ: 39(3)
ῥαββι, ῥαββουνι: p. 3 n. 2, 38
ῥαβδοῦχος: 5(3a)
ῥαθυμεῖν: 26
ῥαίδη, s. ῥέδη
ῥαίνειν, ῥαντίζειν: redupl. 68; pass. w. acc. 159(3)
ῥαπίσμασιν λαμβάνειν: 5(3b), 198(3)
Ῥαχάβ, Ῥαάβ: 39(3)
Ῥαχήλ: 39(3)
ῥέδη (ῥαίδη): 5(1d), 41(1)
ῥεῖν: fut. 77
ρερ-: redupl. of ρ- 68
ῥηγνύναι, ῥήσσειν (ῥάσσειν): 73, 92, 101
ῥῖγος: 13
ῥίπτειν, -εῖν: redupl. 68; 101; ῥῖψαν 13; intr. 308
ῥομφαία: ἐν ῥ. 195(1a)
ῥοῦς: 52
Ῥοῦφος: 41(1)
ρρ: from ρε 34(3)
ρσ–ρρ: 2, 34(2)
ῥύεσθαι: 101; pass. 311(2); constr. w. 180
ῥύπος: ὁ 51(2)
Ῥώμη: art. 261(1)
ῥωννύναι: redupl. 68; 92, 101; also s. ἔρρωσο

σ: f. which (σ)ϛ before β and μ 10; movable σ 21; = Hebr. ᵊ, ᵗ, ᵚ, ᵚ 39(4)
σαβαχθανί (-κτ-): 39(2)

σάββατον: 39(2); dat. plur. -ασιν 52; sg. and plur. 141(3); ὀψὲ σαββάτων 164(4); (δὶς τοῦ) σαββάτου 186(2); (ἐν) τοῖς σάββασιν, τῷ σαββάτῳ etc. 200(3)
-σαι (second sg. mid.-pass.): 87
Σαλαμίν, -μίνη: 46(4), 57
Σαλίμ: 56(3)
σάλος: 51(2)
σάλπι(γ)ξ: 46(4)
σαλπίζειν: ἐσάλπισα etc. 71; σαλπίσει impersonal 129
Σαλώμη: 53(3)
Σαμάρεια, -ίτης: 38; -ίτης art. 262(3)
Σαμψώ(ν): 39(5, 8)
-σαν (ending): impera. 84(1); impf. and second aor. 84(2, 3); opt. 84(4)
Σαούλ, Σαῦλος: 53(2)
Σαπφ(ε)ιρα (-ρος): 38; -μφ- 39(7); -πφ- and -φφ- 40; gen. -ης 43(1)
σαρδ(ι)όνυξ: 115(1)
Σάρεπτα, -φθα: 39(2), 56(2)
σαρκικός, σάρκινος: 113(2)
σάρξ: without art. 258(2); πᾶσα σ. 275(4); τὸ κατὰ σάρκα 160, 266(2); κατὰ σ. w. Ἰσραήλ, κύριος etc. 272
Σά(ρ)ρα: 40
Σαρ(ρ)ωνα: 56(2)
σατανᾶς: also σαταν 58; decl. 55(1b); art. 254(1)
Σαῦλος, Σαούλ: 53(2)
σβεννύναι: 92
σεαυτοῦ (not σαυτοῦ): 31(1), 64(1), 283; position 284(2)
Σεβαστός: 5(3a)
σειρ-, σιρ-: 23
Σεκουνδος: accent 41(3)
σελήνη: w. and without art. 253(1)
σϛμ-: 10
σημαίνειν: ἐσήμανα 72; constr. w. 397(3)
σήμερον: not τήμερον 34(1); ἡ σ. (ἡμέρα) 241(2)
-σία: compounds in 119(3)
σιγᾶν: ingressive aor. 331
σικάριος: 5(1b)
σίκερα: 38, 58
Σιλουανός, Σιλᾶς: 41(2), 55(1b), 125(2); Σιλέας 53(2), 125(2)
Σιλωάμ: ὁ 56(4)
σιμικίνθιον: semicinctium 5(1d), 41(1)
Σίμων, Συμεών: 38, 53(2d)
Σινᾶ (not Σεινα): 38, 56(3)
σίναπι: 42(4)
σινιάζειν: 108(3)
σιρ-, σειρ-: 23
Σιράχ: 39(3)
σιρικόν: sericum 41(1), 42(4)
-σις: subst. in 109(4)
σιτιστός: 112
σιτομέτριον: 111(4)
σῖτος: plur. σῖτα 49(3)
Σιών (not Σειών): 38, 56(3)
σιώπα πεφίμωσο: 461(1)
σκάνδαλον: p. 3 n. 5

297

INDEX OF GREEK WORDS AND FORMS

σκεδαννύναι: 92
-σκειν: vbs. in, meaning 331
σκέπτεσθαι, σκοπεῖν: 101
Σκευᾶς: 125(2)
σκεῦος: 5(1); w. gen. of quality 165
σκληροκαρδία, -κάρδιος: 120(4)
σκοπεῖν: 101
σκορπίζειν: f. σκεδαννύναι 92
σκότος: τό, not ὁ, 51(2)
-σμός: 109(4)
σμύρνα: 10, 43(2)
Σόδομα, -ων: 38, 57
Σολομών, -μῶνος and -μῶν, -μῶντος: 53(1), 55(2)
σός: 285(1)
σουδάριον: *sudarium* 5(1*d*)
Σουσάννα: 40, 53(3)
σπᾶν, -ᾶσθαι: 310(1)
Σπανία: 41(1)
σπεῖρα: 5(3*a*), p. 5 n. 7; -ρης 43(1)
σπεκουλάτωρ: 5(1*b*), 109(8)
σπέρμα: w. *constructio ad sensum* 134(1)
σπερμολόγος: 119(1)
σπεύδειν: constr. w. 392(1*a*); σπεῦσον κατάβηθι 461(1)
σπιλάδες: 45
σπίλος: accent 13
σπλαγχνίζεσθαι: 108(3); constr. w. 176(1), 229(2), 233(2), 235(2)
σπόγγος, σφ-: 34(5)
σπουδάζειν: fut. 77; constr. w. 392(1*a*)
σπουδαῖος: comp. 102(1), 244(2)
σπυρίς, σφ-: 34(5)
σσ–ττ: 2, 34(1)
στάδιον: plur. -οι and -α 49(3)
στάμνος: ἡ 49(1)
στάνειν: f. ἱστάναι 93
στατίων: p. 5 n. 1
στέγη and στέγος: 51(1)
στεῖρα: dat. -ᾳ 43(1)
στερεός: 34(3)
Στεφανᾶς: 125(1)
στήκειν: f. ἑστηκέναι 73
στηρίζειν: dental and guttural 71, 74(1); στ. τὸ πρόσωπον τοῦ w. inf. 400(7)
στοά: 30(2)
Στοϊκός, Στωϊκός: 35(1)
στοιχεῖν: w. dat. 198(5)
στόμα: without art. 259(1); Hebraistic circumlocutions 140, 173(1), 217(3), 234(4), 259(1)
στρατεία: 23; w. *constructio ad sensum* 134(1)
στρατευόμενος: 413(1)
στρατηγός: 5(3*a*)
στρατοπέδαρχος or -άρχης: 50
στρέφειν: intr.? 308
στρῆνος: τό and ὁ 51(2)
στρουθίον: 111(3)
στρωννύειν: 92
Στωϊκός, Στοϊκός: 35(1)

σύ: use of the nom. 277(1, 2), possessive gen. 278, emphatic oblique cases 279; f. any third person 281; position of the possessive μου, σου, ἐμοῦ 284(1, 2)
συγγένεια: 110(2)
συγγενής: dat. plur. -εῦσιν 47(4), 48; w. gen. 194(2); fem. -ίς 59(3)
συγκαθῆσθαι: constr. w. 202
συγκακοπαθεῖν: constr. w. 202
συγκακουχεῖσθαι: constr. w. 202
συγκαλεῖν, -εῖσθαι: 316(1)
συγκατατίθεσθαι: constr. w. 202
συγκληρονόμος: w. gen. 182(1), 194(2)
συγκοινωνός: w. gen. 182(1)
συκῆ: 45
συκομορέα: 25, 45
συλλαλεῖν: constr. w. 202
συλλέγειν: 101 s.v. λέγειν 'to collect'; impersonal third plur. 130(2)
συλλυπεῖσθαι: constr. w. 196
συμβαίνειν: constr. w. 189(3); συνέβη 393(5), 408
συμβουλεύειν, -εσθαι: constr. w. 392(1*a*)
συμβούλιον: 5(3*a*), 111(4); σ. λαμβάνειν (ποιεῖν) 5(3*b*)
σύμβουλος: w. gen. 194(2)
Συμεών, s. Σίμων
συμμέτοχος: w. gen. 182(1), 194(2)
σύμμορφος: w. gen. 182(1), 194(2); w. dat. 194(2)
σύμπας: 275
συμφέρει: constr. w. 151(1), 393(1), 409(3); συμφέρον scil. ἐστίν 127(2); subst. w. gen. 187(8), 413(3)
σύμφορον: w. gen. 187(8), 413(3)
συμφυλέτης: 111(2)
συμφωνεῖν: constr. w. 179(1), 202, 227(2), 409(3)
συμψέλ(λ)ιον: p. 5 n. 1, 41(2)
σύν: 221; assimilation of the ν 19; not ξύν 34(4); along w. μετά w. gen. 221, 227(2); σὺν χειρί 217(2); οἱ σὺν αὐτῷ 266(1); σὺν καί 442(13); σύν in compound subst. and adj. 116(2), w. dat. and gen. 182(1), 194(2); compounds w. σύν, constr. w. 202
συνάγειν: intr. 308
συναίρειν λόγον: 310(1)
συναιχμάλωτος: w. gen. 194(2)
συναναβαίνειν: constr. w. 202
συναντᾶν: fut. 77
συναντιλαμβάνεσθαι: 170(3), 202
συναρμολογεῖν: 119(1)
συναρχία: 13
συνειδέναι: -ειδυίης 43(1)
συνέπεσθαι: constr. w. 193(1)
συνεργεῖν: 148(1)
συνεργός: w. gen. 194(2)
συνέρχεσθαι: τινί 'to accompany someone' 202
συνετίζειν: 108(3)
συνευδοκεῖν: constr. w. 392(3)
συνζητεῖν: non-assimilation of ν 19(2)
σύνζυγε: non-assimilation of ν 19(2)
-σύνη: subst. in 110(2)
συνήθειά ἐστίν τινι: 189(1); constr. 393(3)

298

συνιέναι, συνίειν: 94(2); aor. act. 95(1); constr. w. 173(5)

συνιστάναι: 93; constr. w. 157(4), 197, 397(4), 406(1)

συντίθεσθαι: constr. w. 392(1a), 400(7)

σύντροφος: w. gen. 194(2)

συνχύν(ν)ειν: 73

Συρία: w. and without art. 261(6)

Συροφοινίκισσα, -φοίνισσα: 111(1), 115(1)

συσχηματίζεσθαι: pass. 314

σφάζειν or σφάττειν: 71

σφόγγος, σπ-: 34(5)

σφυδρόν: f. σφυρόν 34(6)

σφυρίς, σπ-: 34(5)

σῴζειν: -ω- and -ῳ- in the tenses 26; constr. w. 180

σῶμα: combined w. gen. of quality 165

Σωσθένης: acc. -ην 46(1)

σωτηρία: art. 258(1)

σωτήριος: ἡ 59(2); constr. w. 187(8); -ον 113(1)

τ: = Hebr. ט, ת 39(2)

ταλιθα: 38

ταμεῖον: f. -ιεῖον 31(2)

τάσσειν: aor.-fut. pass. 76(1); constr. w. 392(1d), 409(1)

-τατος: superl. in 60(1)

ταῦτά: crasis 18

τάχα: 102(2); w. indic. instead of potential opt. 385(1)

ταχινός: 113(3)

ταχύς: adv. -ύ and -έως 102(2); ἐν τάχει 219(4); comp. τάχιον 61(1), meaning 244(1), θᾶττον, θᾶσσον 61(1), 244(2); ὡς τάχιστα 60(2), 244(1), 453(4)

τε: 442f.; τε (...) καί, τε...τε etc. 444, 445(2, 3); in the period 464

τέκνον: τέκνα w. sg. and plur. pred. 133(1); τέκνον, τεκνίον w. μου 192; art. 257(3)

τελεῖν: fut. τελέσω 74(1); w. ptcp. 414(2)

τέλειος, -ε(ι)οῦν: 30(2)

τελευτᾶν: intr. 480(2)

τέλος: τὸ τέλος 'finally' 160; εἰς τ. 207(3)

τελώνιον: -εῖον 13; 111(4)

-τέος: verbal adj. 65(3), 358(2)

τέρας: plur. τέρατα 47(1)

Τέρτυλλος: 41(1)

τεσσαρακονταετής: 13, 124

τέσσαρες: -ερα 29(1); acc. -αρες 46(2); τέτρασι 63(1)

τεσσαρεσκαιδέκατος: 63(2)

τεσσεράκοντα: 29(1)

τέταρτον: τό (scil. μέρος) 241(7)

τετρ(α)αρχεῖν: 124; constr. w. 177

τετρ(α)άρχης: 50, 124

τετράμηνος: ἡ 241(3)

τηλαυγής: 119(4)

τηλικοῦτος: neut. -ον and -ο 64(4); ὁ τ. 274

τηρεῖν: 83(1); constr. w. 149; pres. and aor. 337(2)

-τήριον: subst. in 109(9), 113(1)

-της: nomina agentis in 109(8); in compounds 119(2)

τί, τι, s. τίς, τις

Τιβέριος: 41(1)

τιθέναι: 94(1), 95(1), 96, 97(2); act. and mid. 316(1); constr. w. 157(1), 392(1e, 3); τ. τὰ γόνατα 5 (3b)

τίκτειν: aor. pass. 76(2); fut. 77

τιμᾶν: aor. impera. 337(2)

τιμή: gen. of price 179(1)

τιμιώτατος: 60(1)

τίνειν: τείσω etc. 23

τίς: 64(3) (τοῦ, τῷ are lacking); syntax 298; w. partitive gen. and ἐξ (ἀπό, ἐν) 164(1); f. πότερος 298(1); f. ὅστις 298(4), 303, 376; τίς ἤμην etc. 298(5); τίς γάρ 446; τί(ς) ἄρα 440(2); τί τὸ ὄφελος p. 2 n. 4, 127(3); τί οὖν p. 2 n. 4, 299(3); τί γάρ (μοι) 127(3), 299(3); τί πρὸς ἡμᾶς, σέ 239(6), 299(3); τί ἐμοὶ (ἡμῖν) καὶ σοί 127(3), 299(3); τί as pred. to ταῦτα 131, 299(1); τί (pred.) ἐγένετο 131, 157(1), 299(2); τί 'why?' 299(4); τί ὅτι (τί γέγονεν ὅτι), ἵνα τί 299(4), 300(2a); τί 'how!' 299(4); τί ἐροῦμεν 366(2); position 475(1)

τις: 301; w. partitive gen. and ἐξ (ἐν) 164(1); εἷς τις 247(2), 301(1); τινὲς οἱ 412(4); οὐ (μὴ)...τις 431(2); εἴ τις 475(2); τι 'something (special)' pred. 131, 137(2), τις similarly 131; τι adv. 137(2); παρά τι 236(4); position 473(1)

τίς ποτε: 'any body, somebody' 303

τίτλος: 5(1)

τοι: only in combinations 107

τοιγαροῦν: 107, 451(3)

τοίνυν: 107, 451(3)

τοῖος: 64(4)

τοιόσδε: 64(4), 289

τοιοῦτος: 290(3), 304; neut. -ον and -ο 64(4); ὁ τ. 274, 304; ἥτις f. ἡ τοιαύτη 293(4); pleonastic τοιαύτη after οἷα 297

τολμᾶν: constr. w. 392(1a)

τολμηροτέρως: 102(1)

τόπος: ποίῳ τόπῳ 199

-τος: verbal adj. in 65(3), 112; in compounds 117; w. gen. 183

τοσοῦτος: neut. -ον and -ο 64(4); ὁ τ. 274; τοσούτῳ...ὅσῳ 304; elliptical τοσοῦτο δέ 481

τότε: 105, 459(2); ἀπὸ τ. 203, 459(3)

τοὐναντίον: 18

τοὔνομα: 18

τουτέστιν, τοῦτ' ἔστιν: 12(3), 17, 132(2)

τρέμειν: w. ptcp. 415

-τρια: subst. in 109(8)

τρίβειν: -ῐ- 13

τριετία: 5(3a)

τρίζειν: trans. 148(1)

τρίμηνος: ἡ 241(3)

τρίς: ἐπὶ τρίς 248(2)

τρίτον: τρ. τοῦτο 'for the third time' 154, 248(4); (τὸ) τρ., ἐκ τρίτου 'now for the third time' 248(4); τὸ τρ. scil. μέρος 241(7); without art. 256

-τρον: 35(3)

INDEX OF GREEK WORDS AND FORMS

ὦ (ὤ): w. voc. 146; w. gen. of cause and vbs. of emotion 176(1)

ὧδε: 'here (hither)' 103; ὧδε λοιπόν 451(6)

ὠδίν: 46(4)

ὠθεῖν: augm. 66(2)

-ωλός: adj. in 112

-ων: comp. in, -ονες, -ους etc. 47(2); acc. -ων f. -ω 47(2)

-ών: subst. in 111(6), 143

ὠνεῖσθαι: 66(2), 101

ᾠόν: 26

ὥρα: w. ἐστίν to be supplied 127(2); ὥραν ἑβδόμην and the like f. time when 161(3); ὥρας gen. of time 186(2); dat. and ἐν 200(2); ἐν αὐτῇ (ἐκείνῃ) τῇ ὥρᾳ 288(2), 459(3); ellipsis of 241(3), 256; art. 256; w. attraction in rel. clause 294(5); constr. 382(1), 393(3), 408, 409(3)

-ως: adv. in 102(1)

ὡς: 203; w. pred. 157(3–5), 453(4); ὡς τάχιστα 244(1), 453(4); ὡς, ὡς ὅτι in declarative clauses 386(1), 388, 396, 425(3), 428(5) (negation); w. inf. =ὥστε? 391(1); w. inf. absolute 391a; comp. 453; causal 453(2); w. ptcp. 416(1, 3), 425(3, 4); οὐχ ὡς 425(3); ὡς οὐ 430(3); position w. neg. 433(3); exclamatory 436; ὡς ἐπί versus 453(4); temporal 455(2, 3); position 474(1), 475(1); ὡς= ἕως 455(3)

ὡσάν (ὡς ἄν [ἐάν]): 367, 425(5), 453(3), 455(2)

ὡσαύτως: 12(1)

ὡσεί: 157(5), 425(3), 453(3)

ὥσπερ: 107, 425(3), 453

ὡσπερεί: 107, 453(3)

ὥστε: 391, 406(3), 408, 455(3)

ὠτίον (ὠτάριον): besides οὖς 111(3)

ωυ: in Μωυσῆς 38

ὠφέλεια, -λία: 23

ὠφελεῖν: constr. w. 151(1), 159(2)

ὠφέλιμος: constr. 187(8)

ὤφθην, s. ὁρᾶν

III. INDEX OF REFERENCES

(1) *The New Testament*

Matthew	§§	Matthew (*cont.*)	§§	Matthew (*cont.*)	§§
1: 2ff.	260(2)	5: 17	445(2)	6: 27	247(2), 417
1: 6	162(4), 260(2)	5: 18	247(2), 474(1)	6: 28	476(2)
1:11, 12	166	5: 19	107, 488(1c)	6: 30	372(1a)
1: 16	260(2)	5: 20	185(1), 246	6: 34	176(2), 337(3)
1: 18	416(2), 423(4), 434(1)	5: 21	362	6: 37	366(2)
1: 20	336(3), 423(1)	5: 24	336(3)	7: 2	130(1)
1: 21	157(2)	5: 25	353(1), 369(3)	7: 6	111(3), 214(6), 369(2)
1: 22	343(3)	5: 26	5(1)	7: 9f.	469
1: 23, 25	157(2)	5: 28	333(2), 402(5)	7: 13f.	492
2: 2	253(5)	5: 29	442(1)	7: 14	299(4)
2: 3	56(4), 275(2)	5: 31	130(1)	7: 15	293(2)
2: 4	323(2)	5: 34ff.	445(1)	7: 23	187(4), 412(5)
2: 6	264(6)	5: 37	60(3), 185(1), 432(1)	7: 24	293(2), 466(3)
2: 8	420(2)	5: 38	480(5)	7: 25	126(3), 202 s.v. προσ-, 492
2: 9	215(2), 253(5)	5: 39	380(2)		
2: 10	153(1)	5: 39ff.	337(2)	7: 27	126(3), 492
2: 13	321	5: 40	466(4)	8: 1	423(1)
2: 16	62	5: 41	380(2)	8: 2	372(1a)
2: 20	141	5: 43f.	362	8: 4	336(3)
2: 22	177, 324	5: 45	129, 182(4), 309(1), 492	8: 8	442(2), 473(1)
3: 4	209(4), 277(3)	5: 48	362	8: 9	101 s.v. ἔρχεσθαι, 336(1)
3: 7	149	6: 3	423(3)	8: 12	62
3: 9	392(1a)	6: 5	98, 362	8: 14	471(5)
3: 14	326	6: 7	219(2)	8: 19	107, 247(2)
4: 2	474(1)	6: 8	293(5)	8: 20	368
4: 15	161(1)	6: 9	277(1)	8: 22	488(1c)
4: 16	466(4)	6: 11	123(1)	8: 27	298(3), 444(3), 456(2)
4: 23	150	6: 12	453(2)	8: 28	291(3), 423(1)
4: 25	479(1)	6: 13	263(1)	8: 32	225
5	362	6: 15	445(2)	8: 34	328
5: 1	423(1)	6: 17	277(1)	9: 5	320
5: 3–17	462(2)	6: 18	414(3)	9: 6	470(3), 483
5: 13	273(1), 390(3)	6: 25	131, 337(3)	9: 9	308
5: 15	5(1), 442(2)	6: 26	246	9: 10	423(1)

INDEX OF REFERENCES

INDEX OF REFERENCES

INDEX OF REFERENCES

Luke (*cont.*)

	§§
11: 3	123(1), 337(4)
11: 5ff.	366(1), 442(3)
11: 6	379
11: 7	104(2), 205
11: 8	372(3), 428(1), 439(3)
11: 11	469
11: 13	437
11: 18	372(3), 408
11: 24	134(3)
11: 28	450(4)
11: 31	173(1)
11: 33	5(1), 138(2)
11: 35	370(3)
11: 37	404(2)
11: 38	317
11: 39	184
12: 4	60(3)
12: 6	247(2)
12: 8	220(2), 380(3)
12: 15	149
12: 16	101 s.v. λέγειν, 473(1)
12: 20	189(2)
12: 23	131
12: 24	246
12: 25	417
12: 28	474(5c)
12: 30	254(3)
12: 31	449(1)
12: 36	368, 423(6)
12: 40	294(5)
12: 47	154
12: 48	154, 295, 466(3)
12: 49	299(4), 360(4)
12: 51	448(8)
12: 52f.	235(4)
12: 54f.	323(1)
12: 56	449(1)
12: 58	5(3b), 342(1), 369(3), 455(2)
12: 59	5(1)
13: 2	245(3)
13: 4	245(3), 297
13: 7	144, 322, 442(14)
13: 8	383(2)
13: 9	206(1), 454(4), 480(6)
13: 16	144
13: 24	465(2)
13: 25	476(2)
13: 28	382(4)
13: 33	495(2)
13: 34	47(4)
13: 35	382(2)
14: 1	404(2)
14: 4	170(2)
14: 5	164(1), 471(2)
14: 8	337(3)
14: 8f.	370(2)
14: 10	369(2)
14: 18	157(3), 241(6)
14: 18f.	471(1)
14: 19	157(3), 323(3), 471(1)
14: 21	460(3)

Luke (*cont.*)

	§§
14: 29	423(1)
14: 30	414(2)
14: 31	339(2b)
14: 32	155(2)
15: 6	316(1)
15: 7	245(3)
15: 8	5(1c)
15: 9	316(1)
15: 10	214(6)
15: 12	308
15: 13	433(3)
15: 15	247(2)
15: 16	18, 169(3)
15: 17	172
15: 18	214(6)
15: 19	247(2)
15: 20	423(2)
15: 21	214(6)
15: 22	207(1)
15: 23	420(3)
15: 26	247(2), 299(1), 386(1)
15: 29	322
15: 30	290(6)
16: 1	193(4), 290(1), 425(3)
16: 2	299(1)
16: 4	180(1)
16: 8	176(1)
16: 10	272
16: 20	347(1)
16: 21	111(3)
16: 23	162(8)
16: 24	172
16: 25	289
16: 26	104(1), 235(3), 437
16: 31	101 s.v. πείθειν
17: 2	159(4), 245(3), 372(3), 393(1)
17: 4	252, 266(2)
17: 6	372(1a)
17: 7f.	448(4)
17: 8	298(4), 383(2)
17: 9	76(1), 427(2)
17: 10	76(1)
17: 11	222, 261(4)
17: 12	104(3), 423(1)
17: 15	198(3)
17: 22	382(1)
17: 24	241(1)
17: 27	101 s.v. γαμεῖν
17: 29	129
17: 31	380(2), 469
17: 33	380(3)
17: 35	418(2)
18: 1	402(5)
18: 2, 4	445(4)
18: 5	207(3)
18: 7	365(4)
18: 9	412(4)
18: 10	390(1)
18: 11	290(6)
18: 12	186(2)
18: 13	101 s.v. ἱλάσκεσθαι, 314

Luke (*cont.*)

	§§
18: 14	185(3), 291(2)
18: 18	247(2), 473(1)
18: 22	189(3)
18: 25	24
18: 29	460(3)
18: 29f.	365(3)
18: 36	386(1)
18: 40	423(2)
18: 41	366(3), 465(2)
19: 2	277(3), 290(1)
19: 4	186(1), 484
19: 11	419(4), 435(b)
19: 13	285(2), 383(1)
19: 15	298(5), 404(2), 442(5)
19: 17	102(3)
19: 19	98
19: 20	306(2)
19: 23	360(2)
19: 29	143
19: 40	65(1b), 77, 373(2)
19: 42	439(2), 482
19: 43	442(4)
19: 48	392(1a)
20: 2	101 s.v. λέγειν
20: 3	247(2)
20: 7	406(2)
20: 10	369(2)
20: 11f.	435(a)
20: 13	424
20: 14	260(1)
20: 16	384
20: 19	239(6), 345
20: 20	157(2), 391(3), 406(1)
20: 22	5(1), 409(3)
20: 25	451(1)
20: 26	170(2)
20: 27	429
20: 32	62
20: 33	164(1)
20: 34, 35	101 s.v. γαμεῖν
20: 36	118(1), 445(1)
20: 37	234(3)
21: 5	109(3)
21: 6	466(1)
21: 11	443(1), 488(2)
21: 14	392(3)
21: 15	442(16)
21: 24	383(2)
21: 33	365(1)
21: 36	97(1)
21: 37	143, 205
22: 8	420(2)
22: 10	423(1)
22: 11	378, 484
22: 15	198(6)
22: 19f.	339(2b)
22: 23	386(1)
22: 26	480(5)
22: 30	369(3)
22: 34	383(3), 429
22: 35	154
22: 37	145(2)

307

Romans (*cont.*)

	§§
3: 30	107, 456(3)
4: 1	480(5)
4: 8	365(3)
4: 9	481
4: 10	496(1)
4: 13	399(1)
4: 16	107
4: 17	294(2)
4: 18	434(1)
4: 19	103, 427(1)
4: 20	187(6), 196
5: 2	343(2)
5: 3 ff.	493(3)
5: 6	255(3), 476(1)
5: 7	102(2), 349(1), 385(1)
5: 8	394
5: 9	219(3)
5: 12	235(2)
5: 13	258(2)
5: 14f., 16	488(3)
5: 18	481
6: 4	272, 337(1)
6: 5	194(2)
6: 6	400(8)
6: 10	154, 188(2)
6: 11	157(3), 188(2), 406(1)
6: 12f.	337(1)
6: 14	258(2)
6: 15	75, 299(3)
6: 17	294(5), 327
6: 21	284(3)
7: 3	182(3), 189(2), 349(1), 400(8)
7: 4	188(2), 189(2)
7: 5	269(2)
7: 7	360(1), 428(2), 443(3), 452(3)
7: 7–8: 2	281
7: 18	399(1)
7: 25	281
8: 2	281
8: 3	219(2), 263(2), 480(6)
8: 7	452(3)
8: 9	219(4)
8: 10, 11	372(2b)
8: 12	190(1), 400(2)
8: 13	372(2a)
8: 16	463
8: 18	239(8), 474(5a)
8: 20	222
8: 24	442(14)
8: 28	148(1), 413(3)
8: 29	182(1)
8: 29f.	493(3)
8: 31	496(2)
8: 32	439(3)
8: 33ff.	490
8: 34	351(2), 495(3)
8: 36	157(5)
8: 39	269(2)
9: 1	463
9: 3	211, 272, 359(2)

Romans (*cont.*)

	§§
9: 4	141(8), 460(3)
9: 5	266(2)
9: 6	304, 480(5)
9: 10	479(1)
9: 11	446, 478
9: 12	61(1)
9: 17	290(4)
9: 19	475(2)
9: 20	146(1b), 434(2), 450(4)
9: 21	393(3)
9: 22	165, 263(2)
9: 22f.	467
9: 23	165
9: 24–9	477(2)
9: 25	219(1), 426, 430(3)
9: 30	163, 272, 447(8)
9: 33	187(6)
10: 1	272, 447(4), 463
10: 5	474(5c)
10: 8	130(3)
10: 11	187(6)
10: 14	77, 493(3)
10: 14f.	366(1)
10: 15	470(1)
10: 16	448(3)
10: 18	427(2), 450(4)
10: 18f.	448(3)
10: 20	191(3), 220(1)
11: 2	219(1)
11: 4	53(4), 448(3)
11: 6	456(3)
11: 7	171(2)
11: 8	109(4), 393(6), 400(2)
11: 10	400(2, 4)
11: 13	474(4)
11: 17	120(3), 488(2)
11: 18	483
11: 19	488(2)
11: 20	119(4), 196
11: 21	370(1)
11: 22	456(3), 469, 475(2), 477(2)
11: 24	120(3)
11: 25	188(2), 275(4)
11: 30	196
11: 31	196, 284(2)
11: 33ff.	146(2)
11: 36	223(2), 275(7)
12: 1	223(4), 480(6)
12: 3	223(4), 488(1b)
12: 5	305
12: 6ff.	454(3)
12: 7	258(1), 446
12: 9ff.	258(1), 468(2)
12: 10	150
12: 12	196
12: 15	389, 488(3)
13: 2	188(2)
13: 3	471(3)
13: 5	127(2)
13: 6	290(4)
13: 7	481

Romans (*cont.*)–1 Corinthians

	§§
13: 8	399(1)
13: 9	64(1)
13: 11	442(9), 480(5)
13: 13	200, 337(1), 425(4)
14: 2	397(2)
14: 4	73, 188(2), 412(5)
14: 6	188(2)
14: 7	272
14: 7f.	188(2)
14: 11	188(2), 454(5)
14: 13	399(3)
14: 14	291(4)
14: 19	266(3)
14: 20	223(3)
14: 21	338(1), 399(3), 480(1)
14: 23	344
15: 2	332(1)
15: 12	254(3)
15: 13	404(1)
15: 15	334
15: 17	160
15: 22	400(4)
15: 23	109(5)
15: 24	455(2)
15: 26f.	452(2)
15: 27	113(2)
15: 30	223(4)
16: 1	93
16: 2	277(3)
16: 3ff.	293(4)
16: 7	125(2), 293(4)
16: 8	125(1)
16: 10, 11	162(5)
16: 13	284(2)
16: 19	447(5)
16: 20	384
16: 21	268(1)
16: 25	201
16: 27	467

1 Corinthians

1: 9	223(2)
1: 10	223(4)
1: 11	162(5)
1: 13	229(1), 440
1: 18	190(1), 271
1: 24	127(5)
1: 24f.	477(2)
1: 25	263(2)
1: 25–9	490
1: 27f.	138(1), 263(4)
1: 29	369(4)
1: 30	444(4)
1: 31	481
2: 2	442(9)
2: 4	47(4), 112, 474(4)
2: 6	447(8)
2: 7	220(2)
2: 8	360(4)
2: 9	p. 3 n. 4
2: 13	183
2: 14	190(1)

(2) *The Apostolic Fathers*

INDEX OF REFERENCES

(5) *The Septuagint*